# THE OXFORD HANDBOOK OF

# PUBLIC POLICY

# THE
# OXFORD
# HANDBOOKS
# OF
# POLITICAL
# SCIENCE

GENERAL EDITOR: ROBERT E. GOODIN

The *Oxford Handbooks of Political Science* is a ten-volume set of reference books offering authoritative and engaging critical overviews of all the main branches of political science.

The series as a whole is under the General Editorship of Robert E. Goodin, with each volume being edited by a distinguished international group of specialists in their respective fields:

### POLITICAL THEORY
*John S. Dryzek, Bonnie Honig & Anne Phillips*

### POLITICAL INSTITUTIONS
*R. A. W. Rhodes, Sarah A. Binder & Bert A. Rockman*

### POLITICAL BEHAVIOR
*Russell J. Dalton & Hans-Dieter Klingemann*

### COMPARATIVE POLITICS
*Carles Boix & Susan C. Stokes*

### LAW & POLITICS
*Keith E. Whittington, R. Daniel Kelemen & Gregory A. Caldeira*

### PUBLIC POLICY
*Michael Moran, Martin Rein & Robert E. Goodin*

### POLITICAL ECONOMY
*Barry R. Weingast & Donald A. Wittman*

### INTERNATIONAL RELATIONS
*Christian Reus-Smit & Duncan Snidal*

### CONTEXTUAL POLITICAL ANALYSIS
*Robert E. Goodin & Charles Tilly*

### POLITICAL METHODOLOGY
*Janet M. Box-Steffensmeier, Henry E. Brady & David Collier*

This series aspires to shape the discipline, not just to report on it. Like the Goodin–Klingemann *New Handbook of Political Science* upon which the series builds, each of these volumes will combine critical commentaries on where the field has been together with positive suggestions as to where it ought to be heading.

# THE OXFORD HANDBOOK OF

# PUBLIC POLICY

*Edited by*

MICHAEL MORAN
MARTIN REIN
*and*
ROBERT E. GOODIN

OXFORD
UNIVERSITY PRESS

# OXFORD

UNIVERSITY PRESS

Great Clarendon Street, Oxford OX2 6DP

Oxford University Press is a department of the University of Oxford.
It furthers the University's objective of excellence in research, scholarship,
and education by publishing worldwide in

Oxford New York

Auckland  Cape Town  Dar es Salaam  Hong Kong  Karachi
Kuala Lumpur  Madrid  Melbourne  Mexico City  Nairobi
New Delhi  Shanghai  Taipei  Toronto

With offices in

Argentina  Austria  Brazil  Chile  Czech Republic  France  Greece
Guatemala  Hungary  Italy  Japan  Poland  Portugal  Singapore
South Korea  Switzerland  Thailand  Turkey  Ukraine  Vietnam

Oxford is a registered trade mark of Oxford University Press
in the UK and in certain other countries

Published in the United States
by Oxford University Press Inc., New York

British Library Cataloguing in Publication Data
Data available

Library of Congress Cataloguing in Publication Data
Data available

Typeset by SPI Publisher Services, Pondicherry, India
Printed in Great Britain
on acid-free paper by
Biddles Ltd., King's Lynn, Norfolk

ISBN 0–19–926928–9   978–0–19–926928–0
1 3 5 7 9 10 8 6 4 2

# Contents

# PART IV PRODUCING PUBLIC POLICY

# PART V INSTRUMENTS OF POLICY

# PART VI CONSTRAINTS ON PUBLIC POLICY

# PART VII POLICY INTERVENTION: STYLES AND RATIONALES

# PART VIII COMMENDING AND EVALUATING PUBLIC POLICIES

## PART IX  PUBLIC POLICY, OLD AND NEW

# About the Contributors

Graham Allison is Douglas Dillon Professor of Government, Director of Belfer Center for Science and International Affairs, and Faculty Chair of the Caspian Studies Program at the Kennedy School of Government, Harvard University.

Eugene Bardach is Professor of Public Policy in the Richard and Rhoda Goldman School of Public Policy, University of California, Berkeley.

Johanna Birckmayer is a Senior Research Scientist at the Pacific Institute for Research and Evaluation (PIRE) in Calverton, Maryland.

Davis B. Bobrow is Professor of Public Policy and International Affairs and Political Science at the University of Pittsburgh.

Mark Bovens is Professor of Legal Philosophy and of Public Administration at Utrecht University and Research Director of the Utrecht School of Governance.

Bea Cantillon is Professor of Social Policy, and Director of the Centre for Social Policy, University of Antwerp.

Tom Christensen is Professor of Political Science, University of Oslo.

Neta C. Crawford is Associate Professor (Research) in the Watson Institute for International Studies at Brown University.

Peter deLeon is Professor of Public Policy at the University of Colorado, Denver.

John D. Donahue is Raymond Vernon Lecturer in Public Policy and Director of the Weil Program in Collaborative Governance at the Kennedy School of Government, Harvard University.

Yehezkel Dror is Professor of Political Science at Hebrew University, Jerusalem, and Founding President, The Jewish People Policy Planning Institute. He received the 2005 Israel Prize in Administrative Sciences for his theoretic and applied work on strategic planning.

John S. Dryzek is Professor of Social and Political Theory and Political Science at the Research School of Social Sciences, Australian National University.

Amitai Etzioni is University Professor at George Washington University.

John Forester is Professor of City and Regional Planning, Cornell University.

Richard Freeman is Senior Lecturer in the School of Social and Political Studies, University of Edinburgh.

**Barry L. Friedman** is Professor of Economics at the Heller School for Social Policy and Management, Brandeis University.

**Archon Fung** is Associate Professor of Public Policy, Kennedy School of Government, Harvard University.

**William A. Galston** is Saul I. Stern Professor of Civic Engagement at the School of Public Policy, University of Maryland, and was Deputy Assistant to the President for Domestic Policy during the first Clinton administration.

**Robert E. Goodin** is Distinguished Professor of Social and Political Theory and Philosophy at the Research School of Social Sciences, Australian National University.

**Maarten Hajer** is Professor of Public Policy and Political Science, University of Amsterdam.

**Dirk Haubrich** is Research Officer in Philosophy at the Department of Politics and International Relations, University of Oxford.

**Colin Hay** is Professor of Political Analysis at the University of Birmingham.

**Matthew Holden, Jr.** is Henry L. and Grace M. Doherty Professor Emeritus in the Woodrow Wilson Department of Politics, University of Virginia.

**Christopher Hood** is Gladstone Professor of Government, University of Oxford.

**Ellen M. Immergut** is Professor of Political Science at Humboldt University, Berlin.

**Helen Ingram** is Professor of Planning, Policy, and Design and Political Science, and Drew, Chace, and Erin Warmington Chair in the Social Ecology of Peace and International Cooperation at the University of California, Irvine.

**Mark A. R. Kleiman** is Professor of Public Policy and Director, Drug Policy Analysis Program, UCLA School of Public Affairs.

**Rudolf Klein** is Emeritus Professor of Social Policy, University of Bath.

**Sanneke Kuipers** is Postdoctoral Fellow in the Department of Public Administration, University of Leiden.

**David Laws** is a Principal Research Scientist in the Department of Urban Studies and Planning, Massachusetts Institute of Technology.

**Giandomenico Majone** is Professor of Public Policy Emeritus, European University Institute.

**James G. March** is Professor of Education and Emeritus Jack Steele Parker Professor of International Management, of Political Science, and of Sociology, Stanford University.

**Theodore R. Marmor** is Professor of Public Policy and Management and Professor of Political Science, Yale University.

**Michael Moran** is W. J. M. Mackenzie Professor of Government, University of Manchester.

**Johan P. Olsen** is Research Director of ARENA Center for European Studies and Professor of Political Science, University of Oslo.

**Edward C. Page** is Sidney and Beatrice Webb Professor of Public Policy, Department of Government, London School of Economics.

**Frances Fox Piven** is Distinguished Professor of Political Science and Sociology at the Graduate School and University Center, CUNY.

**John Quiggin** is Australian Research Council Federation Fellow in Economics and Political Science, University of Queensland.

**Martin Rein** is Professor of Sociology in the Department of Urban Studies and Planning, Massachusetts Institute of Technology.

**R. A. W. Rhodes** is Professor of Political Science, Research School of Social Sciences, Australian National University.

**Anne L. Schneider** is Professor in the School of Justice Studies, Arizona State University.

**Colin Scott** is Reader in Law at the London School of Economics.

**Tom Sefton** is Research Fellow at the Centre for Analysis of Social Exclusion (CASE), London School of Economics.

**Henry Shue** is Senior Research Fellow in Politics, Merton College, Oxford.

**Kevin B. Smith** is Professor of Political Science, University of Nebraska, Lincoln.

**Lawrence Susskind** is Ford Professor of Urban and Environmental Planning, Massachusetts Institute of Technology, and Director of the Public Disputes Program in the Program on Negotiation at Harvard Law School.

**Steven M. Teles** is Assistant Professor of Politics, Brandeis University.

**Paul 't Hart** is Senior Fellow in the Political Science Program, Research School of Social Sciences, Australian National University, and Professor of Public Administration at the Utrecht School of Governance, Utrecht University.

**Karel Van den Bosch** is Project Leader at the Centre for Social Policy, University of Antwerp.

**Carol Hirschon Weiss** is Beatrice B. Whiting Professor of Education Policy, Harvard University.

**Richard Wilson**, Lord Wilson of Dinton, Master of Emmanuel College, Cambridge, was Secretary of the Cabinet and Head of the Home Civil Service from 1998 to 2002.

**Christopher Winship** is the Diker-Tishman Professor of Sociology and a member of the faculty in the John F. Kennedy School of Government, Harvard University.

**Jonathan Wolff** is Professor of Philosophy, University College London.

**Oran R. Young** is Professor at the Bren School of Environmental Science and Management at the University of California (Santa Barbara) and co-director of the Bren School's Program on Governance for Sustainable Development.

**Richard J. Zeckhauser** is Frank Plumpton Ramsey Professor of Political Economy at the Kennedy School of Government, Harvard University.

# PART I

# INTRODUCTION

# CHAPTER 1

........................................................................

# THE PUBLIC AND ITS
# POLICIES

........................................................................

ROBERT E. GOODIN

MARTIN REIN

MICHAEL MORAN

THIS *Oxford Handbook of Public Policy* aspires to provide a rounded understanding of what it is to make and to suffer, to study and to critique, the programs and policies by which officers of the state attempt to rule. Ruling is an assertion of the will, an attempt to exercise control, to shape the world. Public policies are instruments of this assertive ambition, and policy studies in the mode that emerged from operations research during the Second World War were originally envisaged as handmaidens in that ambition.[1] There was a distinctly "high modernist" feel to the enterprise, back then: technocratic hubris, married to a sense of mission to make a better world; an overwhelming confidence in our ability to measure and monitor that world;

* We are grateful to Rod Rhodes for invaluable comments on an earlier draft.

[1] In recommending continuation of wartime research and development efforts into the postwar era, Commanding General of the Army Air Force H. H. ("Hap") Arnold had reported to the Secretary of War in the following terms: "During this war the Army, Army Air Forces and the Navy have made unprecedented use of scientific and industrial resources. The conclusion is inescapable that we have not yet established the balance necessary to insure the continuance of teamwork among the military, other government agencies, industry and the universities." Just hear the high modernist ring in the bold mission statement adopted by Project RAND in 1948, as it split off from the Douglas Aircraft Company: "to further and promote scientific, educational and charitable purposes, all for the public welfare and security of the United States of America" (RAND 2004).

and boundless confidence in our capacity actually to pull off the task of control (Scott 1997; Moran 2003).

High modernism in the US and elsewhere have amounted to rule by "the best and the brightest" (Halberstam 1969). It left little room for rhetoric and persuasion, privately much less publicly. Policy problems were technical questions, resolvable by the systematic application of technical expertise. First in the Pentagon, then elsewhere across the wider policy community, the "art of judgment" (Vickers 1983) gave way to the dictates of slide-rule efficiency (Hitch 1958; Hitch and McKean 1960; Haveman and Margolis 1983).

Traces of that technocratic hubris remain, in consulting houses and IMF missions and certain other important corners of the policy universe. But across most of that world there has, over the last half-century, been a gradual chastening of the boldest "high modernist" hopes for the policy sciences.[2] Even in the 1970s, when the high modernist canon still ruled, perceptive social scientists had begun to highlight the limits to implementation, administration, and control.[3] Subsequently, the limits of authority and accountability, of sheer analytic capacity, have borne down upon us.[4] Fiasco has piled upon fiasco in some democratic systems (Henderson 1977; Dunleavy 1981, 1995; Bovens and 't Hart 1996). We have learned that many of tools in the "high modernist" kit are very powerful indeed, within limits; but they are strictly limited (Hood 1983). We have learned how to supplement those "high modernist" approaches with other "softer" modes for analyzing problems and attempting to solve them.

In trying to convey a sense of these changes in the way we have come to approach public policy over the past half-century, the chapters in this *Handbook* (and still more this Introduction to it) focus on the big picture rather than minute details. There are other books to which readers might better turn for fine-grained analyses of current policy debates, policy area by policy area.[5] There are other books providing more fine-grained analyses of public administration.[6] This *Handbook* offers instead a series of connected stories about what it is like, and what it might alternatively be like, to make and remake public policy in new, more modest modes.

This Introduction is offered as a scene setter, rather than as a systematic overview of the whole field of study, much less a potted summary of the chapters that follow. Our authors speak most ably for themselves. In this Introduction, we simply do likewise. And in doing so we try to tell a particular story: a story about the limits of high ambition in policy studies and policy making, about the way those limits have been appreciated, about the way more modest ambitions have been formulated, and about the difficulties in turn of modest learning. Our story, like all stories, is contestable. There is no single intellectually compelling account available of the state of either policy making or the policy sciences; but the irredeemable fact of contestability is a very part of the argument of the pages that follow.

---

[2] For a remarkable early send-up, see Mackenzie's (1963) "The Plowden Report: a translation."

[3] Pressman and Wildavsky 1973; Hood 1976; van Gunsteren 1976.

[4] Majone and Quade 1980; Hogwood and Peters 1985; Bovens 1998.

[5] The best regular update is probably found in the Brookings Institution's "Setting National Priorities" series; see most recently Aaron and Reischauer (1999).

[6] Lynn and Wildavsky 1990; Peters and Pierre 2003.

# 1. POLICY PERSUASION

We begin with the most important of all limits to high ambition. All our talk of "making" public policy, of "choosing" and "deciding," loses track of the home truth, taught to President Kennedy by Richard Neustadt (1960), that politics and policy making is mostly a matter of persuasion. Decide, choose, legislate as they will, policy makers must carry people with them, if their determinations are to have the full force of policy. That is most commonly demonstrated in systems that attempt to practice liberal democracy; but a wealth of evidence shows that even in the most coercive systems of social organization there are powerful limits to the straightforward power of command (Etzioni 1965).

To make policy in a way that makes it stick, policy makers cannot merely issue edicts. They need to persuade the people who must follow their edicts if those are to become general public practice. In part, that involves persuasion of the public at large: Teddy Roosevelt's "bully pulpit" is one important lever. In part, the persuasion required is of subordinates who must operationalize and implement the policies handed down to them by nominal superiors. Truman wrongly pitied "Poor Ike," whom he envisaged issuing orders as if he were in the army, only to find that no one would automatically obey: as it turned out, Ike had a clear idea how to persuade up and down the chain of command, even if he had no persuasive presence on television (Greenstein 1982). Indeed Eisenhower's military experience precisely showed that even in nominally hierarchical institutions, persuasion lay at the heart of effective command.

Not only is the practice of public policy making largely a matter of persuasion. So too is the discipline of studying policy making aptly described as itself being a "persuasion" (Reich 1988; Majone 1989). It is a mood more than a science, a loosely organized body of precepts and positions rather than a tightly integrated body of systematic knowledge, more art and craft than genuine "science" (Wildavsky 1979; Goodsell 1992). Its discipline-defining title notwithstanding, Lerner and Lasswell's pioneering book *The Policy Sciences* (1951) never claimed otherwise: quite the contrary, as successive editors of the journal that bears that name continually editorially recall.

The cast of mind characterizing policy studies is marked, above all else, by an aspiration toward "relevance." Policy studies, more than anything, are academic works that attempt to do the real political work: contributing to the betterment of life, offering something that political actors can seize upon and use. From Gunnar Myrdal's *American Dilemma* (1944) through Charles Murray's *Losing Ground* (1984) and William Julius Wilson's *Truly Disadvantaged* (1987), policy-oriented research on race and poverty has informed successive generations of American policy makers on both ends of the political spectrum, to take only one important example.

Beyond this stress on relevance, policy studies are distinguished from other sorts of political science, secondly, by being unabashedly value laden (Lasswell 1951; Rein

1976; Goodin 1982). They are explicitly normative, in embracing the ineliminable role of value premisses in policy choice—and often in forthrightly stating and defending the value premisses from which the policy prescriptions that they make proceed. They are unapologetically prescriptive, in actually recommending certain programs and policies over others. Policy studies, first and foremost, give *advice* about policy; and they cannot do that (on pain of the "naturalistic fallacy") without basing that advice on some normative ("ought") premisses in the first place.

Policy studies are distinguished from other sorts of political science, thirdly, by their action orientation. They are organized around questions of what we as a political community should *do*, rather than just around questions of what it should *be*. Whereas other sorts of political studies prescribe designs for our political institutions, as the embodiments or instruments of our collective values, specifically *policy* studies focus less on institutional shells and more on what we collectively *do* in and through those institutional forms. Policy studies embody a bias toward acts, outputs, and outcomes—a concern with consequences—that contrasts with the formal-institutional orientation of much of the rest of political studies.

These apparently commonplace observations—that policy studies is a "persuasion" that aspires to normatively committed intervention in the world of action—pose powerful challenges for the policy analyst. One of the greatest challenges concerns the language that the analyst can sensibly use. The professionalization of political science in the last half-century has been accompanied by a familiar development—the development of a correspondingly professional language. Political scientists know whom they are talking to when they report findings: they are talking to each other, and they naturally use language with which other political scientists are familiar. They are talking to each other because the scientific world of political science has a recursive quality: the task is to communicate with, and convince, like-minded professionals, in terms that make sense to the professional community. Indeed some powerful traditions in purer forms of academic political science are actually suspicious of "relevance" in scholarly enquiry (Van Evera 2003). The findings and arguments of professional political science may seep into the world of action, but that is not the main point of the activity. Accidental seepage is not good enough for policy studies. It harks back to an older world of committed social enquiry where the precise object is to unify systematic social investigation with normative commitment—and to report both the results and the prescriptions in a language accessible to "non-professionals." These can range from engaged—or not very engaged—citizens to the elite of policy makers. Choosing the language in which to communicate is therefore a tricky, but essential, part of the vocation of policy analysis.

One way of combining all these insights about how policy making and policy studies are essentially about persuasion is through the "argumentative turn" and the analysis of "discourses" of policy in the "critical policy studies" movement (Fischer and Forrester 1993; Hajer 1995; Hajer and Wagenaar 2003). On this account, a positivist or "high modernist" approach, either to the making of policy or to the understanding of how it is made, that tries to decide what to do or what was done through vaguely mechanical-style causal explanations is bound to fail, or anyway be radically incomplete.

Policy analysts are never mere "handmaidens to power." It is part of their job, and a role that the best of them play well, to *advocate* the policies that they think right (Majone 1989). The job of the policy analyst is to "speak truth to power" (Wildavsky 1979), where the truths involved embrace not only the hard facts of positivist science but also the reflexive self-understandings of the community both writ large (the polity) and writ small (the policy community, the community of analysts).

It may well be that this reflexive quality is the main gift of the analyst to the practitioner. In modern government practitioners are often forced to live in an unreflective world: the very pressure of business compresses time horizons, obliterating recollection of the past and foreshortening anticipation of the future (Neustadt and May 1986). There is overwhelming pressure to decide, and then to move on to the next problem. Self-consciousness about the limits of decision, and about the setting, social and historical, of decision, is precisely what the analyst can bring to the policy table, even if its presence at the table often seems unwelcome.

Of course, reason giving has always been a central requirement of policy applica-tion, enforced by administrative law. Courts automatically overrule administrative orders accompanied by no reasons. So, too, will their "rationality review" strike down statutes which cannot be shown to serve a legitimate purpose within the power of the state (Fried 2004, 208–12). The great insight of the argumentative turn in policy analysis is that a robust process of reason giving runs throughout all stages of public policy. It is not just a matter of legislative and administrative window dressing.

Frank and fearless advice is not always welcomed by those in positions of power. All organizations find self-evaluation hard, and states find it particularly hard: there is a long and well-documented history of states, democratic and non-democratic, ignoring or even punishing the conveyor of unwelcome truths (Van Evera 2003). Established administrative structures that used to be designed to generate dispas-sionate advice are increasingly undermined with the politicization of science and the public service (UCS 2004; Peters and Pierre 2004). Still, insofar as policy analysis constitutes a profession with an ethos of its own, the aspiration to "speak truth to power"—even, or especially, unwelcome truths—must be its prime directive, its equivalent of the Hippocratic Oath (ASPA 1984).

## 2. Arguing versus Bargaining

Our argument thus far involves modest claims for the "persuasion" of policy studies, but even these modest ambitions carry their own hubristic dangers. Persuasion; the encouragement of a reflexive, self-conscious policy culture; an attention to the language used to communicate with the world of policy action: all are important. But all run the risk of losing sight of a fundamental truth—that policy is not only about arguing, but is also about bargaining. A policy forum is not an academic seminar. The danger is that we replicate the fallacy of a tradition which we began by rejecting.

Policy analysts, particularly those who see themselves as part of a distinct high modernist professional cadre, often take a technocratic approach to their work. They see themselves as possessing a neutral expertise to be put to the service of any political master. They accept that their role as adviser is to advise, not to choose; and they understand that it is in the nature of advice that it is not always taken. Accepting all this as they do, policy advisers of this more professional, technocratic cast of mind inevitably feel certain pangs of regret when good advice is overridden for bad ("purely political") reasons.

Politics may rightly seem disreputable when it is purely a matter of power in the service of interests. When there is nothing more to be said on behalf of the outcome than that people who prefer it have power enough to force it, one might fatalistically accept that outcome as politically inevitable without supposing that there is anything at all to be said for it normatively. Certainly there is not much to be said for it normatively, anyway, without saying lots more about why the satisfaction of those preferences is objectively desirable or why that distribution of power is proper.

Nor is this account necessarily incompatible with some conception of democratic policy making. Indeed some democratic theorists try to supply the needed normative glue by analogizing political competition to the economic market. The two fundamental theorems of welfare economics prove Adam Smith's early speculation that, at least under certain (pretty unrealistic) conditions, free competition in the marketplace for goods would produce maximum possible satisfaction of people's preferences (Arrow and Hahn 1971). Democratic theorists after the fashion of Schumpeter (1950) say the same about free competition in the political marketplace for ideas and public policies (Coase 1974). "Partisan mutual adjustment"—between parties, between bureaucracies, between social partners—can, bargaining theorists of politics and public administration assure us, produce socially optimal results (Lindblom 1965).

Of course there are myriad assumptions required for the proofs to go through, and they are met even less often in politics than economics. (Just think of the assumption of "costless entry of new suppliers:" a heroic enough assumption for producers in economic markets, but a fantastically heroic one as applied to new parties in political markets, especially in a world of "cartelized" party markets (Katz and Mair 1995).) Most importantly, though, the proofs only demonstrate that preferences are maximally satisfied in the Pareto sense: no one can be made better off without someone else being made worse off. Some are inevitably more satisfied than others, and who is most satisfied depends on who has most clout—money in the economic market, or political power in the policy arena. So the classic "proof" of the normative legitimacy of political bargaining is still lacking one crucial leg, which would have to be some justification for the distribution of power that determines "who benefits" (Page 1983). The early policy scientists clearly knew as much, recalling Lasswell's (1950) definition of "politics" in terms of "who gets what, when, how?"

The success of that enterprise looks even more unlikely when reflecting, as observers of public policy inevitably must, on the interplay between politics and markets (Lindblom 1977; Dahl 1985). The point of politics is to constrain markets: if markets operated perfectly (according to internal economic criteria, and broader social ones), we would let all social relations be determined by them alone. It is only because markets fail in one or the other of those ways, or because they fail to provide the preconditions for their own success, that we need politics at all (Hirsch 1976; Offe 1984; Esping-Andersen 1985; World Bank 1997). But if politics is to provide these necessary conditions for markets, politics must be independent of markets—whereas the interplay of "political money" and the rules of property in most democracies means that politics is, to a large extent, the captive of markets (Lindblom 1977).

Tainted though the processes of representative democracy might be by political money, they nonetheless remain the principal mechanism of public accountability for the exercise of public power. Accountability through economic markets and informal networks can usefully supplement the political accountability of elected officials to the electorate; but can never replace it (Day and Klein 1987; Goodin 2003).

Another strand of democratic theory has recently emerged, reacting against the bargaining model that sees politics as simply the vector sum of political forces and the aggregation of votes. It is a strand which is easier to reconcile with the "persuasive" character of policy studies. Deliberative democrats invite us to reflect together on our preferences and what policies might best promote the preferences that we reflectively endorse (Dryzek 2000). There are many arenas in which this might take place. Those range from small-scale forums (such as "citizen's juries," "consensus conferences," or "Deliberative Polls" involving between 20 and 200 citizens) through medium-sized associations (Fung and Wright 2001). Ackerman and Fishkin (2004) even make a proposal for a nationwide "Deliberation Day" before every national election.

Not only might certain features of national legislature make that a more "delibera-tive" assembly, more in line with the requirements of deliberative democracy (Steiner et al. 2005). And not only are certain features of political culture—traditions of free speech and civic engagement—more conducive to deliberative democracy (Sunstein 1993, 2001; Putnam 1993). Policy itself might be made in a more "deliberative" way, by those charged with the task of developing and implementing policy proposals (Fischer 2003). That is the aim of advocates of critical policy studies, with their multifarious proposals for introducing a "deliberative turn" into the making of policies on every-thing from water use to urban renewal to toxic waste (Hajer and Wagenaar 2003).

Some might say that this deliberative turn marks a shift from reason to rhetoric in policy discourse. And in a way, advocates of that turn might embrace the description, for part of the insight of the deliberative turn is that reason is inseparable from the *way* we reason: rhetoric is not decoration but is always ingrained in the intellectual content of argument. Certainly they mean to disempower the dogmatic deliverances of technocratic reason, and to make space in the policy-making arena for softer and less hard-edged modes of communication and assessment (Young 2000; Fischer 2003). Reframing the problem is, from this perspective, a legitimate part of the process: it is important to see that the problem looks different from different perspectives, and that different people quite reasonably bring different perspectives to bear (March 1972; Schön and Rein 1994; Allison and Zelikow 1999). Value clarification, and re-envisioning our interests (personal and public), is to be seen as a legitimate and valued outcome of political discussions, rather than as an awkwardness that gets in the way of technocratic fitting of means to pre-given ends. Thus the deliberative turn echoes one of the key features of the "persuasive" conception of policy studies with which we began: reflexivity is—or should be—at the heart of both advice and decision.

These conceptions, true, are easier to realize in some settings than in others. The place, the institutional site, and the time, all matter. National traditions clearly differ in their receptivity to deliberation and argument. The more consultative polities of Scandinavia and continental Europe have always favoured more consensual modes of policy making, compared to the majoritarian polities of the Anglo-American world (Lijphart 1999). Votes are taken, in the end. But the process of policy development and implementation proceeds more according to procedures of "sounding out" stakeholders and interested parties, rather than majorities pressing things to a vote prematurely (Olsen 1972*b*). Of course, every democratic polity worth the name has some mechanisms for obtaining public input into the policy-making process: letters to Congressmen and congressional hearings, in the USA; Royal Commissions and Green Papers in the UK; and so on. But those seem to be pale shadows of the Scandinavian "remiss" procedures, inviting comment on important policy initiatives and actually taking the feedback seriously, even when it does not necessarily come from powerful political interests capable of blocking the legislation or derailing its implementation (Meijer 1969; Anton 1980).

Sites of governance matter, as well. The high modernist vision was very much one of top-down government: policies were to be handed down not just from superiors to subordinates down the chain of command, but also from the governing centre to the governed peripheries. New, and arguably more democratic, possibilities emerge when looking at governing as a bottom-up process (Tilly 1999). The city or neighborhood suddenly becomes the interesting locus of decision making, rather than the national legislature. Attempts to increase democratic participation in local decision making have not met with uniform success, not least because of resistance from politicians nearer the center of power: the resistance of mayors was a major hindrance to the "community action programs" launched as part of the American War on Poverty, for example (Marris and Rein 1982). Still, many of the most encouraging examples of new deliberative processes working to democratize the existing political order operate at very local levels, in local schools or police stations (Fung 2004).

Meshing policy advice and policy decision with deliberation is therefore easier in some nations, and at some levels of government, than others. It also seems easier at some historical moments than others: thus, time matters. Until about a quarter-century ago, for example, policy making in Britain was highly consensual, based on extensive deliberation about policy options, albeit usually with a relatively narrow range of privileged interests. Indeed, the very necessity of creating accommodation was held to be a source of weakness in the policy process (Dyson

1980; Dyson and Wilks 1983). Since then the system has shifted drastically away from a deliberative, accommodative mode. Many of the characteristic mechanisms associated with consultation and argument—such as Royal Commissions—are neglected; policy is made through tiny, often informally organized cliques in the core executive.

The shift is partly explicable by the great sense of crisis which engulfed British policy makers at the end of the 1970s, and by the conviction that crisis demanded decisive action free from the encumbrances of debates with special interests. The notion that crisis demands decision, not debate, recurs in many different times and places. Indeed "making a crisis out of a drama" is a familiar rhetorical move when decision makers want a free hand. Yet here is the paradox of crisis: critical moments are precisely those when the need is greatest to learn how to make better decisions; yet the construction of crisis as a moment when speed of decision is of the essence precisely makes it the moment when those advocating persuasion and reflexivity are likely to be turned away from the policy table.

All is not gloom even here, however. The analysis of crises—exactly, particular critical events—can be a powerful aid to institutional learning (March, Sproull, and Tamuz 1991). Moreover, there are always multiple "tables"—multiple forums—in which policies are argued out and bargained over. "Jurisdiction shopping" is a familiar complaint, as lawyers look for sympathetic courts to which to bring their cases and polluting industries look for lax regulatory regimes in which to locate. But policy activists face the same suite of choices. Policies are debated, and indeed made, in many different forums. Each operates according to a different set of rules, with a different agenda, and on different timelines; each responds to different sets of pressures and urgencies; each has its own norms, language, and professional ethos. So when you cannot get satisfaction in one place, the best advice for a policy activist is to go knocking on some other door (Keck and Sikkink 1998; Risse, Ropp, and Sikkink 1999).

Place, site, and moment often obstruct the "persuasive" practice of the vocation of policy studies. Yet, as we show in the next section, there is overwhelming evidence of powerful structural and institutional forces that are dragging policy makers in a deliberative direction. These powerful forces are encompassed in accounts of networked governance.

## 3. NETWORKED GOVERNANCE

Policy making in the modern state commonly exhibits a contradictory character. Under the press of daily demands for action, often constructed as "crises," decision makers feel the need to act without delay. Yet powerful forces are pushing systems increasingly in more decentralized and persuasion-based directions.

Of course, even in notionally rigid high modernist hierarchies, the "command theory" of control was never wholly valid. "Orders backed by threats" were never a good way to get things done, in an organization any more than in governing a country. Complex organizations can never be run by coercion alone (Etzioni 1965). An effective authority structure, just like an effective legal system, presupposes that the people operating within it themselves internalize the rules it lays down and critically evaluate their own conduct according to its precepts (Hart 1961). That is true even of the most nominally bureaucratic environments: for instance, Heclo and Wildavsky (1974) characterize the relations among politicians and public officials in the taxing and spending departments of British government as a "village community" full of informal norms and negotiated meanings: an anthropologically "private" way of governing public money.

Thus there have always been limits to command. But the argument that, increasingly, government is giving way to "governance" suggests something more interesting, and something peculiarly relevant to our "persuasive" conception of policy studies: that governing is less and less a matter of ruling through hierarchical authority structures, and more and more a matter of negotiating through a decentralized series of floating alliances. The dominant image is that of "networked governance" (Heclo 1978; Rhodes 1997; Castels 2000). Some actors are more central, others more peripheral, in those networks. But even those actors at the central nodes of networks are not in a position to dictate to the others. Broad cooperation from a great many effectively independent actors is required in order for any of them to accomplish their goals.

To some extent, that has always been the deeper reality underlying constitutional fictions suggesting otherwise. Formally, the Queen in Parliament may be all powerful and may in Dicey's phrase, "make or unmake any law whatsoever" (Dicey 1960/1885, 39–40). Nonetheless, firm albeit informal constitutional conventions mean there are myriad things that she simply may not do and retain any serious expectation of retaining her royal prerogatives (unlike, apparently, her representative in other parts of her realm) (Marshall 1984). Formally, Britain was long a unitary state and local governments were utterly creatures of the central state; but even in the days of parliamentary triumphalism the political realities were such that the center had to bargain with local governments rather than simply dictate to them, even on purely financial matters (Rhodes 1988).

But increasingly such realities are looming larger and the fictions even smaller. Policy increasingly depends on what economists call "relational contracts:" an agreement to agree, a settled intention to "work together on this," with details left to be specified sometime later (Gibson and Goodin 1999). Some fear a "joint decision trap," in circumstances where there are too many veto players (Scharpf 1988). But Gunnar Myrdal's (1955, 8, 20) description of the workings of the early days of the Economic Commission for Europe is increasingly true not just of intergovernmental negotiations but intragovernmental ones as well:

If an organization acquires a certain stability and settles down to a tradition of work, one implication is usually that on the whole the same state officials come together at regular intervals. If in addition it becomes repeatedly utilized for reaching inter-governmental agreements in a given field, it may acquire a certain institutional weight and a momentum. Certain substitutes for real political sanctions can then gradually be built up. They are all informal and frail. They assume a commonly shared appreciation of the general usefulness of earlier results reached, the similarly shared pride of, and solidarity towards, the "club" of participants at the meetings, and a considerable influence of the civil servants on the home governments in the particular kind of questions dealt with in the organizations. . . . Not upholding an agreement is something like a breach of etiquette in a club.

And so it has gone in the later life of the European Community, and now the European Union (Héritier 1999).[7]

Within these networks, none is in command. Bringing others along, preserving the relationship, is all. Persuasion is the way policy gets made, certainly in any literal "institutional void" (Hajer 2003) but even within real institutions, where authority is typically more fictive than real (Heclo and Wildavsky 1974).

If this is bad news for titular heads of notionally policy-making organizations, it is good news for the otherwise disenfranchised. The history of recent successes in protecting human rights internationally is a case in point. Advocacy coalitions are assembled, linking groups of powerless Nigerians whose rights are being abused by the Nigerian government with groups of human rights activists abroad, who bring pressure to bear on their home governments to bring pressure to bear in turn on Nigeria (Risse, Ropp, and Sikkink 1999; Keck and Sikkink 1998). Networking across state borders, as well as across communities and affected interests within state borders, can be an important "weapon of the weak" (Scott 1985).

The change has invaded areas hitherto thought of as the heartland of hierarchy and of authoritative decision by the rich and powerful.

Bureaucratic organizations, paradigms of Weberian hierarchy, are yielding to "soft bureaucracy" (Courpasson 2000). And in the world of globally organized business, Braithwaite and Drahos (2000) paint a picture of a decentered world, where networks of bewildering complexity produce regulation often without the formality of any precise moment of decision.

The rise of networked governance in turn accounts for a related turn that is central to the practice of the "persuasive" vocation: the self-conscious turn to government as steering.

---

[7] For example, "it is rare in [European] Community environmental policy for negotiations to fail. . . . An important factor seems to be the dynamics of long-lasting negotiations: i.e., the 'entanglement' of the negotiations which ultimately exerts such pressure on the representatives of dissenters (especially where there is only one dissenting state) that a compromise can be reached . . . [O]n the whole, no member state is willing to assume the responsibility for causing the failure of negotiations that have lasted for years and in which mutual trust in the willingness of all negotiators to contribute to an agreement has been built up" (Rehbinder and Stewart 1985, 265).

## 4. ROWING VERSUS STEERING

High modernist models of policy making were, first and foremost, models of central control. On those models, policy makers were supposed to decide what should be done to promote the public good, and then to make it happen.

This ambition became increasingly implausible as problems to which policy was addressed became (or came to be recognized as) increasingly complex. Despite brave talk of ways of "organizing social complexity" (Deutsch 1963; La Porte 1975), a sense soon set in that government was "overloaded" and society was politically ungovernable (King 1975; Crozier, Huntington, and Watanuki 1975). Despite the aspiration of constantly improving social conditions, producing generally good outcomes for people without fail, a sense emerged that society is now characterized by increasingly pervasive risks, both individually and collectively (Beck 1992).

Even when policy makers thought they had a firm grip on the levers of power at the center, however, they long feared that they had much less of a grip on those responsible for implementing their policies on the ground. "Street-level bureaucrats"—police, caseworkers in social service agencies, and such like—inevitably apply official policies in ways and places at some distance from close scrutiny by superiors (Lipsky 1980). Substantial de facto discretion inevitably follows, however tightly rule bound their actions are formally supposed to be. But it is not just bureaucrats literally on the streets who enjoy such discretion. Organization theorists have developed the general concept of "control loss" to describe the way in which the top boss's power to control subordinates slips away the further down the chain of command the subordinate is (Blau 1963; Deutsch 1963). It can never be taken for granted that policies will be implemented on the ground as intended: usually they will not (Pressman and Wildavsky 1973; Bardach 1977, 1980).

One early response to appreciation of problems of control loss within a system of public management was to abandon "command-and-control" mechanisms for evoking compliance with public policies, in favor of a system of "incentives" (Kneese and Schultze 1975; Schultze 1977). The thought was that, if you structure the incentives correctly, people will thereby have a reason for doing what you want them to do, without further intrusive intervention from public officials in the day-to-day management of their affairs. This thinking persisted into the 1980s and 1990s: it lay, for instance, behind the mania for "internal markets" in so many of the state-funded health care systems of Europe (Le Grand 1991; Saltman and von Otter 1992). The trick, of course, lies in setting the incentives just right. Allowing the Nuclear Regulatory Commission to fine unsafe nuclear power plants only $5,000 a day for unsafe practices, when it would cost the power company $300,000 a day to purchase substitute power off the grid, is hardly a deterrent (US Comptroller General 1979).

Appreciation of the incapacity of the center to exercise effective control over what happens on the ground through command and control within a hierarchy has also led to increasing "contracting out" of public services, public–private partnerships, and arm's-length government (Smith and Lipsky 1993; Commission on Public–Private Partnerships 2001). The image typically evoked here is one of "steering, not rowing" (Kaufmann, Majone, and Ostrom 1985; Bovens 1990).

Twin thoughts motivate this development. The first is that, by divesting themselves of responsibility for front-line service delivery, the policy units of government will be in a better position to focus on strategic policy choice (Osborne and Gaebler 1993; Gore 1993). The second thought is that by stipulating "performance standards" in the terms of contract, and monitoring compliance with them, public servants will be better able to ensure that public services are properly delivered than they would have been had those services been provided within the public sector itself.

This is hardly the first time such a thing has happened. In the early history of the modern state, under arrangements that have come to be called "tax farming," rulers used to subcontract tax collections to local nobles, with historically very mixed success. Fix the incentives as the prince tried, the nobles always seemed to be able to figure out some way of diddling the crown (Levi 1988). Those committed to steering, by monitoring others' rowing, would like to think they have learned how better to specify and monitor contract compliance. But so too has every prince's new adviser.

The history of "steering and rowing" crystallizes the contradictory character of the modern "governance" state, and illuminates also the complex relations between "governance" and the conception of policy studies as a persuasive vocation. On the one hand, powerful, well-documented forces are pushing policy systems in the direction of deliberation, consultation, and accommodation. "High modernism" is accompanied by high complexity, which requires high doses of voluntary coordination. And high modernism has also helped create smart people who cannot simply be ordered around: rising levels of formal education, notably sharp rises in participation in higher education, have created large social groups with the inclination, and the intellectual resources, to demand a say in policy making. These are some of the social developments that lie behind the spread of loosely networked advocacy coalitions of the kind noted above.

Modern steering may therefore be conceived as demanding a more democratic mode of statecraft—one where the practice of the persuasive vocation of policy studies is peculiarly important. But as we have also just seen, "steering" can have a less democratic face. It echoes the ambitions of princes, and a world of centralized scrutiny and monitoring prefigured in Bentham's (1787) Panopticon. The earliest images of the steering state, in Plato's *Republic*, are indeed avowedly authoritarian; and the greatest "helmsman" of the modern era was also one of its most brutal autocrats, Mao Zedong.

As the language of "steering" therefore shows, the legacy of "networked governance" is mixed, indeed contradictory, inscribed with both autocracy and democracy. This helps explain much of the fixation of the new public management on monitoring and control.

For all the borrowing that new public management, with its privatization and outsourcing, has done from economics, the one bit of economics it seems steadfastly to ignore is the one bit that ought presumably to have most relevance to the state as an organized enterprise: the economic theory of the firm (Simon 2000).

Two key works emphasize the point. One is Ronald Coase's (1937) early analysis of why to internalize production within the same firm, rather than just buying the components required from other producers on the open market—the "produce/buy decision." The answer is obvious as soon as the question is asked. You want to internalize production within the firm if, but only if, you have more confidence in your capacity to monitor and control the quality of the inputs into the production process than the quality of the outputs (the components you would alternatively have to buy on the open market). You produce in-house only when you are relatively unconfident of your capacity to monitor the quality of the goods that external producers supply to you.

One implication of this analysis for contracting out of public services to private organizations is plain: for the same reason that a private *organization* is formed to provide the service, the public should be hesitant to contract to them. For the same reason the private organization does not buy in the outputs it promises to supply, preferring to produce them in-house, so too should the public organization: contracts are inevitably incomplete, performance standards underspecified, and the room for maximizing private profits at the cost of the public purposes is too great. Indeed this problem of what may summarily be called "opportunism" lies at the heart of the way the new institutional economics addresses the firm (Williamson 1985, 29–32, 281–5). There then follows another obvious implication: if we do contract out public services, it is better to contract them out to non-profit suppliers who are known to share the goals that the public had in establishing the program than it is to contract them out to for-profit suppliers whose interests clearly diverge from the public purposes (Smith and Lipsky 1993; Rose-Ackerman 1996; Goodin 2003).

The second contribution to the theory of the firm that ought to bear on current practices of outsourcing and privatizing public services is Herbert Simon's (1951) analysis of the "employment relationship." The key to that, too, is the notion of "incomplete contracting." The reason we hire someone as an employee of our firm is that we cannot specify, in detail in advance, exactly what performances will be required. If we could, we would subcontract the services: but not knowing exactly what we want, we cannot write the relevant performance contract. Instead we write an employment contract, of the general form that says: "The employee will do whatever the employer says." Rudely, it is a slavery contract (suitably circumscribed by labour law); politely, it is a "relational contract," an agreement to stand in a relationship the precise terms of which will be specified later (Williamson 1985). Indeed as North points out, there are even elements of the relational in the master–slave relationship (1990, 32). But the basic point, once again, is that we cannot specify in advance what is wanted: and insofar as we cannot, that makes a powerful case for producing in-house rather than contracting out. And that is as true for public organizations as private, and once again equally for public organizations contracting with private *organizations*. For the same reasons that the private contractors employ people at all, for those very same reasons the state ought not to subcontract to those private suppliers.

The more general way in which these insights have been picked up among policy makers is in the slogan, "privatization entails regulation." A naive reading of the "downsizing government" program of Reagan and Thatcher and their copyists world-wide might lead one to suppose that it would have resulted in "less government:" specifically, among other things, "less regulation" (after all, "deregulation" was one of its first aims). But in truth privatization, outsourcing, and the like actually requires more regulation, not less (Majone 1994; Moran 2003). At a minimum, it requires detailed specification of the terms of the contract and careful monitoring of contract compliance. Thus, we should not be surprised that the sheer number of regulations emanating from privatized polities is an order of magnitude larger (Levi-Faur 2003; Moran 2003).

The paradoxes of privatization and regulation thus just bring us back to the beginning of the growth of government in the nineteenth century. That came as a pragmatic response to practical circumstances, if anything against the ideological current of the day. No political forces were pressing for an expansion of government, particularly. It was just a matter of one disaster after another making obvious the need, across a range of sectors, for tighter public regulation and an inspectorate to enforce it (MacDonagh 1958, 1961; Atiyah 1979). Over the course of the next century, some of those sectors were taken into public hands, only then to be reprivatized. It should come as no surprise, however, that the same sort of regulatory control should be needed over those activities, once reprivatized, as proved necessary before they had been nationalized. There was a "pattern" to government growth identified by MacDonagh (1958, 1961); and there is likely a pattern of regulatory growth under privatization.

# 5. POLICY, PRACTICE, AND PERSUASION

To do something "as a matter of policy" is to do it as a general rule. That is the distinction between "policy" and "administration" (Wilson 1887), between "legislating" policy and "executing" it (Locke 1690, ch. 12). Policy makers of the most ambitious sort aspire to "make policy" in that general rule-setting way, envisioning administrators applying those general rules to particular cases in a minimally discretionary fashion (Calvert, McCubbins, and Weingast 1989). That and cognate aspirations toward taut control from the center combine to constitute a central trope of political high modernism

One aspect of that is the aspiration, or rather illusion, of total central control. All the great management tools of the last century were marshaled in support of that project: linear programming, operations research, cost–benefit analysis, management by objectives, case-controlled random experiments, and so on (Rivlin 1971; Self 1975; Stokey and Zeckhauser 1978).

One non-negligible problem with models of central control is that there is never any single, stable central authority that can be in complete control. For would-be totalitarians that is a sad fact; for democratic pluralists it is something to celebrate. But whatever one's attitude toward the fact, it remains a hard fact of political life that the notional "center" is always actually occupied by many competing authorities. A Congressional Budget Office will always spring up to challenge the monolithic power of an Executive Branch General Accounting Office, just as double sets of books will always be kept in all the line departments of the most tightly planned economy.

In any case, total central control is always a fraud or a fiction. In the terms of the old Soviet joke, "They pretend to set quotas, and we pretend to meet them." The illusion of planning was preserved, even when producers wildly exceeded their targets: which surely must, in truth, have indicated a failure of planning, just as much as missing their targets in the other direction would have been (Wildavsky 1973). Every bureaucrat, whether on the street or in some branch office, knows well the important gap between "what they think we're doing, back in central office" and "what actually happens around here." And any new recruit incapable of mastering that distinction will not be long for that bureau's world—just as any landless peasant who supposes that some entitlement will be enforced merely because it is written down somewhere in a statute book will soon be sadly disappointed (Galanter 1974).

One solution is of course to abandon central planning altogether and marketize everything (Self 1993). The "shock treatment" to which the formerly planned economies of central Europe were subjected at the end of the cold war often seemed to amount to something like that (Sacks 1995; World Bank 1996). But as we have seen above, even the more moderate ambitions of privatization and creating managed markets in the established capitalist democracies, led to anything but a more decentralized world: they created their own powerful incentives to monitor and control.

More modestly, there are new modes of more decentralized planning and control that are more sensitive to those realities. "Indicative planning" loosens up the planning process: instead of setting taut and unchanging targets, it merely points in certain desired directions and recalibrates future targets in light of what past practice has shown to be realistic aspirations (Meade 1970).

More generally, policy makers can rely more heavily on "loose" laws and regulations. Instead of tightly specifying exact performance requirements (in ways that are bound to leave some things unspecified), the laws and regulations can be written in more general and vaguely aspirational terms (Goodin 1982, 59–72). Hard-headed political realists might think the latter pure folly, trusting too much to people's goodwill (or, alternatively, putting too much power in the hands of administrators charged with interpreting and applying loose laws and regulations). But it has been shown that, for example, nursing homes achieve higher levels of performance in countries regulating them in that "looser" way than in countries that try to write the regulations in a more detailed way (Braithwaite et al. 1993).

An interesting variation on these themes is the Open Method of Coordination practiced within the European Union. That consists essentially in "benchmarking." In the first instance, there is merely a process of collecting information on policy performance from all member states on some systematic, comparable basis. But once that has been done, the performance of better-performing states will almost automatically come to serve as a "benchmark" for the others to aspire to—voluntarily initially, but with increasing amounts of informal and formal pressure as time goes by (Atkinson et al. 2002; Offe 2003).

Another aspect of "political high modernism" is the illusion of instrumental rationality completely governing the policy process. That is the illusion that policy makers begin with a full set of ends (values, goals) that are to be pursued, full information about the means available for pursuing them, and full information about the constraints (material, social, and political resources) available for pursuing them.

"Full information" is always an illusion. Policy, like all human action, is undertaken partly in ignorance; and to a large extent is a matter of "learning-by-doing" (Arrow 1962; Betts 1978). In practice, we never really have all the information we need to "optimize." At best, we "satisfice"—set some standard of what is "good enough," and content ourselves with reaching that (Simon 1955). In the absence of full information about the "best possible," we never really know for certain whether our standard of "good enough" is too ambitious or not ambitious enough. If we set educational standards too high, too many children will be "left behind" as failures; if too low, passing does them little pedagogic good.

The failure of instrumental reason in the "full information" domain is unsurprising. Its failure in the other two domains is perhaps more so. Policy makers can never be sure exactly what resources are, or will be, available for pursuing any set of aims. It is not only Soviet-style planners who faced "soft budget constraints" (Kornai, Maskin, and Roland 2003). So do policy makers worldwide. In the literal sense of financial budgets, they often do not know how much they have to spend or how much they are actually committing themselves to spending. Legislating an "entitlement" program is to write a blank check, giving rise to spending that is "uncontrollable" (Derthick 1975)—uncontrollable, anyway, without a subsequent change in the legislation, for which political resources might be lacking, given the political interests coalesced around entitlements thus created (Pierson 1994). In a more diffuse sense of social support, policy makers again often do not know how much they have or need for any given policy. Sometimes they manage to garner more support for programs once under way than could ever have been imagined, initially; and conversely, programs that began with vast public support sometimes lose it precipitously and unpredictably. In short: perfect means–ends fitters, in "high modernist" mode, would maximize goal satisfaction within the constraints of the resources available to them; but public policy makers, in practice, often do not have much of a clue what resources really will ultimately be available.

Policy makers also often do not have a clear sense of the full range of instruments available to them. Policies are intentions, the product of creative human imagination.

Policy making can proceed in a more or less inventive way: by deliberately engaging in brainstorming and free association, rather than just rummaging around to see what "solutions looking for problems" are lying at the bottom of the existing "garbage can" of the policy universe (Olsen 1972*a*; March 1976; March and Olsen 1976). But creative though they may be, policy makers will always inevitably fail the high modernist ambition to some greater or lesser degree because of their inevitably limited knowledge of all the possible means by which goals might be pursued in policy.

Perhaps most surprising of all, policy makers fail the "high modernist" ambition of perfect instrumental rationality in not even having any clear, settled idea what all the ends (values, goals) of policy are. Much is inevitably part of the taken-for-granted background in all intentional action. It might never occur to us to specify that we value some outcome that we always enjoyed until some new policy intervention suddenly threatens it: wilderness and species diversity, or the climate, or stable families, or whatever. We often do not know what we want until we see what we get, not because our preferences are irrationally adaptive (or perhaps counter-adaptive) but merely because our capacities to imagine and catalog all good things are themselves strictly limited (March 1976).

The limits to instrumental rationality strengthen the case made in this chapter for policy studies as a persuasive vocation, for they strengthen the case that policy is best made, and developed, as a kind of journey of self-discovery, in which we have experientially to learn what we actually want. And what we learn to want is in part a product of what we already have and know—which is to say, is in part a product of what policy has been hitherto. Recognizing the limits to instrumental rationality also strengthens the case for a self-conscious eclecticism in choice of the "tools of government" (Hood 1983; Salamon 2002). These "tools" are social technologies, and thus their use and effectiveness are highly contingent on the setting in which they are employed. That setting is also in part a product of what has gone before. In other words, policy legacies are a key factor in policy choice—and to these we now turn.

# 6. POLICY AS ITS OWN CAUSE

It may truly be the case that "policy is its own cause." That is the case not just in the unfortunate sense in which cynics like Wildavsky (1979, ch. 3) originally intended the term: that every attempt to fix one problem creates several more; that every "purposive social action" always carries with it certain "unintended conse-quences" (Merton 1936). Nor is it simply a matter of issues cycling in and out of fashion, with the costs of solving some problem becoming more visible than the benefits (Downs 1972; Hirschman 1982). It can also be true in more positive senses.

As we experiment with some policy interventions, we get new ideas of better ways to pursue old goals and a clearer view of what new goals we collectively also value.

From an organizational point of view, solving problems can be as problematic as not solving them. The March of Dimes had to redefine its mission or close up shop, after its original goal—conquering polio—had been achieved. What Lasswell (1941) called the US "Garrison State" had to find some new *raison d'être* once the cold war had been won. Policy is its own cause in cases of successes as well as failures: in both cases, some new policy has to be found, and found fast, if the organization is to endure.

Policy successes can cause problems in a substantive rather than merely organizational sense. Longevity, increasing disability-free life years, is a central goal of health policy and one of the great accomplishments of the modern era. But good though it is in other respects, increasing longevity compromises the assumptions upon which "pay-as-you-go" pension systems were predicated, giving rise to the "old-age crisis" that has so exercised pension reformers worldwide (World Bank 1994).

Policy can be its own cause both directly and indirectly. A policy might successfully change the social world in precisely the ways intended, and then those changes might themselves either prevent or enable certain further policy developments along similar lines. This is the familiar story of "path dependency:" the subsequent moves available to you being a function of previous moves you have taken. Sometimes path dependency works to the advantage of policy makers: once village post offices are set up to deliver the Royal Mail across the realm, the same infrastructure is suddenly available also to pay all sorts of social benefits (pensions, family allowances, and such like) over the counter through them; there, the latter policy is easier to implement because of the first (Pierson 2000). Sometimes path dependency works the other way, making subsequent policy developments harder. An example of that is the way in which pensions being paid to Civil War veterans undercut the potential political constituency for universal old-age pensions in the USA for fully a generation or two after the rest of the developed world had adopted them (Skocpol 1992). Policy is its own cause due to such path dependencies, as well.

# 7. CONSTRAINTS

Policy making is always a matter of choice under constraint. But not all the constraints are material. Some are social and political, having to do with the willingness of people to do what your policy asks of them or with the willingness of electors to endorse the policies that would-be policy makers espouse.

Another large source of constraints on policy making, however, is ideational. Technology is at its most fundamental a set of ideas for how to use a set of resources to achieve certain desired outcomes. The same is true of the "technology of policy" as it is of the more familiar sorts of "technology of production." Ideas of how to pursue important social goals are forever in short supply (Reich 1988).

Occasionally new policy ideas originate with creative policy analysts. Take two examples from the realm of criminology. One idea about why the long, anonymous corridors of public housing complexes were such dangerous places was that common space was everybody's and nobody's: it was nobody's business to monitor, protect, and defend that space. If public housing were designed instead in such a way as to create enclaves of "defensible space," crime might be reduced (Newman 1972). Another idea is that "broken windows" might signal that "nobody cares" about this neighborhood, thus relaxing inhibitions on further vandalism and crime. Cracking down on petty misdemeanors might reduce crime by sending the opposite signal (Wilson and Kelling 1982).

More often, however, policy making is informed by "off the shelf" ideas. Sometimes these are borrowed from other jurisdictions. In times gone by—the times of mimeographed legislative proposals being dropped into the legislative hopper—policy borrowing could be traced by tracking the typographical errors in legislative proposals in one jurisdiction being replicated in the next (Walker 1969). In other cases, the borrowing is from casebooks and classrooms of Public Policy Schools, or under pressure from the World Bank and the International Monetary Fund (Stiglitz 2002).

March and Olsen (1976; Olsen 1972a) famously capture this proposition with their "garbage can model" of public policy making. Policy choice is there characterized as the confluence of three streams: problems looking for solutions; solutions looking for problems; and people looking for things to do. The first stream, but only that one, lines up with the hyper-rationalism of political high modernism. The latter stream represents the desperation of post-polio March of Dimers and the post-cold war Garrison State, looking for things to do once their original missions had been accomplished. The middle stream—solutions looking for problems—captures the paucity of policy ideas that serves as a major constraint on high modernist policy making.

High modernist policy making is supposed to be a matter of instrumentally rationally fitting means to ends. But often the means come first, and they get applied (inevitably imperfectly) to whatever end comes along which they might remotely fit. Take the case of the cruise missile. That technology originally developed as an unarmed decoy to be launched by bombers to confuse enemy radar as they penetrated enemy airspace; but when the Senate insisted that surely some of those missiles should be armed, the air force dropped the scheme rather than acquiesce in the development of unmanned weapons systems. There was a subsequent attempt to adapt the technology jointly by the air force for use on "stand-off bombers" (firing the missiles while still in friendly airspace) and by the navy for use on submarines; but given the differences between launching through an airplane's "short range attack missile" launcher and a submarine's torpedo tube, that joint venture came to naught.

So the original plan was shelved. But the idea was kept on the shelf; and several years later, in a window of strategic opportunity opened up by the SALT I agreements, the cruise missile was suddenly resurrected, this time as a ground-based missile system installed on the edge of the Evil Empire (Levine 1977).

Equally often, certain sorts of means constitute a "good fit" to certain sorts of ends, only under certain conditions which themselves are subject to change. Those often unspoken "background conditions" constitute further constraints to policy making. Consider, for example, the peculiarly Australian style of "worker's welfare state," which made good sense under the conditions of its introduction at the beginning of the twentieth century but no sense under the conditions prevailing by that century's end: if you have, as Australia initially had, full employment and an industrial arbitration system that ensured that everyone in employment earned enough to support a family, then you need no elaborate scheme of transfer payments to compensate people for inadequacies in their market income; but once you have (as under Thatcherite Labor and even more right-wing coalition governments) eviscerated both full employment and industrial arbitration schemes, and with them any guarantee of a "living wage" from market sources, the traditional absence of any transfer scheme to compensate for inadequacies in market income bites hard (Castles 1985, 2001).

The largest constraint under which public policy operates, of course, is the sheer selfishness of entrenched interests possessed of sufficient power to promote those interests in the most indefensible of ways. Politics, Shapiro (1999) usefully reminds us, is ultimately all about "interests and power." Anyone who has watched the farm lobby at work, anywhere in the world, would not doubt that for a moment (Self and Storing 1962; Smith 1990; Grant 1997). Neither would anyone conversant with the early history of the British National Health Service and the deeply cynical maneuvering of physicians to avoid becoming employees of the state (Marmor and Thomas 1972; Klein 2001).

Moralists hope for more, as do conscientious policy analysts. But at the end of the day, politics may well end up being purely about "who gets what, when, how" as the first self-styled policy scientist long ago taught us (Lasswell 1950).

Even those most political of constraints might be of indeterminate strength, though. Consider for example the growth of "alternative medicine" in the USA. Professional medicine, especially in the USA, is a powerfully organized interest (Marmor 1994). Ordinarily we expect its practitioners to be able to see off any challengers with ease. Certainly they successfully froze chiropractors out, when they tried to horn in on the business of osteopaths, for example. Somehow, however, "alternative medicine" has managed to become sufficiently established—despite the political power of conventional medical practitioners—to appear now as an option in Americans' Health Maintenance Organizations and to be eligible for reimbursement by health insurance schemes. It may just be a case of the political power of the insurance industry, weary of ever-escalating medical costs, having been mobilized against the political power of physicians, with practitioners of alternative medicine being the incidental beneficiaries. But, *ex ante*, that would have been a surprising and unexpected source of political support for the alternative medicine movement: *ex ante*, one could scarcely have guessed that the power of organized medicine was as fragile as it turned out to be in this respect.

Of course, "constraints" are not immutable. Indeed, one person's constraint may be another person's opportunity. From Kingdon's windows of opportunity (1984) to Hall's political power of economic ideas (1989) we see how the story is more than one about constraints: it is also about opportunities for change. These we now examine.

# 8. CHANGE, CONSTRAINT, AND DEMOCRATIC POLITICS

The story of policy is in part a story about constraints. But it is also a story about change, and that is what we now examine. Policies change for all sorts of reasons. The problems change; the environments change; technologies improve; alliances alter; key staff come and go; powerful interests weigh in. For those sadly in the know, all those are familiar facts of the policy world.

But for those still inspired by democratic ideals, there is at least sometimes another side to the story: policies can sometimes change because the people subject to those policies want them to change. There is a mass mobilization of groups pressing for reform—workers pressing for legislation on hours and wages, racial or religious minorities pressing for civil rights, women pressing for gender equity. What is more, there is powerful comparative evidence that social and cultural developments are promoting the spread of these mass groups (Cain, Dalton, and Scarrow 2003).

Advocacy groups are always an important force, even in routine policy making (Sabatier and Jenkins-Smith 1993). And they are becoming more so, in networked transnational society (Keck and Sikkink 1998; Risse, Ropp, and Sikkink 1999). But they are often treated as "just another interested party"—like physicians vis-à-vis the NHS—speaking for narrow sectoral interests alone, however much they might pretend otherwise. Even (or perhaps especially) self-styled "public interest lobbies" like Common Cause are often said to lack any authority to speak with any authority about what is "in the public interest:" "self-styled" is importantly different from "duly elected," as members of Congress regularly remind Common Cause lobbyists (McFarland 1976; Berry 1977).

Social movements are advocacy coalitions writ large. They bring pressure to bear where politically it matters, in terms of democratic theory: on elected officials. Sometimes the pressure succeeds, and Voting Rights Acts are legislated. Other times it fails, and the Equal Rights Amendment gets past Congress but is stymied by political countermobilization in statehouses (Mansbridge 1986). Sometimes there is no very precise set of legislative demands in view, as with the "poor people's movement" of the early 1970s (Piven and Cloward 1979), and the aim is mostly just to alter the tone of the national debate.

There is always an element of that, in any social movement. Even social movements ostensibly organized around specific legal texts—the proposed Great Charter or Equal Rights Amendment—were always about much more than merely enacting those texts into law. Still, for social movements to have any impact on policy, they have to have some relatively specific policy implications. Every social movement, if it is to make any material difference, has to have a determinate answer to the question, "What do we want, and when do we want it?"

A full discussion of social movements would take us deep into the territory covered by other *Handbooks* in this series. But there are some things to be said about them, purely from a policy perspective. Consider the question of why social movements seem eventually to run out of steam. Many of the reasons are rooted in their political sociology: they lose touch with their grass roots; they get outmaneuvered in the centres of power; and so on (Tarrow 1994). But another reason, surely, is that they sometimes simply "run out of ideas." They no longer have any clear idea what they want, in policy terms. Winning the sympathies of legislators and their constituents counts for naught, if movements cannot follow up with some specific draft bill to drop into the legislative hopper.

That was at least part of the story behind the waning of the civil rights and feminist movements in the USA as sources of demand for legislative or administrative change. At some point there was a general sense, among policy makers and mass publics, that there was simply not much more that could be done through legislation and public administration to fix the undeniable problems of racial and sexual injustice that remained. The policy-making garbage can was simply empty of the crucial element of "ideas."

Even more narrowly focused advocacy coalitions experience the same phenomenon of "running out of steam" for the lack of further ideas. Consider the case of the "safety coalition" so prominent in US policy making in the 1960s (Walker 1977). It first mobilized around the issue of coal mine safety. That was a problem that had been widely discussed both in technical professional journals and in the wider public for some time; everyone had a pretty clear understanding of the nature of the problems and of what might constitute possible solutions. Having successfully enacted coal mine safety legislation, the safety coalition—like any good denizen of the policy-making garbage can—went looking for what to do next. Auto safety emerged. There, the issue was less "ripe," in the sense that there had been less discussion both in technical journals and in the public press. Still, auto safety legislation was enacted. What to do next? The safety coalition then seized upon "occupational health and safety," an issue about which there had been very little public discussion and little technical scientific discussion. A law was passed, but it was a law with little general backing that in effect discredited the safety coalition and inhibited it from playing any serious role in public policy discussions for more than a decade to come. It revived, in a different guise, only after the accident at the Three Mile Island nuclear reactor.

# 9. Puzzles, Problems, and Persuasion

Policy gets made in response to problems. But what is perceived as puzzling or problematic is not predetermined or fixed for all time. The public's policy agenda shifts as "personal troubles" shift into and out of the realm of perceived "social problems" (Mills 1959). In part, this is a matter of a gestalt shift as to "whose problem it is." And in part it is a matter of transforming sheer "puzzles" into "actionable problems:" if no solution can be envisaged, then for all *practical* purposes there simply is no problem.

The "progressive agenda" had the state assuming increasing responsibility for personal troubles (Rose-Ackerman 1992; Crenson 1998). The watch-cry of the opposite agenda is "personal responsibility," with the state washing its own hands of responsibility for "personal troubles" ranging from health to income security (Wikler 1987; Schmidtz and Goodin 1998). "Deinstitutionalization"—the decanting of asylums' inmates into cardboard boxes across America—is perhaps the saddest instance (Dear and Wolch 1987; Mechanic and Rochefort 1990). But in a way this twentieth-century morality play was just a re-enactment of the earlier processes by which seventeenth-century poor laws emerged as a solution to the public nuisance of vagrancy, only to be shifted over subsequent centuries to punitive regimes of workhouses in hopes of forcing the undeserving poor to take more responsibility for their own lives (Blaug 1963).

Policy is sometimes simply overtaken by events. Whole swathes of policy regulating obsolete technologies become redundant with technological advances. Military strategies designed to contain one opponent become redundant, or worse, when one's opponent shifts.

Policy disputes are often resolved by reframing. Lincoln's great genius, on one account, was reframing the argument over slavery: not as one over abolitionism; but rather as one over the extension of slavery to new territories, and the dangers for free white men in having to compete there against cheap slave labour (Hofstadter 1948, ch. 5).

Policy proposals gain political traction by "hitching a ride" on other policies more in tune with general social values. Described as "a free lunch," proposals for giving everyone a guaranteed basic income are politically dead in the water (Moynihan 1973). Described as "participation income," paying people for socially useful work— or better still, as a form of "workfare"—the same policies might be real runners, politically (Atkinson 1996; Goodin 2001).

Policy disputes are as often resolved by some telling new fact. The rights and wrongs of policies of nuclear deterrence had been hotly contested, both morally and strategically, for more than a quarter-century; but the unthinkable became truly unthinkable when Carl Sagan pointed out the risk that any large-scale use of nuclear weapons might initiate a "nuclear winter" destroying all life even in the country initiating the attack (Sagan 1983–4; see also Sagan and Turco 1990). Or again: the rights and wrongs of banning smoking in public places had been hotly contested for years; but once the risks of "passive smoking" became known, it ceased being a matter of moral dispute and became a straightforward issue of preventing public assaults (Goodin 1989).

Issues cease being issues for all sorts of reasons: some good, some bad. "Benign neglect" might have been the best way of treating all sorts of issues, ranging from race to abortion (Luker 1984). Making public policy can often be a mistake. But making an issue of child abuse and neglect was almost certainly not a mistake (Nelson 1984). The difference between those cases is that in the former there was a real risk of countermobilization undoing any good done by making de facto policies more public, whereas in the latter there seems little risk of countermobilization by or even on behalf of child abusers.

Thinking about the way issues become, or fail to become, policy "problems" takes us right back to the heart of the argument about the persuasive vocation of policy studies. We have argued that the grounds for this persuasive conception are formidable. They include the limits of instrumental rationality; the importance of deliberation in policy formation; the overwhelming evidence of the way modern governing conditions demand a style of policy making that maximizes consultation and voluntary coordination.

"High modernism" is an anachronism. Running modern government by its dictates is like trying to assemble motor cars on a replica of one of Ford's 1920s assembly lines—a recipe for defective production, when interacting components are not fully decomposable (Simon 1981).

But the pursuit of this persuasive vocation is a hard road to follow. It demands a unique combination of skills: the skills of "normal" social science allied to the skills of "rhetoric" in the best sense of that much misused word. And the persuasive vocation must be practised in a hostile world. There is hostility from pressed decision makers who feel impelled to make rapid decisions in the face of urgency or even crisis; hostility from the still powerful administrative doctrines associated with the high modernist project; and hostility from entrenched powers and interests threatened by more reflective and inclusive modes of decision. Intellectually anachronistic doctrines continue to flourish in the world of policy practice for a whole range of reasons, and all are applicable to the case of high modernism. Within bureaucracies and in the vastly rewarding consulting industries that have grown up around the New Public Management there is a huge investment—intellectual and financial—in the modernistic drive for measurement and hierarchical control (Power 1997). Individual crazes still sweep across policy worlds because they offer possibilities of evading democratic control: the enthusiasm for evidence-based policy making in arenas like health care is a case in point (Harrison, Moran, and Wood 2002). And in the promotion of one key variant of high modernism—globalization—key global management institutions like the World Bank and the IMF continue to promote standardized reform packages (Rodrik 1997; Stiglitz 2002; Cammack 2002).

So, in the end, the persuasive appeal comes back to power and interests. Which is to say, politics. Just as the founders of the policy sciences told us from the start.

Policy analysts use the imperfect tools of their trade not only to assist legitimately elected officials in implementing their democratic mandates, but also to empower some groups rather than others. Furthermore, policy is never permanent, made once and for all time. Puzzles get transformed into actionable problems, and policies get made on that basis. But that gives rise to further puzzlement, and the quest for ways of acting on those new problems. The persuasive task of policy making and analysis alike lodges in these dynamics of deciding which puzzle to solve, what counts as a solution, and whose interests to serve.

# References

AARON, H. J., and REISCHAUER, R. D. (eds.) 1999. *Setting National Priorities*. Washington, DC: Brookings Institution Press.

ACKERMAN, B. A., and FISHKIN, J. S. 2004. *Deliberation Day*. New Haven, Conn.: Yale University Press.

ALLISON, G. T., and ZELIKOW, P. 1999. *The Essence of Decision*, 2nd edn. Reading, Mass.: Longman.

AMERICAN SOCIETY FOR PUBLIC ADMINISTRATION (ASPA) 1984. *Code of Ethics*. Washington, DC: ASPA.

ANTON, T. J. 1980. *Administered Politics: Elite Political Culture in Sweden*. Boston: Martinus Nijhoff.

ARROW, K. J. 1962. The economic implications of learning by doing. *Review of Economic Studies*, 29: 155–73.

—— and HAHN, F. 1971. *General Competitive Analysis*. San Francisco: Holden-Day.

ATIYAH, P. S. 1979. *The Rise and Fall of Freedom of Contract*. Oxford: Clarendon Press.

ATKINSON, A. B. 1996. The case for a participation income. *Political Quarterly*, 67: 67–70.

—— CANTILLION, B., MARLIER, E., and NOLAN, B. 2002. *Social Indicators: The EU and Social Inclusion*. Oxford: Oxford University Press.

BARDACH, E. 1977. *The Implementation Game: What Happens after a Bill Becomes a Law*. Cambridge, Mass.: MIT Press.

—— 1980. On desiging implementable programs. In Majone and Quade 1980, 138–58.

BECK, U. 1992. *The Risk Society*, trans. M. Ritter. London: Sage.

BENTHAM, J. 1843/1787. Panopticon: or, the Inspection-House: Containing the idea of a new principle of construction applicable to penitentiary-houses, prisons, houses of industry, work-houses, poor-houses, manufactories, mad-houses, hospitals, and schools; with a plan of management adapted to the principle. In *The Works of Jeremy Bentham*, ed. J. Bowring, vol. iv. Edinburgh: William Tait.

BERRY, J. M. 1977. *Lobbying for the People*. Princeton, NJ: Princeton University Press.

BETTS, R. K. 1978. Analysis, war & decision: why intelligence failures are inevitable. *World Politics*, 31: 61–89.

BLAU, P. M. 1963. *The Dynamics of Bureaucracy*, 2nd edn. Chicago: University of Chicago Press.

BLAUG, M. 1963. The myth of the old poor law and the making of the new. *Journal of Economic History*, 23: 151–84.

BOVENS, M. A. P. 1990. The social steering of complex organizations. *British Journal of Political Science*, 20: 91–117.

—— 1998. *The Quest for Responsibility: Accountability and Citizenship in Complex Organizations*. Cambridge: Cambridge University Press.

—— and 'T HART, P. 1996. *Understanding Policy Fiascos*. New Brunswick, NJ: Transaction.

BRAITHWAITE, J., and DRAHOS, P. 2000. *Global Business Regulation*. Cambridge: Cambridge University Press.

—— MAKKAI, T., BRAITHWAITE, V., and GIBSON, D. 1993. *Raising the Standard*, Final Report of the Nursing Home Regulation in Action Project to the Department of Health, Housing and Community Services. Canberra: AGPS.

CAIN, B., DALTON, R., and SCARROW, S. (eds.) 2003. *Democracy Transformed? Expanding Political Opportunities in Advanced Industrial Democracies*. Oxford: Oxford University Press.

CALVERT, R., McCUBBINS, M. D., and WEINGAST, B. R. 1989. A theory of political control and agency discretion. *American Journal of Political Science*, 33: 588–61.

CAMMACK, P. 2002. The mother of all governments: the World Bank's matrix for global governance. Pp. 36–53 in *Global Governance: Critical Perspectives*, ed. R. Wilkinson and S. Hughes. London: Routledge.

CASTELLS, M. 2000. Materials for an exploratory theory of the network society. *British Journal of Sociology*, 51 (1): 5–24.

CASTLES, F. G. 1985. *The Working Class and the Welfare State: Reflections on the Political Development of the Welfare State in Australia and New Zealand, 1890–1980*. Sydney: Allen and Unwin.

—— 2001. A farewell to Australia's welfare state. *International Journal of Health Services*, 31 (3): 537–44.

COASE, R. H. 1937. The nature of the firm. *Economica*, 4: 386–405.

—— 1974. The market for goods and the market for ideas. *American Economic Review (Papers & Proceedings)*, 64 (2): 384–402.

COMMISSION ON PUBLIC–PRIVATE PARTNERSHIPS 2001. *Building Better Partnerships*. London: Institute for Public Policy Research.

COURPASSON, D. 2000. Managerial strategies of domination: power in soft bureaucracies. *Organization Studies*, 21: 141–61.

CRENSON, M. A. 1998. *Building the Invisible Orphanage: A Prehistory of the American Welfare System*. Cambridge, Mass.: Harvard University Press.

CROZIER, M., HUNTINGTON, S., and WATANUKI, J. 1975. *The Crisis of Democracy*. New York: New York University Press.

DAHL, R. A. 1985. *A Preface to Economic Democracy*. Berkeley: University of California Press.

DAY, P., and KLEIN, R. 1987. *Accountabilities: Five Public Services*. London: Tavistock.

DEAR, M. J., and WOLCH, J. R. 1987. *Landscapes of Despair: From Deinstitutionalization to Homelessness*. Princeton, NJ: Princeton University Press.

DERTHICK, M. 1975. *Uncontrollable Spending for Social Services Grants*. Washington, DC: Brookings Institution.

DEUTSCH, K. 1963. *The Nerves of Government*. Glencoe, Ill.: Free Press.

DICEY, A. V. 1960/1885. *Introduction to the Study of the Law of the Constitution*, 10th edn. London: Macmillan.

DOWNS, A. 1972. Up and down with ecology: the issue-attention cycle. *Public Interest*, 28: 38–50.

DRYZEK, J. S. 2000. *Deliberative Democracy and Beyond*. Oxford: Oxford University Press.

DUNLEAVY, P. 1981. *The Politics of Mass Housing 1945–75*. Oxford: Clarendon Press.

—— 1995. Policy disasters: explaining the UK's record. *Public Policy and Administration*, 10: 52–70.

DYSON, K. 1980. *The State Tradition in Western Europe*. Oxford: Martin Robertson.

—— and WILKS, S. (eds.) 1983. *Industrial Crisis: A Comparative Study of the State and Industry*. Oxford: Martin Robertson.

ESPING-ANDERSEN, G. 1985. *Politics against Markets*. Princeton, NJ: Princeton University Press.

ETZIONI, A. 1965. *A Comparative Analysis of Complex Organizations*. New York: Free Press.

FISCHER, F. 2003. *Reframing Public Policy: Discursive Politics and Deliberative Practices.* Oxford: Oxford University Press.

—— and FORESTER, J. (eds.) 1993. *The Argumentative Turn in Policy Analysis and Planning.* Durham, NC: Duke University Press.

FRIED, C. 2004. *Saying What the Law Is.* Cambridge, Mass.: Harvard University Press.

FUNG, A. 2004. *Empowering Democracy.* Chicago: University of Chicago Press.

—— and WRIGHT, E. O. 2001. Deepening democracy: innovations in empowered participatory governance. *Politics & Society,* 29 (1): 5–41.

GALANTER, M. 1974. Why the "haves" come out ahead: speculations on the limits of legal change. *Law & Society Review,* 9: 95–160.

GIBSON, D. M., and GOODIN, R. E. 1999. The veil of vagueness. Pp. 357–85 in *Organizing Political Institutions: Essays for Johan P. Olsen,* ed. M. Egeberg and P. Lægreid. Oslo: Scandinavian University Press.

GOODIN, R. E. 1982. *Political Theory & Public Policy.* Chicago: University of Chicago Press.

—— 1989. *No Smoking.* Chicago: University of Chicago Press.

—— 2001. Something for nothing? Pp. 90–8 in P. Van Parijs et al. *What's Wrong With a Free Lunch?,* ed. J. Cohen and J. Rogers. Boston: Beacon.

—— 2003. Democratic accountability: the distinctiveness of the Third Sector. *Archives européennes de sociologie,* 44: 359–96.

GOODSELL, C. T. 1992. The public administrator as artisan. *Public Administration Review,* 52: 246–53.

GORE, A. 1993. *From Red Tape to Results: Creating a Government that Works Better and Costs Less,* Report of the National Performance Review. Washington, DC: Government Printing Office.

GRANT, W. 1997. *The Common Agricultural Policy.* New York: St Martin's.

GREENSTEIN, F. I. 1982. *The Hidden-Hand Presidency: Eisenhower as Leader.* New York: Basic Books.

HAJER, M. A. 1995. *The Politics of Environmental Discourse.* Oxford: Clarendon Press.

—— 2003. Policy without polity? Policy analysis and the institutional void. *Policy Sciences,* 36: 175–95.

—— and WAGENAAR, H. (eds.) 2003. *Deliberative Policy Analysis.* Cambridge: Cambridge University Press.

HALBERSTAM, D. 1969. *The Best and the Brightest.* New York: Random House.

HALL, P. (ed.) 1989. *The Political Power of Economic Ideas.* Princeton, NJ: Princeton University Press.

HARRISON, S., MORAN, M., and WOOD, B. 2002. Policy emergence and policy convergence: the case of 'scientific-bureaucratic' medicine in the United States and the United Kingdom. *British Journal of Politics and International Relations,* 4(1): 1–24.

HART, H. L. A. 1961. *The Concept of Law.* Oxford: Clarendon Press.

HAVEMAN, R. H., and MARGOLIS, J. (eds.) 1983. *Public Expenditure & Policy Analysis.* Boston: Houghton Mifflin.

HECLO, H. 1978. Issue networks and the executive establishment. Pp. 87–124 in *The New American Political System,* ed. A. King. Washington, DC: American Enterprise Institute.

—— and WILDAVSKY, A. 1974. *The Private Government of Public Money.* London: Macmillan.

HENDERSON, P. D. 1977. Two British errors: their probable size and some possible lessons. *Oxford Economic Papers,* 29: 159–205.

HÉRITIER, A. 1999. *Public Policy-Making and Diversity in Europe: Escaping Deadlock.* Cambridge: Cambridge University Press.

HIRSCH, F. 1976. *Social Limits to Growth.* Cambridge, Mass.: Harvard University Press.

HIRSCHMAN, A. O. 1982. *Shifting Involvements: Private Interest and Public Action.* Oxford: Martin Robertson.

HITCH, C. J. 1958. Economics and military operations research. *Review of Economics & Statistics,* 40: 119–209.

—— and MCKEAN, R. N. 1960. *The Economics of Defense in the Nuclear Age.* Cambridge, Mass.: Harvard University Press.

HOFSTADTER, R. 1948. *The American Political Tradition and the Men Who Made It.* New York: Knopf.

HOGWOOD, B., and PETERS., B. G. 1985. *The Pathology of Public Policy.* Oxford: Clarendon Press.

HOOD, C. 1976. *The Limits of Administration.* London: Wiley.

—— 1983. *The Tools of Government.* London: Macmillan.

KATZ, R., and MAIR, P. 1995. Changing models of party organization and party democracy: the emergence of the cartel party. *Party Politics,* 1: 5–28.

KAUFMANN, F.-X., MAJONE, G., and OSTROM, V. (eds.) 1985. *Guidance, Control and Evaluation in the Public Sector.* Berlin: W. de Gruyter.

KECK, M., and SIKKINK, K. 1998. *Activists beyond Borders: Advocacy Networks in International Politics.* Ithaca, NY: Cornell University Press.

KING, A. 1975. Overload. *Political Studies,* 23: 284–96.

KINGDON, J. 1984. *Agendas, Alternatives and Public Policies.* Boston: Little, Brown.

KLEIN, R. 2001. *The New Politics of the NHS,* 4th edn. Harlow: Prentice Hall.

KNEESE, A. V., and SCHULTZE, C. L. 1975. *Pollution, Prices and Public Policy.* Washington, DC: Brookings Institution.

KORNAI, J., MASKIN, E., and ROLAND, G. 2003. Understanding the soft budget constraint. *Journal of Economic Literature,* 41 (4: Dec.): 1095–136.

LA PORTE, T. R. (ed.) 1975. *Organized Social Complexity.* Princeton, NJ: Princeton University Press.

LASSWELL, H. D. 1941. The garrison state. *American Journal of Sociology,* 46: 455–68.

—— 1950. *Politics: Who Gets What, When, How?* New York: P. Smith.

—— 1951. The policy orientation. In Lerner and Lasswell 1951, 3–15.

LE GRAND, J. 1991. Quasi-markets and social policy. *Economic Journal,* 101: 1256–67.

LERNER, D., and LASSWELL, H. D. (eds.) 1951. *The Policy Sciences.* Stanford, Calif.: Stanford University Press.

LEVI, M. 1988. *Of Rule and Revenue.* Berkeley: University of California Press.

LEVI-FAUR, D. 2003. The politics of liberalization: privatization and regulation-for-competition in Europe's and Latin America's telecoms and electric industries. *European Journal of Political Research,* 42 (5): 705–40.

LEVINE, H. D. 1977. Some things to all men: the politics of cruise missile development. *Public Policy,* 25: 117–68.

LIJPHART, A. 1999. *Patterns of Democracy.* New Haven, Conn.: Yale University Press.

LINDBLOM, C. E. 1965. *The Intelligence of Democracy.* New York: Free Press.

—— 1977. *Politics and Markets.* New York: Basic Books.

—— 1979. Still muddling: not yet through. *Public Administration Review,* 39: 517–26.

LIPSKY, M. 1980. *Street Level Bureaucracy.* New York: Russell Sage.

LOCKE, J. 1690. *Second Treatise of Government,* ed. P. Laslett. Cambridge: Cambridge University Press, 1960.

LUKER, K. 1984. *Abortion and the Politics of Motherhood.* Berkeley: University of California Press.

LYNN, N. B., and WILDAVSKY, A. (eds.) 1990. *Public Administration: The State of the Discipline.* Chatham, NJ: Chatham House.

MacDonagh, O. 1958. The nineteenth-century revolution in government: a reappraisal. *Historical Journal,* 1: 52–67.

—— 1961. *A Pattern of Government Growth, 1800–1860.* London: MacGibbon and Kee.

McFarland, A. S. 1976. *Public Interest Lobbies.* Washington, DC: American Enterprise Institute.

Mackenzie, W. J. M. 1963. The Plowden Report: a translation. *Guardian,* 25 May. Reprinted pp. 238–51 in Mackenzie, *Explorations in Government.* London: Macmillan, 1975.

Majone, G. 1989. *Evidence, Argument, and Persuasion in the Policy Process.* New Haven, Conn.: Yale University Press.

—— 1994. Paradoxes of privatization and deregulation. *Journal of European Public Policy,* 1 (1: June): 53–69.

—— and Quade, E. S. (eds.) 1980. *Pitfalls of Analysis.* Chichester: Wiley, for International Institute for Applied Systems Analysis.

Mansbridge, J. J. 1986. *Why We Lost the ERA.* Chicago: University of Chicago Press.

March, J. G. 1972. Model bias in social action. *Review of Educational Research,* 42: 413–29.

—— 1976. The technology of foolishness. In March and Olsen 1976, 69–81.

—— and Olsen, J. P. 1976. *Ambiguity and Choice in Organizations.* Bergen: Universitetsforlaget.

—— Sproul, L. S., and Tamuz, M. 1991. Learning from samples of one or fewer. *Organization Science,* 2: 1–13.

Marmor, T. R. 1994. *Understanding Health Care Reform.* New Haven, Conn.: Yale University Press.

—— and Thomas, D. 1972. Doctors, politics and pay disputes: "Pressure Group Politics" revisited. *British Journal of Political Science,* 2: 421–42.

Marris, P., and Rein, M. 1982. *Dilemmas of Social Reform,* 2nd edn. Chicago: University of Chicago Press. First pub. 1967.

Marshall, G. 1984. *Constitutional Conventions.* Oxford: Clarendon Press.

Meade, J. E. 1970. *The Theory of Indicative Planning.* Manchester: Manchester University Press.

Mechanic, D., and Rochefort, D. A. 1990. Deinstitutionalization: an appraisal of reform. *Annual Review of Sociology,* 16: 301–27.

Meijer, H. 1969. Bureaucracy and policy formulation in Sweden. *Scandinavian Political Studies,* 4: 102–16.

Merton, R. K. 1936. The unintended consequences of purposive social action. *American Sociological Review,* 1: 894–904.

Mills, C. W. 1959. *The Sociological Imagination.* New York: Oxford University Press.

Moran, M. 2003. *The British Regulatory State: High Modernism and Hyper-Innovation.* Oxford: Oxford University Press.

Moynihan, D. P. 1973. *The Politics of a Guaranteed Income: The Nixon Administration and the Family Assistance Plan.* New York: Random House.

Murray, C. 1984. *Losing Ground: American Social Policy, 1950–80.* New York: Basic.

Myrdal, G. 1944. *An American Dilemma.* New York: Harper and Row.

—— 1955. *Realities and Illusions in Regard to Inter-Governmental Organizations.* L. T. Hobhouse Memorial Trust Lecture, No. 24; delivered at Bedford College, London, 25 Feb. 1954. London: Oxford University Press.

Nelson, B. J. 1984. *Making an Issue of Child Abuse: Political Agenda Setting for Social Problems.* Chicago: University of Chicago Press.

Neustadt, R. E. 1960. *Presidential Power.* New York: Wiley.

—— and May, E. R. 1986. *Thinking in Time.* New York: Free Press.

NEWMAN, O. 1972. *Defensible Space: Crime Prevention through Urban Design.* New York: Macmillan.

NORTH, D. 1990. *Institutions, Institutional Change and Economic Performance.* Cambridge: Cambridge University Press.

OFFE, C. 1984. *Contradictions of the Welfare State.* Cambridge, Mass.: MIT Press.

—— 2003. The European model of "social" capitalism: can it survive European integration? *Journal of Political Philosophy,* 12: 437–69.

OLSEN, J. P. 1972*a*. Public policy-making and theories of organizational choice. *Scandinavian Political Studies,* 7: 45–62.

—— 1972*b*. Voting, "sounding out" and the governance of modern organisations. *Acta Sociologica,* 15: 267–84.

OSBORNE, D., and GAEBLER, T. 1993. *Reinventing Government.* New York: Plume/Penguin.

PAGE, B. I. 1983. *Who Gets What from Government?* Berkeley: University of California Press.

PETERS, B. G., and PIERRE, J. (eds.) 2003. *Handbook of Public Administration.* Thousand Oaks, Calif.: Sage.

—— —— 2004. *Politicization of the Civil Service in Comparative Perspective: The Quest for Control.* London: Routledge.

PIERSON, P. 1994. *Dismantling the Welfare State? Reagan, Thatcher, and the Politics of Retrenchment.* New York: Cambridge University Press.

—— 2000. Increasing returns, path dependence and the study of politics. *American Political Science Review,* 94 (2: June): 251–68.

PIVEN, F. F., and CLOWARD, R. A. 1979. *Poor People's Movements: Why They Succeed, How They Fail.* New York: Vintage Books.

POWER, M. 1997. *The Audit Society: Rituals of Verification.* Oxford: Oxford University Press.

PRESSMAN, J. L., and WILDAVSKY, A. 1973. *Implementation.* Berkeley: University of California Press.

PUTNAM, R. D. 1993. *Making Democracy Work: Civic Traditions in Modern Italy.* Princeton, NJ: Princeton University Press.

RAND CORPORATION 2004. History and mission. Available at: www.rand.org/about/history (accessed 10 July 2004).

REHBINDER, E., and STEWART, R. 1985. *Environmental Protection Policy.* Berlin: Walter de Gruyter.

REICH, R. B. (ed.) 1988. *The Power of Public Ideas.* Cambridge, Mass.: Ballinger.

REIN, M. 1976. *Social Science and Public Policy.* Harmondsworth: Penguin.

RHODES, R. A. W. 1988. *Beyond Westminster and Whitehall.* London: Unwin Hyman.

—— 1997. *Understanding Governance: Policy Networks, Governance and Accountability.* Buckingham: Open University Press.

RISSE, T., ROPP, S. C., and SIKKINK, K. (eds.) 1999. *The Power of Human Rights: International Norms and Domestic Change.* Cambridge: Cambridge University Press.

RIVLIN, A. M. 1971. *Systematic Thinking for Social Action.* Washington, DC: Brookings Institution.

RODRIK, D. 1997. *Has Globalization Gone Too Far?* Washington, DC: Institution of International Economics.

ROSE-ACKERMAN, S. 1992. *Rethinking the Progressive Agenda.* New York: Free Press.

—— 1996. Altruism, nonprofits and economic theory. *Journal of Economic Literature,* 34: 701–28.

SABATIER, P. A., and JENKINS-SMITH, H. C. (eds.) 1993. *Policy Change and Learning: An Advocacy Coalition Approach.* Boulder, Colo.: Westview.

SACKS, J. 1995. Shock therapy in Poland: perspectives of 5 years. *Tanner Lectures on Human Values*, 16: 265–90.

SAGAN, C. 1983–4. Nuclear war and climate consequence: some policy implications. *Foreign Affairs*, 62: 257–92.

—— and TURCO, R. 1990. *A Path Where No Man Thought: Nuclear Winter and the End of the Arms Race*. New York: Random House.

SALAMON, L. (ed.) 2002. *The Tools of Government: A Guide to the New Governance*. Oxford: Oxford University Press.

SALTMAN, R., and VON OTTER, C. 1992. *Planned Markets and Public Competition: Strategic Reform in Northern European Health Systems*. Buckingham: Open University Press.

SCHARPF, F. W. 1988. The joint decision trap: lessons from German federalism and European integration. *Public Administration*, 66: 239–78.

SCHMIDTZ, D., and GOODIN, R. E. 1998. *Social Welfare & Individual Responsibility*. Cambridge: Cambridge University Press.

SCHÖN, D. A., and REIN, M. 1994. *Frame Reflection: Toward the Resolution of Intractable Policy Controversies*. New York: Basic.

SCHULTZE, C. L. 1977. *The Public Use of Private Interest*. Washington, DC: Brookings Institution.

SCHUMPETER, J. A. 1950. *Capitalism, Socialism and Democracy*, 3rd edn. New York: Harper and Row.

SCOTT, J. C. 1985. *Weapons of the Weak*. New Haven, Conn.: Yale University Press.

—— 1997. *Seeing Like a State*. New Haven, Conn.: Yale University Press.

SELF, P. 1975. *Econocrats and the Policy Process: The Politics and Philosophy of Cost–Benefit Analysis*. London: Macmillan.

—— 1993. *Government by the Market?* London: Macmillan.

—— and STORING, H. 1962. *The State and the Farmer*. London: Allen and Unwin.

SHAPIRO, I. 1999. Enough of deliberation: politics is about interests and power. Pp. 28–38 in *Deliberative Politics*, ed. S. Macedo. New York: Oxford University Press.

SIMON, H. A. 1951. A formal theory of the employment relationship. *Econometrica*, 19: 293–305.

—— 1955. A behavioral theory of rational choice. *Quarterly Journal of Economics*, 69: 99–118.

—— 1981. *The Sciences of the Artificial*, 2nd edn. Cambridge, Mass.: MIT Press.

—— 2000. Public administration in today's world of organizations & markets. *PS: Political Science & Politics*, 33 (4: Dec.): 749–56.

SKOCPOL, T. 1992. *Protecting Soldiers and Mothers: The Political Origins of Social Policy in the United States*. Cambridge, Mass.: Harvard University Press.

SMITH, M. 1990. *The Politics of Agricultural Support in Britain: Development of the Agricultural Policy Community*. Aldershot: Dartmouth.

SMITH, S. R., and LIPSKY, M. 1993. *Non-Profits for Hire: The Welfare State in an Age of Contracting*. Cambridge, Mass.: Harvard University Press.

STEINER, J., BÄCHTIGER, A. B., SPÖRNDLI, M., and STEENBERGEN, M. R. 2005. *Deliberative Politics in Action: Cross-national Study of Parliamentary Debates*. Cambridge: Cambridge University Press.

STIGLITZ, J. E. 2002. *Globalization and its Discontents*. London: Penguin

STOKEY, E., and ZECKHAUSER, R. 1978. *A Primer for Policy Analysis*. New York: Norton.

SUNSTEIN, C. R. 1993. *Democracy and the Problem of Free Speech*. New York: Free Press.

—— 2001. *Republic.com*. Princeton, NJ: Princeton University Press.

TARROW, S. G. 1994. *Power in Movement: Social Movements, Collective Action and Politics*. New York: Cambridge University Press.

TILLY, C. 1999. Power—top down and bottom up. *Journal of Political Philosophy*, 7: 330–52.

UNION OF CONCERNED SCIENTISTS (UCS) 2004. *Scientific Integrity in Policymaking: An Investigation into the Bush Administration's Misuse of Science.* Available at: www.ucsusa.org/global_environment/rsi/page.cfm?pageID=1322 (accessed 10 July 2004).

US COMPTROLLER GENERAL 1979. *Higher Penalties Could Deter Violations of Nuclear Regulations.* Report to the Congress EMD-79-9. Washington, DC: General Accounting Office.

VAN EVERA, S. 2003. Why states believe foolish ideas: non-self-evaluation by states and societies. Ch. 19 in *Perspectives on Structural Realism*, ed. A. K. Hanami. New York: Palgrave.

VAN GUNSTEREN, H. 1976. *The Quest for Control.* London: Wiley.

VICKERS, G. 1983. *The Art of Judgment: A Study of Policy Making.* London: Harper and Row.

WALKER, J. L. 1969. The diffusion of innovations among the American states. *American Political Science Review*, 63: 880–99.

—— 1977. Setting the agenda in the U. S. Senate: a theory of problem selection. *British Journal of Political Science*, 7: 423–46.

WIKLER, D. 1987. Personal responsibility for illness. Pp. 326–58 in *Health Care Ethics*, ed. D. van de Veer and T. Regan. Philadelphia: Temple University Press.

WILDAVSKY, A. 1973. If planning is everything, maybe it's nothing. *Policy Sciences*, 4: 127–53.

—— 1979. *Speaking Truth to Power: The Art and Craft of Policy Analysis.* Boston: Little, Brown.

WILLIAMSON, O. E. 1985. *The Economic Institutions of Capitalism: Firms, Markets, Relational Contracting.* New York: Free Press.

WILSON, J. Q., and KELLING, G. L. 1982. Broken windows. *Atlantic Monthly*, 249 (3): 29–38.

WILSON, W. 1887. The study of administration. *Political Science Quarterly*, 2 (2: June): 197–222.

WILSON, W. J. 1987. *The Truly Disadvantaged: The Inner City, the Underclass and Public Policy.* Chicago: University of Chicago Press.

WORLD BANK 1994. *Averting the Old Age Crisis: Policies to Protect the Old and Promote Growth.* New York: Oxford University Press

—— 1996. *World Development Report 1996: From Plan to Market.* Oxford: Oxford University Press for the World Bank.

—— 1997. *The State in a Changing World: World Development Report 1997.* Washington, DC: World Bank.

YOUNG, I. M. 2000. *Inclusion and Democracy.* Oxford: Oxford University Press.

ZOLBERG, A. 1972. Moments of madness. *Politics & Society*, 2: 183–208.

# PART II

## INSTITUTIONAL AND HISTORICAL BACKGROUND

CHAPTER 2

............................................................................................................

# THE HISTORICAL
# ROOTS OF THE FIELD

............................................................................................................

## PETER DELEON

## 1. INTRODUCTION

............................................................................................................

By most accounts, the academic discipline generally referred to as the study of public policy grew out of the approach called the policy sciences.[1] The policy sciences approach has been primarily credited to the work of Harold D. Lasswell, writing in the late 1940s and early 1950s, most prominently articulated in his essay, "The policy orientation," which was the opening chapter to Lasswell and Daniel Lerner's *The Policy Sciences* (1951a; also see Lasswell 1949, 1971).[2] The policy sciences orientation was explicitly focused on the rigorous application of the sciences (hence, the plural usage of "sciences") to issues affecting governance and government. As Fischer (2003: 3) has recently observed:

Specifically, Lasswell wanted to create an applied social science that would act as a mediator between academics, government decision-makers, and ordinary citizens by providing object-ive solutions to problems that would narrow or minimize ... the need for unproductive political debate on the pressing policy issues of the day.

............................................................................................................

[1] One must immediately acknowledge that this reference, and indeed much of this essay, is "Ameri-can-centric," in that it mainly addresses the contemporary study of public policy in its American context. This emphasis in no way is intended to minimize the contributions of public policy scholars in European and Asian nations, who have made important contributions to the study of public policy.

[2] While this acknowledgement is generally accepted, its recognition is by no means universal; Beryl Radin traces the development of policy analysis in *Beyond Machiavelli* (2000) without mentioning Lasswell; rather, she singles out Yehezkel Dror (see Dror 1971) as the principal early contributor to the field.

In addition, Lasswell and his colleagues (e.g. Lasswell and Kaplan 1950) articulated a clear understanding of the necessity of overlaying the approach with the democratic ethos and processes, or what he defined as the "policy sciences of democracy," which "were directed towards knowledge needed to improve the practice of democracy" (Lasswell 1951*a*, 15). The distinctly democratic orientation grew directly out of Lasswell's animus towards the totalitarian regimes that were present in the world community during the interwar period (see Lasswell 1951*b*).

But if the rigorous study of public policy within the academy to provide advice to policy makers has a relatively short lineage, the concept has a lengthy history. Rulers have been the recipients of advice—often solicited—since at least the recording of history, a veritable cottage industry (see Goldhamer 1978 for details). At times ritualized—a priesthood grew around the prophetic rituals of the Greek Oracle at Delphi—and, more usually, personal or idiosyncratic—European diplomats during the seventeenth and eighteenth centuries were remarkably cosmopolitan in their allegiances—advisers to whomever was in power were rarely lacking. However, there is a clear distinction between the earlier purveyors of policy advice and the policy sciences, namely that policy advice to rulers rarely relied on extensive research, invariably was not recounted in policy memoranda (nor memoirs), nor subjected to protocols of "scientific" enquiry. A major exception, of course, was the remarkable Italian Renaissance diplomat Niccolò Machiavelli, but even *The Prince* (1950/1515) was more of a generalized set of observations than recommendations to any specific ruler or context. A more modern precursor might have been the "brains trust" assembled by President Franklin Roosevelt to help his administration counter the 1930s Great Depression, but this could easily be attributed to the unique confluence of conditions and personalities.

The turn of the twentieth century saw the beginnings of academic study of issues of public salience within the disciplines of political science and public administration, which some (e.g. Heineman et al. 2002) have suggested were the precursors of public policy studies. Later, political science and public administration perspectives rather naturally were directly extended into the public arena, as were relevant aspects found in the disciplines of law, history, sociology, psychology, public health (for instance, in the field of epidemiology), and anthropology. However, the policy sciences approach and its authors have deliberately distinguished themselves from these early academic contributions by posing three defining characteristics that, in combination, transcend the contributions ascribed to the individual disciplines:

1. The policy sciences are explicitly *problem oriented*, quite consciously addressing public policy problems and recommendations for their relief, while openly rejecting the study of a phenomenon for its own sake; the societal or political question of "so what?" has always been at the heart of the policy sciences' approach. Likewise, policy problems are seen to occur in a specific context, a context that must be carefully considered in terms of both the analysis and subsequent recommendations. For these reasons,
2. The policy sciences are distinctively *multidisciplinary* in their intellectual and practical approaches. The reasoning is straightforward: almost every social or

political problem has multiple components that are tied to the various academic disciplines without falling clearly into any one discipline's exclusive domain. Therefore, to gain a complete appreciation of the phenomenon, many relevant orientations must be utilized and integrated. Finally,

3. The policy sciences' approach is consciously and explicitly *value oriented*; in many cases, the central theme deals with the democratic ethos and human dignity.[3] This value orientation, first argued during the emphasis on behavioralism, i.e. "objectivism," in the social sciences, recognizes that no social problem nor methodological approach is value free. As such, to understand a problem, one must acknowledge its value components. Similarly, no policy scientist is without her or his own values, which also must be recognized, if not resolved, as Amy (1984) has discussed.[4] This realization will later surface at the heart of the post-positivist orientation.

Moving the policy sciences from the halls of academe to the offices of government largely occurred on the federal level during the 1960s (see Radin 2000), such that by the 1980s, virtually every federal office had a policy analysis branch, often under the title of a policy analysis and/or evaluation office. Since then, many states (including those with memberships in interstate consortia, such as the National Conference of State Legislatures) have moved in a similar direction, with the only constraints being financial. In addition, for-hire "think tanks" have proliferated seemingly everywhere (and of most every political orientation). Every public sector official would seemingly agree that more pertinent information on which to base decisions and policies is better than less. As such, there has seemingly been a widespread acceptance of the public policy approach and applications.

Concomitantly, virtually every American university has developed a graduate program in public affairs (or retooled its public administration program) to fill the apparent demand for sophisticated policy analysts. Yet the turn of the twenty-first century has hardly ushered in a Golden Age of Policy Advice. With every nook and cranny of government engaged in policy research and evaluation, why do policy scholars often voice the perception that their work is not being utilized? Donald Beam has characterized policy analysts as beset with "fear, paranoia, apprehension, and denial" and states that they do not "have as much confidence . . . about their

---

[3] H. D. Lasswell and Abraham Kaplan (1950, pp. xii, xxiv) dedicate the policy sciences to provide the "intelligence pertinent to the integration of values realized by and embodies in interpersonal relations," which "prizes not the glory of a depersonalized state of the efficiency of a social mechanism, but human dignity and the realization of human capabilities."

[4] A moment should be set aside to distinguish "policy analysis" (and the policy analyst) from the "policy sciences" (and its analogous policy scientist). Many (e.g. Radin 2000; Dunn 1981; Heineman et al. 2002) prefer the former. DeLeon (1988, 9; emphasis added) indicated that "Policy analysis is the most noted derivative and application of the tools and methodologies of the policy sciences' approach . . . [As such], policy analysis is generally considered a more discrete *genus* under the broader umbrella of the policy sciences *phylum*." For the purposes of this chapter, they are largely interchangeable. Fischer (2003, na. 1 and 4, pp. 1 and 3, respectively) is in agreement with deLeon in this usage.

value in the political process as they did 15 or 20 years ago" (Beam 1996, 430–1). Heineman and his colleagues (2002, 1, 9) are equally distressed in terms of policy access and results:

despite the development of sophisticated methods of inquiry, policy analysis has not had a major substantive impact on policymakers. Policy analysts have remained distant from power centers where policy decisions are made .... In this environment, the values of analytical rigor and logic have given way to political necessities.

We need not necessarily agree with all of these claims, but, in general, one can assert that the Lasswellian charge for the policy sciences has not been realized. This chapter attempts to understand this shortfall by tracing the political and cognitive evolutions of the policy sciences, and, in tandem, to offer some advice as to how the policy sciences might achieve some of their earlier goals. To these ends, let us first review the development of the policy sciences' approach, followed by an understanding of the disjunction between the goals of the policy sciences and the policy world, and, lastly, indicate some ways in which the two can become more in tune with each other.

## 2. THE DEVELOPMENT OF THE POLICY SCIENCES

In general, two paths have been proposed to outline the development of the policy sciences. Although they do not stand in opposition to one another, the respective chronologies of Beryl Radin (2000) and Peter deLeon (1998) offer contrasting emphases. Radin (2000) draws upon the heritage proffered by American public administration; for instance, in her telling, policy analytic studies represent a continuation of the early twentieth-century Progressive movement (also see Fischer 2003) in the United States, in particular, its emphases on scientific analysis of social issues and the democratic polity. Her depiction particularly characterizes the institutional growth of the policy approach, metaphorically relying on the (fictional) histories of an "old school" economist cum policy analyst (John Nelson) juxtaposed with a "younger," university-trained policy analyst (Rita Stone). Through them, she casts an institutional framework on the policy studies approach, indicating the progression from a limited analytic approach practiced by a relatively few practitioners (nominally from the RAND Corporation in California, which was the training ground for defense-turned-health analyst Nelson) to a growing number of government institutions and universities. Radin notes the emergence of analytic studies from the RAND Corporation to Robert McNamara's US Department of

Defense in the early 1960s under the guise of "systems analysis" and the Programmed Planning and Budget System (PPBS).[5]

From its apparent success in the Defense Department, PPBS, under President Lyndon Johnson's executive mandate, spread out into other government offices, such as the Department of Health, Education, and Welfare in the mid-1960s. Although PPBS never again enjoyed the great (and, to be fair, transitory) success that it did in the Defense Department (see Wildavsky 1979a), the analytic orientation was soon adopted by a number of federal offices, state agencies, and a large number of analytic consultant groups (see Fischer 1993; Ricci 1984).[6] Thus, Radin (2000) views the growth of the policy analyses as a "growth industry," in which a few select government agencies first adopted an explicitly innovative analytic approach, others followed, and an industry developed to service them. Institutional problems, such as the appropriate bureaucratic locations for policy analysis, arose but were largely overcome. In much the same theme, Gilmore and Halley (1994) address policy research issues as a function of intergovernmental relations. However, Radin's (2000) analysis pays hardly any attention to the hallmarks of the policy sciences approach: there is little direct attention to the problem orientation of the activity and the normative groundings of policy issues (and recommendations) are largely overlooked. As such, her analysis describes the end product of a movement towards institutional analysis, generally portraying a very positive image of the dissemination of the profession and its practitioners.

DeLeon (1988) offered a parallel but somewhat more complicated model, in which he linked analytic activities tied to specific political events (what he terms "supply," that is, events that provided analysts with a set of particular conditions to which they could apply their skills) with an evolving requirement for policy analysis within political circles and government offices ("demand," which represents a growing requirement for the product of policy analytic skills). His underlying assumption was that "supply" and "demand" are mutually dependent and, if the study of public policy is to be intellectually advanced and be utilized by policy makers, both must be present. In particular, he suggested the following political events as having been seminal in the development of the policy research, in terms of "lessons learned:"[7]

*The Second World War*, during which the United States marshaled an unprecedented number of social scientists—economists, political scientists, psychologists, etc.—to support the war effort. These activities established an important illustration of the ability of the social sciences to focus problem-oriented analysis on urgent

[5] See Hitch and McKean (1960) for an authoritative explanation.
[6] Radin (2000, 55) traces the development of the policy orientation through six "representative" analytic offices, chosen specifically to reflect the divergence of the approach: the Office of the Assistant Secretary for Planning and Evaluation in the US Department of Health and Human Services; the California Legislative Analyst's Office; the Center for Budget and Policy Priorities; the Congressional Research Service; the Heritage Foundation; and the Twentieth Century Fund.
[7] These are elaborated upon in deLeon 1988.

public issues, in this case ensuring victory over the Axis powers. In fact, Lasswell and Abraham Kaplan spent the war employed by the Library of Congress studying the use of propaganda techniques. This realization led directly to the postwar formation of the National Science Foundation (although more concerned at first with the physical sciences) and the Council of Economic Advisors, as well as research facilities such as the RAND Corporation (Smith 1966) and the Brookings Institution (Lyons 1969). However, in general, while the "supply" side of the policy equation was seemingly primed, there was little activity on the "demand" side, perhaps because of the post-Second World War society's desire to return to some semblance of "normalcy." As a result, the policy approach was more or less quiescent until the 1960s, and President Lyndon Johnson's declaration and implementation of

*The War on Poverty.* In the early 1960s, largely spurred by the emerging civil rights demonstrations, Americans took notice of the pervasive, debilitating poverty extant in "the other America" (Harrington 1963) and realized that, as a body politic, they were remarkably uninformed. Social scientists moved aggressively into this knowledge gap with unbridled enthusiasm but lacking consensus, producing what Moynihan (1969) called "maximum feasible misunderstanding." A vast array of social programs was initiated to address this particular war, with important milestones being achieved, especially in the improved statistical measures of what constituted poverty and evaluation measures to assess the various anti-poverty programs (see Rivlin 1970) and, of course, civil rights. Walter Williams (1998), looking back on his days in the Office of Economic Opportunity (OEO), has suggested that these were the "glory days" of policy analysis. Other OEO veterans, such as Robert Levine (1970), were more reserved, while some, such as Murray (1984), went so far as to indicate that with the advent of the anti-poverty, anti-crime, and affirmative action programs, the American poor was actually "losing ground." At best, policy analysts were forced to confront the immense complexity of the social condition and discover that in some instances, there were no "easy" answers. DeLeon (1988, 61) later summarized the result of the War on Poverty as "a decade of trial, error, and frustration, after which it was arguable if ten years and billions of dollars had produced any discernible, let alone effective, relief."[8] One reason for the noted shortcomings was that the attention of the American public and its policy makers was sorely distracted by

*The Vietnam War.* In many senses, the Vietnam War brought the tools of public policy analysis, including applied systems analytic techniques, to life-and-death combat situations, a condition exacerbated by the growing civil unrest as to its conduct of the war and, of course, the loss of life suffered by its participants. The war was closely monitored by the Defense Secretary McNamara's office, with intense scrutiny from Presidents Kennedy, Johnson, and Nixon; these analysts were, in the words of David Halberstam, "the best and the brightest" (1972). But it became increasingly obvious that analytic rigor—specified in metrics such as "body counts," ordnance expended, and supplies moved—and "rational" decision making were not only misleading in terms of the war's progress, but were surely not indicative of the

---

[8] For details regarding the War on Poverty, see Aaron 1978; Kershaw and Courant 1970; Nathan 1985.

growing rancor that the war generated among American citizens. Too often there was evidence that the "hard and fast" numbers were being manipulated to serve military and political purposes. Moreover, systems analysis was neither cognitively nor viscerally able to encompass the almost daily changes in the war's activities occurring in both the international and the domestic arena. At the time, Colin Gray (1971) argued that systems analysis, one of the apparent US advantages of defense policy making, turned out to be a major shortcoming of the American war effort and was a partial contributor to the ultimate US failures in Vietnam. Finally, and most tellingly, Defense Department analysis could not appreciate the required (and re-spective) political wills necessary to triumph, or, in the case of this war, outlast the opponent. Frances FitzGerald's *Fire in the Lake* (1972) foretold the imminent Ameri-can military disaster as a function of the almost unlimited resources (including human lives) that the North Vietnamese were willing to expend in what they saw as the defense of their nation. In the latter years of the war, as the USA struggled to maintain its commitments, the Vietnam policies of President Richard Nixon segued unmistakably into

*The Watergate scandals.* The sordid events surrounding the re-election of President Nixon in the early 1970s, his administration's heavy-handed attempts to "cover up" the tell-tale incriminating signs, and his willingness to covertly gather evidence on Vietnam War protester Daniel Ellsberg led to the potential impeachment of an American president, averted only because President Nixon chose to resign in igno-miny rather than face congressional impeachment proceedings (Olson 2003). The overwhelming evidence of wrongdoing in the highest councils of the US government clearly brought home to the public that moral norms and values were central to the activities of government; to amass illegal evidence (probably through unconstitu-tional means) undermining those norms was an unpardonable political act. The Ethics in Government Act (1978) was only the most visible realization that normative standards were central to the activities of government, validating, as it were, one of the central tenets of the policy sciences. Regardless, however, few will ever forget the President of the United States protesting, "I am not a crook," and its effect on the public's trust in its elected government, a condition soon to be exacerbated by

*The energy crisis of the 1970s.* If the early 1960s' wellspring of analytic efforts was the War on Poverty and the late 1960s' was Vietnam, the energy crises of the 1970s provided ample grounds for the best analytic efforts the country could bring to bear. With highly visible gasoline shortages and record high energy prices throughout the nation, the public was inundated with multiple policy descriptions and formulas as to the level of petroleum reserves (domestic and worldwide) and competing energy sources (e.g. nuclear vs. petroleum vs. solar), all over differing (projected) time horizons; finally, as a backdrop framing these issues, hung the specter of threatened national security (for example, see Deese and Nye 1981; Stobaugh and Yergin 1979). With this plethora of technical data, seemingly the analytic community was prepared to bring light out of the darkness. But this was not to be the case; as Weyant was later to note, "perhaps as many as two-thirds of the [energy] models failed to achieve their avowed purposes in the form of direct application to policy problems" (quoted in Weyant 1980, 212). The contrast was both striking and apparent: energy policy was awash in technical considerations (e.g. untapped petroleum reserves and complex technical modeling; see Greenberger, Brewer, and Schelling 1983) but the basic decisions were decidedly political (that is, *not* driven by analysis), as President Nixon declared "Project Independence," President Carter intoned that energy independence represented the "moral equivalency of war" (cattily acronymed into MEOW), and President Ford created a new Department of Energy (see Commoner 1979). There was seemingly a convergence between "analytic supply" and "government demand," yet the inherent complexity of the issues effectively resolved little, that is, no policy consensus was achieved, a condition that did little to enshrine the policy sciences approach with either its immediate clients (government officials) or its ultimate beneficiaries (the citizenry).

Since these historical events were first proposed as events that shaped the development of the policy sciences (deLeon 1988), there have been more than twenty-five years in which numerous political events have occurred that, in retrospect, might have affected the development of public policy studies. These include at least three declared wars in which the United States military has invaded nations, revolutionary legislation to reform regulatory and welfare policies, and a presidential impeachment by the US Congress. While one might make cases for these and (possibly) other events, sufficient evidence and analytic "distance" need to be accumulated before these can be examined through the "supply" and "demand" metaphor.

To summarize: These larger constellations of public events have manifested themselves in a general constellation in the way in which the American people view their government and its processes and, as a result, the role that public policy research could play in informing government policy makers. From the immense national pride that characterized the victory over totalitarian forces in the Second World War, the American public has suffered a series of disappointments and disillusionments in the public policy arena, ranging from what many consider to be a problematic War on Poverty to an ongoing policy stalemate in energy policy to a failed war in South-East Asia to the resignation of a twice-elected president. Thus, there should be little surprise when scholars like E. J. Dionne write *Why Americans Hate Politics* (1991) or Joseph Nye and colleagues edit a book *Why Americans Don't Trust Government* (1997). Most damaging, of course, to the policy sciences' tradition is Christopher Lasch's pointed and hardly irrelevant question: "does democracy have a future?...It isn't a question of whether democracy *can* survive...[it] is whether democracy *deserves* to survive" (Lasch 1995, 1, 85; emphases added),

One needs to be balanced. The picture of post-Second World War American public policy hardly represents a crown of thorns. In many ways, the American quality of political life has benefited directly and greatly from public policy making, ranging from the Marshall Plan (which effectively halted the march of European communism after the Second World War) to the GI Bill (which brought the benefits of higher education to an entire generation of American men) to Medicare/Medicaid (1964) to the American civil rights movements to a flowering of environmental programs to (literally) men on the moon. However, as Derek Bok (1997) has pointed out,

American expectations and achievements have hardly produced universal progress compared to other industrialized nations, with crime, the environment, health care, and public education being only four examples. What motivated the spread of the public policy orientation was the expectation that well-trained, professional analysts, appropriately focused, would produce an unbroken succession of policy successes. As Richard Nelson (1977) wondered, if America could put a man on the moon, why was it unable to solve the problems of the urban ghetto? Nelson suggested, and the narratives above second, that the promise of the policy sciences has not been fulfilled. All of which leads one to ask a series of questions, assuming, naturally, that this promise is still worthwhile, i.e. not impossible: Why are some examples of policy research more successful than others? Or, is there a public policy "learning curve?" What does it resemble and to whom? What is its trajectory? And where is it going?

Finally, it is important to observe that political activities and results are not synonymous with the practice of the public policy or the policy sciences. But they certainly reside in the same policy space. For the policy sciences to meet the goals of improving government policy through a rigorous application of its central themes, then the failures of the body politic naturally must be at least partially attributed to failure of, or at least a serious shortfall in, the policy sciences' approach. To ask the same question from an oppositional perspective: Why should the nominal recipients of policy research subscribe to it if the research does not reflect the values and intuitions of the client policy maker, that is, in their eyes, does not represent any discernible value added? To this question, one needs to add the issue of democratic governance, a concept virtually everybody would agree upon until the important issues of detail emerge (see deLeon 1997; Barber 1984; Dahl 1990/1970), e.g. does direct democracy have a realistic place in a representative, basically pluralist democracy?

# 3. "... Miles to Go Before I Sleep"

Robert Frost, in his "Stopping in the Woods on a Snowy Evening" (published in 1923), was certainly not concerned with the relevance of the public policy in general and, in particular, the institutional viability of the policy sciences. Still, in writing

> The woods are lovely, dark and deep,
> But I have many promises to keep
> And miles to go before I sleep,

he does provide an allusion to what ails the contemporaneous relationship between policy makers and their would-be advisers, a relationship tempered by the history of the policy sciences and their applications, one rife with institutional complexity, with much to promise, and "miles" to go before those promises are realized. What necessary services or goods are policy makers asking from their policy advisers and how can the policy scientist best (as a function of quality and integrity) respond? Inherent in this question is a principal assumption: policy advisers, in the words of Aaron Wildavsky (1979b), must "speak truth to power." That is, without access to and the ear of policy makers, the policy sciences lose their sine qua non; they have been, from their earliest iteration, an applied (inter)discipline: if they need to re-ask Robert Lynn's question, *Knowledge for What?* (1939); if the study of public policy becomes irrelevant through lack of application or, to borrow deLeon's metaphor, if (policy) advice does not match (political) consent, then—let us be candid—the policy sciences have failed to meet the challenges spelled out by Lasswell, Dror, and the other pioneers in their efforts.

There are two possible explanations that might address this worrisome condition. The first, and more optimistic reading is that the policy research community is still maturing in terms of a necessary set of skills and applications. Brewer and Lövgren (1999, 315) allude to this possibility during a Swedish symposium on environmental research:

While the demand for interdisciplinary work is large and apparently growing, our capacity to engage in it productively is not keeping pace. This is not to say that genuine knowledge about complex problems and the requisite theories, methods, and practices to confront them is unfamiliar. Instead, we seem to be facing numerous challenges—intellectual, practical, and organization—that impede our efforts to engage problems effectively.

This explanation suggests that with a bit more theory and practice, typically through a greater application of interdisciplinary activity, more receptive client organizations, and a few more tractable problems, there is little wrong with the policy sciences approach that a normal cognitive maturation process might not remedy. However, in fairness, this promise was laid out by the policy sciences' originating fathers (and others; see Merton 1936) more than a half-century ago and is still awaiting consummation. Moreover, the extant public policy theories are at best only "under construction" rather than in the testing stage (see Sabatier 1999). Few public policy scholars today deride the value of an interdisciplinary approach (e.g. see Karlqvist 1999 and Fischer 2003); in the hands of a careful student of democratic practices, like Robert Putnam in *Making Democracy Work* (1993), it clearly is of great worth and value. However, even if this interdisciplinary possibility is widely seen as both valid and persuasive, then it is still imperative to measure out other ameliorative elements of the policy sciences besides an interdisciplinary approach, a compliant client, or a few more methodological tools.

An alternative (and admittedly more pessimistic) reading is that the policy sciences approach is losing whatever currency it once held among policy makers, policy scholars, and the cognizant publics. If so, one needs to explore possible reasons. To borrow a phrase used by Martin Rein and Donald Schön (1993), in a political system characterized by pluralism, there is an inherent-bordering-upon-intractable problem in reaching a consensus on "framing" the analysis (also see Schön and Rein 1994). In Rein and Schön's (1993, 146) description, "framing is a way of selecting, organizing, interpreting, and making sense of a complex reality to provide guideposts for knowing, analyzing, persuading, and acting." John Dryzek (1993, 222) agrees with Rein and Schön in terms of framing's centrality but also comments on the difficulty in framing policy discourse: "each frame treats some topics as more salient than others, defines social problems in a unique fashion, commits itself to particular value judgments, and generally interprets the world in its own particular and partial way..... [Not surprisingly] frames are not easily adjudicated." (A thought problem for the enthusiast: How have "framing" problems affected the US commitment to the recurrent Middle East crises, to say nothing of the shortcomings of the American public education system or US environmental/energy policy?) In an American political and social system often defined by polar politics and overwhelming complexity that result in a general lack of consensus, reaching agreements on how best to frame policy issues could be tantamount to impossible or, more likely, something to be "put aside" until the next political crisis forces a temporary consensus, which, of course, dissipates when the crisis passes. To pose the question frankly: again, in an applied context, what "value added" does the study of public policy and the policy sciences bring to a political policy-making process that is often and decidedly unanalytic?

Once we have asked these questions, of course, we should not necessarily subscribe to a counsel of despair or unnecessarily rend our collective sackcloth. But it is important to recognize that the policy sciences as a fruitful exercise for future policy makers is not a foregone conclusion, as we have enumerated above, and not necessarily as it has been traditionally presented. If for no other reason, time and conditions have changed. In all likelihood, Lasswell and his colleagues never considered their framework to be forever sacrosanct or beyond amendment. Douglas Torgerson (1986, 52–3; emphasis in original) speaks to this issue:

The dynamic nature of the [policy sciences] phenomenon is rooted in an internal tension, a *dialectic opposition between knowledge and politics.* Through the interplay of knowledge and politics, different aspects of the phenomenon become salient at different moments...the presence of dialectical tension means that the phenomenon has the potential to develop, to change its form. However, no particular pattern of development is inevitable.

What then might be some signposts for the continued development and application of the policy sciences, or what Dan Durning (1999) has described as "The transition from traditional to postpositive policy analysis?" A more precise criterion as well as introducing a new approach is offered by Maarten Hajer and Hendrik Wagenaar (2003a: 4; emphasis in original): "*What kind of policy analysis might be relevant to understanding governance in an emerging social network society?*" Furthermore, Hajer and Wagenaar (2003a: 15) speak directly to the normative compass of the policy sciences: "Whatever we have to say about the nature and foundation of the policy sciences, its litmus test will be that it must 'work' for the everyday reality of modern democracy." Who and what, in Laurence Lynn's (1999) expression, warrants "a place at the [public policy] table" and why? One can posit that the traditional public policy analytic mode, primarily based on a social welfare model (for example, see Weimer and Vining 2005) has not proven particularly successful when applied to the political arena (as, indeed, the post-positivists argue; see below), an arena marked more by backroom compromise than theoretic-elegant solutions. Thus, we are enjoined to consider a broader set of approaches and methodologies beyond those adopted whole cloth from microeconomics and operations research. As such, we need to examine thoughtfully various aspects of the post-positivist research orientations.

Hajer and Wagenaar (2003a) have presented an innovative central concept to the policy sciences methodological tool kit; that is, the idea of *social networks* under a democratic, participative regime.[9] This orientation is reflected in three conditions. First, increasingly, observers of public policy issues no longer look at specified governmental units (say, the Department of Commerce for globalization issues or the Department of Education's mission to "leave no child behind") per se. Rather, they tend to examine *issue* networks, including governmental units on the federal *and* state *and* municipal levels; these are constantly seen to be interacting with important non-profit organizations (NPOs) on both the national and the local levels, and various representations from the private sector as well (Heclo 1977; Carlsson 2000). Research in health care, education, social welfare, the environment, indeed, even national security (in terms of protecting the citizen against terrorist threats; see Kettl 2004) suggests the rise of the social network phenomenon. All of these actors are engaging in what Hajer (1993) called "policy discourses," hopefully, but not always, of a cooperative nature. Second, of equal importance to the policy sciences, they must continue to expound a democratic orientation, or what Mark Warren (1992) has termed an "expansive democracy," one featuring an enlarged component of public participation, often in the direct democratic vein and, more commonly now, without the traditional political party serving as an intermediary; the alternative is what Dryzek once balefully referred to as "the policy sciences of tyranny" (Dryzek 1989, 98), when bureaucratic and technological elites assume governance roles (see Fischer 2003). Third, and in conjunction with the first two, the policy sciences need to assimilate the decentralization tendencies of political systems that are so vital to contemporary public management processes, often under the heading of the "new" public management (e.g. Osborne and Gaebler 1992), but also an integral part of the participatory policy analysis themes (deLeon 1997; Mayer 1997; Fischer 2000).

In many ways, the inclusion of a post-positivist orientation in public policy theory and practice could mark a fractious transition within the community of policy researchers, for a number of reasons. There is the potential for an internecine brouhaha between the positivist and post-positivist advocates. Historically, the public policy "track record" has characteristically been based on a social welfare economics, i.e. a largely empirical, analytic approach; there are significant intellectual investments (to say nothing of a large education infrastructure) supporting this endeavor. However, there are numerous scholars who suggest that the prevailing quantitative orientation is precisely the problem and the positivist approach should

---

[9] Scott (1991) and Wasserman and Faust (1994) offer thorough introductions to social network analysis.

be held intellectually accountable for the shortcomings observed. Many scholars of the post-positivist bent—Frank Fischer (2003), John Dryzek (1990, 2000), Ronald Brunner (1991), Maarten Hajer (1993; with Wagenaar 2003a)—have identified what they claim to be serious epistemological failures of the positivist approach, assumptions, and results, offering historical examples (above) that seem to be supportive. Dryzek (1990, 4–6) has been particularly scathing in his assessments of positivism, especially what he (and others) call "instrumental rationality," which, he claims:

destroys the more congenial, spontaneous, egalitarian, and intrinsically meaningful aspects of human association ... represses individuals ... is ineffective when confronted with complex social problems ... makes effective and appropriate policy analysis impossible ... [and, most critically] is antidemocratic.

But, as Laurence Lynn (1999) has convincingly argued, many lucid and powerful (and in some cases, unexpected) insights have been gleaned from the collective analytic (read: positivist) corpus conducted over the past fifty years (such as in the field of criminal justice, public transportation, and social welfare policy) and there is little reason to suspect that future analysts would want to exorcize these modes. Alice Rivlin (1970) suggested years ago that we might not have arrived at many definitive answers to vexing public problems, but policy research has at least permitted us to ask more appropriate questions. This capability should not be treated lightly, for asking the right questions is surely the first step in deriving the right answers.

Neither side of this divide, then, is without valid debating points as they set forth the future directions for the study of public policy. More important, however, is that the scholars of the positivist and post-positivist persuasions should not intellectually isolate themselves from one another. Few social welfare or health policy economists would deny that there are important variables outside the economic orbit in most social transfer equations; why else would they concern themselves about issues of equity? Similarly, few proponents of an "interpretative analysis" would simply eliminate the calculation of expenses deriving from differing bond rates underlying urban renewal opportunities from their analysis. The policy problem—as any analyst of most any stripe will agree—must be defined in terms of what methodologies are relevant by the context (see deLeon 1998), not by an analyst's preferred methodologies, as Lynn (1999) implies in his criticism of the post-positivist approach. The alternative diagnosis comes dangerously close to Abraham Kaplan's (1964) famous "law of the instrument:" when all you have is a hammer, the whole world looks like a nail.

In this case, social network theory might not only describe a new conceptual approach to viewing the policy world, but it also provides an intellectual bridge that both sides of the positivist–post-positivist divide can accept. And, to be sure, there are already some "bridging" methodologies, such as Q-sort (Durning 1999) and social network analysis, that both camps can possibly share.[10] But the key to the continued development of the policy sciences and public policy research community in general is the ability to countenance and assimilate new concepts as *a function of the problem*

---

[10] Steven Brown (1980) is arguably the best reference for those wishing to engage in Q-sort analysis.

*statement,* i.e. the problem context, as their analytic lodestone. This suggests a willingness to utilize whichever approach is best suited for the analysis at hand. A favorable harbinger in this regard is the recognition of a more ecumenical set of methodological approaches and the importance of process *and* substance, as evidenced in the more recent policy analysis textbooks (e.g. Weimer and Vining 2005; MacRae and Whittington 1997).

The democratic theme, a central part of the policy sciences' Lasswellian heritage, has been emphasized of late in terms of "participatory policy analysis" (PPA), or the active involvements (or "discourse" or "deliberation" or "deliberative democracy") of citizens in the formulation of policy agenda.[11] James Fishkin (1991, 1995) has engaged in a series of carefully structured public deliberations as a means to bring public awareness and discursive involvement to political policy making. But the deliberative role in public policy making has also been derided as being simply "too cumbersome" or "too time intensive;" in the problematic search for consensus, its products are too ambiguous; some characterize it as little more than a publicity exercise in which the opposing group that has the more robust vocal chords or tenacity or resources is the invariable winner; deLeon (1997) has suggested that there are contingencies in which technical expertise and/or expediency are crucial for decision making; and, as Lyons and his colleagues (1992) have written, participatory policy analysis does not necessarily result in greater citizen participation, knowledge of the problem, or even satisfaction; indeed, James Madison's *Federalist Papers* (number 10) carefully warned about the dangers of popular participation in government.

There are, in short, many obstacles to participatory policy analysis that would caution its universal dissemination. However, it does need to be recognized that there have been some instances in which PPA has performed admirably, mostly, of course, on local levels (for examples, see Kathlene and Martin 1991; Gutmann and Thompson 1996; deLeon 1997) and in many cases of environmental mediations (Beierle and Cayford 2002; Fischer 2000). In short, the democratic ethos is such a fundamental bedrock of the American polity that it is difficult to countenance an ideology or orientation that could supplant it (Dahl 1998). In that regard, there appear to be ample grounds for a more systematic examination and application of PPA.

Lastly, in both the public and private sectors, the American polity is undergoing the decentralization of the nation's political processes. The current literature on public management talks extensively about the "devolution" of power from the federal government down to state and municipal governments, a phenomenon manifested by the Welfare Reform Act and the Telecommunication Act (both 1996). To some, for instance, centralized government regulation has become little more than an antiquated (perhaps dysfunctional) concept, as easily abandoned as the bustle. If these trends continue, various aspects of the policy sciences—such as PPA and social network theories—are certain to become more pivotal in addressing the potential effects of decentralized authority; e.g. what measures would be necessary to ensure public accountability? One obvious concern is that policy researchers will

---

[11] See Dryzek 1990, 2000; Renn et al. 1993; Elster 1998; Forester 1999; Fischer 2003; deLeon 1997.

need to assimilate a new set of analytic skills dealing with education and negotiation and mediation, that is, helping to forge policy design and implementation rather than advise policy makers, which raises another recurring dilemma, impartiality.

# 4. CONCLUSION

The policy sciences were developed in part as the "policy sciences of democracy... directed towards knowledge to improve the practice of democracy" (Lasswell 1951*a*, 14) and in recognition of providing "intelligence pertinent to the integration of values realized by and embodied by interpersonal relations [such as] human dignity and the realization of human capacities" (Lasswell and Kaplan 1950, 15). These represent their conceptual bedrock. But, having said this, the world has surely changed since the early 1950s. With these changes, it would be quixotic to suggest that the policy sciences as an intellectual orientation have remained somehow constant. To this end, we have offered some new approaches that could be readily incorporated into the body of the policy sciences' approach.

As we have pointed out, then, some changes are necessary to "improve" the policy sciences' processes and the results; stasis is hardly an option. However, to surrender the hallmarks of the policy sciences' approach would be tantamount to giving up the (relevance) candle to satisfy the (Lasswellian) flame. For these reasons, a continuing dialogue is necessary to assure that both the candle and the flame will endure and shed light on their appointed subjects.

## REFERENCES

AARON, H. J. 1978. *Politics and the Professors: The Great Society in Perspective.* Washington, DC: Brookings Institution.

AMY, D. J. 1984. Why policy analysis and ethics are incompatible. *Journal of Policy Analysis and Management,* 3 (4: Summer): 573–91.

BARBER, B. 1984. *Strong Democracy: Participatory Politics for a New Age.* Berkeley: University of California Press.

BEAM, D. R. 1996. If public ideas are so important now, why are policy analysts so depressed? *Journal of Policy Analysis and Management,* 15 (3: Fall): 430–7.

BEIERLE, T. C., and CAYFORD, J. J. 2002. *Democracy in Practice: Public Participation in Environmental Decisions.* Washington, DC: Resources for the Future.

BOK, D. 1997. Measuring the performance of governing. Ch. 2 in *Why People Don't Trust Government,* ed. J. S. Nye, Jr., P. D. Zelikow, and D. C. King. Cambridge, Mass.: Harvard University Press.

Brewer, G. D., and Lövgren, K. 1999. The theory and practice of interdisciplinary research. *Policy Sciences*, 32 (4: Dec.): 315–17.

Brown, S. R. 1980. *Political Subjectivity: Applications of Q Methodology in Political Science.* New Haven, Conn.: Yale University Press.

Brunner, R. D. 1991. The policy movement as a policy problem. *Policy Sciences*, 24 (1: Feb.): 295–331.

Carlsson, L. 2000. Policy networks as collective action. *Policy Studies Journal*, 28 (3): 502–27.

Commoner, B. 1979. *The Politics of Energy.* New York: Alfred A. Knopf.

Dahl, R. A. 1990/1970. *After the Revolution.* New Haven, Conn.: Yale University Press.

—— 1998. *On Democracy.* New Haven, Conn.: Yale University Press.

Deese, D. A., and Nye, J. (eds.) 1981. *Energy and Security.* Cambridge, Mass.: Ballinger.

deLeon, P. 1988. *Advice and Consent: The Development of the Policy Sciences.* New York: Russell Sage Foundation.

—— 1997. *Democracy and the Policy Sciences.* Albany, NY: SUNY Press.

—— 1998. Models of policy discourse: insights vs. prediction. *Policy Studies Journal*, 26 (1: Spring): 147–61.

Dionne, E. J. 1991. *Why Americans Hate Politics.* New York: Simon and Schuster.

Dror, Y. 1971. *Design for the Policy Sciences.* New York: American Elsevier.

Dryzek, J. S. 1989. The policy sciences of democracy. *Polity*, 22 (1, Fall) 97–118.

—— 1990. *Discursive Democracy: Politics, Policy, and Political Science.* Cambridge: Cambridge University Press.

—— 1993. Policy analysis and planning: from science to argument. Pp. 213–32 in *The Argumentative Turn in Policy Analysis and Planning*, ed. F. Fischer and J. Forester. Durham, NC: Duke University Press.

—— 2000. *Deliberative Democracy and Beyond.* Oxford: Oxford University Press.

Dunn, W. N. 1981. *Public Policy Analysis.* Englewood Cliffs, NJ: Prentice Hall.

Durning, D. 1999. The transition from traditional to postpositivist policy analysis: a role for Q-methodology. *Journal of Policy Analysis and Management*, 18 (5: Summer): 389–410.

Elster, J. (ed.) 1998. *Deliberative Democracy.* New York: Cambridge University Press.

Fischer, F. 1993. Policy discourse and the politics of Washington think tanks. Pp. 21–42 in *The Argumentative Turn in Policy Analysis and Planning*, ed. F. Fischer and J. Forester. Durham, NC: Duke University Press.

—— 2000. *Citizens, Experts, and the Environment: The Politics of Local Knowledge.* Durham, NC: Duke University Press.

—— 2003. *Reframing Public Policy.* Oxford: Oxford University Press.

Fishkin, J. S. 1991. *Democracy and Deliberation.* New Haven, Conn.: Yale University Press.

—— 1995. *The Voice of the People: Public Opinion and Democracy.* New Haven, Conn.: Yale University Press.

Fitzerald, F. 1972. *Fire in the Lake.* Boston: Little, Brown.

Forester, J. 1999. *The Deliberative Practitioner: Encouraging Participative Planning Processes.* Cambridge, Mass.: MIT Press.

Gilmore, R. S., and Halley, A. A. (eds.) 1994. *Who Makes Public Policy?* Chatham, NJ: Chatham House.

Goldhamer, H. 1978. *The Adviser.* New York: American Elsevier.

Gray, C. 1971. What has Rand wrought? *Foreign Policy*, 4 (Fall): 111–29.

GREENBERGER, M., BREWER, G. D., and SCHELLING, T. 1984. *Caught Unawares: The Energy Decade in Retrospect.* Cambridge, Mass.: Ballinger.

GUTMANN, A., and THOMPSON, D. 1996. *Democracy and Disagreement.* Cambridge, Mass.: Harvard University Press.

HAJER, M. A. 1993. Discourse coalitions and the institutionalization of Prace: the case of acid rain in Great Britain. Pp. 43–76 in *The Argumentative Turn in Policy Analysis and Planning,* ed. F. Fischer and J. Forester. Durham, NC: Duke University Press.

—— and WAGENAAR, H. 2003*a*. Introduction. Pp. 1–33 in *Deliberative Policy Analysis: Understanding Governance in the Network Society,* ed. M. A. Hajer and H. Wagenaar. Cambridge: Cambridge University Press.

—— —— (eds.) 2003*b*. *Deliberative Policy Analysis: Understanding Governance in the Network Society.* Cambridge: Cambridge University Press.

HALBERSTAM, D. 1972. *The Best and the Brightest.* New York: Random House.

HARRINGTON, M. 1963. *The Other America: Poverty in the United States.* New York: Macmillan.

HECLO, H. 1977. *A Government of Strangers.* Washington, DC: Brookings Institution.

HEINEMAN, R. A., BLUHM, W. T., PETERSON, S. A., and KEARNY, E. N. 2002. *The World of the Policy Analyst,* 3rd edn. Chatham, NJ: Chatham House.

HITCH, C. J., and MCKEAN, R. N. 1960. *The Economics of Defense in the Nuclear Age.* Cambridge, Mass.: Harvard University Press.

KAPLAN, A. 1964. *The Conduct of Inquiry.* San Francisco: Chandler.

KARLQVIST, A. 1999. Going beyond disciplines: the meaning of interdisciplinary. *Policy Sciences,* 32 (4: Dec.): 379–83.

KATHLENE, L., and MARTIN, J. A. 1991. Enhancing citizen participation: panel designs, perspectives, and policy formation. *Journal of Policy Analysis and Management,* 10 (1: Winter): 46–63.

KETTL, D. F. 2004. *Homeland under Stress: Homeland Security and American Politics.* Washington, DC: CQ Press.

KERSHAW, J. A., with COURANT, P. N. 1970. *Government against Poverty.* Chicago: Markham, for the Brookings Institution.

LASCH, C. 1995. *The Revolt of the Elites and the Betrayal of Democracy.* New York: W. W. Norton.

LASSWELL, H. D. 1949. *Power and Personality.* New York: W. W. Norton.

—— 1951*a*. The policy orientation. Ch. 1 in *The Policy Sciences,* ed. D. Lerner and H. D. Lasswell. Palo Alto, Calif.: Stanford University Press.

—— 1951*b*. *The World Revolution of our Time: A Framework for Basic Policy Research.* Palo Alto, Calif.: Stanford University Press. Reprinted as ch. 2 in *World Revolutionary Elites,* ed. H. D. Lasswell and D. Lerner. Cambridge, Mass.: MIT Press, 1965.

—— 1971. *A Pre-View of Policy Sciences.* New York: American Elsevier.

—— and KAPLAN, A. 1950. *Power and Society.* New Haven, Conn.: Yale University Press.

LEVINE, R. A. 1970. *The Poor Ye Need Not Have With You: Lessons from the War on Poverty.* Cambridge, Mass.: MIT Press.

LYND, R. S. 1939. *Knowledge for What? The Place for Social Science in the American Culture.* Princeton, NJ: Princeton University Press.

LYNN, L. E., Jr. 1999. A place at the table: policy analysis, its postpositivist critics, and the future of practice. *Journal of Policy Analysis and Management,* 18 (5: Summer): 411–24.

LYONS, E. M. 1969. *The Uneasy Partnership.* New York: Russell Sage Foundation.

LYONS, W. E., LOWRY, D., and DEHOOG, R. H. 1992. *The Politics of Dissatisfaction.* Armonk, NY: M. E. Sharpe.

MACHIAVELLI, N. 1950/1515. *The Prince and The Discourses.* New York: New American Library.

MACRAE, D. Jr., and WHITTINGTON, D. 1997. *Expert Advice for Policy Choice.* Washington, DC: Georgetown University Press.

MAYER, I. 1997. *Debating Technologies: A Methodological Contribution to the Design and Evaluation of Participatory Policy Analysis.* Tilburg: Tilburg University Press.

MERTON, R. K. 1936. The unanticipated consequences of purposive social action. *American Sociological Review,* 1 (4: Dec.): 894–904.

MOYNIHAN, D. P. 1969. *Maximum Feasible Misunderstanding: Community Action in the War on Poverty.* New York: Free Press.

MURRAY, C. 1984. *Losing Ground.* New York: Basic Books.

NATHAN, R. P. 1985. Research lessons from the great society. *Journal of Policy Analysis and Management,* 4 (3: Spring): 422–6.

NELSON, R. N. 1977. *The Moon and the Ghetto.* New York: W. W. Norton.

NYE, J. S. Jr., ZELIKOW, P. D., and KING, D. C. (eds.) 1997. *Why People Don't Trust Government.* Cambridge, Mass.: Harvard University Press.

OLSON, K. W. 2003. *Watergate: The Presidential Scandal that Shook America.* Lawrence: University Press of Kansas.

OSBORNE, D., and GAEBLER, T. 1992. *Reinventing Government.* Reading, Mass.: Addison-Wesley.

PUTNAM, R. D. 1993. *Making Democracy Work.* Princeton, NJ: Princeton University Press.

RADIN, B. A. 2000. *Beyond Machiavelli: Policy Analysis Comes of Age.* Washington, DC: Georgetown University Press.

REIN, M., and SCHÖN, D. 1993. Reframing policy discourse. Pp. 145–66 in *The Argumentative Turn in Policy Analysis and Planning,* ed. F. Fischer and J. Forester. Durham, NC: Duke University Press.

RENN, O., WEBBER, T., RAKEL, H., DIENEL, P., and JOHNSON, B. 1993. Public participation in decision making: a three-step procedure. *Policy Sciences,* 26 (3: Aug.): 189–214.

RICCI, D. M. 1984. *The Transformation of American Politics: The New Washington and the Rise of Think Tanks.* New Haven, Conn.: Yale University Press.

RIVLIN, A. M. 1970. *Systematic Thinking for Social Action.* Washington, DC: Brookings Institution.

SABATIER, P. A., (ed.) 1999. *Theories of the Policy Process.* Boulder, Colo.: Westview Press.

SCHÖN, D., and REIN, M. 1994. *Frame Reflection: Towards the Resolution of Policy Controversies.* New York: Basic Books.

SCOTT, J. 1991. *Social Network Analysis: A Handbook.* London: Sage.

SMITH, B. L. R. 1966. *The RAND Corporation.* Cambridge, Mass.: Harvard University Press.

STOBAUGH, R., and YERGIN, D. (eds.) 1979. *Energy Futures.* New York: Random House.

TORGERSON, D. 1986. Between knowledge and politics: the three faces of policy analysis. *Policy Sciences,* 19 (1: July): 33–60.

WARREN, M. 1992. Democratic theory and self transformation. *American Political Science Review,* 86 (1: Mar.): 8–23.

WASSERMAN, S., and FAUST, K. 1994. *Social Network Analysis: Methods and Applications.* Cambridge: Cambridge University Press.

WEIMER, D. L., and VINING, A. 2005. *Policy Analysis: Concepts and Practice.* Upper Saddle River, NJ: Prentice Hall.

WEYANT, J. P. 1980. Quantitative models in energy policy. *Policy Analysis*, 6 (2: Spring): 211–34.
WILDAVSKY, A. 1979*a*. *The Politics of the Budgetary Process*, 3rd edn. Boston: Little, Brown.
—— 1979*b*. *Speaking Truth to Power*. Boston: Little, Brown.
WILLIAMS, W. 1998. *Honest Numbers and Democracy*. Washington, DC: Georgetown University Press.

CHAPTER 3

# EMERGENCE OF SCHOOLS OF PUBLIC POLICY: REFLECTIONS BY A FOUNDING DEAN

## GRAHAM ALLISON

I AM grateful to have been the fifth in a succession of deans of Harvard University's Graduate School of Public Administration, housed in the Lucius N. Littauer Center of Public Administration building. But I am honored to have been designated as the "Founding Dean" of the modern John F. Kennedy School of Government in recognition of my role in leading the School in the period in which it emerged as a major institution. Formally, the School's name was changed in 1966 to honor President John F. Kennedy, a Harvard graduate in the class of 1940. But when I became dean in March 1977, the School had no buildings, fewer than a dozen full-time faculty, a student body of just 200 who took classes mostly from other faculties, no research centers, and no executive education programs.

At the 1977 meeting of Harvard's Overseers Visiting Committee to the School at which President of the University Derek Bok announced my appointment, I responded with remarks later published under the title "Seven initiatives for the John F. Kennedy School of Government." There I reminded the audience of British historian Lord Acton's image of a "remote and ideal objective" that captivates the imagination by its splendor and simplicity and thereby evokes an effort that cannot be commanded by lesser and more proximate goals.

* The author expresses special appreciation for the extraordinary research in preparation of this chapter to Micah Zenko, and to my colleague Mark Moore for a thoughtful review and suggested revisions of the first draft.

At that event I articulated what came to be known as our "canonical objectives" for the Kennedy School of Government in the decade ahead:

- To become a *substantial professional school* that does for the public sector much of what Harvard's Schools of Business, Law, and Medicine do for their respective private professions.
- To become the *hub* of a university-wide Program in Public Policy and Management, mobilizing the rich intellectual resources in all the faculties of the University and focusing them on critical issues of public policy.

Those with first-hand knowledge of the Kennedy School in 1977 understood how well the stated objectives met Acton's test of remoteness. Toward these objectives, I stated seven specific initiatives for the School in the years immediately ahead:

- Completing and occupying the new building: When efforts to build the John F. Kennedy Presidential Library in Cambridge failed, Harvard, nonetheless, managed to hold on to the three acres of land facing the Charles River. In eighteen months, we built the major building for the Kennedy School. The classrooms, offices, and other facilities gave us a physical identity and allowed us rapidly to expand the student body and faculty.
- Consummating the marriage between the Institute of Politics and the School: The Institute aspired to become Harvard's link between the rough and tumble of elective politics and the academy, but remained isolated in the "little yellow house" at 79 Mount Auburn Street. The new building allowed us to bring the Institute within the walls of the Kennedy School, assuring interaction.
- Establishing Executive Programs in Public Policy and Management: Taking a page from the Business School's advanced management programs, we developed our own curriculum and programs for training senior government executives.
- Building mutually rewarding relations with other faculties in the University: To become the hub of public policy research at Harvard, we had to establish alliances with other major faculties and institutes from which they gained.
- Consolidating the core curriculum: In training future government leaders, we decided that formal analytical tools would be the foundation of our instruction (economics, statistics, and decision theory), but that beyond this base, preparation for leadership in government required inventing new courses in organization, politics, and management.
- Creating centers of competence in public policy research and analysis: To assure that our faculty and curricula were grounded in real-world problems of public policy, the invention of what we called "problem-solving research centers" would assemble critical masses of faculty and researchers from the School and the University to identify ways to resolve significant public policy challenges. Policy analyses of significant challenges that drew upon insights from faculty across the University should also be an important product of the School.

- Communicating the mission of the School effectively and concisely: On the eve of the Reagan revolution, government was coming to be seen more as a problem then as a solution. We needed to articulate both the necessity for competent government, and the case for the School's programs for training competent and effective public servants.

Twelve years later, when I stepped down as Dean of the School, the Kennedy School had 750 full-time graduate students, 700 participants in a dozen executive programs, and nine problem-solving research centers. At least in the specific case of Harvard's School of Public Policy and Government, I count myself proud to have been "present at the creation."

This chapter thus offers an insider's view of the emergence of one school of public policy, together with reflections on developments in the larger enterprise of which it is a part. The first section of the chapter presents a brief historical overview of this field, beginning with its roots as a distinct profession reflected in Woodrow Wilson's seminal article, "The study of administration," published in 1887, to the works of E. Pendleton Herring and the "policy sciences" of Harold D. Lasswell, to the growth of professional graduate schools in the 1970s when a number of first-class programs of public policy emerged. This is not meant to be an exhaustive history of the discipline, but rather to note key thematic shifts within the fields of public administration and public policy in the century ending with the 1980s.

Section 2 offers a personal perspective on the emergence of the Kennedy School of Government. Celebrating my tenure when I retired in 1989, President Derek Bok called the School "one of the brightest stars in Harvard University's crown." As he said: "I can't think of anything in Harvard's history that is comparable to the extent of growth and development that has taken place under one brief span of a single dean's leadership" (Lambert 2003). From last place in all measures of performance among Harvard's ten independent faculties in 1977, by 1989, the School was widely recognized as the fourth among the University's major professional schools, alongside the schools of Business, Law, and Medicine.

# 1. HISTORICAL ROOTS OF SCHOOLS OF PUBLIC POLICY

## 1.1 Early Schools of Public Administration

The American post-Reconstruction period was characterized by a diversification and expansion of the administrative tasks of the federal government. Faced with the unification of the continent, economic industrialization, and the emergence of international commerce, America required increased capacity at the national level to meet these challenges. New responsibilities led to the federal regulation of the transcontinental railroads, the development of a national Postal Service, and the marshaling of a professional standing army. As summarized by Stephen Skowronek in his history of this era, this national transformation required *Building a New American State* (Skowronek 1982). Skowronek described the transformation: "To cope with categorically new demands for national control, the nature and status of the state in America had to be fundamentally altered. National administrative expansion called into question the entire network of political and institutional relationships that had been built up over the course of a century to facilitate governmental operations." Nothing less than "an extended assault on the previously established governmental order" would be required (Skowronek 1982, 9, 35).

To staff an enlarged and empowered federal government, a new vanguard of specialized workers was necessary. Previously, government employment was only secured through patronage—the primary reward system of political party incumbency. Passage of the Pendleton Act in 1883 established the federal civil service, and weakened the political party machines. In theory, the Pendleton Act guaranteed that bureaucrats would be hired on the basis of merit and professionalism—as determined by competitive exams—and would receive protection from partisan influence.

Among the first academics to wrestle with the development and complexity of the new American state was the future President Woodrow Wilson. In 1886, Wilson delivered a lecture at Cornell University, "The study of administration," later published in the *Political Science Quarterly* (Wilson 1887). With his essay, Wilson sought to refocus political science away from the noble but perennial chestnuts about political ends to more mundane, operational questions about how government can be practically administered. He recognized the necessity for more practical knowledge in the modern era because, in his words, "It is getting harder to run a constitution than to frame one." Publication of Wilson's essay is generally regarded as "the beginning of public administration as a specific field of study" (Carroll and Zuck 1985).

Wilson was the first to articulate clearly his now famous dichotomy between "politics" and "administration." In keeping with the spirit of neutral bureaucrats envisioned by the progressive reform movement in the Pendleton Act, according to Wilson, "administration lies outside the proper sphere of *politics*. Administrative questions are not political questions. Although politics sets the tasks for administration, it should not be suffered to manipulate its offices." While elected officials should establish the "broad plans of governmental action," Wilson's role for the disinterested public administrator was almost to mechanistically implement the "systematic execution of public law."

Anticipating Fredrick Taylor's principle of eliminating all unnecessary movement from manufacturing processes, Wilson also called for the scientific management of government. Modern public administrators needed to understand "first, what government can properly and successfully do, and secondly, how it can do these proper things with the utmost possible efficiency and at the least possible cost either of money or energy." Recognizing that models of efficient government would not be found at home, Wilson also declared that America's public administrators should look beyond our borders to borrow from the forms and practices of government employed by European states. He urged identifying the best practices in governing extracted from the politics surrounding them, or from the particular policy results. As Wilson evocatively described his goal: "If I see a murderous fellow sharpening a knife cleverly, I can borrow his way of sharpening the knife without borrowing his probable intention to commit murder with it; and so if I see a monarchist dyed in the wool managing a public bureau well, I can learn his business methods without changing one of my republican spots."

In the late nineteenth century, graduate programs in training public administrators emerged at a handful of schools, notably: the Institute of Public Administration at Columbia University, the Maxwell School of Citizenship and Public Affairs at Syracuse University, the Wharton School at the University of Pennsylvania, the Training School for Public Service at the New York Bureau of Municipal Research, the Public Administration Clearing House in Chicago, and Johns Hopkins University (Blunt 1988). In 1939, 150 scholars from these fledgling institutions broke away from the American Political Science Association to form the American Society for Public Administration, the first stand-alone organization in the United States dedicated to improving government performance (Guy 2003, 641–55).

The curricula of these early public administration programs focused on providing the future administrator with a tool kit of business-oriented techniques for effectively managing government programs. Courses included: budgeting and accounting methods, finance, standardization of procedures, performance assessments, and industrial organization (Moscher 1975; Stivers 2003, 37). Wider considerations of the efficacy of policies and the needs of the citizenry were not much researched or debated by these early administrators. Such judgements would emerge through the constitutionally established political process with mandated check and balances—the province of elected officials, not federal administrators.

## 1.2 The Postwar Boom in Public Administration

With the New Deal and the Second World War the size of the federal government expanded exponentially. Until 1920 federal domestic spending never reached 1 per cent of gross domestic product. By 1930, it had tripled to 3 per cent. Two decades later the national budget accounted for 15 per cent of all US economic activity (OMB 2004, table 1.2). By 1950, even after the postwar demobilization, the federal government had a net gain of one million civil servants, doubling the 1939 total (Porter 1994, 279–85). The growth of the welfare state through New Deal programs, and postwar social policies, created more interest groups and constituencies invested in protecting and expanding their benefits. Inverting Wilson's hierarchy of politics before administration, programs now shaped politics (Lowi 1972, 299).

This second wave of public administrators, autonomous from the influence of partisan politics, developed a strong sense of proprietorship for the programs they managed. Scholars of public administration recognized this desire of government employees to protect their programs and meet the demands of affected constituents. The classic treatise on the subject of administrators as arbiters of the public interest was E. Pendleton Herring's 1936 work, *Public Administration and the Public Interest.* Herring introduced the subject of administrative discretion, in which "Congress passes a statute setting forth a general principle ... The bureaucrat is left to decide as to the conditions that necessitate the law's application" (Herring 1936, 7). The bureaucratic decision maker, therefore, was given the additional burden of interpreting the public interest, a task that could not be accomplished in a value-free manner. Herring recognized this potential shortcoming, but contended that well-educated bureaucrats were best positioned to manage societal shifts and the evolving needs of targeted interest groups. As Herring described in stark terms: "Public administration in actual practice is a process whereby one individual acting in an official capacity and in accordance with his interpretation of his legal responsibility applies a statute to another individual who is in a legally subordinate position. The public as such is not concerned in this process" (Herring 1936, 25).

Harold Lasswell sought to go beyond Herring to what he called the "policy sciences." The policy sciences approach sought to employ all of the available tools of social science to understand all relevant inputs in a policy issue area, including knowledge of the policy-making process itself. In practice, Lasswell's goal was for a more muscular and integrated version of Wilson's appeal for the scientific management of government. By understanding the larger picture of policy-making, the policy sciences method sought to ultimately "diminish the policy-makers' errors of judgment and give greater assurance that the course of action decided upon will achieve the intended goals" (Rothwell 1951). Recognizing the interdisciplinary nature of this endeavor, Lasswell and his colleagues called for the merger of the discipline of political science with insights from sociology, economics, business, law, and also to reach out to physicists and biologists (Lasswell 1951, 3–15). Public administrators were to be educated in this approach through taking courses in a range of traditional academic disciplines, and also through a mix of historical case studies, simulation exercises, and professional on-the-job training (Lasswell 1971, 132–59). While Lasswell's project to rationalize further the policy process was well received in some parts of the scholarly community, his ambitious concept was never much embraced in the curricula of public policy programs.

## 1.3 From Public Administration to Public Policy

In 1960 John Kennedy was elected President of the United States. In staffing his administration, Kennedy sought the "best and the brightest:" from Harvard, Dean of

Arts and Sciences McGeorge Bundy and economist John Kenneth Galbraith; from the RAND Corporation, Charles Hitch and Alain Enthoven; and from the world of business and industry, most notably, the president of the Ford Motor Company Robert McNamara. These "new frontiersmen" brought with them a confidence that intelligence and the most advanced techniques for optimizing choices could improve the performance of government. Nowhere was the impulse to clarify policy options through quantification more pronounced than in the Secretary of Defense McNamara's Pentagon. McNamara's "whiz kids" implemented the Policy Planning Budgeting System (PPBS), which applied a cost–benefit analysis framework developed at RAND for decisions about weapons acquisition and war fighting (Enthoven and Smith 1971). President Lyndon Johnson regarded PPBS as so success-ful that he ordered all federal agencies to adopt it in 1965.

Taking into account the highly specialized skills required to develop and oversee the PPBS, the federal government required a new cadre of rigorously trained analysts (Stokes 1996, 160). To meet this demand, major universities responded by establish-ing programs training students in public policy analysis (Crecine 1971, 7–32). Between 1967 and 1971, graduate programs at the master's or doctoral level in public policy were created at: the Institute of Public Policy Studies, University of Michigan; the Kennedy School at Harvard; the Graduate School of Public Policy, University of California, Berkeley; the School of Urban and Public Affairs, Carnegie-Mellon University; the RAND Graduate School; the Department of Public Policy and Management, University of Pennsylvania; the School of Public Affairs, University of Minnesota; the Lyndon B. Johnson School of Public Affairs, University of Texas; and the Institute of Policy Science and Public Affairs, Duke University (Fleischman 1990, 734; Walker 1976, 127–52).

In 1972, the Board of Trustees of the Ford Foundation, under the leadership of McGeorge Bundy, decided to focus on "helping establish or strengthen first-class programs of advanced, professional training for young people aimed at public service" (Bell 1981, 1). Over the following five years, the Ford Foundation provided multi-million-dollar general-support grants to eight grantee programs that were developing a concentration on graduate training in public policy. The Ford Foun-dation also awarded grants for summer conferences, seminars, and working papers that supported the self-study of America's experience in public administration for models that could be applied for aiding economic development in Third World countries (Riggs 1998, 23–4). The Foundation's initial seed money proved crucial in nurturing the incipient development of a new field in an era marked by deep distrust of government (Miles 1967, 343–56).

A key innovation within these programs was a shift in focus from "public administration" to "public policy." Emphasizing policy, the schools addressed ends as well as means. This refocus required a greater understanding of the complex social and political environment within which policy is shaped and implemented. It also required training policy analysts—not simply public administrators—who could inform decision makers about the consequences of alternative policy choices. The insights involved budgetary cost and efficacy, but also issues of social equity, civil rights, and quality of life (Fredrickson 1971, 364). Where traditional schools of public administration sought to train competent, neutral managers, schools of public policy faced the difficult task of identifying what specifically makes a good analyst. As the founder of the Graduate School of Public Policy at the University of California, Berkeley, Aaron Wildavsky, argued, policy analysis requires a balance of technical competence and a list of commonsense intangibles, such as persuasion, argumentation, intuition, and creativity (Wildavsky 1979; 1976, 127–52).

Not directly addressed in these early stages in the development of schools of public policy was the crucially important question of what role students of these schools would play in *making* public policy as well as advising about it or administering the organizations that implemented policies. On one hand, the schools of public policy wanted to distinguish themselves from the schools of public administration that had focused on the narrow questions of efficient administration of public policies established elsewhere by others. They did so by insisting on the relevance of analytic techniques to efforts made to develop and evaluate particular public policies and programs, by training students in the use of these techniques, and by championing the role of powerful staff offices in government agencies which hired individuals who could perform these tasks, and would allow them to become influential in public policy making and implementation.

But left open, however, were the answers to two further important questions: first, the extent to which schools of public policy intended to train individuals to participate effectively in the governmental process as policy makers as well as policy analysts; and if so, how individuals trained to be policy analysts, or policy makers (and whose expertise lay either in substantive knowledge or in abstract analytic techniques) who claimed to be useful in revealing the social or public value of governmental action, would relate to the political processes that were an inevitable part of policy making in a democratic society. The crucial question of where politics fitted into the making of policy, and how students prepared for work in government should both understand and engage in the politics that surrounded their work, had been avoided since Wilson established the distinction between policy and administration. The Progressives had enlarged the prerogatives of technically trained bureaucrats without seriously engaging the question of how increasingly powerful civil servants at national, state, and local levels should relate to what we eventually began to describe as their "political authorizing environment." If schools of public policy intended to train only policy analysts who were concerned about the ends of government, then they need not be deeply concerned about influencing the politics surrounding the politics of their issues—only understanding them well enough to ensure that their advice was not completely irrelevant. If, however, they intended to train individuals who could become influential as leaders and managers of policy-making processes, and saw their graduates not only in elected roles, but in activist roles within government as policy entrepreneurs and innovators, then the schools would have to take seriously the questions about what individuals who sought to be policy leaders and entrepreneurs should know and do. And that might well be different from what policy analysts and putatively neutral bureaucrats seeking efficiency and effectiveness in the achievement of established missions needed to know (Moore 1995).

Seeing to solidify its identity as a stand-alone field, emerging public policy schools also created professional associations. In 1970, the former Council on Graduate Education for Public Administration was renamed the National Association of Schools of Public Policy and Administration (NASPAA). The creation of the NASPAA's Commission on Peer Review and Accreditation in 1983 provided a mechanism for the systematic self-evaluation of the field. The Commission became the specialized accreditor for over 135 graduate programs in public policy, public affairs, and public administration. In this capacity, NASPAA developed a core curriculum for public administration programs, with required courses in quantitative methods, public budgeting and management, organizational theory, and personnel administration (Henry 1990, 3–26). In 1995, NASPAA founded the *Journal of Public Affairs Education* as its publication for peer-reviewed articles on pedagogical and curricular issues. The Association for Public Policy Analysis and Management (APPAM) was formed in 1979 to support academic institutions training students for distinctive professional careers as policy analysts (Guy 2003, 649). In 1981, APPAM merged two journals, *Policy Analysis* and *Public Policy*, into the *Journal of Policy Analysis and Management*, which served as an outlet for multidisciplinary research into public policy issues, and as a sounding board for shifts in the profession.

## 2. LESSONS FROM THE KENNEDY SCHOOL OF GOVERNMENT

Seventy years ago Harvard had no school dedicated solely to the study of public administration or for training students for careers in public service. Early in the twentieth century, Harvard president Charles M. Eliot proposed a school of business and public service. Lawrence Lowell, an influential Boston Brahmin, lecturer in the Government department, and future president of Harvard, found Eliot's scheme of little use. Lowell stated frankly: "We should be holding ourselves out as training men for a career that does not exist, and for which, if it did exist, I think our training would very likely not be the best preparation" (Bell 1980: 7). The opposition led by Lowell triumphed, and Eliot's proposed business and public service school was a false start. With the public service component explicitly dropped, in 1908, the Harvard Business School was created, the first Masters of Business Administration degree-granting program in the world (Cruikshank 1987).

At Harvard's Tercentenary in 1936, the major new initiative announced by the University was the creation of a Graduate School of Public Administration (GSPA). To make that new school of public administration possible, Lucius N. Littauer, a wealthy glove manufacturer and former member of Congress, provided a gift of $2 million—at that point the largest single contribution the University had received from an individual donor. The goal of the new school was to engage Harvard faculty members, primarily from the departments of Economics and Government, in training future civil servants. This concept was greeted with skepticism by many Harvard faculty and administrators, who saw this as a further threat to the University's intellectual standards, in their views compounding the mistake made in establishing the Business School (Roethlisberger 1977). In the early years of the GSPA, the School had no unique identity of its own, no set curriculum, and no faculty members dedicated solely to Littauer's vision of a school for "public service" (John F. Kennedy School of Government 1986, 19). Faculty from the Economics and Government departments enrolled students admitted to the School in their departmental courses, but the Law School and Business School were less hospitable to this questionable venture. Thus, when James Bryant Conant retired as president of Harvard in 1953, he identified the GSPA as his "greatest disappointment" (John F. Kennedy School of Government 1986, 36).

Conant's successor as Harvard president, Nathan Marsh Pusey, also recognized that the GSPA was an institution lacking in strategic vision, or sense of purpose. For a time, Pusey considered closing the School down. As Edith Stokey, a lecturer on public policy, former secretary of the Kennedy School from 1977 to 1993, described the GSPA in the early 1950s: "There was an institution, but it didn't have a curriculum of its own" (Lambert 2004, 5). Candidates for master's or doctorate degrees in public administration were left on their own in assembling a curriculum from the other parts of the University. Don K. Price, Jr., soon after becoming dean of the GSPA in 1966, received both an ultimatum and marching orders from Pusey: "Build it up or I will abolish it" (Lambert 2004, 5).

The GSPA's low status within the Harvard community was a major handicap. Thus, the desire of the Kennedy family to memorialize President John F. Kennedy after his assassination in 1963 played an essential part in the School's turnaround. In 1966 the GSPA was officially renamed the John F. Kennedy School of Government, and the Institute of Politics was created. Under that banner, Harvard recruited Richard Neustadt—a distinguished political scientist and author of *Presidential Power*—to become director of the new Institute of Politics within the new School. In time, Neustadt recruited an all-star cast of professors from faculty from across the University, including Francis Bator, Joseph Bower, Charles Christenson, Philip Heymann, Ernest May, Fredrick Mosteller, Howard Raiffa, and Thomas Schelling, to build a new curriculum for a new Public Policy Program.

Planning the new curriculum for KSG students involved a core of eight professors remarkable for their individual commitment and congeniality, and for their unimpeachable academic reputations. Five senior professors—Bator and Schelling in Political Economy, Mosteller in Statistics, Neustadt in Public Administration, Raiffa in Operations Research—and three junior faculty—Richard Zeckhauser and Henry Jacoby of Economics, and myself of Government—designed the core courses that have been the foundation of a KSG education to this day. That core curriculum initially consisted of eight required core courses: two semesters of economic analysis, two semesters of statistical analysis, two semesters of operations research, and two semesters of what we described as political and institutional analysis. In addition, students were required to participate in a colloquium in which they were asked to apply these abstract techniques to real-world problems. Eventually, influenced by the powerful presence of Larry Lynn who had become the paragon of policy analysis and program evaluation, the relatively informal colloquium was replaced by a regular two-semester-length course called Workshop in which students were asked to perform the professional tasks the school was preparing them to do: namely, offer thoughtful analyses of whether and how the assets of government could be deployed to deal with problematic conditions in the society.

Obviously, the curriculum stressed teaching students the tools of social sciences— economics, statistics, and quantitative analysis. It did so for at least three reasons. First, it was these tools that were new to the practice of government, and to the field of public administration. Second, these tools provide the basis for students to participate in the compelling discussion about what the ends of government should be, and whether government was actually achieving those ends, rather than the more prosaic discussion of what form government organizations should take, and how they should design their administrative systems to ensure reliable bureaucratic control. Third, these tools came from demanding social science disciplines, and helped give the curriculum of the fledgling public policy schools a certain kind of legitimacy in the academic world in which they were struggling for academic respect.

What was relatively de-emphasized (to make room for teaching these new techniques) was courses focused on the leadership of public organizations. Of course, it was obvious that a curriculum that sought to train public sector (by which we meant government) officials could not focus on abstract techniques of social science alone. There had to be some attention given to the application of these techniques to the messy, real-world problems that the students would actually confront in their jobs. (This was the point of the Workshop course.) And there also had to be at least some familiarization of the students with the ways in which real governments actually made and implemented policy—if for no reason other than that individuals being trained to do policy analysis had to understand the context in which their proposals would be considered and enacted. (This was the focus of the courses that Richard Neustadt and I designed to go alongside the analytic courses. My own *Essence of Decision: Explaining the Cuban Missile Crisis* served, in effect, as the text for the basic political and institutional analysis course, and has been adopted for analogous courses in other schools of public policy, business, and other professional training programs.) But the important unanswered question that remained was both how much effort should be devoted to helping students understand, predict, and intervene to change the policy-making processes of government, and from what positions in and outside of government itself we imagined them doing this work.

Eventually, we concluded that we had to train individuals to manage public organizations as well as to offer policy advice. This was, to some degree, forced on us by the fact that the School had a mid-career program that attracted experienced public officials, and what they came expecting to learn was how to manage and lead their organizations—not simply how to analyze policies. It was also necessitated by the fact that, for important strategic reasons, we committed ourselves to offering executive programs in addition to our degree programs. The executives who came for these courses knew that there were lots of good ideas around, and that their problem was more often helping the government reach a choice about what to do, and effectively implement that choice, rather than developing a strong analytic case for a certain line of action. They wanted training in management and leadership, not in policy analysis.

In this setting, in 1977 President Bok asked me to become dean of the Kennedy School. I resisted on four grounds: I was too young—at thirty-seven I would be the youngest dean in Harvard's history; I hoped to join the newly elected Carter administration; I felt the next dean should be first and foremost a fundraiser; and I worried that the School lacked a coherent mission and strategy for the decades ahead. After months of perseverance and pressure from President Bok and fellow colleagues, I relented and accepted the job. But I did so with trepidation.

As a young faculty member, I had often cited George Bernard Shaw's quip about the doers and the teachers. Those who can, do; those who cannot, teach (about what those who can do). As someone who aspired to have a foot in the world of doers as well as teachers, I found this bifurcation uncomfortable. I must confess that while I spend most of my time teaching and writing about what others do, in the case where as a dean I was a doer, I never seriously wrote or thought about that. Thus what follows are reflections of one dean, organized around lessons learned, that, I hope, may be relevant for other deans and faculty members facing similar challenges.

As the historical records make plain, the goal of Mr Littauer and his associates in creating the School was to establish an independent professional school of government along the lines of other major professional schools. In fact, as has happened in other universities, the gift was immediately captured by the parent departments of Economics and Government in the faculty of Arts and Sciences. The funds were used first to build a building that was occupied by these departments, and then to fund faculty members in these departments. The trade-off was that a dean and one administrator enrolled a number of mid-career students who took seats in other courses otherwise offered in the departments of Economics and Government. On occasion, the dean's fund permitted him to provide small grants for research or other expenses of the faculty involved.

Thus, lesson 1: *Even in a university with powerful, independent professional schools like Harvard's schools of Business, Medicine, and Law, a new professional school is a foreign object in the mainstream of the academy.* As a consequence, it is likely to be regarded with suspicion and hostility. It may be rejected. If not, and especially if it comes with scarce resources, it will likely be captured. Thus, in a Harvard-like context during the 1930s—or even today—the most likely fate for what Mr Littauer imagined would be its capture by strong established departments, particularly Economics and Government.

A special feature of Harvard is that its most sacred and ancient principle maintains "ETOB:" every tub on its own bottom. According to this principle, deans of independent schools at Harvard are semi-autonomous barons—required to raise whatever funds they spend, but given wide authority to spend their school's funds as they choose. This principle obviously has great disadvantages—without funds it is not possible to build a school, appoint faculty, or enroll students. Alternatively, the advantage of the system is independence.

From 1972 to 1977, the Kennedy School was part of a university-wide fundraising campaign headed by President Bok. The good news is that we were included as a party. The bad news was that the campaign failed to raise funds for the School. That fact is a strong reminder of the limits of the conception of the School at the time. The concept of that campaign was, as its title stated: the "campaign for public service." It featured four schools of public service—the Education School, the School of Public Health, the Design School, and the new Kennedy School. It sought to raise funds for those concerned about public service as reflected in these four "serving professions." But in part as a result of this concept, and in part because there was no real taste for fundraising at the School, after four years the campaign had raised only $1 million. Because its accumulated reserves and Ford Foundation grant had been running down, the Kennedy School was in serious deficit. Its financial viability was uncertain.

In 1977, the Kennedy School was, in sum, long on promise (given the Harvard setting, name, and history), but short on performance—a largely unseized opportunity. One of my favorite quotations comes from the German philosopher Nietzsche: "The most common form of human stupidity is forgetting what one is trying to do." As noted above, in my "inaugural" remarks to the Visiting Committee, I laid out my vision of what the Kennedy School could become:

- To become a *substantial professional school* that does for the public sector much of what Harvard's Schools of Business, Law, and Medicine do for their respective private professions.
- To become the *hub* of a university-wide Program in Public Policy and Management, mobilizing the rich intellectual resources in all the faculties of the University and focusing them on critical issues of public policy.

Each word in this mission statement was carefully chosen. Each of the terms mattered significantly to the School, its faculty, the various Harvard constituencies, and over time the broader public. The term "*substantial* professional school" signaled two things: a school like Harvard's major professional schools—of Business, Law, and Medicine—and not its minor schools of which there were considerably more. And a *professional* school, focused on serving the profession rather than part of the Arts and Sciences or academic tradition that forms the dominant culture at Harvard. The second part of the mission, namely the *hub* of the university-wide program, was our way of addressing and overcoming what had been a flawed concept of a four-legged stool for public service. It also reminded us that issues of public policy touch competences in many of the faculties of the

University. A new school should not aspire to duplicate these strengths but rather to mobilize and focus them on important questions of public policy.

The mission statement was repeated over and over, at the first faculty meeting each year and in all of our literature—to the point that most faculty members could recite it in unison. It helped to focus all our minds. Lesson 2, therefore, *underlines the importance of a vision and mission.*

In the Kennedy School's 1978–9 Official Register, which we used to recruit students and new faculty members, I developed the case for our vision under the banner "Excellence in Government:"

The challenge of the modern world is government. The dynamics of national politics, the realities of international affairs, and the increasing complexity of society—all fuel a growing demand for government action on behalf of genuinely urgent and worthy causes. Government must act to ensure legitimate economic, social, and security objectives. But the dramatic growth of government and the often indiscriminate character of governmental action can threaten the very values government would guarantee. The urgent challenge, therefore, is to define a viable role for responsible, democratic government.

The authors of the American Constitution articulated the fundamental dilemma of responsible government. In the first instance, they instituted government as society's chief agent for the common good. Without government, who would:

- Establish justice?
- Ensure domestic tranquility?
- Provide for the common defense?
- Promote the general welfare?
- Secure the blessings of liberty?

The American Bicentennial provided a fitting occasion to pause and review the record. Measured by the yardstick of other human endeavors, this system of government, for all its current shortcomings, must be judged an extraordinary success. At the same time, the makers of the Constitution were acutely conscious that in establishing a government powerful enough to serve the commonwealth they were creating enormous risks of irresponsibility. Such a government might exercise authority capriciously, intrude unnecessarily, chose improper means, or simply fail to do its job effectively.

To cope with this fundamental dilemma, the men who met in Philadelphia fashioned something new. On the one hand, the American Constitution *makes* government responsible for defense, law, order, and liberty. On the other, it *holds* government responsible by limiting authority (the Bill of Rights shields civil liberties, including private property, from arbitrary governmental actions); sharing power among separated institutions (functions overlap, as does power, to provide checks and balances); and enthroning the people as the ultimate source of legitimacy (government derives its just power from the consent of the governed). The final guardian of government's responsibility—both positive and negative— was neither the Constitutions nor some higher authority. That duty rests squarely on the shoulders of the informed citizenry and requires their steady participation in the business of the nation.

The basic dilemma of responsible government persists. Twentieth-century developments have only exaggerated its proportions. Events, both international and domestic, require more from government; rising expectations encourage citizens to demand *much* more. Modern governments must, of necessity, assume greater responsibilities than their eighteenth-century predecessors. But a government that pledges to meet all aspirations must fail. And, it can fall too easily into inept and abusive practices. How then, can we hope to develop more responsible government? Significant progress must be made on several related fronts:

### A Clearer Philosophy of the Aims and Limits of Government in a Mixed-Enterprise Society.

The expansion of the size and role of government over the last 60 years has not been informed by a coherent view of the strengths and weaknesses of government. Rather, government's growth has resulted from a combination of sharpened sensitivities and a political process in which problems, once formulated, readily attract advocates of government as a solution. As a result, with minimal appreciation of the limits of legal compulsion, and frequent neglect of the consequences when government oversteps itself, new government programs have arisen and old programs have expanded.

What we now require is harder thought about the role and size of government, and the impact of government's expanse on the balance between the public and private sectors. We need a clear contemporary philosophy of government that appreciates the genius of a mixed-enterprise society committed to individual rights, concerned for the common good, and driven by private action determined by private initiative. Government's role in setting the ground rules, refereeing the game, and intervening for special purposes is essential. Still more important, however, are the actions of private individuals, business firms, associations, and even universities in creating products and jobs, wealth and capital, knowledge, inspiration and, ultimately, values.

### A New Profession of Elected, Appointed and Career Officials.

The nation needs officials with stronger analytical skills, managerial competence, ethical sensitivity, and institutional sense. The complexity of national issues and the claims upon government have steadily outdistanced the capacity of Congress and the Executive Branch to respond. Although critics bemoan government's inability to cope more effectively with issues like inflation, unemployment, energy and economic growth, we must acknowledge the extraordinary difficulty of government's task. Because the problems are so unwieldy and the implications of government's actions so far-reaching, no sector in our society can rival government in its need for the ablest and best-trained minds. And yet, the training provided public servants has been clearly less adequate and more haphazard than that traditionally afforded businessmen, doctors, and lawyers.

Here, universities have a major responsibility. What is needed is nothing less than the education of a new profession. This profession should include persons elected to public office, individuals appointed to executive positions, and career civil servants promoted through the ranks. But whether they serve in legislatures, executive department, or nonprofit institutions, all should be distinguished for their analytic skills, managerial competence, ethical sensitivity, and institutional sense.

### A Deeper Understanding of Major Substantive Policy Issues

Problems, portrayed as crises, attract advocates of governmental solutions. Health, welfare, cities, unemployment, energy—the list goes on. To act wisely on these issues, society must know more. We need first-class centers of problem-solving research dedicated to developing solid data bases, sorting the facts, analyzing the options, and raising the level of governmental and public discussion of major public choices. *Before* government acts, the informed public must be able to look to such centers of competence for intelligent presentations of the issues. Moreover, problem-solving research centers should provide a much greater sensitivity to the ways in which the various private institutions in society operate and, thus, a more sophisticated appreciation of the likely effects of government's interventions. Leading universities have been reluctant to organize themselves seriously for public problem solving. Society can no longer afford this reluctance.

The story of government initiatives of the past decade has too often been one of unintended and unanticipated negative consequences swamping the positive results of programs whose intent may have been worthy, but whose intellectual underpinnings were regrettably weak. U.S. legislation regulating pensions to assure workers of a secure income at retirement is one obvious example: it has led many smaller companies to eliminate pension plans altogether. Avoiding traps like this will require major intellectual investments in improved understanding of both the substantive public policy issues and the operations of business, labor, and other major private institutions of society.

In meeting the challenge of government, Harvard should have a special contribution to make. From its origin in 1636, it has been at the forefront of American universities in its ready acceptance of the obligation to promote excellence in government. Eight signers of the Declaration of Independence—including three of the more prominent leaders of the American Revolution, Samuel Adams, John Hancock, and John Adams—were educated at Harvard. In the last two centuries, Harvard graduates have served as President of the United States for more than one year in four.

The challenge posed by government today, however, is unprecedented. Government's present power, for good or for ill, is unparalleled. Informed citizens cannot escape the implication of Edmund Burke's timeless observation: "All that is required for the forces of evil to triumph in this world is for enough good men to do nothing." It is not only the right, it is the duty of concerned Americans to contribute in whatever measure they can to make government more responsible, competent, and effective.

In the future, as in the past, Harvard University's contribution will take various forms. But the University has concluded that "business as usual" will no longer suffice. Society requires excellence in government: a level of performance at least equal to that of the major private professions. To date, however, society has not been prepared to make an equivalent commitment to education for government. Over the past 70 years, we have invested in professional education for business managers—with handsome returns. If we want managerial competence in government equal to the most outstanding performance in business, we will have to mount a comparable effort to train government managers.

Harvard University has undertaken this major new commitment: to build a substantial professional School of Government that will attempt to serve the public sector in many of the ways Harvard's Schools of Business, Law, and Medicine serve their respective private professions. Specifically, the mission of the School is:

- To develop a clearer philosophy of government in a mixed-enterprise society by giving prominence throughout the University to the central questions about government.
- To train a new profession of government leaders with the analytical skills, managerial competence, ethical sensitivities and institutional sense required for distinguished public service.
- To clarify major issues of public choice through sustained, problem-solving research that mobilizes the intellectual resource of the entire University.
- To provide students who are training for other professions with some understanding of the problems of government.
- To serve as a focal point at which to bring together leaders from government, business and other parts of the private sector to work on major issues of national policy.

The strategy for building a school of public policy that reflected my "Excellence in Government" vision was detailed in a chart, first unveiled in 1978 and revised each year thereafter, where we presented the strategic vision of the school. This strategy organized activity in three major divisions: graduate degree programs, executive programs, and problem-solving research centers. It is worth noting that when I first drew this chart, it was more in the realm of an aspiration than a description of the KSG as it then existed. In fact, I think it would be fair to say that much of the consciousness of the Faculty of the school was focused on one or two lines within the box that lumped degree programs together: namely, the newly created MPP program, and the associated Ph.D. in public policy program. The mid-career MPA program was languishing. And there were no problem-solving research centers or executive programs. Thus, to claim that these were to become important elements of the future Kennedy School was to challenge the KSG to innovate and develop along a path that no school of public administration and no school of public policy had yet followed.

Although there were clear risks in advancing down these paths, I was convinced that the School could not become a "substantial professional school" without developing the capacities suggested by these (then) empty boxes. The school needed to be exposed to the real, practical demands of the world it hoped to influence. And the challenge to give plausibly effective answers to urgent policy issues, and to find the means to help high-level officials who faced the problem of making the government work, was the kind of cold water bath the School needed. It also seemed clear to me that the development of these programs would help the School solve what otherwise seemed an insurmountable financial problem that stood between it, and becoming a school that had sufficient scale to cover many disciplines, many subject matters, and to invest in new ideas as well as to work with already established knowledge and pedagogy.

To move down this path of innovation, we created an organizational structure that ensured that each division, and each program within a division, had a mission, a strategy, and resources. Resources consisted of: core faculty, money to permit the appointment of faculty, space, and a central management team. Thus, lesson 3: *the necessity for a coherent strategy* that could meet the goals of mission impact, financial sustainability, and continued academic legitimacy all at the same time.

The MPP program was the flagship for which we developed a core curriculum. It focused on core skills in analytics, management, major challenges of public policy, and values. This program grew from twenty to over 200 pre-career students per year. The MPA program, with an average student age of thirty-five, was in effect a stepchild of the School. But over time, curricula developed for new public policy courses were adopted for MPAs. Indeed, the MPA program provided the arena within which a great deal of curriculum innovation could occur that focused not only on applied policy areas such as international relations, international development, energy and environment, poverty reduction, etc., but also on our emergent ideas about public management and leadership.

For the academic programs, the School's objective was to provide teaching comparable to the best at Harvard. That meant Harvard's Business School. Lesson 4 *recognizes the validity of the question about "value added."* The Harvard Business School formula has been caricatured: recruit people so talented that nothing the faculty can do to them will so handicap them that they will achieve success—for which the School can take credit. The Kennedy School took a page from that book and recruited the best students possible, while we also tried to remember, at least from time to time, the question of what value was being added. The value added lay primarily in the new curriculum we developed in various areas, and the new pedagogic strategies we taught ourselves or invented. We became the largest developer of cases in public policy and public management, and began using these materials to ensure that the process of applying the abstract ideas of our core courses happened in the core courses as well as in the courses that required students to make applications. We experimented with new pedagogies focusing on simulations and the use of the class as a "case in point" that helped to engage the students more deeply and more personally in the learning process.

Taking a clue from the Business School, Executive Programs became a necessary pillar of the strategy. The basic concept for the Executive Programs was to engage faculty in a process from which they were sure to learn as well as teach. In my management terms, I put the Executive Programs under faculty education. When faculty taught adults who were doing important jobs and whose opinions they valued, they had to learn about the jobs these people did. Thus, the Executive Programs became the major anchor to the profession for the faculty. Most of the demand for executive programs was for help in public management, including the politics of policy making and the management of government organizations. Unfortunately, many of the faculty members, especially those trained in economics, were unable or unwilling to teach in these programs and thus missed this magnetic pole. On the other hand, those faculty who accepted this challenge developed important ideas that helped answer the questions about how appointed and career managers in government could appropriately engage their political authorizers, and offer the kind of leadership that created significant innovations in government. Lesson 5: *Executive Programs provide a visible and essential relationship with the market—and the surest way continually to educate the faculty about the market a professional school is meant to serve.*

As dean, I often cited a remark made by the dean of Harvard's Medical School on the occasion of its hundredth birthday in 1884. That acting dean was none other than Oliver Wendell Holmes, father of the famous jurist who bore the same name with a "junior." At the celebration, he commented: if the entire medical establishment (by which he meant the Harvard Medical School and its affiliated hospitals in Boston) were put onto a ship, taken out into Boston Harbor, and sunk, it would be better for the health of the citizens of the Commonwealth—and worse for the fishes. It is interesting to consider whether Holmes's quip was essentially correct. There is a branch of the history of science that poses a question of various medical diseases: when did the prevailing treatment for such diseases become therapeutic? That is, at what point was a patient more likely to be helped than harmed by submitting to a prevailing medical practice. Recall George Washington's experience when he once had a fever and called a doctor to Mount Vernon. The doctor came, put the leeches upon him, and he died. As it turns out, for a substantial number of diseases, prevailing practice was in fact harmful or at least neutral for most of history. Only in the twentieth century, with the discovery of penicillin, were great leaps forward made.

What relevance could this have for schools of public policy? I believe that we should ask Holmes's question: when, in the treatment of various maladies suffered by the body politic, did the prevailing treatment become therapeutic? Or, when might it do so? If one asks about the treatment prescribed and administered after the Second World War, it is clearly not unrelated to the long peace and ultimate victory in the cold war—a period more than three times as long as the intermission between the First and Second World Wars. In other arenas, however, we are clearly doing less well.

The Kennedy School's problem-solving research centers assemble a critical mass of researchers, senior and junior, and challenge them to advance policy-relevant knowledge. In some cases such research can identify emerging threats or opportunities, for example, terrorism. In others, it analyzes the dynamics of trends in an arena. But in every case, a distinctive feature of problem-relevant research is seriousness about disciplined prescriptions as well as diagnosis.

Lesson 6: *taking practice seriously and capturing lessons learned.* If schools of public policy observe practice over a broad number of cases, they will find that some people are skinning cats more effectively than others. By the "look-see" method, we should then be able to identify successes and failures, begin to extract at least some elements of the recipe, and pass that on. That should be one foundation of our research. Thus we established the Kennedy School Case Program that quickly grew to become the largest collection of public policy and management cases in the world. Moreover, beyond that, as Howard Raiffa has argued, "frontiers of application" should spur inventive theoretical applications.

Lesson 7: *core faculty is essential.* A small number of quality people can set the tone. Commitment is contagious. The School had the good fortune of the outstanding "founding fathers" mentioned above, who were assembled in 1969. That group, led by Raiffa, established the standards for faculty appointments, which moved beyond the metric used by faculty of Arts and Sciences departments. The five criteria adopted by the faculty and applied today in Kennedy School hiring decisions are: (1) quality of mind; (2) research and written product; (3) teaching; (4) demonstrated attainments in public policy and management; and (5) institutional citizenship. Finding individuals who achieve the requisite distinction on all five dimensions has remained a great challenge.

Lesson 8: *fundraising is mostly a matter of hard work.* I often thought of it in terms of dollars per hour. I started off earning about $100 an hour. As I got better, I got to the rate of $1,000 an hour. By the end I was earning about $10,000 an hour. But that means that raising $1 million takes one hundred hours, $10 million a thousand hours, or roughly half a year. Over my twelve years as dean, I spent approximately half my time fundraising as the School's endowment grew from $20 million to $150 million.

Lesson 9: *most academics fail to appreciate the ways in which space shapes activity.* The Kennedy School had the good fortune to build a number of new buildings, thanks to our success in fundraising. This helped us deliberately shape our identity. Central to this effort was the creation of the Kennedy School Forum, a multistoried atrium that serves as our town square and food court by day, but becomes the

University's premier location for public debates each evening. Seating 750, in a cross between a New England town meeting hall and the Greek *agora*, the Forum provides for the Kennedy School and other University students what has been called an "extra course." A regular visitor to the Forum will encounter, and often have an opportunity to question, scores of heads of state and former presidents and prime ministers, political candidates, and policy advocates of all stripes.

Lesson 10: *the centrality of the management team cannot be overemphasized.* To the extent that people can become part of such a team, they multiply the effects of any dean. The temptation is to imagine that one can do it oneself or do better than one's colleagues. But even if one's performance was consistently better than other members of one's team in any specific task, the multiplication that comes from a second person and third and fourth far exceeds what any single person can do him- or herself.

Lesson 11: *in any ambitious pursuit, mistakes are inevitable.* We can think of Type 1 and Type 2 errors—sins of omission and commission. I think the sins of omission are more common in academic administration and that we should worry less about the mistakes of commission. I certainly tried to err on the side of commission—and committed my share.

Lesson 12: *on the press, I never truly figured out how to deal with it.* Over time, we created a Center for Press, Politics, and Public Policy, in order better to understand the role of the press in government. Its role in the building of a school of public policy could also be much better understood. A popular song advises: "Don't piss into the wind." Few of those engaged in trying to build schools of government have taken that advice. Obviously, this has been a hostile environment for government from Nixon and Watergate to Carter, who was perhaps the most viscerally anti-government of recent presidents, and Reagan. As was so often the case, Ronald Reagan said it best in his inaugural address: "Government is not the solution to the problem; government is the problem."

The Kennedy School never effectively targeted this hostility or found any way to deal with it. Nor, unfortunately, has the profession.

Finally, lesson 13 is *the satisfaction of institution building.* Most deans complain a lot. I certainly did. But through that experience, and looking back, one has to be grateful for the satisfactions provided by the opportunity to build and shape an institution whose impact extends beyond one's own reach and perhaps even beyond one's own time.

## REFERENCES

ALLISON, G. 1971. *Essence of Decision: Explaining the Cuban Missile Crisis.* New York: HarperCollins.

BELL, P. 1980. Recommendations for future foundation support of programs in public policy. Ford Foundation Archives.

—— 1981. Graduate training programs in public policy supported by the Ford Foundation. Ford Foundation Archives.

BLUNT, B. E. 1988. Development in public administration pedagogy: 1880 to the present. Pp. 601–31 in *Handbook of Public Administration*, ed. J. Rabin, W. B. Hildreth, and G. J. Miller. New York: Marcel Dekker.

CARROLL, J., and ZUCK, A. 1985. *"The Study of Administration" Revisited: Report on the Centennial Agendas Project*. Washington, DC: American Society for Public Administration.

CRECINE, J. P. 1971. University centers for the study of public policy: organizational viability. *Policy Sciences*, 2(1): 7–32.

CRUIKSHANK, J. L. 1987. *A Delicate Experiment: The Harvard Business School, 1908–1945*. Cambridge, Mass.: Harvard University Press.

ENTHOVEN, A., and SMITH, K. W. 1971. *How Much is Enough? Shaping the Defense Program, 1961–1969*. New York: Harper and Row.

FLEISCHMAN, J. 1990. A new framework for integration: policy analysis and public management. *American Behavioral Scientist*, 33(6): 733–54.

FREDRICKSON, H. G. 1971. Toward a new public administration. Pp. 309–31 in *Toward a New Public Administration: The Minnowbrook Perspective*, ed. F. E. Marini. New York: Harper-Collins.

GUY, M. E. 2003. Ties that bind: the link between public administration and political science. *Journal of Politics*, 65(3): 641–55.

HENRY, N. L. 1990. Root and branch: public administration's travail toward the future. Pp. 3–26 in *Public Administration: The State of the Discipline*, ed. N. B. Lynn and A. Wildavsky. Chatham, NJ: Chatham House.

HERRING, E. P. 1936. *Public Administration and the Public Interest*. New York: McGraw-Hill.

JOHN F. KENNEDY SCHOOL of GOVERNMENT 1986. *The John F. Kennedy School of Government*. Cambridge, Mass.: Ballinger.

LAMBERT, C. 2003. Despite a myriad of challenges 25 years ago, the Kennedy School has prevailed. *Kennedy School Bulletin*, Autumn; available at: www.ksg.harvard.edu/ksgpress/bulletin/autumn2003/features/against_odds.html.

—— 2004. The origins of the John F. Kennedy School of Government. Unpublished.

LASSWELL, H. D. 1951. The policy orientation. Pp. 3–15 in *The Policy Sciences*, ed. H. D. Lasswell and D. Lerner. Palo Alto, Calif.: Stanford University Press.

—— 1971. *A Pre-View of Policy Sciences*. New York: Elsevier.

LOWI, T. J. 1972. Four systems of policy, politics, and choice. *Public Administration Review*, 32(4): 298–310.

MILES, R. E., Jr. 1967. The search for identity of graduate schools of public affairs. *Public Administration Review*, 27(4): 343–56.

MOORE, M. 1995. *Creating Public Value: Strategic Management in Government*. Cambridge, Mass.: Harvard University Press.

MOSCHER, F. C. (ed.) 1975. *American Public Administration: Past, Present, Future*. Birmingham: University of Alabama Press.

NEUSTADT, R. E. 1960. *Presidential Power: The Politics of Leadership*. New York: Wiley.

OFFICE of MANAGEMENT AND BUDGET 2004. *Summary of Receipts, Outlays, and Surpluses or Deficits as Percentages of GDP: 1930–2008*. Washington, DC.

PORTER, B. D. 1994. *War and the Rise of the State: The Military Foundations of Modern Politics*. New York: Free Press.

RIGGS, F. W. 1998. Public administration in America: why our uniqueness is exceptional and important. *Public Administration Review*, 58(1): 22–31.

ROETHLISBERGER, F. J. 1977. *The Elusive Phenomenon: An Autobiographical Account of my Work in the Field of Organizational Behavior at the Harvard Business School*. Cambridge, Mass.: Harvard University Press.

ROTHWELL, C. E. 1951. Foreword. Pp. vii–xi in *The Policy Sciences*, ed. H. D. Lasswell and D. Lerner. Palo Alto, Calif.: Stanford University Press.

SKOWRONEK, S. 1982. *Building a New American State: The Expansion of National Administrative Capacities, 1977–1920*. Cambridge: Cambridge University Press.

STIVERS, C. 2000. *Bureau Men, Settlement Women: Constructing Public Administration in the Progressive Era*. Lawrence: University of Kansas Press.

STOKES, D. E. 1996. "Presidential" address: the changing environment of education for public service. *Journal of Policy Analysis and Management*, 15(2): 158–70.

WALKER, J. L. 1976. The curriculum in public policy studies at the University of Michigan. *Journal of Urban Analysis*, 4(1): 3–28.

WILDAVSKY, A. 1976. Principles for a graduate school of public policy. *Journal of Urban Analysis*, 3(1): 127–52.

—— 1979. *Speaking Truth to Power: The Art and Craft of Policy Analysis*. New Brunswick, NJ: Transaction Books.

WILSON, W. 1887. The study of administration. *Political Science Quarterly*, 2(2): 197–222.

YATES, D. C. 1977. The mission of public policy programs: a report on recent experience. *Policy Sciences*, 8(3): 363–73.

# CHAPTER 4

# TRAINING FOR POLICY MAKERS

## YEHEZKEL DROR

THIS chapter discusses training for policy makers by focusing on a politically incorrect subject, namely training of rulers in grand-policy thinking. But the analysis and recommendations apply with some adjustments to all types and levels of policy makers.

The importance of rulers and their quality is widely recognized, but needs and possibilities for improving them are not only ignored, but taboo. If rulers would in the main perform well this would not matter much. However, it is enough to observe governments and their heads in action to reach the conclusion that even the best of rulers often fail to cope adequately with increasingly fateful choices. And the few very good rulers, too, make grievous mistakes the costs of which are constantly increasing because of the growing future-shaping power of human action. Therefore, steps to improve the performance of the highest strata of policy makers are imperative.

The performance of rulers depends on a range of intrinsic and extrinsic variables. The required qualities are multidimensional, ranging from moral character to political skills. Ways to improve them vary, from improving governance systems within which they operate as a whole to trying to improve their characters, stimulate their "emotional intelligence" (Goleman, Boyatzis, and McKee 2002), and restructure advisory systems. However, given institutional rather than revolutionary leadership, where other qualities are crucial, grand-policy training may often be a very cost-effective approach.

The required performance of rulers and their relative importance depend on situations. However, a core function of all rulers is to fulfill a major and often critical role in decision making and in particular grand-policy crafting.

Governmental decisions can be divided into relatively routine decisions dealing with current issues, which are not expected to make much of a difference; and what

I call "grand policies" which aim at massive effects on the future. Grand policies consist of various combinations of single critical choices and long-term strategies. Critical choices are illustrated by dropping the nuclear bombs on Japan, approving a large infrastructure project, or joining the European Union. Long-term strategies include moving from a command to a market economy, giving priority to the young in public health services, trying to promote democracy in the Middle East, and efforts to become a learning society.

Most choices need improvement. However, grand policies exert more influence on the future and are more intricate. Therefore, a high priority task is to upgrade grand-policy crafting qualities of rulers. Doing so depends on availability of knowledge on which effective grand-policy training of rulers can be based. The basis thesis of this chapter is that such knowledge is available, in part readily so and in part in raw form which can be reprocessed. This proposition will be supported by presentation of a prototype core curriculum for grand-policy training of rulers together with selective references to pertinent knowledge and some comments on training modalities.

# 1. Core Curriculum

The proposed core curriculum is equivalent in content to a preferable model of cognitive capacities of a high-quality ruler in his grand-policy crafting roles. It includes twenty closely linked and in part overlapping themes or subjects, presented concisely, together with select references as mentioned and comments on mentors and didactics adding to what has been postulated above.

A special form of "grand policies" deals with institution building and structural change. Going back to classical views of rulers as "law givers," revamping institutions and building new ones is a major modality of "grand policy." Illustrations include constitution writing, building new governance structures such as the European Union, changing global governance, and building a market economy. Throughout the training, this grand-policy form should be taken into account with attention to the importance of institutions (North 1990) and institutional design (Goodin 1998) within the various subjects.

## 1.1 Separating Politics and Policy

The first imperative is the capacity to make a clear analytic distinction between policy and politics. These closely interact, often overlap, and in part cannot be separated even analytically. The absence of different terms for "politics" and "policy" in most languages other than English reflects the difficulties of that distinction. Furthermore, modern democratic politics often pushes rulers in the direction of subordinating policy to politics and marketing, with rulers often giving priority to "blowing of bubbles" over weaving the future. But grand-policy quality depends on the ability of rulers to differentiate between policy and politics and giving priority to policy requirements before making unavoidable compromises with political reality. Training should clarify and emphasize this distinction.

However, political feasibility must not be neglected. A grand-policy option which cannot be implemented in the foreseeable future because of lack of essential political support or other crucial resources is not one to be chosen, though crafting it as a contingency policy to be realized when conditions change is often to be recommended. Therefore, political feasibility and ways to increase it should be included in the curriculum within the broader context of feasibility testing and policy resources amplification as a whole—but without going into the substance of power mobilization and political marketing.

Here, training is sure to run into a difficulty. Participants will wish to discuss politics and marketing. There is no lack of good literature dealing with policy making in its political context which can be referred to (Stone 2001). Having mentors who know politics and who demonstrate this knowledge from time to time, but without being distracted from the main curriculum, can help a lot.

## 1.2 Value Clarification and Goal Setting

Grand policies are value based, goal directed, and goal seeking. If the values are superficial and slogan-like and the goals are misperceived then choices will be counter-productive. Hence the importance of improving value clarification and goal setting. However, value judgement is a subjective process entrusted by the basic norms of democracy to elected politicians, subject to legal review and sometimes public override. Improving their value judgement and goal setting must not undermine their prerogative and duty to make legitimate value judgements, but rather help them clarify their values and operationalize their goals.

This raises a serious moral problem concerning training of evil rulers which will make them more effective in doing evil (Kellerman 2004, ch. 10). Therefore mentors need a professional code by which to train. Given Western democracies this is not an acute problem, though one to be kept in mind.

Relevant issues to be taken up in grand-policy training include, for instance:

1. Moral and political tensions between following values and desires of the public as against advancing values which the ruler, after full consideration and soul searching, regards as normatively and realpolitically correct (including the tangential issue of how far educating the public to higher values is part of his mission).

2. Tragic choices between meeting present needs as against trying to take care of future generations, including coping with the congenital defect of democracy of future generations not voting now, though heavily impacted by present decisions.

3. Relations between moral intentions, rule-based value judgements (including legal approaches), and consequentialism.

4. Serving individuals as supreme values by themselves as against advancing the thriving of societies.

5. Psychological and moral contradictions between intensely believing in select values and knowing that one's beliefs are largely a product of personal circumstances which one did not choose, such as the period, culture, and family into which one is born.

6. Related, the tension between looking on values as a sociocultural fact and believing in them. And between trying to adopt a cold stance and an attitude of clinical concern on one hand and intensely striving to realize values to which one is deeply committed on the other.

7. Taking into account future unpredictable values, including providing open options for future generations to realize whatever values they may have, as against trying to fortify present values against change.

8. The dilemma between clarifying the value and goal priorities on which a decision is based as against maintaining coalitions and mobilizing support by keeping values and goals ambiguous and opaque.

9. The increasingly acute dilemma between advancing the interests of one's country and taking into account the good of humanity as a whole, what I call *raison d'humanité* (Dror 2002, ch. 9).

10. The problematic of applying value judgements and goal priorities to specific situations as an iterative process.

11. On a different level, but at least to be posed: the personal dilemma between fulfilling one's mission and advancing values on one hand and taking care of one's career on the other.

Such subjects are to be taken up with the help of a broad set of value clarification and moral reasoning approaches. Examples include the following:[1]

- Socratic dialogue, helping self-clarification of values.
- Select basic normative frames, such as religious, Kantian, and utilitarian.
- Soft psycho-didactics, facilitating differentiation between motifs and drives on one hand and values on the other.
- Exposition of often neglected value and goal dimensions, such as preferences in time stream, attitudes to risks, and elasticity as a goal.
- Philosophic discourse posing categorical imperatives, clarifying values (such as in political philosophy), and presenting ways of helping value judgements.

[1] See Boyce and Jensen 1978; Levi 1986.

- Logical and behavioral contradictions between values.
- Sensitivity testing to identify and clarify value choices and goal priorities necessary in specific choice contexts.
- Concept packages provided by jurisprudence and philosophy helping to enrich value thinking and deal with value conflicts, including use of decision rules.
- Discourse on especially problematic value judgement situations, such as "moral bad luck" (Statmen 1993) and "tragic choice" (Calabresi and Bobbit 1979).
- Welfare economics ideas and theorems salient to value consideration, such as Pareto optimum and the Arrow paradox.
- Construction of value and goal taxonomies and hierarchies.
- Goal-costing and microeconomics methods for considering costs–benefits of alternative value and goal mixes.
- Critical clarification of substantive values of high importance in many grand-policy spaces, such as human rights and duties, equity, reducing poverty, environmental values, animal rights, "fairness," communitarianism, "just war," and so on.

Training in value clarification and goal setting is very demanding, in terms of contents and interface with senior decision makers alike. Resistance to being told how to think on values and goals can be overcome by focusing on helping participants to make their own judgement, without presuming to tell them what their values should be. Helpful are uses of court judgements and, especially, literary texts with discussion of the ethical issues raised in them (Nussbaum 1995).

## 1.3 Creatively Weaving the Future

Grand policies are instruments aiming at—to use a striking term coined by Plato in *The Statesman*—"weaving the future" through creatively combining present contradictory materials and processes into making a better future. More specifically, grand policies try to reduce the probability of bad futures, to increase the probability of good futures, as their images and evaluations change with time, and to gear up to coping with the unforeseen and the unforeseeable.

To introduce a different metaphor, in grand-policy crafting rulers perform as both composers and conductors, with composing being much more difficult, original, personal, and important than conducting, however essential the latter is to realization of the compositions, giving them varied interpretations, and adjusting them to changing situations.

The metaphor is revealing, though a ruler is very different from a composer in working within organizations and composing and conducting in union as well as competition and also conflict with peers, advisers, organizations, and societies. The freedom of innovation enjoyed by a great composer creating on his own is larger by many orders of magnitude than the constrained space of creation open to rulers. Still, creation is at the core of grand-policy crafting, all the more so in our epoch when rapid change makes the wisdom of the past into the stupidity of the future, and invention of new options fitting radically novel situations and values is a must. The ruler should in part operate as a creator (as well as transformer and change agent) and his mind pictures and "inner visibility" (Panek 2004) are of profound importance, on a minor scale "on line with the mind-music Beethoven heard when he was deaf" (Gelernter 2004). If the ruler himself cannot be a real creator, at least he should facilitate policy option creativity and be eager to consider and absorb new ideas after open-minded but critical evaluation.

To go one step further, high-quality grand-policy crafting in an epoch of transformations requires visions up to elements of utopian thinking. This is crucial for revolutionary rulers, but also increasingly essential for institutional rulers—who, whether they like it or not, face quasi-revolutionary situations sure to characterize the twenty-first century. Grand-policy training cannot make rulers into visionary leaders. But training can achieve awareness of the importance and nature of the future-weaving mission of rulers with its creative elements.

On a more operational level, to be emphasized and illustrated is the scarcity of promising options for main policy issues and therefore the practical need for option invention, to be sought, encouraged, and pushed by rulers. No less important is the negative necessity to engage in iconoclasm of policy orthodoxies. "More of the same," however politically convenient and organizationally attractive, is frequently worse than doing nothing. Encouraging rulers to be skeptical about accepted "solutions" is therefore an important part of the training.

## 1.4 Time Horizons

Grand policies aim at long-term impacts. But this general statement needs specification so as to help rulers to adopt preferable time horizons adjusted to the features of different policy spaces.

Four main criteria are relevant:

1. Value preferences which postulate the relative importance given value-wise to results at different points in the future, with care to be taken to avoid errors such as discounting results in time stream as if one deals with old-fashioned portfolio investments.
2. The life cycles of relevant policy spaces and the time needed for a decision to reach its main impact.
3. Predictability, with uncertainty and inconceivability usually increasing with the length of time horizons.

4. Political and personal cycles, to assure sufficient time for a grand policy to have a meaningful impact.

For most grand policies medium- and long-range effects should be aimed at, ranging from about five years to multiple generations. The life cycles of most grand policies usually have a similar range. But predictability rapidly decreases, with the outlook beyond five years and more becoming increasingly uncertain and dense with inconceivability. And political and personal cycles in democracies range from four to ten years.

It is the contradictions between long-term values and long implementation cycles on one hand and unpredictability and short political and personal cycles on the other which constitute a main cause of the fragility of grand policies. Uncertainty sophistication, as discussed later, can help, as can political stratagems and governmental structures facilitating policy continuity. But the dilemma is serious, often undermining the very significance of grand policies and making them less attractive to rulers.

Training can expose these problems, suggest treatments, and illustrate coping practices, such as multiphased time horizons divided into five-year intervals with a maximum, in most cases, of twenty-five years. Other possibilities include increasing policy continuity between governments by building consensus and institutionalizing grand policies.

Relevant experiences and ideas are available in literature dealing with planning and strategy (Ansoff 1979; Steiner 1997).

## 1.5 Thinking-in-History

The basic reasoning of grand-policy crafting is one of intervening with historic processes so as to achieve desired impacts on the future. This requires, first of all, "thinking-in-history" with emphasis on macro and deep history. Required are mapping of the evolutionary potential of the past as evolving into the future, designation of policy spaces where interventions are necessary to prevent the bad and achieve the good, identification of main drivers of the future, and pinpointing of a subset of such drivers which can be influenced by deliberate governmental action and thus serve as policy instruments.

All this should be seen within an overall view of human history as shaped by a dynamic mixture, which is changing non-linearly, between necessity, contingency, mutations, and random events—as influenced by human deliberate or unintended interventions.

This formulation fully exposes the presumptuous nature of grand-policy crafting and the dangers of unintended and bad results even when choices are based on the best knowledge and the highest cognitive qualities that human beings can achieve. Therefore, it is only the near-certainty that ongoing historical processes may well result in very bad and also catastrophic futures and the expectation that well-considered governmental, selective, and carefully considered interventions with historical processes have a good chance to avoid some of the bad and achieve more of the good that justify grand-policy crafting and implementation.

The proposed view of historic processes and the conjecture on the potentials for the better of grand policies are foundational for training. Foci of attention include:

1. The dependence of all choice on assumptions concerning causal relations between what is done now and what will happen in the future.
2. The both doubtful and complex nature of such assumptions, requiring on the emotional and personality levels a good measure of skepticism combined with decisiveness; and on the level of cognitive processes a lot of uncertainty sophistication as epitomized in the perception of choices as "fuzzy gambles," discussed later.
3. The moral and realpolitical imperative to seek the best possible groundings for grand policies, in terms of reliance on whatever salient knowledge is or can be made available, serious pondering, and optimal reasoning and choice processes.

Participants should be provided with at least a window into thinking-in-history and its requirements of lifelong reading and both abstract and applied thinking. A preliminary step is to alert them to the dangers of wrongly applying history to current issues, as first pointed out by Nietzsche. These include wrong reliance on historical analogs (May 1972; Neustadt and May 1986) and fixation on surface events without understanding their embedment in deeper processes.

Some classical writings do try to base statecraft on the study of history, as illustrated by the meditations of Machiavelli and *The Peloponnesian War* by Thucydides. These should be referred to, with participants asked to read, if possible before the training activity, one or two books providing a vista of long-term history (Denemark et al. 2000; Gernet 1996), a text or two on the dynamics of history (Hawthorn 1991), and another book or two in philosophy of history and historiography (Braudel 1980). More realistic when maximum reading requirements are limited is demonstrating thinking-in-history and exercising it by application to select grand-policy spaces.

## 1.6  Understanding Reality

Understanding reality as in between the past and the future is of paramount importance while being very error prone. To improve the "world in the mind" (Vertzberger 1990) of rulers so as better to fit reality and its dynamics is therefore a main training task.

It is inherently impossible for human beings to take a "view from nowhere" (Nagel 1986). But the propensities to misread reality because of cultural and personal blinders and motivated irrationality (Pears 1984) can be counteracted and participants can be helped to exit misleading "boxes" and "frames" distorting their perceptions of the world.

A lot is known on factors distorting social imagery, cognitive maps, and reference theories of rulers. There is also quite some knowledge available on the difficulties of improving reality images through providing new information. The rich literature on intelligence failures and distortions can serve as a solid basis for training (Codevilla 1992). Findings dealing with dramatic recent intelligence failures, such as on the terror attack on the USA (National Commission on Terrorist Attacks 2004), can serve as excellent training material to 'open the minds' of rulers in ways very helpful to grand-policy crafting.

Very important is enrichment of the concept packages of rulers so as better to perceive and process reality. Thus, the concept of "second strike capacity," very novel at its time, was crucial in providing understanding of new strategic realities produced by nuclear weapons. Therefore, adding to the mental vocabulary of rulers concepts such as "soft power" (Nye 2004), "inconceivability" (Dror 1999), "fuzzy gambling" as discussed later, "virtual history" (Ferguson 1997), thought experiment (Sorensen 1992), "distant proximities" (Rosenau 2003), and many more can help to improve mental images of reality in ways improving grand-policy thinking. But relevant literature is dispersed over a large range of disciplines, illustrating the need for multidisciplinary bases for grand-policy training of rulers and its dependence on very knowledgeable mentors.

It is easy to present rulers with descriptions and analysis of select aspects of the world (such as some chapters in Lord 2003). Taking up one critical but often misunderstood dimension in order to illustrate needs and possibilities to arrive at deeper understanding can be quite useful, with "globalization" being a good example. But grand-policy training for rulers should provide them with insights, understandings, frames, theories, approaches, reasoning modalities, etc. which will stand the test of time and be applicable to a large variety of changing situations, not monographic knowledge sure to be outdated soon.

Quite different is the question whether one should include in the program exploration of fundamental, very stable parts of reality, such as "human nature" and its competing explanations in terms of fixed essence as against cultural formation (Ridley 2003) and the nature of "evil" (Bernstein 2002). It might be a good idea to expose participants to such problems so as to open their minds, perhaps by guest lectures and short readings. But overloads must be avoided and many important subjects not directly related to grand-policy thinking as such must necessarily be excluded from most training programs for rulers.

## 1.7 Foresight

Understanding historical processes, including their inherent uncertainties and inconceivabilities, is an essential foundation. But directly needed for grand-policy crafting is foresight, the ability to foresee alternative futures and the likely consequences of different interventions with historical processes—so as to decide what to do now and what to plan to do in the future, subject to revisions depending on actual development.

To put it into a literary form, which may be insight providing to participants, foresight (and understanding reality) aim to reduce regret "if only we could know!," as central in the view of one interpretation to the works of Chekhov (Kataev 2002).

However, the dependence of choice on foresight is, as already indicated, the main cause of policy fragility. Our epoch is one of ruptures in historical continuity together with a lot of invariance. Therefore, it is very likely that future historical processes, also in the near future, will be in part radically different from what we know from the past, so that even perfect understanding of the past—which does not exist—cannot provide reliable knowledge on the impacts of different grand policies on the future.

Still, quite some foresight is possible thanks to the relative stability of some main historical structures and processes and some understanding of change. These are the grounding of four main outlook approaches:

1. Extrapolation, with past and present facts and dynamics being projected into the future.
2. Theories and qualitative and sometimes quantitative models based on them from which conditional predictions can be derived by changing the time parameters.
3. Intuitive knowledge, whether professional, local, or naive, which provides subjective images of the future based on tacit knowledge and pattern recognition, expertise, and experience.
4. Imagination, whether "wild" or based on various forms of intuition and experience.

The trouble is that the three first families depend on the past, either directly or as processed into theories and experience. The nature of imagination is not clear and may in part transcend the past, but its validity cannot be evaluated. Therefore basing policies on imagination concerning likely futures (as distinct from utopias which present ideal futures relevant to value clarification) is reckless, however stimulating the images of the future of some thinkers may be.

In terms of both ontology and epistemology, because of the contingent and mutative nature of future-shaping processes and the limits of human understanding of such processer, the future has to be viewed as largely underdetermined by the past. And, the less the future is determined by the past the less can it be foreseen, both inherently and because of the dependence of foresight, including also highly structured outlook and forecasting methods, on the past—with the hypothetical exception of wild imagination, with its many dangers.

We must not have an exaggerated view of future-shaping processes as being chaotic, as there is a lot of continuity. However, the twenty-first century will be characterized by many discontinuities and reality-mutating events, making the future in part inconceivable. The conclusion is that the best foresight is in large parts doubtful as a basis for choice. But choice is unavoidably based on foresight, however in need of skepticism. It follows that grand-policies are largely in their very nature and essence "fuzzy gambles." This is a critical conclusion for the training of rulers.

Explaining the problematic nature of outlook is not difficult, all the more as reality provides many striking illustrations. But care must be taken to avoid too extreme a conclusion, making rulers doubt equally all outlooks and motivating them to trust their own intuition more than professional guesstimates of alternative futures. Over-chaotic views of the future will also result in recklessness or unwillingness to adopt long-term policies when clearly essential. Worst of all is the escape of rulers from uncertainty into fixed and arbitrary assumptions, as if the future is subject to their commands, or reliance on astrology and similar stupidity.

Therefore, care must be taken to balance presentation of uncertainty and inconceivability with emphasis on the many important features of reality and its dynamics which are invariable within policy-relevant timespans, making carefully prepared foresight useful though doubtful.

A special problem is posed by circumstances in which "confidence" is more important than foresight, namely revolutionary situations when it is necessary to trust that God or History are on one's side, so that the effects of "self-fulfilling" prophecy can be mobilized to make the nearly impossible a little less impossible though still very unlikely. But in most situations overdoses of "confidence" (Kanter 2004) are very dangerous, realistic guesstimation being instead required together with prudence and also doubts and skepticism, combined with decisiveness.

There is no scarcity of literature on which exploration of foresight approaches as well as critical examination of predictions can be based (CIA 2004; Lempert, Popper, and Bankes 2003; Molitor 2003).

## 1.8 Cogitating, Feeling, and Dreaming in Terms of Alternative Futures and their Drivers

At the core of the curriculum and summing up much of it are thinking, feeling, imagining, dreaming, speculating, guesstimating, and planning in terms of alternative futures, rise and decline, realistic visions and nightmares, etc., together with their drivers and policy instruments.

Rulers need to be trained and habituated to exercise all their mental facilities to play with and consider in-depth alternative trajectories into the future and the actions they need to take, to reiterate a key formulate, in order to improve the probability of the desirable ones, decrease the probability of the undesirable ones, and gear up to coping with the inconceivable sure to come.

The vast difficulties of doing so are brought out by "if–then" historical speculations, nowadays called "virtual history" (Ferguson 1997). To take a relatively simple example, let us assume that Hitler had been assassinated in 1938. It is very likely that the *Shoah* would never have happened and that Hitler would be remembered mainly as a great German statesman, a "second Bismarck." But what European, Jewish, and global history would have been like is a matter for wild speculation, with available understanding of historical processes being very inadequate for providing supportable conjectures.

This is the case concerning the past, when we know many facts. All the more difficult is consideration of alternative futures, which is a kind of futuristic virtual history dealing with the question: If I do so-and-so what is the future likely to be? Or, more sophisticatedly: If I do so and so, what is the likely range of possible futures? But, however doubtful and in part speculative, this is the stuff on which grand policies are unavoidably based.

Cogitating, feeling, and dreaming in terms of alternative futures and their drivers as central to policy making involve five main elements:

1. As indicated, the hub around which all choice circulates is "alternative futures," a concept first worked out by Bertrand de Jouvenel (Jouvenel 1967) and called by him "futuribles." The ruler's mind has to imagine and think in terms of alternative futures of main policy spaces and all of them together, consider which ones have to be prevented and which ones have to be facilitated, identify main drivers which will further the prevention and realization of the various alternative futures, and select a subset of the drivers which can serve as policy instruments to be integrated into grand policies, including institutional ones.

2. The need is not only for deliberate and disciplined thinking in terms of alternative futures and their drivers, but for exercising one's entire mind. Imagining alternative futures, dreaming about them, and speculating on them are essential for injecting much-needed creativity and for tuning the ruler's entire mind to operating in terms of alternative futures.

3. Imagining, dreaming, speculating, guesstimating, and finally planning and crafting of grand policies require multiple frames so as not to get lost in the kaleidoscopic, multifarious labyrinths of the future. The most demanding but often critical frame is rise and decline of nations, regions, communities, and humanity. However speculative in part, it provides a basis for deep and holistic thinking on alternative futures.

4. Concrete and directly guiding grand policies are realistic visions and nightmares. These are specified alternative images of near and middle-range futures to be approximated or prevented. To check realism and to derive from them policies, they should be linked to present dynamics by scenarios and roadmaps.

Realistic visions and methods for working them out are well recognized in business literature (Hamel and Prahalad 1994) and practice. Military experience is relevant to considering "worst-case" nightmares and their shortcomings. Some countries have prepared realistic visions. All of these provide good bases for training.

More difficult is facilitation of thinking in terms of "rise and decline." Classical writings by Gibson, Toynbee, and Sprengler are in part stimulating, but training should critically discuss modern literature and apply it to select grand-policy domains (Kennedy 1987; Olson 1982; Tainter 1988).

## 1.9 Critical Mass Interventions with Historic Processes

The applied purpose of thinking-in-history, cogitating in terms of alternative futures, etc. and the main rationale of grand policies are to design, plan, and implement interventions with historical processes so as to try and weave a better future. Such interventions with historical processes are, on the most fundamental level, based on a philosophy or theory of history and of reality as a whole (McCall 1994), which—as mentioned—regards the future as produced by a dynamic non-linearly changing mix between (1) necessity, that is, deterministic processes, whether simple or probabilistic (taking the form of stochastic chains); (2) contingencies, that is, pre-fixed sets of alternative futures without predetermined probabilities; (3) mutations, that is, radical shifts and ruptures in continuity leading into what prospectively are largely inconceivable directions, as a result of processes which may or may not be predetermined or indeterminate to various degrees; and (4), in part overlapping the last category, what from a human perspective are random events, such as the idiosyncratic behavior of a powerful ruler.

Given such an image of historic processes, there is scope for human weaving of the future to the extent that a human agency controls resources which can have impact on future-making processes.

As already emphasized, the future-shaping power of human decisions and actions, including by governments and rulers, is increasing by orders of magnitude, mainly as a result of science and technology. However, this conclusion has to be reconsidered within a broader canvas of the potential for human free will to shape the future as in being between values and desires as independent drivers on one hand and stubborn facts of reality as limiting free will and future-shaping possibilities on the other. An extreme idealistic view of human nature and history would grant to freely chosen human values and desires very much influence on the future, while an extreme materialistic view would minimize the existence of free human choice and its impact on the future. Between such extreme positions, the proposed view recognizes the rapidly increasing weight of human action as decided in part by free human choice in influencing the future, but regards this influence as constrained by limits on free choice and historic events and processes beyond human influence. Furthermore, and this is very important, there is a world of difference between the overall impact of human action on human futures and human impacts on the future which are purposeful and are more or less in line with what is aimed at by partly free choice. Much of the growing impact of human action on the future is not intended and even less of the impact fits freely chosen values and goals of human agencies entitled according to accepted ideologies to engage in future shaping, such as legitimate governments and rulers.

Furthermore, not only are many impacts unintended but they are also undesired, with a rapidly increasing risk of unintended very bad impacts resulting from the growing gap between rapidly increasing human power to influence the future, and more or less stable human capacities to exercise these powers so as to prevent the bad and achieve the good.

It is this widening gap between growing impact power and relatively stable decision-making quality which poses the main challenge to grand-policy training of rulers and makes it into an endeavor which may have macro-historic significance.

However "philosophic," these perspectives should be discussed with participants as basic to serious grand-policy thinking. This, together with explanation of the purposes of the training as providing perspectives, understandings, and approaches, not techniques.

On a more applied level, the main purpose of training of rulers can be reformulated as augmenting their capacity to weave the future according to their clarified values and prioritized goals, insofar as legitimate within accepted constitutional norms. An important element of this capacity is their understanding of the potential as well as limits of their ability to achieve desired impacts on the future, including much uncertainty on what the limits of their effective choice are—as evidenced by the many historical cases of very large impacts which could not be expected in advance together with the many cases when effects which were reasonably expected and aimed at were not realized.

Training of rulers should provide them with an understanding of this complex relation between their future-shaping power and their actual impact on the future. Furthermore, participants should realize that to a meaningful though limited extent their impact on the future depends on their personal capacities, including the quality of their grand-policy thinking at the augmentation of which the training is directed.

Given such an understanding of historical processes, effective efforts to shape the future through intervention in historical processes must meet six conditions:

1. A will to shape the future.
2. Some operational notions of what constitute "good" or "bad" futures.
3. Adequate understanding of historical processes, so that the chances of interventions having effects for the better are higher than the risks of bad outcomes.
4. Capacities to translate the understandings into grand policies.
5. Sufficient resources—political, economic, human, etc.—to achieve critical masses of intervention in historical processes so as to have a substantive impact on them.

6. Implementing capacities adequate to translating the grand policies into effective action and applying the resources effectively and efficiently.

The need for "critical intervention mass," including often but not always "large-scale" policies (Schulman 1980), needs emphasis, all the more so as it is often ignored in theory and practice alike. Political and other pressures together with resource limitations frequently result in dispersal of limited resources over many policies with the result that often minimum critical mass thresholds are not reached and as a result policies do not have the desired effects. Hence the need to set priorities and focus resources on a limited number of grand policies so as to achieve adequate intervention masses, together with ways to make this feasible—such as by nominal allocation of limited resources to other policies so as to meet demands without really expecting much impact, while concentrating main efforts on a limited number of grand policies.

Critical mass thresholds vary with the rigidity or fragility of given historic processes and the extent of change aimed at in historic trajectories. Thus, in some cases relatively minor interventions can operate as a "tipping points" while in others only large-scale interventions provide a chance to achieve desired impacts.

Crises sometimes provide unique opportunities to have significant impact with limited intervention masses, as will be discussed later. Even more special a case is the "throwing of surprises at history" as a way to try and achieve major impacts with limited resources by creating a "fulcrum" effect. Illustrations include sudden devaluations and surprise attacks or agreements.

Discussing with participants situations when throwing of surprises at history is justified despite its risks, to avert great dangers or avail oneself of short windows of opportunity, is a good way to clarify the idea of critical mass interventions with historical processes. It also illustrates a special type of grand policy taking the form of critical choice, and brings out the problematic of taking risks as against that of being prudent together with the importance of creativity.

Crucial to effective interventions with history are the causal assumptions on which they are based. Required is explication of such assumptions, critical examination of their bases and validity, and clarification of their quantitatively and qualitatively probabilistic nature at best, and their being often guesstimates and speculations.

Especially difficult for many participants to absorb, as distinct from abstractly understanding, is the unavoidable conclusion that the most "practical" decision maker depends unavoidably on multiple and often quite hypothetical conjectures, assumptions, theories, and speculations. Not less difficult is the required thinking in terms of quantitative and qualitative uncertainties and inconceivability. And hardest of all to accept and act upon is the simple but striking conclusion that all major choices, including grand policies, are in their very nature and essence "fuzzy gambles," with rulers being in crucial respects gamblers with history, often for high and also fateful stakes.

# 1.10 Fuzzy Gambling Sophistication

All that has been said leads to the conclusion that grand policies are in their very nature "fuzzy gambles," that is, gambles without fixed rules the very nature of the outcomes of which is in large part ambiguous, indeterminate, and unknowable in advance. Therefore, to re-emphasize a crucial point which is central to grand-policy training of rulers, one of their most critical tasks is to engage in fuzzy gambling, often for very high stakes. They need not delve into the philosophic, psychological, and methodological aspects of fuzzy gambling and its improvements, but they definitely need awareness of this essential nature of their choices and its problems and familiarity with ways of coping—in short, they need "fuzzy gambling sophistication."

This conclusion is intellectually irrefutable, but very hard to accept emotionally and anathema politically. It may also be dangerous to explain it to decision makers with low tolerance of ambiguity, as it can cause recklessness, an illusionary subjective sense of certainty, and reliance on false prophets and seers.

Particularly challenging are:

1. Required value judgements on preferred mixes of risks, qualitative uncertainties, and inconceivability.
2. Findings in decision psychology indicating that human thinking on uncertainty is very error prone.
3. Irrationality of public attitudes to risk, making it politically dangerous for rulers to explain truthfully the fuzzy gambling nature of their grand policies.
4. Failures and misuses of security intelligence and other types of estimations and outlooks caused by wrong expectations of getting reliable predictions combined with politically convenient readings of ambiguities.
5. Vexing situations where contingencies with very low or unknowable likelihood but very high impact potential are faced.
6. Available methods for improving fuzzy gambling (Dewar 2002; Dror 2002, ch. 15) are in part very useful. But some are misleading and many are complex, demanding, and in part counter-intuitive. Also, while in the main not being quantitative, they are not easy to explain to rulers who are innumerate (Paulos 1988).

All these and additional difficulties are aggravated by standard proposals for coping with uncertainty in much of policy analysis and risk analysis literature, which are wrong. In particular the recommendation to rely on subjective probabilities multiplied by not less arbitrary utilities in order to calculate "expected value" and thus arrive at an "optimal" answer is totally incorrect. This is the case unless relevant historical processes behave stochastically and subjective probabilities approximate objective probabilities, two assumptions which are a phantasm when complex situations are faced.

The nature of choice by rulers as fuzzy gambling was well recognized by Machiavelli in putting the relations between "fortune," "opportunity," "prudence," and "virtue" at the center of his statecraft recommendations. Useful knowledge does exist. Memoirs of rulers and writings by historians who explicate the "throwing of dices" nature of major decisions are helpful to make the subject concrete and palatable to rulers. Therefore, training can do a lot to improve fuzzy gambling sophistication, though this subject should be handled gingerly.

Thus:

1. Rulers should be made fully aware both of the nature of their decisions as fuzzy gambles and of possibilities to improve them together with the impossibility of unmaking their "fuzzy gambling" nature.
2. Training in this matter must also take up emotional aspects, emphasizing the need to accept and tolerate ambiguity.
3. Presenting main error propensities of the human mind in processing uncertainty and explaining counter-measures can help a lot.
4. A number of practical recommendations should be presented and exercised, such as not thinking of complex issues in terms of "solutions" but "treatments;" considering expected results of alternative options always both optimistically and pessimistically; reading contrary opinions of experts not in terms of one being correct and the other false, but as demonstrating uncertainty; persistently asking "what next?" and "what if?"; working with multiple assumptions; testing options for sensitivity to uncertainty; paying attention to low-probability, high-impact contingencies; creatively imagining possible surprise events; and seeking elasticity.
5. Value clarification and goal-setting dimensions should be expanded to include judgement on different mixes of diverse uncertainties.
6. The likelihood of inconceivable events and dynamics should be emphasized with ways to prepare for them, leading to crisis coping as the ultimate way to upgrade fuzzy gambling.
7. The political and public aspects of the fuzzy gambling nature of decisions should be considered, with the dilemma between speaking truth and demonstrating confidence being put forth clearly, though left for the trainees to ponder.
8. The difficulties posed by the fuzzy gambling nature of choices to evaluation by results, learning from consequences, and being judged by the public for what happens in fact should be explained and their practical implications explored.

## 1.11 Crisis Coping

The ultimate way to handle the unforeseen, unforeseeable, and inconceivable is crisis coping. New forms of terror attack epitomize the need for improved crisis coping, but crises also take the form of natural disasters, economic meltdowns, social unrests, and more. In major crises rulers usually are the ultimate decision makers, by action or default. But, unless they have a personal background of crisis coping, they are ill prepared for their lead roles and can easily do a lot of harm.

A major reason for being unprepared is the lack of readiness by senior politicians to take part in crisis exercises, as essential for preparing oneself for crisis coping. The formal reason they frequently give is that they do not want to reveal their hand prematurely, but the real reason is that experienced politicians will not volunteer to be tested. All the more essential in training is sensitizing of rulers to the need to prepare for crisis coping, including also unconventional uses of crises as opportunities to do what otherwise is impossible.

Participants can be introduced to crisis coping by short and long crises exercises dealing with hypothetical but realistic situations. Computer simulations and games can help. Crisis-coping exercises are not only important by themselves, but also provide opportunities to apply and absorb other main grand-policy thinking subjects in stimulating ways which will engage the full attention of participants.

There is plenty of literature available on crisis coping, in both security and civilian contexts, theoretic and applied (Rosenthal, Boin, and Camfort 2001). Good historical examples can serve as interest-evoking introductions (Frankel 2004; Lukacs 1999). Some of the ideas on crisis handling in business enterprises are in part applicable, but especially pertinent are the few books focusing on the role of leadership in crisis (Carrel 2004). Persons with experience in crisis coping can help as can visits to crisis management units and special demonstration runs to be evaluated later.

## 1.12 Holistic View

Rulers need to adopt holistic views of main policy spaces and of their policy cosmos as a whole, so as to set well-considered priorities for grand-policy crafting, understand cross-impacts, and try to achieve synergism.

The need for "holistic governance" is increasingly recognized, at least in theory (Perri 6 et al. 2003), but the best frame for comprehensive grand-policy thinking is provided by the systems approach. Its central ideas are quite clear: overall performance is not a simple additive function of the output of components. Therefore the interaction of components has to be carefully considered so as to prevent negative effects and achieve overall system improvement. Main implications are also clear, such as the advantages of self-managing systems, the need for overall systems understanding and management when self-management does not work, systems costing, and so on—all within appropriate timeframes.

Especially pertinent are implications for the mission of rulers: they are in charge of overall governmental and societal perspectives; and, when self-management does not work, of systems redesign, oversight, and management. Furthermore, it is up to them to assure holistic governance and to achieve themselves an overall systems perspective of main grand policies as an interactive set.

Within this subject, attention should also be devoted to budgeting. Though most attempts to do so have failed, important lessons can be derived for innovative uses of revised policy-linked budgeting as an instrument for achieving some parts of a holistic view.

The systems approach is well developed in the literature (Checkland 1981; Jervis 1997) as well as in some policy-making practice. Explaining and demonstrating its principles to experienced participants is not difficult, but really to make holistic perspectives a part of their thinking exercises, case studies and projects serve best.

More difficult is the issue of a "national overall grand policy" which tries to set an integrated trajectory for most policy spaces. Illustrations include preparing a country for joining the European Union, moving from a Communist regime and command economy to a democratic regime and market economy, waging a life-or-death war, and some overall modernization directions, as in Singapore (Yew 2000). The question if and when having an overall grand policy is advisable, is central for training of rulers in countries engaging in radical but not revolutionary self-transformation. If answered positively, much of the grand-policy training should refer to crafting such an overall grand policy and its derivative policy-space-specific "sub-"grand policies.

There is nearly no relevant literature, other than outdated and often misleading "development policy" treatises. But treatments of "rise and decline" and some multinational documents, such as the "Lisbon Agenda" the European Union, can serve to introduce the subject.

## 1.13 Penetrating Complexities

Nearly all the curriculum subjects appear to add complexity which may well make the task of grand-policy crafting seem impossible and discourage participants. To overcome this barrier and help in dealing with real difficulties, a deeper look at complexity is necessary.

Let me start with what is quite useless for coping with the quandaries which rulers face. The so-called sciences of complexity (Waldrop 1992), however intellectually interesting and in part stimulating, are not really helpful. Chaos theory, catastrophe theory, and similar fashionable approaches supply some valuable concepts, such as the popularized and often exaggerated "butterfly effect," but applying them to real-life high-level policy issues does not yield much. Large-scale computer simulations do help with some aspects of important policy spaces, such as macroeconomy and environment, but are of limited help for most grand-policy issues (La Porte 1975).

However, it is often possible to cut through soaring complexity by seeking and identifying the kernel or cluster of kernels and thus making the situation more comprehensible without falsification of its essence (Slobodkin 1992). Thus, in the Kyoto Agreement the core issue is readiness to pay economic prices for reducing a probabilistic danger. In the European Union core issues are striving for a federated Europe or an alliance of partly sovereign states; wishing to preserve some cultural homogeneity or taking Turkey in; and global standing and policy. And so on: in quite a number of very complex and multifaceted policy issues one of two hard kernels can be identified. Multiple factors have to be taken into account, but many quandaries are in essence less complex than appears before penetration to their kernel.

In seeking to distill the essence from complexity there is much danger of oversimplification, to which top politicians are prone. But, if done with care, complexity can often be handled better by getting to the kernels than by use of refined methods which either make complexity completely unmanageable or wrongly simplify it behind a veneer of advanced methodologies and abstruse calculations and simulations.

However, methods for doing so are scarce. No general approach to penetrate complexity is known and perhaps none is possible, with each policy space to be handled according to its unique characteristics. But examples can clarify the proposed approach and participants can try to penetrate complexity in closely monitored projects, with much care taken to avoid oversimplification.

## 1.14 Basic Deliberation Schema

Let me conclude the core curriculum with a basic deliberation and choice schema. In many training activities it might be good to start with this scheme so as to apply it throughout the activity. However, I present it here as an illustration of tools helping to get to the kernel of complex grand-policy choices.

The structure of the basic deliberation scheme is as follows:

*values-goals*
*options* outlook on expected impacts of options on values-goals

However rudimentary, this schema serves as a useful format for summing up options and presenting them for overall judgement. It also brings out and reiterates a number of important points (Dror 1983, part IV), such as:

- Avoidance of discussing choice in terms of "rationality" in its usual narrow meanings, because of the importance of extra-rational elements, especially values and innovative options. But more advanced notions of higher rationality, such as self-binding (Elster 2000), should be presented and applied.
- Division of labor within grand-policy crafting, with value and goal judgement being a prerogative and duty of the ruler; outlook being a matter for professionals; and options being open to innovators whoever they may be.

- Outlook must never to be put into a singular form, with at least optimistic and pessimistic outlooks being a must, and further refinements to be added such as dependence on events and surprise-proneness.
- All elements have to be phased in time to take into account different time horizons fitting the subject.

This schema, in different forms, is well known in policy analysis and related literature (Weimer and Vining 1998). Teaching it is not problematic, but rulers have to be habituated to demanding its use from their staffs and absorbing and also applying it into their own grand-policy thinking.

## 1.15 Integration and Absorption

It is essential to achieve at least some intellectual and behavioral integration of the various subjects, so as to upgrade grand-policy thinking as a whole and make it into "knowledge-in-action" (Schön 1983).

It is an open question whether the various aspects, approaches, and frames of grand-policy thinking, as in part presented in the curriculum, form a single paradigm or whether they constitute multiple perspectives sharing a world of discourse but different in groundings and nature. Whatever the ultimate answer to this question may be, as matters stand now there exists no unified prescriptive theory fitting grand-policy thinking as a whole, a fact which makes integration difficult. And the ideas, theories, and perspectives which are best suited to serve as a grounding for grand-policy thinking belong to the philosophy of practical reason starting with Aristotle's *Nicomachean Ethics*, as receiving renewed attention in the philosophy of praxis (Bourdieu 1998; Bratman 1987; Velleman 2000), of reasoning (Gilbert 1986), and of judgement (Lycan et al. 1988), together with cognitive sciences (Robinson-Riegler et al. 2003).

I am of the opinion that parts of philosophy and of cognitive sciences can provide strong groundings for a unified prescriptive theory of choice on which much improved versions of grand-policy and policy analysis as a whole can be based (Dror 1988). However, this is not a ready basis for grand-policy training. Mainstream policy analysis literature (representative is Radin 2000) fully reflects the lack of a strong theoretic basis, a weakness which is epitomized by the inapplicability of most of it to grand-policy thinking. It is therefore not an accident that very little of that literature has been cited as providing knowledge relevant to the proposed curriculum. Thus, nearly completely ignored in mainstream policy analysis literature are thinking-in-history and alternative futures, value clarification, and "rise and decline" frames. And a number of crucial subjects are often mistreated, such as deep uncertainty. Most of the bulk of policy analysis literature fits some types of micro-decisions but not grand-policy crafting, though some books (Dunn 2004; Rosenhead 1989) include important relevant ideas and methods. And when that literature presumes to suggest a dominant paradigm, such as an economic or "rational" one, it is a very narrow and largely misleading one when applied to complex choice.

The absence of an encompassing paradigm is in part compensated for by a number of core ideas and leitmotifs around which training can be structured, in particular thinking in terms of alternative futures and intervening in historic processes. But, at least in training activities, the main burden of integrating the material and applying it selectively to different policy spaces is one of "praxis:" participants have to integrate the material in their cognitive processes and develop the skill to apply different approaches selectively to a variety of grand-policy issues.

Some texts may help after critical discussion, such as writings on political judgement (parts of Steinberger 1993) and the documents of the strategy unit of the British Prime Minister (www.strategy.gov.uk) which, in addition to their intrinsic quality, are very credible to rulers as used in practice at a top policy level. But the main way to help participants integrate the material in ways conductive to their praxis is by case studies, exercises, and projects in which a variety of approaches are applied with the help of mentors and tutors having both extensive theoretic knowledge and high-level policy experience.

Another perspective helping with integration is that of creative professionalism. Professionalism involves applying general theories, abstract thinking, and comparative knowledge to concrete issues. Creative professionalism adds innovation, creativity, and "artistry," in line with the composer metaphor. It is up to the mentors to facilitate such thinking throughout the training.

Also useful is integration of the material on the level of "common errors to be avoided." During the presentation of the curriculum, error propensities specific to each subject will have been mentioned. Pulling them together and supplementing them with additional typical policy-making mistakes (Baron 1998: Bovens and 't Hart 1996) can assist participants in gaining an overview on an additional level. Examples added from other domains, such as technology (Perrow 1984) and medicine (Rosenthal and Sutcliffe 2002), can be very helpful.

However, as noted, in training of high-level policy makers integration is to be achieved on the level of praxis with the help of active learning and, especially, extensive group exercises and projects closely monitored by highly qualified mentors.

## 2. TRAINING REQUIREMENTS

In grand-policy training of rulers didactic methods and substantive contents are closely intertwined. To help participants improve both knowledge-based systematic but 'open' thinking and creative design (Schön 1987), extensive use of active learning methods, such as case studies, interactive computer programs and games, syndicate discussions, individual and group exercises, and projects, is essential. Guided reading on one hand and individual tutoring and coaching are also essential.

Preparation of suitable texts, case studies, exercises, and projects is a main challenge facing the still very small epistemic community of policy scholars, policy analysis professionals, and governance practitioners eager to advance grand-policy training of rulers.

The demanding nature of grand-policy thinking together with the difficulties of telling senior participants "how to think" require highly qualified mentors who combine much theoretic and factual knowledge with high-level policy experience. Finding such mentors and getting them to devote sufficient time to prepare for grand-policy training of rulers is a major difficulty.

Selection of participants is very important, because not all will resonate with the proposed training. And needed are alternative training arrangements of different length, various categories of participants, and different foci so as to fit opportunities and demand.

Most difficult is getting senior policy makers to participate in the proposed type of activities. Directing training at junior policy makers on the way up is more feasible and a very useful endeavor in the longer run. But top-level politicians too can and should be motivated to participate in compact workshops. This requires at least some highly reputed mentors, attractive settings, and good presentation. And getting the support of at least a few rulers who will themselves participate in a training activity is critical.

However, all this is secondary to the need to recognize the imperative of upgrading the quality of top-level decision makers and the possibility to do so in part by grand-policy training.

## References

ANSOFF, H. I. 1979. *Strategic Management*. New York: Wiley.

BARON, J. 1998. *Judgment Misguided: Intuition and Error in Public Decision Making*. New York: Oxford University Press.

BERNSTEIN, R. J. 2002. *Radical Evil: A Philosophical Interrogation*. Cambridge: Polity Press.

BOURDIEU, P. 1998. *Practical Reason*. Stanford, Calif.: Stanford University Press.

BOVENS, M. and 'T HART, P. 1996. *Understanding Policy Fiascoes*. New Brunswick, NJ: Transaction.

BOYCE, W. D., and JENSEN, L. C. 1978. *Moral Reasoning: A Psychological-Philosophical Integration*. Lincoln: University of Nebraska Press.

BRATMAN, M. E. 1987. *Intention, Plans, and Practical Reason*. Cambridge, Mass.: Harvard University Press.

BRAUDEL, F. 1980. *On History*. Chicago: University of Chicago Press.

CALABRESI, G. and BOBBIT, P. 1979. *Tragic Choices*. New York: Norton.

CARREL, L. F. 2004. *Leadership in Krisen: Ein Handbuch für die Praxis*. Zurich: Verlag Neue Zürcher Zeitung.

CHECKLAND, P. 1981. *Systems Thinking, Systems Practice*. Chichester: John Wiley.

CIA 2004. *Mapping the Global Future.* Washington, DC: National Intelligence Council. December. Available at: www.cia.gov/NIC_globaltrend2020.html.

CODEVILLA, A. 1992. *Informing Statecraft: Intelligence for a New Century.* New York: Free Press.

DENEMARK, R. A., FRIEDMAN, J., GILLS, B. K., and MODELSKI, G. 2000. *World System History: The Social Science of Long-Term Change.* London: Routledge.

DEWAR, J. A. 2002. *Assumption-Based Planning: A Tool for Reducing Avoidable Surprises.* Cambridge: Cambridge University Press.

DROR, Y. 1983. *Public Policymaking Reexamined,* enlarged edn. New Brunswick, NJ: Transaction Books.

—— 1988. Notes towards a philosophy of policy-reasoning. Pp. 117–71 in *Between Rationality and Cognition,* ed. M. Campanella. Turin: Albert Meynier.

—— 1999. Beyond uncertainty: facing the inconceivable. *Technological Forecasting and Social Change,* 62 (1–2: Aug./Sept.): 151–3.

—— 2002. *The Capacity to Govern: A Report to the Club of Rome.* London: Frank Cass.

DUNN, W. N. 2004. *Public Policy Analysis: An Introduction,* 3rd edn. Upper Saddle River, NJ: Pearson Prentice Hall.

ELSTER, J. 2000. *Ulysses Unbound: Studies in Rationality, Precommitment, and Constraints.* Cambridge: Cambridge University Press.

FERGUSON, N. (ed.) 1997. *Virtual History: Alternatives and Counterfactuals.* London: Picador.

FRANKEL, M. 2004. *High Noon in the Cold War: Kennedy, Khrushchev, and the Cuban Missile Crisis.* New York: Presidio.

GELERNTER, D. 2004. Review of "The Invisible Century by Richard Panek." *New York Times,* 11 Aug.; available at: http://query.nytimes.com/gst/fullpage.html/?res=9A04E7D71E3CF932 A2575BCOA9629

GERNET, J. 1996. *A History of Chinese Civilization,* 2nd edn. Cambridge: Cambridge University Press.

GILBERT, H. 1986. *Change in View: Principles of Reasoning.* Cambridge, Mass.: MIT Press.

GOLEMAN, D., BOYATZIS, R., and McKEE, A. 2002. *Primal Leadership: Realizing the Power of Emotional Intelligence.* Boston: Harvard Business School.

GOODIN, R. E. (ed.) 1998. *The Theory of Institutional Design.* Oxford: Oxford University Press.

HAMEL, G., and PRAHALAD, C. K. 1994. *Competing for the Future.* Boston: Harvard Business School Press.

HARMAN, G. 1986. *Change in View: Principles of Reasoning.* Cambridge, Mass.: MIT Press.

HAWTHORN, G. 1991. *Plausible Worlds: Possibility and Understanding in History and the Social Sciences.* Cambridge: Cambridge University Press.

JERVIS, R. 1997. *System Effects: Complexity in Political and Social Life.* Princeton, NJ: Princeton University Press.

JOUVENEL, B. DE. 1967. *The Art of Conjecture.* New York: Basic Books.

KANTER, R. M. 2004. *Confidence: How Winning Streaks and Losing Streaks Begin and End.* New York: Crown Business.

KATAEV, V. 2002. *If Only We Could Know! An Interpretation of Chekov.* Chicago: Ivan R. Dee.

KELLERMAN, B. 2004. *Bad Leadership: What It Is, How It Happens, Why It Matters.* Boston: Harvard Business School Press.

KENNEDY, P. 1987. *The Rise and Fall of the Great Powers.* New York: Random House.

LA PORTE, T. R. (ed.) 1975. *Organized Social Complexity.* Princeton, NJ: Princeton University Press.

LEMPERT, R. J., POPPER, S. W., and BANKES, S. C. 2003. *Shaping the Next One Hundred Years: New Methods for Quantitative, Long-Term Policy Analysis.* Santa Monica, Calif.: RAND Corporation.

LEVI, I. 1986. *Hard Choices: Decision Making under Unresolved Conflict*. Cambridge: Cambridge University Press.

LORD, C. 2003. *The Modern Prince: What Leaders Need to Know Now*. New Haven, Conn.: Yale University Press.

LUKACS, J. 1999. *Five Days in London: May 1940*. New Haven, Conn.: Yale University Press.

LYCAN, W. G., SOSA, E., DANCY, J., HALDANE, J., HARMAN, G., and JACKSON, F. 1988. *Judgment and Justification*. Cambridge: Cambridge University Press.

McCALL, S. 1994. *A Model of the Universe: Space-Time, Probability, and Decision*. Oxford: Clarendon Press.

MAY, E. R. 1972. *Lessons of the Past: The Uses and Misuses of History in American Foreign Policy*. New York: Oxford University Press.

MOLITOR, G. T. T. 2003. *Power to Change the World: The Art of Forecasting*. Washington, DC: World Future Society.

NAGEL, T. 1986. *The View from Nowhere*. New York: Oxford University Press.

NATIONAL COMMISSION ON TERRORIST ATTACKS, 2004. *The 9/11 Commission Report: Final Report of the National Commission on Terrorist Attacks upon the United States*. New York: Norton.

NEUSTADT, R. E., and MAY, E. R. 1986. *Thinking in Time*. New York: Free Press.

NORTH, D. C. 1990. *Institutions, Institutional Change and Economic Performance*. Cambridge: Cambridge University Press.

NUSSBAUM, M. C. 1995. *Poetic Justice: The Literary Imagination and Public Life*. Boston: Beacon Press.

NYE, J. S., Jr. 2004. *Soft Power: The Means to Success in World Politics*. New York: PublicAffairs.

OLSON, M. 1982. *The Rise and Decline of Nations: Economic Growth, Stagflation, and Social Rigidities*. New Haven, Conn.: Yale University Press.

PANEK, R. 2004. *The Invisible Century: Einstein, Freud and the Search*. New York: Viking.

PAULOS, J. A. 1988. *Innumeracy: Mathematical Illiteracy and its Consequences*. New York: Hill and Wang.

PEARS, D. 1984. *Motivated Irrationality*. Oxford: Clarendon Press.

PERRI 6 et al. 2003. *Towards Holistic Governance: The New Reform Agenda*. London: Palgrave Macmillan.

PERROW, C. 1984. *Normal Accidents: Living with High-Risk Technologies*. New York: Basic Books.

RADIN, A. B. 2000. *Beyond Machiavelli: Policy Analysis Comes of Age*. Washington, DC: Georgetown University Press.

RIDLEY, M. 2003. *Nature Via Nurture: Genes, Experience, and What Makes Us Human*. New York: HarperCollins.

ROBINSON-RIEGLER, G. L., ROBINSON-RIEGLER, B., and ROBINSON-RIEGLER, G. L. 2003. *Cognitive Psychology: Applying the Science of Mind*. London: Allyn & Bacon.

ROSENAU, J. 2003. *Distant Proximities: Dynamics beyond Globalization*. New Haven, Conn.: Yale University Press.

ROSENHEAD, J. (ed.) 1989. *Rational Analysis for a Problematic World: Problem Structuring Methods for Complexity, Uncertainty and Conflict*. Chichester: Wiley.

ROSENTHAL, M., and SUTCLIFFE, K. M. (eds.) 2002. *Medical Error: What Do We Know? What Do We Do?* San Francisco: Jossey-Bass.

ROSENTHAL, U., BOIN, U. A., and COMFORT, L. K. (eds.) 2001. *Managing Crises: Threats, Dilemmas, Opportunities*. Springfield, Ill.: Charles C. Thomas.

SCHÖN, D. A. 1983. *The Reflective Practitioner: How Professionals Think in Action.* New York: Basic Books.

—— 1987. *Educating the Reflective Practitioner: Towards a New Design for Teaching and Learning in the Professions.* San Francisco: Jossey-Bass.

SCHULMAN, P. R. 1980. *Large-Scale Policy Making.* New York: Elsevier.

SLOBODKIN, L. B. 1992. *Simplicity and Complexity in Games of the Intellect.* Cambridge, Mass.: Harvard University Press.

SORENSEN, R. A. 1992. *Thought Experiments.* Oxford: Oxford University Press.

STATMEN, D. (ed.) 1993. *Moral Luck.* Albany: State University of New York Press.

STEINBERGER, P. J. 1993. *The Concept of Political Judgment.* Chicago: University of Chicago Press.

STEINER, G. A. 1997. *Strategic Planning.* New York: Free Press.

STONE, D. 2001. *Policy Paradox: The Art of Political Decision Making,* rev. edn. New York: Norton.

TAINTER, J. A. 1988. *The Collapse of Complex Societies.* Cambridge: Cambridge University Press.

VELLEMAN, J. D. 2000. *The Possibility of Practical Reason.* Oxford: Clarendon Press.

VERTZBERGER, Y. Y. I. 1990. *The World in their Minds: Information Processing, Cognition, and Perception in Foreign Policy Decisionmaking.* Stanford, Calif.: Stanford University Press.

WALDROP, M. M. 1992. *Complexity: The Emerging Science at the Edge of Order and Chaos.* New York: Simon and Schuster.

WEIMER, D. L., and VINING, A. R. 1998. *Policy Analysis: Concepts and Practice,* 3rd edn. Englewood Cliffs, NJ: Prentice Hall.

YEW, L. K. 2000. *From Third World to First: The Singapore Story: 1965–2000.* New York: HarperCollins.

# PART III

# MODES OF POLICY ANALYSIS

# CHAPTER 5

# POLICY ANALYSIS AS PUZZLE SOLVING

## CHRISTOPHER WINSHIP

> Politics finds its sources not only in power but also in uncertainty—men
> collectively wondering what to do.
>
> (Heclo 1974)

## 1. INTRODUCTION

IN her book *The Struggle for Water: Politics, Rationality, and Identity in the American Southwest*, Wendy Espeland describes the incommensurability of both the world views and the goals of the United States Bureau of Reclamation and the Yavapai Indians. Over many years, the Bureau of Reclamation developed a plan to build the Orme Dam in Arizona. The dam, however, would flood the ancestral lands of the Yavapai Indians. Because of the considerable economic value of the dam, the Bureau of Reclamation was willing to pay almost any amount to the Yavapai to compensate them for their loss of land. The Yavapai, however, were not interested at any price. "The land is our mother. You don't sell your mother" (Espeland 1998, 183).

Conflicts over policy ends are ubiquitous. Most obviously, different groups give different priority to alternative goals. Some may see economic growth as deserving precedence, others, a clean environment. Some may prefer safer streets, others greater protection for human rights. Conflicts over ends may exist for single individuals or

* The author would like to thank Xav Briggs, Peter Bearman, Wendy Espeland, John Forester, David Gibson, Neil Gross, Rachel McCleary, Martin Rein, Henry Richardson, Adam Seligman, and Michael Moran for useful suggestions. I am particularly grateful to Bob Goodin and David Thacher for their extensive comments. The usual disclaimer applies.

unitary actors as well (Schelling 1980). Schools may be committed to treating children equally, but recognize that equity, because there are differences in ability and familial resources, requires them to treat students differently (Jencks 1988). Hospitals, because of limited resources, may be forced to ration their services, but may lack a rationale for which individuals should be given priority (Elster 1993).

Traditional policy analysis with its focus on choosing the best means to obtain a well-specified end has little if anything to say about how to deal with conflicting ends (Thacher and Rein 2004; Richardson 2000).[1] Its unitary focus on appropriate or efficient means assumes that the policy analyst or society more generally has complete knowledge of what constitutes the social good. As the philosopher Elijah Millgram (1997) has argued, there is no reason to assume that actors, much less society, have fully worked out the comparative attractiveness of all possible alternatives. To quote Thacher and Rein (2004, 458): "When a policy actor encounters a new situation in which its goals conflict, it may find that its preferences are simply unfinished. Existing models of policy rationality have great difficulty accommodating such situations."

What policy analysis needs is a mode of analysis, an alternative to instrumental rationality, which can deal with conflicting policy ends. Policy scholars, however, have made only limited efforts in this regard. Some have attempted to deal with the problem of conflicting ends within the traditional instrumental framework examining value trade-off (Barry and Rae 1975; Bell, Keeney, and Raiffa 1977; Keeney and Raiffa 1976). In contrast, Schön and Rein (1994) examine situations where actors resolve "intractable policy controversies" by "reframing" their understanding of the policy problem. In the tradition of Habermas, Fischer and Forrester (1993), Forester (1999), Fischer (2003), and Hajer and Wagenaar (2003) argue for the importance of deliberative processes for resolving conflicts about ends. Thacher and Rein (2004) develop an empirical approach examining how policy makers in fact deal with conflicting ends. Specifically, they examine three strategies: cycling, where actors focus sequentially on different values; firewalls, where different institutions are assigned different value domains; and casuistry, where actors use specific and relevant past cases to suggest courses of action.

The goal of this chapter is to describe an alternative form of rationality that complements standard instrumental rationality. In doing so, I propose an approach to policy analysis for dealing with multiple and conflicting ends. However, rather than trying to develop an elaborate theory, I analyze the phenomena of puzzle solving—jigsaw puzzles, Scrabble, crossword puzzles, or Rubik's cubes.[2] These are all examples of puzzles that one tries to solve for fun. They have in common that the goal is to try to figure out a way to assemble a set of pieces into some type of coherent pattern. I primarily focus on the example of an individual or a group attempting to put together a jigsaw puzzle, though, as discussed below, in certain cases, other types of puzzles may have properties more consistent with the properties of particular policy problems.

---

[1] In negotiation theory this is thought of as the problem of deep value differences. The critical point is that interests, but not values, can be negotiated (Forester 1999).

[2] I am in debt to David Gibson for suggesting that I consider multiple types of puzzles.

I use the example of a jigsaw puzzle (and puzzles more generally) to demonstrate how conflicting ends might be dealt with. The different pieces of the puzzle represent different ends. The policy goal is to find a way to fit the pieces together forming a coherent whole. I describe this process as "puzzling."[3] The purpose of the example is twofold. First, it is to draw an analogy between a particular type of policy process and a much more familiar, easily understood, and concrete practice, putting a jigsaw puzzle together. The example, however, is both more and less than a metaphor. It is more in that I make the strong claim that the rationality involved in solving a jigsaw as well as other types of puzzles is an example of the rationality needed to deal with conflicting policy ends. It is less in that the similarity between a jigsaw puzzle and specific policy problems may be in some cases less than perfect. Other examples of puzzles (crossword puzzles, Scrabble, Rubik's cubes, etc.) can then be looked to that involve the same type of rationality. Second, I examine the different issues involved in assembling a jigsaw puzzle in order to elucidate their importance in policy analysis. That is, I analyze the specifics of putting together a jigsaw puzzle in order to help us understand the problems involved in the form of policy analysis that is of concern here.

Puzzling represents a type of rationality distinctly different from standard instrumental rationality. Although there is a specified end, with a puzzle, one may have no idea of what that end will look like. Puzzling conceptually precedes standard rationality. It is a process of determining what options, *if any*, there are.[4] Standard rationality then involves choosing among alternative options if in fact alternative options exist.

## 2. Puzzling about Policy Ends

What type of policy process should be pursued when ends conflict? Consider the example of a jigsaw puzzle with either a few or hundreds of pieces.[5] How does one attempt to put together such a puzzle? At the simplest level the answer is trial and error. But trial and error can work in a number of different ways. At one extreme, one

---

[3] As should be clear, I am not using the term "puzzling" in its usual senses, though the situations that I examine also may involve puzzling in more conventional terms. For example, the Orme Dam conflict, briefly described above, was certainly puzzling for the engineers in that they were baffled for many years about how the disparate ends of the Bureau and Yavapai Indians could be aligned. In addition, the engineers puzzled about this explicitly, in that they analyzed various options in detail. These are both examples of puzzling in a more conventional sense (*The American Heritage College Dictionary* 2002).

[4] Bardach (2000, ch. 3) and MacRae and Whittington (1997, ch. 3) discuss how policy analysis can generate options.

[5] Chase (1982) uses the metaphor of a jigsaw puzzle to suggest how multiple contests between chickens result in linear hierarchies. Bearman, Faris, and Moody's (1999) paper could also be thought of as an instance of puzzling in that there are linked events and the problem is how to see them as a coherent whole, a historical case. Grofman (2001) discusses scholarly analysis as a problem of puzzle solving.

may literally take a single piece and successively determine whether it mates with other pieces. Crossword puzzles are examples where this is often the sole strategy that is used. At the other extreme, one may guess at the overall properties of the puzzle. For example, if one assumed that the overall shape was that of a rectangle, one might pick out all of the pieces with at least one straight edge. An intermediate strategy would be to put together pieces that looked similar, for example, in either color or pattern. This might be done with or without an assumption of what those pieces would represent. For example, one might assume that the picture contained a sky and decide to sort out all blue or blue and white pieces and then attempt to fit them together. Alternatively, one might just sort all black pieces into a single pile.

A conventional puzzle that is easily put together, however, provides a poor analogy to a difficult policy issue in need of solution. But just as policy issues may be difficult to solve, puzzles can be particularly difficult to assemble, potentially for multiple reasons. What the assembled puzzle should look like may be unknown. Pieces may not fit together uniquely. This is the case with Rubik's cubes where all pieces potentially can mate with each other. Shape, color, and the observed patterns on individual pieces may or may not provide clues as to which pieces should be put together with which or they may not. A good guess about the correct organizing principles of a puzzle may be enormously helpful; a bad guess may lead one grossly astray.

There is also no reason why there might not be more than one way of assembling the puzzle; that is, there may be more than one solution to the puzzle/policy issue. The final assembled puzzle might also not be of a conventional shape—say a rectangle—or it may not even have smooth edges. In both cases Scrabble might be a better example than a jigsaw puzzle. In Scrabble there are multiple potential arrangements of letters into words, with different arrangements being of different shapes and representing different "solutions." However, that a jigsaw puzzle should have a single solution or be of a specific shape is simply conventional. If a puzzle does not have a unique solution or is not of a conventional shape, knowing when it has been completed or correctly assembled may be far from clear.[6]

Assembling a puzzle may be a particular challenge if there are missing or extraneous pieces. In the worst case, pieces from two or more puzzles may be mixed together. Here, beliefs about what pieces are in the puzzle and which are not will evolve and change over time. More generally, if pieces do not uniquely mate with each other, the puzzle may go through different stages of assemblage with different subcomponents appearing to cohere. If we fail to find a way to put the subcomponents together, we may discover that certain individual pieces that we thought matched, in fact do not. As a result, we may have to disassemble some subcomponents in order to assemble others. Similarly, we may find that pieces which appear quite different, in fact go together. As a consequence, our conception of what the puzzle will look like when it is fully assembled may change radically with time.

[6] This observation is due to a comment made on an earlier draft by Henry Richardson.

Different strategies for assembling a puzzle are also likely to work better or worse in different situations. If there are missing or extraneous pieces, attempting to fit a single piece to others may lead to a dead end if the initially chosen piece does not in fact belong to the puzzle. Attempts to match a single piece with others may also be ineffective if a single piece can mate with multiple other pieces. Here matching on color or pattern as well as shape may be critical. Alternatively, strong assumptions about what the overall structure or subcomponents of the puzzle consist of may be effective if they are correct or at least nearly so, but may be disastrous if they are wrong. Ideally, in the end, we should succeed in putting all the pieces together. Of course, if the puzzle is difficult, this may not be the case. Alternatively, if the final shape of the puzzle is complex we may not be certain about whether it is fully assembled. As such, a claim that the puzzle is complete may be provisional.

To stretch our example but make it more useful, individuals also may be differentially committed to having specific pieces in the puzzles, convinced that they belong or, as in a game of Scrabble, they may "possess" different pieces. As a result, there may be conflict about which pieces do in fact belong and, if individuals are inflexibly committed having to a piece in the puzzle that in fact does not belong, it may never be possible fully to assemble the puzzle. Thus, at any particular time, our puzzle will only be partially assembled and, in fact, it may never be fully assembled.

# 3. Searching for Coherence: An Alternative

Why is the example of assembling a difficult puzzle potentially useful? In his work on deliberating about final ends, the philosopher Henry Richardson has argued for a type of rationality that differs from and complements the standard model of instrumental rationality found in means–ends policy analysis. What I argue is that the model of assembling a puzzle, what I have termed "puzzling," represents a concrete, but general and generic model of just such a type of rationality. Although it is true that there is an end that is being pursued—to have an assembled puzzle—what the assembled puzzle will look like may be totally unknown. As such, there is no way to know what strategy, i.e. what means, represents the best approach to finding a solution.

The key idea in Henry Richardson's rich and insightful book, *Practical Reasoning about Final Ends* is coherence as an end. By coherence, he means the achievement of a situation in which multiple and potentially conflicting ends are in fact compatible.[7]

---

[7] Richardson's analysis of coherence has important connections to coherence theories of truth (Davidson 1984, 1986, 2001; Hurley 1989). Space limitations prevent me from analyzing these connections.

Richardson argues that when we have multiple conflicting ends that are incommensurable, the solution is not to choose among them and/or impose some metric that makes them commensurable, but rather to find a way that all the ends can be realized simultaneously. To quote Richardson, "Pursuing practical coherence among one's various commitments ... is the best way to discover what we ought to do" (Richardson 1997, 28). In colloquial terms, the goal is to find a way "for us to have our cake and eat it too."[8]

Richardson suggests that coherence may not be an ultimate end, but may be an intermediate end that is pursued for the sake of other ends. There may be specific ends that we are committed to and the search for coherence involves finding a way to pursue those ends simultaneously. Richardson argues that coherence is critical for two reasons. First, it is essential for effective action; that is, to create a workable situation. If a proposed solution meets everyone's end, we will not need to choose among competing ends, and action will be possible. Richardson states that coherence is also important in that it allows for consistency in one's actions. For example, if an academic department can successively hire individuals who are both strong teachers and strong scholars, it can avoid being seen as oscillating between the different values of research and teaching as it makes appointments.

A key component of Richardson's argument is Dewey's theory of holism. Richardson describes this as the recognition of and a commitment to a strategy that seeks coherence through analysis and evaluation at multiple levels. In seeking to make different ends compatible, one approach is to work on a dyadic level, trying to resolve the conflicts between pairs of ends. Alternatively, one may consider the problem more holistically, seeking an overall structure that will allow all or most of the ends to be simultaneously achievable. Finally, one may consider subgroups of ends, and seek ways to make them compatible. Having then worked at one level, one may then evaluate one's progress by examining the degree of coherence at another. For example, if one has been working by trying to mate a single piece to others, one may evaluate the success of one's efforts by examining the overall coherence of one's efforts. Richardson talks about this as bi-directionality or in Rawls's words "working from both ends" (Richardson 1997, 141).

Richardson discusses both the problem of a single individual deliberating about final ends and the more difficult problem of groups of individuals deliberating about shared final ends. It is the latter situation that is of interest to us. In this context, he points out that the goal of coherence is closely related to Rawls's idea of an "overlapping consensus" (Rawls 1987, 1989). The goal of aligning all ends across all individuals is almost certainly unachievable. What is desired, however, is finding areas of agreement or potential compatibility such that it is possible to have an

---

[8] There are important similarities between Richardson's model of coherence and the concept in negotiation theory of an integrative solution (Raiffa 1982; Bazerman and Neale 1992; Lewicki, Saunders, and Minton 1997). An integrative solution is one that turns a dispute into a win–win situation as opposed to a zero-sum game. Thus, parallel to Richardson's model, the goal is not to figure out appropriate trade-offs between different goals, but rather to figure out how simultaneously to achieve all opposing parties' goals. Vickers's (1965) idea of 'integrative decisions' in public administration also is closely related.

"overlapping consensus." If this consensus is broad enough, it may be sufficient to support social life, i.e. there may be enough coherence in different individuals' and groups' ends that coordination of action and the pursuit of joint activities may be achievable.

# 4. Puzzling out Coherent Wholes

Return now to the example of a jigsaw puzzle. The different pieces should be thought of as specific ends. The goal is not to choose a single piece, but rather to see if it is possible to fit the pieces together. That is, the goal is to fit the pieces together into a coherent whole. What that coherent whole will look like in the end may well be unknown. Some pieces may be abandoned because it is eventually determined that they do not fit. We may, however, insist that particular pieces be included, and as such, the inclusion of these pieces will drive the process of assembling the puzzle. These pieces are final ends that we are inflexibly committed to. It is also possible that we may discover that to put the puzzle together we need to include new pieces/ends that have not been considered before and/or that we may need to look at the puzzle in a different way. Finally, it may or may not be clear when the puzzle is finally assembled.

The puzzle example is important for several reasons. First, it shows in a concrete fashion how we can pursue an end that is in great part largely unknown. At a general level the end is to put the puzzle together. We, however, may have little or no idea what the puzzle will look like when it is put together. In the process of assembling the puzzle we may believe that we know what the final assembled picture will look like. But, of course, as the process proceeds, our beliefs about what is the final end we are pursuing may well be revised as our understanding of what pieces fit together changes. In addition, as our thinking changes, our belief about which specific pieces belong in the puzzle or which pieces fit together may change. This is analogous to Richardson's discussion of the specification of ends (Richardson 1997). Thus, the puzzle example shows how in a quite rational deliberative process, both general ends and specific ends may come to be revised.[9]

Second, the puzzle example is useful in illustrating the variety of different strategies that we may use in trying to assemble a puzzle or evaluate our progress in doing so. In this way, it illustrates Dewey's theory of holism. As noted above, at times we may focus at the micro level of trying to find the pieces that fit with one particular piece. At other times, we may focus on placing pieces we believe are likely to go together into groups. At still other times, our assumptions about the overall structure of the picture may drive our strategy of how to sort pieces.

---

[9] See Wildavsky 1979 for a discussion of how policy objectives come to be revised.

If the puzzle example helps elucidate Richardson's model of deliberation, we need to also examine where it differs. For Richardson deliberation about final ends is explicitly about reasoning, as it is for Dewey (Richardson 1997, 83). Puzzling in the sense in which I mean it may or may not involve reasoning. When puzzling involves making and changing assumptions about the overall nature of the puzzle or its subparts, then reasoning is obviously involved. However, when puzzling is done simply by trying to fit a single piece to others, reasoning may be only involved in the most primitive sense—we use reason to recognize whether specific pieces fit together or not. Potentially, it is possible that intentionality, in the sense that we are actively seeking to assemble a puzzle, may not exist. We may simply recognize in passing that specific pieces fit together.[10] The difference between Richardson and the puzzle example is important. What the puzzle example points to is that blind action can lead to coherence. I illustrate this below in my discussion of the empirical case of the Ten Point Coalition.

## 5. Two Policy Examples

*Water rights.* As already briefly discussed, Espeland (1998) examines a many-decade dispute over the plan to build the Orme Dam in central Arizona. Her story is a classic example of conflicting non-commensurable ends that result from non-commensurable world-views, and the importance of flexibility and intransigence. I continue the discussion in more detail here.

The original site proposed by the Bureau of Reclamation was at the confluence of two rivers, making it most attractive from a design perspective. The proposed dam also would be appealing aesthetically, adding one more grand dam to the process of civilizing the southwest. However, if the dam were built in the proposed location it would flood the ancestral lands of the Yavapai Indians.

Because the dam would greatly benefit fast-growing Phoenix and local farmers, the Bureau was willing to pay the Indians handsomely for their land. The Indians, however, were not willing to sell the land at any price, as the land was intimately connected to their identities as Indians. Their view was summarized in their statement: "The land is our mother. You don't sell your mother" (Espeland 1998, 183).

Over time new engineers joined the Bureau. These engineers framed the problem of dam building differently (Schön and Rein 1994). Unlike the "old guard" engineers,

---

[10] Cohen and March's garbage can model could be thought of as a puzzling process. Here individuals with solutions search for problems, and coherence potentially can be achieved in windows of opportunity when a solution fits to an available problem. In the garbage can model there is individual intentionality—individuals trying to find problems for their solutions—but there is no sense of group intentionality (see Cohen and March 1974; Kingdon 1984).

the new group was not particularly interested in building grand dams. Rather, they had been schooled in cost–benefit analysis and economic decision models. Because of their different orientation, they were willing to consider alternative plans that involved multiple dams in different locations. In this process they discovered a plan that avoided flooding the Yavapai's land, but that had the same cost–benefit properties, resolving the dispute. Eventually, it was this plan that was adopted.

Espeland emphasizes that the Bureau and the Indians did not come to any agreement about how to analyze or evaluate the problem of where the dam should be built. In fact, the Indians totally rejected the cost–benefit perspective that the engineers used, which assumed that all options were commensurable. The world-views of the Indians and the engineers remained totally divergent. Rather what they agreed upon was a solution, although the solution was satisfactory for quite different reasons for the two groups. She also points out that resolution totally failed to satisfy the old guard engineers' desires for another grand dam.[11]

For our purposes, Espeland's story is of interest as it is explicitly about a conflict in which an attempt to create commensurability, i.e. buy the Yavapais at some price, fails. It is not possible to solve the problem by evaluating the different components of any solution along a single dimension, though one group, the new engineers themselves, precisely evaluated alternatives in this way. Rather what needed to be found was a solution that allowed the Yavapai Indians to keep their land and at the same time create the needed water resources for local farmers and a quickly expanding Phoenix.

Espeland's story nicely illustrates how coherence in the sense of Richardson (or similarly Rawls's overlapping consensus) can be a central goal. As Richardson points out and the puzzle example illustrates, a solution is only achieved by changing the components of the problem. The new cohort of engineers brought in a new way of thinking about the evaluation of dam sites with the result that new plans were considered. The goals of the original engineers for a grand dam, however, were abandoned. Coherence may often be partial. As a result of new and different perspectives, new pieces are put on the table and potentially added to the puzzle and other pieces, originally thought as essential components (e.g. that the dam be grand), are abandoned. The example also illustrates how the flexibility of one group and the inflexibility of another led to a solution, but a very specific solution.

*Cops and ministers.* In a series of papers Jenny Berrien and Chris Winship (1999, 2002, 2003; Winship 2004) describe how during the 1990s the Boston police department and a group of black inner city ministers known as the Ten Point Coalition put together a partnership to deal with the problem of youth violence in Boston's inner city. Initially, both groups had an extremely hostile relationship, particularly so between one key minister, the Reverend Eugene Rivers, and the police. By the late

---

[11] For discussions of the importance of partial agreements, see Sunstein 1995; Jonsen and Toulmin 1988; Forester 1999.

1990s, however, Boston had become a model for other cities, both nationally and internationally, for how clergy and the police can work together to deal with youth violence. By 2004 over 400 cities had visited Boston to learn about "the Boston Model."

Several things in particular are of interest about this story. First is that both the police and ministers initially had quite different goals. The police saw their job as responding to reports of crime and ensuring that justice was carried out with respect to each crime. The ministers saw themselves as providing "safe houses for decent people" and fighting the police department's maltreatment of Boston's poor black community. Initially, Reverend Rivers was a court advocate for youth who were arrested on drug charges and, as a result, there was strong suspicion that he was a drug dealer himself. In the end, however, both groups came to see their goal as "keeping the next kid from being killed." Initially, neither group saw this as their goal. Multiple times the ministers made clear that when they started to walk the streets at night after an attempted stabbing in a church during a gang funeral, they had no idea what their goal was. They just knew that they had to be "present" in the streets at night even though they were not sure what it was they were trying to accomplish. In the sense described above, they were involved in blind action.

Second, the story is of interest, as the two groups did not come to a common understanding through a series of meetings. To put it in metaphorical terms, there was no "table" in this story around which the two groups sat and worked out a way to work with each other. Rather, the two groups worked out their relationship over time around a series of incidents. In terms of the puzzle example, they found ways to put particular singular pieces together without any conception of what the overall puzzle or even large subparts would look like. The search for coherence was entirely at the micro level. There are multiple examples of this. We discuss one.

In 1991, Reverend Rivers's house was shot up with a bullet barely missing his six-year-old son's head. Rivers was in a difficult situation. He could move his young family out of the tough inner city neighborhood where they lived and he worked. In doing so, he would lose much of his credibility on the street. He had been shot at and ran. Or he could work with the police to apprehend the shooter. He chose to work with the police.

Some police initially thought that Rivers had arranged the shooting himself in order to discredit the belief among street cops that he was a drug dealer. The two cops that Rivers had the most difficult relationship with volunteered to investigate. They volunteered so that they could find out what the real story was. Rivers and the cops suddenly found that they needed to work together. After six months the shooter was arrested. He had actually intended to shoot up the house of a drug dealer next door to Rivers's, but had missed. The shooter was eventually tried and sent to jail with the full support of Rivers.

This incident was critical for two reasons. First, it forced the police and Rivers to work together on the very basic task of finding the shooter. They had to work together to figure out a shared puzzle—who had shot up the Rivers's house.

However, they didn't remotely have any overall agreement about how to deal with the problem of Boston's inner city youth violence. Second, it laid the foundation for a much more general goal that would emerge later of "keeping the next kid from being killed." As a result of the shooting, Rivers was suddenly saying that some kids were so out of control that they needed a prison minister. There was now at least some agreement between Rivers and the police—some kids did need to be in jail.

What this incident and the more general Ten Point story illustrates is how a vision of a common goal (keeping the next kid from getting killed) emerged not by debating or discussing what that vision should be, but rather by having that vision emerge out of a set of common joint actions. Karl Weick (2001, 17) argues that "people commit to and coordinate instrumental acts (means) before they worry about shared goals." Clearly that is what occurred here. The critical work was done at the micro level over a number of years and this then led to an understanding between the two groups that they had a partnership and a common goal.[12]

# 6. Puzzling about Policy

How can we succinctly describe the common element in our two empirical cases? I would suggest that what actors are doing is "puzzling." What they are trying to figure out is how to rectify a set of seemingly conflicting policy ends. As the example of a jigsaw puzzle (or Scrabble, or a crossword puzzle, or Rubik's cube) suggests, they are trying to figure out how it might be possible to fit the pieces of their puzzle, that is, their various ends, together into a single coherent whole.

It is important to recognize that puzzling as we have described it represents a process that is rational, but rational in a way quite different from standard analysis of means. The key difference is that standard rationality involves choosing among a set of possible options. Puzzling involves discovering which options are possible—what are the possible ways that seemingly conflicting ends can be simultaneously pursued. Put in other terms, puzzling involves discovering the ways, if at all, in which disparate pieces may be put together. Both processes are systematic. Standard rationality involves the analysis of the desirability of different possible alternatives. Puzzling involves determining what the alternatives, if any, are. Thus, puzzling might be said to conceptually precede standard rational analysis. It is a process of determining what options there are. Standard rationality then involves choosing among those options.

---

[12] For a discussion of the importance of retrospective sense making for institutions, see Weick 1979, 2001.

How might one puzzle well? Clearly, the most important ability is good perception—the ability to discern which pieces fit together.[13] Aristotle thought that discernment could be learned. It is not a technical knowledge (*techne*), but rather a type of practical knowledge (phronesis) that is learned through experience (Nussbaum 1990; Dunne 1993). In our context, it is through experience that one learns to recognize specific patterns that potentially can be assembled together. Leifer (1991) argues and provides evidence that what differentiates chess masters from lesser players is precisely differences in the ability to recognize patterns, not differences in how many moves forward individuals can see.

Are there are general rules for puzzling well? A few. As we have discussed earlier, inflexible commitment to specific pieces being included can lead to dead ends if in fact those pieces do not belong to the puzzle. In the Orme Dam case, the Yavapai Indians were inflexibly committed to keeping their ancestral dams. With the arrival of a new cohort of engineers, however, the Bureau of Reclamation was able to consider alternative project designs and dam sites. These engineers were then able to come up with a design that met the goals of the Bureau and did not involve flooding the Yavapai lands. If both the Bureau and the Indians had stayed committed to their original positions, they would have been permanently stuck in a dead end. The willingness of the Bureau's new engineers to search for new solutions kept this from happening. Flexibility and avoiding permanent commitments are virtues in puzzle solving. As James Scott argues in *Seeing Like a State* (1998), it may be better to have a plan that is flexible and allows for change than to have the "right" plan.

Our empirical examples have also highlighted the importance of searching at different levels—Dewey's theory of holism. The Orme Dam case illustrates how an overall reframing of the project by the Bureau led them to consider a different set of solutions. In contrast, the case of the Boston police and the Ten Point ministers demonstrates how work at the most micro of levels—literally figuring out how to work together on a day-to-day, situation-by-situation basis—was what created a foundation for a broad-based approach to youth violence. In order to succeed, it may be critical to search at different levels. Furthermore, there is no a priori reason to believe that searching at one level of generality is more likely to be successful than at another.

Finally, the Boston case shows that action that may not be rational in terms of any short-term goal may in fact lead to policy solutions. In terms of the puzzle example, simply by randomly moving the pieces around people may come to recognize new possibilities in terms of which pieces might fit together.[14] This suggests that both patience and a tolerance for uncertainty and for a lack of specific direction may be important to the discovery of which ends can be successfully pursued simultaneously.

---

[13] I am grateful to Rachel McCleary for making this point.
[14] For a related discussion of how a seemingly arational process of wandering can lead to new options or solutions, see Thacher and Rein's (2004, 466–7) discussion of cycling.

If one is patient, new possibilities in the form of new options or new information may appear. Wandering aimlessly and patience may in fact lead to the discovery of a solution. To coin a saying worthy of Yogi Berra: "If you don't know where you are going, you might actually get there."

# REFERENCES

*The American Heritage College Dictionary* 2002. Boston: Houghton Mifflin.

BARDACH, E. 2000. *A Practical Guide for Policy Analysis: The Eightfold Path to More Effective Problem Solving*. New York: Chatham House.

BARRY, B., and RAE, D. 1975. Political evaluation. Pp. 337–401 in *The Handbook of Political Science*, ed. F. I. Greenstein and N. W. Polsby, vol. i. Reading, Mass.: Addison-Wesley.

BAZERMAN, M. H., and NEALE, M. A. 1992. *Negotiating Rationally*. New York: Free Press.

BEARMAN, P., FARIS, R., and MOODY, J. 1999. Blocking the future: new solutions for old problems in historical social science. *Social Science History*, 23(4): 501–33.

BELL, D. E., KEENEY, R. L., and RAIFFA, H. (eds.) 1977. *Conflicting Objectives in Decisions*. New York: Wiley.

BERRIEN, J., and WINSHIP, C. 1999. Boston cops and black churches. *Public Interest*, 136 (Summer): 52–68.

—— —— 2002. An umbrella of legitimacy: Boston's police department–Ten Point Coalition collaboration. Pp. 200–28 *in Securing our Children's Future: New Approaches to Juvenile Justice and Youth Violence*, ed. G. Katzman. Washington, DC: Brookings Institution Press.

—— —— 2003. Should we have faith in the churches? The Ten-Point Coalition's effect on Boston's youth violence. Pp. 249–76 in *Guns, Crime, and Punishment in America*. New York: New York University Press.

CHASE, I. D. 1982. Dynamics of hierarchy formation: the sequential development of dominance relationships. *Behaviour*, 80: 218–40.

COHEN, M. D., and MARCH, J. G. 1974. *Leadership and Ambiguity: The American College President* New York: McGraw-Hill.

DAVIDSON, D. 1984. *Inquiries into Truth and Interpretation*. Oxford: Oxford University Press.

—— 1986. A coherence theory of truth and knowledge. Pp. 307–19 in *Truth and Interpretation: Perspectives on the Philosophy of Donald Davidson*, ed. E. LePore. Oxford: Basil Blackwell.

—— 2001. *Subjective, Intersubjective, Objective*. Oxford: Oxford University Press.

DUNNE, J. 1993. *Back to the Rough Ground*. Notre Dame, Ind.: University of Notre Dame Press.

ELSTER, J. 1993. *Local Justice*. New York: Russell Sage.

ESPELAND, W. N. 1998. *The Struggle for Water: Politics, Rationality, and Identity*. Chicago: University of Chicago Press.

FISCHER, F. 2003. Beyond empiricism: policy analysis as deliberative. Pp. 209–27 in *Deliberative Policy Analysis*, ed. M. A. Hajer and H. Wagenaar. Cambridge: Cambridge University Press.

—— and FORESTER, J. (eds.) 1993. *The Argumentative Turn in Policy Analysis*. Durham, NC: Duke University Press.

FORESTER, J. 1999. Dealing with deep value differences. Pp. 463–93 in *The Consensus Building Handbook*, ed. L. Susskind, S. McKearnan, and J. Thomas-Larmer. Thousand Oaks, Calif.: Sage.

—— 2001. *The Deliberative Practitioner*. Cambridge, Mass: MIT Press.

GROFMAN, B. (ed.) 2001. *Political Science as Puzzle Solving*. Ann Arbor: University of Michigan Press.

HAJER, M., and WAGENAAR, H. (eds.) 2003. *Deliberative Policy Analysis*. Cambridge: Cambridge University Press.

HECLO, H. 1974. *Modern Social Politics in Britain and Sweden: From Relief to Income Maintenance*. New Haven, Conn.: Yale University Press.

HURLEY, S. L. 1989. *Natural Reasons*. New York: Oxford University Press.

JENCKS, C. 1988. Whom must we treat equally for educational opportunity to be equal? *Ethics*, 98: 518–33.

JONSEN, A., and TOULMIN, S. 1988. *The Abuse of Casuistry: A History of Moral Reasoning*. Berkeley: University of California Press.

KEENEY, R. L., and RAIFFA, H. 1976. *Decisions with Multiple Objectives: Preferences and Value Tradeoffs*. New York: Wiley.

KINGDON, J. 1984. *Agendas, Alternatives, and Public Policies*. Boston: Little, Brown.

LEIFER, E. 1991. *Actors as Observers: A Theory of Skill in Social Relationships*. New York: Garland.

LEWICKI, R., SAUNDERS, D., and MINTON, J. 1997. *Essentials of Negotiation*, 2nd edn. Boston: McGraw-Hill.

MACRAE, D., and WHITTINGTON, D. 1997. *Expert Advice for Policy Choice: Analysis and Discourse*. Washington, DC: Georgetown University Press.

MILLGRAM, E. 1997. Incommensurability and practical reasoning. Pp. 151–69 in *Incommensurability, Incomparability, and Practical Reason*, ed. R. Chang. Cambridge, Mass.: Harvard University Press.

NUSSBAUM, M. 1990. *Love's Knowledge: Essays on Philosophy and Literature*. New York: Oxford University Press.

RAIFFA, H. 1982. *The Art and Science of Negotiation*. Cambridge, Mass.: Harvard University Press.

RAWLS, J. 1987. The idea of an overlapping consensus. *Oxford Journal of Legal Studies*, 7: 1–25.

—— 1989. The domain of the political and overlapping consensus. *New York University Law Review*, 64: 233–55.

RICHARDSON, H. S. 1990. Specifying norms as a way to resolve concrete ethical problems. *Philosophy and Public Affairs*, 19: 279–310.

—— 1997. *Practical Reasoning about Final Ends*. Cambridge: Cambridge University Press.

—— 2000. The stupidity of the cost–benefit standard. *Journal of Legal Studies*, 29: 971–1003.

SCHELLING, T. 1980. The intimate contest for self-command. *Public Interest*, 60: 94–118.

SCHÖN, D. A., and REIN, M. 1994. *Frame Reflection: Toward the Resolution of Intractable Policy Controversies*. New York: Basic Books.

SCOTT, J. 1998. *Seeing Like a State*. New Haven, Conn.: Yale University Press.

SUNSTEIN, C. R. 1995. Incompletely theorized agreements. *Harvard Law Review*, 108: 1733–72.

THACHER, D., and REIN, M. 2004. Managing value conflict in public policy. *Governance*, 17: 457–86.

VICKERS, G. 1965. *The Art of Judgment*. New York: Harper and Row.

WEICK, K. 1979. *The Social Psychology of Organizing*. New York: McGraw-Hill.

—— 2001. *Making Sense of the Organization*. Oxford: Blackwell.

WILDAVSKY, A. 1979. *Speaking the Truth to Power: The Art and Craft of Policy Analysis.* Boston: Little, Brown.

WINSHIP, C. 1994. The end of a miracle? Crime, faith, and partnership in Boston in the 1990's. Pp. 171–92 in *Long March Ahead: African American Churches and Public Policy in Post-Civil Rights America,* ed. R. D. Smith. Durham, NC: Duke University Press.

CHAPTER 6

# POLICY ANALYSIS AS CRITICAL LISTENING

## JOHN FORESTER

## 1. INTRODUCTION

In public policy work, we interview people all the time. We try to find out what happened at yesterday's meeting, and we find ourselves asking questions to find out what Harry's done now, what Sue's up to, or how Chris reacted to our new proposal. To work on any new project we may have to "talk to" many different people, and in doing so, we need to listen as much as, or more than to talk as we try to find out about others' perspectives and experiences, their needs and interests, their weak or strong support, and always, too, as we're trying to get a better grasp of the organizational, legal, and practical world we're in with them.

To make new things happen, to find out what we can do effectively in politically uncertain and fluid settings, we need to learn—and to learn, we very often need to ask questions and listen carefully. When we do this, we're "planners" and policy analysts in the most general sense: exploring what's possible, finding out about what we can and can't do. In what follows, I use the term "planners" to refer very generally to all those who need to learn about their environments—public or private, social or natural—in order to change them. As we shall see, "planning for change" not only requires learning in pragmatic and politically astute ways, but in social and political environments, it requires skillful and sensitive interviewing too. But such interviewing, it turns out, is not so simple.

In the world of social science, interviewing can often be formal, but in the world of policy analysis and planning, interviewing may just as often be informal;

* My thanks for help and comments on earlier drafts to Jennie Cameron, Stephen McFarland, David Laws, and Sarah Slack, and for quite extensive suggestions, thanks too to Stephen Atkinson, Sarah Dooling, and Lynne Manzo—who, of course, bear no responsibility for the missteps that remain.

no less serious, but more subtle. In the world of social science, clipboards may be appropriate ritual objects; in the world of policy and planning analysis, though, a cup of coffee or something stronger might help an informative conversation along. Social scientists work to analyze—to understand, and perhaps to explain—"what's going on," and although we as policy and planning analysts certainly share that aspiration, we have to do more: we have to assess what's possible in a future political world, what might yet work for better or worse in a politically reconstructed world that does not yet exist! So let's consider how change agents—entrepreneurs, organizers, managers, policy analysts, activists of many kinds—"planners" we shall call them generically— can do this work of interviewing and practical learning and do it well (Schön 1983; Greenwood and Levin 1999; Forester 1999a; cf. Wildavsky 1989).

In public and private sectors alike, planners often work in between diverse "stakeholders." The head of a hospital department wants to improve care and cut costs, and she works in between higher-level administrators and all those working in her department. The manager of a regional parts supply office works in between local customers and more central suppliers. One of the governor's policy advisers wants to get an economic development taskforce going once again, this time to make a difference in the legislature. The director of a community center works between staff, board members, funders, city officials, community residents, interested academics, and yet others. And so on. Call them "administrators," "managers," "policy staff," "community leaders," or "organizers," but they all try carefully to shape future action: they are all "planners" faced with daunting but intriguing challenges.

Not only must these planners try to protect fragile relationships in often contested, fluid, and ambiguous situations, but they also have to bring about sanity and confidence, some practical order, light as well as heat, from the chaos. Often blessed with a bit of thick skin, they will try to respond to others' felt needs, interests, and desires even as these often conflict. Trying to do their work within and through these webs of relationships, these planners must work to understand many points of view, many perspectives, many senses of what counts, what's valuable—for both technical and political reasons.

Technically, understanding multiple perspectives may enhance planners' own understanding of a particular case because the planners themselves have no special access to truth, full or perfect information. Politically, understanding and being able to integrate many perspectives enables planners to address questions of feasibility and power as well.

So planners have to learn through conversations every day—about people, places, and projects—and to do that, they will find themselves doing many different kinds of interviews. A few interviews will be formal, carefully arranged and recorded. But many more will be much more informal: side conversations before, during, or after meetings; impromptu telephone conversations, ad hoc office visits, "getting a heads-up," "checking in," "seeing how you're doing," and so on.

But this inevitably intermediating role that's played by planners can make their interviews quite special. These interviews search not only for attitudes and relationships that now exist but for possibilities that do not yet exist—so that where some social scientists might be wary of exploring hypotheticals, "What if ...?" questions, those same questions are often crucial, if not altogether essential, for planners.

But in a political world, we know, what any party believes to be possible at all depends on their assumptions about other parties. So planners' and policy analysts' interviews are more typically inter-views: the planners and analysts seek to understand what this neighbors' representative fears about what this developer proposes, what this politician wants as it overlaps and partially contradicts what that politician wants, how this group's concern for "environmental quality" avoids another group's claims regarding affordable housing, and so on. Exploring the stakes and issues in between stakeholders, then, planners' interviews can subtly foster virtual argumentative spaces in which stakeholders not only stake out but explore future possibilities; not only set out positions but clarify, reformulate, and probe the diverse interests they seek to satisfy—and the practical ways they might really satisfy them (Forester 2004b, c; 2005).

So planners listening to contradictory arguments find themselves between views, needing to understand them all in order to work with them, sometimes to mediate between them, sometimes simply to acknowledge them, sometimes simply to be able to craft practical responses that will actually address citizens' real interests. This work is not simple, even though we have been exhorted since elementary school to "listen to others." Planners, mediators, negotiators, and organizers all stress the significance of astute listening to their practice as they face situations full of conflict, ambiguity, posturing, and differences of culture, class, race, gender, and values (Forester 1999a).

We can now explore this work of inter-viewing and listening to multiple parties— from the planners' "in-between" standpoint—in two ways. First, if briefly, we can note the conceptual problems that arise: what, for example, does it mean for an attentive listener or interviewer to be responsibly "rational" in a very messy world of complexity, incommensurability, emotion, conflicting obligations, and the need to improvise when simply following rules, even optimizing, won't do?

Second, we can address at greater length in what follows the practical problems analysts face here. How in actual cases can planners learn, diagnose, inter-view— under the realistic but daunting conditions of unequal power relationships, diverse forms of conflict, and sheer organizational messiness, each of which involve distinct challenges of their own?

Assessing relations of power often reveals shifting interdependencies, and thus spaces of negotiation, and in turn, contingently shifting degrees of participation and thus possibilities of future cooperation and collaboration—possibilities that understandably skeptical, fearful, and distrusting parties may hardly think to be possible at all.

Assessing conflict carefully can reveal multiple perspectives articulated in complex rhetorical ways, including many postures and styles, all framing future possibilities of action and interaction quite selectively. Assessing organizational messiness and complexity reveals not only unique particulars and encompassing general norms, but uncertainties and ambiguities as well as layers of distrust and fear, anger and division, interests and desires, too. Here we find that planners' interviews echo—and can learn from—the work that public dispute mediators do both in the early stages they call "conflict assessment" and in the actual process of mediating as well.

## 2. Inter-viewing in Everyday Policy, Planning, and Public Management Practice

We can begin with four simple examples to suggest the challenges and possibilities of listening and learning in such planning and change-oriented interviews. We then turn, in the following three sections, to consider: (i) what's at stake as planners listen and inter-view well or poorly; (ii) what makes such work difficult; and finally, (iii) what helps.

Consider first, then, a city planner's short story of his own earlier blindness, his own dawning recognition of what was involved in really listening to the people with whom he'd been working (for a time as a social worker). Jim (as we can call him) says:

First I thought I could at least be polite, that I'd be dealing with the poorest and the most downtrodden of society, that even if I didn't have the power to do much, I could be polite. But then I saw that some people were just so personally obnoxious that it was the most I could do to be business-like. Being polite to them was more than I could do. Then, some people just expected the agency to give them hell, and they acted like it.

There was one woman—she was just impossible to deal with. She just yelled and screamed and pounded her fists on my desk—and nothing I could say did anything. There wasn't anything I could do; I'd try to talk to her, but she'd yell and demand this and that—she was just irate.

Then once I couldn't take it anymore. I threw my casebook down on the floor, slammed my fist, and yelled right back at her. What happened? She had a big smile on her face, and in the first calm and steady voice I'd ever heard out of her, she said, "Well, there! You'll be all right yet!"

I was astonished. It seemed I hadn't really been paying attention to her, taking her seriously, really listening to her, until then. (Forester 1989, 112)

Now what's Jim telling us? We notice his early orientation to rules, manners, and politeness—all as a hedge against his own powerlessness, "even if I didn't have the power to do much," in the face of the overwhelming need of "the poorest and the most downtrodden of society," as what he could do "at least"—all of which reflects Jim's preoccupation with Jim himself, and perhaps the inadequacy of his position, rather than any specific recognition of particular people and their particular situations. Jim's demeanor begins with manners but retreats to being "business-like" as he came to work with people "so personally obnoxious that it was the most I could do to be business-like." Here the conventions of civil deference and regard, being polite, called for more than he could give, and the impersonality of being business-like provided him with a style of work and, it seems, protection.

But then, he tells us, one woman taught him a lesson by provoking him to drop that armor of being business-like, to tell her what he really thought. He slammed his fist, threw the book, yelled back—and what happened? For the first time, perhaps, he became—to the woman in front of him—not just a bureaucratic functionary but a real person: and with "a big smile on her face, and in the first calm and steady voice I'd ever heard out of her, she said, 'Well, there! You'll be all right yet!' "

What had happened here? Jim believes he had not been seen to be really paying attention before. He wonders if he had been, then, even with the best of intentions, giving others the impression that he was not taking them seriously, not recognizing their own dignity—so he suspects, no wonder they were angry, and not just with the agency but with him! One part of listening to others and learning from others then, he tells us, involves expressing a real regard for the other, taking them seriously, showing a concern that fits the gravity of the situation at hand: No visible respect, no success interviewing!—as we shall see (Slack 2003).

Consider a second example now as a community organizer-turned-city planner warns us of the constant danger of professional blindness in a world of structured inequalities, felt commitments, and economic conflicts. Sue speaks of working in between landowners, shopkeepers, and local residents involved in a local street-widening project, and she tells us:

In the middle, you get all the flak. You're the release valve. You're seen as having some power—and you do have some ....

Look, if you have a financial interest in a project, or an emotional one, you want the person in the middle to care about your point of view—and if you don't think they do, you'll be angry!

[I asked her then, "So when planners try to be 'professional' by appearing detached and objective, does it get people angry at them?" and she responded,]

SURE! (Forester 1989, 97)

Notice that Sue begins by locating herself in the structure of the situation: when planners are in the middle, both sides imagine that the planner has some influence, some power, and thus that they on each side are vulnerable and at risk in some ways. She tells us too that social and political-economic structures organize investment and attachment—so landowners will be concerned about the value of their real estate; homeowners and residents who have lived in the area for many years may well have attachments to and affection for their neighborhood in other less commercial, less economic ways (and of course they may well also be concerned about economic value).

But each of these parties will face risk, and each of these parties will demand recognition, Sue tells us: "You want the person [the planner] in the middle to care about your point of view." Sue does not say, or even seem to feel, that everyone wants the planner to agree with them, for she implies that the parties recognize complexity, that they do recognize many views and competing concerns (cf. Sanoff 1999). Still, she suggests, the landowners, shopkeepers, and residents alike want the planner at least to "care about [their] point of view," thus to recognize it, to acknowledge its claims, to understand it (even if it is just one view of many), to consider it seriously, to respect it. Not least of all, she warns us—"and if you don't think they do [care, thus understand and respect, even if not agree!], you'll be angry," an anger that all too many planners and professionals have faced, even despite their best intentions (Susskind and Field 1996).

But then in a wonderfully illuminating moment, too, Sue speaks to the difficulties any of us create if we imagine professional rationality to be detached and uninvolved. Asked, "So when planners try to be 'professional' by appearing detached and objective, does it get people angry at them?" she responded quickly and emphatically, "SURE!"

Here we find in a few lines a damning indictment of traditional ideas of professional rationality that make no place for emotional sensitivity and responsiveness, no place for the moral resonance of professional attentiveness—in speech or writing— with the character of situations they face (Benhabib 1990; Slack 2003). But more: we see here too the immediate emotional reaction confronting planners, administrators, managers, organizers...who fail to be sensitive and responsive to citizens' felt attachments and concerns: these citizens will be angry, and rightfully so (Forester 1999a, ch. 2).

Sue teaches us, as Martha Nussbaum (1990) does, that a rationality that makes no place for such emotional responsiveness is an impoverished rationality, one not only partially blinded to what comes before it but one that's actually counter-productive, fueling anger and resentment and thus exacerbating rather than working to respond sensitively to civic problems at hand. Such an emotionally flat rationality is a weaker, thinner rationality, not one more robust and capable, but one more blind rather than more perceptive.

Listen now as another planning consultant ("public manager") tells us about the deceptively simple but politically complex process of learning via interviews in a contentious comprehensive planning process in a busy East Coast transportation corridor. An organizer turned mediator says:

While I love [doing] surveys...I know that for purposes of conflict resolution surveying absolutely is no substitute for personal contact. Interviewing is partially information gathering, but it's sixty percent relationship building. You are introducing yourself and inviting people to trust you.

It's a negotiation in itself. And if they trust you, to share information with you, and you treat that information with the respect that you promise, it's then not a very large leap to say, "Now, will you trust me to put together a meeting where you won't get beaten up?"

Here we see that interviewing and asking questions reach far beyond information gathering—and we glimpse not just the qualities of sharing information, manifesting respect, earning trust, building relationships, but then all of this in the service of convening conversations, "a meeting," in which parties' fears of aggression, distrust, and disrespect (where they "won't get beaten up"!) can be overcome in the pursuit of practical learning and actual civic deliberation. Here the work of interviewing no longer remains prior to—but is thoroughly interwoven with—planning and acting and implementation, because as it builds relationships and trust and encourages future collaboration, it enacts a future-oriented planning imagination and directs practical attention as well (Forester 2006; Umemoto 2001).

Finally, listen to a European port city's planning director and public administrator who contrasts two very different styles of interviewing. Rolf Jensen suggests that he tried to wean his own staff from a conventional, "old fashioned way" to a more exploratory, diagnostic, even deliberative style of planning and policy analysis. He begins by illustrating his staff's earlier practice:

For instance, when [our planners] did urban renewal, and they talked about public partici-pation, it was in the more old fashioned way. You go out with a sketch and say look, "This is what I think is good for you," and some [people] will not be able to understand the sketch at all, and they'd think, "Well, what should I comment on? What should we do? I won't say anything."

And some will say, "This portion is really good; but this portion we don't think is good at all." And the planners would say, "Why do you think so?" And the people would say, maybe, "We're lacking trees," or "There's not enough place for the kids." And the planner would go back, and he would say, "Well, I think they still could use the space for the kids over there," or the planner might change the plan and then go back again.

But it's not really a negotiated process at all. You listen to something, and you decide what you will hear and not hear, and what you will do and not do. When you've done that a couple of times, then you say, "Well, I've done participation. Now, here's a plan as a result of that process." And I don't think I'm exaggerating. That was about the way it was done. *So I wanted to do it differently.*

This planning director continues to describe another way that planners could work with others, encourage "participation," and learn in the process:

[There] was a [land-use] issue that was hard to solve. So we created a special group, trying to come up with schemes for this area, and then the planner would be just a mediator in that group. The planner would let the parties argue, and try to find solutions; they would work with colored pens and papers; they could write; they could do whatever they liked. They had what you might call workshops together, in which the basic task of the planner was to get the parties to understand each other—because in [this country's] tradition, many times, you just present the maps, and that's it: "Take my demand or not!"—[It's] a sort of power play.

We tried to conceive from the first day that we are here to listen. We are here to try to understand. But we are also here to try to tell you a story—in other words why we are concerned about certain things . . . if you do that, you gain two things.

First of all, the other party recognizes you too as a party . . .

But also, secondly, you might be able to help that party to come up with other demands.

This happened both when we as planners met with individual groups and met altogether— all the time! That attitude we used over and over and over again: never presenting a sketch as the sketch. Always saying, "Look, the sketch is not important, but what I've been trying to find a solution to, through this sketch, is this and that and that and that and that and that." In other words, it was the intentions and the characteristics with the sketch that was important, not the sketch itself.

It was important as a way of asking questions, and as a way of controlling questions to the parties: "Does that serve your needs?" "Is this something that you can live with?" Or, "What is really burning you if you look at this sketch?" (Forester 1994, 1999)

Here we find a full-fledged sense that planners' ways of asking questions embodies their overall planning strategies: collecting information and then making their own decisions or, instead, involving affected people more directly and intimately in framing options and choices in varied processes of discussion and dialogue. This planner's account of learning through "the sketch" acknowledges that sketches are also ways to control questions, to focus attention selectively, but we can see the sketch too as a door to newly imagined options and possibilities. In the contrast between the old-fashioned way and the more deliberative strategy, we see the significance of the planners' learning with others, the significance of planners both informing and learning from the views and cares of stakeholders.

In applied settings, in the face of complex projects and policy and project disputes, planners' interviews, we will see, need to reach far beyond traditional survey research interviews, and far even beyond ethnographic interviews, in part because planners must try not only to explain, not only to understand, but also to imagine, clarify, and refine—actually design!—future action. So they must try both to probe and to organize possibilities and thus too, profoundly, in revealing those possibilities, they work to organize hope. We will see this more clearly as we explore now just how much is at stake in planners' practical interviews.

# 3. What are the Stakes: How Much More than "the Facts?"

So let's consider how much we can learn from these interviews—or miss! In practice, it turns out, we can not just learn reflectively—as we reframe our assumptions and expectations—but we can learn deliberatively with others as well: we can reformulate our strategies (how we might act), our relationships (who "we" are), and our interests (what we really care about) too. If we appreciate these many ways that we can learn, we will see much more clearly too what planners and policy analysts might miss in their meetings, what they might not "get," what they actually might never know that they've missed!

We can explore "what's at stake" in good interviewing, what's to be learned or missed, first by asking what's to be learned about the other person, the interviewee; second, by asking what can be learned about the possible relationships between interviewers and interviewees, and perhaps others; and third, by asking what can be learned about the interviewer's own actions. Consider each briefly in turn.

## 3.1 Learning about the Other

### Information

We often interview people to get basic information about what they do, their behavior. "How often do you use the park?" we might ask, or "When you take your children to the doctor, do you use the bus, take a car, get a ride from a friend?" And so forth. We look for the facts of the matter, even if we know that the facts never speak for themselves. And sometimes, of course, we wonder not just about others' behavior but about their preferences—and these concerns are among the classic concerns of survey research (e.g. Judd, Smith, and Kidder 1991).

### Preferences

Beyond some "baseline" facts, then, we may look for subjective desires of the people we interview: "How do you feel about that undeveloped land nearby? Would you welcome a housing project built there? Do you want a park for local children to play in? Given a choice between leaving the land as-is or building A, B, or C, what do you prefer?" And so on, as discussed in standard discussions of survey research (Judd, Smith, and Kidder 1991, 230–3).

### Values

But preferences are just one form of subjective orientations that we might wish to explore. What about "values?" We say typically that we "hold" preferences, but we "cherish" values. We take values to make up part of who we are, what we stand for, what makes us distinctive—in ways that mere preferences do not. When we cannot have one preference, we typically try to substitute another satisfaction in its place. But when we cannot honor a value or lose the valued object, we don't simply look for other satisfactions but we grieve, we feel a deep loss for the intrinsic good that we've lost (Nussbaum 1986). Asking about values, probing for what can be deeply meaningful in a person's life, accordingly, involves an intimacy and requires a degree of respect that asking about preferences typically does not—and so treating another's cherished values as merely strategic preferences can get interviewers in a good deal of trouble (Forester 1999*b*).

### Identity

We might wish to know not only what community members value deeply, but how they imagine themselves, how they understand themselves as members of a community of place or faith or commitment. Here we explore not only elements of commitment, but the ways that history, tradition, and long practice have shaped (even tacit) senses of "who we are" or "who I am"—so that in turn we may regard certain Others as "foreign" or "strange," or to be feared or presumed as not interested in certain issues, or presumed not to be open to dialogue, discussion, or cooperative relationships.

So in interviews that assess the social structuring of controversies or disputes, we need to examine how citizens' identities might shape strong presumptions of yet other citizens. Jones calls herself "an outsider" and speaks of Smith as "an insider," for example, and this sense of political identity might help to explain both their never having spoken face to face, despite their deep concerns with neighborhood issues, and the yet unexplored possibilities of their meeting and perhaps even collaborating.

## Local Knowledge

We certainly might want to know not just what a community member desires, prefers, wants, or values, but what special knowledge they bring to the situations at hand. That "local knowledge" forms the expertise about their own lives that they have in the case at hand, the expertise they bring as perceptive people having lived and worked where they have, having had the problems and meaningful experiences that they uniquely and particularly have had.

We should explore this knowledge not as an either–or alternative to the specialized, professional knowledge that others might bring to bear, but as an additional source of insight, suggestion, suspicion, or consideration, as an additional source of relevant enquiry and research. To miss this local knowledge would assure our blindness to the particular cases in front of us. Listening only to the special knowledge of professionals, we might find ourselves generally correct but particularly, in this specific case, irrelevant (Corburn 2005).

# 3.2  Learning about Possible Relationships

## Needs for Recognition

How we do an interview can profoundly shape, and be just as important as, what we learn from it. If our approach to interviewing makes community members feel used, manipulated, taken advantage of, disrespected, or not really heard, our interviews will do far more harm than good. Part of what's at stake in many interviews, then, is the opportunity for the interviewee to be heard: to be listened to, to gain the recognition of the interviewer as having value and dignity, having a "voice" deserving to be heard (Stein and Mankowski 2004), having an experience that will be taken seriously (whether or not others subsequently agree or disagree)—and, not least of all, having a clear sense from the interviewer how his or her comments might inform future planning or decision making.

So the interviewer who cares more about organizing the clipboard and interview questions than respecting the interviewee may well do damage and learn little in the interview conversation too. In contrast, the interviewer who asks questions with respect and pays attention to the tone and pace and experience of the interviewee gives something back as well as takes information and insight from the interview conversation. As interviewers enact respect or disrespect in asking questions, they satisfy or frustrate interviewees' needs for recognition, and the success of their interview can easily hang in the balance (Arnstein 1969).

### Distrust

Along with that dignity, respect, and recognition at stake in every interview come matters of trust and the dangers of distrust. Depending upon the way an interviewer acknowledges what's been said as worthy of attention, as deserving of respect, as tied to the person speaking and their vulnerability and safety, the interviewer can earn the trust or distrust of those with whom they speak. The interviewer who shows up unannounced, a stranger, with few connections to the community—who appears ready to vanish just as quickly and never to be in touch again—will hardly inspire trust and confidence that they'll either understand really what they've been told or act in accord with its insight. A South African public official put this nicely once when he said, "Show up [for the first time] in my community to do interviews with a tape recorder and you could get hurt!"

### Value, not only "Values"

In many interviews, especially when the subject matter can be complex or controversial, the words spoken are just doorways to deeper worlds of issues and concerns. Interviewers in applied settings are often looking not just for answers to questions, not just for bits of information, but also for clues to what really matters, to what needs to be worried about, what needs to be attended to, what needs to be honored or protected or explored further—so that some actual action can follow. Good listeners know that what's significant to a speaker will often be implicit, so interviewers need to listen as much or more for revealing metaphors as for any clear declarations of values.

Here the interviewer needs to reach well beyond the literal words and well beyond the simple facts at hand to ask about "the facts that matter," to probe as they wonder, "what's being disclosed here as really significant?" Here interviewers try to learn about underlying value, what matters, as well as about the more superficial, if also important, rhetorically espoused "values," preferences, or commitments.

### Co-invention

Interviews provide opportunities, too, not just for information gathering but for cooperation, collaboration, even co-invention. An interviewer's question can prompt fresh thoughts—responses that suggest, "I've never thought of it that way before." An interviewer might ask about a possible line of action, about options, "Would there be any other way to approach this, any other way to explore getting time off?" and find that the question prompts a new thought, "Well, maybe if I offered to help before-hand ..."

Here the interview becomes not just an exchange, a quid pro quo, not just a back and forth conversation, but actually a process of collaboration and co-creation. By exploring possible moves, efforts, suggestions, enquiries, or questions that might be asked of still others, both sides can enquire together to explore new options or new ways of understanding issues at hand.

## 3.3 Learning about the Interviewer's Own Influence

### Emotional Responsiveness

If interviewers display no emotion at all as they listen and pose questions, they can be seen as callous, arrogant, egotistical, disinterested, and disrespectful, or worse. So in our opening quotations above, for example, we see that only when professionals show that they take seriously the experience of those with whom they're speaking will they be likely to have productive conversations—and actually showing that may only be possible through their own emotional responsiveness that they as interviewers bring to bear, that they themselves express.

Being responsive need not mean being wholly deferential, being cowed or intimi-dated or hopelessly distracted, but it might well mean being led to new questions, being led to even more important areas of conversation than the interviewer imagined initially. In part the promise of every interview lies in such discovery, in surprise, in the interviewee at times showing the questioner altogether new issues, new domains to explore, new matters of significance and relevance that ought to be "looked into." Such responsiveness, Sarah Dooling suggests, requires a quality of presence that works "from a place of curiosity and hope," as well as from "a place of political savvy and strategic caution" (personal communication, May 2004).

So emotional responsiveness on the interviewer's part offers opportunities as well as dangers, opportunities for discovery as well as dangers of getting lost. Such responsiveness challenges interviewers to show that when they ask questions, they hope not just to fill out boxes on a clipboard but to show that they "can relate" to the experience, or at least to this telling of the experience, of the interviewee.

### Relationship Building

Interviewers who can't inspire a minimum of trust may not just lose their interviews, for worse still can happen. Instead of being asked to leave, interviewees might ask them to stay and give them a taste of the game they seem to be playing. So a distrusted interviewer might evoke stories and tales designed for many purposes— many purposes that the interviewer may never discover.

Distrusted interviewers may be told "just what they want to hear," whether or not it has any relationship to any real world. They may evoke feigned cooperation just because the interviewee is more worried about his or her own safety than with helping the interloping interviewer: the interviewee might wonder, "Who will find out, and how might I suffer, if I say really what I feel here?"

Similarly, when interviewers can inspire trust and ensure the safety of those they're talking to, they can build relationships that they might build upon in the future. Not least of all, the interviewer might be able to come back, to keep in touch, to learn in the future. So the organizer turned mediator and public manager above told us, "If they trust you, to share information with you, and you treat that information with the respect that you promise, it's then not a very large leap to say, 'Now, will you trust me to put together a meeting where you won't get beaten up?' "

Curiously, a sense of humor can help both to level and to build collaborative working relationships across the interviewer–interviewee divide. Humor can play an ironic role, not just because everyone might laugh, but because they might laugh together: because humor creates a temporary common ground from which new relationships can arise—new relationships of those who come to see something surprising together, and to see in doing so that they share the possibility of viewing the world together, recognizing similar experiences in the world, finding some experiences similarly strange, or surprising, or wacky, or contradictory, or ambiguous, and evoking similarly "a laugh" (Forester 2004a).


## Discovery and Humility

Finally, interviewees often promise to break the presumptions and ordinary expectations of their interviewers. People just say the strangest and most wonderful things. Or they do it in the most unexpected ways. Robert Coles writes of interviewing African-American families with children who'd been the object of the most vicious, hateful heckling as they went daily to school, and Coles tells us of the astounding graciousness and generosity with which he, a stranger and an outsider, a white professional psychiatrist, was received and welcomed.

Humility is a virtue in interviewing not only as a corrective to the dangers of the arrogance that those of us with our important questions can have, the arrogance of those of us who "need to know," as we're on some "official mission" to "find out," but humility counts too because as interviewers we are so ridiculously finite, so merely mortal, so imperfect, so far really from any full rationality or omniscience, that we need to be as open to surprise and discovery as anyone else in the world (Woodruff 2001). Or more: Humility can help us because we may too often already have our sights set, our blinders in place, our presumptions operating even when we think we know to hold our "biases" aside.

So the wonder of words, and the wonder of each new meeting, lies in part in the discoveries we can share in inter-views, if we listen for far more than words, for far more than intentions too (Coles 1989; Reich 1994).

# 4. But what Obstacles make Interviewing Tough?

Talking about interviews is easy, but conducting them can be much tougher. Who are you, after all, to interview someone else? What will they think, once you start to ask questions? How badly have they felt treated by other interviewers—and how will that predispose them to treat you? What are you doing for them? Will they have any reason to trust you? Let's review several of the obstacles that you might face.

## 4.1  How Do You Look Before You Ever Open Your Mouth?

Consider all the non-verbal signals you send when you approach another person to "do" an interview. How do you dress (casually, formally, officially)? How do you smell (full of aftershave or perfume)? How do you arrive (by bus, by foot, by car, whose car)?

The South African official who warned us about the dangers of bringing a tape recorder to interviews unannounced was not alone. Speaking of her experiences as a young planner in Jerusalem, Sarah Kaminker recalled walking in neighborhoods with official-looking maps and having people stream out of their houses, once with rocks. Another planner spoke of introducing herself in a community meeting, and she recalled how she was then greeted as the representative of the city's powerful planning agency: "A guy got up in the back of the room and started yelling at me that his family had lost their home because of what we had done—but I hadn't even been born when that had happened!"

In such cases, these planners teach us, interviewers often send signals before they ever open their mouths. They way they dress, drive, equip, and identify themselves shapes the expectations of others, expectations for which the interviewers have some responsibility too.

## 4.2  "Mere Words" Matter

If interviewers use language that interviewees find strange, overly formal, obscurely technical, ambiguous, or arrogant, their interviews will fail. The language of our questions will shape not just the language of answers but perhaps whether any answers will be forthcoming at all.

In a striking story of intercultural negotiations, Shirley Solomon quotes a Native American tribal leader's experience of the silencing effects of the formal procedures and language of Robert's Rules of Order: He says, "In those meetings where it's Robert's Rules of Order, I know that I either have nothing to say or what I have to say counts for nothing" (Forester and Weiser 1995).

The point here reaches far beyond "Robert's Rules" or parliamentary or other formal procedures. The language of our questions, and the language in which we might presume a conversation to unfold, can discourage, intimidate, humiliate, or otherwise silence many people with important experiences and knowledge to share. If we neglect these languages of interviewing and instead assume some supposedly "neutral" terminology, we risk not only keeping ourselves stupid but undermining future cooperation and weakening our future relationships as well.

## 4.3  Safety Matters

When those asking the questions and those being asked have histories between them, histories of distrust and inequality, interviews will be more complicated than they would otherwise be. Those asking the questions sometimes think that their own "good intentions" should be enough to pave the way to successful interviews, but they can face rude surprises. Ken Reardon writes of taking planning students to East St Louis to interview community leaders about prospective local projects they might work on—only to find that they would be interviewed in turn, if not grilled, and then told pointedly by community leaders of the long history that residents had suffered as objects of previous generations of university researchers (Reardon et al. 1993).

In any situation of conflict, too, parties will be reluctant to "tell all" to third-party mediators for just the same reasons that very few of us "tell all" to many others: we very reasonably worry about how others will use the information we might disclose, especially if others might come to see us in some partial light or take advantage of that information. Even "students" can have difficulties doing interviews if community residents fear that their words will not be accurately reported or that the confidentiality they've assumed (or have been promised) could be violated.

The more general point is simple enough: the more afraid interviewees feel about having their words used against them, the more limited will be the utility of the interview results. Interviewers need to know that these issues reach far beyond their ostensible "good intentions," of course, for they conduct their interviews on institutional stages, in historically and politically staged contexts that frame every word they speak.

## 4.4 Theoretical Blinders

Interviews can run aground on other rocks too: the interviewer's theoretical frame-work may be so selective, so narrow, that he or she cannot grasp effectively, much less adequately report, what's been said or what's significant about it (Umemoto 2001).

Robert Coles puts this beautifully, quoting William Carlos Williams here: "Who's against shorthand? No one I know. Who wants to be shortchanged? No one I know" (Coles 1989, 29).

We do interviews to learn, but we need to ask questions to help others help us, and sometimes our preoccupations, our own selective attention can work not just to focus attention too partially, but to mislead us as well. We might "frame" a question as a matter of time and resources, for example, and not really hear an answer that hints that the problem of limited resources is really humiliation, not economic capacity.

So in a mediation once I asked a young man, as I tried to check what I thought I'd heard, "So, because you're working, you don't have much *time* to do the things that your father's talking about here?"—and when he replied, "Yeah, right, it's hard to do," I missed the significance of his answer altogether. But his father who was sitting across the table didn't miss a thing and exclaimed: "Oh! (I get it!) This is hard for you! Sure, of course; Yes, I can see that it is..." and their whole conversation then turned from arguing and bickering to a real search for cooperation. The point, it turned out, was not about time at all, but about the father's pressure, the son's pride and embarrassment to admit that what the father was asking was difficult because of his job's demands, the father's having been fooled by the son's brave face—and only now, with the son hinting and the father seeing past the blinders of my question about "time," were the father and son able to try together not only to address the supposed "issues" at hand but to improve their relationship as well.

## 4.5 Presumptions Can Blind Interviewers and Interviewees Alike

Robert Coles warns us that patients can have presumptions about what their doctors wish to hear, and so what those doctors learn through their questions can be limited accordingly. Similarly, professionals of all kinds bring presumptions of what others know or don't know, what they will be able or unable to respond to, what they will be willing or unwilling to talk about, and so what they (or we) learn will be shaped accordingly.

Lawyer-turned-mediator Gordon Sloan suggests the influence that such presump-tions can have. Talking to parties participating in a Vancouver Island land use mediation that he had convened, he found many parties telling him that they were quite willing to talk to others, but they then said quite confidently of their adversar-ies, "But they'll never talk to us!"

Sloan tells us, instructively, that he found himself saying then to several of these parties, "Funny thing: that's exactly what they said about you!" and found them responding, in surprise, "They did?!?" (Forester and Weiser 1995).

Here presumptions reach past what gets asked to the very possibility of discussion and dialogue in the first place!

## 4.6  Professional Education as a Source of Blinders and Bias

Our own training encourages us to pay attention selectively, to ask some questions and not others, to see some responses as relevant and not others, to treat some claims and some emotions as significant and others as less so. So in the first part of this chapter we read one planner's warning: if we work with people who've invested years of work and commitment in their neighborhoods, and our own professional self-image leads us to suppress *showing that we care* about those places, those commitments, and that real work, we can very well then seem not to be sensitive, impartial, and professional, but callous, unfeeling, and distant—and if we seem to be blind and unresponsive, we will inspire not confidence and reassurance but resentment (Sandercock 2003; Krumholz and Forester 1990, 256).

If our training misleads us to think of emotion as simply a distraction from rationality—as if irrelevant facts could not be just as distracting—that very training will have saddled us with a terribly thin, emaciated idea of rationality, as Martha Nussbaum has so often argued (1990). We can learn through emotions as well as from facts, which explains why in the face of complex problems we might seek counsel from those capable of feeling as well as thinking. Consider the risks of taking advice—about anything important in your life—from someone with lots of brains but with no emotional sensitivity, no emotional awareness or responsiveness.

## 4.7  Impatience

It can be hard to listen sensitively, or be difficult emotionally to spend the time required to understand someone, when as interviewers we're itching to "get to the point" (or to the next interview!). So having patience as an interviewer can be an art form. New questions can so easily derail a train of thought, and part of the wonder of doing any good interview is enabling surprise, enabling the person being interviewed to bring something wholly new into the conversation: a distinct turn of phrase, a way of putting something, a new idea, an angle that's important, a sense that "I've never really thought of it that way before" (Weiss 1994).

But interviewers may think, after all, that they "don't have all day," and they have others to talk to and other work to do (and so do the interviewees, of course!)—and so interviewers have to be careful: if they show signs of impatience, they're likely not only to shorten the interview, but to get canned and ready-made answers instead of the thoughtful, if less crisp, responses that will really be fresh and instructive.

## 4.8 The Fear of Loss of Control

Not only can patience be in short supply, but so can confidence. When an interviewee seems to be wandering, interviewers have a judgement call to make: do I interject or interrupt to "bring them back" to the topic at hand, or not? Questions often provoke unintended responses, and these can be the most interesting of all or be the most irrelevant—and good interviewers must know the difference!

Questions can provoke strong emotions too, and when they do, in unanticipated ways, interviewers will wonder what they've been missing, what they should have known but didn't, and more: they will wonder if the strong emotions they've provoked will threaten (or help to redirect) the flow and direction of the interview itself.

The more an interview matters, at times, the more emotional the response of those questioned may be. Asked about grievances or the responsibility of others or promises made or betrayed, respondents may quite reasonably become angry, cynical, distressed, disgusted, perhaps prone to go off on a screed that can threaten all but the most experienced interviewer.

So control can often be an issue negotiated all the way along an interview. Like their interviewees, interviewers too have purposes and limited time and limited capacities to understand and assess what they hear—and so they might reasonably fear losing control of interviews when respondents have very strong views or stronger emotions.

## 4.9 Posturing Threatens Successful Interviews

Sound bites threaten interviews no less than they subvert substantive political discussion. If interviewers hope to explore fresh material rather than pre-scripted "pat" answers, then they have to be careful not simply to evoke respondents' "posturing" instead of their more candid replies.

Parties can posture for many reasons. They may distrust the interviewer and so fall back on tried and true answers. They may worry that the interviewer will reveal sensitive information and so not disclose anything that's not already "canned." They may have little time and rely on "tried and true" answers. They may presume that the interviewer wants well-rehearsed, well-thought-out, and prepared answers, and so posturing becomes a way to appear 'prepared' and in control. In these ways and others, interviewees can withhold fresh and thoughtful responses, and their interviewers can learn little, perhaps and very likely never knowing what they are missing.

# 5. So, to Overcome these Obstacles, What can Help us to Inter-view Well?

So you're going to do a series of interviews, and you're reasonably a bit apprehensive about how they might go. What can you do to avoid some of the obstacles just discussed? What can you do to learn a good deal rather than wasting your time? There's a good deal you can do, so consider first at least these dozen or so suggestions:

## 5.1 Think about Ceremony and Rituals of Indirection that Allow Talk

Conversation just doesn't happen. Especially when controversial issues are involved, interviewers may need to build relationships if they're going to be able to ask good questions and get good answers. Tel Aviv public official Baruch Yoscovitz put this wonderfully once when he described the experience of a Japanese planning colleague who'd worked on a major transportation infrastructure project in metropolitan Tokyo (Forester, Fischler, and Shmueli 2001, 39). "How'd you manage to do it?" Yoscovitz recalls asking. He found the answer striking: "Over two thousand cups of tea."

Curiously here, the rituals of meals, breaking bread or sharing tea, allow interviewees to see what sort of person they may be dealing with in the interviewer: is this someone who just wants to "hit and run," to ask pre-scripted questions quickly and leave, or does this person bring a broader agenda? Given our situation, what's appropriate here? And in these same rituals, of course, interviewers may build trust and rapport and learn as well.

## 5.2 Remember that People Care about Much More than they Say

If we know not to take people "literally," as if everything they mean could possibly be expressed in their words, we know to look beyond words, to take what we hear as indications, metaphors, expressions, practically produced accounts in specific (interview-structured) situations. So we know that what we hear is almost always provisional, not the "last word," always incomplete. Once we understand that speakers very often care about much more than they can put into words, we can treat their words as doors to yet other of their concerns, beliefs, worries, commitments, and more—even as we must also be careful about reading too much into what they've said (Spirn, personal communication, 2003).

Just as we must listen for more than mere "words," so do we read quotes not just for "words" but also for meanings and implications, clues and cues, hints and tips to matters of concern far more complex than any simple sentences might literally render. If we resist being too literal as we listen to answers, we might remember the saying that "a picture's worth a thousand words"—and apply that thought to the many pictures that our interviewees paint in our conversations.

## 5.3  Recognize Emotions as Modes of Vision Tied to Cognition (No More Distracting than "Facts"!)

We should listen carefully to the emotional tone of what we hear, and we should appreciate emotions as being equally capable of either distracting us from *or* leading us to "the truth of the matter" at hand (including a party's strategic posturing!). At the risk of repeating a suggestion made above: if we think about it for a moment, we can see that anyone with a deeply hidden agenda can use an appeal to "the facts" to distract others just as much as they ever might use "emotion" for the same ends. But more ironically: the appeal to "facts" might distract us even more subtly (as if "the facts" were simply, out of any context, free of any selectivity, independent of any language of representation, just "the facts").

So instead of assuming either that "the facts" ever speak for themselves or that emotions of fear or anger or suspicion have little to teach us in a specific case, we should try sensitively to learn through such emotions rather than try pre-emptively and blindly to suppress them as "non-rational," "misleading," or "distracting." We can learn through another's fear or anger, for example—if we listen closely—for fear and anger are typically related to evaluative judgements and cognitions: a resident fears losing their neighborhood's "character" if "other people" start to come in, and a sensitive listener might now probe for issues of class or racial stereotypes associated with the fear of "other people." Or a resident's anger at "City Hall" might be understood to involve not just what "City Hall" allowed to happen last time, but the lack of any recognition on officials' parts respecting residents or concerning what actually happened.

Emotions can disclose important information, but interviewers have to listen sensitively so they can probe—or they will just miss the cues, miss the tips, and learn less than they very well might in the practical case at hand.

## 5.4  Realize that Messiness Matters, and Details Help

Mediators need to do careful interviews with parties before they might ever bring them together to try to settle a few of their differences. One mediator—call her Mary—shared a time-tested strategy she has often used: to do a good interview, she remembers to let her interviewees get past their first fifteen minutes, past their tried and true routines, their favorite summaries of "what it's all about"—so she can, then, learn a lot from the details of their less rehearsed and less reductive accounts.

Mary teaches us that interviewers can be held hostage to these summary stories, the favorite phrasings, the practiced simplifications of interviewees, so we ought deliberately to press for further elaboration, for the details, for unexpected angles that can reveal both new information and also at times a better understanding on the part of the interviewees themselves. So we might often ask, for example, "Can you say a bit more about how that happens?" or "Can you give me an example of that?"

## 5.5  Moving Beyond the Rush to Interpretation

Robert Coles warns young doctors that patients may often only tell them what they think the doctors wish to hear. So too in social research can interviewers miss important insights if they fail to appreciate the preconceptions that their interviewees have of the interview process and the interviewer's purposes. Coles warns us to beware of "the rush to interpretation," our own temptations to interpret too quickly, to jump to premature conclusions because of our own lack of time, our own anxiety about getting "the point," our own over-confidence, or simply our own inability to listen well.

The same problem arises in the world of public policy. So students of the field pass along "Goldberg's Rule:" Instead of asking someone, "What's the problem?" ask them instead, "What's the story?"—so you find out not just one narrow perspective on "the" problem at hand, but a broader fabric of relevant details that might do justice to the complexity of what's actually going on (Forester 1999a).

## 5.6  Moving Beyond Contextual Blinders

Recalling their interviews, mediators of public disputes have said some strange things about the parties to those disputes. Sometimes, mediators suggest, parties seem not to have thought very thoroughly about their own "interests" in a given case and seem instead to focus their attention much more narrowly on goals, objectives, positions, or outcomes they hope to achieve.

What sense can that make? If the parties themselves haven't thought these things through, who in the world has? But now, if we don't treat these mediators as blind or condescending here, we can actually learn from these curious comments: parties understandably express "what they want" within the contexts of what they take to be possible, within the frameworks of relationships and institutional possibilities that they take for granted as "realistic."

So too if we were interviewees: our answers would depend on some institutional context we assumed, on some set of possibilities we took to be plausible. So we might believe "the City Council will never allocate funds to honest work on race relations," and so we might not "waste time talking about irrelevancies," things that will never happen (Forester 2005).

The challenge for interviewers here is a complex and theoretically intriguing one: in a world in which everyone has limited vision, limited rationality, we may need to call into question taken-for-granted assumptions that severely restrict what might actually be thought to be politically possible. So interviewers can try to be explicit about contingencies: "If, somehow, the City Council were to consider funding for work on race relations," for example, "what would you recommend? If that were possible, what might you support? Advise?"

Mediators face a related difficulty when they do interviews: parties may fear being exploited if they reveal what really matters to them. Of course, when parties who are interdependent all do this, when they all misrepresent what they care about, they set themselves up ironically and tragically for failure. They make it much more difficult to "trade" across their different priorities. So failing to take advantage of mutually beneficial exchanges—actually possible and mutually beneficial reciprocity, each giving what matters less to them in order to get in return what matters more to them—they reach lose–lose agreements: agreements, but agreements that are "lousy" for both parties relative to what they really might have achieved if they had taken advantage of their differences in priorities, concerns, worries, fears, or "interests" (Susskind et al. 1999; Forester 1999a).

The more general problem for interviewing is this: if interviewees fear being exploited in any way for being truthful, the interviewer may not learn very much, not even that (or why) the interviewee is perhaps quite rightly afraid. What can interviewers do? They can bring a keen sense of politics to their interviews and a practical awareness of the political settings that frame and loom behind them.

If interviewers seem oblivious to those institutional contexts, as if their "good intentions" alone were all that mattered, they will not likely inspire confidence and trust. But they can try to build trust and protect their interviewees in many ways: acknowledging political contexts, clarifying just how they will use interview materials, at times ceasing to take notes or turning off tape recorders, perhaps bringing trusted third parties along, and perhaps most importantly creating their own track record of living up to their word, building relationships over time.

## 5.7 Take Small Steps, Make Small Offers

Imagine that someone wants to interview you about your childhood. If they begin by asking, "Were your parents successful?" what's likely to happen? You might ask in turn, "Well, what in the world do you mean by 'successful'?" Or if you defer to the interviewer and accept her terms, you might now feel put in a bind, as if you had to decide upon a first "yes or no" answer, "successful" or not, and then give subsequent answers that would back up that first answer.

Interviewers might do much better, it would seem, to ask for evidence rather than for summary judgements: to ask for information or stories that might support overall judgements (perhaps about anyone's "success") later in the research process. This means that as interviewers, we have to resist the temptation to ask our interviewees to do our work for us.

So if we want to find out what sort of parents (or alternatively, residents, neighbors, activists, patients, and so on), for example, Sue and Chris are, we'll do far better to ask them for evidence (How do you spend time with your children? How do you respond to your children when they ...?) rather than to ask them point blank, "What sort of parents (and so on) are you?"

In part, this means interviewers must build trust; they must take small steps with interviewees to show that they are interested in the details of experience that matter, not just in easy summary judgements. Small steps build confidence; they invest time and attention; small steps are far less threatening (and less obscure) than big overall questions that overreach and so eventually underachieve. Asking, "How does this political process work?" might ask for such a summary account, and it might signal such ignorance of the process that the question itself may prompt a far more reductive response than the interviewer really wants (and than the interviewee would be willing to give).

Big questions need to be broken into pieces, so interviewers can ask interviewees to walk with them in small steps rather than to jump in front of them in big leaps. Interviewers who ask smaller questions will threaten less, build trust and confidence more, and produce surprising results as well.

## 5.8 Deflecting the Blame Game: Probe Possibilities Too

As Mary suggested above, interviewers, like mediators, can be held hostage to familiar but reductive rationalizations, whether we call them "scripts" or "raps" or "bones to pick" or "spiels" or "homilies" or political doctrines. But they can do better, too, not only by asking for details and examples, but by asking their interviewees for positive suggestions, for proposals, for offers, for possible solutions to problems at hand. This move accomplishes several objectives at once: it moves beyond a "blame game," it searches for value to be protected and honored, and it asks the interviewee to take responsibility as an agent not just to lay blame, but to imagine constructive alternatives too.

Mediators find this "future orientation" to be axiomatic, for the blame game escalates easily and displaces contingent and constructive offers, "What if we tried X, Y, Z? Could we do A, B, C?" Similarly, interviewers can probe not only for the allocation of blame, but for the suggestion of possibilities too—and enrich their research results by doing so.

In a land use case a mediator we'll call "Monica" put this search for proposals this way:

Whenever somebody put something negatively, I would just try to find a positive idea there.

I'd try to turn it around to a positive idea. So someone would rant and rave, somebody could become angry about houses being built in cornfields, let's say—they didn't want to see that, and they mentioned something about a land trust in the course of talking. So I'd pick out that idea, and I'd say, "So are you saying it would be good if we had a local land trust that could try to protect some of this land?" and they'd say, "Yes."

So it was really a question, whenever anybody spoke negatively, of trying to turn it around into a positive suggestion, or just coming back with, "Well, what would you like to see happen?"

That set the tone for our meetings, and it really set the tone for our organization as a whole about what we're trying to do—which is find positive solutions.

## 5.9 Let a Sense of Humor Break Presumptions

Having a sense of humor does more than produce smiles and laughter. It conveys to interviewees that an interviewer has a sense of perspective about her work, that she is not so earnest, so narrow-minded, or so grimly serious that the interviewee must worry from the very beginning, for example, about giving "inadequate," "wrong", or "stupid" answers. Bringing a sense of humor does not only lighten the work for the interviewer, but sharing that sense of multiple perspectives encourages interviewees, too, to share the contradictions and complexities, the riddles and peculiarities they see in cases at hand.

Sharing a sense of humor signals to the person being interviewed that the interviewer is not in full control of the situation; he or she doesn't know all the answers; he or she is prepared for the unexpected, for multiple meanings and views, for not just a soberly serious attitude but for the contributions that a playful approach might make as well.

Having a sense of humor in this way can help build trust and ease the anxieties of interviewer–interviewee relationships; it can align questioner and respondent together collaboratively in the face of ambiguous and puzzling, complex, and contentious subjects. Not least of all, having a sense of humor can make it possible for both interviewee and interviewer to face very difficult, even painful subjects, recognizing them and yet not being held hostage to them (Forester 2004a; Sclavi 2003).

## 5.10  Take a Walk!

Still another approach to interviewing takes a less conversational and more physical, even more ambulatory, form. Talk less about issues in the abstract, and instead get out and move around more and look at the setting or city or neighborhood or view corridor or open space together. As you do things together, you will learn things, and sometimes talking may only come after walking, traveling, touring, moving through space together, going door to door or site to site together. In Tony Gibson's memorable phrase describing participants working together on community planning strategies and physical models: "Eyes down (to the work), hands on, rubbing shoulders, a lot less big mouth" (Gibson 1998).

## 5.11  Pre-brief and De-brief

It might help to realize that interviews live in our imaginations not only before we "do them," but after we have "done them" too. So it can help, early on, to talk to trusted and informed others about what we're getting into—what we might ask or not ask, do or not do. Similarly, we might discuss what we've heard and what we think we've learned with others after the fact, for often others will bring other perspectives, insights, and knowledge to bear on what we've heard, and we will learn even more than we first thought as we "go over" what we've heard with others.

# 6. Conclusions

So inter-viewing means listening to and learning from others and doing that with their cooperation, even collaboration. To interview well is to act practically, responding to the particulars of the person to whom you're talking in the unique situation of your conversation. In more philosophical terms, doing an interview requires a form of practical rationality, a context-sensitive rationality that's finely aware of details and richly responsible to encompassing histories of obligations and responsibilities (as Martha Nussbaum (1990) might put it).

In interviewing well, we try to explore possibilities of understanding the world in new ways. We are asking questions not simply to confirm our suspicions, but ideally to be surprised and to be taught, to be shown in new ways the world about which we care. In policy and planning situations, interviews often involve the sense of future as well as the perception of the past, and in conversations of depth, we can come to see both past and future in new ways—so that we reconstruct the past as hardly so "past" after all, for we may come to interpret that past as we have never before beheld it and acted upon it.

So too in interviewing do we necessarily probe matters of fact and value together, even simultaneously. We probe, after all, the facts that matter, the facts that we take to be worth asking about, the facts that our interviewees find worthwhile noting, drawing our attention to, telling us how much they count.

In planning and policy contexts, then, inter-viewing to explore future possibilities reaches far beyond traditional interviews that might collect multiple-choice answers to pre-scripted questions. Policy and planning interviewing values objectivity not as opposed to subjectivity but as building upon it, as established by inter-subjective confirmation, by public scrutiny rather than private bias. In the policy and planning fields, interviewers dispense with the fictions that salient knowledge could be adequately pre-scripted, and so in these fields, open-ended interviews become essential to open up possibilities of action and design, negotiation and conflict resolution, collaboration and modes of recognition that lie beyond the initial presumptions of the interviewers. In planning and policy contexts, interviewing becomes exploratory, normatively inquisitive, action-oriented collaborative research.

Interviewing, we see, begins with a form of relationship in which strangers often approach each other to talk. In the course of such talk, we can transform relationships (for better or worse), so that interviewers can often create trust and rapport, can make their presence well worth the time of the interviewee. In other cases, of course, interviewers damage relationships by being presumptuous, condescending, threatening, callous, disrespectful, short, confounding, or worse.

When we consider the harm interviewers can do, we can see vividly how the work of interviewing involves an ethics that involves the treatment of others to whom we talk. The ethical considerations that become immediately relevant involve issues of respect, recognition, and emotional sensitivity. So interviewing combines matters of epistemology and ethics: interviewers must care deeply not only how they can know about the world, but also about how they can treat others with or from whom they hope to learn about and perhaps change the world.

Interviewing requires us to listen far beyond the literal words we hear, far beyond the "facts of the matter," so that we assess meaning and significance, so that we assess emotional nuances and feelings as well as factual accuracy, so that we take our conversations not as last words about complex matters but as first words that open them up for us.

Lastly, the challenges of interviewing make clear to us a deep insight of Hannah Arendt's: our work of social enquiry must have a moral resonance with the subject matter, the experiences, the political and moral complexities that we wish to explore (Benhabib 1990; Slack 2003). This sounds simple enough, but perhaps no challenge in social enquiry is more daunting. Pre-scripted questionnaires will hardly do. Just how can one person ask insightfully about another's experience of family or neighborhood or community disintegration, or about the humiliations, perhaps due to racism or sexism or job loss or incapacities, of another's loved one(s)?

Just how can we ask sensitively, not stupidly, about one another's real and precious hopes, or tragic losses?

For all those concerned with matters of public policy possibilities, the work of interviewing is inescapable, ever-present throughout organizational and political life. Technical and non-technical work alike will depend deeply on the skills and insights we bring to our interviews, so we have our work cut out for us.

## References

ARNSTEIN, S. 1969. A ladder of citizen participation. *AIP Journal* (July): 216–24.

BENHABIB, S. 1990. Hannah Arendt and the redemptive power of narrative. *Social Research*, 57: 167–96.

COLES, R. 1989. *The Call of Stories*. Boston: Houghton Mifflin.

CORBURN, J. 2005. *Street Science*. Cambridge Mass.: MIT Press.

FORESTER, J. 1989. *Planning in the Face of Power*. Berkeley: University of California Press.

—— 1994. Profile: Rolf H. Jensen on "dispute resolution as a strategy of urban planning." Dept. of City and Regional Planning, Cornell University.

—— 1999a. *The Deliberative Practitioner*. Cambridge, Mass.: MIT Press.

—— 1999b. Dealing with deep value differences. Pp. 463–93 in *The Consensus-Building Handbook*, ed. L. Susskind, S. McKearnan, and J. Thomas-Larmer. Thousand Oaks, Calif.: Sage.

—— 2004a. Critical moments in negotiations: on humor, recognition and hope. *Negotiation Journal*, 20 (2: Apr.): 221–37.

—— 2004b. Planning and mediation, participation and posturing: what's a deliberative practitioner to do? Prepared for the Annual Symposium of the Interdisciplinary Ph.D. Program in Urban Design and Planning University of Washington, Seattle, 15 Apr.

—— 2004c. Community planning and the art of consensus-building. Prepared for the Safe and Strong Communities Symposium, Sydney, July.

—— 2005. Challenges of public learning and process design: if parties often misrepresent their interests, how can we evaluate negotiated policy agreements? Pp. 150–63 in *Adaptive Governance of Natural Resources*, ed. J. Scholz and B. Stiftel. Washington, DC: Resources for the Future Press.

—— forthcoming 2006. Rationality and surprise: the drama of mediation in rebuilding civil society. In *Engaging Civil Societies in Democratic Planning and Governance*, ed. P. Gurstein and N. Angeles. Toronto: University of Toronto Press.

—— FISCHLER, R., and SHMUELI, D. (eds.) 2001. *Israeli Planners and Designers: Profiles of Community Builders*. New York: State University Press of New York.

—— and WEISER, I. (eds.) 1995. Profiles of environmental/community mediators. Typescript, City and Regional Planning Department, Cornell University.

GIBSON, T. 1998. *The Do-ers Guide to Planning for Real*. London: Neighborhood Initiatives Foundation.

GREENWOOD, D., and LEVIN, M. 1999. *Introduction to Action Research: Social Research for Social Change*. Thousand Oaks, Calif.: Sage.

JUDD, C. M., SMITH, E. R., and KIDDER, L. H. 1991. *Research Methods in Social Relations*, 6th edn. Orlando, Fla.: Harcourt Brace Jovanovich.

KRUMHOLZ, N., and FORESTER, J. 1990. *Making Equity Planning Work: Leadership in the Public Sector.* Philadelphia: Temple University Press.

NUSSBAUM, M. 1986. *The Fragility of Goodness.* Cambridge: Cambridge University Press.

—— 1990. *Love's Knowledge.* New York: Oxford University Press.

REARDON, K., WELSH, J., KREISWORTH, B., and FORESTER, J. 1993. Participatory action research from the inside. *American Sociologist,* 24 (1): 69–91.

REICH, R. 1994. *The Power of Public Ideas.* Boston: Ballinger.

SANDERCOCK, L. 2003. *Cosmopolis II.* New York: Continuum.

SANOFF, H. 1999. *Community Participation Methods in Design and Planning.* New York: John Wiley and Sons.

SCHÖN, D. 1983. *The Reflective Practitioner.* New York: Basic Books.

SLACK, S. 2003. Personal correspondence. E-mail, 11 March.

SCLAVI, M. 2003. *Art of Listening and Possible Worlds* (Arte di ascoltare e mondi possibili. Come si esce dalle cornici di cui siamo parte). Milan: Bruno Mondadori.

STEIN, C., and MANKOWSKI, E. 2004. Asking, witnessing, interpreting, knowing: conducting qualitative research in community psychology. *American Journal of Community Psychology,* 33 (1/2): 21–35.

SUSSKIND, L., and FIELD, P. 1996. *Dealing with an Angry Public.* New York: Free Press.

—— MCKEARNAN, S., and LARMER, J. T. (eds.) 1999. *The Consensus Building Handbook: A Comprehensive Guide to Reaching Agreement.* Thousand Oaks, Calif.: Sage.

UMEMOTO, K. 2001. Walking in another's shoes. *Journal of Planning Education and Research,* 21: 17–31.

WEISS, R. 1994. *Learning from Strangers.* New York: Free Press.

WILDAVSKY, A. 1989. The open-ended, semi-structured interview. Pp. 57–101 in *Craftways: On the Organization of Scholarly Work.* New Brunswick, NJ: Transaction.

WOODRUFF, P. 2001. *Reverence: Renewing a Forgotten Virtue.* New York: Oxford University Press.

# CHAPTER 7

---

# POLICY ANALYSIS AS POLICY ADVICE

---

## RICHARD WILSON

POLICY analysis and advice, and the decisions based on them, should in an ideal world be united in one smooth continuous process: research, analysis, options, consultation, proposals, and decisions, all guided and informed by advice at each stage. This simple sequential model is one which many policy advisers themselves have in mind in setting out on the path leading to a decision.

In practice the world inside government is not always as simple as that. The policy process can be more tortuous. The steps may come in the wrong order and some may be omitted. External factors may have an unpredictable impact on what happens. Even a strong Minister may be swayed late in the day by a word from an influential outsider or a media report or a new statistic. Policy analysis is usually an important part of policy formulation, but it is not necessarily the whole story. This chapter explores why.

The chapter is written from the viewpoint of a practitioner who has worked inside government departments and the Cabinet Office since the 1960s, in a position of both giving and receiving advice. It takes no account of experience elsewhere.[1] Every country does these things in its own way, influenced by its own administrative culture and conditions. This is a local account, hopefully with relevance to others.[2]

---

[1] For corresponding accounts of US practitioners, see e.g. Eizenstadt 1992; Schultze 1992; Neustadt 2001; Barber 2001. For more analytic accounts drawn from a US experience see e.g. Neustadt 1960, 2001; Neustadt and May 1986; Wildavsky 1979; Porter 1983, 1997.

[2] For other academic accounts of the British case, see e.g. Brittan 1964, 1969; Heclo and Wildavsky 1974.

# 1. WHAT IS "POLICY?"

The word "policy" is imprecise and usually used loosely by those who make it. It may indicate an overall objective ("we will take effective action to combat the terrorist threat," in the words of the 1997 New Labour manifesto (Labour Party 1997, 35) ) or a guiding principle ("we will be tough on crime and tough on the causes of crime" (1997, 5) ) or a specific action which will be taken to help reach the objective ("we will halve the time it takes persistent juvenile offenders to come to court" (1997, 5) ).

Definitions of policy are sometimes crafted for a particular purpose. For instance, a Government White Paper on Modernising Government in 1999 said: "policy making is the process by which governments translate their political vision into programmes and actions to deliver 'outcomes'—desired changes in the real world."[3] The National Audit Office, which audits public expenditure on behalf of the UK Parliament, similarly said: "Policy is the translation of government's political priorities and principles into programmes and courses of action to deliver desired changes" (National Audit Office 2001). These definitions were intended to give a signal to particular audiences, and are incomplete. For instance, "policy" may relate to the principles and priorities which a government adopts in relation to an issue, and not to their translation into action: see above. And not all policies are about bringing about change. In some cases the objective of policy is continuity. To take a random example, the British government has declared, as a matter of policy, its joint commitment with China to stability, prosperity, and a high degree of autonomy for Hong Kong.[4]

In other cases "policy" is used with other meanings for other purposes. For instance, Michael Howard, the then Home Secretary, faced demands in Parliament for his resignation following a serious lapse in prison security for which he had dismissed the director general, Derek Lewis. He said:

I am personally accountable to the House [of Commons] for all matters concerning the Prison Service. I am accountable and responsible for all policy decisions relating to the service. The director general is responsible for day-to-day operations.[5]

Here the Minister was proposing a distinction between policy and day-to-day operations as a basis for defining personal responsibility. The distinction was not new. Similar distinctions had been drawn in other contexts, for instance in the relationship between governments and nationalized industries.

The distinction needs to be used with care. Policy making and day-to-day operations are not separate spheres of influence but inextricably linked. The policy maker may, for instance, regard it as morally and politically unacceptable for inmates of a prison, who are there for punishment and correction, to have television sets in their cells, and may decide that they should be withdrawn as a matter of policy. The person

---

[3] Cm 4310.    [4] Prime Minister, press conference, 10 May 2004.
[5] Hansard, 19 Oct. 1995, col. 518.

in charge of day-to-day operations, on the other hand, may regard withdrawal as an operational matter which may lead to disturbance, rioting, and even a loss of control in prisons. Different roles may have different objectives and priorities and ultimately the policy maker has to be responsible for operations as well as policy. But day-to-day operations can of course be delegated within that framework.

Another way of putting the point is that there are different levels of policy making. At the highest level, governments define their policy objectives and how they will be achieved. But at lower levels there is often a myriad of intermediate policy decisions about the interpretation and implementation of policy which is the stuff of daily life in government departments including day-to-day operations; and it is where success and failure often lie.

It can be argued for instance that the chances of successfully introducing the poll tax (community charge) were dramatically reduced by an intermediate policy decision (see Butler, Adonis, and Travers 1994). The Conservative manifesto in the general election in 1987 included a commitment to the tax. The intention was to introduce it alongside its predecessor system, the rates, and to phase out the rates over four years, an arrangement known as "dual running." Then in late 1987, after brief discussion, it was decided to abandon dual running and introduce the tax in one go in April 1990. This intermediate policy decision was arguably as important as the policy itself but it was taken quickly and with only a small fraction of the care and thought.

In this chapter policy means the actions, objectives, and pronouncements of governments on particular matters, the steps they take (or fail to take) to implement them, and the explanations they give for what happens (or does not happen). Policy advice means the advice which is given to governments in connection with these things, including how to achieve a policy goal, once it has been decided upon.

## 2. THE EXERCISE OF POWER

Policy in government is fundamentally about the exercise of power by the state. Policy advice is advice about how that power should be exercised, and to the extent that it actually influences what governments say or do it may itself represent the exercise of informal power. Policy analysis is about providing a basis for the exercise of power, and may or may not be powerful, depending on how far it actually influences what happens. The policy process does not exist in a vacuum, nor does it operate in a world of pure rationality. It can only be seen and understood in a political context.

This is why the relationship between policy analysis and policy advice is rarely straightforward. Power—and therefore control over policy—never remains constantly in one place with one person: it is a matter of degree, dependent very much on time and circumstance. This applies even at the highest levels of government

Policy advice must take account of these things and therefore goes wider than policy analysis. It includes "the art of the possible," the art of judging what can be achieved within the constraints which limit a government's freedom of maneuver (see e.g. Vickers 1983). These constraints are many and varied. Lack of resources, lack of legal power, lack of parliamentary support, public opposition on moral or other grounds, opposition from elsewhere in government, opposition from powerful vested interests such as the trade unions in the 1960s and 1970s or the media today, the reaction of financial markets, lack of technical know-how: these and many similar factors curb the policy options open to governments.

# 3. THE POLITICAL CONTEXT

There are many ways in which context may affect the policy processes of government.

The chances of a policy analysis being accepted may depend in part on who carries it out and for whom. For instance, where the analysis is the work primarily of people at the centre of government working for a Prime Minister or a Chancellor of the Exchequer who is strongly placed in relation to his colleagues, with a large majority in the legislature, the chances are that policy decisions will be in line with the analysis although this is not always the case. Reports from influential inquiries or bodies such as Royal Commissions set up by government are also more likely to carry weight than analyses volunteered unasked, particularly if the group or individual concerned has an obvious interest in the outcome, unless of course it suits the convenience of government to cite them in support.

Where analysis is the subject of dispute within government and differing advice is being given in different quarters to different ministers, a policy analysis which lends weight to a particular viewpoint is more likely to have an effect than one which further muddies the water. So too is a report which is clearly authoritative and independent, in particular on a scientific or social issue of current concern. So too is a report which is clearly expressed and can be grasped by a busy Minister or official reading late at night in the back of a car.[6]

Much of government is about reconciling conflicting points of view held by different groups and individuals outside government. Policy analyses which command wide support among experts or others, and are well documented and supported by authoritative evidence, are more likely to have an impact than analyses which are disputed by other authorities and supported only by one strand of opinion. But even where there is consensus it may not prevail if political conviction and belief points to another course as the best for the long term, as the

[6] For a more general analysis of these phenomena, see Majone 1989.

Thatcher government demonstrated with macroeconomic policy and the trade union reforms of the early 1980s, and as Prime Minister Blair showed over military action in Iraq from 2003.

In practice, if an issue is highly contentious, too many views may come from too many quarters—experts, businessmen, quangos, people inside government, Parliament, the media, pressure groups, and so on—for any rules or generalizations to apply. The issues simply have to be thrashed out in whatever Cabinet Committee or other forum the Prime Minister of the day uses to debate them.

For example, in the late 1970s, the government was faced with a decision on the choice of thermal reactor for the next generation of nuclear power station orders in England and Scotland, a highly technical issue involving many scientific, safety, environmental, and commercial factors. Passions ran high and reached the front pages of newspapers. Opinion was divided between those who favoured the British Advanced Gas-cooled Reactor (AGR), the American Pressurized Water Reactor (PWR), no new nuclear orders, or something else. The policy process was a model of its kind. A technical assessment of the options was prepared at a cost of some millions of pounds; the Secretary of State launched a process of public consultation and personally took evidence from as many groups as possible, including his own civil servants; and the Central Policy Review Staff (see below) prepared their own analysis. In the end there was no obvious "right" answer, no consensus, no determining factor, no greater agreement when everyone had had their say than at the outset of the process. The final decision, taken by the Cabinet after prolonged debate, was a compromise: one AGR for England, one AGR for Scotland and a design study for a PWR which was later built at Sizewell. Sometimes in government there are no "right" decisions, just decisions. (For an academic study of some of these episodes, see Williams 1980.)

Good timing can be a key factor in the influence which a policy analysis may have. There are some fundamental issues such as, say, the elimination of poverty which governments are most likely to be prepared to tackle at the beginning of their period of office or later on when they begin to be accused of running out of steam. Attempts to persuade governments to tackle such issues at other times when there is no public pressure to do so are likely to end up in the long grass however rational the case for addressing them, unless of course they are taken up by a policy unit or individuals close to a strong Prime Minister—as with Prime Minister Thatcher on global warming, for instance—or Chancellor of the Exchequer.

Governments are more open to new thinking at some times than at others. Where consideration of a policy issue is still at an early stage and thinking is still fluid, it is easier to influence it than later when thinking has hardened. The chances of influencing thinking are even greater if a review has been running for a while without making progress and no one knows what to do (which may not always be apparent from the outside). The review of the National Health Service in 1988 which lasted a year had reached few conclusions after six months' work. It had been initiated with no idea of where it would lead and found itself conducting an exercise which required original thinking with relatively little ready-made analysis available to assist.

This happens in government from time to time, particularly in fields which are peculiarly the business of government such as health or social security or rail privatization.

Other things being equal, proposals which involve an increase in taxation, the introduction of legislation, or new public expenditure are less likely to be accepted than proposals which are self-financing (or even better, raise money) or which can be implemented within the existing law. The parliamentary timetable has room for only a limited number of major bills in each session, generally fifteen to twenty: competition among departments for one of those slots is intense and begins well over a year before the session begins.[7]

These are all examples of extraneous factors which may influence the effectiveness of policy analysis and the content of policy advice.

## 4. Poor Decision Making

No amount of good policy process can remedy the wrong political judgement. Those involved in the community charge, referred to above, regarded it as a model of policy analysis. One of the ministers most closely involved, William Waldegrave, said later:

> In the way the policy was originated, formulated and carried through it was a model of how ... modern policy should be formulated. There was a project team. There were outsiders. There was published analysis and enormous consultation. There was modelling of outcomes using the latest technologies. What there wasn't (it is now generally alleged) was a correct political judgement by the Cabinet of the day. That was nothing to do with the civil service and the outside experts who had performed exactly what their democratically elected masters had asked of them ... In the end there is no magic wand which can ensure that human decision-makers avoid mistakes.[8]

Whether it was in fact a model of policy analysis has been questioned: it has for instance been pointed out that the then Chancellor of the Exchequer, Nigel Lawson, composed a devastating critique of the tax which anticipated virtually all the key weaknesses, including the serious distributional impact the tax was likely to have (Butler, Adonis, and Travers 1994). But the central point, that good decisions require good judgement as well as good policy analysis and advice, is a fair one. Where the exercise of power is too concentrated in a department or in government or in one individual this increases the risk of poor decisions.

---

[7] Rose 1986; van Mechelen and Rose 1986. On the timetable imperative in government, see Cabinet Office 2004.

[8] W. Waldegrave, speech to Social Market Foundation conference on 'Reforming the role of government', 1 Dec. 1993, p. 7.

Ultimately, however good the policy process, the quality of the policy decision boils down to the quality of the judgement of the person or people making it. What constitutes "good judgement" is easier to say with the benefit of hindsight. At the time, when everything is still uncertain, good judgement requires personal qualities which comprise the ability to weigh up competing factors with confidence, the courage to work for the long term while managing the immediate politics, an instinct for which objections or difficulties to take seriously, and an understanding of people and human behaviour. Plus good political nous. Plus the qualities specified in Rudyard Kipling's "If." Plus luck.

Those who provide policy advice, whether inside or outside government, need to cultivate these qualities too. The key to conveying policy advice—assuming it is sound—is first, to do so within a relationship of trust; and second, to frame it in terms which are clear and succinct and engage the reader at the right level in the right tone, not labouring things he already knows but focusing on what he wants to know and what he needs to know, even if it is unwelcome, refreshing the issues with a new perspective and crystallizing the key facts and arguments.

# 5. FROM GENERALISTS TO MANAGERS

Over the last thirty years there has been a movement away from civil servants giving policy advice as generalists towards a more rigorous and professional approach to policy making in which policy advice goes wider than traditional concepts of policy analysis and embraces risk, management, and results.[9]

The importance of taking account of management in policy making had always been recognized: Sir Edward Bridges as Secretary of the Cabinet in 1950 described it as "a cardinal feature of British Administration." But in practice it was often overlooked amid the other pressures of decision taking.

Historically the word "policy" has had deep cultural significance in the British civi service. For many years the service was divided into three main classes: administrative, executive, and clerical. Everyone wanted to be in the administrative class. This was where the fun was. In the words of a leading reference book of 1957 it "consists largely of university graduates, advises Ministers on policy, deals with any difficulties arising from current policy and forecasts the probable effects of new measures and regulations."[10] The key word here was policy: the skill of the senior administrator lay in the giving of policy advice to the Minister, including a lucid account of the evidence, options, and arguments and a recommendation about the way forward, although the culture of the service constantly reminded people that the

---

[9] On the corresponding phenomenon in the USA, see Rivlin 1971. On the pitfalls of such approaches see Majone and Quade 1980.

[10] *Whitakers Almanack* 1957, 353.

true power lay with Ministers and the democratically elected government, not officials.

Below the administrative class was the executive class, "responsible for the day-to-day conduct of government business within the framework of established policy."[11] Unusually the word "executive" acquired a faintly pejorative flavour in this context: the superior importance of "policy" was a glass ceiling for people who lacked policy experience when they appeared before promotion boards. The role of the professional, scientific, and technical classes, experts such as doctors, lawyers, and engineers, was famously to be "on tap but not on top." The clerical class was at the bottom of the pile.

The first dent in this cultural attachment to "policy" came with the Report of the Fulton Committee into the Civil Service in 1968 which criticized the "cult of the generalist" (Fulton 1968). Although its proposals never got off the ground at the time, the report laid the seeds of subsequent reforms.

The introduction of financial management under Prime Minister Thatcher, coupled with decentralization of managerial responsibility to "Next Steps agencies," led to recognition of the importance of management as well as policy skills and the need to design policies which took account of the needs of management. (On the "Next Steps" principles, see Jenkins, Caines, and Jackson 1988.) The Major government introduced the requirement that policies on public services should include standards for performance, with complaints and remedies where standards were not met, through the "Citizen's Charter" (Major 1999, 251).

These reforms culminated under the Blair government that was returned in 1997 in a drive to concentrate the civil service still more intently on achieving results and improving public services ("delivery") and on producing better policies rooted in evidence-based analysis, well designed and capable of successful implementation. Numerous publications testify to this drive. *Adding it up*, a report by the Performance and Innovation Unit in January 2000, called for good analysis to be placed at the heart of policy making. *Better Policy-Making*, a report by the Centre for Management and Policy Studies in November 2001, reported examples of the most innovative approaches to policy making in central government. *Modern Policy-Making: Ensuring Policies Deliver Value for Money*, a report by the National Audit Office in November 2001, examined specific examples of cases where policy analysis and advice had resulted in poor design and implementation of policy, and identified nine key characteristics of modern policy making.

These reports had an aspirational flavour, and no doubt benefited from hindsight. But they also reflected the trend away from reliance on generalists. In an address to the civil service on 24 February 2004, the Prime Minister called for:

a more strategic and innovative approach to policy. Strategic policy making is a professional discipline in itself involving serious analysis of the current state of affairs, scanning future trends and seeking out developments elsewhere to generate options; and then thinking

[11] Ibid.

through rigorously the steps it would take to get from here to there. I find too often that civil servants have not put forward a proposal either because they thought it would not be acceptable politically or because it simply seemed too radical.... don't be afraid to recommend ideal solutions that look impractical; it is my job and the job of ministers to decide whether something can and should be done ...Large bureaucracies tend to be risk averse. Failures that result from taking risks are too often punished more severely than failures which result from inaction. The Civil Service needs to encourage and reward lateral thinking. (Blair 2004)

Whether it is reasonable to blame civil servants for taking a realistic view of the world in which they work and the likely consequences if things go wrong, including criticism from Parliament and the media, is another matter. Although it may sound like a joke in *Yes Minister* (Lynn and Jay 1984) more than one Minister has found himself saying, when a policy went wrong: "I know I want people to take more risks but I didn't mean *that* sort of risk."

## 6. DECLINE OF THE GENERALIST: DOES IT MATTER?

It has been argued that the rise of managerial advice and many of the reforms in the 1980s and early 1990s actually stripped away analytic capacity at the centre of government (Dunleavy 1995). Some deplore the exit of the generalist; some applaud it; some dispute whether it has happened. It is very hard to demonstrate, one way or the other.

The numbers prove nothing. There were 2,700 people dealing with policy in the administrative civil service in the mid-1950s. Fifty years later there were 3,800 people in the senior civil service, a narrower, more senior grouping covering both senior policy advisers and senior managers.

To the extent that management reforms required the senior civil service to give greater time and effort to management they implicitly reduced the effort devoted to policy advice within government. The cull of the most senior grades in 1995–7, which led to a reduction of over 20 per cent in the most senior posts, led to a loss of corporate memory, temporarily at least. The list of skills and competences expected of people in senior positions is now more than any single person could hope to acquire in a lifetime, with policy skills only one of many specialisms, and has led to greater emphasis on the importance of teams who between them have all the skills needed to run a big department. Certainly there has been a rebalancing of what is required of senior civil servants with a new and healthy respect for a wider range of professional skills.

But does this mean that policy making is necessarily worse? It can be argued that the old cultural attachment to "policy" described above bears out the model of

"bureaushaping," in which civil servants monopolize the intellectually interesting activity of giving advice to ministers while offloading less intellectually
engaging activities, such as managing policy delivery, to other agencies (see Dunleavy
1991). This creates a pleasant and intellectually stimulating activity but at the
price of detaching policy from the question of whether it can be implemented successfully and efficiently and whether it actually works. There has been
sufficient evidence of the failures of policy advice over the years (see Dunleavy 1995;
Hennessy 1997) and more recent successes, for instance in the field of macroeconomics over the last twenty years compared with the previous twenty years, to
suggest that it is worth striving for better and more professional models of policy
making.

Some commentators worry that "detached from their civil service advisers, Ministers will be able to exercise more arbitrary power given their discretion within the
law" (Foster and Plowden 1996, 178). But arbitrary action, detached from advice, has
always been a hazard, as the Suez venture illustrated. The only duty on Ministers is
"the duty to give fair consideration and due weight to informed and impartial advice
from civil servants, as well as to other considerations and advice, in reaching
decisions" (Cabinet Office 1996). It is the duty of the civil service to give such advice,
but to extend this to acting as a block on government action risks giving the civil
service an independent constitutional role which it does not have.

The end of generalists as a class was a necessary step on the path to better
policy making. Whether the generalist will ever be dispensed with completely is
open to question. Certainly the skills will continue to be needed. But the determined
trend away from the generalist as a class is unmistakable over the period.

# 7. What Prime Ministers Want

One major influence on policy making in government is intervention by Number 10.
Prime ministers want success for their government and re-election; and they may not
see these things as flowing naturally from the sum total of the successes of their
colleagues, unaided by the centre.

Although usually powerful, prime ministers in Britain have relatively few formal
executive powers other than the power to recommend the Queen to appoint and
dismiss ministers and the power to chair and sum up meetings without a vote. Most
executive powers, including legal powers and expenditure, are vested in secretaries of
state or other bodies such as local government. Prime ministers are therefore driven
to searching for ways of intervening effectively.

The extent of their interventions differs; but regardless of political party, they tend
to be reluctant simply to rely passively on their ministerial colleagues to serve up

papers for collective discussion in their own time and on the basis of their own analyses. Most business and most policy has to be left to departments: the volume is far too great to be run from the centre. But there tends to be a restless wish on the part of prime ministers to improve policy decisions and the policy analysis available when decisions are taken.

One reason for this restlessness, obviously not stated, may be a lack of confidence in a colleague or his officials, because of political differences or poor performance or a lack of new ideas coming forward, or for whatever reason. One response in such cases may be a reshuffle of ministers and the astute appointment of permanent officials to key posts in the department when vacancies arise, not out of a wish to politicize but to improve the performance of the department. An alternative response may be the appointment of an adviser in Number 10 to shadow the policies of the department. Both sorts of appointment are better done with the consent, however grudging, of the Minister concerned. The danger otherwise is that, rather than improve policy, there will be tensions which boil over publicly. A famous example concerns Prime Minister Thatcher's appointment of Sir Alan Walters as her economic adviser—an appointment that set up such tensions with the Treasury that it led in 1989 to the resignation of her Chancellor, Nigel Lawson, a resignation that in turn contributed to the chain of events that led to Thatcher's own deposition as Prime Minister in 1990.

A third response may be reorganization of departmental responsibilities. One executive power which prime ministers do have is the power to decide the machinery of government. Some avoid using the power on the grounds that the short-term costs of upheaval are certain whereas the long-term benefits are uncertain and may be small. Thatcher took this view and reorganized very little. Prime Minister Heath on the other hand instituted a major reorganization within months of taking office, making an explicit link between organization and policy:

government departments should be organised by reference to the task to be done or the objective to be attained, and this should be the basis of the division of work between departments rather than, for example, dividing responsibility between departments so that each one deals with a client group. The basic argument for this functional principle is that the purpose of organisation is to serve policy.[12]

Prime Minister Blair similarly carried out a major reorganization of departments at the beginning of his second term of office. But whether the "functional principle" remains so strong and so clear-cut when the "delivery" of high-quality services to different client groups is a top policy priority is an open question. As the focus of government policy becomes increasingly centered on client groups, the functional principle may begin to fall away.

[12]  White Paper, Cmnd 4506, Oct. 1970, Reorganization of central government.

# 8. POLICY UNITS

More fundamentally, all prime ministers are concerned to ensure that departmental policies are scrutinized critically and that the government as a whole has a coherent strategic approach to policy in a "joined-up" way. Cabinet Office secretariats can coordinate papers across departments but they do not have the capacity for independent research, nor indeed is it easy for them to recommend courses of action which are strongly opposed by departments and their Ministers. In such circumstances they can at most draw attention to unpopular options and rehearse the arguments. So the pressure is to create units specifically for policy analysis and advice.

There is another factor. Prime ministers tend to lack the resources to take on a Cabinet colleague and his experts in a major argument about policy. There are ways round the problem, including force of personality and low cunning, but another approach is to develop an alternative source of expertise at the centre.

For these reasons, therefore, successive prime ministers have experimented with policy units. In the White Paper of October 1970[13] Prime Minister Heath set up the Central Policy Review Staff (CPRS, often called the Think Tank) in the Cabinet Office to enable ministers to:

work out the implications of their basic strategy in terms of policies in specific areas, to establish the relative priorities to be given to the different sectors of their programmes as a whole, to identify those areas of policy in which new choices can be exercised and to ensure that the underlying implications of alternative courses of action are fully analysed and considered.

The CPRS had a considerable impact. Under its first head, Lord Rothschild, it developed a style of short papers submitted to Cabinet, expressed in pithy English, usually thinking the unthinkable, which delighted some and infuriated others. One Secretary of State was so irritated by its work that in 1976 he expressly instructed his permanent secretary that when studies on departmental business were undertaken by the CPRS and officials were informed, Ministers should be informed immediately to allow their view to be taken into account by the CPRS. This is another example of the way in which institutional factors may have an effect on policy analysis.

The CPRS was wound up by Prime Minister Thatcher in 1983 when it was perceived to have ceased to be as effective as it was. Thatcher's own account is of interest:

a government with a firm philosophical direction was inevitably a less comfortable environment for a body with a technocratic outlook. And the Think-Tank's detached speculations, when leaked to the press and attributed to ministers had the capacity to embarrass. The world had changed, and the CPRS could not change with it. For these and other reasons, I believe that my later decision to abolish the CPRS was right and probably inevitable. And I have to say that I never missed it. (Thatcher 1993, 30)

[13] Ibid.

In place of the CPRS Thatcher set up a smaller Policy Unit in Number 10, staffed by a mixture of civil servants and special advisers. The location was significant. Whereas the CPRS had submitted its policy advice to the whole Cabinet openly, the Policy Unit worked directly for the Prime Minister who was the only person who saw its work unless she chose to show it to others. At meetings she would have two briefs before her: one from the Policy Unit and one from the relevant secretariat of the Cabinet Office. The support was to the Prime Minister rather than the Cabinet.

The coming to power of the Blair government in May 1997 marked a further step in the use of central units. This had been foreshadowed by Peter Mandelson, a close political ally of Blair, in 1996, drawing on his perception of how Thatcher had run her governments:

Margaret Thatcher's success lay in her ability to focus on a set of clear goals and make everything (and everyone) conform to these priorities... she lost a lot of blood (most of it other people's) on the way. Tony Blair's aim must be to achieve a similar level of policy fulfilment without the accompanying costs and damage to relations inside and outside government ... a prime minister needs support in taking the initiative and imposing a clear strategy on the government, and this support has to be found among the prime minister's personal advisers in No.10 .... The answer lies in a more formalised strengthening of the centre of government. (Mandelson and Liddle 2002, 236, 239, 240)

The result was experimentation with many different forms of policy unit—the Social Exclusion Unit, the Performance and Innovation Unit, the Centre for Management and Policy Studies, and latterly the Strategy Unit in the Cabinet Office and the Policy Directorate in Number 10—and an expansion of the role of the center.

There was also an increasing role for the Treasury in policy analysis and advice, reflecting the strength of the Chancellor of the Exchequer's personal position within the government. This was more often effected directly, using public expenditure as a lever, rather than through the creation of units. Policy making at the centre was in practice now shared between the Treasury and the Prime Minister's Office, with the Cabinet Office providing support both to Number 10 and the Cabinet collectively.

The Blair and Thatcher governments in their different ways illustrate the importance of the political context in which the policy process takes place, and the impact which Number 10 can have on it.

# 9. The Challenge for Policy Units

The challenge for policy units, once established, is to maintain a high quality of work and to nurture their influence, so that their advice continues to be accepted.

Policy units at the centre have developed their own capacity to do research and analysis, rather than just relying on departments. The CPRS moved into the field by the mid-1970s, for instance with their controversial review of Overseas Representation. In the 1980s the Policy Unit under the leadership of Lord (Brian) Griffiths played a major role in the formulation of radical new policies, in particular on education and the national curriculum. By the late 1990s the Performance and Innovation Unit was carrying out substantial research of its own, through teams assembled for the purpose.

Because they are dealing with subjects which cut across government or which are new, policy units often find themselves dealing with subjects which are under-researched or not researched at all. With limited resources, it is difficult for them to do all their research themselves, particularly in view of the critical scrutiny their evidence will receive if their recommendations are controversial. It is also dangerous for them to come up with controversial conclusions if some of the hostility is likely to be from within government. They have the protection of the prime minister; but if they get things wrong, it can seriously damage their reputation and credibility. There is therefore a real incentive for policy units to find allies in the outside world who can help with the research and occasionally trail ideas to test the waters of public opinion. This is where think tanks, pressure groups, and voluntary bodies can gain a foothold.

The other main challenge for policy units is the pressure to be sucked into immediate issues and troubleshooting at the price of losing their role in providing more reflective, long-term advice. It is a tension which reflects the pressures on prime ministers. However important the long-term policy, it can easily seem less urgent and, by implication, less important, than immediate crises and the battle for political survival.

The performance of policy units is difficult to sustain at a high level over time. Most have a finite lifespan after which their usefulness gradually declines. But while they are at their peak they can play a formidable role in the policy process.

# 10. The Departmental Point of View

It should not be assumed that this mistrust of departments is always justified. From the point of view of departments, policy analysis by the centre is liable to be shallow and to lack a proper understanding of the factors which must shape policy. The classic statement of the case for the departmental point of view was put by Lord Bridges:

In most cases the departmental philosophy is the result of ... the slow accretion and accumulation of experience over the years.... They are the expression of the long continuity of experience which can be one of the strongest qualities of an institution, if well organised. Again they are broadly based, and the resultant of protests and suggestions, and counter suggestions, from many interests, of discussion and of debates in which many types of mind have taken part. They represent an acceptable point of view after the extreme divergencies have been rooted out. (Bridges 1950, 16–17)

It is of course these extreme divergencies that some prime ministers want to see before they are rooted out.

The best answer in an imperfect world is likely to be a creative tension between departments and the centre of government in which neither is ever certain of winning. Where the balance of power lies in practice depends on circumstance and may be a matter of some delicacy. There is always the risk that a strong Secretary of State will object vigorously to an infringement of his or her responsibilities. There is also always the risk that a department, weakly placed, will lose control of its policy to the centre as happened, for instance, with the review of the National Health Service (NHS) conducted in 1988. Support for the ministerial group chaired by the Prime Minister was coordinated centrally, and few people in the department or the NHS knew about the group's radical conclusions until shortly before they were announced, arguably a factor which handicapped their implementation. Policy analysis and policy advice are not only about the exercise of power *by* governments; they are about the exercise of power *within* governments.

## 11. CONCLUSION

Governments tend to assume that the government machine can achieve successfully whatever it sets its hand to. In practice performance across government tends to be variable and patchy, with different parts performing well at different times. The same applies to the policy process. There have been big strides towards improving the quality and professionalism of the policy process in government over the years, but there is still a long way to go and performance is variable and patchy. And, however good the analysis and advice, policy making still remains an uncertain business, often a long way from the smooth continuous process envisaged at the opening of this chapter.

## REFERENCES

BARBER, B. 2001. *The Truth of Power: Intellectual Affairs in the Clinton White House.* New York: Norton.

BLAIR, T. 2004. PM speech on reforming the Civil Service, 24 Feb. Available at: www.number-10.gov.uk/output/Page5399.asp.

BRIDGES, S. E. 1950. *Portrait of a Profession.* Cambridge: Cambridge University Press.

BRITTAN, S. 1964. *Treasury under the Tories, 1951–64.* Harmondsworth: Penguin.

—— 1969. *Steering the Economy.* London: Secker & Warburg.

BUTLER, D., ADONIS, A., and TRAVERS, T. 1994. *Failure in British Government: The Politics of the Poll Tax.* Oxford: Oxford University Press.

CABINET OFFICE 1996. *The Civil Service Code.* Available at: www.cabinetoffice.gov.uk/central/1999/cscode.htm.

—— 2004. *Guide to Legislation.* Available at: www.cabinet-office.gov.uk/legislation/legguide/docs/legguide/pdf.

CENTRE FOR MANAGEMENT AND POLICY STUDIES 2001. *Better Policy Making.* London: Cabinet Office.

DUNLEAVY, P. 1991. *Democracy, Bureaucracy and Public Choice.* Hemel Hempstead: Harvester-Wheatsheaf.

—— 1995. Policy disasters: explaining the UK's record. *Public Policy and Administration,* 10 (2): 52–70.

EIZENSTADT, S. E. 1992. Economists and White House decisions. *Journal of Economic Perspectives,* 6 (Summer): 65–71.

FOSTER, C., and PLOWDEN, F. 1996. *The State under Stress.* Buckingham: Open University Press.

FULTON, L. 1968. *Committee on the Civil Service,* i: *Report of the Committee 1966–68.* Cmnd. 3638. London: HMSO.

HECLO, H., and WILDAVSKY, A. 1974. *The Private Government of Public Money.* London: Macmillan.

HENNESSY, P. 1997. *Muddling Through: Power, Politics and the Quality of Government in Post War Britain.* London: Indigo.

JENKINS, K., CAINES, K., JACKSON, A. 1988. *Improving Management in Government: The Next Steps.* London: HMSO.

PARTY, L. 1997. *New Labour Manifesto, 1997 General Election: Because Britain Deserves Better.* London: Labour Party.

LYNN, J., and JAY, A. (eds.) 1984. *The Complete Yes Minister: The Diaries of a Cabinet Minister, by the Right Hon. James Hacker MP.* London: BBC.

MAJONE, G. 1989. *Evidence, Argument and Persuasion in the Policy Process.* New Haven, Conn.: Yale University Press.

—— and QUADE, E. (eds.) 1980. *Pitfalls of Analysis.* Chichester: Wiley, for International Institute of Applied Systems Analysis.

MAJOR, J. 1999. *The Autobiography.* London: HarperCollins.

MANDELSON, P., and LIDDLE, R. 2002. *The Blair Revolution Revisited.* London: Politico's; originally pub. as *The Blair Revolution,* 1996.

NATIONAL AUDIT OFFICE 2001. *Modern Policy-Making: Ensuring Policies Deliver Value for Money.* HC289 Session 2001–2 (1 Nov.).

NEUSTADT, R. E. 1960. *Presidential Power: The Politics of Leadership.* New York: Wiley.

—— 2001. The weakening White House. *British Journal of Political Science,* 31: 1–11.

—— and MAY, E. R. 1986. *Thinking in Time.* New York: Free Press.

PERFORMANCE AND INNOVATION UNIT, 2000. *Adding it up.* London: Cabinet Office.

PORTER, R. B. 1983. Economic advice to the President: from Eisenhower to Reagan. *Political Science Quarterly,* 98 (Fall): 403–26.

—— 1997. Presidents and economists: the Council of Economic Advisers. *American Economic Review, Papers & Proceedings,* 87 (2: May): 103–6.

RIVLIN, A. 1971. *Systematic Thinking for Social Action.* Washington, DC: Brookings Institution.

ROSE, R. 1986. Law as a resource of public policy. *Parliamentary Affairs,* 39 (3): 297–314.

SCHULTZE, C. 1992. *Memos to the President: A Guide through Macroeconmics for the Busy Policymaker.* Washington, DC: Brookings Institution.

THATCHER, M. 1993. *The Downing Street Years.* London: HarperCollins.

VAN MECHELEN, D., and ROSE, R. 1986. *Patterns of Parliamentary Leadership.* Aldershot: Gower.

VICKERS, S. G. 1983. *The Art of Judgment: A Study of Policy Making.* London: Harper and Row.

*Whitaker's Almanack* 1957. Library edn. London: n.p.

WILDAVSKY, A. 1979. *Speaking Truth to Power: The Art and Craft of Policy Analysis.* Boston: Little, Brown.

WILLIAMS, R. 1980. *The Nuclear Power Decisions.* London: Croom Helm.

# CHAPTER 8

## POLICY ANALYSIS FOR DEMOCRACY

### HELEN INGRAM
### ANNE L. SCHNEIDER

## 1. INTRODUCTION

Much of what is taught to policy analysts in many policy programs ill equips them to deal with the issues related to the quality of democracy. Traditionally, policy analysis served democracy by concentrating on the efficiency and effectiveness with which stated policy goals were delivered (Bardach 2000; Weimer and Vining 1999). Using tools from macroeconomics, policy analysts have conducted increasingly sophisticated means–ends assessments and theories of the proper role of government vis-à-vis markets (Ostrom 1990; Lindblom 1977). Where political science has a substantial foothold in policy programs, policy analysts have attended to political feasibility and support, responsiveness of policy to citizens, evaluation of the ways in which policies are constructed to reach agreement, and how implementing agencies relate to constituencies, and to each other (Dye 1998; deLeon and Steelman 1999; Ingram and Smith 1993). Today, assuming that efficiency, effectiveness, and political feasibility are the only measures policy analysts should apply in measuring the various policies' contribution to democracy is clearly inadequate.[1] There is an accumulation of both theoretical and empirical work demonstrating that public policies, and the elements in their designs, have important effects on citizenship, justice, and discourse.[2] The importance of public policy in creating a more just

[1] See Stone 1997; Fischer 1990, 1995; deLeon 1997.
[2] See Schneider and Ingram 1993, 1997; Mettler and Soss 2004; Landy 1993; Soss 1999.

society is apparent worldwide. Issues of distributive justice and responsive leadership cannot be left only to academic enquiry, but must become more central in the work of the policy analyst (Page 1983; Denhardt and Denhardt 2003). Moreover, the context in which policy analysis is taking place is changing in important ways that make the relationship of policy to democracy especially salient.

Our initial theme is to suggest that the contexts for most public policies are undergoing rapid changes, which require a focus on the democracy gap that has previously received scant attention from policy analysts. We will then explore briefly the meanings of conditions for democracy. We will next posit some possible linkages between democratic conditions and public policy content or design. The bulk of the chapter will be in developing these linkages as a subject matter for policy analysis. Finally, we will examine how the purposes and tools of contemporary policy analysts need to change to serve democracy better. While our principal focus will be on developments in the United States, which is the case we know best, we will refer to parallel developments elsewhere as appropriate.

## 2. CONTEMPORARY CONTEXT FOR PUBLIC POLICY

The public opinion context in which policy analysis now takes place is extraordinarily critical about government and public policy not only in the United States, but also in other Western democracies.[3] In the United States, a large proportion of the public no longer believes that government is able to fulfill the promises embodied in policy goals (Skocpol 2003). Rather than being viewed as the principle collective problem solver, often government is perceived to be as much part of the problem as solution (Savas 2000; Rauch 1994; Kennon 1995). Moreover, the motives of government officials are not trusted. Many people do not believe that government is trying to help people like themselves, and believe instead that the interests of the elite and the members of the government are placed above the interests of ordinary citizens (Dionne 1991; Greider 1992; Sandel 1996).

Despite nearly forty years of seemingly aggressive attempts on the part of government to alleviate gender, racial, and ethnic bias and unequal treatment, disparities remain. In fact, race and gender have not disappeared as issues in most modern democracies but instead are masked beneath rhetoric that may not mention either one. In the United States, but also in many other Western democracies, a number of policy issues have become exceptionally divisive along these cleavages, including crime, public schools, welfare, and immigration. In these issues, political support is

[3] See Anderson and Guillory 1997; Norris 1999; Karp, Banducci, and Bowler 2003; Verba et al. 1993.

too often built by appealing to thinly veiled symbols that represent some groups in highly negative terms as unworthy and undeserving. Such portrayals are justification for provision of benefits to positively constructed groups and burdens upon those who are stigmatized as dependent or deviant. In our other work, we have called this degenerative politics because the result is to perpetuate and aggravate divisions among citizens by providing them consistently with quite different treatment at the hands of government (Schneider and Ingram 1997; Ingram and Schneider 2005). The consequence is an American democracy that espouses ideals of equal protection and treatment under the law, while actual treatment by policy of citizens is noticeably and unfairly unequal. There is great variety throughout Western democracies in how much importance is placed on equality or fairness as an outcome of public policy, and in the extent to which governmental practice approaches the ideals of the society. Nevertheless, the US experience toward greater justice and equality is an uneven one and some social issues emerge again and again as if there is no way to solve them "once and for all" (Sidney 2003).

Concern about the vitality of civic society, social capital, and political participation is evident in the United States and the democracies of the Western world.[4] Robert Putnam's often-cited thesis that each generation born in the USA since 1920 has shown less interest in civic participation than the one before has generated numerous calls for civic renewal and numerous policies at the federal and local levels to re-engage citizens in the work of democracy (Putnam 2000).

One of the consequences of the disquiet with politics and government in the United States is that governance structures have altered dramatically with decentralization, devolution, and the emergence of a variety of public–private partnership models (Rosenau 2000; Reeves 2003; Salamon 2002). Among the most salient of these changes is that non-profit organizations now play a critical role in policies as widely divergent as private prisons, charter schools, police, fire, substance abuse, and environmental clean-up (Rosenau 2000). Not only is measuring the efficiency and effectiveness of such programs increasingly difficult, lines of democratic control and accountability are different and less direct (Goodin 2003).

# 3. RELATIONSHIP OF POLICY TO DEMOCRACY

Even as democracy becomes the apparent political system of choice for many nations throughout the world, in the United States it remains an unfinished, open-ended

---

[4] Skocpol and Fiorina 1999; Putnam 2000; LeDuc, Niemi, and Norris 1996; Blais and Dobrzynska 1998; Karp and Bowler 2001; Lijphart 1999; Nevitte and Kanji 2002.

project. As Dryzek (1996, 1997) has argued, democratic governance is in large part striving to expand the franchise, scope, and authenticity of democracy. Franchise refers to the numbers of participants in any political setting. Scope concerns the domains of life under democratic public control. Authenticity is the degree to which democratic control is substantive, informed, and competency engaged (Dryzek 1997). No one of these proposed enlargements ought to take place at the expense of the other: expanded franchise must not lead to superficial deliberation that hurts authenticity. Of course, there are many forces apart from policy, such as interest groups, political parties, leadership, and the press, that affect the democratic enterprise. However, since the important work of Lowi (1964) and Wilson (1986) that connected the content of policy with patterns of politics, a substantial literature has developed tracing the consequences of public policies to politics and to democracy. Figure 8.1 lays out some pathways through which public policy content may influence the character of democracy.

The third set of boxes in the figure identifies some critical conditions for democracy: There need to be open arenas for public discourse in which all relevant points of view are expressed; citizens ought to view their role as citizens as important, as involving obligations as well as rights, and they must be convinced that government has the interest and capacity to solve public problems; citizens themselves should be supportive of policies and positively involved in producing shared goals; and there must be means to hold government accountable for its actions. These important conditions for democracy are directly related to consequences flowing from policy designs: The framing of issues; how targets are constructed; the structure of implementation and delivery systems; and transparency of governmental actions and citizen access to information. The pathways are not meant to be exhaustive but only suggestive. Also, we recognize that a complete causal model would be recursive, showing how changes in the framing of issues impact policy designs, for example; but our focus here is on how policy itself addresses the conditions of democracy.

The relationships shown in Fig. 8.1 reflect an interest in how policy design, or content, affects the framing of problems and citizen identities through language, symbols, and discourse. The central contention here is that policy analysis must probe how the elements of design found in policy content impact framing, constructions, implementation, and information/transparency, and through these the opportunities offered to citizens. These linkages must become part of what policy analysts do if they wish to understand how and why policy impacts democracy and if they wish to design policy that will better serve democracy. Policy is not a black box from which the analyst can understand outputs or outcomes on the basis of inputs such as citizen demand, support, and resources. Nor is policy a simple extension of culture or public opinion. The ways in which the elements of design (goals, target populations, rationales and images, implementation structures, rules, tools) are configured within policy set the stage for what follows.

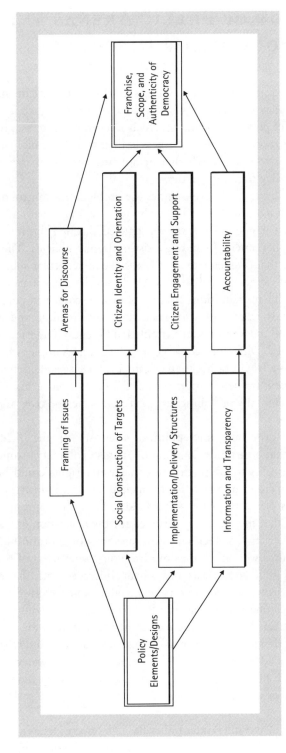

**Figure 8.1.** Linking policy design to democracy

# 4. CREATION OF PUBLIC ARENAS AND OPEN FORUMS FOR DISCOURSE

Robust democracy requires open public forums in which citizens can and should be asked to confront policy problems that affect them directly. In such forums people are encouraged to face policy problems not solely as clients or interest groups, but as citizens who can incorporate the view of others in their own "civic discovery" of what constitutes the collective welfare. Whether or not such arenas emerge is at least in part a function of policy framing and design.

It is a political truism that whoever defines the problem has control of the design of solutions (Bardach 1981; Rochefort and Cobb 1994; Baumgartner and Jones 1993). Problems do not just happen. They are constructed through the interaction of a variety of political phenomena including existing public policies. The definitions embodied in policies that characterize what is at stake in particular subject areas can lead to processes of democratic discovery or drastically limit participation and debate. Different problem definitions locate political discourse in particular value contexts and elicit particular kinds of participants, participation, and institutional response. According to the way an issue is framed, different boundaries of interest or jurisdiction are created. Different people get involved, for example, when domestic violence is defined as a health rather than criminal justice issue. Different values are at stake when an issue is framed in moral rather than economic terms. Framing also affects participants' empathy or willingness to see other perspectives and the likelihood of compromise.

As an example, historians and political scientists in the field of water policy have argued that a misunderstanding of Spanish colonial customary law led western states of the USA to adopt the idea that water rights could be owned as property for growing crops, and later for municipalities and industries. It followed that since water was property, water rights holders were the appropriate decision makers. That meant that the arenas constructed for the discussion of water matters became irrigation districts that focused upon questions of allocation and delivery. Left out of such forums were non-consumptive, non-owner users of water such as recreationists and wildlife enthusiasts and others concerned with the myriad ways water affects the environment. As time passed, water policy evolved to give water other associated meanings: water as product and water as commodity. Water reclamation policy treated water as the output of water development processes of dams and diversions designed to reduce risks, to secure supplies, and to spread water rights allocations to additional users. The arenas in which water development decisions were made not surprisingly consisted of existing and prospective water rights owners as well as producers and managers of large-scale engineering works.

Most recently federal and state water policy has redefined water as a commodity to increase flexibility and efficiency of water reallocations. The discourse in arenas so

constructed is between willing buyers and sellers. This does not mean that environmentalists have had no voice in water resource arenas. In fact, they have exerted
considerable veto power through policies that require environmental assessments
and protect endangered species. However, they certainly have not been participants
in public forums with anything like an equal footing, largely because of the way the
issue has been framed in policy. Moreover, water quantity has tended to be separated
from water quality, and from other issues such as riparian habitat for birds and other
wildlife and the rights of indigenous peoples. The importance of water to a sense of
community and place has been marginalized.

Over the past decade, a competitive frame for considering water has taken hold,
which has variously called itself ecosystems or watershed approaches. The impetus
for framing water differently came largely from the grass roots, but supportive
embodiments in federal agency programs and policies have been important (Yafee
1998). At present, seventeen federal agencies have endorsed ecosystems approaches
(Michaels 1999). State-level laws authorizing watershed planning such as the Massachusetts Watershed Initiative and the Oregon Plans have also been critical. The most
distinguishing mark of this new way of looking at water is that it reintegrates water
into the broad ecological and social processes from which it was disembodied by
property, product, and commodity framing. Watershed planning embraces equal
concern between healthy ecosystems and communities, and envisions them as closely
related (Johnson and Campbell 1999). Watershed associations, the arenas for public
discourse associated with this emergent framing, involve a wide range of stakeholders
including local property holders and citizen coalitions, county state and federal
agencies, scientists, corporations, environmental organizations, and the general
public. Boundaries for involvement are broadly open and inclusive, encompassing
all those who are affected by and have knowledge about particular watersheds.
Decision rules vary, but emphasis is placed on consensus building. Those involved
accept the equal standing of different kinds of information ranging from laboratory
science to detailed experiential understanding based upon long-standing familiarity
with place. The watershed management vision includes specific attention to representation, assistance for weaker parties, full and fair opportunity for all participants
to participate in the negotiation processes, and respect for cultural values (Johnson
and Campbell 1999). Whatever the ambiguities of the watershed approach, and it is
not without its inconsistencies (Blomquist and Schlager 2000), the consequence for
democracy appears to be quite positive.

Another example of how a policy can frame an issue in a way which has adverse
effects on discourse is the Superfund legislation. Mark Landy (1993) has argued that
the goal of the Act, which insists on cleaning up all toxic and hazardous waste dumps
to all applicable standards, does not encourage people to think intelligently about the
issue. It appears to establish a total freedom from risk, but there are far too many sites
and the cost of clean-ups is too high for this goal to be obtainable. Because federal
dollars, supposedly recovered from polluters, carry most of the burden, citizens are
not encouraged to deliberate over which allocations of clean-up efforts are most
desirable. As a consequence, precious environmental protection resources are

misallocated and citizen cynicism that laws do not live up to promises is perpetuated (Landy 1993; Hird 1994).

One of the proposals to redefine the issue and to encourage deliberation begins by making distinctions between different kinds of inactive and abandoned hazardous waste sites (Hird 1994). Older sites at which dumping was legal at the time and where there were no strong connections linking the site to original polluters should be removed from Superfund jurisdiction and made eligible for funding from a National Environmental Restoration Fund. Such sites along with other salient environmental problems such as asbestos removal, radon or lead remediation, or other environmental hot spots are to be relabeled and reframed as environmental restoration problems. Such reframing allows numbers of chronic, long-term risks to community and health to be seen in the same light and considered together. Hird argues that a new kind of arena for discourse then becomes possible. Each state, according to the proposal, would establish a committee of citizen representatives, some of whom live near the waste sites, but also including governmental officials and scientists to decide how the fund allocated by the federal government to the state would be spent (Hird 1994). Citizens would be encouraged through this policy change to engage in discourse about relative risk and values of restored lands in different places. Rather than asserting some absolute right, citizens would deliberate about the value added to different areas by different kinds and levels of restoration.

Similar dynamics are found in many social policies. Traditional societies, for example, conceptualized crime as a violation against an individual and his or her family and tribe. The appropriate enforcers were the victim and victim's family. In some cultures, the prescribed punishment was decided through negotiations between the victim's family and the offender's family. The arenas for discourse belonged to the individuals and groups to which they were culturally tied. In contrast, modern Western societies view crime as an offense against the state. This construction of crime results in enforcement belonging to the state, and the state (not the victim) being the appropriate decision maker regarding the amount and type of punishment or rehabilitation. In addition to changing who the relevant decision makers are, this change (as well as in many other social policies) places decision-making authority within a highly specialized body of knowledge and prescribes what kinds of training are needed if one is to participate. One of the results is that participation becomes increasingly the province of highly specialized knowledge groups. Ordinary citizens scarcely participate at all in dialogue about appropriate responses to crime, or even what sorts of things ought to be considered "crimes." Because these policies lend themselves to highly divisive social constructions of the target populations (a point we will return to below), policy entrepreneurs and those intent on finding issues to be used for political advantage manipulate public opinion, rendering intelligent discourse almost non-existent. Arenas of discourse become contaminated and used as "wedge issues" dominated by negative, divisive, and harmful social constructions of social groups and events.

There have been numerous attempts to reform criminal justice policy and bring it into the province of rational discussion where responses to behavior that is harmful to others or to the society are more uniform and more proportionate to the harm that is done. The juvenile court, for example, is an invention of public policy that traces to the late 1800s where youthful offenders—for whom the harsh penalties of the times seemed too extreme—were separated by policy from "hardened criminals" thereby permitting more lenient and humane responses to the former and continuing with the harshness directed at the latter. These changes also shifted the forms of knowledge specialization such that the juvenile court became dominated by "treatment" philosophies of social workers, psychologists, and educators who believed in rehabilitation. From the 1970s onward, this type of policy separation has continued such that "status offenders" are now separated from "serious juvenile offenders," with different decision makers and arenas for each. Another innovation is to reframe "crime" from being exclusively a legal problem dealt with by police and courts after the fact to a community development issue or a public health problem (Thornton et al. 2000; Howell 1995). This shifts the prevention activities from police and courts, with programs such as "scared straight," or DARE, to those in which ordinary citizens in the community have a greater opportunity for participation.

Experiments with restorative justice both in the United States and elsewhere offer an interesting case in point (Braithwaite 2002; Bazemore et al. 1998; Schneider and Warner 1987; Galaway and Hudson 1996). Restorative justice approaches reconceptualize the offender, not as an incorrigible deviant who is a danger to society, but as a virtuous person who has made a mistake for which he or she needs to be held accountable (Braithwaite 2002; Bazemore et al. 1998; Schneider and Warner 1987). These approaches also reframe the appropriate response, rejecting both the medical model in which agents of the state "treat" the offender and the deterrence model in which the state punishes the offender. Instead, the principle of justice is a responsibility model in which offenders are expected to restore victims and the community even as they restore themselves to a contributing member of the society. Restorative justice involves a process through which victim, offender, and community participate in determining the measure of responsibility and accountability. This reverses the modernist trend toward statist responses to crime in favor of responses that permit those who have been harmed (local community and direct victim) to participate within regulations enforced by the state. The victim, offender, and community are all to be restored through a process that brings understanding to the offender of the harm done and that negotiates a sanction all believe to be fair. By reframing the issue and changing the social construction of the offender, restorative justice programs change the decision-making arena, the decision makers, and the results of the decisions.

These examples of how policy designs frame issues and thereby shape the decision-making arenas and the types of knowledge that are brought to bear only hint at the large number of similar issues begging for intelligent policy analysis. What is the impact of the creation of special districts for particularized service delivery? What have been the impacts of the social justice statements now required in many policy areas in Australia? What are the impacts of the movement away from geographically based to service-based jurisdictional lines? Public policies in many US states provide for citizen initiatives and referendum in a form of direct democracy that is increasingly being used. This enlarges the franchise of democracy in that it opens to the voting public direct legislative authority; but what are the actual impacts on authenticity—on informed discourse and intelligent policy with predictable results (Broder 2000)? Policies that have constructed various types of arenas for public participation in no way anticipated the emergence of the Internet and the ability of people to communicate so quickly over such large distances and with so many others of similar beliefs. How is this affecting the framing of issues, the emergence of social movements, and the formation of entirely new arenas for discourse (Margolis and Resnick 2000)? There is some evidence to suggest that transnational environmental movements encompassing grass-roots groups with shared interests on different sides of international borders are being enabled to act in concert through information shared and networks built in the cyberspace (Doughman 2001; Levesque 2001). Indigenous people are communicating worldwide and taking their case for indigenous rights increasingly into international arenas.

# 5. Identity and Orientation of Citizens

The skepticism and negative attitudes of citizens toward government and public policy are among the growing challenges to American democracy. While there are many causes, the experiences citizens have with public policy are among them. Public policies do more than simply deliver services or implement goals. They also carry messages. The ways in which various publics are treated by policy—whether their views of problems are recognized as legitimate or ignored; whether they are targeted for burdens or benefits; the rules to which they are subjected such as means testing; and the reception they encounter in interaction with implementing agencies—all teach lessons related to democracy (Schneider and Ingram 1997, 2005; Esping-Andersen 1990, 2002).

There is mounting evidence, particularly from the social welfare field, that implicit messages delivered by policy have significant consequences for the construction of citizenship and the role of government (Mettler and Soss 2004). Policies sometimes implicitly signal who is important to national welfare and who is not. In her book *Divided Government*, Suzanne Mettler (1998) argued that New Deal social policies treated white males very differently from women and men of color. Policy sent messages that white males were the significant economic and political actors. While white males were brought under the mantel of national citizenship through social security, white women were included only as widows, and minority domestics and farm workers were ignored until much later. The welfare of women and children was assigned by New Deal policies to the states with varying levels of benefits and state agencies favoring intrusive, paternalistic rules. As a result, a kind of two-tiered, dual citizenship resulted, under which women, and men of color, were treated as second-class citizens not fully incorporated into the mainstream of economic and political life.

Policies carry messages by socially constructing the intended targets in positive and negative terms. In our writing, we have argued that different targets for policy are treated differently and come away with quite distinct identities as citizens and sharply contrasting orientations toward government (Schneider and Ingram 1993; Sidney 2003). Advantaged populations are powerful and positively constructed as good and deserving citizens. They mainly receive benefits from government, and are treated with respect and governmental outreach so that their interests are portrayed as the same as public interests. Advantaged populations view themselves as efficacious and their participation is reinforced. In contrast, other groups whose constructions are not so positive receive fewer benefits and more burdens and pick up messages that their problems are not public but private or of their own making. Only conditional benefits are allocated to them by government, and then only upon successful application. Government is likely to treat them with pity, disrespect, or hostility.

Contemporary experience with welfare policies suggests that the messages damaging to democracy persist. One study of some welfare mothers in Phoenix, whose comments in focus groups were recorded, illustrates messages sent and orientations toward government affected (Luna 2000). Long waits for, and the unreliability of, service and seemingly capricious decisions, led welfare clients to believe that agency officials regarded them as unimportant, dishonest, and unworthy. For example, one mother said:

They're [the welfare case workers] telling me "you have 30 to 45 days to get your case done." I told her I have rent to pay. I need my necessities. They can't understand that. They shrug their shoulders and say, "well they still have 30 to 45 days, and they have other clients." I understand that, but I complied and I did my part like you wanted me to. I was preapproved. All you need to do.... They're the ones who have the computer. You just put it in and send it. But they want to prolong it.

Another woman added: "They act like it's coming out of their pocket. They act like when they get their check, they are going to each of their clients' houses and say, 'ok, here's your fifty, here's your fifty,' and they ain't giving me a dime."

These comments echo many heard by Joe Soss who interviewed clients in a mid-size Midwestern city (Soss 1999). He found that clients of the means-tested program, then the AFDC, believed by overwhelming percentages that government employees are autonomous, that is, "Governmental officials do whatever they want, whenever they want" (Soss 1999, 369). In addition, he found that only 8 per cent of AFDC recipients believe that government listens to people like them. Such attitudes substantially affect the willingness of target groups to participate in politics. Verba, Schlozman, and Brady (1995; Verba et al. 1993) found that public assistance clients were under-represented in every political activity measured. There is real evidence, therefore, that the social constructions built into policies contribute importantly to the existing democracy gap. Those who would seem to have most to gain from participation in the design of the welfare system are the least likely to become engaged. Moreover, the differences in messages received from policy by different racial and gender groups fuel the cleavages within American society and lower the possibility of the citizens' empathy being important to democratic discourse.

A far more encouraging picture of how policy can overcome negative identity conferred by broad social norms is found in the Head Start program. Soss (1999) found that single welfare mothers who had previous experience in the Head Start program developed political orientations and efficacy virtually identical to other citizens, whereas welfare recipients without this type of experience were the least likely to engage in political activity. The Head Start program requires parent participation in shaping the child's education and through this type of policy design emboldens those who otherwise remain very passive in their role as citizen.

# 6. ENGAGEMENT AND SUPPORT

Public policies that serve democracy need to garner support, stimulate civic engagement, and encourage cooperation in the solution of problems.

It is difficult for public policies to achieve goals without sufficient support. Hostile legislators and non-compliant agents and targets can often thwart policy intent. Further, the extent of policy support is an important measure of representation and responsiveness. Policies also can greatly affect the extent of civic volunteerism and civil society. Governmental action can displace private charities and crowd out community problem solving (Skocpol 2003).

The structures of implementation and service delivery embodied in policy have a profound impact upon citizen engagement. The dangers of large-scale bureaucracy to democracy have been thoroughly researched and are widely appreciated (Wood 1994). Public agencies tend to substitute organizational goals in the place of policy intent. Caseworkers in some agencies tend to believe that they must break the rules in some (or many) instances if they are to do what is fair and helpful for their clients (Maynard-Moody and Musheno 2003). The development of specialized areas of policy leads to the dominance of expert knowledge over ordinary grass-roots experiential knowledge and the demise of local knowledge and contextual experience. There is an emphasis in most public agencies of process over content—a reliance on rule compliance rather than tailoring the rules to ensure delivery of desired goals within the local context. Efforts to overcome rules that actually thwart policy success are the source of much of the red tape associated with large hierarchical organizations. Specialists in public agencies are very much a part of the narrowly based, self-serving iron triangles that bring together legislative interests, agencies, and powerful interest groups who are the agency clients. Partly under the banner of strengthening democracy, decentralization, devolution, and contracting out predominate in contemporary policy designs (Minow 2002, 2003; Smith and Lipsky 1993). While these designs arguably may bring implementation and service delivery structures closer to local people, their actual impact upon democracy varies widely.

Studies of partnerships between government and non-profits and their effects upon the authenticity and responsiveness of volunteer organizations deliver mixed results. Some scholars provide examples of governmental actions that spur citizen mobilization and voluntarism (Baker 1993; Marston 1993) or that permit neighborhood-based organizations to carry out missions of providing services to the "poorest of the poor" who often are overlooked by more highly specialized service delivery agencies (Camou 2005). Others find that government funding of non-profits leads to professionalization of staffs, lowered dependence upon volunteers and community ties, and competition among non-profits for particular service niches (Lipsky and Smith 1990; Smith 1998). Studies by Jurik and Cowgill (2005) found that even a non-profit fully devoted to serving the very poor through a micro enterprise loan program, over time, shifted their construction of who the appropriate clients would be to mirror the expectations of the business culture in which they were operating and dependent on for funding. Much would seem to depend upon the particular policy design and the resulting nature of the public–private partnership within particular contexts.

Public–private partnerships take a variety of forms other than government funding of non-profit organizations for service delivery. Some of this activity involves significant public investment in infrastructure (such as ball fields, airports, shopping malls), research and development of innovation, or even new products (Reeves 2003; Rosenau 2000).

Other public–private partnerships have been used to avoid prolonged and debilitating conflict. The Environmental Protection Agency, for example, used a tool described as "civic environmentalism" to avoid a Superfund designation which might have put an end to a revitalization plan in downtown Wichita, Kansas. A plan was negotiated between state and local government officials, the business community, and residents to allow the city to take over clean-up operations of a contaminated site involving many businesses and large acreage. Banks agreed not to deny loans based solely on the contamination of property; the city's liability was limited to what it could collect from responsible parties and property taxes; the polluter agreed to pay for part of the clean-up; and the state government agreed to pass a law creating a special redevelopment district (Knopman, Megan, and Landy 1999). Weale discusses a similar British-based controversy on efforts to democratize decisions about risk (Weale 2001).

Contracting, vouchers, and other partnerships are often successful in building public support for services to dependent groups lacking in political power. Contracting for services with private organizations continues to expand throughout the USA. The contract agency provides a service for government using government funds. In the process, the contract agency becomes a client of government with keen interest in perpetuating and raising funding for the program. Providers band together in supportive associations and supporters also include board members and staffs of private organizations. Since service providers have roots in the community, local support for programs often rises. Similarly, housing vouchers often win the support of landlords for low-income housing programs, which they bitterly opposed when delivery was through public housing (Smith and Ingram 2002).

This same dynamic can work against deviant or dependent groups who lack political power, however, when discipline or punishment is being delivered rather than benefits. Studies of private prisons indicate that this policy design builds a powerful, private sector constituency that competes with public sector prisons for "clients." Prisoners become commodities, and those who advocate expansion in the scope and harshness of punishment have gained a powerful economic ally. When prison policy shifts toward entitlement funding, based on the number of prisoners, there are both public and private sector advocates to continue increasing the number of prisoners. These dynamics are at least partly responsible for the fact that the United States in 2004 had the highest rate of imprisonment in the world (Schneider 2005).

Service learning programs can facilitate civic engagement and support. In the case of Americorps, students prepay some of their college tuition while at the same time becoming actively engaged in community problem solving. The evaluations of the impact of Americorps upon participants' attitudes and behavior are still preliminary, but there is some evidence that service increases the propensity of Americorps' alumni toward greater participation in voluntary associations (Simon and Wang 2000).

# 7. ACCOUNTABILITY

Accountability is critical to democratic governance, and is quite different from political support. The traditional notion of accountability through politically elected and appointed officials operates poorly in an era of decentralization, devolution, and public–private partnerships. In these new patterns of governance, the public must become more directly involved in holding governance structures accountable. There must be accountability built among partners in complex implementation or service delivery relationships. This implies transparency in transactions and full disclosure of interests. From the perspective of democracy, it is important that actors be held accountable not just for the delivery of programmatic goals, but also for fair and equitable actions.

Accountability of the contemporary implementation and service delivery structures is especially difficult because of the complexity of structures, the diffusion of responsibility, lack of understandable information, and competing values among implementers. Goodin (2003) contends that there are different types of accountability mechanisms that need to be used for markets, the state, and the non-profit sector—actions, results, and intentions, respectively. He also argues that the mechanisms of accountability differ, with hierarchy the dominant model for the state, competition for the market, and cooperative networking for the non-profit sector. For public agencies, the implementation literature makes clear that slippage is most apt to occur in long policy-delivery chains (Pressman and Wildavsky 1973). It is possible for the proximate beneficiary of policy to gain resources such as funds for job training, drug treatment, or health services, without delivering full value to the ultimate targets. Child welfare agencies, for example, provide keen support for the programs through which they get funding, but have resisted evaluations and performance measures and remain a deeply troubled area of public policy around the USA (Smith and Ingram 2002).

There are ongoing experiments to improve accountability in the emerging organizational context. The Emergency Planning and Community Right to Know Act of 1986 introduced an interesting model for lowering the transaction costs of obtaining information critical to citizen education, mobilization, and participation. Under the legislation, industries must make public the amounts and location of releases of a large number of potentially damaging toxic substances. The Act is not without flaws, but it has spurred citizen protests and helped to create a sense of community with common stakes among all residents affected by exposure to dangerous substances. "Benchmarking" is a technique increasingly used to improve non-profit performance in delivery of services. It entails investigating the "best practices" in a particular area and then using those criteria to measure performance. "Organizational report cards" have been used to provide information to the public in modes that are easily understandable (Smith and Ingram 2002). The extent to which such accountability mechanisms actually work in practice is in need of analysis.

There is likely to be a direct relationship between the social construction and power of the target groups and the imposition of successful accountability mechanisms. For instance, it has been forcefully argued that the social construction of criminals as deviants suggests that attempts to hold private prisons accountable will be difficult. There is simply insufficient interest in the welfare of or fairness to inmates (Schneider 1999). Moreover, it is probably easier to hold implementation structures accountable for efficiency and effectiveness than for democratic values such as due process, openness, and diversity of clients served. It is much simpler to hold charter schools to some standard of student performance on tests than it is to assure that such schools reflect the diversity of value perspectives in American society.

# 8. CHALLENGE FOR THE POLICY ANALYST

Exploring the kinds of questions and linkages suggested here requires that the policy analyst must evaluate government and governance structures quite differently from simply measuring effectiveness and efficiency. Analysts need to be especially attentive to ancillary effects of actions beyond goal fulfillment. Government must be measured by its ability to intervene strategically in the complex networks of policy delivery systems to encourage better access to information, to correct for power imbalances and damaging stereotypes and social constructions among stakeholders, and to create arenas and spheres of public discourse. Policy analysts must be prepared to unmask framing of problems and social constructions of targets that are degenerative and damaging to democracy. Policy analysts may also be called upon to suggest alternative policy tools, rules, and implementation structures that facilitate the conditions for democracy.

Policy analysts will need to hone skills beyond quantitative policy analysis and system modeling to incorporate these criteria into policy assessments. Additional attention should be given to in-depth interviewing skills including various kinds of narrative analysis. The use of stories, for example, of how street-level policy workers assess client identities and deliver policy that they view as "fair" (Maynard-Moody and Musheno 2003) offers rich insights into the day-to-day work of policy implementers that would be invaluable in helping structure public organizations to release the tension between rule-boundedness and discretionary judgements. Ethnographic and participant observation are vital elements of the policy analyst's work yet are paid scant attention in most policy analysis methodological texts. Participatory policy analysis has been used very effectively not only to assess how and why a program is having certain kinds of impacts, but in designing better alternatives. Further, we need to recognize that policy analysis is inherently a normative exercise and that the values of democracy are in need of particular analytical attention. Thus, interpretative methodologies must be incorporated into the tool kit of the policy analysts.

## REFERENCES

ANDERSON, C. J., and GUILLORY, C. A. 1997. Political institutions and satisfaction with democracy: a cross-national analysis of consensus and majoritarian systems. *American Political Science Review*, 91 (1: Mar.): 66.

BAKER, S. G. 1993. Immigration reform: the empowerment of a new constituency. Pp. 136–62 in *Public Policy for Democracy*, ed. H. Ingram and S. R. Smith. Washington, DC: Brookings Institution.

BARDACH, E. 1981. Problems of policy definition in policy analysis. Pp. 161–71 in *Research in Public Policy Analysis and Management*, vol. i. Greenwich, Conn.: JAI Press.

—— 2000. *A Practical Guide for Policy Analysis: The Eightfold Path to More Effective Problem Solving*. New York: Chatham House.

BAUMGARTNER, F. R., and JONES, B. D. 1993. *Agendas and Instability in American Politics.* Chicago: University of Chicago Press.

BAZEMORE, G., FRANKEL, E., GLYNN, P., and HALEY, J. O. 1998. Restorative justice and earned redemption: communities, victims, and offender reintegration. *American Behavioral Scientist,* 41 (6): 768–842.

BLAIS, A., and DOBRZYNSKA, D. 1998. Turnout in electoral democracies. *European Journal of Political Research,* 33 (2): 239–61.

BLATTER, J., and INGRAM, H. (eds.) 2001. *Reflections on Water: New Approaches to Transboundary Conflicts and Cooperation.* Cambridge, Mass.: MIT Press.

BLOMQUIST, W., and SCHLAGER, E. 2000. Political pitfalls of integrated watershed management. Paper presented at the Western Political Science Association Meeting, San Jose, Calif., Mar.

BRAITHWAITE, J. 2002. *Restorative Justice and Responsive Regulation.* New York: Oxford University Press.

BRODER, D. S. 2000. *Democracy Derailed: Initiative Campaigns and the Power of Money.* New York: Harcourt.

CAMOU, M. 2005. Deserved in poor neighborhoods: a morality struggle. Pp. 197–218 in *Deserving and Entitled: Social Construction and Public Policy,* ed. A. L. Schneider and H. Ingram. Stoneybrook: State University of New York.

DAY, P., and KLEIN, R. 1987. *Accountabilities: Five Public Services.* London: Tavistock.

DELEON, P. 1997. *Democracy and the Policy Sciences.* Albany, NY: SUNY Press.

—— and STEELMAN, T. A. 1999. The once and future public policy program. *Policy Currents,* 9 (2: June): 1–8.

DENHARDT, J. V., and DENHARDT, R. B. 2003. *The New Public Service: Serving, Not Steering.* New York: M. E. Sharpe.

DIONNE, E. J. 1991. *Why Americans Hate Politics.* New York: Simon and Schuster.

DOUGHMAN, P. 2001. Discourses and water in the U.S.–Mexico border region. Pp. 189–212 in *Reflections on Water: New Approaches to Transboundary Conflicts and Cooperation,* ed. J. Blatter and H. Ingram. Cambridge, Mass.: MIT Press.

DRYZEK, J. S. 1996. Political inclusion and the dynamics of democratization. *American Political Science Review,* 90: 475–87.

—— 1997. *Democracy in Capitalist Times: Ideals, Limits, and Struggles.* New York: Oxford University Press.

DYE, T. 1998. *Understanding Public Policy.* Upper Saddle River, NJ: Prentice Hall.

ESPING-ANDERSEN, G. 1990. *The Three Worlds of Welfare Capitalism.* Cambridge: Polity Press.

—— with GAILLIE, D. et al. 2002. *Why We Need a New Welfare State.* New York: Oxford University Press.

FISCHER, F. 1990. *Technocracy and the Politics of Expertise.* Newbury Park, Calif: Sage.

—— 1995. *Evaluating Public Policy.* Chicago: Nelson Halls.

—— 2003. *Reframing Public Policy: Discursive Politics and Deliberative Practices.* Oxford: Oxford University Press.

—— and FORESTER, J. (eds.) 1993. *The Argumentative Turn in Policy Analysis and Planning.* Durham, NC: Duke University Press.

GALAWAY, B., and HUDSON, J. (eds.) 1996. *Restorative Justice: International Perspectives.* Monsey, NY: Criminal Justice Press.

GOODIN, R. E. 2003. Democratic accountability: the distinctiveness of the third sector. *Archives européennes de sociologie,* 44: 359–96.

GREIDER, W. 1992. *Who Will Tell the People? The Betrayal of American Democracy.* New York: Simon and Schuster.

HIRD, J. A. 1994. *Superfund: The Political Economy of Environmental Risk.* Baltimore: Johns Hopkins University Press.

HOOD, C., ROTHSTEIN, H., and BALDWIN, R. 2001. *The Government of Risk.* Oxford: Oxford University Press.

HOWELL, J. C. (ed.) 1995. *Guide for Implementing the Comprehensive Strategy for Serious, Violent, and Chronic Juvenile Offenders.* Washington, DC: Office of Juvenile Justice and Delinquency Prevention, US Department of Justice, 95–6.

INGRAM, H., and SCHNEIDER, A. 2005. The social construction of public policy. Pp. 1–34 in *Deserving and Entitled: Social Construction and Public Policy,* ed. A. L. Schneider and H. Ingram. Stoneybrook: State University of New York.

—— and SMITH, S. R. (eds.) 1993. *Public Policy for Democracy.* Washington, DC: Brookings Institution

JOHNSON, B. R., and CAMPBELL, R. 1999. Ecology and participation in landscape-based planning within the Pacific Northwest. *Policy Studies Journal,* 27 (3): 502–29.

JURIK, N., and COWGILL, J. 2005. The construction of client identities in a post welfare social service program: the double bind of microenterprise development. Pp. 173–96 in *Deserving and Entitled: Social Construction and Public Policy,* ed. A. L. Schneider and H. Ingram. Stoneybrook: State University of New York.

KARP, J. A., BANDUCCI, S., and BOWLER, S. 2003. To know it is to love it? Satisfaction with democracy in the European Union. *Comparative Political Studies,* 36 (3: Apr.): 271–92.

—— and BOWLER, S. 2001. Coalition government and satisfaction with democracy: an analysis of New Zealand's reaction to proportional representation. *European Journal of Political Research,* 40 (1: Aug.): 57–79.

KENNON, P. 1995. *The Twilight of Democracy.* New York: Doubleday.

KEOHANE, R. O. 2003. Global governance and democratic accountability. Pp. 130–59 in *Taming Globalization: Frontiers of Governance,* ed. D. Held and M. Koenig-Archibugi. Oxford: Polity Press.

KNIGHT, R. L., and LANDES, P. B. 1998. *Stewardship across Boundaries.* Washington, DC: Island Press.

KNOPMAN, D. S., MEGAN, S. M., and LANDY, M. K. 1999. Civic environmentalism: talking tough land use problems with innovative governance. *Environment,* 41 (10: Dec.): 24–32.

LANDY, M. 1993. Public policy and citizenship. Pp. 19–44 in *Public Policy for Democracy,* ed. H. Ingram and S. R. Smith. Washington, DC: Brookings Institution Press.

—— and LEVIN, M. A. 1995. *The New Politics of Public Policy.* Baltimore: Johns Hopkins University Press.

LEDUC, L., NIEMI, R. G., and NORRIS, P. (eds.) 1996. *Comparing Democracies: Elections and Voting in Global Perspective.* Thousand Oaks, Calif.: Sage.

LEVESQUE, S. 2001. The Yellowstone to Yukon conservation initiative: reconstructing boundaries, biodiversity and beliefs. Pp. 123–62 in *Reflections on Water: New Approaches to Transboundary Conflicts and Cooperation,* ed. J. Blatter and H. Ingram. Cambridge, Mass.: MIT Press.

LIJPHART, A. 1999. *Patterns of Democracy: Government Forms and Performance in Thirty-Six Countries.* New Haven, Conn.: Yale University Press.

LINDBLOM, C. E. 1977. *Politics and Markets: The World's Political Economic Systems.* New York: Basic Books.

LIPSKY, M., and SMITH, S. R. 1989. When social problems are treated as emergencies. *Social Service Review,* 63 (Mar.): 5–25.

LOWI, T. J. 1964. American business, public policy, case studies, and political theory. *World Politics,* 16: 677–715.

Luna, Y. 2000. The social construction of welfare mothers: policy messages and recipient responses. Paper presented at the Western Political Science Association Meeting, San Jose, Calif., Mar.

Margolis, M., and Resnick, D. 2000. *Politics as Usual: The Cyberspace "Revolution."* Thousand Oaks, Calif.: Sage.

Marston, S. A. 1993. Citizen action programs and participatory politics in Tucson. Pp. 119–35 in *Public Policy for Democracy*, ed. H. Ingram and S. R. Smith. Washington, DC: Brookings Institution.

Maynard-Moody, S., and Musheno, M. 2003. *Cops, Teachers, and Counselors: Stories from the Front Lines of Public Service.* Ann Arbor: University of Michigan Press.

Mettler, S. 1998. *Dividing Citizens: Gender and Federalism in New Deal Public Policy.* Ithaca, NY: Cornell University Press.

—— and Soss, J. 2004. The consequences of public policy for democratic citizenship: bridging policy studies and mass politics. *Perspectives on Politics,* 2(1): 55–74.

Michaels, S. 1999. Configuring who does what in watershed management: the Massachusetts Watershed Initiative. *Policy Studies Journal,* 27(3): 565–77.

Minow, M. 2002. *Partners, Not Rivals: Privatization and the Public Good.* Boston: Beacon Press.

—— 2003. Public and private partnerships: accounting for the new religion. *Harvard Law Review,* 166(1): 1–41.

Nevitte, N., and Kanji, M. 2002. Authority orientations and political support: a cross-national analysis of satisfaction with governments and democracy. *Comparative Sociology,* 1(3–4): 387–412.

Norris, P. 1997. Representation and the democratic deficit. *European Journal of Political Research,* 32(2: Oct.): 273–82.

Ostrom, E. 1990. *Governing the Commons: The Evolution of Institutions for Collective Action.* Cambridge: Cambridge University Press.

Page, B. 1983. *Who Gets What from Government.* Berkeley: University of California Press.

Pressman, J. L., and Wildavsky, A. 1973. *Implementation: How Great Expectations in Washington are Dashed in Oakland: or, Why It's Amazing that Federal Programs Work at All, This Being a Saga of the Economic Development Administration as Told by Two Sympathetic Observers Who Seek to Build Morals on a Foundation of Ruined Hopes.* Los Angeles: University of California Press.

Putnam, R. D. 2000. *Bowling Alone: The Collapse and Revival of American Community.* New York: Simon and Schuster.

Rauch, J. 1994. *Demosclerosis: The Silent Killer of American Government.* New York: Times Books.

Reeves, E. 2003. Public private partnerships in Ireland: policy and practice. *Public Money and Management,* 23 (3: July): 163–70.

Rochefort, D. A., and Cobb, R. W. 1994. *The Politics of Problem Definition: Shaping the Policy Agenda.* Lawrence: University Press of Kansas.

Rosenau, P. V. (ed.) 2000. *Public Private Policy Partnerships.* Cambridge, Mass.: MIT Press.

Salamon, L. (ed.) 2002. *The Tools of Government: A Public Management Handbook for the Era of Third-Party Government.* New York: Oxford University Press.

—— and Anheier, H. K. 1997. *Defining the Nonprofit Sector: A Cross-national Analysis.* Manchester: Manchester University Press.

Sandel, M. J. 1996. *Democracy's Discontent: America in Search of a Public Philosophy.* Cambridge, Mass.: Belknap Press of Harvard University.

Savas, E. S. 2000. *Privatization and Public–Private Partnerships.* New York: Seven Bridges.

SCHNEIDER, A. L. 1999. Public–private partnerships in the U.S. prison system. *American Behavioral Scientist*, 43(1: Sept.): 192–208.

—— 2005. Why does the US have the highest imprisonment rate in the world? Henry J. Bellman Public Policy Lecture, University of Oklahoma, Norman.

—— and INGRAM, H. 1993. Social construction of target populations. *American Political Science Review*, June: 334–46.

—— —— 1997. *Policy Design for Democracy*. Lawrence: University of Kansas Press.

—— —— (eds.) 2005. *Deserving and Entitled: Social Construction and Public Policy*. Stonybrook: State University of New York Press.

—— and WARNER, J. S. 1987. The role of restitution in juvenile justice systems. *Yale Law and Policy Review*, 5(2: Spring/Summer): 382–401.

SIDNEY, M. S. 2003. *Unfair Housing: How National Policy Shapes Community Action*. Lawrence: University Press of Kansas.

SIMON, C., and WANG, C. 2000. Americorps, social capital, and institutional confidence. Paper presented at the Annual Meeting of the Western Political Science Association, San Jose, Calif., Mar.

SKOCPOL, T. 2003. *Diminished Democracy: From Membership to Management in American Civic Life*. Norman: University of Oklahoma Press.

—— and FIORINA, M. R. (eds.) 1999. *Civic Engagement in American Democracy*. Washington, DC: Brookings Institution Press and Russell Sage Foundation.

SMITH, S. R. 1998. Civic infrastructure in America: government and the non-profit sector. *Report from the Institute for Philosophy & Public Policy*, 18(3: Summer; available at: www.puaf.umd.edu/IPPP/Summer98/table_of_contents.htm).

—— and INGRAM, H. 2002. Implications of choice of policy tools for democracy, civic capital and citizenship. Pp. 565–84 in *The Tools of Government: A Public Management Handbook for the Era of Third-Party Government*, ed. L. Salamon. New York: Oxford University Press.

—— and LIPSKY, M. 1993. *Nonprofits for Hire: The Welfare State in the Age of Contracting*. Cambridge, Mass.: Harvard University Press.

SOSS, J. 1999. Lessons of welfare: policy design, political learning, and political action. *American Political Science Review*, 93(2: June): 363–81.

STONE, D. 1997. *Policy Paradox: The Art of Political Decision Making*. New York: W. W. Norton.

STRANG, H., and BRAITHWAITE, J. (eds.) 2001. *Restorative Justice and Civil Society*. Cambridge: Cambridge University Press.

THORNTON, T. N., CRAFT, C. A., DAHLBERG, L. L., LYNCH, B. S., and BAER, K. 2000. *Best Practices of Youth Violence Prevention: A Sourcebook for Community Action*. Atlanta: Centers for Disease Control and Prevention, National Center for Injury Prevention and Control, 161–93.

VERBA, S., SCHLOZMAN, K. L., and BRADY, H. E. 1995. *Voice and Equality: Civic Voluntarism in American Politics*. Cambridge, Mass.: Harvard University Press.

—— —— —— and NIE, N. H. 1993. Citizen activity: who participates? What do they say? *American Political Science Review*, 87 (2: June): 303.

WEALE, A. 2001. Can we democratise decisions on risk and the environment. *Government and Opposition*, 36(3): 355–78.

WEIMER, D. L., and VINING, A. R. 1999. *Policy Analysis: Concepts and Practice*, 3rd edn. Upper Saddle River, NJ: Prentice Hall.

WILSON, J. Q. 1986. *American Government: Institutions and Policies*. Lexington, Mass.: D. C. Heath.

WOOD, D. B. 1994. *Bureaucratic Dynamics: The Role of Bureaucracy in a Democracy.* Boulder, Colo.: Westview Press.

YAFEE, S. 1998. Cooperation: a strategy for achieving stewardship across boundaries. Pp. 299–324 in *Stewardship across Boundaries*, ed. R. L. Knight and P. B. Landres. Washington, DC: Island Press.

.........................................................................................

# CHAPTER 9

# POLICY ANALYSIS AS CRITIQUE

.........................................................................................

## JOHN S. DRYZEK

POLICY analysis encompasses a variety of activities concerned with the creation, compilation, and application of evidence, testimony, argument, and interpretation in order to examine, evaluate, and improve the content and process of public policy. This chapter will look at one such activity, that of critique. Critique is treated not just as one thing that policy analysts might choose to do, but as rightly basic to their whole enterprise. Public policy processes feature communication in context with practical effect, and such communication is always amenable to critique oriented to change for the better. Critical policy analysis therefore constitutes a program for the foundations of the field. All policy analysis should have a critical component, if only to establish that the social problem at hand is not defined in such a way as to advantage particular interests in indefensible ways.

## 1. CRITIQUE AND ITS OPPOSITES

.........................................................................................

The place of critical policy analysis can be approached through reference to two of its opposites: technocracy and accommodation.

The intent of technocratic policy analysis is to identify cause and effect relationships that can be manipulated by public policy under central and coordinated control. At its most ambitious, technocratic analysis could be allied to the nineteenth century positivism of Comte and Saint-Simon, who sought the establishment of a set of causal laws of society that provided points of leverage for policy makers in pursuit of social perfection. Those dreams may be long dead, and positivism long rejected even by philosophers of natural science, but the terms "positivist" and "post-positivist" still animate disputes in the policy field (for example, Durning 1999; Lynn 1999). And the idea that policy analysis is about control of cause and effect lives on in optimizing techniques drawn from welfare economics and elsewhere (Stokey and Zeckhauser 1978), and policy evaluation that seeks only to identify the causal impact of policies. Technocratic analysis implicitly assumes an omniscient and benevolent decision maker untroubled by politics (Majone 1989 refers to "decision-ism"). However, the viewpoint of analysis is not necessarily the same as that of any identifiable real-world decision maker, for two reasons. First, a single locus of decision making may not exist. Second, technocratic analysis often proceeds from its own frame of reference which may embody values different from those of policy makers. For example, cost–benefit analysis is committed to economic efficiency, a value generally held in poor regard by those steeped in the politics of public policy.

It should be stressed that technocratic analysis is not the same as quantitative and statistical analysis. Technocracy can use statistics—but so can critique. There is a long tradition of social reformers gathering statistics concerning poverty, malnutrition, and illness, which can then be presented to indict a social system (Bulmer 1983). Only hardline followers of Michel Foucault would condemn any gathering of social statistics as oppression, treating descriptive statistics as constitutive of the normal-izing gaze of a state that constructs populations as objects to be managed.

Accommodative policy analysis seeks to attach itself to the frame of reference of the policy maker. As such it is a loyalist endeavor in which the successful policy analyst is one who adopts views about the definition of problems, goals, and acceptable solutions from his or her organizational environment. Within these constraints the analyst will still try to bring some distinctive expertise to bear. Explicit advocacy of this orientation is rare (but see Palumbo and Nachmias 1983), though it does capture aspects of the working life of many analysts (Meltsner 1976), and some of the activities of management consultants.

Critical policy analysis can be positioned in terms of explicit rejection of both technocratic and accommodative images (Bobrow and Dryzek 1987, 161–8).

# 2. CRITIQUE AND ITS POLITICS

For all their differences, technocratic and accommodative images of policy analysis both assume that the key contribution of analysis to improving the condition of the world is the enlightenment of those in positions of power so they can better manipulate social systems. In contrast, critical policy analysis specifies that the key task of analysis is enlightenment of those suffering at the hands of power in the interests of action on their part to escape suffering. By definition, a critical theory is directed at an audience of sufferers in order to make plain to them the causes of their suffering. It is validated through reflective acceptance on the part of the audience, and, ultimately, action based on this acceptance (Fay 1987).

Many theories fall under this general critical conception. For example, the Marxist critique of capitalist political economy was directed at the emancipation of the working class, and unmasked ideological and material forces that oppressed the proletariat. When it comes to public policy, it is not hard to show that policies justified as being in the public interest often have benefits skewed toward dominant classes, be they tax cuts for the rich, subsidies for agribusiness, or public transport systems that serve wealthy suburbs while bypassing the urban poor. The Frankfurt School (Adorno, Horkheimer, and Marcuse) developed critical theories of modernity in its entirety, especially in terms of its rationality that destroys the more congenial aspects of human association. Feminist critique highlights the oppressive but often unnoticed effects of patriarchy. Though often a bit weak on how suffering might be overcome, the work of Michel Foucault showed how power could be pervasive and constitutive of oppressive discourses about criminality, health, madness, and sexuality. In radical environmental thought, attempts have been made to link the liberation of human and non-human nature. The critical legal studies movement in the United States has tried to show how ostensibly neutral laws, rules, and associated practices systematically oppress disadvantaged categories of people.

These examples might suggest that critical policy analysis is tied to a radical leftist agenda. Two responses are possible here. The first is that technocratic and accommodative policy analyses also have ideological associations. The center of gravity of technocratic analysis is center-left, in that much of it believes in the possibility of benign active government. Accommodation is center-right, in that it adjusts itself in conservative fashion to the prevailing distribution of political power, though this judgement would have to be qualified if a power center such as an elected government had leftist inclinations.

A second response is that the logical structure of critique is content free. Only when the content is filled in does it happen to be the case that particular critiques—or at least the kind of broad-gauge theories just mentioned—turn out to have radical left associations. At least one important—indeed, foundational—policy field application lacks any such association, and to this I now turn.

## 3. CRITIQUE IN THE ORIGINS OF THE POLICY SCIENCES

This foundational application can be found in the policy sciences movement that began in the 1940s, whose most important figure was Harold Lasswell (see especially Lerner and Lasswell 1951). Lasswell was committed to the idea of a "policy science of democracy." But he doubted that control by existing political elites, or indeed any political elites, could bring this about, because of the psychopathology he believed often accompanied individual pursuit of political power. Lasswell hoped that policy scientists could rise above this sort of motivation, and come to resemble psychological clinicians in their extraordinary self-understanding and commitment to a code of professional ethics (Lasswell 1965, 14). He explored innovations such as the decision seminar, a forum for social learning that would provide an information-rich and interactive environment transcending politics and policy as usual. The audience for Lasswellian critique ranged from existing policy elites to society as a whole. The substantive content was equally wide ranging; most famously, he warned about the need to act against development of a "garrison state" (1941), as alleged pursuit of national security led to restrictions on freedom and democracy. Such a warning is no less pertinent today than in the 1930s when Lasswell first made it. The garrison state would be forestalled by wide recognition of the validity of the warning, and resistance based on that knowledge.

In common with the critical theories already mentioned, Lasswell was concerned about some very large matters: the "progressive democratization of mankind" (1948, 221) versus the garrison state. However, policy analysis as critique can concern itself with more limited issues. The idea is to identify and uncover influences on policy content from dominant ideologies, discourses, or material forces. The policy in question could be (say) a matter of a nation's economic strategy under sway of market liberalism, such that there appears to be no alternative to policies of deregulation, free trade, capital mobility, and privatization. Such influence might be a matter of material forces—if a government is punished for its deviation with capital flight, disinvestment, and attacks on its currency. Or it could be matter of the discourse of globalization: these material forces may not be especially powerful, but all key actors believe they are, and so act accordingly. Hirst and Thompson (1996) try to explode claims about both the novelty and material reality of globalization, treating globalization as more an ideological matter of imposing the market liberal "Washington Consensus" on the world. On their account governments in fact retain substantial scope for policies that pursue social justice, and can implement interventionist economic policies without the dire consequences predicted by economic globalization advocates. Alternatively, the influence of globalization on policy might plausibly come from some mixture of material and discursive forces, in which case the first task of the critical analysis is to ascertain the mix of the material and the discursive, and the processes through which they constitute one another.

# 4. The Linguistic Turn and its Critical Twist

Policy making in large part involves the construction of meaning through language, and policy analysis is itself a symbolic activity. Fischer and Forester (1993) speak of an "argumentative turn" in policy analysis and planning. Logically prior is a "linguistic turn" that recognizes the importance of language in constituting both policy analysis and policy making, because argument is just one specific kind of language. The language of policy might be highly formalized in (say) optimizing techniques; or it might be informal speech embodying only everyday experiential knowledge, or it might be some mix. At any rate, language is never a neutral medium. The idea of critical policy analysis fits well with this linguistic turn, and, with the waning of material critique of the kind that helped define Marxism, most critical policy analysis is today joined to this kind of linguistic orientation to the policy world. Marxists and others attuned to material critique might well bemoan this turn, just as they bemoan the preoccupation of the multicultural left (especially in the United States) with questions of recognition of oppressed minorities (including wealthy ones) to the exclusion of distribution.

In the wake of the linguistic turn, the first task of any piece of policy analysis is the explication of the meanings that are or were present in any particular policy setting. The task is primary because these meanings condition problem definition, which in turn determines (for example) the kind of data or evidence that is relevant. Often key meanings are submerged or taken for granted, and tracing their origins, interconnections with other meanings, and consequences can be quite demanding. A family of techniques covering interpretation, narrative analysis, and discourse analysis is available here.

Interpretive policy analysis (Yanow 1996) focuses most directly on meanings as constructed by participants in particular policy processes. Public policies themselves are not approached as means for the achievement of some goal, but, rather, "modes for the expression of human meaning" (Yanow 2003, 229). The approach can be anthropological, treating policy processes as cultural practice. Classic anthropology of British, and of US federal, budgeting can be found in the studies of Heclo and Wildavsky (1974) and Wildavsky (1974), who elucidate the informal understandings shared by participants that make the process work. Participants share all kinds of assumptions about baselines, the need to come in high but not too high when requesting funds, and so forth that violate the notionally rationalistic and goal-oriented aspects of budgeting. The way meanings are created in implementation can produce consequences not intended by policy makers. Yanow (2003, 241) points to the example of remedial educational programs that require teachers to line up and so identify children in need of help, thus highlighting and reinforcing the very categories of problematic family background and poverty whose consequences the policy was designed to combat.

Narrative analysis (Roe 1994) focuses mainly on stories that are told by participants in policy processes. The language of policy, in common with the language of many social settings, features the telling of stories much more than it features argument, deductive logic, or still less quantitative optimization. The effect of a good story is to convince its audience that an issue ought to be framed in a particular way. The facts never "speak for themselves." For example, a story about rape and murder amid ethnic conflict could be told by a nationalist demagogue in terms of violated ethnic innocence and collective ethnic guilt of its perpetrators. The same facts could also support a story of violation of basic human rights and universal principles of humanity. The action consequences of each story would be vastly different.

Discourse analysis focuses on larger systems of meaning in which stories are often embedded, and which condition policy content. For example, Hajer (1995) traces the emergence of a discourse of ecological modernization in Dutch environmental policy that sees pollution abatement as instrumental to economic development, and does not require conclusive scientific proof of a hazard before acting. He contrasts this with a "traditional-pragmatic" discourse that dominated British environmental policy, emphasizing end-of-pipe regulation rather than redesign of production processes, and requiring scientific proof of damage from a pollutant before policy action. In each case, analysis is needed to uncover dominant discourses, which may be so dominant as to be taken for granted by actors who treat them as natural, and are thus unaware of their existence.

The explication of meaning is a necessary but of itself insufficient step on the road to critique. If policy analysis is in large part concerned with evaluating and improving the content and process of policy, then interpretation, narrative, and discourse analysis of themselves fall short. They may indeed produce better descriptions and understandings of the way the world works, but they may also leave the world pretty much as they find it, even if their results are widely disseminated and accepted. For example, a discourse analysis might lay bare the dominant discourses in a policy area—but then conclude this dominance is immutable. This is quite a common position to hold in, for example, explications of the impact of discourses of globalization in economic policy, which provide little room for maneuver on the part of national governments. Some kinds of interpretative analysis may even support an accommodating image of policy analysis. This is a particular danger for analyses based on depth interviews of elites, which may end up reproducing the world view of these elites.

# 5. SOURCES OF CRITICAL STANDARDS

The impetus of critique is also toward evaluation and improvement, not just description and explication. Critical policy analysis in linguistic mode can hold up the results yielded by interpretation, narrative, and discourse analysis to critical standards. Where, then, might these standards come from? There are several possible answers, all of which begin from the fact that any meanings uncovered are likely to be contestable, if not actually contested (Fischer 2003, 46). The possibility of contestation arises from the identification of contingency in interpretation, narrative, and discourse. For contingency implies there is some alternative, however repressed or marginalized it might be by dominant understandings.

One standard can be found in the critical communications theory associated with Jürgen Habermas (1984). Habermas's own critical theory of society is grounded in the implicit claims to truth, sincerity, comprehensibility, and appropriateness attached to utterances in intersubjective communication. In this light, a social situation can be described as communicatively rational to the extent it is constituted by the reflective understanding of competent actors. Communication among them ought to be free from deception, self-deception, strategizing, and the exercise of power. The normative principles of communicative rationality can be applied to evaluate both the content of understandings that back a particular policy or position, and the process that produces policies (Healey 1993).

When it comes to the content of understandings, critical policy analysis deploying principles of communicative rationality is in a position to unmask ideological claims—ideology here being understood in the pejorative sense as the specification of false necessities. "Globalization" is often used in this ideological sense, as specifying a set of policies that governments must pursue unless they want to be left behind. Other ideological claims might be based on the inevitability of technological change that must be accepted rather than questioned, though this sort of ideology is weaker today than in the 1950s. On the other hand, the kind of ideology that legitimizes all kinds of repressive measures in the name of "war against terror" has grown stronger after 2001. Violations of communicative rationality can also come in more mundane form, operating through interest rather than ideology. For example, tobacco companies long denied the seriousness of the damage of their products to human health, suppressing results of their own studies in clear violation of the "sincerity" aspect of communicative rationality.

Communicative rationality is not problem free as a critical standard. Rigidly applied, it might rule out the tacit knowledge and common sense of ordinary people and policy actors, or the traditional, non-scientific understandings of indigenous peoples about their land. Young (1996) points out that seemingly neutral rules of dialogue can in practice discriminate against those not versed in the finer points of rational argument (though Young's point will not ring true to those who have actually observed communicative exercises involving lay participants). The solution here may be expansion of communicative rationality beyond Habermas's own narrow and unnecessary emphasis on argument to encompass other forms of communication such as Young's own trio of greeting, rhetoric, and storytelling, or beyond to gossip and jokes. All kinds of communication can be assessed in terms of their capacity to induce reflection, their non-coerciveness, and their ability to connect the particular experience of an interlocutor to some more general principle (Dryzek 2000, 68–71).

Communitarians would have a different problem, believing that communicative rationality is too open and ungrounded in the reality of particular societies. Communitarians would stress the particular standards embodied in a society's traditions—for example, the regime values embodied in the United States constitution. While conservative, this position does enable a kind of critique—for example of policies that violate the spirit of the constitution (this is of course the basis for legal challenges to policy decisions, but it could also be the basis for policy analytic challenges). Communitarian standards and communicative rationality could be thought of as different levels of evaluation (Fischer 1980). Perhaps the regime values of one's society can sometimes be treated as unproblematic standards—but sometimes they too may be in need of critical scrutiny. For example, the US constitution originally sanctioned racism and slavery, eventually challenged on the basis of more universalistic principles (though those principles were derived from a variety of sources, including religious ones, so it was never just a matter of anything like communicative rationality being brought to bear).

A more hands-off approach to critical standards is also possible: one could let them emerge in the contestation of different understandings. For example, in criminal justice policy, the recent development of restorative justice approaches challenges more traditional understandings based on (respectively) the psycho-pathology of the criminal mind, the rational choices of criminals as they calculate the costs and benefits of particular crimes, and the miserable social conditions that drive some individuals into a life of crime. Restorative justice postulates community reintegration as both a core value in itself and instrumental to the rehabilitation of offenders and reduction of crime rates. This challenge has to be met by more traditional discourses of criminal justice; adherents of these discourses may on reflection choose to reject the challenge or modify their own normative stance in response to it, but they can hardly ignore it. From such contestation some degree of agreement on standards might emerge—or it might not. But even if it does, the conditions of emergence are crucial, and themselves need to be held up to some critical standard. So the hands-off approach is ultimately not quite sufficient.

Finally, an agonistic approach to the generation of critical standards would insist that opinions are different and will always remain so because they are grounded in different identities and experiences. Agonism's procedural standards specify a particular kind of respectful orientation that treats others as adversaries rather than enemies, and interaction with them as critical engagement rather than strategizing (Mouffe 1999). However, agonism as usually presented lacks connection to collective decision making of the sort that helps define the field of public policy, focusing instead on the nature of interpersonal and intergroup relationships.

# 6. Critique of Processes
## and Institutions

Irrespective of where one looks for its standards, critique need not stop at the content of policies and their underlying understandings, and can extend to questions of the procedure through which policies are produced. Communicative rationality in particular is readily applied in procedural terms (Bernstein 1983, 191–4), providing criteria for how disputes across competing interpretations might be resolved, while respecting a basic plurality of interpretations. The criteria can then be deployed to evaluate prevailing policy processes. For example, it is possible to criticize legal processes for their restrictions on the kinds of arguments that can be made. Kemp (1985) discusses legalistic public inquiries on nuclear power issues in the UK which ruled out arguments that questioned the economic benefits of nuclear energy while allowing economic arguments in favor, featured disparities in financial resources available to proponents and objectors, and allowed proponents to invoke the Official Secrets Act at key points to silence debate.

Critical policy analysis can also inform the design or creation of alternative processes. Such designs might range from Lasswell's decision seminar to more recent experiments in informed lay citizen deliberation—such as citizen's juries, consensus conferences, and deliberative opinion polls. Fung (2003) refers to such exercises as "recipes for public spheres," though each is just one moment in the life of a larger public sphere where public opinion is created. Discursive designs can also involve partisans rather than lay citizens in processes such as mediation, regulatory negotiation, impact assessment, and policy dialogues (Dryzek 1987a). Because they involve partisans, these sorts of processes can feature the exercise of power and strategic action; critical policy analysis can try to move them in a more communicative direction. A commitment to critique means that "design" should itself be a communicative process involving those who will participate in the institution in question and be the subjects of any decisions it reaches. Innes and Booher (2003, 49) show how participants in a discursive process for water management in California created new institutions and procedures that were more open and cooperative and so capable of responding more effectively to changing circumstances. Institutional design of this sort could never resemble engineering.

Participants in institutional reconstruction should also be alive to the degree seemingly discursive innovations can be introduced for thoroughly strategic reasons. For example, such designs have found favor in health policy in the United Kingdom. Their bureaucratic sponsors can present the recommendations of bodies such as citizens' panels as the true face of public opinion, and so circumvent troublesome lobby groups that also claim to represent public interests (Parkinson 2004). Yet such forums once established can escape and sometimes dismay their sponsors.

In its commitment to institutions that try to overcome power inequalities and engage citizens in effective dialogue, critical policy analysis joins recent democratic theory in its overarching commitment to deliberation. Democratic theory took a "deliberative turn" around 1990, under which legitimacy is located in the capacity and opportunity of those subject to a policy decision to participate in deliberation about its content (Chambers 2003). Thus can the Lasswellian aspiration of a "policy science of democracy" now be redeemed—if not quite in the way Lasswell himself saw the matter. Critical policy analysis looks beyond technocracy and thin liberal democracy to a deeper democracy where distinctions between citizens, representatives, and experts lose their force (deLeon 1997). Such a project can expect resistance from both practitioners of technocratic policy analysis and powerful interests that have a stake in perpetuating the political-economic status quo. However, important actors may (as I have noted) sometimes find it expedient to sponsor discursive exercises, providing an opening for more authentic democratization.

# 7. FROM WEBERIAN HIERARCHY TO NETWORKED GOVERNANCE

Recognizing this institutional agenda, a technocratic policy analyst might accept its attractions in terms of democratic values, yet resist it on the grounds of the sheer complexity of policy problems in the contemporary world. The Weberian argument is that intelligence for complex problems has to be coordinated by the apex of a hierarchy that can organize expertise and coordinate responses across the aspects of a complex issue. The apex should divide complex problems into sets and subsets, each of which is allocated to a subordinate unit in an administrative organization chart. Weber himself believed that bureaucracy flourishes in the modern world precisely because it is the best organizational means for the resolution of complex social problems (though he was also alive to the pathologies of bureaucracy, and its suppression of the more congenial aspects of human society). Intelligent problem decomposition—and administrative organization—here means minimizing inter-actions across the sets and subsets into which complex problems are divided. The apex of the hierarchy can then piece together the parts provided by each of the subunits in order to craft overall solutions.

At a theoretical level, an anti-Weberian argument can be mustered to the effect that this approach works only for what Simon (1981) calls "near-decomposable" problems. Higher orders of complexity mean that the density of interactions across the bound-aries of sets and subsets requires that no intelligent decomposition and bureaucratic division of labor exists, and so the coordinating capacities of the apex of the hierarchy are overwhelmed (Dryzek 1987b). Better, then, to accept these sorts of interactions rather than repress them, and promote decentralized communication across diverse competent individuals concerned with different aspects of an issue. While it is possible to adduce examples on both sides of this dispute, some recent developments in practice support the anti-Weberian side, particularly when it comes to "new governance" and networked problem solving (Rhodes 2000). Networks themselves are not necessarily democratic, and can indeed facilitate escape from accountability to a broader public by hiding power and responsibility. But whether or not they are democratic, networks are non-hierarchical, and often defended precisely for their capacity to handle complex problems. Critical policy analysis can remind proponents of new governance of the need for undistorted communication and actor competence in networks (Hajer and Wagenaar 2003), and for resistance to the efforts of new public managers to control networks. This kind of critical analysis is at home in the network society, even as it must often struggle against anti-democratic and exclusionary tendencies in networks themselves. In contrast, technocratic policy analysis flounders in the network society, because its implicit audience is a system controller at the apex of a hierarchy. One defining feature of a network is the absence of any sovereign center; problem solving involves many actors in different jurisdictions. These actors might be politicans and bureaucrats; they might also be corporations, transnational organizations, lobby groups, social movements, and citizens. "Speaking truth to power," as Wildavsky (1979) characterizes the main task of policy analysis, becomes very different when power itself is dispersed and fluid (Hajer 2003, 182). Analysts become interlocutors in a multidirectional conversation, not whisperers in the ears of the sovereign.

# 8. Tasks for the Critical Policy Analyst

The foregoing discussion suggests the following tasks for the analyst under the general heading of critique:

- Explication of dominant meanings in policy content and process.
- Uncovering suppressed or marginalized meanings.
- Identification of what Lindblom (1990) calls "agents of impairment" that suppress alternative meanings. These agents might include ideologies, dominant discourses, lack of information, lack of education, bureaucratic obfuscation, restrictions on the admissibility of particular kinds of evidence and communication, and processes designed to baffle rather than enlighten.
- Identification of the ways in which the communicative capacities of policy actors might be equalized.
- Evaluation of institutions in terms of communicative standards.
- Participation in the design of institutions that might do better.
- Criticism of technocratic policy analysis. Even ostensibly useless technocratic policy analysis draws on and reinforces a discourse of disempowerment of those who are not either experts or members of the policy-making elite. The cumulative weight of such analysis may reinforce the idea that public policy is only for experts and elites (Edelman 1977; Dryzek 1990, 116–17).

To what extent can these tasks be addressed in policy studies curriculum design? One reason for the persistence of technocratic policy analysis is that its techniques can be taught as items in a tool kit. Once analysts find themselves in policy-making processes they can display this tool kit as a badge of professional respectability. But what analysts actually do in practice is often more consistent with the communicative image that is one starting point of critical policy analysis. They ask questions, draw attention to particular issues, investigate and develop stories, make arguments, and use rhetoric to convince others of particular meanings (Forester 1983). So curriculum design for critical policy analysis might begin with specifying that analysts preach what they practice.

Critical policy analysis too has its techniques and logics, not least interpretative, narrative, and discourse analysis. These too can be taught, as can logics of policy evaluation that retain a critical awareness of different sorts of values and world-views that can be brought to bear (Fischer 1995). However, critical analysts also need to reflect on what tools should be used in what circumstances, and to what effect. Analysts should be aware of the context to which they contribute—and help constitute (Torgerson 1986, 41). Forester (1981) recommends a code of communicative ethics for all policy actors, including analysts, that forbids manipulation, hiding and distorting information, deflecting attention from important questions, and the displacement of debate by the exercise of power or claims to expertise. These requirements are inconsistent with the way professions often work—especially when it comes to forsaking the mystique which is one source of professional power (Torgerson 1985, 254–5).

# 9. Conclusion

Critical policy analysis is, then, a demanding vocation. Its practitioners cannot easily seek professional advancement on the basis of their privileged mastery of a set of tools. Their craft promises to make life difficult for occupants of established centers of power. But despite the forces that stand in its way, policy analysis as critique can draw comfort from the fact that, unlike its technocratic opposite, it fits readily into an emerging network society of decentralized problem solving. And in a democratic world, it can draw strength from its capacity to help realize the idea of a policy science of democracy.

## References

Bernstein, R. J. 1983. *Beyond Objectivism and Relativism*. Philadelphia: University of Pennsylvania Press.

Bobrow, D. B., and Dryzek, J. S. 1987. *Policy Analysis by Design*. Pittsburgh, Pa.: University of Pittsburgh Press.

BULMER, M. 1983. The British tradition of social administration: moral concerns at the expense of scientific rigor. Pp. 161–85 in *Ethics, the Social Sciences, and Policy Analysis*, ed. D. Callahan and B. Jennings. New York: Plenum.

CHAMBERS, S. 2003. Deliberative democratic theory. *Annual Review of Political Science*, 6: 307–26.

deLEON, P. 1997. *Democracy and the Policy Sciences*. Albany: State University of New York Press.

DRYZEK, J. S. 1987a. Discursive designs: critical theory and political institutions. *American Journal of Political Science*, 31: 656–79.

—— 1987b. Complexity and rationality in public life. *Political Studies*, 35: 424–42.

—— 1990. *Discursive Democracy: Politics, Policy and Political Science*. New York: Cambridge University Press.

—— 2000. *Deliberative Democracy and Beyond: Liberals, Critics, Contestations*. Oxford: Oxford University Press.

DURNING, D. 1999. The transition from traditional to postpositivist policy analysis: a role for Q methodology. *Journal of Policy Analysis and Management*, 18: 389–410.

EDELMAN, M. 1977. *Political Language: Words That Succeed and Policies That Fail*. New York: Academic.

FAY, B. 1987. *Critical Social Science: Liberation and its Limits*. Ithaca, NY: Cornell University Press.

FISCHER, F. 1980. *Politics, Values, and Public Policy: The Problem of Methodology*. Boulder, Colo.: Westview.

—— 1995. *Evaluating Public Policy*. Chicago: Nelson-Hall.

—— 2003. *Reframing Public Policy: Discursive Politics and Deliberative Practices*. Oxford: Oxford University Press.

—— and FORESTER, J. (eds.) 1993. *The Argumentative Turn in Policy Analysis and Planning*. Durham, NC: Duke University Press.

FORESTER, J. 1981. Questioning and organizing attention: toward a critical theory of planning and administrative practice. *Administration and Society*, 13: 161–205.

—— 1983. What analysts do. Pp. 47–62 in *Values, Ethics, and the Practice of Policy Analysis*, ed. W. N. Dunn. Lexington, Mass.: Lexington Books.

FUNG, A. 2003. Recipes for public spheres: eight institutional design choices and their consequences. *Journal of Political Philosophy*, 11: 338–67.

HABERMAS, J. 1984. *The Theory of Communicative Action I: Reason and the Rationalization of Society*. Boston: Beacon Press.

HAJER, M. A. 1995. *The Politics of Environmental Discourse: Ecological Modernization and the Policy Process*. Oxford: Oxford University Press.

—— 2003. Policy without polity? Policy analysis and the institutional void. *Policy Sciences*, 36: 175–95.

—— and WAGENAAR, H. (eds.) 2003. *Deliberative Policy Analysis: Understanding Governance in the Network Society*. Cambridge: Cambridge University Press.

HEALEY, P. 1993. Planning through debate: the communicative turn in planning theory. Pp. 233–53 in *The Argumentative Turn in Policy Analysis and Planning*, ed. F. Fischer and J. Forester. Durham, NC: Duke University Press.

HECLO, H., and WILDAVSKY, A. 1974. *The Private Government of Public Money*. London: Macmillan.

HIRST, P., and THOMPSON, G. 1996. *Globalization in Question: The International Economy and the Possibilities of Governance*. Cambridge: Polity Press.

INNES, J. E., and BOOHER, D. E. 2003. Collaborative policy making: government through dialogue. In Hajer and Wagenaar 2003, 33–59.

KEMP, R. 1985. Planning, public hearings, and the politics of discourse. Pp. 177–201 in *Critical Theory and Public Life*, ed. J. Forester. Cambridge, Mass.: MIT Press.

LASSWELL, H. D. 1941. The garrison state. *American Journal of Sociology*, 46: 455–68.

—— 1948. *Power and Personality*. New York: Norton.

—— 1965. *World Politics and Personal Insecurity*. New York: Free Press.

LERNER, D., and LASSWELL, H. D. (eds.) 1951. *The Policy Sciences*. Stanford, Calif.: Stanford University Press.

LINDBLOM, C. E. 1990. *Inquiry and Change: The Troubled Attempt to Understand and Shape Society*. New Haven, Conn.: Yale University Press.

LYNN, L. E., Jr. 1999. A place at the table: policy analysis, its postpositive critics, and the future of practice. *Journal of Policy Analysis and Management*, 18: 411–24.

MAJONE, G. 1989. *Evidence, Argument, and Persuasion in the Policy Process*. New Haven, Conn.: Yale University Press.

MELTSNER, A. J. 1976. *Policy Analysts in the Bureaucracy*. Berkeley: University of California Press.

MOUFFE, C. 1999. Deliberative democracy or agonistic pluralism? *Social Research*, 66: 745–58.

PALUMBO, D. J., and NACHMIAS, D. 1983. The preconditions for successful evaluation: is there an ideal paradigm? *Policy Sciences*, 16: 67–79.

PARKINSON, J. 2004. Why deliberate? The encounter between deliberation and new public managers. *Public Administration*, 82: 377–95.

RHODES, R. A. W. 2000. Governance and public administration. Pp. 54–90 in *Debating Governance*, ed. J. Pierre. Oxford: Oxford University Press.

ROE, E. 1994. *Narrative Policy Analysis*. Durham, NC: Duke University Press.

SIMON, H. A. 1981. *The Sciences of the Artificial*, 2nd edn. Cambridge, Mass.: MIT Press.

STOKEY, E., and ZECKHAUSER, R. 1978. *A Primer for Policy Analysis*. New York: Norton.

TORGERSON, D. 1985. Contextual orientation in policy analysis: the contribution of H. D. Lasswell. *Policy Sciences*, 18: 241–61.

—— 1986. Between knowledge and politics: three faces of policy analysis. *Policy Sciences*, 19: 33–59.

WILDAVSKY, A. 1974. *The Politics of the Budgetary Process*, 2nd edn. Boston: Little, Brown.

—— 1979. *Speaking Truth to Power: The Art and Craft of Policy Analysis*. Boston: Little, Brown.

YANOW, D. 1996. *How Does a Policy Mean? Interpreting Policy and Organizational Actions*. Washington, DC: Georgetown University Press.

—— 2003. Accessing local knowledge. In Hajer and Wagenaar 2003, 228–46.

YOUNG, I. M. 1996. Communication and the other: beyond deliberative democracy. Pp. 120–35 in *Democracy and Difference*, ed. S. Benhabib. Princeton, NJ: Princeton University Press.

# PART IV

PRODUCING PUBLIC
POLICY

C H A P T E R  1 0

# THE ORIGINS OF POLICY

## EDWARD C. PAGE

## 1. POLICY, DIVERSITY, AND HIERARCHY

Where do policies come from? Take the 1889 *Invaliditäts- und Alterssicherungsgesetz*, one of the key pieces of Bismarck's social legislation. We might say that it "originated" in the Imperial Office of the Interior. We might seek its origins in its antecedents such as in earlier voluntary schemes of insurance, in the reforms set in train earlier by the 1883 *Krankenversicherungsgesetz*, in Bismarck's state-building strategy, in the Kaiser's notion of a "social emperorship," or even in a longer tradition of social responsibility among German monarchs found in Frederick the Great among others. The measure can be explained as part of a wider strategy of heading off working-class discontent and thus viewed as a product of capitalism in general, as the consequences of a particular transition from a pre-industrial to an industrial society (Moore 1967), or as a response to emerging socialism. We may even agree with Dawson (1912, 1) that it is "impossible to assign the origins of the German insurance legislation, definitely to any one set of conditions or even to a precise period." None of these answers is clearly right or wrong (for a discussion of the novelty of Bismarck's social legislation, see Tampke 1981; for a comparative discussion, see Heidenheimer, Heclo, and Adams 1990). They appear to be answers to slightly different questions.

Insofar as they arise from conscious reflection and deliberation, policies may reflect a variety of intentions and ideas: some vague, some specific, some conflicting, some unarticulated. They can, as we will see, even be the unintended or undeliberated consequences of professional practices or bureaucratic routines. Such intentions, practices, and ideas can in turn be shaped by a vast array of different environmental circumstances, ranging from an immediate specific cue or impetus to a more general spirit of the time or even a belief in a self-evident universal truth. How can we talk about the origins of something as diverse as policy?

The core simplification used in the study of the origins of policy is the analogy of the business meeting. Policies first come into being through being put on an agenda—a notional list of topics that people involved in policy making are interested in, and which they seek to address through developing, or exploring the possibility of developing, policies. Kingdon's (1995) approach to understanding the development of agendas and approaches associated with it (Cobb and Elder 1978; Cohen, March, and Olsen 1972; Baumgartner and Jones 1993), have served to shape thinking about the early origins of policy. Such authors are well aware of the limitations of the agenda analogy for describing the origins of policy because of the possibility of infinite regress: for any idea, proposal, or practice there is an idea, proposal, or practice that helped give rise to it. The value of the notion of agendas is that it provides a framework that allows one to outline the proximate causes that lead to attention being devoted to an issue: how an issue comes to emerge from relative obscurity to becoming something that is being discussed as a serious contender for legislation or some other policy measure.

However, there are two limitations to using the agenda literature to help understand the origins of policy. First, because the analyses on which the leading studies are based are concerned with legislative policy making, they cannot be expected to throw light on policies that have been developed, or better that emerge, without having been the subject of deliberation or without the formal approval of legislative and executive authorities. Second, and perhaps most importantly, the dominant theoretical models have been developed primarily to apply to the United States, and this makes their direct application as generalized descriptions of policy development problematic. The model Kingdon (1995) proposes is highly pluralistic with a plurality of different "important people" in the legislative branch (Congressmen and -women, congressional staffers) and outside (interest groups, consultants, and parties) all with roles to play in placing items on the political agenda. What makes this highly distinctive, from a European perspective, is not the range of people involved, but the fact that the system lacks the hierarchy found in systems of fused legislative and executive branches with party government. As Kingdon (1995, 76) points out:

A complex combination of factors is generally responsible for the movement of a given item into agenda prominence. For a number of reasons a combination of sources is virtually always responsible. One reason is the general fragmentation of the system. The founders deliberately designed a constitutional system to be fragmented, incapable of being dominated by any one actor. They succeeded. Thus a combination of people is required to bring an idea to policy fruition.

However, the same degree of fragmentation found in the US system does not always prevail in executive-dominated systems with party government (whether in coalitions or majorities) where it is possible for one group—those around the chief executive—if not to dominate the entire system then to have a disproportionate effect on what issues get consideration. In addition, the core executive also has a powerful influence on, if not control of, the process by which alternatives are discussed. We will examine the implications of this more fully below, but if the agenda model has largely been developed as a US model we might expect it to be somewhat less useful as a framework for offering an account of how policies develop elsewhere. Consequently the discussion below is hardly pointing out issues that Kingdon and other US theorists dealing with agendas do not appreciate; rather it is highlighting points, some of which are discussed as possibilities in the US system, as having much greater importance outside the USA for telling the story of how policies come into existence.

What is the significance of executive dominance in a party system for the agenda model? Executive dominance does not mean that interest groups are powerless, that governments do not come to rely on the advice and suggestions of such groups, or that individual members of legislatures never develop significant policy initiatives or propose private members' legislation in much the same way as the US agenda literature suggests (see Richardson and Jordan 1979). Rather it means that for the most part those seeking to influence policies, and above all agendas, have to convince one audience above all which has disproportionate influence on the policy process: the political members of the core executive. In some polities the system of policy development has a degree of hierarchy within it that, while not absent in the USA, is entirely routine in most European countries. As Rose (1980, 305) put it in a slightly different context, in European countries there is both government and subgovernment, in the United States there is subgovernment without government (see also Heclo 1978; Truman 1971). Once executive-dominated governments are committed to agendas, they have the constitutional and political capacity to stick with them. They can *commit* to courses of action. Indeed, once commitments have been made in such systems it can be hard to stop the momentum they generate.

The greater potential for hierarchical structuring of the policy process in systems outside the USA means that governments are more easily able to make general commitments that shape a range of policies—from the commitment to a meta-agenda of broad approaches they seek to develop (albeit that they may face severe political opposition such as in the case of "Agenda 2010" in Germany or "Agenda 2006" in France) to the micro-detail of how clauses within legislation are structured and those delivering the policies are instructed to go about their work (as, for example, with the ability of UK Ministers to instruct immigration officials to interpret regulations in a particular way). Thus in such systems it is important to examine the origins of policy in venues somewhat removed from legislative policy making, the focus of US accounts of agendas. This chapter sets out four levels of abstraction and discusses how policies can emerge at each level, and each level has distinctive characteristics.

## 2. Clarifying the Differences in Policy Origins

One of the basic problems involved in setting out the origins of policy is that we do not know precisely what a policy is. The term "policy" can refer to a constructed unity imposed on diverse and disparate measures—we may look at the totality of measures on, say, education and talk of the "education policy" of a particular country. A book on "education policy" is further unlikely to exclude the institutions that shape and deliver it. Or the term "policy" may refer to a particular law or measure—perhaps even a government circular or some other "soft law" instrument. Even if we insist on defining policy narrowly, as a particular law or other instrument, it is likely that several distinct measures, not even necessarily related, will be bundled together such that the description of it as a policy is dubious—"omnibus" bills in the USA or "portmanteau" bills in the UK combine diverse measures in one law.

As suggested in the introduction to this chapter, policies can be described at a variety of degrees of specificity—any one of Bismarck's social policy laws might be seen itself as a collection of specific measures, as a policy in its own right, or as part of a body of measures and laws that is much larger. To help remove this level of ambiguity about what constitutes a policy it is worth considering what we mean by "policy" (though we must avoid elaborate discussion of the many meanings of the term—for a useful discussion see Hogwood and Gunn 1984, 13 ff.). Policies can be considered as *intentions* or *actions* or more likely a mixture of the two. It is possible for a policy to be simply an intention. The proposals of a party unlikely to gain office or participate in a coalition are "policies" even though they have no chance of being put into action. Moreover, it is possible for a policy to be simply an action or a collection of actions. Where, for example, immigration officials do not look closely at dubious applications for entry into a country we might describe immigration *policy* as "lax."

We can, on this basis, specify four levels of abstraction at which policies can be viewed. Intentions and actions can each be divided into two distinct groupings of things, each of which can be described as "policy." Intentions can be relatively broad. A range of terms can be used to describe intentions. Policy intentions might take the form of *principles*—general views about how public affairs should be arranged or conducted. Candidates for principles might include privatization, deregulation, consumer choice, care in the community, services "free at the point of delivery," or "best available technology." Such principles need not necessarily be easily defined or even coherent, but should be a set of ideas that are capable of application in some form or another to diverse policy topics. Something as broad as an ideology—a body of ideas that incorporate discrete principles—might also be interpreted as an even broader statement of intentions. Notoriously difficult to define in precise terms, we know that ideologies such as socialism are capable of generating an array of different principles—public ownership, the role of party in government, workers' rights, and so on. We can include, albeit at a somewhat different level of aggregation, other ideas that contain bundles of different principles as ideologies: Thatcherism, Reaganomics, New Public Management, and "the Third Way."

The intentions might not be quite so broad—they may refer less to an overarching set of principles or even ideology and more to goals related to the specific issue or problem that a policy seeks to address. Let us call these rather specific intentions "policy lines" since they refer to strategies (or lines) to take in regulating or dealing with particular topics. Typically laws contain several lines. Taking the UK's Adoption and Children Act 2002 as an example, one policy sought to increase the number of potential adoptive parents, another line on "intercountry adoption" addressed the problems posed by lax adoption laws in other countries. Yet another line was to develop registers of adoption agencies, and there were several other distinct lines in this broad law.

When we move to actions, there are also two levels at which we may conceptualize policies. *Measures* are the specific instruments that give effect to distinct policy lines: the legal requirements to be met by people entering the country with children not their own is one measure, inserting a new clause in the law prohibiting homosexuality as a barrier to adoption is another. Measures have attracted some attention in the literature as the tools of government (Hood 1983). They are not invariably laws. "Tools" include financial incentives, forms of exhortation or recommendation, or the direct deployment of public personnel—nodality, authority, treasure, and organization in Hood's (1983) NATO scheme.

*Practices* are the behavior of officials normally expected to carry out policy measures. The term includes implementation in its narrow sense: how officials at ports of entry treat families returning to the UK and how adoption counselors change the way they place children. While this aspect of policy is treated as "implementation" of policy (see Pressman and Wildavsky 1973), practices are not invariably implementation in the sense that they are produced by the measures that seek to give effect to policy. In fact, a large part of the study of implementation looks at how a policy interacts with existing practices within an organization to shape its implementation. Indeed, in the original implementation study, the US Economic Development Administration's general desire to spend its money shaped its plans to spend money aimed at increasing the employment of ethnic groups. Herbert Kaufman's (1960) classic study of the forest ranger highlighted the fact that it was the set of norms and practices of the employees of the forestry service that shaped the character of the service, and these norms were not "implementing" any particular piece of legislation.

# 3. Policy Origins and Levels of Abstraction

## 3.1 Overview

It is possible for the origins of policy to be discussed at each of these four levels of abstraction, and for some policies concentrating on one level offers a more plausible account of policy origins than concentrating on another. While we will examine this proposition in detail, let us outline some initial justification for it. As regards *principle*, we might reasonably say that the range of initiatives adopted in the United States in the area of "workfare" after the 1980s suggests that the origins of policy can be reasonably sought in thought about the relationship between social welfare and the obligations of recipients. Of course, how and why that thought was taken up in federal and state legislation is an important part of the story, but since we are interested in origins, it is reasonable to start with principle as an important part of the origin (King 1999). Much of the work surrounding agenda setting concentrates on the origins of what I have termed *policy lines*—specific sets of intentions relating to a particular issue. Kingdon's (1995) empirical analysis in his seminal book on the subject takes as its base policy lines such as proposals or federal funding of health maintenance organizations or the deregulation of freight transport.

*Measures* might at first appear as unlikely candidates for the origins of policy, but they are in fact common stimuli to developing policy—the specific measures developed in connection with some policies can lead to the development of different policies. This argument was given particular prominence in Wildavsky's (1980, 62–85) elaboration of "policy as its own cause" according to which "policies tend to feed on each other: the more there are, the more there have to be to cope with the new circumstances, effects on other policies and unexpected consequences. New legislative amendments and new administrative regulations become a growth industry as each makes work for the other." Elaborating on Wildavsky's ideas, Hogwood and Peters (1983, 1) argue that true innovation in policy development is rare and that "most policy making is actually policy succession: the replacement of an existing policy, program or organization by another." This is in part a result of the "crowding" of the "policy space," by which they mean that increasing aspects of human interaction have become subject to some form of public policy. In consequence "the problem to be tackled by a 'new' policy proposal may not be the absence of a policy, but problems resulting from existing policies or unforeseen adverse consequences arising from the interaction of different programs" (Hogwood and Peters 1983, 3). Specific measures can initiate new policy lines or measures. The ill-fated poll tax had an impact on the British local government system long after it had gone: "The long term harm done to local government by the poll tax system is not in the poll tax itself, but in the raft of measures that accompanied its rise and fall. Three stand out in particular: the nationalization of the business rate, the enforcement of universal capping of councils' spending and the establishment of the Local Government Commission" (Butler, Adonis, and Travers 1994) which led to the large-scale restructuring of local government. *Practices* may also be origins of policy, not least because the behavior of some officials or politicians can lead to the development of policies aimed at remedying them—the development of affirmative action and gender and minority employment programs can be seen in part as a response to the practices established in personnel recruitment in earlier times.

We may well find all four levels of abstraction as significant parts of the story of many "policies"—Pressman and Wildavsky's (1973) discussion of the Economic Development Administration's program for Oakland explains the policy as a mix of principles, lines, measures, and actions. Moreover, it may be possible to construe almost any "policy" as involving all four levels; for example, increasing the cost of posting letters by 10 per cent might be seen as a reflection of the principle or even ideology that people should pay for services they receive as well as a measure designed to raise income. Yet for the purpose of offering an account of the *origins* of policies it is unlikely that all four levels will be helpful, although it cannot be stated in the abstract what determines how helpful any level or combination will be. Nevertheless, we can point to some distinctive features about each level as regards its role in the origin of policy.

## 3.2 Principles

Principles are generally easy to grasp: privatization, the reduction of the role of the state, the development of choice or even slightly lower-order principles such as the compilation of performance league tables and "naming and shaming" are ideas capable of application to a wide array of contexts and can be enacted in a wide variety of different types of measures. In what ways can principles be the origin of a policy? In many respects we might find that principles themselves are artefacts—*post hoc* labels or rationalizations given to an array of different practices, measures, or policy lines. For example, the development of "privatization" as a general doctrine after 1979 was shaped in the UK in part by the experience of one particular policy line—the sale of council houses—and became a progressively more generalized doctrine. Similarly, "new public management" as a general principle was a name applied to a variety of distinct emerging practices in public sector reform (Pollitt and Bouckaert 2000).

In the origins of policy, principles are particularly powerful as cross-sectoral and cross-national spreaders and generalizers of policy initiatives, possibly more than as actual originators. Cross-sectorally the popularity of policy principles can send powerful signals to policy makers and officials involved in developing policy that policy lines, measures, and practices consistent with such principles have political support. Even the most politically unappealing of policy lines can get additional support through its relationship to a government-supported principle—in Britain the land registration reforms of 2002 built on twenty years of attempts to change the system, but such reforms had found it hard to gain the support necessary to find parliamentary time and resources. The fact that the reform could be linked success-fully to a New Labour theme of "modernization" (mainly through one particular policy line—putting land registration on the Web) was decisive in securing its place on the parliamentary timetable (see Page 2003). The favor with which measures are likely to be met by political leaders can also serve as a powerful cue for officials developing them much lower down in the hierarchy. In my study of delegated legislation in the United Kingdom, I showed how such officials took general signals that "deregulation" was good as cues to develop and shape particular measures to relieve regulatory burdens. While, for example, the gambling industry is often assumed to be a powerful lobby, it was bureaucratic initiative rather than industry pressure that led Customs and Excise to reduce regulatory practices in the 1997 Gaming Duty Regulations (Page 2001, 71).

Borrowing from other jurisdictions is commonly argued to have become more important in recent decades as an explanation of policy origins (see Dolowitz and Marsh 1996 for an overview), and studies of borrowing and related concepts tend to underline the power of principles in the spread of policies. Hintze's (1962/1924, 216) suggestion that the turn of the nineteenth century marked the decisive break after which European countries started consciously to learn from each other might question the timing of this common argument, but it affirms the power of principles and ideas in the process since he goes on to say that the modern development of municipal government, for example, is "strongly, indeed decisively, influenced by theories as they emerged above all in France" among the enlightenment thinkers of the late eighteenth century. More recently Walker's (1969, 882) pioneering study of patterns of innovations in US states shows how *ideas* spread, "not the detailed characteristics of institutions created in each state to implement the policy" (see also Gray 1973; Collier and Messick 1975; for an overview of the "diffusion of innovation" literature see Rogers 2003).

The role of principles in the spread of policies is demonstrated especially strongly in studies of cross-national policy "transfer" or, more accurately, policy learning. As Rose (1993, 2005) shows, lesson drawing in public policy requires a precise under-standing of how a policy works in another jurisdiction, a clear and rigorous defini-tion of the lessons to be drawn, and a "prospective evaluation" of the requirements to make the policy work in the jurisdiction hoping to apply the lesson. Yet studies of cross-national policy borrowing in practice have tended to emphasize the import-ance of "labels" as what travels. Perhaps the clearest illustration of this feature of principles as the source of policy is found in Mossberger's (2000) study of the adoption of UK-style Enterprise Zones (EZs) in the United States. The idea of EZs was to remove taxation and regulatory burdens in particular geographic areas in order to stimulate firms to locate and/or start up there, inspired, in turn, by the notion of "freeports" as found in Hong Kong. What actually emerged in the UK was a system of rather limited tax exemptions and a simplification of regulatory procedures rather than more substantial liberalization. However, this did not prevent the idea attracting lots of attention in the United States and the EZ principle was applied in some form in most US states. But Mossberger found that different states had borrowed not a set of specific measures or even policy lines modeled on UK practice, but diverse sets of initiatives with "wide differences in program designs and goals." The idea of the EZ thus "represented a policy label, because it loosely categorized what was in reality a variety of policy solutions, and because it symbolized state intentions to assist distressed areas" (Mossberger 2000, 128).

Such "labels" are what tend to travel best—zero tolerance policing, workfare programs, "evidence-based policy," and "new public management" are examples of principles that have managed to start governments in one country developing policies that appear to have originated in another. Even the injunctions from international organizations, such as the World Bank, which are argued to have an increasing role in shaping domestic policy, frequently on closer inspection contain broad labels rather than specific measures to be implemented. Walt, Lush, and Ogden (2004) highlight the difficulties for policies framed as anything other than general principles to travel. The Directly Observed Treatment Shortcourse (DOTS) was an effective intervention against tuberculosis. Conscious effort was put into simplifying DOTS as a "one size fits all" set of procedures pushed by the World Health Organization (WHO) that individual countries should adopt. The DOTS strategy was forced to reject the strict adherence to its procedures and became a more general principle of ensuring that drug treatments are administered under observation. The strategy gained greater acceptance once the WHO guidelines were loosened.

Domestically, we would expect principles to play a more consistent role in the development of public policy in systems of party government with a fusion of executive and legislative power, as found in many European countries but notably not in the United States. Certainly, general principles can be found at the heart of policy programmes in the USA since their domestic impact depends to a substantial degree on the ability to mobilize legislative and executive power in support of them. General principles can clearly be found to underpin policy development in the USA—the "New Deal," the "Great Society," and "New Federalism"—as well as in US foreign policy. Moreover, Kingdon's (1995, 9–10) own study shows how agendas (as with deregulation) gain momentum and develop into principles applied to different policy areas. However, themed programmes of domestic legislative and other measures are more easily pursued by governments which, through parties, control the executive and legislative process.

## 3.3 Policy Lines

The development of policy lines is perhaps the level of abstraction for which our knowledge is most extensive, as much discussion of the policy agenda is at this level. The literature on policy agendas tends to present, based on the US example, a highly pluralistic model of how items come to be, from just one of countless issues in the "primeval soup," something that "important people are talking about" (Kingdon 1995). Sometimes agendas might be shaped by routines (such as the budgetary cycle) or by other events very difficult if not impossible for policy makers to alter (such as requirements that laws be re-enacted after a specified time), so here we may concentrate on what Walker (1977) terms the "discretionary" parts of the agenda (see also Hogwood and Gunn 1984, 67). There is substantial agreement on the main features of the process of agenda setting and the things that help account for the creation of policy issues from nonentities. Accounts of agenda setting usually include as a significant variable *the skill of the policy activist or policy entrepreneur* in identifying and exploiting opportunities for a policy. Thus, for example, the US Advisory Committee on Intergovernmental Relations in its mammoth 1980 study of the growth of government identified the "policy entrepreneur" as the main instigator of the growth of the federal role in the federal system. In one of its studies it identifies Senator Magnuson as one of the main reasons for the expansion of the federal involvement in fire prevention and firefighting in two laws in 1968 and 1974 (ACIR 1980, 75).

*The character of the policy area*—its intrinsic ability to engage the interest of wider audiences and publics—is a second variable accounting for the rise of an issue to the policy agenda. As Hogwood and Gunn (1984, 68) argue, features of a problem commonly argued to shape whether a new issue reaches the agenda include, as well as the magnitude of its effects, its "particularity," referring to the degree to which a particular issue stands for a more general problem (in the way that, for example, saving the whale stands for saving the planet from ecological disaster), its emotional appeal (some problems, such as suffering endured by children, are traditionally more promising material from which to create a case for sympathy from publics and policy makers), and the ease with which it can be linked, either in substance or semantically, with other items already on the political agenda (see also Cobb and Elder 1977; see Nelson 1984, 127 for a discussion of child abuse policy and its links with civil rights, welfare rights, and the feminist agenda).

*Chance* and the impact of events is central to many discussions of the political agenda. Downs (1972) goes so far as to place a major event as *the* decisive factor in putting items on the political agenda. His "issue attention cycle" postulates that an issue moves from a *pre-problem stage* which "prevails when some highly undesirable social condition exists but has not yet captured much public attention, even though some experts or interest groups may already be alarmed by it" to *alarmed discovery and euphoric enthusiasm* when:

following some dramatic series of events (like the ghetto riots in 1965 to 1967) or for other reasons, the public suddenly becomes both aware of and alarmed about the evils of a particular problem. This alarmed discovery is invariably accompanied by euphoric enthusiasm about society's ability to "solve this problem" or "do something effective" within a relatively short time. (Downs 1972, 39)

The subsequent stages stress fatalism ("realizing the cost of significant progress," "gradual decline of intense public interest," and "the post-problem stage"), but the model places events as the main method of placing items on the agenda. For Kingdon (1995, 94–100) such events are described as "focusing events" and are not the sole route by which items reach the policy agenda. Moreover he highlights the importance of the skills of the policy activist. However, his memorable analogy of policy activists as surfers with their surfboards at the ready to "ride the big wave" as it comes along (Kingdon 1995, 165) also points to the importance of features, like sea tides and conditions outside the control of individuals, as shaping what hits the political agenda. Ideas, issues, and events mingle to provide opportunities, "windows," for policy action which need to be identified and handled skillfully by anyone who wants to shape public policy.

Such trajectories for policy lines becoming agenda items stress the competitiveness of the process. Chance plays a part, but the skill of entrepreneurs to seize the moment and persuade others, or maneuver their issue into prominence before the moment is lost, is also prominent in such accounts. However they might have to be modified somewhat in political systems where there is a stronger monopoly of political authority as found in systems of party government with a fused legislative and executive power. The United States is one of the few countries with a clear separation of legislative and executive power. Policy entrepreneurship in the USA might be accurately described as mobilizing the support of a diverse and internally differen-tiated legislature as well as executive. Moreover, it is possible to identify similar processes of interest groups struggling to place items on the agenda via contacts with the executive or even through private members' legislation in executive-dominated systems such as the UK (see Norton 1993; Richardson and Jordan 1979; Griffith 1974) or other European countries (see Richardson 1982). Yet entrepreneurship in such fused executive-legislative systems under party government generally means getting the support or acquiescence of leading figures within the governing party—an "executive mentality" permeates the system (Judge 1993, 212). As Mayntz and Scharpf (1975, 136–7) suggest, in Germany interest groups "rarely offer fullfledged program proposals or try to initiate policy. This may not hold for some ... but most interest organizations tend to react to the initiatives or proposals ... rather than tak[e] ... the initiative themselves." In the German "active policy making structure" the federal ministries "are the most important ... policy makers. ... [T]he federal bureaucracy also controls, collects and processes most of the information relevant to policy decisions" (Mayntz and Scharpf 1975, 131). This is not to suggest a monocratic "coordinated" central government. As Hayward and Wright (2002, 272) point out in the case of France, "governing from the centre(s) should not be confused with obsessively integrated government," even though the "core executive" (or as Hay-ward and Wright prefer, "core executives") is the prime arena for the "initiation, agenda-setting and formalization stages of decision making."

If we examine the development of one legislative initiative in the UK—the development of Anti-Social Behaviour Orders (ASBOs)—one can offer an example of a less competitive agenda process of the kind found commonly outside the United States. ASBOs allow courts to require individuals to submit to conditions (such as restricted movement) even though they may not be guilty of a criminal offence. As Burney (2002, 470) describes it, the idea arose from a series of publicized prosecu-tions which "created the paradigm of the neighbourhood blighted and terrorised by the outrageous behaviour of one or two families, groups or individuals, apparently beyond the reach of the law." The issue became Labour policy following a speech by Jack Straw (later to become Home Secretary) to the Labour Party Conference in 1996, and ASBOs were introduced in the Crime and Disorder Act 1998 soon after New Labour was elected in 1997.

In some senses it is possible to see the agenda-setting model in this development: a clear public concern, the activities of several groups (above all the Social Landlords' Crime and Nuisance Group). But this policy was maintained and driven by the party in government to the extent that it is extremely difficult to envisage that any group would be able to mobilize effectively against it. It became anchored, in part, because it reflected a general principle that Labour wanted to project—that New Labour was "tough" on disorder and would no longer "be influenced by 'liberal pressure groups'," but also because the policy line itself had become such an object of commitment within the party that the process of deliberation became exceptionally heavily skewed in support of Labour's stated position:

The headline horrors still dominated the debate: the original cases cited in the Labour Party document of 1995 were recycled in Home Office guidance ... published four years later without any further attempt at assessment of the nature, extent and severity of the kind of behaviour being targeted. Such information as there was came almost entirely from a housing management perspective. (Burney 2002, 472)

Moreover, through the toughening and extension of the system, including through the the Anti Social Behaviour Act 2003, ASBOs and their development can be accurately viewed as primarily a New Labour phenomenon—a desire to use the tool as a means of cracking down on anti-social behaviour—rather than a response to group or any distinct public pressures.

Party government makes the agenda-setting process less competitive in the sense that once a party, or a leading group or individual within it, has become converted to a particular policy, it can retain its importance as the validity of the line as a means of addressing a problem becomes an issue of faith which can take over as the impetus for its development.

## 3.4 Measures

The idea that policies can originate in measures might seem implausible. The form of measures that can initiate a policy discussed in the early part of this section might be interpreted as something of a sleight of hand—"policy as its own cause" refers to policy creating unanticipated problems or consequences that then have to be addressed by other policies. While the initial push that started the policy process rolling might have been the measures passed in pursuit of an earlier policy, the manner in which the issue gets handled may, in fact, be at the level of policy lines, principles, or even ideologies—the "bonfire of controls" or initiatives seeking to rid us of "red tape" on which governments occasionally embark may be stimulated by the accumulated mass of measures generated in the pursuit of diverse policies in the past, but the idea gains momentum primarily as a principle (of reducing regulatory burdens) that governments seek to apply across different policy areas. While measures may be an impetus to policy development elsewhere, in what sense can policies be seen to originate as distinct measures?

Despite recognition that "implementation" can shape policy, the notion that there is some funnel of causality in the development of public policy still obtains when it comes to understanding how the precise measures designed to give effect to the intentions behind policy lines are elaborated: first the broad principles of policy are settled and then the specifics are progressively narrowed down (Hofferbert 1974). Devising the measures to give effect to established policy lines, according to this view, becomes closer to a routine, mechanical even, working through the logical consequences of a policy commitment and translating it into specific laws or other measures and securing the necessary budgetary, manpower, or other resources to carry it through. It is, of course, difficult to find a clear statement that the development of measures—the design and application of tools of government (Hood 1983)—is generally regarded as unimportant. The main justification for stating this is the almost complete absence in the literature on public policy of empirical evidence about how the basic tools of government are used by those whom one might expect to be policy craftsmen and -women (see Page and Jenkins 2005). Between a firm commitment by a government to do something about an issue and the set of specific measures to do it with—laws, guidance, budgetary allocations, and the like—is a huge gap. Policy announcements and the commitments made by politicians are rarely enough on their own to guide the hand of legal drafters and those with similar policy enactment roles. Despite the assumption in some of the US literature, such as the study by Huber and Shipan (2002), that politicians shape legislation in detail, to the extent of deciding how much discretion should be left to the bureaucracy in implementing a law, the evidence suggests that politicians rarely get involved in determining the detail of legislation.

If working out the detail of legislation and the other measures needed to give effect to general commitments about policy lines were routine, we would be unable to say that policy starts life here. What have elsewhere been termed "policy bureaucracies" (Page and Jenkins 2005)—parts of the administrative system (whether attached to the legislative, executive, or judicial branch, or even to non-governmental bodies such as interest or professional organizations) given responsibility, among other things, for giving effect to policies—would at best be finishing shops for policy rather than the design studio. Yet they are not. Since relatively little is known about this aspect of the origins of policy, my examples are confined to the UK, although there is little reason to think that the phenomenon of policy starting life as measures developed by "policy bureaucrats," often relatively junior officials, is entirely a UK phenomenon.

Instructions to policy officials to write legislation and other measures to give effect to policy are almost always vague and require the development of lines of policy to enable them to produce the detailed measures required for a coherent law. Talking of the role of the legal drafters of bills to be presented to Parliament, one UK policy bureaucrat who was giving instructions to the lawyer on the policy to be included in the draft pointed out (Page 2003, 662):

It is common for them to come back with a number of questions on the instructions, to clarify just what it is that the policy aims to achieve. It is by no means uncommon for substantial issues of policy to arise at this stage—often generated by a series of "but what if...?" questions through which either the instructions or the early drafts are tested to destruction (an interesting process, though not always a comfortable one). It is largely for this reason that discussions ... on the draft are frequently more than a straight check that he or she has done what we asked.

To develop policy measures, not only do policy lines have to be clarified, in some contexts they have to be developed for the first time. Fundamental policy line issues can develop from the attempt to develop policy measures. In legislation aimed at civil recovery of criminal assets ("civil forfeiture" in US terminology), the details of the whole legal framework for civil recovery (i.e. how to use the civil courts to take away assets believed to be the proceeds of crime even if there has been no criminal conviction) was left to officials to develop and this involved selectively borrowing from practices in Ireland and South Africa, among other places. Deciding the range of assets that could be recovered was one major policy question. As an official involved put it:

We had a broad scheme but we had to make sure that it exempted some things we wanted it to exempt. Crown Property could be by some quirk a part of crime property. We had to think about pensions and pension funds—could they be ransacked for proceeds of crime? These were hugely complex questions. (quoted in Page 2003, 662)

The question of what types of property and assets could be seized required the development of distinct lines of policy as officials sought to devise ways of making the idea of civil forfeiture work.

Indeed the origins of this same piece of legislation, the Proceeds of Crime Act 2002, are to be found in policy officials seeking to develop measures for making earlier legislation on the seizure of criminal assets work (see Page 2003). Developing measures for earlier policy lines can lead to the initiation of other lines. The law started life in 1998 within the Home Office as the Third Report of the Working Group on Confiscation. Some of the officials working on this report recognized that new legislation was needed if the government's intentions of using civil procedures to seize assets were to be achievable. The initiative gained political momentum not least because it was subsequently taken up as a priority by the policy unit close to the Prime Minister (the Performance and Innovation Unit, the report of which was partly written by two of the Home Office officials who had served on the original Working Group and later on the team writing the legislation). The issue, though it started life as the work of policy bureaucrats seeking to develop measures to give effect to a particular policy line, also featured in Labour's 2001 election manifesto.

## 3.5 Activities: Policies without Agendas

The notion of an "agenda" implies that issues are to be subjected to some form of deliberation. However it is possible for policies to be in place without ever being consciously deliberated on. One traditional version of this form of policy is the "non-decision" in the formulation of Bachrach and Baratz (1962). It is quite possible that unconscious (or at least unremarked on) inaction is a form of policy making—the classic case here is Gary, Indiana's failure to introduce pollution legislation despite the high levels of air pollution identified in Crenson's (1971) landmark study *The Un-Politics of Air Pollution*. The cause of this "un-policy" was, according to Crenson, the corporate power of US Steel, a dominant employer in the town, which managed to keep clean air laws off the political agenda. The central problem with this argument is empirical rather than theoretical. The range of items that could potentially be on the political agenda is to all intents and purposes infinite. Determining whether an item is not on the agenda because someone *kept* it off or because it was just one of the multitude that never makes it on to the agenda is difficult, if even possible. As Polsby (1980) shows, Bachrach and Baratz, having raised the issue, went on to demonstrate the issue was incapable of empirical study because once an issue is directly observable as a proposal, failing or refusing to discuss it may be a successful method of opposing something, but it is not a non-decision. Although Crenson's inventive study offers strong circumstantial evidence of a non-decision, by its very nature a non-decision is not directly susceptible to observation. Nevertheless, we must be sensitive to the possibility that items never reach political agendas because of the real or anticipated power of an individual or a group.

Yet "non-policies" are not the only form of policies without agendas. It is also possible to observe policy that has passed through very limited or virtually no deliberative processes because of the absence of any focused discussion as implied in the metaphor of the agenda. If being on the "agenda" of public policy means, at least in part, being subject to deliberation by the formal legislative, executive, and judicial authorities which give public policy programmes legitimacy, it seems hard to envisage public policy which does not pass through an agenda. Nevertheless, such policies exist, especially those shaped by "street level bureaucrats" (Lipsky 1980), including social workers and police officers, who have a degree of discretion in how they carry out their functions. Such policy-shaping activities have been discussed in the US urban literature as "bureaucratic decision rules." Mladenka (1989) points to research indicating that biases in public services can reflect the largely unchallenged norms by which service providers deliver them. For example, library professionals take data on circulation rates as indicators of "need" for their service. Thus larger circulations are taken to mean that demand and therefore "need" is high, and this norm can result in higher financial and staff resources, and more libraries, going to wealthier areas. "First come first served," "oiling the squeaky wheel," and "meeting demand" are further examples of decision rules which have had distributional consequences for urban services. Mladenka's (1989) own research included an examination of how park and recreation services were allocated in Chicago. The city sought to avoid continuing the practices that had allocated disproportionately better services to white neighborhoods by the city's Planning Committee prioritizing neighbourhoods on bases other than demand and putting greater emphasis on regenerating declining areas. Yet the decisions taken in practice largely ignored the prioritization:

On what basis does deviance from the Planning Committee's recommendations occur? Interviews with the superintendent [of the Parks department] did not produce satisfactory answers and justifications were generally vague. When asked why a low-ranked facility was built before one given higher priority, the answer was apt to be "in our judgement that neighbourhood was in most need" or "that area had been without a fieldhouse [sports changing room] for years and was entitled to one". The fact that the Planning Committee's recommendations were based on need factors and levels of existing facilities is ignored when such responses are given. (Mladenka 1989, 576)

The MacPherson Report on the murder of Stephen Lawrence, for example, found "institutional racism" in London's police force and took pains to separate this from any individual racism of members of the Metropolitan Police. Institutional racism was:

The collective failure of an organisation to provide an appropriate and professional service to people because of their colour, culture, or ethnic origin. It can be seen or detected in processes, attitudes and behaviour which amount to discrimination through unwitting prejudice, ignorance, thoughtlessness and racist stereotyping which disadvantage minority ethnic people. (MacPherson 1999, 6.34)

Thus the issue of race in public policy not only shaped the handling of the specific murder case but was also reflected in the way policy was delivered more generally as reflected in, to give two examples cited by MacPherson (1999, 6.45), the ethnic disparity in "stop and search figures" and the under-reporting of "racial incidents."

The idea that activities can be sources of policy is not simply confined to the issue of street-level bureaucracy: It is also possible for higher-level officials and politicians to approve arrangements without debate. A particularly striking instance of policy without agendas can be found in Moran's (2003) elaboration of "club regulation" that emerged in the United Kingdom in the nineteenth century and remained an important mode of governance until the 1960s. "Club regulation" took the form of an elite acquiescence in allowing a large amount of self-regulation, with a light touch by regulatory institutions and legal instruments in issues ranging from factory safety through financial transactions to sport. "Club regulation" in part fits the model of "non-decisions" since it helps explain why other forms of regulation never developed. Moran (2003, 64) argues that, "The rise to hegemonic status of a mandarin, club culture—is connected to one of the great mysteries of the original Victorian regulatory system," that of why despite the early use of independent regulatory commissions they withered away. There developed no widespread use of "powerful regulatory agencies that came to characterize the American regulatory state in the twentieth century." Moran does not have to look far for the main culprit: "Fundamentally what destroyed them was the power of traditional constitutional ideologies, notably those that insisted on the central department with a ministerial head, as the only proper way of organizing public regulation."

# 4. CONCLUSIONS

There is no simple answer to the question of where policies come from. The best we can do is indicate the proximate events leading to the authorization or other form of adoption of policies. Since the procedures leading to authorization and adoption are, at least to a substantial degree, usually institutionally defined, it is not possible to regard the origins of policy in the same way that we might consider the origin of the species in biology as following the same logic or rules whatever the jurisdiction. This chapter has concentrated on outlining the ways that policies can emerge in systems which do not share the basic contours of the US pattern of government. In particular, it suggests that the possibilities for executive dominance of the policy process mean that different kinds of policy origins are more apparent outside the USA than they are in the US-dominated literature on the subject.

To point out the system-specific characteristics of theoretical approaches that have tended to dominate thinking about public policy outside that system is not to criticize them. Rather, it is closer to a criticism of the attempt to adopt them with little systematic adaptation to different kinds of political systems which lack the constitutional, institutional, and political features that underpin them on their native soil. Such criticisms may be extended to a wider range of theoretical approaches, past and current, which have tended to downplay the possibilities for hierarchy introduced by the fused executive-legislative systems dominated by party government characteristic of European government. Thus the "policy communities" of European nations cannot resemble the "issue networks" of US experience from which they have been borrowed (a point raised by Jordan 1981 and Rhodes 1997 among others); "corporatism" in the 1980s sought to extend experiences of some continental European systems prior to the 1960s (including Italy, Austria, and Sweden) with traditions of tripartite bargaining between labour, capital, and government to systems which had never had them (see, for example, Rhodes 1986), and the "community power debate" of the 1960s and early 1970s eventually discovered that the question of "who governs?" could not be posed in quite the same way in Britain as in the USA since the answer was obvious—the institutional leaders of municipal government (Newton 1975). Contemporary theories of delegation and principal–agent relations, with the baggage of legislative influence that seems to be imported along with them, might also be candidates for ideas that are probably more interesting in the US context and in need of substantially more sophisticated adaptation to European conditions than they are subjected to generally.

The recognition that such theories cannot be easily applied outside the USA is quite commonplace, but theoretical frameworks that incorporate hierarchy as a systemic feature—with hierarchy as the central reason why such theories cannot be directly applied in systems with fused executive-legislative branches under conditions of party government—have not generally tended to follow. Instead, theories of policy making tend to treat hierarchy as a variable—something that applies to some sectors or circumstances and not to others, rather than a core systemic feature of government. The central point about systemic hierarchy is not, however, that it is constantly applied, but that it can be *applied at all.* Its presence shapes how decisions are made, whether it is directly exercised or applied or not.

Knowing that governments can, with a secure majority in Parliament, ensure that their proposals can be put into law, whether or not other organized interests oppose them, shapes the strategies and expectations of these groups—Finer (1966, 28–9) for example noted the tendency for group representatives "to be turned into an agency of government administration" by close involvement with government ministries. There is also evidence that interest groups in the UK have relatively low expectations of what they might achieve through their contact with government (Page 2001, 154). The importance of the executive in policy making in such systems also places an emphasis on understanding *intra*-executive processes of government that has generated remarkably little research. While we may know something (albeit often on the basis of dated information—see Aberbach, Putnam, and Rockman 1981) about the people at the top of the executive, we have little on the executive at work and few systematic examinations of the norms and procedures of policy making within the executive comparable with Kingdon's (1995) rich analysis of policy making in the USA. How ministerial agendas are developed, how such agendas are communicated to officials who develop ministries, agencies, departments, and such like what is the role of the officials in developing them, what cues they rely upon, and how partisan priorities impinge on routine policy making, are almost *terra incognita* in the European study of public policy. Studies of executive organizations tend to treat ministries, agencies, departments, and such like as single bodies which develop policies rather than internally differentiated complexes in which bureaucratic norms and procedures, as well as bureaucratic politics, shape what they do.

The origins of public policy are a clear example of this lack of a theoretical framework that recognizes the constitutional peculiarity of the US system, above all by developing the central role played by the executive in the process in other countries. In such systems more attention needs to be paid to the origins of policy, even the proximate origins of policy, in processes somewhat removed from the legislative process that serves as the central arena for Kingdon's (1995) study— whether at the level of principles and ideology or in developing policy lines and measures. The pluralistic agenda-setting models of the USA direct attention away from the rather different process of getting policies started which often has as its focus processes internal to the executive. Curiously, a clearer elaboration of the theoretical and empirical consequences of executive dominance in the policy process offers the possibility of helping explain the more hierarchical, but less studied features of the US system. The secondary legislative process of "administrative regulation" has for some time in the United States been regarded as an important, if understudied feature of the system (see West 1995). Yet while it was generally defined as yet another adjunct to the pluralistic fragmentation of the American policy-making process, where groups that lose out in shaping congressional deliberation can seek to influence the administrative regulations (Lowi 1969), there is increasing appreciation that administrative regulation can offer US executive agencies something like the sort of latitude available to bureaucracies in more hierarchical systems when it comes to shaping, even initiating policies. So, for a change, US political science can learn from studies of European policy processes.

# REFERENCES

ABERBACH, J. D., PUTNAM, R. D., and ROCKMAN, B. A. 1981. *Bureaucrats and Politicians in Western Democracies*. Cambridge, Mass.: Harvard University Press.

US ADVISORY COMMISSION ON INTERGOVERNMENTAL RELATIONS (ACIR) 1980. *The Federal Role in Local Fire Protection, Commission Report A-85*. Washington, DC: Government Printing Office. Available at: www.library.unt.edu/gpo/acir/Reports/policy/A-85.pdf (accessed Dec. 2004).

BACHRACH, P., and BARATZ, M. 1962. Two faces of power. *American Political Science Review*, 56 (4): 947–52.

BAUMGARTNER, F. R., and JONES, B. D. 1993. *Agendas and Instability in American Politics*. Chicago: University of Chicago Press.

BENDOR, J., MOE, T., and SHOTTS, K. 2001. Recycling the garbage can. *American Political Science Review*, 95 (1): 169–90.

BURNEY, E. 2002. Talking tough, acting coy: what happened to the Anti-Social Behaviour Order? *Howard Journal of Criminal Justice*, 41 (5): 469–84.

BUTLER, D. E., ADONIS, A., and TRAVERS, T. 1994. *Failure in British Government: The Politics of the Poll Tax*. Oxford: Oxford University Press.

COBB, R. W., and ELDER, C. D. 1977. *Participation in American Politics: The Dynamics of Agenda-Building*. Baltimore: Johns Hopkins University Press.

COHEN, M. D., MARCH, J. G., and OLSEN, J. P. 1972. A garbage can model of organizational choice. *Administrative Science Quarterly*, 17: 1–25.

COLLIER, D., and MESSICK, R. 1975. Prerequisites versus diffusion: testing alternative explanations of social security adoption. *American Political Science Review*, 69: 1296–315.

CRENSON, M. 1971. *The Un-Politics of Air Pollution: A Study of Non-Decision Making in the Cities*. Baltimore: Johns Hopkins University Press.

DAWSON, W. H. 1912. *Social Insurance in Germany, 1883–1911: Its History, Operation, Results and a Comparison with the National Insurance Act, 1911*. London: Unwin.

DOLOWITZ, D., and MARSH, D. 1996. Who learns from whom: a review of the policy transfer literature. *Political Studies*, 44 (2): 343–57.

DOWNS, A. 1972. Ups and downs with ecology: the issue-attention cycle. *Public Interest*, 28 (Summer): 38–50.

FINER, S. E. 1966. *Anonymous Empire: A Study of the Lobby in Great Britain*. London: Pall Mall Press.

GRAY, V. 1973. Innovation in the states: a diffusion study. *American Political Science Review*, 67 (4): 1174–85.

GRIFFITH, J. A. G. 1974. *Parliamentary Scrutiny of Government Bills*. London: Allen and Unwin.

HAYWARD, J., and WRIGHT, V. 2002. *Governing from the Centre: Core Executive Coordination in France*. Oxford: Oxford University Press.

HECLO, H. 1978. Issue networks and the executive establishment. Pp. 87–124 in *The New American Political System*, ed. A. King. Washington, DC: American Enterprise Institute.

HEIDENHEIMER, A. J., HECLO, H., and ADAMS, C. T. 1990. *Comparative Public Policy: The Politics of Social Choice in America, Europe, and Japan*, 3rd edn. New York: St Martin's Press.

HINTZE, O. 1962/1924. Staatenbildung und Kommunalverwaltung. Pp. 216–41 in *Staat und Verfassung: Gesammelte Abhandlungen zur allgemeinen Verfassungsgeschichte*. Tübingen: Vandenhoeck and Ruprecht.

HOFFERBERT, R. I. 1974. *The Study of Public Policy*. Indianapolis: Bobbs-Merrill.

Hogwood, B. W., and Gunn, L. A. 1984. *Policy Analysis for the Real World*. Oxford: Oxford University Press.

—— and Peters, B. G. 1983. *Policy Dynamics*. Brighton: Wheatsheaf Books.

Hood, C. 1983. *The Tools of Government*. London: Macmillan.

Huber, J. D., and Shipan, C. R. 2002. *Deliberate Discretion? The Institutional Foundations of Bureaucratic Autonomy*. Cambridge: Cambridge University Press.

Jordan, A. G. 1981. Iron triangles, woolly corporatism and elastic nets: images of the policy process. *Journal of Public Policy*, 1 (1): 95–123.

Judge, D. 1993. *The Parliamentary State*. London: Sage.

Kaufman, H. 1960. *The Forest Ranger: A Study in Administrative Behaviour*. Baltimore: Johns Hopkins University Press.

King, D. 1999. *In the Name of Liberalism: Illiberal Social Policy in the USA and Britain*. Oxford: Oxford University Press.

Kingdon, J. W. 1995. *Agendas, Alternatives, and Public Policies*, 2nd edn. New York: Harper Collins.

Lipsky, M. 1980. *Street Level Bureaucracy: The Dilemmas of Individuals in Public Services*. New York: Russell Sage Foundation.

Lowi, T. J. 1969. *The End of Liberalism*. New York: Norton.

MacPherson, S. W. 1999. *The Stephen Lawrence Inquiry: Report of an Inquiry by Sir William Macpherson of Cluny*. Cm 4262–1. London: HMSO, Feb.

Mayntz, R., and Scharpf, F. W. 1975. *Policy-Making in the German Federal Bureaucracy*. Amsterdam: Elsevier.

Mladenka, K. R. 1989. The distribution of an urban public service: the changing role of race and politics. *Urban Affairs Quarterly*, 24: 556–83.

Moore, B. 1967. *Social Origins of Dictatorship and Democracy: Lord and Peasant in the Making of the Modern World*. London: Allen Lane, the Penguin Press.

Moran, M. 2003. *The British Regulatory State High Modernism and Hyper-Innovation*. Oxford: Oxford University Press.

Mossberger, K. 2000. *The Politics of Ideas and the Spread of Enterprise Zones*. Washington, DC: Georgetown University Press.

Nelson, B. J. 1984. *Making an Issue of Child Abuse: Political Agenda Setting for Social Problems*. Chicago: University of Chicago Press.

Newton, K. 1975. Community politics and decision-making: the American experience and its lessons. Pp. 1–24 in *Essays on the Study of Urban Politics*, ed. K. Young. London: Macmillan.

Norton, P. 1993. *Does Parliament Matter?* London: Harvester Wheatsheaf.

Oakeshott, M. 1933. *Experience and its Modes*. Cambridge: Cambridge University Press.

Page, E. C. 2001. *Governing by Numbers: Delegated Legislation and Everyday Policy Making*. Oxford: Hart.

—— 2003. The civil servant as legislator: law making in British administration. *Public Administration*, 81 (4): 651–79.

—— and Jenkins, B. 2005. *Policy Bureaucracy: Government with a Cast of Thousands*. Oxford: Oxford University Press.

Pollitt, C., and Bouckaert, G. 2000. *Public Management Reform: A Comparative Analysis*. Oxford: Oxford University Press.

Polsby, N. 1980. Empirical investigation of the mobilization of bias in community power research. *Political Studies*, 27: 527–41.

Pressman, J. L., and Wildavsky, A. B. 1973. *Implementation: How Great Expectations in Washington are Dashed in Oakland: or, Why It's Amazing that Federal Programs Work at All,*

*This Being a Saga of the Economic Development Administration as Told by Two Sympathetic Observers Who Seek to Build Morals on a Foundation of Ruined Hopes*. Berkeley: University of California Press.

RHODES, R. A. W. 1986. *The National World of Local Government*. London: Allen and Unwin.

—— 1997. *Understanding Governance: Policy Networks, Governance, Reflexivity and Accountability*. Milton Keynes: Open University Press.

RICHARDSON, J. J. (ed.) 1982. *Policy Styles in Western Europe*. London: Allen and Unwin.

—— and JORDAN, A. G. 1979. *Governing under Pressure: Government in a Post-Parliamentary Democracy*. Oxford: Robertson.

ROGERS, E. M. 2003. *The Diffusion of Innovations*, 5th edn. New York: Free Press.

ROSE, R. 1980. Governments against subgovernments: a European perspective on Washington. Pp. 284–347 in *Presidents and Prime Ministers*, ed. R. Rose and E. N. Suleiman. Washington, DC: American Enterprise Institute.

—— 1993. *Lesson Drawing in Public Policy*. Chatham, NJ: Chatham House.

—— 2005. *Learning from Comparative Public Policy: A Practical Guide*. London: Routledge.

TAMPKE, J. 1981. Bismarck's social legislation: a genuine breakthrough? Pp. 71–83 in *The Emergence of the Welfare State in Britain and Germany, 1850–1950*, ed. W. J. Mommsen. London: Croom Helm.

TRUMAN, D. 1971. *The Governmental Process*, 2nd edn. New York: A. A. Knopf.

WALKER, J. L. 1969. The diffusion of innovations among the American states. *American Political Science Review*, 63 (3): 880–99.

—— 1977. Setting the agenda in the US Senate: a theory of problem selection. *British Journal of Political Science*, 7 (4): 423–46.

WALT, G., LUSH, L., and OGDEN, J. 2004. International organizations in transfer of infectious diseases: iterative loops of adoption, adaptation, and marketing. *Governance*, 17 (2): 189–210.

WEST, W. F. 1995. *Controlling the Bureaucracy: Institutional Constraints in Theory and Practice*. Armonk, NY: M. E. Sharpe.

WILDAVSKY, A. B. 1980. Policy as its own cause. Pp. 62–85 in *Policy: The Art and Craft of Policy Analysis*. London: Macmillan.

# CHAPTER 11

# AGENDA SETTING

## GIANDOMENICO MAJONE

THE essence of decision, President John F. Kennedy once observed, remains impenetrable to the observer, often even to the decider himself. This is probably the reason why positive theories of policy making focus on pre- and post-decision processes rather than on the actual moment of choice. Implementation, policy evaluation, learning, and policy dynamics are among the best-researched areas of post-decision analysis. Problem definition, agenda setting, and feasibility analysis are the main, closely interrelated components of pre-decision analysis. Objective conditions are seldom so compelling or unambiguous that they determine the policy agenda. Hence, knowing how a problem has been defined is essential to understanding the process of agenda formation. The purpose of feasibility analysis is to identify the constraints—economic, technological, political, and institutional—that delimit the space of feasible choices. The student of agenda setting attempts to trace the causal paths along which public issues travel, and to predict which issues may eventually reach the decision agenda. A policy idea that fails to meet the feasibility criterion is unlikely to be considered as a serious contender for a place on the public agenda. Methodological differences should not be overlooked, however. Feasibility analysis has a reasonably clear logical structure, and can rely on the theoretical support of well-developed disciplines like decision theory, microeconomics, and modern political economy. In the case of agenda setting, no generally accepted paradigm exists. Even the best-known models are rather ad hoc, largely descriptive, and cover only some aspects of what one could reasonably assume to be part of agenda setting. Because of this methodological deficit, the present treatment is less concerned with those parts of the process that are fairly well understood—such as the role of interest groups, and of political and policy entrepreneurs, or the importance of issue coalitions—than with aspects which have received insufficient attention, or have been largely ignored by the available literature. The hope is that extending the scope of agenda-setting analysis may stimulate the development of a more rigorous approach to this crucially important component of policy analysis.

The chapter is organized as follows. Section 1 discusses the possibility that some individual or institution may hold exclusive power over the agenda—a possibility largely overlooked by analysts outside the rational choice framework. Under rather general conditions, a monopoly agenda setter can achieve almost any desired result. That this is more than a theoretical possibility is shown by the control over legislative proposals exercised by committees of the US Congress, and by the monopoly of policy initiation enjoyed by the Commission of the European Union. Section 2 emphasizes the links between the study of agenda setting and democratic theory. It is suggested that the analyst can find in the literature on the democratic process valuable insights into the dynamics of agenda setting. Two examples are the notion of non-decision, and the model of government by discussion. Another topic discussed in this section is the possibility of ensuring effective democratic control of the agenda of regulatory agencies by means of suitable procedures The next section addresses another issue not sufficiently researched by students of agenda setting: the selection of priorities within the decision agenda. The problem is particularly important in risk regulation, where setting the wrong priorities may entail severe opportunity costs—the number of lives that could have been saved by using the same resources in a different way. The significant risk doctrine, developed by American courts in the 1980s, has played a key role in forcing agencies to prioritize their agenda, and also in favoring the systematic use of risk analysis. The concluding Section 4 emphasizes the growing impact of international factors on the formation of national agendas. There is little empirical evidence that growing economic integration entails a restriction of the agenda of democratic states because of the declining ability of policy makers to produce the public goods people demand. Actually, international pressures may improve the quality of the national agenda. The threat of economic retaliation in cases of serious violations of basic rights, for example, shows that international trade may be used to push the agenda of authoritarian states in a more humanitarian direction.

# 1. Agenda Control

One topic which has not received sufficiently attention by policy analysts is the possibility that some individual or institution may hold exclusive power over the agenda. One of the central results of the analysis of political institutions in a rational choice perspective, the McKelvey–Schofield "chaos theorem," has direct and far-reaching implications for the study of agenda control—a subject which was neither well understood nor frequently studied prior to the publication of this theorem. McKelvey (1976) and Schofield (1976) showed that the absence of a majority-rule equilibrium implies that virtually any policy outcome is possible. Hence, those who control the agenda can engage in all sorts of manipulations. A monopoly agenda setter can achieve almost any outcome she wishes, provided she can appropriately order the sequencing of paired options considered by the voting group operating under majority rule (Shepsle 1979). These results have been exploited to examine the impact of rules and procedures on policy making; to account for the political power of parliamentary leaders, who control the sequence and order of legislative deliberations; and to explain the power of legislative committees (Bates 1990). As noted above, students of agenda setting have largely neglected agenda control, yet no sharp dividing line can be drawn between manipulating and shaping the agenda. Only by paying attention to both aspects of agenda setting can we hope to understand how policy is made or, perhaps even more important, why certain issues never appear on the public agenda.

The importance of agenda control can be grasped intuitively in a simplified situation. Barry Weingast (1996) presents a one-dimensional (single issue) version of the median voter theorem. He supposes that any alternative may be proposed, and that individuals wishing to offer proposals are recognized randomly. Each proposal is pitted in a majority vote against the status quo. The process continues until no more proposals are offered. Elementary geometrical considerations show that the only stable alternative to result from the voting is the median voter's ideal policy. But suppose that an individual (or organization or committee) called the "setter" has monopoly power over the agenda. The setter chooses a proposal, and then the voters vote for either the proposal or the status quo, Q. Now the setter's institutionalized power results in an outcome different from the median voter's ideal policy—unless the setter's ideal policy happens to coincide with that of the median voter. All she has to do is propose the policy that she most prefers from the 'win set' of Q—the set of policy alternatives that command a majority against Q. The full power of agenda control, however, is best appreciated in more complicated, and more realistic, situations. I will briefly mention two examples: the committees of the US Congress; and the monopoly of legislative initiative enjoyed by the Commission of the European Union.

According to the model of an idealized legislative committee system developed by Weingast and Marshall (1988), each congressional committee has jurisdiction over a specific subset of policy issues. Within their jurisdiction, committees possess the monopoly right to bring alternatives to the status quo up for a vote before the legislature; and committee proposals must command a majority of votes against the status quo to become public policy. The agenda power held by committee members implies that successful coalitions must include the members of the relevant committee. Without these members, the bill will not reach the floor for a vote. Thus committee veto power means that, from among the set of policies that command a majority against the status quo, only those that make the committee better off are possible. The ability to veto the proposals of others is a powerful tool used by committees to influence policy in their jurisdiction. According to Weingast and

Marshall, institutionalizing control over the congressional agenda—over the design and selection of proposals that arise for a vote—provides durability and enforceability of bargains in a legislative setting.

The European Union (EU) offers another striking example of agenda control. The European Commission is usually considered the executive branch of the EU, but in fact it plays a very important role also in the legislative process because of its monopoly of policy initiation. This monopoly has been granted by the founding Treaty and is carefully protected by the European Court of Justice. Hence, no national government can induce the Commission to make a specific proposal changing the status quo, unless that proposal also makes the Commission better off. Such tight control of the policy agenda has no analogue either in parliamentary or in presidential democracies. In parliamentary systems, legislators introduce relatively few bills; most legislative proposals are instead presented by bureaucrats to the cabinet, which then introduces them as draft legislation to the parliament. Once legislators receive such proposals, however, they are free to change or reject them. This is not the case in the EU, where as a rule the main legislative body (the Council of Ministers) may modify Commission proposals only under the stringent requirement of unanimity. In the separation-of-powers system of the United States, not only do legislators have the final word over the form and content of bills, but, further, only legislators can introduce bills. In the course of a typical congressional term, members of Congress will introduce several hundred bills on behalf of the president or of executive-branch agencies. During the same period, however, members of Congress will introduce on their own behalf as many as 15,000 or 20,000 bills (McCubbins and Noble 1995).

It is important to understand clearly what is implied by the Commission's monopoly of agenda setting. First, other European institutions cannot legislate in the absence of a prior proposal from the Commission. It is up to this institution to decide whether the EU should act and, if so, in what legal form, and what content and implementing procedures should be followed. Second, the Commission can amend its proposal at any time while it is under discussion in the Council of Ministers, while, as just mentioned, the Council can amend the proposal only by unanimity. Thus if the Council unanimously wishes to adopt a measure which differs from the Commission's proposal, the latter can deprive the legislative branch (the Council of Ministers and European Parliament) of its power of decision by withdrawing its proposal. Finally, neither the Council nor the Parliament nor a member state can compel the Commission to submit a proposal, except in those few cases where the EU Treaty imposes an obligation to legislate. To understand the rationale of this sweeping delegation of agenda control to a bureaucratic body, one has to keep in the mind that in the constitutional architecture of the EU, the Council of Ministers represents the national interests of the member states, while the Commission is supposed to represent the supranational interests of the Union. If also the Council had the right to initiate legislation, it could turn back the clock of European integration for domestic political reasons. In other words, the Commission's control of the legislative and policy agenda serves the purpose of enhancing the credibility of the member states' commitment to the cause of European integration (Majone 1996*b*). In this as in other cases, precommitment is achieved by preventing the final decision makers from engaging in "issue creation." Thus in both cases—the US Congress and the European Union—agenda control turns out to be crucial for understanding policy outputs.

# 2. AGENDA SETTING AND DEMOCRATIC THEORY

Few topics of public policy analysis are more closely linked to the theory and practice of representative democracy than agenda setting and agenda control. Thus, Robert Dahl's normative criterion of a full democratic process is based on the idea of final control of the agenda by the people: "The demos must have the exclusive opportunity to decide how matters are to be placed on the agenda of matters that are to be decided by means of the democratic process" (Dahl 1989, 113). Because of the normative significance of agenda control, one finds valuable insights on our subject in works dealing with the functioning and effects of democratic institutions. A well-known example is the contribution of Bachrach and Baratz (1963) to the problem of non-decisions. The essential insight of the work of these authors was that the power to keep something off the governmental agenda is as important as the power to choose among the few policy options that make the agenda. According to Bachrach and Baratz, economic elites are powerful not because they affect the final choices in government but because they guarantee that these choices are between almost indistinguishable alternatives. It should be noted, however, that also ordinary citizens can keep items off the decision agenda. Thus, legislators often avoid considering specific policy options because they fear retribution by the voters. For example, throughout the 1970s the US Congress refused to consider imposing a high gasoline tax, despite evidence that it would be the least intrusive method for curbing demand for imported oil. Throughout the 1980s, Congress refused to consider any reduction in social security payments for current beneficiaries, despite the massive budget deficit. In these and other cases none of the proposals suggested by the experts made it on to the congressional agenda because legislators believed that the voters would not tolerate the imposition of large and visible costs (Arnold 1990). The same fear of retribution by the voters has induced the German and other European governments to keep necessary welfare reforms off the public agenda for years.

## 2.1 Government by Discussion

Government by discussion—the liberal model of parliamentary democracy—provides another example of the close link between agenda setting and democratic theory. According to this model, as described by Ernest Barker (1958), policy is made through a continuous process of discussion which begins with expressions of general concerns and ends in concrete decisions. Political parties identify issues and formulate programs; the electorate discusses issues and candidates and, after the grand debate of a general election, expresses a majority in favor of one of the programs; the legislative majority translates programs into laws, in constant debate with the opposition; finally, the discussion is carried forward to the cabinet, where it is translated into specific policies. Two principles guide the process through the four stages of discussion: differentiation of function, and the principle of cooperation and interdependence. According to the first principle, each stage has its own organs, specific function, and method of conducting the discussion and bringing it to a conclusion. In the first stage, alternative programs have been formulated by debate in each party. In the second, representatives of the different programs have been selected after debate by the electorate, and authorized by it to form a parliament for further debate, to be conducted in a particular form and for a particular purpose. The purpose of the third, parliamentary, stage is to translate the program endorsed by a majority of the voters into laws, and to control how the executive government transforms general rules of law into a series of particular and separate Acts, which must however be connected to a general program.

The principle of differentiation also implies that each stage is independent in exercising its particular function, but only within limits, and as a part of the entire process of defining the national agenda. The function of political parties must be distinguished from that of the electorate, the functions of both from that of parliament, and the functions of all three from that of the cabinet. However, this differentiation of functions is only one aspect of the process of government by discussion. The other aspect is provided by the principle of cooperation and interdependence. According to this second principle, the different organs and their functions must be interlocked as well as differentiated. Each has to act as part of a system, that is, it has to act with reference to, and in harmony with, the other parts. The balance between differentiation and cooperation is very delicate, and hence it can be maintained only in a polity that shares some basic values and a common political culture (Barker 1958, 57–8).

This is a stylized, normative model of agenda setting and policy making in a democracy. It overlooks the play of power and influence, the uneven distribution of knowledge and manipulation of information, inter-institutional competition and bureaucratic politics, the low level of active citizen participation, the role of the mass media, and a host of other factors that figure prominently in modern theories of agenda setting and policy making. It is also clear that the model has been designed with one particular system in mind: the British political system with its disciplined two-party system, distinctive Parliament–Cabinet relationship, and paradoxical emphasis both on the derivative character of political authority and on its independence from popular preferences. And yet the reader of such works as Cobb and Elder's (1972) *Participation in American Politics* or John Kingdon's (1984) *Agendas, Alternatives and Public Policies* cannot fail to notice striking similarities between the model of government by discussion and these more recent works. If political parties play a more crucial role in Barker's model, this only reflects the realities of the British political system, where policy entrepreneurs are mostly to be found in the political parties or, nowadays, in think tanks closely linked to parties. Similarly, if the process of agenda setting appears to be much less random than, say, in Kingdon's discussion of political and policy windows, this is partly due to the normative character of the model, but especially to the inherent capacity for effective action which is a distinctive characteristic of British government—an effectiveness which no government based on the principle of separation of powers can match.

More important than such differences in emphasis, however, is the basic agreement on the central role of elected officials in the agenda-setting process. Like Barker, Kingdon finds that it is difficult to assign responsibility for the emergence of agenda items solely to interest groups. Rather than structuring the public agenda, interest groups often try to introduce their preferred alternatives once the agenda is already set by some other process or participant. Also the media turn out to be less important than anticipated. They seem to report events rather than having an independent effect on governmental agendas; they can help shape and structure an issue, but they cannot create an issue. Academics, researchers, and consultants affect the alternatives more than the agenda, and affect long-term directions rather than short-term outcomes. The president, his political appointees, and Congress turn out to be central to agenda setting and, with the help of their staffs, also to alternative specification. Kingdon's conclusion that "[t]he model of a democratic government controlled by elected officials is not only our normative idea, but also our dominant picture of empirical reality" (Kingdon 1984, 46) would be fully endorsed by the theorists of government by discussion, from John Stuart Mill to Ernest Barker.

## 2.2 Agenda Setting in the Regulatory State

The modern regulatory state is characterized by an extensive delegation of quasi-legislative powers to independent commissions or agencies. In an increasing number of politically sensitive areas—from telecommunications and public utilities to environmental protection and food safety—policy is made by such non-elected bodies, typically on the basis of a fairly broad legislative mandate. The existing literature on agenda setting has not paid sufficient attention to the implications of delegation of rule-making powers to independent agencies. Kingdon, for example, finds that career civil servants are not particularly important in setting the national agenda, relative to other participants. According to him, "a top-down model of the executive branch seems to be surprisingly accurate. We discovered that the president can dominate his political appointees, and that the appointees can dominate the career civil servants" (Kingdon 1984, 33). However, the independent regulatory commissions and also many single-headed agencies are not, *de jure* or de facto, under the direct control of the president or of his political appointees. Also in Europe, a variety of independent regulatory authorities operate outside the line of ministerial or departmental hierarchy. Whether, or to what extent, legislatures are able to control the agenda of the independent agencies they create is a controversial issue on both sides of the Atlantic. The US Congress, for example, has many means at its disposal to retain influence over agency decisions, but this influence can be offset by presidential opposition, court decisions, or the actions of agency personnel (Bawn 1995).

Until the early 1980s, the thrust of much research on political–bureaucratic relations was that agency bureaucracy has a substantial degree of autonomy in its choice of issues. This autonomy is possible because legislative oversight for purposes of serious policy control is time consuming, costly, and difficult to do well under conditions of uncertainty and cognitive complexity. At any rate, legislators are concerned more with satisfying voters to increase the probability of re-election than with overseeing the bureaucracy they create. As a result, they do not typically invest their scarce resources in general policy control. More recently, however, better theoretical models, largely based on principal–agent theory, and more careful empirical analyses have shown that the variety of control instruments available to political principals is a good deal larger than was previously assumed. This research also threw new light on traditional approaches to the control problem. There are two main forms of control of agency decisions: oversight—monitoring, hearings, investigations, budgetary reviews, sanctions—and procedural constraints. The received view on procedures is that they are primarily a means of assuring fairness and legitimacy in regulatory decision making. This is of course a very important function of procedures, but it has been shown that procedures also serve control purposes.

In an important paper published in 1987, McCubbins, Noll, and Weingast used statutes like the US Administrative Procedure Act (APA) and the Freedom of Information Act (FOIA) as evidence that procedural rules fulfill important control functions, providing cost-effective solutions to problems of non-compliance by agencies. In addition to reducing the informational disadvantage of political executives, stakeholders, and citizens at large, procedures can be designed so as to ensure that the agency's agenda will be responsive to the constituents that the policy is supposed to favor. The procedural requirements under the APA, FOIA, and related statutes reduce an expert agency's discretion in a number of ways. First, agencies cannot present the political principals with a fait accompli. They must announce their intention to consider an issue well in advance of any decision. Second, the notice and comment provisions assure that the agency learns who are the relevant stakeholders, and takes some notice of the distributive impacts associated with various actions. Third, the entire sequence of agency decision making—notice, comment, collection of evidence, and construction of a record in favor of a chosen action—affords numerous opportunities for political principals to respond when the agency seeks to move in a direction that the principals do not approve of. Finally, the broad public participation which the statutes facilitate also works as a gauge of political interest and controversy, providing advance warning about the agency's decision agenda and the likely distributive consequences of agency decisions, in the absence of political intervention.

Moreover, by controlling the extent and mode of public participation, legislators can strengthen the position of the intended beneficiaries of the bargain struck by the enacting coalition. This has been called "deck stacking." Deck stacking enables political actors to cause the environment in which an agency operates to mirror the political forces that gave rise to the agency's legislative mandate, long after the enacting coalition has disbanded. The agency may seek to develop a new clientele for its services, but such an activity must be undertaken in full view of the members of the initial coalition, and following procedures that automatically integrate certain interests in agency decision making. In sum, one important function of procedures is to reduce the risk that the agenda-setting process of regulatory agencies may be captured by interests—whether economic, bureaucratic, or ideological—different from those explicitly acknowledged by the enabling statute. These theoretical insights are supported by a good deal of empirical evidence. In particular, a careful statistical study by Wood and Waterman (1991) of the decisions of seven regulatory agencies from the late 1970s through most of the 1980s found that all seven agencies appeared to be responsive to the preferences of their democratically elected principals. The authors conclude that the evidence for active political control is so strong that controversy should end over whether political control of the regulatory bureaucracy is possible. Instead, research should concentrate on a detailed analysis of the various mechanisms of control.

However, democratic control is only one horn of the dilemma of statutory regulation, the other being the need to preserve the necessary degree of agency discretion. The difficulty of achieving a satisfactory balance is demonstrated by the failure of the American "non-delegation doctrine"—the first attempt to resolve the regulatory dilemma. For several decades this judicial doctrine enjoyed such wide-spread acceptance that it came to be regarded as the traditional model of adminis-trative law. The model conceives of the regulatory agency as a mere transmission belt for implementing legislative directives in particular cases. Hence, when passing statutes Congress should decide all questions of policy and frame its decisions in such specific terms that administrative regulation will not entail the exercise of broad discretion by the regulators (Stewart 1975). The non-delegation doctrine had already found widespread acceptance when the first institutionalization of the American regulatory state, the Interstate Commerce Commission, was established by the 1887 Interstate Commerce Act. The Act, with its detailed grant of authority, seemed to exemplify the transmission-belt model of administrative regulation. However, the subsequent experience of railroad regulation revealed the difficulty of deriving operational guidelines from general standards. By the time the Federal Trade Com-mission was established in 1914, the agency received essentially a blank check author-izing it to eliminate unfair competition. The New Deal agencies received even broader grants of power to regulate particular sectors of the economy "in the public interest." The last time the Supreme Court used the non-delegation doctrine was in 1935, when in *Schechter Poultry* it held the delegation in the National Industrial Recovery Act unconstitutional.

The doctrine against delegation unraveled because the practical case for allowing regulatory discretion is overwhelming. Contrary to Kingdon's findings concerning the limited role of executive-branch bureaucrats in agenda setting, few students of regulation would deny that agencies, in their area of competence, are important participants in the agenda-setting process. For example, the Federal Communications Commission (FCC) began allowing competition to the American Telephone and Telegraph Company (AT&T) in long-distance communications in the late 1950s, several years before pro-competitive deregulation acquired widespread political support in Washington. Also other regulatory commissions played a leading role in the reversal of traditional regulatory policy in America, such as the Civil Aeronautics Board (CAB), the Interstate Commerce Commission (ICC), and the Securities and Exchange Commission (SEC). The CAB not only succeeded in bringing about an almost complete deregulation of the airline industry: even more significantly, its chairman Alfred E. Kahn persuaded Congress to abolish the agency. The ICC did not ask to be abolished, but its staff dropped from 2,000 in 1976 to 1,300 in 1983. Finally, the SEC was a major shaper of the agenda of financial deregulation, especially in securities markets, in the 1970s. In all these cases the chairmen provided powerful leadership in bringing about policy change. This may seem surprising given the collegial nature of the agencies. In fact, after organizational reforms in the 1950s and 1960s, the chairpersons have emerged as the chief executives and dominant figures. As chief executives they expect, and are expected by others, to have a well-defined agenda, and to measure their success by the amount of the agenda they accomplish (Derthick and Quirk 1985, 65).

Perhaps even more surprising was the fact that the staffs of these regulatory commissions actively supported, or at least did not oppose, the pro-deregulation stance of their superiors, even when the consequences of the new policy for the size of the staff and even for the survival of the organization were apparent. It has been suggested that this open-mindedness may be due to the rise of professional policy analysts and regulators, using widely shared standards of argument and problem-solving styles, and to the growing influence of public interest groups, both of which factors balance the influence of bureaucratic ideologies and traditional patterns of behavior. These examples suggest that when American regulators enjoy the support of the courts, of key committees and subcommittees of Congress, and of academic and public opinion, they can be quite important in setting the national agenda, even against the resistance of the regulated industries and of important elements of the executive branch, including the president—for instance, President Reagan as well as the Departments of Defense and Commerce were opposed to the divestiture of AT&T. According to Derthick and Quirk (1985, 91) the regulatory commissions "served as vehicles for converting the disinterested views of experts into public policy, even if the expert views had originated largely as criticisms of their own conduct."

Also in Europe regulators play an increasingly significant role in setting the national agenda in their area of competence (Majone 1996*b*).

## 3. PRIORITIZING THE AGENDA

The systematic study of agenda setting has been greatly facilitated by a number of analytic distinctions, such as that between visible and hidden participants, between agenda setting and alternative specification, or between the governmental agenda and the decision agenda. Another important distinction—between agenda setting and the setting of priorities within a given, or potential, agenda—is the subject of the present section. The significance of the distinction lies in the fact that it may not be good enough for a policy proposal to get onto the decision agenda; even more important is that the proposal should occupy a high position on the agenda. Resource limitations—time, money, personnel, or expertise—usually make it necessary to define priorities within the decision agenda. The notion of priority stems from the commonsense proposition that one should do first things first. From a normative viewpoint, a rational setting of priorities implies that the opportunity costs of alternative proposals are duly taken into account; see below.

Microeconomics has a clear rule for the optimal allocation of resources among different activities: at the margin, the return should be the same across all agenda items. The consistent implementation of this rule in a political–bureaucratic context presents formidable difficulties, but if the stakes are high enough second-best solutions are likely to be found, sooner or later. This may require a good deal of learning about the implications of different criteria and decision rules. That such policy learning is possible is shown by the example of how American courts gradually induced regulators to accept the need for rational priority setting in risk regulation. As already noted in the introduction, a key role in this learning process was played by the "significant risk" doctrine. In order to appreciate the innovative character of this doctrine, however, it is necessary to consider the older approach to risk regulation: the least-feasible-risk criterion.

According to this criterion, human exposure to health risks should be reduced to the lowest possible level. This is a sort of second-best rule. The first-best regulatory policy would be one that ensures a risk-free working and living environment, but because of technical and economic constraints a risk-free environment is unattainable; hence the need of a second-best rule. Thus, Section 6(b)(5) of the 1970 US Occupational Safety and Health Act directs the Occupational Safety and Health Administration (OSHA), in regulating worker exposure to toxic substances, to set standards that "most adequately assure, *to the extent feasible*, ... that no employee will suffer material impairment of health or functional capacity even if such employee has regular exposure to the hazard ... for the period of his working life" (emphasis added). Trade union representatives claimed that this instruction obliged OSHA to mandate the use of whatever available technology an industry could afford without bankrupting itself. Federal courts generally upheld OSHA's standards based on the least-feasible-risk criterion. One striking exception was the benzene standard, which reduced the occupational exposure to this carcinogen from 10 parts per million (ppm) to 1 ppm. In the case *American Petroleum Institute* v. *OSHA* (1978), the Fifth Circuit Court of Appeals held the regulation invalid on the ground that the agency had not shown that the new exposure limit was "reasonably necessary and appropriate to provide safe or healthful employment" as required by the statute. Specifically, the court argued that OSHA had failed to provide substantial evidence that the benefits to be achieved by the stricter standard bore a reasonable relationship to the costs it imposed. The agency, the court reasoned, "must have some factual basis for an estimate of expected benefits before it can determine that a one-half billion dollar standard is reasonably necessary" (cited in Mendeloff 1988, 116–17). What was required was some sort of quantification of benefits as a necessary step to carry out a benefit–cost test of the new standard. Without a quantification of risk, and hence of the expected number of lives saved by the regulation, it is impossible to weigh the benefits against the costs. Unlike other agencies such as the Environmental Protection Agency (EPA) and the Food and Drug Administration (FDA), OSHA had always maintained that quantitative risk analysis is meaningless. OSHA's reluctance to follow the example of the EPA and the FDA reflected trade union pressures, combined with staff preferences for protection to override any interest in the use of more analytic approaches. It was feared that if the agency performed quantitative risk assessments (QRAs), these might be used as a weapon by those who opposed strict standards. On the other hand, an agency like EPA, with a much broader mandate, was aware that not every risk could be reduced to the lowest feasible level.

The Fifth Circuit Court's decision stunned OSHA's leaders, who viewed it as a total challenge to their regulatory philosophy and to their idea of the agency's mission (Mendeloff 1988, 117). They decided to appeal the decision. In *Industrial Union Department (AFL-CIO)* v. *American Petroleum Institute* (1980), a badly split Supreme Court—the nine justices issued five separate opinions—upheld the Fifth Circuit's decision, but not all parts of its argument; in particular, it expressed no opinion about the requirement of a cost–benefit assessment. Justice Powell, concurring in part and concurring in the judgement, did however note that "a standard-setting process that ignored economic considerations would result in a serious misallocation of resources and a lower effective level of safety than could be achieved under standards set with reference to the comparative benefits available at a lower cost" (cited in Mashaw, Merrill, and Shane 1998, 815). Expressing the view of a four-judge plurality (in a separate opinion, Justice Rehnquist provided the fifth vote for overturning the standard) Justice Stevens explicitly rejected the lowest-feasible-risk approach: "We think it is clear that the statute was not designed to require employers to provide absolute risk-free workplaces whenever it is technologically feasible to do so, so long as the cost is not great enough to destroy an entire industry. Rather, both the language and structure of the Act, as well as its legislative history, indicate that it was intended to require the elimination, as far as feasible, of *significant* risks of harm" (cited in Graham, Green, and Roberts 1988, 100; emphasis added).

In other words, zero risk cannot be the goal of risk regulation. Justice Stevens insisted that "safe" is not the same as risk free, pointing to a variety of risks in daily life—ranging from driving a car to "breathing city air"—that people find acceptable. Hence, before taking any decision, the risk from a toxic substance must be quantified sufficiently to enable the agency to characterize it as significant "in an understandable way." From the government's carcinogenic policy the agency had concluded that in the absence of definitive proof of a safe level, it must be assumed that *any* level above zero presents *some* increased risk of cancer. But, the justices pointed out that, "In view of the fact that there are literally thousands of substances used in the workplace that have been identified as carcinogens or suspect carcinogens, the Government's theory would give OSHA power to impose enormous costs that might produce little, if any, discernible benefit" (cited in Mashaw, Merrill, and Shane 1998, 813). Since the government's generic carcinogen policy provided no guidance as to which substances should be regulated first, an important merit of the significant risk doctrine was to raise the crucial issue of regulatory priorities. Most risks are regulated in response to petitions or pressures from labor unions, public health groups, environmentalists, and other political activists, with little analysis by the agency of other possible regulatory targets. Given that resources are always limited, the real (opportunity) cost of a safety regulation is the number of lives that could be saved by using the same resources to control other, perhaps more significant risks. By requiring OSHA to show significant risk as a prelude to standard setting, the justices were insisting on some analysis in priority setting: regulatory priorities should be directed toward the most important risks—which are not necessarily those that are politically most salient.

The significant risk doctrine places a higher analytical burden on regulators than the lowest-feasible-risk approach. Not all potential risks are treated equally; only those substances shown to pose a significant risk of cancer will be regulated, focusing limited agency resources on the most important health risks. In addition, the doctrine, without requiring a formal analysis of benefits and costs, does place a constraint on the stringency of standards. If exposure to a carcinogen is reduced to the point that the residual risk is insignificant, then no further tightening of the standard is appropriate (Graham, Green, and Roberts 1988, 103–5). *Industrial Union Department (AFL-CIO)* v. *American Petroleum Institute* is a landmark case also from the point of view of the methodology of risk analysis. The US Supreme Court not only confirmed the legitimacy of quantitative risk assessment; it effectively made reliance on the methodology obligatory for all American agencies engaged in risk regulation. In most subsequent disputes over regulatory decisions to protect human health, the question has not been whether a risk assessment was required but whether the assessment offered by the agency was plausible. The reasoning that led to the significant risk doctrine may be particularly instructive for those national or supra-national regulators that still follow something like the least-feasible-risk criterion and hence are reluctant to accept the need for setting rational regulatory priorities. For example, it can be shown that the precautionary approach adopted by the European Union is equivalent to that criterion, with the same negative implications for the setting of rational priorities within the regulatory agenda of the EU (Majone 2003).

# 4. Agenda Setting in the Era of Globalization

Growing economic and political interdependence among nations affects the substance and procedures of national policy making, including of course the agenda-setting process. The question which concerns us here is whether it is true that deepening economic integration must result in a more constrained national agenda, and thus in fewer channels for the expression of democratic preferences. An alternative hypothesis is that deepening economic integration may actually improve the quality of policy making by making national leaders more aware of the international impacts of their decisions, more willing to engage in international cooperation, and more open to ideas and suggestions coming from their foreign counterparts, from international institutions, and from non-governmental organizations. It is clear that in an integrating world economy the effectiveness of certain policy instruments may be seriously eroded. For example, the greater the degree of openness of a national economy, the less effective Keynesian demand management will be as an instrument of domestic stabilization policy. This is because some portion of any additional government expenditure will be spent on imports from the rest of the world, so that some of the demand-creating effect of the expenditure is dissipated abroad.

The obsolescence of particular policy instruments or approaches does not, however, imply that democratic polities are no longer able to satisfy the demands of their citizens, as some critics of globalization maintain. In fact, the demand for more transparency in public decision making, the search for new forms of accountability, and the growing reliance on persuasion rather than on traditional forms of governmental coercion can be shown to be related, at least in part, to growing economic and political interdependence (World Bank 1997; Majone 1996a). Moreover, it is sometimes possible to transfer policy-making powers to a higher level of governance, so that what can no longer be done at the national level may be achieved through international cooperation. These, then, are the two polar positions to be discussed in this section: on the one side, the "diminished democracy" thesis, according to which international economic integration, absent a world government, inevitably results in a restricted national policy agenda; on the other side, the more optimistic view which sees international integration and cooperation as an opportunity not only to expand the scope of consumer choice, but also to enrich the national agenda. Globalization, i.e. international economic integration, certainly imposes constraints on national policy makers, but these often turn out to be more enabling than limiting. I conclude that future studies of agenda setting will have to pay much more attention to exogenous influences on national agendas.

## 4.1 The Diminished Democracy Thesis

According to a familiar result of international economics known as the Mundell–Fleming theorem or, more informally, the "open-economy trilemma," countries cannot simultaneously maintain an independent monetary policy, capital mobility, and fixed exchange rates. If a government chooses fixed exchange rates and capital mobility it has to give up monetary autonomy. If it chooses monetary autonomy and capital mobility, it has to go with floating exchange rates. Finally, if it wishes to combine fixed exchange rates with monetary autonomy it has to limit capital mobility (Lindert and Kindleberger 1982). Harvard economist Dani Rodrik has argued that the open-economy trilemma can be extended to what he calls the political trilemma of the world economy (see Fig. 11.1). The elements of Rodrik's political trilemma are: integrated national economies, the nation state, and "mass politics," i.e. a democratic system characterized by a high degree of political mobilization and by institutions that are responsive to mobilized groups. The claim is that it is possible to have at most two of these things. To quote Rodrik: "If we want true international economic integration, we have to go either with the nation-state, in which case the domain of national politics will have to be significantly restricted, or else with mass politics, in which case we will have to give up the nation-state in favor of global federalism. If we want highly participatory political regimes, we have to choose between the nation-state and international economic integration. If we want to keep the nation-state, we have to choose between mass politics and international economic integration" (Rodrik 2000, 180).

Politics would not necessarily shrink under global federalism since economic power and political power would then be aligned: all important political and policy issues would be treated at the global level. A world government is not in the domain of the politically possible, now or in the foreseeable future, but the price of maintaining national sovereignty while markets become international is that politics has to be exercised over a much narrower range of issues: "The overarching goal of nation-states... would be to appear attractive to international markets... Domestic regulations and tax policies would be either harmonized according to international standards, or structured such that they pose the least amount of hindrance to international economic integration. The only local public goods provided would be those that are compatible with integrated markets" (Rodrik 2000, 182).

In essence, this is the diminished democracy thesis which has found wide, if uncritical acceptance among critics of international (or even regional, e.g. European)

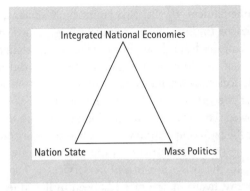

**Fig. 11.1.** Rodrik's political trilemma

(*Source*: Rodrik 2000, 181)

integration. The core of this thesis is an argument about the declining ability of democratic policy makers to produce public policies that depart from market-conforming principles. Typical of this school of thought is the assertion that "European economic integration has significantly reduced the range of policy instruments available, and the range of policy goals achievable, at the national level. To that extent, the effectiveness as well as the responsiveness of government, and hence democratic legitimacy, are seen to have been weakened" (Scharpf 2001, 360). However, numerous empirical studies cast serious doubts on the accuracy of any simple correlation, much less a causal link, between increasing economic integration and a "diminished democracy" syndrome. Thus, a recent econometric analysis using annual data from 1964 to 1993 for sixteen OECD countries finds little evidence that international capital mobility exerted systematic downward pressure on the public sector, the welfare state, and the provisions of public goods (Swank 2001).

According to another version of the diminished democracy thesis, capital becomes more footloose because of increasing economic integration and, as a result, countries begin to compete to attract it by cutting their tax rates. The process may reach a point where a country is forced to provide a lower level of public services than its citizens would otherwise wish. Given this scenario, tax harmonization seems a reasonable proposition. At a minimum, if tax cutting is matched by all nations, no country gains a comparative advantage. In fact, one observes relatively little tax harmonization, even among countries whose economies are undergoing a process of deep integration, such as the members of the European Union. It has often been predicted that a failure to harmonize taxation in the EU will result in destructive competition among member states which will ultimately undermine Europe's generous welfare systems, but after fifty years of European integration, no such "race to the bottom" can be observed. While barriers to trade and to capital mobility have been falling almost continuously since the late 1950s, EU countries have not experienced any significant degree of tax competition and consequent fall in tax rates. On the contrary, the average tax rates were climbing between the mid-1960s and the end of the 1990s both in the original member states—the Benelux countries, Germany, France, and Italy—and in the countries of the European "periphery"—Spain, Portugal, Greece, and Ireland. Moreover, tax rates have always been higher in the richer than in the poorer countries, showing that the growing integration of Europe did not make the richer members of the EU feel constrained by tax competition from low-wage countries. Since the late 1970s the difference between the tax rates of these two groups of countries has narrowed. However, this narrowing has gone in the opposite direction to that predicted by the tax-competition view, with average tax rates in the peripheral countries approaching those of the richer countries. There are also few signs that a race to the bottom in the provision of public services is taking place in the EU. Rather, as in the case of taxation, the race has been in the other direction, with the southern countries upgrading to northern levels of expenditure on service provision (Barnard 2000). In sum, even in a deeply integrated EU, "the nation-state is still the principal site of policy change, and there remains ample scope for political choice... if institutional arrangements and policy mixes are suitably modified, then the core principles of the European social model can be preserved and in many respects enhanced in their translation into the real worlds of European welfare" (Ferrera, Hemerijck, and Rhodes 2001, 164).

A third version of the diminished democracy thesis is that the rules of international trade restrict the autonomy of national policy makers, making it impossible for them to provide the public goods their citizens demand. In fact, members of the World Trade Organization (WTO) not only enjoy domestic policy autonomy but must also respect the exercise of that autonomy by other members. This basic principle is reflected in the most-favored-nation (MFN) principle, the fundamental function of which is to ensure that each WTO member accords access to its markets independently of any of the policies of the trading partner, including domestic policies. For example, the critics assert that under WTO rules a government cannot protect from import competition those domestic industries that have to bear the costs of environmental or other regulations not applied by other countries. As Roessler (1996) has convincingly shown, however, WTO rules do permit member states to take a domestic regulatory measure raising the cost of production in combination with subsidies or tariffs that maintain the competitive position of the domestic producers that have to bear these costs. The only restriction is that if the compensatory measures adversely affect the interests of other WTO members, procedures designed to remove the adverse effects of those measures on third countries must be observed. It is precisely the combination of rigid rules with flexible safeguards that has permitted the liberalization of international trade to proceed so far without any domestic policy harmonization—or undue interference with the national agenda. This subtle compromise makes possible the coexistence of the two apparently opposing principles of domestic policy autonomy and the globalization of trade.

Of course, to say that the rules of the world trade regime, the liberalization of capital markets, and even EU-style deep economic integration do not significantly restrict the national policy agenda is not to imply that domestic policies do not have to be adapted to changing economic, political, and technological conditions. Everywhere welfare states face serious problems, but the causes of the current difficulties are mostly related to factors that have little to do with the growing integration of the national economies: the impact of demographic changes, domestic opposition to high tax rates and excessive bureaucratization, the failure of traditional social policies to respond to new needs and risks generated by socioeconomic and technical change, and ideological and political shifts reflecting all these changes. International economic integration per se does not seem to constrain significantly national agendas. What is even more important, the constraints created by a rule-based approach to economic integration—not only within the WTO and EU frameworks, but also in the North American Free Trade Area (NAFTA), and dozens of similar arrangements throughout the world—may actually improve the transparency, fairness, and credibility of policy making at the national level.

## 4.2 Enabling Constraints

Part of the intuitive appeal of the diminished democracy thesis derives from a misunderstanding of the nature of constraints in general, and of their role in policy making, in particular. Constraints often turn out to be blessings in disguise because once a constraint has been identified it is often possible to take advantage of it (Majone 1989). Learning depends on the recognition and skillful exploitation of constraints. All organisms can learn and adapt only to the extent that their environment is constrained. In this respect the laws of the state are entirely analogous to the laws of nature since they provide fixed features in the environment in which an individual has to move. Similarly, constitutional rules do not merely restrict the substantive and procedural choices of policy makers; they are also enabling in that they can enhance the effectiveness of the policy makers' actions or the credibility of long-term commitments. For example, the principle of separation of powers can enhance governmental authority by, *inter alia*, helping overcome a paralyzing confusion of functions. As a political version of the division of labor, separation of powers is enabling to the extent that specialization enhances sensitivity to a diversity of public problems (Holmes 1995, 165).

Under international economic integration, national policy makers are constrained also by supranational rules, such as the treaties and laws of the European Union, and the agreements and rules of the World Trade Organization or NAFTA. Consider for example the influence of European law on the agenda of national policy makers. The creation of a common European market and the attendant rules of market liberalization meant that governments could no longer pursue protectionist policies vis-à-vis other members of the EU, nor continue to protect public or private monopolies within the national borders. The discipline imposed on state subsidies and on the criteria of public procurement further reduced the discretionary powers of national executives—and the various forms of rent seeking and political corruption which usually accompany administrative decisions in these areas. Similarly, WTO rules have made it increasingly difficult for the European Union and the United States to pursue protectionist policies at the international level, notably in the area of agriculture. NAFTA has strengthened the independent role of national courts, and improved the transparency of national policy making.

It should not be assumed that supranational rules only favor economic interests. European law, for example, has also assisted individuals and public interest groups in their struggle against many forms of discrimination on the grounds of sex, nationality, religion, age, or physical disability. The best instance in the area of individual rights is Article 119 of the founding Treaty of Rome, which requires application of the principle of equal pay for male and female workers, for equal work or work of equal value. The European Court of Justice (ECJ) used this article in the *Defrenne* case (decided in 1976) to determine that the policy of the Belgian airline Sabena—forcing stewardesses to change job within the company (accepting a loss in wages) at the age of forty, but imposing no such requirement on cabin stewards doing the same work—was discriminatory, and required Sabena to compensate Mrs Defrenne's loss of income. In the *Bilka* case of 1986, the Court indicated its willingness, absent a clear justification, to strike down national measures excluding women from any employer-provided benefits, such as pensions. These and many other ECJ rulings show the positive impact supranational law can have on national legislation and legal practice by outlawing direct and indirect discrimination both in individual and in collective agreements. They also suggest that today international courts can have a major influence on the national agenda. For example, in another well-known case (the *Barber* case decided in 1990), the European Court extended the meaning of Article 119 to cover age thresholds for pensions eligibility. Mr Barber, a British national, having been made redundant at age fifty-two, was denied a pension that would have been available immediately to female employees of the same age. Instead, he received a lump-sum payment. The court held that this treatment violated European law since pensions are pay and hence within the scope of Article 119 of the Treaty of Rome. The decision required massive restructuring of pension schemes, and implications for future pension plans in all the member states of the EU are considerable. The issues raised by the *Barber* case became an important item on the agenda of European leaders in preparation for the 1992 Treaty on European Union.

Although the strong institutions of the European Union are not easily replicated at the international level, it is a remarkable fact that the international community and international law today accept the principle that the protection of basic human rights cannot stop at the national borders. Hence the growing acceptance of the principle of "universal jurisdiction," which allows the prosecution of gross human rights violations even in a country where the crime did not take place. Also the threat of trade sanctions has proved to be an effective instrument for protecting basic human rights at the international level. It should be noted that the credibility of this threat is enhanced by the growing integration of national economies. This is another example of enabling constraints, in that the rules of free trade are used by democratic governments and human rights groups to put pressure on authoritarian states, and even to redefine the diplomatic agenda.

## 4.3 Other Exogenous Influences

As shown by the example of the international protection of human rights, international law and judicial decisions are not the only exogenous influences on national agendas. A good deal of the work of international bodies like the Organization for Economic Cooperation and Development, the International Monetary Fund, and specialized agencies of the United Nations like the Food and Agriculture Organization and the World Health Organization is aimed at influencing the process of agenda setting in the member countries. Sometimes the aim is not simply to raise certain issues to the governmental agenda, but even to change the priorities of the decision agenda—as in the case of the AIDS epidemic, or the urgent need for reform of the pension systems of industrialized countries. A significant influence is exercised also by transnational nongovernmental organizations on issues such as human rights or protection of the global environment (Keck and Sikkink 1998; Risse, Ropp, and Sikkink 1999).

Policy externalities and the requirements of information exchange are other influences on the formation of national agendas. Globalization has the effect of strengthening the impact of domestic policies on other countries. Exchanges of information among policy makers of different countries are useful for assessing the extent of policy externalities, understanding the mechanisms through which they are transmitted, and planning remedial action. Students of economic policy coordination have come to the conclusion that the major benefit of discussions among national policy makers derives not from explicit coordination, but rather from making governments aware of the consequences of their actions for other countries. Such awareness is often important in shaping the alternatives for governmental action. An example is the "least-restrictive means" principle of international economic law. This is the requirement that policy objectives be achieved in the manner that imposes least costs on a country's trading partners. National health or safety measures, for example, should be so designed as to minimize negative externalities for other countries. Notice, comments, and publication requirements—on which the WTO system, the European Union, and NAFTA extensively rely—are mechanisms for implementing the least-restrictive means principle. The idea is to give advance warnings of new measures which may have significant transboundary externalities, and to delay their implementation briefly while other countries have an opportunity to comment on them.

Recently, the European Union has introduced a rather elaborate method—known as Open Method of Coordination (OMC)—which, if successful, will have a significant impact on the national agenda of the member states. The new method has been pushed by EU leaders in order to favor some convergence of national policies in areas, such as social policy, employment, and pension reform, that are too politically sensitive to be handled by the traditional, more centralized approach. The OMC is a means of spreading best practice, a learning process that should lead to policy convergence in the long run. Its main elements are: general guidelines for the Union, combined with specific timetables for achieving the short-, medium-, and long-term goals set by the member states themselves; quantitative and qualitative indicators and benchmarks derived from best practice worldwide, but tailored to the needs of individual countries and sectors; policy reform actions of the member states to be integrated periodically into their National Action Plans; periodic monitoring, evaluation, and peer review of the results. The European Council—the highest policy-making institution of the EU—guides and coordinates the entire process. It sets the overall objectives to be achieved, while sector-specific committees of national experts undertake the technical aspects of the work, notably the selection of indicators and benchmarks. The progress made in each area is reviewed annually, during the spring session of the European Council that is devoted to economic and social questions (Scott and Trubek 2002; Borras and Greve 2004).

As was said in the introduction, the aim for this chapter was not to survey the existing literature on agenda setting, but rather to introduce certain themes which that literature has largely neglected. The reasons for the neglect are methodological, conceptual, and substantive. The issue of agenda control, for example, has been investigated mostly by political scientists adopting a rational choice approach to institutional analysis, and the influence of this brand of institutionalism on policy analysis has remained rather limited so far. Yet, the two examples given in Section 1— the control of the legislative agenda by the committees of the US Congress, and the monopoly of legislative and policy initiative by the Commission of the European Union—should suffice to demonstrate the importance of this mode of agenda setting. Another case of neglect due to methodological reasons is the issue of priority setting within a given agenda. As was argued in Section 3, the correct selection of priorities is especially important in areas such as risk regulation, where the opportunity cost of a wrong selection of priorities can be quite high. But risk regulation relies on probabilistic reasoning and on the theory of decision making under uncertainty—methodologies which have not been used even by students of the agenda-setting process who emphasize its random nature. Conceptually, the relevance of agenda setting to the theory and practice of democracy is well understood. Recall that Dahl has made the criterion of full agenda control by the demos a crucial test of full-fledged (rather than merely procedural) democracy. Yet, democratic theory has many other stimulating insights and problems to offer to students of agenda setting. I am thinking in particular of recent discussions about the role of democracy in a world where important decisions are increasingly shifted to the supranational level—what Dahl has called the third transformation of democracy, after the direct democracy of the Greeks and the representative democracy of the modern nation state. In the preceding pages I have argued against the diminished democracy hypothesis—the idea that because of globalization, democratic policy makers are no longer able to provide the public goods the citizens demand. To reject this pessimistic hypothesis is not to suggest that the institutions and processes of democracy do not have to be adapted to the "third transformation," just as representative democracy was an adaptation of direct democracy to the rise of the nation state. From a substantive point of view, I would argue that the greatest payoffs in the future will come from the study of exogenous influences on the domestic agenda, and of agenda setting at the international level. In the past, policy analysis has been state-centric almost by definition, and most of our ideas and techniques of analysis reflect our own national experiences. However, the idea of governance is much broader than that of government, and it is this broader reality that policy analysis in general, and the study of agenda setting in particular, will have to address in order to remain relevant to new generations of private and public policy makers.

# REFERENCES

ARNOLD, R. D. 1990. *The Logic of Congressional Action*. New Haven, Conn.: Yale University Press.

BACHRACH, P., and BARATZ, M. S. 1963. Decisions and nondecisions: an analytical framework. *American Political Science Review*, 57: 641–51.

BARKER, E. 1958. *Reflections on Government*. Oxford: Oxford University Press.

BARNARD, C. 2000. Social dumping and the race to the bottom: some lessons for the European Union from Delaware? *European Law Review*, 6: 57–78.

BATES, R. H. 1990. Macropolitical economy in the field of development. Pp. 31–54 in *Perspectives on Positive Political Economy*, ed. J. E. Alt and K. A. Shepsle. Cambridge: Cambridge University Press.

BAWN, K. 1995. Political control versus expertise: congressional choices about administrative procedures. *American Political Science Review*, 89: 62–73.

BORRAS, S., and GREVE, B. (eds.) 2004. Special issue: the open method of coordination in the European Union. *Journal of European Public Policy*, 11(2).

COBB, R. W., and ELDER, C. D. 1972. *Participation in American Politics: The Dynamics of Agenda Building*. Boston: Allyn & Bacon.

DAHL, R. A. 1986. *Democracy and its Critics*. New Haven, Conn.: Yale University Press.

DERTHICK, M., and QUIRK, P. J. 1985. *The Politics of Deregulation*. Washington, DC: Brookings Institution.

FERRERA, M., HEMERIJCK, A., and RHODES, M. 2001. The future of the European "social model" in the global economy. *Journal of Comparative Policy Analysis*, 3: 163–90.

GRAHAM, J. D., GREEN, L. C., and ROBERTS, M. J. 1988. *In Search of Safety*. Cambridge, Mass.: Harvard University Press.

HOLMES, S. 1995. *Passions and Constraint*. Chicago: University of Chicago Press.

KECK, M., and SIKKINK, K. 1998. *Activists beyond Borders: Advocacy Networks in International Politics*. Ithaca, NY: Cornell University Press.

KINGDON, J. W. 1984. *Agendas, Alternatives, and Public Policies*. Boston: Little, Brown.

LINDERT, P. H., and KINDLEBERGER, C. P. 1982. *International Economics*, 7th edn. Homewood, Ill.: Richard D. Irwin.

McCubbins, M. D., and Noble, G. W. 1995. The appearance of power: legislators, bureaucrats, and the budget process. Pp. 56–80 in *Structure and Policy in Japan and the United States*, ed. P. F. Cowhey and M. D. McCubbins. Cambridge: Cambridge University Press.

—— Noll, R., and Weingast, B. 1987. Administrative procedures as instruments of political control. *Journal of Law, Economics, and Organization*, 3: 243–77.

McKelvey, R. 1976. Intransitivities in multidimensional voting models and some indications for agenda control. *Journal of Economic Theory*, 12: 472–82.

Majone, G. 1989. *Evidence, Argument and Persuasion in the Policy Process*. New Haven, Conn.: Yale University Press.

—— 1996a. Public policy and administration: ideas, interests and institutions. Pp. 610–27 in *A New Handbook of Political Science*, ed. R. E. Goodin and H.-D. Klingemann. Oxford: Oxford University Press.

—— 1996b. *Regulating Europe*. London: Routledge.

—— (ed.) 2003. *Risk Regulation in the European Union: Between Enlargement and Globalization*. Florence: European University Institute.

Mashaw, J. L., Merrill, R. A., and Shane, P. M. 1998. *Administrative Law*, 4th edn. St Paul, Minn.: West Group.

Mendeloff, J. M. 1988. *The Dilemma of Toxic Substance Regulation*. Cambridge, Mass.: MIT Press.

Risse, T., Ropp, S. C., and Sikkink, K. (eds.) 1999. *The Power of Human Rights: International Norms and Domestic Change*. Cambridge: Cambridge University Press.

Rodrik, D. 2000. How far will international economic integration go? *Journal of Economic Perspectives*, 14: 177–86.

Roessler, F. 1996. Diverging domestic policies and multilateral trade integration. Pp. 21–56 in *Fair Trade and Harmonization: Prerequisites for Free Trade?*, vol. ii, ed. J. N. Bhagwati and R. E. Hudec. Cambridge, Mass.: MIT Press.

Scharpf, F. W. 2001. Democratic legitimacy under conditions of regulatory competition: why Europe differs from the United States. Pp. 355–74 in *The Federal Vision*, ed. K. Nicolaidis and R. Howse. Oxford: Oxford University Press.

Schofield, N. 1976. Instability of simple dynamic games. *Review of Economic Studies*, 45: 575–94.

Scott, J., and Trubek, D. M. (eds.) 2002. Special issue on law and new approaches to governance in Europe. *European Law Journal*, 8 (Mar.).

Shepsle, K. A. 1979. Institutional arrangements and equilibrium in multidimensional voting models. *American Journal of Political Science*, 23: 27–59.

Stewart, R. B. 1975. The reformation of American administrative law. *Harvard Law Review*, 88: 1667–813.

Swank, D. 2001. Mobile capital, democratic institutions and the public economy in advanced industrial societies. *Journal of Comparative Policy Analysis*, 3: 133–62.

Weingast, B. R. 1996. Political institutions: rational choice perspectives. Pp. 166–90 in *A New Handbook of Political Science*, ed. R. E. Goodin and H.-D. Klingemann. Oxford: Oxford University Press.

—— and Marshall, W. J. 1988. The industrial organization of Congress. *Journal of Political Economy*, 96: 132–63.

Wood, D. B., and Waterman, R. W. 1991. The dynamics of political control of the bureaucracy. *American Political Science Review*, 85: 801–28.

World Bank 1997. *The State in a Changing World: World Development Report 1997*. Washington, DC: World Bank.

CHAPTER 12

# ORDERING THROUGH DISCOURSE

## MAARTEN HAJER

## DAVID LAWS

## 1. DEALING WITH AMBIVALENCE

Practitioners face "wicked" problems, complex influences, shifting commitments, and moral complexity in their daily efforts to act on policy goals. In many situations, they will not even be able to agree on what the problem *really* is (Rittel and Webber 1973), and turning to the facts may amplify rather than resolve differences in the face of "contradictory certainties" (Schwarz and Thompson 1990).

Much policy analysis tries to reduce conflict and uncertainty and respond to the need for stability by deriving generalizable knowledge and universal principles that can be applied to achieve policy goals across domains and settings. In this chapter, we address a competing tradition that starts with the conflict, ambiguity, and lure of stability that policy actors experience, treats their action as intelligent, and tries to organize scholarship to understand and support the efforts of these policy practitioners. We focus on a central problem that public officials, policy analysts, researchers, and stakeholders face in these circumstances: "How can I make sense of this complex and politically charged world?" This question often takes the form, "How should I act, given this complexity and uncertainty?"

Scholarship on this problem has a long history that dates back at least to C. S. Peirce's call for reflection on the logic by which we fix beliefs (Peirce 1992), Kenneth Burke's effort to model the search for regularity on a grammar (Burke 1969), and Erving Goffman's enquiry into how individuals respond to the question "What is going on here?" in social behaviour (Goffman 1974). Ambivalence, ambiguity, and doubt have inspired a rich body of scholarship ever since March and Olsen (1989).

While it is now sociological common sense that policy practitioners seek stability and act in a social world that is a kaleidoscope of potential realities, the approaches to understand their efforts to make sense of the world vary. We use the term "ordering device" here to connote the *conceptual tools that analysts use to capture how policy actors deal with ambiguity and allocate particular significance to specific social or physical events.* These ordering devices explain how policy makers structure reality to gain a handle on practical questions.

## 2. UNDERSTANDING AMBIVALENCE

Policy makers are supposed to analyse situations and determine how to act. Professionally preoccupied with the quest for order and control (Van Gunsteren 1976), they are likely to be concerned when they experience ambivalence. When a situation is ambiguous, the available tools may not be useful or lead to immediate advice. In *Modernity and Ambivalence*, Zygmunt Bauman (1991) describes the unease that people experience when they cannot "read" a situation and choose readily among alternatives. Bauman defines ambivalence as the "possibility of assigning an object or an event to more than one category" (Bauman 1991). Ambivalence confounds choice as the organizing metaphor for action. This becomes a policy problem when the sovereignty of the state is based on the "power to define and to make definitions stick" (1991, 1–2). Governing, in his account, is in a large part a matter of defining the situation and this, in turn, is a key feature of policy practice. His analysis only raises the salience of the question, however. How do policy makers manage ambivalence in this endeavour?

This question is complex because ambivalence (or ambiguity, we use the terms interchangeably) lends itself to suppression. This is particularly true in policy work. We all know the joke that a good policy adviser has only one hand (so that she cannot say "on the other hand . . ."): politicians look to their policy advisers for clarity, to help them *overcome* ambivalence. This assumes that ambivalence is always a problem, a deficit, a thing to overcome. Yet we might also see ambivalence and doubt as part of a policy domain and engaging them as a key part of good policy work. The appreciation of ambivalence and the capacity to doubt are arguably essential components of a reflective way of acting in the world. Hence good policy work typically takes place between two poles: one pulling in the direction of clarity and the reduction of complexity, the other illuminating precisely that which we do not fully understand.

Robert McNamara's reflections on the Cuban Missile Crisis in *The Fog of War* (Morris 2003) illustrate the kind of struggle that goes on between these poles in policy making. Information was imperfect; conditions were "foggy." The clock was ticking and policy had to be made on the spot (Kennedy 1971). In this fog, McNamara suggests, the Kennedy administration could have read the Cuban situation in two ways, each implying a radically different course of action.

How did policy makers make sense of this ambiguous situation and choose how to act? We would expect them to employ classification and, as Mary Douglas has observed, that "institutions [would] do the classifying" (Douglas 1986). Classification is an *institutional* device for ordering in which perception is guided by routine. In the Cuban Missile Crisis, the Pentagon classified the situation in its established categories. The test of classification in such circumstances is the ability to define a situation persuasively and provide concrete suggestions for action (in this case including a pre-emptive strike against Cuba). In hindsight, the strength of the policy deliberation in this crisis was the ability of Kennedy's advisers to resist the rush to classification; they *acknowledged ambiguity*, kept doubt alive, and worked to "ferret out" the assumptions embedded in routine ways of classifying the situation. This enabled them to "frame" and "reframe," and thereby explore different ways of understanding the situation.

The ability of the Kennedy administration to engage doubt, in this account, prevented a military conflict and allowed them to find a way out of the conflict: in the end both parties (the USA and Soviet Union) could back down without losing face. This could not have been a simple task. Particularly not given the unease, as Deborah Stone and others have underscored, that policy makers experience when objects or situations do not fit in one particular category or understanding (Stone 1997). If a situation is unclear and imbued with ambivalence, the task is seen to be creating order. But if policy makers have the key task of choosing between alternative trajectories of action, then acknowledging and, subsequently, handling ambivalence is essential for prudent action. In this sense, the strength of institutionally embedded systems of classification may also be their weakness. The force of institutional classifications in the face of ambivalence can interfere with responsible judgement. McNamara shows how this extends to even the strongest of policy decisions. They are imbued with ambiguity, and the ability to manage this relationship is what distinguishes the Kennedy administration's efforts in the Cuban Missile Crisis.

In political science the Cuban Missile Crisis is almost automatically associated with Graham Allison's *The Essence of Decision* (Allison 1971; Allison and Zelikow 1999). Allison showed how analysis of the dynamics depends on the analyst's conceptual lens. In so doing, Allison in fact showed how the need to order, and the distinctiveness this imbues analysis with, is not just limited to analysis in the immediate crisis, but extends to the efforts of political scientists to theorize the experience.

## 3. INTERPRETIVE SCHEMATA

McNamara's account highlights the influence of different interpretative schemata in the crisis. He argues that the Pentagon's vigorous interpretation was countered by

Tommy Thompson, the former ambassador to Moscow. Thompson drew on personal knowledge of the Russian leader Khrushchev and argued for a different interpretation. Khrushchev "was not the kind of person" to fit in the story the Pentagon was telling. So what, in the name of policy analysis, was going on in this confrontation? Was it a confrontation between a five-star general with an extraordinary track record and a soft-spoken statesman with personal knowledge of his adversary? Should we understand this as a conflict between two institutionalized ways of making sense of an ambiguous situation? Or should we try to connect bits of both interpretations?

In this tension we can read the outlines of what sociologists have labelled the "actor–structure" problem (Giddens 1979). Should we focus on personality and individual power? Or should we emphasize the (institutional) structures within which individuals operate? It is now widely agreed that this dichotomy is false. Individuals and institutions are both important. The analytic task is to develop concepts that can mediate between actors and structure (March and Olsen 1989). This is what policy academics attempt to do with the three ordering devices we discuss here at some more length: beliefs, frames, and discourses.

We know that what people see is shaped by "interpretative schemata." Cognitive science has shown that people inevitably privilege some attributes over others and influence what is deemed important, exciting, scary, threatening, reassuring, promising, or challenging. Scholarship on interpretative schemata has a long history. An undisputed milestone is the early work of Ludwig Fleck in the 1930s (Fleck 1935). Fleck made the case for a social understanding of cognition suggesting that action is dependent on the way in which "thought collectives" conceive of the world. Each collective has a particular "thought style" that orders the process of cognition, explains new empirical findings ("the facts"), and informs sense making in complex situations. Recognition of Fleck's work grew, particularly when Thomas Kuhn acknowledged his debt to Fleck in his analysis of scientific "paradigms." Kuhn's seminal *The Structure of Scientific Revolutions* combines an appreciation of the social embeddedness of interpretative schemata with the *Gestalt* psychology to make it understandable how, even when people look at the same object, they might see different things. This provides a way to relate individual cognition to social ordering devices (in his case "paradigms") that explains widely distributed patterns in conceiving realities (Kuhn 1970/1962).

The range of concepts that have been coined to understand this process of ordering is broad and includes "appreciative systems" (Vickers 1965), "cognitive maps" (Axelrod 1984), "heresthetics" (Riker 1986), and "frames" (Gamson and Modigliani 1989; Snow and Benford 1992; Schön and Rein 1994). Recent work has investigated the role of "policy narratives," "storylines," or "discourses" in public policy practice (Litfin 1994; Roe 1994; Hajer 1995; Yanow 1996). Rather than spelling out each conceptual approach, we illuminate some key characteristics of this scholarship and where these approaches differ and overlap.

# 4. THREE CONCEPTUAL APPROACHES

For all the differences, the scholarship on these concepts shares a few important characteristics: ordering is related to cognitive commitments; all approaches include an account of how judgement takes place; ordering is seen as involving elements of exchange and coalition building; ordering is tied to action, and the concepts are supposed to help explain dominance, stability, and (limited) policy learning. Accounts of this process overlap in puzzling ways and the supposed variation among these approaches can seem, at times, more like wordplay. We believe, however, that there are important differences among the ordering devices that scholars employ to describe policy practice. We try and make these differences understandable by comparing the approaches in terms of their ontological and epistemological assumptions.

First, we position them on a continuum between an individualist ontology in which ordering is understood in terms of *individual* capacities (e.g. ordering in terms of individual "beliefs") and a *relational* pole that describes ordering in terms of the patterns of social interaction that characterize a particular situation (e.g. some work on frames and some scholarship on discourse). Second, we examine how proponents of different approaches generate and deliver knowledge about the world of public policy. What rules do they, explicitly or implicitly, follow when they try to make sense of the way in which policy makers deal with a complex and ambivalent world? Here we distinguish two empirical orientations: the first directed at creating generalizable knowledge by abstracting from contexts and a second focused on identifying detailed dynamics in policy practice.

# 5. BELIEFS

A prominent example of policy analysis that draws on the concept of belief is the "advocacy coalition framework" (ACF) developed by Sabatier and Jenkins-Smith (1993). Advocacy coalitions consist of "actors from a variety of . . . institutions at all levels of government who share a set of basic beliefs . . . and who seek to manipulate the rules, budgets, and personnel of governmental institutions in order to achieve these goals over time" (1993, 5). The coalition members who come together around the focal point of shared core beliefs coordinate their actions to a "non-trivial degree" (1993, 25).

The ACF approach has inspired and informed a substantial body of policy analysis. Yet precisely how the individual and the interpersonal interrelate and how shifts in belief occur remains opaque. A key feature of the ACF belief system approach is the effort to build a social explanation of policy from an ontology of individuals with clearly defined and stable value preferences that inform their actions and provide a stable basis for association. The pursuit of core values through individual and collective action (via coalitions) produces the distinctive ordering in a policy field and lends stability to a domain. Yet the research focus on strategic behaviour and cognitive learning does not suggest a way of understanding how policy makers deal with ambiguities and how ambiguity might relate to policy change and learning.

Epistemologically, Sabatier and Jenkins-Smith see the ACF as tuned to a Humean search for general laws. They (1993, 231) formulate nine hypotheses designed to test the robustness of the advocacy coalition framework in explaining policy learning and policy change and search for a causal theory, with clearly distinguishable forces of change, that is testable/falsifiable, fertile, and parsimonious (1993, 231). At the same time ACF proponents also speak a dialect of constructivism: they seek to analyse how problems get defined, emphasize the role of perceptions, and underline the inevitable influence of the conceptual lens on analysis (e.g. in the preface to the 1993 book). Yet the individualist ontology, search for general laws, and reliance on hypothesis testing clash with the interpretative elements of the advocacy coalition framework.

# 6. FRAMES

Over the last fifteen years the frame concept has built a remarkable career as an ordering device in public policy scholarship. This is more due to its usefulness in explaining practice patterns that resist other forms of analysis than to its internal consistency or its verifiability. Most frame analysis draws on the work of ethnomethodologists like Garfinkel and Goffman, but seeks to scale this approach up to deal with social and collective behaviour. All frame analysis takes, *to varying degrees*, language, or more specifically language use as the organizing framework for understanding society.

The popularity of frames is rooted in their intuitive appeal. The concept captures something about the dynamics of policy making that makes sense to practitioners and to those who analyse policy practice. In a similar manner, framing has been employed in economics and psychology (Kahneman and Tversky 2000) and social movement research (Gamson and Modigliani 1989; Snow and Benford 1992). Frame analysis highlights the communicative character of ordering devices that connects particular utterances (a speech, a policy text) to individual consciousness and social action (Entman 1993, 51).

What a frame is, is harder to say. Like the play of action they help to explain, frames are recognized, in part, by the way they resist specification. A frame is an account of ordering that makes sense in the domain of policy and that describes the move from diffuse worries to actionable beliefs. In this way frames navigate the relationship between the *"struggle to attain a state of belief"* and the persistent *"irritation of doubt"* (Peirce 1992). Frames mediate this relationship by parsing the "field of experience" in a distinctive way, linking "facts derived from experience," observations, and accepted sources with values and other commitments in a way that guides action. Framing is the process of drawing these relationships and the frame is the internally coherent constellation of facts, values, and action implications.

Schön and Rein (1996) root their account of this process in the way "frame" is used in everyday speech and are tolerant of the play this leaves in the concept. They describe four ways of looking at frames that they treat as "mutually compatible images rather than competing conceptions" (1996, 88). A frame can be understood as "an underlying structure which is sufficiently strong and stable to support an edifice." Thus a house has a frame even if it is not visible from the outside. The idea of structure implies "a degree of regularity, and hence, a lack of adaptability to events as they unfold over time" (1996, 88). A frame can also be seen as a boundary, in the way a picture frame fixes our attention and tells us what to disregard. This boundary helps us freeze the continuous stream of events and demarcate what is inside, and deserving of our attention, from what is outside (1996, 89). Their third image portrays a frame as "a schemata of interpretation that enables individuals" to locate, perceive, identify, and label occurrences within their life space and their world at large "rendering events meaningful and thereby guiding action" (1996, 89). Finally, harkening back to their original formulation, they describe frames as a particular kind of "normative-prescriptive" story that that provides a sense of what the problem is and what should be done about it. These "generic story lines" are important because they "give coherence to the analysis of issues in a policy domain" (1996, 89). In strict terms, a frame is the form of ordering that makes these four views compatible. As a group, they present a picture of framing as an essential act for making sense of a policy field, in which part of making sense is deciding how to act. They also express two representative tensions that distinguish framing as an account of this process. Frames are neither entirely intentional nor tacit and frames conceal as they reveal, in part by the way commitments insulate themselves from reflection.

Snow and Benford define a frame in more or less compatible terms as "an interpretive schemata that signifies and condenses the 'world out there' by selectively punctuating and encoding objects, situations, events, experiences, and sequences of actions within one's present or past environment" (Snow and Benford 1992, 137). Their account extends the play between intention and tacit action that is part of the concept of frame. Frames enable actors to "articulate and align" (ibid.) events and occurrences and order those in a meaningful fashion. Here there is no distance between belief and frame. Yet, actors also retain sufficient leverage over frames (and the distance this implies) to play an active and intentional role in shaping the process. "[W]hat gives a collective action frame its novelty is not so much its innovative ideational elements as the manner in which *activists articulate or tie them together*" (1992, 138; emphasis added). Frames are powerful when they are empirically credible, consistent with experience, and ideationally central (1992, 140).

In these accounts, frames are recognized and active in the relationship among facts, values, and action. The relative strength and stability of the constellations drawn is what helps explain stability and change in a policy domain. In social movement research (see also Poletta, this volume) frame analysts distinguish their approach as an alternative to "resource mobilisation" and "political opportunity structures." They suggest that "non structural" factors account for both the particular arousal of groups and their ability to act collectively. They treat meanings as "social productions," analyse actors as being engaged in "meaning-work," and push to open the process of signification in order to explain action (Snow and Benford 1992). They conceptualize this "signifying work" as *framing* and allocate a central role to frames as the ordering device. This take on frames really is about "framing" as a deliberate act (undertaken by "signifying agents") aimed to make others follow particular patterns of signification (cf. also Steinberg 1998, 845). The balance gives priority to the framing as an intentional, even strategic activity and posits a certain distance between belief and frame.

The effort to describe framing in terms of actors' efforts to name and frame in an ongoing struggle between dominant frames and challengers also draws on this strategic orientation (Gamson and Modigliani 1989). This take emphasizes the importance of institutional sponsors and their strategic employment of frames in the struggle for dominance. It deepens the account of dominance, however, and in the process blurs the line between strategic and interpretative action. This move ties framing back to its roots by emphasizing the problematic character of ordering. The concern with dominance is rooted in an appreciation of the strong and persistent influence of the "irritation of doubt" and of the character of belief as "of the nature of habit" that, together, leave the "fixation of belief" open to "tenacity" and "authority" and make dominance both common and pernicious (Peirce 1992). It explains deference to authority and the willingness to turn aside conflicting evidence and sustain belief: better to accept the dominant framing than to open up a settled question to doubt. As Peirce (1992) put it:

Doubt is an uneasy and dissatisfied state from which we struggle to free ourselves and pass into the state of belief; while the latter is a calm and satisfactory state which we do not wish to avoid, or to change to a belief in anything else. On the contrary, we cling tenaciously, not merely to believing, but to believing just what we do believe. (Available at: www.peirce.org/writings/p107.html)

Gamson and others emphasize that these tendencies contribute to the occurrence and stability of dominant frames. The tendencies are exacerbated because framing takes place in a strategic field of action in which the "fixation of belief" is aligned with the distribution of influence and resources. This shapes a distinctive role for the analyst as an agent in this struggle whose critical perspective is needed to open up dominant frames by challenging their appropriation of interpretation that presents a particular way of linking facts, values, and actions as natural or self-evident.

Schön and Rein's analysis of intractable controversies turned away from this strategic orientation to explore another facet of the play of belief and doubt. It also draws attention to the tenacity characteristic of belief and to the claim that there is no "view from nowhere." Frames are not "out there;" they *are* the sense we make by identifying some features as "symptomatic," relegating others to the background, and "bind[ing] together the salient features...into a pattern that is coherent and graspable" (Rein and Schön 1977, 239). To change, or even reflect on a frame then is to work against habit and further marginalize the already provisional stability beliefs provide. An intractable controversy is one in which frames conflict and in which the conflict further insulates the frames from reflection. Thus we are drawn again to the character of a frame as a way of fixing the play between belief and doubt and to the problematic charter of this process that limits our ability to reflect in action.

These broadly compatible accounts of framing embed a methodological pluralism. Snow and Benford's methods are closer to Sabatier than to Rein and Schön. They formulate highly abstract "propositions" to test relationships between (master) frames and cycles of protest. They treat frames as expressed by individuals, but also rooted in and sustained by social interaction. The confirmation that comes with sharing stabilizes and supports them. Testing can be understood as a distinctive form of sharing. Rein and Schön are not concerned with validating their analysis through hypothesis testing. For them frames are part of an *epistemology of practice* that takes the case as its unit of analysis and is redeemed by its usefulness in explaining reasoning in cases, the commitment to act in complex policy fields, and features like intractable controversy.

The internal unity of fact, value, and action distinguishes framing as an approach to ordering and ties it clearly and closely to ambivalence understood as the play between belief and doubt. This still finesses the question of *why* people deem something empirically credible, etc. and why *frames* are the way to grasp this process. The historical concern with dominance and intractability highlight the dynamic quality of the process by tying these forms of stability to persistent sources of concern (tenacity, authority) with the process of fixing belief itself. Reflection and reframing constitute distinct responses to these tendencies by engaging actors' "limited but not negligible" capacity for reflexivity in the former case and inventiveness in response to the natural instability of beliefs in the latter. It is worth noting that framing has been adopted readily and some of the most interesting expressions as policy analysis have come in practice fields like organizational learning (Argyris 1999) and mediation (Forester 1999). The effort to scale up ethnomethodology remains incomplete and frames' tolerance of methodological pluralism is another distinctive quality of the approach.

# 7. NARRATIVE AND DISCOURSE

In 1964 Clifford Geertz wrote that we had "no notion of how metaphor, analogy, irony, ambiguity, pun, paradox, hyperbole, rhythm, and all the other elements of what we lamely call 'style' operate in relation to how people order their personal preferences and become public or collective forces" (Geertz 1964). In the footsteps of Edelman (1964, 1988) a pack of scholars has picked up the challenge to understand the role of linguisitic and non-linguistic symbols in politics, discourse, and narrative in politics and policy (White 1992; Fischer and Forester 1993).

An important stream in the scholarship on policy and narrative has applied the insights of literary theory and sociolinguistics to the understanding of the dynamics of policy making (Kaplan 1986; Throgmorton 1993). Emery Roe, one of its protagonists, highlights the role of narratives in policy making and demonstrates how narrative analysis can help find ways out of complex policy controversies (Roe 1994). He distinguishes *stories* that "underwrite and stabilize the assumptions for policy-making in situations that persists with many unknowns, a high degree of interdependence, and little, if any, agreement" (Roe 1994, 34); *non-stories*, which are interventions that critique particular stories but do not have the full narrative structure of a beginning, middle, and end; and *meta-narratives*, which are constellation of stories and non-stories that together represent the policy debate. Such distinctions help illuminate what others have called the "discursive space" of controversies: seeing what gets discussed and what is disputed, and which elements go unnoticed.

Narrative analysts have shown that storytelling is a principle way of ordering, of constructing shared meaning and organizational realities (Boyce 1995). Stories can create a collective centering that informs policy actors' choices about what to do and, by providing a "plot" can help define operational solutions. Interestingly, much of this scholarship has taken place in the organizational studies literature (Czarniawska 1997). Here Gabriel (2000) employs the concept of "story-work," pointing out that while people's initial accounts of "facts-as-experience" include ambiguity, this changes over time as people try to discover the underlying meaning of events and negotiate a shared way of understanding. Analytically, narrative functions as the ordering device, suggesting that the telling of stories and the interactive development of plots is the way in which ambiguity is handled in organizational settings. People use "causal stories" (Stone 1989) to order complex realities.

In terms of the ontological premises, this take on policy work emphasizes how stories emerge in an interaction, thus operating with a relational ontology. Individual actors may strategically (seek to) insert a particular story, but whether this will organize a policy domain depends on how others respond to it, twist it, take it up. Narratives are like a ball that bounces backwards and forwards and constantly adapts to new challenges that are raised. Interestingly, narrative scholarship has amended the advocacy coalition framework discussed above. In an empirical study of the highly sensitive debate on tax competition in the EU, Claudio Radaelli combines insights from narrative analysis with the advocacy coalition framework and shows that, contrary to the assumptions of the ACF, it is precisely seemingly superficial policy narratives that have the capacity to change "deep core beliefs" (Radaelli 1999). In a special issue following this initial finding, he and Vivian Schmidt found that in complex policy situations where people have to learn across belief systems, it is discursive "variables" that help explain how preferences change (Schmidt and Radaelli 2004). This confirmed a finding of Hajer who, in a study of environmental discourses in the United Kingdom and the Netherlands, suggested that the complex policy domains were structured by "storylines" that actors from a widely differing background could relate to without necessarily understanding each other exactly (Hajer 1995). More generally, empirical research points out that narrative and discourse fulfill an essential role in structuring relations, in determining whether groups turn into opponents rather than collaborators, whether a confrontation leads to joint governance or to conflict (Healey and Hillier 1996).

Although the demarcation between narrative analysis and discourse analysis is not always clear-cut, the latter often takes a broader perspective suggesting ordering works through linguistic systems, through "vocabularies" or "repertoires" that shape the way in which people perceive and judge concrete situations (Potter and Wetherell 1987). These linguistic regularities even provide stability and organizational orientation as actors collaborate in "interpretative communities" that share a particular way of talking about policy situations or help understanding the social exclusion that is inherent in particular policy categories or vocabularies (Yanow 2003). Where discourse analysis draws on French post-structuralist theory, of which Foucault is the most prominent example, scholarship suggests that language allows us to look at a much more ingrained, well-embedded system of ordering. Here discourse is no longer synonymous with "discussion," but refers to something the analyst infers from a situation. Discourses are then seen as patterns in social life, which not only guide discussions, but are institutionalized in particular practices (Burchell et al. 1991). The idea of a strategic acting subject is corrected by the recognition that discourses come with "subject-positions" that guide actors in their perceptions. Because discourses are embedded in institutional practices, they cannot simply be manipulated. The recent work on discourse analysis combines enduring, even "unthought" or "epistemic," categorizations with the more dynamic narrative and metaphorical dimensions of language use (Hajer 2003; Howarth and Torfing 2004).

To the extent a policy analyst can adopt a reflexive position *outside* the cognitive domain of the policy makers, he or she can get analytic leverage on how a particular discourse (defined as an ensemble of concepts and categorizations through which meaning is given to phenomena) orders the way in which policy actors perceive reality, define problems, and choose to pursue solutions in a particular direction. By analyzing documents, sitting in on or video taping policy interactions, or by means of open-ended or focused interviews, the analyst aims to gain insights into the patterning and to relate these patterns back to the practices in which actors operate when doing their policy work. Elaborating Foucault's lectures on governmentality, the discourse analytical methods have been employed to expose a particular power regime in policy domains (Rose and Miller 1992; Dean 1999). This work on "governmentality" fundamentally connects the way in which actors speak to the practices in which they function and the "mentality" that this work represents.

The discourse-analytical tradition addresses ambiguities head on. Pease Chock on immigration discourses is a case in point (1995), Radaelli (1999) explicitly addresses the issue of ambiguity, and Roe (1994) launches his narrative policy analysis in the context of controversies where actors really do not know where to go. In such situations storytelling becomes the central vehicle of consensus building and policy making (Kaplan 1986; Yanow 1996).

As with the work employing belief and frames, one has to look to how the analytical vocabularies of narrative and discourse are applied to understand how the policy analysis is conducted. Work in which discourses are seen as constraining, and are called upon to explain failure to influence the course of affairs, is markedly different in its analytical orientation from studies that try to illuminate how the very meaning of particular terms and categories is constantly contested and in need of social reproduction, and would even go so far as to illuminate how misunderstandings and ambiguity can facilitate diplomatic success (Radaelli and Schmidt 2004) or explain cross-disciplinary learning (cf. the notion of "communicative miracle" in Hajer 1995). The insistence on the social relationality of power and meanings is typical for the analysis of narrative and discourse. Discourse analysis is most consistently positioned at the relational pole of the analytic continuum. Its epistemology is heavily focused on illuminating mechanisms in policy practice, rather than on trying to generate general laws.

# 8. How Do Policy Makers Know What to Do?

In this chapter we thematized ambivalence in policy-making settings. We argued for a reappreciation of the character and role of ambivalence that treats the relationship with ambiguity as a significant feature of policy work. We examined how the public policy scholarship handles ambivalence by looking at scholarship on interpretative schemata. We distinguished and compared three "ordering devices" that analysts employ to make sense of what guides policy makers in their actions.

The empirical case studies in this literature highlight features whose salience is often less distinct in the dialects of analytic regimes we have discussed. In these cases, beliefs are not stable, discourses are not set in stone, and frames are perhaps best seen as constantly being renegotiated. In case studies that follow policy makers closely in their "work," stability is outside any single actor's reach (Healey 1992; Schön and Rein

1994). Actors are actively "naming" and "framing," but this is only part of what needs to be taken into account. All three approaches we looked into, for example, try to bridge actors and institutional structures to help us understand how ordering takes place in concrete policy contexts.

Epistemological principles and methodological rules should help clarify this process. Yet the work we reviewed seems to force a choice. We can either make sense of the activity of policy makers by spelling out general conditions and defining lawlike regularities, or we can undertake the case study work at a detailed level to show how actors deal with ambiguity *in situ* without worrying about how these findings can be generalized. This poses a nasty dilemma. It seems as if the type of question we raised leaves generalized statements open to critique on the grounds that they do not appreciate the particulars of the situation, but does not describe how case research that is detailed enough to grasp the particular can "scale up." Actually, the situation is more complex.

Policy analysts must also be ready to deal with the problem Steinberg raised in his critique of scholarship on frames that, in its strategic emphasis, treated values, beliefs, or belief systems as exogenous to interaction. This gives little attention to the social production of frames. Steinberg suggest that even ideology can be treated as an endogenous characteristic—"it is possible that ideology is an emergent and inter-actional product of framing and is essentially produced in framing" (1998, 847)—thereby avoiding the "reification" inherent in representing "a frame as a discrete text" distinct from "disparate and discontinuous discourse processes" (1998, 848). This led Steinberg to focus on the discursive production of frames and values, a move that resonates with work in the advocacy coalition framework that describes how policy "narratives" seem to guide actors towards compatible positions. These approaches echo the effort to understand how social actors deal with ambivalent situations triggered by Goffman's organizing question, "What is it that is going on here?" If the problem that policy makers have to face is, how do we "arrive at reasonable, acceptable and feasible judgement under conditions of high uncertainty" (Wagenaar 2004), then it makes sense to treat the seemingly effortless activity of policy makers as a struggle, as work (ibid.). The central questions become how to understand inter-action in context, and how to trace the dynamics that occur in the effort to "fix belief," allocate meaning, and stabilize the situation enough to be able to act.

Such epistemological commitments have important consequences for the methodology of policy analysis. They call for a very precise, almost ethnographic approach. If beliefs-frames-discourses cannot be assumed to be stable, but are always incomplete and constantly shifting, then we need to be able to expose this process of "refracturing." Analytical work can illuminate the *mechanisms* that are used to manage ambivalence, help us see what makes certain frames appear "natural" at a particular moment in time, and make sense of what stabilizes them in a stream of experience that always includes conflicting facts and commitments and produces patterns like dominance and intractability. One might be able to start to understand how stable beliefs, frames, narratives, or discourses can become responsive and resilient in the in face of turbulent social events. Concepts like Law and Latour's use of translation can help, as they start from an assumption of variability and precisely target understanding how knowledge and commitments are constantly renegotiated as they are passed on in time.

This step to treat policy practice as the site at which interpretative schemata are produced and reproduced is a significant one. It builds on the linguistic account of policy making that employs narratives—stories, metaphors, myths—to create an image of the world that is acted upon and that constitutes that world at the same time. If we accept that language interferes, that it is more than a medium of something "outside" it (Fischer and Forester 1993), then analysis of policy work as the way in which practitioners make sense of a world that, as such, entails a kaleidoscope of possible meanings, acquires a concrete focus on the *interaction* among actors and on the way in which they interactively frame a situation.

This does not require a turn away from treating actors as strategic operators, nor is it necessarily a denial of the usefulness of traditional research products, like surveys. It is, however, a claim that to understand how policy makers make sense of a complex world and design actions, we need to look more carefully at concrete interaction. Lester and Piore (2004) suggest what the general outlines of such a take might look like when they compare the competence they observed in engineers and other practitioners involved in technical innovation to language development. They draw on sociolinguistic research and argue that "language evolves from clarity to ambiguity—in precisely the opposite direction of evolution that one finds in analytical problem solving. Language development evolves, in other words, toward the creation of interpretative space" (Lester and Piore 2004, 70–1).

Language provides a model to understand competence in which a central feature of practice, and of the intelligence of action, is precisely the way in which these interpretative spaces are opened, sustained, and how the actors who participate engage ambiguity. As Kenneth Burke put it (in his case in the context of an effort to construct a "grammar of motives"): "what we want is *not terms that avoid ambiguity,* but *terms that clearly reveal the strategic spots at which ambiguities necessarily arise"* (Burke 1969). Or, to tailor it more directly to our purposes, what we want are terms that reveal the particular ways in which coping with and finding the creative potential in these ambiguities is constitutive of good policy practice.

If policy work these days often takes place in settings in which people do not share a past and cannot draw on a shared vocabulary of experience, where they can assume misunderstanding as diverse participants draw on different interpretative schemata in the situation, then the need to understand and contribute to the ability to disentangle the complexities of these exchanges is all the more vital. What is more, analysis becomes part of an effort to provide the sort of interpretative spaces that Lester and Piore describe.

This does not imply, however, a policy science that is nothing more than an accumulation of case studies. It is an approach that generates knowledge on the mechanisms involved, precisely the basis on which many contributions to understanding of the sociopolitical dynamics of public policy have been made (Schön and Rein 1994; Argyris 1999; Yanow 2003). But one of the challenges for the time to come is to show to a much broader community how this tradition can yield practical insights into key policy dilemmas and produce meaningful knowledge that can help us understand controversy, resolve conflicts, and innovate. Such an approach holds particular promise for understanding fields like the transnationalization of society that trigger interplay with established political institutions and for husbanding the development of new practices that respond to contemporary public policy challenges. It is in such a context that the relationship between highly decontextualized propositional knowledge (featured here in the work of Sabatier and Jenkins-Smith, and Snow and Benford) and contributions of work in the practice tradition can begin to be explored. This is also the context in which we might begin a search for regularities modelled on the way one searches for regularities in language use, as a grammar of practice.

This brings us to the policy analyst. Rein and Schön have argued that the prevailing traditions in policy analysis fail to take seriously the way in which cultural variables often hinder the resolution of policy controversies. To mainstream traditions that conceive of cultural values as constant and static, cross-cultural controversies appear intractable. Rein and Schön's interpretative approach illuminated how problems, problem holders, and analysts mutually construct one another. Much like the way symbolical interactionism revolutionized thinking about the relationship between the power of the individual and social institutions in sociological theory, Rein and Schön suggest policy makers' competence can be enhanced through procedural innovations.

This perspective still holds. The very epistemological approach that is assumed in the "policy analysis of practice" we investigated here already calls for direct and often extended engagement with policy makers in their actual work. Being aware of the role of ordering, employing the analytical tools we have discussed, allows for a policy analysis that can provide insights into mechanisms operating in contemporary policy making and also facilitate concrete problem solving. Based on that knowledge new, well-researched books in the Lasswellian tradition of policy sciences (Lasswell 1951) can be written that help us understand *and* respond to the controversies of our time.

# REFERENCES

ALLISON, G. T. 1971. *Essence of Decision: Explaining the Cuban Missile Crisis.* Boston: Little, Brown.
—— and ZELIKOW, P. 1999. *Essence of Decision: Explaining the Cuban Missile Crisis.* Reading, Mass.: Longman.
ARGYRIS, C. 1999. *On Organizational Learning.* Oxford: Blackwell.
AXELROD, R. 1984. *The Evolution of Cooperation.* New York: Basic Books.
BAUMAN, Z. 1991. *Modernity and Ambivalence.* Cambridge: Polity Press.
BOYCE, M. E. 1995. Collective centring and collective sense-making in the stories and story-telling of one organization. *Organization Studies*, 16 (1): 107–37.

BURCHELL, G., et al. (eds.) 1991. *The Foucault Effect: Studies in Governmentality.* London: Harvester.

BURKE, K. 1969. *A Grammar of Motives.* Berkeley: University of California Press.

CZARNIAWSKA, B. 1997. *Narrating the Organization: Dramas of Institutional Identity.* Chicago: University of Chicago Press.

DEAN, M. 1999. *Governmentality: Power and Rule in Modern Society.* London: Sage.

DOUGLAS, M. 1986. *How Institutions Think.* London: Routledge.

EDELMAN, M. 1964. *The Symbolic Uses of Politics.* Chicago: University of Illinois Press.

—— 1988. Skeptical studies of language, the media, and mass culture. *American Political Science Review,* 82: 1334–9.

ENTMAN, R. M. 1993. Framing: toward clarification of a fractured paradigm. *Journal of Communication,* 43 (4): 51–8.

FISCHER, F., and FORESTER, J. (eds.) 1993. *The Argumentative Turn in Policy Analysis and Planning.* Durham, NC: Duke University Press.

FLECK, L. 1935. *Entstehung und Entwicklung einer wissenschaftlichen Tatsache? Einfürung in die Lehre vom Denkstil und Denkkollektiv.* Basel: Suhrkamp Verlag KG.

FORESTER, J. 1999. *The Deliberative Practitioner: Encouraging Participatory Planning Processes.* Cambridge, Mass.: MIT Press.

GABRIEL, Y. 2000. *Storytelling in Organizations: Facts, Fictions, and Fantasies.* Oxford: Oxford University Press.

GAMSON, W. A., and MODIGLIANI, A. 1989. Media discourse and public opinion on nuclear power: a constructionist approach. *American Journal of Sociology,* 95 (1): 1–37.

GEERTZ, C. 1964. Ideology as a cultural system. Pp. 47–76 in *Ideology and Discontent,* ed. D. E. Apter. London: Free Press.

GIDDENS, A. 1979. *Central Problems in Social Theory.* London: Macmillan Press.

GOFFMAN, E. 1974. *Frame Analysis: An Essay on the Organization of Experience.* New York: Harper and Row.

HAJER, M. A. 1995. *The Politics of Environmental Discourse: Ecological Modernization and the Policy Process.* Oxford: Oxford University Press.

—— 2003. A frame in the fields: policy making and the reinvention of politics. Pp. 88–110 in *Deliberative Policy Analysis: Understanding Governance in the Network Society,* ed. M. A. Hajer and H. Wagenaar. Cambridge: Cambridge University Press.

HEALEY, P. 1992. A planner's day: knowledge and action in communicative practice. *Journal of the American Planning Association,* 58 (1): 9–20.

—— and HILLIER, J. 1996. Communicative micropolitics: a story of claims and discourses. *International Planning Studies,* 1 (2): 165–84.

HOWARTH, D., and TORFING, J. (eds.) 2004. *Discourse Theory and European Politics: Identity, Policy and Governance.* London: Palgrave.

KAHNEMAN, D., and TVERSKY, A. (eds.) 2000. *Choices, Values, and Frames.* New York: Russell Sage Foundation.

KAPLAN, T. J. 1986. The narrative structure of policy analysis. *Journal of Policy Analysis and Management,* 5 (4): 761–78.

KENNEDY, R. F. 1971. *Thirteen Days: A Memoir of the Cuban Missile Crisis.* New York: W.W. Norton.

KUHN, T. S. 1970/1962. *The Structure of Scientific Revolutions,* 2nd edn. Chicago: University of Chicago Press.

LASSWELL, H. D. 1951. The policy orientation. Pp. 3–15 in *The Policy Sciences,* ed. H. D. Lasswell and D. Lerner. Stanford, Calif.: Stanford University Press.

LESTER, R., and PIORE, M. 2004. *Innovation: The Missing Dimension.* Cambridge, Mass.: Harvard University Press.

LITFIN, K. T. 1994. *Ozone Discourses: Science and Politics in Global Environmental Cooperation.* New York: Columbia University Press.

MARCH, J. G., and OLSEN, J. P. 1989. *Rediscovering Institutions: The Organizational Basis of Politics.* New York: Free Press.

MORRIS, E. 2003. *The Fog of War.* USA, Sony: 1 hour 43 min.

PEASE CHOCK, P. 1995. Ambiguity in policy discourse: congressional talk about immigration. *Policy Sciences,* 28: 165–84.

PEIRCE, C. S. 1992. The fixation of belief. Pp. 109–23 in *The Essential Peirce,* vol. i, ed. N. Houser and C. Kloesel. Bloomington: Indiana University Press.

POTTER, J., and WETHERELL, M. 1987. *Discourse and Social Psychology: Beyond Attitudes and Behaviour.* London: Sage.

RADAELLI, C. M. 1999. Harmful tax competition in the EU: policy narratives and advocacy coalition. *Journal of Common Market Studies,* 37 (4): 661–82.

—— and SCHMIDT, V. A. 2004. Conclusions. *West European Politics,* 27 (2): 364–79.

REIN, M., and SCHÖN, D. A. 1977. Problem setting in policy research. Pp. 235–51 in *Using Social Research for Public Policy Making,* ed. C. Weiss. Lexington, Mass.: Lexington Books.

RIKER, W. H. 1986. *The Art of Political Manipulation.* New Haven, Conn.: Yale University Press.

RITTEL, H. W. J., and WEBBER, M. 1973. Dilemmas in a general theory of planning. *Policy Sciences,* 4 (2): 155–69.

ROE, E. 1994. *Narrative Policy Analysis: Theory and Practice.* Durham, NC: Duke University Press.

ROSE, N., and MILLER, P. 1992. Political power beyond the state: problematics of government. *British Journal of Sociology,* 43: 173–205.

SABATIER, P. A., and JENKINS-SMITH, H. C. (eds.) 1993. *Policy Change and Learning: An Advocacy Coalition Approach.* Boulder, Colo.: Westview Press.

SCHMIDT, V. A., and RADAELLI, C. M. 2004. Policy change and discourse in Europe: conceptual and methodological issues. *West European Politics,* 27 (2): 183–210.

SCHÖN, D. A., and REIN, M. 1994. *Frame Reflection: Toward the Resolution of Intractable Policy Controversies.* New York: Basic Books.

—— —— 1996. Frame critical policy analysis and frame reflective policy practice. *Knowledge and Policy: The International Journal of Knowledge Transfer and Utilization,* 9 (1): 85–104.

SCHWARZ, M., and THOMPSON, M. 1990. *Divided We Stand: Redefining Politics, Technology and Social Choice.* London: Harvester Wheatsheaf.

SNOW, D. A., and BENFORD, R. D. 1992. Master frames and cycles of protest. Pp. 133–55 in *Frontiers in Social Movement Theory,* ed. A. D. Morris and C. McClurg Mueller. New Haven, Conn.: Yale University Press.

STEINBERG, M. W. 1998. Tilting the frame: considerations on collective framing from a discursive turn. *Theory and Society,* 27 (6): 845–72.

STONE, D. 1989. Causal stories and the formation of policy agendas. *Political Science Quarterly,* 104 (2): 281–300.

—— 1997. *Policy Paradox: The Art of Political Decision Making.* New York: W. W. Norton.

THROGMORTON, J. A. 1993. Survey research as rhetorical trope: electric power planning arguments in Chicago. Pp. 117–44 in *The Argumentative Turn in Policy Analysis and Planning,* ed. F. Fischer and J. Forester. Durham, NC: Duke University Press.

VAN GUNSTEREN, H. 1976. *The Quest for Control: A Critique of the Rational-Central-Rule Approach in Public Affairs.* New York: John Wiley.

VICKERS, G. 1965. *The Art of Judgment: A Study of Policy Making.* London: Chapman and Hall.

WAGENAAR, H. 2004. "Knowing" the rules: administrative work as practice. *Public Administration Review,* 64 (6): 643–55.

WHITE, J. D. 1992. Taking language seriously: toward a narrative theory of knowledge for administrative research. *American Review of Public Administration*, 22: 75–88.

YANOW, D. 1996. *How Does a Policy Mean? Interpreting Policy and Organizational Action.* Washington, DC: Georgetown University Press.

—— 2003. *Constructing "Race" and "Ethnicity" in America: Category-Making in Public Policy and Administration.* London: M. E. Sharpe.

CHAPTER 13

# ARGUING, BARGAINING, AND GETTING AGREEMENT

## LAWRENCE SUSSKIND

## 1. INTRODUCTION

In the public policy-making arena, stakeholders and decision makers are engaged in a never-ending process of trying to influence each other's thinking and behavior. Sometimes, this is accomplished through option one: conversation in which one party seeks to convince another to do something (i.e. lend support, change their mind) on the basis of evidence or argument. More often than not, though, an exchange of views—no matter how elegantly presented—is insufficient to alter strongly held beliefs. Because of this, many parties resort to option two—hard bargaining—in which threats, bluff, and political mobilization are used to gain the outcomes they want. Particularly if political power is unevenly distributed, powerful parties can often use hard bargaining to pursue their objectives. In many democratic contexts, however, confrontations that flow from hard bargaining lead to litigation (or other defensive moves), which typically generates less than ideal results for all parties.

There is a third option: "mutual gains" negotiation, or what is now called consensus building. In this mode, parties seek to make mutually advantageous trades—offering their "votes" in exchange for a modification of what is being proposed or for a promise of support on other issues. So, while arguing and bargaining—the first two approaches to dealing with conflict in the public policy arena—can sometimes produce the desired results, they often generate a backlash or lead to sustained confrontation. Only when parties feel that their core interests have been met, they have been treated fairly, and they know everything possible is being done to maximize joint gains (i.e. through consensus building) will agreements be reachable and durable enough to withstand the difficulties of implementation.

The dynamics of deliberation, bargaining, and consensus building in the public arena have been reasonably well documented (Gutmann and Thompson 1996). These published findings suggest that well-organized dialogue on matters of public policy can improve the climate of understanding and increase respect for differences in perspective, but will not lead to changes in policy or shifts in the balance of political power (Yankelovich 1999; Straus 2002; Isaacs 1999). On the other hand, there is some evidence to indicate that carefully structured consensus-building efforts can produce fairer, more efficient, wiser, and more stable results—even when political power is not distributed evenly (Susskind and Cruikshank 1987; O'Leary and Bingham 2003). That is, that negotiation can actually lead to shifts in policy or political alignments. However, obstacles to the organizational learning required to institutionalize consensus building are substantial, and the documentation that does exist points to a relatively small number of successful consensus-building efforts in the public arena (Schön and Rein 1994). Further, attempts by others elsewhere in the world to capitalize on and apply what has been learned in the United States about negotiation and consensus building are only just beginning (Centre for Democracy and Governance 1998).

Most bargaining and negotiation theory postulates interaction between two parties. In the public policy arena, however, policy-related exchanges involve many (non-monolithic) parties represented by agents (i.e. elected spokespeople or unofficial representatives). As such, multiparty, multi-issue negotiations tend to be much more complicated than negotiation theorists suggest. Indeed, getting agreement in a multiparty situation often requires someone (other than the parties themselves) to manage the complexities of group interaction. This has led to the emergence of a new profession of public dispute mediation (Susskind and Cruikshank 1987). Indeed, in many contentious settings, having wasted time and money on recurring public policy disputes that have not been settled effectively, participants have sought mediator assistance to reach agreements through collaboration.

In this chapter, I will describe the three options that I have dubbed arguing, bargaining, and getting agreement. I will also highlight what appear to be usefully prescriptive norms of behavior for "combatants" in the public policy arena.

## 2. DIALOGUE AND ARGUMENTATION

A distinction is sometimes made by those who focus on discourse between dialogue and discussion. The former refers to the exploration of options while the latter refers to making decisions. Isaacs suggests that dialogue involves listening, respecting what others have to say, suspending judgement (i.e. avoiding the tendency to defend pre-existing beliefs), and voicing reactions. So, the key questions, then, are: how to get others to listen to what we have to say, how to structure a dialogue (or a skillful conversation) to ensure that participants suspend judgement and reflect carefully on what we are saying, and how to control or manage debate to ensure that the most useful exchange of ideas and arguments occurs (Isaacs 1999).

## 2.1 Getting People to Listen

Some people will listen politely to the views of others, no matter how outrageous, because that's what they have been taught to do—as a matter of manners. In most contexts, however, politeness breaks down when passions run high, core values are threatened, or the stakes are substantial. Politeness also breaks down when those speaking are more concerned about the reactions of their constituents or followers to what they are saying than they are about the reactions of their partners in dialogue. In multiparty dialogue, representatives of faction-laden groups play to their supporters. They are more concerned about "looking tough" than they are about convincing the "other side" to go along with their proposals.

Isaacs suggests that the "atmosphere, energy and memories of people create a field of conversation" (Isaacs 1999). Within such fields, he asserts, "dialogue fulfills deeper, more widespread needs than simply 'getting to yes.' " Thus his claim is that the aim of a negotiation may be to reach agreement among parties who differ, but the intent of dialogue is to reach new understandings and, in doing so, to form a totally new basis from which to think and act. In dialogue, Isaacs and others suggest, the goal is not only to solve problems, but to "dissolve them" (Isaacs 1999, 19). The question that must be asked is whether or not dialogue—as opposed to negotiation—can solve problems if nothing is traded and only an understanding of differences (and the basis for them) is enhanced.

## 2.2 Structuring the Conversation

The goal, according to those who see conversation as an end in itself, is to break down politeness and move to a kind of joint enquiry or "generative dialogue." What motivates such a shift, we must ask, if no decision needs to be made, or no agreement must be reached? The moves necessary to accomplish such a transformation hinge on the capacity of the parties to achieve and maintain a substantial level of self-control. In addition, there seems to be an assumption that the participants care more about convincing others of the merits of what they are saying than they do about achieving a particular outcome. Unfortunately, this doesn't seem likely to occur in the world of public policy.

Ground rules for constructive deliberation must be internalized or enforced. If the exchange is one-time only, as it often is in the public policy arena, it seems highly unlikely that this can be accomplished (unless each of the participants is an old hand at such exchanges). The conversation must be managed in a way that constantly reminds the participants to listen to and respect each other's views. Often, this is best achieved with the help of a trained facilitator (or by building the capacity of the participants through training). But this only works as long as everyone buys into the idea. It is not clear how to deal with obstructionists who seek only to achieve what they see as a symbolic victory by bringing the conversation to a close. When a key player in the conversation is either out of control or has decided, for strategic reasons, that bringing the exchange to a halt is his or her objective, there is nothing that even the most skilled facilitator can do.

## 2.3  Avoiding Demonization (and Stressing the Importance of Civility) in Debates over Values

"Interests," as William Ury, an anthropologist and mediator, explains, are "needs, desires, concerns, or fears—the things one cares about or wants. They underlie people's positions—the tangible items they say they want" (Fisher, Ury, and Patton 1983). When conflicts revolve around interests, numerous solutions are possible. Since individuals and groups usually have numerous interests, it is often possible with creativity and hard work to find a deal that satisfies many, if not all of the interests involved. Mutual gains negotiation, or integrative bargaining as consensus building is sometimes called in the theoretical literature, is about advancing self-interest through the invention of packages that meet interests on all sides. However, interests are not always the only thing at stake. Fundamental values may be involved as well.

As mediator Christopher Moore explains, "Values disputes focus on such issues as guilt and innocence, what norms should prevail in a social relationship, what acts should be considered valid, what beliefs are correct, who merits what, or what principles should guide decision-making" (Moore 1986). Values involve strongly held personal beliefs, moral and ethical principles, basic legal rights, and more generally, idealized views of the world. While interests are about what we want, values are about what we care about and what we stand for.

In value-laden debates, to compromise or to accommodate neither advances one's self-interest nor increases joint gains. Compromise, in its most pejorative sense, means abandoning deeply held beliefs, values, or ideals. To negotiate away values is to risk giving up one's identity.

Social psychologist Terrell Northrup details several stages through which value disputes move toward intractability. Intense conflict begins when individuals feel threatened. The threat is perceived as an awful trade-off: either you survive or I do. In order to maintain belief systems in the face of such threats, the first thing parties do is to engage in a process of distortion. This includes building up the perceived legitimacy of their own claim (in their mind) and tearing down the claims of other(s). Then, individuals (and groups) involved in conflict develop increasingly rigid explanations of their own actions and the actions of others. In order to maintain the integrity of our own belief systems, we stereotype others. Behaviors that we find distasteful in ourselves, we project onto our "enemies." As this process continues, our adversaries become dehumanized and are seen not merely as different, but as inhumane. Such reasoning, carried to its radical end, justifies and supports violent behavior (Northrup 1989, quoted in Susskind and Field 1996).

Northrup's final stage, maintaining the conflict, becomes central to each party's identity. To maintain their own values, the groups in conflict must keep the conflict alive. Ironically, this creates an implicit and often tragic agreement among the parties that Northrup labels "collusion." Over time, groups, cultures, and even nations institutionalize behaviors and beliefs which maintain long-standing conflicts. No wonder dialogue, no matter how skillfully managed, is unlikely to produce agreement in situations in which fundamental values are at stake.

Northrup suggests that there are three levels at which conflicts involving fundamental values and identities can be addressed. At the first level, the disputants may agree on peripheral changes that do not eliminate the ongoing hostilities but alleviate specific problems. For example, in the wake of the killing of two employees at a Planned Parenthood Clinic in Massachusetts, Bernard Cardinal Law of Boston called for a temporary moratorium on sidewalk demonstrations and asked protesters to move their vigils inside churches. At this level, both sides held fast to their basic principles. Pro-life Catholics continued to oppose abortion and support demonstrations. Pro-choice groups continued to support a woman's right to choose abortion. However, when the focus shifted to the goal of minimizing violence, it was possible to reach agreement on specific steps that needed to be taken. Unfortunately, such agreements have little effect on basic value conflicts.

Second-level changes alter some aspects of ongoing relationships, but fundamental values are not challenged or transformed at this level either, at least in the short run. Agreements reached at the second level focus on how the parties will relate to one another over time as opposed to merely how one specific situation or problem will be solved. For instance, in Missouri, the director of an abortion clinic, an attorney opposing abortion, and a board member of a Missouri right-to-life group agreed to meet to discuss adoption, foster care, and abstinence for teenagers. Surprisingly, these groups agreed to support legislation to pay for the treatment of pregnant drug addicts. They also established an ongoing dialog that transformed the way they dealt with each other. They began to meet individually, on a personal basis, to work on problems they had in common.

Third-level change is far more difficult. This kind of change involves shifts in the identities that people hold dear. Not only are working relationships changed at this level, but the way people view themselves is altered. Northrup uses the example of psychotherapy to illustrate. In psychotherapy, an individual's core constructs are examined, faulty constructs are discarded, and the individual develops a transformed sense of self over time. Changes at the first and second levels frequently set the stage for third-level changes (Northrup 1989, cited in Susskind and Field 1996).

## 2.4  Can Anyone be Convinced to Do Something That is Not in their Best Interest?

The key question for those who believe that "differences" can be worked out through conversation is whether or not anyone can be convinced to do or support something that is not in their own best interest. It seems unlikely. Rhetorical methods, however, can be very powerful. They basically boil down to (1) argumentation with reference to logic; (2) argumentation with reference to emotion; (3) argumentation with reference to history, expert judgement, or evidence; and (4) argumentation with reference to ideology or values. In each case, the person who is trying to do the convincing is basically asking the object of their persuasion (their audience) to hold predispositions in abeyance and remain open to new ideas, new evidence, or new interpretations.

## 2.5  Influencing the Opinions of Others Through the Use of Rhetoric

It is useful to think of rhetoric in terms of a speaker, an audience, and a message.[1] At the outset, the speaker needs to convince the audience that he or she is trustworthy and knowledgeable. This gives the audience a reason to listen to and, perhaps, believe what the speaker is saying. An audience that ignores the speaker cannot be reached. Thus, establishing some emotional connection with the audience is important. Of course, there is a danger the audience can become too emotionally involved. This can lead to the blind acceptance of arguments. While such persuasiveness might seem advantageous in the short run, concurrence reached in this way will likely be temporary, evaporating once emotions are no longer running high and more thoughtful analysis takes place.

A rhetorical message must be articulated in a language an audience can understand. The most successful rhetoricians try to argue a viewpoint that is usually mildly discrepant with what an audience believes. An audience doesn't want to look foolish—holding an opinion that is demonstrably wrong—but they aren't going to swing across a wide spectrum either. While they usually search for evidence that

---

[1] Many thanks to Noah Susskind for offering suggested language for this section of the chapter.

verifies what they already believe, most people spend more time scrutinizing an argument that differs radically from their own (Kassin 2004). If the speaker is preaching to the choir, the choir tends to expend less effort finding fault with the message.

Context and expectations are obviously important. The choice of a rhetorical approach must match the situation. In some instances, it makes sense to lean more heavily on emotion than on logical proof, while in other situations the reverse is true. If there is a clash of ideas or viewpoints, it sometimes makes sense to build upon an opponent's foundational beliefs, but draw different conclusions— pointing out how the other side has misinterpreted the situation or made incorrect leaps of judgement. Convincing an audience that you are right and your opponent is wrong can take several forms. In a dialogue, one side can try to convince the other that they are being a hypocrite because their beliefs, actions, or conclusions contradict each other. They can claim that the other side's beliefs will lead to dangerous outcomes or that their beliefs are fundamentally wrong. They can take a milder course claiming that the other side's beliefs are correct, but their conclusions are wrong. Finally, they can make reference to a conventional body of wisdom, arguing that everybody agrees that they are right so that their opponent must be wrong.

## 2.6 Using Evidence to Make Arguments on "their Merits"

In the context of public policy debates of various kinds, advocates are very likely to utilize scientific or technical information to bolster their arguments (Ozawa 1991). There are many analytic tools and techniques, including cost–benefit analysis, risk assessment, and environmental impact assessment, that are often used to justify one interpretation of what a particular policy or proposal will or won't accomplish. While these techniques are fairly well developed, they are not immune from criticism. So, if one party doesn't like the evidence offered by an adversary to justify a particular public action, he can either challenge the relevance of that particular technique or suggest that the technique was applied incorrectly. Since almost all such studies hinge, at least in part, on non-objective judgements of one kind or another (i.e. geographic scope of the study, timeframe for the study, etc.), it is possible to accept the relevance and the legitimacy of a study, but show how key assumptions could have been made differently, and if they were, how the results would vary (Susskind and Dunlap 1981).

Advocates of "improved" public discourse press all sides to make arguments "on their merits," that is, to put aside claims based solely on ideology or intuition and to rely, instead, on arguments built on "independent" scientific evidence. Unfortunately, all too often, this leads to the "battle of the printout" as each side appropriates carefully selected expertise to support its a priori beliefs. In the current era, in which relativism appears to trump positivism, the prospect of "dueling experts" leads some to suggest that scientific or technical evidence might just as well be ignored entirely.

## 2.7 The Prospects of Joint Fact Finding

If all the parties in a public policy dispute felt they could rely on a particular bit of shared scientific or technical analysis, and agreed to use it to inform a public decision, it would probably have to be generated in a way that all parties had a hand in formulating, by analysts all sides were willing to accept. That is pretty much the idea behind joint fact finding. Since partisans in public policy disputes are unlikely to defer to experts selected by their opponents, and since the idea of unbiased or independent expertise is more or less unconvincing, the only alternative—if technical input is going to be considered at all—is analysis generated by experts chosen and instructed jointly by the partisans.

Joint fact finding can most easily be understood in the context of the consensus-building process (that will be described in more detail below); however, it can also be presented on its own terms and can be used in a dialogue process that it is not necessarily aimed at achieving agreement, but only at enhancing understanding. Joint fact finding begins with the framing of a set of questions. The choice of analytic methods, the selection of experts, even strategies for handling non-objective judgements (including key parameters like timeframe, geographic boundaries, and strategies for dealing with uncertainty) must all then be made in a credible fashion. While joint fact finding rarely settles policy debates, it ensures that useful information, in a believable and timely form, is considered by the parties (Susskind, McKeavner, and Thomas-Lovmer 1999).

Unfortunately, even when joint fact finding is used as part of carefully structured public deliberations, dialogue—no matter how well facilitated—is unlikely to lead to agreement on public policy choices. Argumentation, no matter how skillfully presented or corroborated by expert advice, will rarely cause partisans in public policy debates to put their own interests (as they see them) aside.

## 3. HARD BARGAINING

Hard bargaining refers to a set of classical negotiation tactics. In an effort to convince someone to do "what you want, when you want, the way you want," hard bargainers try to limit the choices available to their negotiating partners by making threats, bluffing, and demanding concessions. In a hard bargaining context, it also helps to have more "political power" than the other side. These classical negotiating techniques are still very much in vogue even though consensus-building or mutual gains approaches to negotiation have emerged as a highly desirable alternative.

## 3.1  Hard Bargaining in Two-party Situations

Most prescriptive advice about negotiation assumes a two-party bargaining situation modeled on traditional buyer–seller interaction (Cohen 1982). That is, it assumes two monolithic parties engaged in a one-time-only face-to-face exchange in which each party seeks to achieve its goals at the expense of the other. Such a "zero-sum" approach assumes that the only way one side can get what it wants is by blocking the other's efforts to meet its interests. Note that this presumes that each bargainer is monolithic, or at least has the power to commit (regardless of how many people they might represent). So, agents are not involved.

Hard bargaining follows a well-established pattern. First, one side begins with an exaggerated demand (knowing full well that it will not be acceptable to the other). This is followed by an equally exaggerated demand by the other side. Openings are sometimes coupled with bluff and bluster—indicating that if the initial demand is not accepted, negotiations will come to an immediate halt. Of course, this is not true. Concessions continue to be traded as each side reduces its demand in response to reductions offered by the other. Along the way, each attempts to convince the other that the prior concession was the last that will be offered. They also plead their case on occasion, trying to gain sympathy. During such exchanges, little or no attention is paid by either side to the arguments put forward in support of the other's demands. After all, if one side admitted that the other's claims were legitimate, they would have to make the final (and probably the larger) concession. Finally, the parties either slide past an acceptable deal or reach a minimally acceptable agreement.

## 3.2  Using Threats to Win Arguments in the Public Arena

In a public policy context, it is not clear that the use of threats is very effective. Hard bargaining in the public policy arena only succeeds when the other side(s) agree(s) to go along. Threats undermine legitimacy, and in the absence of legitimacy, large numbers of people tend to refuse (actively or passively) to comply with whatever agreement is worked out by their representatives. Since threats are usually viewed as illegitimate (or, at the very least, unfair), this can create opposition and instability, requiring larger investments in enforcement to achieve implementation or compliance with whatever public policy decision is ultimately made. In addition, threats set an undesirable precedent. They encourage retaliation by others the next time around.

In a bilateral context, threats can be aimed directly at a particular party. In a multilateral context (more common in the public arena), threats can cause a backlash in unexpected quarters by contributing to the formation of unlikely blocking coalitions.

## 3.3  Does Bluffing Work?

Bluffing typically involves threats in the absence of power. That is, the one making the bluff knows that they do not have the capacity or the intention to follow through. If they have the power, why bluff? Bluffing is usually a bad idea in a bargaining context. A bluff may be met with resistance on the other side, just to see whether the claim is authentic or not. When it is not real, it undermines future credibility. This is a high price to pay. The negotiation literature dealing with bluffing suggests that it is usually an ineffective practice (Schelling 1980).

## 3.4  Getting the Attention of the "Other Side"

In what is clearly a hard bargaining situation, it may be necessary to take dramatic action (i.e. adopt a flamboyant opening gambit) to get the attention of the other side, especially if there is an imbalance of power and the "less powerful party" is trying to frame the negotiation in a way that is most helpful to them. Less powerful parties may open with a take-it-or-leave it offer, although they should only do this if they really mean to walk away. Sometimes less powerful groups will try to stage a media event to bring pressure on their potential negotiating partners. Of course, this often stiffens the resolve of the party that is the target of such tactics. Sometimes, in a hard bargaining situation, one side will attempt to send what is called a back-channel message to the other side (through a mutually trusted intermediary) to see if they can get a better sense of the "real" Zone of Possible Agreement (ZOPA) or what economists sometimes call "the contract curve." This avoids face-saving problems later when threats are ignored (Raiffa 1985).

## 3.5  The Results of Concession Trading

When hard bargaining involves outrageous opening demands on either side, it is hard to explain to the constituencies represented (who follow the whole process) why the final agreement should be viewed as a victory. It will tend to look like what it is— the minimally acceptable outcome rather than a maximally beneficial one (for either side). Not only that, but an outrageous opening demand can sometimes cause a potential negotiating partner to walk away, figuring incorrectly that there is no Zone of Possible Agreement (ZOPA), when in fact, there is lots of room to maneuver. Exaggerated opening demands sometimes create a test of will (especially when one or both negotiators are trying to prove how tough they are to their own constituents). This can make the negotiation more contentious than it needs to be. Emotions can be triggered. These can outstrip logic, leading to no agreement when in fact, one was possible. There is a good chance, if the parties stop listening to each other entirely, that they will slide right past a minimally acceptable deal because one or both sides assumes that the back-and-forth of concession trading is still not over.

## 3.6 Power and Hard Bargaining

There are many sources of power in negotiation, although in a hard bargaining situation only a few are relevant (Fisher 1983). The first, obviously, is a good "walk away" alternative. The party with the best BATNA (Best Alternative to a Negotiated Agreement) has the most leverage. If one party can muster a coalition, it can sometimes increase its bargaining power by bringing members into a supportive coalition, which can alter the BATNA of the other side (or increase what is available to offer to the other side). I am avoiding reference to physical coercion since it seems out of place in a public policy context, but obviously there may be occasions where decisions are made because people are afraid for their safety. Finally, information can sometimes be used as club. If one side's reputation will be tarnished if critical information is released, then this becomes a source of power in hard bargaining. The key point about hard bargaining is that the parties do not care about the relationships with which they are left once the negotiation is over. Nor do they care about the trust that may be lost between them, or the credibility they lose in the eyes of the public at large. When these matter, hard bargaining must give way to consensus building.

# 4. GETTING AGREEMENT

Whereas hard bargainers assume, in zero-sum fashion, that the best way to get what they want is to ensure that their negotiating partner does not get what he or she wants, consensus building proceeds on a very different assumption: namely, that the best way for a negotiator to satisfy his interests is to find a low-cost way (to him) of meeting the most important interests of his negotiating partner. As the number of parties increases, which it often does in public policy disputes, the same principle applies. Dispute resolution theoreticians have dubbed this the "mutual gains approach" to negotiation (Fisher, Ury, and Patton 1983; Susskind and Field 1996; Lewicki and Literer 1985). So, hard bargaining and consensus building are both forms of negotiation, but consensus building puts more of a premium on (1) maximizing the value (to all sides) of the agreement reached; (2) leaving the parties in a better position to deal with each other in the future and reducing the costs associated with implementing agreements; (3) reducing the transaction costs involved in working out an agreement; and (4) adding to the trust and credibility that the parties have in the eyes of the community at large as a product of the negotiations.

It is easiest to understand consensus building in multiparty situations if we first review the application of "mutual gains" theory to a two-party context.

## 4.1 The Mutual Gains Approach to Negotiation

There are four steps in the mutual gains approach to negotiation. They are depicted in Fig. 13.1.

### Preparation

In a hard bargaining context, negotiators spend most of their preparatory time trying to decide how much to exaggerate their initial demand, what their fall-back proposal will be when the other side objects, and which strategies they can employ to increase their negotiating partner's level of discomfort—so that they will settle for less just to end the exchange. The mutual gains approach, on the other hand, calls on negotiators to (1) clarify (and rank order) their interests; (2) imagine what the interests of their negotiating partners are; (3) analyze their own BATNA and think about ways of improving it before the negotiations begin; (4) analyze their partner's BATNA and think about ways of raising doubts about it if it seems particularly good; (5) generate possible options or packages of options for mutual gain; (6) imagine the strongest arguments (an objective observer might make) on behalf of the package that would be beneficial to the negotiator; and (7) ensure that they have a clear mandate regarding the responsibilities and autonomy accorded to them by their own constituents or organization. This requires a substantial investment of time and energy. Moreover, it usually implies organizational and not just individual effort.

### Value Creation

At the outset of a mutual gains negotiation, it is in the interest of all parties to take whatever steps they can to create value, that is, to "increase the size of the pie" before determining who gets what. The more value they can create, the greater the chances

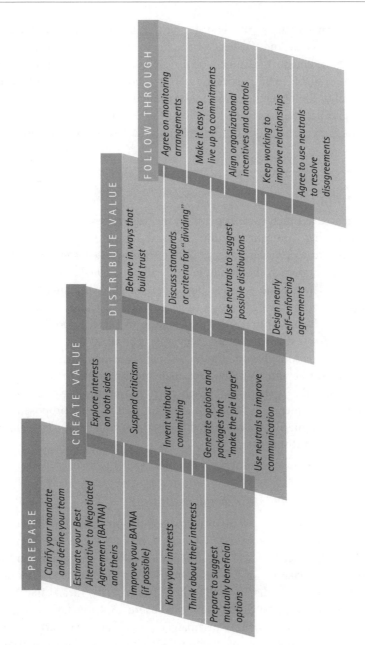

**Fig. 13.1.** Mutual gains approach to negotiation

*Source*: Susskind, Mckearnan, and Thomas-Lamar 1999.

that all sides will exceed their BATNA (and thus find a mutually advantageous outcome). Value creating requires the parties to play the "game" of "what if?" That is, each party needs to explore possible trades to determine which would leave them better off. So, one side might ask the other, "What if we added 'more A' and assumed 'less B' in the package? Would you like that better?" The other might say, "Yes, that's possible, but we would need to actually double the amount of A and not decrease B by more than 10 per cent. And, I'd need to be able to count on some C being included as well." The back-and-forth is aimed, obviously, at finding a package that maximizes the total value available to the parties. By working cooperatively to identify things they value differently, the negotiators can make mutually advantageous trades. For this to work in practice, they need to be willing to "invent without committing," that is, to explore a great many options before going back to their constituents for final approval.

## Value Distribution

Having generated as much value as possible, the negotiators—even in a mutual gains context—must then confront the difficult (and competitive) task of dividing the value they have created. At this stage, gains to one constitute losses to the other. Thus, the mutual gains approach should not be, as it often is, called a "win-win" approach to negotiation. There is no way for both sides to get everything they want in a negotiation. Rather, mutual gains seek to get both (or all) sides as "far above" their BATNA as possible and to maximize the creation of value. In addition, the parties need to be able to explain to others why they got what they got. This entails a discussion of the reasons that the figurative "pie" is being distributed the way it is. Both sides need to be able to go back to their organizations (or constituents) and explain why what they got was fair. Each party has an incentive to propose such criteria so that the others will be able to agree to what is being proposed. No one is likely to accept voluntarily a package that leaves them vulnerable to the charge when they return home that they were "taken."

## Anticipating the Problems of Implementation

Even though the parties to a mutual gains negotiation are almost always satisfied with the outcome (or they would not have agreed to accept it), they still need to worry about the mechanics of implementation. Often, particularly in the public policy world, the make-up of groups changes over time. Indeed, fluctuations in elected and appointed leadership are to be expected. This means that negotiators cannot depend on good relationships alone to ensure implementation of agreements. Instead, prior to signing anything or finalizing a package, the parties must invest time in crafting the best ways of making their agreement "nearly self-enforcing." This may require adding incentives or penalties to the terms of the agreement. In the public policy arena, informally negotiated agreements are often non-binding. However, they can be grafted onto or incorporated into formal administrative decisions, thereby solving the implementation problem, It may also be necessary to identify a party to monitor implementation of an agreement or to reconvene the parties if milestones are not met or unexpected events demand reconsideration of the terms of an agreement. All of this can be built into the agreement if relationships are positive and trust has been built during the earlier stages of the process.

## 4.2 Psychological Traps

Even mutual gains negotiators are susceptible to falling into a range of psycho-logical traps, although they are less likely to be trapped than hard bargainers. These traps go by a variety of names—"too much invested to quit," "reactive de-valuation," "self-fulfilling prophecy," and others (Bazerman and Neale 1994; Kahneman and Tversky 2000). They grow out of the psychological dynamics that overtake people in competitive situations. The best way to avoid or escape such difficulties is to retain perspective on what is happening—perhaps by taking advan-tage of breaks in the action to reflect with others on what has occurred thus far. Substantial preparation is another antidote. Negotiators are less likely to give in to their worst (irrational) instincts if they have rehearsed carefully and tried to put themselves "in the shoes" of the other side (Ury 1991). While there is no guarantee that a mutual gains approach to negotiation will succeed, by its very nature it involves cooperation as well as competition. It also puts a premium on building trust. These are useful barriers to the paranoia that so often overwhelms hard bargainers.

## 4.3 The Impact of Culture and Context

The mutual gains approach to negotiation is viewed somewhat differently in various cultural contexts (Avruch 1998). There are well-documented indigenous dispute-handling techniques used in cultures in Africa, Asia, and Latin America to generate community-wide agreement on a range of public policy matters (Gulliver 1979). Even indigenous peoples in North America share a tradition of community-wide consen-sus building (Morris 2004). There are hard bargaining oriented cultures, however, that are suspicious of the mutual gains approach to negotiation. Even in these cultures, however, while business negotiations retain their hard bargaining character, there is ongoing experimentation with consensus-building approaches to resolving public arena disputes.

## 4.4 The Three Unique Features of Multiparty Negotiation

As noted above, most public policy disputes take place in a multiparty context. There are usually proponents who want to maintain the status quo. Opponents inevitably emerge whose interests run in different directions. These opponents may be unified in their opposition, but more often than not they are likely to have their own (separate) reasons for protesting. Then, one or more government agencies is cast as the decision maker(s) in either a regulatory (administrative), legislative, or judicial role (Susskind and Cruikshank 1987). Indeed, multiple levels and agencies of government can be involved. Ultimately, still other groups are interested bystanders, waiting to see what will happen before they jump in on one side or another.

As the number of parties increases, the complexity of the negotiations increases. Most public policy disputes involve many parties, talking (sometimes at cross-purposes) about a range of issues. Generating agreement in such contested circumstances is not easy. Someone needs to bring the "right" parties to the table. Ground rules for joint problem solving must be agreed upon. Believable information needs to be generated. The conversation needs to be managed, often in the glare of media attention. All the legal and administrative conventions that are already in place, guaranteeing certain groups access to information and others rights as well, have to be observed. Any effort at consensus building has to be superimposed on this underlying legal and administrative structure. Assuming the powers-that-be are willing to go along with an unofficial effort to generate consensus, the three most difficult problems in any multiparty context are: (1) managing the coalitional dynamics that are sure to emerge; (2) coping with the mechanics of the group conversation that makes problem-solving dialogue and decision making so difficult; and (3) dealing with the kaleidoscopic nature of the BATNA problem as alternative packages are proposed (Susskind et al. 2003). When some or all of the parties are represented by lawyers or agents, the difficulties are further increased.

## 4.5 The Steps in the Consensus Building Process

The use of consensus building (i.e. mutual gains negotiation in multiparty situations focused on matters of public policy) is well documented (Susskind, McKearnan, and Thomas-Larmer 1999). Indeed, "best practices" have begun to coalesce (SPIDR 1997). They are perfectly consistent with the spirit of deliberative democracy outlined in the political theory literature (Cohen 1983; Gutmann and Thompson 1996; Barber 1984; Dryzek 2000; Mansbridge 1980; Fung 2004). However, it is important to note that they are meant to supplement representative democratic practices, not replace them (Susskind and Cruikshank 1987). The five steps in the consensus-building process are:

### Convening

Usually, a consensus-building process in the public sector is initiated by an elected or appointed official or by an administrative/regulatory agency. This person or group is called a convener. The convener hires an external neutral, a facilitator or mediator, to help determine whether or not it is worth going forward with a full-fledged collaborative process. As part of that determination, the neutral prepares a Conflict Assessment (sometimes called an Issue Assessment, or just an Assessment). This is a written document with two parts. The first section summarizes the results of off-the-record interviews with all (or most) of the relevant stakeholders in the form of a "map of the conflict" (Susskind et al. 2003, 99–136). The second part, assuming the Assessment results suggest that the key parties are willing to come to the negotiating table, is a prescriptive section with a proposed list of stakeholding groups that ought to be invited (by the convener), a proposed agenda, work plan, timetable, budget, and operating ground rules. By the time this is submitted to the convener, it has usually been reviewed in detail by all the stakeholders who were interviewed. A Conflict Assessment, in a complex public dispute, might be based on fifty to seventy interviews. By the time the convener sends out letters of invitation, it is usually clear that the key groups are willing to attend at least the organizing session. At that point, the participants are usually asked to confirm the selection of a professional "neutral" (i.e. a facilitator or mediator) to help manage the process and to sign the ground rules that will govern the work of the group.

## Signing on

When stakeholder groups agree to participate in a consensus-building process, they are not committing to a particular view of the conflict or a specific agreement architecture. They usually are, however, asked to accept a work plan, a timetable, some way of dividing the costs associated with the process, and as mentioned above, ground rules that oblige them to negotiate "in good faith." When they confirm the selection of a mediator or a facilitator, they are typically asked to agree to an approach to working together, including ground rules restricting interactions with the press, a clear assignment of responsibility for preparing written meeting summaries, and the expectations that each participant will keep his or her constituency informed about the group's progress and prepare appropriately for meetings.

Often, participants are encouraged to select alternates to stand in for them on a continuing basis if they cannot be present.

## Deliberation

Deliberations are guided by the professional neutral following the agreed-upon ground rules and work plan. Often, a consensus-building process will mix some sessions at which information is presented for group review, some at which brainstorming of possible "solutions" or "ideas for action" are discussed, and some at which "outside experts" are invited by the group to answer technical questions (following the joint fact-finding process described earlier). Often, a large group will create subcommittees to do some of these things and bring work products back to the full group for discussion.

Consensus-building deliberations follow the mutual gains approach to negotiation outlined above. Because there are many parties, the process can be extremely complicated.

## Deciding

Consensus-building efforts do not conclude with a vote. Unlike traditional group decision making, governed by majority rule, consensus building seeks to achieve unanimity (but most often settles for overwhelming agreement once all the parties concur that every reasonable effort has been made to respond to the legitimate interests of all the stakeholders). It is up to the neutral to frame the decision-making choices put before the group. These usually take the form of a question, "Who can't live with the following ...?" Those who object are obligated to propose further changes or additions that will make the proposed package acceptable to them without losing the support of the rest of the group. If they cannot suggest such modifications, consensus has been reached. The consensus might not be implementable if a key group, with the power to block, refuses to support the agreement. The decision rule in a consensus-building process is up to the group and must be articulated at the outset of their deliberations.

## Implementing

The product of ad hoc consensus-building efforts (including those initiated by governmental conveners) is invariably a proposal, not a final decision. Whatever is suggested must be acted upon by those with the relevant authority to do so. Thus, the product of most consensus-building efforts, no matter how detailed, is almost always subject to further review and action by elected or appointed officials. Of course, were those officials significantly to modify the proposal, the groups involved would disavow their support. And, the agencies themselves typically participate (usually through their staff) in the entire consensus-building effort. So, whatever their concerns might be, they should have been addressed by the group.

Participants in negotiated agreements try to produce "nearly self-enforcing agreements." This can be done by laying out a range of contingent commitments that will come into play only if hard-to-estimate events occur or milestones are reached. Sequences of reciprocal agreements can be spelled out along with monitoring requirements, incentives for performance, and penalties for non-compliance. All of these must then, of course, be incorporated into official actions (i.e. become additional terms added to a contract, permit, license, or administrative decision).

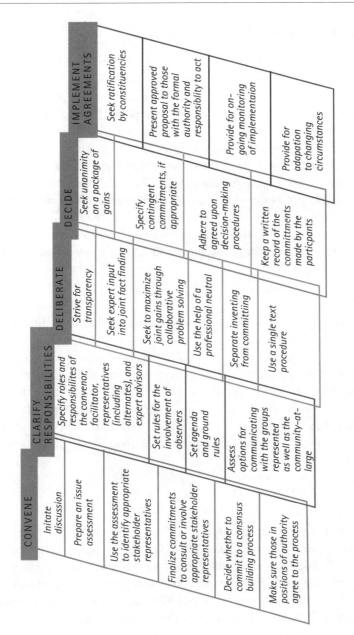

**Fig. 13.2.** Consensus building: essential steps

*Source*: Susskind, Mckearnan, and Thomas-Lamar 1999.

## 4.6 The Role of Professional Neutrals

The person or group selected by the convener is often (but not always) tapped by the full group to serve as the manager of the consensus-building effort, if such a process goes forward. Over the past twenty years, the number of people trained to manage such conflict resolution efforts has increased rapidly. The Association for Conflict Resolution (ACR) is one of several professional associations of neutrals in the United States who do this kind of work (www.acrnet.org). There are degree programs at more than a dozen universities in the United States that offer training in facilitation, mediation, and other dispute-handling skills. The Code of Ethics of the ACR defines a professional neutral as someone who is forbidden from taking sides in a conflict or from trying to impose his or her view of what the "best" outcome ought to be (SPIDR 1986). Public dispute resolution has emerged as a subspecialization within the conflict management field (Carpenter and Kennedy 1988; Dukes 1996).

### Facilitation

A great deal, but not all of the work done by a professional facilitator takes place "at the table"—when the parties are working face to face (Doyle and Straus 1993). Facilitation of consensus-building efforts involving many parties working on complex issues often requires a team to keep track in written form of the commitments made by the group. Although the facilitator must refrain from taking a stand on the issues before the group, he or she often reframes elements of the conversation, drawing attention to emerging agreement or insurmountable disagreements, and reminding the parties of their commitment to the process ground rules.

### Mediation

Much of what happens in consensus building, particularly what often seem like a breakthrough, occurs "away from the table" as the professional neutral meets privately with one or more parties to sound out their willingness to accept an emerging package or to find out what it will actually take to win their support. Mediation includes everything described under facilitation plus all the away from the table activities required at each stage of the consensus-building process. Table 13.1 summarizes these tasks.

## 4.7 Who Can Mediate Public Disputes?

There is some disagreement about the need to involve professionally trained mediators in public dispute resolution efforts. Indeed, some public officials argue that they are in a better position to manage the dispute resolution process—in part

**Table 13.1** Tasks of the mediator

| Phases | Tasks |
| --- | --- |
| **Prenegotiation** | |
| **Getting started** | Meeting with potential stakeholders to assess their interests and describe the consensus-building process; handling logistics and convening initial meetings; assisting groups in initial calculation of BATNAs |
| **Representation** | Caucusing with stakeholders to help choose spokespeople or team leaders; working with initial stakeholders to identify missing groups or strategies for representing diffuse interests |
| **Drafting protocols and agenda setting** | Preparing draft protocols based on past experience and the concerns of the parties; managing the process of agenda setting |
| **Joint fact finding** | Helping to draft fact-finding protocols; identifying technical consultants or advisers to the group; raising and administering the funds in a resource pool; serving as a repository for confidential or proprietary information |
| **Negotiation** | |
| **Inventing options** | Managing the brainstorming process; suggesting potential options for the group to consider; coordinating subcommittees to draft options |
| **Packaging** | Caucusing privately with each group to identify and test possible trades; suggesting possible packages for the group to consider |
| **Written agreement** | Working with a subcommittee to produce a draft agreement; managing a single-text procedure; preparing a preliminary draft of a single text |
| **Binding the parties** | Serving as the holder of the board; approaching outsiders on behalf of the group; helping to invent new ways to bind the parties to their commitments |
| **Ratification** | Helping the participants "sell" the agreement to their constituents; ensuring that all representatives have been in touch with their constituents |
| **Postnegotiation** | |
| **Linking informal agreements and formal decision making** | Working with the parties to invent linkages; approaching elected or appointed officials on behalf of the group; identifying the legal constraints on implementation |
| **Monitoring** | Serving as the monitor of implementation; convening a monitoring group |
| **Renegotiation** | Reassembling the participants if subsequent disagreements emerge; helping to remind the group of its earlier intentions |

*Source*: Susskind and Cruikshank 1987.

because they are accountable to the public and must stand for election (or, if they are an appointed official, work for someone who does). There are others who believe that only former officials (i.e. those who have retired from the public or the private sector) have the clout or standing necessary to pressure unreasonable parties to work out an agreement. The evidence available thus far, however, suggests that professionally trained mediators are usually quite effective (Susskind, Amundsen, and Matsuura 1999). Many of the most experienced public dispute mediators come from a background in planning, public management, or law (Sadigh and Chapman 2000).

# 5. ORGANIZATIONAL LEARNING

One of the striking results of recent efforts to document the successful application of consensus building in the public arena is how few public agencies and units of government, even those with positive experiences to date, have tried to institutionalize mediation or other forms of conflict management into their normal operations (Dukes 1996). Almost two dozen US states have created offices of dispute resolution of various kinds—some in the executive branch, some in the legislative branch, and some in the judicial branch. Yet, most of these offices continue to operate on an experimental basis and have been asked to help with relatively few public policy controversies (Susskind 1986). Only three or four states have amended their zoning enabling acts to encourage consensus building. State and local agencies that confront constant challenges to their facility siting efforts have used consensus building on occasion (some with great success), yet few states have taken steps to shift as a matter of course to collaborative approaches. At the federal level, the results are a bit more impressive. The Administrative Dispute Resolution Act of 1996 requires federal agencies to use more consensus-oriented approaches to meeting their statutory mandates and to use these methods whenever possible.

## 5.1 The Barriers to Organizational Learning

There are a variety of forces working against the move to consensus building in the public policy arena. First, there is a substantial lack of knowledge about these relatively new techniques for getting agreement on public policy matters. A great deal of misinformation has been spread by advocacy groups who mistakenly believe that ad hoc, non-accountable representatives, working behind closed doors, will be given undue power (while key advocates are excluded) if consensus building is allowed. They fail to understand that consensus building guarantees that all relevant stakeholder groups must be given a place at the table and that in terms of both process and outcome, consensus-building efforts must be conducted in the "sunshine." Finally, the product of every ad hoc consensus-building effort must be acted upon by duly elected or appointed officials.

A second obstacle is the unwillingness on the part of elected and appointed officials to give up any measure of control. They rightly see consensus building as an effort to open up the operation of government to closer public scrutiny and more direct involvement of civil society. They know that the presence of a professional neutral, committed to a code of ethics and to non-partisan intervention, means that policy choices will have to be justified in a way that satisfies the interests of the community at large. The usual exercise of power will have to be accompanied by an explicit statement of the reasons why one package of policies or proposals was selected.

Finally, there is no entity responsible for trying to improve the quality of problem solving or group decision making in the public arena. Thus, there is no locus of public learning where the results of a shift to consensus building can be weighed and reviewed.

## 5.2 Dispute Systems Design

In the same way that total quality management (TQM) moved slowly from the private to the public sector, even though the results (in terms of consumer satisfaction) more than justified such a shift, consensus building has been slow to take hold in the public arena. Only a larger-scale, systemic assessment of the gains and losses associated with such a shift will provide sufficiently convincing evidence to allow those who see the benefits to make their case successfully. What needs to be done is to assess the advantages and disadvantages of a consensus-building approach at the systems design level. So, for example, when a stream of similar disputes (in the same locale) is handled in a new way there is a basis for comparison. In Canada, for instance, the Alberta Environmental Appeals Board, which hears hundreds of challenges each year to environmental enforcement efforts undertaken by the Provincial level agency, shifted to a mediated approach (when the litigants were willing). The results suggest that the overall effectiveness and responsiveness of the Appeals Board were improved markedly (Taylor et al. 1999).

## 5.3 Overcoming the Barriers to Organizational Capacity-building

There are a number of strategies that have been used to overcome some of the organizational barriers described above. Training agency personnel so that they are not fearful about more direct involvement of stakeholder representatives in collaborative decision making is an important first step. Senior staff need to set internal policies so that agencies are willing to participate in consensus building, and operational staff need to learn how to function effectively in a mutual gains negotiation. Training also needs to be made available to the full range of stakeholder groups. If they feel they are at a disadvantage because an unfamiliar process has been selected, they will resist. A wide array of public agencies are sponsoring training for non-governmental, business, and other organizations.

Some agencies, such as the US Environmental Protection Agency, have set aside funds to cover the costs of consensus-building experiments. Without additional funds, staff will be disinclined to use existing program money to explore new ways of managing disputes surrounding the drafting of technical regulations. Once funds were set aside that could only be used for negotiated approaches to drafting regulations, internal advocates for such innovative efforts emerged. When word got out within the agency that negotiated rule making not only took less time and cost less money than traditional approaches to rule making, there was a greater willingness (although no great rush) to adopt such a consensus-oriented approach (Freeman 1997). The availability of discretionary grants also attracted the attention of non-government groups that saw an opportunity to generate subsidies for their involvement in rule-making processes that usually offer no support to non-governmental actors.

A third approach to promoting consensus-oriented approaches to public dispute resolution involves establishing a clear locus of responsibility for improving the quality of dispute handling. Federal legislation requires every agency to name a dispute resolution coordinator to look for opportunities to use consensus building in ways that will enhance the efficiency and effectiveness of government (Negotiated Rulemaking Act 1996). Once someone has this responsibility, it is not surprising that opportunities emerge. A number of states have something similar: naming an existing agency or creating a new agency to advocate consensus building. These agencies not only measure their success by the level of use of these new techniques, but they are also available to explain to others who may have reservations why consensus building is appropriate.

A fourth strategy depends on pre-qualifying a roster of approved neutrals. The US Environmental Protection Agency in conjunction with the US Institute for Environmental Conflict Resolution (USIECR) has established a computer-based list of carefully reviewed service providers. By maintaining this list (in an easily computer-accessible form) they have made it easier for stakeholder groups to participate in reviewing and selecting qualified neutrals. By standardizing payment rates for equivalently experienced mediators, the USIECR has eliminated many of the questions that often impede collaborative efforts to employ neutrals.[2]

It is easy for groups of all kinds to find reasons not to support consensus-oriented approaches to resolving public disputes when they are used to hard bargaining or feel qualified only to participate in traditional approaches to dialogue. It will take some time for democratic institutions to extend a full-fledged commitment to consensus-oriented approaches to resolving public disputes.

# 6. CONCLUSIONS

1. Persuasion and hard bargaining do not produce results that are as fair, as efficient, as stable, or as wise as the public often desires when public policy choices must be made. Consensus building or the mutual gains approach to negotiation (as a supplement to, not a replacement for direct democracy) offers some hope of doing better.

2. Dialog can improve understanding if that is the goal, but dialog alone won't produce agreements, especially when values and not just interests are at stake.

3. Hard bargaining will continue to be used in a great many public policy-making situations, in many parts of the world, but the use of this approach ultimately makes it harder to implement agreements (because less powerful parties will feel that they have been unfairly overpowered and seek revenge), undermines trust in government, and often generates suboptimal (i.e. wasteful) agreements.

4. Consensus building puts a premium on mutual gains negotiation and creates a new, important role for an emerging player—the professional neutral (who knows how to use facilitation and mediation techniques)—to generate agreements that meet the interests of all the stakeholders involved.

5. The obstacles to institutionalizing consensus-building techniques in the public policy-making arena are imposing. It is difficult to overcome the resistance of public officials who mistakenly believe that ad hoc consensus-building efforts are a substitute for the legitimate exercise of government or that professional neutrals are a threat to their authority.

6. More participatory and more collaborative approaches to public policy making, built around the mutual gains model of negotiation, can enhance the legitimacy of government and reduce the long-term costs of collective action.

## REFERENCES

AVRUCH, K. 1998. *Culture and Conflict Resolution.* Washington, DC: United States Institute for Peace.

BARBER, B. 1984. *Strong Democracy: Participatory Politics for a New Age.* Los Angeles: University of California Press.

BAZERMAN, M. H., and NEALE, M. A. 1994. *Negotiating Rationally.* New York: Free Press.

CARPENTER, S., and KENNEDY, W. J. D. 1988. *Managing Public Disputes.* San Francisco: Jossey-Bass.

CENTRE FOR DEMOCRACY AND GOVERNANCE 1998. *Alternative Dispute Resolution Practitioners' Guide.* Washington, DC: Centre for Democracy and Governance, Mar.

COHEN, H. 1982. *You Can Negotiate Anything*. New York: Bantam.

COHEN, J. 1983. *On Democracy*. Harmondsworth: Penguin.

DOYLE, M., and STRAUS, D. 1993. *How to Make Meetings Work*. New York: Berkley.

DRYZEK, J. S. 2000. *Deliberative Democracy and Beyond: Liberals, Critics, Contestations*. Cambridge: Oxford University Press.

DUKES, E. F. 1996. *Resolving Public Conflict*. New York: St Martin's Press.

FISHER, R. 1983. Negotiating power. *American Behavioral Scientist*, 27 (2): 149–66.

—— URY, W., and PATTON, B. 1983. *Getting to Yes: Negotiating Agreement without Giving in*. New York: Penguin.

FREEMAN, J. 1997. Collaborative governance in the administrative state. *UCLA Law Review*, 45 (1): 1–99.

FUNG, A. 2004. *Empowered Participation: Reinventing Urban Democracy*. Princeton, NJ: Princeton University Press.

GULLIVER, P. H. 1979. *Dispute and Negotiations: A Cross Cultural Perspective*. New York: Academic Press.

GUTMANN, A., and THOMPSON, D. 1996. *Democracy and Disagreement*. Cambridge, Mass.: Harvard University Press.

ISAACS, W. 1999. *Dialogue and the Art of Thinking Together: A Pioneering Approach to Communicating in Business and in Life*. New York: Bantam Dell.

KAHNEMAN, D., and TVERSKY, A. 2000. *Choices, Values, and Frames*. New York: Cambridge University Press.

KASSIN, S. 2004. *Psychology*, 4th edn. Upper Saddle River, NJ: Pearson–Prentice Hall.

LEWICKI, R. J., and LITERER, J. A. 1985. *Negotiation*. Homewood, Ill.: Richard D. Irwin.

MANSBRIDGE, J. 1980. *Beyond Adversary Democracy*. New York: Basic Books.

MOORE, C. W. 1986. *The Mediation Process: Practical Strategies for Resolving Conflicts*. San Francisco: Jossey-Bass Wiley.

MORRIS, C. (ed.) 2004. Conflict transformation and peacebuilding: a selected bibliography. Retrieved 14 Sept. 2004; available at: www.peacemakers.ca/bibliography/bibintro99.html.

NEGOTIATED RULEMAKING ACT OF 1996, 5 USC 561 et seq. (1996).

NORTHRUP, T. A. 1989. The dynamic of identity in personal and social conflict. Pp. 55–82 in *Intractable Conflicts and their Transformation*, ed. L. Kriesberg, T. A. Northrup, and S. J. Thorson. Syracuse, NY: Syracuse University Press.

O'LEARY, R., and BINGHAM, L. B. 2003. *The Promise and Performance of Environmental Conflict Resolution*. Washington, DC: Resources for the Future.

OZAWA, C. P. 1991. *Recasting Science: Consensual Procedures*. Boulder, Colo.: Westview Press.

RAIFFA, H. 1985. *The Art and Science of Negotiation*. Cambridge, Mass.: Belknap Press.

SADIGH, E., and CHAPMAN, G. 2000. *Public Dispute Mediators: Profiles of 15 Distinguished Careers*. Cambridge, Mass.: PON.

SCHELLING, T. C. 1980. *Strategy of Conflict*. Cambridge, Mass.: Harvard University Press.

SCHÖN, D. A., and REIN, M. 1994. *Frame Reflection: Toward the Resolution of Intractable Policy Controversies*. New York: Basic Books.

SOCIETY FOR PROFESSIONALS IN DISPUTE RESOLUTION (SPIDR) 1986. *ACR'S Ethical Standards of Professional Responsibility*. Retrieved 15 Sept. 2004; available at: www.acrchicago.org/standards.html.

—— 1997. *Best Practices for Government Agencies: Guidelines for Using Collaborative Agreement Seeking Processes*. Washington, DC: Association for Conflict Resolution.

STRAUS, D. 2002. *How to Make Collaboration Work: Powerful Ways to Build Consensus, Solve Problems, and Make Decisions*. San Francisco Berrett-Koehler.

SUSSKIND, L. 1986. NIDR's state office of mediation experiment. *Negotiation Journal,* 2 (3): 323–7.

—— AMUNDSEN, O., and MATSUURA, M. 1999. *Using Assisted Negotiation to Settle Land Use Disputes: A Guidebook for Public Officials.* Cambridge, Mass.: Lincoln Institute of Land Policy.

—— and CRUIKSHANK, J. 1987. *Breaking the Impasse: Consensual Approaches to Resolving Public Disputes.* New York: Basic Books.

—— and DUNLAP, L. 1981. The importance of nonobjective judgments in environmental impact assessments. *Environmental Impact Assessment Review,* 2 (4): 335–66.

—— and FIELD, P. 1996. *Dealing with Angry Public: The Mutual Gains Approach to Resolving Disputes.* New York: Free Press.

—— McKEARNEN, S., and THOMAS-LARMER, J. (eds.) 1999. *The Consensus Building Handbook: A Comprehensive Guide to Reaching Agreement.* Thousand Oaks, Calif.: Sage.

—— MNOOKIN, R., FULLER, B., and ROZDEICZER, L. 2003. *Teaching Multiparty Negotiation: A Workbook.* Cambridge, Mass.: Program on Negotiation.

TAYLOR, M., FIELD, P., SUSSKIND, L., and TILLEMAN, W. 1999. Using mediation in Canadian environmental tribunals: opportunities and best practices. *Dalhousie Law Journal,* 22 (2): 51–124.

URY, W. 1991. *Getting Past No: Negotiating your Way from Confrontation to Cooperation.* New York: Bantam.

YANKELOVICH, D. 1999. *The Magic of Dialogue: Transforming Conflict into Cooperation.* New York: Simon and Schuster.

# CHAPTER 14

.............................................................................................................................

# POLICY IMPACT

.............................................................................................................................

## KAREL VAN DEN BOSCH

## BEA CANTILLON

## 1. INTRODUCTION

.............................................................................................................................

At a certain level, questions about the impact of policy are easy to answer. Consider the two Korea states, North and South. Fifty years ago, ravaged by war, both were dirt-poor, both had few natural resources, and their prospects were bleak. The North and the South followed policies which were almost diametrically opposed. The former adopted the centralized economic policies of China and the Soviet Union. The latter pursued policies that were more free-market oriented (though certainly not completely laissez-faire), and more open to the outside world. Now, the South is a prosperous country, after nearly a half-century of unprecedented growth (in the context of development since 1950, the economic crisis in 1997 was only a minor setback), while the North is one of the poorest countries on earth, suffering regular famines.

That policy can make a difference is therefore clear. Certainly, mistaken policies can have disastrous results. But the example of the two Koreas also raises two questions of a general nature. The first is: did policy makers really have a choice? Or were policies largely dictated by circumstances, in this case in particular by the cold war and international power relations? Secondly, which South Korean policies were key to the economic success? Or did the precise policies not matter much, as long as they did not impede private enterprise? Both questions ask: do politics matter? but in different ways. The first question does so in the spirit of Castles and McKinlay (1997), who enquire whether policy makers can make real choices, or

* The authors thank the editors of the *Handbook* for very helpful comments, Joanna Geerts and members of the Centre for Social Policy for useful references, and Mieke Augustyns for efficient research assistance.

whether their actions are largely determined by social and economic forces beyond their control (and perhaps even beyond their consciousness). The second question asks whether the policies that are enacted (irrespective of how they are arrived at) make a difference for persons' actual circumstances of living. It is the second question with which we will be concerned in this chapter.

This is of course a very large question, which we cannot possibly do justice to in a short chapter. Let us note the main limitations. In order to maintain coherence, we focus our review on the impact of *public income transfer* programs, mainly because that is the area of research with which we are familiar. However, we believe that at least some of the points made also apply to the study of other areas of public policy. Even in this domain we must be selective as regards topics and studies. We do not even claim that the studies quoted are in some sense the best or the most interesting; we use them to make the points we want to make, with a certain preference for cross-national analyses. While we would have liked to concentrate on the impacts itself, methodological discussions cannot be avoided, as different approaches (sometimes) come up with different answers.

The chapter proceeds as follows. The next section reviews a number of approaches than can be taken in the study of policy impacts. In the third section we look at the impact of tax-and-transfer systems on income inequality and poverty. Though the reduction of inequality and the relief of poverty are not the only explicit goals of public transfer systems, and perhaps not even the main ones (Barr 1992), most of the actual goals would imply some redistribution, and therefore "it seems reasonable to assess welfare state policies in terms of their redistributive impact" (Sefton, this volume). The following section considers the impact of public transfers on various activities, in particular labor market participation and informal care. These are both areas where, it has been argued, welfare state programs have unwanted effects, discouraging people from working, and crowding out informal care by relatives and friends. We will see what the evidence in this regard says. The final section has some concluding remarks.

# 2. Methods to Assess Policy Impact

Analysts use a variety of approaches to assess policy impact. Often, *social experiments* are seen as the ideal way to evaluate policies. In such experiments, persons are randomly assigned either to a "treatment" group, which receives the benefits or services of a certain program, or to a "control group," which does not. Program impacts are measured as the difference between outcome variables (e.g. income labor market participation, skill level) before and after the "treatment," after adjusting for the results in the control group, which are supposed to capture the effects of all other factors apart from the program which might influence the outcomes. Despite their clear attractiveness, social experiments have serious limitations, as emphasized by

Heckman, Lalonde, and Smith (1999). First, they are much better suited for evaluating new measures that are not yet implemented than for ongoing programs. Secondly, social experiments are inevitably limited in scope, in time, and geographically; and subjects are aware of this. Thirdly, while people can be excluded from programs, participation is generally by and large voluntary, so that the "treatment" group is often self-selected to some extent, introducing bias into the impact estimates. Finally, experiments are expensive and time intensive, and put heavy demands on program administrators and fieldworkers; the requirement for rigorous randomization may conflict with the professional attitude of the latter.

A second approach is the *difference-in-difference approach*. Here, outcomes for persons who get some benefit or service in an actual program are compared with those for otherwise similar persons who do not participate in the program. This approach therefore is similar to the experimental method, with the important difference that it concerns actual programs, implying that the researcher has no say in the assignment of cases to the program. The main problem of this approach is of course to find a suitable comparison group. By definition, persons in the comparison group cannot be completely identical to persons in the "treatment" group—if they were, they would also be eligible for the program in question. Sometimes the assumption is made that the control group is not really comparable, but that any developments apart from the introduction of the program would affect both groups equally, so that any difference in outcomes between the groups can be attributed to the program. Thus, Francesconi and Van der Klaauw (2004) use single women without children as a control group in their evaluation of the impact of the Working Families Tax Credit on single mothers. Schoeni and Blank (2000) compare the labor market participation rates of educated women with those of less educated women to assess the impact of welfare reforms in the USA, arguing that those reforms will have little impact on the first group of women. The approach can also be used on cases at a higher level of aggregation, e.g. states in the USA. When some states implement a measure while others do not, or (more often) do so at different times, outcome variables on the state level can be used to gauge the aggregate impact of the program, assuming that state effects are constant across years, and that any period effects are common to all states. The worry of course is that those assumptions are violated. Additional difficulties are that states often do not enact exactly the same program, or that all states implement them at nearly the same time (Blank 2002).

Perhaps the most basic strategy is to compare outcome variables *before and after* the introduction or administration of a benefit or service. If data are available for a number of periods, one can control for other trends such as changes in the unemployment rate when evaluating labor market participation-enhancing programs. While intuitively plausible, the method can be misleading. On the micro level there is the possibility that entry into a program can be the result of a temporary setback, which would remedied even without the program (the "Ashenfelter dip;" see Heckman, Lalonde, and Smith 1999). A person may become unemployed, take part in a job-search program, and find work again, but the last event may not be the result of the program. On the aggregate (state or country) level, the introduction of a program can be endogenous: measures may be enacted precisely because the situation calls for them.

The complement to the before–after approach is the *cross-sectional* method. On the micro level it compares the outcomes for participants with those for non-participants in a program. It can be regarded as a curtailed version of the difference-in-difference method, and given what has been said above, the limitations of this approach are obvious, and need not be spelled out. On the macro level of societies, this approach enjoys great popularity, especially in political science, under the label of the *comparative method* (see e.g. Ragin 1987). The method is plagued by the so-called degrees of freedom problem: while societies differ from each other in innumerable respects, the small number of cases (at best a few dozen, often much less, in most studies) prevents researchers from taking account of more than a few.

All approaches reviewed above have in common that they compare outcomes after a program has been implemented or administered with a situation that existed or had existed in the real world—either the situation of other comparable cases at the same moment who did not participate in the program, or the situation of the same cases before they took part in it. In *model-based* evaluations the comparison is made not with a really existing state, but with a hypothetical or simulated counterfactual one. In this approach researchers use a model to predict the impact of the introduction or administration (or, alternatively, the absence) of a program with particular features on subjects such as persons or organizations. For instance (and to make the abstract description more concrete), Blundell et al. (2000) use survey data, a tax and benefit simulation model, and a labor market behavioral model to predict the impact of the Working Families Tax Credit in the UK on hours of work and labor market participation. The validity of such predictions depends of course crucially on the quality of the data and on, in particular, that of the model and its parameters. Typically for behavioral models, these parameters are estimated using survey data, which makes them subject to sampling variability, and more importantly, to specification error. Moreover, model parameters estimated on the whole population or a large group may not always be applicable to the rather specific groups on which many real-world programs focus.

A particular kind of model is presented by tax and benefit models. These models incorporate, in as much detail as possible, the tax and benefit rules existing in a country, and can calculate disposable income out of gross income or market income for households in a micro database (Sutherland 2001). More interestingly, one can replace some existing rules with alternative ones, and compare the resulting income distribution with the current one, providing a very detailed picture of the impact of the alternative rule. Typically, such models do not incorporate behavioral reactions, and therefore provide only a first-order approximation of the true impact. However, for many purposes this is quite informative.

Independent of these methods, a useful distinction can be made between studies which look at the social impact of large institutions, such as the welfare state as a whole, and research which tries to identify the effects of particular measures or policy reforms. The first kind is often rather academic in nature, while the latter tends to be more policy oriented. "Holistic" studies are generally cross-national, comparing aggregate indicators of programs and society-wide indicators of social outcomes. "Particular" studies are more limited in scope, often considering only one country.

Finally, all methods reviewed only help to discover impacts that the researcher is looking for. Yet, there may be a host of unintended effects that we just have not thought about.[1] Theory and previous studies might help in thinking of unintended conseqences, but otherwise it is just a matter of imagination.

# 3. The Impact of Public Tax-and-Transfer Systems on Income Inequality and Poverty

In this section we will review two "holistic" approaches to the study of the impact of the public tax-and-transfer system on income inequality and poverty, namely the "pre-post taxes and transfers" method, and the (truly) comparative approach. In the third section we look at the impact of US welfare reforms in the Clinton era on a number of outcomes.

## 3.1 The "Pre-post" Approach

The standard method to assess the degree of redistribution effected by taxes and transfers is to compare the distributions of income "pre taxes and transfers," i.e. income when taxes have not been subtracted and without transfers, and "post taxes and transfers," i.e. disposable income. Income "pre taxes and transfers" is variously called market income, factor income, private income, or original income, depending on what is precisely included in transfers.[2] In terms of Section 2, the method can be seen as a rather crude instance of the model-based approach to the measurement of policy impacts. An important element of the standard method is that income is measured on the household level, not on the individual level. The idea is that members of one household pool their resources, so that economic well-being is produced on the household level and equally shared among its members. Of course,

---

[1] For instance, Peltzman (1975) shows that seat belts saved lives of passengers in cars, but (because drivers felt safer and hence free to drive more carelessly) cost about an equal number of lives among pedestrians.

[2] In the literature, the words "before" and "after" are ofen used instead of "pre" and "post." However, since the former terms inappropriately suggest a temporal order, these are avoided here.

larger households need more income than smaller ones to achieve the same level of economic well-being, although they profit from economies of scale in the consumption of housing, heating, and such items. An equivalence scale is therefore used to adjust household incomes.

A fairly large number of studies have employed the standard approach, e.g. Ringen (1989), Mitchell (1991), Deleeck, Van den Bosch, and De Lathouwer (1992). A fairly comprehensive study is provided by Mahler and Jesuit (2004), using data from the Luxembourg Income Study, and covering twelve OECD countries (including the main Anglo-Saxon countries, as well as Scandinavian and northern European nations) for the period 1981–2000. Their main results are consistent with previous studies. First of all, the measured overall impact of taxes and transfers on inequality is large. The Gini coefficient, a commonly used measure of income inequality, is nearly halved in Sweden, and even the limited American welfare state (at least in terms of cash transfers) achieves a reduction of 23 per cent. The impact on income poverty (using a poverty line set at 50 per cent of national median equivalent income) is even more impressive. Pre taxes and transfers between 24 and 32 per cent of all households are in poverty, while "post-government," poverty rates vary between 5 and 17 per cent; on average across countries about two-thirds of market income poor households are lifted above the poverty line by taxes and transfers.

Secondly, although the impact of government income redistribution through taxes and transfers is large in all countries, the variation across welfare states is important. Scandinavian and the Benelux countries achieve the largest reductions in measured inequality: between 40 and 50 per cent. Germany and France score somewhat lower, around 39 per cent, while taxes and transfers in the UK, Australia, and Canada reduce inequality by around 30 per cent. The reduction is smallest in the USA, only 23 per cent. A study by Immervoll et al. (2004) using data from the European Community Household Panel and national data-sets complements this picture, as it provides results for a number of European countries which are not (well) represented in the LIS database, in particular the southern European countries. They find that the tax–benefit system is highly distributive in a number of Scandinavian and European continental countries. Most southern European countries on the other hand have a low degree of redistribution (about 30 per cent reduction in the Gini). Ireland, the UK, and also Spain form a middle group.

Thirdly, most of the redistribution is achieved through transfers—on average across countries they account for 73 per cent of the overall reduction, while taxes account for only 27 per cent. While there is considerable variation across countries in the relative importance of taxes and transfers in fiscal redistribution, the maximum share of taxes is 44 per cent—in the USA. The main factor explaining this variation appears to be the aggregate share of transfers in total household income (or what one could call the size of the overall transfer budget); where this is large, taxes account for only a small part of total redistribution; where this is small, as in the USA, Australia, and Canada, taxes are more important.

The empirical finding that taxes are less redistributive than transfers might be considered surprising, as in many countries most transfers are not explicitly means

tested, while tax systems in all OECD countries are to some extent progressive, meaning that as income rises taxes paid as a proportion of income increase.
However, this progressivity is relatively limited in countries with the highest average
tax rates, such as Sweden and Denmark (Wagstaff et al. 1999). When progressivity is
zero, taxes are proportional to income, and do not effect any reduction in income
inequality (as it is commonly understood and measured). Conversely, several countries with a rather progressive tax structure, such as France and Germany, tend to
enjoy low average tax rate. In those countries, the relatively limited overall size of the
tax intake prevents it from having an important impact on the overall income
distribution. There appears to be some sort of a trade-off between progressivity
and the average tax rate (Verbist 2004). The reason for this trade-off could be that as
the government has to increase taxes to cover its expenses, it becomes increasingly
difficult, politically and economically, to put most of the burden on the highest
incomes, and everyone has to take up their share in the total cost of government
activities. On the other hand, even though in most countries most public *transfers* are
not means tested, they still tend to go to households with no or little other income,
thus considerably reducing measured inequality and income poverty. This point
applies in particular to pensions.

The standard "pre-post" method has a number of shortcomings and problems.
The first is that, as it is commonly applied, it takes only account of cash transfers, and
not of transfers in kind, such as (most importantly) health care and education. This
point is addressed in a paper by Garfinkel, Rainwater, and Smeeding (2004). They
find that "full income," which includes the cash value of in-kind benefits, is less
unequally distributed than disposable income. The difference is largest among
English-speaking nations, especially the USA. After taking account of in-kind benefits (as well as the taxes required to finance them), these countries still have the most
unequal distributions of income, but the differences from the northern continental
European countries and Scandinavia are narrowed substantially. The reasons for this
shift are: first, that some nations, in particular the USA, that spend relatively little on
cash transfers, devote more of their resources to in-kind benefits; and secondly, that
the big spending welfare states rely more heavily on indirect taxes and taxation of
cash benefits than e.g. the USA.

As Garfinkel et al. themselves note, there remain a number of conceptual and
empirical problems in this type of analysis, regarding the incidence and the valuation
of in-kind benefits. One problem is that the equivalence scales typically used are
designed for consumption that is paid out of disposable income. For the analysis of
"full income," a different equivalence scale might be needed, which would reflect the
greater needs of children for education, and of the elderly for health care.

A second problem of the standard method (again, as it is typically applied) is that
the income accounting period is usually only one year. But a large part of social
security can be considered as an institution that forces people to make transfers across
the life cycle (forced savings), rather than between-person or between-household
transfers; this point applies of course in particular to pensions. Actually, in all
countries a large part of the measured reduction in overall inequality is due to

pensions (Mahler and Jesuit 2004). One way to address this point is to look only at the non-elderly (although social insurance systems for sickness, invalidity, and unemployment also incorporate intraperson transfers). The figures of Mahler and Jesuit (2004) indicate that among households headed by persons at working age (25–59), the equalizing impact of public transfers is considerably lower, though still respectable: on average 26 per cent instead of 37 per cent among the population as a whole. (Yet, disposable income inequality among this group is smaller than among the population as a whole.) Moreover, countries that score high on redistribution among the total population are not necessarily those that achieve a large equalizing effect among those at working age.

Unfortunately, data that permit us to analyze the equalizing effect of social transfers on a lifetime basis do not seem to exist. The next best thing is to construct a model, using data from panel surveys, to construct estimates of lifetime earnings and transfers. As data requirements are high, and the construction of such models involves a great deal of researcher time, energy, and intelligence, few such models have been constructed. Nelissen (1993) for the Netherlands and Falkingham and Harding (1996) for Australia and Britain are some of the few. Nelissen (1993, 236) reports that the social security system reduces lifetime income inequality by about 26 per cent in the oldest cohorts studied (born 1930–45), and somewhat less for younger cohorts. Most of the reduction is due to public flat-rate pensions and invalidity benefits; semi-public earnings-related additional pensions actually *increase* lifetime inequality. Falkingham and Harding (1996, 254) find that the net effect of the tax/transfer system in Britain is to reduce the Gini coefficient by 0.082; in Australia the effect is greater, at 0.097. In percentage terms the reduction in inequality represents 25 per cent and 26 per cent. The authors conclude that the primarily social assistance-based system of Australia, with its emphasis on poverty alleviation, in conjunction with a more progressive tax system, results in a greater degree of interpersonal income equalization, while the primarily social insurance-based system of Britain achieves a greater degree of intrapersonal redistribution (Falkingham and Harding 1996, 264). While the figures just quoted cannot be directly compared with the annual redistribution results discussed above, they do indicate that a substantial amount of income redistribution from high- to low-income persons occurs even in a lifetime perspective.

The most basic problem of the "pre-post" method, as many authors have observed, is the assumption that benefits, taxes, and contributions have no feedback effect on the pre-tax, pre-transfer distribution of "market" incomes. This assumption is of course quite unrealistic: without a system of benefits and taxes people would change their work, saving, and family formation behavior. These second-order effects, as well as any macroeconomic "third-order" effects, are disregarded in the standard "pre-post" method. The direction of the resulting bias in the estimate of pre-transfer market income is theoretically indeterminate (Danziger, Haveman, and Plotnick 1981, 979). In the next section we will discuss behavioral responses regarding labor supply; it will turn out that transfer programs are expected to reduce labor supply, especially if they are means-tested. However, the theoretical effect of taxes is ambiguous. Economic theory also cannot predict the direction of the private savings response to transfer programs (Danziger, Haveman, and Plotnick 1981, 982). People may reduce life-cycle and precautionary saving when they can expect pay-as-you-go old-age pensions or unemployment benefits. However, economists have identified a number of other possible mechanisms, making the net result of transfers on saving behavior uncertain. Little theoretical effort appears to have been spent on the effect of public transfers on household formation. Youngsters may leave the parental home earlier if they are eligible for some benefit when they live on their own. Such benefits may also induce more frequent divorce. Conversely, lacking an old-age pension, many elderly persons might choose (or be forced) to live with their children. These examples suggest that a generous system of public transfers will lead to family dissolution, in the sense that the total population will be spread out across a larger number of families of smaller size. However, the net effect of this on pre-transfer income inequality is hard to establish.

Despite these theoretical ambiguities, it seems likely that in the absence of transfers and taxes, income would be less unequally distributed than measured "pre-taxes-and-transfers" income is now. A large proportion of households now have little or no income except from public benefits, especially but not exclusively among the elderly, and this pushes up observed "pre-taxes-and-transfers" income inequality. Obviously, such households would need some form of non-public income if public benefits were abolished. A confirmation of this hunch can be found in the results of Mahler and Jesuit (2004). Observed "pre-taxes-and-transfers" income inequality is actually higher in generous welfare states such as Sweden, the Netherlands, and Belgium than it is in the USA and Australia. Given what we know about these societies (e.g. the fact that wage inequality is relatively low in the Scandinavian and Benelux countries), it appears highly unlikely that market income inequality in the absence of public transfers would be as high as it would be in the United States. The implication of this is that the "pre-post" method almost certainly overstates the equalizing effect of the public tax-and-transfer system. Another implication concerns the general finding reported above that taxes appear to be less equalizing than transfers. This result might well be biased, as the distribution of taxes is compared with the distribution of gross income, which includes transfer payments, and is therefore less unrealistic than the distribution of "pre-tax-and-transfer" incomes (Ringen 1989, 179).

Above we have discussed possible changes in private behavior that would occur if public transfers did not exist. However, it is probable that the institutional context would also be different (Danziger, Haveman, and Plotnick 1981, 979). Employees that cannot look forward to public pensions would demand (larger) company pensions. Perhaps mutual insurance companies would spring up (again). Last (but not least, although rarely mentioned), there would also be political reactions, one of which would be a probably irresistible demand for the reinstatement of public transfers. The last sentence points to the most fundamental problem of the "pre-post" method: we cannot really envisage what a developed democratic society without public transfers would look like. After all, no such society exists, and if any country tried to totally abolish public transfers, it might well prove economically and politically unsustainable. This implies that the question, "what is the impact of public transfers on income inequality," is fundamentally unanswerable, as the proper counterfactual cannot be established (West-Pedersen 1994; Barr 1992, 745). The implication of this is that we cannot measure the impact of any welfare state in an absolute sense; what we could possibly do is to compare the effects of different welfare states.

Given this basic change of strategy, one might try to put the "pre-post" method into a comparative framework. Instead of looking only at one country at a time, one might compare the difference in inequality between pre- and post-transfer distributions across a number of countries. However, the necessary assumption for this approach is that second-order effects are constant across countries, or at least not systematically related to the various systems of public transfers, and this is unlikely to be the case (West-Pedersen 1994, 9). Generous systems will have other effects than strict ones; people will behave differently in response to selective benefits than to universal ones. Therefore, it is at best uncertain whether the cross-national variation in the inequality-reducing effects as measured by the "pre-post" method tells us much about the true comparative redistributive impact of different of tax-and-transfer systems. Given the available data as reviewed above, it seems likely that the inequality-reducing effect of large welfare states is overstated relative to those of smaller welfare states.

## 3.2 The (Truly) Comparative Approach

We turn now to studies where outcomes of different welfare states are compared with each other, instead of with a hypothetical situation. An obvious but not trivial requirement of comparative studies into the impact of tax-and-transfer systems is to characterize the welfare states one wants to study. Several approaches exist. *First,* international reference works such as MISSOC (Mutual Information System on Social Protection in European Union Member States, as well as other European countries; European Commission 2004), enable one to compare particular welfare arrangements, such as the eligibility rules of particular social security benefits. However, one tends to lose sight of the forest because of the trees. A *second* way is the model family method, following which net incomes under a given tax-and-transfer system are calculated for a set of hypothetical families (Bradshaw and Finch 2002; OECD 2002). This approach therefore reflects the fact that household incomes are always income packages, composed of various sources of income and benefits, which may interact in complicated ways. Thus, they can reveal the real net minimum income guarantee available to families. While the results cannot be regarded as indicators of real-world impacts, they can be informative in that they only reflect (explicit or implicit) policy choices. For this reason they can be used to evaluate trends in government policies regarding minimum incomes and replacement rates, and also to compare policies across welfare states. *Third,* analysts

(Titmuss 1974; Esping-Andersen 1990; and many others) have produced social security and welfare state typologies, which depart from institutional characteristics and not from data on outcomes; see below and Sefton, this volume. Yet, many studies prefer a *fourth* approach, and use total expenditure on welfare state arrangements as a proxy for welfare state effort.

Studies using the last method have now established that there is a strong and negative relationship between social expenditure and income poverty (as well as income inequality) (cf. Bradbury and Jäntti 2001; Cantillon, Marx, and Van den Bosch 2003). Scandinavian countries spend the most, and have the lowest levels of poverty; the Anglo-Saxon countries, as well as southern European nations, spend much less, and poverty is much higher in those societies. As Oxley et al. (2001, 392–6) show, some countries achieve better "efficiency" in terms of child poverty reduction (i.e. poverty is reduced more for each euro or dollar spent) through targeting more on low-income groups. However, "effort" and "targeting" are negatively related, and thus "countries with higher 'efficiency' due to targeting have traded a good part of this away by reducing 'effort'."

Incontrovertible and important though this relationship is, it raises a number of questions. Welfare states differ in more respects than the size of total expenditures and the degree of targeting. If those were the only important characteristics, the policy recommendation would be simple: increase expenditure (and/or improve targeting for those countries which already spend a lot). However, if proof were needed that things are not that simple, it is given in a paper by Van den Bosch (2002). Using cross-country micro-data, he simulated an across-the-board increase in benefits within existing systems, such that all countries would spend the same proportion of aggregate income on social transfers. Surprisingly, such a move would *not* lead to a convergence in poverty rates, but rather the reverse, as poverty would increase in some European countries where it is already high.

Also, *societies* which sustain well-developed social support systems are likely to be different from those with smaller welfare states. It is suggestive (as well as perhaps surprising) that across OECD countries social expenditure and the incidence of low pay are strongly negatively related (Cantillon, Marx, and Van den Bosch 2003). Alvarez (2001) calls the finding that wage-egalitarian societies present the highest levels of welfare effort and redistribution "the puzzle of egalitarianism." Part of the reason for this puzzle may be that generous benefits reduce labor supply among those commanding low wages, while the high taxes needed to pay them discourage high wage earners from putting in many hours, leading to a more condensed wage distribution, both from above and from below. But, as Atkinson (1999, 67–8) suggests, another reason may be that some countries are characterized by notions of equity that at the same time support pay norms, collective agreements, and adequate minimum wages, as well as quasi-universal and generous benefits. Politically, such countries could be characterized by strong labor unions (West-Pedersen 1994).

Analysts, especially those favoring the welfare state-type approach, have emphasized a number of methodological shortcomings of total expenditure as a proxy for welfare state effort. They argue that a euro spent on an earnings-related civil servant pension does not represent the same degree of welfare state effort as a euro spent on social assistance. Another simple but important drawback of this line of comparative research of welfare states is that total expenditure is not really an input indicator, certainly not a policy-input indicator, but at best an intermediate indicator. Governments after all do not each year set down the total budget for welfare state expenditure; social security budgets tend to be open ended. Total expenditure is the result of incremental policy making in the past, as well as social and economic developments on which the government has little influence.

Esping-Andersen (1990), Korpi and Palme (1998), and others have tried to characterize welfare states by way of a typology. Having collected a smaller or larger number of indicators of welfare state characteristics, they try to capture similarities and differences into a limited number of types. Mostly this is done analytically, i.e. the authors formulate a number of ideal types, and typecast actual welfare states according to how closely they resemble one of those types. Alternatively, De Beer, Vrooman, and Willeboer Schut (2001) follow an empirical strategy, investigating whether fifty-eight institutional characteristics of welfare states cluster together to form distinct types (though they use indicators that other researchers would regard as outcomes, such as labor market participation rates). While different typologies employ different names, and produce somewhat different country groupings, the basic pattern is always the same; see Sefton, this volume for a description of Esping-Andersen's (1990) typology.

Korpi and Palme (1998, 675) find the expected relation between welfare state type and budget size (which is here regarded as an outcome of institutions, not as a characteristic): welfare states that rely heavily on means testing or on flat-rate benefits tend to have smaller total expenditure levels than welfare states where earnings-related benefits play a larger role. For this reason, the former perform worse in terms of the impact on income inequality and poverty. This leads the authors to formulate the "Paradox of redistribution:" "The more we target benefits at the poor and the more concerned we are with creating equality via equal public transfers to all, the less likely we are to reduce poverty and inequality" (Korpi and Palme 1998, 661).

This being said, welfare state types are not always very distinguishable as regards their impact. Even the correlation between welfare state type and budget size of which Korpi and Palme (1998, 675) make so much is not very strong, and "some countries in the basic security [mainly Anglo-Saxon] and corporatist [mainly European continental] categories have total expenditures levels approximating those in the encompassing group [Scandinavia]." De Beer, Vrooman, and Willeboer Schut (2001, 5) find that "the liberal welfare states perform consistently worse on the indicators for income levelling, income (in)equality and poverty ... There is however no consistent difference between the social-democratic countries and the corporatist countries. [Both] achieve roughly comparable results in terms of income protection by using quite different institutions." The qualification "in terms of income protection" is important here; as regards labor market outcomes social democratic welfare states radically differ from corporatist ones: whereas the former are characterized by high labor market participation, in particular of women, the opposite is true of the latter.

## 3.3  The Impacts of US Welfare Reforms

As each year brings a few or more, smaller or larger, changes in the institutions of each welfare state, and many of these are evaluated in some way, it is impossible and probably fruitless to attempt a review of all "particularistic" studies of separate measures, programs, and reforms. In this section we focus on one particular reform, namely the US social policy reforms during the Clinton presidency in the years after 1993. The reason for this choice is that this reform was radical, wide ranging, and has been well studied, and is therefore a good case to illustrate a number of points. An implication is that we will not only review the impact on poverty and income distribution, since other outcome variables were equally, if not more, important for this reform.

Objectives of the Clinton reform included "to make work pay," and to get people out of welfare and into work. To this end the Earned Income Tax Credit program was greatly expanded. This program provides persons with children who are working with a refundable tax credit for each dollar earned up to a maximum, thereby in effect topping up low earnings. (A refundable tax credit is not just subtracted from taxes to be paid, but actually paid out to households when no taxes are due.) Furthermore, among other reforms, a lifetime limit of five years was set on federal-funded welfare. For further detail, we refer to Blank and Ellwood (2001). The budget implications of the reform were huge: between 1992 and 1999, annual real federal spending on new or expanded programs increased by over $30 billion, which is nearly twice as much as total spending on Aid to Families with Dependent Children (AFDC), the main pre-reform welfare program. As a result, the net gain from working for single mothers on welfare dramatically increased (Blank and Ellwood 2001, 7).

It is instructive to compare the Clinton welfare reform with a simple earnings disregard program, where welfare recipients can keep part of their benefit up to a point if they start earning. This does have the desired effect of creating financial incentives for non-working welfare recipients to enter the labor market, but also creates unwanted incentives for current non-recipients to reduce their work effort (Blank, Card, and Robins 1999, 12). This appears to be one of the key reasons for the disappointing results of the negative income tax experiments of the 1970s. By contrast, the Clinton welfare reforms contained a number of provisions to limit this unwanted side effect, including eligibility restrictions that target benefits to long-term welfare recipients, and hours restrictions that limit benefits to full-time workers (Blank, Card, and Robins 1999, 40).

What was the impact of those changes? Perhaps surprisingly, given the scale and size of the reforms, this question is not easy to answer. Certainly, at the end of Clinton's second term, the number of people on welfare had more than halved compared with the start of his first term. Labor force participation among single women with children increased by more than 10 percentage points in this period. Poverty fell significantly. However, at the same time the US economy went through a period of strong growth and labor force expansion. It turns out to be quite difficult to disentangle the impact of policies from the effects of the booming economy. As Blank and Ellwood (2001, 31) write, it is relatively easy to document that outcomes changed at the same time as policy. To establish causality is another matter.

Researchers have spent considerable effort on doing just that, using a variety of methods and data, but relying mostly on difference-in-difference studies on the state level (see Section 2). These studies indicate that policy changes were important in getting people off welfare. Regarding labor market participation, researchers tend to agree that the Clinton policy changes dramatically increased work by single parents, though it is less clear what was the relative contribution of EITC and other work supports versus welfare reform (Blank and Ellwood 2001, 39).

The focus on labor market participation entails a danger of increased poverty, if earnings are no greater than the welfare income they replace, and if some persons are taken off the welfare books without any alternative source of income. Overall, however, the net effect of the policy reforms appears to be positive: poverty declined, and the income of female-headed families with children rose. At the same time, some single-mother families at the very bottom probably became worse off. The most serious question concerns what will happen if the economy stops growing (Blank and Ellwood 2001, 53–4). The policy changes are such that the welfare system is most effective during an economic upturn (when people find it easy to find a job); how it will perform during a recession remains to be seen.

# 4. The Impact of Income Transfers on Activity

It is often alleged that the welfare state, while perhaps a good thing in principle, has a number of unwanted side effects, which reduce its real impact. The perverse effects of welfare state programs haven been most forcefully put forward by Murray (1984). He argues that in the USA, the numbers of poor stopped shrinking in the early 1970s, and then began growing, despite the combination of economic growth and huge increases in expenditures on the poor. Other basic indicators of well-being also took a turn for the worse in the 1960s, most consistently and most drastically for the poor.

The reason for this turn of events, according to Murray, was precisely the huge expansion of welfare state programs, which encouraged behavior that perpetuated the state of poverty, through early school drop-out, weak attachment to the labor market, and family break-up. These failures were then masked through too generous transfers. While many analysts have argued that Murray's thesis does not fit the facts (e.g. Jencks 1992), much time and energy have been devoted to identifying the possible perverse side effects of welfare state programs. In this section we will look at two such side effects, namely discouraging people from working, and crowding out informal care by relatives.

## 4.1 Impact on Labor Supply

The impact of welfare state programs on labor market participation is the subject of an enormous literature, often of great technical complexity, which is impossible to do justice to in one section of a short chapter. Below, we present certain highlights which give some impression of the variety of issues and results.

The standard economic textbook model (Danziger, Haveman, and Plotnick 1981, 979; Atkinson 1993a) is that persons trade off work against leisure, and that *ceteris paribus* they will prefer leisure over work. Under these assumptions, transfer programs that provide income support without requiring work will unambiguously reduce labor supply through the income effect, that is, people will use the extra income to "buy" extra leisure time. Some persons will work fewer hours, and others will stop working altogether. Transfers that are means tested will have an additional labor supply reducing effect, as for each euro or dollar earned a part of the benefit is withdrawn. The effect of taxes is ambiguous: the fact that taxes reduce net earnings may induce persons either to work more to make up for the lost earnings (income effect), or to work less, as each hour worked brings in less in net earnings (substitution effect).

This bare-bones economic textbook model ignores many dimensions of work and labor supply, as explained by Atkinson (1993a). One is the assumption that people are completely free to choose their hours of work, implying that there is no involuntary unemployment, or compulsory early retirement. Another is the disregard for the institutional context of labor supply decisions, e.g. the presence of collective bargaining, restrictions on laying-off employees, or the fact that real-world tax systems often produce non-linear budget constraints. Income-tested benefits moreover may imply that the budget constraint is non-convex, and effective marginal tax rates may be higher at low earnings than higher up the scale. People living on social assistance may even find themselves in a so-called "poverty trap," as any effort to obtain additional earnings may not bring them any advance in net-income terms. Furthermore, labor market decisions are not made individually, but within families, which may be taxed jointly, and where there is also unpaid but essential household production work to be done. The trade-off is therefore not simply one between net income and leisure, but between consumption goods bought in the market and having more time for household activities, and also between the incomes and non-working time of husband and wife. Moreover, lifetime considerations may be important, as people may work hard during their prime-age years to provide for their (early) retirement.

Thus, economic theory, certainly when some model assumptions are relaxed, cannot provide a clear-cut answer as regards the direction of the effect of real world tax-and-transfer systems, and moreover, theory is silent on the *magnitude* of the effects, which is as important as the direction. Empirical studies only can provide useful answers. There are several approaches in this domain. One is to use real-world socioeconomic experiments, of which the best-known example is probably the New Jersey negative income tax experiment (Pechman and Timpane 1975). The broad conclusion from this and other similar experiments was that there was a noticeable but not massive reduction in work effort (Atkinson 1993*a*, 43). Yet, although the evidence produced by such experiments is unique, it cannot be regarded as conclusive, for the reasons set out in Section 2. Other studies have followed the before-after method, or the modeling approach outlined in Section 2.

Atkinson (1993*b*, 297), reviewing a number of such studies, concludes that, overall, "a number of the effects that have been identified are relatively small in size," and "there are relatively few situations in which a disincentive effect has been clearly established." There is evidence that taxation causes married women to work less, but little evidence of a negative response by prime-age male workers. There is also little clear evidence that *benefits* represent a major discouragement to take up work. One reason for this is that, though the tax-and-transfer system in many countries creates a poverty trap, this may affect relatively few people. Also, transfers may have a positive impact (the so-called entitlement effect), as people keep working or looking for work in order to become or remain eligible for benefits.

Another group for which tax-and-transfer arrangements may have an important effect on labor market participation (apart from married women) is men aged 50–64. In many countries participation rates for this group have fallen drastically during the last four decades. Gruber and Wise (1998) show that, across a number of OECD countries, labor force participation of older persons is strongly related to the implicit social security tax on work. This implicit tax arises because in many countries, staying on for one more year in the labor force for older persons implies a reduction in the present discounted value of total pension benefits during the remaining lifetime. In some cases, this reduction is even larger than the net wages earned during the extra period in work! The "tax force to retire" is especially strong in Italy, Belgium, the Netherlands, Germany, and France. However, as Gruber and Wise note, in some countries (e.g. Belgium) the reduction in labor market participation of older persons was not an unwanted side product; rather, encouraging older workers to leave the labor force was an explicit goal, with a view to easing labor market tension and reducing unemployment among younger workers.

Welfare state arrangements and even public transfers can also help to keep persons *in* work. This was after all one of the objectives of the Clinton social policy reforms discussed in Section 3.3. Another illustration is provided by an interesting cross-national study by Gornick, Meyers, and Ross (1996) on the employment of mothers with young children. Gornick et al. note that easier (cheaper) access to child care will increase mothers' employment rate, either (and equivalently) because it reduces the value of time spent at home, or because it increases the net wage mothers can earn. The effect of paid maternity leave cannot be predicted unambiguously—on the one hand it may strengthen mothers' attachment to paid work, on the other it may induce some women to stay at home (temporarily) who would otherwise have kept on working. The direction and especially the magnitude of these effects is therefore an empirical matter. Gornick et al. look at what they call the "child penalty:" the decrease in the probability of employment of mothers, given the presence of young children, all else equal. Compared with an analysis of employment rates per se, this has the advantage that all kinds of institutional and macroeconomic variables are implicitly controlled, insofar as it can be assumed that these other factors affect mothers of young children and other women, e.g. mothers of teenage children, equally. Gornick et al. compare the "child penalty" with a pair of indices that integrate a range of measures of public support for child care and parental leave. They find that these two are strongly related—in some countries which do not strongly support maternal employment the "child penalty" is as large as 35 (Australia) or 45 percentage points (UK), while in Sweden there appears to be no "child penalty" whatsoever.

## 4.2  The Impact of Welfare State Provisions on Family Care

Some observers maintain that the welfare state not only carries an economic cost in lost hours of work, but also crowds out compassion and activity from private life (Burenstam Linder 1970, quoted in Ringen 1989, 119). One relationship that should be particularly sensitive to such perverse influences is that between the elderly and their children. Formal, social, and emotional ties are less strong than they are between spouses, and between parents and young children within the nuclear family. Old-age care is generally seen as more burdensome than child care (Ringen 1989, 129–30). So what is the evidence as regards the effect of increasing, the supply of public old-age care on family care? According to Ringen (1989, 134) "informal care in the family sector is still the dominant form of old-age care." "There are no signs ... of a decline in family activity, of less vitality or compassion in the sensitive relationships between the elderly and younger family members." However, since Ringen wrote those conclusions, much new research on this topic has been published.

Many writers on this topic take the position that family care and public provisions, far from being substitutes, are actually complements. Several arguments are advanced in this regard. Families will be more willing to provide help when burdens are not too heavy. Also, generous pensions enable the older generation to reciprocate support from the younger generation. Public services may allow families to specialize in psycho-social support rather than instrumental help (Daatland 2001, 18–19). Three kinds of evidence can be called upon to determine whether the substitution or the complement effect predominates. First of all, there are cross-country differences. These indicate that substitution effects are likely, as countries with the highest level of services seem to have the lowest level of family care (Daatland 2001, 19). However, these differences may be due to the more familistic culture of Germany and Italy (which may be associated with both less public care and more private care), compared with the (allegedly) more individualistic societies of Scandinavia. Secondly, there are cross-sectional studies which investigate whether elderly people tend to receive help from one source only, or whether public services and family help appear together. Such studies typically suggest that family care and public provisions are indeed complements, as many elderly persons use both even when controlling for need (e.g. Künemund and Rein 1999, in a five-country study). In a literature review with a focus on longitudinal studies, Penning and Keating (2000) conclude that the findings suggest that formal services are not used to displace or substitute for informal care but rather, that formal services tend to be used to supplement and complement the care provided by the informal network.

Finally, one can follow developments over time: when public services expand, does family care go down, and vice versa? Here the available evidence is mixed. A study by Lingsom (1997, quoted in Daatland 2001) for Norway suggests that this does not happen. Families were not crowded out, nor did they withdraw, when alternative sources of help were available. On the other hand, Johansson et al. (2003) claim that results show that relatives more often provided care to older people half a century ago than in contemporary Sweden. More recently, cutbacks in public services in Sweden have led to a substantial reversal in care patterns. Increased input from families matches the decline of public services. A positive reading of these results would be that even in individualistic Sweden the welfare state has not destroyed the bonds between elderly persons and their children: when needed (again), the latter are ready to provide help.

# 5. CONCLUSION

Since this chapter as a whole is fairly short and rather synthetic in nature, it hardly needs summary. However, we would like to make some general points, first on methodological issues and then on substantive ones.

First, a methodological point that is perhaps rather uncontroversial, but still worth making. Theory, certainly economic theory, is in general insufficient to predict the impact of policies. Theory can guide us as to what to look for, but often the direction of the effects, and almost always their magnitude, can only be established empirically. Often, effects that loom large in the theoretical literature turn out to be insubstantial in the real world.

A second, perhaps less obvious point is that, even though the tool kit of policy analysts contains a variety of methods, it is often very hard to identify, let alone quantify the impact of particular policies with a reasonable degree of accuracy. Even the consequences of the US welfare reform under Clinton turned out to be hard to pinpoint, despite the scope of the reforms, and the wealth of data seemingly available. Social experiments are perhaps inherently the most powerful method, but they are suitable only for programs that are not yet in place, and that can be enacted on a small scale. For larger and existing programs the difference-in-difference method is perhaps the most valid and convincing way to measure policy impacts, whenever it can be applied. The problem of finding a suitable comparison group is often not trivial, though. The fundamental problem seems to be that the impacts of policy changes are often small compared with those of exogenous social and economic developments. It then becomes difficult to tease out the message from the noise.

Thirdly, macro-social comparative studies, which look at large institutions such as welfare states as a whole, have given us important new insights in the past decades. However, the fact that multivariate analysis is nearly impossible with fifteen or twenty cases (rich democratic nations) limits crucially the power of this approach. It therefore has no answer to the basic fact that each welfare state is embedded in a different society, making it very difficult to distinguish impact from association. Welfare state typologies are very useful to get some grasp on the otherwise bewildering variety of institutional characteristics, but appear to have limited potential as predictors of impacts. Perhaps the most fruitful approach is represented by comparative studies which look at the impact of policy packages offered by different welfare states to particular groups, such as mothers with young children, or males at pre-retirement ages. At this middle-of-the-road level, policies can be described, or even quantified with a fair degree of precision; there is often more variety in outcomes; and the relationship between policies and outcomes is more easily established, and easier to interpret.

The main *substantive* conclusion we can draw from the material presented above (despite some methodological reservations) is that policies do have an impact, in the sense of making a difference to people's actual living circumstances. There can be little doubt that large welfare states are more equalizing than smaller welfare states, although it is probable that large welfare states can only flourish in societies that are rather egalitarian in the first place. Their impact is not entirely frittered away through unintended side effects. The experience of US welfare reform under Clinton indicates that a well-designed package of programs can induce people to move off welfare rolls and into work. Comparative research shows that older people retire early when pension and other benefit systems contain clear incentives to do so. Studies suggest strongly that mothers with young children continue working, or return to the labor force after a time, if a package of benefits and services is in place that helps them to do so.

Secondly, the examples just quoted suggest that a large policy impact requires a large program—or package of programs. Measures need to be well designed, well funded, and sustained over time. Attempts to get results "on the cheap" can backfire. The largest example of this is perhaps the "paradox of redistribution" (Korpi and Palme 1998). Welfare states that attempt to target resources onto the poor tend to have lower redistributive budgets, resulting ultimately in more poverty and more income inequality, compared with welfare states that rely on more universal benefits.

The third conclusion is an instance of the previous one, but worth mentioning in its own regard: people react to incentives, provided these are clear and large. Welfare mothers in the USA move back to work if it is made clearly worth their while to do so. Older men in some continental welfare states retire early in great numbers, when the rules of existing pension and other benefit systems minimize the gains of continuing to work (calculated on a lifetime basis).

Fourthly, we do not intend to imply that getting a large impact is just a matter of spending a large amount of money. In all of the examples just quoted the impact was produced by a package of programs, not by just a single measure. Such a package needs to be well designed, so that the different parts work together towards the same objectives. The comparison of the complicated welfare reforms under Clinton with the rather simple negative income tax proposals indicates that real-world policy packages are often quite complex and detailed, and need to be so, in order to contain unwanted side effects, and to keep costs in check.

# REFERENCES

ALVAREZ, P. 2001. *The Politics of Income Inequality in the OECD: The Role of Second Order Effects.* Luxembourg Income Study Working Paper No. 284. Syracuse, NY: Syracuse University.

ATKINSON, A. B. 1993a. Work incentives. Pp. 20–49 in *Welfare and Work Incentives: A North European Perspective*, ed. A. B. Atkinson and G. V. Morgensen. Oxford: Clarendon Press.

—— 1993b. Conclusions. Pp. 289–97 in *Welfare and Work Incentives: A North European Perspective*, ed. A. B. Atkinson and G. V. Morgensen. Oxford: Clarendon Press.

—— 1999. The distribution of income in the UK and OECD countries in the twentieth century. *Oxford Review of Economic Policy*, 15 (4): 56–75.

BARR, N. 1992. Economic theory and the welfare state: a survey and interpretation. *Journal of Economic Literature*, 30: 741–803.

BLANK, R. 2002. Evaluating welfare reform in the United States. *Journal of Economic Literature*, 40: 1105–66.

—— CARD, D., and ROBINS, P. 1999. *Financial Incentives for Increasing Work and Income among Low-Income Families.* NBER Working Paper No. 8437. Cambridge, Mass.: National Bureau of Economic Research.

BLANK, R., and ELLWOOD, D. 2001. *The Clinton Legacy for American's Poor.* NBER Working Paper No. 6998. Cambridge, Mass.: National Bureau of Economic Research.

BLUNDELL, R., DUNCAN, A., McCRAE, J., and MEGHIR, C. 2000. The labour market impact of the working families' tax credit. *Fiscal Studies,* 21 (1): 75–103.

BRADBURY, B., and JÄNTTI, M. 2001. Child poverty across twenty-five countries. Pp. 62–91 in *The Dynamics of Child Poverty in Industrialised Countries,* ed. B. Bradbury, S. Jenkins, and J. Micklewright. Cambridge: Cambridge University Press.

BRADSHAW, J., and FINCH, N. 2002. *A Comparison of Child Benefit Packages in 22 Countries.* UK Department for Work and Pensions, Research Report No. 174.

BURENSTAN LINDER, S. 1970. *Den hjärtlösa välfärdsstaten.* Stockholm: Timbro.

CANTILLON, B., MARX, I., and VAN DEN BOSCH, K. 2003. The puzzle of egalitarianism: the relationship between employment, wage inequality, social expenditure and poverty. *European Journal of Social Security,* 5 (2): 108–27.

CASTLES, F. G., and McKINLAY, R. D. 1997. Reflections: does politics matter. Increasing complexity and renewed challenges. *European Journal of Political Research,* 1 (2): 102–8.

DAATLAND, S. O. 2001. Ageing, families and welfare systems: comparative perspectives. *Zeitschrift für Gerontologie und Geriatrie,* 34: 16–20.

DANZIGER, S., HAVEMAN, R., and PLOTNICK, R. 1981. How income transfer programs affect work, savings and the income distribution: a critical review. *Journal of Economic Literature,* 19: 975–1028.

DAVEY, A., and PATSIOS, D. 1999. Formal and informal community care to older adults: comparative analysis of the United States and Great Britain. *Journal of Family and Economic Issues,* 20 (3): 271–99.

DE BEER, P., VROOMAN, C., and SCHUT, J. M. W. 2001. *Measuring Welfare State Performance: Three or Two Worlds of Welfare Capitalism?* Luxembourg Income Study Working Paper No. 276. Syracuse, NY: Syracuse University.

DELEECK, H., VAN DEN BOSCH, K., and DE LATHOUWER, L. 1992. *Poverty and the Adequacy of Social Security in the E.C.: A Comparative Analysis.* Aldershot: Avebury.

ESPING-ANDERSEN, G. 1990. *The Three Worlds of Welfare Capitalism.* Cambridge: Polity Press.

EUROPEAN COMMISSION 2004. *MISSOC Social Protection in the Member States of the European Union, the European Economic Area and Switzerland.* European Commission, Directorate-General of Employment and Social Affairs.

FALKINGHAM, J., and HARDING, A. 1996. Poverty alleviation vs. social insurance systems: a comparison of lifetime redistribution. Pp. 234–66 in *Microsimulation and Public Policy,* ed. A. Harding. Amsterdam: Elsevier.

FÖRSTER, M. 2000, *Trends and Driving Factors in Income Distribution in the OECD area.* Labour Market and Social Policy Occasional Papers No. 42. Paris: OECD.

FRANCESCONI, M., and VAN DER KLAAUW, W. 2004. *The Consequences of "In-Work" Benefit Reform in Britain: New Evidence from Panel Data.* ISER Working Paper 2004–13. Colchester: ISER, University of Essex.

GARFINKEL, I., RAINWATER, L., and SMEEDING, T. M. 2004. *Welfare State Distribution and the Redistribution of Well-Being: Children, Elders, and Others in Comparitive Perspective.* Luxembourg Income Study Working Paper No. 387. Syracuse, NY: Syracuse University.

GORNICK, J., MEYERS, M., and ROSS, K. 1997. Supporting the employment of mothers: policy variation across fourteen welfare states. *Journal of European Social Policy,* 7 (1): 45–70.

GRUBER, J., and WISE, D. 1998. Social security and retirement: an international comparison. *American Economic Review,* 88 (2): 158–63.

HECKMAN, J., LALONDE, R., and SMITH, J. 1999. The economics and econometrics of active labor market programs. Pp. 1865–2097 in *Handbook of Labor Economics*, vol. iii, ed. A. Ashenfelter and D. Card. Amsterdam: Elsevier.

IMMERVOLL, H., et al. 2004. The effect of taxes and transfers on household incomes in the European Union. Paper accepted for the conference "The distributional effects of government spending and taxation," 15–16 Oct., Levy Institute of Bard College.

JENCKS, C. 1992. *Rethinking Social Policy: Race, Poverty, and the Underclass.* Cambridge, Mass.: Harvard University Press.

JOHANSSON, L., SUNDSTROM, G., et al. 2003. State provision down, offspring's up: the reverse substitution of old-age care in Sweden. *Ageing and Society*, 23 (3): 269–80.

KORPI, W., and PALME, J. 1998. The paradox of redistribution and strategies of equality: welfare state institutions, inequality, and poverty in the western countries. *American Sociological Review*, 63: 661–87.

KÜNEMUND, H., and REIN, M. 1999. There is more to receiving than needing: theoretical arguments and empirical explorations of crowding out. *Ageing and Society*, 19: 93–121.

LINGSOM, S. 1997. *The Substitution Issue: Care Policies and their Consequences for Family Care.* Report 6. Oslo: NOVA

MAHLER, V., and JESUIT, D. 2004. *State Redistribution in Comparative Perspective: A Cross-national Analysis of the Developed Countries.* Luxembourg Income Study Working Paper No. 392. Syracuse, NY: Syracuse University.

MITCHELL, D. 1991. *Income Transfers in Ten Welfare States.* Aldershot: Avebury.

MURRAY, C. 1984. *Losing Ground: American Social Policy 1950–1980.* New York: Basic Books.

NELISSEN, J. H. M. 1993. *The Redistributive Impact of Social Security Schemes on Lifetime Labour Income.* Tilburg: Proefschrift Katholieke Universiteit Brabant.

OECD 2002. *Benefits and Wages.* Paris: OECD.

OXLEY, H., DANG, Th.-Th., FÖRSTER, M. and PELLIZARI, M. 2001. Income inequalities and poverty among children and households with children in selected OECD countries. Pp. 371–405 in *Child Well-Being, Child Poverty and Child Policy in Modern Nations: What do we Know*, ed. K. Vleminckx and T. Smeeding. Bristol: Policy Press.

PECHMAN, J., and TIMPANE, P. M. 1975. *Work Incentives and Income Guarantees.* Washington, DC: Brookings Institution.

PELTZMAN, S. 1975. The effects of automobile safety regulation. *Journal of Political Economy*, 83 (4): 677–726.

PENNING, M., and KEATING, N. 2000. Self-, informal and formal care: partnerships in community-based and residential long-term care settings. *Canadian Journal on Aging*, 19 (Suppl. 1): 75–100.

RAGIN, C. 1987. *The Comparative Method: Moving beyond Qualitative and Quantitative Strategies.* Berkeley: University of California Press.

RINGEN, S. 1989. *The Possibility of Politics: A Study in the Political Economy of the Welfare State.* Oxford: Clarendon.

SCHOENI, R., and BLANK, R. 2000. *What has Welfare Reform Accomplished? Impacts on Welfare Participation, Employment, Income, Poverty and Family Structure.* NBER Working Paper No. W7627. Cambridge, Mass.: National Bureau of Economic Research.

SUTHERLAND, H. 2001. *EUROMOD: An Integrated European Benefit–Tax Model.* Euromod Working Paper No. EM9/01. Cambridge: Department of Applied Economics, University of Cambridge.

TITMUSS, R. 1974. *Income Distribution and Social Change*, London: Allen and Unwin.

VAN DEN BOSCH, K. 2002. Convergence in poverty outcomes and social income transfers in member states of the EU. Paper for the XV World Congress of Sociology, Brisbane, July.

VERBIST, G. 2004. Herverdeling door de fiscus. Effecten van de personenbelasting op de inkomensongelijkheid in België en andere OESO-landen. *Kwartaaltijdschrift Economie*, 3: 284–303.

WAGSTAFF, A., et al. 1999. Redistributive effect, progressivity and differential tax treatment: personal income taxes in twelve OECD countries. *Journal of Health Economics*, 72: 73–98.

WEST-PEDERSEN, A. 1994. *The Welfare State and Inequality: Still no Answer to the Big Questions*. Luxembourg Income Study Working Paper No. 109. Syracuse, NY: Syracuse University.

# CHAPTER 15

# THE POLITICS OF POLICY EVALUATION

## MARK BOVENS
## PAUL 'T HART
## SANNEKE KUIPERS

## 1. EVALUATION BETWEEN "LEARNING" AND "POLITICKING"

In this chapter policy evaluation refers to the *ex post* assessment of the strengths and weaknesses of public programs and projects. This implies we shall not address the voluminous literature on *ex ante* policy analysis, where methods to evaluate policy alternatives are developed and offered to policy makers and other stakeholders as decision-making aids (see, e.g., Nagel 2002; Dunn 2004). We shall argue that policy evaluation is an inherently normative act, a matter of political judgement. It can at best be informed but never fully dominated by scholarly efforts to bring the logic of reason, calculation, and dispassionate truth seeking to the world of policy making. Policy analysis's mission to "speak truth to power" (Wildavsky 1987) is laudable, and should be continued forcefully, but scholars should not be naive about the nature of the evaluation game they participate in (Heineman et al. 1990, 1). In the ideal world of policy analysis, policy evaluation is an indispensable tool for feedback, learning, and thus improvement. In the real world of politics, it is always at risk of degrading into a hollow ritual or a blame game that obstructs rather than enhances the search for better governance.

When public policies are adopted and programs implemented, the politics of policy making do not come to an end. The political and bureaucratic controversies over the nature of the problems to be addressed and the best means by which to do so that characterize the policy formulation and policy selection stages of the policy cycle do not suddenly abate when "binding" political decisions are made in favour of option X or Y. Nor do the ambiguities, uncertainties, and risks surrounding the policy issue at stake evaporate. They merely move from the main stage, where political choices about policies are made, to the less visible arenas of policy imple- mentation, populated by (networks of) bureaucratic and non-governmental actors who are involved in transforming the words of policy documents into purposeful actions. At one time or another, the moment arrives to evaluate what has been achieved. This moment may be prescribed by law or guided by the rhythm of budget or planning and control cycles. It may, however, also be determined by more political processes: the replacement of key officials, elections that produce government turn- overs, incidents or figures that receive publicity and trigger political calls for an investigation, and so on.

Whatever its origins, the ideal-typical structure of a formal evaluation effort is always the same: an *evaluating body* initiates an investigation with a certain *scope* (what to evaluate: which programs/projects, policy outcomes, and/or policy- making processes, over which time period?); it employs some—explicit or implicit —evaluation *criteria*; it gathers and analyzes pertinent *information*; it draws *conclusions* about the past and *recommendations* for the future; and it *presents its findings*. Beneath this basic structure, tremendous variations exist in evaluation practices (Fischer 1995; Vedung 1997; Weiss 1998; Weimer and Vining 1999; Nagel 2002; Dunn 2004). They differ in their analytical rigor, political relevance, and likelihood to produce meaningful learning processes (cf. Rose 1993).

Bodies that conduct evaluations range from scientific researchers acting on their own accord to consulting firms to public think tanks, and from institutionalized watch dogs such as ombudsmen or courts of audit, to political bodies such as parliamentary commissions. Some of these evaluations are discreet and for direct use by policy makers; others occur in a blaze of publicity and are for public consumption and political use. One and the same policy program or episode may be evaluated by several of these bodies simultaneously or over time. It frequently happens that one type of evaluation exercise triggers others. For instance, the crash of a Dutch military cargo plane at Eindhoven airport in 1996 and the subsequent disaster response by the military and local authorities led to no less than fifteen separate investigation efforts by various government bodies, courts, and think tanks. This cascading effect was partly caused by the fact that both the cause of the accident and the adequacy of the response were subject to speculation and controversy, including the taking of provisional disciplinary sanctions against military airport officials. Moreover, different evaluation bodies may even compete overtly: government-initiated versus parliamentary evaluations, different chambers of parliament with different political majorities each conducting their own investigations into some presumed policy fiasco, governmental versus stakeholder evaluations, national versus IGO evaluations, and so on. The Reagan government's so-called Iran-Contra affair (which included the selling of arms to Iran in the hope of securing the release of American hostages held by Shi'ites in Lebanon) set in motion three evaluation efforts: one by a blue-ribbon presidential commission, one by the Senate, and one by the House of Representatives. Not surprisingly, the three reports were all critical of the course and outcomes of the policy, but differed markedly in the attribution of responsibility for what happened (see Draper 1991).

In the ideal world of the positivist social scientist, we stand to gain from this multiplicity: presumably it results in more facts getting on the table, and thus a more solid grasp of what happened and why. In the real world, multiple evaluations of the same policy tend to be non-cumulative and non-complementary. Their methods and findings diverge widely, making it hard to reach a single authoritative or at least consensual judgement about the past and to draw clear-cut lessons from it.

In this chapter we shall approach the politics of policy evaluation in two ways. First we shall elaborate on the roles and functions of policy evaluation in the broader politics of public policy making. Then we shall look at how key schools of policy analysis propose to deal with the essentially contested, inherently political nature of evaluation. Each, we argue, has crucial strengths and shortcomings. In the final section, we offer our own view of how policy analysis may cope with the conundrum of *ex post* evaluation.

# 2. The Politics of Policy Evaluation

It is only a slight exaggeration to say, paraphrasing Clausewitz, that policy evaluation is nothing but the continuation of politics by other means. This is most conspicuous in the assessment of policies and programs that have become highly controversial: because they do not produce the expected results, because they were highly contested to begin with, because they are highly costly and/or inefficient, because of alleged wrongdoings in their implementation, and so on. The analysis of such policy episodes is not a politically neutral activity, which can be done by fully detached, unencumbered individuals (Bovens and 't Hart 1996). The ominous label of "failure" or "fiasco" that hovers over these policies entails a political statement. Moreover, once policies become widely viewed as failures, questions about responsibility and sometimes even liability force themselves on to the public agenda. Who can be held responsible for the damage that has been done to the social fabric? Who should bear the blame? What sanctions, if any, are appropriate? Who should compensate the victims? In view of this threat to their reputations and positions, many of the officials and agencies involved in an alleged fiasco will engage in tactics of impression management, blame shifting, and damage control. The policy's critics, victims, and other political stakeholders will do the opposite: dramatize the negative conse-quences and portray them as failures that should, and could, have been prevented (cf. Weaver 1986; Gray and 't Hart 1998; Anheier 1999; Hood 2002).

The pivotal importance of blaming entails the key to understanding why the evaluation of controversial policy episodes itself tends to be a highly adversarial process. The politics of blaming start at the very instigation of evaluation efforts: which evaluation bodies take on the case, how are they composed and briefed (Lipsky and Olson 1977)? It is highlighted especially by the behaviour of many stakeholders during the evaluation process. To start with, the very decision to have an incident or program evaluated may be part of a political strategy. Penal policy constitutes an interesting example of this. In most countries, prison escapes take place from time to time, and in some periods their incidence increases. But there appears to be no logical connection between objectifiable indicators of the severity of the problem such as their frequency, their success rate, the number of escapees per annum, and the likelihood of major evaluation and learning efforts being undertaken at the political level. In the Netherlands, for example, political commotion about prison escapes rose to peak levels at a time when all penal system performance indicators were exceptionally good after an earlier period of problems and unrest. Rather, the scale, scope, and aims of a post-escape investigation seem to be a function of purely coincidental factors such as the method of escape and the level of violence, as well as the nature of the political climate regarding criminal justice and penal policy at any given time (Boin 1995; Resodihardjo forthcoming).

Even seemingly routine, institutionalized evaluations of unobtrusive policy pro-grams tend to have political edges to them, if only in the more subterraneous world of sectoral, highly specialized policy networks. Even in those less controversial instances, policy evaluations are entwined with processes of accountability and lesson drawing that may have winners and losers. However technocratic and seemingly innocuous, every policy program has multiple stakeholders who have an interest in the outcome of the evaluation: decision makers, executive agencies, clients, pressure groups. All of them know that apart from (post-election) political turnovers or crucial court cases, evaluations are virtually the only moments when existing policy trajectories can be reassessed and historical path dependencies may be broken (cf. Rose and Davies 1994). Evaluations hold the promise of a reframing of a program's rationale and objectives, a recalibration of the mix of policy instruments it relies on, a reorganization of its service delivery mechanisms, and, yes, a redistribution of money and other pivotal resources among the various actors involved in its implementation. Hence in the bulk of seemingly "low-politics program" evaluations, the stakes for the circle of interested parties may be high (Vedung 1997, 101–14; Pawson and Tilly 1997; Radin 2000; Hall and Hall 2004, 34–41).

Astute players of the evaluation game will therefore attempt to produce facts and images that suit their aims. They will produce—or engage others to produce—accounts of policy episodes that are, however subtly, framed and timed to convey certain ideas about what happened, why, and how to judge this, and to obscure or downplay others. They will try to influence the terms of the evaluation, in particular also the choice and weighting of the criteria by which the evaluators arrive at their assessments. Evaluating bodies and professional policy analysts will inevitably feel pressures of this kind building up during the evaluation process. The list of tactics used by parties to influence the course and outcomes of evaluation efforts is long, and somewhat resembles the stratagems of bureaucratic and budgetary politics: evaluators' briefs and modus operandi may be subject to continuous discussion; key documents or informants may prove to be remarkably hard, or sometimes remarkably easy, to encounter; the drafting and phrasing of key conclusions and recommendations may be a bone of contention with stakeholder liaisons or in advisory committees; there may be informal solicitations and *démarches* by stake-holders; reports may be prematurely leaked, deeply buried, or publicly lambasted by policy makers. In short, even the most neutral, professional evaluators with no political agenda of their own are likely to become both an object and, unwittingly or not, an agent of political tactics of framing, blaming, and credit claiming (see Bovens et al. 1999; Brändström and Kuipers 2003; Pawson and Tilley 1997; Stone 1997).

# 3. Dealing with the Political in Policy Evaluation

Policy scientists have long recognized these political ramifications of policy evaluation, but have found it impossible to agree on how to cope with them. The cybernetic notion of evaluation as a crucial, authoritative "feedback stream" that enhances reflection, learning, and thus induces well-considered policy continuation, change, or termination, has ceased to be a self-evident rationale for elaborating evaluation theory and methodology. The political realities have simply been too harsh. "The field of evaluation is currently undergoing an identity crisis," lamented two advocates of the positivist approach to policy analysis twenty years ago (Palumbo and Nachimas 1983, 1). At that time, a multitude of alternative approaches had taken the place of the single methodology and assumption set of the classical, first-generation policy analyst of the science-for-policy kind. The mood of optimism and its belief in planned government intervention that had characterized for instance Johnson's "Great Society Program" in the United States was replaced by a mood of scarcity and skepticism (Radin 2000; see also Rossi and Freeman 1993, 23). The focus in policy analysis shifted from *ex ante* evaluation to *ex post* evaluation, because the creation of large public policies became less fashionable than the scrutiny of existing programs (Radin 2000, 34). As Dye (1987, 372) put it, it became "exceedingly costly for society to commit itself to large-scale programs and policies in education and welfare, housing, health and so on, without any real idea about what works." Instrumental policy evaluation continued to be a stronghold in the field of policy analysis, although it was now increasingly exploited as a tool to measure *ex post* cost–benefit ratios to support retrenchment efforts by New Right governments (Radin 2000; Fischer 1995).

At the same time, the value trade-offs and political controversies involved in the scrutiny of existing public policies raised questions about the neutrality assumptions of policy analysis. The apolitical, quantitative assessments of policy outcomes that were supposed to support optimal decision making in the 1950s and 1960s became the subject of increasing criticism. The judgemental character of policy evaluation provoked discussion about its inherently normative, political nature, and about the initial stubbornness among policy analysts steeped in the rationalistic tradition to deny that evaluating policy impact is "an activity which is knee-deep in values, beliefs, party politics and ideology, and makes 'proving' that this policy had this or that impact a notion which is deeply suspect" (Parsons 1995, 550). A new generation of policy analysts came up, and rejected the fundamental assumption that it is possible to measure policy performance in an objective fashion. Like Hugh Heclo, they argued that "a mood is created in which the analysis of rational program choice is taken as the one legitimate arbiter of policy analysis. In this mood, policy studies are politically deodorized—politics is taken out of policy-making" (Heclo 1972, 131). Several approaches to policy evaluation were developed to "bring politics back in" (Nelson 1977; Fischer 1980; Majone 1989).

The diversity of evaluation approaches that has developed since will be discussed here in terms of two traditions. The dividing line between those traditions will be based on the way norms, values, interests, and power are accommodated in evaluation. The *rationalistic tradition* with its strong emphasis on value neutrality and objective assessments of policy performance tries to save evaluation from the pressures of politics, by ignoring these pressures or somehow superseding them. In contrast, the *argumentative tradition* sees policy evaluation as a contribution to the informed debate among competing interests and therefore explicitly incorporates politics in the *ex post* analysis of policy performance.

## 3.1 Rationalistic Policy Evaluation

The rationalists advocate a rigorous separation of facts and values and explicitly strive to produce apolitical knowledge (Hawkesworth 1988; Lynn 1999; Mabry 2002). Policy analysis is rooted in positivism and strives to produce factual data about societal structures and processes by employing concepts and methods borrowed from the natural and physical sciences. Policy analysis serves to bring about rational decision making in the policy process. Judgements about a program's or project's effectiveness and efficiency have to be based on reliable empirical data. It is the task of the policy analyst to produce information that is free from its psychological, cultural, and linguistic context. Because such information transcends historical and cultural experiences, it is assumed to have political and moral neutrality.

Rational methods can be used to construct theoretical policy optimums (in terms of both efficiency and efficacy); in evaluation one can then measure the distance of actual policy outcomes from this optimum. Evaluation thus yields policy-relevant information about the discrepancies between the expected and factual policy performance (Dunn 2004). According to Berk and Rossi (1999, 3) evaluation research is "essentially about providing the most accurate information practically possible in an even-handed manner." Political decisions and judgements require testimonies based on generally applicable and scientifically valid knowledge for "it is rarely prudent to enter a burning political debate armed with only one case study" (Chelimsky 1987, 27). The effort to "remedy the deficiencies in the quality of human life" requires continuous evaluation directed at the improvement of policy programs, based on valid, reliable empirical information (Rossi, Freeman, and Lipsey 1999, 6).

This form of policy evaluation assumes the existence of an exogenously produced, i.e. given, set of clear and consistent policy goals and/or other evaluation standards. It also assumes intersubjective agreement on which indicators can be identified to measure the achievement of these goals. Some rationalistic evaluators might acknowledge that evaluation is in essence a judgement on the value of a policy or program and therefore goes beyond the realms of empirical science (Dunn 2004), or that policy evaluation takes place in a political context with a multitude of actors and preferences involved. For example, Nagel's (2002) approach to *ex ante* policy evaluation includes political considerations to the extent that it proposes a "win–win analysis" to be made: a survey and assessment of the preferred alternatives of political actors involved to find among them an alternative that exceeds the best initial expectations of representatives of the major viewpoints in the political dispute. But their bottom line is clear: Dunn (2004), for instance, asserts that the outcome of policy evaluation is a value judgement, but that the process of evaluation nevertheless has to provide unbiased information. Likewise, the Rossi et al. (1999) handbook self-consciously advocates the systematic application of social research procedures, emphasizing the analysis of costs and benefits, targets, and effects. Earlier, they did not only argue that evaluation should provide value-neutral information to political decision makers, but also that context-sensitive, biased, and argumentative evaluators are "engaged in something other than evaluation research" (Rossi and Freeman 1993, 33).

A remarkably influential institutionalized manifestation of the rationalistic approach to policy evaluation is the Organization for Economic Co-operation and Development (OECD). The OECD aims to foster good governance by monitoring and comparing economic development, deciphering emerging issues, and identifying "policies that work" (according to its own website at www.oecd.org). Its country reports have gained considerable authority over the years and its standardized comparisons are used as verdicts on national policy performance.

## 3.2 Argumentative Policy Evaluation

This brings us to the other camp. The argumentative critics of the rationalist approach complain that the positivist world view is fundamentally distorted by the separation of facts from values. Policy intervention with respect to social and political phenomena is an inherently value-laden, normative activity which allows but for a biased evaluation (Fischer and Forester 1993; Guba and Lincoln 1989). The so-called "post-positivists" or social constructivists understand society as an organized universe of meanings, instead of a mere set of physical objects to be measured. It is not the objects per se that are measured, but the interpretation of the objects by the scientist. The system of meanings shapes "the very questions that social scientists choose to ask about society, not to mention the instruments they select to pursue their questions" (Fischer 1995, 15). Facts depend on a set of underlying assumptions that give meaning to the reality we live in. These assumptions are influenced by politics and power, and empirical findings based on these underlying assumptions "tend to reify a particular reality" (Fischer 1998, 135). The first evaluation of the "Great Society's" Head Start program for socially deprived children was a measurement of the participating children's cognitive development shortly after the program's implementation. This measurement was a relatively simple quantitative assessment of only one of the program's possible positive effects. It showed a lack of improvement in the children's cognitive capacities and that, compared to the total costs of the government intervention, the program had been an expensive failure. If only the evaluators had accepted the program's underlying assumptions that children would benefit from their participation by gaining social experience that would teach them how to function successfully in middle-class-oriented educational institutions, they would have awaited the results of long-term monitoring. The short-term evaluation outcomes were very welcome to the new Nixon administration as an argument to cut down on Head Start considerably (Fischer 1995). The short-term cost–benefit analysis that befitted Nixon's attack on large-scale government planning efforts served to prove him right.

Likewise, the standardized comparison of budgetary and performance figures employed by think tanks such as the OECD leaves open much interpretative and therefore contested ground. One ground for dispute concerns the construction of the categories. In the OECD's report, the Belgian unemployment rate was put just above 8 per cent of the total labor force; in contrast, the Belgian unemployment agency's (www.rva.be) own reports state that it pays unemployment benefits to more than a million people monthly, i.e. 23.5 per cent of the labor force (Arents et al. 2000). The disparity can only be explained by examining closely the definitions of "unemployment" used in studies such as these.

To post-positivists this is just one example among many. They claim it is an illusion to think that separation between values and facts is possible. Moreover, it is impossible to create a division of labor between politics and science where politicians authoritatively establish policy values and scientists can neutrally assess whether the policy outcomes meet the prior established norms (Majone 1989). Policy analysts should actively engage in and facilitate the debate on values in policy making and function as a go-between for citizens and politicians. By attempting to provide "the one best solution" in *ex ante* policy analysis and the "ultimate judgement" in *ex post* evaluation, the ambition of most (rationalist) policy scientists has long been to settle rather than stimulate debates (Fischer 1998).

The advocates of the argumentative approach see yet another mission for policy analysis, including evaluation. Knowledge of a social object or phenomenon emerges from a discussion between competing frameworks (Yanow 2000). This discussion— or discursive interaction—concerning policy outcomes can uncover the presuppositions of each framework that give meaning to its results from empirical research. Policy analysts can intervene in these discussions to help actors with different belief systems understand where their disagreements have epistemological and ethical roots rather than simply boiling down to different interests and priorities (Van Eeten 1999; Yanow 2000). If evaluations can best be understood as forms of knowledge based on consensually accepted beliefs instead of on hard-boiled proof and demonstration (Danziger 1995; Fischer 1998), it becomes quite important to ascertain whose beliefs and whose consensus dominates the retrospective sense-making process. Here, the argumentative approach turns quite explicitly to the politics of policy evaluation, when it argues that the deck with which the policy game is played at the evaluation can be stacked as a result of institutionalized "mobilization of bias." In that sense evaluation simply mirrors the front end of the policy process (agenda setting and problem definition): some groups' interests and voices are organized "in" the design and management of evaluation proceedings, whereas other stakeholders are organized "out." Some proponents of argumentative policy evaluation therefore argue that the policy analyst should not just help expose the meaning systems by which these facts are being interpreted; she should also ensure that under-represented groups can make their experiences and assessments of a policy heard (Fischer and Forester 1993; Dryzek 2000).

DeLeon (1998) qualifies the argumentative approach's enthusiasm about "consensus through deliberation." He cautions that the democratic ambitions of the post-positivists bear the risk of the tyranny of the majority as much as the shortcomings of positivism. The infinite relativism of the social constructivists makes it difficult to decide just whose voice is most relevant or whose argument is the strongest in a particular policy debate. The evaluation by social constructivists may well recognize the political dimension of analytic assessments of policy outcomes, but it does not by definition lead us to more carefully crafted political judgements.

# 4. Doing Evaluation in the Political World

How then, should we cope with the normative, methodological, and political challenges of policy evaluation? In our view, the key challenge for professional policy evaluators should *not* be how to save objectivity, validity, and reliability from the twin threats of epistemological relativism and political contestation. This project can only lead to a kind of analytical self-deception: evaluators' perfunctory neglecting or "willing away" pivotal philosophical queries and political biases and forces (Portis and Levy 1988). It may be more productive to ask two alternative questions. How can policy analysts maximize academic rigor without becoming politically irrelevant? And how can policy evaluations be policy relevant without being used politically? The first question requires evaluators to navigate between the Scylla of seemingly robust but irrelevant positivism and the Charybdis of politically astute but philosophically problematic relativism. The second question deals with the applied dimension. It alerts evaluators to the politics of evaluation that are such a prominent feature of contemporary policy struggles and of political attempts to "learn" from evaluations.

The approach to evaluation advocated here should be viewed within the context of a broader repositioning of policy science that we feel is going on, and which entails an increased acceptance of the once rather sectarian claim of the argumentative approach that all knowledge about social affairs—including public policy making— is based on limited information and social constructions. If one does so, the hitherto predominantly positivist and social engineering-oriented aims and scope of policy evaluation need to be revised or at least broadened. Befitting such a "revisionist" approach to policy analysis is the essentially incrementalist view that public policy makers' best bet is to devote the bulk of their efforts to enabling society to avoid, move away from, and effectively respond to what, through pluralistic debate, it has come to recognize as important present and future ills (Lindblom 1990). Policy analysis is supposed to be an integral part of this project, but not in the straightforward manner of classic "science for policy." Instead, the key to its unique contribution lies in its reflective potential. We agree with Majone (1989, 182) that:

It is not the task of analysts to resolve fundamental disagreements about evaluative criteria and standards of accountability; only the political process can do that. However, analysts can contribute to societal learning by refining the standards of appraisal and by encouraging a more sophisticated understanding of public policies than is possible from a single perspective.

This also goes for evaluating public policies and programs. Again we cite Majone (1989, 183): "The need today is less to develop 'objective' measures of outcomes—the traditional aim of evaluation research—than to facilitate a wide-ranging dialogue among advocates of different criteria."

In a recent cross-national and cross-sectoral comparative evaluation study, an approach to evaluation was developed that embodies the main thrust of the "revisionist" approach (Bovens, 't Hart, and Peters 2001). The main question of that project, which involved a comparative assessment of critical policy episodes and programs in four policy sectors in six European states, was how the responses of different governments to highly similar major, non-incremental policy challenges can be evaluated, and how similarities and differences in their performance can be explained. A crucial distinction was made between the programmatic and the political dimension of success and failure in public governance.

In a *programmatic* mode of assessment, the focus is on the effectiveness, efficiency, and resilience of the specific policies being evaluated. The key concerns of programmatic evaluation pertain to the classical, Lasswellian–Lindblomian view of policy making as social problem solving most firmly embedded in the rationalistic approach to policy evaluation: does government tackle social issues, does it deliver solutions to social problems that work, and does it do so in a sensible, defensible way (Lasswell 1971; Lindblom 1990)? Of course these questions involve normative and therefore inherently political judgements too, yet the focus is essentially instrumental, i.e. on assessing the impact of policies that are designed and presented as purposeful interventions in social affairs.

The simplest form of programmatic evaluation—popular to this day because of its straightforwardness and the intuitive appeal of the idea that governments should be held to account on their capacity to deliver on their own promises (Glazer and Rothenberg 2001)—is to rate policies by the degree to which they achieve the stated goals of policy makers. Decades of evaluation research have taught all but the most hard-headed analysts that despite its elegance, this method has big problems. Goals may be untraceable in policy documents, symbolic rather than substantial, deliberately vaguely worded for political reasons, and contain mutually contradictory components. Goals also often shift during the course of the policy-making process to such an extent that the original goals bear little relevance for assessing the substance and the rationale of the policy that has actually been adopted and implemented in the subsequent years.

Clearly, something better was needed. In our view, a sensible form of programmatic policy evaluation does not fully omit any references to politically sanctioned goals—as once advocated by the proponents of so-called "goal-free" evaluation—but "embeds" and thus qualifies the effectiveness criterion by complementing and comparing it with other logics of programmatic evaluation. In the study design, case evaluators had to examine not only whether governments had proven capable of delivering on their promises and effectuating purposeful interventions. They were also required to ascertain: (a) the ability of the policy-making entity to adapt its program(s) and policy instruments to changing circumstances over time (i.e. an adaptability/learning capacity criterion); (b) its ability to control the costs of the program(s) involved (i.e. an efficiency criterion). In keeping with Majone's call, these three general programmatic evaluation logics were then subject to intensive debate between the researchers involved in the study: how should these criteria be understood in concrete cases, what data would be called for to assess a case, and what about the relative weight of these three criteria in the overall programmatic assessment? Sectoral expert subgroups gathered subsequently to specify and operationalize these programmatic criteria in view of the specific nature and circumstances of the four policy areas to be studied. The outcomes of these deliberations about criteria (and methodology) are depicted in Fig. 15.1.

The *political* dimension of policy evaluation refers to how policies and policy makers become represented and evaluated in the political arena (Stone 1997). This is the discursive world of symbols, emotions, political ideology, and power relationships. Here it is not the social consequences of policies that count, but the political construction of these consequences, which might be driven by institutional logics and political considerations of wholly different kinds. In the study described above, the participants struggled a lot with how to operationalize this dimension in a way that allowed for non-idiosyncratic, comparative modes of assessment and analysis. In the process it became clear that herein lies an important weakness of the argumentative approach: it rightly points at the relevance of the socially and politically constructed nature of assessments about policy success and failure, but it does not offer clear, cogent, and widely accepted evaluation principles and tools for capturing this dimension of policy evaluation. In the end, the evaluators in the study opted for a relatively "thin" but readily applicable set of political evaluation measures: the incidence and degree of political upheaval (traceable by content analysis of press coverage and parliamentary investigations, political fatalities, litigation), or lack of it; and changes in generic patterns of political legitimacy (public satisfaction of policy or confidence in authorities and public institutions). An essential benefit of discerning and contrasting programmatic and political evaluation modes is that it highlights the development of disparities between a policy-making entity's programmatic and

*The governance of decline: policy making for the steel industry*
Key policy challenge: Coping with the declining global competitiveness of a
once strategically vital and highly unionized industrial sector involving large
numbers of jobs, often concentrated in particular regions

Programmatic assessment criteria:

- The timing of government steel restructuring initiatives relative to other countries
- The financial costs of restructuring the industry
- The economic viability of the industry in the years following restructuring
- The size of employment losses sustained

*Innovation governance—Finance sector*
Key policy challenge: Coping with the impact of technological change and
global trends towards deregulation of the banking and financial services sector

Programmatic assessment criteria:

- Number of bank failures and/or relative asset size of failed banks
  Absolute and relative financial costs of bailouts
- Timing of state intervention

*Reform governance—Health sector*
Key policy challenge: Controlling the modus operandi of the medical
profession, particularly the remuneration and labor conditions of doctors

Programmatic assessment criteria:

- Ability to overcome resistance and achieve intended changes in the targeted
  aspects of the operation of the medical profession
- Duration of reform episode from first plans to actual implementation

*Crisis governance—Blood transfusion sector*
Key policy challenge: Responding to a novel, ill-structured, and increasingly
threatening and urgent problem of the connection between the emerging AIDS
epidemic and the quality of national blood transfusion systems

Programmatic assessment criteria:

- The timing and scope of donor selection measures
- The timing and scope of mandatory blood tests
- The timing of import stops for untreated blood products
- The timing of health treatment of blood products
- The timing and effectiveness of measures to withdraw existing untreated
  products from the market

**Fig. 15.1.** Programmatic policy evaluation: an example (taken from Bovens et al. 2001, 20–2)

political performance. This should not surprise the politically astute evaluator:
political processes determine whether programmatic success, or lack of it, is acknowledged by relevant stakeholders and audiences. The dominant assessment of
many conspicuous "planning disasters"—the Sydney Opera House for example—
has evolved over time, as certain issues, conflicts, and consequences that were
important at the time have evaporated or changed shape, and as new actors
and power constellations have emerged (compare Hall 1982 to Bovens and 't
Hart 1996). In the Bovens et al. study, some remarkable asymmetries between

programmatic and political evaluations were identified. In the banking sector, for example, (de-)regulatory policies and/or existing instruments for oversight in Spain, the UK, France, and Sweden did not prevent banking fiascos of catastrophic proportions (i.e. major programmatic failures); at the same time, the political evaluation of these policies in terms of the evaluation criteria outlined above was not particularly negative. Likewise, in programmatic terms German responses to the HIV problem in the blood supply were at least as bad as those in France; in France this became the stuff of major political scandal and legal proceedings, whereas in Germany the evaluation was depoliticized and no political consequences resulted. These types of evaluation asymmetries defy the commonsense, "just world" hypothesis that good performance should lead to political success, and vice versa. Detecting asymmetries then challenges the analyst to explain these discrepancies in terms of structural and cultural features of the political system or policy sector and the dynamics of the evaluation process in the cases concerned (see Bovens, 't Hart, and Peters 2001, 593 ff.).

Talking not so much about policy analysts but about policy practitioners, Schön and Rein (1994) have captured the approach to policy evaluation advocated here under the heading of "frame-reflection." This implies willingness on the part of analysts to reflect continuously upon and reassess their own lenses for looking at the world. In addition, they need to make efforts to communicate with analysts using a different set of assumptions. In the absence of such a reflective orientation, policy analysts may find that they, and their conclusions, are deemed irrelevant by key players in the political arena. Or they may find themselves set up unwittingly to be hired guns in the politics of blaming. They ought to be neither.

Reflective policy analysts may strive for a position as a systematic, well-informed, thoughtful, and fair-minded provider of inputs to the political process of argumentation, debate, maneuvering, and blaming that characterizes controversial policy episodes. In our view, their effectiveness could be enhanced significantly if they adopt a role conception that befits such a position: explicit about their own assumptions; meticulous in developing their arguments; sensitive to context; and striving to create institutional procedures for open and pluralistic debate. At the same time, since the political world of policy fiascos in particular is unlikely to be supportive of such frame reflection, policy analysts need a considerable amount of political astuteness in assessing their own position in the field of forces and in making sure that their arguments are heard at what they think is the right time, by the right people, and in the right way. Finding ways to deal creatively with the twin requirements of scholarly detachment and political realism is what the art and craft of policy evaluation are all about.

## REFERENCES

ANHEIER, H. K., ed. 1999. *When Things Go Wrong*. London: Sage.

ARENTS, M., CLUITMANS, M. M., and VAN DER ENDE, M. A. 2000. *Benefit Dependency Ratios: An Analysis of Nine European Countries, Japan and the US*. The Hague: Elsevier.

BERK, R. A., and ROSSI, P. H. 1999. *Thinking about Program Evaluation*. Thousand Oaks, Calif.: Sage.

BOIN, R. A. 1995. The Dutch prison system in the 1990s: organizational autonomy, institutional adversity, and a shift in policy. *American Jails*, 9(4): 88–91 (part I), and *American Jails*, 9(5): 87–95 (part II).

BOVENS, M., and 'T HART, P.    1996. *Understanding Policy Fiascoes*. New Brunswick, NJ: Transaction.

—— —— et al. 1999. The politics of blame avoidance. Pp. 123–48 in *When Things Go Wrong*, ed. H. K. Anheier. London: Sage.

—— —— and PETERS, B. G. (eds.) 2001. *Success and Failure in Public Governance: A Comparative Study*. Cheltenham: Edward Elgar.

BRÄNDSTRÖM, A., and KUIPERS, S. L. 2003. From "normal incidents" to political crises: understanding the selective politicization of policy failures. *Government and Opposition*, 38: 279–305.

CHELIMSKY, E. 1987. The politics of program evaluation. *Society*, 25: 24–32.

DANZIGER, M. 1995. Policy analysis postmodernized: some political and pedagogical ramifications. *Policy Studies Journal*, 23: 435–50.

DELEON, P. 1998. Introduction: the evidentiary base for policy analysis: empiricist versus postpositivist positions. *Policy Studies Journal*, 26: 109–13.

DRAPER, T. 1991. *A Very Thin Line: The Iran-Contra Affairs*. New York: Hill and Wang.

DRYZEK, J. S. 2000. *Deliberative Democracies and Beyond: Liberals, Critics, Contestations*. Oxford: Oxford University Press.

DUNN, W. N. 2004. *Public Policy Analysis: An Introduction*, 3rd edn. Upper Saddle River, NJ: Prentice Hall.

DYE, T. R. 1987. *Understanding Public Policy*, 6th edn. Englewood Cliffs, NJ: Prentice Hall.

EDELMAN, M. 1988. *Constructing the Political Spectacle*. Chicago: University of Chicago Press.

FISCHER, F. 1980. *Politics, Values, and Public Policy: The Problem of Methodology*. Boulder, Colo.: Westview.

—— 1995. *Evaluating Public Policy*. Chicago: Nelson Hall.

—— 1998. Beyond empiricism: policy inquiry in postpositivist perspective. *Policy Studies Journal*, 26: 129–46.

—— and FORESTER, J. 1993. *The Argumentative Turn in Policy Analysis and Planning*. Durham, NC: Duke University Press.

GLAZER, A., and ROTHENBERG, L. S. 2001. *Why Government Succeeds and Why it Fails*. Cambridge, Mass.: Harvard University Press.

GRAY, P., and HART, P. 'T. (eds.) 1998. *Public Policy Disasters in Western Europe*. London: Routledge.

GUBA, E. G., and LINCOLN, V. S. 1989. *Fourth Generation Evaluation*. Newbury Park, Calif.: Sage.

HAJER, M., and WAGENAAR, H. (eds.) 2003. *Deliberative Policy Analysis: Understanding Governance in the Network Society*. Cambridge: Cambridge University Press.

HALL, I., and HALL, D. 2004. *Evaluation and Social Research: Introducing a Small-Scale Practice*. Basingstoke: Palgrave.

HAWKESWORTH, M. E. 1988. *Theoretical Issues in Policy Analysis.* Albany: State University of New York Press.

HECLO, H. H. 1972. Review article: policy analysis. *British Journal of Political Science,* 2(1): 83–108.

HEINEMAN, R. A., BLUHM, W. T. et al. 1990. *The World of the Policy Analyst.* Chatham, NJ: Chatham House.

HOOD, C. 2002. The risk game and the blame game. *Government and Opposition,* 37: 15–37.

LASSWELL, H. 1971. *A Pre-View of Policy Science.* New York: Elsevier.

LINDBLOM, C. 1990. *Inquiry and Change: The Troubled Attempt to Understand and Shape Society.* New Haven, Conn.: Yale University Press.

LIPSKY, M., and OLSON, D. J. 1977. *Commission Politics: The Processing of Racial Crisis in America.* New Brunswick, NJ: Transaction.

LYNN, L. E. 1999. A place at the table: policy analysis, its postpositive critics and the future of practice. *Journal of Policy Analysis and Management,* 18: 411–24.

MABRY, L. 2002. Postmodern evaluation—or not? *American Journal of Evaluation,* 23: 141–57.

MAJONE, G. 1989. *Evidence, Argument and Persuasion in the Policy Process.* New Haven, Conn.: Yale University Press.

NAGEL, S. S. 2002. *Handbook of Policy Evaluation.* Thousand Oaks, Calif.: Sage.

NELSON, R. R. 1977. *The Moon and the Ghetto.* New York: Norton.

PAL, L. A. 1995. Competing paradigms in policy discourse: the case of international human rights. *Policy Sciences,* 28: 185–207.

PALUMBO, D. J., and NACHIMAS, D. 1983. The preconditions for successful evaluation: is there an ideal type? *Policy Sciences,* 16: 67–79.

PARSONS, D. W. 1995. *Public Policy: An Introduction to the Theory and Practice of Policy Analysis.* Aldershot: Edward Elgar.

PAWSON, R., and TILLEY, N. 1997. *Realistic Evaluation.* London: Sage.

PORTIS, E. B., and LEVY, M. B. (eds.) 1988. *Handbook of Political Theory and Policy Science.* Westport, Conn.: Greenwood.

RADIN, B. A. 2000. *Beyond Machiavelli: Policy Analysis Comes of Age.* Washington, DC: Georgetown University Press.

RESODIHARDJO, S. L. forthcoming 2006. Institutional crises and reform: constrained opportunities. Ph.D. dissertation, Leiden University.

ROSE, R. 1993. *Lesson-Drawing in Public Policy.* Chatham, NJ: Chatham House.

—— and DAVIES, P. 1994. *Inheritance in Public Policy.* New York: Oxford University Press.

ROSSI, P. H., and FREEMAN, H. E. 1993. *Evaluation: A Systemic Approach,* 5th edn. Newbury Park, Calif.: Sage.

—— —— and LIPSEY, M. R. 1999. *Evaluation: A Systemic Approach,* 6th edn. Thousand Oaks, Calif.: Sage.

SCHÖN, D., and REIN, M. 1994. *Frame Reflection.* New York: Basic Books.

STONE, D. 1997. *Policy Paradox: The Art of Political Decision Making.* New York: W.W. Norton.

THROGMORTON, J. A. 1991. The rhetorics of policy analysis. *Policy Sciences,* 24: 153–79.

VAN EETEN, M. 1999. *Dialogues of the Deaf: Defining New Agendas for Environmental Deadlocks.* Delft: Eburon.

VEDUNG, E. 1997. *Public Policy and Program Evaluation.* New Brunswick, NJ: Transaction.

WEAVER, R. K. 1986. The politics of blame avoidance. *Journal of Public Policy,* 6: 371–98.

WEIMER, D. L., and VINING, A. R. 1999. *Policy Analysis: Concepts and Practice,* 3rd edn. Upper Saddle River, NJ: Prentice Hall.

WEISS, C. H. 1998. *Evaluation: Methods for Studying Programs and Policies.* Upper Saddle River, NJ: Prentice Hall.

WILDAVSKY, A. 1987. *Speaking Truth to Power: The Art and Craft of Policy Analysis.* New Brunswick, NJ: Transaction.

YANOW, D. 2000. *Conducting Interpretative Policy Analysis.* Newbury Park, Calif.: Sage.

# CHAPTER 16

# POLICY DYNAMICS

## EUGENE BARDACH

UNDERSTANDING dynamics is about understanding change, and a concern with policy dynamics has to be, in some measure, about policy change—how to get from here to there in the political process. This concern should be focused on both policy-making and policy-implementing processes. Consider the following questions that call for answers framed at least partially in dynamic terms:

- The federal welfare reform Act[1] of 1996 was something of a backlash against an unpopular program that was seen as encouraging dependency. But was it also:
  - An equilibrating move in a political system that tends to seek the ideological center?
  - An evolutionary move towards economic efficiency that either does or does not have a built-in tropism towards efficiency?
  - A product of successful long-term "learning" processes in the policy-making system?
- Why can't the United States seem to get a rational health care system that provides reasonable quality care at reasonable cost to all Americans? Perhaps one reason is that the dynamics of policy development in this area, begun in the 1930s, have locked us in to a system that depends heavily, but also only partially on employer-based financing.
- Regulatory agencies are often said to become captured by the industries they regulate. How does the process of becoming captured unfold?
- How did the United States Congress come to be such a polarized body? It was not always this way, and the process took place over many years. How did the

---

[1] Formally known as the Personal Responsibility and Work Opportunity Reconciliation Act (PRWORA).

process work? Is the process specific to this institution and its historical context(s), or is the process, at least in part, more generic?

- An entrepreneurial group of legislative staff and legislators with close ties to the powerful Speaker of the California Assembly sought the Speaker's assistance for a major reform in mental health policy only in the closing days of the legislative struggle. Why did they wait? Might they have been better off not waiting so long?

While this chapter does not attempt to answer these questions in particular, it does seek to describe and evaluate a number of conceptual frameworks for answering questions like these.

# 1. Overview

This is not a review essay on the status of a mature field. It does not try to summarize comprehensively the works of others. The study of policy dynamics is not a field at all; and, to the best of my knowledge, no one has previously brought together all the phenomena I canvass here. I have scanned for work in which dynamics and policy both happen to be present, even if the authors did not self-consciously intend to make the connection. I have also not aimed to eliminate subjectivity on my part. Scanning is bound to be subjective, perhaps idiosyncratic, as is interpretation of the results.

My main objective is to stimulate research interest in a neglected phenomenon and, by way of doing so, to present concepts and substantive hypotheses that I have found stimulating or that others might find so.

The most important others are the likely readers of this *Handbook*. I assume the average reader to have a generalist's interest in the policy process. Hence, I have favored breadth over depth. Secondly, I have focused more on the institutional dynamics of the policy-making process than on the evolution of substantive policies themselves, though obviously the two subject matters overlap. This focus has naturally led me to look primarily to the work done by political scientists, though I also mention stimulating contributions by economists and other social scientists.[2] Thirdly, I have tried to point to policy-relevant applications of leading ideas in the study of dynamic social systems, even though such applications are often isolated, pioneering, and not necessarily widely cited by students of the policy process. Fourthly, I occasionally refer to studies or bodies of work that, although not closely related to the policy process, suggest the power of certain approaches to the study of dynamic systems.

---

[2] I am, of course, indebted to the work of Baumgartner and Jones, who have presented a survey on these topics as well (Baumgartner and Jones 2002).

In Section 2, I explain some key concepts in systems analysis that are necessary for understanding dynamics.

Section 3 deals with dynamic processes dominated by negative feedback. They are in some sense equilibrating, or balance seeking. However, in most cases equilibrium is not actually achieved, unless one is willing to call oscillating within some broad or narrow range an equilibrium. They all have to do with what one might think of as "the balance of power."

Section 4 discusses processes dominated by positive feedback. These are the more integrative processes of political life, e.g. consensus building, network construction, community mobilization, collective learning, interorganizational collaboration.

Section 5 briefly describes dynamic processes that unfold in only one direction. That is, they do not involve feedback loops. The processes selected here for discussion involve filtering and chain reactions, or "cascades."

Section 6 concludes with a short wish list for future research.

## 1.1 Do Dynamics Matter Anyway?

As this chapter is devoted exclusively to policy dynamics, it would be easy for both author and reader to be carried away by the putative importance of dynamic processes and process-related tactical skills relative to, say, institutionalized authority or interest group power or interpersonal influence. The conceptual fascination of the subject matter, and some of the exotic models to deal with it, increases the temptation. Not all scholars working in this area have been immune. We should probably believe, though, that in the end, authority, power, and influence all matter more. If you are wrestling Hercules, you will lose eventually, no matter what the sequence of holds and escapes along the way. The assumption behind this chapter is merely that *when* process dynamics are consequential, we need the conceptual tools and empirical knowledge for understanding them.

## 2. "Systems" and "Dynamics"

Not all systems are dynamic, but all dynamics occur within systems. We must therefore say something at the outset about how to understand systems.

Robert Jervis, in *System Effects: Complexity in Political and Social Life*, provides this useful definition of a system: "We are dealing with a system when (a) a set of units or elements is interconnected so that changes in some elements or their relations produce changes in other parts of the system, and (b) the entire system exhibits properties and behaviors that are different from those of the parts" (Jervis 1997, 6).

A closed system is one that is responsive only to changes initiated by its own elements; an open system contains an endogenous core that behaves in many ways like a closed system but can also receive inputs from its environment. In this chapter, I consider only open systems but often focus mainly on the dynamics of their endogenous cores.[3]

To convey the flavor of what counts as what, in Terry Moe's paper on the dynamics of the National Labor Relations Board (NLRB), the endogenous core consists of the Board, the staff, and the millions of employers and workers who are potential complainants, whereas the environment is composed of political officials, judges, and a variety of economic conditions (Moe 1985). In Moe's analysis of who wins and who loses at the NLRB, the workings of the endogenous core have an interesting but minor influence compared to influences from the larger environment. Exogenous influences on the Board, especially by way of presidential appointments, importantly shift its pro- or anti-labor tilt. Then endogenous dynamics take over. Suppose, for instance, the Board shifts its interpretative standards in a direction favorable to labor. This leads to a temporary increase in the win rate. But this increase is only temporary. As the backlog of cases to be settled favorably to labor under the standards diminishes, so too does the average win rate. But the temporarily above-average win rate, in combination with signals about the Board's new interpretative standards, encourages an increase in labor filings. The average quality of the new filings is below the average quality of the old caseload, however, and the win rate at the staff level (as they filter cases up to the board) drops. As staff criteria and labor perceptions of those criteria stabilize, the average merit of cases and the labor win rate converge on some "normal" level. This new level, though, is more pro-labor than it used to be before the shifts in the Board's composition.

## 2.1 Negative and Positive Feedback Loops

The structure of a system consists of (1) its constituent elements, (2) the rules governing their interactions, and (3) the information required by the system to apply the rules. In virtually all dynamic systems of interest to students of policy, "running" the system creates feedbacks that might alter the structure of the system.

By means of feedback loops certain system outputs (whether intermediate or final) influence certain of the system's inputs. For instance, teachers encourage parents to read to their children, and the children's improved performance encourages parents to keep up the good work. The literature on systems dynamics calls such growth-inducing feedback loops "positive" because in conventional loop diagrams such as

---

[3] Richardson usefully distinguishes two meanings, analytical and material, of "closed" system. In a material, or real, sense all systems are open. For analytical purposes, however, it sometimes makes sense to treat certain systems as closed. Jay W. Forrester, a pioneer of at least one wing of contemporary systems analysis, works only on analytically closed systems (Richardson 1991, 297–8).

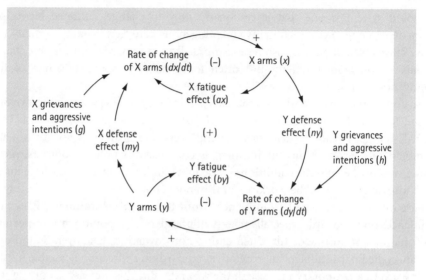

**Fig. 16.1.** Loop structure of Richardson's linear model of an arms race

Fig. 16.1 the product of the components' polarities is positive. "Negative" feedback loops, on the other hand, have balancing, or equilibrating effects, as the product of the polarities is negative. Figure 16.1 diagrams the well-known arms race model of Lewis Richardson. Richardson's algebraic model is given in equations (1) and (2), with $x$ and $y$ representing stockpiles of arms in two nations, $m$ and $n$ being positive "defense" coefficients, and $g$ and $h$ representing "grievances" or "aggressive intentions" (Richardson 1991, 40).

$$dx/dt = my - ax + g \tag{1}$$

$$dy/dt = nx - by + h \tag{2}$$

In the NLRB case, a larger gap between cases filed and cases won increased worker realism, while increased realism fed back and decreased the gap.

## 2.2 "Emergent Properties" and "Developments"

As they run, most complex systems with positive feedback loops create new features, "emergent properties." In the physical world, think of a pot that miraculously emerges from the system of clay, wheel, and potter. In the social world, think of gridlock that emerges from thousands of drivers converging on the same highways or urban streets. As these examples suggest, emergent properties are properties of the system as a whole rather than any of its component parts.

"Emergent properties" can loosely be translated back into more conventional language as "developments." In the course of this chapter I shall refer to many such developments in policy-related systems. I have already mentioned win rates in the NLRB case. Other such examples will be:

- Partial fragmentation of an advocacy coalition following soon after counter-mobilization by its opponents.
- The emergence of a functioning "interagency collaborative" out of a combination of human and non-human assets hitherto relatively independent of one another.
- A variety of momentum processes that go into the creation of electoral bandwagons, the construction of implementation networks, and the development of legislative consensus.
- The "lock-in effect" that comes to hem in social policy by all the policies previously enacted and with which any new policy must be reconciled.

# 3. NEGATIVE FEEDBACK PROCESSES: THE BALANCING OF POWER

I discuss two types of negative feedback, or equilibrating, processes. They are:

- Oscillations occurring within certain—perhaps changeable—limits.[4]
- Efforts being made to maintain a "monopolistic" equilibrium condition, one based on the superior political power of the monopolists. When reformers do manage to succeed, this might be termed a "disequilibrating" process.

I will note preliminarily that I ignore the large domain of processes that either do or might reach a game-theoretical equilibrium. Many of these, such as the Prisoner's Dilemma game, are of great relevance to policy making and implementation and have inspired a large literature. The reason for this omission is that equilibration in these games, if it occurs, is instantaneous; hence, there is no "dynamic" to talk about. For the same reason I also omit effects that compensate for failures to reach an equilibrium, such as discussed in Miller (Miller 1992).

## 3.1 Oscillating Processes

Before turning to domestic policy processes, our main interest, let us consider the classic oscillating system, balance of power politics in the international arena. At its

---

[4] In their generally thorough and insightful work on both positive and negative feedback, Baumgartner and Jones refer occasionally to the "homeostatic" role of negative feedback (Baumgartner and Jones 2002, 8–9). This implies a return to some prior defined state. I do not think this occurs very frequently. All I attribute to negative feedback is system movement in a reactive direction.

core, the process features (1) the rise of a countervailing coalition to challenge any emerging coalition of states and (2) fluidity in coalition formation, so that today's enemy may be tomorrow's ally. The system oscillates between relative peace and near-war, sometimes tipping over into actual war when countervailing threat fails to deter. However, it also tends to preserve most actors' territorial integrity and bars the way to successful total domination (Jervis 1997, 131–3).

Whether or not one thinks the balance of power actually "works"—in Renaissance Italy or in Europe, say, from the seventeenth century until the Second World War—it is clear that it does not work all the time. When rulers are extremely ambitious or miscalculate, or countervailing forces are slow to mobilize, the system will break down. That is, war will occur. These failures do not arise from the dynamics of the system's endogenous core, however, but from exogenous forces in the system's environment, such as leaders' psychology (Napoleon, Hitler) or the influences of domestic politics (public opinion in Neville Chamberlain's England).

*Regulatory agencies.* In domestic politics, the oscillation of regulatory policy is the best illustration of negative feedback. As we have seen in the case of Moe's study of the NLRB, the influence of exogenous factors on the dynamics of the core is a point of great importance and general applicability. Of course, one might say that the oscillations in the political environment are themselves the expression of endogenous processes within a larger system. Like the NLRB, risk regulators such as the Occupational Safety and Health Administration (OSHA) and the Environmental Protection Agency (EPA) are more aggressive regulators when Democrats are in power than when Republicans are. This oscillation between parties, and the interest groups that thrive under their protection, is certainly systematic after a fashion. We shall return to this point below.

Politics aside, the very nature of risk regulation probably guarantees a certain amount of endogenous oscillation independent of that induced by the political environment (Hood, Rothstein, and Baldwin 2001; Bardach and Kagan 2002/1982). All that is required is regulators who wish to adhere to norms about making "good public policy" but who work under conditions of great technical uncertainty. This is a standard condition for almost all risk-regulating agencies. Good scientific information is often lacking about what exposures cause how much damage to what kinds of individuals under which circumstances. Nor do regulators know with certainty whether, in the real world of policy and program implementation, particular remedies will be applied effectively or not. Following Jonathan Bendor, suppose that regulators follow heuristics like "If it seemed to work in the past, keep on doing it" and "If it didn't seem to work, tighten (loosen) the regulatory regime." As long as mistakes appear to happen, the agency will not get trapped in a suboptimal regime, but it will not be able to prevent its oscillating away from an optimal regime either (Bendor 2004, 13–14).

Bendor uses the Food and Drug Administration as his primary illustration, following the work of Paul Quirk (Quirk 1980, ch. 6), and plausibly assumes that the point of optimal stringency lies within the limits of oscillatory movement. But of course, it need not do so. Bardach and Kagan (2002/1982) postulate a regulatory dynamic that has regulatory stringency (in its multiple dimensions) oscillating according to political pressures in the short run and the medium run but over the long run, drifting upward. They refer to a "regulatory ratchet." In any given cycle, stringency may be reduced, but it will not be reduced below its lowest level in the previous cycle. If such a ratchet is indeed at work,[5] it would be a fortunate but only temporary happenstance that the optimum point would be located within the oscillatory limits.

*Spending.* In "The public as thermostat: dynamics of preferences for spending," Christopher Wlezien explicitly tests a negative feedback hypothesis, one based on what he takes to be a theory of democratic accountability, in which the public "would adjust its preferences for 'more' or 'less' policy in response to policy outputs themselves. In effect, the public would behave like a thermostat; when the actual policy 'temperature' differs from the preferred policy temperature, the public would send a signal to adjust policy accordingly, and once sufficiently adjusted, the signal would stop" (Wlezien 1995, 981). Wlezien did find, in regard to defense and to five social programs, that public preferences were a counterweight to budgetary appropriations: whatever direction they had moved in, public opinion wanted them to move back.

*Elections and parties.* Periodic contested elections in a two-party system are, of course, a negative feedback system writ very large. Although in a separation-of-powers system the idea of a "party in power" is sometimes ambiguous, over time grievances build up against whoever is identified as "the party in power," and voters "throw the rascals out." That these grievances may not realistically be attributable to the actions of the party or its standard bearers (Fiorina 1981) is not to the point. The feedback loop from party conduct to voter attributions of responsibility is not the only source of such attributions, and systems can function as smoothly with irrational as rational feedback. The system-like quality of electoral oscillations is not diminished by the lack of uniformity in the intervals between turnovers. The duration of such intervals probably must be explained by exogenous factors, such as business cycles, changing demographics, and random shocks from foreign events or scandals.[6]

Within particular election seasons, negative feedback systems also come into play. Anthony Downs's well-known spatial models of party positioning show that, in a simple single-dimensional (left/right) world of voter preferences, two parties are driven towards the center as they compete for the loyalties of the median voter. This is not a negative but a positive feedback system. However, the process may not move to completion, as the party leaders (candidates) are dragged back from the center by the threat of non-voting (and non-campaigning) from their party's base. Negative

---

[5] For evidence that the ratchet effect occurs, see Ruhl and Salzman 2003.

[6] The duration of intervals might, however, have a statistical regularity such as Zipf's law, which connects the frequency of an event type with the rank of that type in a population of related events. Zipf's law holds for diverse events like the appearances of words in the English language and the population sizes of cities. See Bak 1996, 24–6. For instance, the tenth most frequently used word appeared 2,653 times in Zipf's sample; the twentieth most used word, 1,311 times; and the 20,000th most used word once. Such data fit a straight line on a logarithmic plot with slope near one.

feedback arising from moves too far towards the center or back towards the party's enthusiasts leads to an equilibration of candidates' positions short of the median voter (Shepsle and Bonchek 1997, 114).

*Reform cycles.* Observers have noted episodes of reform—principally anti-corruption, anti-business, and/or anti-government—in American political history. Samuel Huntington speaks of a characteristically American "creedal passion" to create a civic life of democratic and ethical purity erupting every sixty years (Huntington 1981, 147 ff.). This eruption occurs when the "ideals-versus-institutions gap" has grown too large. Although Huntington does claim there is a systematic basis for the sixty-year cycle, he does not explain what it is.

Similarly, McClosky and Zaller, in their much praised *The American Ethos* (1984) postulate that, over decades, there are "swings in the national mood" between support for "a competitive, private economy in which the most enterprising and industrious individuals receive the greatest income" and "a democratic society in which everyone can earn a decent living and has an equal chance to realize his or her full human potential." These values of "capitalism" and "democracy" are in some tension politically and philosophically, they argue. Yet beyond this they do not specify the mechanisms whereby the predominance of one value set begins to retreat in the face of its rival.[7]

In the classic age of interest group theory, David Truman once famously wrote of the "balance wheel" in American politics, which had interest groups who triumphed in one round losing to newly mobilized "potential groups" in the next (Truman 1951, 514). "In a relatively vigorous political system ... unorganized interests are dominant with sufficient frequency ... so that ... both the activity and the methods of organized interest groups are kept within broad limits" (1951: 515). Here indeed is a theory of reform cycles based on negative feedback.

Andrew McFarland has updated Truman and proposed a "reform cycle" theory focused on pro- and anti-business policies and politics from 1890 to at least 1991, the date of his paper (McFarland 1991). His summary:

Economic producer groups have a more stable incentive to participate in issue-area decision making than the reform groups that challenge their control. However, after a few years of the business-control phase of the cycle, unchecked producer groups tend to commit "excesses", violations of widely shared values. This leads to political participation [and policy triumphs] by the reformers [1991, 257]. [But once legislation has been passed, and regulations drawn up] ... the period of high politics is over: the public loses interest, journalistic coverage ceases, Congress and the president turn to other issues..., but the activity of producer groups remains constant, due to their continuing economic stakes... After a few years, another period of producer group power is at hand, leading eventually to new excesses, a new reform period and so forth. (1991, 263–4)

One implication of this theory, says McFarland, is that "across the scope of hundreds of issue areas, business control or reform phases tend to occur at the same time" (1991, 257).

---

[7] McClosky and Zaller greatly overstate the general case for a tension between these two value sets. Exchanging the highly charged "capitalism" for the more neutral "markets," democratic and market institutions are not only compatible but may be mutually required.

That there are indeed waves of "reform" cutting across many issue areas simultaneously is true enough. McFarland points in particular to the Progressive movement (after 1900), the New Deal (in the 1930s), and the 1960s (the civil rights and anti-Vietnam War movements). Whether these represent true cycles in an oscillating system is questionable, however. In McFarland's theory the stimulus for the reform phase of the cycle is "new excesses" by business, implying that it is an *increase* relative to some accepted or acceptable lower level of misconduct that triggers reform. The basic driver of the system is thus varying and objectively perceived levels of business misconduct. It is just as likely to be the case, however, that the actual levels of business misbehavior do not vary greatly over time and that changing social and cultural conditions trigger collective expressions of outrage and demands for "reform." It is noteworthy that since the 1960s, reformist demands have been directed at *both* business and government, that is, at institutions representing hierarchy (Douglas and Wildavsky 1982; Inglehart 1997).[8]

If there were indeed reform cycles in the past, they might have given way since the 1960s to a world of institutionalized "reform" almost on a par with the institutions of business. Critics would say even stronger than those of business. Reformist interest groups abound. In Washington and in some US state capitals, those representing "good government," environmental, gay, women, and safety interests have solid financial bases, professional staffs, and strategic sophistication.[9] Those representing the poor and various minorities are much weaker. All such interests benefit from the "rights revolution" of the last thirty to forty years, however, and have legal protection, at least in principle, against a great many more impositions than in earlier eras. Actual implementation of these rights is, of course, very patchy.

## 3.2 Monopolistic Equilibria and Punctuated Equilibria

Frank R. Baumgartner and Bryan D. Jones have taken an important step beyond the imagery and theory of the oscillating equilibrium (Baumgartner and Jones 1993). They postulate a condition of monopolistic control of the agenda in an issue area by established interests. An older imagery describing the same thing is the "iron triangle" (also "subgovernment") of interest group, executive agency, and congressional appropriations and policy committees. If this triad agreed on policy, no one else could get into the game. And even if they disagreed, they had a stake in keeping others out while they settled matters among themselves. Knowing this, few even tried. Baumgartner and Jones call this condition an equilibrium, even though it does not in fact equilibrate anything. It is an "equilibrium" only in the same sense that death is a state of "peace."

---

[8] Rejecting both cultural and corporate misconduct theories, David Vogel argues that reformist movements flourish when the economy is performing relatively well and become more quiescent when it is deteriorating (Vogel 1989).

[9] See Baumgartner and Jones 1993, 179–89 for useful details.

Nevertheless, the term is usefully applied here because overturning this system of domination, unlike being resurrected from death, is actually possible. Adopting the language of evolutionary biology, they call the overturning process a "punctuation" of the existing equilibrium. In a useful departure from the oscillation imagery, they presume that the forces unleashed by punctuation can start at almost any time and go off in many directions. Once alcohol abuse, for instance, gets on the agenda of social problems that government must somehow attend to, a variety of remedies are considered in a variety of venues. The brewers and distillers lobby cannot suppress all the talk everywhere. Policy approaches run the gamut from supporting research into drunk driving to education against alcohol abuse, to funding treatment. Moreover, institutions are established, such as the National Institute on Alcohol Abuse and Alcoholism, that ensure a continuing level of attention to the issue even after a popular groundswell may have receded (Baumgartner and Jones 1993, 161–4, 84).

Baumgartner and Jones describe two "models of issue expansion." In one case a wave of popular enthusiasm for dealing with a novel problem or opportunity leads to the creation of new policies and institutions. In the other case, there is a "mobilization of criticism," which invades existing monopoly turf and seizes control of the agenda. In both cases, media attention is a central and early developmental catalyst, followed by the attention of elected officials. Although Baumgartner and Jones count both cases as representing "pattern[s] of punctuated change" (1993, 244), the first ought not to count as an instance of "punctuated equilibrium." If there is indeed novelty, there is nothing substantive to punctuate. The punctuated change is only with respect to the pace of change itself.

# 4. POSITIVE FEEDBACK PROCESSES: ENDOGENOUS DEVELOPMENTS

In a purely technical sense positive feedback processes are more interesting than negative feedback processes. They are more complex and are sometimes counter-intuitive. They are also more interesting substantively, in that they are at the heart of all processes of growth and development.[10]

## 4.1 Momentum

Momentum affects many political processes, such as electioneering, legislative coalition building, developing interagency collaboratives, implementing complex pro-

---

[10] It is worth emphasizing that I am referring here to positive and negative feedback *processes* rather than *systems*. Systems often contain both, and which type of feedback dominates is often dictated as much by how an observer defines "the system's" boundaries as by ontological realities, such as they may be.

gram designs, energizing social movements, building community consensus, and diffusing innovations. The central structural fact about a momentum process is that every step in the process has a dual aspect. On the one hand, it is a movement in the direction of a goal; more indirectly, it creates a stimulus or an opportunity that encourages others to move towards the goal as well. In the simplest case, a band-wagon, every new supporter is an increment towards getting enough support to win according to the rules of the game; but it is also an addition to the signal that observers on the sidelines should regard this as the winning side.

A more complicated dynamic involves not merely signaling but interacting as well. Each new recruit to the cause becomes an asset in the emerging advocacy coalition as well, a potential proselytizer. Thus, in a community consensus-building process, each new recruit is both a confidence-building signal on a broadcast channel, so to speak, and a persuader and reinforcer to those with whom she communicates in a network of narrowcast channels. To take another example, implementing a complex program design, or building an interagency collaborative, is even more complicated. Each new institutional actor that begins to play its required role becomes (1) a bandwagon signal, (2) a persuader and reinforcer for others who are more reluctant, and (3) another node in a communications network that creates more capacity both to mobilize and to work through further implementation details. The constructive role of momentum building and of emergent new communications capacity was underappreciated in the pioneering work on implementation by Pressman and Wildavsky (Pressman and Wildavsky 1979), who assumed that all institutional actors made decisions independently of one another, whereas in most cases positive de-cisions by some increase the likelihood of positive decisions by others.

Momentum dynamics are at the heart of the very complex phenomenon of revolutions. Susanne Lohmann has postulated a model of "informational cascades" to illuminate mass protest activities leading to regime collapse and applied it persuasively to East Germany in the period 1989–91. The model incorporates: (1) "costly political action" by individuals that expresses dissatisfaction with the regime; (2) the public receiving "informational cues" from the size of the protest movement over time; and (3) loss of support and regime collapse "if the protest activities reveal it to be malign" (Lohmann 1994, 49).

## 4.2 Selective Retention

From biological evolution, selective retention is familiar as a competitive process. This model obviously applies to the results of electoral competition as well. A less obvious application of the model is to agenda setting. John Kingdon has applied the model, however, to remarkable effect (Kingdon 1995).[11] Separate streams carrying problems, policies, and politics course through a community of political elites, intersecting haphazardly if not exactly randomly. Elements of each stream may

---

[11] He calls it a "garbage can model," but this counts as a type of evolutionary model.

combine with one another and flourish ("coupling," for Kingdon) should they be lucky enough to pass through a "window of opportunity," itself created by a confluence of macro and micro events. The result is that within the relevant subset of political actors, a certain problem, and a certain set of candidate policies, gets to be discussed, that is, treated as an "agenda" issue.[12]

## 4.3 Path-dependent Shaping of Policy Options

Today's policy options are a product of policy choices made previously—"the path"—sometimes decades previously. Hence the concept of "path dependency." Those earlier choices may have both a constraining, or "lock-in" effect and an opportunity-enhancing effect.

The current health care delivery system in the United States is an example of both such effects. Rationalizing the current system is constrained by the extensive system of employer-financed health insurance for employees plus the tax-exempt status of such insurance for the recipients. If employers could not offer this benefit, to keep employee total compensation at the same level they would have to increase the employee's *after-tax* income. This would cost employers more than they presently pay in insurance premiums. The public treasury also has a stake in the present employer-based system to the extent that any shift from employer financing to government financing would be a budgetary burden. Here we have two serious institutional barriers to shifting away from employer-based and tax-subsidized financing. The scheme overall rose to prominence in the 1930s, following the market-place's invention of group-based health insurance and employers' perception that offering such insurance as a fringe benefit might foster worker allegiance and retard unionization (Hacker 2002, 199–202).

The evolved system, or the installed base as some would put it, constrains radical departures from it. Hence the lock-in effect. On the other hand, what started as an afterthought in the collective mind evolved into a full-fledged policy system, a very extensive system of health insurance for the working population and their families. As is the case with most tax-expenditure-financed policies, it multiplied by stealth far more than an on-budget financing scheme would probably have done. Hence what I called above the opportunity-enhancing effect.

Policy reforms are a special but nevertheless representative case of policy evolution processes in general, and Eric Patashnik has followed the course of three reforms over the years following adoption: airline deregulation in 1978, the 1986 tax reform (which lowered rates and broadened the base), and the Federal Agricultural Improvement and Reform Act (FAIR) in 1996 (Patashnik 2003). Although the rates have stayed low, the tax base has shrunk again, as special interests never laid to rest, chipped away at it.

---

[12] To this model, True, Jones, and Baumgartner add what they call a "serial shift" in attention. This involves both a shift in the object of attention and a self-reinforcing process of attention growth from disparate quarters (True, Jones, and Baumgartner 1999, 103).

Similarly, the subsidies ended by FAIR have made a return. But the new flexibility given to farmers over planting decisions has been retained, since farmers made large investments in the expectation of continuation. These investments warded off any serious thoughts of diminishing the flexibility. Thus, reform got "locked in." Or perhaps one might better say that would-be meddlers got "locked out" (Schwartz n.d.). What is the difference between reforms that stick and those that don't? Those that stick develop constituencies that will be greatly aggrieved if the reforms don't stick.[13] Airline deregulation was successfully maintained because it created almost overnight a number of winners in the newly competitive airline industry who have resisted—or locked out—efforts to roll back the deregulation.[14]

What is the explanation for path dependency? In an influential line of thinking, nicely expressed in a paper by Paul Pierson (2000), the explanation lies in "increasing returns." In the context of production this means higher returns to the next increment of investment virtually without limit (without the normal process of diminishing returns setting in), as in the case of a software firm that creates larger network economies among its product users the larger the network grows. Pierson applies the idea to policy-making systems: it is easier politically to try to modify something already in place than to set out on a new course even if the new course is believed technically superior; and in any case, preferences endogenously shift towards the current policy configuration, giving it an automatically increasing return. Hence, there is a positive feedback loop. Pierson's conclusions are reasonable, but it is unnecessary and generally misleading to invoke increasing returns as an explanatory model. The imagery behind increasing returns is endogenously expanding opportunity, whereas the appropriate imagery for the policy-making process is typically endogenously increasing constraint (lock-in/out). Even in the case of opportunity-enhancing effects (e.g. tax expenditures facilitating the expansion of subsidized health care), the increasing returns model would still be misleading if in fact the marginal returns function were conventionally shaped (rising and then falling) and the observer accidentally focused only on the rising portion.[15]

The particular paths that policy has taken in certain spheres of regulatory policy bear special mention. Government regulation, market structure, common law rules,

---

[13] On the importance of constituencies as barriers to terminating policies in general, see Bardach 1976.

[14] For other examples of constituency creation that is intended to lock in policies, see Glazer and Rothenberg 2001, especially 78, 114. The 1977 Clean Air Act amendments forced expensive scrubbers on the coal-burning utilities partly because, once the capital investments had been made, the industry would have little incentive to press for revisions in the direction of regulatory leniency. Glazer and Rothenberg also conjecture that military service academies plus minimum years-of-service requirements following graduation is a better way to subsidize officer training than to provide higher salaries during a career. The higher-salaries strategy would be subject to policy reversals down the line; and, unwilling to take this risk, potential recruits might not sign up.

[15] One of the virtues of the "path" metaphor is that it reminds us that the character of the path depends on the distance from which it is observed. The same path that looks full of twists and turns to a pedestrian might look perfectly straight to an airplane passenger passing over it. The federal welfare reform Act of 1996 looks like a revolution close up (end welfare as an entitlement, require work as a condition of receipt, time limits on receipt), but from a distance it looks like a modest recalibration of some of the mutually interdependent terms in a fairly stable social insurance contract (Bardach 2001*b*).

and trade and professional association oversight often co-evolve. They are partial functional substitutes for one another in market conditions of information asymmetry combined with high transaction costs in common law enforcement. Thus, the regulation of milk and dairy products began in the early part of the twentieth century because consumers were uninformed and ill effects sometimes hard to attribute definitively or cheaply. As small retail groceries with open milk bins gave way to large supermarket chains, milk in cartons, better refrigeration, and the ability to monitor the quality of dairy farm conditions, the utility of government regulation declined. Dairy farms have in effect become vertically integrated into the operations of large buyers with a reputation to protect. In California, government inspectors have effectively been made into paid agents of the large buyers in all but name.[16]

## 4.4 Trial-and-error Learning

The policy process is in some sense a trial-and-error problem-solving process. Problems arise, citizens complain, and policy makers offer a policy solution. The solution works imperfectly (or not at all), the facts become known, and a new policy solution is devised. It too is imperfect, and the process then continues.

Although it is common to conceptualize trial-and-error learning as a negative feedback process (deviations from the goal stimulating adjustments that get closer to the goal), learning in complex and ambiguous problem situations is better thought of as a positive feedback process. The positive feedback element under these conditions has to do with the constantly improving store of information and analytical understanding about both the nature of the problem to be solved and the workability of potential solutions. By what mechanisms does this learning process work? And how well?

*System-wide learning.* Based on the literature, it is hard to answer these questions. Most of the literature on social and organizational learning refers to the private sector. It therefore assumes substantial goal consensus within the organization (profit maximization, typically). Rational analysis (variously interpreted), open communication, and open-mindedness are thought to be critical (Senge 1990).[17] The policy process, however, institutionalizes value conflict as well as consensus formation. Learning is undoubtedly present, and emerges from the work of advocacy coalitions (Sabatier and Jenkins-Smith 1993). However, it is typically much more effective in policy domains that lend themselves to technical analysis (e.g. worker safety and

---

[16] See Roe 1996 for an interesting evolutionary story about how government regulation of the securities market arose as a functional substitute for oversight by strong national banking firms, which failed to emerge because Andrew Jackson vetoed the rechartering of the Second Bank of the United States.

[17] Even under these conditions, it is hard for learning that occurs in small groups within an organization to diffuse to other units (Roth 1996).

environmental issues[18] more than child abuse prevention). Learning is also selective. What is learned is smoothed so as not greatly to deform the learner's preconceptions. Learning is also a matter of cultural, not merely cognitive change (Cook and Yanow 1996), and may be inhibited across the cultural communities existing within the borders of advocacy coalitions. If the policy-making *system* learns at all, and learns how to increase overall welfare rather than simply a partisan version of it, how might that happen?

One possibility is that turnover within elites brings to the fore, temporarily, a faction that learned something complementing and/or correcting what its predecessor took for granted. It is the Bendor process of oscillation enacted on a larger scale. Whether the temporary learning survives the next turnover, however, is a different question. In the political process it sometimes happens that new elites cast down the work of their predecessors simply because it was the work of their predecessors. One constraint on such a process is the presence of technically minded professionals in the orbit of the political elites. Nearly any agency or legislative body has at least some such individuals who will be a ballast for technical rationality.[19] And forums that manage to cut across opposed advocacy coalitions may be able to give technical rationality a better hearing than it otherwise might receive (Sabatier and Jenkins-Smith 1999, 145–6).[20]

*Interjurisdictional learning.* If a technical solution to a problem has been tried somewhere else and seems to work, it should have a leg up on ideas still untried. And if that somewhere else is a nearby jurisdiction, such as a neighboring state or city, so much the better. A momentum effect is likely at work: "the probability that a state will adopt a program is proportional to the number of interactions its officials have had with officials of already-adopting states" (Berry and Berry 1999, 172); and the potential for such interactions goes up as a function of the number of already-adopting states. In any case, there is by now solid evidence for the realism of regional diffusion models (Walker 1969; Berry and Berry 1999, 185–6). In the realm of public administration, a diffuse philosophy called "New Public Management," which is highly results oriented and sympathetic towards competitive outsourcing, entrepreneurial management, and other practices normally associated with business, has picked up momentum across many jurisdictions in the USA and also internationally (Barzelay 2001; Hood 1998; Hood and Peters 2004).[21]

---

[18] See, for instance, Perez-Enriquez 2003; Taylor, Rubin, and Hounshell 2004. In the latter case, one must think of private sector entities (utilities and technology firms) as part of the relevant policy system.

[19] This does not mean they are without flaws and prejudices of their own. But on balance, across all agencies, and in the long run these flaws and prejudices are probably less harmful than those of the political elites whom the technical cadres serve.

[20] For an interesting exception to all the above—a case where two ideologically opposed legislators set out on what proved to be a successful mission to learn jointly about welfare policy—see Kennedy 1987.

[21] It started in the UK and in Australia and New Zealand in the early 1980s.

## 4.5 Complex Systems

Complex systems are hard to predict because they are hard to understand. The primary source of the complexity is the multiplicity of interactions within the system, or as Jervis calls them, "interconnections" (Jervis 1997, 17).[22]

The creator and guiding spirit of the "system dynamics" school of systems modeling since the early 1960s has been Jay W. Forrester, now emeritus of the Sloan School of Management at MIT. According to Forrester (Forrester 1968) and his interpreter George P. Richardson (Richardson 1991, 300), systems with multiple, non-linear, and high-order feedback loops are "complex." Cause and effect are not closely related in time and space, and are often counter-intuitive. They are also "remarkably insensitive to changes in many system parameters" (Richardson 1991, 301), presumably because their behavior is dominated by the structural interconnections between their components and between components and the emergent system itself.

*Compensating feedback.* Forrester and his disciples have long been interested in policy issues. They have concluded that "compensating feedback" mechanisms hidden in complex systems would often defeat policy interventions. For instance, in *Urban Dynamics* Forrester argued that government-sponsored low-income housing and a jobs program for the unemployed would create a poverty trap, expand the dependent population within the city, and diminish the city's prospects, while tearing down low-income housing and declining business structures would create jobs and boost the city's overall economy (Forrester 1969).[23] A systems dynamics study of heroin use in a community concluded that a legal heroin maintenance scheme for addicts would not stop heroin addiction because reduced demand from one subgroup would simply induce new users into the market to take up the slack, and pushers would more aggressively recruit new suppliers (Richardson 1991, 307–8).

Such studies are conducted by means of computer simulation. Although the model structure and parameters can be calibrated against reality to some extent, typically model construction requires a lot of guesswork. Hence, although it is quite possible that the models in these and other such cases were sufficiently realistic to give good projections, it is also possible that they were not, as critics have typically alleged. In any case, it is generally accepted that complex systems are indeed hard to predict, and often counter-intuitive and insensitive to their precise parameters.

*Agent-based models.* The systems dynamics school populates its models with "level" variables, feedback loops connecting these levels, and "rate" variables governing the feedback flows. It is in a sense a "top-down" approach to systems modeling, since the modeler must know, or assume, a lot about the structure and the parameter values. Robert Axelrod has pioneered a "bottom-up" approach to the modeling of systems, populating his models with a variety of independent agents who interact

[22] Robert Axelrod and Michael D. Cohen write, "a system should be called complex when it is hard to predict not because it is random but because the regularities it does have cannot be briefly described" (Axelrod and Cohen 1999, 16).

[23] Forrester was inspired to study the problem of the urban economy by a former mayor of Boston, John Collins, who occupied an adjacent office at the Sloan School for a time.

according to certain strategies. He has relied on computer simulation to project the emergence of empires, cultures, cabinets, business alliances, cooperative norms, metanorms, and perhaps everything in between (Axelrod 1984, 1997). In agent-based models, the relative densities of different types in the population change, as do the frequency of different strategies in use. Selection rules then allow these changing densities to propagate still further changes in the population (Axelrod and Cohen 1999, 3–7). When the community of agents seek to adapt to one another (even if that means "try to dominate"), Axelrod and Cohen speak of a "Complex Adaptive System" (1999, 7).

In their 1999 book Axelrod and Cohen sought to give advice to organizational managers (primarily) about how to "harness complexity." Perhaps the most valuable advice, in the authors' view and in mine, was the least specific: get comfortable with "the ideas of perpetual novelty, adaptation as a function of entire populations, the value of variety and experimentation, and the potential of decentralized and over-lapping authority" (Axelrod and Cohen 1999, 29).

*Simulation as a policy design tool.* Almost any policy of significant scope and purchase will be intervening in a complex social, economic, political, and cultural system. Given its record of providing deep insights into the nature of complex systems, computer simulation is plausibly of some value as an aid for projecting the efficacy of alternative policy proposals or designs. The efforts appear to be fragmentary but growing.

One example is the work done, in the Forrester systems analysis tradition, by a group based at the State University of New York at Albany modeling alternative welfare-to-work program designs (Zagonel et al. 2004). For instance, they compared an "Edges" and a "Middle" policy and a Base Case fit to actual 1997 data. The Middle policy was designed to intensify investment in and emphasis on assessment, monitoring, and job finding. The Middle policy was implemented primarily by the social services agency. The Edges policy focused on what happened to clients before and after they entered the social services caseload. The relevant services were prevention, child support enforcement, and self-sufficiency promotion, functions not typically under the direct control of social services. The model contained various agency and other resource stocks. Somewhat surprisingly to the analysts, the Middle policy did not do well at all compared to the Edges policy in terms of reducing caseloads:

To summarize the mechanism at work here, the Middle policy is great at getting people into jobs, but then they lose those jobs and cycle back into the system because there aren't enough resources devoted to help them stay employed. The Edges policy lets them trickle more slowly into jobs but then does a better job of keeping them there.

Another example is climate change models. Robert J. Lempert, Steven W. Popper, and Steven C. Bankes of the RAND Corporation are developing a computer-based tool for projecting the effects of various interventions to manage climate change as well as other such problems of large scale and long duration. They call the project "long-term policy analysis (LTPA)" (Lempert, Popper, and Bankes 2003, xii). Central to the generic LTPA problem is the inevitability of surprise and the consequent "deep uncertainty" about what to model and how to model it. They propose four key elements of a high-quality LTPA:

- Consider large *ensembles* (hundreds to millions) of scenarios.
- Seek *robust*, not optimal strategies.
- Achieve robustness with *adaptivity*.
- Design analysis for *interactive exploration* of the multiplicity of plausible futures. (2003, xiii)

They note that none of the computer models available for modeling climate change were suitable for their own work because the models "strive[d] for validity through as precise as possible a representation of particular phenomenology" (2003, 82). What they chose instead was almost the opposite, a simple systems-dynamics model, Wonderland, which provided the flexibility they needed "for representing crucial aspects of the robust decision approach—e.g., consideration of near-term adaptive policies and the adaptive responses of future generations" (2003, 82).

## 4.6 Chaos Theory

Even if most complex systems are insensitive to their parameter values, as Forrester contends, this is not true of all of them. System outputs that increase as a multiplicative function of their own growth and of the difference between their actual growth and their potential growth are an important exception. They exhibit four types of behavior depending on how intensively they react to this product, expressed by the parameter $w$ in equation (3):[24]

$$y_{t+1} = wy_t(1 - y_t) \tag{3}$$

At low levels of reactivity, they approach a point equilibrium; at higher levels they oscillate stably; at still higher levels they are oscillating and explosive; and at the highest levels they show no periodic pattern at all and appear to be random— "chaotic"—even though their behavior is in fact completely determined (Kiel 1993; Baumol and Benhabib 1989). The set of points towards which any such system moves over time is said to be an "attractor."[25]

The time profile of such a system can also shift dramatically as its behavior unfolds. For this reason the behavior of the system will look very different depending on where in its course one first views the behavior, i.e. the first-observed value of $y$. Hence, the system is said to be sensitive to its "initial condition,"[26] although a more

---

[24] This is "[t]he most widely used mathematical formula for exploring [the] behavioral regimes [of interest]...a first-order nonlinear difference equation, labeled the logistic map" (Kiel and Elliott 1996a, 20).

[25] For a discussion of the properties of five basic different attractors, see Daneke 1999, 33, and also Guastello 1999, 33–5.

[26] This sensitivity is often called "the butterfly effect" because the flapping of a butterfly's wings in Brazil could, by virtue of its happening within a chaotic system (weather), set off storms in Chicago.

meaningful characterization would usually be "the point at which we choose to start graphing it."

*How much of the world really fits?* It is still open as to whether chaos models realistically describe many phenomena of interest to students of policy or the policy process. I suspect it will always be difficult to choose between models of endogenously induced chaotic change and more commonsensical models of exogenously induced multivariate but linear change laced with pure randomness.[27] Chaos models can only be applied to substantially closed systems with a relatively long history, and it is not clear that such phenomena exist in great abundance. Macroeconomic systems are the most obvious (Baumol and Benhabib 1989).[28]

Unfortunately, because "chaos" is often used loosely, it may describe *any* non-linear complex process. For instance, Berry and Kim (1999) entitle a paper "Has the Fed reduced chaos?" when they mean by "chaos" a series of changing oscillating equilibria in two historical periods from the end of the Civil War through 1950. An even greater danger is that the "sensitivity to initial conditions" of chaos models will be applied to systems that are merely linear and therefore, in principle, much more manageable. Hamilton and West (1999), for instance, analyze a twenty-seven-year time series of teenage births in Texas and claim to find a pattern behind which lies a non-linear dynamic system, the character of which they do not explicitly define and for which they provide no plausible behavioral theory. Yet they conclude by warning that "a small change in school policy, health care accessibility or welfare eligibility can, due to feedback in the system, result in large changes in teen births." Were it only true in social policy that small changes *could* issue in large results! It is more likely that "compensating feedback" (see above) finds a way to dampen results.

*Self-organizing systems.* Decentralized systems with rich interactions and good information flow among the components are capable of evolving high degrees of internal coordination and productivity. They are "self-organizing." It is possible that their richest possibilities for attaining a high degree of self-organization occur when their interactions have reached "the edge of chaos" (Kauffman 1995). However, this proposition may apply most effectively to inanimate or at any rate non-human systems. Human beings may be able purposively to create the requisite interaction, variety, and communication in a complex adaptive system without having to push themselves to such a danger point. It is noteworthy that Axelrod and Cohen, in *Harnessing Complexity*, hardly refer to chaos or its edge (Axelrod and Cohen 1999, xv, 72).

---

[27] The interaction of chaotic systems and exogenous disturbances is also possible, of course. The result is "nonlinear amplification that alter[s] the qualitative behavior of the system." These are called "symmetry-breaking" events (Kiel and Elliott 1999, 5).

[28] See also the persuasive efforts by Courtney Brown to apply chaos models to electoral phenomena, particularly to the rise of the Nazi Party in the 1930s (Brown 1995, ch. 5). Less persuasive are the political chapters contained in Kiel and Elliott 1996*b*.

## 4.7 Qualities-based Sequencing

So far we have been discussing what might be called the dynamics of quantities: the feedback loops tell us that the more (or less) of $x$, then the more (or less) of $y$. But there is no reason to eschew qualitative models where they are appropriate. The basic idea behind these can be summed up as: Sequence Matters.

In an earlier work (Bardach 1998) I have conceptualized the emergence of a well-functioning interagency collaborative—an "ICC"—as the result of a *building* process.[29] The process has a dynamic aspect, in that sequence makes a difference, just as in building a house it is only the erection of a frame that then permits one to install a roof, or the creation of a wall that will then constitute a medium for the making of doors and windows. Considered in feedback loop terms, each step feeds back into the emergence of a new state that affords a previously non-existent opportunity to reach the next-most state.

*Opportunities.* These states are qualitative. In the ICC case, they are defined by the variety of organizational and political building blocks that have been assembled on the way to building a functional collaborative. These would include, for instance: a workable operating system, a culture of pragmatism, a threshold quantity of real resources, a degree of political latitude, and a number of others. The full set is displayed in Fig. 16.2[30]. The sequence in which these elements are assembled makes a difference to how well the building process works.

Figure 16.2 in effect puts forward a hypothesis: it is more efficient and less risky to put the building blocks in place in the depicted sequence—starting from the bottom and moving upward—than it is to assemble them in any other sequence.[31] Space does not afford the opportunity to explain just why this developmental sequence might be more efficient and less risky than some alternative sequence of interest.[32] One example, concerning just one pairing in the sequence, must suffice, namely the proposition that trust should precede the acceptance of leadership rather than the other way around. Leadership is extremely useful for solving communications and other problems in an emerging collaborative (as indicated by the platforms above it in Fig. 16.2). It can be fragile, though, because the institutional partners in a typical

---

[29] "ICC" stands for Interagency Collaborative Capacity. It is a more precise term than "collaborative" because at any given moment in the evolution of the "collaborative" it may not be capable of doing much and the participants may be doing more arguing than collaborating. "Capacity" may be large or small, growing or shrinking; hence it can be construed as a continuous variable, which is analytically useful.

[30] Slightly modified from Bardach 1998, 274.

[31] The process of trying to execute better rather than worse sequences I call "platforming." I leave aside complexities such as the relatively weak but non-trivial interdependence between platforms supporting the two different legs of the structure.

[32] See Bardach 2001a for further details. Nor is it clear which of all the alternative sequences should be held up to comparison. I acknowledge that empirical evidence bearing on the efficiency and risk properties of this sequence matter is fragmentary and merely suggestive (Bardach 1998, ch. 8). The main point, though, is not to assert the truth of this particular developmental hypothesis but to illustrate the nature of reasoning about how sequence might matter.

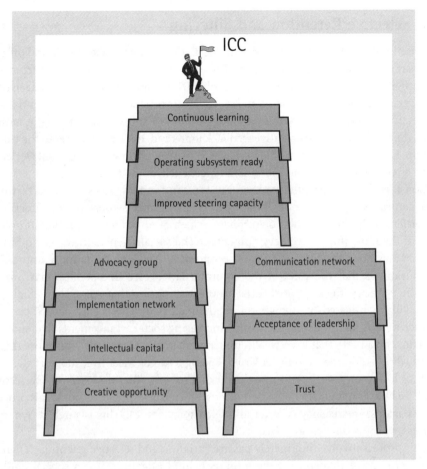

**Fig. 16.2.** Each new capacity a platform for the next

collaborative are moderately suspicious of one another. Thus, leadership will function best if a prior base of trust can be established.[33]

## 5. DYNAMICS WITHOUT FEEDBACK LOOPS

Not all dynamics processes involve feedback loops. Some unfold in only one direction.[34]

---

[33] There is more to the dynamics of ICC construction than platforming, I would note. Building momentum of various kinds is also significant (Bardach 1998, 276–92).

[34] Some systems dynamics theorists would question this possibility. They would say that nothing fails to produce feedback of some kind, however indirect. This is true. Nevertheless, as mentioned earlier, to

## 5.1 Selective Retention and Filtering

We discussed selective retention above, in the section on positive feedback, and offered the example of agenda setting. In the Kingdon model, agendas emerged from the agglutination of policies, politics, and problems as they intersected and survived a chancy competitive process. One could see the entire process as composed essentially of a selective retention subsystem and an agglutination subsystem. The agglutination subsystem is dominated by positive feedback loops and gives its character to the whole system. However, it is also possible to view selective retention as a process that works, in some circumstances, without the benefit of feedback loops at all.

Consider, for instance, the evolution of the common law rules of property, torts, and contracts, which, if not "policy" in a traditional sense, are the functional equivalent of "policy" in their own sphere, which often overlaps with that of policy. One of the most impressive developments in the social sciences in the last quarter-century has been the field of law and economics. And one of its most impressive conclusions is that the rules of the common law evolve in a welfare-maximizing fashion.[35] Briefly, the argument turns on the assumption that relatively inefficient[36] laws will be litigated at a higher rate than efficient laws. This occurs because inefficient laws fail to sustain the wealth-increasing social arrangements that efficient laws do, and a party that loses wealth under an inefficient legal rule loses more than a party who loses under an efficient rule. Facing a larger incentive, more of the first kind of losers sue, and spend more on trying to win, than do losers of the second kind. So long as judges are not biased *against* efficiency in their decisions, this process selects against inefficiency (Cooter and Ulen 1997, 375–6). This is surely a dynamic process, but it is one without feedback.[37]

This process involves not merely passive variation and selective retention. There is also a propulsive element, i.e. the motives behind litigation. It is a special kind of evolutionary process, therefore, a filtering process. Many potential common law rules pass through the filter of judicial consideration, attached, as it were, to litigants' claims; but the filter retains (in the long run) only the more efficient of these, while the rest wash into history. Another such filtering dynamic is the well-known Peter Principle, whereby people "rise to the level of their incompetence." The dynamic involves promotion in a hierarchy based on demonstrated competence in a particular position. Once one demonstrates incompetence in a position, advancement ends and the incumbent just sits there, being incompetent. (Of course, if promotion depends on expected rather than demonstrated competence, the Peter Principle does not

draw the boundaries around a particular system or process is ultimately an analytical, not an ontological decision. There is no analytical barrier to defining a dynamic process as single directional.

[35] Such claims are not generally made about statutory law, however, nor should they be.

[36] "Inefficient" in the technical economic sense of the term.

[37] In fact there is an element of positive feedback, since common law rules do not get transformed overnight. They get eroded and refashioned, at both the extensive and the intensive margin; and each instance of eroding and refashioning feeds into the legal culture to facilitate further change. However, we focus here only on the filtering subsystem.

apply.) A special case of a filtering process is stranding, e.g. the progressive concentration of less motivated, and perhaps less apt students in certain public schools as the wealthier and more education-oriented families in the catchment area move away or opt for private schools.

## 5.2  Event Cascades

What I shall call "event cascades" are another significant class of one-way dynamic processes. These are sequences of events that have a built-in, or structural dynamic, like the stones in a rockslide that come from above and dislodge stones below, or the workings of a Rube Goldberg machine. Discrete events trigger subsequent discrete, and substantially irreversible events through the medium of a structure that links them. Here is an example in political life from Winston Churchill, describing changes in British naval technology before the First World War (quoted in Jervis 1997, 129, though he does not call this an event cascade): "From the original desire to enlarge the gun we were led on step by step to the Fast Division, and in order to get the Fast Division we were forced to rely for vital units of the Fleet upon fuel oil. This led to the general adoption of oil fuel and to all the provisions which were needed to build up a great oil reserve. This led to enormous expense and to tremendous opposition on the Naval Estimates.... Finally we found our way to the Anglo-Persian Oil agreement and contract which ... has led to the acquisition by the Government of a controlling share in oil properties and interests."

No doubt it is a lot easier to describe such an event cascade once it has occurred than to model the process that produces it and to use the model to predict the result beforehand. One could conceptualize the process as the actualization of one chain of events out of a host of potential events probabilistically linked in a Markov matrix. The empirical challenge would entail defining the universe of potential events contained in the Markov matrix and then stipulating each of their contingent probabilities. Most event chains through such a matrix would have close to no probability of being actualized. A few would probably stand out as very likely candidates; and a very few would be intriguing long shots. The event chain from the British decision to enlarge a warship's guns to a transformation of British Middle East policy might not have been apparent to decision makers *ex ante*; but in Churchill's account, it seems *ex post* to have been a near certainty.

# 6.  FUTURE RESEARCH

I conclude with suggestions for future research. If the study of policy dynamics were "a field," these thoughts would be cast as a proposed research agenda. But the phenomena that ought to be studied through a "dynamics" lens are varied and do not congeal as one field. Nor, with the important exception of computer simulation, is there or ought there to be a widely utilized methodology.[38] At the conceptual level, our understanding is so rudimentary that it makes sense to let dozens of flowers bloom—agent-based models, systems dynamics models, chaos models, cascade models, punctuated equilibrium models, and path dependency models, to mention only the principal models already discussed. All are promising in their own way, and one can only urge work on all of them.

I am, however, ready to urge particular attention to two phenomena that I take to be of unusual substantive significance and which require a dynamic approach: (1) understanding a process Aaron Wildavsky once labeled "policy as its own cause," and (2) bringing more rigor to the study of what scholars loosely call "stages" or "phases" in various processes, particularly that of legislative coalition building.

## 6.1 Policy as its Own Cause

Aaron Wildavsky in 1979 wrote of "the growing autonomy of the policy environment" (Wildavsky 1979, 62), because policy "solutions create their own effects, which gradually displace the original difficulty," and "big problems usually generate solutions so large that they become the dominant cause of the consequences with which public policy must contend." His prime example was Medicare and Medicaid, which succeeded in expanding access for the poor and elderly but at the same time made access more difficult for others and increased costs for everyone. The whole system started to behave unpredictably:

For each additional program that interacts with every other, an exponential increase in consequence follows. These consequences, moreover, affect a broader range of different programs, which in turn, affect others, so that the connection between original cause and later effect is attenuated. One program affects so many others that prediction becomes more important and its prospects more perilous, because effects spread to entire realms of policy.

*Social policy.* A quarter-century ago, Wildavsky was writing about the *social* effects of policies, and sounding very much like Jay Forrester and his students in his concern over the sheer complexity of things. Today there is a second, if not third generation of problems that arise from the complexity of interactions, and these are the problems of making policy adjustments in an environment already dense with interconnected policies. In social policy, for instance, eligibility for one program is sometimes

---

[38] One of several reasons why our understanding of dynamic processes is not far advanced is that their internal behavior is too hard to grasp with language, pictures, or mathematics. Computer simulation is the solution to this problem, as work in the agent-based models and the Forrester-type "systems dynamics" traditions attests. To be sure, there are uncertainties over how to validate computer models, but computer simulation is a powerful tool that deserves to be wielded more extensively by scholars interested in dynamics.

conditioned on eligibility for another, so that reasonable cutbacks (or expansions) in the latter have unexpected and undesirable effects in the former. As these interdependencies multiply, it becomes more difficult for responsible policy makers to consider adjustments of any kind. The gridlock is worsened when low-level adjustments are also delayed pending higher-level and more comprehensive reforms that policy makers signal are "imminent." This is not just a locked-in or locked-out effect, but a locked-up effect.

The important questions for study here concern just how prevalent these phenomena are and what mechanisms are at work. Of interest also is the question of what exactly happens should one of these cascades actually be set in motion. Do negative feedback loops kick in at some point to dampen the disequilibrating consequences?

*Regulatory policy.* In the regulatory sphere, J. B. Ruhl and James Salzman have written of "the accretion effect" on emerging bodies of regulatory rules (Ruhl and Salzman 2003). Various mechanisms cause rules to accumulate but only rarely to diminish. Ruhl and Salzman claim, with some evidence, that this accretion has a negative effect on compliance, vastly increases the compliance burden on companies (in the environmental area), and diminishes the legitimacy of the regulatory regime. They present a further claim which is more interesting and more speculative. It concerns what they call "the properties of dynamic conflicting constraints" (2003, 811), which cause improved compliance with one rule to decrease the likelihood of compliance with another. They appeal to the theory of complex dynamic systems to explain why this should happen. Despite a few examples, however, they do not provide evidence of a widespread problem. This is a tantalizing theoretical as well as practical issue, and more systematic research would be welcome.

## 6.2 "Phases" and "Stages"

There is no shortage of the word "dynamics" in the titles of works about one or another aspect of the policy process.[39] Usually, the implications are that important developments happen in "stages" or "phases," that earlier stages somehow condition later ones, and that later stages have been conditioned by earlier ones. For instance, in conventional accounts of "the dynamics of the legislative process," successive majorities must be sought in subcommittees, committees, and full chambers; and a compromise at one stage may reduce or enhance a bill's prospects at a later stage. In the course of interagency collaboration, to take another example, Barbara Gray has written that there are three phases: problem setting, direction setting, and structuring (Gray 1985, 916–17). A paper on the development of buyer–seller relationships posits

---

[39] "Dynamics" is often a virtual synonym for complex phenomena that are slightly mysterious and that may or may not actually be "dynamic" once properly understood.

that they "evolve through five general phases identified as (1) awareness, (2) exploration, (3) expansion, (4) commitment, and (5) dissolution ... Each phase represents a major transition in how parties regard one another" (Dwyer, Schurr, and Oh 1987, 15). A controversy swirls over whether the idea of "stages of the policy process" is or is not analytically useful (deLeon 1999). The most recent list of candidate stages is: initiation, estimation, selection, implementation, evaluation, and termination (deLeon 1999, 21).[40]

I acknowledge that any such list of phases or stages is bound to be at least in part a product of the observer's theoretical notions, for developments of this sort are in no way "natural kinds." Nevertheless, these developmental categories do not seem to me well enough grounded empirically. The developments in question ought to be expressions of *endogenous* systems processes, and it is not clear to what system these processes might belong. Is it possible to conceptualize developmental phases of this sort that will prove analytically useful?

*What is analytically useful?* By social scientific standards a conceptual scheme is analytically useful to the extent that it permits one to generate propositions about the world that are insightful, interconnected, explanatory, and realistic. In the case of trying to conceptualize endogenously connected developmental phases, it is hard to know how to apply this standard because the idea of offering a satisfying "explanation" is elusive—a point I shall not elaborate upon here. A satisfactory alternative, however, is to use a practical standard that is in all respects but the demand for explanatory power like the social scientific standard. In place of explanatory power, the practically based standard asks whether the conceptual scheme could produce an *intertemporal map of the foreseeable risks and opportunities that might emerge*; for with such a map anticipatory strategies can be canvassed.

I made an unsophisticated effort to model the endogenous emergence of such risks and opportunities in *The Skill Factor in Politics* (Bardach 1972, 241–60). The generic model tracked "Support" (a continuous variable) through time in a legislative contest over a reformist policy proposal. The time path of Support rose and fell as a function of: (1) mobilization on the part of an advocacy coalition, (2) lagged resistance on the part of opponents, (3) differential adherence by a small pool of neutrals, (4) concessions and sweeteners that alter the evolving shape of the legislative proposal, (5) the emergence of intracoalition tensions and resultant defections in response to the changing shape of the proposal, (6) the uncertainties, and struggles over various arena and scheduling parameters, and (7) the intersection of the current contest, in its endgame phase, with a variety of unrelated issue agendas, actors, and influence patterns. The model was intended to map foreseeable risks and opportunities that a hypothetical entrepreneur would try to anticipate and prepare for.

---

[40] DeLeon credits Garry Brewer with this list. Brewer derived it from Harold Lasswell's seven stages: intelligence, promotion, prescription, invocation, application, termination, and appraisal.

So far as I am aware, neither this model nor any model aiming to accomplish the same objectives has found a place in the literature on legislative dynamics. I do not hold a particular brief for my own effort. But I do think the objective would be scientifically useful as well as of practical worth to a would-be legislative entrepreneur, and that others should try their hand at the problem.

# References

AXELROD, R. 1984. *The Evolution of Cooperation.* New York: Basic Books.
—— 1997. *The Complexity of Cooperation: Agent-Based Models of Competition and Collaboration.* Princeton, NJ: Princeton University Press.
—— and COHEN. M. D. 1999. *Harnessing Complexity.* New York: Free Press.
BAK, P. 1996. *How Nature Works: The Science of Self-Organized Criticality.* New York: Copernicus.
BARDACH, E. 1972. *The Skill Factor in Politics: Repealing the Mental Commitment Laws in California.* Berkeley: University of California Press.
—— (ed.) 1976. Special issue on termination of policies, programs, and organizations. *Policy Sciences,* 7 (June).
—— 1998. *Getting Agencies to Work Together: The Practice and Theory of Managerial Craftsmanship.* Washington, DC: Brookings Institution.
—— 2001*a*. Developmental dynamics: interagency collaboration as an emergent phenomenon. *Journal of Public Administration Research and Theory,* 11 (2): 149–64.
—— 2001*b*. Exit "equality," enter "fairness." In *Seeking the Center: Politics and Policymaking at the New Century,* ed. M. A. Levin, M. K. Landy, and M. Shapiro. Washington, DC: Georgetown University Press.
—— and KAGAN. R. A. 2002/1982. *Going by the Book: The Problem of Regulatory Unreasonableness.* Somerset, NJ: Transaction.
BARZELAY, M. 2001. *The New Public Management: Improving Research and Policy Dialogue.* Berkeley: University of California Press.
BAUMGARTNER, F. R., and JONES, B. D. 1993. *Agendas and Instability in American Politics.* Chicago: University of Chicago Press.
—— —— 2002. Positive and negative feedback in politics. In *Policy Dynamics,* ed. F. R. Baumgartner and B. D. Jones. Chicago: University of Chicago Press.
BAUMOL, W. J., and BENHABIB, J. 1989. Chaos: significance, mechanism, and economic applications. *Journal of Economic Perspectives,* 3 (1): 77–105.
BENDOR, J. 2004. *Bounded Rationality: Theory and Policy Implications.* Berkeley: Goldman School of Public Policy.
BERRY, F. S., and BERRY, W. D. 1999. Innovation and diffusion models in policy research. In *Theories of the Policy Process,* ed. P. A. Sabatier. Boulder, Colo.: Westview Press.
BERRY, J. L., and KIM, H. 1999. Has the Fed reduced chaos? In *Nonlinear Dynamics, Complexity and Public Policy,* ed. E. Elliott and L. D. Kiel. Commack, NY: Nova Science.
BROWN, C. 1995. *Serpents in the Sand: Essays on the Nonlinear Nature of Politics and Human Destiny.* Ann Arbor: University of Michigan Press.
COOK, S. D. N., and YANOW, D. 1996. Culture and organizational learning. In *Organizational Learning,* ed. M. D. Cohen and L. S. Sproull. Thousand Oaks, Calif.: Sage.

COOTER, R., and ULEN, T. 1997. *Law and Economics*, 2nd edn. Reading, Mass.: Addison-Wesley.

DANEKE, G. A. 1999. *Systemic Choices: Nonlinear Dynamics and Practical Management.* Ann Arbor: University of Michigan Press.

DELEON, P. 1999. The stages approach to the policy process. In *Theories of the Policy Process*, ed. P. A. Sabatier. Boulder, Colo.: Westview Press.

DOUGLAS, M., and WILDAVSKY. A. 1982. *Risk and Culture: An Essay on the Selection of Technical and Environmental Dangers.* Berkeley: University of California Press.

DWYER, R. F., SCHURR, P. H., and OH, S. 1987. Developing buyer–seller relationships. *Journal of Marketing*, 51: 11–27.

FIORINA, M. P. 1981. *Retrospective Voting in National Politics.* New Haven, Conn.: Yale University Press.

FORRESTER, J. W. 1968. *Principles of Systems.* Cambridge, Mass.: Wright-Allen Press.

—— 1969. *Urban Dynamics.* Cambridge, Mass.: MIT Press.

GLAZER, A., and ROTHENBERG, L. S. 2001. *Why Government Succeeds and Why it Fails.* Cambridge, Mass.: Harvard University Press.

GRAY, B. 1985. Conditions facilitating interorganizational collaboration. *Human Relations*, 38 (10): 911–36.

GUASTELLO, S. J. 1999. Hysteresis, bifurcation structure, and the search for the natural rate of unemployment. In *Nonlinear Dynamics, Complexity and Public Policy*, ed. E. Elliott and L. D. Kiel. Commack, NY: Nova Science.

HACKER, J. S. 2002. *The Divided Welfare State: The Battle over Public and Private Social Benefits in the United States.* New York: Cambridge University Press.

HAMILTON, P., and WEST, B. J. 1999. Scaling of complex social phenomena such as births to teens: implications for public policy. In *Nonlinear Dynamics, Complexity and Public Policy*, ed. E. Elliott and L. D. Kiel. Commack, NY: Nova Science.

HOOD, C. 1998. *The Art of the State: Culture, Rhetoric, and Public Management.* Oxford: Oxford University Press.

—— and GUY, P. 2004. The middle aging of new public management: into the age of paradox. *Journal of Public Administration Research and Theory*, 14 (3): 267–82.

——ROTHSTEIN, H., and BALDWIN, R. 2001. *The Government of Risk: Understanding Risk Regulation Regimes.* Oxford: Oxford University Press.

HUNTINGTON, S. P. 1981. *American Politics: The Promise of Disharmony.* Cambridge, Mass.: Harvard University Press.

INGLEHART, R. 1997. Postmaterialist values and the erosion of institutional authority. In *Why People Don't Trust Government*, ed. J. S. J. Nye, P. D. Zelikow, and D. C. King. Cambridge, Mass.: Harvard University Press.

JERVIS, R. 1997. *System Effects: Complexity in Political and Social Life.* Princeton, NJ: Princeton University Press.

KAUFFMAN, S. 1995. *At Home in the Universe: The Search for the Laws of Self-Organization and Complexity.* New York: Oxford University Press.

KENNEDY, D. 1987. California Welfare reform. Kennedy School of Government Case Program, Case # C16-87-782.0.

KIEL, L. D. 1993. Nonlinear dynamical analysis: assessing systems concepts in a government agency. *Public Administration Review*, 53 (2): 143–53.

—— and ELLIOTT, E. 1996a. Exploring nonlinear dynamics with a spreadsheet: a graphical view of chaos for beginners. In *Chaos Theory in the Social Sciences: Foundations and Applications*, ed. L. D. Kiel and E. Elliott. Ann Arbor: University of Michigan Press.

—— —— (eds.) 1996b. *Chaos Theory in the Social Sciences.* Ann Arbor: University of Michigan Press.

—— —— 1999. Nonlinear dynamics, complexity and public policy: introduction. In *Nonlinear Dynamics, Complexity and Public Policy*, ed. E. Elliott and L. D. Kiel. Commack, NY: Nova Science.

KINGDON, J. W. 1995. *Agendas, Alternatives, and Public Policies*, 2nd edn. New York: Harper-Collins.

LEMPERT, R. J., POPPER, S. W., and BANKES, S. C. 2003. *Shaping the Next One Hundred Years: New Methods for Quantitative, Long-Term Policy Analysis*. Santa Monica, Calif.: RAND Pardee Center.

LOHMANN, S. 1994. The dynamics of informational cascades: the Monday demonstrations in Leipzig, East Germany, 1989–1991. *World Politics*, 47 (1): 42–101.

McCLOSKY, H., and ZALLER, J. 1984. *The American Ethos: Public Attitudes toward Capitalism and Democracy*. Cambridge, Mass.: Harvard University Press.

McFARLAND, A. S. 1991. Interest groups and political time: cycles in America. *British Journal of Political Science*, 21 (3): 257–84.

MILLER, G. J. 1992. *Managerial Dilemmas: The Political Economy of Hierarchy*. New York: Cambridge University Press.

MOE, T. M. 1985. Control and feedback in economic regulation: the case of the NLRB. *American Political Science Review*, 79 (4): 1094–116.

PATASHNIK, E. 2003. After the public interest prevails: the political sustainability of policy reform. *Governance*, 16 (2): 203–34.

PEREZ-ENRIQUEZ, B. 2002. *Economics and Politics of Global Environmental Commodities Market*. Berkeley: University of California Press.

PIERSON, P. 2000. Increasing returns, path dependence and the study of politics. *American Political Science Review*, 94 (2): 251–67.

PRESSMAN, J. L., and WILDAVSKY, A. 1979. *Implementation*, 2nd edn. Los Angeles: University of California Press.

QUIRK, P. J. 1980. Food and drug administration. In *The Politics of Regulation*, ed. J. Q. Wilson. New York: Basic Books.

RICHARDSON, G. P. 1991. *Feedback Thought in Social Science and Systems Theory*. Philadelphia: University of Pennsylvania Press.

ROE, M. J. 1996. Chaos and evolution in law and economics. *Harvard Law Review*, 109: 641–68.

ROTH, G. 1996. From individual and team learning to systems learning. In *Managing in Organizations that Learn*, ed. S. A. Cavaleri and D. S. Fearon. Cambridge, Mass.: Blackwell.

RUHL, J. B., and SALZMAN, J. 2003. Mozart and the Red Queen: the problem of regulatory accretion in the administrative state. *Georgetown Law Journal*, 91 (3): 757–850.

SABATIER, P. A., and JENKINS-SMITH, H. C. (eds.) 1993. *Policy Change and Learning: An Advocacy Coalition Approach*. Boulder, Colo.: Westview Press.

—— —— 1999. The advocacy coalition framework: an assessment. In *Theories of the Policy Process*, ed. P. A. Sabatier. Boulder, Colo.: Westview Press.

SCHWARTZ, H. n.d. *Down the Wrong Path: Path Dependence, Increasing Returns, and Historical Institutionalism*. Charlottesville: University of Virginia Department of Politics.

SENGE, P. M. 1990. *The Fifth Discipline: The Art and Practice of the Learning Organization*. New York: Doubleday.

SHEPSLE, K. A., and BONCHEK, M. S. 1997. *Analyzing Politics: Rationality, Behavior, and Institutions*. New York: W. W. Norton.

TAYLOR, M. R., RUBIN, E. S., and HOUNSHELL, D. A. 2005. Regulation as the mother of invention: the case of $SO_2$ control. *Law & Policy*, 27 (2): 348–78.

TRUE, J. L., JONES, B. D., and BAUMGARTNER, F. R. 1999. Punctuated-equilibrium theory: explaining stability and change in American policymaking. In *Theories of the Policy Process*, ed. P. A. Sabatier. Boulder, Colo.: Westview Press.

TRUMAN, D. B. 1951. *The Governmental Process.* New York: Knopf.

VOGEL, D. 1989. *Fluctuating Fortunes: The Political Power of Business in America.* New York: Basic Books.

WALKER, J. L. 1969. The diffusion of innovations among the American states. *American Political Science Review,* 63: 880–99.

WILDAVSKY, A. 1979. *Speaking Truth to Power: The Art and Craft of Policy Analysis.* Boston: Little, Brown.

WLEZIEN, C. 1995. The public as thermostat: dynamics of preferences for spending. *American Journal of Political Science,* 39 (4): 981–1000.

ZAGONEL, A. A., ROHRBAUGH, J., RICHARDSON, G. P., and ANDERSEN, D. F. 2004. Using simulation models to address "what if" questions about welfare reform. *Journal of Policy Analysis and Management,* 23(4): 890–901.

# CHAPTER 17

## LEARNING IN PUBLIC POLICY

### RICHARD FREEMAN

## 1. INTRODUCTION

We do little that we have not learned. As we learn to breathe, to eat, to walk and talk, learning seems essential to living. But what, in fact, is learning? The irony is that the importance and ubiquity of what we might think of as learning in turn makes it difficult to define. What does it mean to learn, and how do we do it?

Our commonsense assumptions about learning are those we have from school. It seems to have something to do with teaching, with lessons, with doing well or badly. And then, on reflection, we seem to learn as much by informal as by formal processes: we learn from experience (which is sometimes gained by experiment), and from others, including our parents and peers. Often, the two are mutually reinforcing: we learn from others' experience, and it is our parents and peers who help us make sense of our own.

These processes have their corollaries in public policy, both as a practical activity and a field of study. Policy makers compare current problems to previous ones, networking with others both in their own and in other jurisdictions. By the same token, we might think of the collective process of agenda setting as one in which a polity learns as much as decides what it wants, and implementation as the process by which agencies and employees learn how to deliver it.

* This chapter is a product of some of the processes it describes. I have been lucky to be included in a community of scholars working in this and related fields, and am particularly grateful to the editors of this volume and to Elizabeth Bomberg for comments on a preliminary draft. The errors and omissions which remain testify only to my own failure to learn.

Something similar is true of those reading and writing about politics and public policy. We think in ways that previous work has made available, and draw where we can on related fields. In substantive terms, too, we deploy history and comparison in developing explanations of what governments and others do and the effects it has. More fundamentally, perhaps, learning is not only the what and the how of public policy but also its why. Public policy is an applied science, and learning is much of its rationale. Policy has always been explored and explained with a sense that doing so might be useful, that it might provide lessons for government.

How government learns became an explicit subject of study in the 1960s, in what was felt across countries to be a period of extensive social and political, economic, and technological change. The interest in learning was the result of two sometimes complementary and sometimes seemingly contradictory impulses. One was a sense of uncertainty about what government should do. Few of the prevailing assumptions about public administration and the environment in which it operated felt secure or were expected to hold. Writing at the end of the decade, Donald Schön argued that "The task which the loss of the stable state makes imperative, for the person, for our institutions, for society as a whole, is to learn about learning" (Schön 1973, 28).

The other prompt to think seriously about learning was a recognition of similarity in problems, policies, and programs across countries. Government had grown in the 1960s: most advanced industrial countries now had large-scale welfare programs, for example, and were beginning to face problems in their financing and management. While uncertainty suggested governments needed to learn, similarity indicated that they seemed to be doing so. But how, and why, and to what effect?

In turn, this sense of instability and the learning it necessitates has since been intensified by an awareness of global change—change which has prompted, arguably, more similarity and more uncertainty. Increased interdependence between countries has made for greater degrees of both competition and collaboration. Global trends appear to create unprecedented opportunities for learning as well as a pressing need to take them. Learning has quickened to the extent that living has.

The purpose of this chapter is to take stock of different ways of thinking about learning in public policy. In doing so, it immediately faces a problem, which is that—insofar as learning is both essential and ubiquitous—the relevant literature is voluminous, eclectic, and multidisciplinary.[1] While the chapter necessarily concentrates on studies of and for policy, it is worth noting at the outset how much of that work has drawn (and might still draw) on research in educational theory, social psychology, organizational sociology, and the sociology of organizations, among other fields. That said, the chapter preserves a distinction between learning and the concept of policy transfer, which has more recently become established in the vocabulary of public policy.[2]

---

[1] Wayne Parsons, in his encyclopedic treatment of the field, suggests that thinking of government as learning or information processing is "perhaps the most diverse of all analytical frameworks" (Parsons 1995, 35).

[2] Transfer remains a broader concept than learning in that it is designed to include "forced" processes such as colonization and the sorts of constraints imposed by conditionality, for example. For an

The chapter begins with the sense of similarity and the literature on convergence and diffusion between countries. This is important for making a distinction between learning and other processes of development. I then turn to Heclo's landmark study of political learning, or what he describes as "collective puzzling," discussing the way his work has been taken up in accounts of the role of ideas in policy making as it unfolds over time. It outlines a third and very different literature about learning as part of the ordinary business or practice of policy making. Tensions within each body of research are as important as differences between them.

On this basis, it becomes possible to distinguish different models or ways of thinking about learning, described as mechanistic and organic in turn. The chapter abstracts from what has gone before, what appear to be some of the elements of a theory of learning. The intention is not to posit any theory as such, but to highlight the essential issues which any account of learning must address. I conclude with reflections on the role of comparison in the process of learning across space and time. The underlying argument of the whole is that it is the way we think about learning which determines how well we do it.

# 2. CONVERGENCE, DIFFUSION, AND LEARNING

In general terms, convergence refers to a pattern of increasing similarity in economic, social, and political organization between countries, essentially driven by the process of industrialization and its consequences. What was at issue in the early historical literature was whether public policy was simply a functional byproduct of those changes, or whether more specific explanations were required to take account of actors and interests, ideas and institutions.[3] To the extent that it may be attributed to structural factors, the implications of convergence theory are determinist: convergence does not in itself require attention to be paid to political actors or agents, or to contact or communication between them. To the extent that it can account for emergent similarity without such contact or communication, its significance here is as a counterfactual.

Classically, the idea of diffusion refers to a pattern of successive or sequential adoption of a practice, policy, or program either across countries or across subnational jurisdictions such as states and municipalities (Eyestone 1977). Like convergence,

introductory framework, see Bennett 1991 as well as Dolowitz and Marsh 1996, 2000; for a critique, see James and Lodge 2003.

[3] Convergence was a strong feature of an early phase of comparative welfare state research, including Rimlinger 1971, Wilensky 1975, and Flora and Heidenheimer 1981. For an introductory account of this literature, see Williamson and Fleming 1977; for more recent and stimulating discussion of social policy, see Visser and Hemerijck 2000.

this sequence may be explained in two ways, either because countries C and D reached a requisite level of development sometime after countries A and B, or because C and D borrowed or learned from A and B—or, as seems likely, something of both. In different versions, convergence in public policy may or may not be taken as expressing under-lying changes in economic, social, and political structure (Bennett 1991), while a distinct body of work on the American states pointed to the importance of interaction between policy elites in different jurisdictions (Walker 1969; Gray 1973; Collier and Messick 1975).

Meanwhile, a sociological tradition of diffusion research has been primarily inter-ested in the take-up of information and ideas, practices and technologies among individuals, and principally among networks of peers. Its essential elements remain those identified in Ryan and Gross's early study of the use of hybrid seed-corn among Iowa framers in the 1940s (Ryan and Gross 1943; Rogers 1962, 2003). Drawing together a range of empirical work in rural sociology, medical sociology, anthropol-ogy, communication studies, marketing, and geography, Rogers defines diffusion as the process by which "(1) an *innovation* (2) is *communicated* through certain *channels* (3) *over time* (4) among the members of a *social system*" (Rogers 2003, 11; emphasis in original). The typical pattern of diffusion, in which a few adopt an innovation in its early stages, the bulk of a population follows, and some lag behind, is known as the "S-curve."

Rogers is important for attending to communication between practitioners, though his understanding of the nature and process of communication is contested. In essence, this concept of diffusion (which, here, is equivalent to learning) assumes a relationship between someone who knows, and someone who doesn't. Individual A, who knows about a new artefact or technology, or procedure—or policy—commu-nicates it to B; if it is communicated more or less successfully, then learning can be said to have taken place.[4] For present purposes, this might be better described as a theory of teaching rather than learning.

It is this which Donald Schön criticizes as the "centre–periphery model" (Schön 1973).[5] For it assumes that "The innovation to be diffused exists, fully realized in its essentials, prior to its diffusion," and that "Diffusion is the movement of an innov-ation out to its ultimate users" (1973, 77). This makes for the further assumption that "Directed diffusion is a centrally managed process of dissemination, training, and provision of resources and incentives" (1973, 77). However, systemic resistance to change ("dynamic conservatism") implies that diffusion is "more nearly a battle than a communication" (1973, 90) and as such subject to various forms of failure. Part of the problem is that the introduction of a new product or procedure according to the centre–periphery model assumes relative stability in other aspects of a social (and/or

---

[4] "The essence of the diffusion process is the human interaction in which one person communicates a new idea to a new person" (Schön 1973, 90).

[5] Schön is best known for work on learning in organizations (Argyris and Schön 1978) and in individual professional practice (Schön 1983). Work on the state, which preceded it (Schön 1973), seems somewhat forgotten.

technological, economic, and political) system. But Schön is interested in learning and change under conditions of instability, uncertainty, and complexity.

He presents a historical case study of the emergence of the granite industry in New England, in which each significant development represented "a complex reconfiguration of related systems" (1973, 100). This leads, in turn, to the formulation of an alternative model of diffusion:

> [F]or innovations... which precipitate system-wide changes, the process of diffusion is a battle for broad and complex transformation. And within such a process, the assumptions underlying the classical diffusion model do not hold: The innovation process does not by any means entirely antedate the diffusion process; it evolves significantly within that process. The process does not look like the fanning out of innovation from a single source. Many sources of related and reinforcing innovations are likely to be involved. And the process does not consist primarily in centrally managed dissemination of information. (1973, 101)

As he goes on to explain in respect of network forms of organization (his examples are business systems and social movements): "It [diffusion] has no clearly established centre... Neither is there a stable, centrally established message... the system of the movement cannot be described as the diffusion of the established message from a centre to a periphery" (1973, 105–6).

This is a long way from more positivist constructions to be found elsewhere. For Eyestone, for example, "A state's propensity to adopt a policy probably depends on three factors: some intrinsic properties of the policy, a state's politics, and emulative (interaction) effects. Of these, only the policy itself can be assumed to be invariant over time" (Eyestone 1977, 442). For Schön, not only is the policy not invariant, it is virtually invented in the process of diffusion.[6]

Schön then develops a discussion of "government as a learning system," exploring the ways in which new ideas come to prominence, gain acceptance, and come to be implemented. He notes that the new idea is often fluid, mutable, changing itself and its environment as it moves. Ideas move in the form of metaphors, as in the concept of community advocacy, for example, which carries a legal idea into the civil, public, political domain. Governments invariably struggle with implementation because they hold a centre–periphery model of diffusion or learning, which rests in turn on a theory of the stable state. Underlying their thought and action is a rational experimental model of knowledge and its use, which assumes that knowledge derived

---

[6] This sense of the object of interest being in a continual process of invention or construction features strongly in the sociology of science and technology, and specifically in studies led by "Actor-network theory" (ANT) or what is also known as the "sociology of translation" (for an accessible introduction, see Law 1997). Bruno Latour (1996) contrasts translation with diffusion, arguing that "the initial idea barely counts" (Latour 1996, 119). From this, several things follow: the object (a technology, or perhaps a program or policy) has no autonomous power of its own; there is nothing intrinsically necessary or inevitable about it; it is not driven, promulgated, marketed, or championed by an "inventor." It moves only if it interests groups of actors (only if it "interests interests"); the means by which it does that is referred to as translation. The object translates interests into new terms, and new interests remake the object: there is "no transportation without transformation." Only at the end of the process of transfer (and not at the beginning, as the diffusion model would have it) is the object realized: "(I)nterpretations of the project cannot be separated from the project itself" (Latour 1996, 172).

from experiment can and should be applied to the next comparable instance. But "the loss of the stable state means that it won't be the same next time" (Schön 1973, 188).

# 3. PUBLIC POLICY AS COLLECTIVE PUZZLING

Heclo picks up the historians' interest in learning in his account of the development of social policy in Britain and Sweden. Drawing on different elements of the convergence literature, he describes socioeconomic developments as well as political factors such as elections, parties, and interest groups, arguing that the problem is not to choose between variables, but to work out how they fit together. In doing so, he establishes analytic themes which structure much of the rest of this discussion.

Heclo formulates what now stands as the original construct of political learning: "Politics finds its sources not only in power but also in uncertainty—men collectively wondering what to do... Governments not only 'power'... they also puzzle. Policy making is a form of collective puzzlement on society's behalf; it entails both deciding and knowing... Much political interaction has constituted a process of social learning expressed through policy" (Heclo 1974, 305–6). And if forced to choose between the various factors he has considered, Heclo says that it is civil servants who were crucial to the development of policy in both Britain and Sweden. This is partly to do with the permanence of their position in the political process: it is civil servants' influence, almost by definition, which is the most consistent factor in policy making. But they also have particular functions: "To officials has fallen the task of gathering, coding, storing and interpreting policy experience" (Heclo 1974, 303).[7]

What we know about learning refers for the most part to individuals, while our understanding of how groups learn remains, as Heclo puts it, "fragmentary." This is a significant weakness, because while social learning is created "only by individuals," "alone and in interaction these individuals acquire and produce changed patterns of collective action" (Heclo 1974, 306). These interactions, and through them the process of learning, are inescapably complex (Heclo refers to a "cobweb of inter-action"; 1974, 307, 316). "A better image for social learning than the individual is a maze where the outlet is shifting and the walls are being constantly repatterned; where the subject is not one individual but a group bound together; where this group disagrees not only on how to get out but on whether getting out constitutes a satisfactory solution; where, finally, there is not one but a large number of such

---

[7] Heclo's claim is endorsed by Bennett's more recent work in the very different field of data protection: "(C)onvergence is primarily a result of this constant communication among members of a policy community from nations sharing the same technological problems and the same concerns for privacy... Policy convergence is at least as attributable to the actions and preferences of an international policy community of public, or quasi-public, officials, as it is to anything else" (Bennett 1992, 151, 225).

groups which keep getting in each other's way. Such is the setting for social learning" (Heclo 1974, 308).

Nevertheless, learning is not random. It is shaped by three things: by individuals, by organizations and the relationships between them, and by the impact of previous policy. Heclo notes that some of the principal agents of change are often in some sense marginal to the organizations, administrations, or communities in which they work, "talented amateurs... rather than established professionals and experts" (Heclo 1974, 309). Crucially, they are networked across countries; what they think and know comes from being informed about and paying attention to what goes on elsewhere (1974, 310–11).

Heclo relates organizational interrelationships to the "internal set" of stimulus–response theory. The way an organism, organization, or system responds to an external stimulus is determined in part by the way it is configured internally. Here, this refers to ways of thinking as well as prominent organizational actors and the relationships between them. Interestingly, the internal set seems to be as much a way of accounting for resistance to change, or non-learning, as it is for learning itself.

Perhaps the principal condition both of and for current decisions is previous policy. Policy makers rarely find themselves in uncharted territory. They are much more often confronted by the legacy of previous decisions and the problems they have addressed, solved, and sometimes reproduced. They must take into account the constraints set by apparently unrelated decisions in connected fields. A key feature of Heclo's learning theory is not only the way in which initial perceptions and dispositions shape a specific response to a stimulus, but the way in which this response is reinforced by the effects it produces. "What one learns depends on what one does... In both its self-instruction and self-delusions, the cobweb of socioeconomic conditions, policy middlemen, and political institutions reverberates to the consequences of previous policy in a vast, unpremeditated design of social learning" (Heclo 1974, 316). Seen like this, public policy making is a continuous process of iteration and reiteration.

## 3.1 The Advocacy Coalition Framework

In developing his advocacy coalition framework, one of the more prominent new theories of the policy process to emerge in the 1980s and 1990s, Sabatier set out to formalize some of Heclo's precepts.[8] The concept of the advocacy coalition serves to aggregate large numbers of actors and organizations at different levels of government into manageable units of analysis. Particular features of the framework are the way it takes account of the impact of technical information on decision making, its attention to the evolution of policy over time in a given domain, and its conception of public policies and programs as belief systems (Sabatier and Jenkins-Smith 1999).

[8] See Sabatier 1987, 1988; Sabatier and Jenkins-Smith 1993, 1999.

In many respects, then, it casts the theory of public policy making as a theory of learning.

A belief system is organized in three tiers: what Sabatier terms a "deep core" of normative belief or ideology which can be expected to hold across domains; a "policy core" of more specific commitments within a domain; and then non-essential or secondary matters of detail. What holds a coalition together is agreement over a policy core, and the only way this core can change is as an effect of some external and fundamental shock. Within a domain, however, learning takes place between coalitions as a result of differences in their belief systems. The likelihood of learning is inversely related to the level of commitment to a belief, such that secondary aspects of a policy or program are more likely to be revised or amended in the light of new evidence than elements of the policy core. The process of learning is facilitated by the existence of a professional forum in which members of different coalitions may exchange views and interpretations of both problems and solutions.

Frank Fischer (2003) presents a social constructionist critique of the advocacy coalition framework, drawing on Maarten Hajer's work on discourse coalitions (Hajer 1995). His argument is that belief systems are not pre-existing and empirically verifiable in the way Sabatier and colleagues might claim, but are instead better understood as narratives or storylines. A common interpretation of a problem and appropriate solutions to it is not the basis for membership of a coalition, but something which its various members produce together, through their communications and interactions. Indeed, a common storyline is likely to be more powerful and effective the more it is susceptible to a variety of interpretations.

## 3.2 Social Learning

Peter Hall's influential treatment of what he calls "social learning" is based on a study of economic policy making in Britain in the 1970s and 1980s (Hall 1993).[9] He is interested in the "interpretative framework" of policy, meaning the common understanding of its goals and instruments as well as the nature of the problems to which policy is addressed. Drawing on Kuhn (1962), he refers to this as a "paradigm," and the question he asks is why it changes or shifts, that is, how and why a policy community learns to think differently. For what is at issue in Heclo's largely technocratic model of policy learning is the idea of the relative autonomy of the state from societal pressure. Is "learning" really confined to a ministerial and administrative elite?

---

[9] Hall's work has inspired and influenced a small literature on macroeconomic policy learning in the UK, as James and Lodge (2003) point out.

Hall's argument is that the shift from Keynesianism to monetarism was not made on rational or scientific grounds alone. Since there was certainty about neither approach, policy change was necessarily experimental. Hall describes what he terms first-, second-, and third-order change: the first applies to policy settings (adjusting tax rates, for example); the second to the instruments of policy making (such as the use of cash limits, or targets for M3); and the third to the underlying assumptions and ultimate goals of policy itself (growth rather than employment). While first- and second-order change represent "normal" policy making (like Kuhn's "normal science"), third-order change constitutes a paradigm shift.

What is important about third-order change is not just its scale but the way it occurs, and it is this that is understood as "social learning." For Hall, the "collectivity" which "puzzles" is much broader than that suggested by Heclo (1974).[10] The significance of the "social" epithet is that third-order change in economic policy making was widely debated and socially embedded. Decisions about policy instruments and the way they should be set were indeed a largely technocratic affair, a process conducted in Whitehall. But once the Treasury began to lose its authority, "The ensuing struggle to replace one policy paradigm with another was a societywide affair, mediated by the press, deeply imbricated with electoral competition, and fought in the public arena ... Only some kinds of learning seem to take place inside the state itself. The process of learning associated with important third order changes in policy can be a much broader affair subject to powerful influences from society and the political arena" (1993, 287–8).

What is also important in Hall's framework is the way in which a paradigm serves to make sense of the world, to identify certain phenomena as problematic, and to suggest certain courses of action in response to them. He cites Anderson to the effect that "the deliberation of public policy takes place within a realm of discourse ... policies are made within some system of ideas and standards which is comprehensible and plausible to the actors involved," commenting that "Like a *Gestalt*, this framework is embedded in the very terminology through which policy makers communicate about their work, and it is influential precisely because so much of it is taken for granted and unamenable to scrutiny as a whole" (1993, 279).[11]

---

[10] In truth, much of this is prefigured in Heclo, whose contention is that it is the administrative elite which constitutes only what he calls the "institutional" agent of learning. For this to have political impact, new ideas must be taken up by some "popularly organized group" (Heclo 1974, 319).

[11] A previous study (Hall 1989) was concerned with the introduction and establishment of Keynesian economic thinking across countries. "When an evocative set of ideas are introduced into the political arena, they do not simply rest on top of the factors already there. Rather, they can alter the composition of other elements in the political sphere, like a catalyst or binding agent that allows existing ingredients to combine in new ways ... Keynesian ideas did not simply reflect group interests or material conditions: they had the power to change the perceptions a group had of its own interests, and they made possible new courses of action that changed the material world itself" (Hall 1989, 367, 369).

## 4. Learning in Practice

Other writers on learning in public policy have sought to work closer to the ground, to think about policy making from within.[12] Writing as much for as about learning, for example, Richard Rose (1991, 1993, 2000, 2005) thinks of it in terms of "lesson-drawing" and is both rigorous and prescriptive about what it should mean. Lesson drawing is not about reasoning from first principles, or about the way in which "big ideas" take hold of a polity. It is instead "both a normative and a practical activity" (Rose 1993, 11). A lesson is "an action-oriented conclusion about a programme or programmes in operation elsewhere" (1991, 7).

Furthermore, "A lesson is not a disjointed set of ideas about what to do. It requires a cause-and-effect model showing how a program designed on the basis of experience elsewhere can achieve a desired goal if adopted in the advocate's own jurisdiction" (1993, 13). "The process of lesson-drawing starts with scanning programmes in effect elsewhere, and ends with the prospective evaluation of what would happen if a programme in effect elsewhere were transferred here in future" (1991, 3). Policy makers are likely to begin by searching for information near at hand; some "subjective identification" with counterparts elsewhere is likely to be significant (1991, 14). The next stage of the process consists in modeling or abstracting from extant programs in order to appreciate their essential components: in order to serve as material for transfer, foreign experience must be abstracted from the context in which it is embedded. Then, a program may be simply *copied* from one elsewhere or *emulated*, which means adjusting it in some way to new domestic circumstance. Combining elements of more than one program in more than one other place amounts to *hybridization* or *synthesis*, while drawing on experience elsewhere as intellectual stimulus for what amounts to a new program is described as *inspiration* (Rose 1991, 21–2).

Rose acknowledges that learning from others is inevitably shaped by other factors such as political power, expert opinion, and the values of policy makers (Rose 1993). Yet however contingent the political process, it is in his account separate and separable from policy substance. Lessons are prior to the learning of them, and the assumption is that they are or should be logical, rational, and real. This leaves the sense that learning can only be properly done in rare and straitened circumstances. In practice, in normal conditions of uncertain knowledge and unstable preferences, most learning inevitably appears as some impoverished approximation to an ideal.

But these are precisely the conditions that others take as their starting point. For there is a key distinction to be made between knowing that and knowing how (Brown

---

[12] The classic practical injunction on learning from history is Neustadt and May's *Thinking in Time* (1986). For a practical resource on learning from abroad, see the UK government's policy hub at www.policyhub.gov.uk/bpmaking/icpm_toolkit/beyond_the_horizon_ICPM_home.asp, accessed 10 Sept. 2004.

and Duguid 2000).[13] To know *that* depends on the accumulation and assimilation of information; knowing *how* comes through practice. Simply, we learn by doing as much as by reading, thinking, or being told. What this implies is what Scott describes as an epistemological *metis* (Scott 1998, ch. 9), local, vernacular, practical. It has something in common with Lindblom and Cohen's (1979) "ordinary" knowledge. Yet we know surprisingly little about what bureaucrats and administrators do when they are doing their job, let alone about the ways they think and learn. We necessarily have recourse to theory and to other studies of workplace learning. These suggest two things: first that learning in practice is ad hoc, in the sense of being context or problem specific, and second that it is collaborative.[14]

It is ad hoc, not least because policy makers and administrators are continually confronted by problems and policies that appear to be new and different from those they have known before. And this newness presents not only in agenda-setting and decision-making stages of the policy process, but in implementation, too. We might think of implementation as a process of learning rather than carrying out instructions (Pressman and Wildavsky 1984; Schofield 2004): in the process of implementation, administrators and professionals alike discover not only how to put policy into practice but what a policy really means or entails. Their learning is reactive but ingenious.[15]

## 4.1 Communities of Practice

Improvisation of this kind is ordinarily collaborative (Brown and Duguid 2000, 103 ff.). Collaboration and improvisation in turn are carried on by telling stories, by exchanging ideas, suggestions, theories, by developing a common sense of the nature and origins of as well as possible solutions to a problem. In public policy as much as anywhere else, solving problems is an embedded, social process as much as a

---

[13] The distinction is Ryle's (1949, ch. 2). In their study of government learning, Etheredge and Short (1983) similarly distinguish between intelligence and effectiveness.

[14] Wagenaar and Cook review ideas about practice in public policy: "Practice . . . is an important and distinct dimension of politics, with its own logic (pragmatic, purposeful), its own standards of knowing (interpretative, holistic, more know-how than know-that), its own orientation towards the world (interactive, moral, emotional), and its own image of society (as a constellation of interdependent communities)" (Wagenaar and Cook 2003, 141). "Situated learning" is a theory of knowledge acquisition which emphasizes learning in context and through interaction and collaboration: on workplace learning, see Lave and Wenger 1991, Wenger 1998, Brown and Duguid 2000; and for an interesting discussion of global change in similar terms, Tenkasi and Mohrman 1999. On the productive efficiency of learning by doing, see Arrow 1962.

[15] Policy makers and administrators have much in common with Lévi-Strauss's *bricoleur* (Lévi-Strauss 1966, 16–22). The *bricoleur*, in contrast to the scientist or engineer, picks up objects (tools and materials or, here, policies, programs, and instruments) as he goes, keeping them until he recognizes an opportunity to use them. The way they are used and the effects they have are in part determined by the way they have been used before, but they rarely work in the same way twice. Not only are the properties of the policy object uncovered in use, but the opportunity to use them is itself invariably made to fit.

rational, scientific one. We learn with others as much as from others.[16] Geoffrey Vickers, for example, thinks his way into a seat at the table around which the members of a Royal Commission are discussing their views and findings (1965, ch. 3).[17] Part of their judgement, of course, is shaped by what they know and by the moral and intellectual positions they have already established individually. But these norms are revised and refined in the process of applying them to the specific problem, and in the course of discussion and debate, that is "by the impact, attrition and stimulus of each commissioner on the others" (Vickers 1965, 64).

Brown and Duguid (2000, 141 ff.) go on to describe what they call "networks of practice," which are something like occupational groups: people who do similar things, who are linked to each other in some way (by their training, or through the associations to which they belong) but do not necessarily know each other. Beyond that, working together on the same task establishes more intense "communities of practice" (Wenger and Snyder 2000). Networks and communities have complementary qualities. Networks have reach but little reciprocity; they are good at sharing knowledge, but less good at producing (or applying) it. Communities are inevitably limited in their scope or reach, but collaboration and reciprocity are tightened, meaning that new knowledge is quickly propagated.

Key individuals, or "brokers," are often critical to communication and learning between communities, occupying ambivalent positions both central and marginal to the communities and contexts within which they work. A broker depends on the trust or complicity of others—"at just that point, the intercommunal boundary, where trust can be hardest to win" (Brown and Duguid 2001, 60). Importantly, trust is earned or realized in practice, in carrying negotiation back and forth. Nevertheless, in many respects he or she will operate in the margins, his or her status uncertain and often threatening. For the broker is to some degree a stranger, relativizing and calling into question what is locally taken to be common sense (Schütz 1964). The stranger may be a source of contagion as well as valuable new resources.

Almost by definition, community makes for a greater degree of equity or reciprocity in learning, but it also makes for a different order of communication. To begin with, partners to a conversation or dialog (in effect, a relationship) talk about each other, about the things they have brought separately to that situation. Over time, they come to talk increasingly about things they have thought of through their talking; the dialog becomes self-generating. Participants in a dialog are not only learning from each other, but also learning something new. There are good reasons, therefore, to think we might learn best from friends (Forester 1999, 31–8).[18] Friends

---

[16] It is also the case that much learning may be done vicariously (McKendree et al. 1998). We learn often by observing or fringing on dialogues and exchanges conducted by others.

[17] Vickers is the more interesting to this discussion because he writes as an experienced practitioner: he was a soldier and officer, solicitor, senior civil servant, and company director, and a member of the London Passenger Transport Board, the National Coal Board, and the Medical Research Council.

[18] This sort of affinity is one of the reasons Dolowitz, Greenwold, and Marsh (1999) give for Britain's predominant reference to the USA as a source of transfer and learning.

relate appropriate information and experience, knowing what is appropriate to us because they know us. They help us to see ourselves in context, to understand not how things are, but how we are. They recognize complexity, instead of proffering simple solutions. They help us to deliberate, to mull over, to wonder about alternatives. They recognize the emotions, feelings, and values which inform our decisions. "The type of friendship from which we should consider learning is not the friendship of long affection and intimacy, but the friendship of mutual concern, of care and respect for the other's practice of citizenship, their full participation in the political world. This is the friendship of appreciation of the hopes and political possibilities of the other, the friendship recognizing, too, the vulnerabilities of those hopes and possibilities" (Forester 1999, 36).

## 5. THE ELEMENTS OF LEARNING

Implicit in the different literatures reviewed here are two different ways of thinking about learning, one largely positivist and the other constructionist. They might be described as mechanistic and organic in turn.[19] The first model, the positivist or mechanistic, assumes that a thing exists in time and space, and is picked up and carried over—transferred—and used in another time and/or place. What matter are the vectors, levers, couplings, and communications by which this is achieved. Transfer, whether of knowledge, technology, or public policy, is an act of engineering. To the extent that it acknowledges that rationality is bounded, that action is constrained by institutions, and that as a result policies adopted from elsewhere are also invariably adapted, it may be called a qualified mechanism. The second model, constructionist or organic, treats policy as emergent. Policy does not exist somewhere else in finished form, ready to be looked at and learned from, but is finished or produced in the act of looking and learning. Learning is the output of a series of communications, not its input; in this sense it is generated rather than disseminated. The difference between the two models is that between a sense of learning being complicated, and its being complex.

These models are worth exploring in part because they point to a possible tension between policy makers' espoused theory of learning and their theory in use.[20] The difference between them is between the rational, legal, and scientific discourse in which policy makers and administrators are often trained, and the social, managerial, and political ways of knowing which are the currency of their daily practice. Sometimes,

---

[19] I have taken this terminology from Burns and Stalker (1961), though its more general use in social science originates in Durkheim. There is something of the same idea in James March's distinction between "exploitative" and "exploratory" learning (March 1991).

[20] The distinction is Argyris and Schön's (1978).

policy is designed on the basis of evidence from experience or elsewhere. Usually, too, conflicting evidence and argument makes some compromise necessary. Often, however, policy makers collaborate, exchanging information about problems and policies which are similar in essential respects, but different enough to provoke reflection and creative thinking (or "collective puzzling").[21] An interesting implication of this is that the concept of learning does not necessarily entail its habitual corollary, that of teaching. Standard images of cross-national "policy borrowing," "import," and "export" risk obscuring much of the mutualism of learning processes.

To the extent that studying learning begs familiar questions about the ways in which ideas are manifested in behavior (Majone and Wildavsky 1979), the distinction drawn here has its methodological corollary, too, which is that learning will be interpreted as much as explained. Vickers (1965, 187) posits a "point of acceptance," when what is known is realized, when insight comes to be supported by commitment, when the assimilation of information turns into the reformulation of belief, when a "potential fact" becomes a "potential act." As he acknowledges, this psychological change is both "theoretically obscure" and "one of the most familiar facts of experience." Heclo, similarly, notes that learning will be "easier to illustrate than to prove conclusively" (Heclo 1974, 321).

## 5.1 Agency and Interaction

The study of learning makes certain assumptions about agency, that learning is an active process. But who learns? There is some agreement in the literature that learning is something that individuals and only individuals do. But it is also something they do in the course of interaction with others, in groups, networks, communities, and organizations: learning is a social process (Bandura 1977).[22]

This conception is the more valuable because it highlights the difficulty and fragility of learning. Learning is difficult precisely because it is interactive, "because so many men must do it together" (Pressman and Wildavsky 1984, 125). By the

---

[21] Vickers's distinction between compromise and "integrative" decision making is significant here. An integrative solution to a problem is one which wholly satisfies the different claims of parties to it. This is possible to the extent that their different ways of seeing the problem are changed, which in turn "enlarges the possibilities of solution beyond those which existed when the debate began" (Vickers 1965, 208).

[22] "Thus judgment and decision, though mental activities of individuals, are also part of a social process. They are taken within and depend on a net of communication, which is meaningful only through a vast, partly organized accumulation of largely shared assumptions and expectations, a structure constantly being developed and changed by the activities which it mediates. The individual decider can no more be studied in isolation than the individual decision. The mental activity and the social process are indissoluble" (Vickers 1965, 15). The social process of thinking and the way it threatens common assumptions about the individual, rational self is Mary Douglas's theme in *How Institutions Think* (Douglas 1986).

same token, some situations and contexts are more conducive to learning than others, and a powerful claim can be made that social entities such as groups, organizations, and states which cultivate learning have more prospect of success than others.[23]

The notion of agency implicit in action and interaction means little without some associated concept of autonomy. On this basis, John Forester (1985) sets out the kinds of interaction that might constitute learning from those which don't. What is at issue for him is the relative legitimacy of different interactions. The conditions for learning ("some enhanced competence for action and self-understanding;" 1985, 265) are essentially the same as those for Habermas's "ideal speech situation," namely that the validity of a statement may be assessed without coercion or threat.[24] The significance of this is that we might come to think of learning as a function of a particular kind of relationship, rather than simply of the capacity of different parties to it.

Learning ordinarily takes place in conditions of complex interdependence, in which the thoughts and actions of any given agent change the context or environment in which others must think and act. "(A) communicated prediction changes the situation," as Vickers puts it (1965, 84), simply because others assess our predictions and adjust their actions according not only to the likely accuracy of our predictions, but also according to their own, different predictions of our behaviour. It is this awareness of complex interdependence which informs contemporary ideas of governance as steering, and which is expressed for example in the European Union's "open method of coordination."[25] It is also the logic of policy or program development and management by benchmarking. Benchmarking—"learning by monitoring" (Sabel 1994)—emerged in fast-developing areas of industry and commerce where no objective standards of evaluation exist, or where those standards change quickly. It works not by the imposition of standards but by the construction and subsequent discussion and interpretation of norms: "(G)uidance is neither precise nor persuasive enough to determine action. Individuals must interpret the general rules and expectations to bring them to bear on their actual situation. These reinterpretations proceed through argumentative encounters in which the individual attempts to establish an equilibrium between his or her views and social standards by recasting them both" (Sabel 1994, 156).

[23] This proposition is the basis of what has become an extensive literature on organizational learning: for introductions, see Weick and Westley 1996; Levitt and March 1998.

[24] By the same token, learning does not mean life without conflict. Learning takes place in the pursuit of different preferences and purposes: where conservatives will want to learn how to do better with existing programs, reformers will want to learn about new programs, or how to change or expand existing ones for somewhat different ends (Browne and Wildavsky 1983, 245).

[25] On governance, see Rhodes 1996 and Kooiman 2003; on the open method of coordination, a special issue of the *Journal of European Public Policy*, 11 (2), 2004.

## 5.2 Cognition and Communication

Learning begins in uncertainty: if there were no uncertainty, there would be no need for puzzling. This uncertainty is in part a function of inadequate information. Policy makers are ordinarily bound to act in circumstances in which their information, their imagination, and their resources are inevitably incomplete. As a result, their rationality is limited, contingent, or in Simon's phrase, "bounded."[26]

The issue is more subtle and more fundamental than just not knowing enough. Following Heclo (above), what we are able to do is in part determined by what we have done before. Our prior decisions shape the domain in which future ones will be taken. We learn from the past and from our experience, not least because the past is in some degree the source of our problems. But what is important here is that this is a mental as much as a material or empirical process, or what we might call a "path dependence of the mind." For what we learn is in part determined by what we have learned before. Learning is a process of making sense of the world around us, and we tend to do so in terms with which we are already familiar. What we learn is a function of what we know already.

Vickers calls this an "appreciative system:" "a set of readinesses to distinguish some aspects of the situation rather than others and to classify and value these in this way rather than that" (1965, 67). It has equivalents in Heclo's "internal set," in what Schön and Rein (1994) call a "frame" and Young (1977) an "assumptive world;" it is close to Schotter's conception of institutions as "machines for thinking" (Schotter 1981; Douglas 1986). What is important for students of learning is that these various "readinesses," which themselves have to be learned, are "limiting, as well as enabling" (Vickers 1965, 68). For they shape and determine what we don't see as well as what we do.[27]

This implies that learning is not simply an interpretative act, a process of registering and taking account of the world; it is, in a fundamental way, about creating the world. It is an active process of *making* sense (Weick 1995). Similarly, just as we shop in order to discover what we want (and we might think of some kinds of political learning as "policy shopping"), so we read in order to discover what we think, not just what any given author thinks (Brown and Duguid 2000). What emerges is a conception of learning as an act of imagination, invention, and persuasion as much as (or as well as) comprehension, deduction, and assimilation.

Wildavsky, similarly, thinks of implementation as exploration, or hypothesis testing (Browne and Wildavsky 1983, 254). We make predictions and act accordingly, adjusting our actions according to whether or not our predictions appear in fact to have been true. The problem is that the hypothesis alters the basis on which it will be

---

[26] In her study of employment policy in the USA from the New Deal to the 1970s, Margaret Weir (1992) describes the institutional processing of new ideas as one of "bounded innovation."

[27] See also March's account of "model bias in social action" (March 1972). Analytically, non-learning is as interesting as learning. For instances in public policy, think of the way in which decision making is often constrained (and distorted) by the need to conform to and reproduce the established norms and assumptions of a deliberating group. This is what Janis has described as "groupthink" (Janis 1982).

subsequently revised. This means that public policies and the environments in which they operate are engaged in a process of mutual adaptation over time, which means in turn that "(I)mplementation is shaken from its safe cognitive anchorage in prior objectives and future consequences" (Pressman and Wildavsky 1984, xvii). Implementation is "not about getting what you once wanted but ... about what you have since learned to prefer" (Browne and Wildavsky 1983, 234).

Cognition or "appreciation," meanwhile, is as much a product of communication as of perception. "(A)ll perception and all response, all behaviour and all classes of behaviour, all learning and all genetics ... all organization and all evolution—one entire subject matter—must be regarded as communicational in nature" (Bateson 1973, 253). Attention to communication is important only to the extent that it does not imply the exact reproduction of a message intended by a speaker in the mind of a listener: what is understood by the listener is always and inevitably the result of a process of interpretation. The reproduction of the message is always to some degree imperfect: as the sociologists of science put it, "information is transformation" (Callon and Latour 1981, 300); what we think of as transfer is invariably an act of translation.

The central issue can be simply stated. We communicate by means of signs (words and pictures, sounds and images). The relationship between the sign and what it signifies is neither determined nor mechanical. What things mean is a matter of convention (a social construct) and it is invariably inexact. Meaning may be shared, but it is not identical. This fundamental epistemological uncertainty, this requirement that every utterance be accompanied by some hermeneutic move on the part of the reader or listener, is a source of innovation and creativity as well as error and failure. Translation—the processing of what you say into terms that I understand—is ubiquitous and imperfect.

The elements of learning distinguished here are intended as no more than a heuristic, a formal separation of concepts which are practically and essentially interconnected. Beyond them, it is worth drawing attention to two background themes, not only because they are important here but also because they are sometimes neglected in other accounts of policy making. First, there is much in the treatment of policy learning as it has unfolded over three or more decades which calls on systems theory. Heclo's concept of learning is derived from stimulus–response theory, and both he and Schön draw on Deutsch's cybernetic model of government (Deutsch 1963). Heclo, for example, cites Polanyi's " 'spontaneous order', an order attained by allowing each part to interact on its own initiative" (Heclo 1974, 320). Vickers acknowledges making use of "concepts and ways of thought which, though common today in a wide variety of sciences, have so far penetrated only patchily into the thought of laymen—concepts which can perhaps be comprehended with least danger of misconception under the name of general system theory" (Vickers 1965, 16). Wenger (2000) offers a more explicit articulation of the community of practice in terms of systems theory, focusing on the learning which takes place at and across boundaries between communities.

Second, there is a further reach back to phenomenology and the roots of American pragmatism, as developed by James, Peirce, and perhaps most interested in problems of learning, John Dewey. It is this that leads Heclo to assert that "Apart from the policy process there were no 'problems', only conditions" (Heclo 1974, 288) and Schön to suggest that "diagnosis comes about through intervention" (Schön 1973, 199). It is the dominant strain in Weick's (1995) *Sensemaking in Organizations*, and Brown and Duguid's (2000) *Social Life of Information*. Weick builds on Graham Wallas's classic citation of a child's remark: "How can I know what I think till I see what I say?" (Wallas 1926; Weick 1995, 12), explaining that what he calls sense making is about "the ways people generate what they interpret ... the invention that precedes interpretation" (Weick 1995, 13–14).

# 6. Learning by Comparison

This chapter began by noting the ordinary experience of learning from others and from the past. It concludes here with reflections on the way in which learning, in both time and space, turns on comparison. For we learn from (and with) others with whom we identify in some way: because they are like us, or perhaps because we would like to be like them, or because their problems seem to be like ours. By the same token, we find it difficult to learn from those we think (or would like to think) are very different.

This is a different way of thinking about comparison from that which is usual in studies of public policy. More formally, comparison may be a source of explanation, of accounting for why things happen in one country and not in others, or why they happen in different ways. Used like this, to distinguish some causal variables from others, it is the closest the policy sciences come to experimental logic. At the same time, comparison may serve as a means of evaluation, a way of judging policy or practice and asking how it might be improved.

In practice, of course, such lessons are difficult to draw and difficult to apply. The contexts in which policy is made and implemented are complex, such that the relationship between policy cause and outcome or effect is often unclear. However compelling they may be, explanations and evaluations remain understandings of what has happened before, elsewhere. Where they work, where we can marshal enough evidence to be confident that they have general validity, and where they are flexible enough to be portable from one place to another, we might go with them. But often we can't. Comparative analysis as classically conceived is a rich, valuable, but in itself insufficient guide to policy.

But much of the learning considered here is based on a different order of comparison, one which is prior to the other two. For comparison is predicated on description and redescription, cognition and recognition, categorization and classification, and understanding its implications is necessarily an interpretative process. To compare something with something else entails the logically prior recognition or assumption that they are comparable. It is to use the juxtaposition of things to make sense of them, both separately and together.

Comparison entails the use or production of categories to describe cases, which is something we usually do no more than half-consciously. Cross-national talk, for example, requires a more creative, slightly more abstract grammar and vocabulary than the ones we might ordinarily use to discuss situations we know and are familiar with with those who also inhabit them. Comparison is realized in what might be described as a "third code," or a language of translation. This is partly why it often seems difficult, alien, disorienting, as well as exhilarating.

Vickers (1965) describes the formidable challenge presented by the Robbins Report on higher education in the UK. What it did was to review the position of an array of institutions of "higher education," in the process defining and constructing this new, tertiary sector. What was at issue was the function and purpose of different teacher training and other technical colleges as well as the relations between them. Defining this set of organizations involved "a mental adjustment of a peculiarly difficult and complex kind," which was in essence one of recategorization. It meant taking parts of the state system of education out of that category and grouping them with universities, which had always insisted on a separate, special identity. Inventing or constructing higher or tertiary education in turn implied some more explicit relationship to schools, the secondary tier. As throughout his work, Vickers connects the administrative problem to a psychological insight: "(I)n reorganizing institutions, it is easiest to subdivide, more difficult to combine and most difficult to carve up and regroup the constituents in a going concern. The difficulty illustrates and is perhaps related to the more basic psychological difficulties attending the growth of the categories which underlie our judgments of reality ... The report ... is not merely a plan for a reorganization of our institutions. It is also a plea for the reorganization of our thought" (Vickers 1965, 59–60).

## REFERENCES

ARGYRIS, C., and SCHÖN, D. 1978. *Organizational Learning*. London: Addison-Wesley.

ARROW, K. 1962. The economic implications of learning by doing. *Review of Economic Studies*, 29 (3): 155–73.

BANDURA, A. 1977. *Social Learning Theory*. Englewood Cliffs, NJ: Prentice Hall.

BATESON, G. 1973. The logical categories of learning and communication. In *Steps to an Ecology of Mind*, ed. G. Bateson. London: Granada.

BENNETT, C. J. 1991. Review article: what is policy convergence and what causes it? *British Journal of Political Science*, 21 (2): 215–33.

—— 1992. *Regulating Privacy: Data Protection and Public Policy in Europe and the United States*. Ithaca, NY: Cornell University Press.

BROWN, J. S., and DUGUID, P. 2000. *The Social Life of Information*. Boston: Harvard Business School Press.

—— —— 2001. Structure and spontaneity: knowledge and organization. In *Managing Industrial Knowledge: Creation, Transfer and Utilisation*, ed. I. Nonaka and D. J. Teece. London: Sage.

BROWNE, A. and WILDAVSKY, A. 1983. Implementation as exploration. Reprinted in *Implementation: How Great Expectations in Washington are Dashed in Oakland*, ed. J. L. Pressman and A. Wildavsky, 3rd expanded edn. Berkeley: University of California Press, 1984.

BURNS, T., and STALKER, G. M. 1961. *The Management of Innovation*. London: Tavistock.

CALLON, M. and LATOUR, B. 1981. Unscrewing the big Leviathan: how actors macro-structure reality and how sociologists help them to do so. In *Advances in Social Theory and Methodology: Toward an Integration of Micro and Macro-Sociologies*, ed. K. D. Knorr-Cetina and A. V. Cicourel. London: Routledge and Kegan Paul.

COLLIER, D., and MESSICK, R. 1975. Prerequisites versus diffusion: testing alternative explanations of social security adoption. *American Political Science Review*, 69: 1296–315.

DEUTSCH, K. W. 1963. *The Nerves of Government: Models of Political Communication and Control*. New York: Free Press.

DOLOWITZ, D., GREENWOLD, S., and MARSH, D. 1999. Policy transfer: something old, something new, something borrowed, but why red, white and blue? *Parliamentary Affairs*, 52 (4): 719–30.

—— and MARSH, D. 1996. Who learns what from whom: a review of the policy transfer literature. *Political Studies*, 44 (2): 343–57.

—— —— 2000. Learning from abroad: the role of policy transfer in contemporary policy making. *Governance*, 13 (1): 5–24.

DOUGLAS, M. 1986. *How Institutions Think*. Syracuse, NY: Syracuse University Press.

ETHEREDGE, L. S., and SHORT, J. 1983. Thinking about government learning. *Journal of Management Studies*, 20 (1): 41–58.

EYESTONE, R. 1977. Confusion, diffusion and innovation. *American Political Science Review*, 71: 441–7.

FISCHER, F. 2003. *Reframing Public Policy: Discursive Politics and Deliberative Practices*. Oxford: Oxford University Press.

FLORA, P., and HEIDENHEIMER, A. J. (eds.) 1981. *The Development of Welfare States in Europe and America*. New Brunswick, NJ: Transaction.

FORESTER, J. 1985. The policy analysis–critical theory affair: Wildavsky and Habermas as bedfellows? In *Critical Theory and Public Life*, ed. J. Forester. Cambridge, Mass.: MIT Press.

—— 1999. *The Deliberative Practitioner: Encouraging Participatory Planning Processes*. Cambridge, Mass.: MIT Press.

GRAY, V. 1973. Innovation in the states: a diffusion study. *American Political Science Review*, 67: 1173–85.

HAJER, M. 1995. *The Politics of Environmental Discourse*. Oxford: Oxford University Press.

HALL, P. A. (ed.) 1989. *The Political Power of Economic Ideas: Keynesianism across Nations*. Princeton, NJ: Princeton University Press.

—— 1993. Policy paradigms, social learning and the state: the case of economic policymaking in Britain. *Comparative Politics*, 25: 275–96.

HECLO, H. 1974. *Modern Social Politics in Britain and Sweden: From Relief to Income Maintenance*. New Haven, Conn: Yale University Press.

JAMES, O., and LODGE, M. 2003. The limitations of "policy transfer" and "lesson drawing" for public policy research. *Political Studies Review*, 1: 179–93.

JANIS, I. 1982. *Groupthink: Psychological Studies of Policy Decisions and Fiascoes*. Boston: Houghton Mifflin.

KOOIMAN, J. 2003. *Governing as Governance*. London: Sage.

KUHN, T. S. 1962. *The Structure of Scientific Revolutions*. Chicago: Chicago University Press.

LATOUR, B. 1996. *Aramis, or the Love of Technology*. Cambridge, Mass.: Harvard University Press.

Lave, J., and Wenger, E. 1991. *Situated Learning: Legitimate Peripheral Participation*. Cambridge: Cambridge University Press.

Law, J. 1997. Traduction/trahison: notes on ANT. Department of Sociology, Lancaster University; available at: www.comp.lancs.ac.uk/sociology/papers/law-traduction-trahison.pdf (accesed 19 Aug. 2004).

Lévi-Strauss, C. 1966. *The Savage Mind*. London: Weidenfeld and Nicolson.

Levitt, B., and March, J. 1998. Organizational learning. *Annual Review of Sociology*, 14: 319–40.

Lindblom, C. E. and Cohen, D. K. 1979. *Usable Knowledge: Social Science and Social Problem Solving*. New Haven, Conn.: Yale University Press.

McKendree, J., Stenning, K., Mayes, T., Lee, J., and Cox, R. 1998. Why observing a dialogue may benefit learning. *Journal of Computer Assisted Learning*, 14 (2): 110–19; available at: www.hcrc.ed.ac.uk/gal/vicar/VicarPapers/JCAL98.RTF.

Majone, G., and Wildavsky, A. 1979. Implementation as evolution. Reprinted in *Implementation: How Great Expectations in Washington are Dashed in Oakland*, ed. J. L. Pressman and A. Wildavsky, 3rd expanded edn. Berkeley: University of California Press, 1984.

March, J. G. 1972. Model bias in social action. *Review of Educational Research*, 42: 413–29.

—— 1991. Exploration and exploitation in organizational learning. *Organization Science*, 2 (1): 71–87.

Neustadt, R., and May, E. 1986. *Thinking in Time: The Uses of History for Decision Makers*. New York: Free Press.

Parsons, W. 1995. *Public Policy: An Introduction to the Theory and Practice of Policy Analysis*. Aldershot: Edward Elgar.

Pressman, J. L. and Wildavsky, A. 1984. *Implementation: How Great Expectations in Washington are Dashed in Oakland*, 3rd expanded edn. Berkeley: University of California Press.

Rhodes, R. 1996. The new governance: governing without government. *Political Studies*, 44: 652–67.

Rimlinger, G. 1971. *Welfare Policy and Industrialization in Europe, America and Russia*. New York: Wiley.

Rogers, E. 1962. *Diffusion of Innovations*. New York: Free Press.

—— 2003. *The Diffusion of Innovations*, 5th edn. New York: Free Press.

Rose, R. 1991. What is lesson-drawing? *Journal of Public Policy*, 11 (1): 3–30.

—— 1993. *Lesson-Drawing in Public Policy*. Chatham, NJ: Chatham House.

—— 2000. What can we learn from abroad? *Parliamentary Affairs*, 53: 628–43.

—— 2005. *Learning from Comparative Public Policy: A Practical Guide*. Abingdon: Routledge.

Ryan, B., and Gross, N. C. 1943. The diffusion of hybrid seed-corn in two Iowa communities. *Rural Sociology*, 8: 15–24.

Ryle, G. 1949. *The Concept of Mind*. London: Hutchinson.

Sabatier, P. 1987. Knowledge, policy-oriented learning and policy change. *Knowledge*, 8: 649–92.

—— 1988. An advocacy coalition framework of policy change and the role of policy-oriented learning therein. *Policy Sciences*, 21: 129–68.

—— and Jenkins-Smith, H. (eds.) 1993. *Policy Change and Learning: An Advocacy Coalition Approach*. Boulder, Colo.: Westview.

—— —— 1999. The Advocacy Coalition Framework: an assessment. In *Theories of the Policy Process*, ed. P. Sabatier. Boulder, Colo.: Westview.

SABEL, C. 1994. Learning by monitoring: the institutions of economic development. In *The Handbook of Economic Sociology*, ed. N. J. Smelser and R. Swedberg. Princeton, NJ: Princeton University Press.

SCHOFIELD, J. 2004. A model of learned implementation. *Public Administration*, 82 (2): 283–308.

SCHÖN, D. A. 1973. *Beyond the Stable State: Public and Private Learning in a Changing Society*. Harmondsworth: Penguin.

—— 1983. *The Reflective Practitioner: How Professionals Think in Action*. London: Temple Smith.

—— and REIN, M. 1994. *Frame Reflection: Toward the Resolution of Intractable Policy Controversies*. New York: Basic Books.

SCHOTTER, A. 1981. *The Economic Theory of Social Institutions*. Cambridge: Cambridge University Press.

SCHÜTZ, A. 1964. The stranger: an essay in social psychology. *American Journal of Sociology*, 49 (6): 499–507. Reprinted in *Alfred Schütz: Collected Papers, ii: Studies in Social Theory*, ed. A. Brodersen. The Hague: Nijhoff, 1976.

SCOTT, J. C. 1998. *Seeing Like a State: How Certain Schemes to Improve the Human Condition have Failed*. New Haven, Conn.: Yale University Press.

TENKASI, R. V., and MOHRMAN, S. A. 1999. Global change as contextual collaborative knowledge creation. In *Organizational Dimensions of Global Change: No Limits to Cooperation*, ed. D. L. Coopernider and J. E. Dutton. Thousand Oaks, Calif.: Sage.

VICKERS, G. 1965. *The Art of Judgment: A Study of Policy Making*, London: Chapman and Hall.

VISSER, J., and HEMERIJCK, A. 2000. Learning and mimicking: how European welfare states adjust. Manuscript.

WAGENAAR, H., and COOK, S. D. N. 2003. Understanding policy practices: action, dialectic and deliberation in policy analysis. In *Deliberative Policy Analysis: Understanding Governance in the Network Society*, ed. M. A. Hajer and H. Wagenaar. Cambridge: Cambridge University Press.

WALKER, J. L. 1969. The diffusion of innovations among the American states. *American Political Science Review*, 63: 880–99.

WALLAS, G. 1926. *The Art of Thought*. New York: Harcourt Brace.

WEICK, K. E. 1995. *Sensemaking in Organizations*. Thousand Oaks, Calif.: Sage.

—— and WESTLEY, F. 1996. Organizational learning: affirming an oxymoron. In *Managing Organizations: Current Issues*, ed. S. R. Clegg, C. Hardy, and W. R. Nord. London: Sage.

WEIR, M. 1992. Ideas and the politics of bounded innovation. In *The New Institutionalism: State, Society and Economy*, ed. S. Steinmo, K. Thelen, and F. Longstreth. New York: Cambridge University Press.

WENGER, E. 1998. *Communities of Practice: Learning, Meaning and Identity*. Cambridge: Cambridge University Press.

—— 2000. Communities of practice and learning systems. *Organization*, 7 (2): 225–46.

—— and SNYDER, W. M. 2000. Communities of practice: the organizational frontier. *Harvard Business Review* (Jan.–Feb.): 139–45.

WILENSKY, H. L. 1975. *The Welfare State and Equality: Structural and Ideological Roots of Public Expenditure*. Berkeley: University of California Press.

WILLIAMSON, J. B., and FLEMING, J. J. 1977. Convergence theory and the social welfare sector: a cross-national analysis. *International Journal of Comparative Sociology*, 18 (3–4): 242–53.

YOUNG, K. 1977. Values in the policy process. *Policy and Politics*, 5: 1–22.

CHAPTER 18

# REFRAMING PROBLEMATIC POLICIES

## MARTIN REIN

PUBLIC policies are often problematic because the ends they seek are themselves problematic. The defining challenge of public policy lies not in finding the best means to given ends, but rather in reframing ends so as better to cope with unavoidable problems of vagueness and conflicts among the ends themselves. Those problems are largely neglected in the standard instrumentalist approach to policy research.

Two weaknesses of the instrumental conception of policy knowledge are particularly important. First, lopsided attention to instrumental knowledge can have the effect of obscuring the value choices facing public policy, hiding them in the tools of the policy analysts' trade. Instrumentalism cannot completely bypass value choices. Instead it makes those choices silently, in its decisions about what to measure, how to specify models, and how to quantify outcomes (Rein 1976).

Second, instrumentalism has had mixed success on its own terms. Instrumentalism presupposes strong causal reasoning to demonstrate that specific variables lead to particular normatively desirable outcomes. Social science has had very little success establishing that type of relationship. Most evaluative studies simply do not reveal any strong and unambiguous effects and outcomes. The literature is littered with only modest effects, with most of the variance in the dependent variable usually

* I want to extend special thanks to David Thacher and Chris Winship for our discussions about the issues raised in this chapter. Nancy Borofsky and Bob Goodin were especially helpful during the final stages.

remaining unexplained (Rein and Winship 2000). In the meantime, the values themselves, as well as conflicts among them, usually remain unexplored.[1]

I begin by exploring various different types of situations that threaten instrumental means–end rationality. Starting with two of the most familiar—namely, the conflict of values and the ambiguity of ends—I then proceed to extend the list and consider other dynamics that are less well known. The problematic ends thus revealed are not free standing but rather, are interdependent and mutually reinforcing. I end by surveying various ways of socially coping with these problematic ends, concluding with an extended discussion of "secondary reframing" as a way of avoiding problematic ends and unwanted clients. Choice is always choice under some description: institutions frame policy problems and choices in that way; and reframing, looking at the problem through a different frame, can shift how we perceive the policy problem and how we respond to it.[2]

# 1. PROBLEMATIC ENDS: SIX EXAMPLES

## 1.1 Conflicting Aims

What does the term "values" mean in practice? "Values" are the ultimate ends of public policy—the goals and obligations that public policy aims to promote as desirable in their own right, rather than as some clear means to some other specific objective. Goals like safety, equality, prosperity, freedom and self-governance, family autonomy (to name a few) can all have this character. Each of these ends can be its own justification, at least to some people at some times.

For example, at some level most of us believe in some form of equality. We cling to it as an ideal, even if only modest instrumental benefits can be claimed for it, or even if these benefits turn out to be an illusion. As Isaiah Berlin (1981, 102) puts it, "Equality is one of the oldest and deepest elements in liberal thought ... Like all

---

[1] Consider racial integration. *Brown v. the Board of Education* was based on the evidence suggesting that segregated schools "damage the personality of minority group children" and "decrease their motivation and thus impair their ability to learn." This established the instrumental case for the desegregation of schools. But thirty years later, experience and further research showed that the benefits were minor and the community opposition among both black and white parents strong. The instrumental argument crowded out the case for desegregation on the grounds it was an important societal value, the right thing to do in a democracy. Most important, it obscured the opposition of the affected groups, who (leaving the less noble values that motivated their opposition aside) did not believe that either goal—desegregation as an end in itself, or the improvement of education for minority children—should outweigh neighborhood autonomy and cohesion (Rein and Winship 2000, 44).

[2] On this see Schön and Rein 1994 and cognate work across a range of disciplines, e.g. March 1972; Axelrod 1976; Sen 1980; Douglas 1986; Kahneman and Tversky 2000; Allison and Zelikow 1999.

human ends it cannot itself be defended or justified, for it is itself that justifies other acts [as] means taken towards its realization."

Of course, the value of equality still needs specification if it is to serve as a guide for action through public policy. For example, equality has been broadly interpreted as "equal opportunity" rather than "equal outcomes." But even on this interpretation, equality conflicts with other values such as "family autonomy." After all, parents want to give their children an *un*equal opportunity of access to resources, in order that they will be in a better position to compete and to do well in the labor market. The value of equal opportunity is in conflict with the autonomy of the family to protect and to advance their children's career in whatever way they can (Fishkin 1983; Swift 2003).

Another example is the conflict between participation and deliberation, seen in the American attempt, four decades ago, to promote the participation of the poor as a way to reduce poverty. Community Action programs were designed to reduce the apathy of the poor by encouraging participation that challenged the performance of local public institutions. Here, the conflict soon became visible and the program to promote participation dramatically changed. In the *Dilemmas of Social Reform*, Marris and Rein (1982, 1) tersely state the problem as follows: "A reformer in America faces three crucial tasks. He must recruit a coalition of power sufficient for his power; he must respect the democratic tradition which expects every citizen, not merely to be represented, but to play an autonomous part in the determination of his own affairs; his policies must be demonstrably rational." The imperatives for power, participation, and rationality all conflict with each other, in practice.

Participation has evolved over time from an action-oriented concept to a more passive mode. Confrontation, viewed as building power in order to confront inept bureaucrats, has faded as a meaningful public approach to promote participation. Modern-day advocacy takes the different form of collaboration (coalition building, partnerships, building trust, citizen juries); but through this evolution of the meaning of the term, the idea of some form of citizen participation is now widely accepted. Hence, the conflict was mitigated by sanitizing the form of participation and thus, hopefully, reducing the potential conflict between participation and deliberation.

## 1.2 Ambiguity and Vagueness

Ambiguity is so widespread in the legislative and administrative process that a large body of literature on the subject has emerged (March and Olsen 1976; Goodin 1982, ch. 4). Even the courts sometimes make use of it to reach a decision (Sunstein 1996; White 2002).

But we still seem to be undecided about the virtues of ambiguity in political and legal decision making. The former head of the French government is widely credited with the skeptical comment, "if we extricate ourselves out of ambiguity we do so at our own cost." Thus there is a mixed message in the literature: in some situations clarity can be costly and the only pragmatic course to follow is by the use of ambiguity, viewed as a strong precondition to achieve some measure in building a political coalition to promote collective action.

More than the vagueness of ends and means can be found in the academic public policy literature. There is also an interesting use of ambiguous concepts and theories. Some examples are the use of ideas like "sustainability," the "informal sector," and "organizational learning." These concepts are hard to define but nevertheless can be useful in both mobilizing action and charting a course for research and enquiry. The world of action and research are linked, because once a vague concept is accepted in the field of practice, and resources become available, then the academic community becomes involved in the evaluation of outcomes and in the design of future policy.

## 1.3 Abstract Ends

Maybe the classic statement can be found in the writing of Selznick (1957), who says: "Means tyrannize when the commitments they build up divert us from our true objectives. Ends are impotent when they are so abstract and unspecified that they offer no principles of criticism and assessment."

## 1.4 Unwanted Precarious Ends

"Unwanted ends" are ones that are imposed on an organization, requiring that the organization pursue goals that extend beyond the original mandate of the organization. They create an organizational "triple bottom line:" maintaining fiscal solvency; realizing the primary mission; and dealing with the imposed and unwanted mission, which they are obliged to follow, since some regulatory oversight is imposed by an outside agency. These new and imposed values become what Selznick (1965, 126) called " 'precarious values', defined as values that are not well integrated into the agency's core mission." It is precisely this loose coupling with the primary mission of the organization that makes those ends "precarious."

David Miller (2001) formulates the problem in more normative terms, as a conflict about "distributive responsibility." This frames the problem at an earlier stage. There can be broad agreement that we should collectively intervene in this situation, but what is unresolved is the distribution of responsibility for that intervention. Who is responsible for covering the financial and organizational costs of the decision to actually do something? We can agree to name a problem as a "humanitarian crisis;" we can collectively agree that the genocide must be stopped. But we can't agree at what cost, to be incurred by whom. We seem willing only to define the problem, not to agree on a principle distributing responsibility for action. Many social welfare problems also take this form.

There are, of course, many other examples of posing issues of how to distribute responsibility. Consider the situation where the government cuts back on the funding of non-profit organizations and these organizations, over time, find that they increasingly lack the necessary funding to carry out their missions. They are then forced to seek other resources if they are to survive. Some turn to the market as a source of income; others seek to pass on the cost to the consumer if the form of co-payment. Weisbrod (1998) offers a telling analysis of the dilemmas of practice that emerge when public policy shifts its distribution of responsibility, by focusing on how non-profit organizations deal with their double bottom line of promoting financial stability and commitment to their mission.

This situation could provide an entrée for government to impose values on the reluctant non-profit agencies. For example, local government might insist that non-profit agencies accept a large portion of the poor welfare mothers or the homeless or prisoners released from incarceration in their caseload. That can then create a Selznick-type problem of "precarious values," depending on how the situation is resolved. Who has the responsibility of caring for prisoners released from incarceration and unable to find their footing in their local community? Organizations eager to maintain clear and simple goals have developed strategies of restructuring to deal with these unwanted, and often alien, imposed ends.

Thacher (2004) ponders one of the serious dilemmas of a strategy of imposing punishment when the law is broken: what if no institutions will take the responsibility for what happens after the sentence is fulfilled? The graduates of these programs, with no place to go, then create a new category of "institutional orphans," who are unwanted clients. Those caught between the punishment and rehabilitation system are often simply ignored, responsibility for them being distributed to no one who effectively accepts it.

## 1.5  Unattainable Objectives

The child welfare system provides a good example of the pursuit of desirable but unattainable ends. The desirable end is for children to live in "normal" families, defined as ones who accept broad social norms of child rearing. Efforts are made to realize this goal by removing neglected and abused children into alternative care, such as foster care or sometimes adoption.

The experience shows that many of these children in care do not in fact return to their original families. The child welfare system of foster care and adoption has not developed effective means to create a substitute living arrangement for these children. Many of these children spend large parts of their lives moving from one foster home to another, or from adoptions back to foster care. We seem not to be able to return these children to "normalized" living arrangements (Steiner 1981). So normalization is perhaps not an attainable objective, in child welfare organizations that pursue their mission with insufficient resources and periodic shifts in direction.

These children eventually come of age and leave foster care to be absorbed, as best they can, into the community. A recent study of youth aging out of foster care shows that "overall 19% of the study group experienced a stay on Shelters" and the numbers are higher for some subgroups depending on race and gender (Youth Aging Out of Foster Care 2002). The adjustment of many of these children to the community is clearly wanting. But this does not mean that public policy can give up on the self-evident objective of rehabilitation or normalization of these children.

We do not have a viable alternative. Placing unwanted children in institutions seems not to be the way to go forward. The cost of building and maintaining such institutions is alarmingly high and there is no evidence that is a very effective way to go. One can read accounts that date back 100 years to see that we have not made much progress (Rothman 1971; Crenson 1998). Hence we call this a "problematic end," since we have not devised a way to attain that end (a system of normalization) for a substantial portion of this group.

## 1.6 Missing Ends

An interesting example of "missing ends" is found in an essay by Russell Baker (2004). Here in brief is the argument. Since the end of the cold war, Washington has been suffering from "the sense of pointlessness." "Government is about raising money to get elected and then reelected to service those that put up the money," but it is unclear what form that service should now take. To deal with this problem Washington has invented something called "spinning" which the press converts into what is "spun" by cunning spin doctors who create urgent problems they can then solve.

There are of course other examples in the political science literature on symbolic politics. There, action is taken for show, with little commitment to act on these symbolic intensions. Edelman's work on *The Symbolic Uses of Politics* (1964; see also Edelman 2001) is an early example of this political form.

# 2. INSTITUTIONAL STRUGGLES TO DEAL WITH PROBLEMATIC ENDS

One might think that the best way to deal with these troublesome "problematic ends" is, at the conceptual level, to clarify the fuzzy ideas. If the ends are confusing, contradictory, and conflicting, then the starting point must surely be first to clarify the muddle and substitute clear, disciplined thinking. What is needed is an intellectual search for more coherent policies that seeks to redefine the goals being sought. Henry Richardson's (1997) writing on practical reasoning develops a compelling argument to support the case for coherence.

We consider next some illustrative examples of an institutional approach to coping with the problematic ends discussed above. The central idea is to approach problematic ends as a puzzle that demands finding a plausible and coherent solution (Winship, this volume). It is a "practice worry"[3] where the main focus is on the question of action, "What is to be done?" This does not rule out clarification of ends, but it extends the search for coherence and clarity to consider practical and programmatic redesigns of existing practice.

The best way to illustrate this intuition is to provide several concrete examples of these pragmatic institutional approaches. Each is briefly discussed to illustrate different approaches that we find in practice.

Gibson and Goodin (1999) view ambiguity as an ally in policy development. They call their approach "the veil of vagueness," in contrast to Rawls's famous "veil of ignorance." Rawls's idea is that if individual players did not know crucial facts about their identity and place in society, they could devise through a deliberative process a set of fundamental principles of justice as fairness. But real-world political actors cannot do this. The authors propose an alternative model, a "veil of vagueness," which can work in two different ways: the "vagueness of ends" and the "vagueness of means" respectively. First, vagueness can cloak the nature of the agreement: ambiguity or abstraction can facilitate agreement getting; practitioners who disagree at some level can often agree at some higher level of abstraction about what should be done; in broad, vague terms, most members of society can agree what is in the "public interest." Second, vagueness can be used to mask the subsequent steps in the process by which a final agreement will eventually be reached.

Joshua Cohen (1996, 2004) proposes a second, very different approach to the puzzle of how problematic ends can be dealt with in practice. He makes a forceful argument that the values of "deliberation" and "participation," the two foundational pillars on which of theory of democracy rests, not only can in practice pull in different directions; furthermore, improving the quality of participation may come at the cost of public deliberation. In brief, the theory of democracy rests on two potentially conflicting imperatives. Cohen believes that there is no intellectual way to resolve these deep value conflicts by climbing the ladder of abstraction in search of resolution at an abstract level of reasoning. It is an illusion to believe that more thought and deeper conceptual clarification of the sources of the conflict can resolve the conflict. A solution can only be realized through an institutional or a procedural approach. What is called for is "practice experimentation," an idea in the spirit of what Dewey calls "inquiry and institutional innovation." What is needed is thought combined with action, and a willingness to consider doing something different and non-conventional.

---

[3] For an elaboration of this concept, see Rein 1983.

Popular devices such as referenda certainly encourage direct citizen participation. But at the same time, "requiring a yes/no vote may discourage reasoned discourse in legislation." A good example of how the referendum can be disruptive is the experience of a small country like Switzerland. A small but determined group can undo a legislative initiative that has been the result of a long deliberative process (Neidhart 1970). Something like this occurred in pension policy that eventually led to mandating private pensions rather than increasing the value of pensions in the public sector. This might in the end prove to be a judicious outcome, but the process was created by a referendum designed to block legislative intent.[4]

A theory of practical reasoning must always involve the combination of thought in action and enquiry into the process and the outcomes of this enquiry. This is in fact what we actually do in practice. Consider the third example of, and the institutional approach to, how to deal with value conflicts. Thacher and Rein (2004) identify three practical strategies that societies have used for concretely dealing with them:

1. *casuistry*, which involves seeing how similar conflicts are actually dealt with and resolved in practice;
2. *cycling*, which emphasizes first one value and then another; and
3. the art of *separation* (Walzer 1983, 1984), which assigns responsibilities for each value to different institutional structures.

The principle of casuistry is common practice among legal scholars. Following this approach they ask, "what is this a case of?" They then rely upon the repertoire of case law to see how the case was handled in past practice, letting earlier decisions provide a guide for what to do in the present, on the assumption that the two cases are similar in important ways. The drawback to this approach is that in most fields of public policy no such written record exists and the repertoire of experience is only available in the lived experience of the practitioners, who often cannot fully articulate what the intuition is that guides their action (Neustadt and May 1986; Thacher and Rein 2004; Searle 2001). Cycling and separation can also fail to provide a complete solution. But they do illustrate how, in the real world, institutions cope with value conflict.

Another example of how the legal system makes use of ambiguity in its decisions involves the Environmental Protection Agency (EPA) mandate to implement the Clean Air Act. In *Whitman v. American Trucking Association* (1999), the US Supreme Court decided unanimously that the non-delegation doctrine (Alexander and Prakash 2003) was satisfied so long as the EPA had provided an "intelligible principle" governing the writing of administrative guidelines; there was no danger of passing undue vagueness on to other agencies of government (White 2002).

Another approach to dealing with problematic ends builds on the intuition (Winship, this volume) that the precondition for dealing with disagreements must also be

---

[4] This is of course a one-dimensional account of the effects of referrenda: some can stimulate a national conversation, such as that over the monarchy/republic in Australia, or the series of referenda that eventually radically changed Irish abortion law.

based on a widely shared agreement as to what are the choices over which we might be disagreeing. Institutionally, the key to acting on this insight is a pre-negotiation stage that creates a template about the naming and framing of what is to be addressed and what is to be ignored in an actual negotiation. The institutional solution is the invention of an "art of convening" that generates a way to map the terrain of what is discussable and non-discussable in the later stage of direct negotiations (Raiffa, Richardson, and Metcalfe 2003).

One can hire an outsider, a trusted person to map actionable terrain. The aim is not to reach a philosophical clarification of what is at issue but rather to define a practical way to deal with this specific situation. It is a case of "learning by monitoring:" "an institutional device for churning, amidst the flux of economic life, the pragmatic trick of simultaneously defining a collective-action problem and a collective actor with a natural interest in solving it" (Sabel 1994, 272).

# 3. Secondary Reframing: The Case of Offloading Unwanted Clients

While some institutional approaches try to adapt a practical way to cope with the problematic ends that they confront in their practice, other institutions act in ways that exacerbate them. The strategies of offloading and secondary reframing that I review next are not really new, but are much older ideas that can be recognized under different names.[5]

The basic intuition is illustrated by the following example. Suppose a government does not wish to make the level of its unemployment of older workers politically visible, as a problem of "people without jobs sufficient to provide an adequate income to live on." It may try to mask or hide the phenomenon by "renaming" it, and by giving it a somewhat different name shifting the problem a different institutional spheres. I call this the "transfer" from one policy domain to another. One well-known way of dealing with the problem of older workers is to pass it on to another institutional domain as a problem, not of the weakness of the labor market, but of "disability" or where the institutional rules permit, as a problem of "ageing" and "retirement" (Kohli et al. 1991). In Germany the formal retirement age is sixty-five, but the average age of actual entry in the Old Age Pension System was around age fifty-five (Schön and Rein 1994, ch. 4). In the Netherlands, where the pension system had rigid rules of entry by age, in practice flexibility was established by using the disability system as the port of entry into retirement for those below the age of

---

[5] On framing and reframing more generally, see Schön and Rein 1994.

sixty-five, No one seriously believes that a healthy and affluent country of 15 million people also has a population close to one million disabled persons, even though that is the number receiving public and private disability benefits.

This attempt to reframe the mission of a policy domain occurs not only at the national level but also at the local level, where a different dynamic of "offloading" is visible. Consider next the flow across domains of "security" and "services" in the case of prison incarceration, mental illness, or homelessness. In the United States and other advanced industrial societies, we find that the local jail is the largest manager of care for the mentally ill.[6] No one seriously believes that the best way to deal with the mentally ill is to place them in local jails or prisons. Instead, it is an institutional process of "secondary reframing" that leads to such problematic ends.

Some providers of homeless shelters anecdotally report that the proportion of formerly incarcerated people in shelters is as high as 70 per cent. Furthermore, a national survey shows that—judging from the fact that it is now increasingly "people leaving state prisons, as opposed to city jails, who are entering the shelter system"— "the bouts of correctional involvement are no longer the result of vagrancy or the benevolent sheltering function of local jails" (Cho 2004, 1–2). Cho's diagnosis is that this institutional failure derives from "the growing fragmentation of government . . . stemming from isolated policy making." He goes on to argue that homeless shelter is a default category, the last residual institution that manages to provide some care and service when the others have turned away.[7]

The conventional approaches for coping with these problems usually consist of three main ideas: more resources are needed; less organizational fragmentation is needed; or more coordination is needed. Resource scarcity suggests that the problem derives from a passive process that no one intended and no one wanted, but no one noticed or was capable of altering. But this type of reframing can also be a byproduct of an intended process of the administrative classification of individuals based on the "primary cause" of their condition. In other words, secondary reframing can be partly created by a process of categorization (Douglas 1986, ch. 8).

Here I want to stress three less well-known interpretations of the mechanisms in play (Rein 2000):

1. Professional and institutional "creaming."
2. The institutional dynamics of "offloading."
3. A professional commitment to "ideals," in which the commitment to "do good" is not balanced with an equally strong commitment to responsibility in a way that requires a realistic assessment of what is doable (Weber 1919).

---

[6] "There are now far more mentally ill in the nation's jails and prisons (200,000) than in the state hospitals (61,700). With 3,000 mentally ill inmates, Riker's Island in New York has, in effect, become the state's largest psychiatric facility" (Winship, this volume).

[7] His paper explores three strategies for dealing with the default: "frame reflection, transformative learning and boundary spanning," categories that he developed from the literature on collaborative learning and policy making, and from his engagement in a program in New York designed to cope with the problem.

## 3.1 Creaming

"Creaming" is a mechanism whose importance has long been recognized in the administration of professional programs in many domains. Creaming involves both a passive process of drift through indifference and an active process where professionals "pass over" or reject unwanted clients, either at the initial point of contact or intake or some time after some service has begun through a process known as "information and referral." In this process of "creaming," one could identify specific actions of agents that make the phenomenon happen, namely, the passing on clients that they cannot or do not want to handle "on their watch." There is an impressive body of literature which identifies "creaming" as one of the most important keys to understanding how, perversely, those most in need are not served by a program that takes that objective as its main mission.

In one of the earliest sociological studies of creaming, "Creaming the poor," Miller, Roby, and Steenwijh (1970) focus on the dynamics of organizational exclusion, and how it came about organizationally and became normal professional practice. Miller and his colleagues studied a French religious organization called in the 1960s "Aide à Toute Détresse' ("Help for All in Need"); under its new name, the "Fourth World Movement," the organization is still alive and active today with a worldwide agenda. I recently discovered another service organization with a similar mission.

The Alliance for the Mentally Ill is an advocacy group in Boston formed by the families of the mentally ill, whose goal is to challenge the "resource scarcity" view of drift. This is a group of parents who had family members with severe mental illness and which is committed to an alternative, non-creaming agenda. They argued that professional mental health practice is organized to serve the "worried well." The Alliance sponsors propose an alternative frame: mental illness is a brain disease; the condition requires treatment by drugs and not conventional therapy; and the mentally ill require lifelong chronic care, even though the severity of the condition fluctuates periodically. The Alliance strongly objects to the priority allocation of resources to the "worried well," and aspires to become an important political force pressing the mental health community to reform present practice, committing itself to the care of the severely mental ill and eschewing the current professional practice of creaming. The Alliance has had some success in creating "continuity of care" by creating therapeutic teams (consisting of members of several professional groups including nurses, social workers, rehabilitation counselors, and so on), with the same team being available, in principle, to the severely mentally ill for their lifetime.

## 3.2 Offloading

In this section I want to call attention to "offloading," and its two different types, "diversion" and "shedding," without an explicit organizational commitment to redefine who it services. "Diversion" is illustrated by the professional movement to promote diversion in the criminal justice domain. This example illustrates an active, self-reflective dimension of getting other domains to help in solving a "practice problem." That is in contrast to the other common form of "shedding," or aggressively offloading, which is an only partially visible policy that operates in the twilight, without discussion or debate.

The mechanism of diversion can be seen as an opposite one to that involved in the earlier example of prisons as temporary guardians of the mentally ill. The strategy of diversion involves an explicit decision to divert clients away from the criminal justice system into or back to the mental health system. This is an instance of an intentional rather than passive policy of dealing with clients that overlap both the health and security domains. The difference between offloading and diversion may be difficult to distinguish in the complicated world of practice, with its demands for a quick decision.

Police are almost always accused of excessive use of authority in carrying out their law-enforcement mandate. This antagonism can create community backlash, with the public charge of "police harassment" taking on strong racial overtones. When this occurs in minority communities with a predominately white police force, the charge of harassment can undermine the legitimacy of the police. The police then have a strong incentive to reduce the tension by passing on responsibility and authority to non-police domains.

There is a fundamental, and to a degree inescapable conflict between strategies designed to cut street crime (saturation patrols, close surveillance) and those designed to minimize tensions (avoid "street stops," reduce surveillance, ignore youth groups). Ultimately, the best way to minimize tensions is to find non-police methods for reducing street crime. To the extent that better economic opportunities, speedier court dispositions, more effective sentencing decisions, and improved correctional methods can reduce street crime, the burdens on the police and the tensions between police and citizen can be greatly reduced.[8]

The basic idea is that the domains overlap and are linked in ways that require a broader policy focus, not on the autonomy of a single domain to realize its unique mission, but on the interdependencies and linkage across domains. Accordingly, only some diversion strategies might be an appropriate forum to address problems of professional practice in the criminal justice domain.

While it is difficult to see the general case for actively managing mental illness in prisons and homeless shelters, the case can certainly be made in specific situations. Consider where two very different labels can be aptly applied to describe the same condition. A phenomenon need not be either A or B; it can be, or it can represent the so-called "missing middle" by being both A and B. The behavior of a mentally ill person, in a specific situation, may both signal a deep mental disorder and express itself in law-violating behavior.

The practical question becomes: what is the appropriate strategy for dealing with this person, at this specific time, and in this situation? This way of viewing the

---

[8] This is a restatement of the writing of James Q. Wilson (1972, 139).

process of is as "redefining the case," not as one of offloading or diversion. It is as a more practical matter of "reclassification," based on professional discretion. That does not need to presume that there exists a deliberative forum for a practitioner to make a reflective decision about which is the more appropriate classification and hence which is the more appropriate course of action to follow. Such a system can also be regulated, if there are standards that could be applied in this situation, which has in the legal context been dubbed an "intelligibility principle."

## 3.3 Idealization

There is a subtle tension between an idealized commitment to goals of "doing good" and an idealized goal of "being responsible." The commitment to the good can have the unintended effect of initiating a dialectic that resulted in its opposite, the creation of "evil." Max Weber creatively transformed this dialectic into an important insight about policy and practice, when he articulated a very useful distinction between the ethics of conviction and the ethics of responsibility in his famous essay on "Politics as a vocation" (1919).[9] The ethics of conviction insists that it is our duty to do certain things that we believe are the right things to do, regardless of whether these right actions actually have the effect of producing good results. "Here I stand, I can do no other." The crucial point is that one must do the right thing regardless of its consequences. The ethic of responsibility contrasts sharply; it insists that "it is irresponsible to settle on what one ought to do apart from what others are likely to do as a result .... so this ethic is equivalent to consequentialism." Weber thus argued that doing right things can actually lead to intentional or non-intentional evil, at some later stage in the process.

The challenge then is how to strike a balance between these two ethics. We need to know how to make moral judgements about choice or balance in concrete situations, so that it can actually lead to something constructive. After all, the concrete judgements might be based on the overselling of the idealized vision, or the failure to enquire about the internal contradictions of the two idealized norms, or the inability to take seriously and to reflect on current actual practice and to learn from practice the history of past failures.

Many mental health workers practice within the context of institutional policies that give prominence to their role in the social control of the behavior of the poor (such as protecting public housing from irresponsible tenants who damage property (e.g. continuously clogging toilets), protecting the integrity of the rationing system that is designed to develop queues so as to allocate scarce housing to families that are in greatest need, and discouraging practices like social workers advising their clients to enter a haveless shelter with their children in order to jump the queue). However, in their own view, their everyday practice of mental health can occur in a policy

---

[9] This interpretation draws freely on the discussion in Larmore (1987, 144–50).

environment that can be antagonistic to their idealized, preferred practice. Not infrequently their practice is guided by the idealized logic of a mental health frame that enjoins them to "help" their clients get what they need, based on need and without attention to actual constraints. This definition of their mission sets the stage for an idealized practice that fails to recognize the conflict between the ethics of commitment and of responsibility.

# 4. CONCLUSION

Thus, at least three quite different mechanisms might plausibly account for secondary reframing, leading one domain to take on the functions of another. These are, of course, not necessarily alternative interpretations, and the relative importance of each varies depending on the specific domain under consideration.

- The first and most conventional interpretation is that of resource scarcity: drift across domains occurs because the domain lacks the personnel and the material resources to provide the appropriate service within the domain. Since these are largely public programs, the main causal agent becomes the failure of government to allocate the needed resources.
- Secondly, "creaming" occurs when professionals keep the clients they want, especially those that can be most successfully helped, and the unwanted population drifts or is actually pushed into other domains.
- A third mechanism arises from an active process of offloading. The simple case is when behavior poses multiple and overlapping problems, and "naming" the appropriate category requires professional judgement. But there are other cases where "secondary renaming" originates from positive motives, as in the case of diversion programs designed to separate the system to promote security (like courts and prisons) and the system designed to promote mental health. In general, the commitment to prevention is an example of an active design, believed to offer the best chance of reducing a specific problem by moving to a different domain than that of the presenting problem.[10]
- The fourth and perhaps least understood mechanism is that of an idealized practice which neglects to balance the practical consequences of an "ethics of

---

[10] Delinquency prevention offers an example, where a federal anti-delinquency program assumed that apathy and blocked opportunity caused crime. This program allocated Community Action funds to local communities to empower the poor, to overcome apathy, and to create new programs that provided employment and training opportunities as a way of overcoming blocked opportunity. But the responsible outcome can be different from the idealized desire "to do good" and "to help."

conviction" with an "ethic of responsibility." This occurs, for example, where the risks of offloading are widely understood but seldom acknowledged in the vocabulary of professional practice.

The challenge we now face is how to reduce secondary reframing and the problems it creates by permitting creaming, offloading, and idealization. The problem of idealization may be more ellusive, because we do not yet have any deep understanding of the underlying dynamics at play. But regulatory agencies with oversight responsibility for social policy might be able to take first steps to deal with creaming and offloading by formulating some "intelligible principles" to guide the conduct of those to whom they delegate tasks of service delivery. This chapter is a preliminary attempt to lay the intellectual framework. What is now needed is a detailed, well-documented study of practice, which offers concrete examples of how all these processes are actually played out in everyday practice in the administration of social and other public services.

# REFERENCES

ALEXANDER, L., and PRAKASH, S. 2003. Reports of the non-delegation doctrine's death are greatly exaggerated. *University of Chicago Law Review*, 70: 1297–329; available at: http://papers.ssrn.com/sol3/papers.cfm?abstract_id=449020 (accessed 10 Dec. 2004).

ALLISON, G. T., and ZELIKOW, P. 1999. *The Essence of Decision*, 2nd edn. Reading, Mass.: Longman.

AXELROD, R. 1976. *Structure of Decision: The Cognitive Maps of Political Elites.* Princeton, NJ: Princeton University Press.

BAKER, R. 2004. In Bush's Washington. *New York Review of Books*, 18 (8: 13 May).

BERLIN, I. 1981. *Concepts and Categories.* London: Penguin.

CHO, R. 2004. Putting the pieces back together: overcoming fragmentation to prevent post-incarceration homelessness. Working paper, Corporation for Supportive Housing; available at: www.csh.org/index.cfm?fuseaction=Page.viewPage&pageId=641&nodeID=81 (accessed 10 Dec. 2004).

COHEN, J. 1996. Procedure and substance in deliberative democracy. Pp. 95–119 in *Democracy and Difference*, ed. S. Benhabib. Princeton, NJ: Princeton University Press.

—— 2004. Participation and deliberation. Available at: http://lawweb.usc.edu/cslp/conferences/democracy_workshops/cohen.pdf.

CRENSON, M. A. 1998. *Building the Invisible Orphanage: A Prehistory of the American Welfare System.* Cambridge, Mass.: Harvard University Press.

DOUGLAS, M. 1986. *How Institutions Think.* Syracuse, NY: Syracuse University Press.

EDELMAN, M. 1964. *The Symbolic Uses of Politics.* Urbana: University of Illinois Press.

—— 2001. *The Politics of Misinformation.* Cambridge: Cambridge University Press.

FISHKIN, J. S. 1983. *Justice, Equal Opportunity and the Family.* New Haven, Conn.: Yale University Press.

GIBSON, D., and GOODIN, R. E. 1999. The veil of vagueness: a model of institutional design. Pp. 357–85 in *Organizing Political Institutions*, ed. M. Egeberg and P. Lægreid. Oslo: Scandinavian University Press.

GOODIN, R. E. 1982. *Political Theory & Public Policy.* Chicago: University of Chicago Press.

KAHNEMAN, D., and TVERSKY, A. (eds.) 2000. *Choices, Values and Frames.* Cambridge: Cambridge University Press.

KOHLI, M., REIN, M., GUILLEMARD, A. M., and VAN GUNSTEREN, H. (eds.) 1991. *Time for Retirement: Comparative Studies of Early Exit from the Labor Force.* Cambridge: Cambridge University Press.

LARMORE, C. E. 1987. *Patterns of Moral Complexity.* Cambridge: Cambridge University Press.

MARCH, J. G. 1972. Model bias in social action. *Review of Educational Research,* 42: 413–29.

—— and OLSEN, J. P. 1976. *Ambiguity and Choice in Organizations.* Bergen: Universitetsforlaget.

MARRIS, P., and REIN, M. 1982. *Dilemmas of Social Reform: Poverty and Community Action in the United States,* 2nd edn. Chicago: University of Chicago Press.

MILLER, D. 2001. Distributing responsibilities. *Journal of Political Philosophy,* 9: 452–70.

MILLER, S. M., ROBY, P., and STEENWIJH, A. A. V. 1970. Creaming the poor: help to the worse off. *Trans-Action,* 7 (8: June).

NEIDHART, L. 1970. *Direkte Demokratie: Ein Vergleich der Einrichtungen und Verfahren in der Schweiz und Kalifornien, unter Berücksichtigung von Frankreich, Italien, Dänemark, Irland, Österreich und Australia.* Bern: Haupt.

NEUSTADT, R. E., and MAY, E. R. 1986. *Thinking in Time.* New York: Free Press.

RAIFFA, H., RICHARDSON, J., and METCALFE, D. 2003. *Negotiation Analysis: The Science and Art of Collaborative Decision-Making.* Cambridge, Mass.: Harvard University Press.

REIN, M. 1976. *Social Science and Public Policy.* Harmondsworth: Penguin.

—— 1983. *From Policy to Practice.* London: Macmillan.

—— 2000. Primary and secondary reframing. *Cybernetics and Human Knowing,* 7(2–3): 89–103.

—— and WINSHIP, C. 2000. The dangers of strong causal reasoning. Pp. 26–54 in *Experiencing Poverty,* ed. J. Bradshaw and R. Sainsbury. Aldershot: Ashgate.

RICHARDSON, H. S. 1997. *Practical Reasoning about Final Ends.* Cambridge: Cambridge University Press.

ROTHMAN, D. 1971. *The Discovery of the Asylum: Social Order and Disorder in the New Republic.* Boston: Little, Brown.

SABEL, C. 1994. Learning by monitoring: the institutions of economic development. Pp. 137–65 in *The Handbook of Economic Sociology,* ed. N. J. Smelser and R. Swedberg. Princeton, NJ: Princeton University Press.

SCHÖN, D. A., and REIN, M. 1994. *Frame Reflection: Toward the Resolution of Intractable Policy Controversies.* New York: Basic Books.

SEARLE, J. R. 2001. *Rationality in Action.* Cambridge, Mass.: MIT Press.

SELZNICK, P. 1957. *Leadership in Administration.* Berkeley: University of California Press.

—— 1965. *TVA and the Grassroots,* 2nd edn. Berkeley: University of California Press.

SEN, A. 1980. Description as choice. *Oxford Economic Papers,* 32: 353–69.

STEINER, G. Y. 1981. *The Futility of Family Policy.* Washington, DC: Brookings Institution.

SUNSTEIN, C. R. 1996. Leaving things undecided. *Harvard Law Review,* 110: 4–101.

SWIFT, A. 2003. *How Not to be a Hypocrite.* London: Routledge.

THACHER, D. 2004. Prisoner reentry and the professionalization of housing. Paper presented at the American Society of Criminology, Nov.

—— and REIN, M. 2004. Managing value conflict in public policy. *Governance,* 17: 457–86.

WALZER, M. 1983. *Spheres of Justice.* Oxford: Martin Robertson.

—— 1984. Liberalism and the art of separation. *Political Theory,* 12: 415–30.

WEBER, M. 1919. Politics as a vocation. Pp. 77–128 in *From Max Weber*, ed. H. Gerth and C. W. Mills. New York: Oxford University Press, 1946.

WEISBROD, B. 1998. *To Profit or Not to Profit*. Cambridge: Cambridge University Press.

WHITE, D. J. 2002. The non-delegation doctrine revisited: *Whitman v. American Trucking Associations. University of Cincinnati Law Review*, 71: 359–82.

WILSON, J. Q. 1972. *The Police and the Community*. Baltimore: Johns Hopkins University Press.

YOUTH AGING OUT OF FOSTER CARE 2002. *Preventing Homelessness at an Early Stage: Summary*. New York: Youth Aging Out of Foster Care.

# PART V

## INSTRUMENTS
## OF POLICY

CHAPTER 19

....................................................................................................................

# POLICY IN PRACTICE

....................................................................................................................

DAVID LAWS

MAARTEN HAJER

THIS chapter is about practice, so we start with an example. A group of environmental regulators in the USA responding to "practice worries" (Rein 1983) recently tried to render their sense of competence. They contrast a zone of (relative) stability accounting for 20 per cent of problems and opportunities with a zone of uncertainty that accounts for the remaining 80 per cent. Loosely defined up-coming problems (climate change), remainders from established practice (noise, odor, non-point pollution), new claims (environmental justice), and competing frames (industrial ecology, natural capital, eco-metrics) together disrupt the stability of conventions and crowd them to the margins of attention. The tension between the known and unknown, the conventional and the chaotic, belief and doubt, is recognizable as a moment in practice, imbued with risk and opportunity. It has generated the unsettled effort to name and, thereby, tame doubt by remaking practice.

We could tell similar stories about the efforts of transportation and land use planners in the Netherlands or about public health officials in the UK. The actors' movements in these stories narrate a complex and unstable landscape. They must continuously try to make sense of changing conditions, to reinterpret the relationship between how they act and what they know, and to gain perspective on the improvisations they find themselves involved in. Stability is provisional, persistently marginalized by conflicts and uncertainties that have slipped through the conventions of politics and science.

By speaking of the efforts of these environmental regulators in terms of "practice worries," "stories," "doubt," and "coping" we have already begun to speak the language of policy practice that we develop in this chapter. We root our discussion in the study of public policy and then turn to three adjacent fields where the

observation of practice has pushed change. These developments deepen the distinctiveness and broaden the relevance of policy practice for policy analysis and the study
of public policy.

# 1. A PRACTICE TRADITION?

The initiative of the regulatory practitioners may be less surprising to students of
public policy than to other observers of governance. The activities of "street-level
bureaucrats" and other policy practitioners have long attracted and frustrated the
attention of policy analysts. Practitioners' efforts to make policy work evoke and
animate the distinctive moral and technical complexity of their policy domain and
the persistent uncertainty that attends action. They fix our gaze and elude our
grasp.

Much of the early attention to the efforts of social workers, lawyers, planners and
urban designers, regulators, teachers, and administrators came through studies of
implementation. Pressman and Wildavsky, for example, proposed to "begin at the
end" and focus "on that part of a public program following the initial setting of goals,
securing of agreement, and committing of funds" (Pressman and Wildavsky 1973).
Their initial account of the EDA's effort to promote economic development in
Oakland could not escape the constant intrusions of context and persistent need to
adapt that made "joint action" insuperably complex. The very notion of design failed
along the "tortured path" that Pressman and Wildavsky traced in a narrative of
inversion in which "great expectations are dashed" and the only refuge is
"amaz[ement that] anything works at all."

The chaos they found frustrated not only the designs of policy makers, but also
their own effort to theorize the experience in Oakland. Wildavsky addressed this
tension by revising the original account in four chapters appended to the second and
third editions. Expanding "the task of evaluation beyond the mere measurement of
outcomes to their causes" preserved the priority of analysis as that which "provides
the intelligence to make sense out of what is happening" (1973, xv).[1] The terms of the
new account—evolution, learning, and exploration—suggest a different view. They
render implementation as a context-rich domain in which action implies adaptation
and learning in an encounter with the unknown. In this domain "baseline goals are
often resculpted at the very scene of implementation," the implementer becomes "a
source of new information," and "a case can be made for the reconceptualization of

---

[1] Pressman and Wildavsky treat implementation and evaluation as "two sides of the same coin,
implementation providing the experience that evaluation interrogates and evaluation providing the
experience to make sense of what is happening" (1973, xv).

implementation as an exploratory rather than an unquestioning, instrumental, and even subservient type of process" (1973, 256).

Lipsky was more direct (Lipsky 1980). He argued that "the decisions of street-level bureaucrats, the routines they establish, and the devices they invent to cope with uncertainties and work pressures, effectively *become* the public policies they carry out" and that "public policy is not best understood as made in legislatures or top-floor suites of high-ranking administrators, because in important ways it is actually made in the crowded offices and daily encounters of street-level workers" (Lipsky 1980, xii; author's emphasis). He discarded the evaluative focus and tried to grasp why "organizations often perform contrary to their own rules and goals" by looking at "how the rules are experienced by workers in the organization and to what other pressures they are subject" (Lipsky 1980, xi).

Marris and Rein (1967) describe policy shaped by practitioners struggling to cope with moral dilemmas raised by their efforts to act on policy goals. Schön's reflective practitioners manage the relationship with the unknown by learning to value surprise as a source of insight and spark for development (Schön 1983). Stone describes policy in the interplay between "paradox" and "reason" (Stone 1997). Understanding practice demands acceptance of such tensions in order to find the intelligence at work in action.

The unity of practice in the face of these persistent tensions is derived from its character as "a way of acting and thinking at once" (Flyvbjerg 2001). One frequently used metaphor is the judgement the expert practitioner displays in coping with a fluid and complex world (Schön 1983; Roe 1998). Another is the limited capacity of actors to manage their own competence, which "naturalizes its own arbitrariness" and eludes reflection "like a fish in water" (Bourdieu 1977). Some accounts emphasize the "critical capacity" of "people who are doing things together ... who have to coordinate their actions, realize that something is going wrong; that they cannot get along any more; that something has to change" (Boltanski and Thévenot 1999), and other practitioners' ability for "moral improvisation," "learning about value," and "knowing the rules" (Forester 1999; Wagenaar 2004).

Wenger (1998) emphasizes the social character of human enterprise. It is interaction (as opposed to individual reflection) that generates learning: "As we define these enterprises and engage in their pursuit together, we interact with each other and with the world and we tune our relations with each other and with the world accordingly. In other words, we learn" (Wenger 1998). This "collective learning" draws together "the pursuit of our enterprises" with their "attendant social relations" (ibid.). Thus practices are defined and developed socially and should be understood as "the property of a kind of community created over time by the sustained pursuit of a shared enterprise" (Wenger 1998). It is this collective construction that "make[s] the job possible by inventing and maintaining ways of squaring institutional demands with the shifting reality of actual situations" (1998, 46).

Doing—the central thread of practice—is never "not just doing in and of itself," in Wenger's account but is always "doing in a historical and social context that gives structure and meaning to what we do" (1998, 47). These relationships, among actors and between doing and its context, "include ... both the explicit and the tacit." They include "what is said and what is left unsaid; what is represented and what is assumed. [They include] the language, tools, documents, images, symbols, well-defined roles, specified criteria, codified procedures, regulations, and contracts that various practices make explicit for a variety of purposes ... [and also] all the implicit relations, tacit conventions, subtle cues, untold rules of thumb, recognizable intuitions, specific perception, well-tuned sensitivities, embodied understandings, underlying assumptions, and shared world views" (Wenger 1998).

This notion of practice as a site of joint action and learning constituted around shared problems and a competence that resists reflection, provides the starting point for study. In the sections that follow we trace developments in three adjacent fields that account for (1) the fluid organizational arrangements, (2) the situated character of knowledge and variety of forms it takes, and (3) the democratic, even constitutional significance of the interactions among policy practitioners, citizens, private managers, and elected representatives that play out in the domain of practice.

## 2. Organizations and Institutions

In Lipsky's account of policy practice, one of the primary activities of street-level bureaucrats was to manage their relationship with organizational hierarchy. Because the organizations he studied were dependent on the judgement, creativity, and initiative of front-line practitioners to reconcile the categories and demands of policy with the resource limits, competing imperatives, and unruly cases that characterize the work environment in a public bureaucracy, the authority of hierarchy was incomplete and relationships were dynamic. The boundaries within which authority and control were negotiated were relatively stable, however. The implementation of policy in practice took place in the context of the stable container of the public bureaucracy and its relationship to its clients.

The stability of these relationships can no longer be assumed. The *site* and *scope* of policy practice has become part of what has to be explained and this lends new significance to the concept of policy practice (Hajer and Wagenaar 2003). The fluid interorganizational or "cross-boundary" character of policy making has attracted attention at least since Heclo (1978) described the "loose-jointed play of influence ... in political administration" and highlighted the "webs of influence [that] provoke and guide the exercise of power" (Heclo 1978). Attention to the role of actors from outside the formal state apparatus in policy work and to the open and fluid patterns of association that often characterize their participation is a persistent concern in the study of public policy today.

"Network" is the conceptual device used to capture the horizontal—as opposed to vertical-linkages that increasingly tie participants together in subsystems and policy communities (Rhodes 1997). No single actor, public or private, can have all the knowledge and information needed; no actor has sufficient overview to make the application of instruments effective; and no single actor has sufficient action potential to dominate a particular governing model. In this context governing and governance are interpreted in practice-compatible terms as dynamic, complex, and diverse. Society is not managed or controlled by a central intelligence; rather, controlling devices are dispersed and intelligence is distributed among a multiplicity of action units (Marin and Mayntz 1991).

Similar developments have attracted attention in efforts to explain economic behavior. The study of production practices regularly turns up patterns of association and collaboration that do not fit easily in the established organizational categories of hierarchy—embodied in the organizational structures of the firm—and market. Production in "craft industries" like construction, publishing, and film making, in successful regional economies, and even in core industries like automobile manufacturing seemed to many analysts, to operate on logic of production in which the key feature was coordination across organizational boundaries in "extensive collaborative subcontracting agreements" (Powell 1990).

In light of this accumulating evidence, it became more and more difficult to sustain the belief that "the bulk of economic exchange fits comfortably at either of the poles of the market–hierarchy continuum" or that the patterns of behavior observed in these cases could be explained as some hybrid of them (Powell 1990). The network metaphor provided a way to make sense of the observed patterns of mutual reliance across organizational boundaries in which economic exchange "entail[s] indefinite, sequential transactions within the context of a general pattern of interaction" (Powell 1990, 301). Networks provided a way to sustain (and explain) cooperation in settings where expectations were not stable, where the environment might fluctuate suddenly, where "know how" is important, and where adaptation to the changing demands of the market is a central attribute of success. Several characteristics differentiated networks from markets and organizational hierarchies:

- "Cooperation can be sustained over the long run as an effective arrangement;"
- "networks create incentives for learning and the dissemination of information, thus allowing ideas to be translated into action quickly;"
- "the open-ended quality of networks is most useful when resources are variable and the environment is uncertain;"
- "networks offer a highly feasible means of utilizing and enhancing such intangible assets as tacit knowledge and technological innovation" (Powell 1990, 322).

The "dominant" account of networks, in policy as well as economic behavior, focuses on "the way in which the network resolves certain problems of cooperative behavior among purposive rational actors seeking to maximize their individual economic well-being" (Piore 1992). This account provides valuable insights where sustained coordination of action is the central challenge and means–ends relationships are relatively stable, understood, and sufficient. Axelrod and Ostrom were among the first to clarify the implications of such patterns of cooperation for public policy (Axelrod 1984; Ostrom 1990). Over the last ten years the idea of organization by cooperation impacted on the policy literature at the cost of straightforward "command-and-control" and pure market-based mechanisms. Key in these new approaches is the realization that effective policy making nowadays requires cooperation *across* organizational boundaries (Rhodes 1997; Pierre and Peters 2000).

Cooperation across such boundaries involves interactions among actors from widely differing backgrounds, with markedly distinct value preferences. This extends the challenge of cooperation to include questions about how a shared base for exchange can be created and maintained. If formal organizations achieve cooperation through standard procedures and "rationalized myths" (Meyer and Rowan 1977) then how can policy makers provide the mutual confidence, stability, and functionality of interorganizational cooperative arrangements?

Expectations of reciprocity suddenly seem thin in the face of conflicts rooted in distinct histories and organizational identities that must continually be adapted to one another and to a volatile environment. They appear even thinner in circumstances of deep value difference, such as in multicultural settings, where policy making becomes a form of "joint governance" that must "recogniz[e] that some persons will belong to more than one political community, and will bear rights and obligations that derive from more than one source of legal authority" (Shachar 2001). Here networks raise the possibility that governance can be based in the development of *situated* organizational logics, shared experience, and joint deliberation in between the "standing" organizations. In the face of potentially incommensurable values and latent conflicts of interest, the search is for a "repertoire of techniques of accommodation" that allow for joint problem solving. This helps explains the renewed interest for specific "on-site" techniques for governing, be it the literature on negotiation, conflict resolution, or consensus building (Susskind et al. 1999). Each provides an account of how actors negotiate difference, cope with uncertainty, and otherwise make sense of the world as they act, that responds to the demands and logic of practice in a network.

Such discussions of networks deepen the account of cooperation and contribute to the burgeoning literature on trust (Misztal 1996; Warren 1999) that now seems essential to explain public policy making. Trust, in these accounts, is not embedded in constitutional rules of organizations, but must be won continuously in concrete policy making processes. Policy practitioners become institutional theorists who not only have to master the content of their field of action, but also have to be experts in process: able to develop, maintain, and operate the complex policy networks that are an indispensable part of their operational work.

Sabel ties cooperation to learning to provide a clear account of how repeated interaction in networks unites interpretative activity and efforts to further ends. The driving force in the "principles of decentralized coordination" that operate in the firm (understood as "a federation of work groups, a team of collaborators, or a policy community"), is a "joint exploration of collaborative possibilities" that is tied to joint evaluation of experience in a system that Sabel calls "learning by monitoring" (Sabel 1994). The ability of actors to initiate and sustain instrumental cooperation is tied to their commitment to figure out jointly how to make sense of changing experience and take advantage of the opportunities it provides. In the fluid world of decentralized production:

the rules of unbalanced growth transform ... a chain of exchanges ... into a continuous discussion of joint possibilities and goals, where the parties' historical relation defines their mutual expectations. Just as in a discussion, the parties suppose their understanding of their situation is limited. Therefore they jointly specify what they believe they understand so as to expose and begin exploring the limits of that understanding. Just as in a discussion, they must accept the possibility that their views of themselves, of the work, and the interests arising from both—their identities, in short—will be changed unexpectedly by those explorations. (Sabel 1994, 247–8)

The picture of firms having to turn this "pragmatic trick" again and again to sustain provisional stability in the persistently turbulent interorganizational fields in which they function raises strong, if surprising resonances with the position of staff in a regulatory or social service agency for whom the traditional bases for stability and security have lost their purchase. Like the managers and blue-collar workers terrified at continued competition, these policy practitioners may be pushed to face up to the daunting prospect of moving from an old pattern of organization to a new one.

For those willing to take the plunge, the details of cooperation in the new decentralized production arrangements bear as much counsel as the broad outlines. The self-governance of work groups and the ability to federate local units into broader production arrangements in which they reinvent themselves through sustained interaction suggest, as Sabel points out, a pragmatic strategy for problem solving, interpretation, and learning that has potential for organizational renewal that democrats would be wise try to understand in a period when the state is caught in such disarray. Sabel finds in the new pragmatism employed by these firms a social process that is not just about solving economic problems but one that has direct implications for democratic renewal (see below).

# 3. KNOWLEDGE

The relationship of policy practice to knowledge has become more complex and problematic since the time, not that long ago, when social scientists might meaningfully ask whether social science could "lift all but the most fundamental moral issues out of ideological debate" (Rein 1976).[2] Giving up on the belief that natural and social scientific knowledge can help us make better policy decisions is as unattractive to policy practitioners today as it was in the earlier days of policy science. Yet science has become a more contested terrain and a less stable toehold for the policy practitioner looking for footing amidst the chaotic flux of everyday life. At times the tables may even turn completely and policy practitioners may find themselves making the case to preserve some measure of regard for the facts. The distinction between theory and practice that animates the "applied science" model (in which theory developed in science guides and liberates practice) collapses in such circumstances. The best way to preserve regard for facts now seems to be to moderate the claim that knowledge can by itself guide policy making and liberate it from struggles among competing claims. There are at least five ways in which these claims must be moderated; each entails practical considerations for policy practitioners.

First, the activities of scientists are themselves conceived of in the model of practice (Latour and Woolgar 1986; Latour 1987). Second, the "application" of knowledge in policy must face the fact that scientific knowledge is contested. The stability and credibility that may once have been available by insulating knowledge development from practice have been problematized by practical challenges and by work in the sociology of science. Not only does the social penetrate the practice of the scientist (Latour 1987), it is *instrumental* in the way in which scientific progress functions. Even the "crucial experiment" was staged (Shapin and Schaffer 1985). Third, the neutrality of knowledge in policy design and practice has become problematic in light of scholarship that has highlighted the differences between academic and policy-oriented, "regulatory" research (Jasanoff 1990a,b). The latter is organized and carried out under different circumstances from the former, has to answer a different set of questions, and operates in a different timeframe. Fourth, scholars have observed that analytical scientific techniques often fail to capture the problems that people experience and thus provide "bad" input for policy (Fischer 2000). Finally, the domain of knowledge is not confined to the one demarcated by scientists, but is fundamentally open and relational. The experience of AIDS activists is one of many cases that illustrate the influence that non-scientists can have by contesting the organization of research and the interpretation of findings in policy commitments (Epstein 1996). In another, citizens developed the capacities to analyze health problems they were facing and their "popular epidemiology" soon started to produce scientifically valuable outcomes.

In this context, it has become customary to conceive of the relationship between science and policy in terms of "negotiated knowledge" (Nowotny, Scott, and Gibbons 2001). Knowledge is seen as the product of interaction among researchers and between researchers and non-researchers. Shackley and Wynne, for instance, describe how advisory scientists working on the issue of what is colloquially called the "greenhouse effect" have to negotiate their work and credibility both in the circles of their own scientific communities as well as in the world of policy makers (Shackley

---

[2] Incidently, Rein is summarizing these ambitions which he goes on to critique.

and Wynne 1996). Nowotny, Scott, and Gibbons argue that this scholarship in science studies demands that scientific authority find a different footing. It must be localized and contextualized, rather than universalized. It is precisely when knowledge is linked to the particular circumstances of a particular case that it can uphold its claims (Nowotny, Scott, and Gibbons 2001).

The insights of science studies link knowledge to the practices in which it is produced. Latour's *Science in Action* can be read as an argument against cognitive explanations and in favor of a form of practice-based reasoning (Latour 1987). He describes how new ideas about the natural and social order are not cognitive or discursive productions but are co-produced by the very techniques and practices that made them conceivable. Scientific knowledge, then, no longer provides a way to "stop" a debate by invoking the external authority of scientists, but comes to be seen as the product of an interaction in which (a variety of) scientific inputs help guide policy deliberation.

As knowledge and policy become more intertwined, conducting policy work in the old institutional set-up becomes counter-productive. Both environmental impact assessment and regulatory standard setting in the USA have long histories in which "advocacy science" has escalated in the context of legal forums, producing ever thicker analyses that diminished in value as they grew in volume. Similarly, it is easy to see how as seemingly straightforward a technique as cost–benefit analysis can contribute to the reproduction of one way of conceiving of value (Porter 1995) that features some aspects but at the cost of others. Here the very settings influence the knowledge that can be meaningfully produced; or to put it differently, practice guides knowing. Policy practitioners have responded by designing institutional settings in which knowledge can be negotiated directly in the context of a case.

Policy makers also confront the heterogeneity of science in conventional settings. The disciplinary organization of science, criticized by Lasswell in the early postwar years (Lasswell 1951), frustrates practitioners who start from a concern with problems that raise recurring concerns about how to "integrate" the relevant knowledge of, say, hydro-geologists, soil scientists, and ecologists, as well as economists and sociologists. Concerns about knowledge integration have even begun to be reflected in patterns of organization within universities where programs and centers organized around functional problems like migration, labor, sustainability, or transportation anticipate the demands of policy makers by bringing together researchers from different disciplinary backgrounds and, in the best cases, addressing the problems of knowledge integration this creates.

When it comes to policy problems, scientific work is nearly always heterogeneous. Consequently, the complexity of delivering useful knowledge requires cooperation. If we want to give the idea of science-for-policy a new lease for life one needs to be able to think how meaningfully coordinated communication is possible. Transdisciplinarity was an effort to tie integration across disciplinary boundaries (Weinberg 1972), but there is an extra value in case-based, problem-driven conversations "between science and society" (Scholz and Tietje 2002). Recently, the science studies literature has highlighted how "methods" are used to translate between divergent viewpoints and diverging social worlds. Leigh Star's "boundary-objects" facilitate those sustained efforts to develop a conversation using an array of knowledge inputs. Such boundary objects "have different meanings in different social worlds but their structure is common enough to more than one world to make them recognizable, a means of translation" (Star and Griesemer 1989). Later the concept has been applied in a more diverse way, pointing at the material components that are featured in this practice and by which this integration of insights takes place (be it a map, minutes, a text that is drafted). These objects guide cognition and influence the ultimate success of a particular initiative.

Policy analysis as a form of "problem-oriented" learning is well embedded in the "policy science" perspective promoted by Lasswell (Lasswell 1951; Torgerson 1985). It not only problematized the disciplinary organization of knowledge, but extended the search for workable solutions to include the participation of actors who bring domain-specific "contextual" knowledge to the table. Finding a way to engage the managers, production workers, and tradespeople who have detailed knowledge about the systems in which change is being pursued is a key challenge for policy practitioners. The insights of such practitioners, rather than just the commitments of top-level executives, are essential to achieve policy goals like reducing the use of toxic chemicals in manufacturing, managing agricultural waste, or providing greater security in the food system. Case reports of patients are essential (if often neglected or disdained) in recognizing and reasoning about threats to environmental health; the participation of citizens who can speak knowledgeably about the "habits" of inner city residents, particularly prominent ethnic subgroups, is likewise found to be essential to promoting environmental health (Ozonoff 1994; Corburn 2005). This broadening of the "peer community," to the "policy community" and the emergence of practice as the container for the complex conversation that takes place, raises both epistemological and practical questions that have become prominent concerns in the contemporary design of policy-making arrangements (Nicolini et al. 2003).

The sociological scholarship on "risk" in modern society has brought these issues into sharp relief. Work on "risk society" demonstrates the limits on our ability to "know" dangers and capture risks analytically. Knowing, the argument goes, is always related to not-knowing and to reflexivity about the conditions under which beliefs are developed (Lash et al. 1996). The considerations that generate these demands are not limited to the kind of probabilistic statements about outcomes that have characterized decision making under uncertainty. Rather than thinking about "residual" risk and "acceptability levels" the awareness of uncertainty (in this broad sense) informs policy-making arrangements. Uncertainty thus ceases to be the kind of marginal concern signified by error bars and becomes a constitutive characteristic of knowledge and of policy choices. This holds on a grand scale for projections about the scale and distribution of the impacts of global warming, but also for efforts to understand the effects of chronic low-level exposure to air pollution on respiratory function and the impacts of offshore windmills on birds and fish. As authors like Brian Wynne have shown, policy and science in these settings (alone and together) do not give attention to sources of uncertainty broadly, but typically elevate attention to a limited domain of uncertainties and neglect others (Wynne 1996). These questions become practical considerations when the behavior of, say, radiocaesium in the Cumbrian soils of the United Kingdom does not meet expectations, upsetting the organization of policy arrangements. Or, with a disastrous consequence in the case of BSE (the disease that devastated the UK cattle population in the 1990s), when policy advice is sound, but simply does not consider what it will mean to implement recommendations in a local setting. In the BSE case, the crucial problem arose in slaughterhouses where the recommended strict separation of spine tissue and red meat was hardly implementable because the spine was used as a "clothes hanger" in the carving process.

Natural resource managers increasingly view policy choices in similar terms as "genuine projections into the unknown" (Piore 1996), where management regimes address systems that are too complex to allow any confidence in the prediction of future states, where the systems are already in flux, and where management, no matter how responsible, contributes to this uncertainty. In these settings questions about knowledge become centrally questions about the relationship between different ways of knowing, the shadow cast by not knowing, and the organization of the settings in which these questions can be analysed, debated, and provisional decisions and judgements can be reached. A primary response to this is either to make the negotiation of knowledge explicit or to build a "vital social discourse" around the employment of knowledge in policy practice (Functowicz 1993).

It is where the literature on policy practice has been heading for a while. "Rather than asking how organizational practitioners might make better use of normal social science, or how normal social scientists might make their research results more palatable to practitioners, I have considered these practitioners as causal inquirers in their own right and asked how a different kind of social science might enhance the kinds of causal inquiry they conduct in their everyday practice" (Schön 1995, 96).

# 4. DEMOCRATIC PRACTICE

The initiatives of policy practitioners have generally raised questions about the legitimacy of policy. Discretion is a practical necessity, but the same judgements of practitioners that are necessary to make policy work strain the roots of state legitimacy in representative institutions. Recent developments in democratic theory provide a new take on these relationships. Instead of asking how can the provisional legitimacy of administrative action be enhanced, they raise the question of how policy practice can contribute to the broader legitimacy of the state and buttress the increasingly provisional legitimacy of representative institutions.

This reorientation is often preceded by a historical analysis that emphasizes the limits on the effectiveness and legitimacy of the modern representative welfare state, occasioned by the globalization of economic institutions that limits the ability of the state to manage production and provide security for workers, and the increasing diversity of the social basis of association and patterns of associative activity (Cohen and Rogers 1995). The reorientation itself hinges on two shifts. The first begins with a restatement of democratic legitimacy as arising from the collective authorization of citizens (Cohen 1997). It is completed with an account of collective authorization through a process of reciprocal reason giving, as opposed to voting or preference aggregation (Cohen 1989). The second is to see in the interaction of policy practitioners, citizens, and other stakeholders over how to act on policy goals the potential for democratic conversations that can meet the test as deliberation (Gutmann and Thompson 1996). The process of making policy workable and more effective could also provide an avenue to enhance the legitimacy of the state. The combination of these shifts produces a directly deliberative vision of democracy in which policy practice plays a foundational, rather than derivative role (Cohen and Sabel 1997).

This vision is persuasive in part because it refuses to accept the distinction between theory and practice that has long characterized the discussion of policy practice. This is possible in part because "[t]he gap between the theory and practice of deliberative democracy is narrower than in most conceptions of democracy. To be sure its highest ideals make demands that actual politics may never fulfil. But its principles modulate their demands in response to the limits of political necessity: they speak in the idiom of 'insofar as' or 'to the degree that' " (Gutmann and Thompson 1996). Moreover, "the theory of deliberative democracy partly constitutes its own practice: the arguments with which democratic theorists justify the theory are of the same kind that democratic citizens use to justify decision and policies in practice. In contrast to some forms of utilitarianism, deliberative democracy does not create a division between reasons that are appropriate in theory and those that are appropriate in practice. In contrast to some other conceptions of democracy, deliberative democracy does not divide institutions into those in which deliberation is important and those in which it is not. This continuity of theory and practice has implications for the design of institutions in modern democracies" (Gutmann and Thompson 1996, 357–8).

In the context of this close association between theory and practice it is natural to see a potential "communicative power" in the interactions among practitioners and citizens and to wonder whether it might "pick...up some of the work of the administrative state" and in the process start to rebuild the ties of solidarity that have atrophied in the face of broader structural shifts (Cohen and Rogers 1995). This focuses attention on trying to understand these policy practices as a form of deliberative organization that might "harness ... the distinctive capacity of associations to gather local information, monitor compliance, and promote cooperation among private actors by reducing its costs and building the trust on which it typically depends" (Cohen and Rogers 1995). While the solidarity developed through these problem-oriented interactions would differ from the more organic sources found in family, in shared culture, and even in the shared economic and social circumstances that tied workers together, "the bonds arising from participation in such arenas in the solution of large and commonly-recognized problems, need not be trivial or weak" (Cohen and Rogers 1995, 148). Indeed, if the prescription is apt, the solidarities arising from these particularistic interactions might "comprise ... a form of solidarity operative in civil society; transparently not 'natural' or 'found' or particularistic, not based in direct participation in the national project of citizenship, but definitely founded on participation in deliberative arenas designed with a cosmopolitan intent" (Cohen and Rogers 1995, 148–9). This rendering has fixed attention on practices as forms of democratic experimentalism that can be analyzed as institutional designs (Fung and Wright 2001) and has further problematized the organizational boundaries between governmental practices and other settings in which citizens engage one another and other policy actors (Mansbridge 1999).

# 5. Conclusion

The developments highlighted in the preceding sections will, at least in part, be familiar to many students of policy making and reflective practitioners. The role of networks, the shift from government to governance, the problems with a straightforward science-for-policy scheme, the emerging practices of deliberative democracy, and the way in which a deliberative rendering opens a direct link between policy studies and democratic theory are all widely narrated and discussed. We have tried to connect these discussions to the long-standing policy concern with policy practice. The fluidity of organizational relationships, the importance of repeated and overlapping forms of interaction among diverse and changing groups of actors, the potential for learning inherent in these relationships, the need to negotiate knowledge *in situ*, and the democratic character and significance of the interactions that occur around action, are already available in the experience of action and the domain of practice. In general terms, the concept of practice highlights the *negotiated character* of public policy and does so in a way that relates individual action to institutional contexts.

These discussions also suggest that the concept of practice may allow for a better grasp of the "units" at which learning and innovation take place: where results can be secured and monitored and where we should locate the flexibility and robustness of a deliberate response to public problems. We have also tried to highlight how the concept of policy practice actually helps understand how to conceive of public policy making in an unstable world. If we can usefully reconceive the world of standing organizations in terms of the networks of practices that essentially exist in and in between these organizations, then perhaps the understanding of policy practices as the locus of public intelligence can also help find solutions that lie beyond the reach of isolated institutions.

## REFERENCES

AXELROD, R. 1984. *The Evolution of Cooperation.* New York: Basic Books.

BOLTANSKI, L., and THÉVENOT, L. 1999. The sociology of critical capacity. *European Journal of Social Research,* 2 (3): 359–77.

BOURDIEU, P. 1977. *Outline of a Theory of Practice.* Cambridge: Cambridge University Press.

COHEN, J. 1989. Deliberation and democratic legitimacy. Pp. 17–34 in *The Good Polity: Normative Analysis of the State,* ed. A. Hamlin and P. Pettit. Oxford: Basil Blackwell.

—— 1997. Procedure and substance in deliberative democracy. Pp. 407–37 in *Deliberative Democracy,* ed. J. Bohman and W. Rehg. Cambridge, Mass.: MIT Press.

—— and ROGERS, J. (eds.) 1995. *Associations and Democracy.* London: Verso.

—— and SABEL, C. 1997. Directly-deliberative polyarchy. *European Law Journal,* 3 (4): 313–40.

CORBURN, J. 2005. *Street Science: Community Knowledge and Environmental Health Justice.* Cambridge, Mass.: MIT Press.

EPSTEIN, S. 1996. *Impure Science: Aids, Activism, and the Politics of Knowledge.* Los Angeles: University of California Press.

FISCHER, F. 2000. *Citizens, Experts, and the Environment: The Politics of Local Knowledge.* Durham, NC: Duke University Press.

FLYVBJERG, B. 2001. *Making Social Science Matter: Why Social Inquiry Fails and How it can Succeed Again.* Cambridge: Cambridge University Press.

FORESTER, J. 1999. *The Deliberative Practitioner: Encouraging Participatory Planning Processes.* Cambridge, Mass.: MIT Press.

FUNCTOWICZ, S. J. R. R. 1993. Science for the post-normal age. *Futures,* 25 (7): 739–56.

FUNG, A., and WRIGHT, E. O. 2001. Deepening democracy: innovations in empowered participatory governance. *Politics and Society,* 29 (1): 5–41.

GUTMANN, A., and THOMPSON, D. 1996. *Democracy and Disagreement.* Cambridge, Mass.: Belknap Press.

HAJER, M. A., and WAGENAAR, H. (eds.) 2003. *Deliberative Policy Analysis: Understanding Governance in the Network Society.* Cambridge: Cambridge University Press.

HECLO, H. 1978. Issue networks and the executive establishment. Pp. 87–124 in *The New American Political System,* ed. A. King. Washington, DC: American Enterprise Institute for Public Policy Research.

JASANOFF, S. 1990a. *The Fifth Branch: Science Advisers and Policy Makers.* Cambridge, Mass.: Harvard University Press.

—— 1990b. *Risk Management and Political Culture.* New York: Russell Sage Foundation.

LASH, S., SZERSZINSKI, B., et al. (eds.) 1996. *Risk, Environment and Modernity: Towards a New Ecology.* London: Sage.

LASSWELL, H. D. 1951. The policy orientation. Pp. 3–15 in *The Policy Sciences,* ed. H. D. Lasswell and D. Lerner. Stanford, Calif.: Stanford University Press.

LATOUR, B. 1987. *Science in Action.* Cambridge, Mass.: Harvard University Press.

—— and WOOLGAR, S. 1986. *Laboratory Life: The Construction of Scientific Facts*. Princeton, NJ: Princeton University Press.

LIPSKY, M. 1980. *Street-Level Bureaucracy: Dilemmas of the Individual in Public Services*. New York: Russell Sage Foundation.

MANSBRIDGE, J. 1999. Everyday talk in the deliberative system. Pp. 211–39 in *Deliberative Politics: Essays on Democracy and Disagreement*, ed. S. Macedo. Oxford: Oxford University Press.

MARIN, B., and MAYNTZ, R. (eds.) 1991. *Policy Networks: Empirical Evidence and Theoretical Considerations*. Frankfurt: Campus Verlag.

MARRIS, P., and REIN, M. 1967. *Dilemmas of Social Reform: Poverty and Community Action in the United States*. New York: Atheston Press.

MEYER, J. W., and ROWAN, B. 1977. Institutionalized organizations: formal structure as myth and ceremony. *American Journal of Sociology*, 83 (2): 340–63.

MISZTAL, B. 1996. *Trust in Modern Societies: The Search for the Bases of Social Order*. Cambridge: Polity Press.

NICOLINI, D., GHERARDI, S., et al. (eds.) 2003. *Knowing in Organizations: A Practice-Based Approach*. Armonk, NY: M. E. Sharpe.

NOWOTNY, H., SCOTT, P., and GIBBONS, M. (eds.) 2001. *Rethinking Science: Knowledge and the Public in an Age of Uncertainty*. Cambridge: Polity Press.

OSTROM, E. 1990. *Governing the Commons: The Evolution of Institutions for Collective Action*. Cambridge: Cambridge University Press.

OZONOFF, D. 1994. Conceptions and misconceptions about human health impact analysis. *Environmental Impact Assessment Review*, 14 (5–6): 499–515.

PIERRE, J., and PETERS, B. G. (eds.) 2000. *Debating Governance: Authority, Steering, and Democracy*. Oxford: Oxford University Press.

PIORE, M. 1992. Fragments of a theory of technological change and organizational structure. Pp. 430–44 in *Networks and Organizations: Structure, Form, and Action*, ed. N. Nohria and R. G. Eccles. Boston: Harvard Business School Press.

—— 1996. Review of the *Handbook of Economic Sociology. Journal of Economic Literature*, 34: 741–54.

PORTER, T. M. 1995. *Trust in Numbers: The Pursuit of Objectivity in Science and Public Life*. Princeton, NJ: Princeton University Press.

POWELL, W. W. 1990. Neither market nor hierarchy: network forms of organization. *Research in Organisational Behavior*, 12: 295–336.

PRESSMAN, J. L., and WILDAVSKY, A. 1973. *Implementation: How Great Expectations in Washington are Dashed in Oakland; or, Why it's Amazing that Federal Programs Work at All, this being a Saga of the Economic Development Administration as Told by Two Sympathetic Observers who Seek to Build Morals on a Foundation of Ruined Hopes*. Los Angeles: University of California Press.

REIN, M. 1976. *Social Science and Public Policy*. Harmondsworth: Penguin.

—— 1983. *From Policy to Practice*. Armonk, NY: M. E. Sharpe.

RHODES, R. A. W. 1997. *Understanding Governance: Policy Networks, Governance, Reflexivity, and Accountability*. Buckingham: Open University Press.

ROE, E. 1998. *Taking Complexity Seriously: Policy Analysis, Triangulation and Sustainable Development*. Boston: Kluwer Academic.

SABEL, C. 1994. Learning by monitoring: the institutions of economic development. Pp. 137–65 in *The Handbook of Economic Sociology*, ed. N. J. Smelser and R. Swedberg. Princeton, NJ: Princeton University Press.

SCHOLZ, R. W., and TIETJE, O. 2002. *Embedded Case Study Methods: Integrating Quantitative and Qualitative Methods*. Thousand Oaks, Calif.: Sage.

SCHÖN, D. A. 1983. *The Reflective Practitioner: How Professionals Think in Action*. New York: Basic Books.

—— 1995. Causality and causal inference in the study of organizations. Pp. 69–101 in *Rethinking Knowledge: Reflections across the Disciplines*, ed. R. Goodman and W. R. Fisher. Albany, NY: SUNY Press.

SHACHAR, A. 2001. *Multicultural Jurisdictions: Cultural Differences and Women's Rights*. Cambridge: Cambridge University Press.

SHACKLEY, S., and WYNNE, B. 1996. Representing uncertainty in global climate change science and policy: boundary-ordering devices and authority. *Science, Technology and Human Values*, 21 (3): 275–302.

SHAPIN, S., and SCHAFFER, S. 1985. *Leviathan and the Air-Pump: Hobbes, Boyle, and the Experimental Life*. Princeton, NJ: Princeton University Press.

STAR, S. L., and GRIESEMER, J. R. 1989. Institutional ecology, "translations" and boundary objects: amateurs and professionals in Berkeley's Museum of Vertebrate Zoology, 1907–39. *Social Studies of Science*, 19: 387–420.

STONE, D. 1997. *Policy Paradox: The Art of Political Decision Making*. New York: W. W. Norton.

SUSSKIND, L., MCKEARNAN, S., et al., (eds.) 1999. *The Consensus Building Handbook: A Comprehensive Guide to Reaching Agreement*. Thousand Oaks, Calif.: Sage.

TORGERSON, D. 1985. Contextual orientation in policy analysis: the contribution of Harold D. Lasswell. *Policy Sciences*, 18: 241–61.

WAGENAAR, H. 2004. "Knowing" the rules: administrative work as practice. *Public Administration Review*, 64 (6): 643–55.

WARREN, M. E. 1999. *Democracy and Trust*. Cambridge: Cambridge University Press.

WEINBERG, A. 1972. Science and trans-science. *Minerva*, 10: 209–22.

WENGER, E. 1998. *Communities of Practice: Learning, Meaning, and Identity*. Cambridge: Cambridge University Press.

WYNNE, B. 1996. May the sheep safely graze? A reflexive view of the expert–lay knowledge divide. Pp. 44–83 in *Risk, Environment and Modernity: Towards a New Ecology*, ed. S. Lash, B. Szerszinski, and B. Wynne. London: Sage.

CHAPTER 20

.....................................................................................................

# POLICY NETWORK ANALYSIS

.....................................................................................................

## R. A. W. RHODES

Tis all in pieces, all cohærence gone.

(John Donne (1611), "The First Anniversary. An Anatomy of the World,"
1985 edition, 335 line 213)

## 1. INTRODUCTION: THE UBIQUITY OF NETWORKS

.....................................................................................................

Network analysis comes in many guises. It is common to all the social science disciplines. The vast literature ranges from social network analysis (Scott 2000) to the network society created by the information revolution (Castells 2000), from the actor-centered networks of technological diffusion (Callon, Law, and Rip 1986) to cross-cultural analysis (Linn 1999). This chapter focuses on that species of network analysis most common in political science—policy network analysis.

Few social science disciplines can ever agree on the meaning of an idea. So, a policy network is one of a cluster of concepts focusing on government links with, and dependence on, other state and societal actors. These notions include issue networks (Heclo 1978), iron triangles (Ripley and Franklin 1981), policy subsystems or sub-

\* I would like to thank Chris Ansell, Mark Bevir, Jenny Fleming, Johan Olsen, and the editors for their comments and advice.

governments (Freeman and Stevens 1987), policy communities (Richardson and Jordan 1979), and epistemic communities (Haas 1992). I discuss these terms below. All are varieties of networks, so I use "policy network" as the generic term.

This buzzing, blooming confusion of terms has not detained us for long. Defining policy networks will take no longer. Policy networks are sets of formal institutional and informal linkages between governmental and other actors structured around shared if endlessly negotiated beliefs and interests in public policy making and implementation. These actors are interdependent and policy emerges from the interactions between them. There could be many qualifications to this definition, but it will do as a starting point for my exploration.

Section 2 of this chapter reviews the literature on policy network analysis, distinguishing between descriptive, theoretical, and prescriptive accounts. It identifies three descriptive uses of the term: networks as interest intermediation, as interorganizational analysis, and as governance. It then summarizes the two main theoretical approaches—power dependence theory and rational choice—before looking at the instrumental, interactive, and institutional approaches to managing networks. Section 3 looks at the debates and challenges in the literature. It focuses on the difficulties of synthesizing the findings from the proliferating case studies, and on the critics of the "new governance." It reviews the various answers to the question of why networks change, looking at the advocacy coalition framework, the dialectical model, strategic relational theory, and the interpretative turn. It concludes with the observation that the study of policy networks mirrors general trends in political science in its concern with ethnographic methods and the impact of ideas. Finally, it looks at the problems of managing the institutional void, especially the difficulties posed by mixing governing structures, the diffusion of accountability, enhancing coordination, and devising new tools.

# 2. THE LITERATURE ON POLICY NETWORK ANALYSIS

The term policy network is used in three main ways in the literature: as a description of governments at work, as a theory for analyzing government policy making, and as a prescription for reforming public management.

## 2.1 Networks as Description

When describing government policy making, the term policy network refers to interest intermediation, interorganizational analysis, and governance.

## Networks as Interest Intermediation

The roots of the idea of a policy network lie, in part, in American pluralism and the literature on subgovernments. For example, Ripley and Franklin (1981, 8–9) define subgovernments as "clusters of individuals that effectively make most of the routine decisions in a given substantive area of policy." They are composed of "members of the House and/or Senate, members of Congressional staffs, a few bureaucrats and representatives of private groups and organizations interested in the policy area." The emphasis in this literature is on a few privileged groups with close relations with governments; the resultant subgovernment excludes other interests and makes policy. Some authors developed more rigid metaphors to characterize this relationship. Lowi (1964) stressed the *triangular* nature of the links, with the central government agency, the Congressional Committee, and the interest group enjoying an almost symbiotic interaction. This insight gave birth to the best-known label within the subgovernments literature, the "iron triangle" (see Freeman and Stevens 1987, 12–13 and citations).

The literature on policy networks develops this American concern with the oligopoly of the political marketplace. Governments confront a multitude of groups all keen to influence a piece of legislation or policy implementation. Some groups are outsiders. They are deemed extreme in behavior and unrealistic in their demands, so are kept at arm's length. Others are insiders, acceptable to government, responsible in their expectations, and willing to work with and through government. Government needs them to make sure it meets its policy objectives. The professions of the welfare state are the most obvious example. Over the years, such interests become institutionalized. They are consulted before documents are sent out for consultation. They don't lobby. They have lunch. These routine, standardized patterns of interaction between government and insider interests become policy networks.

There are many examples of the use of policy networks to describe government policy making.[1] Marsh and Rhodes (1992) define policy networks as a meso-level concept that links the micro level of analysis, dealing with the role of interests and government in particular policy decisions, and the macro level of analysis, which is concerned with broader questions about the distribution of power in modern society. Networks can vary along a continuum according to the closeness of the relationships in them. Policy communities are at one end of the continuum and involve close relationships; issue networks are at the other end and involve loose relationships (and on the influence of this approach see Börzel 1998; Dowding 1995; LeGalès and Thatcher 1995; Richardson 1999).

A policy community has the following characteristics: a limited number of participants with some groups consciously excluded; frequent and high-quality interaction between all members of the community on all matters related to the policy issues; consistency in values, membership, and policy outcomes which persist over

---

[1] On Australia see Considine 1994, Davis et al. 1993; on Canada see Coleman and Skogstad 1990, Lindquist 1996; on the UK see Rhodes 1988, Richardson and Jordan 1979; on continental Europe see LeGalès and Thatcher 1995, Marin and Mayntz 1991; on the USA see Mandell 2002, O'Toole 1997.

time; consensus, with the ideology, values, and broad policy preferences shared by all participants; and exchange relationships based on all members of the policy community controlling some resources. Thus, the basic interaction is one involving bargaining between members with resources. There is a balance of power, not necessarily one in which all members equally benefit but one in which all members see themselves as in a positive-sum game. The structures of the participating groups are hierarchical so leaders can guarantee compliant members. This model is an ideal type; no policy area is likely to conform exactly to it.

One can only fully understand the characteristics of a policy community if we compare it with an issue network. McFarland (1987, 146), following Heclo's (1978) use, defines an issue network as "a communications network of those interested in policy in some area, including government authorities, legislators, businessmen, lobbyists, and even academics and journalists ... [that] ... constantly communicates criticisms of policy and generates ideas for new policy initiatives." So, issue networks are characterized by: many participants; fluctuating interaction and access for the various members; the absence of consensus and the presence of conflict; interaction based on consultation rather than negotiation or bargaining; an unequal power relationship in which many participants may have few resources, little access, and no alternative. The study of interest groups understood variously as issue networks, policy subsystems, and advocacy coalitions is probably the largest American contribution to the study of policy networks. They are seen as an ever-present feature of American politics (and for surveys of the literature see Baumgarten and Leech 1998 and Berry 1997).

Obviously the implication of using a continuum is that any network can be located at some point along it. Networks can vary along several dimensions and any combination of these dimensions; for example, membership, integration, resources. Various authors have constructed continua, typologies, and lists of the characteristics of policy networks and policy communities (see for example Van Waarden 1992). This lepidopteran approach to policy networks—collecting and classifying the several species—has become deeply uninteresting.

## Networks as Interorganizational Analysis

The European literature on networks focuses less on subgovernments and more on interorganizational analysis (see for example Rhodes 1999/1981). It emphasizes the structural relationship between political institutions as the crucial element in a policy network rather than the interpersonal relations between individuals in those institutions. At its simplest, interorganizational analysis suggests that a "focal organization attempts to manage its dependencies by employing one or more strategies, other organizations in the network are similarly engaged." A network is "complex and dynamic: there are multiple, over-lapping relationships, each one of which is to a greater or lesser degree dependent on the state of others" (Elkin 1975, 175–6).[2]

---

[2] See also Benson 1975; Crozier and Thoenig 1976; Hanf and Scharpf 1979; Thompson 1967.

The most impressive attempt to apply this variant of network analysis to politics and policy making is the several collaborations of David Knoke, Edward Laumann, and Franz Pappi (see especially Knoke 1990; Knoke et al. 1996; Laumann and Knoke 1987). Their "organizational state" approach argues that "modern state–society relationships have increasingly become blurred, merging into a mélange of inter-organizational influences and power relations." These interorganizational networks "enable us to describe and analyze interactions among all significant policy actors, from legislative parties and government ministries to business associations, labor unions, professional societies, and public interest groups" (Knoke et al. 1996, 3). The key actors are formal organizations, not individuals. In their analysis of national labor policy in America, Germany, and Japan, Knoke et al. 1996 compiled the list of key actors by, for example, searching public documents such as the *Congressional Information Service* volumes for the number of times they testified before the relevant congressional or Senate committee, including only organizations with five or more appearances. The individuals in these organizations responsible for governmental policy affairs were then interviewed on such matters as the informant's perception of the most influential organization, the communication of policy information, and participation in the policy area. Knoke et al. then use the techniques of network analysis to map the links between organizations, employing classic network measures such as centrality and density (for an introduction to such techniques see Scott 1991, and for a compendium see Wasserman and Faust 1994).

Knoke et al. argue that their data not only describe the power structure of their chosen policy area but also explain the different policy outcomes. The value of this species of network analysis lies in its use of the structural properties of networks to explain behavior and outcomes. Unfortunately, little work in this idiom is explanatory. Instead, it describes power structures and network characteristics. Moreover, "it has not yet produced a great deal that is novel" (Dowding 2001, 89–90 and n. 2). It is hard to demur from this judgement when Knoke et al. (1996, 210, 213) conclude that "the state clearly constitutes the formal locus of collective decision making that affects the larger civil society within which it is embedded," or that "the more central an organization was in either the communication or the support network, the higher was its reputation for being influential" (see also Thatcher 1998, 398–404).

## Networks as Governance

The roots of policy network analysis lie, finally, in the analysis of the sharing of power between public and private actors, most commonly between business, trade unions, and the government in economic policy making (Atkinson and Coleman 1989; Jordan 1981). Initially, the emphasis fell on corporatism, a topic worthy of an article in its own right (see Cawson 1986; Schmitter and Lehmbruch 1979). There was also the long-standing and distinctive Scandinavian analysis of "corporate pluralism" (Rokkan 1966; Heisler 1979), which continues under such labels as "the segmented state" (Olsen 1983, 118) and "the negotiated economy" (Nielsen and Pedersen 1988). Latterly, the main concern has been with governance by (and through) networks, on trends in the relationship between state and civil society government rather than policy making in specific arenas. Thus, governance is a broader term than government with public resources and services provided by any permutation of government and the private and voluntary sectors (and on the different conceptions of governance see Kjær 2004; Pierre 2000).

There are several accounts of this trend for Britain, continental Europe, and the USA. Thus, for Britain, there has been a shift from government by a unitary state to governance by and through networks. In this period, the boundary between state and civil society changed. It can be understood as a shift from hierarchies, or the bureaucracies of the welfare state, through the marketization reforms of the Conservative governments of Thatcher and Major to networks and the emphasis on partnerships and joined-up government.[3]

There is also a large European literature on "guidance," "steering," and "indirect coordination" which predates both the British interest in network governance and the American interest in reinventing government. For example, Franz-Xavier Kaufmann's (1986) edited volume on guidance, steering, and control is truly Germanic in size, scope, and language. It focuses on the question of how a multiplicity of interdependent actors can be coordinated in the long chains of actions typical of complex societies (see also Bovens 1990; Luhmann 1982; van Gunsteren 1976).

For the USA, Osborne and Gaebler (1992, 20, 34) distinguish between policy decisions (steering) and service delivery (rowing), arguing bureaucracy is a bankrupt tool for rowing. In its place they propose entrepreneurial government, with its stress on working with the private sector and responsiveness to customers. This transformation of the public sector involves "less government" or less rowing but "more governance" or more steering. In his review of the American literature, Frederickson (1997, 84–5) concludes the word "governance is probably the best and most generally accepted metaphor for describing the patterns of interaction of multiple-organizational systems or networks" (see also Kettl 1993, 206–7; Salamon 2002). Peters (1996, ch. 1) argues the traditional hierarchic model of government is everywhere under challenge. He identifies four trends, or models of governance, challenging the hierarchic model—market, participative, flexible, and deregulated governance. Fragmentation, networks, flexibility, and responsiveness are characteristics of flexible governance. In sum, talk of the governance transformation abounds even if the scope, pace, direction, and reasons for that change are matters of dispute (for a survey see Pierre 2000).

## 2.2 Policy Networks as Theory

There is a large theoretical literature on policy networks in Britain (see Rhodes 1988, 1997a, 1999/1981), the rest of Europe (see Börzel 1998; Kickert, Klijn, and Koppenjan

---

[3] See for example Ansell 2000; Bevir and Rhodes 2003; Rhodes 1997a, 2000; Stoker 2004; and for a review of the literature and citations, see Marinetto 2003.

1997), and the USA (see O'Toole 1997; Salamon 2002). There are two broad schools of thought, depending on how they seek to explain network behavior: power dependence or rational actor.[4]

## Power Dependence

The power dependence approach treats policy networks as sets of resource-dependent organizations. Their relationships are characterized by power dependence; that is, "any organization is dependent on other organizations for resources," and "to achieve their goals, the organizations have to exchange resources." So, actors "employ strategies within known rules of the game to regulate the process of exchange." Relationships are a "game" in which organizations maneuver for advantage. Each deploys its resources, whether constitutional-legal, organizational, financial, political, or informational, to maximize influence over outcomes while trying to avoid becoming dependent on the other "players." So, behavior in policy networks is gamelike, rooted in trust and regulated by rules of the game negotiated and agreed by network participants. Variations in the distribution of resources and in the bargaining skills of participants explain both differences in outcomes in a network and variations between networks. Finally, the networks have a significant degree of autonomy from government (Rhodes 1997a, ch. 2; 1999/1981, ch. 5).[5]

## Rational Choice

The rational choice school explains how policy networks work by combining rational choice and the new institutionalism to produce actor-centered institutionalism. The best example is the Max-Planck-Institut's notion of "actor-centered institutionalism." For Renate Mayntz, Fritz Scharpf, and their colleagues at the Max-Planck-Institut, policy networks represent a significant change in the structure of government. They are specific "structural arrangements" that deal typically with "policy problems." They are a "relatively stable set of mainly public and private corporate actors." The links between network actors serve as "communication channels and for the exchange of information, expertise, trust and other policy resources." Policy networks have their own "integrative logic" and the dominant decision rules stress bargaining and sounding out. So, as with the power dependence approach, the Max Planck school stresses functional differentiation, the linkages between organizations, and dependence on resources (Kenis and Schneider 1991, 41–3).

---

[4] Bob Goodin pointed out correctly that theories of complexity are also relevant to the study of network (personal correspondence). See, for example, La Porte 1975; Luhmann 1982; Simon 1981/1969. Such ideas exercised some influence on the "governance club" research program at Erasmus University, Rotterdam (see for example Kickert, Klyn, and Koppenjan 1997). They have not been a major influence on the rest of the network literature.

[5] The analysis of "power dependence" is not limited to the study of networks. More generally see: Blau 1964; Emerson 1962; Keohane and Nye 1977, 1987; Pfeffer and Salancik 1978.

To explain how policy networks work, Scharpf (1997, chs. 2, 3) combines rational choice and the new institutionalism to produce actor-centered institutionalism. The basic argument is that institutions are systems of rules that structure the opportunities for actors (individual and corporate) to realize their preferences. So, "policy is the outcome of the interactions of resourceful and boundedly-rational actors whose capabilities, preferences, and perceptions are largely, but not completely, shaped by the institutionalised norms within which they interact" (Scharpf 1997, 195).

Networks are one institutional setting in which public and private actors interact. They are informal institutions; that is, informally organized, permanent, rule-governed relationships. The agreed rules build trust and foster communication while also reducing uncertainty; they are the basis of non-hierarchic coordination. Scharpf uses game theory to analyze and explain these rule-governed interactions.

In the UK, there have been vigorous exchanges between the two schools (see for example Dowding 1995, 2001 versus Marsh 1998, 12–13, 67–70; Marsh and Smith 2000). It is a case of "ne'er the twain shall meet." The two sides have irreconcilable differences of both theory and method. The disagreements are as basic as the deductive, positivistic, quantitative approach of economics versus the inductive, interpretative, qualitative approach of sociology. For insiders, harmony is not threatening to break out any time soon. To outsiders, the debate seems like a spat. The outsiders could well be right.

## 2.3 Policy Networks as Reform

The spread of networks and the recognition that they constrain government's ability to act has fueled research on how to manage networks. The goal is now "joined-up government" or a "whole-of-government" approach. Networks are no longer a metaphor or a site for arcane theoretical disputes but a live issue for reforming public sector management. Here I concentrate on the public sector literature.[6]

Kickert, Klijn, and Koppenjan (1997, 46) identify three approaches to network management in the public sector: the instrumental, interactive, and institutional. The instrumental approach focuses on how governments seek to exercise legitimate authority by altering dependency relationships. The key problem with the instrumental approach is the cost of steering. A central command operating code, no matter how well disguised, runs the ever-present risks of recalcitrance from key actors, a loss of flexibility in dealing with localized problems, and control deficits.

The interaction approach stresses management by negotiation instead of hierarchy. The trick is to sit where the other person is sitting to understand their objectives and to build and keep trust between actors. So, chief executive officers in the public sector must have "strong interpersonal, communication and listening

---

[6] On the private sector, see Child and Faulkner 1998, ch. 6; Ford et al. 2003; Pfeffer and Salancik 1978.

skills; an ability to persuade; a readiness to trade and to engage in reciprocal rather than manipulative behavior; an ability to construct long-term relationships" (Ferlie and Pettigrew 1996, 88–9). The key problem of the interactive approach is the costs of cooperation. Network management is time consuming, objectives can be blurred, and outcomes can be indefinite. Decision making is satisficing, not maximizing.

The institutional approach focuses on the institutional backcloth, the rules and structures against which the interactions take place. The aim is incremental changes in incentives, rules, and culture to promote joint problem solving. The institutional approach has one major, even insurmountable problem; incentives, rules, and culture are notoriously resistant to change because networks privilege a few actors, who equate their sectional interest with the public interest. They are well placed to protect their sectional interests.

The literature specifically on managing networks grows apace in both America and Europe. Salamon (2002) provides a comprehensive review of the tools available for America's new governance, covering the "classic" instruments such as grants, regulation, and bureaucracy but laying great emphasis on the collaborative nature of modern governing and the need to switch from hierarchy and control to enabling and the indirect management of networks.[7]

What do you do if you have to run a network? Painter, Rouse, and Isaac-Henry (1997, 238) provide specific advice on game management. They conclude that local authorities should: conduct an audit of other relevant agencies; draw a strategic map of key relationships; identify which of their resources will help them to influence these other agencies; and identify the constraints on that influence. As with all new trends, there is an upsurge of advice from both academics and consultants. So the ten commandments of networking include: be representative of your agency and network, take a share of the administrative burden, accommodate and adjust while maintaining purpose, be as creative as possible, be patient and use interpersonal skills, and emphasize incentives (Agranoff 2003, 29). It is certainly not "rocket science" (Perri 6 et al. 2002, 130) and this list of lessons gives credence to that claim. Wettenhall (2003, 80) reviews the literature on partnerships, joined-up government, and the new governance. He concludes these terms have "become the dominant slogan in the turn-of-the-century discourse about government" (see, for example, Cabinet Office 2000; Cm 4310 1999; MAC 2004). So any disapproving reader dismissing this literature should pause to note it is well on the way to becoming the new conventional wisdom in public sector reform. Those of more caustic disposition, having paused, might move on by noting that network management is an ephemeral mix of proverbs and injunctions.[8]

---

[7] See Agranoff 2003; Kettl 2002; Kickert, Klyn, and Koppenjan 1997; McGuire 2002; Mandell 2002; O'Toole 1997; Osborne 2000; Perri 6 et al. 2002.

[8] The literature may be preoccupied with adducing lessons for would-be managers but it also analyzes network management as, for example, brokerage. See Bardach 1998; Carpenter, Esterling, and Lazer 2004; Fernandez and Gould 1994; Taylor 1997.

## 3. DEBATES AND CHALLENGES

Paralleling the earlier discussion, this section looks at the debates and challenges that confront policy network analysis. In turn, I examine some descriptive, theoretical, and prescriptive pitfalls.

### 3.1 Describing Governance

The notion of a policy network can be dismissed as mere metaphor. It is not a metaphor because there is no analogy. Policy making *is* a set of interconnected events and communicating people. It is no more a metaphorical term than bureaucracy. The term's resonance and longevity stems from the simple fact that for many it represents an enduring characteristic of much policy making in advanced industrial democracies.

In his review of British studies of pressure groups and parties, Richardson (1999, 199) claimed that Dowding's (1995) critique of policy networks marked the "intellectual fatigue" of the approach. The sheer number and variety of articles published since this "watershed," including Richardson's (2000) own prize-winning paper on networks and policy change, testifies to the continuing utility of the term. Not only are there innumerable case studies of British policy networks but casting the net wider, beyond the confines of political science, policy networks are staples in, for example, criminology (Loader 2000; Ryan, Savage, and Wall 2001). The international relations literature on networks expanded, with Haas's (1992) notion of epistemic communities influential. They are transnational networks of knowledge-based experts with an authoritative claim to policy-relevant knowledge within their domain of expertise. The distinguishing features of these networks are their shared beliefs and professional judgements. Directly analogous to Haas's network of experts are Keck and Sikkink's (1998, 1) transnational advocacy networks of activists. For example, the UN, domestic and international non-governmental organizations, and private foundations form an international issue network to counter the "forgetfulness" of governments. The network is an alternative channel of communication that argues, persuades, lobbies, and complains to inject new ideas and information into the international debate on human rights (see also Risse, Ropp, and Sikkink 1999; Sikkink 1993).

Transnational networks are also a feature of policy making in the European Union (EU). For Peterson (2003, 119, 129), "policy network analysis is never more powerful as an analytical tool than when it is deployed at the EU level" and "few... would deny that governance by networks is an essential feature of the EU."[9] Policy network

---

[9] See also Ansell 2000; Andersen 1990; Josselin 1997; Kassim 1993; Mazey and Richardson 1993; Rhodes, Bache, and George 1996.

analysis has also colonized intergovernmental relations in and between states, most notably federal–state relations (Galligan 1995; Rhodes 1988; Wright 1978).

Finally, there is governance in a globalizing world. It comes in several varieties. Keohane's (2002, 204, 210–12, 214) version of global governance is one of "networked minimalism." In other words, there is no hierarchy but a network of nation states, private firms, NGOs, and subunits of government, which pursues "minimal rather than ambitious objectives." The nation state will remain the "primary instrument of domestic and global governance" but "it is not the only important actor" (see also Slaughter 2003). Rosenau (2000, 172–3) provides a more dramatic vision of a "multi-centric" world composed of diverse transnational collectivities that both compete and cooperate and do not lend themselves to hierarchic control or hegemonic coordination. The world is a network and networks are the world.

In short, I doubt there could be a clearer example of "have theory will travel" and, therefore, there is a problem. There is no synthesis of the findings of this diverse literature. Indeed, a synthesis may not be possible. The key question would be, "what type of network emerges in what conditions with what policy outcomes?" There have been many willing to tell us how to answer this question (Dowding 1995; Thatcher 1998). Only a few brave souls have tried to give an answer, and even then they confine their analysis to either comparing several policy sectors in a single country or a single policy sector in several countries (see for example Considine 2002; Marsh 1998).

When seeking to compare policy networks across countries, the problems are probably insurmountable. Policy networks are but political science writ small. The problems that bedevil comparative government also plague policy networks. They were devastatingly summarized by MacIntyre (1972, 8):

There was once a man who aspired to be the author of the general theory of holes. When asked "What kind of hole—holes dug by children in the sand for amusement, holes dug by gardeners to plant lettuce seedlings, tank traps, holes made by roadmakers?" he would reply indignantly that he wished for a *general* theory that would explain all of these. He rejected *ab initio* the—as he saw it—pathetically commonsense view that of the digging of different kinds of holes there are quite different kinds of explanations to be given.

Such "modernist-empiricism" (Bevir 2001, 478) treats policy networks as discrete objects to be measured, classified, and compared. It may not be one of "the more dangerous kinds of practical joke" (MacIntyre 1972, 26) but it is only one way of studying networks.

The story about the rise and rise of governance raises a second issue. This "new orthodoxy" does not carry all before it. Marinetto (2003) disputes the "Anglo-Governance School's" claim there has been a loss of central control. He suggests that it exaggerates the ruptures in history, arguing there has been a long-standing tension between centralization (government) and fragmentation (governance) in Britain. In a similar vein, Holliday (2000) insists Britain still has a strong core executive, the center has not been hollowed out, networks have not spread, and the center can and does exercise effective control. Whether the Anglo-Governance School has "to undergo an intellectual crisis wrought by the growing weight of criticism" and the extent to which this "critical response is underway, albeit gradually" will become clear over the next few years (Marinetto 2003, 605–6). I too expect to see "alternative ways of conceptualising the institutions, actors and processes of change in government," to listen to a new generation of stories about governance, and to ponder another round of debate about whether changes are epiphenomena of present-day government policy or more deep-seated ruptures. Stick around long enough and the aphorism "what goes around comes around" sounds like a balanced summary of fads and fashions in the social sciences rather than irony or even cynicism.

## 3.2 Explaining Change

The most common and recurrent criticism of policy network analysis is that it does not, and cannot, explain change (for a summary of the argument and citations, see Richardson 2000). So, policy network analysis stresses how networks limit participation in the policy process; decide which issues will be included and excluded from the policy agenda; shape the behavior of actors through the rules of the game; privilege certain interests; and substitute private government for public accountability. It is about stability, privilege, and continuity.

There have been several attempts to analyze change and networks but I must make two preliminary points. First, it is no mean feat to describe and explain continuity and stability in policy making. Second, the analysis of change may be a recurring problem but, and this point is crucial, it is not specific to the study of networks. Just as there are many theories of bureaucracy, so there are many theories of policy networks. There is no consensus in the political science community about how to explain, for example, political change, only competing epistemological positions and a multitude of theories. Students of policy networks can no more produce an accepted explanatory theory of change than (say) students of bureaucracy, democracy, or economic development. Debates in the policy network literature mirror the larger epistemological and ontological debates in the social sciences.

Of the several efforts to build the analysis of change into policy networks, three have attracted attention: advocacy coalitions, the dialectical model, and decentered analysis.

The advocacy coalition framework (ACF) has four basic premisses. First, "understanding the process of policy change...requires a time perspective of a decade or more." Second, "the most useful way to think about policy change...is through a focus on 'policy subsystems'." Third, "those subsystems must include an intergovernmental dimension." Finally, "public policies...can be conceptualized in the same manner as belief systems, that is, sets of value priorities and causal assumptions about how to realize them" (Sabatier and Jenkins-Smith 1993, 16). Sabatier argues that coalitions try to translate their beliefs into public policy. Their belief systems determine the direction of policy. Their resources determine their capacity to change government programs. Resources change over time, most commonly in response to changes external to the subsystem. Most distinctively, Sabatier distinguishes between core and secondary beliefs and argues that coalitions have a consensus on their policy core that is resistant to change. In sharp contrast, secondary aspects of the belief system can change rapidly (paraphrased from Sabatier and Jenkins-Smith 1993, 25–34). Moreover, these beliefs are central to understanding the actions of policy makers who are not necessarily motivated by rational self-interest. However, as Parsons (1995, 201) succinctly points out, the model works well for the federal and fragmented government of America, but there is little evidence that it travels well.

The dialectical model proposed by Marsh and Smith (2000) suggests that change is a function of the interaction between the structure of the network and the agents operating in it, the network and the context in which it operates, and the network and policy outcomes. They see networks as structures that can constrain or facilitate action but do not determine actions because actors interpret and negotiate constraints. Exogenous factors may prompt network change but actors mediate that change. So we must examine not only the context of change but also structure, rules, and interpersonal relationship in the network. Finally, not only do networks affect policy outcomes but policy outcomes feed back and affect networks. This dialectical model provoked heated debate and lectures on how to do political science, but little convergence and a mere tad of insight (compare Marsh and Smith 2000, 2001, with Dowding 2001).

Grappling with the same issues as the formation, evolution, transformation, and termination of policy networks, Hay and Richards's "strategic relational theory of networks" is a sophisticated variation on the dialectical theme. To begin with, they avoid the ambiguities of, and controversies surrounding the term "dialectical." They argue individuals seeking to realize certain objectives and outcomes make a strategic assessment of the context in which they find themselves. However, that context is not neutral. It too is strategically selective in the sense that it privileges certain strategies over others. Individuals learn from their actions and adjust their strategies. The context is changed by their actions, so individuals have to adjust to a different context. So a networking is "a practice—an accomplishment on the part of strategic actors . . . which takes place within a strategic (and strategically selective context) which is itself constantly evolving through the consequences (both intended and unintended) of strategic action" (Hay and Richards 2000, 14; see also Hay 2002).

A different challenge comes from those who advocate an interpretative turn and argue that policy network analysis could make greater use of such ethnographic tools as: studying individual behavior in everyday contexts; gathering data from many sources; adopting an "unstructured" approach; focusing on one group or locale; and, in analyzing the data, stressing the "interpretation of the meanings and functions of human action" (paraphrased from Hammersley 1990, 1–2). The task would be to write thick descriptions or our "constructions of other people's constructions of what they are up to" (Geertz 1973, 9, 20–1; and for a similar recognition that the political ethnography of networks is an instructive approach, see Heclo and Wildavsky 1974; McPherson and Raab 1988).

Bevir and Rhodes (2003, ch. 4) argue for the decentered study of networks, for a shift of topos from institution to individual, and a focus on the social construction of policy networks through the ability of individuals to create meaning. Bang and Sørensen's (1999) story of the "Everyday Maker" provides an instructive example of a decentered account of networks. They interviewed twenty-five active citizens in the Nørrebro district of Copenhagen to see how they engaged with government. They identify the "Everyday Maker," who focuses on immediate and concrete policy problems at the lowest possible level. Thus, Grethe (a grass-roots activist) reflects that she has acquired the competence to act out various roles: contractor, board member, leader. There has been an explosion of "issue networks, policy communities, ad hoc policy projects, and user boards, including actors from 'within,' 'without,' 'above,' and 'below' traditional institutions of democratic government." So the task of the "Everyday Maker" is "to produce concrete outcomes" (Bang and Sørensen 1999, 332). Political activity has shifted from "formal organizing to more informal networking" (Bang and Sørensen 1999, 334). Politics is no longer about left and right but "dealing with concrete problems in the institutions around which... everyday life... is organized" (Bang and Sørensen 1999, 336). In short, they draw a picture of Nørrebro's networks through the eyes of its political activists, constructing the networks from the bottom up.

This discussion highlights two points. First, the trend in the study of policy networks to ethnographic methods mirrors general trends in political science. Fenno (1990, 128) observed, "not enough political scientists are presently engaged in observation." That was then. Now there is a growing interest in the interpretative turn in political science. Any discussion of this turn would take us too far afield. However, it is worth noting that the origins of network analysis lie in social anthropology, which examines who talks to whom about what in (say) a Norwegian village. So this point is perhaps best expressed as an overdue return to roots.

Second, all three approaches to network change are part of a broader trend in political science to exploring the impact of ideas on policy making. Again, it would take us too far afield to cover this topic, but Sabatier's (Sabatier and Jenkins-Smith 1993) work on advocacy coalitions stands alongside that of, for example, Kingdon (1984) on policy ideas and policy agendas. The link between changing policy networks, new ideas, and setting policy agendas is exploited to great effect in Richardson (2000).

## 3.3 Managing the Institutional Void

If we live in a world of "polycentric networks of governance," then the task facing politicians, managers, and citizens is to manage "the institutional void," that is, to make and implement policy when there are no generally accepted rules and norms for conducting policy making (Hajer 2003, 175). Hajer's vivid metaphor may overstate the extent of change but it does dramatize the problems of managing the network state. Four such problems recur: the mix of governing structures, the diffusion of accountability, enhancing coordination, and devising new tools.

## Managing the Mix

In a world of policy networks where every service is a mix of bureaucracy, markets, and networks, we need to understand when these governing structures for allocating resources work. We need to be clear about what we mean when we call for effective service delivery because the criteria of effectiveness vary. For example, the competition that characterizes markets conflicts with the cooperation so characteristic of networks. Flynn et al. (1996, 136–7) argue that trust became important in the British National Health Service because of the difficulties in specifying contracts and participants' experience of assertive purchasers whose style "engenders or exacerbates suspicious attitudes and feelings of mutual distrust." So, market relations had "corrosive effects" on "professional networks which depend on cooperation, reciprocity and interdependence." I would belabor the obvious if I gave examples of bureaucratic failures. The apt conclusion is not that contracts or bureaucracies or networks fail, but that they all do (Jessop 2000). Not every day or every week or for every policy. The key is to understand the conditions under which each works and a core lesson of that analysis is, "it is the mix that matters." We need to know how to manage not only each governing structure but also the relationship between them.[10]

## Diffuse Accountability

Conventional notions of accountability do not fit when authority for service delivery is dispersed among several agencies. Bovens (1998, 46) identifies the "problem of many hands" where responsibility for policy in complex organizations is shared and it is correspondingly difficult to find out who is responsible (see also van Gunsteren 1974, 3). He also notes that fragmentation, marketization, and the resulting networks create "new forms of the problem of many hands" (Bovens 1998, 229). For example, Hogwood, Judge, and McVicar (2000) show that agencies and special purpose bodies have multiple constituencies, each of which seeks to hold them to account. There is no system, just disparate, overlapping demands. In a network, the constituent organizations may hold the relevant officials and politicians to account but to whom is the set of organizations accountable? As Mulgan (2003, 211–14) argues, buck passing is much more likely in networks because responsibility is divided and the reach of political leaders is much reduced. However, all is not doom and gloom. Following Braithwaite (2003, 312), policy networks can be seen as an example of "many unclear separations of powers" in that the several interests in a network can act as checks and balances on one another. However, it is more common for networks

---

[10] See for example Considine and Lewis 1999; Thompson et al. 1991; Powell 1991; Rhodes 1997b; Simon 2000.

to be closed to public scrutiny, a species of private government. The brute fact is that multiple accountabilities weaken central control (Mulgan 2003, 225).[11]

## Enhancing Coordination

Weakened accountability is not the only consequence of networks. The spread of networks also undermines coordination. Despite strong pressures for more coordination, the practice is "modest." It is "largely negative, based on persistent compartmentalisation, mutual avoidance and friction reduction between powerful bureaus or ministries;" "anchored at the lower levels of the state machine and organised by specific established networks;" "rarely strategic, so almost all attempts to create proactive strategic capacity for long-term planning...have failed;" and intermittent and selective in any one sector, improvised late in the policy process, politicized, issue oriented, and reactive (Wright and Hayward 2000, 33). And that it is before we introduce networks into the equation. Networks make the goal ever more elusive. As Peters (1998, 302) argues, "strong vertical linkages between social groups and public organizations makes effective coordination and horizontal linkages within government more difficult." Once agreement is reached in the network, "the latitude for negotiation by public organizations at the top of the network is limited." However, these remarks presume hierarchy is the most important or appropriate mechanism for coordination. Lindblom (1965) persuasively argued many years ago that indirect coordination or mutual adjustment was messy but effective. The San Francisco Bay Area public transit system is a multiorganizational system (or network) and Chisholm (1989, 195) shows that only some coordination can take place by central direction and so "personal trust developed through informal relationships acts a lubricant for mutual adjustment." In sum, coordination is the holy grail of modern government, ever sought, but always just beyond reach, and networks bring central coordination no nearer. However, they do provide their own messy, informal, decentralized version.

## Devising New Tools

The mainstream literature (for example Salamon 2002) encourages a tool view of how to manage networks; if learning the skills of indirect management is itself a major challenge, it is not the only one confronting would-be network managers. The epistemological debate extends to the question of how to manage networks. An interpretative approach encourages us to replace the toolbox approach with storytelling. Although the label varies—the argumentative turn, narratives—there is now a growing literature on storytelling as a way of managing the public sector.[12] Van Eeten, van Twist, and Kalders (1996) make the important point that this latest

[11] On the need to rethink accountability in the nation state see Behn 2001; and on accountability in a globalizing world see Keohane 2002, 219–44; 2003.

[12] See Bevir, Rhodes, and Weller 2003; Hummel 1991; Rein 1976; van Eeten, van Twist, and Kalders 1996; Weick 1995.

intellectual fashion has its feet firmly on the ground because managers use stories not only to gain and pass on information and to inspire involvement, but also as the repository of the organization's institutional memory. In sum, as Hummel (1991, 103–4) argues, "managers communicate first and foremost through stories." He asks, "how could it be otherwise?" When managers confront a problem, their people tell them what is going on. So, managers "could do worse than hone their skills in story-telling and story-validating." Management is just as much about interpretation as rational calculation.

# 4. Conclusions

In the 1970s, debate raged about the future of public policy making and policy analysis. Was it a distinctive field of study or just good old public administration under a new and fashionable label? It staked a claim to be a distinct field of study. Now we no longer discuss the question. Policy analysis is established. In this sense, there is no longer a debate about the future of policy networks. The story of policy networks follows the same trajectory as public policy making. The subject is here to stay—a standard topic in any public policy-making textbook (Parsons 1995) or textbooks on British government (Richards and Smith 2002).

What was all the excitement about? It is not just the story of the rise of an idea. It is about a new generation of political scientists. "Young—well youngish—Turks" carved out a reputation for themselves by challenging their elders and betters. Sound and fury are essential to such uprisings. In Britain, added edge came from the challenge to the Westminster model, which had run out of steam as a way of understanding the changes in British government. The debate was not only about networks but also about how to study British government. It should be no surprise, therefore, that the recurrent problems of the policy network literature, for example in explaining change, mirror issues in broader political science. The rise of governance was our story of how British government had changed. It was not the story in the graduate and postgraduate texts on which we were raised. We abandoned the eternal verities of the British constitution. In sharp contrast to the fuddy-duddies, we could explain both continuity and change. Of course, we were wrong but we weren't about to admit it. Anyway the spats were fun!

The story of policy networks is a story of a success. The "Young Turks" won their elevation to the professorial peerage, ran out of steam, and moved on. A flood of doctorates and case studies followed. It is no longer an innovative idea but a commonplace notion in almost every nook and cranny of both political science texts and British government textbooks in particular. It is ripe for challenge. Controversies in policy network analysis now parallel controversies in political science, whether they are about how to explain political change or the uses of ethnographic methods. Of course, we also respond to debates and problems in the "real" world. Much of the literature reviewed in this chapter sees networks as an effective way of managing complex problems in health and education. However, Al Qaeda and the war on terror have focused attention on "dark networks" (Raab and Milward 2003), a term that also encompasses drug smuggling, the arms trade, and failed states. Fieldwork may not be an option but the problems of policing dark networks cannot be ignored. Policy network analysis has become one more locus for the endless debates about how we know what we know in the social sciences. I doubt the founders could have hoped for more. I am sure their expectations were less.

# REFERENCES

AGRANOFF, R. 2003. *Leveraging Networks*. Arlington, Va.: IBM Endowment for the Business of Government.

ANDERSON, J. J. 1990. Sceptical reflections on a Europe of regions: Britain, Germany and the ERDF. *Journal of Public Policy*, 10: 417–47.

ANSELL, C. 2000. The networked polity: regional developments in western Europe. *Governance*, 13 (3): 303–33.

ATKINSON, M. M., and COLEMAN, W. D. 1989. Strong states and weak states: sectoral policy networks in advanced capitalist economies. *British Journal of Political Science*, 19: 47–67.

BANG, H. P., and SØRENSEN, E. 1999. The everyday maker: a new challenge to democratic governance. *Administrative Theory and Praxis*, 21: 325–41.

BARDACH, E. 1998. *Getting Agencies to Work Together: The Theory and Practice of Managerial Craftsmanship*. Washington, DC: Brookings Institution Press.

BAUMGARTEN, F. R., and LEECH, B. L. 1998. *Basic Interests: The Importance of Groups in Politics and in Political Science*. Princeton, NJ: Princeton University Press.

BEHN, R. D. 2001. *Rethinking Democratic Accountability*. Washington, DC: Brookings Institution.

BENSON, J. K. 1975. The interorganizational network as a political economy. *Administrative Science Quarterly*, 20: 229–49.

BERRY, J. M. 1997. *The Interest Group Society*, 3rd edn. New York: HarperCollins.

BEVIR, M. 2001. Prisoners of professionalism: on the construction and responsibility of political studies. *Public Administration*, 79: 469–509.

—— and RHODES, R. A. W. 2003. *Interpreting British Governance*. London: Routledge.

—— —— and WELLER, P. 2003. Comparative governance: prospects and lessons. *Public Administration*, 81: 191–210.

BLAU, P. M. 1964. *Exchange and Power in Social Life*. New York: Wiley.

BÖRZEL, T. J. 1998. Organizing Babylon: on the different conceptions of policy networks. *Public Administration*, 76: 253–73.

BOVENS, M. A. P. 1990. The social steering of complex organizations. *British Journal of Political Science*, 20 (1): 91–117.

—— 1998. *The Quest for Responsibility: Accountability and Citizenship in Complex Organizations*. Cambridge: Cambridge University Press.

BRAITHWAITE, J. 2003. On speaking softly and carrying big sticks: neglected dimensions of a republican separation of powers. *University of Toronto Law Review*, 47: 305–61.

CABINET OFFICE 2000. *Wiring it up*. London: Cabinet Office.

Cmd 4310 1999. *Modernising Government.* London: HMSO.

CALLON, M., LAW, J., and RIP, A. (eds). 1986. *Mapping the Dynamics of Science and Technology,* London: Macmillan.

CARPENTER, D. P., ESTERLING, K. M., and LAZER, D. M. J. 2004. Friends, brokers, and transitivity: who informs whom in Washington politics? *Journal of Politics,* 66: 224–46.

CASTELLS, M. 2000. Materials for an exploratory theory of the network society. *British Journal of Sociology,* 51: 5–24.

CAWSON, A. 1986. *Corporatism and Political Theory.* Oxford: Blackwell.

CHILD, J., and FAULKNER, D. 1998. *Strategies of Co-operation: Managing Alliances, Networks and Joint Ventures.* Oxford: Oxford University Press.

CHISHOLM, D. 1989. *Coordination without Hierarchy: Informal Structures in Multiorganizational Systems.* Berkeley: University of California Press.

COLEMAN, W. D., and SKOGSTAD, G. 1990. *Policy Communities and Public Policy in Canada.* Toronto: Copp Clark Pitman.

CONSIDINE, M. 1994. *Public Policy: A Critical Approach.* Melbourne: Macmillan.

—— 2002. The end of the line? Accountable governance in the age of networks, partnerships, and joined-up services. *Governance,* 15: 21–40.

—— and LEWIS, J. 1999. Governance at ground level: the frontline bureaucrat in the age of markets and networks. *Public Administration Review,* 59: 467–80.

CROZIER, M., and THOENIG, J.-C. 1976. The regulation of complex organised systems. *Administrative Science Quarterly,* 21: 547–70.

DAVIS, G., WANNA, J., WARHURST, J., and WELLER, P. 1993. *Public Policy in Australia,* 2nd edn. St Leonards: Allen and Unwin.

DONNE, J. 1985/1611. *The Complete English Poems of John Donne,* ed. C. A. Patrides. London: John Dent, Everyman's Library.

DOWDING, K. 1995. Model or metaphor? A critical review of the policy network approach. *Political Studies,* 43: 136–58.

—— 2001. There must be an end to confusion. *Political Studies,* 49: 89–105.

ELKIN, S. L. 1975. Comparative urban politics and inter-organizational behaviour. Pp. 158–84 in *Essays on the Study of Urban Politics,* ed. K. Young. London: Macmillan.

EMERSON, R. E. 1962. Power-dependence relations. *American Sociological Review,* 27: 31–41.

FENNO, R. F. 1990. *Watching Politicians: Essays on Participant Observation.* Berkeley: Institute of Governmental Studies, University of California.

FERLIE, E., and PETTIGREW, A. 1996. Managing through networks: some issues and implications for the NHS. *British Journal of Management,* 7: 81–99.

FERNANDEZ, R. M., and GOULD, R. V. 1994. A dilemma of state power: brokerage and influence in the national health policy domain. *American Journal of Sociology,* 99 (6): 1455–91.

FLYNN, R., et al. 1996. *Markets and Networks: Contracting in Community Health Services.* Buckingham: Open University Press.

FORD, D., GADDE, L.-E. HÅKANSSON, H., and SNEHOTA, I. 2003. *Managing Business Relationships,* 2nd edn. Chichester: Wiley.

FREDERICKSON, H. G. 1997. *The Spirit of Public Administration.* San Francisco: Jossey-Bass.

FREEMAN, J. L., and STEVENS J. P. 1987. A theoretical and conceptual re-examination of subsystem politics. *Public Policy and Administration,* 21: 9–25.

GALLIGAN, B. 1995. *A Federal Republic.* Cambridge: Cambridge University Press.

GEERTZ, C. 1973. *The Interpretation of Cultures.* New York: Basic Books.

HAAS, P. M. 1992. Epistemic communities and international policy coordination. *International Organization,* 46: 1–35.

HAJER, M. 2003. Policy without a polity? Policy analysis and the institutional void. *Policy Sciences*, 36: 175–95.

HAMMERSLEY, M. 1990. *Reading Ethnographic Research: A Critical Guide*. Harlow: Longman.

HANF, K., and SCHARPF, F. W. (eds). 1979. *Interorganizational Policy Making*. London: Sage.

HAY, C. 2002. *Political Analysis*. Houndmills: Palgrave.

—— and RICHARDS, D. 2000. The tangled webs of Westminster and Whitehall. *Public Administration*, 78: 1–28.

HECLO, H. 1978. Issue networks and the executive establishment. Pp. 87–124 in *The New American Political System*, ed. A. King. Washington, DC: AEI.

—— and WILDAVSKY, A. 1974. *The Private Government of Public Money*. London: Macmillan.

HEISLER, M. 1979. Corporate pluralism revisited: where is the theory? *Scandinavian Political Studies*, 2: 277–92.

HOGWOOD, B. W., JUDGE, D. and McVICAR, M. 2000. Agencies and accountability. Pp. 195–222 in *Transforming British Government, i: Changing Institutions*, ed. R. A. W. Rhodes. London: Macmillan.

HOLLIDAY, I. 2000, Is the British state hollowing out? *Political Quarterly*, 71: 167–76.

HUMMEL, R. P. 1991. Stories managers tell: why they are as valid as science. *Public Administration Review*, 51: 31–41.

JESSOP, B. 2000. Governance failure. Pp. 11–32 in *The New Politics of British Local Governance*, ed. G. Stoker. Houndmills: Macmillan.

JORDAN, A. G. 1981. Iron triangles, woolly corporatism and elastic nets. *Journal of Public Policy*, 1: 95–123.

JOSSELIN, D. 1997. *Money Politics in the New Europe*. Houndmills: Macmillan.

KASSIM, H. 1993. Policy networks, networks and European policy-making: a sceptical view. *West European Politics*, 17: 15–27.

KAUFMANN, F.-X., MAJONE, G. and OSTROM, V. (eds.) 1985. *Guidance, Control and Evaluation in the Public Sector*. Berlin: W. de Gruyter.

KECK, M. E., and SIKKINK, K. 1998. *Activists beyond Borders: Advocacy Networks in International Politics*. Ithaca, NY: Cornell University Press.

KENIS, P., and SCHNEIDER, V. 1991. Policy networks and policy analysis: scrutinizing a new analytical toolbox. Pp. 25–59 in *Policy Networks: Empirical Evidence and Theoretical Considerations*, ed. B. Marin and R. Mayntz. Frankfurt: Campus Verlag.

KEOHANE, R. O. 2002. *Power and Governance in a Partially Globalized World*. London: Routledge.

—— 2003. Global governance and democratic accountability. Pp. 130–59 in *Taming Globalization: Frontiers of Governance*, ed. D. Held and M. Koenig-Archibugi. Cambridge: Polity Press.

—— and NYE, J. S. 1977. *Power and Interdependence*. Boston: Little, Brown.

—— —— 1987. Power and independence revisited. *International Organization*, 41: 725–53.

KETTL, D. F. 1993. *Sharing Power: Public Governance and Private Markets*. Washington, DC: Brookings Institution.

—— 2002. Managing indirect government. Pp. 490–510 in *The Tools of Government: A Guide to the New Governance*, ed. L. M. Salamon. Oxford: Oxford University Press.

KICKERT, W. J. M., KLIJN, E.-H., and KOPPENJAN, J. F. M. (eds.) 1997. *Managing Complex Networks: Strategies for the Public Sector*. London: Sage.

KINGDON, J. W. 1984. *Agendas, Alternatives and Public Policies*. Boston: Little, Brown.

KJÆR, A. M. 2004. *Governance*. Cambridge: Polity Press.

KNOKE, D. 1990. *Political Networks: The Structural Perspective*. New York: Cambridge University Press.

—— Pappi, F. U., Broadbent, J., and Tsujinaka, Y. 1996. *Comparing Policy Networks: Labor Politics in the U.S., Germany and Japan*. New York: Cambridge University Press.

La Porte, T. R. (ed.) 1975. *Organized Social Complexity*. Princeton, NJ: Princeton University Press.

Laumann, E., and Knoke, D. 1987. *The Organizational State*. Madison: University of Wisconsin Press.

LeGalès, P., and Thatcher, M. (eds.) 1995. *Les Réseaux de politique publique: Débat autour des policy networks*. Paris: Editions L'Harmatton.

Lindblom, C. E. 1965. *The Intelligence of Democracy*. New York: Free Press.

Lindquist, E. A. 1996. New agendas for research on policy communities: policy analysis, administration and governance. Pp. 219–41 in *Policy Studies in Canada: The State of the Art*, ed. L. Dobuzinskis, M. Howlett, and D. Laycock. Toronto: University of Toronto Press.

Linn, N. 1999. Social networks and status attainment. *Annual Review of Sociology*, 61: 900–7.

Loader, I. 2000. Plural policing and democratic governance. *Social and Legal Studies*, 9: 323–45.

Lowi, T. 1964. How the farmers get what they want. *Reporter*, May: 34–6.

Luhmann, N. 1982. *The Differentiation of Society*. New York: Columbia University Press.

McFarland, A. 1987. Interest groups and theories of power in America. *British Journal of Political Science*, 17: 129–47.

McGuire, M. 2002. Managing networks: propositions on what managers do and why they do it. *Public Administration Review*, 62: 599–609.

Macintyre, A. 1972. Is a science of comparative politics possible? Pp. 8–26 in *Philosophy, Politics and Society*, ed. P. Laslett, W. G. Runciman, and Q. Skinner, 4th series. Oxford: Basil Blackwell.

McPherson, A., and Raab, C. 1988. *Governing Education*. Edinburgh: Edinburgh University Press.

Management Advisory Committee (MAC) 2004. *Connecting Government: Whole of Government Responses to Australia's Priority Challenges*. Canberra: Commonwealth of Australia.

Mandell, M. P. (ed.) 2002. *Getting Results through Collaboration: Networks and Network Structures for Public Policy and Management*. Westport, Conn.: Quorum.

Marin, B., and Mayntz, R. (eds.) 1991. *Policy Networks: Empirical Evidence and Theoretical Considerations*. Frankfurt: Campus Verlag.

Marinetto, M. 2003. Governing beyond the centre: a critique of the Anglo-Governance School. *Political Studies*, 51: 592–608.

Marsh, D. 1998. *Comparing Policy Networks*. Buckingham: Open University Press.

—— and Rhodes, R. A. W. (eds.) 1992. *Policy Networks in British Government*. Oxford: Clarendon Press.

—— and Smith, M. 2000. Understanding policy networks: towards a dialectical approach. *Political Studies*, 48: 4–21.

—— —— 2001. There is more than one way to do political science: on different ways to study policy networks. *Political Studies*, 49: 528–41.

Mazey, S., and Richardson, J. (eds.) 1993. *Lobbying in the European Community*. Oxford: Oxford University Press.

Mitchell, J. C. (ed.) 1969. *Social Networks in Urban Situations*. Manchester: Manchester University Press.

Mulgan, R. 2003. *Holding Power to Account: Accountability in Modern Democracies*. Houndmills: Palgrave Macmillan.

Nielsen, K., and Pedersen, O. K. 1988. The negotiated economy: ideal and history. *Scandinavian Political Studies*, 11: 79–101.

Olsen, J. P. 1983. *Organized Democracy*. Oslo: Universitetsforlaget.

OSBORNE, D., and GAEBLER, T. 1992. *Reinventing Government.* Reading, Mass.: Addison-Wesley.

OSBORNE, S. (ed.) 2000. *Public–Private Partnerships: Theory and Practice in International Perspective.* London: Routledge.

O'TOOLE, L. 1997. Treating networks seriously: practical and research based agendas in public administration. *Public Administration Review,* 57: 45–52.

PAINTER, C., ROUSE, J., and ISAAC-HENRY, K. 1997. Local authorities and non-elected agencies: strategic responses and organizational networks. *Public Administration,* 77: 225–45.

PARSONS, W. 1995. *Public Policy.* Aldershot: Edward Elgar.

PERRI 6, LEAT, D., SELTZER, K., and STOKER, G. 2002. *Towards Holistic Governance: The New Reform Agenda.* Houndmills: Palgrave.

PETERS, B. G. 1996. *The Future of Governing: Four Emerging Models.* Lawrence: University of Kansas Press.

—— 1998. Managing horizontal government: the politics of coordination. *Public Administration,* 76: 295–311.

PETERSON, J. 2003. Policy networks. Pp. 117–35 in *European Integration Theory,* ed. A. Wiener and T. Diez. Oxford: Oxford University Press.

PFEFFER, J., and SALANCIK, G. R. 1978. *The External Control of Organizations: A Resource Dependence Perspective.* New York: Harper and Row.

PIERRE, J. (ed.) 2000. *Debating Governance.* Oxford: Oxford University Press.

POWELL, W. 1991. Neither market nor hierarchy: network forms of organization. Pp. 265–76 in *Markets, Hierarchies and Networks: The Coordination of Social Life,* ed. G. Thomson et al. London: Sage.

RAAB, J., and MILWARD, H. B. 2003. Dark networks as problems. *Journal of Public Administration Theory and Research,* 13: 413–39.

REIN, M. 1976. *Social Science and Public Policy.* Harmondsworth: Penguin.

RHODES, R. A. W. 1988. *Beyond Westminster and Whitehall.* London: Unwin-Hyman.

—— 1997a. *Understanding Governance.* Buckingham: Open University Press.

—— 1997b. It's the mix that matters: from marketisation to diplomacy. *Australian Journal of Public Administration,* 56: 40–53.

—— 1999/1981. *Control and Power in Central-Local Government Relationships,* rev. edn. Aldershot: Ashgate.

—— (ed.) 2000. *Transforming British Government,* i: *Changing Institutions;* ii: *Changing Roles and Relationships.* London: Macmillan.

—— BACHE, I., and GEORGE, S. 1996. Policy networks and policy making in the European Union: a critical appraisal. Pp. 367–87 in *Cohesion Policy and European Integration,* ed. L. Hooghe. Oxford: Clarendon Press.

RICHARDS, D., and SMITH, M. J. 2002. *Governance and Public Policy in the UK.* Oxford: Oxford University Press.

RICHARDSON, J. 1999. Pressure groups and parties and social movements: a "haze of common knowledge" or the empirical advance of a discipline? Pp. 181–222 in *The British Study of Politics in the Twentieth Century,* ed. J. Hayward, B. Barry, and A. Brown. Oxford: Oxford University Press for the British Academy.

—— 2000. Government, interest groups and policy change. *Political Studies,* 48: 1006–25.

—— and JORDAN, G. 1979. *Governing under Pressure: The Policy Process in a Post-Parliamentary Democracy.* Oxford: Martin Robertson.

RIPLEY, R., and FRANKLIN, G. 1981. *Congress, the Bureaucracy and Public Policy.* Homewood, Ill.: Dorsey Press.

RISSE, T., ROPP, S. C., and SIKKINK, K. (eds.) 1999. *The Power of Human Rights: International Norms and Domestic Change.* Cambridge: Cambridge University Press.

ROKKAN, S, 1966. Norway: numerical democracy and corporate pluralism. Pp. 70–115 in *Political Oppositions in Western Democracies,* ed. R. A. Dahl. New Haven, Conn.: Yale University Press.

ROSENAU, J. 2000. Governance in globalizing space. Pp. 167–200 in *Debating Governance,* ed. J. Pierre. Oxford: Oxford University Press.

RYAN, M., SAVAGE, S. P., and WALL, D. S. (eds.) 2001. *Policy Networks in Criminal Justice.* Houndmills: Palgrave.

SABATIER P., and JENKINS-SMITH, H. C. 1993. *Policy Change and Learning: An Advocacy Coalition Approach.* Boulder, Colo.: Westview.

SALAMON, L. M. (ed.) 2002. *The Tools of Government: A Guide to the New Governance.* Oxford: Oxford University Press.

SCHARPF, F. W. 1997. *Games Real Actors Play: Actor-Centered Institutionalism in Policy Research.* Boulder, Colo.: Westview.

SCHMITTER, P. C., and LEHMBRUCH, G. (eds.) 1979. *Trends towards Corporatist Intermediation.* London: Sage.

SCOTT, J. 2000. *Social Network Analysis: A Handbook,* 2nd edn. London: Sage.

SIKKINK, K. 1993. Human rights, principled issue-networks and sovereignty in Latin America. *International Organization,* 47: 411–41.

SIMON, H. A. 1981/1969. *The Sciences of the Artificial,* 2nd edn. Cambridge, Mass.: MIT Press.
—— 2000. Public administration in today's world of organizations and markets. *PS: Political Science & Politics,* 33 (4): 749–56.

SLAUGHTER, A.-M. 2003. Everyday global governance. *Daedalus,* 132 (1): 83–91.

STOKER, G. 2004. *Transforming Local Governance.* Houndmills: Palgrave Macmillan.

TAYLOR, A. 1997. "Arm's length but hands on:" mapping the new governance. The Department of National Heritage and cultural policies in Britain. *Public Administration,* 75: 441–66.

THATCHER, M. 1998. The development of policy network analyses. *Journal of Theoretical Politics,* 10: 389–416.

THOMPSON, G., et al., (eds.) 1991. *Markets, Hierarchies and Networks: The Coordination of Social Life.* London: Sage.

THOMPSON, J. D. 1967. *Organizations in Action.* New York: McGraw-Hill.

VAN EETEN, M. J. G., VAN TWIST, M. J. W., and KALDERS, P. R. 1996. Van een narratieve bestuurskunde naar een postmoderne beweerkunde? *Bestuurskunde,* 5: 168–89. English translation supplied by Mark van Twist.

VAN GUNSTEREN, H. 1976. *The Quest for Control.* London: Wiley.

VAN WAARDEN, F. 1992. Dimensions and types of policy networks. *European Journal of Political Research,* 21: 29–52.

WASSERMAN, S., and FAUST, K. 1994. *Social Network Analysis: Methods and Applications.* Cambridge: Cambridge University Press.

WEICK, K. E. 1995. *Sensemaking in Organizations.* London: Sage.

WETTENHALL, R. 2003. The rhetoric and reality of public–private partnerships. *Public Organization Review,* 3: 77–107.

WRIGHT, D. S. 1978. *Understanding Intergovernmental Relations.* North Scituate, Mass.: Duxbury Press.

WRIGHT, V., and HAYWARD, J. E. 2000. Governing from the centre: policy coordination in six European core executives. Pp. 27–46 in *Transforming British Government,* ii: *Changing Roles and Relationships,* ed. R. A. W. Rhodes. London: Macmillan.

# CHAPTER 21

........................................................................................................

# SMART POLICY?

........................................................................................................

## TOM CHRISTENSEN

## 1. INTRODUCTION

........................................................................................................

The traditional state or "old public administration" takes the form in many countries of a centralized and integrated state that combines conscious structural design with a integrated culture (Olsen 1988).[1] Its strength lies in its capacity to act and its ability to accommodate simultaneously various legitimate considerations and create trust (Egeberg 2003). Its potential weaknesses are domination by a few elite groups, excessive complexity, and problems of effectiveness, efficiency, and accountability (Weaver and Rockman 1993).

When New Public Management (NPM) arrived in the early 1980s, initially most systematically in Australia and New Zealand, but also in the UK and USA, it was presented as a kind of antithesis to the centralized state model.[2] It was labeled a "supermarket state" because it focused on the service-providing functions of government (Olsen 1988). NPM emphasizes cost efficiency, markets, competition, contracts, devolution, decentralization, etc. (Self 2000). It may be viewed as a new technical instrument—an optimal means, inspired by new institutional economic theory, of organizing government and solving the efficiency problems of governments all over the world—or else as a "shopping basket" of reforms with heterogeneous and inconsistent features (Pollitt 1995). While it contains some core concepts and ideas, its incorporation of both centralizing and decentralizing elements, whether connected to new institutional economic theory or management theory,

[1] This is of course a simplification, since states will vary in their degree of centralization and cultural homogeneity. However, these are some core features of the old type of state.

[2] See Pusey 1982; Hilmer 1993; NZ Treasury 1987; Boston et al. 1996; Considine and Lewis 1999; Considine 2001, 2002.

makes it potentially difficult to use to solve a priori problems (Boston et al. 1996; Christensen and Lægreid 2001, 19–20; Kettl 1997).

A third perspective, adding to the traditional and supermarket ones, sees NPM as a new "corporate culture" concerned less with internal problems and rights and more with external needs and the interests of the consumer (McKevitt 1998). A fourth perspective sees NPM more as a new ideology than a specific reform program (Christensen and Lægreid 2003b). According to this perspective, the primary effect of NPM reforms is to further neoliberal ideology and symbols rather than to produce actual reforms. Reform ideas are easier to spread than reform practice, so when political leaders state their intention to implement reforms, they often engage in "double-talk" or "hypocrisy," trying to balance talk and action (Brunsson 1989). Thus NPM reform processes and effects are open to a variety of interpretations and have different meanings for different actors and stakeholders.

This chapter focuses on "smart policy"—the term used by reform entrepreneurs espousing the instrumental-technical perspective on NPM to describe its alleged enhancement of *effectiveness* and *efficiency*. We discuss whether this is a defendable position, addressing the following questions: First, what are the main ideas and practical reform elements in NPM? Second, what are the main preconditions for smarter policy? Is smarter policy made *feasible* by NPM reforms? Is this primarily a question of rational calculation—more unambiguous means–end thinking—or political-administrative control, or a combination of both (Dahl and Lindblom 1953, 57)? Is it (eventually) *desirable* to produce smarter policy through NPM? What are the normative pros and cons? Does NPM create more polarization between actors? Third, what do we know about the effects of NPM? How easy is it to show that these type of reforms result in smarter policy? Is the effect of smarter policy demonstrable in some dimensions but not in others? Fourth, does joined-up government as a new reform element show the limits of trying to be smart, or does it make policy even smarter?

# 2. Main Features of New Public Management

NPM is presented by its supporters primarily as an efficiency instrument (Self 2000). It is often promised that NPM will result in more efficiency overall, but the preconditions for or indicators of this are seldom discussed. Efficiency and rationality are effects that are generally taken for granted, and the appeal of these values for most actors makes them potentially strong symbols (March 1986, 30–2). NPM's preoccupation with efficiency reveals a view of the public sector primarily as a service provider and not related to a strict command structure, while other legitimate aspects of governmental activity are assigned a secondary role. The implementation of NPM reforms in New Zealand has shown that service provision can be defined very widely and in a quantitative way, de-emphasizing both traditional control and regulation functions and qualitative aspects of service provision (Gregory 2001, 247–9).

The efficiency perspective also embraces the assumption that the public sector can learn from the private sector, often in an unconditional and one-dimensional way (Self 2000). This involves the deployment of competition and market mechanisms—competitive tendering, consumer choice, or benchmarking—and the use of contracts, in such arrangements as the contracting out of services, leadership contracts, or other relational contracts (Martin 1995). Other elements borrowed from the private sector in the name of efficiency include the unambiguous definition of goals and the means or instruments to achieve them, monitoring and evaluation of results, and the use of incentives (Sahlin-Andersson 2001, 48–52). Moreover, it is considered desirable to have a less ambiguous division between politics and administration, more transparent decision-making processes, and clearer criteria for accountability. NPM also pays more attention to consumer interests, advocating more direct consumer access to service providers and more direct influence on the organization, pricing, and quality of services, etc. (Fountain 2001).

The NPM-oriented reforms in the UK under the Conservative governments seem to appear in three phases and combine marketizing and minimizing (Pollitt and Bouckaert 2004). First, there were cuts in the number of civil servants, then from 1982/3 decentralized management and budgets became popular together with more emphasis on audit (the three Es—economy, efficiency, and effectiveness), reform of the NHS, and privatization programs from the mid-1980s. From 1987 stronger market mechanisms were used (education, health, and care), the purchaser/provider split established, performance indicators used more, and further privatization decided. The largest reform was, however, the Next Steps program from 1988/9, establishing 140 executive agencies (70 per cent of the non-industrial central civil service) subordinate to the ministries/departments (Goldsworthy 1991; Trosa 1994). In early 1990s the increased consumer-orientation resulted in the Citizens' Charter (UK Prime Minister 1991, 1994), but also different types of competitive tendering and contracting out. Further, in the mid-1990s, some ministries/departments were downsized after management reviews. When Blair became prime minister not much was reversed of the reforms; they were only somewhat modified in a rather loose package of partly old reforms. He emphasized more professional management, efficient service delivery, more coordination through partnership and joined-up government, and more evaluation.

The Reinventing Government program introduced in the USA in the 1990s (Osborne and Gaebler 1993) was viewed both as one in a series of many rationally oriented reforms in US history (Downs and Larkey 1986) and as a US version of NPM (Aberbach and Rockman 2000, 135). Reinventing Government was related to the Performance Management Review (PMR) initiated by Al Gore (1993) and contained four main elements (Aberbach and Rockman 2000, 143–7): First, cutting red tape—i.e. streamlining public administration and removing rules and other obstacles to efficiency. This was problematic, since rules are important instruments in the US public sector and politicians are constantly producing new ones. Second, an increased consumer focus—implying more competition and use of business methods. This principle disregards the citizenship role and neglects the problems of heterogeneous consumer interests and providers, focusing primarily on profit. Third, empowering leaders and employees—meaning more delegation and decentralization. The problem here was to delegate authority without undermining central political control. Fourth, cutting back to basics—related to cutting programs and costs. However, the definition of a basic program or task is probably more a political than an administrative question (Fredrickson 1996).

Neither NPM nor the Reinventing Government reform nor the varied UK reforms pay much heed to the diverse features of the public sector and civil service (cf. Allison 1983). First, efficiency is only one of many considerations in the public sector, and often not the most important one. The definition and furthering of collective goals by political executives, and the decision-making efficiency and political loyalty connected to these goals, are important, as are the professional competence of civil servants, the protection of people's rights, the obligations of politicians, civil servants, and citizens, and concern for the interests of affected parties and interest groups, etc. (Egeberg 2003). Second, public goals are often multiple and ambiguous, because there are so many different stakeholders, interests, and considerations, and public administration is often correspondingly multistructured, multifunctional, and multicultural. Third, public organizations are path dependent and attend to particular complex historical traditions (Peters 1999; Selznick 1957). The roots of public organizations and the context in which they were established create different trajectories and determine the routes taken. Public organizations may be "historically inefficient" related to reform efforts because they care more about integrative cultural features and informal norms and values than aggregative features and instrumental goals (March and Olsen 1989). These features may potentially limit the implementation of NPM and hence of "smart policy."

When NPM took hold in New Zealand and Australia in the 1980s, the reforms were said to be theory driven and therefore "pure" and consistent (Pusey 1982; Boston et al. 1996, 16–35). However, since then many researchers and studies have shown that while the basic ideas of NPM may be fairly consistent, its implementation in practice contains many contradictions (Pollitt 1995). NPM is inspired by a combination of new institutional economic theory, which advocates centralizing elements and contract features, and management theory, which espouses devolution, decentralization, delegation, empowerment of managers and users, etc., which points in a rather different direction (Yeatman 1997). The balance between these two elements will vary between countries, but the management elements seem to have gained the upper hand in many political-administrative systems (Christensen and Lægreid 2001, 28). NPM treats the roles of political and administrative leaders ambiguously, saying on the one hand that political leaders cannot be trusted, because they promise too much, particularly when running for election, and thus produce inefficiency, showing an anti-political element. On the other hand, NPM assigns political leaders a central role in ensuring that goals are fulfilled, results met, and incentives used, suggesting that they can be trusted. In accordance with the management ideal, administrative leaders are delegated functions and authority, can choose how goals are to be attained, and also control others on behalf of the political executive. However, they are also more subject to control by political leaders than they were before, for example through contracts of various kinds. These inconsistencies may be one major reason why several studies have concluded that NPM produces more, not less complexity and bureaucracy (Pollitt and Bouckaert 2004).

# 3. PRECONDITIONS FOR SMARTER POLICY

Two main components determine the success of smarter policy in practice: *feasibility* and *desirability* (March and Olsen 1983; Pollitt and Bouckaert 2004, 26). Feasibility concerns the quality of the organizational thinking behind NPM and the potential for controlling the reform process and its implementation. Desirability is about what kind of society and political-administrative system is preferable.

Feasibility may be connected to what Dahl and Lindblom (1953, 58) labeled *rational calculation*, i.e. the quality of the organizational or means–end thinking. Do the main ideas of NPM draw a strong enough connection between economic/management ideas and organizational solutions to further smart policy? Boston et al. (1996, 16–35) show that the basic economic ideas in NPM may translate into a number of different organizational forms—i.e. contrary to the arguments of many reform entrepreneurs, the ideas of NPM do not offer one "best solution." What is more, NPM encompasses many different economic theories, which further complicates the feasibility question. Added to this is the inconsistency between the economic and management theories shown above. A reasonable conclusion is, therefore, that the theories and ideas behind NPM are underdeveloped and do not provide a satisfactory basis for organizational solutions and concrete reform efforts.

Another aspect of the feasibility question is whether it is possible to isolate efficiency or make it so dominant that all other factors are unimportant. This seems highly unlikely, since political-administrative systems embrace a great many other legitimate considerations. Hesse, Hood, and Peters (2003) draw a distinction between effects connected to main goals (efficiency) and side effects, and consider whether reforms bring about the intended result, the opposite result, or no change at all. Thus, the ideal situation would be reforms that are unambiguous in their ideas and solutions and produce the expected efficiency gains while yielding one or more positive side effects, such as political-democratic control. The second best result would be the fulfillment of the main goals with neutral or no side effects, or else limited negative side effects. The worst-case scenario would be failure to achieve the main goal and negative side effects.

A third aspect of rational calculation concerns the question of effectiveness. How easy is it to get public decision makers to define their goals and the means of achieving them less ambiguously and to obtain and evaluate information about the results (Pollitt and Bouckaert 2004)? While the pressure exerted by NPM in this direction may help to increase awareness (Christensen and Lægreid 1998), public goals are by nature complex and ambiguous, simply because so many different and inconsistent interests and considerations need to be balanced. Therefore, while NPM may go some way to simplifying and clarifying the goal structure, much ambiguity and complexity will remain. While many NPM entrepreneurs find this frustrating, skeptics point out that it is an inherent feature of the system, not a sign of a public "disease."

Summing up, there are few general reasons to believe that NPM-related thinking will easily lead to increased efficiency and effectiveness and therefore smarter policy, particularly when NPM reforms are broad-ranging and ambitious. The preconditions for smarter policy may be more favorable if reform is narrow, related to one sector, public institution, or function, or if it is related to functions that inherently are easy to quantify (e.g. technical functions) or targeted by elites as quantifiable (Christensen and Lægreid 2001, 310–11).

A second aspect of the feasibility question concerns political, administrative, or social control (Dahl and Lindblom 1953, 58). How easily will different stakeholders, inside and outside the public apparatus, accept the organizational thinking behind the reforms and the efforts to implement them? The first problem will probably be disagreement about the goals, i.e. some actors will oppose putting so much emphasis on efficiency. Second, even if there is agreement about general goals there may be strong disagreement about means, such as whether policy instruments like competitive tendering are really the best ones. In both cases curtailment or modification of the reforms would be the probable result. Third, there might be general problems of enacting hierarchical control in reform processes. Members of the cabinet may disagree about the reforms, there may be a tug of war between sectors and ministers, political executives holding responsibility for reforms may lack the necessary authority, and political and administrative leaders may conflict over the reforms. Tensions may exist between different governmental levels, the opinion of international actors may have to be taken into account, or more broadly speaking, interest groups or ad hoc groups may try to stop or modify reforms.

Comparative studies of NPM reforms seem to show that controlling and implementing such processes is generally more easy in Anglo-Saxon countries, where the dominant party, often through some kind of political entrepreneurship, can "crash through" the reforms, while in other types of parliamentary system with coalition governments the control is much more problematic and negotiations and compromises more evident (Christensen and Lægreid 2001; Pollitt and Bouckaert 2004).

Summing up, viewed from the control angle the best scenario would probably be support by most actors for means–end thinking, a strongly united political and administrative leadership, and acceptance of their authority by most other actors (March and Olsen 1983). The worst-case scenario would be loose organizational thinking criticized by most actors, internal conflicts in the leadership, and strong resistance to reform from many different actors. In reality several studies of

NPM-related reform processes have shown mixed results with regard to feasibility features (Christensen and Lægreid 2001; Pollitt and Bouckaert 2004; Rhodes and Weller 2001).

If the two main aspects of feasibility—organizational thinking and control—are combined it becomes clear that the ideal preconditions for smarter policy are unambiguous means–end thinking, expected effects, and strong control of the reform process. Generally speaking it is easier to exercise control than to produce carefully thought-out and well-planned reforms (March and Olsen 1983). In most countries it is accepted that political and administrative leaders will control NPM-like reforms as they do with other reforms. However, reform entrepreneurs often have problems presenting unambiguous and consistent reforms, because political-administrative systems are complex and not easily understood or changed. Generic solutions and reforms alleged to fit any political-administrative system are often offered as an answer to this complexity and ambiguity. The advantage of decontext-ualized solutions of this kind is their strong symbolic potential (Meyer and Rowan 1977; Røvik 1996); the obvious disadvantage is that in the process of being adapted to a particular context they become dependent on unique combinations of national structures and cultures. The most successful NPM entrepreneurs manage to balance decontextualization and contextualization.

Most NPM-related reform processes, like other public change processes, are characterized by "bureaucratic politics" (Allison 1971; Allison and Zelikow 1999) or Realpolitik (March and Olsen 1983)—i.e. a struggle between elite actors with differ-ent interests and definitions of reform. One way of resolving this situation is to have strong coalitions dominating the reforms, something that is more feasible in Anglo-Saxon countries, where power relationships are more potentially instrumental (Hal-ligan 2001; Hood 1996). This may create problems of legitimacy, however. This happened in New Zealand in 1984 when Roger Douglas forced through reforms. Later on, probably as a reaction to this, a referendum about the election system produced a majority in favor of an MMS system that created more small parties and undermined conditions for future reforms (Goldfinch 1998, 197–8).

A second way is for competing actors to engage in a lengthy negotiation process and finally reach a compromise between efficiency-oriented interests and traditional and path-dependent considerations. The inclusion of a greater number of actors in the process has the advantage of enhancing the legitimacy of reforms (Mosher 1967). A disadvantage might be that the eventual compromise deviates from the reform vision of the political and administrative leadership and produces a certain amount of ambiguity and eventually inadequate reform responses. A third way is sequential attention to goals and quasi-solution of conflicts (Cyert and March 1963), meaning that different considerations and interests are catered for at different points in time, as in the negotiation process in the US Congress. While this accommodates many interests, it may create inconsistency.

The question of *desirability* is at the heart of the normative issue (Goodin and Wilenski 1984; Le Grand 1991). NPM reforms may be feasible, but whether they should be furthered or implemented depends on basic ideological and cultural norms (Self 2000, 159–69). Does NPM represent a normative trend with the potential to create new types of leaders, citizens, public systems, and societies, or is it a less fundamental reform model, aimed at modifying only certain aspects of traditional public sector models?

The debate about NPM reform processes often takes place at the symbolic or ideological level (Brunsson 1989). Advocates of NPM gather support for reforms by stressing all the worst things about the traditional centralized state, particularly its legitimacy and efficiency problems. Myths and symbols are used to convince people that NPM-related reforms have all the instrumental answers to the pressing problems of a modern state (Christensen and Lægreid 2003b). Skeptics and opponents of NPM see this primarily as a neoliberal crusade, undermining and destroying traditional and well-functioning public systems. NPM ideas are presented as highly problematic and their potentially negative effects exaggerated, while the old public administration is held up as heroic and flawless. The result is normative polarization. While supporters of NPM often claim that there are objective reasons to say that the old public administration has failed concerning efficiency and caring for clients/users, opponents fiercely deny this and underline that empirical evidence for this is loose and that "if it ain't broken, don't fix it."

The "ideological war" over NPM, part of a continuous normative conflict, is being waged chiefly between neoliberal parties, which argue that these reforms are desperately needed and desirable, and socialist parties or left-leaning social democratic parties supported by the trade unions, which perceive NPM reforms as extremely damaging (Hirschman 1982; Self 2000). It is also manifest, however, in the conflicts within social democratic and labor parties, particularly in Europe, many of which have moved to the right in the last two decades and helped to open the way for NPM reforms. The modernizers have claimed that accepting some features of NPM is necessary to survive, while the opponents have accused the modernizers of selling off the "family silver." Among scholars the debate has been fierce, with symbolic overtones (Callinicos 2001; Giddens 2002)

Another indicator is the increased attention to evaluation processes. Evaluation has become much more popular and is used by reform advocates, who often have the upper hand in the modern reform processes, as a political-symbolic instrument to brand most reforms as successes, and to underline the need for continued reforms (Boyne et al. 2003; Christensen, Lægreid, and Wise 2003). The opponents of NPM have tried to come up with counter-symbols and counter-expertise to undermine the reform process.

The desirability question may also be connected to informal cultural norms and values in political-administrative systems. Supporters of NPM often argue that traditional and centralized government is rule oriented and introverted and that it is insufficiently oriented towards the environment and the consumers of public services. Opponents of NPM counter that these reforms are incompatible with legitimate traditional norms and values, and it is necessary to care more for traditional bureaucratic norms and values (cf. March and Olsen 1989; Selznick 1957). They believe NPM creates actors who are rational and strategic in a one-dimensional sense. They often cite increasing problems of accountability in crisis situations and problems of corruption under NPM, as seen in New Zealand (Gregory 1998, 2001). A third position is to emphasize that NPM reforms are quite often about a new balance of old and new cultural elements, not substituting the new for the old ones. Gains (2004) shows, for example, that the working of the Next Steps agencies in the UK have been characterized by an ambiguous and flexible combination of old and path-dependent elements, like ministerial responsibility, together with new features like hands-off management and performance indicators and result orientation.

# 4. SMART POLICY AND THE EFFECTS OF NPM

If we look at the effects of NPM—how easy is it to show that NPM has led to smarter policy, i.e. more efficiency and effectiveness? Is it possible to answer this question in a general way or do we need to analyze different dimensions and reform elements?

Since NPM introduced a large number of reform elements at the same time, some of which point in different directions, it is clearly impossible to make a general analysis of the effects of reform on efficiency. Instead, the effects of different reform elements need to be analyzed individually. NPM aimed to produce more efficiency via several structural changes, like increased structural devolution (vertical differentiation) and increased horizontal specialization (single-purpose organizations) (Boston et al. 1996, 354–9; Christensen and Lægreid 2001, 133–42). This seems generally to have produced more bureaucracy and probably less efficiency. NPM has probably simplified the jobs of leaders of subordinate organizations, like agencies and state-owned companies, because they have fewer considerations to attend to, but at the same time the roles of top leaders have become more complex and potentially inefficient. In a few countries, like New Zealand and the UK, there has been a conscious attempt to reduce personnel, but this is not the main picture (Gregory 2001).

The most likely area for efficiency gains is public service provision, particularly where competitive tendering is used. Several studies have been conducted in this area, mainly by economists. Their overall conclusion is that NPM leads to savings and efficiency gains, often of around 20 per cent or more (Domberger and Rimmer 1994). More sophisticated studies put this figure rather lower, however (Hodge 1999). There are also problems of measurement, and savings will vary according to the type of service, the market situation, and "purchaser competence." The main finding seems to be that savings result from increased competition as such, irrespective of whether the service is public or private, but this is disputed (Hodge 2000; Savas 2000).

One crucial question is whether increased efficiency through competitive tendering has been obtained at the expense of other considerations. In the old public administration many considerations other than purely commercial ones were coupled to service provision, such as more general societal considerations or issues of sector policy. Many of these involved additional expense and have now been removed from the services. They are often defined as non-commercial and as something that involves extra payment (Christensen and Lægreid 2003a; Self 2000). Clearly a narrower and commercial definition of a public service potentially may make it more efficient. Examples of this are when regional considerations in communications policy are weakened by the introduction of competition, or when the interests of weak clients in educational, health, or social services are formally de-emphasized or taken care of in other ways. In this latter respect NPM understandably increases social differences (Podder and Chatterdjee 1998; Stephens 2000).

Another broader socioeconomic perspective on efficiency in public service provision concerns the fate of the workforce under NPM. In many countries, particularly Australia and New Zealand, efficiency gains were obtained by reducing the number of people working in public services, particularly in telecommunications and transport (Mascarenhas 1996, 272–314). Where the workforce is rather old or unskilled, these people may well end up in various pension programs, casting doubt on the overall economic gains of NPM.

It is often said that the increased consumer orientation of NPM will eventually lead to both increased quality and more efficiency. The argument is that the consumer knows best how to improve services and that increased consumer participation and influence will enhance service provision (McKevitt 1998, 37–67). There are few studies to show whether increased consumer orientation will lead to smarter policy. One factor undermining this argument is that consumer experience of and hence attitudes to public service provision vary considerably, so increased efficiency for one set of consumers may run counter to the interests of others (Aberbach and Rockman 2000, 145).

Another question is whether consumers really influence public service provision under NPM. While certain strong and coordinated groups of consumers may do so, possibly to the detriment of others, the overall picture is that service providers think primarily about profit. Allowing consumers too much participation or influence takes time and resources and is therefore not efficient (Fountain 2001, 56, 61, 64). In this respect the consumer orientation of NPM may have symbolic overtones. Nevertheless, certain consumer-oriented structural reform efforts look more promising in terms of efficiency than others. One example is the "one-stop shop" or "one-window" programs established first in Australia (Centrelink) (Halligan 2004; Vardon 2000) and later in Western Europe (Hagen and Kubicel 2000). They seem to make a difference for users with a complex problem profile and represent potential administrative efficiency gains, but may also create cultural conflicts and increase organizational complexity.

The other dimension of smarter policy is effectiveness. Does NPM make it easier to formulate, pursue, and fulfill collective public goals? One way to answer this rather complicated question is to ask whether public employees are more conscious of goals, means and results than before. Some studies show this to be the case (Christensen and Lægreid 1998). The crucial question, however, is whether this increased con-sciousness will change the behavior of civil servants.

Another aspect of effectiveness is whether NPM increases political control of decision-making process in the public sector, i.e. whether hierarchical control is easier to enact. Several comparative studies covering many countries seem to show that this is not the case (Christensen and Lægreid 2001; Pollitt and Bouckaert 2004). NPM generally weakens central political control, partly as a result of increased structural devolution and partly because of the management elements in the reform. Formal changes give subordinate leaders and institutions increased authority and there is often normative pressure to keep political executives from interfering. The focus has been on frame steering or steering of strategy and basic principles rather than of minor, individual cases, and new formal control systems have replaced old informal ones. Political executives now tend to find themselves losing influence while keeping formal responsibility and thus get the blame, particularly in crisis situations (cf. Brunsson 1989).

NPM entrepreneurs seem to represent an anti-political tendency, whereby public decision making and service provision are deemed to work better if politicians are kept at a distance (Self 2000). Their focus is often on managerial control and effectiveness in single organizations, not on political-democratic control overall. This anti-political tendency seems paradoxical, since NPM reforms in many coun-tries seem to be driven by political executives. How could political executives consciously undermine their own position? One answer to this is that they, on an ideological basis, firmly believe that the working of the political-administrative system is better off with a political hands-off approach, so in their minds this is not anti-political. Another answer is that political executives too easily accept the NPM arguments about this and don't imagine the negative effects on political control. A study of a center government in Norway in the late 1990s shows quite clearly that this cabinet underestimated the undermining of political control result-ing from NPM, and was reluctant to accept the implications (Christensen and Lægreid 2002). Features like this seem in some European countries to result in efforts to bounce back and install more traditional control again, i.e. devolution and deregulation are followed by centralization and reregulation (Pollitt and Talbot 2004); this is also the case in New Zealand now (Gregory 2003).

A crucial question when political control is weakened through NPM reforms is: who gains influence? A preliminary answer would be that administrative leaders are delegated more authority (Rhodes and Weller 2001). As long as administrative leaders primarily see their role as controlling on behalf of political leaders and there is mutual trust and a close relationship between these two groups of actors, this does not amount to much weakening of overall political control. If, however, administrative leaders see their role as more formal and strategic and have a con-frontational and mistrustful attitude towards the political executive, political control may be weakened and there may be a tendency to try to pass on blame and accountability, particularly in times of crisis (Dunn 1997). Administrative leaders close to ministers are often subject to cross-pressure and attend more to political signals, while agency leaders, who are further removed from political executives structurally, seem to care less about political considerations (Christensen and Lægreid 2001).

The increased structural devolution and much narrower commercial focus entailed in NPM seem to have profoundly changed the role of executives in state-owned companies (Spicer, Emanuel, and Powell 1996; Zuna 2001), making them more autonomous and less subject to central political control. State business executives, who are often recruited from the private sector, tend to think it is appropriate for politicians to control and steer once a year at the formal business meeting. NPM supporters welcome this change, arguing that it makes public commercial leaders more competent and companies more efficient and thus able to contribute more to the collective purpose. Critics, however, argue that public commercial leaders often develop various rational strategies to avoid control and regulation. Bevan and Hood (2004) labels one such group of actors "reactive gamers," subordinate leaders who share some main goals with political leaders but also try to avoid control and make failures look like successes. Another group is known as "rational maniacs," meaning that they do not act in the collective interest and are rational in extremely self-interested and occasionally illegitimate and criminal ways. Rational maniacs are insensitive to many legitimate considerations and relevant contexts. Examples of this were seen when corruption increased in New Zealand after NPM was introduced (Gregory 2001).

Another reform feature of structural devolution is creating more autonomous agencies subordinate to ministries. The largest and earliest effort of this kind was the "Next Steps" reform in UK, establishing over 100 executive agencies subordinate to the ministries, based on principles of structural disaggregation, task-specific organizations, performance contracts, and deregulation/self-regulation (Talbot 2004). This way of organizing was certainly not new, since Sweden has had agencies like this since the seventeenth century, and the USA also for quite a long time. The effects of such a reform seem to have been varied and not dramatic concerning political control (Hogwood 1993; Rhodes 1997). Variation is evident since these agencies have quite different size, functions, and connection to the ministries, and the control not so much undermined since the ministries and Parliament have several potential instruments of control.

Pollitt and Talbot (2004) show, however, in a broad comparative book, that the last decade has brought a NPM-inspired further wave of agencification and autonomization in many countries. This wave has on the one hand increased the autonomy of the agencies, several of them regulatory agencies, and therefore also weakened the control of central political executives, but on the other hand also resulted in more efforts at controlling the agencies with new means, i.e. deregulation has been followed by reregulation. The total result of this development is not easy to sum up, but there seems to be an overall weakening of political control.

The structural devolution and withdrawal of political executives brought about by NPM seem to have increased accountability problems and left a power vacuum. This has influenced the role of elected bodies at various levels, often producing "double-bind" situations for the executive political leadership. If political executives make an effort not to interfere in the activities of agencies and public companies, they are often criticized for being too passive, especially in conflict situations (Christensen and Lægreid 2003*b*). If, on the other hand, they yield to pressure to interfere from elected political bodies and the media, they are accused of being too active and of breaking the formal rules of devolution and management reforms. At the same time, parliaments all over the world, often inspired by NPM, are strengthening their formal control of the executive, through various forms of audit organization, open hearings, parliamentary commissions, etc., potentially creating capacity problems for the political executive (Christensen, Lægreid, and Roness 2002; Pollitt et al. 1999).

Summing up the effects of NPM concerning the first aspect of smarter policy—efficiency—there seem to have been efficiency gains in public service provision. The crucial question, however, is whether the price paid for this is politically acceptable. This will vary from one country to another, depending on how much attention is paid to individual interests versus collective considerations, how much emphasis is put on equality and equity, whether there is a strong *Rechtsstaat* tradition, etc.

The analysis of the second dimension of smarter policy—effectiveness—shows that political executives are losing control through NPM; thus collective, hierarchically defined effectiveness seems to decrease. Nevertheless, the reforms may lead to more effectiveness in individual administrative bodies and public companies that have fewer political considerations and signals to attend to. This can, however, quite easily lead to "local rationality" (Allison 1971)—a typical feature of the NPM transformation from an integrated to a disintegrated and fragmented state.

# 5. Joined-up Government—Showing the Limits of Being Smart?

The concept of a "joined-up government" (JUG)—sometimes also called "whole of government"—approach involves governments paying more attention to coordination in an attempt to increase and improve it (Pollitt 2003). JUG is used mainly in countries where NPM has found extensive implementation, such as the UK and other Anglo-Saxon countries, and as such must be seen as a program for dealing with some of the problems created by NPM. JUG may be seen as an overall concept for the public sector, but it is most relevant to service-providing functions and is based on the idea that public problems often cut across sectors.

JUG has a horizontal and a vertical dimension. It includes better instruments for communication and contact, political and administrative taskforces, public committees, and intra- or interadministrative program, project, or working groups as well as stronger structural measures, whereby sectors and policy areas are merged or reorganized in other ways. JUG is a rather new label, and as such may be seen as one of many modern slogans and fads, but its thinking and instruments are actually quite old. Gulick (1937), a representative of the Scientific Administration school that sought to change the structure of the federal bureaucracy in the USA, stresses that there is an inner dynamic between specialization according to purpose, process, clients, and geography, and coordination based on organization or ideas. NPM revives some of these ideas in a more extreme version, leading to horizontal and vertical fragmentation and disintegration and thus creating a need for the increased coordination envisaged by JUG.

The horizontal dimension of JUG may relate to both the efficiency and the effectiveness aspects of smart policy. Efficiency may increase if sectors, policies, programs, and projects are coordinated better, for example by reducing overlap, contradictions, and duplication, thus potentially saving resources. The effectiveness and goal attainment of government may be enhanced by better coordination of policy and program goals, of the interests of different governmental stakeholders, and of the activities of service providers.

Attending more to the vertical dimension of JUG may make political signals to subordinate institutions or levels less ambiguous, thus allowing them to pursue central political aims more effectively, and also lead to more consistent use of the new formal control instruments typical of NPM. Another way in which JUG could modify some of the main ideas of NPM would be to bring subordinate organizations, like agencies and government companies, closer to the political leadership. It could use new laws or less ambiguous directives to make it easier for political leaders to interfere in individual cases, particularly potentially controversial ones. A further possibility would be increased cultural cooperation. However, all these measures would probably bring greater effectiveness than efficiency gains.

There are few studies showing the effects of JUG measures. The best-case scenario would be smarter policies produced by more and easier coordination between sectors, programs, and actors and across political and administrative levels and institutions and the creation of synergies. The worst-case scenario would be the erection of new structural barriers between policies and programs, making the political-administrative system even more bureaucratic, complex, and ambiguous, and decreasing efficiency and effectiveness. Pollitt (2003) points out that new coordinated "silos" can cut across existing sector- or policy-oriented ones, resulting in more problems of complexity and accountability. JUG may also create more myths and symbols, because it is "an idea whose time has come" (Røvik 1996).

In some countries joined-up *government* is coupled to joined-up *governance*, meaning better coordination between the government and society, interest groups or voluntary associations, business organizations, etc. In certain policy areas, like health and social services, some of these groups have for a long time been important in implementing governmental policy. There is now renewed interest in this aspect, as in the UK, where "New Labour" is talking about a more holistic and network-oriented approach to public policy, to be realized, for example, through public–private partnerships (Newman 2001).

A good illustration of the dynamics between NPM and JUG is New Zealand, where worries about the fragmentation of central government increased in the late 1990s. This led to a quest for more joined-up government, which materialized in a public report in 2001 that talked about a "whole of government" perspective (as in Australia). The report discussed "putting public service back together again" (Gregory 2003). The measures proposed were creating interagency "circuit-breaker" teams to solve problems of service delivery, establishing "super networks" better to integrate policy, delivery, and capacity building, and a careful process of structural consolidation.

Summing up, JUG represents a continuation of the age-old government dilemma of specialization versus coordination and will probably eventually lead to renewed demands for specialization. At the same time, it must be seen as a modern reaction to the problems of fragmentation and disintegration produced by NPM reforms. The *raison d'être* for JUG is the realization that policy can only be made smarter if the effects of NPM are counteracted or modified in certain ways. The goals involved are so ambitious and the policy areas so broad and complicated that the prospect of rich rewards also entails a high risk of failure and negative political consequences. In this respect a more pragmatic style of joined-up government is a viable alternative.

# 6. CONCLUSION

This chapter has discussed whether and how NPM-related reforms have contributed to more efficiency and effectiveness—smarter policy—in the public sector. First, the one-dimensional focus on efficiency, the tension between efficiency and other legitimate considerations in the public sector, and the internal inconsistency of the reform measures were discussed. Second, it was shown that feasibility related to both efficiency and effectiveness is difficult to obtain overall in large and complex reforms like NPM but more likely in individual institutions engaging in systematic and unambiguous reforms. Concerning desirability, normative conflicts and polarization over the reforms were identified. However, the ideological dominance of NPM supporters has helped to further NPM in many countries. Third, the effects of NPM were analyzed. NPM has not led to smarter policy overall. However, there have been some efficiency gains in public service provision and an increase in effectiveness in certain public organizations, albeit with some problematic and controversial side effects. Overall political control is undermined by NPM, structural and cultural fragmentation and disintegration have increased, as have social costs and inequality, and these are reasons why NPM reforms have been modified in some countries, trying to control more again.

Fourth, efforts to increase coordination in the form of joined-up government may be seen as a reaction to the fragmentation and disintegration in the modern NPM state. Whether JUG's enhanced focus on coordination and collaboration will produce smarter policy is not easy to judge and has yet to be seen. It may potentially increase efficiency and effectiveness through fewer duplications and more synergies, but it may also increase costs by adding layers of new leaders and coordinating jobs, and make decision-making structures more complex.

It is a parallel literature about smart practice that is of relevance to discussing smart policy. This literature, primarily connected to a seminal book by Bardach (1998), is generally sympathetic towards the principles of NPM, but talks quite a lot about some different features. Bardach (2004) is preoccupied with "inter-agency collaborative capacity" and "craftmanship thinking" as a combination of creativity and public spirtedness. He sees these features as major preconditions for smart practice. And Barzelay (2004) stresses the vertical integrative efforts and hands-on attitudes of political and administrative leaders as supporting successful innovation. These are ideas pretty similar to some of the JUG thoughts, and they are different from the core of NPM concerning devolution and fragmentation.

If we take a broader view of NPM and smart policy, the main trends seem to be that NPM has peaked, after some fifteen to twenty years of dominance, and some of the core Anglo-American NPM countries, like New Zealand, are heading in another direction (Gregory 2003). An indication of this is also that the main reform entrepreneur, the OECD, is not that eager any longer and is talking more about other concepts or recipes for reform (Christensen and Lægreid 2004; Sahlin-Andersson 2001). Some of the latecomers, like the Scandinavian countries and some continental European countries are still heading in a NPM direction, but in a more reluctant and modified way, attending more to reform symbols than to NPM practice.

The variations between countries concerning the history of NPM and smart policy seem to be explained by combining a rather complex set of perspectives/theories: One set of factors connects to the environment (Olsen 1992). Some of the countries most eagerly pursing the NPM path experienced strong pressure from both the technical environment, for example through economic crises, and the institutional environment, through critique towards the government for inefficiency and lack of responsiveness (whether true or not). But NPM seems to have had problems delivering better overall efficiency and overall results, something that has led the front runners to hesitate more and partly turn around.

A second set of explanatory factors concerns the cultural-historical constraints and norms (Christensen and Lægreid 2001). Countries with a strong *Rechtsstaat* tradition, like the Scandinavian countries and Germany, have been far more reluctant to take on board NPM than the Anglo-American countries, many of which put less emphasis on equality and equity. Even though consistent pressure over some time has gradually changed this variety, and made countries more similar in this respect, some of this division is still evident and persistent.

A third important set of factors concerns structural and instrumental factors. Countries with a Westminster type of parliamentary system have always had a much stronger potential for implementing substantial reform than systems with a more heterogeneous parliamentary structure, like the Scandinavian countries or many continental European countries, not to mention fragmented presidential systems like the USA (Pollitt and Bouckaert 2004). The neoliberal wave behind NPM also occurred first in these countries. A rather homogeneous administrative system in some of these countries may also further NPM. Combining these three sets of explanatory factors shows quite clearly the variety in the use and implementation of NPM and smart policy. External crises, two-party systems, and reform-compatible culture explain why Anglo-American countries have been the reform entrepreneurs, but also why some of them now are able to turn around or modify the path chosen, when NPM cannot deliver smart practice.

## References

ABERBACH, J. D., and ROCKMAN, B. A. 2000. *In the Web of Politics: Three Decades of the U.S. Federal Executive.* Washington, DC: Brookings Institution Press.

ALLISON, G. T. 1971. *Essence of Decision.* Boston: Little, Brown.

—— 1983. Public and private managers: are they fundamentally alike in all unimportant respects? In *Public Management. Public and Private Perspectives,* ed. J. L. Perry and K. L. Kraemer. Palo Alto, Calif.: Mayfield.

—— and ZELIKOW, P. 1999. *Essence of Decision* 2nd edn. Reading, Mass.: Longman.

BARDACH, E. 1998. *Getting Agencies to Work Together: The Practice and Theory of Management Craftsmanship.* Washington, DC: Brookings Institution.

—— 2004. Implementing innovation across agency lines. Paper presented at the 20th Anniversary Conference of the Structure and Organization of Government Research Committee of the International Political Science Association, "Smart practices toward innovation in public Management." Vancouver, 15–17 June.

BARZELAY, M. 2004. Narratives, arguments, and institutional processualism: learning about implementing presidential priorities from *Brazil in Action.* Paper presented at the 20th Anniversary Conference of the Structure and Organization of Government Research Committee of the International Political Science Association, Vancouver, 15–17 June. Available at: http://faculty.arts.ubs.ca/campbell/sog-conf/papers/sog2004-barzelay.pdf (accessed 22 Mar. 2006).

BEVAN, G., and HOOD, G. 2004. Where soft theory meets hard cases: the limits of transparency and proportionality in health care regulations. Working paper presented at the ASPA conference, Portland, 27–30 Mar. Available at: www.lse.ac.uk/. . ./europeanConferenceOnHealth Economics2004/EHPGPAPERS/EHPG4BevanHood.doc (accessed 22 Mar. 2006).

BOSTON, J., MARTIN, J., PALLOT, J., and WALSH, P. 1996. *Public Management: The New Zealand Model.* Auckland: Oxford University Press.

BOYNE, G. A. 1998. Competitive tendering in local government: a review of theory and evidence. *Public Administration,* 76 (Winter): 695–712.

—— FARRELL, C., LAW, J., POWELL, M., and WALKER, R. M. 2003. *Evaluating Public Management Reforms.* Buckingham: Open University Press.

BRUNSSON, N. 1989. *The Organization of Hypocrisy: Talk, Decisions and Actions in Organizations.* Chichester: Wiley.

CALLINICOS, A. 2001. *Against the Third Way: An Anti-Capitalist Critique.* Cambridge: Polity Press.

CHRISTENSEN, T., and LÆGREID, P. 1998. Administrative reform policy: the case of Norway. *International Review of Administrative Sciences,* 64: 457–75.

—— —— (eds.) 2001. *New Public Management: The Transformation of Ideas and Practice.* Aldershot: Ashgate.

—— —— 2002. *Reformer og lederskap: Omstilling i den utøvende makt* (Reforms and Leadership: Renewal in the Executive Power). Oslo: Scandinanian University Press.

—— —— 2003*a*. Administrative reform policy: the challenges of turning symbols into practice. *Public Organization Review: A Global Journal,* 3: 3–27.

—— —— 2003*b*. Coping with complex leadership roles: the problematic redefinition of government-owned enterprises. *Public Administration,* 81 (4): 803–31.

—— —— 2004. Regulatory agencies—the challenges of balancing agency autonomy and political control. Revised paper presented at the 20th Anniversary Conference of the Structure and Organization of Government Research Committee of the International Political Science Association, "Smart practices toward innovation in public management." Vancouver, 15–17 June.

—— —— and RONESS, P. G. 2002. Increasing parliamentary control of the executive? New instruments and emerging effects. *Journal of Legislative Studies,* 8 (1: Spring): 37–62.

—— —— and WISE, L. C. 2003. Evaluating public management reforms in central government: Norway, Sweden and the United States of America. In *Evaluation in Public Sector Reform: Concepts and Practice in International Perspective,* ed. H. Wollmann. Cheltenham: Edward Elgar.

CONSIDINE, M. 2001. *Enterprising States: The Public Management of Welfare-to-Work.* Cambridge: Cambridge University Press.

—— 2002. The end of the line? Accountable government in the age of networks, partnerships and joined-up services. *Governance,* 15 (1: Jan.): 21–40.

—— and LEWIS, J. M. 1999. Governance at ground level: the frontline bureaucrat in the age of markets and networks. *Public Administration Review,* 59 (6: Nov.–Dec.): 467–80.

CYERT, R. M., and MARCH, J. G. 1963. *A Behavioral Theory of the Firm.* Englewood Cliffs, NJ: Prentice Hall.

DAHL, R. A., and LINDBLOM, C. E. 1953. *Politics, Economics, and Welfare.* New York: Harper and Row.

DOMBERGER, S., and RIMMER, S. 1994. Competitive tendering and contracting in the public sector: a survey. *International Journal of the Economics of Business,* 1 (3): 439–53.

DOWNS, G. W., and LARKEY, P. D. 1986. *The Search for Government Efficiency: From Hubris to Helplessness.* Philadelphia: Temple University Press.

DUNN, D. D. 1997. *Politics and Administration at the Top: Lessons from Down Under.* Pittsburgh, Pa.: University of Pittsburgh Press.

EGEBERG, M. 2003. How bureaucratic structure matters: an organizational perspective. In *The Handbook of Public Administration,* ed. B. G. Peters and J. Pierre. London: Sage.

FOUNTAIN, J. E. 2001. Paradoxes of public sector customer service. *Governance,* 14: 55–73.

FREDRICKSON, H. G. 1996. Comparing the reinventing movement with the New Public Administration. *Public Administration Review,* 56 (3: May–June): 263–70.

GAINS, F. 2004. Adapting the agency concept: variations within "Next Steps." In *Unbundled Government: A Critical Analysis of the Global Trend to Agencies, Quangos and Contractualism,* ed. C. Pollitt and C. Talbot. London: Routledge.

GIDDENS, A. 2002. *Where Now for New Labour?* Cambridge: Polity Press.

GOLDFINCH, S. 1998. Remaking New Zealand's economic policy: institutional elites as radical innovators 1984–1993. *Governance,* 11 (2): 177–207.

GOLDSWORTHY, D. 1991. *Setting up Next Steps.* London: HMSO.

GOODIN, R. E., and WILENSKI, P. 1984. Beyond efficiency: the logical underpinnings of administrative principles. *Public Administrative Review,* 44: 512–17.

GORE, A. 1993. *From Red Tape to Results: Creating a Government that Works Better and Costs Less.* Report of the National Performance Review. Washington, DC: Government Printing Office.

GREGORY, R. 1998. Political responsibility for bureaucratic incompetence: tragedy at Cave Creek. *Public Administration,* 76 (Autumn): 519–38.

—— 2001. Transforming governmental culture: a sceptical view of New Public Management. In *New Public Management: The Transformation of Ideas and Practice,* ed. T. Christensen and P. Lægreid. Aldershot: Ashgate.

—— 2003. All the king's horses and all the king's men: putting New Zealand's public sector back together again. *International Public Management Review,* 4 (2): 41–58.

GULICK, L. 1937. Notes on the theory of organizations. With special reference to government. In *Papers on the Science of Administration,* ed. L. Gulick and L. Urwin. New York: A. M. Kelley.

HAGEN, M., and KUBICEL, H. (eds.) 2000. *One-Stop Government in Europe: Results from 11 National Surveys.* Bremen: University of Bremen.

HALLIGAN, J. 2001. The process of reform in the era of public sector transformation. In *New Public Management: The Transformation of Ideas and Practice,* ed. T. Christensen and P. Lægreid. Aldershot: Ashgate.

—— 2004. Advocacy and innovation in inter-agency management: the case of Centrelink. Paper presented at the 20th Anniversary Conference of the Structure and Organization of Government Research Committee of the International Political Science Association, Vancouver, 15–17 June. Available at: http://faculty.arts.ubs.ca/campbell/sog-conf/papers/sog2004-haligan.pdf (accessed 22 Mar. 2006).

HESSE, J. J., HOOD, C., and PETERS, B. G. (eds.) 2003. *Paradoxes in Public Sector Reform.* Berlin: Duncker & Humblot.

HILMER, F. 1993. *National Competition Policy.* Canberra: Australian Government Publishing Service.

HIRSCHMAN, A. 1982. *Shifting Involvements.* Princeton, NJ: Princeton University Press.

HODGE, G. A. 1999. Competitive tendering and contracting out: rhetoric or reality? *Public Productivity & Management Review,* 22 (4: June): 455–69.

—— 2000. *Privatization: An International Review of Performance.* Boulder, Colo.: Westview.

HOGWOOD, B. W. 1993. Restructuring central government: the "Next Steps" initiative. In *Managing Public Organizations,* ed. J. Kooiman and K. Eliassen, 2nd edn. London: Sage.

HOOD, C. 1996. Exploring variations in public management reform of the 1980s. In *Civil Service Systems,* ed. H. A. G. M. Bekke, J. L. Perry, and T. A. J. Toonen. Bloomington: Indiana University Press.

KETTL, D. F. 1997. The global revolution in public management: driving themes, missing links. *Journal of Policy Analysis and Management,* 16 (3): 446–62.

LE GRAND, J. 1991. *Equity and Choice.* London: HarperCollins.

McKEVITT, D. 1998. *Managing Public Services.* Oxford: Blackwell.

MARCH, J. G. 1986. How we talk and how we act: administrative theory and administrative life. In *Leadership and Organizational Culture: New Perspectives on Administrative Theory and Practice,* ed. T. J. Sergiovanni and J. E. Corbally. Urbana: University of Illinois Press.

—— and OLSEN, J. P. 1983. Organizing political life: what administrative reorganization tells us about government. *American Political Science Review,* 77: 281–97.

—— —— 1989. *Rediscovering Institutions: The Organizational Basis of Politics.* New York: Free Press.

MARTIN, J. 1995. Contracting and accountability. In *The State under Contract,* ed. J. Boston. Wellington: Bridget Williams.

MASCARENHAS, R. C. 1996. *Government and the Economy in Australia and New Zealand: The Politics of Economic Policy Making*. San Francisco: Austin and Winfield.

MEYER, J. W., and ROWAN, B. 1977. Institutionalized organizations: formal structure as myth and ceremony. *American Journal of Sociology*, 83 (Sept.): 340–63.

MOSHER, F. (ed.) 1967. *Governmental Reorganizations*. Indianapolis: Bobbs-Merrill.

NEWMAN, J. 2001. *Modernising Governance: New Labour, Policy and Society*. London: Sage.

NEW ZEALAND, TREASURY 1987. *Government Management*. Wellington: Government Printer.

OLSEN, J. P. 1988. Administrative reform and theories of organization. In *Organizing Governance: Governing Organizations*, ed. C. Campbell and B. G. Peters. Pittsburgh, Pa.: University of Pittsburgh Press.

—— 1992. Analyzing institutional dynamics. *Staatswissenschaften und Staatspraxis*, 2: 247–71.

OSBORNE, D., and GAEBLER, T. 1993. *Reinventing Government*. New York: Plume/Penguin.

PETERS, B. G. 1999. *Institutional Theory in Political Science: The "New Institutionalism."* London: Pinter.

PODDER, N., and CHATTERJEE, S. 1998. Sharing the national cake in post-reform New Zealand: income inequality in terms of income sources. Paper presented to the New Zealand Association of Economists Conference, Aug.

POLLITT, C. 1995. Justification by works or by faith. *Evaluation*, 1 (2): 133–54.

—— 2003. Joined-up government. *Political Studies Review*, 1 (1): 34–49.

—— and BOUCKAERT, G. 2004. *Public Management Reform: A Comparative Analysis*, 2nd edn. Oxford: Oxford University Press.

—— and TALBOT, C. (eds.) 2004. *Unbundled Government: A Critical Analysis of the Global Trend to Agencies, Quangos and Contractualism*. London: Routledge.

—— GIRRE, X., LONSDALE, J., MUL, R., SUMMA , H., and WAERNESS, M. 1999. *Performance or Compliance? Performance Audit and Public Management in Five Countries*. Oxford: Oxford University Press.

PUSEY, M. 1982. *Economic Rationalism in Canberra*. Melbourne: Cambridge University Press.

RHODES, R. A. W. 1997. Reinventing Whitehall 1979–1995. In *Public Management and Administrative Reform in Western Europe*, ed. W. Kickert. Cheltenham: Edward Elgar.

—— and WELLER, P. (eds.) 2001. *The Changing World of Top Officials: Mandarins or Valets?* Buckingham: Open University Press.

RØVIK, K. A. 1996. Deinstitutionalization and the logic of fashion. In *Translating Organizational Change*, ed. B. Czarniawska and G. Sevon. New York: De Gruyter.

SAHLIN-ANDERSSON, K. 2001. National, international and transnational construction of New Public Management. In *New Public Management. The Transformation of Ideas and Practice*, ed. T. Christensen and P. Lægreid. Aldershot: Ashgate.

SAVAS, E. S. 2000. *Privatization and Public Private Partnership*. New York: Chatham House.

SELF, P. 2000. *Rolling Back the State: Economic Dogma and Political Choice*. New York: St Martin's Press.

SELZNICK, P. 1957. *Leadership in Administration*. New York: Harper and Row.

SPICER, B., EMANUEL, D., and POWELL, M. 1996. *Transforming Government Enterprises*. St Leonards: Centre for Independent Studies.

STEPHENS, R. 2000. The social impact of reform: poverty in Aotearoa/New Zealand. *Social Policy and Administration*, 4 (1: Mar.): 64–86.

TALBOT, C. 2004. The agency idea: sometimes old, sometimes new, sometimes borrowed, sometimes untrue. In *Unbundled Government: A Critical Analysis of the Global Trend to Agencies, Quangos and Contractualism*, ed. C. Pollitt and C. Talbot. London: Routledge.

TROSA, S. 1994. *Next Steps: Moving On*. London: Cabinet Office.

UNITED KINGDOM PRIME MINISTER 1991. *The Citizens' Charter*. London: HMSO.

UNITED KINGDOM PRIME MINISTER 1994. *The Citizen's Charter: Second Report.* London: HMSO.

VARDON, S. 2000. Centrelink: a three-stage evolution. In *The Howard Government,* ed. G. Singleton. Sydney: University of New South Wales Press.

WEAVER, B. K., and ROCKMAN, B. A. (eds.) 1993. *Do Institutions Matter? Government Capabilities in the United States and Abroad.* Washington, DC: Brookings Institution.

YEATMAN, A. 1997. The reforms of public management, DC: an overview. In *Managerialism: The Great Debate,* ed. M. Considine and M. Painter. Melbourne: Melbourne University Press.

ZUNA, H. R. 2001. The effects of corporatisation on political control. In *New Public Management: The Transformation of Ideas and Practice,* ed. T. Christensen and P. Lægreid. Aldershot: Ashgate.

C H A P T E R  2 2

...........................................................................................................

# THE TOOLS OF GOVERNMENT IN THE INFORMATION AGE

...........................................................................................................

## CHRISTOPHER HOOD

WHAT does the arrival of contemporary information-age technology mean for older, horse-age and railway-age, ways of thinking about the instruments used by government for public policy? Do we need completely new ways of conceiving those instruments in the twenty-first century? Or on the contrary, do the older questions and conceptions of government tools have just as much if not more analytic value in an age of changing technology? This chapter argues the case for the latter proposition. It begins by briefly reviewing some of the standard strains in the policy instruments literature of the last two decades, and then explores the case of e-government and information-age technology to assess how far such developments radically challenge earlier ways of thinking about the instrumentalities of the state, and what we can learn about information-age technology in government through the lenses of conventional tools of government analysis.

# 1. TOOLS OF GOVERNMENT ANALYSIS:
# THREE CONVENTIONAL STRAINS

The tools or instruments of government have been analyzed in at least three main ways in the public policy literature over the past twenty years or so, and changing forms of information technology present different analytic issues for each of those conventional approaches. One such approach, possibly the best known, is to conceive of instruments as institutions, in the sense of forms of organization available to government, such as public corporations, independent or private sector contractors, and various forms of public–private partnership. Perhaps the leading contemporary exponent of this approach is Salamon (2002; originally Salamon and Lund 1989), who argues that new types of institutional forms for public policy are central to the "new governance" paradigm of recent decades. How far those public–private institutional forms are as truly distinctive to the modern era as Salamon (2002, 2) claims is debatable—after all, apparently commercial and independent forms of organization have long been extensively used by governments in the world of espionage, black propaganda, and other forms of unconventional warfare (see Mackenzie 2002) and church organizations have traditionally been important in education, welfare, and population registration in many European states. But that is not the central issue here.

A second well-established approach focuses on the politics of instrument selection, in the sense of the interests or ideas that shape the choice of tools. For this approach it is not crucial whether government instruments are viewed as institutions or other forms of action: the key question concerns what political, ideological, or cognitive processes lead to the choice of one policy instrument rather than another. A striking instance of this kind of approach is the exploration by Ackerknecht (1948) and more recently by Baldwin (1999) of the extent to which differences between authoritarian and liberal state regimes shaped the choice between "sanitarian" and "quarantinist" tools to tackle the serious problem of contagious disease in nineteenth-century European states. But in the general public policy literature, this approach is perhaps best exemplified in the work of Linder and Peters (1989, 1992, 1998), who have classified various ways of understanding the link between policy problems and selection of instruments, ranging from contingency to "constitutivism."

A third set of approaches to the instruments of government has tended to be institution free and to focus more on cataloguing the tool kit in a generic way than on the politics of instrument choice. This approach can be partly traced back to Dahl and Lindblom's (1953) pioneering analysis of the array of socioeconomic instruments used by government, though that is a hybrid of institutional and institution-free analysis. More strongly institution-free approaches come in at least three varieties. Some, notably Elmore's (1987) approach (elaborated by Schneider and Ingram 1990), have a strong purposive or managerial theme and focus on broad (and not neces-sarily government-specific) "intervention strategies" that include capacity building, symbolism, and system changing. Another fairly well-known approach of this type is the "carrots, sticks, and sermons" categorization of policy instruments, developed by Vedung (Bertelmans-Videc, Rist, and Vedung 1998), on the basis of a well-known trichotomy of types of organizational control originally developed by the famous organizational sociologist Etzioni (1961) over thirty years before. Le Grand's (2003) "knights, knaves and pawns" analysis of motivations in public policy might be argued to be of a similar kind. A third is my own analysis of the instruments available to government for gathering information and affecting behaviour at the point where government comes into contact with citizens (Hood 1983).

The latter analysis differs from the "carrots, sticks, and sermons" approach insofar as it is concerned with the instruments specifically available to government (rather than those employable in any organization), is concerned with both information-gathering and behaviour-modifying/enforcement tools (rather than with the latter alone), and is based in cybernetics, the science of general control systems, rather than organizational sociology. (For classic applications of cybernetics to government and organization, see Deutsch 1963; Beer 1966; Steinbruner 1974; Dunsire 1978.) The key claim is that the instruments specific to government for information gathering and behaviour modification—universal aspects of control—have to be based on some combination of at least four basic social resources, namely "nodality," "authority," "treasure," and "organization." Nodality denotes the capacity of government to operate as a central point (not necessarily *the* central point) in information networks. Authority denotes government's legal power and other sources of legitimacy. "Treasure" denotes its assets or fungible resources, and "organization" denotes its capacity for direct action, for instance through armies, police, or bureaucracy.

This three-part classification of approaches does not cover all the possible ways of conceiving the instrumentalities of the state. And there are certainly some approaches, such as Dahl and Lindblom's (1953) early account of the socioeconomic instruments of public policy, as already mentioned, which cut across the three types (mixing institutional forms and generic forms of action, in that case). But the trichotomy perhaps captures enough of the conventional forms of "instruments" analysis to allow us to explore how far such conventional analysis is radically superseded by the information age, and how far it can be fruitfully drawn upon to understand information-age government tools.

# 2. INFORMATION AGE TECHNOLOGY AND GOVERNMENT: TRANSFORMATION OR DYNAMIC CONSERVATISM?

The idea that information-age technology is destined to have radically transformative effects on the way government operates has been advanced both by scholars and by governments themselves. In the academic world, numerous cyber-scholars (such as Taylor 1992, 377–8) have berated their colleagues in public administration and public policy for neglecting or seriously underestimating the extent to which information and communications technology alter the way that government works. Some, such as Frissen (1996, 1998), have gone so far as to argue that such technology heralds an entirely new form of state—in his case, a "virtual state" in which the new techno-culture produces "fragmented, decentred and non-hierarchical" structures and processes (Frissen 1998, 41). Over a decade ago, Taylor and Williams (1991, 172) claimed: "A new public administration is being forged and new information flows, and the computer networks which facilitate and mediate them, are fundamental to the innovation process." Scholars such as Bellamy and Taylor (1998) have argued in similar vein that the separation of front- and back-office functions in government, facilitated by developments in information and communications technology, is fundamental to changing government's modus operandi. More broadly, the advent of microprocessors brought a range of prophets who argued that the new technology would decentralize power and control in society, and would thus help to usher in a less hierarchic society (for an early analysis of the "neutrality" debate see Ward 1989).

In rather darker vein, civil libertarian critics have made much of information and communications technology developments that are said to be bringing about a quantum extension in government's powers to detect and punish, through applications such as satellite and CCTV cameras linked to computers, new ways of monitoring telephony and computer use, high-security identity systems, and compulsory tagging of various kinds of individuals. Brin's (1998) *Transparent Society*, developing earlier "surveillance society" analyses (such as Rule 1973; Bunyan 1976; Ackroyd et al. 1977; Hewitt 1982, ch. 2), makes much of the potentially radical implications of surveillance technology that can continuously pinpoint the whereabouts of individuals in spaces as small as a single square metre—an application being developed at the time of writing for surveillance of convicted paedophiles and those who have been convicted of domestic violence who are legally restrained from approaching those they have abused.

Politicians and public service reform visionaries such as Osborne and Gaebler (1992) have likewise made much of the potentially transformative effects of information and communications technology on public service delivery. Every self-respecting government today has to have a relentlessly upbeat vision of the future that involves information and communications technology decisively improving the way it interacts with citizens. Perhaps the best-known example of that sort of techno-vision is the 1993 Clinton–Gore "National Performance Review" of the US federal government, which claimed (Gore 1993, 112): "With computers and telecommunications we need not do things as we have in the past. We can design a customer-driven electronic government that operates in ways that, 10 years ago, the most visionary planner would not have imagined." The NPR made much of the ways that information and communications technology could transform government purchasing systems, advice and information systems, methods of funds transfer, "smart cards" to entitle citizens to use a range of related public services, and electronic interactions between citizens and government on matters such as filing of tax returns. And that vision has been widely echoed in other countries, for example in the UK government's *Modernizing Government* White Paper of 1999 (Cabinet Office 1999), almost to the point of cliché.

Against these transformative visions of the effect of information and communications technology on government instrumentalities and operations, numerous scholars have offered more sceptical analyses more redolent of Schön's (1971) idea of "dynamic conservatism"—that is, the sort of change that allows underlying social relationships to remain the same. Numerous scholars have argued that technologies in government tend to mirror and reproduce the cultures they develop within, contrary to expectations that they can usher in quite new social or organizational climates (see Kraemer and King 1986; Hood 2000; and for the broader "radical science movement" argument that science and technology are shaped by social systems, see Rose and Rose 1976). Indeed, contrary to Frissen's "end-of-hierarchy" analysis of the effects of ICT, Holliday (2001) has argued that central agencies in government are quite capable of using ICT developments to maintain and consolidate their power. For Holliday (2001), "the sole novelties [in the command structure of the state] introduced by the information and communications technology revolution are to be found in the expanded networks that can now be constructed around issues, and in the expanded array of resources on which actors are able to draw in seeking to secure their goals." Other scholars have highlighted the extent to which technological possibilities for enhancing government's surveillance capacity can be countered by the resourcefulness of opportunists or principled adversaries of government, as with the use of caller ID and other devices in the 1980s to avoid government surveillance of telephones through wiretapping (Chan and Camp 2002, 26). Margetts (1999) and other scholars have shown how far short government's actual information and communications technology operations often fall of what Margetts calls the "hyper-modernist" promises and visions of the new techno-future, to the point of introducing major new sources of government waste and failure.

Some of these differences in perspective might be put down to the difference between the analysis of implementation after the fact and the forward-looking analysis of potential. Some might be put down to the difference between the effects of information and communications technology on government's internal organization and its effects on the way government interacts with citizens. And some of those differences in perspective might depend on the time period that is taken, since many claim that the age when information and communications technology development mainly affected government's internal organization started to change decisively with later stages of such development, particularly web-based technology and tracking systems (see Margetts 2003, 371). Against that argument, it might be questioned whether the Internet really *is* so different, given that it too has been attended by the same contradictory "transformation" and "dynamic conservatism" views that surrounded the development of microprocessors in an earlier generation: in the early years of Internet expansion it "brought much social commentary telling us how the web was about to sweep away the old regime ... The pendulum swung back quickly, however" (Healy 2002, 480).

However, to the extent that the advent of the web did make a real difference to the instruments used by government at the point where it interacts with citizens, the notion that decisive change began with web technology would echo the argument of the veteran management guru Peter Drucker (1999, 49), who drew a parallel with the course of the nineteenth-century Industrial Revolution to argue that the first effect of the "informational revolution" has been to find new ways of making existing products, though it might later lead to qualitatively new products such as the railroads: "Like the Industrial Revolution two centuries ago, the Informational Revolution so far—that is, since the first computers in the mid-1940s—has only transformed processes that were here all along."

Drucker's argument certainly seems plausible for the case of taxation, where up to now the information and communications technology revolution has tended to consist more in changing the way that established taxes are paid (for instance through new filing or payment systems) and weakening some types of taxes that are vulnerable to avoidance through the Internet (such as betting taxes), than in collecting radically new types of taxes. In principle, Internet service providers could be the oil companies of the information age, a key point for tax collection, and in principle "virtual stamps" on email could be a twenty-first century fiscal innovation to match the invention of stamp taxes in the seventeenth century. But in line with Drucker's claim, such fiscal innovation has so far been marked by its absence rather than its presence (see Hood 2003).

However the difference between the "transformational" and "dynamic-conservatism" perspectives on the effect of information and communications technology on government's instruments might be accounted for, the question stated at the outset remains. That is, are the conventional ways of understanding government's tools that were described in the previous section still adequate for the understanding of government's operations in the information age?

# 3. Applying Conventional Analysis to Information-Age Tools of Government: Three Sets of Issues

The three ways of analyzing government's instruments that were identified earlier each raise different issues for the way government works in the cyber-age. For the Salamon-type instruments-as-institutions approach, the central issue is how far information-age technology reshapes or extends the range of alternative institutional arrangements available to government. There are several possible mechanisms through which that could happen. One is by the development of computational power that reduces the transaction costs of choice or trading in such a way as to open up institutional possibilities that go beyond traditional forms such as regulated private monopolies or state enterprise. And in some cases, that does seem to have happened. For instance, Foster (1992, 73) claims that spot markets for electricity were not possible when electricity grids were first introduced in countries such as the UK in the 1920s (because of limited detection tools in calibrating a good that cannot be readily stored), meaning that the only real institutional alternatives for provision of electricity in those technological conditions were monopoly public trading corporations or regulated monopoly private providers, as in the traditional US style. However, Foster argues, the requisite computing power for creating a new kind of market had developed by the 1980s, offering the possibility for "a truly commercial electricity market buying and selling through the grid" that considerably extended the range of institutional alternatives. The capacity for utility consumers (for water, gas, telephones, etc.) to choose among alternative providers could also be argued to have been heavily shaped by the same sort of information technology developments.

Another way that information-age technology could reshape the institutional tools of government is by new forms of communication that shrink the effects of geographical distance for organizations. The development of this kind that has been most discussed by students of government, as noted earlier, is the capacity of information and communications technology to allow "back-office" functions to be physically separated from "front-line" activity (see for instance, Bellamy and Taylor 1998). And a further potential route might be found in the ability of information-age technology to reshape the case-handling, filing, and memory functions that were once distinctive to public bureaucracies, paving the way for new forms of privatization and outsourcing to global corporations, perhaps in conjunction with modern target systems (see Dunleavy 1994; Cairncross 2005, 19).

The second, politics-of-instruments approach to analyzing the tools of government that was identified earlier can also be applied to government policy instrumentalities in the information age, even though information-age technology is not central to Linder and Peters's original analysis. For instance, we have already noted that IT developments have tended to be presented as a remedy for all the traditional shortcomings of government bureaucracy in politicians' visions of re-engineered public services, at least since the Clinton–Gore "National Performance Review" in the United States a decade or so ago. Evidently, information-age technology was widely viewed as a solution looking for problems, to the extent that it offered an important new form of what Linder and Peters (1992) confusingly call "instrumentalism" in the choice of methods of policy delivery (they use the word instrumentalism to denote obsession with a single tool, such as price mechanisms or participative decision styles, as a panacea for all problems).

However, it is debatable how far such solution-for-every-problem attitudes towards information and communications technology are best understood as a contemporary manifestation of the recurring utopian belief, going back at least to Saint-Simon, that new technology can usher in radically improved social and governance arrangements. Dunlop and Kling (1991, 16–17) have claimed that there is a recurring strain of utopian thought that "places the use of some specific technology—computers, nuclear energy, or low-energy, low-impact technologies—as the central enabling element of a utopian vision." Such visions, according to Dunlop and Kling, typically assume the use of technology in social contexts where the users are highly cooperative and sabotage, conflict, politics, and adversarial legalism scarcely exist. On the face of it many contemporary visions of better governance and a new social order through information and communications technology (though not the dystopian visions) do seem to fit that pattern fairly closely, as has already been noted.

On the other hand, the solution-for-every-problem view of the implications of information and communications technology for the tools of government might involve something more than utopian optimism. That is, it might be best understood as a reflection of a new information-industrial complex with large corporate interests at stake in the outsourcing and computerization of government's once-distinctive information-collecting, filing, and case-handling operations. From a Linder–Peters perspective, some parallel could be drawn with the military-industrial complexes that grew up in the nineteenth century as governments moved away from direct production of military *matériel* in arsenals and government dockyards to outsourced production of armaments, though the parallel is certainly far from exact. Indeed, in a different policy domain, the nineteenth century saw widespread abandonment of tax farming in favour of direct bureaucratic tax collection (see Ardant 1965; Levi 1988). Though Linder and Peters stop rather short of such an analysis of the way ideology and interest shape instrument choice in the information age, it would seem to be central to the understanding of modern executive government.

Indeed, the same sort of analysis could be used to explain how it was that, having created the Internet in the 1970s as a largely unintentional result of research sponsored in universities and defence establishments, government came to apply its authority tools to the Internet in rather traditional ways as the medium became commercialized. That is, government chose to use its authority to control content and to underpin ever-more draconian copyright and intellectual property controls (see Healy 2002, 490), rather than to give effect to the early libertarian visions of the Internet as a sphere that was immune to government regulation (2002, 481) and therefore destined to bring about a new kind of society free of traditional restrictions on the use of information. Explaining that choice is the sort of question that is eminently suited for the politics-of-instrumentality approach.

For the third set of approaches to analyzing the tools of government—the classification of forms of action for the purpose of exploring alternatives and combinations—the question is how far the repertoire of instruments identified by such approaches has been rendered obsolete by information-age technology. At one level, it seems undeniable that contemporary cyber-technology is transforming both the instrumentalities and the issues faced by contemporary government in important ways, just as much if not more than with the advent of railroads 150 years ago. Many of the examples given in my own 1983 book (Hood 1983) are undeniably as obsolete now as steam cars or seaplanes or transatlantic liners. There is no question that the cyber-age has produced some particularly dramatic changes in the information-gathering tools available to government, with the near-universal ownership of cell phones giving government the opportunity to track the position of almost every cell-phone-using individual, and rapidly to put together information from different sources on any given individual. Indeed, Margetts (1999) has shown how information technology has significantly changed the way that government applies all its tools for gathering information and modifying behaviour.

However, this sort of technology-free approach to understanding government's policy tools is arguably more rather than less applicable to an age of fast-changing technology, for at least three reasons. One is that there are sharp limits to "virtualizing" government, particularly for those situations that most call for government action, where normal facilities or civilities have broken down, the chips are down, and the stakes are high. *Pace* Frissen and those who think like him, even in a world where much is digitized and "virtual," many of those virtual processes ultimately depend for their efficacy on processes that are unavoidably physical rather than virtual. That is not to deny that there are *some* wholly virtualized government services. For instance, one of the most unexpectedly popular uses of government-sourced information in recent years is the runaway growth of interest in searching for family history on the Internet through official records such as censuses, wills, tax records, registers of births, deaths, and marriages in a way that was much more difficult and costly for those would-be family historians in a pre-digital era. But only some of government's operations are like that. Sometimes the scope for virtuality is limited by the need to build non-virtual elements into administrative processes as a defence against online fraudsters, as applies to many commercial transactions. And the limits of virtuality show up sharply with those types of government operations that involve unavoidably physical operations, especially for disaster-relief activity or at the coercive end of government's relationship with citizens, when government faces principled or opportunistic recalcitrance. The tool kit of government always has to include instruments that are anything but virtual, and indeed too much of a focus on the virtual part will tend to take away from those ways in which government has to relate to citizens outside the cyber-world.

Indeed, a second reason why conventional technology-free analyses of the tools of government are still useful in a world of changing technology is that only analysis of such a kind can enable us to pinpoint what exactly changes in government's operations in the information age. For instance, in policy domains such as the handling of crime and public order, the collection of taxes, and the handling of contagious diseases—all part of government's "defining" policy operations (Rose 1976)—it is the "detector" or information-gathering part of those operations that have changed more as a result of information-age technology than the "effector" part of the operation. For crime and public order policing, dramatic new surveillance technology has developed, as already mentioned, and the information age in principle allows information to be put together from many different sources, such that the traditional instrument of the periodic census may be becoming outdated (though data protection laws often sharply limit the ability of governments to use the dramatic "joining-up" potential of information and communications technology across different information sources—see Raab 1995).

In tax collection, too, the information and communications technology age lends itself to new surveillance techniques, such as the cameras linked to computers that lie behind London's congestion charge system introduced in 2003, and direct tax filing and payment systems through the Internet are dramatically changing traditional tax administration. In contagious disease control, information and communications technology has also led to new kinds of detectors, for instance in new kinds of animal identification for control of animal-borne disease by microchips embedded in the flesh (a technique that was originally adopted to control "ringing" of racehorses and later spread to control of dogs and other animals (see Lodge and Hood 2002, 6)). But in all of those cases, the effecting end of the process—"boots on the ground" to tackle rioters, the physical tracking down of tax non-payers to haul them off to justice, the burning or burying of infected animals, or the enforcement of quarantine systems—depend on processes that have been decidedly less transformed by the information age—and indeed often turn out to be the weak points of information-age government.

Third, at the level of basic social resources, it is not clear that the advent of information-age technology brings fundamentally new instruments to government of the same order as nodality, authority, treasure, and organization, any more than the railroad age brought fundamentally new principles to the law (see Holmes 1920, 196). While the technology of the cyber-age dramatically changes the way that executive government is internally organized, and how information and control operates within it, at some level it does not alter the basic levers that are available to government to obtain information from or change the behaviour of citizens.

# 4. CONCLUSION

Information and communications technology developments have undoubtedly changed the way that government works and will continue to do so. But the advent of a new information age does not necessarily mean that we need completely new ways to analyze and understand the instruments of government. Conventional ways of analyzing those instruments can serve to identify what changes information and communications technology brings to institutional arrangements, to the politics of instrument choice, and to the forms of policy intervention available to government. We do not need to invent new analytic frameworks to explore such questions (for an analogous argument, see Barzelay 2000). Indeed, only by applying technology-neutral analytic frameworks can we identify what precisely alters when technology changes. Margetts (1999) has used precisely such a framework to show how information and communications technology has changed the way that government in the UK and USA applies all its detecting and effecting tools, produced new ways for the resources of nodality, authority, treasure, and authority to be applied, and produced new ways of linking detecting and effecting tools.

Margetts's use of that kind of analysis is, however, unusual, and serious application of the conventional lines of analysis of government's tools to the information age has been relatively little developed up to now. Yet it is only by applying that sort of approach that we can test the claims of those who see e-technology as heralding a quantum transformation in the working of government against the claims of those who see it as another form of "conservative change." (Such debates throw up in an exaggerated form all the difficulties historians face in identifying and accounting for administrative revolutions in government (see McDonagh 1958).) And what that analysis shows is that while all of the tools of government as identified in conventional classificatory analysis have been, and are being reshaped by information and communications technology developments, those changes do not appear to have been all of the same order. Particularly dramatic changes have taken place in the application of information and communications technology to government's detection tool kit and especially to its active detectors. And within the set of government's effecting tools, information and communications technology developments have brought particularly dramatic changes to the way that government nodality works in information dissemination and in the way that government organization has been reconfigured. By comparison, information and communications technology developments for the tools of authority and treasure seem to have followed the path noted by Drucker, amounting to new ways of making existing products or instruments. And, as Margetts (2003) points out, developments up to now seem to have brought about neither the utopian nor dystopian visions of technological transformation in the way government relates to citizens.

## References

ACKERKNECHT, E. H. 1948. Anticontagionism between 1821 and 1867. *Bulletin of the History of Medicine*, 22 (5: Sept./Oct.): 562–93.

ACKROYD, C., MARGOLIS, K., ROSENHEAD, J., and SHALLICE, T. 1977. *The Technology of Political Control*. London: Pelican.

ARDANT, G. 1965. *Théorie sociologique de l'impôt*. Paris: SEVPEN.

BALDWIN, P. 1999. *Contagion and the State in Europe 1830–1930*. Cambridge: Cambridge University Press.

BARZELAY, M. 2000. *The New Public Management*. Berkeley: University of California Press.

BEER, S. 1966. *Decision and Control*. London: Wiley.

BELLAMY, C., and TAYLOR, J. A. 1998. *Governing in the Information Age*. Buckingham: Open University Press.

BERTELMANS-VIDEC, M.-L., RIST, R. C., and VEDUNG, E. 1998. *Carrots, Sticks and Sermons: Policy Instruments and their Evaluation*. New Brunswick, NJ: Transaction.

BRIN, D. 1998. *The Transparent Society*. Reading, Mass.: Addison-Wesley.

BUNYAN, T. 1976. *The History and Practice of the Political Police in Britain.* London: Friedmann.

CABINET OFFICE 1999. *Modernizing Government.* Cm 4310. London: HMSO.

CAIRNCROSS, F. 2005. The death of distance. *Oxford Forum,* 1 (Spring): 18–19.

CHAN, S., and CAMP, L. J. 2002. Law enforcement surveillance in the network society. *IEEE Technology and Society Magazine,* Summer: 22–30.

DAHL, R., and LINDBLOM, C. 1953. *Politics, Economics and Welfare.* New York: Harper and Row.

DEUTSCH, K. W. 1963. *The Nerves of Government.* Glencoe, Ill.: Free Press.

DRUCKER, P. F. 1999. Beyond the information revolution. *Atlantic Monthly,* 284 (4): 42–7.

DUNLEAVY, P. J. 1994. The globalization of public service production: can government be "best in world?" *Public Policy and Administration,* 9 (2): 36–64.

DUNLOP, C., and KLING, R. (ed.) 1991. *Computerization and Controversy: Value Conflicts and Social Choices.* Boston: Academic Press.

DUNSIRE, A. 1978. *Control in a Bureaucracy: The Execution Process,* vol. ii. Oxford: Martin Robertson.

ELMORE, R. F. 1987. Instruments and strategy in public policy. *Policy Studies Review,* 7 (1): 174–86.

ETZIONI, A. 1961. *A Comparative Analysis of Complex Organizations.* New York: Free Press.

FOSTER, C. D. 1992. *Privatization, Public Ownership and the Regulation of Natural Monopoly.* Oxford: Blackwell.

FRISSEN, P. H. 1996. *De Virtuele Staat: Politiek, Bestuur, Technologie: Een Postmodern Verhaal.* Amsterdam: Academic Service.

—— 1998. Public administration in cyberspace. Pp. 33–46 in *Public Administration in an Information Age: A Handbook,* ed. I. T. Snellen and W. B. Van de Donk. Amsterdam: IOS Press.

GORE, A. 1993. *From Red Tape to Results: Creating a Government that Works Better and Costs Less.* Report of the National Performance Review. Washington, DC: Government Printing Office.

HEALY, K. 2002. Survey article: digital technology and cultural goods. *Journal of Political Philosophy,* 10 (4): 478–500.

HEWITT, P. 1982. *The Abuse of Power: Civil Liberties in the United Kingdom.* Oxford: Martin Robertson.

HOLLIDAY, I. 2001. Steering the British state in the information age. *Government and Opposition,* 36 (3): 314–29.

HOLMES, O. W., Jr. 1920. The path of the law. Pp. 167–202 in *Collected Legal Papers.* London: Constable.

HOOD, C. 1983. *The Tools of Government.* London: Macmillan.

—— 2000. Where the state of the art meets the art of the state. *International Review of Public Administration,* 5 (1): 1–12.

—— 2003. The tax state in the information age. Pp. 213–33 in *The Nation-State in Question,* ed. T. V. Paul, G. J. Ikenberry, and J. A. Hall. Princeton, NJ: Princeton University Press.

KRAEMER, K. L., and KING, J. L. 1986. Computing and public organizations. *Public Administration Review,* 46: 488–96.

LE GRAND, J. 2003. *Motivation, Agency and Public Policy: Of Knights and Knaves, Pawns and Queens.* Oxford: Oxford University Press.

LEVI, M. 1988. *Of Rule and Revenue.* Berkeley: University of California Press.

LINDER, S. H., and PETERS, B. G. 1989. Instruments of government: perceptions and contexts. *Journal of Public Policy,* 9 (1): 35–58.

—— —— 1992. The study of policy instruments. *Policy Currents,* 2: 1–7.

—— —— 1998. The study of policy instruments: four schools of thought. In Peters and van Nispen 1998: 33–45.

LODGE, M., and HOOD, C. 2002. Pavlovian policy responses to media feeding frenzies? Dangerous dogs regulation in comparative perspective. *Journal of Contingencies and Crisis Management,* 10 (1): 1–13.

McDONAGH, O. 1958. The nineteenth-century revolution in government: a reappraisal. *Historical Journal,* 1 (1): 52–67.

MACKENZIE, W. J. M. 2002. *The Secret History of SOE: The Special Operations Executive 1940–1945.* London: St Ermin's Press.

MARGETTS, H. Z. 1999. *Information Technology in Government: Britain and America.* London: Routledge.

—— 2003. Electronic government: a revolution? Pp. 366–76 in *The Handbook of Public Administration,* ed. B. G. Peters and J. Pierre. London: Sage.

OSBORNE, D., and GAEBLER, T. 1992. *Reinventing Government.* Reading, Mass.: Addison-Wesley.

PETERS, B. G., and VAN NISPEN, F. K. M. (eds.) 1998. *Public Policy Instruments: Evaluating the Tools of Public Administration.* Cheltenham: Edward Elgar.

RAAB, C. 1995. Connecting Orwell to Athens? Information superhighways and the privacy debate. Pp. 195–211 in *Orwell in Athens: A Perspective on Informatization and Democracy,* ed. W. B. van de Donk, I. Snellen, and P. Tops. Amsterdam: IOS Press.

ROSE, H., and ROSE, S. P. R. (eds.) 1976. *The Political Economy of Science.* London: Macmillan.

ROSE, R. 1976. On the priorities of government: a developmental analysis of public policies. *European Journal of Political Research,* 4 (3): 247–89.

RULE, J. B. 1973. *Private Lives and Public Surveillance.* London: Allen Lane.

SALAMON, L. M., with ELLIOTT, O. V. (eds.) 2002. *The Tools of Government: A Guide to the New Governance.* Oxford: Oxford University Press.

—— and LUND, M. S. 1989. *Beyond Privatization: The Tools of Government Action.* Washington, DC: Urban Institute Press.

SCHNEIDER, A., and INGRAM, H. 1990. Behavioral assumptions of policy tools. *Journal of Politics,* 52 (2): 510–29.

SCHÖN, D. 1971. *Beyond the Stable State.* London: Temple Smith.

STEINBRUNER, J. D. 1974. *The Cybernetic Theory of Decision.* Princeton, NJ: Princeton University Press.

TAYLOR, J. A. 1992. Information networking in public administration. *International Review of Administrative Sciences,* 58: 375–89.

—— and WILLIAMS, H. 1991. Public administration and the information polity. *Public Administration,* 69 (2): 171–90.

WARD, H. 1989. The neutrality of science and technology. Pp. 157–92 in *Liberal Neutrality,* ed. R. E. Goodin and A. Reeve. London: Routledge.

# CHAPTER 23

POLICY ANALYSIS AS
ORGANIZATIONAL
ANALYSIS

BARRY L. FRIEDMAN

ORGANIZATIONAL analysis has become a major concern of policy analysis. The interest in organizations emerged out of studies of implementation. As evaluations of policies began to show program failures, the question arose as to whether the failures were a result of flawed policy design or perhaps just good policies that were implemented poorly. The focus on implementation in turn led to an interest in the organizations implementing policy. It came to be recognized that policy analysts could not ignore implementation and the behavior of implementing organizations. But Pressman and Wildavsky (1973, xvii) in their pioneering study went a step further and warned that "the separation of policy design from implementation is fatal." For Pressman and Wildavsky they are linked, and in a way that highlights the importance of organizations. In the program they studied, the policy itself was complex and involved many organizations in the implementation, each with its own motivations. The complexity in policy created complexity in the interactions among the multiple organizations, which ultimately resulted in an ineffective policy. The link was that policy complexity created organizational complexity. Since their work, many more links have emerged between policy design and implementing agencies. The design determines or at least influences the constraints faced by implementing organizations and the opportunities or discretion they have within the constraints.

Linkages can also run from organizations to policy design. Some of the original implementation studies began with discrete legislative actions. When the analysis is set up in this way, the causation necessarily starts with policy design and policy goals, which may then be subverted by organizations as part of the implementation process. However, Lipsky (1980, xii) argued that "the decisions of street-level bureaucrats, the routines they establish, and the devices they invent to cope with uncertainties and work pressures, effectively *become* the public policies they carry out." More generally, public policies are determined by a combination of legislative actions and actions of implementing organizations and the street-level bureaucrats within them. Along with the policy initiatives that begin in government, there is feedback from agencies leading to modifications in policy and even initiatives by the agencies themselves. Through expanded purchases of service, government programs have come to use non-profit and for-profit organizations in addition to government agencies as implementing organizations. There are non-profits in particular that design services that go beyond governmental policy in order to fill social gaps that they perceive. With government in some countries trying to cut back on its social programs, it is essential for policy analysis to consider not only what government does but also what is done or not done outside of government. Taking this broader view, organizations may have substantial impacts both on the design of public programs and on the social policy environment outside of government.

The causal influences in both directions create the links that connect policy and implementing organizations. These links in turn depend on the behavior of the organizations. The stronger the links, the more intertwined policy analysis is with organizational analysis. Thus, organizational analysis is a useful, often essential component of policy analysis. This chapter focuses on organizational analysis and the insights it can provide into policy analysis.

# 1. FROM IMPLEMENTATION STUDIES TO ORGANIZATIONAL ANALYSIS: A REVIEW

Organizational elements emerged in studies of implementation, but have gradually been elaborated into a more complex and complete organizational analysis. The top-down approach was one of the first systematic forms of implementation analysis, and organizational issues play an important role here. It begins with policy formulated at the top so that it focuses primarily on one-way links from policy to implementing organizations. Beginning from the top, its approach to organizations tends to be hierarchical. An early study by Hood attempted to characterize perfect implementation as beginning with a unitary administrative system, operating with single-line authority and having perfect communication and obedience (1976, 6). More generally, the top-down approach was used to analyze implementation situations and to prescribe remedies for difficulties, knowing that the complete control described by Hood was impossible. Early top-down work included van Meter and van Horn

(1975), Sabatier and Mazmanian (1979), and Gunn (1978). The hierarchical view focused on structures such as channels of communication and mechanisms for controlling organizations. It was generally recognized that implementing organizations need appropriate forms of discretion, but that it should to be controlled (Younis and Davidson 1990, 8; Sabatier 1986, 22–3). Indeed, one of the links between policy and organizations comes from identifying necessary forms of discretion and building them into the organizational structure. It has been argued that implementation and organization may differ by policy type and that the relationship with relevant actors should be different in different policy types (Ripley and Franklin 1982, 198). On the other hand, critics have argued that discretion extends beyond that which is required programmatically (Burke 1990) and the undesired forms may be difficult to control (Rhodes and Marsh 1992).

There were attempts to be more explicit about the nature of the discretion in implementing organizations. The most notable was the focus within organizations on the discretion available to street-level bureaucrats, those who directly deliver the services to clients. To an extent, the discretion results from features of the policy being implemented. Lipsky (1980, 14–15) argues that many service needs are too complicated to be reduced to precise instructions. Depending on the service, street-level bureaucrats may be given discretion to respond to unique individual circumstances. On the other hand, he also argues that street-level officials may be subject to voluminous, contradictory rules, in effect leaving them with the discretion to decide which to follow. The first source of discretion may promote the goals of the policy, while the second may thwart them, but both result in opportunities for a degree of street-level independence. Lipsky and others (Prottas 1979) have explored how street-level bureaucrats use their discretion and how they relate to managers in implementing organizations. They generally conclude that the kinds of hierarchical controls envisioned in top-down models are likely not to work. However, managers at times do attempt to tighten controls, and the result may be a reduction in the quality of service (Lipsky 1984).

The bottom-up approach, including the work on street-level bureaucracies, enriched the understanding of relationships within organizations and in particular the importance of the level where services are actually provided. Elmore (1978) also rejected hierarchical models, but suggested several alternative models including street-level bureaucracy, an organizational development model, and a conflict bargaining model. Bottom-up models also rejected the view that policy design was the exclusive prerogative of the legislative process. Lipsky argued that street-level actions effectively determined important features of the policy. Elmore (1979) argued that policy should be formulated through a process of backward mapping in which the capabilities and resources of street-level officials are assessed first in order to design programs that will work. There was a normative element in these arguments, so they did not yet provide a fully developed view behaviorally of how organizations affect policy and the reverse, but they were a step toward articulating these relationships.

Later work considered different degrees of street-level discretion and differing capabilities to control it (Burke 1987; Thompson 1982). There was also interest in combining top-down and bottom-up approaches. Sabatier (1986) incorporated street-level elements into a top-down structure with feedbacks from below; Mazmanian and Sabatier (1989, 40) showed in a formal way many of the cross-influences between policy, organizations, and outcomes; while Elmore (1985) combined his bottom-up concept of backward mapping with forward mapping to accommodate the interests of central policy makers. Eclectic approaches became common. Later summaries synthesized the approaches in various ways.[1] From the point of view of organizational analysis, syntheses allow in one way or another for both hierarchical and bottom-up organizational structures and for varying mixes of the two in different situations.

While the street-level approach was important to understanding relationships within an organization, other studies emphasized interorganizational relationships. This approach began with the insight that many governmental programs are carried out by multiple organizations, each with limited tasks, carrying out a part of the implementation and each with different, possibly conflicting interests (Hanf 1978). Since conflicts are likely in the presence of multiple organizations, studies looked at interorganizational mechanisms for dealing with the conflicts and the implications of these mechanisms for policy. Stoker (1989) emphasized the importance of cooperation and identified implementation regimes based on how likely they would be to achieve cooperation. Goggin et al. (1990, 33) emphasized the role of the communications system linking the multiple organizations in a framework that combined top-down and bottom-up elements; Ostrom (1998, 13) elaborated further on how communications can affect implementation.

Network theory is one approach to interorganizational relationships that has received increased attention. The idea is not new (Hanf, Hjern, and Porter 1978). A network is the set of relationships among the multiple organizations involved in a program. Since the members may forge their own relationships, networks are sometimes presented as a bottom-up alternative to a hierarchical system in a multiple organization setting. O'Toole (1997) argued that networks have become more common in public administration. Within government, there are more inter-agency efforts; non-profits and for-profits have become implementers; and all may network with each other. Considine and Lewis (1999) sought to evaluate empirically whether networking behavior exists among organizations providing services. They studied organizations providing employment services to the unemployed in Australia, where many private agencies have contracts. They concluded that networked systems do exist among some agencies, but even in this homogeneous service area, it is not the only approach. Salamon (2002) also argued that government increasingly operates through other organizations including non-profits and for-profits to carry out its policies, and these organizations may network with each other even while each pursues its own interests and values. Traditional hierarchical command and control

---

[1] See Lester et al. 1987; Goggin et al. 1990; Ryan 1995.

structures are not likely to be effective in managing such networks, but central authorities still have an interest in accountability. Salamon proposed a new governance paradigm in which central authorities as well as managers within the networks need to rely on negotiation, persuasion, and tools such as incentives to achieve public goals. While traditional control mechanisms sought to prescribe particular actions, central authorities might seek indirect means to alter the behavior of the network and the organizations within it under the new governance paradigm. It opens the possibility that policy might affect organizational structure and not just specific procedures.

Along with the new governance paradigm and its focus on effective management, there has also been concern over accountability in the presence of networks and government contracting with the private sector. One concern is the accountability of private agencies to the democratically set goals of the public policies they implement. Another concern is the possibility that contracting might subject non-profits to political control and reduce their effectiveness in meeting their traditional goals related to individual and community needs. There have been explorations of the balance between these concerns (Smith and Lipsky 1993; Minow 2002; Goodin 2003). Considine (2002) studied accountability empirically in agencies providing employment services across four countries. He considered more than one kind of accountability including vertical accountability: top-down to superiors in the chain of command and bottom-up to the preferences of clients. He also considered horizontal accountability to other organizations and actors in a network. He found that one kind of accountability tends not to preclude another. Being in a network does not prevent attention to vertical accountability, but horizontal accountability was relatively more important in non-profits than in government agencies.

Although organizations have long been of interest in policy analysis, they were often viewed through the lens of implementation, sometimes as an obstacle to policy, sometimes as a force to be controlled in carrying out policy. Some studies had a hierarchical approach, but this was challenged first by the idea of street-level bureaucracy and then in a multi-organizational context by network theory. The bottom-up approaches opened the possibility that organizations may not only be an obstacle, but also could play a positive role in the design of policy. The next two sections explore further aspects of organizations that can make a contribution to policy analysis.

## 2. INNOVATION AND THE INFLUENCE OF ORGANIZATIONS ON POLICY

There was a presumption particularly in the earlier top-down literature that public policy is the prerogative of government. Of course, studies recognized that there are feedbacks from organizations to policy. Organizations lobby, do research, and discover flaws in policies, all of which may result in modifications. But there is also a normative argument that democratic accountability requires that democratic legis-lative processes should formulate policy. However, as a practical matter there are agencies outside of government that seek social change, that innovate and design policies in line with their own views, and in so doing affect the social policy environment.

In a democratic process, program adoption depends on majority rule. A minority can achieve some of its objectives by forming alliances, logrolling, or other political maneuvering, but it may not get all the programs it would like. A strictly democratic process serves the needs of minorities imperfectly, but pluralistic interests can be met if minorities can develop their own programs outside of government. Is it feasible for groups to organize outside of government? If not, the case for government action would be practical more than normative. Government has strong advantages as a provider of social programs, given its power of compulsion and especially taxation. Many public programs can be considered public goods or else services provided publicly because of positive externalities. A market would underproduce these services, and one response is public provision. The standard argument is that in the presence of positive externalities, a free-rider problem is likely, and individuals will not contribute to the service voluntarily. It would take the compulsion powers of government to make sure that the service is provided. This would suggest that government is needed as the provider. Of course, the government decision to provide the service and the level of support depend on a democratic decision.

In fact, however, the free-rider problem is not insurmountable. There is a long tradition of non-profit organizations successfully mobilizing resources to pursue a mission not funded by government. Religious and other affinity groups and cultural organizations may not win majority support and would not work in the market, but are able to organize as non-profits. There have long been charities that provided hospitals or orphanages without direct support from government. Many succeeded as non-profits in spite of potential free-rider problems. Although government has a clear advantage in organizing and funding social programs, experience suggests that it is not a necessity. Determined minorities can organize to get services they want. One factor strengthening the determination of organizations to develop programs has been the attempt by governments in some countries to cut back on the services they provide. In a time of government cutbacks, the minorities that succeed tend to be those that believe in a service even though it does not get a legislative majority. Normatively, it is not clear why the government should have a monopoly in deciding on social services. Practically, a government monopoly is not necessary as long as the free-rider problem is not important. Governments also have weaknesses as providers (Ostrom and Walker 1997, 36). However, for private organizers to succeed, they need good management skills. The design of overall social policy, public and private, depends on the behavior of the thousands of private organizations that initiate and provide their own services.

For the traditional charity, a key skill for survival is fundraising. This in turn depends on strategic management skills including the ability to define a mission that would appeal to donors. It also depends on the marketing skills to sell the concept to those who might contribute. The growth of government programs opened new opportunities. An agency could obtain funding by contracting with government, provided it was willing to provide the kind of service the government prescribed. But it could also leverage off the funding base from the government contract to pursue its own mission and develop its own services. An agency could turn to the market to sell services or to sell a product that could cross-subsidize a service that did not pay for itself. Social entrepreneurship has become a growing movement in which organizations seek profits to be used to pursue social goals (Dees, Emerson, and Economy 2002). Some social enterprises are non-profits with for-profit subsidiaries, and some are organized outright as for profits. And non-profit agencies get indirect support from government in the form of tax exemption and deductibility for donors if they satisfy basic requirements. Strategic and financial skills are necessary to decide among all these possibilities.

Although data on privately initiated social services are not currently available, a few figures can illustrate the extent of the private and public parts of the US social system. In 1994 (more recent data are under revision), social welfare expenditure of government amounted to 21.8 per cent of GDP and private expenditures were 13.5 per cent (US Social Security Administration 2002, 132). Of the private expenditures, 80 per cent are employee benefits. These include the pensions and health insurance provided by employers. The remaining private expenditures include education and welfare services of non-profits. Within the non-profits, data are available on the "independent sector," organizations covered under sections 501(c)(3) and 501(c)(4) of the Internal Revenue Code, or over 75 per cent of the whole sector. In 1996 it produced 6.7 per cent of GDP (including an imputation for the value of volunteer time estimated at one-third of the total) or $434 billion. It owned about 5 per cent of the wealth of the private sector. It employed almost 12 per cent of the labor force, including volunteers (Steuerle and Hodgkinson 1999, 77). Of course, some of the product of the sector comes from contracts with government. Considering the sources of revenue of the independent sector, in 1997, 31 per cent came from government contracts and grants; 20 per cent from private contributions; 38 per cent from private payments for dues and services; and 11 per cent from income on investments (Urban Institute 2002, xxxii). One further source of financing that does not appear in these figures comes from the fact that private giving is tax deductible, so that the government indirectly finances a portion of it. It is estimated that the tax expenditure on charitable giving deductions is nearly 10 per cent of the amount of the contributions themselves (Brody and Cordes 1999, 145).

This analysis suggests an area for policy analysis that originates in organizational analysis. Among the issues to consider, the first is to assess what is being done privately. The data available currently are limited. What is the extent of social policy initiated by private actors? What kinds of services are being provided privately? There are areas where government would seem to have a clear advantage such as income maintenance programs. But even here, there are private counterparts coming not so much from non-profits as from the employee benefits of all employers, and this area of private provision is large. Programs to monitor behavior such as child protection services are established by government even when contracted out, but an agency contracting with government may also choose to initiate on its own other services for children. On the other hand, community development programs are a natural area for innovation by non-profits, and job training and development programs for disadvantaged workers are a favorite of social enterprises.

Another area is to determine why the private services develop. This involves looking into the organizations initiating services and understanding their behavior, their financing opportunities, their evaluation of social needs, and their ability to mobilize support and to organize and sustain services. Many organizations try, but do not succeed, so what distinguishes successes from failures? Another issue is evaluative. With so many social decisions dispersed over so many actors, each with their own values and priorities, how effective is policy overall? Would it be better to rely on larger government programs instead? In dealing with this question, the issue of democratic accountability is one evaluative stance among many. Of course, this question must deal also with the political reality of what government is willing to do.

# 3. Organizational Challenges and Responses and Policy Analysis

Much literature has focused on the challenge to policy of organizational discretion. This may be the most important, but there are other challenges that can also affect policy. Another challenge comes from the information problems that arise in the many services that have outcomes that are complex and difficult to measure. This problem is a challenge for managers, clients, funders, and policy makers, and the responses of all these parties can affect policy outcomes. Another challenge that can interact with the information challenge results from managing the multiple services that organizations choose to offer. Diversification clearly serves the business and mission interests of many organizations. The last section considered the diversification by agencies that wanted to innovate into areas to further their vision of social change. Some non-profits use one service to cross-subsidize another that does not pay for itself (James 1986), and many agencies provide multiple services in an attempt to meet the multiple needs of their clients. But the way organizations manage their multiple services can have adverse outcomes in an area like pricing. After introducing information problems, this section considers the responses of organizations to the combination of information problems and diversification in two areas, pricing and quality control. Government also may respond to the information problems. The section concludes by considering implications for policy analysis.

*Information problems.* Many information problems are asymmetric where one party, for example the provider, has information that the other, the client, lacks.

A parent leaving her child in day care does not see what happens after she drops off her child, and a person placing an older relative in a nursing home does not know how the relative is treated if the relative cannot communicate. There is a potential market failure, allowing the provider to take advantage of the client. But there is also an information problem for services when the lack of information is symmetric and both sides lack the information. In this case, it may be difficult for all parties to specify, measure, and agree on the outcomes of a service. It also may be difficult for all parties to assess the contribution of the provider to the outcome. Whether the information problem is asymmetric or symmetric, it may create organizational challenges.

Hansmann (1980) argued that the contract failure resulting from asymmetric information provided a rationale for the existence of non-profit organizations. He argued that the non-profit structure, which does not allow for the distribution of profits, could allay the fears of clients that providers would take advantage of them. However, even he acknowledged that in many services 'for-profit' and 'non-profit' organizations coexist, and clients do not automatically opt for the non-profit choice. The information problem is inherent in the services, and is usually not solved by organizational form alone. No matter what the organizational form, managers need to respond to it in a number of areas. We consider responses related to pricing and quality control.

*Pricing.* Although some non-profit services are funded by donations, many services of non-profits and for-profits alike are purchased either by clients or third-party payers and so need to be priced. In an ordinary market where there are no information problems, buyers can assess the output and pay for it. However, in many service markets, there is uncertainty about the outcome. For example, the desired outcome from health services is health, but health is a concept so broad and so difficult to specify that it does not provide an easy basis for pricing. Moreover, not everyone treated will get healthy, or the improvement may come slowly. The client and provider may not agree on whether the healthy state has been achieved. Similarly with education, one intended outcome is higher earnings and a better career. But it may take years after graduation before the outcome is known. Providers have a strong interest in charging for services delivered rather than for outcomes.

Because it is difficult to define an outcome unit that can be priced, agencies tend to seek other units instead. Common measures are numbers of visits or hours or months of service. These are concrete and can be measured and priced. Organizations tend to call these their "outputs" which are distinguished from outcomes. Of course, in a production sense these outputs are really more like inputs that go into producing the ultimate outcomes. The pricing problem is more or less resolved by input-based pricing in principle. Operationally, however, there are problems also in defining the inputs. For example, the US Medicare program pays one price for all the inputs needed to provide a complete service that it defines (diagnostic-related group), while many hospitals charge uninsured patients separately for each detailed input.

One factor affecting both the definition of input and the level of the pricing is market power of the payer relative to the provider. In the presence of multiple payers, those with the least power are at a disadvantage. Government has the power to define the input package and set the price it will pay for the clients it covers, and some large insurers do the same. However, US hospital patients without health insurance have no market power, and hospitals pass on to them the highest rates. Another pricing problem is that payers focused on inputs try to control specific costs such as indirect cost rates. For a diversified agency with multiple funders, its cost accounting may have to focus on managing the differing indirect rates, perhaps to the extent of expanding activities with higher rates at the expense of those with lower rates. Not only may this deflect attention from assessing the costs of each activity accurately, but it may also begin to affect the strategic direction of an agency if it decides that it must limit sales to payers with restrictive indirect cost rules. Thus, there is interplay between mission, accounting, financing, and pricing that affects the behavior of provider agencies.

*Quality control.* Difficulties in measuring outcomes matter for provider organizations, clients, funders, and public policy. All of these parties may take actions to improve information about the outcomes. For the provider, measuring actions and outcomes is a standard task in operations management. If more complex information is needed, the agency can conduct an evaluation, often calling on an outside evaluator for help. If the agency can measure a problem, it may be able to find ways to manage it and improve performance. Performance and accountability have also become major concerns of donors and of government agencies contracting for services. They conduct evaluations or encourage the provider to do so. Government agencies and others conduct research on measuring outcomes in particular service areas. They use the results to rate providers and to set regulations. In any one service area, quality improvement can be viewed as a process of trial and error. There are initiatives from both government and the organizations themselves, with the possibility of some missteps, but also an opportunity for improvements in quality over time.

One illustration shows also initiatives from clients when providers and public policy both fall short in meeting needs. Personal care services for people with disabilities were designed without considering the preferences of those receiving them. Both providers and government policy focused on the services themselves rather than on their effects on the lives of the consumers, an outcome not measured and not recognized. The impetus for change came from a movement for consumer direction among the consumers themselves. The solution in this case was a new structure allowing consumers who wanted to do so to hire, pay, and fire their own workers.

*Implications for policy analysis.* One lesson is that policy analysis needs to consider not only what government does, but also what it does not do. A gap analysis is often relevant. Organizations enter the analysis to the extent that they provide services to those not covered in government programs, for example the hospitals or clinics that provide care to the uninsured, since their behavior can affect the outcomes for the uninsured. But government can also affect the outcomes for those it does not cover, as when its pricing policies induce hospitals to shift costs to others, including the uninsured. Another lesson is that organizational analysis may have to go into detailed aspects of management such as pricing and quality control in order to find behavior that matters for policy analysis. And one more lesson is that in the presence of information problems, both policy and organizations may not get it right initially, as illustrated in the cases of pricing and quality control. Subsequent responses may involve missteps, but also the possibility of learning leading to improved outcomes. In the presence of uncertainty, an action does not always have a unique, predictable outcome. Rather, the organizational analysis provides the tools for searching for those areas where organizational actions have a consequence for public policy.

# 4. CONCLUSION

Some early policy analyses began with a single government program and, of course, found that implementing organizations could affect the outcomes. As policy formulation itself came under the purview of policy analysis, there was recognition that organizations could play a role in this also. This chapter has emphasized that in addition to feedback effects, private organizations are playing an innovating role in developing programs to further their vision of social change. As government has attempted to cut back social programs, private organizations have stepped in to meet needs. Policy analysis cannot be restricted to activities originating only in government. Influences run both ways: not only does the private sector innovate, but government programs can affect social programs run privately, sometimes adversely, because of the responses of organizations. Thus, a complete policy analysis must consider social policy innovations in and out of government as well as the influence of both government and organizations on policies, whether initiated by government or privately.

To study organizations, the literature focused on discretion by organizations as a major challenge in implementing public policy. Various organizational and policy responses to this challenge have been examined, including looking inside organizations at street-level bureaucrats and across organizations at the networks formed by multiple organizations. While discretion may be the most important challenge, there are others, and this chapter looked in particular at the information problems that arise in the many services that have outcomes that are complex and difficult to measure. For organizational analysis the task is to identify how organizations respond to the information problem. They may do so in many detailed ways that can influence policy outcomes, and we illustrated the case of pricing and quality control operations. Since government also responds, the outcome depends on the interplay between governmental and organizational actions.

Organizations implement governmental policies at the same time that they innovate, manage multiple programs, and respond to various challenges. While they need to cooperate with government on the services they contract with it, they often do not act as servants of government. Rather, organizations and government are intertwined in the design and implementation of policy. To recognize this, policy analysis must also be intertwined with organizational analysis.

# REFERENCES

BRODY, E., and CORDES, J. J. 1999. Tax treatment of nonprofit organizations: a two-edged sword. Pp. 141–75 in *Nonprofits and Government: Collaboration and Conflict*, ed. E. T. Boris and C. E. Steuerle. Washington, DC: Urban Institute Press.

BURKE, J. 1987. A prescriptive view of the implementation process: when should bureaucrats exercise discretion? *Policy Studies Review*, 7 (1): 217–31.

BURKE, J. 1990. Policy implementation and the responsible exercise of discretion. Pp. 133–48 in *Implementation and the Policy Process: Opening up the Black Box*, ed. D. Palumbo and D. Calista. New York: Greenwood Press.

CONSIDINE, M. 2002. The end of the line? Accountable governance in the age of networks, partnerships, and joined-up services. *Governance: An International Journal of Policy, Administration, and Institutions*, 15 (1): 21–40.

—— and LEWIS, J. 1999. Governance at ground level: the frontline bureaucrat in the age of markets and networks. *Public Administration Review*, 59 (6): 467–80.

DEES, J. G., EMERSON, J., and ECONOMY, P. 2002. *Strategic Tools for Social Entrepreneurs: Enhancing the Performance of your Enterprising Nonprofit*. Hoboken, NJ: Wiley.

ELMORE, R. 1978. Organizational models of social program implementation. *Public Policy*, 26: 185–228.

—— 1979. Backward mapping: implementation research and policy decision. *Political Science Quarterly*, 94: 606–16.

—— 1985. Forward and backward mapping: reversible logic in the analysis of public policy. Pp. 33–70 in *Policy Implementation in Federal and Unitary Systems*, ed. K. Hanf and T. A. J. Toonen. Dordrecht: Martinus Nijhoff.

GOGGIN, M., BOWMAN, A., LESTER, J., and O'TOOLE, L., Jr. 1990. *Implementation Theory and Practice: Towards a Third Generation*. Glenview, Ill.: Scott, Foresman.

GOODIN, R. 2003. Democratic accountability: the distinctiveness of the third sector. *Archives européennes de sociologie*, 44 (3): 359–96.

GUNN, L. A. 1978. Why is implementation so difficult? *Management Services in Government*, 33: 169–176.

HANF, K. 1978. Introduction. Pp. 1–15 in *Interorganizational Policy Making*, ed. K. Hanf and F. Sharpf. London: Sage.

—— HJERN, B., and PORTER, D. 1978. Local networks of manpower training in the Federal Republic of Germany and Sweden. Pp. 303–44 in *Interorganizational Policy Making*, ed. K. Hanf and F. Sharpf. London: Sage.

HANSMANN, H. B. 1980. The role of nonprofit enterprise. *Yale Law Journal*, 89: 835–98.

HOOD, C. 1976. *The Limits of Administration*. London: Wiley and Sons.

JAMES, E. 1986. How nonprofits grow: a model. Pp. 185–95 in *The Economics of Nonprofit Institutions*, ed. S. Rose-Akerman. Oxford: Oxford University Press.

LESTER, J., BOWMAN, A., GOGGIN, M., and O'TOOLE, L., Jr. 1987. Public policy implementation: evolution of the field and agenda for future research. *Policy Studies Review*, 7 (1): 200–16.

LIPSKY, M. 1980. *Street-Level Bureaucracy*. New York: Russell Sage Foundation.

—— 1984. Bureaucratic disentitlement in social welfare programs. *Social Service Review*, 58: 3–27.

MAZMANIAN, D. A., and SABATIER, P. A. 1989. *Implementation and Public Policy*. Lanham, Md.: University Press of America.

MINOW, M. 2002. *Partners, Not Rivals: Privatization and the Public Good*. Boston: Beacon Press.

OSTROM, E. 1998. A behavioral approach to the rational choice theory of collective action. *American Political Science Review*, 92 (1): 1–22.

OSTROM, E. and WALKER, J. 1997. Neither markets nor states: linking transformation processes in collective action arenas. Pp. 35–72 in *Perspectives on Public Choice: A Handbook*, ed. D. Mueller. Cambridge: Cambridge University Press.

O'TOOLE, L., Jr. 1997. Treating networks seriously: practical and research-based agendas in public administration. *Public Administration Review*, 57 (1): 45–52.

PRESSMAN, J., and WILDAVSKY, A. 1973. *Implementation*. Berkeley: University of California Press.

PROTTAS, J. 1979. *People Processing: The Street-Level Bureaucrat in Public Service Bureaucracies*. Lexington, Mass.: Lexington Books.

RHODES, R. A. W., and MARSH, D. 1992. Thatcherism: an implementation perspective. Pp. 1–10 in *Implementing Thatcherite Policies: Audit of an Era*, ed. D. Marsh and R. A. W. Rhodes. Buckingham: Open University Press.

RIPLEY, R., and FRANKLIN, G. 1982. *Bureaucracy and Policy Implementation*. Homewood, Ill.: Dorsey Press.

RYAN, N. 1995. Unravelling conceptual developments in implementation analysis. *Australian Journal of Public Administration*, 54 (1): 65–80.

SABATIER, P. 1986. Top-down and bottom-up approaches to implementation research: a critical analysis and suggested synthesis. *Journal of Public Policy*, 6 (1): 21–48.

—— and MAZMANIAN, D. 1979. The conditions of effective implementation: a guide to accomplishing policy objectives. *Policy Analysis*, 5 (4): 481–504.

SALAMON, L. 2002. The new governance and the tools of public action: an introduction. Pp. 1–47 in *The Tools of Government*, ed. L. Salamon. Oxford: Oxford University Press.

SMITH, S., and LIPSKY, M. 1993. *Nonprofits for Hire*. Cambridge, Mass.: Harvard University Press.

STEUERLE, C. E., and HODGKINSON, V. A. 1999. Meeting social needs: comparing the resources of the independent sector and government. Pp. 71–98 in *Nonprofits and Government: Collaboration and Conflict*, ed. E. T. Boris and C. E. Steuerle. Washington, DC: Urban Institute Press.

STOKER, R. 1989. A regime framework for implementation analysis: cooperation and reconciliation of federalist imperatives. *Policy Studies Review*, 9 (1): 29–49.

THOMPSON, F. 1982. Bureaucratic discretion and the National Health Services Corp. *Political Science Quarterly*, 97 (3): 427–45.

URBAN INSTITUTE 2002. *The New Nonprofit Almanac*. Washington, DC: Urban Institute Press.

US SOCIAL SECURITY ADMINISTRATION 2002. *Social Security Bulletin: Annual Statistical Supplement*. Washington, DC: Government Printing Office.

van Meter, D., and van Horn, C. 1975. The policy implementation process: a conceptual framework. *Administration and Society*, 6 (4): 445–88.

Younis, T., and Davidson, I. 1990. The study of implementation. Pp. 3–14 in *Implementation in Public Policy*, ed. T. Younis. Dartmouth: Aldershot.

# PUBLIC–PRIVATE COLLABORATION

## JOHN D. DONAHUE
## RICHARD J. ZECKHAUSER

## 1. INTRODUCTION

Economists most frequently contribute to public policy analysis through efforts to identify government's proper goals (the domain of welfare economics) and to guide the allocation of resources across competing claims (the domain of cost-effectiveness analysis). Yet a complementary and equally important analytic task is to inform the choice and management of *means*. Once retraining for trade-displaced workers is identified as a goal that warrants major spending, for example, the analyst's job is by no means done. Should government run training programs itself, contract with a community organization, issue vouchers to displaced workers, or use a tax incentive to induce firms to provide training? What principles tell us whether direct government supply, delegation to private non-profits, or for-profit provision is the best approach to park management, foreign aid, or renal dialysis?

Good governance requires choosing the right implementation model as well as the right ends. The richer the repertoire of alternative models, the more important is analytic work to guide the assignment of tasks. As government increasingly shares the collective-action stage with private actors, both for-profit and not-for-profit, addressing this assignment problem—who should do what?—becomes both more complex and more consequential. This chapter examines a particular form of public–private collaboration that we term "collaborative governance," here defined as:

The pursuit of authoritatively chosen public goals by means that include engaging the efforts of, and sharing discretion with, producers outside of government.

Finer points of definition and distinction are developed below, but some basics are required at the outset. Collaborative governance is distinguished from simple contracting and from philanthropy in the allocation of operational discretion. A pure service contract vests all discretion with the government. Pure voluntary provision vests all discretion with the donor. Strategic interaction, at both extremes, is relatively sparse. In what we term collaborative governance, by contrast, each party has a hand in defining not only the means by which a goal is achieved but the details of the goal itself. This yields relationships that promise to augment the capacity (whether financial, productive, or both) available for public missions and to increase the flexibility with which such missions are pursued, but at the price of more ambiguous lines of authority and far greater strategic complexity.

While the evidence is spotty, arrangements involving non-governmental actors appear to account for a growing share of authoritatively designated public action in the United States, and there is reason to believe that the more narrowly defined category of collaborative governance is growing as well. Although the data for other countries are sketchier still, collaborative governance appears to be a widely shared trend in the developed world, and in some developing nations.

This chapter first offers a brief overview of relevant literatures, then documents the magnitude of private involvement in public undertakings—for present purposes construed, of necessity, more broadly than collaborative governance—using a variety of metrics. Next it more carefully distinguishes collaborative governance from other categories of public–private interaction to situate it on a spectrum of collective-action models. Finally, it probes some of the dynamics of shared discretion in the pursuit of public goals, and notes the implications for government's role, and in particular the analytical and managerial demands on the public sector, when missions are advanced through collaborative means.

# 2. A Brief Survey of Related Literatures

Though our conception of collaborative governance—and the specific term—may be unfamiliar, a good deal of work from several disciplines (including political science, economics, public management, and administrative law) illuminates the phenomenon. In political science, antecedent literatures include work on the dynamics of coalitions, as well as studies of political pluralism (Dahl 1961).[1] The concept of social

---

[1] Dahl's book with Lindblom (Dahl and Lindblom 1953) draws an interesting distinction between "polyarchy-controlled" institutions and "price-system controlled" institutions. Their treatment of polyarchy-controlled institutions deals with government agencies; collaborative governance imports private institutions into this domain.

capital has been invoked to illuminate the mechanisms of adhesion within collaborations and the features of cultural settings that improve or worsen the odds for joint undertakings. A well-developed literature on networks speaks to relevant themes.[2] Mancur Olson's *Logic of Collective Action* offers a simple though elegant analytical framework for the formation and evolution of collaborative efforts (Olson 1965). Robert Axelrod has examined conditions and behaviors conducive to cooperation (Axelrod 1984). In an article cited in several salient literatures, William Ouchi examines normative consensus among actors in collective endeavors and the resulting congruence of goals as a broad-spectrum (though far from universally available) remedy to the defects of both market-based and rule-based social coordination (Ouchi 1980). The extensive theoretical and empirical literature on corporatism is also germane.[3] Pathological forms of interaction between government and the private sector—from classic corruption to National Socialism and crony capitalism—warrant attention as well. The empirical record here is lamentably extensive, but fortunately well documented (e.g. Steffens 1904).

Legal scholars have extensively explored topics related to collaborative governance. Mark Freedland has attempted to impose some analytical discipline on the Public Finance Initiative, a British effort to enlist private capital into the provision of public services that began in the 1980s under the Conservative government of Margaret Thatcher and was embraced and extended under its Labour successors (Freedland 1999, 145–68). Jody Freeman has used the same term we employ (though her definition differs somewhat from ours) in a 1997 article that casts collaborative governance as a generic label for a range of regulatory reform initiatives that include the Environmental Protection Agency's Project XL and the Occupational Safety and Health Administration's Maine 200 experiment. The common characteristics of these initiatives include agency discretion, negotiation over rules and their application, and far more scope for conditional regulatory forbearance than is permitted by conventional administrative approaches. Yet Freeman sees the conventional insistence on clear-cut lines of political accountability as a shibboleth blocking bolder experimentation, and calls for greater tolerance of agency discretion and the development of a richer, more subtle repertoire of accountability mechanisms (Freeman 1997). Martha Minow has examined the involvement of both for-profit and non-profit private entities in education, health care, welfare, legal services, and other public undertakings. She calls on scholars to "make sure that our system displays ... conflicts and tensions—between public and private, religious and secular, profit and non-profit—rather than papers them over" (Minow 2002, 171). (We endorse this goal, and aim to advance it.)

[2] A classic in this literature is Knoke and Kuklinski 1982; an influential recent contribution is Rowly 1997. In an example of the network literature with particular relevance to collaborative governance, McGuire (1993) argues that an informal network—originating mostly in elite law schools (non-profit), seasoned in court clerkships or stints in the Solicitor General's office (government), and currently or prospectively members of top DC law partnerships (private)—holds special expertise and exercises special influence over the institution at the pinnacle of the judicial branch.

[3] The Carnegie Endowment's Marina Ottaway (2001) explicitly characterizes (and critiques) the Global Compact—which stands as the poster child for collaborative governance on the international plane—as a linear descendant of classic corporatism.

Pertinent intellectual traditions in economics include game theory (particularly analyses of coalitions and bargaining) and the transactions-cost-based theories of economic structure rooted in work by Coase in the 1930s (Coase 1937). A sophisticated and diverse literature on the principal–agent relationship clarifies both the definition of collaborative governance we offer (and its distinction from other collective-action models) and the dynamics of particular collaborations (Pratt and Zeckhauser 1985). The portfolio of concepts and analytical methods clustered under the label of "the new institutional economics," most closely associated with Oliver Williamson, illuminates the structure, function, and vulnerabilities of cross-sectoral productive arrangements. Julian Le Grand has employed Williamson's concept of "quasi-markets" to analyze the private provision of education, health, housing, and other social services in post-Thatcher Britain (Le Grand 1991, 1256–67). Work by sociologist Victor Nee crosses over into the economics arena, drawing upon and complementing concepts developed by Williamson and Olson, among others (Nee 1998).

The literature on corporate alliances and strategic partnerships—an area of enquiry by economists, business scholars, and organizational experts—is surprisingly rich in material related to collaborative governance arrangements (Olson and Zeckhauser 1966; Sandler 1992). This literature has been especially lively since the late 1980s, in parallel with the ferment of real-world experimentation with new models of interaction among firms. A 1988 volume edited by Farok Contractor and Peter Lorange marked an early effort to apply social science concepts to a private sector phenomenon, corporate alliances, that has some clear affinities to collaborative governance (Contractor and Lorange 1988). Bruce Kogut arrayed some key analytical frameworks for studying corporate alliances in a seminal journal piece from the late 1980s (Kogut 1988). A special edition of *Organization Science* has been devoted to contemporary work on the empirics and analytics of business collaborations and strategic alliances (Koza and Lewis 1998; Arino and De La Torre 1998; Madhok and Tallman 1998; Smith, Carroll, and Ashford 1995).

In the public management literature, concepts related to collaborative governance are now firmly wedged in the mainstream. The "new public management" centers on indirect, collaborative arrangements for accomplishing public work. Eugene Bardach has done extensive empirical and conceptual work on collaboration between government agencies, with some lessons applicable to cross-sectoral collaboration as well (Bardach 1998). Several decades of commentary on "public–private partnerships" offers antecedents for the study of collaborative governance (Brooks, Liebman, and Schelling 1984). Steven Rathgeb Smith and Michael Lipsky have examined in detail the contractual enlistment of non-profits in the implementation of social welfare policies in the United States (Smith and Lipsky 1993). Donald Kettl, in a recent *Public Administration Review* piece, summarizes a generation-long transformation by which "to a large and growing degree . . . governments share responsibility with other levels of government, with private companies, and with nonprofit organizations" (Kettl 2000). Lester Salamon's ambitious edited volume, *The Tools of Government: A Guide to the New Governance* is predicated on the notion that arrangements of the sort we term collaborative governance are becoming the norm. "What is distinctive about many of the newer tools of public action is that they involve the sharing with third-party actors of a far more basic governmental function: the exercise of discretion over the use of public authority and the spending of public funds" (Salamon 2002; Kelman 2002; Posner 2002; Groenbjerg and Salamon 2002).

# 3. DIRECT AND INDIRECT GOVERNMENT ACTION

Private engagement in governmental undertakings is neither new nor rare. Indeed, it is difficult to imagine any plausible blend of state and market organization that has not been applied in practice at some time and place. Those inclined to view public affairs as (until recently) the state's exclusive domain might contemplate imperial Roman tax administration, for example (which was delegated to private revenue agents) (Finer 1999), or the fabled history of the British East India Company (which frequently functioned as an extension of the British government), or J. P. Morgan's personal crusades against financial panics (which anticipated those of Alan Greenspan by roughly a century) (Means 2001, 128–30). The less familiar story of the St Louis Missouri River Fur Company is also instructive. This private company was formed in 1808 with William Clark, the former co-leader of the Voyage of Discovery, as a lead partner. The following year Meriwether Lewis (previously Clark's compatriot, and then governor of the Louisiana Territories) hired the company to carry out a mission of armed diplomacy to the Mandan Indians. The contract—with the explicit authorization of President Thomas Jefferson—featured performance incentives that seem remarkably up to date (Ambrose 1997).

Virtually every nation's armamentarium of collective-action models is forged from a blend of state and market components, but the preferred alloy varies substantially by place and (our point here) by time. Prominent private roles are the historical norm, but they seem novel against the backdrop of the extraordinary consolidation of central state authority, particularly in the United States, in the mid-twentieth century.

US federal government spending accounted for less than 4 per cent of gross domestic product in 1930. Within fifteen years, the New Deal and the Second World War had driven the federal share to over 44 per cent. But even after this wartime surge ebbed, federal spending rarely fell below 15 per cent of GDP, and the average for the second half of the century was 19.8 per cent (Office of Management and Budget 2004a). This was not merely a matter of the armed forces (and their civilian entourage) expanding to fight wars hot and cold. Excluding the military and the entire civilian defense establishment, the number of executive-branch workers roughly tripled (from around 400,000 to around 1.2 million) between 1940 and 1978 (Office of Management and Budget 2004b). Quantitative expansion forced

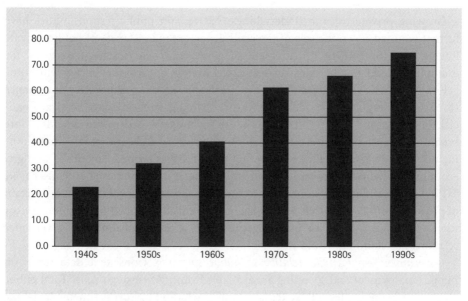

**Fig. 24.1.** Grants, benefit payments, interest, and other financial transfers as share of federal outlays: averages by decade, 1940–2000

qualitative evolution as the mid-century heyday of the central state etched enduring patterns into organizational structures, administrative procedures, and the mindsets of scholars and practitioners.

The central state's ascendancy was relatively brief; a counter-trend was apparent well before the end of the last century. While total US government spending has retreated only modestly from early 1980s levels which approached a third of GDP, this relative stasis in the *level* of public spending concealed the erosion of the mid-century model. The ideological counter-attack spearheaded by Thatcher and Reagan is too familiar to warrant review here, but other factors were at work. Some aspects of the central state's eclipse cannot easily be calibrated. Public trust—and with it, government's moral authority—suffered in the wake of Vietnam and Watergate, for example, and the end of the cold war undercut (briefly, it now appears) the rationale for maintaining a massive defense capacity. Other aspects, though, are fairly clear. One was a shift in government power away from Washington and toward the cities and states. Federal outlays constituted around three-fourths of US public spending from 1947 through 1960, but from 1999 onward accounted for less than two-thirds (Office of Management and Budget 2004c). Another was the escalating share of financial transfers—as distinct from concrete programmatic activities—within federal budgets. Social insurance payments, intergovernmental grants, debt service, and other rearrangements of purchasing power grew from just over 20 per cent of federal spending during the 1940s to reach an average of around 75 per cent in the century's final decade (Office of Management and Budget 2004d) (Fig. 24.1).

Growing private roles in undertakings that remain public responsibilities have further whittled down the role of the central state. Many instances of public–private interaction (government procurement of goods and many clear-cut services, for example) should not be construed as collaborative governance, as we will argue below. Moreover, some areas that are properly considered collaborative governance (for example, regulatory models that feature shared discretion) leave no clear financial footprints and hence will not show up in budget-based measurements. More broadly, there are systematic difficulties—both practical and conceptual—in delimiting public and private realms within what one of us has termed America's "mongrel economy" of hybrid organizations and ambiguous responsibilities (Zeckhauser 1986, 73). Yet it is useful to seek some sense of the scale and contours of the broader terrain of privately performed public work—against the shifting context of the public sector itself—as a prerequisite to mapping the more specific collaborative governance relationships standing within it.

*Government employment relative to public spending.* Consistent data series on public employment and spending are available from 1962 through 2002. Total public sector employment (federal, state, and local) including uniformed members of the armed services peaked at nearly 20 per cent of economy-wide employment in the late 1960s. (When the armed services are excluded from both public and overall payrolls the peak comes lower and later—around 17 per cent of the workforce in the mid-1970s.) The government's share of the workforce broadly declined in later decades. In the late 1990s it was just over 16 per cent or, excluding the military, just over 15 per cent. (Its share increased somewhat by both measures in the early 2000s.) Government employment is much more useful as a gauge of indirect production, however, in combination with government spending. If government is relying less on its own workers to accomplish public missions, the public share of employment should decline relative to the public share of the economy.

Total government spending was around one-quarter of GDP in the mid-1960s, but rose to more than 30 per cent for most years from the mid-1970s through the mid-1990s. Spending slipped to 28 per cent of GDP in 2000 and 2001. So the size of the public workforce relative to the government's weight in the economy indeed has been somewhat lower in recent decades. Figure 24.2 tracks the trend. If the public workforce moved in lockstep with public spending, Fig. 24.2 would feature two flat lines (one for all public employment, including the armed forces, and the other for civilian employment alone.) Through most of the 1960s each 10 per cent of the economy claimed by government required over 7 per cent of the workforce. Since the early 1980s government's share of the workforce has been less than 60 per cent as great as its share of the economy, representing a fall of 15 per cent in the ratio of the public workers to government's share of the economy. This offers a coarse indicator of the rise of indirect governmental action, though the shift is modest and a mild counter-trend seems to have been at work since the mid-1990s.

*Government outlays for employees and outside services.* The relationship between public employment and spending provides only a crude gauge of indirect governance, since the relationship is affected by changes in government's missions, not just

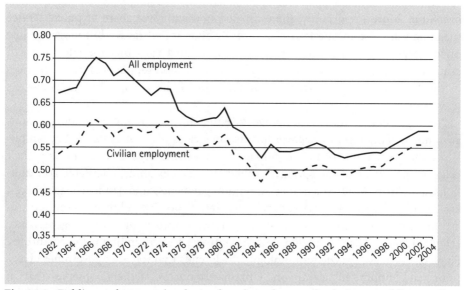

**Fig. 24.2.** Public employment (as share of total employment) relative to public spending (as share of GDP), 1962–2002

*Source*: OMB Fiscal 04 budget, historical tables 17.5 and 15.3; CEA ERP table B-36.

how government pursues those missions. In particular, the relative growth of "check-writing" activities (especially social security, Medicare, grants to other governments, and debt service) should depress the workers-to-spending ratio because check writing requires few workers per dollar of expenditure. Such a shift would not signal a rise in indirect governance. A more precise measure would be to compare governmental spending on employee compensation with spending (through grants or contracts) to acquire the services of agents outside government. Unfortunately, no official data series tracks this relationship, even in the densely documented United States.

A recent study attempts to estimate the share of governmental spending on services devoted to the procurement of external services (rather than to employee compensation) over the last four decades of the twentieth century (Minicucci and Donahue 2004). It employs National Income and Product Account (NIPA) data from the Commerce Department's Bureau of Economic Analysis to make its estimates. The NIPA figures require extensive refinement to permit valid inferences about direct and indirect service spending. They do, however, allow discrimination between activities under the control of state, federal, or local governments and transfer payments or intergovernmental grants for which the choice of direct or indirect production is not generally meaningful.

The results of the study indicate a tilt away from direct governmental production. However, the trends differ over time (with a mild shift *toward* direct government service delivery in the 1960s and 1970s, and toward outside providers thereafter) and by level of government. The state and local sectors rely less on outside service suppliers than does the federal sector, but their reliance grows more rapidly over time. More importantly, the estimated non-employee share of public service spending was close to one-fourth in 1959. By 2000 it had risen—but remained just under 32 per cent. In other words, the conventional view that the late twentieth century witnessed a transformative shift toward outside suppliers of public services in the United States is correct about the sign of the change, but overstates its magnitude.

*Tax expenditures.* As an alternative to either hiring employees or paying non-governmental organizations, governments can seek to advance a mission by manipulating the tax system to induce individuals or private organizations to alter their behavior in service of the specified public goal. For example, charitable contributions, employee health insurance premium payments, and student-loan interest are all subsidized at a taxpayer's marginal rate. "Tax expenditures"—the term of art for such provisions—form an important category of indirect governance (Howard 2002). There is a good deal of controversy surrounding tax expenditures. Some critics challenge the terminology, which tends to imply that government has a prior and unlimited claim on citizens' resources. Others observe that if a legally binding obligation is cancelled, conditional on the debtor's undertaking some specified action, the transaction is indeed equivalent to spending. At a less epistemological level, the efficiency, transparency, and fairness of tax expenditures also engender lively debate. We do not address these debates here—though we endorse their importance—but concern ourselves merely with matters of scale.

In the United States, the president is required by law to identify and estimate the scale of tax expenditures, including preferential tax rates, credits, deferrals, exclusions, exemptions, and deductions. The Office of Management and Budget (OMB) presents such an account as part of the Analytical Perspectives addendum to each year's budget (OMB 2003). The staff of the Congressional Joint Tax Committee prepares its own annual tally of federal tax expenditures, using generally similar concepts and data (Joint Committee 2002). For most purposes and most years the two reports differ little; the OMB data are employed here. OMB presents estimates of specific tax preferences—for example, allowing members of the clergy to exclude parsonage allowances from their taxable income—and groups them into general purposes (such as "National Security," "Energy," and "Education") roughly analogous to the accounting categories OMB employs for direct spending. Tax expenditures are measured both in terms of their estimated revenue loss and in terms of their "outlay equivalent."[4]

For five civilian agencies—the Departments of Commerce, Education, Energy, Health and Human Services, and Housing and Urban Development—it is possible to compare direct departmental outlays with concurrent tax expenditures directed to

---

[4] The chapters in *The Tools of Government: A Guide to the New Governance* (Oxford University Press, 2002) by Ruth Hoogland De Hoog and Lester M. Salamon "Purchase-of-Service Contracting," pp. 319–39; Steven J. Kelman, "Contracting," pp. 282–318; and Paul L. Posner, "Accountability Challenges of Third-Party Government," pp. 523–51 are particularly germane to our topic. Also see Kirsten A. Groenbjerg and Lester M. Salamon, "Devolution, Marketization, and the Changing Shape of Government," in Salamon, ed. *The State of Non-Profit America* (Brookings Institution Press, 2002), pp. 447–70.

parallel missions. We have developed scale comparisons of outlays and tax expenditures, at five-year intervals, for 1975 through projections for 2005. As recently as 1975,
tax expenditures for these five major areas of federal activity were only 38 per cent as
great as direct outlays. By 1980 tax expenditures had risen to 92 per cent of direct
outlays, and they have stayed at rough parity ever since (OMB 2004e). In Fiscal Year
2000 (when the weighted average for the five departments was 90 per cent) tax
expenditures were 18 per cent as large as direct outlays for the Department of Energy,
38 per cent for Health and Human Services, and 49 per cent for Education. At the
Department of Housing and Urban Development, tax expenditures exceeded outlays
by a factor of four; at Commerce, by a factor of seventeen. Again, we do not address
the merits of using the tax code as a lever for collective action, but merely observe
that in at least some domains of the US federal government this approach is
quantitatively significant.

# 4. RATIONALES AND RISKS OF INDIRECT
# GOVERNMENT ACTION

## 4.1 Motives for Private Involvement in Public Missions

Non-governmental actors are appropriately enlisted into public undertakings to
improve performance in the creation of public value. This core rationale applies
whether the mode of engagement is collaborative governance or more familiar forms
of contracting and voluntarism. Private entities may offer advantages over governmental organizations in several (partly overlapping) dimensions.

*Resources.* Perhaps the simplest rationale for collaboration with the private sector
is invoked when government itself lacks the resources—or the ability to mobilize
the resources—required to accomplish some mission. In principle, to be sure,
"governmental resources" is both an imprecise and an elastic category. At least in
liberal democracies government "owns" things only as the citizens' steward, rather
than on its own account. Its command of resources is not measured by its net worth
or collateral available to support debt (as for a family or a firm) but rather in terms of
the citizens' tolerance for taxation, including the future taxation implicit in public
debt. So a declaration that government's resources are inadequate to realize some
public goal translates to one or more of the following:

- Citizens are unwilling to provide, through taxation, revenues to fund this
  particular undertaking—a situation that, if it strictly applied, would raise
  questions about whether the mission is accurately labeled as a "public goal."
- Citizens are not asked to provide designated resources for this particular goal,
  so we cannot assess their willingness to pay for it, but their tolerance of

taxation in the aggregate is exhausted, or nearly so. That is, they do not want to spend more government dollars the way those dollars will likely be spent. If it cannot be established that this enterprise should take precedence over alternative and pre-existing claims on funds, or if such a judgement does not result in the reallocation of tax revenues, then a ceiling on overall taxation can be a binding constraint against this undertaking.

- Procedural impediments (budget rules, debt limits) preclude incremental funding for this goal independent of its merits and resources cannot be or are not diverted from other purposes.
- Citizens *are* willing to devote resources to the mission, but not enough to accomplish it with public funds alone. Only if costs borne by government can be lowered through an infusion of non-governmental resources, or by improving operational efficiency through private involvement, does it meet the net benefits test from the public perspective.
- Some aspects of a public project provide benefits that are so narrowly directed to particular groups that the electorate believes the prime beneficiaries should pay at least a share, and is unwilling to fund the endeavor except on these terms.

*Productivity.* A second generic rationale for indirect government production is that external agents command productive capacity that government lacks. No one proposes the government build its own trucks. The same logic may apply to operating nursing homes. By collaborating with firms or non-profit organizations, government can tap their efficiency edge to improve performance or lower costs or both, relative to acting alone. One variant of this rationale emphasizes particular instances of technical know-how, proprietary intellectual capital, or other potentially transferable capacity that happens to reside in the private sector instead of in government. The more interesting variant emphasizes productivity advantages inherent in the private form of organization. Potential reasons for such advantages are familiar—the focused incentives of the profit motive (with respect to for-profits) and procedural flexibility (with respect to both for-profits and non-profits), the ability to harvest economies of scale and scope by operating beyond jurisdictional boundaries, and the prospect that the quality of performance will affect the odds of expansion, merger, or extinction. The more important and more "embedded" are private productivity advantages, the stronger the rationale for delegated, collaborative, or otherwise shared production.

*Information.* Even if government's resources are no more constrained, and its productivity no lower, than the private sector's, private involvement may be warranted when it is impossible or prohibitively costly for government to acquire pertinent information (Coglianese, Zeckhauser, and Parson 2004). The types of information needed to carry out public tasks—such as the cheapest way to reduce pollution from a particular industrial process or the most effective way to endow workers with a particular skill—are often embodied in private organizations and cannot simply be purchased like a computer, a truck, or a software program.

*Legitimacy.* Private involvement may enhance the perceived legitimacy of an undertaking if a particular task is seen as inappropriate for government to pursue on its own. Suppose we had irrefutable evidence that persuading substance abusers to seek the aid of a higher power in overcoming their addictions would yield significant public benefits. We might still prefer government to encourage and even fund groups such as Alcoholics Anonymous to do this work, rather than establish a Department of Prayer. The legitimacy may flow in the opposite direction. A grant from the National Endowment for the Arts—while unlikely to be munificent—helps non-profit arts organizations demonstrate their gravitas to potential donors. Of course, government activities that might be quite acceptable in one culture or at one time may seem beyond bounds in another time or place. If government is held in systematically low esteem by the citizenry—as say in failed states or corrupt regimes—collaboration with the private sector can shore up legitimacy independent of any task-specific factors.

As these examples illustrate, the rationales for private involvement shift with time and locale. The potential gains from sharing responsibilities with firms or non-profits are contingent on the government's relative weaknesses, whether in resources, productivity, information, or legitimacy. As rewards at the top of the labor market have soared in the United States, for example, government has had increasing difficulty recruiting and retaining talented employees for most of the past generation, particularly for technically trained and higher-level positions (Donahue forthcoming). Were this personnel deficit somehow to be reversed, it would substantially reorder many metrics of relative capacity. The potential payoff from contracting, collaboration, or other forms of delegation will vary across tasks, over time, and from one polity to another.

## 4.2 Risks of Private Involvement in Public Missions

Indirect government action can expand the resources, improve the efficiency, or boost the legitimacy of an undertaking (compared to the baseline of purely governmental activity). However, it also introduces a range of potential losses, which are commonly called "agency costs." That is, the private sector agents supposedly acting at government's behest may not faithfully fulfill the public's mission. We emphatically do not mean to suggest that direct government action escapes agency costs—elected officials and government workers can and do pursue their own agendas at the expense of citizens' interests—but relationships that reach across sectoral boundaries summon distinctive categories of agency costs:

- *Diluted control.* With the exception of the simplest forms of service contracting, indirect action explicitly diminishes government's monopoly of authority for defining the mission, directing the means, or both. Beyond this open and accepted dilution of autonomy, indirect action also involves the risk of unanticipated or unrecognized losses of control.

- *Higher spending.* Indirect production can sometimes prove more costly than anticipated, and can turn out to be more expensive than direct production. This can be because of an erroneous prediction of private productivity advantages; because of transactions costs; because the dilution of control leads to a different and more costly definition of the mission; or because private actors exploit and extract resources from their governmental partner. (Only the latter two categories are agency losses, strictly speaking, but all can show up as burdens on public budgets.)
- *Reputational vulnerability.* Most forms of indirect action expose the government to some risk that the actions of its agents will adversely affect its reputation. (Private partners, of course, face similar vulnerabilities with respect to both the government and other private participants in joint undertakings.) The overstretched US military has relied extensively on private contractors for logistical, security, translation, and other functions in Iraq during and subsequent to the 2003 invasion. In legal and budgetary terms there is a clear difference between a US soldier and a US military contractor. But Iraqis and Islamic observers of the conflict make no such distinction. The vividly publicized abuse of Iraqi detainees at Abu Ghraib prison seriously damaged the United States' image in the eyes of the Islamic world, probably for decades. Multiple reports have suggested that private contractors at Abu Ghraib were responsible for at least some of the abuses (Cushman 2004).
- *Diminished capacity.* In some cases opting for indirect production may discourage or even preclude the maintenance of capacity for direct governmental action. Any contractor knows that today's contract tends to build market power on a contract for tomorrow. To the extent that government becomes dependent on private capabilities, it puts itself in a disadvantaged position in future rounds of negotiation with its agents. Whether "path dependency" presents trivial or profound barriers to reverting to a direct delivery model, and whether reliance on external capacity entails minor or major future costs, will depend on the details of each case.

# 5. MAPPING COLLABORATIVE GOVERNANCE

Where does collaborative governance fit within the sprawling spectrum of models for structuring collective action? Our goal is to draw boundaries that impose precision without stumbling into obscurity or marginal relevance. One step toward anchoring collaborative governance is to read "governance" as dealing with public purposes that are conventionally associated with government. The orchestration of essentially individual purposes—however valuable, however far-flung and

intricate—is something different. (There is an element of circularity in this conception, of course, since "publicness" is defined in part by reference to the capacities and
shortfalls of market-based collective action.) Beyond this imprecise boundary condition there are many potential dimensions along which collaborative governance
can be defined. Here are six that we find instructive:

*Formality.* A collaborative relationship can be institutionalized on a spectrum
ranging from formal contracts (or the equivalent) through informal agreements to
tacit understandings. Many important collaborative governance relationships are
informal. For example, the "military-industrial complex" identified by Eisenhower
capitalizes on military contracts, but its principal instruments—e.g. lobbying efforts,
historical precedent, personal relationships—do not appear on paper. While collaborations cemented solely by gentlemen's agreements and implicit cultural codes may
be important, they are hard to analyze, or even recognize. Hence, we focus on those
characterized by some element of formality.

*Duration.* At one extreme are governance arrangements meant to be permanent
(or at least indefinitely enduring); at the other extreme are ad hoc collaborations that
dissolve as soon as a crisis is resolved or a goal achieved. Short-lived arrangements
often arise in dramatic contexts and hence figure prominently in lists of familiar
collaborations. Other things being equal, however, longer-lived collaborations seem
more likely to prove consequential.

*Focus.* Collaboration can be narrowly structured to meet a single shared challenge, or
can be more broadly designed to address a range of concerns common to the collaborating parties. The focus may be broadened chronologically, taking up new missions as
old ones are fulfilled, or simultaneously with the pursuit of a portfolio of undertakings.

*Diversity of participants.* A minimum level of diversity among participating institutions—at least one public and one private player—is a threshold requirement for
collaborative governance. Beyond this baseline, collaborations can display more or
less internal diversity. For example, private players can be for-profit or non-profit, or
(as with the US hospital sector) an assortment including both. A joint effort among
"summit" institutions within a single country (the federal government, Wal-Mart, and
the United Way in the USA, for example) features less diversity than, say, a collaboration
among the Calcutta municipal authorities, Toshiba, and Médecins sans Frontières.

*Stability.* A collaboration will be stable if its members share objectives, and potentially volatile to the extent members' norms or interests diverge. In less stable collaborations, tugs of war over the division of the pie may impede enlarging the pie, implying
that significant energies must be devoted to maintaining the collaboration itself.

*Discretion.* Whose hand is on the tiller when it comes to validating the mission,
assessing results, triggering adjustment, and so on? In other words, who is leveraging
whom? A two-part test seems warranted here. First, to count as collaborative
*governance,* a large share of discretion must rest with a player who is answerable to
the public at large. While the specification of ends is a strategically complex matter, as
later sections explore, authorized units of government will normally have the final
word on the objectives to be pursued and the criteria by which progress is to be
assessed. Where government is absent, weak, or undemocratic (not a clean criterion,

we recognize) this condition is unlikely to hold, so that our conception of collaborative governance is chiefly a phenomenon of relatively healthy polities. Second, each of the collaborating parties must possess a degree of discretion. If private participants merely carry out government's instructions—conveyed through fully specified contracts or other means—the relationship is something other than collaborative governance.

Indeed, the allocation of discretion is the most useful discriminant for separating collaborative governance from other forms of public–private interaction. Consider, on the one hand, corporate charitable contributions. Companies enjoy broad discretion over their philanthropic giving, and their choices are presumptively defined as "the public good" for tax purposes. There are limits, to be sure. Charitable deductions cannot, under current law, exceed 10 per cent of taxable corporate income (a constraint that rarely binds). No deductions can be claimed for gifts to political parties, or to the CEO's shiftless cousin. But while shareholders might quibble over grants to the chairman's alma mater, or the local polo league, or exotic religious sects, the government has no standing to complain short of trying to discredit the charity itself. The public sector is a party to the undertaking—surrendering revenue it would have otherwise received—but is a passive and silent partner. No doubt this arrangement permits occasions of waste or triviality, but there are strong reasons for protecting donors' discretion against governmental second-guessing on the merits of the mission—for example, so that government does not find itself in the position of declaring which religions are acceptable and which are not. (The Comptroller of Texas attempted to strip Unitarianism—one of America's oldest denominations–of its status as a tax-exempt church in 2004, on the grounds of excessive heterodoxy, but reconsidered after mild local protests and louder national ridicule (Herman 2004).)

Consider, conversely, a municipal government contracting with a private waste management company. The company's mission—to pick up the garbage and dump it at the landfill—is explicit, complete, and controlled by the government, and its motive is to maximize the revenue (less costs) it receives in return. If, upon contract renewal, the government wants the garbage to be collected on Fridays instead of Wednesdays, or incinerated instead of buried, it is at liberty to alter the mandate and the company's only legitimate claim is fair payment for the work. The private player is a pure agent, and discretion rests with the government. Denying the agent initiative—e.g. the right to shop for the cheapest disposal option—obviates some of the reasons for engaging private agents in the first place. But in many arenas of public–private interaction such one-sided discretion is both customary and prudent.

We do not address the myriad complexities that attend pure voluntarism or pure contracting. Nor do we suggest that binary assignments of discretion—wholly private or wholly public—are the normal case. Our goal is to demarcate the domain within which collaborative governance resides, and to underscore that the sharing of discretion both enriches the potential of public–private interaction and renders it much more complex, not just in application but analytically, in ways we will seek to describe once a few examples introduce somewhat more concreteness into the discussion.

# 6. ILLUSTRATIVE EXAMPLES

A virtually endless list of examples could be offered of arrangements that qualify as collaborative governance. We outline a few here, selected by the rather rudimentary choice criterion that they illustrate different aspects of collaborative governance.

*New York City's Park Department.* By the early 1980s New York City was losing the struggle to maintain its public parks. The Parks Department—while not particularly dysfunctional, by most accounts—was overmatched by its mission. As New York's mid-1970s fiscal crisis constrained the Department's resources, squalid and often dangerous parks became symbols of a city in decline. Improvisation under pressure eventually produced a strategy of enlisting private involvement in park upgrades, maintenance, and management.

Such involvement came in a wide range of forms, including conventional voluntarism ("friends of the park" groups clearing litter or supervising playgrounds in a neighborhood park) and conventional outsourcing (contracting out particular maintenance tasks) but also more complex arrangements featuring the sharing of discretion. In New York's most famous park, informal groups of concerned citizens coalesced—with the active encouragement of Department officials—into the Central Park Conservancy, a private non-profit that was given formal responsibility for managing the park in the late 1990s. The restoration and management of Bryant Park was delegated to a "business improvement district" authorized to collect special levies from surrounding businesses. Adrian Benepe, Parks Commissioner under Mayor Michael Bloomberg, declared such "partnerships" to be the linchpin of his management strategy. He and his senior staff often spent more time orchestrating the contributions of various non-governmental actors than they did managing the Department's workforce. While New York City did not cede formal ownership of any park, it delegated much of the responsibility for managing the system to private players (Donahue 2004; Rogers 1986).

*Management-based regulation.* Across a range of arenas the classic approach to regulation—in which government specifies what must be done to forestall safety, environmental, or economic harms—is yielding to approaches that grant regulated firms a degree of discretion. The trend is heterogeneous and carries various labels, but Cary Coglianese's term "management-based regulation" captures the central thrust (Coglianese and Nash 2001). Government regulators' recognition that they suffer a deficit of information, relative to regulated firms, is the fundamental motive for sharing regulatory discretion with firms' managers.

In the environmental arena, a conventional regulatory approach might specify the technologies for processing waste water before it can enter a river. A management-based approach would set maximum levels for each contaminant, but allow firms to decide the best way to meet the standards. In worker safety, the federal Occupational Safety and Heath Administration (OSHA) has experimented with approaches that rely on companies to develop their own worker safety plans and tolerates technical deviations from OSHA rules in otherwise effective plans (Donahue 1999).

A comparable model for food safety regulation, the Hazard Analysis and Critical Control Point protocol released by the Food and Drug Administration in 2001, deals with the heterogeneity of the food-processing industry—and the FDA's scant familiarity with most firms' operations—by identifying generic "critical control points" but leaving it up to firms how to assure safety at each of these points (Coglianese and Lazer 2002). While flat generalizations about the broad and varied terrain of regulation are notoriously perilous, we perceive a widespread migration toward regulatory models featuring efforts to forge common goals, the sharing of discretion, and strategically charged interaction—in a word, collaboration.

*Smallpox vaccinations for "first responders."* The specter of "bioterrorism" surged to the forefront of American anxieties in the wake of the September 2001 terror attacks, and a deliberate release of the smallpox virus was a grim but conceivable scenario. Smallpox had been effectively eradicated roughly two decades earlier. Routine vaccinations had ceased, so most Americans were vulnerable to this highly contagious and devastating disease. Late in 2002 the Bush administration announced a plan of selective immunization to reduce the devastation should a smallpox attack occur. General immunization was rejected since vaccination carried a significant risk of complications. Instead, the administration planned to vaccinate military personnel bound for overseas conflicts and about ten million "first responders"—physicians, nurses, firefighters, police officers, and others who were both likely to be exposed early in a bioterrorism attack and whose services would be especially critical in limiting the extent of any smallpox outbreak. The short-term goal was a million vaccinations by the end of summer 2003.

The federal government took a direct approach to vaccinating the military: Service members selected for vaccination, including the commander-in-chief, met with military physicians or nurses and rolled up their sleeves. The civilian side of the effort was considerably more complex. Rather than delivering vaccinations through the Public Health Service, Centers for Disease Control, or some other federal entity, Washington relied on hospitals and other mostly private medical organizations to nominate half a million doctors, nurses, and emergency medical technicians for the initial wave of first responder vaccinations.

Within weeks half a million military service members had been vaccinated, but the civilian campaign was slow to start and quick to stall. Hospital directors and individual medical personnel compared the aggregate and abstract benefits of readiness to respond against the more immediate and focused risks of inoculation. A doctor or nurse receiving the vaccination would almost certainly suffer some discomfort; might miss some days of work; and faced an unknown but real risk of serious health complications. Moreover, recently vaccinated health workers could pass on the vaccinia virus—the mild but not innocuous relative of smallpox used to confer immunity—to patients or family members for whom this infection could be damaging or even deadly. As private players balanced the costs of vaccination (to themselves, their families, and the missions of their organizations) against the public benefits of preparedness against terrorism, many opted against it. Some hospitals explicitly and publicly declared they would not participate in the government's campaign. Many more private institutions and individuals quietly opted out. By midsummer fewer than 40,000 civilians had been vaccinated. Within a few months the inoculation campaign was quietly halted.

*Federal programs for worker training.* The Workforce Investment Act of 1998 governs the use of federal funds for a range of job training efforts, including programs for young people, workers who have been displaced by technological change or foreign competition, and currently employed workers seeking additional skills. To an even greater extent than its predecessor legislation, this law envisages a collaborative approach to human-capital investment. It embodies the presumption that government has a strong interest in worker training, but tends to be badly positioned to carry out training itself. The usual public sector operational deficiencies—amply revealed in previous attempts at federal training programs—argue against setting up a network of government training centers.

But even if government were able to deliver high-quality, low-cost training on its own, it suffers from severe informational handicaps relative to private players. Effective workforce development requires fine-grained information about current and future skill requirements, and about the potential of particular workers, that government generally lacks. Thus the Act mandates the extensive involvement of private entities, both for-profit and non-profit. Each state and locality is required to establish a governing body, with a majority of business representatives, to oversee federally funded training activities. The private sector is extensively involved not just in governance but also in delivery. Community colleges and other non-profit educational institutions are eligible to deliver training, but so are for-profit training providers. Moreover, private firms are explicitly granted eligibility to deliver on-the-job training to individual workers and (under certain circumstances) to use public money to upgrade the skills of their overall workforce. While this collaborative approach to workforce development has its strengths and weaknesses, there is an apparently durable bipartisan consensus behind this general strategy (Donahue, Lynch, and Whitehead 2000).

*Program for a new generation of vehicles.* During his 1992 campaign for president, Bill Clinton called for increasing federal fuel economy standards from about 28 to 40 miles per gallon, within only eight years. Clinton's election—and that of his running mate Al Gore, whose best-selling book *Earth in the Balance* had called the conventional car "a mortal threat to the security of every nation" (Gore 1992, 325)—was greatly regretted, therefore, by US automakers. The industry had narrowly managed to block legislation in the previous Congress raising mileage standards, and braced for tougher rules under Clinton. Yet the new administration preferred to avoid a head-on confrontation with the auto industry. Moreover, once in office Clinton and Gore realized that reducing climate-damaging emissions (rather than just slowing their growth) would require mileage improvements far beyond what government could force upon an unwilling industry.

A series of overtures by technical experts in government and business led to high-level discussions over collaboration to reinvent the automobile, and early in the Clinton administration the president and vice president, along with the CEOs of the

three major US automakers, formally unveiled the Partnership for the Next Generation of Vehicles. The mission was to put into production within a decade cars with
up to triple the fuel economy of 1993 models with no sacrifice in cost or performance
(Clinton Administration et al. 1993). The means were thoroughly collaborative. An
undersecretary of commerce and senior vice presidents from Ford, GM, and Chrysler
were assigned to co-chair the initiative's steering group. Working teams of government and industry scientists and technicians, with full access to the national laboratories and research facilities of the Departments of Energy and Defense, the National
Aeronautics and Space Administration, and other federal agencies, would push for
breakthroughs in engine design, new materials, emissions control, and alternative
fuels. A new unit in the Commerce Department—with a direct line to the White
House, and in consultation with industry—would coordinate roughly $300 million
in annual federal research and development spending (Buntin 1997). While the
Clinton administration did not promise to forgo seeking statutory increases in
mileage standards, it made it clear that the Partnership was its preferred strategy
for progress on clean cars.

By mid-2000 Washington had invested about $800 million in PNGV, and the auto
industry nearly $1 billion. Ford, Chrysler, and GM had all developed "concept cars"
that approached or exceeded the goal of 80 miles per gallon for a family sedan,
though none were ready for mass production (Hyde 2000). But Honda and Toyota—
which were not participants in PNGV—were preparing to market "hybrid" vehicles
with mileage of around 60 mpg at a modest price premium over conventional cars.
When George W. Bush defeated Al Gore in the 2000 election, the new administration
announced its skepticism toward PNGV, and its first budget proposal cut funding
sharply (Pickler 2001). Within a year the Bush administration cancelled PNGV,
calling instead for a long-term effort to develop hydrogen-fueled cars (Garsten 2002).

We offer these illustrations not as authoritative type specimens, but simply
as opportunistically selected samples from a very large population. Nor (for the
moment) do we attempt to describe their dynamics or evaluate their success. Their
chief purpose is to render somewhat less abstract the conceptual discussion to follow.


## 7. THREE FORMS OF DISCRETION

We now turn to a more detailed discussion of discretion, the most useful dimension
by which collaborative governance is distinguished from other forms of collective
action. We call it philanthropy when private players enjoy full discretion over the
definition and pursuit of the public interest. We call it contracting when discretion
rests with the government, and private players are simple agents. The murky middle
ground, in which both parties exercise discretion, is the domain of collaborative
governance. We distinguish among three kinds of discretion—involving production,

payoffs, and preferences—that shape the potential, the risk, and the strategic complexity of collaboration.

*Production discretion.* A fundamental motive for indirect governmental action is the realistic prospect of efficiency gains (relative to direct provision) through engaging private capacity. This motive does not on its own call for collaborative governance; government can harness private efficiency advantages, while avoiding the complexities of shared discretion, through simple procurement contracts. If government requires a truck, a bus route, or a software package, and recognizes that acquiring it from the private sector is likely to be more efficient than producing it internally, it can specify its requirements, invite competing bids, and choose the provider who promises to deliver on the best terms (Donahue 1989). The chosen contractor is permitted a good deal of latitude over how to meet the terms of the deal. Indeed, the expectation of efficiency through flexibility in production forms much of the rationale for outsourcing. But the definition of ends remains government's prerogative. Effective contracting is not a trivial task. The government runs the risk of error in determining its requirements; of mishandling the translation of these requirements into contractual terms, the choice among competitors, or the monitoring of a provider's performance; and of deceit or incompetence on the part of providers. The challenges, however, are relatively straightforward—more tactical than strategic.

Yet it is sometimes impractical, unwise, or flatly impossible for government fully to specify its goals. For example, the Department of Homeland Security has little understanding about what combination of ambulance drivers, nurses, and emergency room technicians would be most valuable to blunting a smallpox outbreak in Muncie, Indiana, so it lets administrators at Ball Memorial Hospital set priorities for vaccinating "first responders." The Occupational Safety and Health Administration may focus on trash compactors as the greatest danger in grocery stores, but the manager of the local Safeway may know that reducing the risk of loading-dock workers' slipping on spilled produce would deliver greater safety gains. A local job-training official might prescribe on-the-job training in statistical process control for Betty, but her employer may know that Betty is bad at math but good with people—and that in eighteen months the assembly line will be moved to Pakistan while the local office concentrates on marketing. No government agency is likely to match an automaker's judgement over the relative promise of innumerable changes in fuel, engines, design, and materials to boost mileage and hold down the costs of new-generation vehicles. In these and myriad other cases, public goals can be advanced more efficiently if private players are allowed some discretion not just over the means, but over the precise ends to be pursued.

When government yields a share of such discretion, it has crossed the line from simple delegation to collaborative governance. The boundary between "means discretion" and "ends discretion" tends to be imprecise, both in theory and in practice. The distinction is a useful one, however (also both in theory and in practice), and we suspect that a significant quotient of shared discretion characterizes many of today's more consequential areas of public—private interaction. In all but the most straightforward undertakings, private agents' participation in specifying what is to be produced greatly enhances the potential for efficiency improvements. Yet it also amplifies government's challenge of ensuring accountability, in ways to be clarified through describing two other forms of discretion that tend to be unwelcome concomitants of production discretion.

*Payoff discretion.* Suppose that granting production discretion to private collaborators can frequently increase the efficiency of governance and create more value than either direct government production or contractual delegation with tightly defined goals. Dealing with the *distribution* of that augmented pool of value would still ensure that shared discretion remained a troublesome issue. The allocation of payoffs is a perennial problem of collective action, of course. But with both direct government production and ends-specified delegation it is a bounded problem. Government workers would prefer higher pay and more flexible schedules; their managers prefer leaner budgets and predictable staffing. Government contractors prefer rich profit margins and broad-minded evaluations; contract officers prefer low costs and rigorous compliance with specifications. The division of payoffs is a bargaining game, with the outcome dependent on each party's negotiating skill, will, and leverage.

Matters become far more complicated when collaborations feature a choice among alternative production points that lead to different distributions of value. An automaker, for example, would favor a new-generation car campaign that relies heavily on reformulated fuel (at the oil industry's expense) rather than redesigned engines. To the extent that new kinds of engines are part of the mix, the automaker would like to maximize the government's share of the research and development investment. For a given level of priority on new engines and a given share of the spending burden, a company that has already made progress on diesel-electric hybrids would like the campaign to anchor on that design. Similarly, it may be a good thing for Betty, her employer, and society at large for Betty to be trained in marketing. But her employer's share of the payoff will be larger if the government pays the entire cost, if actual marketing assignments as well as classroom work count as "training," and if the focus is on skills peculiar to the employer's market niche instead of more general capabilities that could tempt Betty to switch jobs if she doesn't get a big raise.

When production alternatives entail different immediate distributions of value, the inevitable entanglement of payoff discretion with production discretion renders government vulnerable whenever it lacks full information about the efficiency and payoff characteristics of each alternative. At best, government must expect collaboration to yield results that are better for the private players but worse for it than would be the case if all information were fully shared. At worst, collaboration may lead to a choice of ends and a net pool in public value that are inferior to what could be obtained through direct governmental production. This risk is not unrecognized, of course, and is why governments are usually chary about sharing discretion. Unfortunately, conventional tactics for limiting government's vulnerability to payoff discretion—such as tight performance goals, ceilings on agents' payoffs, or aggressive expost auditing—frequently have the side effect of sacrificing efficiency gains available through production discretion. In theory, the government and private parties could contract around conflicts on the distribution of payoffs—agreeing to rebalance benefits through other deals—but in practice money tends to stick where it starts.

For example, if an automaker gets what turns out to be an unduly generous tax incentive to develop its new-generation car, it is unlikely to lose most of that advantage in other dealings with the government.

*Preference discretion.* Payoff discretion describes leverage over the distribution of value where that value is manifested in, or can be translated into monetary terms. Preference discretion is a related but broader concept, rooted in the recognition that payoffs come in various forms that collaborators may value differentially. Preference discretion arises more commonly with non-profit collaborators but is not unique to them (nor are non-profits immune to manipulating collaborations to reap narrow material payoffs.) Collaborators' preferences are rarely aligned in all respects. Even in a fond marriage you may prefer to go out to a Mexican place while your spouse would rather have sushi. It is in the very nature of the *public* missions to which collaborative governance applies that there be multiple definitions of the good and varying preference differences among collaborators, whether on the margins or at the core. Such differences come in many forms, including:

*Focused philanthropy.* Few lovers of mankind are wholly undiscriminating in their ardor. Even when motives are sincerely altruistic, the satisfactions of selflessness are likely to be more intense for some benefits, or some beneficiaries than for others. A donor may be more inclined to support research on a specific disease that has claimed a parent than to donate to medical science in general. A community organization may be zealous about offering effective, low-cost training to those who need it most, conditional on their belonging to the neighborhood or ethnic group that stirs the founder's loyalties. A park volunteer may be willing to devote endless hours to nature programs for preschoolers, while athletic programs for teenagers leave her cold.

*Semi-private goods.* Economists recognize that the notion of a "public good" is a convenient but potentially misleading shorthand. Even apparent public goods—that cleanly meet the standard criteria of non-rivalry and non-exclusivity—rarely spread their benefits uniformly. Forestalling global warming through cleaner cars is good for everyone, but benefits today's kindergarteners more than today's octogenarians. At the margin, a plant manager crafting a pollution reduction plan might care more about curbing the soot that befouls his town and his company's image than the chlorofluorocarbons that invisibly degrade stratospheric ozone. A benefactor of Central Park might esteem flower beds in general, but think most highly of those visible from her terrace.

*Divergent values.* Preferences can be not just different but antagonistic. It may be integral to a training provider's mission that trainees absorb religious tenets along with workplace skills, even if government funders insist on separating church and (however mediated) state. Since a recent recipient of a smallpox inoculation risks transmitting a dangerous or even fatal vaccinia infection to immuno-compromised patients, such as transplant recipients or the HIV-positive, many medical personnel saw their duty to prepare for a hypothetical smallpox attack to be in conflict with their core value of protecting their patients. Robert Goodin has observed that steadfastness with respect to value preferences can be considered the core "asset" of non-profit organizations, one that they cannot lightly compromise in joint undertakings with the state (Goodin 2003, 359–96).

Preference discretion would not impede accountable collaboration were it not entangled with production discretion. Government cannot be sure that a collaborator is guided by his expertise, or by his interests, as he seeks to shape the ends of the collaboration. For example, as the Central Park Conservancy matured from an adjunct to the mainstay of park management, ball-fields were sodded over and impromptu football throwing restricted in favor of "passive recreation" on well-tended grounds. This may be because the Conservancy recognizes that it is inefficient to squander space within Olmstead's urban jewel on activities that can be pursued elsewhere. Or it may be because the Conservancy's managers—like the Conservancy's major donors, and perhaps unlike many other New Yorkers—place a higher value on strolling along manicured paths than on playing ball. This is not a disagreement about the most effective means to reach consensual ends—such as whether low-fat or low-carb is the better watchword for lowering weight—but a disjuncture in underlying preferences.

The central task for government officials attempting to create public value through collaborative arrangements is to maximize the efficiency gains of production discretion, net of the losses associated with payoff and preference discretion. Figure 24.3 offers a graphic illustration of this task. In Fig. 24.3, the value gained through collaboration (relative to direct production or discretion-free contracting) rises as private players are granted more production discretion. That discretion is exercised by choosing superior means for reaching a particular point, or by achieving production points unavailable to government acting on its own or through agents bound by tight contractual specifications. The gains of production discretion flatten out as the potential of agents' productive and informational superiority is progressively exhausted. At that point, E—as discretion expands into areas where agents are less deft and worse informed than government—payoffs begin to diminish.

Beneficial production discretion, alas, generally brings with it undesirable payoff and preference discretion. To simplify, we illustrate solely with the losses from payoff

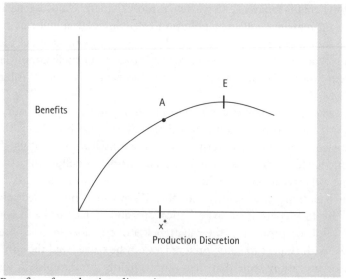

**Fig. 24.3.** Benefits of production discretion

discretion. Losses from preference discretion (when scaled to represent net departures from government's preferred position) would be additive. The ratio between production and payoff discretion is by no means a constant. Figure 24.4 shows two different trajectories of the relationship between these two types of discretion. Some payoff discretion is unavoidable, as shown by the vertical interecepts of the production possibility curves. Curve I illustrates a situation in which relatively little additional payoff discretion is incurred at the early stages of the range. The balance becomes somewhat worse as government continues to loosen constraints on private collaborators. Curve II illustrates a less fortunate marginal relationship between production and payoff discretion; it rises more steeply than does curve I.

Figure 24.4 might be thought of as illustrating two different arenas of collaborative governance, one with an inherently favorable relationship between good and bad discretion and the other a more troublesome entanglement. Curve I might illustrate an "adopt a highway" program in which local businesses take responsibility for clearing litter from a stretch of road in exchange for signs that publicize their civic-mindedness (as well as their donuts or pet-care services.) Curve II might depict an on-the-job training program in which rightward movement corresponds to weakening restrictions on employers' discretion to choose which workers to train, in which skills, and by what means. In the one case, the nature of the task presents private agents with limited opportunities to expropriate payoffs or insinuate preferences as they are given progressively more production discretion. In the other case, such temptations are pervasive.

Alternatively, and just as validly, Curves I and II can be thought of as referring to the same collaboration, but with more- and less-sophisticated governmental efforts to structure and manage the relationship. Curve II, in this version, would represent a feebly designed adopt-a-highway or on-the-job training program. Curve I would represent the same endeavor, but with more astute measures to harvest the gains while avoiding the losses that come with private discretion. In the highway case, for

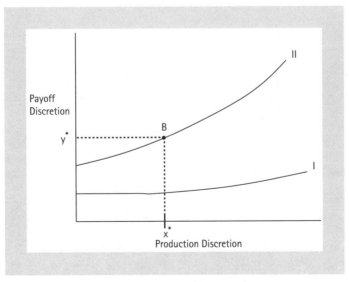

**Fig. 24.4.** Payoff discretion as a function of production discretion

example, signs identifying benefactors might be smaller but more frequent to solidify the link between a company's image and the condition of a given stretch of roadway. In the training case, government might gauge the outcomes of employers' discretion by measuring trainees' before-and-after test scores or hourly earnings.

Figure 24.4 showed how payoff discretion rises with the level of production discretion. Figure 24.5 shows how much this costs. The value lost through payoff discretion grows as government loosens the reins, with the rate of loss accelerating as government exercises less control over collaborators' ability to claim larger payoffs or substitute their preferences for the public's.

The optimum is derived from the three functions represented on Figs. 24.3, 24.4, and 24.5. It is found at x*, implying that payoff discretion will be at y*, and that the program will operate at points A, B, and C. The technically minded reader will note that the marginal benefit (MB) of greater production discretion, the slope at A in Fig. 24.3, just equals the marginal cost (MC). The latter is the product of the slopes at points B and C in Figs. 24.4 and 24.5. That product represents the increase in payoff discretion from a unit increase in production discretion times the marginal cost of that increase.

In general, we would also expect preference discretion to enter the picture, and its level will be positively related to production discretion. The efficiency condition would then be:

MB of production discr. = MC of payoff discr. + MC of preference discr.

As these illustrations hint, the outcomes for the public of collaborative governance can range from spectacular to calamitous, depending on government officials' ability to determine when collaboration is a promising approach; to judge how much discretion to cede to private agents; and to fine-tune the terms of the collaboration to maximize the benefits less the costs associated with shared discretion.

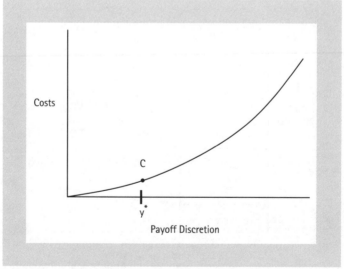

**Fig. 24.5.** Costs of payoff discretion

# 8. COLLABORATIVE GOVERNANCE AND GOVERNMENT'S ANALYTICAL IMPERATIVES

Not only is the orchestration of collaborative governance a challenge of a high order, but it is also a fundamentally different sort of challenge from those posed by managing bureaucracies, and distinct as well from writing and monitoring clear-cut contracts. To fulfill the functions that we rather casually summarize in the preceding paragraph, government officials must:

- gauge the expected efficiency differential between direct government performance and delegation to the private sector of a particular function;
- evaluate the net public benefits of different levels and variants of an undertaking;
- estimate the probable balance between value gained and value lost for each increment of private discretion, in order to judge how fully specified the terms of a delegated task should be;
- appreciate the objectives, constraints, and internal dynamics of potential collaborators in sufficient detail to predict the gains from production discretion and the degree and nature of risks associated with payoff and preference discretion;
- discriminate among potential collaborators according to how they are likely to employ any discretion granted, and how likely they are to comply with measures to curb their discretion;
- structure, implement, and uphold a regime of rules that loosely constrain productive discretion and tightly constrain payoff and preference discretion;
- alter the terms of the collaboration as public priorities change or new evidence comes to light;
- and do all of this even when, as will frequently be the case, the private parties in a collaboration outmatch the public parties in resources, political influence, and popular esteem.

We do not mean to imply that government must be confident of performing all of these tasks with uniform perfection before contemplating collaborative arrangements. The parallel requirements of public management for direct governmental action, after all, are seldom realized in full. We conclude with three observations relevant to our prospects for collecting the benefits while avoiding the risks of collaborative governance.

First, the growing practical importance of collaborative governance has outstripped our capacity to understand, categorize, make predictions about, and prescribe improvements to such arrangements. Our analytical apparatus—anchored in traditional, more crisply defined concepts such as market failure and public goods—lags behind practitioners' exuberant improvisation. This intellectual lag has ample precedent; governments were improvising policies to enhance public welfare, for example, before welfare economics was invented to steer such efforts. With the recognition of this new category of collective action, scholars once again have their work cut out for them.

Second, orchestrating collaborative arrangements calls upon skills that are frequently found among corporate executives, venture capitalists, or senior consultants, but less so among front-line public managers. We are not currently accustomed to selecting, compensating, or evaluating government workers on the basis of such competencies. The requisite skill set, we emphasize, is predominantly *analytical.* The functions described above have relatively little to do with classic public administration and a great deal to do with economics, institutional analysis, game theory, decision analysis, and other relatively advanced tools for predicting and influencing outcomes. The need for analytical sophistication, moreover, extends quite deeply into government. It applies at the level of implementation (not just policy making) and continuously (not just at the start of an initiative). When the menu of implementation models was short and simple, government could get by with a small pool of analytical talent near the top. Collaborative governance confronts the public sector with different analytical imperatives—fine-grained, ongoing, distributed deeply through government—for which we are not yet ready.

Finally, although there are major gaps in the data, it seems inescapable that collaborative governance is an increasingly consequential category of collective action wherever there is a public entity robust enough to hold up government's side. Our empirical references have been anchored on the United States, with which we are most familiar, but parallel developments appear to be under way in nearly all OECD countries and in many developing and transitional nations as well. As demands for the creation of public value outpace governments' capacity to deliver it unaided—in health care, education, environmental preservation, employment and social welfare, and even security—the collaborative impulse intensifies. This form of governance (though it entails undeniable risks) promises great benefits, on balance, when employed advisedly and managed adroitly. This presents scholars and practitioners with an urgent agenda—to develop analytical frameworks and management tradecraft that can bolster the benefits and curb the costs of the collaborative approach to governance.

## References

AMBROSE, S. E. 1997. *Undaunted Courage: Meriwether Lewis, Thomas Jefferson, and the Opening of the American West.* New York: Touchstone.

ARIÑO, A., and TORRE, J. D. L. 1998. Learning from failure: towards an evolutionary model of collaborative ventures. *Organization Science*, 3: 306–25.

AXELROD, R. 1984. *The Evolution of Cooperation.* New York: Basic Books.

BARDACH, E. 1998. *Getting Agencies to Work Together: The Practice and Theory of Managerial Craftsmanship.* Washington, DC: Brookings Institution.

BROOKS, H., LIEBMAN, L., and SCHELLING, C. (eds.) 1984. *Public Private Partnership: New Opportunities for Meeting Social Needs.* Cambridge, Mass.: Ballinger.

BUNTIN, J. 1997. From confrontation to cooperation: how Detroit and Washington became partners. Kennedy School of Government Case Study. Cambridge, Mass.: Harvard University.

CLINTON ADMINISTRATION AND US COUNCIL FOR AUTOMOTIVE RESEARCH 1993. Partnership for a new generation of vehicles: a declaration of intent. Joint Press Release, Sept.

COASE, R. 1937. The nature of the firm. *Economica*, 4: 386–405.

COGLIANESE, C., and LAZER, D. 2002. Management-based regulatory strategies. Pp. 201–24 in *Market-Based Governance: Supply Side, Demand Side, Upside and Downside*, ed. J. D. Donahue and J. S. Nye, Jr. Washington, DC: Brookings Institution Press.

—— and NASH, J. 2001. *Regulating from the Inside.* Washington, DC: Resources for the Future Press.

—— ZECKHAUSER, R. J., and PARSON, E. 2004. Securing truth for power: informational strategy and regulatory policy-making. Kennedy School of Government Working Paper RWP04-021, May.

CONTRACTOR, F., and LORANGE, P. (eds.) 1988. *Cooperative Strategies in International Business.* Lexington, Mass.: Lexington Books.

CUSHMAN, J. H. 2004. Private company finds no evidence its interrogators took part in abuse. *New York Times* (13 Aug.): 8.

DAHL, R. A. 1961. *Who Governs?* New Haven, Conn.: Yale University Press.

—— and LINDBLOM, C. 1953. *Politics, Economics, and Welfare.* New Brunswick, NJ: Transaction.

DONAHUE, J. 1989. *The Privatization Decision: Public Ends, Private Means.* New York: Basic Books.

—— 1997. *Disunited States.* New York: Basic Books.

—— (ed.) 1999. *Making Washington Work.* Washington, DC: Brookings Institution Press.

—— 2004. *Parks and Partnership in New York City A: Adrian Benepe's Challenge.* Cambridge, Mass.: Harvard University, Kennedy School of Government Case Program.

—— forthcoming. *The Problem of Public Jobs: American Inequality and the Warping of Government Work.*

—— LYNCH, L., and WHITEHEAD, R. W., Jr. 2000. *Opportunity Knocks: Training the Commonwealth's Workers for the New Economy.* Boston: Massachusetts Institute for a New Commonwealth.

ELSTER, J. 1989. *The Cement of Society: A Study of Social Order.* New York: Cambridge University Press.

FINER, S. E. 1999. *History of Government.* New York: Oxford University Press.

FREEDLAND, M. 1999. Public law and private finance: placing the private finance initiative in a public law frame. Pp. 145–68 in *Regulation and Deregulation: Policy and Practice in the Utilities and Financial Services Industries*, ed. C. McCrudden. Oxford: Clarendon Press.

FREEMAN, J. 1997. Collaborative governance in the administrative state. *UCLA Law Review*, 45 (1: Oct.): 1–99.

GARSTEN, E. 2002. Bush abandons high-mileage program for hydrogen fuel-cell. *Associated Press State and Regional Wire Service*, Business News section, 9 Jan.

GOODIN, R. E. 2003. Democratic accountability: the distinctiveness of the third sector. *Archives européennes de sociologie*, 44 (3): 359–96.

GORE, A., Jr. 1992. *Earth in the Balance.* New York: Houghton Mifflin.

GROENBJERG, K. A., and SALAMON, L. M. 2002. Devolution, marketization, and the changing shape of government. Pp. 447–70 in *The State of Non-Profit America*, ed. L. Salamon. Washington, DC: Brookings Institution Press.

HERMAN, K. 2004. Unitarians get religious status after intercession. *Austin American-Statesman* (25 May): B-1.

HOWARD, C. 2002. Tax expenditures. Pp. 410–44 in *Tools of Government*, ed. L. Salamon and O. V. Elliot. New York: Oxford University Press.

HYDE, J. 2000. GM says Precept concept car achieves 80 mpg in tests. *Associated Press State and Regional Wire Service*, Business News section, 20 Oct.

JOINT COMMITTEE ON TAXATION OF THE US CONGRESS 2002. *Estimates of Federal Tax Expenditures for Fiscal Years 2003–2007.* Report prepared for the Committee on Ways and Means and the Committee on Finance, US Government Printing Office.

JONES, C., HESTERLY, W., FLADMOE-LINDQUIST, K., and BORGATTI, S. 1998. Professional service constellations: how strategies and capabilities influence collaborative stability and change. *Organization Science*, 9 (3): 396–410.

KELMAN, S. J. 2002. Contracting. Pp. 282–318 in *The Tools of Government: A Guide to the New Governance*, ed. L. Salamon. Oxford: Oxford University Press.

KETTL, D. 2000. The transformation of governance: globalization, devolution, and the role of government. *Public Administration Review*, 60 (6: Nov.–Dec.): 488–97.

KHANNA, T., SIMESTER, D., and ANDERSON, E. 1988. The scope of alliances. *Organization Science*, 9(3): 340–55.

KOGUT, B. 1988. Joint ventures: theoretical and empirical dimensions. *Strategic Management Journal*, 9: 319–32.

KOZA, M. P., and LEWIS, A. Y. 1998. The co-evolution of strategic alliances. *Organization Science*, 9 (3: Mar.) 255–64.

LE GRAND, J. 1991. Quasi-markets and social policy. *Economic Journal*, 101 (127: Sept.): 1256–67.

McGUIRE, K. T. 1993. Lawyers and the U.S. Supreme Court: the Washington community and legal elites. *American Journal of Political Science*, 37 (2: May): 365–90.

MADHOK, A., and TALLMAN, S. B. 1998. Resources, transactions and rents: managing value through interfirm collaborative relationships. *Organization Science*, 9 (3: May–June): 326–39.

MEANS, H. 2001. *Money and Power: The History of Business.* New York: Wiley.

MINICUCCI, S. M., and DONAHUE, J. D. 2004. A simple estimation method for aggregate government outsourcing. *Journal of Policy Analysis and Management*, 23 (3: Summer): 489–508.

MINOW, M. 2002. *Partners, Not Rivals: Privatization and the Public Good.* Boston: Beacon Press.

NEE, V. 1998. Norms and networks in economic and organizational performance. *American Economic Review*, 87(4): 85–9.

OFFICE OF MANAGEMENT AND BUDGET 2003. Analytical perspectives. *The Budget of the United States, Fiscal Year 2004*, Section 6. Washington, DC: Government Printing Office.

—— 2004a. Fiscal 2004 budget, Historical Table 1–2. At: www.whitehouse.gov/omb/budget/fy2004/sheets/hist01z2.

—— 2004b. Fiscal 2004 budget, Historical Table 17.1. At: www.whitehouse.gov/omb/budget/fy2004/sheets/hist17z1.xls.

—— 2004c. FY 2004, Historical Table 15.3. At: www.whitehouse.gov/omb/budget/fy2004/sheets/hist15z3.xls.

OFFICE OF MANAGEMENT AND BUDGET 2004d. FY 2004, Historical Table 6.1. At: www.whitehouse.gov/omb/budget/fy2004/sheets/hist06z1.xls.

—— 2004e. Outlays by agency: 1962–2008. *Budget of the United States, Fiscal Year 2004*, Historical Table 4.1. At: www.whitehouse.gov/omb/budget/fy2004/sheets/hist04z1.xls.

OLSON, M. 1965. *The Logic of Collective Action: Public Goods and the Theory of Groups*. Cambridge, Mass.: Harvard University Press.

—— and ZECKHAUSER, R. 1966. An economic theory of alliances. *Review of Economics and Statistics*, 48 (3: Aug.): 266–79.

OTTAWAY, M. 2001. Corporatism goes global: international organizations, NGO networks and transnational business. *Global Governance*, 7(3): 265–92.

OUCHI, W. G. 1980. Markets, bureaucracies, and clans. *Administrative Science Quarterly*, 25 (1: Mar.): 129–41.

PERRY, J. L., and RAINEY, H. G. 1988. The public–private distinction in organization theory: a critique and research strategy. *Academy of Management Review*, 13(2): 182–201.

PICKLER, N. 2001. Partnership may not reach goals for affordable "super car" by 2004. *Associated Press State and Regional Wire Service*, Business News section, 13 Aug.

POSNER, P. L. 2002. Accountability challenges of third-party governance. Pp. 523–51 in *The Tools of Government: A Guide to the New Governance. Accountability Challenges of Third-Party Government*, ed. L. Salamon. Oxford: Oxford University Press.

PRATT, R., and ZECKHAUSER, R. (eds.) 1985. *Principals and Agents: The Structure of Business*. Cambridge, Mass.: Harvard Business School Press.

PUTNAM, R. 1993. *Making Democracy Work: Civic Traditions in Modern Italy*. Princeton, NJ: Princeton University Press.

—— 2000. *Bowling Alone: The Collapse and Revival of American Community*. New York: Simon and Schuster.

ROGERS, E. 1986. *Rebuilding Central Park: A Management and Restoration Plan*. Cambridge, Mass.: MIT Press.

ROWLEY, T. 1997. Moving beyond dyadic ties: a network theory of stakeholder influences. *Academy of Management Review*, 22(4): 887–910.

SALAMON, L. M. (ed.) 2002. *The Tools of Government: A Guide to the New Governance*. Oxford: Oxford University Press.

SANDLER, T. 1992. *Collective Action, Theory and Applications*. Ann Arbor: University of Michigan Press.

SMITH, K. G., CARROLL, S. J., and ASHFORD, S. J. 1995. Intra- and interorganizational cooperation: toward a research agenda. *Academy of Management Journal*, 38 (1: Feb.): 7–23.

SMITH, S. R., and LIPSKY, M. 1993. *Nonprofits for Hire: The Welfare State in the Age of Contracting*. Cambridge, Mass.: Harvard University Press.

STEFFENS, L. 1904. *The Shame of the Cities*. New York: McClure, Philips.

WILLIAMSON, O. 1975. *Markets and Hierarchies*. New York: Free Press.

—— 2000. The new institutional economics: taking stock, looking ahead. *Journal of Economic Literature*, 38 (Sept.): 595–613.

ZECKHAUSER, R. J. 1986. The muddled responsibilities of public and private America. P. 45–76 in *American Society: Public and Private Responsibilities*, ed. R. Zeckhauser and W. Knowlton. Cambridge, Mass.: Ballinger.

# PART VI

## CONSTRAINTS ON PUBLIC POLICY

CHAPTER 25

# ECONOMIC CONSTRAINTS ON PUBLIC POLICY

## JOHN QUIGGIN

## 1. INTRODUCTION

Economics is commonly described as "the science of allocating scarce resources." By contrast, a popular description of politics is "the art of the possible." Both of these descriptions refer to the same central feature of human existence: our wants generally exceed our capacity to satisfy them. However, economic and political approaches to the problem of scarcity are quite different.

In the standard mainstream economic view, the problem of allocating limited resources has a well-defined optimal solution, for any given initial allocation of property rights. Moreover, this solution can be achieved, or at least approximated, by allowing individuals to trade freely in markets, perhaps with the assistance of governments to correct a variety of market "failures" or "imperfections."

The political view, and particularly the "pragmatic" view associated with the characterization of politics as the art of the possible, is rather different. The gap between wants and resources is expressed in the form of demands on governments. The political problem is that of achieving "bargained consensus," at least among those groups with a capacity to obstruct or veto an agreement. The art of the

* I thank Nancy Wallace, Bob Goodin, and Mick Moran for helpful comments and criticism. This research was supported by an Australian Research Council Federation Fellowship.

politician consists partly in leading parties from initially disparate positions to sustainable compromise, and partly in finding policy innovations that permit the achievement of seemingly irreconcilable goals.

In the practice of this art, the ambiguity of the term "possible" is crucial. On the one hand, it refers to limitations in a manner similar to that of the economist. There is a bounded set of possibilities, and the problem is to choose between them. On the other hand, there is a deep-seated notion of limitless possibility, that if we only set our minds to it, we can achieve anything.

One way in which the conflict between the two views may be usefully examined is by considering economic constraints on public policy. Constraints play a central role in economic thought: the problem of how best to allocate scarce resources is commonly represented, in mathematical terms, as one of maximizing an objective function subject to one or more resource constraints. This approach is not always congenial to political practitioners, who frequently suggest that alleged constraints are being used to promote the adoption of particular policies on the grounds that "there is no alternative."

In this chapter, a variety of perspectives on the role of economic constraints are considered. First, the relationship between economic constraints and accounting identities, such as those derived from government budgets and national accounts, is examined. The relationship between budget balance constraints and external balance constraints is considered with reference to notions of "crowding out" and "twin deficits." The idea that globalization has tightened the constraints on governments is critically assessed and found to be largely baseless. Second, the dual relationship between constraints and trade-offs is considered. The presence of a constraint implies a trade-off and vice versa. This relationship provides the basis for a consideration of how public policy can respond to constraints and trade-offs.

## 2. IDENTITIES AND CONSTRAINTS

An important set of constraints on public policy arise from a range of economic and accounting identities.

## 2.1 The Budget Balance Constraint

To take a simple example, a government's budget balance is the difference between revenue (mainly from taxation) and public expenditure, being a surplus if this is positive, and a deficit if (as is more common) this is negative.

Surveys of public opinion commonly show that majorities of respondents support increases in public expenditure, reductions in taxation, and improvements in the budget balance.[1] Politicians therefore have incentives to support all three, but they are not mutually consistent.

A variety of accounting devices, such as the treatment of the proceeds of asset sales as if they were current income, may be and have been used to provide the appearance of stable budget balance even while expenditure is rising and revenue is declining. Such expedients are inevitably doomed to failure in the long run.

In the long term, the budget balance constraint is simpler: appropriately measured, government consumption and payments of benefits must equal government income. Borrowing allows higher consumption in the present at the expense of lower consumption or higher taxes in the future, but the requirement for long-run balance cannot be avoided.

A number of issues arise here. The first is that, given a positive real rate of interest, a given amount of consumption or income now can be traded for a larger amount in the future. This means that, to compare streams of consumption and income, it is necessary to convert them to a present value using standard discounting procedures.

The second issue, which follows logically from the first, is that in evaluating budget balances, it is necessary to focus on current consumption and current income, excluding capital transactions and the associated flows of interest payments, of which the most important are interest payments on public debt. These payments are taken into account in present value calculations, and treating them as part of current debt would lead to double counting.

A third, and much trickier issue concerns the treatment of risk. In general, a risky stream of income is less valuable than a riskless stream with the same expected value, and this fact needs to be taken into account in evaluating budget constraints. This problem raises complexities that are beyond the scope of this chapter, but are addressed in Quiggin (2004).

Next, it is important to consider ways in which it might seem possible to avoid the long-run balanced budget constraint. Historically, the most popular strategy has been the use of the government's capacity to create money by resort to the printing press (or in the days of metallic money, through debasement of coinage). Although the relationship is neither instant nor automatic, this method of finance invariably leads to inflation.[2] Inflation reduces the value of existing holdings of money, and also of outstanding obligations such as government bonds, and is therefore best seen as a tax on holders of such assets. Over the long run, benefits from taxing bondholders through inflation are cancelled out by compensating increases in nominal interest rates, so the only real benefit is that derived directly from the issuance of money. The resulting revenue is called seignorage.

---

[1] This does not necessarily mean that individual respondents are acting inconsistently. Suppose for example, that one-third of respondents favour lower taxes and improved budget balance, one-third favour higher expenditure and improved budget balance, and one-third favour lower taxes and higher public expenditure. Then there is a majority in favour of all three proposals, even though no individual supports all three.

[2] In fact, some economists use the term "inflation" to refer to expansion of the monetary base, rather than to the ensuing increase in the general price level. This is the interpretation that fits most naturally with the ordinary meaning of the term.

If inflation is regarded as a tax, it is evident that the availability of this option does not lead to any relaxation of the balanced budget constraint. Considered as a source of revenue, inflation taxes may be compared with other taxes to determine what rate of inflation is socially optimal. The general consensus of economic opinion at present is that modest, but positive rates of inflation, of around 1 to 2 per cent annually, are optimal. The resulting seignorage amounts to around 0.5 per cent of GDP for the United States (much of this associated with offshore holdings of dollars) and less for other developed countries. This is small in relation to other sources of revenue such as income and sales taxes and can therefore be disregarded for most purposes.

A second strategy aimed at avoiding the balanced budget constraint is the sale of assets, most notably through the privatization of government business enterprises. This expedient was particularly popular in the 1980s and 1990s. Although there has been a variety of arguments put forward in support of privatization, one of the most consistent themes in the case for privatization has been the claim that the sale of public assets can reduce government debt without the need for higher taxes or lower public spending.

This claim is fallacious. Selling an income-earning asset such as a government business enterprise means forgoing the stream of earnings generated by that asset. Selling a service-generating asset such as a publicly owned building means that it is necessary to pay for, or do without, the services that the asset previously generated. If the asset has the same value in private and public ownership, the revenue realized by selling it will be equal to the present value of the income and services generated by the asset. In this case, the budget balance constraint is unaffected by asset sales. This fact is recognized in the accrual accounting systems now in use in many jurisdictions. However, under the cash accounting systems used until the 1990s, the proceeds of asset sales were treated as if they were current income.

Asset sales produce a net benefit if the proceeds from the sale are greater than the value of the asset in continued public ownership. It makes sense, therefore, for governments to manage their assets actively, and dispose of unused assets. A common example is the sale of land acquired for some public purpose that is no longer relevant.

On the other hand, if assets are sold for less than their value in continued public ownership, a net loss results. Most privatizations undertaken in developed countries have produced a net loss of this kind. The privatization of British Telecom set the pattern. Half of this enterprise was sold at a price equivalent to only two years' earnings. Subsequent privatizations have produced smaller losses in most cases, but the general pattern of losses has not changed. As a result, some advocates of privatization have revised their views (Nellis 1999).

The British experience is instructive. The Thatcher government sold assets and used the proceeds to cut taxes substantially, while making only modest cuts in aggregate public expenditure. Under the cash accounting system the asset sales allowed the government to record a surplus. By the early 1990s, however, with the tax cuts still in place and with no more assets left to sell, the surpluses turned into large deficits, exacerbated by the economic downturn beginning in 1990. By 1993–4, the deficit approached nearly 8 per cent of GDP. The resulting increase in debt implied a requirement for higher taxes and lower public expenditure to cover interest payments.

If in an appropriate sense, budgets must balance in the long run, it is natural to consider a requirement that governments should maintain balanced budgets at all times, at least on an annual basis. Such requirements have been adopted by many governments, either as a constitutional or legislative constraint, or as a matter of policy. There are, however, strong arguments against a requirement for annual balanced budgets.

In the absence of specific policy changes, tax revenue will decline during recessions and public expenditure (for example on unemployment benefits) will rise. The shift in the budget balance partly offsets the decline in national income during a recession, helping to reduce the impact on aggregate (public and private) consumption. This automatic stabilizing effect reduces the severity of recessions.

In addition to these direct effects, Keynesian models of the economy imply that there is a second-round effect arising from the stimulus to private demand generated by public sector payments. Hence, Keynesians usually favour additional discretionary fiscal policies to stimulate demand during recessions.

Although highly successful in the decades immediately following the Second World War, Keynesian fiscal policies have had mixed success since then. Critics of Keynesian economics generally prefer rule-based approaches in which tax rates and policy programs are fixed so as to maintain budget balance over the course of the economic cycle. Even without discretionary intervention, however, a rule-based approach implies that the budget will not be balanced on an annual basis.

The most appropriate interpretation of this constraint is a version of what has been referred to as the "golden rule," namely that, over the course of the economic cycle the net worth of the public sector, expressed as a proportion of GDP, should remain constant.

## 2.2 The External Balance Constraint

The second major constraint with which policy makers have to deal relates to external balance, that is, to international flows of goods, services, and capital. National accounts incorporate identities relating to external balance, and these constraints correspond to constraints on economic policy.

The most important identity is that the balance of payments on current account (the difference between the values of exports and imports of goods and services plus the difference between outgoing and incoming flows of income payments) is equal and opposite to the balance of the capital account (the difference between outgoing and incoming flows of capital in the form of debt and equity investment). So, for example, a country like the United States, which consistently has a deficit on the current account, must *by definition* have a surplus on the capital account. It follows that the simplistic assumption that deficits are invariably bad and surpluses invariably good is self-contradictory; each surplus has its corresponding deficit.[3]

Just as with government budgets, the accounting identities imply a long-run constraint that, appropriately measured, imports and exports must balance. Although the long-term external balance constraint cannot be avoided, the force with which it bears on national governments varies greatly depending on the settings of policy.

## 2.3 The Twin Deficits and Crowding Out

The budget balance and the external balance, combine with the consumption and investment of the private sector to form the national income identity:

Income = Consumption + Investment + Govt spending + Exports − Imports

Again, it is important to emphasize that this is an identity, true by virtue of the definitions of the terms, and not because of any particular economic theory. This identity can be rearranged in various ways. The most useful involves taking taxation revenue into account as a transfer from households to governments. Rearranging, it is then possible to show that the government budget deficit must be equal to the sum of Imports − Exports (the trade deficit) and Private Saving (after-tax income less consumption) − Investment. When a government increases spending or cuts taxes, leading to a higher budget deficit, one or other of these must change as well since the accounts must balance.

The "twin deficits" hypothesis is that the adjustment will take the form of more borrowing from abroad, that is, an increase in the capital account surplus and, therefore, the current account deficit. Hence the budget deficit and the current account deficit are "twins." This hypothesis seems to fit the data on some occasions, such as Australia and the United States in the 1980s, but there are some obvious exceptions. In the late 1990s, the US budget went from deficit to surplus, but the current account kept on increasing.

An alternative view is that balances of trade in goods and services, and on the current account, are determined mainly by factors specific to the traded goods sector. If this is the case, then increases in the government budget deficit must be matched, in equilibrium, by increases in private saving. We can write:

Saving = Income − Tax − Consumption − Investment

If taxes are assumed to be set by government, an increase in savings can be realized by changes in any of the other three variables. Views about the desirability or otherwise of budget deficits depend in part on which variable is seen as likely to adjust.

---

[3] Because the measures of international flows are imperfect, the accounts do not, in general, balance automatically and must be reconciled by the inclusion of a "statistical discrepancy."

The most pessimistic view, called "crowding out," is that investment will decline as private savings are used to fund the budget deficit.[4] The neutral position, called Ricardian equivalence, is that consumption will adjust. In this story, people realize that the budget deficit will imply higher taxes in future, and increase saving now. Few economists find this story plausible, although it is consistent with an extreme version of the rationality postulate commonly adopted by economists. The optimistic position is that income will increase, partly offsetting the original increase in the budget deficit as tax revenue rises and also allowing for higher private savings.

There are two reasons why the optimistic position may be justified. The first is derived from Keynesian macroeconomics and the other from "supply-side" micro-economic theories.

The Keynesian argument for deficits, discussed above, assumes that there are lots of unemployed workers, idle factories, and so on. The extra demand produced by tax cuts or government spending is met by hiring more workers and reopening factories, which in turn stimulates "multiplier" effects. In a very simplistic model, sometimes referred to as the "pump-priming" model, the growth is sufficient to wipe out the original increase in the budget deficit.

Most economists are Keynesian in the short run, but believe some mixture of crowding out and twin deficit models applies in the long run. As already discussed, this suggests the ideal policy called the "golden rule," namely, running deficits during recessions and surpluses during booms so as to achieve budget balance over the course of the cycle.

The "supply-side" argument based on the (in)famous Laffer curve applies only to cuts in taxes. It's claimed that the extra incentives provided by the tax cuts will stimulate more work effort, higher investment, and so on, thereby raising income and in the extreme case, wiping out the original increase in the budget deficit, as in the "pump-priming" story. Few serious economists accept this strong claim. Evidence on whether there is any relationship between tax rates and growth in national income is mixed, but there is a broad consensus that it is unwise to rely on incentive effects when projecting the likely consequences of tax cuts.

## 2.4 Globalization and Constraints on Public Policy

It is commonly supposed that "globalization" has tightened the constraints on public policy, and particularly on economic policy. This idea has two parts. The first is that globalization and, in particular, the massive growth in international flows of capital observed over the past three decades is the inevitable outcome of technological change, and particularly of the striking innovations in computing and telecommunications that have taken place in recent years.

---

[4] As the argument above shows, the twin deficits hypothesis and the crowding out hypothesis are logically contradictory. Nevertheless some critics of budget deficits have pushed both theories, and some have managed to believe both simultaneously.

However, recent improvements in communications are merely a continuation of a long-standing trend. For most of the twentieth century, the cost of telecommunications services has declined at a real rate of 4 to 5 per cent per year. For long-distance services the decline has been even more rapid—around 10 per cent per year. Over a period of 100 years, the compound effect yields a reduction in costs by a factor of 1 million or more.

As far as long-term financial transactions are concerned, however, the innovations of the twentieth century are not particularly important. An order to buy or sell assets worth billions of dollars can be transmitted just as effectively in a fifteen-word telegram as in a fifteen-minute telephone conversation, even though the bandwidth requirements differ by a factor of 1 million. Instantaneous communications within and between developed countries have been available since the nineteenth century.

Computers and telecommunications have permitted an increase in the complexity of financial transactions and in the volume of short-term capital flows. The increase in the ratio of the volume of financial transactions to the volume of real transactions has been widely noted with respect to international markets. It is important to observe, however, that a similarly massive increase in financial "churning" has taken place in domestic financial markets, such as stock markets.

Communications technology has been improving steadily for the last 150 years. International capital flows have shown nothing like the same steady growth. At least in relation to long-term capital flows, global capital markets were about as integrated in the late nineteenth century as in the late twentieth. Capital markets were radically disrupted by war and depression in the first half of the twentieth century. The Bretton Woods system that prevailed from 1945 to the early 1970s involved tight restrictions on capital flows, which were seen as disruptive and a threat to macroeconomic policies aimed at maintaining full employment.

It was only with the breakdown of the Bretton Woods system and the associated Keynesian macroeconomic policies that barriers to international capital flows were removed, and the massive growth of the late twentieth century began. While developments in capital markets, such as the growth of the offshore "eurodollar" market, helped to undermine the Bretton Woods system, the critical problem was the failure of domestic macroeconomic policies to respond adequately to "stagflation," the combination of high unemployment and high inflation.

The idea of globalization as a constraint on policy options has been popularized by Friedman's (1999) colourful metaphor of the "Golden Straightjacket." To fit into the Golden Straitjacket, a country must adopt the following (rather redundantly expressed) golden rules:

- making the private sector the primary engine of its economic growth;
- maintaining a low rate of inflation and price stability;
- shrinking the size of its state bureaucracy;
- maintaining as close to a balanced budget as possible, if not a surplus;
- eliminating and lowering tariffs;

- getting rid of quotas and domestic monopolies;
- increasing exports;
- privatizing state-owned industries and utilities;
- deregulating capital markets and the domestic economy;
- opening banking and telecommunications to private ownership and competition; and
- allowing citizens to choose from an array of competing pension options.

This set of rules has also been referred to as the "Washington Consensus." This term, coined by Williamson (1990), refers to the advocacy of these policies by the World Bank, International Monetary Fund, and US Treasury, all of which are located in Washington, DC. The policies formed the basis of the conditions imposed on developing countries seeking assistance in dealing with the global debt crisis of the 1980s. The successful resolution of this crisis (at least in most middle-income developing countries) helped to create the consensus described by Williamson, which was particularly strong in the early 1990s.

In many accounts the question of whether the policies of the Washington Consensus are actually beneficial is, strictly speaking, irrelevant, since there is no alternative option. This is the point of the "straitjacket" part of Friedman's metaphor. Like other proponents of globalization, Friedman argues that governments must adopt the policy agenda of the Washington Consensus or face the wrath of the "Electronic Herd" of global financial traders. The only alternative is to create a closed society like that of North Korea.

There is little evidence to support Friedman's claims. It is true that policies of the kind listed above have been widely adopted in the past twenty-five years, but this is more a reflection of changing ideas than of the constraints imposed by global financial markets. Britain and the United States implemented much of the policy agenda described above in the 1980s, under the Thatcher government and Reagan. European governments have been much slower to follow suit. That has not prevented foreign exchange markets from bidding the euro up to unprecedently high levels against the US dollar.

Moreover, contrary to what might be expected from Friedman's arguments, the correlation between exposure to global trade and the ratio of government expenditure to GDP is positive, not negative. European countries have high ratios of trade to national product, and large government sectors. The United States and Japan have relatively small governments and relatively small exposure to trade. This may be coincidence or it may reflect a demand for government intervention to compensate for exposure to external shocks. Either way, it is inconsistent with the idea that globalization necessitates small government.

The actual relationship is more complex and interesting. In macroeconomic terms, the choices available to governments can be described in terms of the "impossible trinity." A government cannot simultaneously pursue an independent macroeconomic policy, maintain a fixed exchange rate, and allow free international capital movements. The analysis of the problem was first undertaken by Mundell (1963), though the origins of the phrase "impossible trinity" remain obscure.

Over the last century, governments have responded to this trilemma in very different ways. The economy of the nineteenth century, like that of the late twentieth century, was one of unrestricted capital flows, and tight constraints on government policies. As noted above, a radically different system was adopted in 1945. The Bretton Woods system relied on fixed exchange rates and restrictions on international capital flows. With these restrictions in place, the main policy instrument used to stabilize the economy, avoiding recessions and excessive booms, was fiscal policy. In periods of depressed activity, governments stimulated demand by cutting taxes and increasing public expenditure. The opposite measures were used to restrain potentially inflationary booms. Monetary policy played a subordinate role.

The abandonment of controls on capital flows and the shift to floating exchange rates in the 1970s had mixed effects on the scope for fiscal and monetary policy. As the impossible trinity argument shows, with no controls on capital flows, governments can adopt an independent monetary policy only if they are prepared to abandon any control over the exchange rate.

Few governments or central banks have been willing to disregard the exchange rate, often seen as an indicator of national economic worth, but Australian experience suggests that this is probably the optimal response. The willingness of the Reserve Bank to accept a sustained depreciation in the value of the Australian dollar, rather than raising interest rates to support the currency, was the main reason why Australia, unlike New Zealand, suffered little or no adverse effect from the Asian crisis in 1998. Similarly, Britain's forced exit from the European Monetary System in 1992, following the speculative attack on the pound by George Soros and others, is generally regarded, in retrospect, as highly beneficial.

The impact of globalization on the scope for fiscal policy is complex and, in some respects, paradoxical. In some important respects, the removal of controls on capital flows makes it easier for governments to adopt a flexible fiscal policy. In a closed economy, attempts to stimulate economic activity through tax cuts or higher public spending, financed by the issue of government bonds, tend to raise interest rates and may therefore "crowd out" private investment (including the purchase of homes and consumer durables).

By contrast, in the absence of controls on international movements of capital, interest rates are set on world markets. Provided that budget deficits are not so large or sustained as to raise concerns that governments may repudiate their debt or resort to inflationary financing, budget deficits have no direct effect on interest rates.

The main problem with globalization is not that it imposes tight constraints on governments, but that it makes national economies vulnerable to sudden shifts in sentiment. Until 1997, for example, Asian economies were seen as miraculously good performers, in spite of well-known deviations from standard Western investment practices in favour of relationships based on personal connections. Before 1997, the relationship-based approach was generally referred to in favourable terms, but it has subsequently become known as "crony capitalism." When relatively minor economic difficulties emerged in Thailand, there was a sudden panic and investors sought to pull funds not only out of Thailand, but out of all the major economies in Southeast Asia (as well as Korea and Taiwan).

One of the few Southeast Asian economies to emerge relatively unscathed from this process was that of Malaysia. Following the logic of the impossible trinity, Malaysian Prime Minister Mahathir imposed temporary controls on capital movements, thereby permitting the maintenance of the exchange rate for the Malaysian ringgit and the pursuit of an independent (in this context, non-contractionary) monetary policy.

An even more clear-cut example was that of Argentina. Following the international debt crisis of the 1980s, Argentina was the leader among South American countries in adopting the policies of the Washington Consensus. To demonstrate its unwillingness to pursue an independent monetary policy, with the associated potential for irresponsibly inflationary policy, the Argentine government handed over control of monetary policy to a currency board, which was required to maintain a fixed exchange rate with the US dollar, regardless of the impact on the domestic economy. All controls on capital flows were lifted, and public assets were privatized on a large scale.

The result was rapid capital inflow which permitted the government to run large budget deficits, partly disguised by the use of privatization proceeds to fund current expenditure. Laudatory articles about the success of the Argentine experiment with currency boards were still appearing in the financial press in 2001, when sentiment suddenly shifted.

In November 2001, there was a run on the Argentine peso and the government fell, as did a string of successors. In 2002, Eduardo Duhalde became Argentina's fifth president in two weeks. Convertibility of the peso was suspended and banks were closed, leading to widespread economic distress. Output fell by as much as 20 per cent, comparable to the Great Depression. Stability was restored only with the election, in 2003, of the Kirchner administration, which repudiated both the Washington Consensus and most of the debts incurred by its predecessors.

In both the Asian and Argentine cases, there was no obvious trigger for the crisis and even in retrospect, it is not clear which events were crucial. In a globalized economy, governments face vaguely defined constraints, but the penalty for violating those constraints, usually unwittingly, can be very severe.

## 3. CONSTRAINTS AND TRADE-OFFS

One of the crucial ideas in economics is the duality between quantities and prices. One manifestation of this duality is the fact that a quantitative constraint, such as a budget constraint, can be expressed in relative price terms as a trade-off between the goods that are subject to the constraint.

The simplest example is a household's budget constraint. The fact that the household's expenditure must equal its income (net of saving or borrowing) means that there is a trade-off between any two items of consumption, given by their relative market prices. The example can be taken further when we consider the possibility of varying hours of work. There is a trade-off between leisure and items of consumption, given by the marginal post-tax wage rate and the price of the consumption items.

Constraints on government policy can similarly be expressed in terms of trade-offs. In all its various forms, the long-term balanced budget constraint means that higher spending and lower taxes today must be traded off against lower spending and higher taxes in the future. Within each period, there is a trade-off between taxes and public expenditure.

Unlike household budget constraints, policy constraints are non-linear; that is, the associated prices are not fixed. The higher the ratio of taxation revenue to GDP, the greater the marginal cost in terms of economic disincentives, taxpayer non-compliance, and political resistance.

## 3.1 Dealing with Constraints and Trade-offs

If a policy issue is considered in terms of a constraint, and an associated trade-off, three questions naturally arise. First, is the constraint binding, or is it possible to do more of everything? Second, how costly is it to relax the constraint? Third, given a binding constraint, what is the optimal trade-off?

Consider, for example, the problem of determining government expenditure, subject to a balanced budget constraint. To determine whether the constraint is binding, it is obviously necessary to measure the budget balance appropriately, as has been discussed above. It is also necessary to look for policy options that may allow for more spending on all objectives, without violating the constraint.

On the revenue side, a tax reform that increased the efficiency with which taxes are collected might allow for an increase in revenue with no increase in the effective burden of taxation. The replacement of retail turnover taxes by value-added taxes is commonly regarded as such a reform.

On the expenditure side, reorganization of government activities may eliminate duplication and waste, allowing provision of more services for the same cost. Of course, it is much easier for politicians to promise to cut duplication and waste than to actually do so.

A movement of the kind discussed above is referred to by economists as a potential Pareto improvement, since, assuming the extra resources are allocated appropriately, at least some people can be made better off while no one is made worse off. Examples of potential Pareto improvements are rare, and actual Pareto improvements even rarer.

A binding constraint is associated with a "shadow price," which corresponds to the cost of relaxing the constraint. In the case of the budget constraint on government expenditure the shadow price is the cost (economic, political, and social) of increasing tax revenue. From the Second World War to the 1970s, this shadow price was low enough to permit a gradual increase in the ratio of public expenditure to national income, with a corresponding increase in tax revenue. The "Tax Revolts" of the late 1970s brought this growth to an end but did not, in most countries, reverse it.

Finally, given a fixed constraint, it is necessary to choose the best available allocation of resources, given the trade-offs imposed by that constraint. There are a variety of institutional approaches to this problem. Businesses, including commercialized government businesses, use market prices as the basis for determining trade-offs, since this is the approach that maximizes profits. Governments can influence these trade-offs through taxes, subsidies, and community service obligations.

In many cases, market prices are not an appropriate guide to public policy. The techniques of benefit–cost analysis provide a formal basis for making trade-offs in such cases. Using benefit–cost analysis, seemingly disparate kinds of benefits and costs can be reduced to common terms (usually present-day money terms) for the purpose of making trade-offs between them.

The benefits of different health care for example, can be converted into the common currency of quality-adjusted life years (QALYs), and then compared against alternative life-saving interventions, such as improvements in road safety. These can then be traded off against alternative uses of public funds, giving rise to implicit values for QALYs and "statistical lives" (typical values are \$100,000/QALY and \$5 million/life). Loomes and McKenzie (1989) give a good survey of the QALY method and its competitors.

The most ambitious version of benefit–cost analysis, the "total valuation" framework (Randall and Stoll 1983), asserts that all social values can be reduced to aggregates of individual willingness to pay for benefits and willingness to accept costs. This assertion seems to assume a population made up entirely of classical utilitarians, however.

In practice, most political actors have conceded some role for benefit–cost analysis, but hardly any have accepted its more ambitious claims, let alone those of the "total valuation" school. In the real world, trade-offs are, inevitably, a mixture of economically based attempts at the scientific allocation of scarce resources and political exercises in the art of the possible.

# References

BAKER, D., EPSTEIN, G., and POLLIN, R. (eds.) 1998. *Globalization and Progressive Economic Policy*. Cambridge: Cambridge University Press.

BHAGWATI, J. 2004. *In Defense of Globalization*. Oxford: Oxford University Press.

DORFMAN, R., SAMUELSON, P., and SOLOW, R. 1958. *Linear Programming and Economic Analysis*. New York: McGraw-Hill.

FÄRE, R., et al. 1993. Derivation of shadow prices for undesirable outputs: a distance function approach. *Review of Economics and Statistics*, 75: 374–85.

FELDSTEIN, M., and HORIOKA, C. 1980. Domestic saving and international capital flows. *Economic Journal*, 90 (358): 314–29.

FINER, S. 1955. The political power of private capital, part 1. *Sociological Review*, 3: 279–94.

—— 1956. The political power of private capital, part 2. *Sociological Review*, 4: 5–30.

FRIEDMAN, T. 1999. *The Lexus and the Olive Tree: Understanding Globalization*. New York: Farrar Straus Giroux.

GARRETT, G., and MITCHELL, D. 1995. Globalisation and the welfare state: income transfers in the industrial democracies, 1965–1990. Paper presented to the conference on Comparative Research on Welfare Reforms, Pavia, Sept.

GIDDENS, A. 2000. *Runaway World: How Globalization is Reshaping our Lives*. New York: Routledge.

KOOPMANS, T. 1975. Concepts of optimality and their uses. Nobel Memorial Lecture, 11 Dec., Stockholm.

KORNAI, J., MASKIN, E., and ROLAND, G. 2003. Understanding the soft budget constraint. *Journal of Economic Literature*, 41 (4): 1095–136.

KOTLIKOFF, L., and BURNS, S. 2004. *The Coming Generational Storm: What You Need to Know about America's Economic Future*. Cambridge, Mass.: MIT Press.

LINDBECK, A. 1997. The Swedish experiment. *Journal of Economic Literature*, 35 (3): 1273–319.

LINDBLOM, C. E. 1977. *Politics and Markets*. New York: Basic Books.

LOOMES, G., and MCKENZIE, L. 1989. The use of QALYs in health care decision making. *Social Science and Medicine*, 28: 299–308.

MITCHELL, D. 1995. Is there a tradeoff between the efficiency and effectiveness goals of income transfer programs. *Journal of Income Distribution*, 5 (1): 111–35.

MUNDELL, R. 1963. Capital mobility and stabilization policy under fixed and flexible exchange rates. *Canadian Journal of Economics and Political Science*, 29: 475–85.

NELLIS, J. 1999. Time to rethink privatization in transition economies? *Finance and Development*, 36 (2): 16–19.

QUIGGIN, J. 1995. The suboptimality of efficiency. *Economics Letters*, 47: 389–92.

—— 1995. Does privatisation pay? *Australian Economic Review*, 2nd quarter (110): 23–42.

—— 2004. *Risk, Discounting and the Evaluation of Public Investment Projects*. Canberra: Bureau of Transport Economics.

RANDALL, A., and STOLL, J. 1983. Existence value in a total valuation framework. Pp. 265–74 in *Managing Air Quality and Scenic Resources at National Parks and Wilderness Areas*, ed. R. Rowe and L. Chestnut. Boulder, Colo.: Westview.

SHEIL, C. (ed.) 2001. *Globalisation: Australian Impacts*. Sydney: University of New South Wales Press.

STIGLITZ, J. 2003. *Globalization and its Discontents*. New York: W. W. Norton.

WEISS, L. 1998. *The Myth of the Powerless State: Governing the Economy in a Global Era*. Cambridge: Polity Press.

WILLIAMSON, J. 1990. What Washington means by policy reform. Pp. 7–33 in *Latin American Adjustment: How Much has Happened?*, ed. J. Williamson. Washington, DC: Institute for International Economics.

# CHAPTER 26

# POLITICAL FEASIBILITY: INTERESTS AND POWER

## WILLIAM A. GALSTON

My topic is political feasibility, understood both in its general sense and more particularly, as shaped by the interests of individuals within a society and the distribution of power among them. I divide my discussion into four sections: some broad reflections on the concept of political feasibility; a historical/analytical examination of shifting conceptions of power; a exploration of the role of organized interests within the institutional and cultural context of US politics; and finally, a glance at the collapse of President Clinton's proposal for universal heath care—as a case study of the boundaries of the possible.

## 1. POLITICAL FEASIBILITY: GENERAL COMMENTS

I begin with some broad observations on the concept of political feasibility. To begin: this concept is nested within some broader ideas of possibility, some of which are outside the domain of politics. For example, if a policy proposal is logically or mathematically impossible (as many covertly are), then it cannot be politically feasible. Similarly infeasible are policies that contradict well-established natural scientific laws—the bizarre episode of Lysenkoist agriculture during Stalin's regime, for example. Nor can an option pass the test of political feasibility if it violates key findings from other social sciences such as economics or psychology.

Human nature as expressed through motives for action provides another core constraint on political feasibility. As the history of the twentieth century demonstrated, there are limits to human malleability. The effort to produce the "new Soviet man" ran aground, as did Maoist cultural revolutions in China, Cambodia, and elsewhere. While many individuals are capable of devotion to their fellow citizens and to the common good some of the time, and a few are capable of that behavior most of the time, any political program predicated on the belief that most citizens are capable of it most of the time is bound to run aground.

The refusal to assume pervasive altruism or civic devotion is the hallmark of American constitutionalism. In the words of George Washington: "A small knowledge of human nature will convince us that, with far the greatest part of mankind, interest is the governing principle; and that almost every man is more or less, under its influence. Motives of public virtue may for a time, or in particular circumstances, actuate men to the observance of a conduct purely disinterested; but they are not of themselves sufficient to produce persevering conformity to the refined dictates and obligations of social duty"(quoted in Morgenthau 1978, ch. 1). In *Federalist* 51 James Madison drew out the implications for political institutions: "The interest of the man must be connected with the constitutional rights of the place. It may be a reflection on human nature that such devices should be necessary to control the abuses of government. But what is government itself but the greatest of all reflections on human nature?" While government is the greatest, it is anything but unique. Madison mused that "this policy of supplying, by opposite and rival interests, the defect of better motives, might be traced through the whole system of human affairs, private as well as public" (Rossiter 1961, 322).

If anything, the focus on the omnipresence of self-interest understates the motivational difficulty. Albert Hirschman (1977) has traced the effort of social theorists, starting in the seventeenth century, to replace the politics of the passions (aristocratic as well as religious) with the politics of the interests. Commercial society, it was hoped, would mute aggression and reduce violence. Fear for one's life and livelihood would tame the unruly excesses of the human spirit. This thesis culminated in the Edwardian confidence that the spread of trade and commercial relations had rendered war among developed nations unthinkable. The First World War delivered what turned out to be a permanent blow to this shallow optimism. Many young men eagerly embraced warfare as an antidote to the stifling constraints of bourgeois life. Courage, sacrifice, brutality, and death were the coin of the military realm.

Few religious thinkers of any depth were surprised. In the words of Jean Bethke Elshtain (2003, 152), "Augustinians are painfully aware of the temptation to smash, destroy, damage, and humiliate .... Violence unleashed when what Augustine called the *libido dominandi,* or lust to dominate, is unchecked is violence that recognizes no limits."

But a dark view of human nature can be just as superficial and one-sided as its opposite. A realistic appraisal stands removed from cynicism as well as wishful thinking. As a great modern Augustinian and democrat put it, "Man's capacity for justice makes democracy possible; but man's inclination to injustice makes democracy necessary" (Niebuhr 1944, xii).

Let me now move a step closer to my topic. The concept of political feasibility is embedded rather than free standing. The question is almost always, feasible where? And feasible when?[1] Public culture varies from place to place, as do political institutions; policies that are feasible in parliamentary democracies with statist beliefs may well prove impractical in regimes, such as the United States, with divided powers and anti-statist inclinations. Similarly, policies that are not feasible now may be feasible later, or might have been feasible before earlier decisions closed off options. (This is one of the implications of path dependency in human affairs.)

Political realists take pride in seeing the world "as it is," not as some might wish it to be, undistorted by hope, fear, credulity, or abstract theory. This is not a simple matter, however, because any clear-sighted view of the world must take into account the effects of human imagination and creativity, often characteristic of great leaders, as well as the element of plasticity in our collective life. An example of the former: after the first Zionist Congress in 1897, Theodore Herzl remarked that he had just re-established the Jewish state and that while no one could see that today, in fifty years the matter would be clear to all. His famous slogan, "If you will it, it is no fairy-tale," turned out to be more realistic in the long run than the sensible but blinkered doubts of the skeptics.

An example of the latter: the economist and social choice theorist Kenneth Arrow has shown that in many circumstances, the distribution of opinion in democratic publics does not dictate a single determinate outcome but rather admits of many potential majorities, each of which expresses a different ensemble of policy prefer-ences. In such circumstances, which may not be rare, the influence of institutional structures and of entrepreneurial leaders can be decisive.[2]

In short, the field of political action, while bounded, is not fixed, but rather includes a range of possibilities. The passage of time and the mutability of belief, along with the variety of institutions and leadership, expand the range of feasible outcomes. A thin line separates the visionary from the crank, and no algorithm defines the location of that line.

In ordinary political discourse, the concept of feasibility plays three distinct roles: forward looking, as a guide to action; present regarding, as excuse; and backward looking, as explanation. When considering whether to undertake particular initia-tives, political agents often do (and always should) ask themselves whether the goals they seek are feasible. When groups pursue a goal believing it is possible when it isn't, the opportunity cost is typically high; not only are they are likely to be disillusioned, but also they will have forgone other, more attainable goods.

We are all too familiar with the use of feasibility as excuse. A subordinate goes to a supervisor (or a citizen to a public official, or a newly elected member of Congress to the chair of a committee) with a request; the supervisor replies, "I'd love to help you

---

[1] See, e.g., Przeworski 1987; Huitt 1968; Majone 1975; Wildavsky 1979, esp. ch. 2; Meltsner 1972; Moynihan 1973; Philbrook 1953; Goodin 1982, ch. 7.

[2] Cf. Arrow 1963; Riker 1983, 1986; Mackie 2004.

out, but it's just not possible." Sometimes what the supervisor says is true, and when so, unobjectionable as well as dispositive. Often, however, feasibility is invoked as a way to evade a truth uttering which will entail costs for the supervisor: "You (the supplicant) aren't significant enough to help;" or "Honoring your request would divert resources from projects I (the supervisor) regard as more important;" or "Doing what you ask would require me to initiate a conflict I would rather avoid."

Feasibility, finally, can be used to explain why a political initiative didn't succeed: Although we didn't know it at the time (the story might go), the deck was stacked against us. Our opponents had us outnumbered and had used their superior resources to obtain the support of the decisive actors. No matter how well we played our hand, we were bound to lose. Like feasibility as excuse, feasibility as explanation is often valid, but its truth is hard to assess. Critics will often say that if you had played your hand differently, the results would have been different. Unfortunately, history is not a laboratory experiment; you cannot replay it, changing the variable whose impact you wish to assess. In the game of bridge, some contracts can be assessed definitively as doomed on their face, such that not even the world champion could fulfill them. In the world of public affairs, such judgements will usually be contestable, and at best matters of greater and lesser probability rather than certainty.

## 2. POLITICAL FEASIBILITY AND POWER

Questions of political feasibility are often translated into the language of power, a concept that theorists and researchers have debated for centuries. Within contemporary social thought and social science, this discussion has proceeded through a number of distinct phases. Led by Robert Dahl, the early behavioralists focused on power over individual, empirically observable decisions. Critics of this approach, such as Peter Bachrach and Morton Baratz (1970), emphasized the processes by which key issues are excluded from the decision-making agenda. In turn, Steven Lukes (1974) criticized both of these approaches as resting on an unexamined conception of human wants. A truly "radical" understanding of power would develop an objective conception of human interests and assess the extent to which the influence of processes within a given society unequally hindered certain groups from realizing those interests.

Lukes's influential thesis sparked two lines of critique and development. Some theorists noted that Lukes had failed to provide an account of how real human interests could be identified and sought to remedy this deficiency. (Jürgen Habermas's (1984, 1987) "ideal speech situation" is the most influential proposal in this vein.) Other theorists argued that Lukes had overemphasized individual human agency at the expense of the social structures that shape individual wants and decisions and had failed to clarify the relation between structure and agency. The work of Anthony Giddens (1984) exemplifies the efforts of many thinkers to overcome this dualism: agency produces structures, which in turn condition agency.

Most recently, Michel Foucault's influential work has shifted the debate over power in two ways. First, he replaces the duality of structure and agency with a conception of discursive practices that form the ensemble power/knowledge. As Stewart Clegg (1989, 158) puts it, "Foucault seeks to show how relations of 'agency' and 'structure' have been constituted discursively, how agency is denied to some and given to others ... The focus is upon how certain forms of representation are constituted rather than upon the 'truth' or 'falsity' of the representations themselves."[3] Second, and relatedly, Foucault rejects the focus of classical political theory on "sovereign" power in favor of discursive practices that pervade and "discipline" the entire social field. Because power does not have a definable center, it cannot be overthrown through regicide or its equivalent, but only resisted at specific points in the social field. We can best understand power, therefore, by studying "micropolitics" rather than institutions, structures, or causal relations.[4]

Against this backdrop of competing approaches, I want to investigate two conceptions of power—effective agency and domination—in somewhat greater depth. Many scholars trace this discussion in its modern form to Thomas Hobbes, who devoted a portion of chapter 10 of *Leviathan* to this topic. Hobbes defines the "power of a man" as his "present means, to obtain some future apparent good." Some means—such as strength, good looks, intelligence, charm, and the like—are aspects of an individual's natural endowment. Other means—wealth, fame, friends—are gained through the exercise of such endowments. The essential point is that these means are resources that determine the extent to which an individual has the *power to* attain particular ends.

Many reject this way of framing the issue on the ground that the most relevant understanding of power is as *power over* others. The underlying argument is that in our political and social life, our ability to attain our ends is thwarted, not only by the lack of personal resources, but also by the conflicting ends and intentions of other agents. It is this intuition that leads Brian Barry (1989) to argue that an individual has power if he has the "ability to overcome resistance or opposition."[5] In a similar vein, Robert Dahl (1957) argues that "A has power over B to the extent that he can get B to do something that B would not otherwise do."[6] The modern origin of this way of thinking is Max Weber's (1947, 152) definition of power as "the probability that one

---

[3] Clegg 1989, 158. The preceding three paragraphs summarize the account that Clegg (1989, chs. 3–6) offers in his useful survey.

[4] This brisk canter through decades of complex disputation is all that space permits. Clegg (1989) offers a wealth of detail as well as a superb bibliography.

[5] Quoted and discussed in Morriss 2002, xxxiii. Morriss's volume complements that of Clegg by providing a comprehensive bibliography of the analytical philosophical literature on conceptions of power.

[6] Quoted and discussed in Morriss 2002, 13.

actor within a social relationship will be in a position to carry out his own will despite resistance, regardless of the basis on which this probability rests."[7]

It is common to associate "power over" with coercion, but as Weber's definition makes clear, the scope of the concept is much wider, because the basis on which A exerts power over B may have little or nothing to do with compulsion. Consider a familiar micro-example: the organizer of a conference asks a prominent expert to write and present a paper, but the expert declines. The organizer then offers the expert $5,000, and he assents. Without resorting to coercion, the organizer has gotten the expert to do something that he or she otherwise would not have done. In this sense, the phrase "bargaining power" is more than metaphorical.

Bargaining situations illustrate, as well, that power relations can be reciprocal: B can have power over A at the same time that A has power over B.[8] It may still make sense to claim that A has *more* power over B than B has over A, as indicated by (say) the division between the parties of the advantages accruing from agreement.[9]

For the most part, earlier generations of scholars distinguished between economic and sociopolitical relations: economics was considered to be the sphere of free exchange among symmetrically situated agents, while society involves power-based transactions among unequal agents. Since the 1960s, however, theorists such as John Harsanyi (1962) and Thomas Schelling (1960) have argued for a more integrated view of power and exchange. The reason is this: to the extent that A's resistance to B's will is a function of incentives for compliance, B can reasonably hope to gain A's cooperation by changing the balance between gains (or losses) from compliance as opposed to continued resistance. To recognize this is to narrow the gap between the activity of exchange and the employment of power.

This is not to say, however, that the two concepts are wholly congruent. While some theorists have tried to model authority ("legitimate" power) as exchange, the thesis seems forced. To be sure, legitimacy depends on performance: over time, troops are likely to challenge the authority of military leaders who prove cowardly and incompetent, especially when these faults subject soldiers to unnecessary risks. Day to day, however, the authority of commanders does not depend on exchange. When soldiers receive orders from sources they regard as legitimate, they comply without asking for anything in return. At the level of individual events, the structure of power relations may look nothing like exchange.

Political power is located somewhere between economic exchange and military obedience. During the 1952 presidential transition between Harry Truman and the President-Elect, Dwight Eisenhower, the outgoing president mused that Eisenhower would enter the Oval Office with false expectations. "Poor Ike," Truman exclaimed, "he'll sit here and say Do this, do that. And nothing will happen" (Neustadt 1960). Put more formally, Truman was suggesting that while military leaders can get their way by invoking their authority, a president who wants to succeed must have an

---

[7] For an important recent elaboration of Weber's thesis with particular attention to various forms and sites of power, see Poggi 2001.

[8] For an elaboration of this point, see Baldwin 1989, 113–20.

[9] This is not to say that power can be precisely measured. See Baldwin 1989, 24–9.

answer to the recalcitrant committee chair who asks, "What's in it for me?" During 1993, for example, President Clinton offered inducements to many congressional Democrats to gain their support for controversial proposals such as his deficit-reduction plan and the North American Free Trade Agreement. This kind of political power is at its core transactional and rests on the supply of tradeable resources at an official's disposal.

On the other hand, public officials often attain their objectives by exercising non-exchange-based forms of power. For example, their offices come equipped with formal authority. Many senior officials have subordinates whom they can hire and fire at will and who are expected to obey their superior's decisions. Many officials also enjoy substantive authority, based on factors such as the process by which they were selected or their personal characteristics. It is difficult for most people to walk into the Oval Office without being reminded that unlike every other public official in the United States, the president occupies his office pursuant to a decision made by the people as a whole. This creates an aura of legitimacy, which is magnified when the president displays unusual insight into issues or the motivations of other political actors.[10]

To summarize: the distinction between power to and power over suggests two ways in which considerations of power influence political feasibility. It may be the case, first, that attaining a particular end requires resources of a kind or quantity that the agent does not possess and cannot mobilize. In addition (or alternatively), it may be the case that attaining this end requires the agent to overcome the implacable opposition of pivotal individuals or groups, a task to which the agent's full armory of carrots, sticks, authority, and persuasion proves unequal.

## 3. Political Feasibility and Interests

All individuals have interests, but not all interests have a significant impact on politics. In polities larger than face-to-face communities, interests must be organized to be effective. And once organized groups in the aggregate achieve a certain density in the relevant political space, they have a significant impact on the domain of political feasibility.

These bland propositions cover over a number of complications. Let me cite just two. First, the existence of a number of individuals with similar interests does not guarantee that organized groups will emerge to promote those interests. As Mancur Olson (1965) argued four decades ago, in groups of any size, organization is costly, and incentives to free-ride are high. For interest groups to form, leaders who receive

---

[10] Some philosophers analyze the formal/substantive distinction as the different between being "in authority" and "an authority." For a seminal discussion along these lines, see Friedman 1990.

some combination of material and psychic rewards from organizational activities must come forward (Frohlich, Oppenheimer, and Young 1971).

Second, political institutions shape the formation and efficacy of interest groups, not just vice versa. Since the seminal arguments of James Madison in *Federalist* 10, it has been clear that the basic structure of the US constitution was designed to encourage the multiplication of interest groups as a check on the tyrannical potential of any single entity. That the self-interested pursuits might not serve the common good was equally clear, but the effort to cure the "mischiefs of faction" by suppressing the liberty of groups was bound to be worse than the disease.[11]

Not only institutions, but also public policies affect interest groups. The enactment of a law creates new opportunities for self-interested activities, and groups emerge to take advantage of them. The larger the scope of the legislation, the larger and more influential these groups are likely to be. Since 1960, the number of Americans receiving social security benefits has roughly tripled, to over 40 million. The American Association of Retired Persons (AARP), founded in 1958, now has more than 30 million members (Rauch 1999, 43). In an important study, Andrea Louise Campbell (2003) has demonstrated the extraordinary organizational and participatory impact of social security on older Americans.

The point is this: any discussion of organized interests and their impact on political feasibility is bound to be context dependent. This section traces, and tries to explain, some trends in US interest group politics over roughly the past half-century. The story would be different in other advanced democracies, let alone other regime types.

While Americans have always formed groups to express their views and promote their interests, the pace of interest group formation has dramatically accelerated in recent decades. Since 1955, the number of registered associations has more than quadrupled, from under 5,000 to more than 20,000. During that same period, membership in the American Society of Association Executives has risen tenfold, from under 2,500 to almost 25,000. In just twenty years (1975–95), the number of lobbyists registered with the US Senate more than tripled, from 3,000 to 10,000 (Rauch 1999, 42, 45, 87). Since 1972, the number of Washington lawyers, many of whom lobby on behalf of interest groups, has surged from 12,000 to 76,000.[12] Jeffrey Berry's characterization of these trends as the "advocacy explosion" (Berry 1997, ch. 2) seems factual rather than hyperbolic.

As interest groups have proliferated, their composition has changed. Two shifts are especially noteworthy. Starting with the civil rights movement, citizens' organizations have sprung up to advocate policies affecting racial and ethnic minorities, women, consumers, individuals with disabilities, gays and lesbians, the environment, and a host of other groups and causes. During the 1960s and 1970s, most of these

---

[11] For a good summary of Madison's thought on these points, see Berry 1997, 2–4, 236–7.

[12] Berry 1997, 25; updated information for 1995–2004 provided by the Washington DC Bar Association.

groups tilted toward the liberal side of the political spectrum. Since the election of Ronald Reagan, however, conservative citizens' groups have begun to change the balance of advocacy. Many of them came into being to oppose decisions of the US Supreme Court on issues such as school prayer and abortion as well as broader cultural trends (which opponents regard as permissive, indecent, or relativistic) in modern American society. During this same period, businesses formed organizations to resist what they regarded as burdensome regulations pushed by liberal citizens' groups.[13]

There is no single explanation for these changes, but rather a number of mutually reinforcing factors. The standard list includes at least the following: an expansion in the scope of government, which increased the number of issues and demographic sectors the public sector affects, as well as the sheer quantity of resources in play; the centralization of political authority at the national level, which increased incentives for interest groups to fund headquarters organizations with permanent staff and lobbyists; a shift in governance toward detailed regulations, which increases the effectiveness of groups with highly focused interests; the post-1954 legitimization of civil rights and other group enpowerment causes; the emergence of post-material issues and an agenda of cultural issues, which catalyzed the formation of new kinds of groups; relatedly, the increasing cultural and demographic diversity of the US population; and the post-1968 changes in US political parties, which diminished the power of elected officials and local party organizations while enhancing the intra-party power of single-issue groups.[14]

Whatever the causes of the interest group explosion may be, its effects are clear. First, it becomes harder to pass broad legislation in the public interest, both because more centers of power must be brought together into a winning coalition and because more groups can exercise an effective veto. Consider the issue of health care, to which I will return in the next section. Between 1984 and 1993, the number of Washington-based groups focusing on health care tripled from under 300 to over 800, with the bulk of the increase occurring well before the election of Bill Clinton and the epic struggle over his health care proposal.

A second effect of interest group proliferation: it becomes harder to terminate programs that are ineffective or have outlived their useful life, because the most affected groups can band together to defend them. As a result, it is harder than it once was to clear enough fiscal and policy space for new ideas to flourish.

---

[13] It is hard to deny that a regulatory explosion took place during this period. In the nearly two decades between the beginning of the Truman administration and the end of the Kennedy administration, the number of pages of federal regulations barely budged. In the next thirty years from 1963 to 1993, total pages rose from 15,000 to about 70,000 and have continued to climb (Rauch 1999, 59).

[14] In *The Rise and Decline of Nations*, Mancur Olson (1982) argued that in stable, free societies, there is a general tendency for increasing numbers of interest groups to form over time, much as barnacles encrust a ship. Even if this is true, however, it does not explain why the slope of the US curve has tilted up so sharply during the past four decades.

And third, it becomes easier for well-organized, highly focused groups to achieve, and then defend, legislative and regulatory outcomes that serve their narrow interests. It is at least suggestive that the interest group explosion has coincided with declining public trust in the efficacy or integrity of government and an increasing disposition to believe that elected officials respond to well-placed insiders at the expense of the public interest.

I conclude this section with a brief reflection on two ways in which the literatures of power and interests overlap. First, some critics of the interest group pluralism that dominated US political science in the 1950s and 1960s focused on the inequalities of power that group-based representation produced. Not only do these groups tend to defend the status quo, but also some interests will be under-represented or even voiceless in the political process. Groups representing the powerful will tend to be powerful; groups representing the weak and poor will themselves be weak and short of resources. In the 1960s, these considerations led some national policy makers to conclude that government should act affirmatively to create and empower groups that would advocate for under-represented populations. Today, these considerations fuel proposals to loosen legal and regulatory restraints on the advocacy activities of non-profit organizations.

Second, as we have already noted, other critics of interest group pluralism argued that the heart of the difficulty was not the asymmetrical power of the groups themselves, but rather a flawed understanding of interests. It was a methodological mistake, they argued, to study the desires the public expresses without attending to the processes by which these desires are formed. The power (wherever it may lie) to shape individuals' definitions of their own interests is more fundamental than the processes that represent and aggregate these interests. As Steven Lukes (1974, 23) puts it, "A may exercise power over B by getting him to do what he does not want to do, but he also exercises power over him by influencing, shaping or determining his very wants. Indeed, is it not the supreme exercise of power to get another or others to have the desires you want them to have?"

Lukes's thesis, with its roots in the Marxist tradition and echoes of Plato's *Republic*, has the merit of drawing our attention to the possibility that publicly articulated interests may represent, not the exercise of power, but rather its effect. It has the disadvantage of plunging us back into theses concerning "false consciousness" and "real interests" that empowered vanguard parties and disfigured the politics of the twentieth century. The lesson seems to be that while it may be necessary as a theoretical matter to raise questions about the sources of expressed interests, it is important not to leap to conclusions about the substance of individuals' real interests or about the processes through which they are determined.[15]

---

[15] Recall the old joke: One comrade declares that "Capitalism is the oppression of man by man;" the other replies, "Yes, and communism is just the reverse."

# 4. A CASE STUDY: PRESIDENT CLINTON'S FAILED HEALTH CARE INITIATIVE

During the 1992 presidential campaign, Bill Clinton had promised that if elected, he would present a plan to the US Congress that would guarantee high-quality, affordable health for all Americans. In the fall of 1993, he fulfilled that promise. At the time, most political observers believed that before Congress adjourned for the 1994 midterm election campaign, it would enact a plan (perhaps different from the president's proposal) to guarantee universal health care. In the end, of course, that did not happen. No approach ever crystallized a consensus among Democrats, and after some initial hesitation the Republican Party united against the entire effort. By September of 1994, Senate majority leader George Mitchell felt impelled to declare the death knell for health care reform, setting the stage for catastrophic Democratic losses in congressional elections that November.

Surveying the rubble, many journalists emphasized the impact of personalities and focused on what they regarded as tactical errors. It is more illuminating, however, to view the failure of Clinton's health care reform through this chapter's two prisms of power and interests.

Consider, first, the power that President Clinton had at his disposal. He had the formal powers of his office, of course, plus a substantive grasp of the issues and a legendary ability to charm and persuade. But he lacked a crucial form of power—namely, tradeable political resources. He had inherited a huge budget deficit, which he and his advisers regarded as an obstacle to sustained economic growth. To put this problem on the path toward solution, therefore, his first budget featured an austere spending plan as well as controversial tax increases on energy and upper-income Americans. In that context, the president's ability to "wheel and deal" by offering members traditional inducements such as public works projects in their districts was very limited.

Nor did President Clinton have a crucial resource on which many prior presidents (and his immediate successor) were able to rely: unity within his own party in Congress. Some Democrats, such as the chair of the Senate Finance Committee, did not believe that health care deserved a high priority in the president's legislative agenda. Others who agreed with the president about the importance of the issue disagreed with him about how to approach it. (These divisions enhanced the power of the unified minority party.)

This leads us from "power to" to "power over." President Clinton had taken office with the backing of only 43 per cent of the American people. Every congressional Democrat had run ahead of the president in his or her state or district. Few believed that they owed their electoral success to his efforts. On the contrary: Democrats in the House of Representatives were entering their twentieth consecutive Congress as the majority party, a status they did not believe was in jeopardy. Not only did the president have few positive inducements to offer, he also lacked the form of power over others that flows from the ability to make credible threats. In addition, he lacked formal power over independent actors such as the Congressional Budget Office, which had the responsibility for estimating the costs and consequences of all legislative proposals.

In a democracy, of course, there is another form of power, one that flows from the people. Here again President Clinton labored under a disadvantage. On the one hand, the American people said they wanted action on health care; on the other, their confidence in government as an instrument of positive and effective change was at an all-time low.[16] When opponents of the president's health care proposal invoked the cost and bureaucratic complexity of government programs, therefore, they tapped into a well of public mistrust that the president and his allies proved unable to counteract.

The landscape of interests did not offer brighter vistas for the president's proposals. The existing system of employer-provided health insurance, supplemented by public programs such as Medicare and Medicaid and charity care for the uninsured, had developed over half a century from its somewhat accidental inception during the Second World War. Predictably, substantial organized interests had come into being to defend those who benefited from that system. At the same time, the New Deal system of stable party competition with legislative deals struck among a handful of party leaders had given way to a new fragmented politics dominated by a multiplicity of smaller power centers within Congress and the proliferation of narrow interest groups seeking to influence the course of legislation.[17] As we have already seen, the number of health-focused interest groups with headquarters in Washington had surged during the 1980s. In the end, the combination of party and interest group fragmentation defeated the administration's efforts to assemble a majority coalition for reform.

While I have stressed the significance of changes in structures of power and interests in the United States, there is as well an enduring political reality stressed by analysts from Machiavelli to Dahl: the forces of the status quo enjoy a systemic advantage over the forces of change. Those who benefit from the status quo know who they are, can calculate what they have to lose, and have strong incentives to organize to protect themselves against losses. By contrast, the beneficiaries of broad change are a diffuse group. They can only project or imagine (not experience) the impact of the proposed change on their lives, and many will be disposed to doubt that the promised benefits will reach them at all. For these reasons, among others, they are harder to organize than are those who seek to protect what they already have.

During the New Deal, the majority of Americans were have-nots who had suffered losses as government failed to act effectively in the face of private sector collapse. In those circumstances, Franklin Roosevelt's invocation of activist government yielded an affirmative response from a sustainable public majority. Sixty years later, most

---

[16] For more on this structural problem, see Skocpol 1996, 19, 130.
[17] For more on these developments, see Skocpol 1996, 84–9. More generally, see Neustadt 2001.

Americans were health "haves" rather than have-nots. They had something to lose, and reasonably enough, they weighed the prospective advantages of government action against its possible costs. By contrast, the health have-nots tended to be those who lacked resources in other areas as well. Their political voice was even more muted than their numbers would have dictated. In contemporary circumstances, unless a majority of the middle and professional classes in the United States believe that their interests coincide with those of the working class and the poor, the basic structure of power and interest groups will tilt strongly against redistributive reform.

# REFERENCES

ARROW, K. J. 1963. *Social Choice and Individual Values*, 2nd edn. New Haven, Conn.: Yale University Press.

BACHRACH, P., and BARATZ, M. 1970. *Power and Poverty*. New York: Oxford University Press.

BALDWIN, D. A. 1989. *Paradoxes of Power*. Oxford: Blackwell.

BARRY, B. M. 1989. Power: an economic analysis. Pp. 222–69 in B. M. Barry, *Democracy, Power and Justice*. Oxford: Oxford University Press.

BERRY, J. M. 1997. *The Interest Group Society*, 3rd edn. New York: Longman.

CAMPBELL, A. L. 2003. *How Policies Make Citizens: Senior Citizen Activism and the American Welfare State*. Princeton, NJ: Princeton University Press.

CLEGG, S. 1989. *Frameworks of Power*. London: Sage.

DAHL, R. A. 1957. The concept of power. *Behavioral Science*, 2: 201–15.

ELSHTAIN, J. B. 2003. *Just War against Terror: The Burden of American Power in a Violent World*. New York: Basic Books.

FRIEDMAN, R. B. 1990. On the concept of authority in political philosophy. Pp. 77–85 in *Authority*, ed. J. Raz. New York: New York University Press.

FROHLICH, N., OPPENHEIMER, J. A., and YOUNG, O. R. 1971. *Political Leadership and Collective Goods*. Princeton, NJ: Princeton University Press.

GIDDENS, A. 1984. *The Constitution of Society*. Oxford: Polity Press.

GOODIN, R. E. 1982. *Political Theory and Public Policy*. Chicago: University of Chicago Press.

HABERMAS, J. 1984, 1987. *The Theory of Communicative Action*, trans. T. McCarthy, 2 vols. Boston: Beacon Press.

HARSANYI, J. C. 1962. Measurement of social power, opportunity costs and the theory of two-person bargaining games. *Behavioral Science*, 7: 67–80.

HIRSCHMAN, A. O. 1977. *The Passions and the Interests: Political Arguments for Capitalism before its Triumph*. Princeton, NJ: Princeton University Press.

HUITT, R. K. 1968. Political feasibility. Pp. 263–76 in *Political Science and Public Policy*, ed. A. Ranney. Chicago: Markham.

LUKES, S. 1974. *Power: A Radical View*. London: Macmillan.

MACKIE, G. 2004. *Democracy Defended*. Cambridge: Cambridge University Press.

MAJONE, G. 1975. The notion of political feasibility. *European Journal of Political Research*, 3: 259–74.

MELTSNER, A. J. 1972. Political feasibility and policy analysis. *Public Administration Review*, 32: 859–67.

MORGENTHAU, H. J. 1978. *Politics among Nations: The Struggle for Power and Peace*, 5th edn. New York: Knopf.

MORRISS, P. 2002. *Power: A Philosophical Analysis*, 2nd edn. Manchester: Manchester University Press.

MOYNIHAN, D. P. 1973. Politics as the art of the impossible. Pp. 248–58 in D. P. Moynihan, *Coping*. New York: Random House.

NEUSTADT, R. E. 1960. *Presidential Power*. New York: John Wiley.

—— 2001. The weakening White House. *British Journal of Political Science*, 31: 1–11.

NIEBUHR, R. 1944. *The Children of Light and the Children of Darkness*. New York: Scribner's.

OLSON, M., Jr. 1965. *The Logic of Collective Action*. Cambridge, Mass.: Harvard University Press.

—— 1982. *The Rise and Decline of Nations*. New Haven, Conn.: Yale University Press.

PHILBROOK, C. 1953. "Realism" in policy espousal. *American Economic Review*, 43: 846–59.

POGGI, G. 2001. *Forms of Power*. Cambridge: Polity Press.

PRZEWORSKI, A. 1987. The feasibility of universal grants under democratic capitalism. *Theory & Society*, 15: 695–708.

RAUCH, J. 1999. *Government's End: Why Washington Stopped Working*. New York: Public Affairs.

RIKER, W. H. 1983. *Liberalism against Populism*. San Francisco: W. Freeman.

—— 1986. *The Art of Political Manipulation*. New Haven, Conn.: Yale University Press.

ROSSITER, C. (ed.) 1961. *The Federalist Papers*. New York: New American Library.

SCHELLING, T. C. 1960. *The Strategy of Conflict*. Cambridge, Mass.: Harvard University Press.

SKOCPOL, T. 1996. *Boomerang: Clinton's Health Security Effort and the Turn against Government in U.S. Politics*. New York: Norton.

WEBER, M. 1947. *The Theory of Social and Economic Organization*, trans. A. M. Henderson and T. Parsons. New York: Free Press.

WILDAVSKY, A. 1979. *Speaking Truth to Power*. Boston: Little, Brown.

CHAPTER 27

........................................................................................................

# INSTITUTIONAL CONSTRAINTS ON POLICY

........................................................................................................

## ELLEN M. IMMERGUT

SOCIAL scientists became interested in studying the impact of institutional constraints on public policies for both practical and theoretical reasons. First, in the late 1960s and early 1970s, a wave of ambitious policy making—like Lyndon Baines Johnson's "Great Society" initiative in the United States or the expansion of the powers of the federal government through constitutional reform in Germany—met with disappointment. Despite unprecedented popular support for using the tools of government to improve societies, many of these programs did not achieve their ends. The problems to be addressed were not solved; the monies that had been allocated were in some cases not even spent (Pressman and Wildavsky 1984). Second, as scholars sought to understand the roots of these policy failures, their theoretical attention turned away from societies, and towards institutions. As the following sections of this chapter will detail, there is thus a historical and theoretical affinity between policy studies and institutional theory. Institutions have affected policies, and policies have changed our understandings of institutions. Indeed, policy studies have led to an institutionalist interpretation of politics, and new theories about democratic governance.

# 1. The Impact of Policy Studies on Institutionalist Theory

In the 1950s and 1960s, both political science and policy studies might have been termed "society centered." Politics were often understood as a "vector-sum" of group pressures or as the outcomes of long-term societal trends summarized by the shorthand term "modernization." On this view, various societal interests competed for governmental resources by forming interest groups, and by using any available channel of access to government in order to press for policy concessions. As long as the "multiple memberships" of group adherents (members of a parent–teacher organization, for example, might belong to several different religions or ethnic backgrounds) restrained group leaders from becoming too extreme, and as long as "potential interests" (citizens that could potentially mobilize to defend an interest, especially that of the overarching constitutional framework or "rules of the game") restrained both groups and government from departing from the rules of the game, interest group lobbying could produce both democratic and effective public policies. Indeed, by providing a mechanism for representing the interests of citizens to government, the "governmental process," as Truman called it, both tamed democracy and provided for responsive government, attuned to changing problems caused by economic and social development (1971/1951; see also Dahl 1961). The pluralist model thus assumed an efficient transmission of preferences from citizen to state, and viewed political decisions and outcomes as the result of a natural equilibrium of citizen and group preferences. The pluralists saw the state and other institutions as neutral arbiters of interest group competition, and expected rapid adaptation to a changing environment.

Critics attacked the "pluralist" view of public policy for not addressing inequalities in power that preceded the onset of the interest group process, such as the "privileged position of business" (Lindblom 1977), the tendency of political decision making to be restricted to a "power elite" occupying the "command posts" of both government and the "military-industrial complex" (Mills 1956), and the importance of non-decisions—the areas of policy that never even make it onto the political agenda (Connolly 1969; Crenson 1971; Lukes 1974). Similarly, a renewed interest in class relations and the "capitalist state" led to the suspicion that interest group bargaining might simply serve to hide the more significant power relations—in this case related to the economic system—that could better explain patterns of policy, and perhaps thus the failures of the 1960s reform era (Offe 1984; Alford and Friedland 1985).

Crenson's book, *The Un-Politics of Air Pollution* (1971) provides a good example of this "third face" of power, as Lukes has called it. In Gary, Indiana—the location of the headquarters of US Steel—there were no complaints in the early 1950s about air pollution, whereas across the river in East Chicago, Illinois, complaints by house-wives about dirty laundry evolved into a full-scale social movement that successfully pressured local government to enact legislation to introduce air pollution controls. If we assume an efficient policy process, and imputed preferences from the political process, we would conclude that citizens in Gary were less interested in clean air than those in East Chicago. Crenson argues that it is more plausible to assume that the large number of persons employed by US Steel made citizens in Gary hesitate to make a stink about air pollution, as air pollution controls might cause a loss of jobs for the city. In other words, issues of importance to citizens do not automatically lead to the formation of protest or interest groups. Consequently, we cannot assume that public policies have merit because they were produced by a democratic process; instead, we must judge both the quality of political participation in policy decision making and the resulting public policies by independent, substantive standards, such as environmental quality or social justice.

In contrast to the pluralist and structural power views of public policy, an alternative approach looked to features of government and the polity to explain both the enactment and implementation of public policies. In part inspired by neo-Marxist theories of the capitalist state, the "state-centered" approach took its main guidance from the works of Weber, Hintze, and Tocqueville (Skocpol 1985). On this view, states should be conceptualized both as actors and as structures. As actors, individual bureaucrats and politicians within the state acted according to their ideas regarding good government, and their interests in advancing their own careers or the stature of their agency. As structures, states shaped the policy-making process by their organization, and hence the access of various groups and social strata to governmental decision making, as well as the pattern of policy implementation. Skocpol has pointed out several different mechanisms by which states might shape public policies. The career paths of politicians may make some policies (but not others) attractive to the particular politicians in strategic locations in the polity for launching policy initiatives. This, was the case for example in the legislation of the New Deal. Labor legislation such as the Wagner Act guaranteeing the right to union representation was more central than many aspects of the welfare state that could not pass through the gauntlet of congressional committees unless slimmed down to exclude many basic social rights, such as health care and the right to live according to a national or universal standard of "decency and health" (Skocpol 1980). Such political decisions continued to set constraints on future public policies by affecting states' strategic capacities and establishing policy legacies. In the United States and Britain, Keynesian policies were impeded, because state capacities for economic modeling and access to economic expertise were less institutionalized than in the Swedish case, for example (Weir and Skocpol 1985). In a similar vein, Zysman (1983) points out that national industrial policies depend upon a particular organization of the banking system: if firms depend upon equity markets for capital, governments do not have the capacity for governing industrial development; if firms, by contrast, rely on national or regional banks, governments can promote particular investment policies and hence, influence industrial development.

Previous policies also impart a lasting legacy to policy making by affecting the views and opinions of both citizens and the political elite. The subordination of US Civil War pensions to patronage politics and the spoils system created a suspicion of social programs amongst American policy activists who might otherwise have fought for an expanded welfare state during the Progressive era (Orloff and Skocpol 1984). More generally, as Pierson (1994) has argued, pension policies create lock-in effects because citizens must plan for retirement far ahead, and are thus not inclined to support radical changes in these public programs, such as converting public plans to private insurance or vice versa.

Past policies may also help to "socialize" or "privatize" conflict, as Schattschneider (1960) put it, by encouraging groups to organize, and to view their problems as legitimate grievances, which deserve public, and hence governmental solutions. The impact of government policies on the organization and mobilization of interests was termed by Skocpol (1985, 21) a "Toquevillian" view of the role of the state. A classical example was provided by Selznick in *TVA and the Grassroots* (1984/1949). Selznick argued that the TVA's decision to implement its "grassroots philosophy" by signing agreements with local farmers' organizations diverted the organization from its original aims. For example, TVA agricultural demonstration programs funded mainly the distribution of phosphates rather than nitrates, a decision that benefited large farmers, but left tenant farmers out in the cold, because their strips of land were not large enough for the use of phosphates, as this required crop rotation. To be sure, phosphates were preferable from an environmental point of view. However, in the land use policy of the TVA, the interests of large farmers rather than the environment were decisive: following protests by landowning farmers the TVA radically reduced the strips of land surrounding the electric power reservoirs that were incorporated into the public domain for conservation purposes. Thus, by trying to co-opt the influential farmers belonging to the American Farm Bureau Federation into its very organizational structure—with the aim of being better able to actually implement its policies—the TVA surrendered its ability to make independent policy decisions, and tipped the balance of power away from environmentalists and the poor, and towards the wealthier farmers. Later research on the TVA pointed to yet another instance of political bias: to avoid conflict with influential local parties, the dormitories of the TVA were strictly segregated, a racial policy not in line with federal guidelines.

Similarly, social policies have affected the balance of the "democratic class struggle" by giving organizations representing working-class interests both moral and economic resources. Universal social policies, for example, encourage solidarity (and therefore collective action) across occupational categories, whereas programs organized around more narrow occupational groupings undercut broader class mobilization. In addition, to the extent that social protection becomes enshrined as a social "right," political mobilization aimed at expanding or maintaining social policies gains in legitimacy (Esping-Andersen and Korpi 1984; Klass 1985). Unemployment insurance administered through unions—the "Ghent" system—was used as a selective incentive to attract members, and thus led to higher rates of union membership in countries that organized unemployment policy in this way (Rothstein 1992).

Urban policies that encouraged class segregation, as in Britain, ultimately encouraged political organization based on class identities, whereas those based on ethnic identities resulted in a bifurcation of politics and class, with class important at the workplace and ethnic identity in politics, as in the United States (Katznelson 1985). Similarly, British colonial rule in what later became southwest Nigeria privileged tribal or ethnic identities at the expense of religious cleavages (Laitin 1985).

This interplay between state and society—and indeed the networks of relationships that link social interests to the polity—was a central focus of neocorporatist theorists. These scholars argued that institutionalized relationships between government and interest groups created entry barriers for new groups and new political issues. Consequently, interest group negotiations took place within nationally distinct institutions of interest intermediation that changed the array of organized interests as well as their impact on government policies. In some countries, but not in others, interest groups were functionally specialized, centrally organized, and enrolled high numbers of members. This allowed them to play a useful role in both preparing and implementing legislation, such as public health insurance, and in promoting more informal policies, such as incomes policies to control inflation (Schmitter and Lehmbruch 1979; Berger 1981; Goldthorpe 1984; Katzenstein 1985; Maier 1987).

Thus, research on public policies—the welfare state, urban policies, tax policy, economic policy, health policy, environmental policy—helped reawaken interest in institutions. As study after study showed that policy outcomes could not be accounted for by the preferences of citizens, the balance of interest group opinion, or larger social structural forces or actors (such as "classes"), scholars' attention turned to how the organization of the polity affected policy making and implementation (Hall 1986; Scharpf 1997; Czada, Héritier, and Keman 1998; Peters 1998, 2001). Moreover, as such a variety of factors outside of the strict purview of government were relevant, the emphasis on the state gave way to a more general "institutionalist" perspective that viewed governmental institutions as "political configurations," and broadened the scope of the analysis to include more non-governmental factors (Immergut 1992a, 3 ff., 24–8; Skocpol 1992, 41 ff., 47 ff.; Thelen and Steinmo 1992; Hall and Taylor 1996; Immergut 1998). These studies differed with regard to which institutions precisely were most relevant in a particular case, ranging from the impact of the electoral system on party competition (Steinmo 1993), the relationship between legislatures and the courts (Hattam 1993), and "political opportunity structures" (Kitschelt 1986), to a much broader set of institutional effects, including standard operating procedures, windows of opportunity, and norms and ideas (Weir 1992). Nevertheless, these studies share a common conclusion: that institutions and institutional effects unbalance the purported level playing field of the pluralist model, and so channel policy decisions onto some paths but not others, as in models of path dependency (Pierson 2000).

## 2. THE IMPLICATIONS OF INSTITUTIONALIST THEORY FOR PUBLIC POLICY STUDIES

If policy studies have improved our understanding of institutions, can an institutionalist perspective help us to improve public policies? In any given area, policy analysis depends upon a host of information and technical knowledge that does not necessarily have anything to do with institutions, politics, or society. Yet, the decisions about what do to about this information is a *political* or *social* or *public* choice, to use some of the terms that are commonly used. Once we have defined public policy as "collective choice" we face a number of questions to which political science and social science have quite a bit to say: Who shall make these choices? What procedures should be used to make these choices? How are we to distinguish "good" from "bad" choices?

The institutionalist model of democratic choice seeks to improve the *substance* of public policy choices by improving the *procedures* used to make these choices. Many institutionalists, such as Lowi, write of going beyond "process" or "bargaining" to "procedures," and to replace "what is merely popular" with what is "truly public" (1979, 61, 63, 297). To some extent, this is just a play on words, but the point that is expressed is that one must look more critically at the political process, and if necessary, adjust the rules of the game in order to improve the normative quality of the results. Institutionalist scholars seek procedures that allow for meaningful political participation, such as supports for political arenas that allow for goal-setting discussions to take place, or judicial procedures that allow citizens to press for justice. Elster (1986) describes the institutionalist vision of democratic choice as a "forum" in which decisions are made and interests defined through adversarial discussion, as opposed to a "market" where interests or preferences are aggregated; the former relies on a logic of "arguing;" the second on a logic of "bargaining." March and Olsen (1986) likewise discuss the difference between merely "aggregating" versus truly "integrating" preferences.

Lowi's (1979) work on "juridical democracy" provides a good illustration of this approach. Lowi argues that with the expansion of the role of the president and the executive administration in US politics since the New Deal has come an unacknowledged constitutional change, which he refers to as the "Second Republic." American political debates are disconnected from these realities of executive power and interventionist government, pretending to revolve around the poles of "more" or "less" government, when in fact, both major parties support more government spending, but differ mainly on the purposes to which it should be put. The consequence is a tendency to devolve government power to administrative discretion and negotiations with private interest groups. As in Max Weber's classic work on the proper relationship between politics and administration (1978/1918; see also Aberbach, Putnam, and Rockman 1981), Lowi urges the legislature to wrest power away from administrative agencies by making laws with clear purposes that allow politicians to monitor the activities of the administration. More broadly, these political representatives should be engaged in political deliberation to produce a "public philosophy" which drawing on the work of Lippmann, Lowi defines as "any set of principles and criteria above and beyond the reach of government and statesmen by which the decisions of government are guided and justified" (1969, 82). Such a public philosophy "will emerge from a kind of political discourse in which few of us have engaged during the false consensus of our generation" (1979, 298) and requires "meaningful adversary proceedings ... [with] conflict among political actors at the level where each is forced regularly into formulating general rules, applicable to individual acts of state and at one and the same time ethically plausible to the individual citizen" (1969, 84).

Thus, like Weber, Lowi believes that legislative power should be firmly in the hands of the legislative branch of government, and that politicians should decide on the *ends* of policy through public debate. Here, Lowi makes it clear that what is important is reaching agreement on the substantive aims of politics through a deliberative and adversarial process, by which the quality of political participation and political discussion rather than the breadth of participation is what counts: "The juridical approach does not dictate a particular definition of justice, of virtue, or of the good life.... It does not reduce the virtue of political competition, but only makes access to some areas of government a bit more difficult to acquire" (1979, 311). Thus, the title of the book has a double meaning. *The End of Liberalism* means both that the previous classical liberal era of big versus small government is over, and that political representatives must engage in a new debate about the goal or "end" of government in this new era, or "Third Republic." In a similar vein, Selznick complained that because the substantive content of the TVA's grass-roots philosophy was never clearly defined, its leaders had the scope to choose a means of policy decision making and implementation that devolved public power to private groups and thereby allowed agriculture interests to hijack the agency. As he wrote, "Means tyrannize when commitments they build up divert us from our true objectives. Ends are impotent when they are so abstract and unspecified that they offer no principles of criticism and assessment" (1984/1949, iv).

The American "War on Poverty" can serve as a case in point for this institutionalist perspective. In contrast to the New Deal, which introduced its social policies by a law (the Social Security Act of 1935) that provided relatively clear guidelines as to which social risks were to be insured by government, the War on Poverty proposed a strategy of "maximum feasible participation" ("maximum feasible misunderstanding" in Moynihan's (1969) famous phrase). The idea was to fight poverty by politically empowering the poor and other disadvantaged groups. This strategy was legitimized by the pluralist philosophy of government, which hoped that by correcting unequal access to the interest group process, government outcomes would be made more in line with the public interest. However, the result was much money misspent and few results. Substantive justice would have been better served, according to Lowi, by deliberating in Congress about the ends and means of anti-poverty policy, and then drafting a new law. Formal procedures and not informal processes are thus the route to defining the substantive goals of public policy, and choosing the means for reaching these goals.

Even Lowi admits, however, that not every single detail of public policy can be made a matter of a legislative decision. Therefore, he urges that better procedures be used for administrative policy making as well. To govern fully according to the rule of law means, according to Lowi, to force administrative agencies to deliberate about the rules they are implementing and to forbid them from granting exceptions to the rules to particular groups. If necessary, the agencies should refer the case to Congress to ask for a reinterpretation or revision of the original law. Much as a case brought before a court of law serves to improve the definition of justice and the legal rules themselves, administration of laws should lead to the adoption of better rules, and in many cases, better laws. Nonet (1969) used the case of deliberations about workmen's compensation to show how such an approach can lead to "administrative justice." Many nations have introduced courtlike procedures for adjudicating about bio-ethics.

Thus, by critiquing procedures for democratic choice, institutionalist research can provide guidelines for drafting policy procedures involving not just making laws but the administrative decision making that inevitably follows. Indeed, many policy solutions entail introducing a set of guidelines for administrative decision making rather than directly legislating a policy outcome. The implication of the institutionalist perspective is that the quality of administrative decision making depends upon the procedures for decision making themselves. However, the impact of institutions also depends upon their social and political context.

Here, a classic policy study may serve as illustration. As a result of their path-breaking study of the implementation of the Economic Development Act in Oakland, California, Pressman and Wildavsky (1984) came to the conclusion that implementation requires agreement at many points in a chain of decision making. Even if the probability of agreement at each decision point is quite high, say 0.9, the effect of multiple decision points (N) will be to reduce the probability of a final agreement by the formula $(0.9)^N$. The types of decision points that caused problems in Oakland were things like negotiations with interest group and community leaders about plans to build a new airport to create jobs and the criteria for distributing small business loans. By the time local administrators had met with interested parties in multiple rounds of meetings, it became increasingly difficult to spend the allocated funding at all, let alone developing substantively rational criteria for placing people in jobs or supporting small businesses. The explanation advanced by Pressman and Wildavsky is typical of an organization theory approach: the organizational procedures for decision making (and not political disagreements or differences in political power) are responsible for the policy outcomes. Their own evidence, however, points to the importance of more *political* factors. The Washington, DC, headquarters of the Economic Development Administration (EDA) purposely chose Oakland, California, for its pilot development program, because of its weak local political structure. Rather than having a directly elected mayor, Oakland was run by a City Council with an appointed city manager. Further, local interest groups were weak and poorly organized. The theory was that this would make it difficult to mobilize local resistance to EDA plans. The consequence, however, was that it was difficult to find local leaders that could organize meetings and help get things done. Had the EDA chosen a city with an effective political machine, like Chicago, the impact on local employment might have been far greater. Indeed, in their study of social assistance, Piven and Cloward point out that the "street-level bureaucrats" of the city of Chicago distributed welfare payments to recipients effectively during the 1950s and 1960s, whereas in New York, it took political pressure from newly organized groups representing the poor to open up city administration to these under-represented citizens (1971, n. 41, 335–6; Lipsky 1980). Thus, in practice, the impact of the procedures for implementation depends upon local political structures and patterns of political mobilization and not simply the formal rules.

# 3. INSTITUTIONAL CONSTRAINTS ON PUBLIC POLICY

Given that institutional rules and procedures have a large impact on both the politics of policy making and the implementation of various policy designs, what lessons can we learn from the institutionalist perspective for policy design? Research on the exact impact of institutional procedures on policy decision making and the interaction effects of institutional rules with political, social, and even historical contexts is still in its infancy. What has been learned so far?

One approach has consisted of typologies for comparing political systems. Lijphart (1984, 1999) divides democracies into two types: majoritarian and consensus democracies. The political institutions of majoritarian systems provide for the creation of strong majorities and provide few constraints on government actions, whereas consensus democracies focus on including minorities and providing those minorities with institutional mechanisms for blocking majority decisions. He determines whether the political system of a given nation belongs to the first or second type by considering a number of variables that he groups into two dimensions, the "executive-party" dimension and the "federalism-unitary" dimension. The executive-party dimension is measured by indicators such as the frequency with which one governing coalition is in power, the number of political parties and the types of divisions or 'cleavages' that characterize them (socioeconomic, religion, language, ethnicity), the average duration of governments, and the disproportionality of the electoral system. The more these indicators show a pattern of concentrated government power, the more "majoritarian" the ranking of the political system on the executive-party dimension. The federal-unitary dimension is characterized by bicameralism, tax decentralization, and constitutional rigidity, all of which Lijphart uses to indicate federalism. He finds a statistical association between consensus democracy and higher levels of economic growth, lower inflation rates, more encompassing welfare states, and greater levels of citizen satisfaction with democracy, causing him to conclude that "consensus democracy tends to be the 'kinder, gentler' form of democracy" (1999, 275).

However, as Lijphart himself is well aware, we find consociational political institutions in "divided societies," as he puts it—those divided for example, by ethnic or religious cleavages (1969). These divisions are the historical reason for various sorts of veto powers for minorities. Consequently, it may not be the *political institutions* that result in the kinder, gentler democracies, but perhaps the *"divided" societies* that have these sorts of political institutions may have also tended to develop integrative social institutions of various types, precisely to overcome the divisions that led to political blockages. This "chicken-and-egg" problem in institutional development is often referred to as the problem of "endogeneity."

Powell (2000) has produced a similar typology based on the formal constitutional rules for electing representatives and making policy decisions, in which he refers to the "majoritarian" and "proportional" visions of democracy. The "majoritarian" vision calls for electoral rules that allow a majority of voters to elect a government, and for that government to enact policies without institutional impediments. The majoritarian vision allows a political party to assume governmental power and to enact its political program with full accountability to the voters. The proportional vision by contrast is more concerned with minorities that might never be represented in a majoritarian system, and calls for proportional representation, coalition governments, and mechanisms of power sharing, such as bicameralism, and the representation of the opposition in parliamentary standing committees.

Persson and Tabellini (2002) divide electoral rules and political regimes into two types: majoritarian versus proportional electoral systems; and presidential versus parliamentary regimes. They focus on the individual incentives of politicians as the link between formal political institutions and political behaviour. They argue that in single-member district electoral systems, politicians in a political party must focus on maximizing the number of districts they win; this means focusing on policies targeted to voters in a particular district, such as employees of a particular company that might be given a government contract, or other types of "pork barrel" policies. Lowi has referred to these policies as "distributive" (1964, 1972). Under proportional representation, by contrast, politicians need to maximize votes and not districts; for this purpose, redistributive policies that appeal to broad strata of voters, such as national health insurance or public pension plans, are better.

Attempts to characterize political systems in terms of discrete political institutions share three problems, however. First, no political system is an ideal-type combination of these various institutions, but a conglomeration of institutional details that come together as a semi-coherent whole. Second, the functioning of political institutions depends upon the exact distribution of votes amongst political parties in elections, and the ways in which institutional rules and procedures convert those vote shares into distributions of parliamentary seats and shares of governmental power, as well as the decision-making rules for making governmental and legislative decisions. Third, these approaches consider the institutions as interdependent variables, but institutions are not political actors. Instead institutions in combination with particular distributions of votes should be viewed as incentive structures, and hence as intervening variables, and not as actors.

Immergut (1990, 1992b) characterizes political systems in terms of their "veto points" which are formed by the combination of constitutional rules and political majorities at any given point in time. A "veto point" is defined as a political arena with the jurisdictional power to veto a government legislative proposal, in which the probability of veto is high. This model assumes that politicians within the executive or legislative branch have decided to propose legislation, and considers the points in the subsequent chain of decision making in which veto is likely. Although it is tempting to overextend this model to call any locus of political disagreement a "veto point," the original intent was to present a restricted definition. If, for example, a law must be passed in the two chambers of a bicameral parliament, and the second chamber is controlled by a different majority from the first chamber, then disagreement between the two chambers and hence, second chamber veto of first chamber decisions is likely. Under these conditions, the second chamber should be considered a veto point. Other examples of potential veto points are: constitutional courts, presidents, and referenda. In the European legislative process, the European Parliament (EP) has only been a veto point since the co-decision procedure was introduced by the Treaty of Maastricht (1993).

Tsebelis has incorporated the "veto points" model into a more general "veto players" theory (1995, 1999, 2002). Veto players theory also focuses on the policy-making capacities of executive governments, but defines "veto player" positively as any institutional or partisan actor whose agreement is necessary for approval of legislation. The institutional veto players are identical to the veto points. But the veto players theory goes further by also considering the members of the governmental coalition as veto players, as the members of the different parties in the coalition must all agree in order for legislation to be proposed. Tsebelis also considers the policy distances and policy cohesion of the various veto players. The veto players theory says that policy change will be made more difficult as the number of veto players increases, and also their policy distance and cohesion.

Attempts to test these theories about the impact of institutions on policies and policy making have resulted in mixed conclusions. Armingeon (2002) tests variables from Lijphart's typology and comes to the conclusion that one must distinguish between different dimensions of "consensus" democracy: corporatism (the organization of interests), consociationalism (need for agreement amongst relatively large numbers of parties), and counter-majoritarian institutions (institutions for blocking majority decisions). Huber, Ragin, and Stephens (1993) and Schmidt (2002) find support for the impact of constitutional structures and both veto points and veto players on social policy, but find that one must examine interaction effects between partisanship and political structures. In a study of attempts to renegotiate the policies of coordinated market economies, Immergut and Kume (2006) and collaborators find that "public beliefs" set limits to the ability of policy makers to transform their institutions of social and political coordination. Thus, in moving from studying past policies to examining newer patterns of politics and policies, political institutional theories have begun to move from a focus on institutional blockages to look more at processes of political competition and public persuasion.

# 4. CONCLUSION

This chapter has examined the impact of research on public policies on the development of institutional theory and conversely, the implications of institutional theory for the development of public policies. Research on the impact of institutional rules and procedures on public policies has relevance as well for policy solutions that are based on procedural methods. As contemporary policy makers increasingly abandon their faith in policies constructed and implemented by government, they turn ever increasingly to policy solutions based on "starting a process," "creating a network," or "indicating a procedure." It is precisely here that institutional analysis in offering a basis for critique and prescription has most to offer, even though research on the impact of rules and procedures on politics and policies is still in a relatively early phase.

## REFERENCES

ABERBACH, J. D., PUTNAM, R. D., and ROCKMAN, B. A. 1981. *Bureaucrats and Politicians in Western Democracies*. Cambridge, Mass.: Harvard University Press.

ALFORD, R. R., and FRIEDLAND, R. 1985. *Powers of Theory: Capitalism, the State, and Democracy*. Cambridge: Cambridge University Press.

ARMINGEON, K. 2002. The effects of negotiation democracy: a comparative analysis. *European Journal of Political Research*, 41: 81–105.

BERGER, S. (ed.) 1981. *Organizing Interests in Western Europe: Pluralism, Corporatism and the Transformation of Politics*. Cambridge: Cambridge University Press.

CONNOLLY, W. E. (ed.) 1969. *The Bias of Pluralism*. New York: Atherton Press.

CRENSON, M. A. 1971. *The Un-Politics of Air Pollution: A Study of Non-Decisionmaking in the Cities*. Baltimore: Johns Hopkins University Press.

CZADA, R., HÉRITIER, A., and KEMAN, H. 1998. *Institutions and Political Choice: On the Limits of Rationality*. Amsterdam: VU University Press.

DAHL, R. A. 1961. *Who Governs? Democracy and Power in an American City*. New Haven, Conn.: Yale University Press.

ELSTER, J. 1986. The market and the forum: three varieties of political theory. Pp. 103–32 in *Foundations of Social Choice Theory*, ed. J. Elster and A. Hylland. Cambridge: Cambridge University Press.

ESPING-ANDERSEN, G., and KORPI, W. 1984. Social policy as class politics in post-war capitalism: Scandinavia, Austria, Germany. Pp. 179–208 in *Order and Conflict in Contemporary Capitalism: Studies in the Political Economy of Western European Nations*, ed. J. H. Goldthorpe. Oxford: Clarendon Press.

EVANS, P. B., RUESCHEMEYER, D., and SKOCPOL, T. (eds.) 1985. *Bringing the State Back in.* Cambridge: Cambridge University Press.

GOLDTHORPE, J. H., (ed.) 1984. *Order and Conflict in Contemporary Capitalism: Studies in the Political Economy of Western European Nations.* Oxford: Clarendon Press.

HALL, P. A. 1986. *Governing the Economy: The Politics of State Intervention in Britain and France.* Oxford: Oxford University Press.

—— and TAYLOR, R. C. R. 1996. Political science and the three new institutionalisms. *Political Studies*, 44: 936–57.

HATTAM, V. C. 1993. *Labor Visions and State Power: The Origins of Business Unionism in the United States.* Princeton, NJ: Princeton University Press.

HUBER, E., RAGIN, C. C., and STEPHENS, J. D. 1993. Social-democracy, Christian democracy, constitutional structure, and the welfare-state. *American Journal of Sociology*, 99: 711–49.

IMMERGUT, E. M. 1990. Institutions, veto points, and policy results: a comparative analysis of health care. *Journal of Public Policy*, 10: 391–416.

—— 1992a. *Health Politics: Interests and Institutions in Western Europe.* Cambridge: Cambridge University Press.

—— 1992b. The rules of the game: the logic of health policy-making in France, Switzerland and Sweden. In Steinmo, Thelen, and Longstreth 1992: 57–89.

—— 1998. The theoretical core of the new institutionalism. *Politics & Society*, 26: 5–34.

—— and KUME, I. (eds.) 2006. Crises of governance: institutions and the politics of change in Japan and Europe (special issue). *Governance*, 19.

KATZENSTEIN, P. J. 1985. *Small States in World Markets: Industrial Policy in Europe.* Ithaca, NY: Cornell University Press.

KATZNELSON, I. 1985. Working-class formation and the state: nineteenth-century England in American perspective. In Evans, Rueschemeyer, and Skocpol 1985: 257–84.

KITSCHELT, H. 1986. Political opportunity structures and political protest: anti-nuclear movements in four democracies. *British Journal of Political Science*, 16: 57–85.

KLASS, G. M. 1985. Explaining America and the welfare state: an alternative theory. *British Journal of Political Science*, 15: 427–50.

LAITIN, D. D. 1985. Hegemony and religious conflict: British imperial control and political cleavages in Yorubaland. In Evans, Rueschemeyer, and Skocpol 1985, 285–316.

LIJPHART, A. 1969. Consociational democracy. *World Politics*, 21: 207–25.

—— 1984. *Democracies: Patterns of Majoritarian and Consensus Government in Twenty-One Countries.* New Haven, Conn.: Yale University Press.

—— 1999. *Patterns of Democracy: Government Forms and Performance in Thirty-Six Countries.* New Haven, Conn: Yale University Press.

LINDBERG, L. N., et al. (eds.) 1975. *Paradigms of Relation between State and Society.* Lexington, Mass.: Heath.

LINDBLOM, C. E. 1977. *Politics and Markets: The World's Political-Economic Systems.* New York: Basic Books.

LIPSKY, M. 1980. *Street-Level Bureaucracy: Dilemmas of the Individual in Public Services.* New York: Russell Sage Foundation.

LOWI, T. J. 1964. American business, public policy, case-studies, and political theory. *World Politics*, 16: 677–715.

Lowi, T. J. 1969. The public philosophy: interest-group liberalism. Pp. 81–122 in *The Bias of Pluralism*, ed. W. E. Connolly. New York: Atherton.

—— 1972. Four systems of policy, politics and choice. *Public Administration Review*, 32: 298–310.

—— 1979. *The End of Liberalism: The Second Republic of the United States*. New York: W. W. Norton.

Lukes, S. 1974. *Power: A Radical View*. London: Macmillan.

Maier, C. S. (ed.) 1987. *Changing Boundaries of the Political: Essays on the Evolving Balance between the State and Society, Public and Private in Europe*. Cambridge: Cambridge University Press.

March, J. G., and Olsen, J. P. 1986. Popular sovereignty and the search for appropriate institutions. *Journal of Public Policy*, 6: 341–70.

Mills, C. W. 1956. *The Power Elite*. Oxford: Oxford University Press.

Moynihan, D. P. 1969. *Maximum Feasible Misunderstanding*. New York: Free Press.

Nonet, P. 1969. *Administrative Justice: Advocacy and Change in a Government Agency*. New York: Russell Sage.

Offe, C. 1984. *Contradictions of the Welfare State*. Cambridge, Mass.: MIT Press.

Orloff, A. S., and Skocpol, T. 1984. Why not equal protection? Explaining the politics of public social spending in Britain, 1900–1911, and the United States, 1880s–1920. *American Sociological Review*, 49: 726–50.

Persson, T., and Tabellini, G. 2002. Political institutions and policy outcomes: what are the stylized facts? Available at: ftp://ftp.igier.uni-bocconi.it/homepages/tabellini/tp0208161.pdf.

Peters, B. G. 1998. Political institutions, old and new. Pp. 205–20 in *A New Handbook of Political Science*, ed. R. E. Goodin and H.-D. Klingemann. Oxford: Oxford University Press.

—— 2001. *Institutional Theory in Political Science: The "New Institutionalism."* London: Continuum.

Pierson, P. 1994. *Dismantling the Welfare State? Reagan, Thatcher and the Politics of Retrenchment*. Cambridge: Cambridge University Press.

—— 2000. Increasing returns, path dependence, and the study of politics. *American Political Science Review*, 94: 251–67.

—— (ed.) 2001. *The New Politics of the Welfare State*. Oxford: Oxford University Press.

Piven, F. F., and Cloward, R. A. 1971. *Regulating the Poor: The Functions of Public Welfare*. New York: Vintage.

Powell, B. G. 2000. *Elections as Instruments of Democracy: Majoritarian and Proportional Visions*. New Haven, Conn.: Yale University Press.

Pressman, J. L., and Wildavsky, A. 1984. *Implementation*. Berkeley: University of California Press.

Rothstein, B. 1992. Labor-market institutions and working-class strength. In Steinmo, Thelen, and Longstreth 1992: 33–56.

Scharpf, F. W. 1997. *Games Real Actors Play: Actor-Centered Institutionalism in Policy Research*. Oxford: Westview.

Schattschneider, E. E. 1960. *The Semisovereign People: A Realist's View of Democracy in America*. New York: Holt, Rinehart and Winston.

Schmidt, M. G. 2002. Political performance and types of democracy: findings from comparative studies. *European Journal of Political Research*, 41: 147–63.

Schmitter, P. C., and Lehmbruch, G. (eds.) 1979. *Trends towards Corporatist Interest Intermediation*. London: Sage.

Selznick, P. 1984/1949. *TVA and the Grass Roots: A Study of Politics and Organization*. Berkeley: University of California Press.

SKOCPOL, T. 1980. Political response to capitalist crisis: neo-Marxist theories of the state and the case of the New Deal. *Politics and Society*, 10: 155–201.

—— 1985. Bringing the state back in: strategies of analysis in current research. In Evans, Rueschemeyer, and Skocpol 1985: 3–37.

—— 1992. *Protecting Soldiers and Mothers: The Political Origins of Social Policy in the United States.* Cambridge, Mass.: Harvard University Press.

STEINMO, S. 1993. *Taxation and Democracy: Swedish, British and American Approaches to Financing the Modern State.* New Haven, Conn.: Yale University Press.

—— THELEN, K., and LONGSTRETH, F. (eds.) 1992. *Structuring Politics: Historical Institutionalism in Comparative Analysis.* Cambridge: Cambridge University Press.

THELEN, K., and STEINMO, S. 1992. Historical institutionalism in comparative politics. In Steinmo, Thelen, and Longstreth 1992: 1–32.

TRUMAN, D. B. 1971/1951. *The Governmental Process: Political Interests and Public Opinion*, 2nd edn. New York: Alfred Knopf.

TSEBELIS, G. 1995. Decision making in political systems: veto players in presidentialism, parliamentarism, multicameralism and multipartyism. *British Journal of Political Science*, 25: 289–325.

—— 1999. Veto players and law production in parliamentary democracies: an empirical analysis. *American Political Science Review*, 93: 591–608.

—— 2002. *Veto Players: How Political Institutions Work.* Princeton, NJ: Princeton University Press.

WEBER, M. 1978/1918. Parliament and government in a reconstructed Germany. Pp. 138–462 in *Max Weber: Economy and Society*, ed. G. Roth and C. Wittich. Berkeley: University of California Press.

WEIR, M. 1992. *Politics and Jobs: The Boundaries of Employment Policy in the United States.* Princeton, NJ: Princeton University Press.

—— and SKOCPOL, T. 1985. State structures and the possibilities for "Keynesian" responses to the Great Depression in Sweden, Britain, and the United States. In Evans, Rueschemeyer, and Skocpol 1985: 107–63.

ZYSMAN, J. 1983. *Governments, Markets and Growth: Financial Systems and the Politics of Industrial Change.* Ithaca, NY: Cornell University Press.

.........................................................................................................

# CHAPTER 28

# SOCIAL AND CULTURAL FACTORS: CONSTRAINING AND ENABLING

.........................................................................................................

## DAVIS B. BOBROW

When a pickpocket looks at a king all he sees is pockets.

(Senegalese saying)

understanding how it is that men's notions, however implicit, of the "really real" and the dispositions these notions induce in them, color their sense of the reasonable, the practical, the humane, and the moral.

(Clifford Geertz 1973, 124)

## 1. INTRODUCTION

.........................................................................................................

Public policy never begins with a blank slate whether we are talking about how and why it is made or whether it plays out in terms of wanted or unwanted consequences. Policy makers, implementers, target populations, and their audiences already hold and use a complex of "notions" to arrive at choices and evaluations (as Geertz suggests). Those "notions" affect what is treated as more or less relevant, important,

---

* I am indebted to my two favorite anthropologists, Gail Benjamin and Riall Nolan, for their suggestions.

and desirable—from information to material assets to institutions to skills to normative judgements. They "load the dice" with regard to public policy indicators, focal situations, issue categories, cause and effect judgements, strategic repertoires, and success criteria. They even define what is for people, public policy and politics (Hudson 1997; Thompson, Grendstad, and Selle 1999). Notions in use amount to constraints on and enablers for public policy.[1]

How well we explain the occurrence and consequences of one or another policy or policy problem depends significantly on how well we understand the notions used by actors involved with it. How effectively we shape policy seldom will be greater than our understanding of the notions used by those who matter for policy adoption and implementation (Elmore 1985). For example, law enforcement attempts to curtail gang-related crime in Chicago ghettos would benefit from recognizing that for the residents, both gangs and the police are sources of protection *and* exploitation (Akerlof and Yellen 1994). How accurately we predict the effects of chosen policies depends on understanding of the notions used by those populations the policies seek to influence. Such understandings often amount to awareness of what is "local knowledge" for the various parties to public policy and policy processes, be they White House staffs or impoverished female heads of households.

Meeting those challenges encounters at least two major complications. One is that of variety: "what men believe is as various as what they are—a proposition that holds with equal force when it is inverted" (Geertz 1973, 124).[2] In the Senegalese saying, what is for some a ruler is for others a set of professional opportunities. A statement or act or material object is then subject to alternative interpretations and thus diverse implications for action and evaluation. The second is a less than total overlap between what people alone and in groups say, what they do, and what they believe (assume, know, or think). There often may be a very substantial difference between what they say to "insiders" (persons they classify as ongoing members of their identity or membership group) and to outsiders. What people actually do can vary as they think their actions are or are not observed by insiders or outsiders. The outsider is faced with the task of seeing behind "veils" and "masks" whether those are worn because of conscious deception or just acceptance of cultural notions—and often less well prepared to do so accurately than are insiders.

Later sections will briefly discuss these complications, and note some ways to cope with them. Those ways feature approaches central in social science fields other than political science—ethnography, sociology, social psychology, cognitive linguistics, and organizational behavior. Yet, as the next section reports, the concepts and

[1] The premiss is not that cultural notions matter *instead* of material and institutional factors (as discussed in Snyder 2002). Rather, it is that such notions lead to important, choice-mediating interpretations of those other sorts of factors, interpretations which provide conditions conducive to their continuity or change.

[2] What level of aggregation is useful or distorting is a recurrent concern, and has raised doubts about looking for and relying on a common characterization of large sets of people categorized by a particular nationality, religion, or even profession (for critical examples of the last, see Kier 1995; Zhang 1992). Charges of excessive aggregation have been leveled at modal personality, national character, and civic culture studies.

methods involved have a substantial history of use by eminent political scientists concerned with public policy. This chapter does not call for doing what is unprecedented in understanding cultural and social constraints and enablers on public policy.[3] It does call for greater attention to the pursuit and application of such understandings, and making such activities as standard a part of the analysis and design of public policies as applied micro- or macroeconomics or law.[4]

# 2. SOME INTELLECTUAL HISTORY

The sort of political science concerned with public policy in light of cultural and social factors was a feature of the Chicago school which emerged between the First and Second World Wars (Almond 2002, 23–108), and exemplified in the work of Harold Lasswell (e.g. Lasswell 1971, 1951; Lasswell and Fox 1979; Lasswell and Leites 1949). That prominence reflected strong professional relationships with notable sociologists, social psychologists, anthropologists, and linguists. The appeals of policy alternatives and their consequences were shaped by belief systems encoded in symbols. Symbol manipulation was a major part of politics. Political capital included intangible assets such as social status and rectitude as well as material assets such as instruments of coercion and wealth. Indeed the legitimacy and influence of the material was partly a function of the non-material assets accorded by association with and propagation of symbols.

   Political appraisals and policy assessments then needed to be informed by three types of inventories of markers for intangibles, and methods to take those inventories. One was of symbol usage and the associations thus invoked. The relevant symbols might be words, but they also might be physical icons and sites used in public rituals. A second was of social memberships and origins (life histories) of policy elites. The premiss was that shares of representation in policy processes served to constrain and enable in one or both of two ways. A predominant share might make some particular set of "notions" prevalent in policy processes. It also might indicate that a broader population viewed those thought to hold certain "notions" as particularly relevant, capable, and normatively sound players of central roles in public policy. A third inventory focused on symbols and complexes of "notions" in and about primary social membership groups. That required identifying primary membership groups for actors in the aspect of public policy under consideration.

---

   [3] The distinction between social and cultural factors is not useful as the level of modernization distinctions between the sets of people analyzed by sociologists and anthropologists has eroded.

   [4] Positively, recent "behavioral economics" innovates by probing relevant populations to get at their "notions" and related actions rather than assuming fit with an assumed model.

For Lasswell and his associates, new sorts of knowledge were needed to cope with stunning failures in domestic public policy, and with grave challenges from foreign "others" to favored conceptions about and even the existence of a just and humane world. The inventories would show variety from place to place and time to time. They would be useful for monitoring and countering politically malign actors, and designing strategies to improve and protect a valued political order.

Unsurprisingly, the landmark *The Policy Sciences* (Lerner and Lasswell 1951) included chapters by anthropologists (Kluckhohn on culture and Mead on national character), a sociologist (Shils on primary groups), and a social psychologist (Stouffer on how to discern what is really going on in large organizations). After the Second World War, work by Lasswell's students and their students evolved in several directions with a common intent of arriving at more systematic policy and political system implications. Those efforts sought to organize notions used in official speech by policy elites into operational codes (e.g. Leites 1951; George 1969) and notions expressed by mass populations into profiles of national civic cultures (e.g. Almond and Verba 1963). Subsequent work presented alternative models of political cultures about major policy matters such as budgets and risk management (e.g. Wildavsky 1987, 1988; Thompson, Ellis, and Wildavsky 1990; Douglas and Wildavsky 1982); sweeping characterizations of particular national and regional political systems (e.g. Pye 1988; Pye and Pye 1985); thematic inventories of the notions and related actions of politicians in for them important situations (e.g. Fenno 1990 on US legislators); and reconstructions of the strategic rationales and related actions of ordinary (or even marginal) populations in encounters with public sector policies and institutions (e.g. Scott 1985, 1990 on Malaysian peasants).

It is important to note the scope of this legacy. The actors have ranged from elites to marginal populations, in the USA and abroad. The units have ranged from whole nations to small groups. The methods have ranged from at-a-distance analysis of public documents and interviews with émigrés to large-scale opinion surveys and direct observation (with more or less participation), and sometimes gone further to construct typologies and models. Both quantitative and qualitative tools have been used. To say that policy analysis needs to consider cultural and social factors as constraints and enablers is not to commit to a single methodology or type of data. It is, however, to commit to empirical enquiry, i.e. to beginning if not ending with "thick description" of what people say and do. For those an analyst holds to be of political and public policy interest, "If something is important to them, it becomes important to you. Their view of the world is as important as your view of that world" (Fenno 1990, 113–14).

Work in the Lasswellian tradition does not focus mostly on the texts of a few intellectuals. It does not assume that populations marginal to prevailing systems of power and wealth are especially worthy (or unworthy) of study or of public policy "voice." Priorities should depend on what are crucial roles in the policy process and in its consequences, matters which differ across policy issues, options, and salient events. Deciding whose notions most call for understanding should not be confounded with moral judgements about who holds meritorious notions. Finally, the

Lasswellian tradition recognizes that the cultural and social information it would have us gather can be used for "emancipatory" or oppressive purposes.

## 3. Coming to Terms With Variety

General laws of political behavior have obvious appeals. Yet public policy in application is less a general than a specific matter in terms of its when and where, who to whom, the options considered, and the consequences of options chosen. Accordingly, most general laws, be they of rational choice utilitarianism, prospect theory anchoring and loss aversion (Levy 1997), or social affiliation and identity (Sen 1977), provide only containers lacking situationally relevant operational content.[5] Applying the containers of utility, costs, and benefits involves imputing what the relevant actors treat as having more or less utility, cost, or benefit. Similar imputations, filling in, are required to get at what anchors are used and losses focused on, or what social affiliations are given great weight.

Policy-relevant applications of such laws involve accurately recognizing what participants pull from their containers to assess cause and effect relations between alternative courses of action in a situation and likely consequences. Excessively general, ahistorical labeling does little to illuminate why some population behaves as it does or what would lead it to act differently. Consider the variety of significations attached in different countries to visits by their heads of state and ordinary citizens to war casualty memorial sites, and even more distinctions between indigenous and foreign interpretations of such commemorative activities (as with domestic and international controversy about Japan's Yasukuni Shinto Shrine; Nelson 2003).

A similar need to specify content in use applies to make informative such broad "classical" cultural and social categories as class, race, ethnicity, religion, nationality, age, or generation. Doing that will often reveal that the category may be a useful summary of aggregate outcomes, but not of much which bears on achieving changes in outcomes. Thus, Thompson and Wildavsky (1986) called for a shift "from economic homogeneity to cultural heterogeneity in the classification of poor people." Suppose the category is being used to anticipate how those placed in it will respond to different policy treatments or interventions. Suppose further that the members of the category have more than one behavioral choice open to them during the time period during which a policy is supposed to accomplish its desired consequences. For

---

[5] To recognize a dimension of possible difference is of course to recognize one of possible similarity. That still leaves a need for content to substantiate contentions about the predominance of similarity or difference (as argued in Johnston 1995).

example, in the context of US election-related quarantine policies toward Castro's Cuba, it matters if relevant voters in Florida think of themselves as primarily Hispanic Americans or as Cuban Americans, and give more weight to ties with relatives in Cuba or to a vision of regime change there.

Realizing the policy maker's anticipations (Cuban-American votes) depends then on the "notions" of the targets with respect to: (a) their giving membership or identity primacy to the general category over subdivisions of it and over other categories; and (b) their "notions" as they lead them to recognize and evaluate alternatives open to them as category members. The targets are not clay but intentional actors from whom passive compliance and uniform reactions are not givens. Differences in (interpreted) experience with particular public institutions can lead to different general notions of effectiveness in dealing with public institutions and participating in politics more generally (as Soss 1999 found for recipients of two cash-providing US social safety net programs administered in contrasting ways). Specific content will still be needed even if claims are true that we are in an era of new, post-industrial broad categories replacing the "classical" ones (e.g. Clark and Hoffman-Martinot 1998; Inglehart 1990).

Suppose that the use of familiar categories follows less from an intent to shape the ostensible target population and more from judgements about how third parties (e.g. majority populations, taxpayers, allied governments) will react to invocations of a category label—e.g. "welfare cheats" or "the deserving poor," "terrorists" or "liberation fighters." Third-party reactions will depend on their "notions" about the members of the target category in relation to the salient situation. Other policy elites, bureaucrats, or populations which can reward or punish the invoker can use notions far different from those of the ostensible target population. When they do, public policies can produce desired behaviors and interpretations by almost everyone but it. The post 9/11 USA Patriot Act arguably has impacted less on those who would commit terrorist actions than on the general population and a host of government agencies. That bears some resemblance to what Edelman (1977) had in mind when he evaluated American anti-poverty programs as "words that succeed and policies that fail."

Talk about cultures or subcultures in relation to public policy usually follows from an image of a set of people whose relevant notions and actions differ from some historical, existing, or imaginable set of people. Differences get our attention when we think they constrain or enable some relative to other policies and policy processes. What contribution such talk will make to the analysis and conduct of public policy depends on awareness of the multiple dimensions of difference the world offers, and on the breadth and depth of efforts to understand how particular differences get applied to specific situations.

Cultures and subcultures and their members can differ in the dimensions of difference their notions identify. They can differ in the number of distinctions made on a given dimension and the distance between points on a dimension, e.g. about what religious or ethnic differences make a marriage mixed. They can differ in the value they place on being different or even unique. They can differ in how situations determine the importance of some aspect of difference. They can differ in what are key markers (signifiers) of any of these facets of difference. They can differ in what are held to be the correlates of commonly identified aspects of difference in terms of behavior, capability, intent, and normative worth. And, of course, they can differ in the degree to which their beliefs about how they are different from others and others different from them are shared by those others.

Whatever the cultural or subcultural content in these respects, it is not completely fixed if the experience of members is itself changing. Yet, in a context of pre-existing variety of notions and salient material context, populations can view that change as amounting to a very different sort of experience. Thus, the turn in US social policy from "welfare" to "workfare" may for those not participating in such programs appear as a well-intentioned offer of an avenue to a better life. At the same time, some participants view it as an ill-intentioned move to "cram down their throat" harsh choices between child rearing and work, or education and income (as with part-time fast-food jobs for Oakland teenagers of color; Stack 2001).

People come to any particular policy situation with a stock of notions about the degree and nature of relevant variety based on their prior actual or virtual experiences (including socialization, accepted history, academic learning). Thus Grammig (2002, 56) reports that a development assistance project was for experts of different nationalities "an empty shell that each participant filled with his own meaning." What is learned about whom usually results from prior judgements about the importance of a culture or subculture and sufficient curiosity to enquire about it. We are more likely to have elaborated profiles of others we have dealt with before and previously treated as important, and less likely to have such about those rarely encountered or thought lacking in wealth, coercive power, status, or rectitude. Of course players in policy systems and policy issues are a heterogeneous lot in terms of who they have encountered and treated as important. In sum, which and how many differences get recognized (or denied) are political and cultural matters. Public policies shape and are shaped by those recognitions, especially with regard to the processing of actual experiences into notion-related interpretative precedents, maxims, fables, and warnings.

Unfortunately, a number of often thought to be general tendencies for public policy get in the way of facing up to variety, and favor downplaying it. Consider three rather common assumptions: (1) *ceteris paribus* public policy tries to keep things simple to avoid overload; (2) politicians try to stay in good standing with their selectorates; and (3) bureaucratic agents try to look good to those who can affect their careers and agency resources.

Keeping things simple works against attending to a plethora of differences which would cast doubt on "one size fits all" policies. It favors attributing to apparently similar verbal or physical acts a standard meaning, and similar intent and affect. It is far easier to treat all welfare recipients as having similar views of work, or all Muslims as having similar notions of what being a "good Muslim" entails. It is far easier to interpret the reasons for poor grades by African-American males as following from factors which would account for poor grades by Caucasian or Asian males. It is far easier to interpret an audible "yes," smile, or even calls by admirals in different countries for a "strong Navy" (Booth 1979, 80–1) as meaning what they mean for us when we engage in such acts. A determined effort to think and act otherwise would compound the work involved in public policy formation, implementation, and evaluation.

Since public policy seldom is a "unitary actor" phenomenon, it usually involves achieving (or at least assuming) somewhat cooperative and communicative relationships between people and groups with less than identical notions. If it cannot be avoided, it can seemingly be made easier by an emphasis on dealing with persons and groups who seem less different from one's own culture or subculture. For example, a retired director of the CIA profiled for me a desirable replacement leader in an Islamic country as someone who "wears Western clothes, drinks whiskey, speaks English." Political legitimacy with indigenous constituencies can be slighted.

Of course, some stark claims of difference can enable policies which the prevailing notions in the adopting policy culture would otherwise deem morally illegitimate or pragmatically counter-productive. If others are inherently different in ways which threaten our culture and its preferred policies and policy processes, anything (or at least almost anything) goes, e.g. American treatment of some Iraqi and Afghan detainees. In such cases, what becomes constrained are policies which treat members of counter-cultures or clashing "civilizations" as our proclaimed notions would have us treat fellow culture members.[6] In its less culturally stressful and physically harsh versions, this makes for policies which deny existence through constructed invisibility (the Israeli tour leader who said, "the population of Israel is three million Jews"). In its often more culturally stressful and physically brutal versions, it can enable policies of genocide, ethnic cleansing, and state and non-state terrorism (e.g. Sluka 2000).

Selectorate-sensitive politicians (i.e. those particularly likely to gain and hold power) are constrained and enabled by the notions used by their selectorates. They tend to more or less proactively accommodate to them either reflexively when they too hold those notions or by consciously opportunistic acts of symbol manipulation (labeling, exemplification, and association). Policy issues and stances, salient events, political parties/movements/factions, and prominent personalities are then subjects for framing and counter-framing in light of judgements about the selectorate's notions. Informative examples are the testimony of expert witnesses for the prosecution and defense in the Rodney King police brutality trial (Goodwin 1994), and the politics of public school "reform" in Nashville (Pride 1995).

When the selectorate is quite uniform in its notions, the constraints and enablers are rather obvious. Politicians and activists compete to seem to fit best with predominant notions, and "expose" rivals as deviating from them. Given widely held notions of a USA under terrorist attack and of government employees as slackers, it was predictable that politicians would compete for authorship of a Department of

---

[6] The fact of harsh treatment of some Americans in American prisons is handled by invisibility, at least among much of the white US population.

Homeland Security. It was also hardly surprising that those of them trying to make establishment contingent on provision of established civil service protections to its employees would come under partisan attack and for the most part fold.

A selectorate rather evenly divided between clashing sets of notions calls for different strategies and tactics to relax the constraint of dissensus. Imagine a US selectorate split between holders of very different notions about the proper role of government derived from equally different notions about the good family (Lakoff 1996). Public policy practitioners may then seek to couch policies in ways which bundle together seemingly incompatible symbols and labels to appeal simultaneously to several sets of notions (e.g. "compassionate conservative"). They may engage in policy turn taking with respect to serial use of different symbolic packages catering to one or another of the competing sets of notions. They may even seek to create a replacement set of notions based on credible constructions of recent experience which promise to replace notions in mutual tension with a "Third Way" (as did President Clinton and Prime Minister Blair in the 1990s). Politicians, and not just ones in democratic societies, have reasons to be practicing ethnographers, or at least to have staff members who are.

Further complications arise when politicians have to appeal to domestic selectorates with one set of notions and also secure favorable treatment from elites and selectorates embedded in different cultures. That dual agenda may motivate policy elites to develop a repertoire with more than one set of culturally appropriate content. They may metaphorically (and sometimes quite literally) don different wardrobes (or dialects) for dealings with local, domestic, or foreign parties. Cosmopolitan US Southern senators have been known to shift into the regional dialect of their constituency when talking with its members. Flights from non-Arab countries to Saudi Arabia shortly before arrival often have returning citizens of considerable standing covering up modish Euro-American clothes.

In a multicultural polity and an internationalized world, politicians with more than a monocultural repertoire can be advantaged—at least if their practices avoid triggering conclusions that they are not really genuine, sincere members of any of the pertinent cultures. Manifesting some characteristics of another culture can lead its members to expect that actor to manifest others. Disappointment may follow, and accusations of "bad faith."[7] Of course, if selectorates in one policy culture have negative notions about another, there are risks of "guilt by association."[8]

Most public policies and policy processes originate in some bureaucratic agency or professional epistemic community, and most depend for stamps of approval (certi-

[7] "Governments like individuals, have great expectations of reasonable behaviour from those they think are like themselves. They will naturally expect them to see the world in the same way and to behave sensibly, which in political practice does not mean behaving with 'good sense', but rather means behaving 'like me' or 'in accordance with my wishes'.... When a close associate fails to act in a desired manner, the disappointment is all the greater" (Booth 1979, 56).

[8] For example, that premiss may have underlain Republican attacks on the US Democratic presidential candidate in 2004, John Kerry, as being "too French." The counter unsurprisingly was to display Kerry in association with symbols thought to be central to the selectorate's notions of genuine membership in American culture such as driving a motorcycle and hunting.

fication) and implementation on one or more bureau or professional communities. Top policy makers and their policies are then enabled and constrained by what members of those groupings hold to be the notions used by their career gatekeepers, and by their convictions about the grounds (notions and situational triggers) which others rely on to determine collective or individual rewards or punishments.[9] When agency is given to a bureau or profession with a distinct set of notions, the chances are that set of notions is privileged *de jure* or de facto. Some policies and policy process routines are then more enabled and some more constrained.

To say that bureaux and professions have "world-views," "standard operating procedures," "folklore," and pantheons of exemplary individuals and events is to say that they have a culture. The centrality of membership in that culture mounts when bureaux and professions have accepted and nearly deterministic cause-and-effect theories, normative criteria of merit, high barriers to entry and exit, and identities framed in terms of contrasts with other bureaux and professions. Consider, for example, the protective "code blue" of silence US policemen sometimes use when challenged by civilians and civilian authorities, or the claims to special turf rights made by "foreign area experts" to keep out international relations "generalists" (Samuels and Weiner 1992). A public health service (e.g. the Centers for Disease Control) is likely to treat the problem of bioterrorism differently from a domestic security service (e.g. the FBI). Economists are likely to treat pollution problems more with an eye to market mechanisms such as permit auctions while lawyers might emphasize regulatory mechanisms such as penalties for breaching emission ceilings.

Suppose an issue is assigned to two bureaux with different established notions, notions which include viewing each other as expansionist, untrustworthy, or less competent rivals. Policies which require generous cooperation are constrained, e.g. think of the FBI and CIA even if both are labeled as belonging to a common membership group (the US "Intelligence Community"). A more subtle form of constraint occurs when some key policy role is assigned to a "subculture" which exists in a low-status way (e.g. civil affairs units in the US military) in a larger organization whose culture centers on quite different missions (e.g. war fighting and deterrence). Unsurprisingly, the assignment is then often followed by resource and promotion starvation (e.g. the fate of enforcement agents in the US Immigration and Naturalization Service or INS; Weissinger 1996).

In any event, for many members of most agencies and bureaux there are widely held views ("conventional wisdom") of what policy-relevant behavior carries high risks. Those views may or may not be transparent to outsiders, especially if they clash with declared norms among members. Privileged bureaux and professions (and indeed "ordinary folks") will go to considerable effort to get around policy emphases and directives which seem to them to pose such risks.

---

[9] Policy systems vary in the extent to which and ways in which they have a common culture across key bureaux, levels of government, and specializations (e.g. as the French try to do with few entry paths into the elite higher civil service or the Chinese Communists used to try to do through party socialization).

# 4. FINDING VARIETY

The arguments to this point are that: (1) cultural variety matters for public policy; (2) there are chronic tendencies to deny it the attention it ought to have; and (3) denial deprives some policy options and policy process alternatives of a level playing field. A superficial acknowledgement of variety will not help much unless acted on to improve the information provided for and actually used in public policy. Those changes are more likely with increased representation and standing in policy processes of those attentive to variety. What sort of repertoire of enquiry would then get greater emphasis?[10]

One priority would be analyzing two aspects of language used by members with each other. The first is that of metaphors which treat some matter as similar to another, and invoke from such similarities guidance about situational interpretations and warranted action (Lakoff and Johnson 1980). For American public policy, for example, one may note the frequent use of conflict metaphors such as the "war on" or the "fight against" (as with the Johnson administration on poverty, the Carter administration on energy dependence, and the Bush II administration on terrorism). For Americans and Japanese, the sheer volume of talk about sport suggests that it is seen as a source of relevant metaphors for much else (Boswell 1990; Whiting 1990). The more frequently similar metaphors and analogies occur in general writing and speech, the more likely they are to be drawn on with respect to public policies and policy processes.

A second focus would be on thorough elicitation of what members of a relevant population use by way of categories of actors and actions, cues to relevant categories, and expectations about the efficacy of particular actions in relation to actors in some category (e.g. Spradley 1970). Rather than imposing categories (as in closed response survey interviews), the emphasis would be on discovering the categories, cues, and expectations held by those whose behavior we are trying to understand and perhaps influence. Special attention would go to matters elaborated with numerous distinctions suggesting importance in the lives of those whose language is under examination.

Language is only one form of behavior open to observation. A variety-finding orientation calls for as much direct observation as possible of what people do in their natural situations, i.e. what for them are real situations involved with the aspect of public policy of interest, and then seeking their rationales for acting as they have done (e.g. DeWalt and DeWalt 2002). The observation should be conducted as unobtrusively as possible (e.g. along the lines of Webb et al. 1966) with the observer as blended into and neutral in the situation as possible. The observer would try to become a watcher and listener *in situ* whether the subject of interest is the campaign behavior of elected politicians in Hong Kong (Beatty 2003), the processing of issues

---

[10] Brief reviews of pertinent methods and applications appear in Schensul et al. 1999*a*, 1999*b*, 1999*c*.

by local office holders in New York state (Sady 1990), or the inferential process of arriving at US intelligence estimates (Johnston 2003). That may or may not involve participation either as part of blending in or as a way to discern notions used by culture members.

Whether the focus is on language or other behaviors, considerable attention should go to associations and evaluations in terms of cultural propriety and likely pragmatic consequences operating for those being observed. That involves eliciting and recognizing what for the members of the culture under examination are codes of conduct, key historical references and myths, understandings (images) of others who matter to them for dealings with public policy, and prototypically successful or unsuccessful courses of action by those held to be similar to themselves. Those may often be surprisingly elaborated and shared, as with homeless alcoholics in Seattle on dealing with the personnel and institutions of the "criminal justice" system (Spradley 1970).

When the behaviors in question involve physical actions and material objects, the discovery process needs to look contextually at when those actions are taken and the full range of uses made of those objects. If we wish to change practices in India about cows, we should engage in a "functional systems analysis" of how cows are used in and adapted to Hindu society and its economy and ecology (Harris 1966). If we wish to understand the extent to which educational administrators are concerned with student demonstrations and physical disruption, or diplomats with their embassies being attacked, we should examine features of newly constructed facilities (as in "riot renaissance" architecture). If we wish to understand and improve the availability of public recreational space for children in New York City, we should look to see where they play (the street) rather than assuming that only parks and playgrounds are sites for play (e.g. Yin 1972).

Fully understanding variety may not be possible, and faces numerous obstacles of access, evidence, and inference. Yet several "best practices" can at least increase understanding. One is to extend the language mapping and other observations across time and situations. For example, a longitudinal study of an "innovative school" found notions, processes, and roles far different from those stressed in the professional literature on school innovation (Smith et al. 1998). A one-time, few-day, and situationally unusual field trip or site visit may produce a "shock of recognition" that variety exists. It is unlikely to create substantial awareness of the notions used by others. Shortcomings are especially likely when the "visitor" deals primarily with stationed officials from his or her own culture rather than those of another. Deliberate steps to "get out of the bubble" need to be taken to avoid pitfalls of "spurious direct encounters" with other cultures at home and abroad.

It also can be helpful to focus on material practices and talk widespread in the population one wishes to understand. For example, insider jokes among them and what for them are popular mass media products should not be slighted in favor of "serious" talk and highbrow products. If we are interested in young Americans, MTV programs may be more informative than the *New York Review of Books*. If we are interested in US legislators and their staffs, their "neighborhood" newspaper (*Roll*

*Call*) may merit as much attention as the *American Political Science Review*. If we are interested in the extent to which upper- and middle-class South Africans are preoccupied with crime, we might gain insight by noting the large amount of attention home design and accessory magazines for that market give to residential alarm systems and security barriers, and the consumer demand for "armed response team" services.

Finally, there is the selection and assessment of informants, individual and group sources thought by outsiders to be "insiders" to a culture of interest and relied on to illuminate it. Some use of informants is hard to avoid, but taking what they communicate at face value is not. It is advisable to rely more on informants with substantial recent experience in the culture of interest than on those who have been "in exile" for several decades. It is advisable to weigh what informants tell us in light of their own likely agendas, interests in our holding particular views of their cultures and taking or avoiding certain interventions in it. All of those cautions should enter into decisions about giving informants and their primary membership groups key roles in relationships between our culture and theirs. Prudential lessons might be drawn from the disappointments of US efforts at regime change which drew on unwarrantedly rosy émigré judgements (the Bay of Pigs in the Kennedy administration and the 2003 invasion of Iraq).

This repertoire deserves a far more prominent place than it usually has in programs to prepare future professionals to analyze and participate in public policy.

# REFERENCES

AKERLOF, G., and YELLEN, J. L. 1994. Gang behavior, law enforcement and community values. Pp. 173–97 in *Values and Public Policy*, ed. H. J. Aaron, T. E. Mann, and T. Taylor. Washington, DC: Brookings Institution.

ALMOND, G. A. 2002. *Ventures in Political Science*. Boulder, Colo.: Lynne Rienner.

—— and VERBA, S. 1963. *The Civic Culture: Political Attitudes and Democracy in Five Nations*. Princeton, NJ: Princeton University Press.

BEATTY, B. 2003. *Democracy, Asian Values, and Hong Kong: Evaluating Political Elite Beliefs*. Westport, Conn.: Praeger.

BOOTH, K. 1979. *Strategy and Ethnocentrism*. New York: Homes and Meier.

BOSWELL, T. 1990. What we talk about when we talk about sports: it's not just who won or lost—it's how we use the game. *Washington Post Magazine*, 12 Aug.: 23–8.

CLARK, T. N., and HOFFMANN-MARTINOT, V. 1998. *The New Political Culture*. Boulder, Colo.: Westview.

DEWALT, K. M., and DEWALT, B. R. 2002. *Participant Observation: A Guide for Fieldworkers*. Walnut Creek, Calif.: AltaMira Press.

DOUGLAS, M., and WILDAVSKY, A. 1982. *Risk and Culture: An Essay on the Selection of Technical and Environmental Dangers*. Berkeley: University of California Press.

EDELMAN, M. 1977. *Political Language: Words That Succeed and Policies That Fail*. New York: Academic Press.

ELMORE, R. F. 1985. Forward and backward mapping: reversible logic. Pp. 33–70 in *Policy Implementation in Federal and Unitary Systems*, ed. K. Hanf and T. A. J. Toonen. Boston: Martinus Nijhoff.

FENNO, R. 1990. *Watching Politicians: Essays on Participant Observation*. Berkeley: University of California at Berkeley Institute of Governmental Studies.

GEERTZ, C. M. 1973. *The Interpretation of Cultures*. New York: Basic Books.

GEORGE, A. 1969. "The operational code:" a neglected approach to the study of political leaders and decision-making. *International Studies Quarterly*, 13: 190–222.

GOODWIN, C. 1994. Professional vision. *American Anthropologist*, 96: 606–33.

GRAMMIG, T. 2002. *Technical Knowledge and Development: Observing Aid Projects and Processes*. London: Routledge.

HARRIS, M. 1966. The cultural ecology of India's sacred cattle. *Current Anthropologist*, 7: 51–9.

HUDSON, V. M. (ed.) 1997. *Culture and Foreign Policy*. Boulder, Colo.: Lynne Rienner.

INGLEHART, R. 1990. *Culture Shift in Advanced Industrial Societies*. Princeton, NJ: Princeton University Press.

JOHNSTON, A. I. 1995. Thinking about strategic culture. *International Security*, 19: 32–64.

JOHNSTON, R. 2003. Developing a taxonomy of intelligence analysis variables. *Studies in Intelligence*, 47: 61–72.

KIER, A. 1995. Culture and military doctrine. *International Security*, 19: 65–93.

LAKOFF, G. 1996. *Moral Politics: What Conservatives Know That Liberals Don't*. Chicago: University of Chicago Press.

—— and JOHNSON, M. 1980. *Metaphors We Live By*. Chicago: University of Chicago Press.

LASSWELL, H. D. 1951. *The Political Writings of Harold Lasswell*. Glencoe, Ill.: Free Press.

—— 1971. *Propaganda Technique in World War I*. Cambridge, Mass.: MIT Press.

—— and FOX, M. B. 1979. *The Signature of Power: Buildings, Communication, and Policy*. New Brunswick, NJ: Transaction.

—— and LEITES, N. 1949. *The Language of Politics: Studies in Quantitative Semantics*. New York: George W. Stewart.

LEITES, N. 1951. *The Operational Code of the Politburo*. New York: McGraw-Hill.

LERNER, D., and LASSWELL, H. R. (eds.) 1951. *The Policy Sciences: Recent Developments in Scope and Method*. Stanford, Calif.: Stanford University Press.

LEVY, J. 1997. Prospect theory and the cognitive-rational debate. Pp. 33–50 in *Decisionmaking on War and Peace*, ed. N. Geva and A. Mintz. Boulder, Colo.: Lynne Rienner.

NELSON, J. 2003. Social memory as ritual practice: commemorating spirits of the military dead at Yasukuni Shrine. *Journal of Asian Studies*, 62: 443–67.

PRIDE, R. A. 1995. How activists and media frame social problems. *Political Communication*, 12: 5–26.

PYE, L. 1988. *The Mandarin and the Cadre: China's Political Cultures*. Ann Arbor: Center for Chinese Studies, University of Michigan.

—— and PYE, M. 1985. *Asian Power and Politics: The Cultural Dimensions of Authority*. Cambridge, Mass.: Harvard University Press.

SADY, R. 1990. *District Leaders: A Political Ethnography*. Boulder, Colo.: Westview.

SAMUELS, R. J., and WEINER, M. 1992. *The Political Culture of Foreign Area and International Studies: Essays in Honor of Lucian W. Pye*. Washington, DC: Brassey's.

SCHENSUL, J. J., et al. 1999a. *Using Ethnographic Data: Interventions, Public Programming, and Public Policy*. Walnut Creek, Calif.: AltaMira Press.

—— et al. 1999b. *Enhanced Ethnographic Methods: Audiovisual Techniques, Focused Group Interviews, and Elicitation Techniques*. Walnut Creek, Calif.: AltaMira Press.

SCHENSUL, J. J., et al. 1999c. *Mapping Social Networks, Spatial Data, and Hidden Populations*. Walnut Creek, Calif. AltaMira Press.

SCOTT, J. C. 1985. *Weapons of the Weak: Everyday Forms of Peasant Resistance*. New Haven, Conn.: Yale University Press.

—— 1990. *Domination and the Arts of Resistance: Hidden Transcripts*. New Haven, Conn.: Yale University Press.

SEN, A. 1977. Rational fools. *Philosophy & Public Affairs*, 6: 317–44.

SLUKA, J. A. (ed.) 2000. *Death Squad: The Anthropology of State Terror*. Philadelphia: University of Pennsylvania Press.

SMITH, L. M., DWYER, D. C., PRUNTY, J. J., and KLEINE, P. F. 1998. *Innovation and Change in Schooling: History, Politics, and Agency*. New York: Falmer Press.

SNYDER, J. 2002. Anarchy and culture: insights from the anthropology of war. *International Organization*, 56: 7–45.

SOSS, J. 1999. Lessons of welfare: policy design, political learning, and political action. *American Political Science Review*, 93: 363–80.

SPRADLEY, J. P. 1970. *You Owe Yourself a Drunk: An Ethnography of Urban Nomads*. Boston: Little, Brown.

—— 1979. *The Ethnographic Interview*. New York: Holt, Rinehart and Winston.

STACK, C. 2001. Coming of age in Oakland. Pp. 179–98 in *The New Poverty Studies: The Ethnography of Power, Politics, and Impoverished People in the United States*, ed. J. Goode and J. Maskovsky. New York: New York University Press.

THOMPSON, M., ELLIS, R., and WILDAVSKY, A. 1990. *Cultural Theory*. Boulder, Colo.: Westview.

—— GRENDSTAD, G., and SELLE, P. (eds.) 1999. *Cultural Theory as Political Science*. New York: Routledge.

—— and WILDAVSKY, A. 1986. A poverty of distinction: from economic homogeneity to cultural heterogeneity in the classification of poor people. *Policy Sciences*, 19: 163–99.

WEBB, E. J., CAMPBELL, D. T., SCHWARTZ, R. D., and SECHREST, L. 1966. *Unobtrusive Measures: Nonreactive Research in the Social Sciences*. Chicago: Rand-McNally.

WEISSINGER, G. 1996. *Law Enforcement and the INS: A Participant Observation Study of Control Agents*. Lanham, Md.: University Press of America.

WHITING, R. 1990. *You Gotta Have Wa*. New York: Vintage.

WILDAVSKY, A. 1987. Choosing preferences by constructing institutions: a cultural theory of preference formation. *American Political Science Review*, 81: 3–21.

—— 1988. A cultural theory of budgeting. *International Journal of Public Administration*, 11: 651–77.

YIN, R. K. 1972. *Participant-Observation and the Development of Urban Neighborhood Policy*. New York: New York City RAND Institute, R-962.

ZHANG, S. G. 1992. *Deterrence and Strategic Culture: Chinese–American Confrontations, 1949–1958*. Ithaca, NY: Cornell University Press.

CHAPTER 29

# GLOBALIZATION AND PUBLIC POLICY

## COLIN HAY

## 1. INTRODUCTION

VIRTUALLY no topic in contemporary public policy is more contested or more potentially consequential than the impact of globalization. The balance of opinion would certainly suggest that there is a strong prima facie case for seeing globalization and public policy as antagonistic—the extent of globalization, for many, being an index of the retrenchment of public policy, at least at the national level. A variety of more or less plausible mechanisms for this tension between globalization and public policy can be pointed to. In particular, globalization is seen to challenge the public nature of (domestic) public policy by summoning a series of non-negotiable, external, and largely economic imperatives that must be appeased in a technically proficient manner if good economic performance is to be maintained, whatever the cost in terms of democratic accountability. Similarly, globalization is seen as the enemy of policy, public or otherwise, in the sense that it is seen to dictate policy choices whilst itself being beyond the capacity of domestic political actors to control. Yet none of this is uncontested. In this chapter my aim is to unpack the notion of globalization, considering the diverse ways in which globalization might be seen as antithetical to public policy, before turning to a review of the empirical evidence and the debate that it has generated. I conclude by suggesting that although globalization and public policy can be seen as antithetical in a variety of respects, this is less a consequence of the direct and necessary constraints globalization is seen to impose than it is a consequence of more political and contingent factors—in short, the constraints of globalization are as much as anything else, what political actors make of them. I also suggest that if globalization is antithetical to public policy, then it is only antithetical to public policy at the domestic level; arguably it merely reinforces the need for effective and democratic public policy at the transnational level (see also Goodin 2003). If it is problematic or at least premature to suggest that domestic public policy is a casualty of globalization, it is no less problematic to overlook the opportunities and need for public policy at the transnational level that globalization generates.

In most conventional treatments, globalization and public policy are counter-posed. Invariably, in such accounts, globalization is seen to intensify the competitive struggle amongst nations for global market share, driving states to subordinate public policy considerations to economic imperatives, thereby exposing their public sectors to an exacting "competitive audit." Yet, however familiar, this is by no means the only mechanism by which globalization might be seen as in tension with public policy. Indeed, at least four rather different sources of such tension might be identified:[1]

1. Globalization is held to necessitate a certain privatization and technicization of "public policy," rendering it less publicly accountable. Here it is the distinctly "public" character of public policy that is potentially seen as a casualty of globalization. By virtue of "time-space compression" and the complex interdependencies that ensue, globalization is seen to render policy deliberations so technical and involved as to necessitate significant changes in the conduct—and notably the legitimization—of public policy. In the face of the speculative dynamics unleashed by financial market integration, for in-stance, it is argued that monetary policy must be removed from political control and rendered both predictable and rules bounded rather than discre-tionary. Globalization, and the complexities and interdependencies which are seen to characterize it, are here associated with powerful tendencies to depoliticization, privatization, and technicization (see also Berman and McNamara 1999). If valid, this is a very important development, for it implies that in a context of globalization public policy cannot be held to account publicly (and hence democratically) to the extent to which we have become accustomed. Such claims rest on the notion of a significant and perhaps growing trade-off, in a context characterized by complex interdependencies between effectiveness and accountability in public policy and that we should resolve any such trade-off in terms of the former. It is suggestive, moreover, of a potentially troubling explanation for the growing and widely identified lack

---

[1] It is important to acknowledge at the outset that these four sources of tension are by no means mutually compatible; indeed, different authors have placed rather different emphasis upon them. Thus, for some neo-Ricardians, an increasingly integrated global economy intensifies the international division of labour, driving a process of divergence (reflecting specialization). For others, however, globalization unleashes vicious competitive dynamics which drive economies, at pain of poor performance, to race to adopt the most optimal policy stance, thereby driving a process of convergence. There is no obvious reconciliation between such contending theoretical predictions; and neither is clearly borne out by the available empirical evidence.

of trust in public officials and associated discontent and disengagement with formal politics (see, for instance, Dalton 2004; Dalton and Wattenberg 2000).

2. Globalization is seen to necessitate an internalization by the state of the preferences of capital and an associated squeezing of the "fiscal space" for public policy. This is perhaps the most conventional sense in which globalization is seen to be antithetical to public policy.[2] As will be discussed in more detail in later sections, the mechanism invoked here is relatively simple. Globalization is treated as synonymous with the mobility of capital. In order to retain high levels of investment, on which economic growth and high levels of employment are predicated, states must increasingly provide an investment climate conducive to profit maximization or more to the point, conducive to the *anticipation* by potential investors of profit maximization. They must, in short, internalize the preferences of capital.[3] Such preferences are conventionally assumed to be for a lightly regulated marketplace relatively free from public policy interventions and characterized by low levels of taxation.[4] The mobility of capital is, then, seen both directly and indirectly, to exert strong downward pressures on public policy—directly, since globalization enhances the effective bargaining power of capital and capital is seen to exert a strong preference for market mechanisms as opposed to public

[2] Whilst this notion of globalization as antithetical to the public accountability of domestic policy is a familiar one with powerful resonances in much contemporary public discourse, it is by no means expressive of a consistent orthodoxy. International institutions (like the World Bank and the IMF) here speak with forked tongues—on the one hand advocating powerfully the need for central bank independence from political influence whilst, on the other, emphasizing the importance of good governance and democratic accountability as preconditions of economic modernization. What is clear, however, is that the prevailing wisdom in international institutions, as elsewhere, would seem to be that economic globalization necessitates a certain subordination of domestic political considerations (including accountability to public opinion) to harsh economic imperatives. Good governance and democratic accountability are, in this sense, secondary considerations.

[3] Of course, it is not only capital that is mobile in a globally integrated market. Insofar as labor is both mobile and scarce—and in some sectors of the international economy it is certainly both—its preferences, too, must be accommodated if the supply of this essential factor of production is to meet demand. With a few rare exceptions, however, the mobility of labor has not featured prominently in accounts of the economic imperatives issuing from globalization (though see, for instance, Rogowski 1989). This is largely because of the emphasis placed in the existing literature upon the differential mobility of capital and labor. Yet two further factors are also likely to have proved significant—first, the stigmatized and rather undifferentiated public discourse which surrounds immigration in most of the world's leading economies and the rather greater political clout and influence of those advocating ostensibly capital-friendly reforms. The latter, of course, are more likely to stress the mobility of capital and the imperatives issuing from it than those issuing from the mobility of labor.

[4] The notion that capital is motivated politically by strong deregulatory preferences is, of course, a crude generalization and one, as we shall see in later sections, that is difficult to reconcile with the expressed preferences of capital (as revealed by its investment behaviour). Regulation may well bring with it a certain sense of security on the part of (say, financial) investors, suggesting at minimum the existence of complex trade-offs in capital's own assessment of the merits of regulation versus deregulation. The simple point is, however, that in most stylized accounts of globalization such complex trade-offs are simply not acknowledged and capital's preferences are assumed both simple and fixed.

regulation; and indirectly, since globalization effectively squeezes the fiscal base out of which public policy is funded.

3. More generally, globalization is seen to diminish the policy-making capacity and autonomy of the nation state, resulting in a displacement of functions from public to quasi-public bodies (such as independent central banks) and from national to transnational institutions (such as those associated with the process of European integration and more obviously global institutions such as the IMF, the WTO, and the World Bank)[5]. Clearly this third sense in which globalization and public policy-making capacity at the national level are seen to be antithetical is not unrelated to the points already discussed—indeed the displacement of functions from public to quasi-public bodies almost directly parallels the privatization and technicization of policy discussed above. Yet the emphasis is, again, slightly different. Here commentators highlight what they identify as an increasing disparity between the level at which policy problems emerge and/or must effectively be dealt with and the still predominantly national/domestic character of the institutions from which such responses are initially sought. In short, they note, in a context of globalization, the nation state's increasing lack of fitness for purpose. Of course, to identify a proliferation of global/transnational problems which the nation state is not well placed to deal with is not necessarily to point to a shortfall in public policy, especially if global/transnational policy-making capacity is enhanced in parallel with the proliferation of problems at this level. Yet it is the gap between the pace at which the problems proliferate and the policy-making capacity increases that prompts contemporary concerns. Invariably, it seems, global problems have failed to generate coordinated global solutions—environmental degradation providing an ever more alarming case in point. As this already serves to indicate, many of the contemporary challenges for public policy are to devise proficient and democratic institutions of global governance—an effective policy-making capacity for dealing with problems of global public policy.

4. Globalization is seen as driving a process of convergence, thereby diminishing both variations between states in public policy and the significance of variations in public policy as variables in the explanation of comparative performance. Questions of convergence, divergence, or continued diversity have provided a key focus for public policy analysis in an era of globalization, provoking considerable controversy.[6] In most conventional accounts, for reasons already discussed, globalization is seen to promote convergence, as states have come to internalize the preferences of capital, thereby embracing

---

[5] On the role of the latter in "global business regulation" see, especially, the exemplary and exhaustive discussion in Braithwaite and Drahos (2000).

[6] Compare Berger and Dore 1996; Garrett 1998; Gray 1998; Hall and Soskice 2001; Weiss 1998.

neoliberal policies. Yet in recent years a rather more institutionally differentiated view has developed. This so-called "varieties of capitalism" perspective is associated most clearly with what Peter A. Hall and David Soskice (especially 2001) call "dual" rather than simple convergence. It sees globalization as an agent of convergence, but suggests that it is likely to have different impacts on coordinated and liberal market economies, reinforcing rather than undermining their distinctiveness (see also Garrett 1998). Yet even in this more subtle, differentiated, and increasingly influential perspective globalization heavily circumscribes public policy makers' autonomy. In liberal market economies, for instance, it essentially imposes on them market-conforming policies, raising questions again about the extent to which public policy can be held to account publicly/democratically.

As this already serves to indicate, the dominant themes in the existing literature on globalization and public policy all point to an adversarial relationship between globalization and public policy—in which the former is seen to select strongly for the depoliticization, privatization, and technicization of the latter. In this context, it is perhaps hardly surprising that commentators like David Marquand should point to a contemporary "decline of the public" (2004). Yet before rushing to endorse such a pessimistic conclusion it is important to acknowledge that most of the themes of the literature already discussed rest on strong assumptions as to the nature, extent, and consequences of globalization. Whether acknowledged as such, these are unavoidably empirical claims and, moreover, empirical claims that do not always stand up to a close consideration of the available evidence.

Indeed, although the contemporary period is invariably referred to as one of globalization, and although globalization is invariably seen as placing stringent constraints on the size of the public sector, in aggregate terms states consume a larger share of global GDP than at any previous point in their history (Garrett 2001; see also Hirst and Thompson 1999). Of course, such evidence is not in itself sufficient to refute the globalization thesis, nor is it especially difficult to see how the globalization thesis might accommodate such ostensibly unsupportive data (for a more sustained discussion see Hay 2005). Yet it certainly suggests the importance of a rather more detailed consideration of the empirical evidence than characterizes much (though by no means all) of the current literature. The frequently hyperbolic nature of much of the globalization debate and its tendency to extrapolate wildly from anecdotal illustrations where empirical evidence is appealed to at all necessitates a more thoroughgoing empirical review.

This is the aim of the later sections of this chapter. However, before turning to the evidence, it is first important to consider the concept of globalization itself.

# 2. What is Globalization?

Given the now habitual contextualization of public policy in terms of the constraints, pressures, and more rarely, opportunities associated with globalization, one might be forgiven for expecting a clear (if implicit) consensus on the meaning of the term. Nothing could be further from the truth. Whether globalization is occurring or not is highly contested; and indeed, what would count as evidence of globalization in the first place is scarcely less contested. The result is considerable confusion as analysts, who may in fact agree to a far greater extent than they assume on what is really going on, mistake semantic differences for more substantive analytical disagreements.

As this suggests, the question "what is globalization?", however straightforward, is one that invariably lacks a straightforward answer; indeed, it is one that is surprisingly rarely posed. A variety of effects follow from this—not the least of which is the tendency of proponents of the globalization thesis ("radicals" in Giddens's (1999) terminology) and their critics ("skeptics" in the same terms) to talk past one another.[7] Whether globalization is happening and whether the consequences often attributed to it *should* be attributed to it depend on what globalization is taken to imply—and it is here that the major differences often lie. Unremarkably, skeptics tend to adopt more exacting definitional standards than radicals, pointing almost in the same breath to the disparity between the real evidence (such as it is) and the rigors of such an exacting definitional standard. Radicals by contrast set for themselves a rather less discriminating definitional hurdle, with the effect that they interpret the very same evidence that leads skeptics to challenge the globalization thesis as seemingly unambiguous evidence *for* the thesis. What makes this all the more confusing is the seeming reluctance of authors on either side of the exchange to define clearly and concisely their terminology.

However frustrating this may be, it is not perhaps as surprising as it might at first seem. For radicals especially—and they are, if anything, rather more guilty of a failure to provide a precise minimal definitional standard—globalization is multifaceted and complex. Accordingly, it does not avail itself easily of a simple definition. Such authors, perhaps understandably, tend to be reluctant to frame their understanding of globalization in discriminating terms and/or in terms that might easily be operationalized empirically. Insofar as they define globalization at all, then, it is often defined in an anecdotal manner—Giddens, for instance, introduced his 1999 Reith Lectures on globalization not with a definition but with the story of an anthropologist friend watching *Basic Instinct* on video in Central Africa (1999; see also Hay and Watson 1999). After a few more anecdotes, Giddens's audience probably gained a pretty good sense of what he was talking about; what they probably did not get was a

---

[7] The archetypal "radical" account is probably that of John Gray (1998); the archetypal "skeptic" account probably that of Hirst and Thompson (1999).

sense of a precise analytical concept that could be operationalized empirically to achieve significant analytical purchase on the social and political processes it sought to describe and illuminate.

One way to get at underlying or implicit understandings of globalization in such accounts is to look at the assumptions made by their proponents in deriving the consequences and effects they attribute to it. This is perhaps rather easier when it is the economic consequences of globalization that are being considered—for here the assumptions made by radicals are quite often both stark and stylized. The so-called "business school" variant of the radical or "hyper"-globalization thesis is a case in point (as is its practical political expression within the so-called "Washington Consensus"). Here globalization is essentially synonymous with economic openness—in neoclassical economic terms, with a perfectly clearing and fully integrated global market. The effects of globalization appealed to in this literature are, in effect, logical correlates of such assumptions (albeit without the algebraic/formal modelling associated with the open economy neoclassical international macroeconomics from which these assumptions are drawn). This is an important point, for whatever one thinks of it, the global economy today is *not* a perfectly clearing and fully integrated market. In this sense many of the predictions/diagnoses of the hyper-globalization literature are predicated on unrealistic and implausible assumptions—assumptions used in economic theory not for their accuracy but for their heuristic value (in modeling a perfectly integrated market) and as simplifying distortions necessary to facilitate the formal modeling. Yet important though this is, it does not get us closer to a definition of globalization. For radicals do not offer perfect market integration on a global scale as a definition of globalization—though this *is* invariably how they operationalize the term. The question of how perfectly integrated globally a market must be to warrant analysis in such terms is, again, rarely posed; and consequently, the question of when the degree of integration in the world economy is sufficient to justify the label globalization is rarely, if ever answered.

Having failed to find many clear statements of what globalization actually is, it is time to attempt an alternative strategy. Like so many contested terms in the social sciences, globalization is perhaps better understood in negative rather than positive terms—in terms of what it is not.

This strategy immediately bears fruit as a number of "others" can relatively easily be identified—terms presented alongside globalization, often in the same breath, yet starkly counterposed to it. Amongst such conceptual pairings the following are perhaps the most obvious:

(i)   nation vs. global (referring to the level at which the center of gravity of the world system might be seen to lie and the primary character of the cultures, economies, and polities within that system);

(ii)  international vs. global (referring to the character of supranational decision-making processes and specifically, the extent to which these might be seen as trans- rather than merely international in form);

(iii)  regionalization vs. globalization (referring to the precise geographical scope and character of any particular process of integration);

(iv)  protectionism/closure/internal orientation vs. globalization as external orientation (referring to a policy-making orientation and a set of policies consistent with such an orientation).

This immediately reveals a range of rather different senses of globalization or, better perhaps, a range of *dimensions* of the concept. Moreover, looking at globalization in terms of such conceptual pairings is suggestive of a range of continuous (and not necessarily orthogonal) axes along which progress towards (or retrenchment from) globalization might be gauged. Such an approach encourages us to conceive of globalization in rather more fluid and dynamic terms, as a (potential) outcome of a set of tendencies to which there are counter-tendencies (see also Hay and Marsh 2000). Yet whilst this might seem to lessen the importance somewhat of a precise and easily empirically operationalizable definition of globalization, it does not diminish the significance of the question, "how global does it have to be to count as evidence of globalization?"—indeed, it merely projects this question onto a number of distinct dimensions.

The high stakes of such controversies are well illustrated by the debate which still rages on the geographical character of trade within the world system today.[8] For many of those who counterpose regionalization and globalization, deepening intra-regional integration is not, in and of itself, evidence of globalization. For such authors, contemporary patterns of trade integration do not seem to provide strong prima facie evidence for trade globalization—with the most recent data showing that for most of the world's leading regional economies, the pace of intra-regional trade integration far outstrips that of inter-regional trade integration. As a consequence, they conclude, the world economy, though ever more integrated in terms of trade, is becoming ever more regionalized and in that sense, less globalized (Hay 2005, 2004; Hirst and Thompson 1999). Yet such an interpretation rests on a semantic distinction. The same evidence can be described rather differently. For those who see trade openness and globalization as synonymous, the precise geographical character of patterns of trade integration is not the issue—this is, by definition, globalization. And even amongst those who seek to differentiate clearly between regionalization and globalization, there are those who would interpret precisely the same data as evidence of both globalization and regionalization. Such commentators emphasize, in so doing, not the higher *relative* pace of intra- as opposed to inter-regional integration, but the *absolute* increase in both intra- and inter-regional integration (for instance Perraton et al. 1997).

Yet, tempting though it may well be to dismiss the issue in such terms, this is not merely a question of semantics—there is much of substance at stake here. For if, on the basis of a detailed assessment of the trading relations of the EU economy, for

---

[8]  See, for instance, Frankel 1997; Hay 2004; Hirst and Thompson 1999; Perraton et al. 1997.

instance, we identify regionalization where once we saw globalization, we may come to view the competitive imperatives such economies face by virtue of trade integration rather differently. It matters whether Britain and France compete increasingly with their European partners or whether they must increasingly compete in a genuinely global market for traded goods. The semantics matter because they may potentially obscure, in a rather amorphous conception of globalization, the quite specific competitive challenges our economies now face.

# 3. The Impact of Globalization

In terms of public policy, as already indicated, globalization is invariably seen as a constraint rather than an opportunity. Its impact, if we can indeed speak of powerful globalization tendencies, is then frequently seen in terms of the imposition of external imperatives—most notably perhaps that of competitiveness. However vague and implicit notions of globalization may be in the existing literature, a clear and relatively well-conserved set of mechanisms of constraint on domestic policy-making autonomy is appealed to in the existing literature. These are principally, but not exclusively economic and rely centrally on notions of mobility. Four such sources of external imperatives can be identified, each worthy of more sustained reflection.

1. *Trade.* The free mobility of goods leads to pressures to enhance economic competitiveness.
2. *Foreign direct investment.* The free mobility of investment capital (and in many accounts, already invested capital) leads to pressures to enhance and retain "locational competitiveness."
3. *Finance.* The free mobility of virtual/digital capital leads to an essentially constant audit by international investors of monetary and fiscal policies and the institutions (for instance, independent central banks) responsible for their delivery.
4. *Environment and "the global commons."* The mobility of pollutants and the global nature of "high consequence risks" (Giddens 1990)—leads to the need to pool sovereignty in institutions of effective global governance.

In what follows I consider each as a mechanism, assessing the plausibility of the assumptions and the evidential basis for both the assumptions and the consequences inferred from them to discern the likely consequences for public policy arising from each.

## 3.1 Trade Integration

Most accounts of the economic consequences of globalization start from a consideration of trade integration. Pointing to a near exponential rise in openness (conventionally expressed in terms of imports plus exports as a share of GDP) since the 1960s, they seek to derive a series of competitive imperatives for the domestic economy and domestic policy makers from heightened trade integration.

In rather stylized terms, such accounts frequently counterpose the supposedly closed national economies of the advanced liberal democracies until the 1960s and 1970s with the open integrated world economy which, they suggest, has developed subsequently. In the former, closed national economic world, competitiveness is of no great consequence, since only a relatively small proportion of GDP is traded and domestic consumption can be assumed to be satisfied by domestic production thereby facilitating a series of domestic management techniques such as Keynesianism.

Under (stylized) open economy conditions things look very different. Keynesianism is no longer effective since the injection of demand into the domestic economy will only serve to boost imports, precipitating a worsening of the balance of payments situation. More significantly still, domestic economic growth is now predicated upon success in international markets—in other words, competitiveness. Competitiveness, moreover, is frequently understood in rather narrow and cost-centered terms—the capacity to produce, distribute, and ultimately sell a given commodity in international markets for less than the competition. Consequently the imperatives of competitiveness that (global) trade integration brings tend to be seen in terms of cost-saving measures—the elimination of burdensome regulations, the reduction in non-wage labor costs (such as those out of which welfare states are funded), and the exertion of downward pressure on labor costs (by, for instance, scaling back workers' bargaining power and removing the institutional settings in which it might be exercised).

The mechanism is a clear one, lubricated by the heightened mobility of goods in a more globally integrated world market (an improvement in the aggregate terms of trade within the world economy). Yet, compelling and influential though it is, the necessity of the competitiveness-enhancing cost-saving "race to the bottom" that it predicts is not so easily reconciled with the empirical evidence. As already noted, state-related activity continues to account for a high and in fact rising share of global GDP, suggesting at minimum that in the face of such competitive imperatives public institutions funded out of taxation receipts have proved remarkably resilient. Moreover, as a growing body of literature testifies, there is a positive and indeed, strengthening relationship between public spending and economic openness—the most open economies in the world are also those, in statistical terms, with the largest public sectors (Rodrik 1996). That historical relationship (as famously revealed by Cameron 1978) shows no signs of being eroded. Finally, however high contemporary levels of trade integration are, a significant body of scholarship suggests that such levels are by no means unprecedented. Indeed, it suggests, there is still some way to go before pre-First World War levels of trade integration, at least for the world's leading economies, are exceeded (Bairoch 1996; Hirst and Thompson 1999).

The empirical evidence also suggests a number of reasons why the anticipated deregulatory "race to the bottom" is at best a simplifying distortion of a far more complex reality. First, as already noted, markets, not least those for traded goods, are far from perfectly integrated—and on balance, distortions from perfect market integration tend to serve to protect the most advanced and affluent economies (those with the largest public sectors) from competitive undercutting. Second, it is only a relatively small proportion of potentially tradeable commodities whose cost is determined to a significant extent by direct labor costs and indirect non-wage labor costs (such as payroll taxes). Consequently, the competitive undercutting predicted in the globalization thesis, even though it certainly goes on, is more confined to certain sectors of the world market than the model assumes. Third, to a very considerable extent the advanced capitalist economies compete less in terms of cost than they do in terms of the distinct qualities of the goods they export. And quality competitiveness, in contrast to cost competitiveness, is often enhanced and supported by high levels of public spending. Fourth, as already noted, regionalization tendencies that are often ignored in the overly general literature on globalization may alter significantly the real terms of competition that economies face, giving rise to rather different competitive dynamics from those assumed to drive a deregulatory race to the bottom.

## 3.2 Foreign Direct Investment

Scarcely less significant in accounts of the consequences for public policy of globalization is the role of foreign direct investment and the (assumed) mobility of international investors. The significant, indeed at times exponential growth in both the accumulated stock of invested foreign capital (total fixed capital formation) and fresh foreign direct investment is seen, in conventional accounts of globalization, to impose upon domestic policy makers a series of additional competitive imperatives. Here it is not so much the competitiveness of the domestic economy qua domestic economy that is the focus of attention (important though this is), but the "locational competitiveness" of the economy as a site for new or continued investment.

The picture created is of potentially footloose and fancy-free investors choosing from a vast array of potential investment locations the one that offers them the best anticipated return on their investment—that is, until a new and better opportunity arises elsewhere. In order to attract investors in the first place, then, governments must essentially internalize and approximate as closely as possible in terms of their exhibited policy choices the preferences of mobile capital. Those preferences, in turn, are anticipated to be for attractive investment incentives at the point of initial investment, flexible labor markets, low rates of corporate taxation, a flexible regulatory regime, and lax environmental standards. Big government and the taxation receipts out of which a generous welfare state might be funded are rendered increasingly anachronistic—a guarantee of disinvestment and economic crisis.

Equally intuitive though such a view is, it is again at some considerable odds with the available empirical evidence. A number of points might again be noted. First, the mobility of invested capital is grossly exaggerated in such stylized accounts which invariably discount the costs borne by investors of carrying through an "exit" threat to the point of disinvestment. Having invested and often built plant in a particular economy, foreign direct investors acquire a variety of generally irredeemable sunk costs. For, to relocate production is, essentially, to sacrifice the lion's share of the capital value of the initial investment (assuming no new investor is prepared to take the place of the old), whilst bearing the significant costs of building and equipping new plant, to say nothing of the intervening period of non-production. For this reason, whilst it may well be rational for hypothetically mobile investors to threaten "exit" whenever they wish to bargain for concessions and/or changes in policy from their host government, it is seldom in their interests to exercise their hypothetical mobility even in the absence of such concessions. This is presumably why it is that the much-vaunted exit option is in fact rather less frequently exercised than the model of free capital mobility would predict.[9] Second, there is quite simply no inverse relationship, such as the model would lead us to anticipate, between volumes of inbound foreign direct investment and levels of corporate taxation, environmental and labor market regulations, generosity of welfare benefits, or state expenditure as a share of GDP.[10] This would merely seem to underline the point of the previous section that competitive advantage is not necessarily secured by cost minimization strategies. Finally, as is again now well documented, the vast majority of the world's outward foreign direct investment (over 90 per cent between 1980 and 1995) is sourced from within the so-called "triad" (of North America, Europe, and Pacific Asia) and the vast majority (between 75–80 per cent over the same period) of inward foreign direct investment is invested within the triad (Brewer and Young 1998, tables 2.7, 2.8; Hay 2004, fig. 7). This staggering concentration of foreign direct investment is hardly consistent with the predictions of the simple globalization model, a point reinforced by the observation that the most significant factor determining investment location is not the availability of investment incentives but geographical proximity and access to a sizeable market (Cooke and Noble 1998).

[9] It may, of course, be that the emphasis here on "exit" in much of the literature, radical and skeptic alike, is misplaced or at least exaggerated. For multinational firms, and many such firms now exist, there is no need to exercise exit nor is there often a need to build new plant whenever disinvestment occurs. Such firms, with multiple production sites, can simply juggle production volumes between locations, bargaining with local jurisdiction for policy concessions which might increase the likelihood of them expanding capacity in a particular location. I am indebted to Mick Moran for pointing this out to me.

[10] See Cooke and Noble 1998; Pfaller et al. 1991; Traxler and Woitech 2000; Wilensky 2002; and see also Hay 2005 for a fuller assessment of the empirical evidence.

## 3.3 Financial Market Integration

The third in the triumvirate of sources of external economic constraints on public policy comes from the anticipated consequences of financial market integration. Once again, the assumption in much of the literature is of perfectly clearing and fully integrated global markets—here financial markets, with near instantaneous invest-ment decisions lubricated by new digital technologies operating in an effectively post-geographical environment (O'Brien 1992).[11] In such a context, vast financial resources can be unleashed by institutional investors in speculative attacks on the currencies of states incurring the investors' displeasure. Sterling's forcible ejection from the European Monetary System (EMS) at the hands of George Soros and others is a classic case in point. Within such models, portfolio investors, in particular, are seen to display a clear interest in, and preference for, strong and stable currencies backed both by implacable independent central banks with hawkish anti-inflationary credentials and governments wedded in theory and in practice to fiscal moderation and prudence. Any departure from this new financial orthodoxy, it is assumed, will precipitate a flurry of speculation against the currency and a haemorrhaging of investment from assets denominated in that currency. Governments provoke the wrath of the financial markets at their peril.

Once again, this is a familiar and intuitively plausible proposition that would seem to be borne out by a series of high-profile speculative flurries against "rogue" governments in recent decades. It is, however, an empirical claim and one that a growing body of scholarship reveals to be considerably at odds with the empirical evidence. For capital markets do not seem to be as perfectly integrated as the globalization literature invariably assumes. In particular, the anticipated convergence in interest rates which one would expect from a fully integrated global capital market is simply not exhibited (Hirst and Thompson 1999; Zevin 1992). Moreover, financial integration has also failed to produce the anticipated divergence between rates of domestic savings and rates of domestic investment which one would expect in a fully integrated global capital market—the so-called "Feldstein–Horioka puzzle" (Feld-stein and Horioka 1980; see also Epstein 1996, 212–15; Watson 2001a). Finally, though the liberalization of financial markets has certainly increased the speed, severity, and significance of investors' reactions to government policy, capital market participants appear far less discriminating or well informed in their political risk assessment than is conventionally assumed (Mosley 2003; Swank 2002). Consequently, policy makers may retain rather more autonomy than is widely accepted. Speculative dynamics, it seems, are in fact relatively rarely unleashed against currencies and, at least as far as the advanced liberal democracies are concerned, the range of government policies

[11] This is, of course, to adopt a wholly undifferentiated and correspondingly problematic conception of "financial markets"—a term which can and should be disaggregated. Such a generic category in fact hides very significant variations, for instance between the instrument trading that characterizes foreign exchange markets and the altogether more locationally immobile provision of commercial services like corporate law. The point is, however, that in the somewhat stylized accounts which dominate the existing literature on globalization's impact on public policy, such disaggregation is exceptionally rare (though see, for instance, Mosley 2003; Watson 2001b).

considered by market participants in making investment decisions is, in fact, extremely limited. As Mosley explains:

Governments are pressured strongly to satisfy financial market preferences in terms of overall inflation and government budget deficit levels but retain domestic policymaking latitude in other areas. The means by which governments achieve macropolicy outcomes, and the nature of government policies in other areas, do not concern financial market participants ... [G]overnments retain a significant amount of policy autonomy and political accountability. If, for domestic reasons, they prefer to retain traditional social democratic policies, for instance, they are quite able to do so. (2002, 305)

This important finding is further reinforced by other recent work. On the basis of a detailed statistical analysis, Swank demonstrates that, contrary to the prevailing consensus, "rises in international capital openness, or exposure to international capital markets, do not exert significant downward pressure on the welfare state at moderate levels of budget imbalance [and] when budget deficits don't exist, some expansion of social protection is possible even in the context of international capital mobility" (2002, 94).

Financial markets, it seems, are neither as highly integrated as we are accustomed to thinking, nor as exacting in the audit of fiscal and monetary policy they are frequently assumed to engage in.

## 3.4 Environmental Degradation

Thus far we have focused almost exclusively upon mechanisms identifying *economic* globalization as the key contemporary constraint on public policy-making autonomy. We have also questioned, in so doing, the extent to which contemporary economic trends are well captured by the term globalization. Yet at least equally compelling is a rather more political mechanism which refers unequivocally to issues that are genuinely global in their scope and scale. Strictly speaking this does not so much point to the diminished capacity of public policy makers in an era of globalization, as to the globalization of the problems with which such policy makers are confronted—and their inability to date to deal with such problems.

The classic example here is the problem of high-consequence global environmental risks (Giddens 1990). This is well expressed in the so-called "tragedy of the commons" first identified by Garrett Hardin (1968). Hardin provides an intuitively plausible and all too compelling model of the seemingly intractable problem of environmental degradation in contemporary societies (for a useful extension and updating of Hardin's pioneering work, see Gardiner 2004). The systematic exploitation and pollution of the environment, it is argued, is set to continue since individual corporations and states, despite a clear collective interest, choose not to impose upon themselves the costs of unilateral environmental action. Their logic is entirely rational, though potentially catastrophic in its cumulative consequences. Such actors know that environmental regulation is costly and, particularly in an open international economy, a burden on competitiveness. Accordingly, in the absence of an international agency capable of enforcing the compliance of all states and all corporations, the anticipation of free-riding is sufficient to ensure that corporations and states do not burden themselves with additional costs and taxes. The long-term effects for the environment are all too obvious, preventing as it does a global solution to a genuinely global problem.

The extent to which the narrowly perceived self-interest of states and governments can subvert the development of effective mechanisms and institutions of global governance is well evidenced by the Bush administration's withdrawal from the 1997 Kyoto Protocol (committing signatories to staged reductions in greenhouse gas emissions); and for its critics, by the fact that such a protocol, even if fully implemented, would only serve to reduce slightly the pace of an ongoing process of environmental degradation.

This is a most important example, and a number of broader implications might be drawn from it. First, the "tragedy of the commons" is indicative of a more general disparity between the need for and supply of effective institutions and mechanisms of global public policy. For whilst it is easy to point to genuinely global problems requiring for their resolution coordinated global responses, it is far more difficult to find examples of the latter. Second, whilst the proliferation of genuinely global political problems does point to the incapacity of a system of sovereign states (capable of exercising veto power) to deal with the challenges it now faces, it does not indicate any particular incapacity of domestic public policy to deal with the problems and issues it has always dealt with. This is, then, less a story of a loss of capacity than of the proliferation of issues which domestic policy makers have never had the capacity to deal with. Finally and rather perversely, the disparity between the need for and supply of global solutions to global problems is merely exacerbated by economic globalization. For this has served to drive states, at pain of economic crisis, to elevate considerations of competitiveness over all other concerns, including environmental protection. There is a clear and obvious danger that the narrow pursuit of short-term economic advantage will come at the long-term price of a looming environmental, economic, and political catastrophe.

# 4. Conclusion: From Globalization versus Public Policy to Global Public Policy

I began this chapter by pointing to the pervasiveness in the existing literature of a significant tension between globalization and public policy—such that the extent of globalization is seen as a simple index of the degree of the loss of autonomy of (domestic) public policy makers. In the preceding sections, I have sought to demonstrate that however influential this trade-off is seen to be, it is deeply problematic—both theoretically and empirically. Whether globalization is occurring or not depends both on how exacting a definitional standard one imposes and where one looks to gather evidence. Moreover, in seeking to discern the space for public policy in a more globally integrated environment, the characteristically amorphous and vaguely specified concept of globalization obscures as much as it reveals. For as I have sought to demonstrate, the challenges that public policy makers face from, say, processes of economic integration are specific to the contexts in which those policy makers are located. Overly aggregated and general accounts of globalization can only fail to capture and reflect that specificity; as such, they distort significantly the constraints faced by public policy makers today.

This is an important point, for it reminds us again of the significance of semantics. Whether globalization is happening or not depends on what the term is taken to imply. It has been the argument of this chapter that if we are to develop more complex and differentiated accounts of the various external constraints and challenges (economic and otherwise) that public policy makers face today we need to move beyond the amorphous and anecdotal appeal to terms like globalization. This entails a rather more exacting definitional standard—one that sharpens rather than blunts the analyst's descriptive vocabulary and one that leaves us capable of differentiating, for instance, between globalization and regionalization. If the preceding analysis seems unremittingly skeptical of the globalization thesis, then this is at least in part because of this insistence on a rather more demanding and empirically operationalizable conception of globalization than is often the case in the existing literature. Yet we should not let the appeal to semantic differences blind us to the still very significant differences in interpretations of the constraints imposed on public policy makers in an ever-more interdependent international environment. Even if we settle our semantic differences, there is plenty of scope for controversy.

Yet even if this is accepted, there is a certain danger that we confine ourselves to a consideration of the degree of autonomy of domestic policy makers in an era of complex interdependence or globalization. The casualty in this is an adequate consideration of transnational public policy. For arguably, and as the final section of this chapter hopefully serves to demonstrate, the greatest challenges to public policy today do not come from internalizing domestically the competitive imperatives unleashed by economic globalization. Rather they lie in developing the global and transnational policy-making capacity to deal collectively with the environmental and other consequences of processes of complex economic integration (for an exemplary discussion of the extent to which this has already been achieved within the area of business regulation, see Braithwaite and Drahos 2000). Far too much of the literature to date on globalization and public policy has presented the latter, often in narrowly domestic terms, as a casualty of the former. It is surely now time to re-present and project public policy onto a global stage, as having the potential to hold the process of globalization to account—both publicly and democratically.

# References

BAIROCH, P. 1996. Globalisation myths and realities: one century of external trade and foreign investment. Pp. 173–92 in *States against Market: The Limits of Globalisation*, ed. R. Boyer and D. Drache. London: Routledge.

BERGER, S., and DORE, R. (eds.) 1996. *National Diversity and Global Capitalism*. Ithaca, NY: Cornell University Press.

BERMAN, S., and McNAMARA, K. R. 1999. Bank on democracy: why central banks need public oversight. *Foreign Affairs*, 7: 2–8.

BRAITHWAITE, J., and DRAHOS, P. 2000. *Global Business Regulation*. Cambridge: Cambridge University Press.

BREWER, T. L., and YOUNG, S. 1998. *The Multilateral Investment System and Multinational Enterprises*. Oxford: Oxford University Press.

CAMERON, D. R. 1978. The expansion of the public economy: a comparative analysis. *American Political Science Review*, 72 (4): 1243–61.

COOKE, W. N., and NOBLE, D. S. 1998. Industrial relations systems and US foreign direct investment abroad. *British Journal of Industrial Relations*, 36 (4): 581–609.

DALTON, R. J. 2004. *Democratic Challenges, Democratic Choices: The Erosion of Political Support in Advanced Industrial Democracies*. Oxford: Oxford University Press.

—— and WATTENBERG, M. P. (eds.) 2000. *Parties without Partisans: Political Change in Advanced Industrial Democracies*. Oxford: Oxford University Press.

EPSTEIN, G. 1996. International capital mobility and the scope for national economic management. Pp. 211–24 in *States against Market: The Limits of Globalisation*, ed. R. Boyer and D. Drache. London: Routledge.

FELDSTEIN, M., and HORIOKA, C. 1980. Domestic savings and international capital flows. *Economic Journal*, 90: 201–20.

FRANKEL, J. A. 1997. *Regional Trading Blocs: In the World Economic System*. Washington, DC: Institute for International Economics.

GARDINER, S. M. 2004. Survey article: ethics and global climate change. *Ethics*, 114 (3): 555–600.

GARRETT, G. 1998. *Partisan Politics in the Global Economy*. Cambridge: Cambridge University Press.

—— 2001. Globalization and government spending around the world. *Studies in Comparative International Development*, 35 (4): 3–29.

GIDDENS, A. 1990. *The Consequences of Modernity*. Cambridge: Polity Press.

—— 1999. *The Runaway World*. London: Profile.

GOODIN, R. E. 2003. Globalising justice. Pp. 68–92 in *Taming Globalisation: Frontiers of Governance*, ed. D. Held and M. Koenig-Archibugi. Cambridge: Polity Press.

GRAY, J. 1998. *False Dawn: The Delusions of Global Capitalism*. London: Granta.

HALL, P. A., and SOSKICE, D. (eds.) 2001. *Varieties of Capitalism*. Oxford: Oxford University Press.

HARDIN, G. 1968. The tragedy of the commons. *Science*, 162: 1243–8.

HAY, C. 2004. Common trajectories, variable paces, divergent outcomes? Models of European capitalism under conditions of complex economic interdependence. *Review of International Political Economy*, 11 (2): 235–62.

—— 2005. Globalisation's impact on states. Pp. 235–62 in *Global Political Economy*, ed. J. Ravenhill. Oxford: Oxford University Press.

—— and MARSH, D. 2000. Introduction: demystifying globalisation. In *Demystifying Globalisation*, ed. C. Hay and D. Marsh. Basingstoke: Palgrave.

HAY, C. and WATSON, M. 1999. Globalisation: "sceptical" notes on the 1999 Reith Lectures. *Political Quarterly*, 70 (4): 418–25.

HIRST, P., and THOMPSON, G. 1999. *Globalisation in Question*, 2nd edn. Cambridge: Polity Press.

MARQUAND, D. 2004. *Decline of the Public*. Cambridge: Polity Press.

MOSLEY, L. 2003. *Global Capital and National Governments*. Cambridge: Cambridge University Press.

O'BRIEN, R. 1992. *Global Financial Integration: The End of Geography*. London: Royal Institute for International Affairs.

PERRATON, J., GOLDBLATT, D., HELD, D., and MCGREW, A. 1997. The globalisation of economic activity. *New Political Economy*, 2 (2): 257–78.

PFALLER, A., GOUGH, I., and THERBORN, G. (eds.) 1991. *Can the Welfare State Compete? A Comparative Study of Five Advanced Capitalist Countries*. London: Macmillan.

RODRIK, D. 1996. Why do more open economies have bigger governments? NBER Working Paper No. 5537. Cambridge, Mass.: National Bureau of Economic Research.

ROGOWSKI, R. 1989. *Commerce and Coalitions*. Princeton, NJ: Princeton University Press.

SWANK, D. 2002. *Global Capital, Political Institutions and Policy Change in Developed Welfare States*. Cambridge: Cambridge University Press.

TRAXLER, F., and WOITECH, B. 2000. Transnational investment and national labour market regimes: a case of "regime shopping?" *European Journal of Industrial Relations*, 6 (2): 141–59.

WATSON, M. 2001a. International capital mobility in an era of globalisation: adding a political dimension to the "Feldstein–Horioka Puzzle." *Politics*, 21 (2): 81–92.

—— 2001b. Embedding the "new economy" in Europe: a study of the institutional specificities of knowledge-based growth. *Economy and Society*, 30 (4): 504–23.

WEISS, L. 1998. *The Myth of the Powerless State: Governing the Economy in a Global Era*. Cambridge: Polity Press.

WILENSKY, H. L. 2002. *Rich Democracies: Political Economy, Public Policy and Performance*. Berkeley: University of California Press.

ZEVIN, R. 1992. Are world financial markets more open? If so, why and with what effects? Pp. 43–83 in *Financial Openness and National Autonomy: Opportunities and Constraints*, ed. T. Banuri and J. B. Schor. Oxford: Oxford University Press.

# PART VII

........................................................................

# POLICY INTERVENTION
## STYLES AND RATIONALES

........................................................................

CHAPTER 30

# DISTRIBUTIVE AND REDISTRIBUTIVE POLICY

## TOM SEFTON

## 1. INTRODUCTION

Whenever a government pursues a course of action towards a specific goal, there will inevitably be winners and losers, even if these distributional effects are unintended. In this broadest sense, virtually all government policy can be termed redistributive (Tullock 1997). But for the purposes of this chapter, the focus is on social and welfare[1] policies, where the redistributive motive is most prominent (Hills 2004). Most of the literature in this area is concerned with taxation and spending on cash transfers or in-kind services, though "legal welfare," such as minimum wage legislation, can also have significant distributional effects.

Social and welfare policies are often assessed as if their only purpose were to redistribute from rich to poor. If so, the effectiveness of welfare systems as a whole could be assessed by looking at their impact on overall inequality and poverty. Similarly, in assessing a particular policy or program, the crucial question would be which income groups benefit most. In common with most of the literature on redistributive policy, this chapter is largely concerned with these two types of question.

* I am grateful to the ESRC for funding for part of his time preparing this chapter and to the editors and to John Hills for very helpful suggestions and comments on an earlier draft.

[1] The word "welfare" is used here in the broader sense of social welfare policies, including cash and in-kind transfers from government, not just in the narrower sense often applied in the USA referring only to assistance for certain poor groups. Similarly "social security" refers to all cash transfer programs, not just those for the elderly.

However, it is also important to recognize that redistribution from rich to poor is only one of several dimensions along which redistribution may occur and further-more, that policies with redistributive effects may have dominant objectives other than redistribution. These issues are discussed briefly in the next section along with some of the implications for the analysis of redistributive policy.

In understanding empirical analysis of the redistributive effects of policy, it is also important to realize that this will entail an (often implicit) comparison with a counterfactual world where the policy was not applied. The use of different counter-factuals will change the results. One important aspect of this is that if one is looking at the impact of government spending, one usually has to ask which taxes would be lower in its absence. The answer may be crucial, but not obvious. But beyond this, many other aspects of behaviour may change too: without social insurance systems covering health care, individuals would make more use of private health insurance, with many knock-on effects through the economy. What economists call the "final incidence" of a tax or spending item is very difficult to measure, but cannot be assumed simply to equal the "first round" measurement of who administratively is the recipient or liable (Pechman and Okner 1974).

## 2. ALTERNATIVE FORMS OF REDISTRIBUTION

Low incomes are not the only reason for receiving cash benefits or services in kind. Many welfare policies provide insurance against adverse risks, such as unemploy-ment or ill health, and provide a mechanism for smoothing income over the life cycle—what Barr (2001) refers to as the "Piggy Bank" function. This has received relatively little attention in the literature compared with the "Robin Hood" function (i.e. redistribution from rich to poor), but is arguably as, if not more important. Barry (1990) argues that whilst there is no reason for expecting the welfare state to have a single rationale, if it is to be identified with one objective, it is that of income *maintenance* rather than the relief of poverty.

This has several implications for analysis of redistributive policy. First, a snapshot picture of redistribution can be misleading. Education goes disproportionately on the young, health care and pensions on the old, while the taxes that finance them come mostly from the working generation. Much of the redistribution that appears to be taking place at a given point in time will be canceled out over people's lifetimes. According to Hills and Falkingham (1995), between two-thirds and three-quarters of welfare state spending in the UK in the 1980s and 1990s was life-cycle redistribu-tion—redistribution of individuals' own lifetime incomes across different stages in their own lives, as opposed to redistribution between the "lifetime rich" and "lifetime poor."

Secondly, it may not always be appropriate to judge a particular benefit or service according to whether it benefits the poor more than the rich. Many public health care systems, whether social insurance based or tax funded, seek to provide equal treatment for equal need: as such, they are primarily designed to achieve horizontal redistribution between people with similar incomes, but different medical needs, as opposed to vertical redistribution between people with different incomes, but similar medical needs. Similarly, certain social welfare policies are designed to provide for the extra needs of families with children, to meet the additional costs incurred by disabled people, or to help counter the effect of other forms of disadvantage relating to age or race, for example. The key distributional question in these cases is whether the benefits people receive match their respective needs, irrespective of whether they are rich or poor—or possibly whether they compound disadvantage. Studies of the distributional effects of programs or policies may therefore emphasize the impact on different ethnic groups, age and/or gender groups, geographic areas, or some other relevant breakdown of the population, rather than, or as well as the impact on different income groups (Danziger and Portney 1988).

Nonetheless, even policies that are not primarily designed to redistribute from rich to poor can have a significant redistributional impact for a variety of reasons. Lower socioeconomic groups generally face a greater risk of experiencing the adverse events that social insurance schemes are designed to protect them against: they are more likely to experience extended spells of unemployment, to suffer ill health, or to be injured at work (Burchardt and Hills 1996; Ferrarini and Nelson 2003). Thus, even if all citizens were to participate in these schemes on equal terms (though as we see later on, social insurance schemes and universal public services almost invariably incorporate progressive elements), they would still involve redistribution from higher- to lower-income groups.

Furthermore, poverty alleviation is a *byproduct* of a "well-ordered" welfare state, even if that is not the primary objective of most of the individual policies that make up that system (Barry 1990). In a welfare state that provides a continuing income (above the poverty line) for the unemployed, the sick or disabled, and the retired; that provides an income for those not expected to work because they are looking after young children or adults who need constant care; that offers a universal child benefit set at a level sufficient to meet the costs of raising children; and that covers special expenses associated with personal misfortune, almost all the job of relieving poverty will be done by policies whose rationale is in fact quite different.

Thus, at the very least, redistribution from rich to poor is an important side effect or secondary objective of many social and welfare policies and collectively, they should ideally ensure that poverty is kept to a minimum, even if that is not their primary motivation. On this basis, it is often important to assess such policies in terms of their redistributive impact.

# 3. OTHER AIMS

Two further points should be borne in mind in reading this chapter. First, redistribution is not only about redistributing incomes, but also about redistributing opportunities: access to better education, better job opportunities, and better health that may lead to greater equality in incomes in the long term, as well as being an end in themselves. The appropriate balance between more traditional tax-transfer forms of redistribution and what has been variously termed an "equal opportunity" or "active" welfare state has been the subject of a long-running debate among policy makers and academics (e.g. Haveman 1988; HM Treasury 1999). Most countries still rely mostly on the former to achieve their distributional objectives, but have over time attempted to shift the balance more towards the latter.

Secondly, social spending and taxation are not only (or even primarily) about redistribution in whatever form and therefore, should not be judged solely against this criterion. In particular, there is an efficiency, as well as an equity function to the welfare state. Even if all poverty could be eliminated, there would still be a need for institutions to enable people to insure themselves and to provide important services, such as health care and education. Uncertainty and other forms of imperfect information on the part of insurers mean that important areas of private insurance are likely to be inefficient or non-existent and external benefits may also mean that certain goods or services would be under-provided in a free market. In cases where market failure is costly and government is effective, state intervention can increase efficiency (Barr 2001).

Browning (1975), however, challenges the presumption that in-kind transfers are necessarily more efficient than cash transfers as a method of redistribution whenever there are external benefits associated with the consumption of particular goods. More generally, economists often maintain that the market system is a superior mechanism for allocating resources as there will always be a way of combining the price system (to achieve efficiency) with lump-sum transfers (to achieve distributional objectives). But as Weitzman (1977) points out, this is typically not very useful for policy prescriptions, because the necessary transfers are almost never paid. Furthermore, Arrow (1963) uses the example of the medical care industry to show that in some cases market conditions deviate markedly from those under which the "competitive model" (or free market) can be assumed to produce an efficient allocation of resources.

Another rationale for the in-kind provision of certain goods or services is that taxpayers have an altruistic, but paternalistic concern for the welfare of others; they may be prepared to pay for some kind of redistribution to the poor, but only if it takes the form of providing them with specific services, such as health care, food stamps, or subsidized housing (Le Grand 1982). This is sometimes referred to as the "merit good" argument. Similarly, Weitzman (1977) discusses a particular class of good or service, such as housing, whose just distribution to those having the greatest need for them might be viewed by society as a desirable end in itself. Tobin (1970) refers to this as "specific egalitarianism:" the view that certain commodities should be distributed more evenly than the ability to pay for them. Weitzman argues that the price mechanism of the market will be comparatively less effective in achieving an appropriate distribution of these goods (compared with a crude form of state rationing) when income inequality is relatively high, because those with larger incomes will tend to monopolize consumption of the goods in question.

Whilst these principles help to differentiate between in-kind and cash provision on "efficiency" or other grounds, the patterns of provision observed in different countries are also likely to be strongly influenced by historical circumstances and the power of different actors in the policy process.

# 4. Approaches to Redistributive Policy

Esping-Andersen (1990) provides a useful, though contested typology of welfare states with distinct approaches to redistribution, based on a broader conceptualization of the welfare state which recognizes that the level of social expenditure does not necessarily provide an accurate indication of a state's redistributive effort. This sets redistributive policy into an institutional context, helping to explain the political and economic values that underlie different welfare states. In the context of this chapter, the focus is on the notion of equity that underlies these welfare regimes and how this is reflected in different approaches to redistributive policy.

*Liberal welfare regimes* look to the market as their primary source of "welfare." The main role of the state is to ensure the smooth operation of the market, implying a minimalist role for redistributive policy. The state assumes responsibility only when the family or the market fails and seeks to limit its commitments to providing a safety net for marginal and deserving groups. Entitlement rules should be strict, and benefit levels modest and time limited so as not to crowd out private provision or charity, whilst guarding against the danger of cultivating a dependency culture.

*Social democratic welfare regimes* give a much more prominent role to redistributive policy. Unlike the liberal regime, the underlying assumption is that the outcomes of unfettered capitalism are unfair and, therefore, social democrats are much more prepared to manipulate the market economy to social ends (e.g. via strong employment protection and minimum wage legislation) even at some cost to overall productivity. Redistribution is also to be achieved by taking certain goods and services, such as health, education, and housing out of the capitalist realm and ensuring they are distributed more equally than income or wealth ("decommodification"). Entitlement to certain state benefits is seen as part of the "rights of citizenship" and insurance systems are usually broad and universal. Benefits are typically graduated in proportion to accustomed earnings in order to ensure high replacement rates, even for relatively high earners. Since state services and benefits are tailored to the expectations of middle-income groups, the market is largely crowded out of the welfare sector.

*Corporatist welfare regimes* seek to preserve the existing order and the patterns of distribution within it, in contrast to the social democratic state's explicit attempt to alter the distribution between rich and poor. The corporatist approach to welfare relies on mutual aid to take care of those who fall upon hard times. Social programs are generous, but are funded largely by contributions made over recipients' own working lives. Social entitlements derive principally from employment rather than citizenship (as in the social democratic model) or proven need (as in the classic liberal model). The primary role of the state is to underwrite and facilitate group-based schemes of insurance and arrange residual insurance pools for those who are not part of an established occupational group. The state's emphasis on upholding status differentials dampens its distributional impact (over complete lifetimes, at least), though most corporatist systems contain some weakly redistributive elements.

Such differences are not only seen in the structures that emerged between different nations' welfare regimes in the third quarter of the twentieth century, but also in their responses to fiscal pressures at the end of the century. Such pressures—from aging and slower growth—may have been greater in the more extensive social democratic or corporatist regimes, but so was their political entrenchment, leading to varied responses (Pierson 2001).

Esping-Andersen and others have attempted to classify countries into one of these three regimes, using a whole range of indicators. In practice, few countries match these descriptions in every respect, though most countries tend towards one or other of them. The USA is the clearest example of a liberal welfare regime, the Scandinavian countries come closest to the social democratic model, and the continental European countries, including France, Germany, and Italy, are commonly cited as examples of corporatist regimes.

## 4.1 Universal versus Targeted Welfare

One of the key distinctions between the liberal and social democratic regimes is that the former favors targeted welfare on the poor, whereas the latter favors universal provision of welfare. In practice, however, all welfare states contain a mixture of targeted and universal welfare provision.

"Universalists" advance many reasons for regarding the targeting of welfare as bad policy. Means testing often involves an intrusive enquiry into people's personal and financial circumstances; it can stigmatize the recipients and may be socially divisive; targeted welfare payments may tend to become less generous to the poor over time, because they generally command less political support than universal programs; many of those in need may miss out, because need is often difficult to identify; non-take-up is a greater problem with means-tested benefits, in part because of the stigma or time cost attached to claiming these benefits; means-tested benefits are generally more difficult and expensive to administer; means testing can create a "poverty trap," because benefits are withdrawn as incomes rise; and, since means tests only make sense when applied to the family, they run counter to the desire to have a social security system that promotes greater independence for women (Atkinson 1983, 1993, 1995, part III; Cornia and Stewart 1995).

Supporters of more targeted welfare argue that it is a more efficient way of combating poverty and can be equally effective. By definition, a greater proportion of any expenditure goes towards helping those below the poverty line. Social transfers impose costs on the economy, which are minimized through better targeting. They also dispute or downplay some of the arguments against means testing. Mitchell, Harding, and Gruen (1994), for example, have argued that a well-designed means test need not be stigmatizing; that non-take-up is generally greatest among those entitled to only small amounts; and that the disincentive effects generated by means testing may not be as great as might be thought.

## 4.2 The Efficiency–Equity Trade-off

Another key distinction between liberal and other welfare regimes is that they are more concerned about the potential trade-off between equity and economic efficiency. The principal idea behind the neoclassical critique of the welfare state is that social programs with high replacement rates constitute a powerful disincentive for people to work and to save for old age or insure against other adverse events. These disincentives are expected to reduce employment rates and increase welfare dependency, which are in turn a drag on economic growth (cf. Goodin et al. 1999). At the same time, greater income inequality is a spur to economic growth, because it rewards innovation and effort and increases savings and investment as those with higher incomes tend to save a larger share of their income (see, for example, Welch 1999).

On the other hand, there are theoretical arguments for why greater equality may be good for economic growth. Higher tax rates can increase work effort if there is a large enough "income effect," whereby individuals have to work harder to achieve a given level of post-tax income. Some economists also argue that more equal pay can help to suppress unwanted (but unobservable) uncooperative behaviour at work, such as shirking. More generally, Haveman (1988) argues that the redistribution system reduces economic insecurity and uncertainty, increases economic stability, and facilitates economic change and the production of human capital. As he puts it, each of us feels better knowing we live in a society which protects the weak and moderates the extremes in income and economic power that accompany the operation of free markets. Though harder to quantify, these efficiency gains need to be set against the economic losses generated by any adverse incentives and distortions that the redistribution system creates.

Whilst it is a commonplace contention that high taxes and generous transfers produce work disincentives, a comprehensive review of research on Denmark, Sweden, Germany, and the UK demonstrates that the empirical evidence is much more mixed (Atkinson and Mogensen 1993). Generous early retirement pensions do appear to induce early exit from the labour market; otherwise, the negative effects on labour supply are generally small or insignificant and positive effects are not infrequent for some subgroups such as prime age men. Moreover, findings for one country do not necessarily hold for another, so it is hard to generalize.

Empirical evidence on the relationship between inequality and growth is also inconclusive. Some studies find that countries with more inequality tend to have slower rates of economic growth, whilst others find precisely the opposite, depending on the countries included in the study, the period covered, and the methodology used. Kenworthy (2004), for example, carries out a cross-country analysis and a cross-state analysis (for the USA) and shows that in both cases there is a possible negative effect of inequality on growth, but that the association is weak at best and very sensitive to one or two outliers. He concludes that "although there is surely a point at which the distribution of income might be too egalitarian to be compatible with desirable rates of economic growth, the experience of the past two decades suggests that such a point has yet to be reached." Particular institutions or policies may have growth-impeding effects, but there is no evidence of a general equity–efficiency trade-off over this period.

Similarly Atkinson reviews ten econometric studies of the relationship between the level of social spending in different countries and their economic performance. For comparability, he takes the results of each study to produce its prediction of what would be implied for a country's rate of economic growth if its social spending was smaller as a share of GDP. Four of the studies fitted suggestions that a smaller welfare state would be associated with faster growth. But two found no significant relationship, and four suggested that growth would be *slower* if social spending were reduced. He concludes, "studies of the aggregate relationship between economic performance and the size of the welfare state do not yield conclusive evidence" (Atkinson 1999, 84). The question itself may not be the right one to ask—instead we should be looking at the structure and design of the components of social spending: some may have positive effects on economic performance, for instance education and training; others may have negative effects, for instance because of damaging incentive effects.

# 5. EFFECTIVENESS OF REDISTRIBUTIVE POLICY

The effectiveness of redistributive policy can be examined on two levels: macro-level comparisons of different welfare regimes across countries and micro-level analyses of individual social policies and programs within countries. These two strands of literature are discussed in turn.

## 5.1 Cross-country Comparisons

The effectiveness of different welfare regimes is usually judged in terms of their impact on inequality and poverty, though some of these analyses also take into account other criteria, such as economic efficiency.

Smeeding (2004) compares the level of inequality before and after taxes and benefits in thirteen OECD countries using the most recent data from the Luxembourg Income Study for 2000 (or the mid–late 1990s for some countries). His analysis shows that the high-spending countries in northern and central Europe and Scandinavia have the greatest impact on inequality—a reduction of between 40 and 48 per cent in the Gini coefficient. The Anglo-Saxon nations, excluding the USA, are next with reductions of 24 to 31 per cent; the USA with an 18 per cent reduction is the lowest of the rich OECD nations.

The anti-poverty effect of taxes and transfers shows a similar pattern. In all countries, taxes and transfers reduce income poverty, but the reduction is greater in both absolute and proportional terms in countries with high levels of social spending (as in Scandinavia and northern Europe) or more careful targeting of government transfers on the poor (as in Canada, for example). The USA shows the least anti-poverty effect of these countries—poverty is reduced by 28 per cent in 2000 (from 23.7 to 17.0 per cent), compared to an average reduction of more than 60 per cent for the eight countries included in this analysis.

The Dutch welfare regime—used in Goodin et al. (1999) as an "imperfect" example of a social democratic regime—is also more effective at reducing the length and recurrence of poverty spells through its public transfer program, as well as minimizing the number of such spells in the first place. On an annual basis, around 18 per cent of the US population were poor, whereas it was less than a third of that in the Netherlands (during the late 1980s and early 1990s). These differences are even greater when looked at over an extended time period. Dutch poverty rates dropped to around 1 per cent if incomes are averaged over a five-year period, whereas American rates remained at around 15 per cent. The US welfare regime has no impact (or even a slightly negative one) on working age households. The only sort of poverty the US regime helps to alleviate is among the elderly—and it removes only about half of that, compared to around 90 per cent in Germany and the Netherlands.

Hicks and Kenworthy (2003) use regression analysis to examine the relationship between the characteristics of welfare regimes and various outcome measures, including redistribution. They find that those characteristics associated with "progressive liberalism" (which broadly equates to Esping-Andersen's social democratic model) have a strong and positive effect on inequality and poverty reduction. The estimates for "traditional conservatism" (which broadly equates to Esping-Andersen's corporatist model) are also positive in both cases, but the impact on inequality is not statistically significant and its impact in reducing poverty is weaker than that of progressive liberalism.

## 5.2  Paradox of Redistribution

Contrary to common wisdom, it is now well established that systems which target narrowly to the most needy generally perform rather badly in terms of redistribution or poverty alleviation (Esping-Andersen 1996). Korpi and Palme (1998) called this the "paradox of redistribution:" the more benefits are targeted at the poor, the less likely this is to reduce poverty and inequality. While a targeted program may have greater redistributive effects per unit of money spent, other factors are likely to make universalistic programs more redistributive.

Korpi and Palme put forward several explanations for this counter-intuitive finding. First, an emphasis on targeting may over time undermine broad-based support for social security, because it largely benefits the politically weak poor, and may therefore lead to lower levels of social security expenditure and ultimately to more, not less inequality. Second, the institutional welfare state may "crowd out" even more inegalitarian private alternatives. This might explain, for example, why the lowest inequality in the incomes of older people occurs in the four countries with the most unequal public pensions—Finland, Sweden, Norway, and Germany. Third, most earnings-related social insurance programs have some, often a strong element of redistribution built into them. In a "pure" earnings-related scheme, contributions and benefits are both proportional to earnings, but in practice most schemes have a "floor" below which benefits are not allowed to fall and a "ceiling" above which the percentage of earnings replaced is gradually reduced, favouring lower earners.

Goodin et al. (1999) offer a slightly different explanation for why liberal welfare regimes are less effective at combating poverty. While liberals want their welfare state to help the poor and only the poor, they also want it to do so efficiently and at least cost to overall macroeconomic performance. This "big trade-off" causes them to temper their pursuit of poverty alleviation. Whereas social democratic welfare regimes "err on the side of kindness," the liberal US system is "lean and mean." US welfare programmes are over-tightly targeted, so many poor people receive less than they need and a substantial proportion do not receive any transfer payments.

## 5.3  Caveats

In summary, the evidence strongly suggests that comprehensive, universalistic, and more generous welfare states of the Scandinavian type are considerably more egalitarian in outcome than others. By contrast, the same studies invariably show that the USA, and to a lesser extent other more "liberal" regimes, perform relatively poorly in terms of reducing inequality or poverty compared to other OECD countries. However, there are several caveats which need to be borne in mind.

First, even in the USA, the tax-transfer system has been a powerful instrument for reducing poverty and inequality. Absolute poverty (as measured by the official US poverty line) was between 40 and 60 per cent lower in the mid- to late 1980s than it would have been in the absence of government transfers (Haveman 1988; Danziger 1988). Federal taxes are also progressive, though only mildly so (Pechman and Mazur 1984; Haveman 1988). In a historical context, the period 1960–80 saw the US government transformed from a traditional defense–transportation–natural resources enterprise to a major engine for poverty reduction. Social policies that are redistributional by nature grew from about a quarter to nearly half of federal activities over this period (Haveman 1988). Nevertheless, as he also points out, in spite of the massive increase in taxes and spending, inequality was no lower in 1988 (and is probably higher now) than it was in 1950, because of rising inequality in market incomes.

Secondly, as argued by Alesina and Angeletos (2003), redistribution from rich to poor is more limited in the USA than in continental Europe at least in part because of differences in public attitudes towards the source of income inequality. In a society like the USA, people are much more likely to believe that individual efforts determine income and that poverty is due to lack of effort rather than bad luck or social injustice. Americans accept a larger measure of inequality and choose less redistribution, because they believe that the distribution of incomes produced by the market is closer to what they consider to be a fair outcome. Schwabish, Smeeding, and Osberg (2003) offer a different perspective on the relationship between income inequality and social spending. They argue that cross-national differences in social expenditure are associated with and according to their theory, may be driven by the degree of inequality in the top half of the income distribution, because political influence is concentrated among the rich who stand to benefit less (or lose more) from social and welfare programs the more unequal the society.

Thirdly, and related to the previous point, many defenders of American economic and political institutions argue that inequality plays a crucial role in creating incentives for people to improve their situations through saving, hard work, and investment in education and training. According to this line of argument, wide income disparities may be in the best long-term interest of the poor themselves as the benefits of higher economic growth "trickle down" to the poor. However, Smeeding, Rainwater, and Burtless (2000) conclude that the supposed efficiency advantages of high inequality do not appear to have accrued to low-income residents of the USA, at least so far, but rather to those further up the income scale. Kenworthy (1998) assesses the relationship between the "extensiveness" of social welfare policies and overall poverty rates in fifteen developed countries over the period 1960–91, allowing for the possible impact on long-run economic growth. The results of his multivariate analysis, though not conclusive, suggest that social welfare policies do significantly help to reduce absolute and relative poverty, even when possible indirect, dynamic effects on long-term economic growth are taken into account.

Finally, there are various ways in which the methodology used in comparative studies may exaggerate the differences between countries, making simple comparisons of pre- and post-transfer poverty or inequality potentially misleading. This relates to the problem with establishing incidence discussed at the start. For example, in countries with generous earnings-related social insurance schemes, older people will have had less need to make private provision for their retirement, so they are more likely to have relatively low pre-transfer incomes. A simple comparison of pre- and post-transfer poverty rates will show that government transfers are lifting many older people out of poverty. But, this implicitly assumes that people would not alter their behavior in the absence of social insurance or other government transfer schemes. In practice, many of these older people would have made alternative arrangements and would not in fact have been poor in the absence of government transfers. Similarly, by deducting taxes and national insurance contributions, but not private pension contributions, the "standard approach" to the analysis of income data will exaggerate the disposable incomes of middle- and higher-income groups in countries where pensions are more private than public (Whiteford and Kennedy 1995).

Studies based solely on cash incomes may also give a distorted picture of the impact of social and welfare policies, because governments may seek to achieve their redistributive goals through programs which provide non-cash benefits rather than just through tax-transfer mechanisms. Smeeding et al. (1993) find, however, that the ranking of countries according to levels of cash and non-cash transfers is similar (with the exception of Canada whose non-cash ranking is well above its cash transfer ranking), suggesting that governments have not used cash transfer and non-cash benefit programs as substitutable methods of achieving their social objectives. Non-cash incomes appear to reinforce the distributional impact of conventional tax-transfer mechanisms, rather than acting to offset them in any major way.

## 5.4 Analysis of Individual Programs

Twenty years ago, in his book *The Strategy of Equality*, Julian Le Grand (1982) reached the striking conclusion that "almost all public expenditure on the social services [in the UK] benefits the better off to a greater extent than the poor." Goodin and Le Grand (1987a) extended this analysis to other countries and to include examples of cash payments, as well as in-kind services. Their conclusion has been widely, though not universally accepted. Esping-Andersen (1996), for example, states that "it is now well-established that huge areas of welfare state activity, especially in education and the other in-kind services, are probably of greatest benefit to the middle classes."

If this is so, a large part of social policy would have failed in what many would see as one of its main aims. As we shall see below, this conclusion depends critically on a series of assumptions about how to analyze the distributive impact of social welfare programs, and more fundamentally, on the meaning attached to their redistributive role.

Le Grand (1987) examined the use of various social services in the UK in the 1970s and found that people from lower social classes used fewer health services per ill person, benefited less from subsidies to owner-occupiers and transport-related subsidies, and that their children were less likely to stay on in post-compulsory state education. Of the services he looked at, only subsidies to council tenants and rent rebates were directed primarily at the poor (though his analysis did not cover social care or cash transfers, both of which are also pro-poor). Goodin and Le Grand (1987*b*) used the example of the Australian social security system to argue that even programs that are tightly targeted on the poor at their inception may, over time, be "infiltrated" by the non-poor, defeating or at least defusing their redistributive aims—what they term "creeping universalism." At the same time, those services targeted at the poor have a tendency to be cut first when budgets are under pressure. Hanson (1987) argued that state-funded programs in the USA are particularly vulnerable to these kinds of pressures because "footloose" businesses lobby them to keep taxes low. The neglect of social assistance is easily carried out simply by not adjusting benefit levels for inflation—as a result, the entry point for social assistance (i.e. the maximum permissible income to qualify for AFDC payments) fell from 80 per cent of the official US poverty line in 1968 to 57 per cent in 1981. Thus, governments appear to favor public services that are extensively used by the middle classes and to neglect spending areas that are targeted at the poor.

The authors offered several possible explanations for "middle-class capture." The better off, being generally better educated and more articulate, are more able to manipulate the system to their advantage: to ensure, for example, that their doctor refers them to a specialist or that their children go to the right schools. They are also likely to face lower costs in using services and have greater political influence.

To some extent at least, therefore, inequality in health care and other services reflects inequality in society more generally. On this basis, they argue that governments should intervene directly in the market to ensure it produces the "right" income distribution in the first place, rather than relying on fiscal transfers or in-kind provision of social services to "patch up" the secondary income distribution.

These conclusions have been challenged on at least two grounds. First, some have argued that universal programs are a good thing per se, because they foster social cohesion, whereas targeted programs can be socially divisive. This view seems to be consistent with the founding principles of the British welfare state. According to Marshall, "universal benefits symbolise the fact of social equality by conferring on everyone a badge ... of citizenship." If equality is seen in terms of a common system of provision for all, then equality of entitlement is more important than equality of use or equal use for equal need (Powell 1995). Taking measures to reduce the participation of the middle classes would involve lowering the quality of services to deter middle-class users and/or tightening the conditions for access and risking stigmatizing low-income users, neither of which would seem to be of benefit to the poor.

Secondly, subsequent analyses of the distributional effects of welfare programs—both cash and in-kind—have found that they involve substantial redistribution from low- to high-income groups. It is important to be careful in specifying the precise distributional question being asked. For instance, poorer groups may receive fewer (or lower-quality) services *relative to their* needs than higher-income groups, but may still receive the largest aggregate amounts, simply because their needs are so much greater. Sefton (2002) examines the UK distribution of what he calls the "social wage" (benefits in kind from health care, education, social housing, and social care) between income groups between 1979 and 2000. The results show that the poorest fifth of households receive, on average, around twice the value of services that the richest fifth of households receive. Part of this pro-poor bias is accounted for by the demographic composition of income groups: older people and children, who are the most intensive users of welfare services, are disproportionately represented among lower-income groups. But, a significant pro-poor bias remains even after controlling for demographic factors, because certain services are targeted at poorer households, some services are strongly needs related (which skews them towards lower-income groups), and higher-income groups are much more likely to use private education and health care. Calero (2002) comes to very similar conclusion using Spanish data for 1994. He finds that age determines a considerable part of the distribution of spending on cash benefits and benefits in kind, but that social spending also leads to significant reductions in inequalities between social classes.

Furthermore, neither of these studies takes into account the distributional effects of taxation. Most social spending is financed from general taxation so it is difficult to say definitively which taxes are used to pay for which services. However, on plausible assumptions, allowing for taxation will substantially strengthen the redistributive impact of welfare policies. This is because most forms of taxation are proportional to incomes or progressive. Thus, even if spending on welfare programs were equal across income groups, those on lower incomes would still be net gainers, simply because they pay less tax into the system.

Having said this, some studies of individual policies or programs have shown these are less redistributive than they may appear at first. Gustman and Steinmeier (2000), for example, show that the US social security benefit system is not nearly as progressive as a point-in-time examination of the benefit formula would suggest. Replacement rates are considerably lower for those with relatively high average annual earnings over their lifetime than for those with low average earnings (ranging from 15 up to 90 per cent in 2000), implying substantial redistribution from high to low earners—and indeed this is the case at the level of the individual. However, about half of this redistribution is *within* families—from men to their spouses, especially those who have spent large amounts of time out of the labor market. There is much less redistribution from high- to low-income families. Similarly, Liebman (2002) finds that the extent of income-based redistribution is fairly modest compared to the benefits paid out by the social security system—only between 5 and 9 per cent of the total. Much of the intra-cohort redistribution is related to factors other than income, including from people with low to people with high life expectancies and from single workers and two-earner couples to one-earner couples. Since high-income families tend to have higher life expectancies and receive larger spouse benefits, a substantial part of the progressivity implicit in the basic benefit formula is offset.

# 6. Conclusions

Whilst nearly all acts of government have redistributive effects, most are not primarily about "traditional" redistribution from rich to poor. Even redistributive policies are often concerned with different forms of redistribution and have other objectives besides redistribution. Nonetheless, government tax and transfer policies substantially reduce inequality and poverty in all rich OECD countries, though with varying degrees of success. The outcomes in different countries are shaped by differences in political and economic values, including judgements about the trade-offs between equity and efficiency and the merits of targeted versus universal support, as well as considerations of political economy.

In a broader context, the politics of important areas of public policy may depend as much on who gains from government's activities and their financing as on their success against other, often primary objectives. This is not only true of cash transfer or taxation policies, but applies across most areas of government. When reform is proposed, debate often focuses on who are the losers from any transition from the status quo, rather than on assessing any new structure in its entirety. However, determining who the losers and gainers are usually depends on particular and contestable assumptions about how the world would be in the absence of policy change, as well as the time period over which comparisons are made. Empirical studies in the last twenty or so years have helped to shed light not only on what the redistributive impact of government is, but also on the most appropriate ways of framing the questions.

## References

Arrow, K. 1963. Uncertainty and the welfare economics of medical care. *American Economic Review*, 53 (5): 941–73.

Alesina, A., and Angeletos, G. 2003. Fairness and redistribution: US versus Europe. NBER Working Paper 9502. Cambridge, Mass.: National Bureau of Economic Research.

Atkinson, A. 1983. *The Economics of Inequality*. Oxford: Clarendon Press.

—— 1993. On targeting social security: theory and Western experience with family benefits. Welfare State Programme Discussion Paper 99. London: STICERD, London School of Economics.

—— 1995. *Incomes and the Welfare State: Essays on Britain and Europe*. Cambridge: Cambridge University Press.

—— 1999. *The Economic Consequences of Rolling Back the Welfare State*. Cambridge, Mass.: MIT Press.

—— and Mogensen, G. (eds.) 1993. *Welfare and Work Incentives: A North European Perspective*. Oxford: Clarendon Press.

Barr, N. 2001. *The Welfare State as Piggy Bank: Information, Risk, Uncertainty, and the Role of the State*. Oxford: Oxford University Press.

Barry, B. 1990. The welfare state vesus the relief of poverty. In *Needs and Welfare Provision*, ed. A. Ware and R. Goodin. London: Sage.

BROWNING, E. 1975. The externality argument for in-kind transfers: some critical remarks. *Kyklos*, 28: 526–44.

BURCHARDT, T., and HILLS, J. 1996. *Private Welfare Insurance and Social Security: Pushing the Boundaries*. York: York Publishing Services for the Joseph Rowntree Foundation.

CALERO, J. 2002. The distribution of public social expenditure in Spain: a general analysis with special reference to age and social class. *Social Policy and Administration*, 36 (5).

CORNIA, G., and STEWART, F. 1995. Two errors of targeting. In *Public Spending and the Poor: Theory and Evidence*, ed. D. Van de Walle and K. Nead. Baltimore: Johns Hopkins University for the World Bank.

DANZIGER, S. 1988. Recent trends in poverty and the antipoverty effectiveness of income transfers. In *The Distributional Impacts of Public Policies*, ed. S. Danziger and K. Portney. Basingstoke: Macmillan in association with the Policy Studies Organization.

—— and PORTNEY, K. (eds.) 1988. *The Distributional Impacts of Public Policies*. Basingstoke: Macmillan in association with the Policy Studies Organisation.

ESPING-ANDERSEN, G. 1990. *The Three Worlds of Welfare Capitalism*. Cambridge: Polity Press.

—— 1996. Positive-sum solutions in a world of trade-offs? Pp. 256–67 in *Welfare States in Transition: National Adaptations in Global Economies*, ed. G. Esping-Andersen. London: Sage.

FERRARINI, T., and NELSON, K. 2003. Taxation of social insurance and redistribution: a comparative analysis of ten welfare states. *Journal of European Social Policy*, 13 (1).

GOODIN, R., and LE GRAND, J. et al. 1987a. *Not Only the Poor: The Middle Classes and the Welfare State*. London: Unwin Hyman.

—— —— 1987b. Creeping universalism in the Australian welfare state In R. Goodin and J. Le Grand et al. 1987a.

—— et al. 1999. *The Real Worlds of Welfare Capitalism*. Cambridge: Cambridge University Press. Cambridge.

GUSTMAN, A., and STEINMEIER, T. 2000. How effective is redistribution under the social security benefit formula. NBER Working Paper No. w7597. Cambridge, Mass.: National Bureau of Economic Research.

HANSON, R. 1987. The expansion and contraction in the American welfare state. In R. Goodin and J. Le Grand et al. 1987a.

HAVEMAN, R. 1988. *Starting Even: An Equal Opportunity Program to Combat the Nation's New Poverty*. New York: Simon and Schuster.

HICKS, A., and KENWORTHY, L. 2003. Varieties of welfare capitalism. *Socio-Economic Review*, 1 (1).

HILLS, J. 2004. *Inequality and the State*. Oxford: Oxford University Press.

—— and FALKINGHAM, J. 1995. *The Dynamic of Welfare: The Welfare State and the Life Cycle*. Hemel Hempstead: Prentice Hall.

HM TREASURY 1999. *Tackling Poverty and Extending Opportunity*. The Modernisation of Britain's Tax and Benefit System No. 4. London: HM Treasury.

KENWORTHY, L. 1998. *Do Social-Welfare Policies Reduce Poverty? A Cross-National Assessment*. Luxembourg Income Study Working Paper No. 188.

—— 2004. An equality–growth trade-off? Ch. 5 in *Egalitarian Capitalism*. New York: Russell Sage Foundation.

KORPI, W., and PALME, J. 1998. The paradox of redistribution and strategies of equality: welfare state institutions, inequality, and poverty in the western countries. *American Sociological Review*, 63 (5): 661–87.

LE GRAND, J. 1982. *The Strategy of Equality: Redistribution and the Social Services*. London: Allen and Unwin.

—— 1987. The middle-class use of the British social services. In R. Goodin and J. Le Grand et al. 1987a.

LIEBMAN, J. 2002. Redistribution in the current US social security system. NBER Working Paper No. w8625. Cambridge, Mass.: National Bureau of Economic Research.

MITCHELL, D., HARDING, H., and GRUEN, F. 1994. Targeting welfare. *Economic Record*, 70 (210): 315–40.

PECHMAN, J., and MAZUR, M. 1984. The rich, the poor and the taxes they pay: an update. *Public Interest*, 77.

—— and OKNER, B. 1974. *Who Bears the Tax Burden?* Washington, DC: Brookings Institution.

PIERSON, P. (ed.) 2001. *The New Politics of the Welfare State*. Oxford: Oxford University Press.

POWELL, M. 1995. The strategy of equality revisited. *Journal of Social Policy*, 24 (2).

SCHWABISH, J., SMEEDING, T., and OSBERG, L. 2003. *Income Distribution and Social Expenditures: A Crossnational Perspective*. Luxembourg Income Study Working Paper No. 350.

SEFTON, T. 2002. Recent changes in the distribution of the social wage. CASE Paper 62. London: London School of Economics.

SMEEDING, T. 2004. Public policy, economic inequality, and poverty: the US in comparative perspective. Paper presented at the "Inequality and American politics" conference, Syracuse University, 20 Feb.

—— RAINWATER, L., and BURTLESS, G. 2000. *United States Poverty in a Cross-National Context*. Luxembourg Income Study Working Paper No. 244.

SMEEDING, T., SAUNDERS, P., CODER, J., JENKINS, S., FRITZELL, J., HAGENHAARS, A., HAUSER, R., and WOLFSON, M. 1993. Poverty, inequality, and family living standards impacts across seven countries: the effect of non cash subsidies for health, education and housing. *Review of Income and Wealth*, 39: 229–54.

TOBIN, J. 1970. On limiting the domain of inequality. *Journal of Law and Economics*, 13: 263–78.

TULLOCH, G. 1997. *Economics of Income Redistribution*. London: Kluwer Academic.

WEITZMAN, M. 1977. Is the price system or rationing more effective in getting a commodity to those who need it most? *Bell Journal of Economics*, 8: 517–24.

WELCH, F. 1999. In defence of inequality. *American Economic Review, Papers and Proceedings*, 89 (2).

WHITEFORD, P., and KENNEDY, S. 1995. *Incomes and Living Standards of Older People*. Department of Social Security Research Report No. 34. London: HMSO.

# CHAPTER 31

# MARKET AND NON-MARKET FAILURES

MARK A. R. KLEIMAN

STEVEN M. TELES

## 1. INTRODUCTION

All government action involves coercion, if only the coercive use of the taxing power. Liberal principles therefore dictate that the state should intervene only where voluntary action produces suboptimal results. Such situations are sometimes identified with the "market failures" of the economics textbooks. But not every case where the results of individual choice and voluntary coordination fall short of some ideal involves a market failure as economists use the term: there are also failures of other voluntary institutions, and of the mechanisms of individual choice. These might be called "failures of private choice" or "failures of voluntary action." Simply finding a market (or other private) failure does not, without further analysis, justify government intervention. The costs and risks of coercion are often serious enough to justify tolerating the imperfect voluntary outcomes of private choices.

This chapter explores the implications of these three ideas: deference to voluntary action as a "default option," recognition of the scope of departures from the optimal in private choice, and acknowledgement of the pervasiveness of government failure. Combined, they provide the template for responsible policy analysis, taking account of all consequences foreseeably arising from a recommended course of action.

# 2. Departures from Optimality under Voluntary Action and State Intervention

Markets mediate cooperation for mutual benefit. Under certain highly restrictive assumptions, the market equilibrium can be shown to be a Pareto optimum, a state in which the well-being of any individual cannot be enhanced without worsening the position of at least one other individual (Bator 1959). Where those assumptions do not hold markets are said to "fail:" fail, that is, to produce Pareto-optimal results.

One doctrine of public decision making holds that the state's coercive power should be brought to bear only against such "market failures," and to create the conditions, such as enforceable contracts and property rights, that allow markets to function. (An exception is usually made for "distributional" questions.) But this doctrine is surely too narrow. Markets do indeed mediate cooperation, but so do the non-market institutions sometimes lumped together as "civil society:" families, neighborhoods, professional societies, not-for-profit enterprises, churches, voluntary associations, and less easily pictured phenomena such as norms, practices, and values. These, too, can fail to secure optimal cooperation. It would be perverse, though possible, to use the language of market failure to analyze a litter-strewn neighborhood, a neglected child, dangerously aggressive driving, an ethos hostile to learning, or a culture wanting in altruism or inclined to violence. It would be equally perverse to insist on such an analysis as a prerequisite for treating those conditions as possible targets of public intervention.

The economic analysis underlying the doctrine of market failure assumes an individual capable of maximizing expected subjective utility, subject to constraint: a good steward of his own well-being. That assumption is obviously false for children and the insane. But it is also false for many decisions made by ordinarily competent people about, for example, time management, saving, financial risk taking, diet, exercise, and the use of psychoactive chemicals. And it is not obviously true of the processes by which individuals change their own preferences, by investing in their capacities to appreciate or contribute to music, literature, or painting, or by attempting to increase their self-command or altruism. Nor is it fully consistent with the observed relationships between expenditure and well-being studied by the developing discipline of hedonics (Easterlin 2002; Layard 2005). Thus the scope of suboptimal performance in voluntary individual choice and spontaneous organization is substantially larger than orthodox welfare-economics approaches suggest.

Yet if the scope of potentially justifiable state actions should be broadened to take account of failures of civil society institutions and of individual rationality as well as market failures, it remains true that the scope of actually justified state actions will turn out to be a good deal narrower. Government is not, after all, a frictionless device for correcting for market or other failures. No one claims that it is. But applying this insight demands a step most policy analysts shy away from: comparing the efficiency of the institutions of voluntary choice, left to their own devices, with the efficiency of state action, or with the efficiency of private action as modified by regulation.

We understand government effectiveness to be a function of institutional incentives, material resources, and the sophistication of personnel, mediated by the transaction costs imposed by the institutional and cultural context (in particular the citizenry's willingness to cooperate with government objectives without extensive surveillance or threat). Understanding these constraints on government effectiveness is essential to policy analysis, since analysts have a professional obligation to hold themselves responsible for all of the predictable consequences of their recommendations, and these include both the way that other actors will respond to actual or possible government intervention and the way that governments will, over time, respond to the demand for intervention.

In essence, we accept the basic formulation of the problem of public choice proposed by James Buchanan: "Under what circumstances will collective-governmental supply be more efficient than private or non-collective supply?" This question, Buchanan adds, "the economist must answer on the basis of some comparative analysis of alternative institutions. The results that may be predicted to emerge from publicly organized supply must, in each case, be compared with those that may be predicted to emerge from non-collective, voluntarily organized, market supply" (Buchanan 1999).[1] So finding a hypothetical failure of private action is not sufficient to show that some choice ought to be made publicly rather than privately: the effects of individual choice and voluntary cooperation must be compared with those of government intervention before concluding that identified imperfections need something other than the policy Burke called "salutary neglect" (Burke 1974).

To accept Buchanan's formulation does not dictate accepting his rubric, shared with most other public choice theorists (notably William Riker), for the analysis of the quality of public intervention. The claim that actors in the public arena invariably act entirely for private benefit—that political man is simply economic man acting under different incentives—is neither empirically well supported nor theoretically demonstrable without making untenably restrictive assumptions.

Relaxing the assumption that officials are invariably predatory makes it conceivable that intervention by admittedly flawed government institutions will sometimes yield better results than letting things be. Once we take seriously both sides of the problem—the failures of markets, other means of voluntary cooperation and individual choice on the one hand and, on the other hand, government failures—the optimal scope of government action comes to depend crucially on government competence. The greater the prevalence and degree of suboptimal decision making in administration, the higher ought to be the threshold beyond which the powers of the state are mobilized against market and other private failure. The more competent the government, the greater the scope of interventions with which it can be trusted.

---

[1] But see O'Hare 1989 for an argument that "supply" is only one category of governmental action.

Those who would advise policy makers must take seriously the institutional context of their recommendations. A policy might be desirable in the context of efficient government, low corruption, and informed decision making but disastrous in the absence of these conditions. If the quality of intervention suffers as its scale increases, due to competing demands for the attention of decision makers, the diminished performance on other tasks that would result from adding a new program to the governmental repertoire (Rose and Peters 1975; Douglas 1976; Crozier, Huntington, and Watanuki 1975) may prove as important as the budgetary cost of the new program. In many situations the most pressing agenda for policy analysts will be to alter the context of decision making and administration to expand the scope for efficient government correction of private failures. The likely effect of a given policy choice on the quality of future public decision making and implementation may be among its most important consequences.

# 3. The Classical Market Failures

Markets can be said to "fail" whenever an exchange that would be a Pareto improvement—one that would improve the well-being (as the participants understand it) of all those affected—will not be made by self-interested agents (Bator 1958). A monopolist, for example, sets his price where marginal revenue equals marginal cost, rather than where price equals marginal cost, as a competitive market would require. The profit gain to the monopolist from the higher price is less than the sum of the consumers' surpluses lost due to the combination of higher price and smaller volume: the potential consumers' surpluses from the units not sold at the monopoly price, but which would have been sold at the competitive marginal-cost price, are a deadweight loss. The consumers, if they could costlessly organize without free-rider problems to buy the monopoly from the monopolist, could pay the monopolist a sum greater than the monopoly profit and still increase the welfare of each consumer. But they cannot, and therefore the monopoly price remains in place. The market thus fails to maximize consumers'-plus-producers' surpluses. Here regulation can, in principle, help matters, either by fixing a price for the monopoly good nearer the marginal-cost price or by forcing competition.[2]

However, a good with increasing returns to scale in production—whose marginal cost is falling throughout the relevant range—cannot be efficiently produced by more than one producer. Such a good is therefore a "natural monopoly," and thus a candidate for price regulation or public provision.

The extreme of "natural monopoly" is a situation in which the marginal cost is zero. Zero marginal cost is characteristic of goods that are non-rival in consumption

[2] As William Baumol (2002) has argued, actual competition may not be necessary as long as the market remains "contestable," that is, the possibility of new entry is maintained.

(i.e. use by any one individual does not compete with or interfere with use by others). Knowledge and information, such as in the form of digitally stored text, music, or video, are non-rival in that sense. Other goods, such as pharmaceuticals, have physical embodiments that are rival in consumption, but those physical embodiments are so inexpensive, compared to the development effort required to make the first unit, as to make such goods primarily non-rival "information goods." As the share of total economic activity involving information goods rises, so does the importance of this version of the public goods market failure.

If the marginal cost of production is zero or negligible, then any positive price will create a market distortion. But a price at or near zero will not allow the producer to recoup the cost of development. Thus the market result will not be a Pareto optimum.

It is possible to imagine the potential consumers of a non-rival consumption good forming a cooperative enterprise to develop and produce that good (if we assume away the problem of identifying potential consumers in advance), but again a Pareto optimum will not be achieved. If the good is made available only to those who contribute their pro rata share of the development cost, then there will be lost consumers' surpluses among those who would derive some benefit from consuming the good but not enough benefit to cover their share of the development cost. If the good is made available to all comers, then no self-interested individual will volunteer to pay his share of the costs, preferring to get a "free ride" on the contributions of others.

Non-rival consumption goods share some of the characteristics of what economists call "pure public goods." The market will fail to achieve a Pareto optimum when, for technical or institutional reasons, those who do not pay for some good cannot be prevented from consuming it: when, in economic jargon, the good is "non-excludable."

Ambient air quality is a classic public good. Everyone in a given area necessarily breathes the same outdoor air. If it is polluted, all suffer alike. Rationally self-interested individuals interacting in markets will not in general generate the optimal level of actions to clean the air because whoever initiates such action cannot collect from others the value his efforts create for them. If some potential level of clean-up action would produce more benefit than cost—if the sum of the willingness-to-pay for the improvement of all who breathe the air in question exceeds the cost of the clean-up—then there must be some distribution of those costs would leave every person in the area better off. But, absent coercion, it will not be in the interest of any individual to contribute to the cost of the clean-up. The temptation to "free-ride" tends to defeat the project of voluntary action and by the same token, the project of securing universal agreement for each to pay his or her share conditional on all others doing the same.

Common property resources pose analogous problems. Common property resources are goods that are rival in consumption beyond some point—use by any one consumer interferes with the quantity or quality available for others—but non-excludable for technical or institutional reasons. Thus a common property resource can be thought of as something scarce—or alternatively, subject to crowding—but unowned. On one analysis, the resulting market failure reflects a failure to allocate property rights in the scarce resource. Hardin's example, from which the "commons" problem derives its familiar label, is of villagers with rights to pasture sheep on common pastureland, where the alternative is pasturing the sheep on open wasteland (Hardin 1968). The more sheep that share the common, the worse the pasturage. But as long as the pasturage is even marginally better on the common than on the waste, a selfishly rational villager will continue to move his sheep from the waste to the common. Thus in equilibrium the common will provide no better pasturage than the wasteland, and its aggregate value will be zero. Only if the resource is privately appropriated will the owner have the incentive to ration its use down to the level where the aggregate gain is maximized. Overfishing and traffic congestion provide important contemporary examples of commons problems.

External cost was the first market failure to be identified in the literature. The original doctrine, going back to Pigou, was that whenever the production or consumption of an item imposed costs on (or created benefits for) third parties, markets would fail to produce optimal outcomes: there would be overproduction and over-consumption (Pigou 1912). The reverse would be true for external benefit, as when the benefit that bees produce by pollinating fruit trees accrues to the orchard owner rather than to the beehive owner. In each case, it was assumed that market participants would act solely on their own immediate interests, ignoring the interests of those "external" to the transaction.

Pigou's proposed solution was a set of taxes and subsidies designed to internalize external costs by charging or paying to each external-cost imposer or external-benefit provider a sum equal to that cost or benefit. Pigouvian taxation appears most prominently in contemporary policy making in the "polluter pays" principle.

Coase's essay on "The problem of social cost" (Coase 1960) complicated this analysis by pointing out that externalities could be internalized if those indirectly interested in transactions offered inducements to those directly involved to engage in (desist from) beneficial (harmful) actions, as empirical orchardists hire empirical beekeepers to provide pollination services.

According to Coase, whether the markets for external cost and benefit will find the Pareto optimum depends entirely on the transactions costs involved. If they are small, an externality poses no problem, no matter who has the original property right. But if they are large, as they will be when the number of non-excludable beneficiaries is great enough to create free-rider problems, or the number of potential inflictors of external harm (each of whom may need to be paid for refraining from doing so) is great enough to create a problem of "paying the Danegeld," then the market is less reliable. In such cases, the efficiency of the outcome will depend either on finding the optimal initial allocation of rights—not in itself something the market can be relied on to accomplish—or on interventions such as regulation or Pigouvian taxation. Thus external cost or benefit creates a market failure justifying coercive intervention only in the presence of free riding or other transactional complexity.

The "free ridership" problem thus turns out to be central to the policy analysis of almost any form of market failure; without it, the parties who would benefit from curing such a failure would just contract around whatever institutional problem keeps markets from generating a Pareto-optimal outcome.

Another set of potential market failures arises from uncertainty and imperfect information (and especially asymmetric information, where some participants are known by others to have knowledge not generally available). Diminishing marginal utility (itself implied, absent important "lumpiness," by the capacity to budget rationally) implies risk aversion. Risk aversion, in turn, implies the existence of potential utility gains from risk sharing. Thus an insurance contract, although it seems, if analyzed *ex post*, to be a set of transfers beneficial to those insured who have made claims exceeding their premiums and costly to the rest, can improve the expected utility of every participant (as analyzed *ex ante*), even allowing for the overhead costs of underwriting, marketing, and claims administration. In effect, insurance allows participants to transfer resources from possible future worlds in which they have not suffered losses (and in which their marginal utility of wealth is lower) to possible future worlds in which they have (and their marginal utility of income correspondingly higher).

But contingent-claims markets are subject to two special classes of market failure, known in the specialized vocabulary of underwriting as "adverse selection" and "moral hazard." When, as a result, contingent-claims markets do not work perfectly, those Pareto-improving opportunities are not, in practice, fully available through voluntary cooperation.[3]

Adverse selection results from information asymmetry. If, as is usually true, those who might buy insurance know more about their risks than the underwriter knows, then among any group offered insurance at a given rate the worse risks will tend to buy insurance and the better risks to self-insure. The result may be that those who face comparatively low risks may be unable to buy insurance at anything resembling an actuarially fair premium, and will forgo the benefits of risk spreading. Their departure from the market leaves everyone else, and in particular the next-lowest-risk group, facing higher premiums. If members of that group start to leave in turn, those at slightly higher risk may leave as well, in what has been called the "insurance death spiral."

Moral hazard—the tendency of the insured to be less careful, given that they will not bear the full costs of their losses—can be thought of as a pecuniary version of the external-cost problem. But it too rests on asymmetric information: moral hazard could not exist if the underwriter could perfectly and costlessly observe risky behavior. The inefficiency implicit in moral hazard—people taking risks they wouldn't take except for the fact that other people will help pay for their losses—always reduces the benefits from risk-spreading institutions, and when the losses are great enough compared to the utility gained from risk spreading, makes insurance altogether unavailable

In addition, some risks for which rational consumers would purchase insurance from behind a "veil of ignorance" cannot be insured against by the market because

---

[3] See Zeckhauser 1993.

the outcomes are already known: e.g. being born in socially disadvantaged circumstances or born with disabilities, congenital diseases, or (increasingly) with detectable genetic risk factors for expensive-to-treat diseases.

Information asymmetries also exist, and create losses, outside the contingent-claims markets. Goods whose qualities are better known to their sellers than to their buyers are subject to what Akerlof called "lemons problems" (Akerlof 1970). The market price reflects the lowest-quality variety of the good, because no buyer will pay more knowing that the lowest quality is what he may receive. And therefore only lowest-quality items are in fact sold, because no seller will sell better-quality merchandise at a bad-quality price.[4]

Another information asymmetry, that between principals and their agents, creates "agency losses" (Arrow 1985). Here the problem is that a principal cannot costlessly observe behavior of his agent, as a result of which the principal will make costly efforts to ensure diligence (and perhaps the agent will make costly efforts to seem more diligent than is the case) and full advantage will not be taken of the potential benefits of shifting the risk of bad outcomes from the (presumably more risk-averse) agent to the (presumably less risk-averse) principal. Both sides could benefit from greater transparency, but the principal cannot ensure it and the agent cannot credibly promise it.

Information asymmetry also creates another market failure: costly signaling behavior, such as the acquisition of credentials. A college diploma is statistically correlated with intelligence and diligence, qualities that employers value. So employers prefer to hire college graduates, other things being equal. This gives each job seeker an incentive to seek such a credential, even if the educational activity required to achieve the diploma has (non-signaling) benefits less than its costs.[5]

The private benefit of an activity that generates a market-valued signal will therefore tend to be higher than its social benefit. This might be thought of as an example of an externality; my educational attainment imposes a cost on all my competitors, as theirs does on me. We could, in principle, all be better off if we could agree to limit the arms race in credentials, but the problem of free

----

[4] In many markets, of course, the benefit to sellers of maintaining good reputations will induce at least some of them to make honest revelation of their private information. But the market valuation of E-bay, attributed primarily to its system of reputational ratings, testifies to the large potential losses from information asymmetry, as reflected in the gains from overcoming it.

[5] This intrinsic problem is partially exacerbated, rather than alleviated, by government, in particular by most democratic governments' preference for increasing the number of individuals in higher education. In some cases, it might be efficient for government to create a negative incentive to attend higher education (for example by making the entire subsidy attach to the individual rather than the institution of higher learning, and allowing those individuals to convert their subsidy into other investment goods, such as down payments on a house or start-up investment in a small business). Government could also deal with at least part of the problem by directly capping numbers, although this is only possible in systems (such as that in the United Kingdom) that are almost wholly centralized. Whether the external benefits from education (such as better citizenship) offset the losses due to signaling is a separate enquiry; so is the question whether other market or individual-choice failures (e.g. capital market imperfections making education hard to finance or underappreciation of the value of increased "consumption capital") might tend to lead to underconsumption in education. The general point is that there is no a priori reason to expect private choice to generate an optimal level of investment in higher education or of other goods and services with signaling value.

riding complicates any attempt at voluntary cooperation on that Pareto-improving result.

The "conspicuous waste" that Veblen theorized as emerging from "pecuniary emulation" (Veblen 1899) can be thought of as a market failure due to the signaling value of wealth display. If so, then it is possible (as Robert Frank suggests) that welfare could be improved by inducing everyone to choose, for example, shorter commutes and smaller houses, but that no individual could improve his own well-being by making that choice (Frank 1999).

Any of these market failures can, in principle, create a case for public intervention. On the other hand, public intervention itself, or even its threat can also *create* market failure, as when the moral hazard incident to publicly supplied disaster insurance induces home building in floodplains or on eroding beach fronts, or when the threat of price controls or public food distribution in a food shortage discourages the holding of private inventories. It is not enough, therefore, to show the existence of a market failure by comparison with some imaginary optimum; public intervention will be justified only when the intervention—which implicitly is a decision to treat situations like the one under discussion as matters of public decision for the future—will, on balance, do more good than harm. Intervention that fixes one market failure at the cost of making markets work less well in the future is likely to be more trouble than it is worth.

# 4. BEYOND MARKET FAILURE

The classical market failures, even as expanded by contingent-claims and information issues, do not exhaust the set of circumstances in which voluntary individual action fails to lead to an optimal outcome. There are other failures of spontaneous cooperation—less well catalogued, if not less widely recognized. In addition, a more realistic model of individual decision making and cognition than those found in the elementary economics textbooks implies the possibility of losses from imperfect individual foresight or self-command and thus gains from paternalistic intervention.

After all, the perfectly rational consumer—self-interested, self-controlled, and therefore capable of acting to maximize subjective expected utility subject to constraint—is no more to be met with in real life than the geometer's straight line. Actual human beings report that they have bad habits, succumb to temptations, procrastinate and favor the very near over the slightly more distant future, act badly under pressure, and regret actions motivated by appetites for food, sex, and mood-altering chemicals, aversion to pain, financial loss, or embarrassment (Ainslie 2001). They regard self-control not as an axiom but as a constant struggle. Anticipating actions they know they will later regret, they try sometimes to avoid being put in those situations by creating external constraints on their own choices, as Odysseus had himself tied to the mast.[6] Experimental economists and allied psychologists have made an industry of cataloguing the heuristics and biases that create behavioral gaps between *homo economicus* and *homo sapiens* (Kahneman, Slovic, and Tversky 1990).

The consumer we know from the introductory microeconomics textbook typically gains some consumer surplus from everything he buys; at worst, for the marginal consumer or the marginal unit consumed, that surplus is reduced to zero. But real consumers sometimes make predictably regrettable purchases: purchases that might be thought of as creating consumer's deficits. (The resulting losses have been called "internalities.") In such cases, constraints on choice can be welfare increasing even in the absence of externalities or strategic interactions.

The possibility of beneficial paternalistic intervention is readily agreed to in the cases of children, the insane, and the mentally deficient. Since neither adulthood nor sanity nor normal intelligence comes with a natural bright-line demarcation, it would be surprising if normal healthy adults showed no tendencies for suboptimal action, even evaluated from a purely selfish viewpoint. However, in contrast to the well-worked-out accounts of how to deal with market failures, there is little theoretical discussion of how to deal with failures of individual rationality. That constraint *may* increase welfare does not imply that constraint will *always* increase welfare, even when internalities are present. High cigarette taxes may well improve the welfare of those whom they cause to stop, or not to start smoking but they will hurt those who maintain the habit despite the higher price. As Jonathan Caulkins has remarked, making smokers pay through the nose does not cure the damage smoking does to their lungs.[7] The additional harm done by drug prohibitions to those who become addicted despite them is merely a more dramatic example of the same problem.

Drug addiction lies toward one end of a continuum, rather than being a problem *sui generis* (Kleiman 1992, ch. 2). Some commodities and activities generate relatively little in the way of internalities; others generate more, in patterns that vary across time, age, geography, and ethnicity as well as apparently randomly, from individual to individual. That a particular practice is harmless, or even beneficial to most of its habitués does not ensure that it will not create great misery in others. Of the major drugs of abuse, only nicotine in the form of cigarettes creates more dependent than casual users. Constraints that benefit some actual or potential addicts will impinge on the harmless pleasure of non-addicted users; a war against obesity or compulsive gambling will necessarily inconvenience and annoy those with controlled appetites for food or games of chance. Compulsory saving for old age will help the majority who struggle to curb their spending but complicate the financial planning of the more self-disciplined minority.

As any parent knows, successful paternalistic action is harder than it looks. Constraining choice today to deal with a self-command problem in one domain may have the unwanted side effect of damaging self-command for the future, or in other areas. That is one advantage of non-coercive governmental strategies of

---

[6] For important extrapolations of this insight, see Schelling 1984 and Elster 1979.
[7] The argument, though not the quoted phrase, appears in Kleiman and Caulkins 2001.

information, and persuasion over more directly coercive measures such as prohibitions, regulations, and taxes (O'Hare 1989). The drug wars have provided ample evidence of the risks of paternalistic intervention, including the risk of making those who resist such intervention into social enemies.

But the difficulty of dealing with failures of individual choice through public policy does not make the failures themselves disappear. Sounder policy might arise from a recognition of that fact in theory as well as in practice. Admitting that there are cases where paternalistic intervention is justified might even help the project of creating norms of public action that can constrain the excesses of paternalism.[8]

Behind and alongside the markets stand the institutions of civil society: both observable ones, such as families, neighborhoods, professional organizations, and voluntary civic associations, and less observable ones, such as norms of cooperation and fair dealing. Like markets, they involve the interactions of many people, acting, if not in every case in their own interests, at least from their own viewpoints. Unlike markets, there is not even a prima facie reason to expect them to perform optimally, because civil society lacks anything resembling the price mechanism as a lubricant of interactions, a binding force making it in the interest of each to consider the desires of others, and a readily available source of objective, quantified information about what those desires are. Conscience and reputation can motivate pro-social behavior, and motivate the actions of private approbation and disapprobation, reward and punishment, that motivate pro-social behavior in others.[9] But the mechanisms by which self-reinforcing expectations of good behavior are created and maintained are poorly understood (Fehr and Gächter 2000).

Perhaps as a consequence, no one has catalogued the failures of non-market voluntary cooperative mechanisms, and there exists no set of ready-made solutions for such failures, analogous to Pigouvian taxation as a remedy for external-cost problems or appropriation as a remedy for the overuse of common-property resources. To say that a society with low levels of interpersonal trust would benefit from an increase in its social capital (Banfield 1965; Putnam 2002) is not to describe how such an increase is to be brought about. After all, social capital is a public good, benefiting alike those who contribute to it and those who do not; the effort to create a society whose members are averse to free riding must itself overcome the free-rider problem.

Like interventions to cure market failure, interventions to remedy failures of voluntary cooperation risk side effects. Symptomatic cures can exacerbate underlying conditions. There may be a tension between relieving the distress caused by failures of voluntary cooperation and stimulating the exercise of voluntary cooperation for the future.[10]

Consider the case of a neglected child. To try to state the problem in terms of market failure would be absurd: the situation is hardly illuminated by observing that capital-market imperfections make it impossible for the child to borrow against its

---

[8] For an attempt at an analysis based on this principle, see Kleiman 1992.
[9] As classically argued by Adam Smith (2002).
[10] The clearest statement of this point is by Nathan Glazer (1988).

future earnings to hire appropriate guardianship services, or that agency losses in contracts for such services are likely to be large. But it would be equally absurd to assert that there is, therefore, no failure to be remedied. The rule that assigns guardianship of a child to its parents involves an assumption that the parents will act in its interests. Where that assumption proves inaccurate, the liberal maxim that allows parents wide discretion in its upbringing needs to be modified.[11] The courts and the social welfare agencies can attempt to pressure and help the parents to do a more adequate job; or they can terminate parental custody (in favor of other relatives, of adoptive parents, or of foster parents who take temporary custody on behalf of the state and receive a subsidy); or—in sheer desperation—they can send the child to an orphanage or even a juvenile corrections facility.

As in market failure, dealing with "family failure" requires careful analysis not only of the failure to be remedied but also of the capacities and characteristic failures of the remedial machinery. An intervention that improves the child's immediate condition may be worse than none if it weakens the parents' capacity or inclination to perform their role in the future, or reduces the propensity of other kin or neighbors to encourage parental performance or act as substitute nurturers. The worse the alternatives, the higher the state's tolerance will have to be for poor parental performance. Even if the alternatives were better than they are, the decision to suspend or terminate parental rights is among the most intrusive state actions, raising the question of how much "due process" the natural parents ought to receive before losing custody.

Neighborhoods, too, can fail. In a well-functioning neighborhood, neighbors fulfill both negative and positive duties: not being noisy, not littering, not engaging in assault or theft, acting with ordinary politeness, rendering neighborly services and assistance. But "neighborliness" is not an inevitable outcome of spontaneous, individual behavior. Some neighborhoods develop norms that, while functional at the individual level, are collectively destructive. Elijah Anderson has described how, in some poor neighborhoods, norms of pre-emptive and aggressive violence once established, become difficult even for reluctant inhabitants to resist (Anderson 2000). Starting with a small minority, they can quickly become close to universal in a chain reaction of self-defence. While most people in the neighborhood may wish to move away from a norm of violence and low sociability to one of greater sociability and cooperation, it would be irrational (and possibly suicidal) for any individual to make the first move. Thus neighborhoods, without some exogenous shock (or some terribly brave individual), may continue indefinitely at a low-level equilibrium of collective dysfunction (Platt 1973) or they may just depopulate as whoever can move out does so.

The more dysfunctional the neighborhood, the greater its need for intervention by organs of the state (if only to reconstruct its capacity for spontaneous action). But of course the state's capacity to intervene depends in part on the neighborhood's capacity to express its needs through formal or informal political interactions. Typically, a neighborhood where norms of sociability have broken down will also be handicapped by damaged channels of communication to the state. Precisely where

---

[11] This was accepted even by John Locke (1988).

interventions to overcome failures are most needed they may be least likely to succeed. This is the paradox that plagues efforts at "community policing:" where the police are most needed, the "community" may be hardest to find; heavy-handed enforcement, uninformed by a nuanced understanding of the situation, can make matters worse rather than better.[12]

Beyond families and neighborhoods, norms and expectations shape other behaviors: honesty or its reverse in paying taxes; politeness or its opposite on the highway; love or contempt for learning and the arts; an appetite for, or aversion to violence; respect or disrespect for received moral codes and religious doctrines; acceptance of or hostility to ethnic heterogeneity; attitudes about the proper role and status of women; sexual and reproductive practices; willingness or unwillingness to provide private voluntary support for public goods and the relief of private misfortune; and so on almost without limit.

No sensible person could deny the limits on our knowledge of how such norms change spontaneously or can be changed deliberately. But it would be equally fatuous to deny that the happiness of the people who constitute a society may rise and fall as much with such as with changes in material well-being, or that material well-being itself depends in part on the norm structure and its supporting institutions. Does anyone argue that the divorce rate among couples with young children is a matter of purely private concern or that public policy is incapable of influencing that rate?

If this is right, then one possible justification for government action is that it will tend to move the norms and institutions that support civil society and economic activity in desirable directions, or slow their movement in undesirable directions. That not everyone agrees about what the desirable directions might be gives the politics of virtue much of its hard edge. But it would take a very stubborn brand of liberal agnosticism to deny that some norms are more consistent with well-being than others, or that state intervention can move norms, if only by stating authoritatively which norms are choice-worthy.

# 5. SUBOPTIMAL GOVERNANCE

The foregoing analysis supports an ambitious public agenda. But an analysis that begins and ends with a description of private failures is incomplete. There is no *deus* in the form of an infallible government that can deal with every failure of voluntary behavior in unproblematic fashion, and no *machina* from which to hang it. Just as a serious analysis of market failure expands the governing agenda, often in surprising ways, an analysis of government failures shrinks it back to size. Such expansion and

---

[12] Price (1992) provides a compelling fictional account. There are cases, however, where changes in policing have gone hand in hand with efforts to remedy the relationship between poor communities and the state. See, for example, Fung 2004 and Winship 1999.

contraction do not, however, take us back to where we started, but to very different conclusions about what government should do, where, and how.

Government failure is pervasive (Wolf 1988), but not constant: while many of its causes are intrinsic to government, some vary with the institutional structure, political culture, and level of political and economic development. Even the illustrative list of seven of the causes of government failure presented below suffices to show that government failure is more extensive than most analyses assume: pervasive enough to make us want to move the analysis of the limits of government competence into the core of policy analysis rather than leave it on the periphery.

## 5.1 Cause One: Inadequate Penetrative Capacity

Government agents must learn about the society they want to influence. At the most basic level, they need to know who their citizens are, where they live, and some basic facts about them, such as income and occupation. For more ambitious endeavors, governments may need much more extensive information concerning patterns of social and economic interaction. To regulate companies' environmental impacts, governments need to understand firms' production processes and decision-making structures. To control crime, they need information about the character of criminal enterprises, the social structure of unstable communities, and the interactions between citizens and the formal and informal sources of order. To make old-age policy effective, they must understand how decisions to retire are made, how citizens will respond to incentives to save or policies that make them pay taxes for future benefits, and how the management of private pension systems by corporations, unions, and future retirees will respond to public intervention. In each case, effective intervention requires both extensive information about individuals and a sophisticated understanding of how different social institutions operate and how they will react to government action. "Penetrative capacity" can be defined as the degree to which government is capable of seeing into society and understanding its dynamics.

Penetrative capacity is one of the most important features that make governments "modern." Resistance to government information gathering is among the oldest forms of resistance to modernization (Scott 1985). Shortfalls in penetrative capacity are most likely to lead to government failures in less developed contexts. But while more developed countries are rich in certain penetrative capacities, such as well-developed statistical databases on population and incomes, they may be sorely lacking in less formalized ways of knowing. For example, taking police officers off the sidewalks and putting them in automobiles—undertaken under Progressive influence as a "modernizing" move—may cost them detailed knowledge of neighborhood personalities and dynamics (Kelling and Moore 1988).

Modernized governments, despite plentiful data, may lack nuance, especially as applied to marginalized subgroups: recent immigrants, for example, who often hesitate to share information with outsiders and whose patterns of response may be difficult for outsiders to model accurately. In short, governments in more and less developed countries face different kinds of problems with penetrative capacity, but in both cases they are likely to commit errors arising from inadequate information about societies they seek to govern.

In order to penetrate and reshape societies, governments must have the legitimacy and efficiency to acquire information and mobilize consent, while simultaneously resisting capture by private interests. This trick is not easily pulled off: success in creating what Peter Evans has called "embedded autonomy" is probably the exception rather than the rule (Evans 1995). Where this does not exist, or cannot be generated, the agenda for the state must correspondingly shrink. The importance of penetrative capacity is one reason to take political and institutional context seriously in making policy recommendations. Thus developing countries with simultaneously embedded and autonomous states may successfully manage market-directing policies that would, where those qualities of governance are lacking, lead to results considerably worse than could be achieved by laissez-faire (Wade 1990).

## 5.2 Cause Two: Inadequate Voluntary Cooperation

As many conquerors have found, it can be very difficult to govern effectively a society that does not voluntarily cooperate with its government. Penetrative capacity depends upon citizens' willingness to share information. In its absence, governments have to learn what they need to know by coercion, or by offering expensive incentives. At the least, governments need citizens to fill out census forms, companies to supply information on sales, and sublevel governments to share information about performance. At a more complex level, police forces need citizens to report crimes and provide leads, courts need to count on the veracity of testimony given under oath, and regulators need whistle-blowers to report their employers' violations of securities and environmental laws. Without voluntary cooperation, the costs of penetration can be prohibitive.

Governments also need other forms of voluntary cooperation. Any system of income taxation depends upon citizens accurately to report their income, and to, in the main, pay the taxes they owe without the immediate threat of punishment. The criminal justice system needs to be able to count on most citizens' obeying the law most of the time without calculating the risk of apprehension. Welfare systems need most recipients to be honest in reporting their earnings and family composition. If employers do not internalize the norms of non-discrimination, the difficulty of detecting violators will make equal-opportunity laws nearly unenforceable. In societies where trust in government and moral strictures against non-cooperation are low, government failure will be more pervasive and the scope of market and non-market failures that governments can efficiently correct will be narrow.

Few governments have enough legitimacy among their citizens to generate as much penetrative capacity and voluntary cooperation as officials want. Citizens and wielders of informal power often resist attempts to make society "legible" from the center (Scott 1998). Such resistance is not always bad for the citizenry: higher government penetrative capacity and voluntary cooperation can expand the range of market failures that states can correct, but they can be used also for purely extractive purposes. Where government is fundamentally extractive rather than developmental, keeping its agents in the dark may actually increase overall social wealth by preventing the redistribution of resources from productive to unproductive activities. So whether improvements in government capacity in these areas lead to overall social improvement depends crucially on the honesty of those who operate the state machinery.

## 5.3 Cause Three: Institutional Overhead

Even where society is cooperative and social information plentiful, governments find other ways to fail. Instead of or alongside fixing private failures, officials can choose to serve themselves at the expense of public purposes by pursuing their own agendas without mobilizing consent (which we will call "subversion"), refusing to apply themselves ("shirking"), or using governmental power to enrich themselves or their cronies ("graft"). A well-designed government can reduce some of these problems but it cannot eliminate them all, and its attempts to limit them will likely cause other pathologies.

Typically, economists think of the relationship between higher and lower levels of organizations, such as governments, in terms of principal–agent relationships. Information asymmetry makes it hard for principals (the citizens with respect to elected leaders, or the elected leadership with respect to the bureaucracy, or higher-level officials with respect to lower-level officials) to ensure that their agents will comply with instructions: agents will tend to subvert, shirk, or indulge in graft. Principals thus need to develop mechanisms of enforcement or of incentive, which requires them to have the means to observe their agents' behavior or measure its results.

But those mechanisms are certain to have costs of their own. Making and enforcing detailed rules imposes costs and saps agents' energy and morale. "Red tape" is the other side of the coin of "corruption." Civil service personnel policies, low-bidder procurement regulations, and excessive audit requirements all make the jobs of public managers harder, and often cost much more than they save (Anechiarico and Jacobs 1996). Incentive-based systems encourage deception and performance simulation, in accord with Dukenfield's Law: "Anything worth winning is worth cheating for."

The higher the cost of these mechanisms to check agent misbehavior, the greater the agency losses. The higher the agency losses in government, the smaller the range of failures of voluntary action it can efficiently correct. Societies in which shirking, subversion, and graft are morally acceptable, or at least not highly stigmatized, will find the cost of government very high, and the desirable scope of government activity correspondingly limited.

Inefficiency also arises at the level of decision making. Different systems of government have different numbers of "veto points:" positions from which action can be blocked. Each veto point creates an opportunity for some constituency to ask for some consideration for not using its veto. Where nothing is demanded but appropriate side payments to convert a potential Pareto improvement into an actual Pareto improvement by redistributing some of the gains from the change to those who would otherwise be hurt by it—as in the familiar case of compensation for houses taken to build highways—this process is unproblematic; it can even help forestall projects whose costs in fact exceed their benefits. The problem arises when those who would not lose, and might even gain from the proposed policy use their veto-point position as a mere bargaining tool. At some point, the cost of paying off veto holders or their agents may make a project valuable in itself unfeasible, leaving the private failure it was to fix unremedied. Avinash Dixit refers to these payments as "political transaction costs" (Dixit 1998). Other things being equal, therefore, complex institutions, especially those with separation of powers or multilevel bargaining in government, should have larger political transaction costs.

On the other hand, systems with large numbers of veto points may also be characterized by more extensive deliberation. Every point where change may be stopped or compensation required is also a "deliberation point," where additional facts may be considered, arguments heard, consequences predicted. Systems that attempt to lower the cost of compensating veto players through centralization may be likelier to make big, costly mistakes due to haste, a cramped set of options, and insufficient foresight (Butler, Adonis, and Travers 1994). Thus centralized systems with fewer veto players are likely to have significant costs of decision making as well, but these will be large and relatively infrequent, while in decentralized systems the costs will be relatively small but marbled throughout most decisions. Either way, the process of decision making raises the cost of government intervention to correct private choice failures.

## 5.4 Cause Four: Voter Attention and Inattention

Voting, and related electioneering activity can be thought of as both information-gathering processes and decision processes. But there is no compelling reason to expect that voters will act in the public interest, or even in the interest of the smaller groups with which they identify. The outcome of an election is a public good, and efforts to influence it therefore suffer from free-rider problems.

A purely rational citizen would not even voluntarily vote—let alone engage in more costly political activity—unless under the dictates of conscience or reputation, because his private gain from having his candidate win the election, multiplied by the (vanishingly small) probability of his vote proving decisive, is smaller than his private cost of voting. The public choice literature considers it a paradox that people vote at all (Fiorina 1990).

Even if someone decides to vote, the private return to studying the candidates and issues is so small that a rationally selfish voter would remain "rationally ignorant" and so be unable to cast an informed vote (Downs 1957). If voters are usually uninformed, then elected officials have no strong incentive to serve voters' interests.

Olson (1971) theorized that groups that are comparatively successful in politically mobilizing their members—according to Olson by offering private rewards for participation—tend to overcome their less well-mobilized, even if larger competitors

(Olson 1971). That might not be true of voting, but it is a powerful insight into other forms of electoral activity, including financial contributions. "Private rewards" in Olson's sense need not be pecuniary: someone who attends a political fundraising event in part to meet the other attendees, and to be seen by them, derives a private benefit from attendance, a benefit from which non-contributors are excluded. Those private benefits, which James Q. Wilson calls "solidary benefits," can help overcome the free-riding problem (Wilson 1995). By the same token, the collective interests being pursued can be what Weber called "ideal interests" as well as material interests; the problem of whale lovers organizing to save the whales is analytically similar to the problem of veterans organizing to increase veterans' pensions.

Actual election turnouts disconfirm theories that predict turnouts close to zero, so the equation of *homo politicus* with *homo economicus* seems not to be a correct model of gross voting behavior. But that does not prove that free riding, in the form of rational ignorance, is not a substantial problem in democratic systems. And concern about the nature of the private benefits offered for political contributions is at the center of the ongoing debates about campaign finance reform. Thus there is reason to doubt that any decision-making process with mass voting at its base will produce consistently optimal decisions, or create strong incentives for elected or appointed officials to serve the public interest.

But the consequences of this argument for specific policies are perhaps less sweeping than they might seem. The fact that imbalances of attention frequently lead to policy biased toward the attentive does not mean that policy changes are never made in the interests of large, diffuse groups and against concentrated interests. They often are, as a quite substantial political science literature demonstrates.[13] These analyses demonstrate that what concentrated interests get from their attentiveness— and often their financial contributions—is reduced scrutiny from policy makers (Hall and Wayman 1990). However, when some focusing event or factor leads to heightened scrutiny, many of their advantages disappear.

That suggests that heightened public scrutiny improves decision making on a particular issue. Yet the public (under the spell of rational ignorance) will not attend to everything at once, or to any one thing (a few perennial issues excepted) for very long (Baumgartner and Jones 2005). So what happens after reform happens?

Other things being equal, the answer is that as attention shifts, the underlying, inherent imbalance of power reasserts itself, and the reform is slowly undermined. Eric Patashnik has demonstrated this pattern with such signal "public interest breakthroughs" as the 1986 Tax Reform Act and the 1996 Freedom to Farm Act (Patashnik 2003). Policy remains durable only where institutions or rules are put in place that make reversal difficult, or where exceptionally creative bureaucracies are established to act as policy guardians. Absent these factors, policy-making "regression to the mean" due to systematic inequality in attention should be factored into analysts' recommendations.

[13] Among the most important contributions are Arnold 1992, Landy and Levin 1995, and Baumgartner and Jones 1993.

## 5.5 Cause Five: The Path Dependence of Political Decision Making

The calculation that, given their relative defects, government decision making on some topic would produce better results than purely private choice does not exhaust the room for comparative analysis. The decision to prefer government decision making in the present may make reverting to voluntary decision making difficult in the future, if the original calculation proves incorrect or if the relative efficiency of markets and governments changes. If the recalibration of government response is more sluggish than the private response, and if the character or intensity of the problem varies over time, a policy choice that looks rational in the present may prove suboptimal over the long term. As a general matter, political decision making tends to be more path dependent than market-based decision making, because of the higher costs of mobilizing consent in political—especially democratic—systems.

The extent to which political decision making is path dependent (Pierson 2000, 2004) is largely determined by the design of institutions. Systems with large numbers of veto points usually make it relatively difficult to re-evaluate existing commitments, although they may make it easier to create new, and in some cases competing governmental responses.[14] Systems with fewer veto points generally make it easier to re-evaluate existing commitments, but the limited carrying capacity of the political agenda makes it harder for alternatives to get sustained policy attention.

"Corporatist" systems where decision making occurs largely at the top levels of relatively few organizations may find it easier to engage in incremental adjustment of existing commitments but because of the size of the organized units, difficult to generate support for major reassessment that imposes large costs.[15] Interest group systems, by contrast, may find it hard to adjust incrementally to problems, but because of the relatively small size of their organized units, easier to impose large costs when entrenched interests lose control of the agenda.[16]

Geographically centralized systems that encompass substantial diversity are likely to find it hard to mobilize consent to re-evaluate existing commitments. But where they do, they can impose that choice over a large scale. Geographically decentralized systems need to mobilize less consent to introduce alternative solutions in some locales, and in some cases competition in the market for policies (Wittman 1989) can lead to optimal solutions, but multiple policies in a single national jurisdiction can also lead to redundancy or destructive competition.[17] Moreover, widespread reforms under decentralized systems require political battles across a number of venues,

---

[14] On the character of decision making in systems with multiple entry points, see Baumgartner and Jones 1993.

[15] This is one account of both the spectacular, and highly government-directed Japanese economic success in the period up to the Asian currency crises of 1987 and the extreme difficulty Japan has had in reacting to the resulting banking crisis.

[16] On the relative characteristics of corporatist and interest group systems, see Scheingate 2001.

[17] An argument for the superior decision making of decentralized systems is made by Michael Greve (1999). For an argument about the limits of decentralization, see Teles and Landy 2001.

making it difficult to focus public attention sufficiently to overcome concentrated interests. Systems that delegate a great deal of decision-making authority to bureaucrats tend to have greater flexibility in adapting policies to changing circumstances than those that tightly circumscribe bureaucratic autonomy, but this advantage comes at the risk of bureaucrats' wresting effective agenda control from their political masters and the voters who choose them.

So while some institutional designs may improve the flexibility and reduce the path dependence of governmental responses to private choice failures, all carry risks of their own. While the institutional form matters, and in some cases matters a great deal, almost any form of political decision making involves quite substantial transaction costs in moving from one set of responses to another. But these macro-institutional factors are not the only considerations in explaining the relative stickiness of government solutions. Policies themselves create rules, institutions, and incentives that make them more or less easy to change, and may make reform more or less efficient and timely (Pierson 1994). These factors are, to some degree, under the control of the persons making the original decisions about whether to choose government or private control, though of course their evolution over time is only imperfectly predictable (Volokh 2003). Some decisions that increase adaptability may impose other costs, including difficulty in assembling the coalition necessary to enact the new policy in the first place.


## 5.6 Cause Six: Competition for Technical Expertise

While some public goals can be achieved through means that require only limited sophistication among public employees, others are intrinsically complex and require professionally informed judgement. In any society, at any moment, there is a fixed set of such skilled personnel, distributed between government and the private sector. The range of market failures that a government can effectively remedy will depend, in the first instance, on attracting individuals competent to carry out the task at hand. In other cases, government must attract workers who are not just competent but are competitive with their private sector counterparts. (Regulators must not be too far inferior in skill to those they regulate, or investigators to the crooks they try to catch.)

Attracting skilled individuals to public service becomes a more significant challenge as the scale of modernization increases. As societies become more complex, regulating them becomes harder, increasing the need for highly trained public servants. Yet increased social and economic complexity is also accompanied by increasing premiums for skill in the private sector (Frank and Cook 1995). Where egalitarian impulses, or concerns about the corruption that can result from placing large numbers of high-paying jobs in the gift of elected officials, make it difficult for the public sector to pay competitively, there will be a tendency for skilled personnel to leach out of the public sector, leaving government to select among the least competent or most risk-averse personnel. The result can be a downward spiral, where low salaries lead to poor performance by public agencies, poor performance to public disdain, and public disdain to low salaries. Norms making politicians and "bureaucrats" the bearers of stigma and the butt of jokes make the problem worse and can act as one mechanism of the downward spiral.

Government could respond to this competition by deregulating its own determination of professional salaries: it could empower managers to hire fewer but more highly compensated individuals or to spend more money on salaries and less on other things. While such deregulation almost always creates some risk of encouraging destructive forms of public job seeking, those risks need to be judged against the less visible effects of low overall civil service quality (DiIulio 1994).

The degree to which government is able to organize itself to compete for these highly trained and compensated individuals will substantially determine its ability to correct private choice failures in these areas. Such reforms are almost always difficult for governments to achieve, and competing with the private sector will tend to become more problematic as the level of development increases, sending the top end of private compensation ever higher.

What this suggests is that governments may have to consider the possibility that certain forms of regulation that could potentially correct significant private choice failures are unlikely to be effective given the competition for skilled personnel. What is more, where the regulators are significantly less talented than those they regulate, the presence of any government intervention at all may be worse than a completely unregulated environment. Governments may be better off with a clear, unambiguous policy of laissez-faire than with clumsy attempts to regulate processes that their civil servants cannot understand.

## 5.7 Cause Seven: Weak Administrative Culture

The quality of administrative agencies is not only a function of competition with the private sector for skilled individuals, because agencies are not simply aggregates of individual agents. Agencies are structured in particular ways through a process of historical inheritance that produces a relatively stable administrative culture. Moreover, agencies are embedded in a larger political culture that establishes expectations about how those agencies should operate, their scope for entrepreneurship and leadership within a system of separated powers, the degree to which they focus on problem solving as opposed to distributive politics or patronage, and the degree to which public service is considered an honorable or even respectable occupation.

Both the quality of an agency's administrative culture, and the orientation of the larger political culture that it is embedded in and draws upon, limit the interventions that a political system can contemplate. Lawrence Mead (2004) observes that Wisconsin was as successful as it has been with highly directive welfare reform in large part because it could draw upon a progressive political culture: one with a low tolerance for uncivil behavior, an orientation toward disinterested examination of social problems, and a legacy of efficient and entrepreneurial administrative agencies, connected to high-quality educational institutions designed to produced analytically skilled administrators. This set of inherited attitudes and institutions allowed the state to set ambitious goals for welfare reform, to work through the administrative consequences of those goals, and to make them a reality at the level of the street-level bureaucrat.

Mead shows that a culture of administrative quality is a precondition to making complex policy changes work. Motivating welfare clients actively to seek work and organize other parts of their lives requires that welfare administrators themselves be trained, equipped, and motivated. It requires that outcomes be closely tracked, and those outcomes fed back into an ongoing process of policy and administrative reform. Finally, it requires that the overall political system recognize major policy reform as a long-term process, which depends upon being willing to use bad news to make incremental changes rather than using it to score political or partisan points.

These requirements exceed the administrative and cultural inheritance that most states are able to draw upon. As a consequence most states have settled for less, counting upon changes in the larger economy to do most of the job of driving down welfare rolls, or imposing benefit cut-offs without the benefit of close supervision. Some states have recognized that their administrative culture fell short of their ambitions to replicate Wisconsin-style welfare reform, and have attempted to build up such a culture on the fly. While they have had some success, they have also been pushing against their administrative inheritance, requiring them to engage in "state building" at the same time as they were putting in place a new policy, but without the supportive cultural background that Wisconsin could count on. Their results have been correspondingly modest.

This suggests that policy makers need to recognize that administrative quality, and the cultural background that it rests upon, cannot be assumed, and can be created ad hoc only to a limited degree. Where the inherited administrative culture is weak, policy aspiration must be scaled down correspondingly.

That being so, the impact of a proposed policy change on the administrative culture may be more important, in the long run, than its immediate costs and benefits. A good public manager is not merely a skilled administrator of current policies, but a good steward of his or her agency's capacity to produce public benefit into the future.

# 6. Putting it Together: Policy Making in a World of Imperfect Alternatives

Human beings and the social groups they form are astoundingly self-regulating, capable of remarkable feats of optimization without external direction, especially if the market is allowed to exert its power of making every participant's wants a motive for others to satisfy those wants. That insight remains the key to the fundamentally liberal form of social and political organization that has enjoyed such spectacular success over the past three centuries.

But neither individual nor social self-regulation is perfect. Economists have assembled a growing catalog of market failures; when markets fail (fail, that is, to reach Pareto-optimal outcomes) there may be scope for the coercive powers of government to improve matters. There exists no comparable catalog of the failures of individual self-command, or of the failures of non-market forms of voluntary cooperation, but their existence is hard to deny. Once such failures are recognized, both paternalistic intervention to protect individuals from themselves and interventions designed to rectify the failures of the institutions of civil society appear as justifications for government action on a par with the classical market failures.

Still, no situation is so bad that it can't be made worse. To say that a condition is suboptimal is not to say that coercive intervention by the state will improve matters. State action is subject to its own list of suboptimalities, known in the public choice literature as "government failures." Moreover, coercive intervention can if not carefully designed, worsen the individual and institutional failures whose consequences it sets out to correct. A comprehensive policy analysis therefore requires an analysis of both sets of failures, with an eye not merely to the best resolution of the current controversy but to the "constitutional" consequences of a decision to act, or to let be.

If the foregoing argument is correct, it has important consequences for policy areas beyond the scope of our analysis, and in particular to the problem of distribution.

On the one hand, there are some powerful arguments for increased equality: the diminishing marginal utility of income, the measured impacts on individuals' physical and psychological health of having low relative (as opposed to absolute) income or wealth, the difficulty of maintaining equality of opportunity when children grow up with very different levels of family advantage, the incompatibility of democracy as a political ideal with the differences in political power created by extreme economic stratification, the destructive social tensions extreme stratification can create, and the prospect that reduced stratification might lead to reduced wealth-signaling behavior and thus welfare-enhancing shifts of energy from material acquisition to living well.

But the analytical leverage to be had by a wider recognition of areas where the results of private choice may be suboptimal needs to be accompanied by an assessment of the likely governmental response to the demand for a wider scope of redistribution. Enforcement of a collective decision to reduce working hours, for example, depends upon the supervisory and coercive powers of government, and also perhaps, on the ability of government to hire staff sophisticated enough to detect cheating. Such policies might also be subject to the attention disequilibrium described above—while the public may be highly aroused to create such a policy, those who most immediately feel its costs (such as employers) are likely to sustain their interests in undermining its impact in practice. Unless a means is discovered to maintain the public ardor that created the pressure for the income–leisure swap in the first place, its impact may be severely degraded over time, while imposing administrative costs that could, in the aggregate, make the policy worse in practice than no policy at all.

This analysis touches the very core of political theory. The inheritors of Rawlsian political philosophy rarely consider the shape and character of the political institutions that will be created to bring into practice the distributive preferences deduced from behind the veil of ignorance. But those reasoning about justice in ways intended to connect to the real world need knowledge of the predictable effects of the operation of actual political institutions. (An important exception to the absence of sophisticated analyses connecting political theory and institutional design is Rothstein 1998.) The shape of desirable redistribution may be altered by a recognition not only of what actual political institutions will do with the demand for extensive redistribution, but also what institutions so empowered will be able to do to (and perhaps for) citizens when their scope has been increased. Ultimately, normative political economy must grapple with institutional and political questions.

Public policy, institutional analysis, and political philosophy do not deal with three distinct subject matters; rather, they are three different attempts to deal with the problem of how human beings ought to govern themselves. The world will not be well governed until the statesmen learn to pay attention to the results of careful thought and the thinkers take the problems of statesmanship seriously.

# REFERENCES

AINSLIE, G. 2001. *Breakdown of Will.* Cambridge: Cambridge University Press.

AKERLOF, G. 1970. The market for lemons: quality uncertainty and the market mechanism. *Quarterly Journal of Economics*, 84 (3): 488–500.

ANDERSON, E. 2000. *The Code of the Streets.* New York: Norton.

ANECHIARICO, F., and JACOBS, J. 1996. *The Pursuit of Absolute Integrity: How Corruption Control Makes Government Ineffective.* Chicago: University of Chicago Press.

ARNOLD, D. 1992. *The Logic of Congressional Action.* New Haven, Conn.: Yale University Press.

ARROW, K. J. 1985. The economics of agency. Pp. 37–51 in *Principals and Agents: The Structure of Business*, ed. J. Pratt and R. Zeckhauser. Cambridge, Mass.: Harvard Business School.

BANFIELD, E. 1965. *The Moral Basis of a Backward Society.* Glencoe, Ill.: Free Press.

BATOR, F. M. 1958. The anatomy of market failure. *Quarterly Journal of Economics*, Aug.: 351–79.

—— 1959. The simple analytics of welfare maximization. *American Economic Review*, 47: 22–59.

BAUMGARTNER, F., and JONES, B. 1993. *Agendas and Instability in American Politics.* Chicago: University of Chicago Press.

—— —— 2005. *The Politics of Attention: How Government Prioritizes Problems.* Chicago: University of Chicago Press.

BAUMOL, W. J. 2002. *The Free Market Innovation Machine.* Princeton, NJ: Princeton University Press.

BLACKORBY, C., and DONALDSON, D. 1988. Cash versus kind, self-selection, and efficient transfers. *American Economic Review*, 78: 691–700.

BUCHANAN, J. M. 1999/1968. *The Demand and Supply of Public Goods.* Indianapolis: Liberty Fund.

BURKE, E. 1974. Speech on the conciliation of America. Pp. 66–134 in *Burke's Speeches: On American Taxation, On Conciliation with America, & Letter to the Sheriffs of Bristol,* ed. F. G. Selby. Westport, Conn.: Greenwood Press; first pub. 1780.

BUTLER, D., ADONIS, A., and TRAVERS, T. 1994. *Failure in British Government: The Politics of the Poll Tax.* Oxford: Oxford University Press.

COASE, R. H. 1960. The problem of social cost. *Journal of Law and Economics,* 3: 144.

CROZIER, M., HUNNINGTON, S., and WATANUKI, J. 1975. *The Crises of Democracy.* New York: New York University Press.

DELONG, B. J. 2004. On the maximization of social welfare. In *Brad DeLong's Semi-Daily Journal;* www.j-bradford-delong.net/movable_type/2004_archives/001113.html.

DiIULIO, J. (ed.) 1994. *Deregulating the Public Service: Can Government Be Improved?* Washington, DC: Brookings Institution Press.

DIXIT, A. 1998. *The Making of Economic Policy: A Transaction Cost Approach to Politics.* Cambridge, Mass.: MIT Press.

DOUGLAS, J. 1976. The overloaded crown. *British Journal of Political Science,* 6(4): 483–505.

DOWNS, A. 1957. *An Economic Theory of Democracy.* Boston: Addison-Wesley.

EASTERLIN, R. (ed.) 2002. *Happiness in Economics.* Cheltenham: Edward Elgar.

ELSTER, J. 1979. *Ulysses and the Sirens.* Cambridge: Cambridge University Press.

EVANS, P. 1995. *Embedded Autonomy: States and Industrial Autonomy.* Princeton, NJ: Princeton University Press.

FEHR, E., and GÄCHTER, S. 2000. Fairness and retaliation: the economics of reciprocity. *Journal of Economic Perspectives,* 14: 159–81.

FIORINA, M. 1990. Information and rationality in elections. Pp. 329–42 in *Information and Democratic Processes,* ed. J. Ferejohn and J. Kuklinski. Urbana: University of Illinois Press.

FRANK, R. H. 1999. *Luxury Fever.* New York: Free Press.

—— and COOK, P. 1995. *The Winner-Take-All Society.* New York: Free Press.

FUNG, A. 2004. *Empowered Participation: Reinventing Urban Democracy.* Princeton, NJ: Princeton University Press.

GLAZER, N. 1988. *The Limits of Social Policy.* Cambridge, Mass.: Harvard University Press.

GREVE, M. 1999. *Real Federalism: Why It Matters, How It Could Happen.* Washington, DC: AEI.

HALL, R., and WAYMAN, F. 1990. Buying time? The mobilization of bias in congressional committees. *American Political Science Review,* 84 (3): 797–820.

HARDIN, G. 1968. The tragedy of the commons. *Science,* 162: 1243–8.

JEFFERSON, T. 1813. The natural aristocracy. Letter to John Adams, 28 Oct.

KAHNEMAN, D., SLOVIC, P., and TVERSKY, A. 1990. The causes of preference reversal. *American Economic Review,* 80 (1): 204–17.

KELLING, G., and MOORE, M. H. 1988. The evolving strategy of policing. Pp. 36–55 in *Perspectives on Policing.* Washington, DC: National Institute of Justice.

KELMAN, S. 1986. A case for in-kind transfers. *Economics and Philosophy,* 2: 53–74.

KLEIMAN, M. 1992. *Against Excess: Drug Policy for Results.* New York: Basic Books.

—— and CAULKINS, J. 2001. Noticing the micro-distributional consequences of cigarette taxation and its equivalents. *Journal of Policy Analysis and Management,* 20 (2): 337–48.

LANDY, M., and LEVIN, M. (eds.) 1995. *The New Politics of Public Policy.* Baltimore: Johns Hopkins University Press.

LAYARD, R. 2005. *Happiness.* London: Penguin.

LOCKE, J. 1988. Of paternal power. Pp. 52–3 in *The Second Treatise of Government*, ed. P. Laslett. Cambridge: Cambridge University Press; first pub. 1690.

LOEWENSTEIN, G. 1996. Out of control: visceral influences on behavior. *Organizational Behavior and Human Decision Processes*, 65: 272–92.

MEAD, L. 1997. The rise of paternalism. Pp. 1–37 in *The New Paternalism: Supervisory Approaches to Poverty*, ed. L. M. Mead. Washington, DC: Brookings Institution Press.

—— 2004. *Government Matters*. Princeton, NJ: Princeton University Press.

O'HARE, M. 1989. A typology of governmental action. *Journal of Policy Analysis and Management*, 8 (4): 670–2.

OLSON, M. 1971. *The Logic of Collective Action: Public Goods and the Theory of Groups*. Cambridge, Mass.: Harvard University Press.

PATASHNIK, E. 2003. After the public interest prevails: the political sustainability of policy reform. *Governance*, 16 (2): 203–15.

PIERSON, P. 1994. *Dismantling the Welfare State?* Cambridge: Cambridge University Press.

—— 2000. Increasing returns, path dependency and the study of politics. *American Political Science Review*, 94 (2): 251–68.

—— 2004. *Politics in Time: History, Institutions, and Social Analysis*. Princeton, NJ: Princeton University Press.

PIGOU, A. C. 1912. *Wealth and Welfare*. London: Macmillan.

PLATT, J. 1973. Social traps. *American Psychologist*, 28: 641–51.

PRICE, R. 1992. *Clockers*. Boston: Houghton-Mifflin.

PUTNAM, R. 2002. *Bowling Alone*. New York: Simon and Schuster.

RAWLS, J. 1971. *A Theory of Justice*. Cambridge, Mass.: Harvard University Press.

ROSE, R., and PETERS, B. G. 1975. *Can Government Go Bankrupt?* London: Macmillan.

ROTHSTEIN, B. 1998. *Just Institutions Matter: The Moral and Political Logic of the Universal Welfare State*. Cambridge: Cambridge University Press.

SCHEINGATE, A. 2001. *The Rise of the Agricultural Welfare State*. Princeton, NJ: Princeton University Press.

SCHELLING, T. 1984. *Choice and Consequence*. Cambridge, Mass.: Harvard University Press.

SCOTT, J. 1985. *Weapons of the Weak: Everyday Forms of Peasant Resistance*. New Haven, Conn.: Yale University Press.

—— 1998. *Seeing Like a State*. New Haven, Conn.: Yale University Press.

SMITH, A. 2002. *The Theory of Moral Sentiments*, ed. K. Haakonssen. Cambridge: Cambridge University Press; first pub. 1759.

TELES, S., and LANDY, M. 2001. Beyond devolution: from subsidiarity to mutuality. Pp. 413–27 in *The Federal Vision: Legitimacy and Levels of Government in the US and EU.*, ed. R. Howse and K. Nikolaidis. Oxford: Oxford University Press.

THUROW, L. 1977. Cash vs. in-kind redistribution. Pp. 85–106 in *Markets and Morals*, ed. G. Dworkin, G. Bermant, and P. Brown. Washington, DC: Hemisphere.

VEBLEN, T. 1899. *The Theory of the Leisure Class: An Economic Study of Institutions*. New York: Macmillan.

VOLOKH, E. 2003. The mechanisms of the slippery slope. *Harvard Law Review*, 116: 1026.

WADE, R. 1990. *Governing the Market: Economic Theory and the Role of Government in East Asian Industrialization*. Princeton, NJ: Princeton University Press.

WILSON, J. Q. 1995. *Political Organizations*. Princeton, NJ: Princeton University Press.

WINSHIP, C. 1999. New approaches to urban crime: Boston cops and black churches. *Public Interest*, 136: 52–68.

WITTMAN, D. 1989. Why democracies produce efficient results. *Journal of Political Economy*, 97 (6): 1395–424.

WOLF, C. Jr. 1988. *Markets or Governments: Choosing between Imperfect Alternatives.* Cambridge, Mass.: MIT Press.

ZECKHAUSER, R. 1974. Risk spreading and distribution. Pp. 206–28 in *Redistribution through Public Choice*, ed. H. M. Hochman and G. E. Peterson. New York: Columbia University Press.

—— 1993. Insurance. Pp. 22–6 in *The Fortune Encyclopedia of Economics*, ed. D. R. Henderson. New York: Warner.

# PRIVATIZATION AND REGULATORY REGIMES

## COLIN SCOTT

## 1. INTRODUCTION

Regulation, both as public policy instrument and as field of investigation, was apparently an area of dramatic growth in the last quarter of the twentieth century. The policy boom may be explained in part by a loss of confidence in traditional mechanisms of public ownership in many fields of public service delivery in OECD countries. This disenchantment was combined with a perception that public ownership was a drag on fiscally constrained economies, whereas selling off assets provided positive fiscal benefits. Policies of privatization (defined narrowly in this chapter as transfer of ownership of state assets—see the analytical discussion of wider conceptions of privatization by Feigenbaum, Henig, and Hamnett 1999, 8–11) were accompanied by processes of public management reform within bureaucracies. These reform processes have, in many countries, liberalized some aspects of central public management, while at the same time being accompanied by the creation of new layers of regulation over public sector activities, frequently in new or remodeled free-standing agencies (Hood et al. 2004).

The focus on regulation as the problem of control for sectors where ownership was transferred from public to private sector stimulated the identification of other, long-established policy processes (for example in financial services and health care sectors and over economy-wide issues such as occupational health and safety, consumer protection, and the environment) as also belonging to the set of regulatory activities. Consequently there has been much for scholars in the relatively new field of regulation to examine, even though many of the phenomena were not exactly new.

* I am grateful to Martin Lodge for comments on an earlier version of this chapter.

The central concerns of the public policy literature in understanding this transformation in governance have been with the emergence of the regulatory state (Braithwaite 2000; Majone 1994*b*; Moran 2002, 2003; Sunstein 1990), and with the qualities and problems associated with regulatory agencies (Macey 1992; Thatcher 2002; Thatcher and Sweet 2002). This focus within the political science literature may partly be explained by the interest within the discipline in formal state institutions, which generates a concern to map an apparent shift in power from government departments to autonomous agencies, linked to privatization policies which have swept through the OECD since the early 1980s.

The risk faced by the discipline in focusing on these two linked dimensions of regulation, the regulatory state and agencies, is that this model of regulation as an instrument of governance may obscure as much as it illuminates. More specifically the approach is open to the criticism that it assumes too strongly the transfer and adoption of public policy institutions and processes which it may be argued, are peculiar to the United States and unlikely to be replicated elsewhere. It is ironic that the policy boom in regulation occurred at a time when the agenda in the USA was geared towards attempting to dismantle a good part of its regulatory heritage through programmes of deregulation. Even before regulation as an instrument of government had matured elsewhere, the OECD was calling for extensive regulatory reform (OECD 1997*b*).

One way to reconceptualize the field, developed in this chapter, is to conceive of the institutions, norms, and processes of regulation in a somewhat broader way than is suggested by the American model of public regulation of business by agencies. According to this reconceptualization regulation occurs within "regimes" characterized by diffuse populations of actors and considerable diversity in the norms and mechanisms of control. The concept of regimes facilitates us in making a link between regulation, with its traditional narrow conception of state institutions and laws, and contemporary analysis of governance. A governance narrative emphasizes the fragmentation of regulatory power in contemporary policy processes. This approach is skeptical about the possibility of wholesale delegation of regulatory power to agencies and is more open to the possibility that power may be shared and diffused. As regards state organizations and power, this critique notes that outside the United States delegation to agencies commonly involves the substantial retention of power by ministerial departments (Hall, Scott, and Hood 2000). Second it notes an OECD-wide trend towards exerting a substantial degree of oversight over agencies, not just through the courts, but also through central agencies concerned with the promotion of regulatory efficiency.

The "intra-state diffusion of regulatory power" (Daintith 1997) is accompanied and magnified by further diffusion of key regulatory capacities both to supranational governance organizations (Braithwaite and Drahos 2000) and to a variety of non-state actors (Grabosky 1994). This organizational diffusion is coupled with diversity in mechanisms of control to embrace not only conventional hierarchical methods and official non-legal alternatives (such as soft law), but also modalities rooted in the capacities of both community and competitive processes to exert control. Viewed from this perspective the focus on public regulatory agencies exerting control through legal authority appears incomplete at best, and perhaps seriously misleading for those seeking to understand ideas about regulatory regimes.

## 2. REGULATORY REGIMES AND INTERDEPENDENCE

There is no consensus in policy or academic circles as to what exactly is connoted by the term regulation. Selznick's classic definition—"sustained and focused control exercised by a public agency over activities that are socially valued" (Selznick 1985, 363–7)—is often cited with approval (Majone 1994*b*; Ogus 1994). But the exclusive focus on public agencies, common within American studies of regulation, is problematic when so much regulatory activity is "decentred" (Black 2001*a*). Many regulatory regimes do not focus on a public agency (whether a government department or independent agency) as regulator, and even where they do such agencies may not have a monopoly over regulatory power (Francis 1993, 43–8).

A strength of Selznick's definition is that it comprehends not only oversight by reference to rules (consistent with the *OED* definition of regulation) but also other forms of control. Empirical analyses of regulatory activities within particular domains do, in many cases, point to a diffusion of regulatory capacities among a range of state, non-state, and supranational actors. Resources relevant to the exercise of power within regulatory regimes include legal authority, wealth, organizational capacity, information, and the capacity to bestow legitimacy (cf. Daintith 1997; Hood 1984).

It has often been observed in empirical studies that regulators rarely use their formal powers of enforcement, and are more likely to use strategies based on education, advice, and persuasion to secure some form of compliance (Grabosky and Braithwaite 1986). Such observations have been used to ground a prescriptive theory which suggests that regulators should generally seek to rely on such low-level strategies, at the base of a pyramid of regulatory enforcement, and only escalate to more formal and coercive measures where lower-level strategies have failed (Ayres and Braithwaite 1992). Even in the case of legal authority, power is liable to be fragmented—a factor which creates problems for the rational and instrumental deployment of regulatory pyramids by agencies (Scott 2004). For example, a regulatory agency may have powers to monitor sectors of the market, to collect information, and to initiate enforcement actions. But it is not unusual to find that legislatures or government departments reserve to themselves powers to make or change regulatory rules, in addition to the wider power to change the regime as a whole. Furthermore it is quite common to find that formal sanctions can only be applied with the consent or decision of a tribunal or a court. Within most systems regulatees may wield formal legal power, for example to consent to rule changes, to make enforceable undertakings, or through standing to challenge regulatory decisions by means of litigation. Indeed, the formalization of norms within regulatory regimes, a hallmark characteristic of the transition to the regulatory state (Loughlin and Scott 1997), carries with it the risk of juridification and the displacement of effective social norms by a dependence on legal rules which are incapable of grounding such effective control (Teubner 1998/1987). This kind of challenge in the use of law for regulatory purposes has led both to critiques of inherent "fuzzy legality" (Cohn 2001) and prescriptions for "regulation of self-regulation" (Teubner 1984) and proceduralization as mechanisms for escaping from the adverse effects of legalization (Black 2000, 2001*b*).

In many regimes formal legal authority is shared between national and supra-national governmental organizations, particularly in respect of standard setting. States are key players within "webs of influence" through which supranational regulatory regimes emerge and develop (Braithwaite and Drahos 2000). But that significance does not lie in the capacity of any individual state to determine the direction taken by a regime; rather there is a range of strategies by which governments may respond to forces over which they exert little control.

In some regimes the legal authority component is constituted not by legislation but by contracts, giving regulatory relations more of the flavour of agreements than hierarchical instruments. Some of these instances of "contractual regulation" are individuated in character—taking the form of agreements between two parties, one of whom, for example a major public or private purchaser, is likely to exert greater power in setting the contractual rules of the game (Scott 2002). In other cases the contractual basis is collective. Thus, while some self-regulation (for example as it applies to legal and medical professions) may be authorized by statute, many self-regulatory regimes are underpinned by contracts between the members of a trade association which empower the association to make and enforce rules against their members. An apparent paradox, never fully taken on board by self-regulation skeptics, is that self-regulatory associations typically wield the full array of regulatory powers—rule making, monitoring, and enforcement—within a single organization, untroubled by the kind of regulatory fragmentation more common in public regulatory regimes. Not all self-regulation is characterized by such monopolistic power, and for Ogus (1995) the potential for competition between self-regulatory organizations offers a means of control over their activities. Such competition is liable to be magnified at the international level where national or regional self-regulatory associations find themselves competing both for credibility and for members with other similar bodies.

The other resources relevant to the exercise of power within regulatory regimes are typically more widely distributed than legal authority. It has long been observed by economists that firms are liable to possess more information than consumers and also regulators (defined as "information asymmetry" (Arrow 1963)), pointing up a particular form of weakness in the capacity of agencies to regulate. In sectors characterized by small numbers of large firms regulatees are also likely to have greater wealth and organizational capacity than agencies, giving them greater capacity to participate effectively in regulatory proceedings or to interpret regulatory rules.

It is not straightforward to offer an a priori suggestion as to which actors are likely to have the capacity to bestow legitimacy on a regime. Under different conditions it may be any of government, agencies, regulatees, supranational organization, or NGOs.

Taken together, the observations that resources relevant to the exercise of power within regulatory regimes are typically widely dispersed, and that much regulatory control is not effected through the application of formal legal authority, suggest the "regulatory regime" may be a more appropriate unit of analysis than the regulatory agency. Regime is a concept borrowed from the study of international relations (Krasner 1983) which highlights the "historically specific configuration of policies and institutions which structures the relationship between social interests, the state, and economic actors in multiple sectors of the economy" (Eisner 2000, 1).

Eisner's regimes analysis, rooted in the context of US regulatory policy in the twentieth century, does focus on the regulatory agency as the basic unit of analysis (Eisner 2000, 15). But he shows that the "market regimes" established during the Progressive era (for example for regulation of competition and interstate commerce) have been followed by further waves of regulation, promoting the role of interest groups in "associational regimes" in the New Deal era and "societal regimes" in the postwar period. Eisner characterizes the emergence of controls over regulation and the deregulation movement which developed from the 1970s as an "efficiency regime" (Eisner 2000, 8–9).

The dynamics within the US polity generating these different structures and rationales for regulation have been interpreted as a product of complex interactions between changing environment, interests, ideas, and institutional histories (Hood 1994). The economic theory of regulation (ETR) developed in the work of George Stigler (Stigler 1971) and Samuel Peltzman (Peltzman 1976) in the 1970s, has been highly influential in the development of a somewhat jaundiced explanation for the development of regulatory regimes by reference to the pursuit of interests. The ETR conceives of regulation as a service provided by government for which there is supply and demand akin to a market. Behaviour for firms, bureaucrats, politicians, and others is explained by reference to the standard economic assumption that individuals are in the rational pursuit of their own utility. These actors all seek "rents" as the rewards for their actions. Though hardly tested empirically (or arguably, capable of being tested) the hypothesis that regulation was likely to be supplied by government to favor those interests willing to pay the most (by means of contributions to election funds, and perhaps also bribes) and would thus nearly always favor large firms rather than serve any conception of the public interest has been influential.

It was something of a problem for the economic theory that it struggled to explain the emergence of social regulation in the postwar period which appeared to favor less wealthy and more diffuse interests such as employees and consumers. The interests-based theory was considerably sharpened by political scientist James Q. Wilson in his coalitional theory. Wilson (1980) suggests that political preferences are more complex than simply the aggregate of society's utility functions, and liable to be shaped through political processes which may yield coalitions on particular issues. Thus, it is more than narrowly concentrated interests which shape the initiation and development of regulatory regimes.

Proponents of ETR faced another challenge when, rather against the expectations of their hypotheses, the US federal government began dismantling regulation in such industries as trucking, airlines, and telecommunications in the 1970s. One possible response is to suggest that the political system somehow managed to produce a set of outcomes which heroically challenge the apparent inevitability that public policies will be provided to support wealthy interests. A second possibility, perhaps linked to the first, is that ideas of the kind being developed by proponents of ETR and others had themselves become factors shaping the behaviour of actors in developing deregulatory policies (Derthick and Quirk 1985). Peltzman (1989), however, attempted a bold application of ETR to explain the apparent paradox of deregulation. He suggested that the industries which had been subject to deregulation had each experienced reductions in the rents available to the service providers. Consequently major industry players had less to offer politicians and bureaucrats to reward this behaviour and consequently, at some point, the bias of the regime towards favoring industry incumbents tipped to favour others. Put briefly, "[t]he rents supporting the political equilibrium eroded" (Peltzman 1989). He recognizes that this revised account does not appear to provide a universal explanation for what happened. In telecommunications, in particular, he suggests that regulators could have protected monopoly rents for a longer period than they did, and that deregulation is better explained by reference to changing ideas about the performance of the public function by regulatory officials (Peltzman 1989). The strength of the ETR appears to lie in the influence it has had in causing widespread questioning, in both policy and academic circles, of assumptions that regulation serves the public interest. The case for its capacity to explain dynamic processes of regulatory change is, at best, unproven.

European scholarship on the dynamics of regulatory regimes cannot ignore the powerful influence of the literature which has emerged from the context of American regulatory policies and procedures. Some, such as Giandomenico Majone, embrace the American model and doctrines, advocating, for example, substantial adoption of the US model of independent regulatory agencies and suggesting that a process of convergence is already occurring (Majone and Everson 2001). Others are more skeptical. Leigh Hancher and Michael Moran (Hancher and Moran 1989) challenge assumptions about the risk of regulatory capture, showing that within European political systems the diffusion of power within "regulatory space" reduces the applicability of ideas about either *ex ante* capture of the ETR variety or *ex post* capture of the type posited in Bernstein's life-cycle theory of regulation (Bernstein 1951). The concept of regulatory space provides a powerful metaphor for encouraging closer attention to the attributes, ideas, interests, and capacities of the variety of actors found within regulatory regimes (Hancher and Moran 1989; Lange 2003; Scott 2001; Shearing 1993).

The approach also encourages us to think beyond state organizations as regulators. Thus we can incorporate in models of regulation both professional and industry self-regulation, regulation by contract (by both state and non-state bodies), and the work of private standard-setting organizations such as the national standards organizations established in Germany (DIN), France (AFNOR), the UK (BSI), and the United States (ANSI) in the first quarter of the twentieth century, together with their more recent supranational counterpart, the International Standard Organization (ISO, established in 1946). The tendency to treat international regulatory bodies, whether governmental or non-governmental, as somehow "external" can also be countered by linking the regimes approach to ideas of regulatory space.

# 3. Modalities of Control

It is a weakness within the political science literature on regulation generally that it has paid closer attention to the emergence of regulatory regimes and the policy-making processes surrounding them, at the expense of investigating day-to-day processes of implementation which have largely been the preserve of sociolegal scholarship. In support of closer investigation of how regulatory regimes are implemented, the idea of regulatory space can be given greater analytical clarity by introducing conceptions of control which have been read across from cybernetics. This approach suggests that any viable regulatory regime should have each of the three identifiable components of a system of control (Hood, Rothstein, and Baldwin 2001). Within this analysis any control system must have some rule, goal, standard, or norm (director in cybernetics speak), a mechanism for monitoring or feeding back information about compliance with the rule, goal, standard, or norm (detector), and a means by which deviational performance is realigned (effector). In a classical regulatory analysis these components map onto rules, monitoring, and enforcement. This approach has two particular strengths. First it promotes an analysis which precisely identifies the dispersal of the three components of a regulatory regime around the various actors within the regulatory space. Secondly it encourages us to recognize modalities of control which either supplement hierarchical control (in hybrid forms) or wholly substitute for it. Thus community-based control operates through the emergence of norms in social settings with monitoring through mutual observation of actors within a community and realignment of deviant conduct through the application of social sanctions such as disapproval and ostracization. Within competition-based control, standards emerge through the rivalry of actors jockeying for position in markets or in other settings, information about compliance with the standards is fed back into the system through the implicit monitoring of performance, for example by buyers in markets, and deviant behaviour is realigned by the aggregated decisions of diffuse actors who use information about performance (for example buyers choosing to buy elsewhere, or parents choosing to send their children to different schools).

While the first three modalities of control, hierarchy, competitition, and community, are well established in the literature, albeit with a variety of labels, there is no consensus on the existence of a fourth modality, labelled "contrived randomness" in the work of Christopher Hood (Hood 1998; Hood et al. 1999) and "architecture" by Lawrence Lessig (Lessig 1999). The former concept refers to the deliberate building into regulatory systems of uncertainty as to what the payoffs of regulatee conduct may be, for example by randomly rotating regulatory staff to different positions, or using unannounced inspection visits to detect infractions. Lessig's architecture category traces its lineage back to Bentham's proposals to increase the effectiveness and reduce the cost of incarceration through the design of a prison in the form of a Panopticon in which guards located in a central tower are able to carry out surveillance of all parts of the prison from a single location. More recent applications of the idea have sought to develop architectural solutions to the problem of crime control (Newman 1972) and in Lessig's own work (1999), the design of software code by manufacturers as a means to prevent users from engaging in certain forms of behavior. In each case randomness and architecture are self-enforcing mechanisms rooted in design. Randomness self-enforces through behavioral responses to uncertainty, whereas architecture self-enforces through physical inhibition—the classic example contrasts the efficacy of the concrete parking bollard with the uncertainty as to whether a parking attendant will show up and issue a ticket for an illegally parked car. The weakness of the concrete bollard is that it prevents parking at all times, whereas policy may only require parking restrictions during certain times of the day (the problem of over-inclusiveness).

In practice the "modalities of control" are often found in hybrid forms in particular regulatory regimes. Thus competition policy employs a combination of hierarchy and competition as a means to control the behaviour of market actors. Enforced self-regulation combines hierarchy with the capacities of businesses to regulate themselves. Mandatory product rules which require the implementation of design-based controls over user behaviour, such as automatic cut-out devices, combine hierarchy with architecture. A challenge for regulation scholars is to identify and incorporate into their analyses mechanisms of control which combine the modalities *other than hierarchy* and by doing so move beyond the preoccupation with hierarchical control within state-centric approaches to regulatory governance (Scott 2004).

# 4. Varieties of Regulatory Organization and Style

The emergence of regulation as an international field of public policy and scholarly enquiry carries with it the risk that regulation will be conceived of as a homogeneous and uniform policy instrument involving particular organizational forms and styles. There is much work to be done in building on the pioneering scholarship which has emphasized the nature and extent of variety in these dimensions of regulation. David Vogel's classic comparative study of environmental regulation in the United States contrasted the characteristics of "secrecy, informality, and voluntary compliance" of the British regime with "the more open, legalistic, and adversarial styles of regulation adopted in the United States" (Vogel 1986, 146). Notwithstanding the striking variation in styles, Vogel was not able to detect much difference in the effectiveness of the two regimes, despite the observation that American standards appeared much stricter (Vogel 1986, 161–2).

Though the first of the great federal independent commissions, the Interstate Commerce Commission, was established in the 1880s it was the proliferation of agencies in the New Deal period which gave regulation a central position in American public management and spawned the early classic studies (Bernstein 1951; Cushman 1941; Landis 1938). The 1930s can perhaps be seen as a period of maturing of the regulatory form of governance. By the 1950s most European countries had assigned many of the activities operated through regulated private enterprise in the United States to government-owned enterprises of one kind or another. This was the position in respect of provision of telephone, telegraph, energy, railways, and airlines, for example. This observation was behind contrasting characterizations of the United States as a regulatory state and European countries, by and large, as welfare or provider states (Majone 1994b).

But this distinction between modes of governance is over-simple. The United States Interstate Commerce Commission was modelled on a British organization, the Railways Commission, which when created in 1873, was a landmark institutional reform because of the shift it represented from regulation by government departments and boards and the emergence of a doctrine of independence for regulatory agencies somewhat akin to the doctrine of the independence of the judiciary (Dimock 1933). The Railways Commision was, in essence, a tribunal applying legislative rules through processes of adjudication. But the British had developed other regulatory techniques earlier in the nineteenth century, introducing inspection into many areas of economic life, as with the factories inspectorate, as a means to promoting compliance with statutory norms. Some European countries had traditions of government inspectorates dating back to the eighteenth century—as with the well-known case of the Prussian Polizei (Raeff 1983). Viewed from the vantage point of the twenty-first century, European experimentation with public ownership as a distinctive form of provision may look like a relatively long blip in a history of state–industry relations in which the norm is regulated private provision. For example, the divergent policies and structures of France, Britain, and the USA for the pursuit of railways policy in the nineteenth century were each based on regulated private ownership (Dobbin 1994). The observation that European countries have long traditions of state regulation, and distinct "varieties of regulatory capitalism" (Levi-Faur 2005), suggests that any shift towards regulatory forms of governance is likely to be towards distinctively European forms rather than wholesale adoption of American models. The same arguments might be deployed for other countries such as those of north Asia. Kagan has characterized the American style of regulation in terms of "adversarial legalism" and suggests that Japanese regimes in domains such as pollution control, occupational health and safety, and financial services have a deserved reputation for informality and flexibility in their implementation (Kagan 2000; but cf. Schaede 2000).

Taking one example of regulatory reform, it is easy to represent privatization as a withdrawal of the state from determining key issues of public service provision through transfer of ownership into private hands. But in many cases the central state exerted little control over public enterprises, which were frequently free to develop and execute their own policies. Policies of privatization pursued diverse motivations for governments. The UK government stumbled upon a policy which was initially "pragmatic" (and largely concerned with reducing debt) but became "systemic" in the sense of promoting a long-term shift in the balance of power from government to the private sector (Feigenbaum et al. 1999, 54). A central paradox of privatization is that where the policy has been accompanied by the creation of new regulatory apparatus, as with the utilities sectors in most countries, government may have more information about, and greater practical capacity for control over, privatized enterprises than it did over their public predecessors (Majone 1994a). Thus, Vogel's comparative study of regulatory reform found that privatization and liberalization processes in both Japan and France exhibited tendencies for central government to attempt reinforcement of its capacity for control over the applicable sectors (Vogel 1996, 257). This finding, and the contrast it provides with the disengagement strategies of the United States and (controversially) the United Kingdom, suggests that "the evidence does in fact contradict the popular wisdom that the overwhelming power of international markets has forced national regulators in a common direction" (Vogel 1996, 261–2).

The choice of institutional form for regulation over privatized industries has been a major public policy question. The general arguments in favor of independent regulatory agencies (IRAs) include the following: they reduce the capacity for dominant firms to exploit their de facto regulatory capacities to inhibit or reduce competition, a major factor behind the EU legislative policy which requires separation of regulation and operation of services in the telecoms, postal, and energy sectors; they tend to insulate regulatory decision making to some extent from the agendas of elected politicians. The rise of such "non-majoritarian" institutions for regulation has been a central theme of contemporary public policy approaches to regulation, offering as they do for some, a superior form of economic government for addressing highly complex issues in domains such as utilities regulation, financial services, and biotechnology (Majone and Everson 2001; Thatcher and Sweet 2002). Less attention has been paid to alternative organizational choices, such as the use of government departments or courts as regulators. Contemporary discussions of self-regulation, and in particular of co-regulation, suggest greater attention is now being paid to the question as to how the self-regulatory capacity of industry can be harnessed for public regulatory purposes (Steinberg 2001).

## 5. REGULATORY LEGITIMACY

A focus on regulatory agencies as the main delivery point for regulatory policies has generated a substantial literature on how this organizational form can be rendered legitimate. A central problem is that of delegation from legislatures and/or from the executive. In some systems, notably that of the United States, delegations may be wide, including powers to make regulatory rules and to enforce penalties for breach. It is more common in the OECD to find agencies with more limited delegations, for example of monitoring and investigatory powers, with the application of formal sanctions reserved to courts and tribunals and rule-making powers reserved to ministers and/or the legislature. Given this variation in the extent of delegation it is unsurprising to find that the American literature is particularly concerned with the delegation problem.

A central concern of the new institutional economics literature as applied to regulatory policy has been to find ways to structure delegations to agencies in such a way as to reduce the potential for "bureaucratic drift" (Horn 1995). In other systems, such as the Westminster-type regimes of the UK and Jamaica, there is a pronounced risk of legislative drift, as changes in government create the potential for the rules of a regulatory regime to be changed (Levy and Spiller 1996). Within this literature the central problem of regulatory delegation is not so much the democratic one of how to hold agencies to the will of the elected politicians, but rather the more technocratic issue of creating the "credible commitment" to stability in a regulatory regime that firms proposing to invest can depend on. The point here is that governments cannot rely on coercion to secure their objectives, but rather need to create an environment in which investors are willing to take risks (Gilardi 2002, 875).

Credible commitment is a particular issue for developing countries seeking inward investment in their newly privatized utilities sectors, under conditions where the "institutional endowments" (the courts and the rule of law, stock exchange, markets) may appear to lack stability or reliability (Levy and Spiller 1996). Thatcher's study of delegation to agencies within the UK, Germany, France, and Italy notes the functional reasons for such delegation—permitting politicians to transfer responsibility for politically unpopular decisions, enhancing the credibility of decisions, and enhancing the technical capacity of decision makers in complex areas (Thatcher 2002, 130). But, he suggests that the institutional form chosen for such agencies in each country is the one best calculated to reduce "agency costs"—the risks that agencies will "shirk" or deviate from their missions. The precise patterns were shaped both by institutional learning, but also by the peculiar state traditions of each country. Credible commitment has also been identified as a problem for EU regulation, subject to a degree of supervision by the European Commission, under conditions where that organization is becoming increasingly politicized (Majone 2000). Majone suggests that the solution to this threat is to tackle the substantial political and legal obstacles to create independent agencies at the level of the European Union.

There is a potential for tension between conceptions of legitimacy which empha-size procedural matters and the structures for democratic and fair regulatory deci-sion making, on the one hand, and newer movements which measure the legitimacy of regulation according to substantive measures of effectiveness and efficiency. The tensions are well illustrated by the Australian National Competition Policy (NCP), introduced in the mid-1990s (Morgan 1999). The policy involves a series of reviews by state, territory, and federal governments of all existing legislative instruments having regulatory effects for business, and is complementary to policies of regulatory impact assessment (RIA) for new policy instruments, common to most OECD countries. The NCP significantly cuts across the capacity of state and territory governments to maintain in force regulatory regimes for social and other purposes, by mandating that regulation of business may only be sustained where it addresses market failures.

The turn towards efficiency can, of course, be seen as a ratcheting up of the procedural accountability required within regulatory regimes. Most OECD govern-ments have established central units of some kind charged with overseeing the review by initiators of new regulatory instruments, and this, it is suggested, complements the more traditional political and legal accountability of regulators to legislature and courts for their actions (OECD 1997a). Many find that these traditional accountabil-ity mechanisms are insufficiently robust to address the wide powers granted to regulatory agencies (Graham 2000, 85)

An alternative to the approaches which either suggest that formal accountability mechanisms are always likely to be impossibly weak, or that they should be ratcheted up, is to identify alternative mechanisms which are at least equivalent to formal accountability processes, embedded within relations of interdependence within regulatory regimes (Scott 2000; cf. Stirton and Lodge 2001; Wilks 1998, 140). An advantage of thinking in this broader way about accountability, so as to incorporate the day-to-day constraints on decision making and action which derive from inter-dependence, is that it provides a more ready means through which to consider the legitimacy of non-state and supranational actors who exercise regulatory power. Thus companies, though not subject to parliamentary and judicial oversight in the same form as public agencies, may nevertheless be subject to equivalent constraints through corporate governance regimes or market positioning. Onora O'Neill has introduced the concept of "intelligent accountability" to embrace the idea that institutions might be "allowed some margin for self-governance of a form appropri-ate to their particular tasks, within a framework of financial and other reporting" (O'Neill 2002, 58) This approach is the antithesis of the assumption that organiza-tions, whether public or private, can be subjected to "total control" by regulation.

Regulation in public policy is defined in part by reference to its instrumental qualities. Regulatory regimes, organizations, and norms are targeted at delivering particular outcomes. The instrumental character of regulation is often contrasted with classical legal norms which are applied universally and lack the quality of being targeted (Parker et al. 2004). The claims to instrumentalism of regulation have come under sustained attack from a variety of different disciplinary sources. As noted above, the Economic Theory of Regulation has retained an assumption that regulation can deliver intended outcomes, but suggested that it is instrumental for private rather than public purposes. Within the sociology of law, adherents to the legal theory of autopoiesis suggest that communications between the differentiated subsystems of politics, law, and economics are so problematic that it would be surprising if we often found sufficient alignment (or "structural coupling") between rules set by politicians as they are implemented in the legal system and understood in the economy for regulation ever to be coherent (Teubner 1984). Many variations have been offered on this central problem of control. Some studies focus on the inevitable fiascos and catastrophes associated with some aspects of regulatory policy (Moran 2001, 2003, ch. 7). Classic studies of unintended effects in regulation use the terms "fatal remedies" (Sieber 1981) and "counterproductive regulation" (Grabosky 1995).

One possible response to the problem of instrumentalism is to think of abandoning or scaling down the commitment to regulation, in the manner of the deregulation movement of the 1970s and 1980s. An alternative approach has been to suggest that regulation need not be inherently problematic, but rather that more attention needs to be paid to the difficulties of securing control, with a wider array of more imaginative solutions to the problems presented. Ayres and Braithwaite's theory of responsive regulation (Ayres and Braithwaite 1992) offers an agenda for "transcending the deregulation debate," invoking game theory to show how regulatory responses can be better targeted to the behaviour of regulatees. Other recipes are available for making state agencies more efficient and responsive in carrying out their tasks, invoking the popular public management language of reinvention (Pildes and Sunstein 1995; Sparrow 2000). Other approaches to the development of a "new instrumentalism" look beyond the state, examining the role of firms and trade associations in developing and implementing "smart regulation" (Gunningham and Grabosky 1998) and the potential for building on the compliance function such as to make firms the principal bearers of responsibility for regulatory implementation with an emphasis on "meta-regulation" (Parker 2002).

# 6. CONCLUSIONS

Where should the public policy literature on regulatory regimes go next? For some a central concern is to stimulate more empirical work so as to develop better data to test and inform the building of theories. Such empirical development would likely yield better understanding of the conditions under which regulatory regimes deliver the effects which are intended, but also give a better understanding of regulatory variety and the conditions under which regulatory forms might be effectively transplanted (or not) from one context (whether a domain or a country) to another. In pursuit of regulatory regimes this research should focus not only, and perhaps not mainly on national regulatory agencies, but seek also to encompass government departments, non-state regulatory organizations, and the increasingly significant supranational regulatory organizations, both governmental and non-governmental.

Even if there were some consensus amongst scholars and policy analysts that the broad reconceptualization of regulation as a field of study set out in this chapter is desirable, it is difficult to imagine how institutions and decision makers might respond to a new agenda. On the one hand there is ample evidence of experimentation and innovation in regulatory governance in many OECD countries—the deployment of new instruments, the stimulation of co-regulation, innovative mechanisms for applying sanctions and rewards—some of which appear cognizant of the kind of capacities for regulatory governance which are located outside state organizations. On the other hand it appears to be the case that where issues reach high levels of political salience, often due to crises or scandals (such as the internationally important BSE crisis and Enron scandal), governmental responses frequently (or perhaps invariably?) involve the assertion or reassertion of traditional state regulatory power and the implicit claim that if the matter at hand is very important then it can be tackled only through traditional public regulation of some form—exemplifying the claim that the regulatory state in Britain is a reflection of "high modernism" in contemporary public policy (Moran 2003). Such responses fail to ask the question at to where the capacity to address the target problem might lie.

What kind of narrative can be constructed which might be effective in shifting the conception of regulation at the coalface of public policy closer to the image of effective and legitimate regulation offered in this chapter? One possibility lies in the development of the discourse of "meta-regulation." Meta-regulation is the process of regulating regulatory regimes and it is what governments are doing when they attempt to stimulate or steer self-regulatory regimes towards public ends (as with co-regulation) or when they seek to develop general instruments of control over public regulation (as with regulatory impact analysis and other processes of regulatory review). If the shift from public ownership towards regulation witnessed in many OECD countries exemplifies a shift from rowing to steering, then perhaps the next step in regulatory reform would be to adopt the idea that, as with rowing, some or much of the steering should be left to actors outwith the central state, and for important and politically salient problems and not just trivial ones. This would leave state actors to new modes for engaging in steering of steering, or meta-regulation.

It is not desirable or credible to propagate "the myth of the powerless state" (Weiss 1998), but rather to recognize the power of other key actors. A critical question is whether we should conceive the state as the intelligent and purposive core for any regulatory regime, delegating power (implicitly or explicitly) and continuing to steer other actors, whether non-state, supranational, or both, through processes of meta-regulation for public purposes. Or does the reconception of regulation argued for in this chapter remove the state from a special position, dooming it to compete with others for position and influence within regulatory space? Further thought and research are required to resolve this outstanding question.

# REFERENCES

ARROW, K. 1963. Uncertainty and the welfare economics of medical care. *American Economic Review*, 53 (5): 941–71.

AYRES, I., and BRAITHWAITE, J. 1992. *Responsive Regulation: Transcending the Deregulation Debate*. Oxford: Oxford University Press.

BERNSTEIN, M. H. 1951. *Regulating Business by Independent Commission*. Princeton, NJ: Princeton University Press.

BLACK, J. 2000. Proceduralizing regulation: part I. *Oxford Journal of Legal Studies*, 20 (4): 597–614.

—— 2001a. Decentring regulation: the role of regulation and self-regulation in a "post-regulatory" world. *Current Legal Problems*, 54: 103–46.

—— 2001b. Proceduralizing regulation: part II. *Oxford Journal of Legal Studies*, 21 (1): 33–58.

BRAITHWAITE, J. 2000. The new regulatory state and the transformation of criminology. *British Journal of Criminology*, 40: 222–38.

—— and DRAHOS, P. 2000. *Global Business Regulation*. Cambridge: Cambridge University Press.

COHN, M. 2001. Fuzzy legality in regulation: the legislative mandate revisited. *Law and Policy*, 23: 469–97.

CUSHMAN, R. 1941. *The Independent Regulatory Commissions*. New York: Oxford University Press.

DAINTITH, T. 1997. *Regulation*. Tübingen: Mohr Siebeck.

DERTHICK, M., and QUIRK, P. 1985. *The Politics of Deregulation*. Washington, DC: Brookings Institution.

DIMOCK, M. E. 1933. *British Public Utilities and National Development*. London: Allen and Unwin.

DOBBIN, F. 1994. *Forging Industrial Policy: The United States, Britain and France in the Railway Age*. New York: Cambridge University Press.

EISNER, M. A. 2000. *Regulatory Politics in Transition*, 2nd edn. Baltimore: Johns Hopkins University Press.

FEIGENBAUM, H., HENIG, J., and HAMNETT, C. 1999. *Shrinking the State: The Political Underpinnings of Privatization*. Cambridge: Cambridge University Press.

FRANCIS, J. 1993. *The Politics of Regulation*. Oxford: Blackwell.

GILARDI, F. 2002. Policy credibility and delegation to independent regulatory agencies: a comparative empirical analysis. *Journal of European Public Policy*, 9 (6): 873–93.

GRABOSKY, P. 1994. Beyond the regulatory state. *Australian and New Zealand Journal of Criminology*, 27: 192–7.

—— 1995. Counterproductive regulation. *International Journal of the Sociology of Law*, 23: 347–69.

—— and BRAITHWAITE, J. 1986. *Of Manners Gentle: Enforcement Strategies of Australian Business Regulatory Agencies*. Melbourne: Oxford University Press.

GRAHAM, C. 2000. *Regulating Public Utilities: A Constitutional Approach*. Oxford: Hart.

GUNNINGHAM, N., and GRABOSKY, P. 1998. *Smart Regulation: Designing Environmental Policy*. Oxford: Oxford University Press.

HALL, C., SCOTT, C., and HOOD, C. 2000. *Telecommunications Regulation: Culture, Chaos and Interdependence Inside the Regulatory Process*. London: Routledge.

HANCHER, L., and MORAN, M. (eds.) 1989. *Capitalism, Culture and Regulation*. Oxford: Oxford University Press.

HOOD, C. 1984. *The Tools of Government.* London: Macmillan.

—— 1994. *Explaining Economic Policy Reversals.* Buckingham: Open University Press.

—— 1998. *The Art of the State.* Oxford: Oxford University Press.

—— ROTHSTEIN, H., and BALDWIN, R. 2001. *The Government of Risk.* Oxford: Oxford University Press.

—— SCOTT, C. et al. 1999. *Regulation inside Government: Waste-Watchers, Quality Police, and Sleaze-Busters.* Oxford: Oxford University Press.

—— JAMES, O., PETERS, G., and SCOTT, C. 2004. *Controlling Modern Government.* Cheltenham: Edward Elgar.

HORN, M. 1995. *The Political Economy of Public Administration.* Cambridge: Cambridge University Press.

KAGAN, R. A. 2000. Introduction: comparing national styles of regulation in Japan and the United States. *Law and Policy,* 22: 225–44.

KRASNER, S. D. 1983. *International Regimes.* Ithaca, NY: Cornell University Press.

LANDIS, J. 1938. *The Administrative Process.* New Haven, Conn.: Yale University Press.

LANGE, B. 2003. Regulatory spaces and interactions: an introduction. *Social and Legal Studies,* 12: 411–24.

LESSIG, L. 1999. *Code: and Other Laws of Cyberspace.* New York: Basic Books.

LEVI-FAUR, D. 2005. The global diffusion of regulatory capitalism. *Annals of the American Academy of Political and Social Science,* 598: 12–32.

LEVY, B., and SPILLER, P. (eds.) 1996. *Regulation, Institutions and Commitment.* Cambridge: Cambridge University Press.

LOUGHLIN, M., and SCOTT, C. 1997. The regulatory state. Pp. 205–19 in *Developments in British Politics 5,* ed. P. Dunleavy, I. Holliday, A. Gamble, and G. Peele. Basingstoke: Macmillan.

MACEY, J. R. 1992. Separated powers and positive political theory: the tug of war over administrative agencies. *Georgetown Law Journal,* 80: 671–703.

MAJONE, G. 1994a. Paradoxes of privatization and deregulation. *Journal of European Public Policy,* 1 (1): 53–69.

—— 1994b. The rise of the regulatory state in Europe. *West European Politics,* 17: 77–101.

—— 2000. The credibility crisis of Community regulation. *Journal of Common Market Studies,* 38: 273–302.

—— and EVERSON, M. 2001. Institutional reform: independent agencies, oversight, coordination and procedural control. Pp. 139–83 in *Governance in the European Union,* ed. O. D. Schutter, N. Lebessis, and J. Paterson. Brussels: European Commission.

MORAN, M. 2001. Not steering but drowning: policy catastrophes and the regulatory state. *Political Quarterly,* 72: 414–27.

—— 2002. Review article: understanding the regulatory state. *British Journal of Political Science,* 32: 391–413.

—— 2003. *The British Regulatory State and Hyper-Innovation.* Oxford: Oxford University Press.

MORGAN, B. 1999. Regulating the regulators: meta-regulation as a strategy for reinventing government in Australia. *Public Management,* 1: 49–65.

NEWMAN, O. 1972. *Defensible Space: Crime Prevention through Urban Design.* New York: Macmillan.

OECD. 1997a. *Regulatory Impact Analysis: Best Practices in OECD Countries.* Paris: OECD.

—— 1997b. *Regulatory Reform,* i: *Sectoral Studies.* Paris: OECD.

OGUS, A. 1994. *Regulation: Legal Form and Economic Theory.* Oxford: Oxford University Press.

—— 1995. Rethinking self-regulation. *Oxford Journal of Legal Studies,* 15: 97–108.

O'NEILL, O. 2002. *A Question of Trust.* Cambridge: Cambridge University Press.

PARKER, C. 2002. *The Open Corporation: Self-Regulation and Democracy.* Melbourne: Cambridge University Press.

—— SCOTT, C., LACEY, N., and BRAITHWAITE, J. (eds.) 2004. *Regulating Law.* Oxford: Oxford University Press.

PELTZMAN, S. 1976. Toward a more general theory of regulation. *Journal of Law and Economics,* 19: 211–40.

—— 1989. The economic theory of regulation after a decade of deregulation. Pp. 1–59 in *Brookings Papers on Economic Activity: Microeconomics,* ed. M. N. Baily and C. Winston. Washington, DC: Brookings Institution.

PILDES, R. H., and SUNSTEIN, C. R. 1995. Reinventing the regulatory state. *University of Chicago Law Review,* 62: 1–129.

RAEFF, M. 1983. *The Well-Ordered Police State: Social and Institutional Changes through Law in the Germanies and Russia 1600–1800.* New Haven, Conn.: Yale University Press.

SCHAEDE, U. 2000. *Cooperative Capitalism: Self-Regulation, Trade Associations and the Antimonopoly Law in Japan.* Oxford: Oxford University Press.

SCOTT, C. 2000. Accountability in the regulatory state. *Journal of Law and Society,* 27: 38–60.

—— 2001. Analysing regulatory space: fragmented resources and institutional design. *Public Law,* 329–53.

—— 2002. Private regulation of the public sector: a neglected facet of contemporary governance. *Journal of Law and Society,* 29: 56–76.

—— 2004. Regulation in the age of governance: the rise of the post-regulatory state. Pp. 145–74 in *The Politics of Regulation,* ed. J. Jordana and D. Levi-Faur. Cheltenham: Edward Elgar.

SELZNICK, P. 1985. Focusing organizational research on regulation. Pp. 363–7 in *Regulatory Policy and the Social Sciences,* ed. R. G. Noll. Berkeley: University of California Press.

SHEARING, C. 1993. A constitutive conception of regulation. Pp. 67–79 in *Business Regulation in Australia's Future,* ed. J. Braithwaite and P. Grabosky. Canberra: Australian Institute of Criminology.

SIEBER, S. D. 1981. *Fatal Remedies: The Ironies of Social Intervention.* New York: Plenum.

SPARROW, M. 2000. *The Regulatory Craft: Controlling Risks, Solving Problems and Managing Compliance.* Washington, DC: Brookings Institution.

STEINBERG, P. 2001. Agencies, co-regulation and comitology—and what about politics? A critical appraisal of the Commission's white paper on governance. In *Mountain or Molehill: A Critical Appraisal of the Commission White Paper on Governance,* ed. C. Joerges, Y. Meny, and J. Weiler. Florence: European University Institute; available at: www.jeanmonnetprogram.org/papers/01/012901.html (accessed 12 Aug. 2004).

STIGLER, G. J. 1971. The theory of economic regulation. *Bell Journal of Economics,* 2: 3–21.

STIRTON, L., and LODGE, M. 2001. Transparency mechanisms: building transparency into public services. *Journal of Law and Society,* 28 (4): 471–89.

SUNSTEIN, C. R. 1990. Paradoxes of the regulatory state. *University of Chicago Law Review,* 57: 407–41.

TEUBNER, G. 1984. After legal instrumentalism? Strategic models of post-regulatory law. *International Journal of the Sociology of Law,* 12: 375–400.

—— 1998/1987. Juridification: concepts, aspects, limits, solutions. Pp. 389–440 in *Socio-Legal Reader on Regulation,* ed. R. Baldwin, C. Scott, and C. Hood. Oxford: Oxford University Press.

THATCHER, M. 2002. Delegation to independent regulatory agencies: pressures, functions and contextual mediation. *West European Politics,* 25: 125–47.

THATCHER, M., and STONE SWEET, A. 2002. Theory and practice of delegation to non-majoritarian institutions. *West European Politics*, 25: 1–22.

VOGEL, D. 1986. *National Styles of Regulation: Environmental Policy in Great Britain and the United States.* Ithaca, NY: Cornell University Press.

VOGEL, S. 1996. *Freer Markets, More Rules: Regulatory Reform in Advanced Industrial Countries.* Ithaca, NY: Cornell University Press.

WEISS, L. 1998. *The Myth of the Powerless State.* Cambridge: Polity Press.

WILKS, S. 1998. Utility regulation, corporate governance, and the amoral corporation. Pp. 133–61 in *Changing Regulatory Institutions in Britain and North America*, ed. G. B. Doern and S. Wilks. Toronto: University of Toronto Press.

WILSON, J. Q. 1980. *The Politics of Regulation.* New York: Basic Books.

# CHAPTER 33

# DEMOCRATIZING THE POLICY PROCESS

## ARCHON FUNG

> The danger of modern liberty is that, absorbed in the enjoyment of our private independence, and in pursuit of our particular interests, we should surrender our right to share in political power too easily.
>
> The holders of authority are only too anxious to encourage us to do so. They are so ready to spare us all sort of troubles, except those of obeying and paying! They will say to us: what, in the end, is the aim of your efforts, the motive of your labours, the object of all your hopes? Is it not happiness? Well, leave this happiness to us and we shall give it to you. No, Sirs, we must not leave it to them.
>
> (Benjamin Constant, 1816)

What is the role of citizen participation and deliberation in modern governance and policy making? The tension between expertise and popular voice in contemporary polities remains unresolved by students of politics, policy, and administration. Direct democracy strikes many as both undesirable and unfeasible. It is not desirable because the public virtues of political engagement have no special place in modern values and conceptions of the good life.[1] Even if it were desirable, it is not feasible

\* This chapter emerged from discussions held in a workshop on novel forms of representation organized by Nancy Rosenblum at the Radcliffe Institute for Advanced Study, 21 May 2004. I thank Joshua Cohen, Jane Mansbridge, Martha Minow, Nancy Rosenblum, Richard Tuck, Sidney Verba, and the other participants for their insights during and after that discussion. I would also like to thank Elena Fagotto, Joseph Goldman, and Abigail Williamson for their comments on a previous draft. Their diligent research never fails to spark new ideas, and their enthusiasm and commitment always inspires. I am grateful to Robert Goodin and Michael Moran for very helpful responses to earlier drafts.

[1] See Constant 1995/1816; Kateb 1981; Hibbing and Theiss-Morse 2002; Posner 2003.

because the challenges of complexity and scale rule out familiar kinds of participatory democracy such as the New England town meeting (Bryan 2004; Mansbridge 1980) and the ancient Athenian *ekklēsia* (Sinclair 1988; Ober 1991).

There are grounds for thinking that the first claim is overdrawn—that there are many contexts in which modern citizens desire greater voice over decisions that affect them or are made in their name because that influence is the essence of democracy (Pitkin and Shumer 1982). In the pages that follow, however, I concede this claim arguendo. Everything that follows supposes that most citizens of modern industrial democracies do not value political participation for its own sake. The experiences discussed below illustrate, however, that citizens do participate in substantial numbers given motive and opportunity. Nevertheless, participation requires time and energy that might be better devoted to private aspirations and enjoyments. Citizens' energies should not be consumed by the potentially extravagant demands of participatory governance when public business can be delegated to a class of professional representatives and administrators who reliably advance their interests. But the vision of a responsive and just government run by elites for the benefit of citizens is as utopian as full-blown participatory democracy (Cohen and Fung 2004). In many contexts, the policy-making apparatus of political representation and expert administration—the very machinery developed over the past two centuries to govern well without requiring too much from citizens—exhibits certain acute failures. These failures can be addressed with mechanisms of citizen participation and deliberation. Belying the second skeptical claim regarding the feasibility of participatory democracy, experiences in local governance have combined representative and participatory mechanisms in hybrid configurations that make government more responsive and just than either pure form.

These experiences suggest that the historic antagonism between proponents of representative and participatory democracy confuses more than it illuminates. A contemporary, pragmatic challenge for democratic theory and practice is to identify the contexts in which received governance mechanisms exhibit serious and systematic democratic deficits, and then to devise appropriate institutional remedies. This chapter pursues a part of that challenge by illuminating characteristic deficits of the conventional representative and professionalized policy-making process and then suggesting how novel combinations of representation and administration on one hand, and participation and deliberation on the other, can and in some cases have, addressed those deficits. This exploration surveys several of the ways in which participation and deliberation can address shortcomings of a minimal representative policy process. There are certainly other ways to address those shortcomings that do not involve popular participation; we focus here on the subset of solutions that deepen democratic engagement. Furthermore, important criticisms of participation and deliberation that claim, for example, that such processes exclude particular perspectives or interests, or that they reinforce patterns of domination and inequality, lie outside the scope of this treatment (Fraser 1992; Sanders 1997; Young 2000).

# 1. Democratic Deficits in the Policy Process

As a basis for the discussion that follows, consider a highly stylized view of the policy process in capitalist democracies that connects the interests of citizens to the outcomes of government action. This scheme can be called a *minimal representative policy process*; it has no place for direct citizen participation or deliberation. Though its abstraction begs many important issues, many beginning texts for students of politics and policy feature some variant of this schematic depiction. Figure 33.1 is modified from the variant that appears in Przeworki, Stokes, and Manin's volume on representation and accountability (1999). Briefly, in this scheme citizens have (1) interests and (2) preferences over policy options that they think will advance those interests. They (3) signal these preferences to government by voting in periodic elections for parties and politicians whose programs most closely match their preferences. These electoral signals generate mandates for representative politicians to make (5) policies to advance these interests. Under the separation of powers between legislative and executive functions, (6) agencies staffed by professional administrators are charged with executing these policies, which generate (7) outcomes that advance the (1) interests that begin this process.

The discipline of elections is thought to create two dynamics—representation and accountability—that ensure the integrity of the link between citizens' interests and policy outcomes. Prospectively, citizens' votes select the politicians who they think will represent them—those who will know and champion their preferences (2) by advancing appropriate policies (5). Retrospectively, the requirement that politicians stand periodically for election allows citizens to punish those who have failed to secure satisfactory outcomes (7) by ejecting them from office (3) in favor of others who might do better. These dual mechanisms of representation and accountability may produce responsive and just government with only modest citizen participation in many domains of law and policy under favorable circumstances such as competitive elections, strong parties with clear platforms, vigorous public vetting of contentious policy alternatives, an informed electorate, sufficient insulation of state from

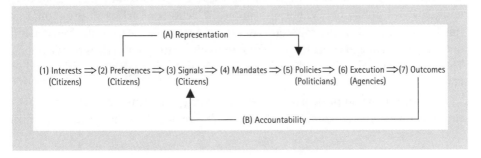

**Fig. 33.1.** The minimal representative policy process

economy, and a capable executive. For many public problems and under less favorable conditions, however, this minimal institution of periodic elections fails to secure a level of political representation and accountability that makes government responsive.

Consider four characteristic difficulties, or democratic deficits that prevent electoral institutions from making government responsive. For many public issues, citizens have *unclear preferences* regarding the public policies that best advance their interests. Or, they have preferences that are *unstable* in the sense they would change easily upon exposure to new information, arguments, or perspectives (D1). When popular preferences are underdeveloped in these ways, then the subsequent consequences of political and policy choice rest on highly unstable foundations. Even when the rest of the electoral and executive machinery has great integrity, "garbage in produces garbage out." When citizens do have stable preferences, electoral mechanisms provide only *blunt signals* to politicians and parties regarding the content of those preferences (D2).[2] Absent a thicker, continuing relationship between political elites and their constituents than that provided by periodic elections, politicians often misunderstand their constituents. This kind of misunderstanding is especially likely on the wide range of issues that do not figure prominently in campaigns leading up to elections. Politicians who do not understand their constituents cannot represent them well. Third, electoral mechanisms may prove too weak to hold the political and administrative machinery of government *accountable* to citizens when they have clear preferences (D3). On many state decisions, the interests of politicians and administrators may differ from those of the majority of citizens. It is difficult for citizens to use elections to compel politicians to act to advance popular interests rather than their elite ends when elections are uncompetitive, when narrow interests oppose diffuse ones, or when outcomes are difficult to monitor and assess. Accountability problems are compounded by the fact of widespread delegation of power and authority to administrative agencies in modern states. Even if citizens can hold politicians accountable, politicians may not be able to control and monitor the administrative apparatuses that implement, and often make policy. Finally, even when electoral devices of representation and accountability allow citizen-principals to control their political and administrative agents, the state itself may lack the capacity to produce outcomes that advance citizens' interests well (D4). In areas such as economic development, for example, successful outcomes depend not only upon law and public policy, but also upon the actions of actors in the economic sphere. In areas such as environment, education, and public safety, outcomes depend upon engagement and contributions from individual citizens as well as public policy. These democratic deficits, and their positions in the policy process are depicted in Fig. 33.2.

The chains between principals (citizens), agents (politicians and administrators), and outcomes in contemporary democracies are long indeed. The four links

---

[2]  See Przeworski, Stokes, and Manin 1999; Goodin 2000.

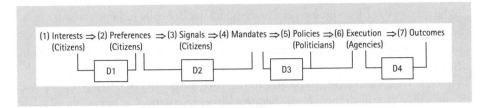

Fig. 33.2. Democratic deficits in the policy process

described above are particularly weak in many contexts. The next four sections describe how participatory and deliberative democratic mechanisms can repair these deficits. Some approaches seek to improve the dynamics of preference formation, representation, and accountability by supplementing elections with direct participation and deliberation. Other approaches seek to reduce the role of political representatives by making agencies and state action more directly responsive to citizens. The case for participation and deliberation below is a tempered and pragmatic one. I do not claim that directly democratic strategies are the only, or best way to address these democratic deficits. Rather, I aim only to articulate the ways in which they can make government more responsive to citizens' interests, and to show how they have been used to do so in actual cases. This analysis suggests that the optimal configurations of decision-making institutions will vary across policy domains, but in many cases should combine both representative and participatory mechanisms.

# 2. DELIBERATIVE PREFERENCE ARTICULATION

On policy matters for which there are prominent, diverse, and developed perspectives in the public debate—for example legalization of abortion or the distribution of wealth—citizens may have policy preferences that are clear and stable. On many other matters—where one or a few perspectives dominate, where misinformation abounds, those that are remote from the perceived interests, where having a sensible opinion requires substantial cognitive and informational investments, or issues that simply fail to capture the attention of many citizens—popular preferences may be unclear or unstable (see D1 in Fig. 33.2 above). The people can hardly be said to rule when policies have such fickle foundations. On such matters, institutions that contribute to the development and stabilization of preferences by making them more clear, coherent, rational, and reasonable therefore deepen democracy and potentially make government more responsive to citizens' interests.

The quality of citizen preferences in democracies depends in large measure upon the quality of the institutions of the public sphere—media and secondary associations—through which political perspectives and debates reach citizens.[3] Beyond general improvements to the public sphere, which lie beyond the scope of this chapter, several innovative efforts aim to improve the quality of citizens' preferences by convening groups of them to deliberate with representatives, other public officials, and each other.

Deliberative Polling® is among the most prominent of these. Its inventor James Fishkin describes the effort this way:

Select a national probability sample of the citizen voting age population and question them about some policy domain(s). Send them balanced, accessible briefing materials to help inform them and get them thinking more seriously about the same subject(s). Transport them to a single site, where they can spend several days grappling with the issues, discussing them with one another in randomly assigned, moderated small groups and putting questions generated by the small group discussions to carefully balanced panels of policy experts and political leaders. At the end, question the participants again, using the same instruments as at the beginning. (Luskin, Fishkin, and Jowell 2002)

Fishkin argues that these deliberations often have profound impacts on the opinions of those that participate. In a 1994 deliberative poll on crime in the UK, for example, participants became much less likely to think that strong punishments deter crime and they became more sympathetic to criminal defendants (Luskin, Fishkin, and Jowell 2002). He shows similar opinion shifts for deliberative polls on issues such as energy utility policy, adoption of the euro in Denmark, and metropolitan governance. These changes may be the result of participants adopting more informed, coherent, and reasonable positions out of their deliberations with one another.

It should be noted that Deliberative Polling is not itself a form of deliberative *democracy* when that term is understood as a method of making social choices. Deliberative democracy is often defined as a system in which citizens make collective decisions by offering reasons that others can accept, or perhaps to illuminate conflicts, rather than, say, simply voting for proposals that best advance their interests. In Deliberative Polling, participants discuss the merits of various positions, but there is no effort to reach consensus or reach a collective choice. Its designers fear that requiring consensus would distort individual preference formation by introducing pressures to conform. This absence of collective decision perhaps makes Deliberative Polling best suited to address the unstable preference deficit of many policy processes.

Deliberative Polling is one member of a family of civic and policy interventions that convene citizens to deliberate with one another in the effort to improve public opinion and action. Its siblings share a commitment to participation and deliberation, but differ in the design of their processes. Citizen Juries for example, also use random selection, but typically convene smaller groups than deliberative polls and meet for several days rather than just a weekend. Citizen Juries also issue collective

---

[3] Treatment of the public sphere generally lies beyond the scope of this article.

findings and recommendations (Smith and Wales 2000; Gastil 2000; Leib 2004). Twenty First Century Town Meetings, invented by an organization called AmericaSpeaks, convene thousands of citizens and organize deliberations through an inventive use of technology and facilitation.[4] They dispense with random selection in favor of open meetings and heavy recruitment from subgroups that are likely to be underrepresented otherwise. The Study Circles sponsored by the Topsfield Foundation are community-wide deliberations on specific issues that occur over several months.[5] Among these efforts, pre- and post-deliberation surveys exist only for Deliberative Polling and so little is known about the extent of changes in participants' preferences and views in other processes. Even the careful research on Deliberative Polling has focused upon the magnitude of opinion change, rather than impact upon the stability, coherence, rationality, or reasonableness of preferences.[6] Though these intentional projects in preference articulation are promising additions to electoral mechanisms, many dimensions of the micro-dynamics of political deliberation remain uncharted.

Efforts such as Deliberative Polling and Citizen Juries typically aim to improve the quality of public opinion on issues that emerge within conventional policy-making institutions. In this way, the agenda of issues that they consider usually comes from policy makers themselves. But the schedule of issues for which citizens have articulated preferences, and those for which they do not, is itself a source of democratic concern. In particular, citizens are more likely to have articulate preferences in areas where they perceive that they have real choices, but less so in areas that they perceive to be outside of their influence. For example, many residents of neighborhoods in urban and suburban America have quite articulated preferences regarding the character of their residence, the school to which they send their children, choice of grocery, and the like. But in other areas, where outcomes are important but depend upon the choices of remote agencies or the market decisions of developers or others—such as whether there is a park in their neighborhood and what it is like, the character of nearby businesses, and how the neighborhood relates to its city or town—residents may have less clear views while those other public and private actors have well-developed preferences. When the actions of those external forces become threatening—gentrification or the construction of "locally undesirable land uses" (LULUs) such as shelters for the homeless or hazardous waste facilities—reactionary "preferences" of rejection commonly emerge.

But the areas of life over which citizens exercise control—and so the depth of citizens' preferences—is itself determined by prior institutional choices. In 1990, the city of Minneapolis, Minnesota initiated a Neighborhood Revitalization Program (NRP) under which $400 million were allocated to some sixty neighborhood associations. In order to spend these funds, neighborhood groups had to develop priorities, plans, and projects, and many did so in a deliberative way that engaged

---

[4] See www.americaspeaks.org.     [5] See www.studycircles.org.
[6] For a more skeptical view about the effects of deliberation upon preference formation, see Cass Sunstein (2002).

many residents. In some neighborhoods, the planning requirement and the resources associated with successful planning encouraged residents to develop much clearer, sometimes shared preferences regarding the character of their neighborhoods. One Minneapolis neighborhood association, for example, developed a comprehensive, professionally executed, long-term plan for the neighborhood that incorporated all major aspects of neighborhood development. Deliberations around the use of NRP funds triggered the desire to articulate neighborhood preferences more clearly:

This area is undergoing major redevelopment right now. People wanted not just to react to proposals [for redevelopment] that will be coming down the pike. They wanted to have a professional set of guidelines that express what the neighbors want, so that when a developer comes along, hopefully at a very early stage before the developer gets too far along, we can hand them this master plan and say to him "this is what we're looking for architecturally and with respect to land use, where we want the green space, where we want residential [units]." It gives a nice vision.[7]

In order to contribute to the articulation of popular preferences, deliberative and participatory efforts should seek to involve as many citizens as possible. One substantial limitation of efforts such as Deliberative Polling and neighborhood associations is that they directly involve only a tiny fraction of relevant constituencies. These efforts all aim to involve others through indirect means such as media coverage, but citizens who participate directly in deliberations—for which preference development may be quite profound—are in all of these cases only tenuously connected to other citizens and the broader public sphere.

## 3. COMMUNICATIVE REAUTHORIZATION

Participatory democrats have criticized representative government on the ground that it relegates most citizens, most of the time, to passive roles of spectator and subject.[8] But other democratic theorists argue that representation should be conceptualized as a relationship in which both parties—constituents and professional politicians—are active participants. It is a mistake to think of those who are represented as passive or dominated. Plotke analogizes political to market representation. "My representative in the market is *authorized* to make certain agreements. In turn I am *obligated* by his or her actions. I communicate with my representative, and I can replace him or her... If x represents y, y is guiding and constraining x, enabling and authorizing him" (Plotke 1997, 28). Similarly, Iris Marion Young argues that "A representative process is worse, then, to the extent that the separation tends

---

[7] Interview with Minneapolis neighborhood association staff member, 7 Apr. 2004.

[8] Introducing a similar line of thought, Rousseau wrote famously that "The people of England regards itself as free; but it is grossly mistaken; it is free only during the election of members of parliament. As soon as they are elected, slavery overtakes it, and it is nothing" (*Social Contract*, book III, ch. 15).

toward severance, and better to the extent that it establishes and renews connections between constituents and representatives, and among members of the constituency" (Young 2000, 130). Jane Mansbridge suggests that political representatives often act in anticipation of what the responses of their constituents will be in the next election, rather than being instructed by the prior one. Such "anticipatory representation," she argues, works better when elections are joined with mutually educative interactions that enable citizens develop their preferences and representatives to gauge them (Mansbridge 2003).

These conceptions of representation provide a contingent argument for direct participation and deliberation. Campaigns and elections provide quite thin, and infrequent signals about citizens' preferences and interests (see D2 in Fig. 33.2 above). Elections fail to give the people voice on new issues that arise between campaign seasons, that lack public salience, or when major decisions have been delegated to independent administrators rather than politicians. When elections fail to articulate citizens' voices, participation and deliberation before and between elections can work to thicken communication between constituents and representatives.

In the United States, common mechanisms to gauge the public temperament include public hearings, notice and comment requirements, focus groups, and surveys. These devices often produce discussion and argument that fails to elicit a rich sense of public sentiments and educates neither citizens nor officials. Public hearings and meetings, for example, typically are organized in ways that allow well-organized opposing sides to testify before decision makers without facilitating exchange (Kemmis 1990). Deliberative practitioners in civil society organizations have responded to the shortcomings of deliberative and participatory techniques for reconnecting constituents to representatives by applying insights from the fields such as alternative dispute resolution, organizational design, and group process facilitation. In some cases, politicians and administrators have adopted their methods to create non-electoral, participatory, and deliberative mechanisms that inform and reauthorize their policy choices.

A small community in Idaho called Kuna, for example, has adopted a kind of two-track policy process.[9] On the minimally participatory electoral track, representatives and administrators dispose of routine matters without elaborate communication or reauthorization from citizens. Where public sentiments are unclear and on issues that are likely to prove controversial, officials and community organizations frequently convene a process of Study Circles in which citizens are invited to learn about the issue in more detail and deliberate with one another and with officials about the merits and costs of various options over the course of several days. Following the national study circles model, participants in these events are given briefing materials and organized into small, facilitated discussion groups. In these groups and in large group discussions composed of the whole, members develop opinions about the issues and options at stake and prepare questions and recommendations for policy makers. These popular deliberations sometimes validate decision makers' views and

[9] Information in this paragraph is drawn from the field research of Joseph Goldman, unpublished.

galvanize community members in favor of certain policy positions. Sometimes, however, the deliberations reveal objections and latent preferences that cause representatives and other officials to modify their proposals. Citizens often come to understand and appreciate the reasons that favor various proposals and positions in their deliberations with officials. Between one and several hundred residents typically participate in these study circles. Over the past five years, Kuna has convened study circles on issues ranging from multimillion-dollar school bonds to student drug testing, local tax policy, and town planning.

A popular deliberative track was also deployed to the very different challenge of rebuilding the area of lower Manhattan destroyed in the 11 September 2001 attacks on New York City (Kennedy School of Government 2003). Two regional agencies—the Port Authority and the Lower Manhattan Development Corporation (LMDC)—were charged with leading the effort to rebuild the World Trade Center site. But multiple and conflicting goals and visions—such as commercial versus residential interests, speedy reconstruction versus deliberate and inclusive consultation, and the desires of the families and friends for the victims to be appropriately honored—would make it impossible for these agencies to meet these challenges through technocratic approaches alone. The regional authorities agreed to join with several civic organizations and convene a series of large-scale public discussions on the site's fate. These public engagement efforts culminated in a large meeting, drawing more than 4,000 participants, held at the Jacob Javitz Convention Center in July 2002 called "Listening to the City." The event was organized by AmericaSpeaks according to their "Twenty First Century Town Meeting" methodology. Instead of the conventional talking heads or public hearing format, the event created hundreds of more intimate, yet focused conversations. The main floor of the convention center contained 500 tables of ten seats each. On each table was a computer that was in turn hooked to a central bank of computers. Throughout the day, discussions from each table were relayed to a central "theme team" that attempted to pick out views and themes recurring for the large group as a whole. In addition to recording table conversations, each participant had his or her own "polling keypad" through which votes and straw polls would be recorded throughout the day. The aim of all of this technology was to create a form of public deliberation that combined the benefits of small group discussion with the power of large group consensus. The consensus of this particular group rejected key elements of the plans that the LMDC and Port Authority had prepared in favor of bolder architecture, greater priority on a memorial for the fallen, reduced emphasis on commercial priorities, and greater attention to affordability and the quality of residential life. The event received substantial media coverage—forty-nine articles in northeast regional newspapers, eighteen of those in the *New York Times*—almost all of it highly favorable.[10] The combination of public feedback and communicative pressure from media and civic

---

[10] Author's Lexis-Nexis search on 25 June 2004 of articles published in 2002 containing "Listening to the City" in northeast regional news sources.

organizations compelled the two agencies to begin the planning process anew and adopt many of the values and preferences articulated at "Listening to the City".

# 4. POPULAR ACCOUNTABILITY

The democratic policy process is more seriously threatened still when the interests of professional representatives depart systematically from that of their constituency and when the electoral mechanism is too weak to compel representatives to respond to the interests of citizens rather than using political power to advance their own ends (see D3 in Fig. 33.2 above). The problem of harnessing the energies of political elites to popular interests is perhaps the central challenge of democratic institutional design. In many sociopolitical contexts, the mechanism of regular elections has been only partly successful in meeting that challenge. Consider two common and systematic obstacles to electoral accountability: administrative delegation and political patronage relationships.

Public bureaucracies conduct much of the business of modern government. The growth in the size, complexity, and insulation of these administrative agencies "poses important problems in a democracy because it creates the possibility that unelected officials can decisively impact policy, potentially in ways that disregard public preferences" (Dunn 1999). Career administrators may enjoy substantial advantages over elected officials and civic organizations in information, capability, and energy (see Friedrich 1940; Stewart 1975; Lowi 1979). Such agencies, furthermore, may have agendas—rooted in organizational needs or professional habits and discourse—that depart from public interests and preferences (see Fischer 2003; Hajer and Wagenaar 2003). Reforms in administrative law, in particular the Administrative Procedures Act regulating federal rule making, create opportunities for affected parties to engage directly with federal agencies in ways that bypass structures of political representation (Stewart 1975; Sunstein 1990).

Participatory and deliberative forums in which citizens engage with each other and with officials can strengthen popular accountability and so address the dilemmas of administrative delegation. The "Listening to the City" case of reconstructing lower Manhattan, discussed above, illustrates this possibility. In the course of the reconstruction planning, the authorized public agencies developed particular policy preferences that seemed related to their organizational priorities. For example, the Port Authority derived revenue from the economic activity at the site, and its directives to planners stressed reconstruction of commercial space. If the results of the deliberations at the public participation events in the summer of 2002 reflected broader sentiments, the Port Authority's agenda and initial plans failed to respond to popular desires. Whereas many public meetings fail to discipline officials, "Listening to the City" did seem to impose accountability upon these agencies. The agencies subsequently altered the guidelines for reconstruction in ways that incorporated the public preferences articulated at the event, and they initiated a public competition for design concepts. The participatory-deliberative event increased official account-ability because it was embedded in larger, highly visible debates about lower Man-hattan occurring in popular media. "Listening to the City" was a large-scale discussion, open to all citizens, without a carefully controlled agenda, and transpar-ent to anyone who cared to report on it. It was not a report from a special agency or press release from particular interest groups. These participatory democratic features of the process endowed its conclusions with a distinctive legitimacy that journalists and their readers found highly compelling. Subsequently, agency officials and their political masters could not ignore them. Political elites could, however, avoid making the same mistake twice. They notably declined to sponsor similar events in later parts of the planning and reconstruction, and subsequent decision making was substan-tially less participatory.

"Listening to the City" illustrates how occasional public deliberation can supple-ment the pre-existing structure of electoral-cum-administrative accountability in episodes where popular accountability is especially threatened. In more challenging contexts, however, electoral mechanisms reproduce and reinforce elite domination rather than checking it, and so popular accountability can only be achieved through thorough-going reforms of a corrupted policy process. The experience of popular participation in public budget decisions in the Brazilian city of Porto Alegre illus-trates this trajectory (Baiocchi 2003; Abers 2000; Avritzer 2002a). In 1989, the left-wing Workers' Party (Partido dos Trabalhadores, or PT) was elected to the mayoralty in part on a platform of empowering the city's community and social movements. Over the next two years, this promise was transformed into policy through a highly innovative mechanism called the Participatory Budget (Orçamento Participativo, or OP). Fundamentally, the policy shifts decision making regarding use of the capital portion of the city's budget from the city council to a system of neighborhood and city-wide popular assemblies. Through a complex annual cycle of open meetings, citizens and civic associations meet to determine local investment priorities. These priorities are aggregated into an overall city budget. The budget must be ratified by the elected city council, but ratification is largely a formality due to the enormous legitimacy generated by the popular process that produces it each year. The rate of participation in the OP has grown substantially since its initiation. By some esti-mates, some 10 per cent of the adult population participates in the formal and informal gatherings that constitute the process. Furthermore, participants are drawn disproportionately from the poorer segments of the population.

One major accomplishment of the OP has been to replace a system of political patronage and clientelism with popular decision-making institutions that make public investments more responsive to citizens' interests. In surveys, the number of civic leaders who admit client–patron exchanges of benefits for political support declined from 18 per cent prior to the OP (Baiocchi 2005, 45–6). Another study by Leonardo Avritzer found that 41 per cent of associations secured benefits by directly contacting politicians prior to the OP, but none relied on such unmediated channels after its establishment (Avritzer 2002*b*). The substantive results of reduced clientelism and enhanced political accountability are striking. Poor residents of Porto Alegre enjoy much better public services and goods as a result of the OP. The percentage of neighborhoods with running water has increased from 75 to 98 per cent, sewer coverage has grown from 45 to 98 per cent, and the number of families offered housing assistance grew sixteenfold since the initiation of the OP (Baiocchi 2003).

To develop participatory institutions that circumvent the representative process may seem an extreme solution to the problem of electoral accountability. For the vast majority of cities in developed countries, where corruption and clientelism are exceptions rather than the norm, such an extravagant participatory reform may be disproportional to the extent of deficits of political accountability that it would address. Where patron–client exchanges are highly stable, entrenched, and reinforcing dynamics of a policy-making process, however, thoroughgoing participatory reform may be an effective corrective.

# 5. Alternative Governance and Public Problem-solving Capacity

A fourth characteristic deficit of the representative policy process grows out of the inability of state mechanisms to solve certain kinds of public problems (see D4 in Fig. 33.2 above). State-centered solutions are limited for some kinds of problems that require cooperation and even collaboration with non-state actors. Some observers have coined the term "governance," in contrast to "government," to mark this decentering of public decision making and action away from the boundaries of formal state institutions. Addressing issues such as public safety in violent neighborhoods, the education of children, and many social services, for example, requires not only the active consent, but sometimes positive contributions (co-production) and even joint decision making (co-governance) by beneficiaries and other affected citizens. More broadly, problems that involve interdependent actors who have diverse interests, values, and experiences, such as in many kinds of natural resource management and economic development problems, have often proven resistant to traditional top-down, state-centered mechanisms and methods (Booher and Innes 2002). Furthermore, the complexity of some social problems, stemming from the multiplicity of causes that span conventional divisions of expertise, the volatility of their manifestations across time, or their diversity across space, can make them intractable to traditional state bureaucracies that organize themselves into separate policy disciplines and that presume a certain stability in their problem environments (Cohen and Sabel 1997).

Direct participation and deliberation can help to transcend these limitations on state capacity. Opening channels of participation to public decision making can bring the energies, resources, and ideas of citizens and stakeholders to bear on complex public problems. Appropriate kinds of deliberation can trigger a search for innovative strategies and solutions (Booher and Innes 1999) and create normative pressure to make collective decisions that are fair and reasonable. Elsewhere, I have characterized such reforms as Empowered Participatory Governance. Such reforms invite citizens to deliberate with each other and with officials to solve concrete, urgent problems (Fung and Wright 2003). To illustrate how Empowered Participatory Governance can expand collective capacities to solve public problems, consider transformations to the Chicago police department (Fung 2004; Skogan et al. 1999; Skogan and Hartnett 1997) in the 1990s. In 1994, the Chicago police department adopted a deep form of community policing. Every month in each of the 280 neighborhood police beats in the city, residents meet with police to deliberate about how to make their neighborhoods safer. They decide which of many local problems should receive concentrated attention and they formulate strategies to address those problems. These neighborhood deliberations produce plans that involve not just police action, but also contributions from other city departments, from private organizations, and from citizens themselves. Such participatory problem solving and cross-agency action marks a substantial departure from traditional, hierarchical police methods that have proven ineffective against problems of chronic crime and disorder. Similar participatory and deliberative governance reforms have also emerged in diverse policy areas such as primary and secondary education, environmental regulation, local economic development, neighborhood planning, and natural resource management (Weber 2003; Sabel, Fung, and Karkkainen 2000). In all of these policy domains, traditionally organized regulatory or service delivery state bureaucracies faced acute performance crises. In some contexts, those crises were addressed through participatory and deliberative reforms that joined the distinctive capacities of citizens and stakeholders to state authority.

Several important differences should be noted, however, in the character of public participation and deliberation that addresses limitations of state capacity. This fourth category of engagement is likely to require more intensive, and therefore less extensive kinds of participation than public engagement to clarify preferences, communicate with officials, or occasionally bolster mechanisms of accountability. In cases like Chicago community policing, residents join with officials in detailed discussions and planning, often over extended periods of time. Citizens who become deeply involved acquire a level of expertise that enables them to interact on a par with professionals. It is unrealistic to expect that a large portion of citizens will invest so deeply in such matters. Furthermore, the particular democratic deficit at issue here is public capacity rather than representation. In such cases, the involvement of a small percentage of citizens or stakeholders—whose involvement generates public goods for the rest—can often make a large difference with respect to problem-solving capacities. Similarly, deliberation in such cases often focuses more upon identifying and inventing effective courses of action rather than upon resolving deep-set conflicts of value that occupy much of the analysis of deliberation in democratic theory.

# 6. CONCLUSION

Should public decision making in modern democracies be organized in participatory and deliberative ways or though political representatives selected through periodic elections? This chapter's answer lacks finality: it depends. It depends first of all upon the nature of a particular public issue that a democratic process addresses. Is that issue one on which citizens have informed and stable preferences, communication between representatives and constituents creates mutual knowledge, representatives' actions are aligned with citizen preferences, and for which public bureaucracies possess sufficient capabilities? If all these questions are answered affirmatively, then the minimal democratic mechanism of elections to select representatives may be sufficient to ensure that the state is responsive to popular interests. There are many other issues, however, for which one or more of these conditions fail to hold. Institutions of citizen deliberation and participation can help to repair such broken links in the minimal representative policy process. Rather than conceiving deliberation and participation as alternatives to representation, it is perhaps more fruitful to explore which combinations of institutions and procedures best advance democratic values such as state responsiveness for various issues and political contexts. The pages above have offered several experiences that illustrate such synergies as a first step toward that fuller exploration.

## REFERENCES

ABERS, R. N. 2000. *Reinventing Local Democracy: Grassroots Politics in Brazil.* Boulder, Colo.: Lynne Rienner.

AVRITZER, L. 2002a. *Democracy and the Public Space in Latin America.* Princeton, NJ: Princeton University Press.

—— 2002b. New public spheres in Brazil: local democracy and deliberative politics. Unpublished manuscript, Fall.

BAIOCCHI, G. 2003. Participation, activism, and politics: the Porto Alegre experiment. Pp. 45–76 in *Deepening Democracy: Institutional Innovations in Empowered Participatory Governance*, ed. A. Fung and E. O. Wright. London: Verso.

—— 2005. *Militants and Citizens: The Politics of Participatory Democracy in Porto Alegre.* Stanford, Calif.: Stanford University Press.

BOOHER, D. E., and INNES, J. E. 1999. Consensus building as role playing and bricolage: toward a theory of collaborative planning. *Journal of the American Planning Association*, 65: 9–26.

—— —— 2002. Network power in collaborative planning. *Journal of Planning Education and Research*, 21: 221–36.

BRYAN, F. 2004. *Real Democracy: The New England Town Meeting and How It Works.* Chicago: University of Chicago Press.

COHEN, J., and FUNG, A. 2004. Radical democracy. *Swiss Journal of Political Science*, 10: 23–34.

—— and SABEL, C. 1997. Directly-deliberative polyarchy. *European Law Journal*, 3: 313–42.

Constant, B. 1995/1816. The liberty of ancients compared with that of moderns. Pp. 309–28 in *Constant: Political Writings*, ed. B. Fontana. Cambridge: Cambridge University Press.

Dunn, D. 1999. Mixing elected and nonelected officials in democratic policy making: fundamentals of accountability and responsibility. Pp. 297–325 in *Democracy, Accountability, and Representation*, ed. A. Przeworski, S. Stokes, and B. Manin. Cambridge: Cambridge University Press.

Fischer, F. 2003. *Reframing Policy Analysis: Discursive Politics and Deliberative Practices.* Oxford: Oxford University Press.

Fishkin, J. 1995. *The Voice of the People.* New Haven, Conn.: Yale University Press.

Fraser, N. 1992. Rethinking the public sphere: a contribution to the critique of actually existing democracy. Pp. 109–42 in *Habermas and the Public Sphere*, ed. C. Calhoun. Cambridge, Mass.: MIT Press.

Friedrich, C. 1940. Public policy and the nature of administrative responsibility. *Public Policy*, 1: 1–24.

Fung, A. 2004. *Empowered Deliberation: Reinventing Urban Democracy.* Princeton, NJ: Princeton University Press.

—— and Wright, E. O. (eds.) 2003. *Deepening Democracy: Institutional Innovations in Empowered Participatory Governance.* London: Verso.

Gastil, J. 2000. *By Popular Demand: Revitalizing Representative Democracy through Deliberative Elections.* Berkeley: University of California Press.

Goodin, R. 2000. Accountability—elections as one form. Pp. 2–4 in *International Encyclopedia of Elections*, ed. R. Rose. Washington, DC: Congressional Quarterly Press.

Hajer, M., and Wagenaar, H. (eds.) 2003. *Deliberative Policy Analysis: Understanding Governance in the Network Society.* Cambridge: Cambridge University Press.

Hibbing, J. R., and Theiss-Morse, E. 2002. *Stealth Democracy: Americans' Beliefs about How Government Should Work.* New York: Cambridge University Press.

Kateb, G. 1981. The moral distinctiveness of representative democracy. *Ethics*, 91: 357–74.

Kemmis, D. 1990. *Community and the Politics of Place.* Norman: University of Oklahoma Press.

Kennedy School of Government 2003. Listening to the city: rebuilding at New York's World Trade Center site. Case 1687.0 and 1687.1.

Leib, E. 2004. *Deliberative Democracy in America: A Proposal for a Popular Branch of Government.* University Park: Pennsylvania State University Press.

Lowi, T. 1979. *The End of Liberalism: The Second Republic of the United States.* New York: Norton.

Luskin, R., Fishkin, J., and Jowell, R. 2002. Considered opinion: Deliberative Polling in Britain. *British Journal of Political Science*, 32: 455–87.

Mansbridge, J. 1980. *Beyond Adversary Democracy.* New York: Basic Books.

—— 2003. Rethinking representation. *American Political Science Review*, 97: 515–28.

Ober, J. 1991. *Mass and Elite in Democratic Athens.* Princeton, NJ: Princeton University Press.

Pitkin, H. F., and Shumer, S. 1982. On participation. *Democracy*, 2: 43–54.

Plotke, D. 1997. Representation is democracy. *Constellations*, 4: 19–34.

Posner, R. 2003. *Law, Pragmatism, and Democracy.* Cambridge, Mass.: Harvard University Press.

Przeworski, A., Stokes, S., and Manin, B. (eds.) 1999. *Democracy, Accountability, and Representation.* Cambridge: Cambridge University Press.

Sabel, C., Fung, A., and Karkkainen, B. 2000. *Beyond Backyard Environmentalism.* Boston: Beacon Press.

—— and LIEBMAN, J. 2003. A public laboratory Dewey barely imagined: the emerging model of school governance and legal reform. *NYU Review of Law and Social Change*, 23(2): 183–304.

SANDERS, L. M. 1997. Against deliberation. *Political Theory*, 25: 347–76.

SANTOS, B. S. 1998. Participatory budgeting in Porto Allegre: toward a redistributive democracy. *Politics and Society*, 26: 461–510.

SINCLAIR, R. K. 1988. *Democracy and Participation in Athens*. Cambridge: Cambridge University Press.

SKOGAN, W. G., and HARTNETT, S. M. 1997. *Community Policing: Chicago Style*. New York: Oxford University Press.

—— —— BOIS, J. D., COMEY, J., KAISER, M., and LOVIG, J. 1999. *On the Beat: Police and Community Problem Solving*. Boulder, Colo.: Westview.

SMITH, G., and WALES, C. 2000. Citizens' juries and deliberative democracy. *Political Studies*, 48: 51–65.

STEWART, R. B. 1975. The reform of administrative law. *Harvard Law Review*, 88: 1667–813.

SUNSTEIN, C. 1990. *After the Rights Revolution: Reconceiving the Regulatory State*. Cambridge, Mass.: Harvard University Press.

—— 2002. The law of group polarization. *Journal of Political Philosophy*, 10: 175–95.

WEBER, E. P. 2003. *Bringing Society Back in: Grassroots Ecosystem Management, Accountability, and Sustainable Communities*. Cambridge, Mass.: Massachusetts Institute of Technology Press.

YOUNG, I. M. 2000. *Inclusion and Democracy*. New York: Oxford University Press.

# PART VIII

## COMMENDING AND EVALUATING PUBLIC POLICIES

# THE LOGIC OF APPROPRIATENESS

## JAMES G. MARCH

## JOHAN P. OLSEN

THE logic of appropriateness is a perspective on how human action is to be interpreted. Action, policy making included, is seen as driven by rules of appropriate or exemplary behavior, organized into institutions. The appropriateness of rules includes both cognitive and normative components (March and Olsen 1995, 30–1). Rules are followed because they are seen as natural, rightful, expected, and legitimate. Actors seek to fulfill the obligations encapsulated in a role, an identity, a membership in a political community or group, and the ethos, practices, and expectations of its institutions. Embedded in a social collectivity, they do what they see as appropriate for themselves in a specific type of situation.

The present chapter focuses particularly on rules of appropriateness in the context of formally organized political institutions and democratic political orders. We ask how an understanding of the role of rule-driven behavior in life might illuminate thinking about political life, how the codification of experience into rules, institutional memories, and information processing is shaped in, and shapes a democratic political system. *First*, we sketch the basic ideas of rule-based action. *Second*, we describe some characteristics of contemporary democratic settings. *Third*, we attend to the relations between rules and action, the elements of slippage in executing rules. *Fourth*, we examine the dynamics of rules and standards of appropriateness. And, *fifth*, we discuss a possible reconciliation of different logics of action, as part of a future research agenda for students of democratic politics and policy making.

* We thank Jeffrey T. Checkel, Robert E. Goodin, Anne-Mette Magnussen, Michael Moran, and Ulf I. Sverdrup for constructive comments.

# 1. THE BASIC IDEAS

A vision of actors following internalized prescriptions of what is socially defined as normal, true, right, or good, without, or in spite of calculation of consequences and expected utility, is of ancient origin. The idea was, for example, dramatized by Sophocles more than 2,000 years ago in Antigone's confrontation with King Creon and by Martin Luther facing the Diet of Worms in 1521: "Here I stand, I can do no other." The tendency to develop rules, codes, and principles of conduct to justify and prescribe action in terms of something more than expected consequences seems to be fairly universal (Elias 1982/1939), and echoes of the ancient perspectives are found in many modern discussions of the importance of rules and identities in guiding human life.

The exact formulation of the ideas varies somewhat from one disciplinary domain to the other, but the core intuition is that humans maintain a repertoire of roles and identities, each providing rules of appropriate behavior in situations for which they are relevant. Following rules of a role or identity is a relatively complicated cognitive process involving thoughtful, reasoning behavior; but the processes of reasoning are not primarily connected to the anticipation of future consequences as they are in most contemporary conceptions of rationality. Actors use criteria of similarity and congruence, rather than likelihood and value. To act appropriately is to proceed according to the institutionalized practices of a collectivity, based on mutual, and often tacit understandings of what is true, reasonable, natural, right, and good. The term "logic of appropriateness" has overtones of morality, but rules of appropriateness underlie atrocities of action, such as ethnic cleansing and blood feuds, as well as moral heroism. The fact that a rule of action is defined as appropriate by an individual or a collectivity may reflect learning of some sort from history, but it does not guarantee technical efficiency or moral acceptability.

The matching of identities, situations, and behavioral rules may be based on experience, expert knowledge, or intuition, in which case it is often called "recognition" to emphasize the cognitive process of pairing problem-solving action correctly to a problem situation (March and Simon 1993, 10–13). The match may be based on role expectations (Sarbin and Allen 1968, 550). The match may also carry with it a connotation of essence, so that appropriate attitudes, behaviors, feelings, or preferences for a citizen, official, or expert are those that are essential to being a citizen, official, or expert—essential not in the instrumental sense of being necessary to perform a task or socially expected, nor in the sense of being an arbitrary definitional convention, but in the sense of that without which one cannot claim to be a proper citizen, official, or expert (MacIntyre 1988).

The simple behavioral proposition is that, most of the time humans take reasoned action by trying to answer three elementary questions: What kind of a situation is this? What kind of a person am I? What does a person such as I do in a situation such as this (March and Olsen 1989; March 1994)?

## 2. THE SETTING: INSTITUTIONS OF DEMOCRATIC GOVERNANCE

Democratic political life is ordered by institutions. The polity is a configuration of formally organized institutions that defines the setting within which governance and policy making take place. An institution is a relatively stable collection of rules and practices, embedded in structures of *resources* that make action possible—organizational, financial and staff capabilities, and structures of *meaning* that explain and justify behavior—roles, identities and belongings, common purposes, and causal and normative beliefs (March and Olsen 1989, 1995).

Institutions are organizational arrangements that link roles/identities, accounts of situations, resources, and prescriptive rules and practices. They create actors and meeting places and organize the relations and interactions among actors. They guide behavior and stabilize expectations. Specific institutional settings also provide vocabularies that frame thought and understandings and define what are legitimate arguments and standards of justification and criticism in different situations (Mills 1940). Institutions, furthermore, allocate resources and empower and constrain actors differently and make them more or less capable of acting according to prescribed rules. They affect whose justice and what rationality has primacy (MacIntyre 1988) and who becomes winners and losers. *Political* institutionalization signifies the development of distinct political rules, practices, and procedures partly independent of other institutions and social groupings (Huntington 1965). Political orders are, however, more or less institutionalized and they are structured according to different principles (Eisenstadt 1965).

This institutional perspective stands in contrast to current interpretations of politics that assume self-interested and rationally calculating actors, instrumentalism, and consequentialism. In the latter perspective rules simply reflect interests and powers, or they are irrelevant.[1] It can never be better to follow a rule that requires actions other than those that are optimal under given circumstances (Rowe 1989, vii); and the idea that society is governed by a written constitution and rules of appropriateness is seen as a possible reflection of the naive optimism of the eighteenth century (Loewenstein 1951). The logic of appropriateness, in contrast, harks back to an older conception that sees politics as rule driven and brands the use of public institutions and power for private purposes as the corruption and degeneration of politics (Viroli 1992, 71).

---

[1] Following the logic of consequentiality implies treating possible rules and interpretations as alternatives in a rational choice problem and it is usually assumed that "man's natural proclivity is to pursue his own interests" (Brennan and Buchanan 1985, ix). To act on the basis of the logic of consequentiality or anticipatory action includes the following steps: (*a*) What are my alternatives? (*b*) What are my values? (*c*) What are the consequences of my alternatives for my values? (*d*) Choose the alternative that has the best expected consequences. To act in conformity with rules that constrain conduct is then based on rational calculation and contracts, and is motivated by incentives and personal advantage.

Rules of appropriateness are also embodied in the foundational norms of contemporary democracies. Subjecting human conduct to constitutive rules has been portrayed as part of processes of democratization and civilization; and legitimacy has come to depend on *how* things are done, not solely on substantive performance (Merton 1938; Elias 1982/1939). For example, an important part of the modern democratic creed is that impersonal, fairly stable, publicly known, and understandable rules that are neither contradictory nor retroactive are supposed to shield citizens from the arbitrary power of authorities and the unaccountable power of those with exchangeable resources. Self-given laws are assumed to be accepted as binding for citizens. A spirit of citizenship is seen to imply a willingness to think and act as members of the community as a whole, not solely as self-interested individuals or as members of particular interest groups (Arblaster 1987, 77). Judges, bureaucrats, ministers, and legislators are expected to follow rules and act with integrity and competence within the democratic spirit. Officialness is supposed to imply stewardship and an affirmation of the values and norms inherent in offices and institutions (Heclo 2002).

In short, actors are expected to behave according to distinct democratic norms and rules and the democratic quality of a polity depends on properties of its citizens and officials. If they are not law-abiding, enlightened, active, civic-minded, and acting with self-restraint and a distance from individual interests, passions, and drives, genuine democratic government is impossible (Mill 1962/1861, 30). Yet, as observed by Aristotle, humans are not born with such predispositions. They have to be learned (Aristotle 1980, 299).

Democratic governance, then, is more than an instrument for implementing predetermined preferences and rights. Identities are assumed to be reflexive and political, not inherited and pre-political (Habermas 1998), and institutions are imagined to provide a framework for fashioning democrats by developing and transmitting democratic beliefs. A democratic identity also includes accepting responsibility for providing an institutional context within which continuous political discourse and change can take place and the roles, identities, accounts, rules, practices, and capabilities that construct political life can be crafted (March and Olsen 1995).

## 3. RULES OF APPROPRIATENESS IN ACTION

The impact of rules and standard operating procedures in routine situations is well known (March and Simon 1958; Cyert and March 1963). The relevance of the logic of appropriateness, however, is not limited to repetitive, routine worlds, and rule prescriptions are not necessarily conservative. Civil unrest, demands for comprehensive redistribution of political power and welfare, as well as political revolutions and major reforms often follow from identity-driven conceptions of appropriateness more than conscious calculations of costs and benefits (Scott 1976; Lefort 1988; Elster 1989).

Rules prescribe, more or less precisely, what is appropriate action. They also, more or less precisely, tell actors where to look for precedents, who are the authoritative interpreters of different types of rules, and what the key interpretative traditions are. Still, the unambiguous authority of rules cannot be taken as given—it cannot be assumed that rules always dictate or guide behavior. Rather, it is necessary to understand the processes through which rules are translated into actual behavior and the factors that may strengthen or weaken the relation between rules and actions. How do actors discover the lessons of the past through experience and how do they store, retrieve, and act upon those lessons? How do actors cope with impediments to learning and resolve ambiguities and conflicts of what the situation is and what experience is relevant; what the relevant role, identity, and rule are and what they mean; and what the appropriate match and action are?

Sometimes action reflects in a straightforward way prescriptions embedded in the rules, habits of thought, "best practice," and standard operating procedures of a community, an institution, organization, profession, or group. A socially valid rule creates an abstraction that applies to a number of concrete situations. Most actors, most of the time, then, take the rule as a "fact." There is no felt need to "go behind it" and explain or justify action and discuss its likely consequences (Stinchcombe 2001, 2).

A straightforward and almost automatic relation between rules and action is most likely in a polity with legitimate, stable, well-defined, and integrated institutions. Action is then governed by a dominant institution that provides clear prescriptions and adequate resources, i.e. prescribes doable action in an unambiguous way. The system consists of a multitude of institutions, each based on different principles. Yet, each institution has some degree of autonomy and controls a specified action sphere. The (living) constitution prescribes when, how, and why rules are to be acted upon. It gives clear principles of division of labor, maintains internal consistency among rules, prevents collisions between divergent institutional prescriptions, and makes the political order a coherent whole with predictable outcomes. Together, a variety of rules give specific content in specific situations both to such heroic identities as statesman or patriot and to such everyday identities as those of an accountant, police officer, or citizen (Kaufman 1960; Van Maanen 1973).

In other contexts actors have problems in resolving ambiguities and conflicts among alternative concepts of the self, accounts of a situation, and prescriptions of appropriateness. They struggle with how to classify themselves and others—who they are, and what they are—and what these classifications imply in a specific situation. The prescriptive clarity and consistency of identities are variables, and so are the familiarity with situations and the obviousness of matching rules. Fulfilling an identity through following appropriate rules often involves matching a changing and ambiguous set of contingent rules to a changing and ambiguous set of situations.

A focus on rules and identities therefore assures neither simplicity nor consistency (Biddle 1986; Berscheid 1994). It is a non-trivial task to predict behavior from knowledge about roles, identities, rules, situations, and institutions, and describing action as rule following is only the first step in understanding how rules affect behavior. As a result, a distinction is made between a rule and its behavioral realization in a particular situation in the study of formal organizations (Scott 1992, 304; March, Schulz, and Zhou 2000, 23), institutions (Apter 1991), and the law (Tyler 1990). The possible indeterminacy of roles, identities, rules, and situations requires detailed observations of the processes through which rules are translated into actual behavior through constructive interpretation and available resources (March and Olsen 1995). We need to attend to the interaction between rules and purposeful behavior and the factors that enhance or counteract rule following and mediate the impact rules have on behavior (Checkel 2001).

Defining a role or identity and achieving it require time and energy, thought and capability. In order to understand the impact of rules upon action, we need to study such (imperfect) processes as attention directing, interpretation of rules, the validation of evidence, codification of experiences into rules, memory building and retrieval, and the mechanisms through which institutions distribute resources and enable actors to follow rules, across a variety of settings and situations.

For example, individuals have multiple roles and identities and the number and variety of alternative rules assures that only a fraction of the relevant rules are evoked in a particular place at a particular time. One of the primary factors affecting behavior, therefore, is the process by which some of those rules rather than others, are attended to in a particular situation, and how identities and situations are interpreted (March and Olsen 1989, 22). Fitting a rule to a situation is an exercise in establishing appropriateness, where rules and situations are related by criteria of similarity or difference through reasoning by analogy and metaphor. The process is mediated by language, by the ways in which participants come to be able to talk about one situation as similar to or different from another, and assign situations to rules. The process maintains consistency in action primarily through the creation of typologies of similarity, rather than through a derivation of action from stable interests or wants.[2]

Individuals may also have a difficult time interpreting which historical experiences and accounts are relevant for current situations, and situations can be defined in different ways that call forth different legitimate rules, actors, and arguments (Ugland 2002). Where more than one potentially relevant rule or account is evoked, the problem is to apply criteria of similarity in order to use the most appropriate rule or account. In some cases, higher-order rules are used to differentiate between lower-order rules, but democratic institutions and orders are not always monolithic, coordinated, and consistent. Some action spheres are weakly institutionalized. In others institutionalized rule sets compete. Rules and identities collide routinely

---

[2] Processes of constructive interpretation, criticism, justification, and application of rules and identities are more familiar to the intellectual traditions of law than economics. Lawyers argue about what the rules are, what the facts are, and what who have to do when (Dworkin 1986, vii). Law in action—the realization of law—involves legal institutions and procedures, legal values, and legal concepts and ways of thought, as well as legal rules (Berman 1983, 4).

(Orren and Skowronek 1994), making prescriptions less obvious. Actors sometimes disobey and challenge some rules because they adhere to other rules. Potential conflict among rules is, however, partly coped with by incomplete attention. For instance, rules that are more familiar are more likely to be evoked, thus recently used or recently revised rules come to attention.

In general, actors may find the rules and situations they encounter to be obscure. What is true and right and therefore what should be done may be ambiguous. Sometimes they may know what to do but not be able to do it because prescriptive rules and capabilities are incompatible. Actors are limited by the complexities of the demands upon them and by the distribution and regulation of resources, competencies, and organizing capacities; that is, by the institutionalized capability for acting appropriately. A separation between substantive policy making and budgeting is, for example, likely to create a gap between prescribed policy rules and targets and the capabilities to implement the rules and reach the targets.

Rules, then, potentially have several types of consequences but it can be difficult to say exactly how rules manifest themselves, to isolate their effects under varying circumstances and specify when knowledge about rules is decisive for understanding political behavior. While rules guide behavior and make some actions more likely than others, they ordinarily do not determine political behavior or policy outcomes precisely. Rules, laws, identities, and institutions provide parameters for action rather than dictate a specific action, and sometimes actors show considerable ability to accommodate shifting circumstances by changing behavior without changing core rules and structures (Olsen 2003).

Over the last decades focus has (again) been on the pathologies and negative effects of rule following, in the literature as well as in public debate in many countries. The ubiquity of rules, precedents, and routines often makes political institutions appear to be bureaucratic, stupid, insensitive, dogmatic, or rigid. The simplification provided by rules is clearly imperfect, and the imperfection is often manifest, especially after the fact. Nevertheless, some of the major capabilities of modern institutions come from their effectiveness in substituting rule-bound behavior for individually autonomous behavior.

Rules, for example, increase action capabilities and efficiency—the ability to solve policy problems and produce services. Yet the consequences of rules go beyond regulating strategic behavior by providing incentive structures and impacting transaction costs. Rules provide codes of meaning that facilitate interpretation of ambiguous worlds. They embody collective and individual roles, identities, rights, obligations, interests, values, world-views, and memory, thus constrain the allocation of attention, standards of evaluation, priorities, perceptions, and resources. Rules make it possible to coordinate many simultaneous activities in a way that makes them mutually consistent and reduces uncertainty, for example by creating predictable time rhythms through election and budget cycles (Sverdrup 2000). They constrain bargaining within comprehensible terms and enforce agreements and help avoid destructive conflicts. Still, the blessing of rules may be mixed. Detailed rules and rigid rule following may under some conditions make policy making and implementation more effective, but a well-working system may also need discretion and flexibility. Consequently, short-term and long-term consequences of rules may differ. Rules may, furthermore, make public debate obligatory, but rule following may also hamper reason giving and discourse.

A one-sided focus on policy consequences may furthermore hide a broader range of effects. Logics of action are used to describe, explain, justify, and criticize behavior and sometimes the primary reason for rules is to proclaim virtue rather than to control behavior directly, making the implementation of rules less important (Meyer and Rowan 1977; Brunsson 1989; March 1994, 76). Rules and institutions of government are, in addition, potentially transformative. More or less successfully, they turn individuals into citizens and officials by shaping their identities and mentalities and making them observe the *normative* power of rules (Mill 1962/1861; Fuller 1971; Joerges 1996).

An important aspect of rules, then, is their possible consequences for the development of a community of rule, based on a common identity and sense of belonging. A key issue of political organization is how to combine unity and diversity and craft a cooperative system out of a conflictual one; and the democratic aspiration has been to hold society together without eliminating diversity—that is, to develop and maintain a system of rules, institutions, and identities that makes it possible to rule a divided society without undue violence (Wheeler 1975, 4; Crick 1983, 25).

The growth and decay of institutions, roles, and identities, with their different logics of action, are therefore key indicators of political change (Eisenstadt 1965; Huntington 1965). Rules also help realize flexibility and adaptiveness as well as order and stability. This is so because part of the democratic commitment is the institutionalization of self-reflection and procedures through which existing rules can legitimately be examined, criticized, and changed.

# 4. THE DYNAMICS OF RULES
# OF APPROPRIATENESS

Why are the rules of appropriateness what they are? Why are specific behavioral prescriptions believed to be natural or exemplary and why do rules vary across polities and institutions? Through which processes and why do rules of appropriateness change? A conception of human behavior as rule and identity based invites a conception of the mechanisms by which rules and identities evolve and become legitimized, reproduced, modified, and replaced. Key behavioral mechanisms are history-dependent processes of adaptation such as learning or selection. Rules of appropriateness are seen as carriers of lessons from experience as those lessons are encoded either by individuals and collectivities drawing inferences from their own and others' experiences, or by differential survival and reproduction of institutions, roles, and identities based on particular rules. Rule-driven behavior associated with successes or survival is likely to be repeated. Rules associated with failures are not.

A common interpretation of rules, institutions, roles, and identities is that they exist because they work well and provide better solutions than their alternatives (Goodin 1996; Hechter, Opp, and Wippler 1990; Stinchcombe 1997, 2001). They are, at least under some conditions, functional and consistent with people's values and moral commitments. In contemporary democracies, this interpretation is reflected in high learning aspirations. Appropriate rules, in both technical and normative terms, are assumed to evolve over time as new experiences are interpreted and coded into rules, or less attractive alternatives are eliminated through competition. Lessons from experience are assumed to improve the intelligence, effectiveness, and adaptability of the polity and be a source of wisdom and progress. The key democratic institution for ensuring rational adaptation of rules is free debate where actors have to explain and justify their behavior in public through reason-based argumentation, within a set of rules defining appropriate debates and arguments.

In practice, however, the willingness and ability of democracies to learn, adapt rules, and improve performance on the basis of experience is limited (Neustadt and May 1986; March 1999). Rules are transmitted from one generation to another or from one set of identity holders through child rearing, education, training, socialization, and habitualization. Rules are maintained and changed through contact with others and exposure to experiences and information. Rules spread through social networks and their diffusion is constrained by borders and distances. They compete for attention. They change in concert with other rules, interfere with or support each other, and they are transformed while being transferred (Czarniawska and Joerges 1995; March, Schulz, and Zhou 2000). Change also takes place as a result of public discourse and deliberate interventions. These dynamics reflect both the effects of change induced by the environment and endogenous changes produced by the operation of the rule system itself.

Yet, as is well known from modern investigations, such processes are not perfect. For example, the encoding of history, either through experiential learning or through evolutionary selection, does not necessarily imply intelligence, improvement, or increased adaptive value. There is no guarantee that relevant observations will be made, correct inferences and lessons derived, proper actions taken, or that imperfections will be eliminated. Rules encode history, but the coding procedures and the processes by which the coded interpretations are themselves decoded are filled with behavioral surprises.[3]

We assume that new experiences may lead to change in rules, institutions, roles, and identities and yet we are not committed to a belief in historical efficiency, i.e. rapid and costless rule adaptation to functional and normative environments and deliberate political reform attempts, and therefore to the functional or moral necessity of observed rules (March and Olsen 1989, 1995, 1998). Democratic institutions,

---

[3] March and Olsen 1975, 1989, 1995, 1998; Levitt and March 1988; March 1994, 1999; March, Schulz, and Zhou 2000; Olsen and Peters 1996.

for example, are arranged to both speed up and slow down learning from experience and adaptation. Democracies value continuity and predictability as well as flexibility and change, and usually there are attempts to balance the desire to keep the basic rules of governance stable and the desire to adapt rules due to new experience. The main picture is also one of renewal and continuity, path departures and path dependencies. Different rules, roles, and identities are evoked in different situations and when circumstances fluctuate fast, there may be rapid shifts within existing repertoires of behavioral rules based on institutionalized switching rules. However, the basic repertoire of rules and standard operating procedures change more slowly.

Change in constitutive rules usually requires time-consuming processes and a strong majority, a fact that is likely to slow down change. The same is true when the basic rules express the historical collective identity of a community and embody shared understandings of what counts as truth, right, and good. Deliberate reform then has to be explained and justified in value-rational terms; that is, in terms of their appropriateness and not solely in efficiency terms (Olsen 1997); and change in entrenched interpretative traditions and who are defined as the authoritative interpreters of different types of rules, are also likely to change relatively slowly.

Core political identities are not primordial and constant. Nevertheless, barring severe crises, processes of identity formation and reinterpretation are likely to be slow. All political rulers try to transfer naked power into authority. Civic virtue and shared internalized principles of rights and obligations[4] and identities are to some degree accessible to political experience, reasoning, and action. They can, for example, be affected through policies of nation building, mass education, and mass media, even if the causal chains are long and indirect. In democracies, where the authority of law is well established, identities may also be fashioned through political and legal debates and decisions (Habermas 1996). Legalization may in some settings be a prelude to internalization of rules of appropriateness, even if they in other settings may substitute for internalized rules.

There is, however, modest knowledge about the factors that govern targets of political identification and codes of appropriate behavior, and where, when, and how different types of actors obtain their identities and codes—for example the relative importance of specific political ideologies, institutions, professions, and educations, and belonging to larger social categories such as nation, gender, class, race, religion, and ethnicity (Herrmann, Risse, and Brewer 2004). Neither is it obvious how well different institutions today embody and encourage democratic identities and make it more likely that citizens and officials act in accordance with internalized democratic principles and ideals. Furthermore, an improved understanding of rule dynamics may require better insight into how the dynamics of change may be related to normal, new, and extraordinary experience in different institutional settings.

---

[4] As observed by Rousseau: "the strongest man is never strong enough to be always master unless he transforms his power into right, and obedience into duty" (Rousseau 1967/1762/1755, 10). In modern society, Weber argued, the belief in legality—the acceptance of the authority of law, legal actors, reasoning, precedents, and institutions—is the most common form for legitimacy (Weber 1978, 37).

*Consider normal experience and routine learning.* Experiences are routinely coded into rules, rules into principles, and principles into systems of thought in many spheres of life. Routine refinement of rules can be imagined to improve their fit to the environment, and one study showed that the stability of rules is related positively to their age at the time of last revision. However, changes in rules can also create problems that destabilize rules, and the current stability of rules is related negatively to the number of times they have been revised in the past (March, Schulz, and Zhou 2000).

In some spheres, i.e. Weberian bureaucracies and court systems, these processes are systematic and institutionalized (Weber 1978; Berman 1983); in other spheres they are less so. Conflict between competing situational accounts, conceptions of truth and justice, and interpretations of appropriate behavior is also routine in contemporary democracies. Democracies are at best only *partly* communities of shared experiences, communication, interpretative traditions, and memory that give direction and meaning to citizens. They are glued together by shared debates, controversies, and contestations and by fairly broad agreement on some basic rules for coping with conflicts.

In fragmented, or loosely coupled systems, competing rules of appropriateness may be maintained over long time periods due to their separateness. As long as rule following meets targets and aspiration levels, rules are unlikely to be challenged, even if they are not in any sense "optimal." Reduced slack resources may, however, call attention to inconsistencies in rules and produce demands for more coordination and consistency across institutional spheres and social groups (Cyert and March 1963). Comparison across previously segmented institutional spheres or groups with different traditions, rules of appropriateness, and taken-for-granted beliefs, may then trigger processes of search and reconciliation or dominance and coercion.

*Consider new experience and settings.* Processes of search and change may also be triggered when an existing order, its institutions, rules of appropriateness, and collective self-understandings, are challenged by new experiences that are difficult to account for in terms of existing conceptions (Berger and Luckmann 1967, 103). Entrenched accounts and narratives then do not make sense. They no longer provide adequate answers to what is true or false, right or wrong, good or bad, and what is appropriate behavior; and there is search for new conceptions and legitimizations that can produce a more coherent shared account (Eder 1999, 208–9).

Account and concepts may be challenged because new institutions and meeting places have developed. An example of a new institutional setting generating increased contact and challenging national traditions is the integration of sovereign nation-states into the European Union. Challenges may also follow from institutional collisions between previously separated or segmented traditions, for example the invading of market rules of appropriateness into institutional spheres traditionally based on different conceptions, such as democratic politics, science, and sport. Increased mobility or massive migration across large geographical and cultural distances may likewise create collisions that challenge established frames of reference and institutionalized routines. Such collisions may generate destructive conflicts, but they may also generate rethinking, search, learning, and adaptation by changing the participants' reference groups, aspiration levels, and causal understandings.

*Consider the unacceptability of the past and institutional emancipation.* Actors are likely to learn from disasters, crises, and system breakdowns—transformative periods where established orders are delegitimized, are challenged, or collapse. Then, institutions and their constitutive rules are discredited as unworkable and intolerable and change initiatives are presented as emancipation from an order that is a dysfunctional, unfair, or tyrannical relic of an unacceptable past, as was, for example, the case when Communist regimes in central and eastern Europe collapsed (Offe 1996; Wollmann 2006).

In situations of disorientation, crisis, and search for meaning, actors are in particular likely to rethink who and what they and others are, and may become; what communities they belong to, and want to belong to; and how power should be redistributed. Often the search for legitimate models and accounts is extended far back to possible glorious periods in own history, or they are copied from political systems that can be accepted as exemplary. Short of revolution or civil war, there may be shifts in cognitive and normative frames, in who are defined as legitimate interpreters of appropriateness, in interpretative traditions, and in the system for collecting, communicating, and organizing knowledge (Eder 1999), as well as in resource distributions and power relations.

*In sum,* an improved theoretical understanding of the dynamics of rules, institutions, roles, and identities requires attention to several 'imperfect' processes of change, not a focus on a single mechanism. Change is not likely to be governed by a single coherent and dominant process. Except under special circumstances, rules of appropriateness develop and change through a myriad of disjointed processes and experiences in a variety of places and situations, even when the result is normatively justified post hoc by rational accounts (Eder 1999, 203). For example, decrees, command, and coercion have a limited role in developing and maintaining legitimate rules, roles, and identities. The internalization of rules and identities is usually not a case of willful entering into an explicit contract either. In practice, processes such as learning, socialization, diffusion, regeneration, deliberate design, and competitive selection all have their imperfections, and an improved understanding of these imperfections may provide a key to a better understanding of the dynamics of rules (March 1981).

Required then is the exploration of the scope conditions and interaction of such processes as purposeful reform, institutional abilities to adapt spontaneously to changing circumstances, and environmental effectiveness in eliminating suboptimal rules, institutions, and identities (Olsen 2001). In the final part, we explore how an adequate understanding of politics may also require attention to the scope conditions and interaction of different logics of behavior.

# 5. RECONCILING LOGICS OF ACTION

Action is rule based, but only partly so. There is a great diversity in human motivation and modes of action. Behavior is driven by habit, emotion, coercion, and calculated expected utility, as well as interpretation of internalized rules and principles. Here, focus is on the potential tension, in the first instance, between the role- or identity-based logic of appropriateness and the preference-based consequential logic; and in the second instance, between the claims of citizenship and officialdom and the claims of particularistic roles or identities.

Democratic governance involves balancing the enduring tensions between different logics of action, for instance between the demands and obligations of offices and roles and individual calculated interests (Tussman 1960, 18). Political actors are also likely to be held accountable for both the appropriateness and the consequences of their actions. A dilemma is that proper behavior sometimes is associated with bad consequences and improper behavior sometimes is associated with good consequences. From time to time, democratic actors will get 'dirty hands.' That is, they achieve desirable outcomes through methods that they recognize as inappropriate. Or, they follow prescribed rules and procedures at the cost of producing outcomes they recognize to be undesirable (Merton 1938; Thompson 1987, 11).

Partly as a result of the tensions between them, there are cycles between logics of action. Compared to the *Rechtsstaat*, with its traditions and rhetoric tied to the logic of appropriateness, twentieth-century democracies (particularly the welfare states of Europe) embraced practices and rhetoric that were more tied to the logic of consequentiality. Consequence-oriented professions replaced process-oriented ones, and effectiveness and substantive results were emphasized more than the principles and procedures to be followed. Governance came to assume a community of shared objectives rather than a community of shared rules, principles, and procedures (March and Olsen 1995).

More recent reforms have continued that trend. Governments in the 1980s generally tried to change concepts of accountability even more toward emphasis upon results and away from an emphasis on the rules and procedures (Olsen and Peters 1996). While several reforms were processual in character, rules were often seen as instrumental rather than having a legitimacy of their own. In particular, they aimed at binding and controlling elected politicians and experts. One reason for the reforms was the conviction that individuals needed better protection against political interventions. A second reason was the conviction that consequence-oriented professions such as medical doctors and teachers in welfare states were ineffectively subjected to public accountability and that obligations to report and being subject to audit had to be expanded (Power 1994).

Nevertheless, there is no uniform and linear trend making rules of appropriateness outdated. Scandals in both the private and public sector have triggered demands for legal and ethical rules and an ethos of responsibility. The European Union is to a large extent a polity based on rules and legal integration; and in world politics there is a trend towards legal rules and institutions, including an emphasis on human rights, even if the trend may be neither even nor irreversible (Goldstein et al. 2000).

Political systems deal with the multitude of behavioral motivations in a variety of ways and one is separating different logics by locating them in different institutions and roles (Weber 1978). Different logics of action are also observed within single institutions. Individual institutions, on the one hand, separate logics by prescribing different logics for different roles. For instance, in courts of law the judge, the prosecutor, the attorney, the witness, and the accused legitimately follow different logics of action. The credence of their arguments, data, and conclusions is also expected to vary. On the other hand, logics also compete within single institutions. In public administration, for example, there have been cycles of trust in control of behavior through manipulation of incentive structures and individual cost–benefit calculations, and trust in an ethos of internal-normative responsibility and willingness to act in accordance with rules of appropriateness. Historically, the two have interacted. Their relative importance, as well as the definition of appropriateness, have changed over time and varied across institutional settings (deLeon 2003).

A theoretical challenge is to fit different motivations and logics of action into a single framework. Specific logics, such as following rules of appropriateness and calculating individual expected utility, can be good approximations under specific conditions. It is difficult to deny the importance of each of them (and others) and inadequate to rely exclusively on one of them. Therefore, a theory of purposeful human behavior must take into consideration the diversity of human motivations and modes of behavior and account for the relationship and interaction between different logics in different institutional settings. A beginning is to explore behavioral logics as complementary, rather than to assume a single dominant behavioral logic (March and Olsen 1998; Olsen 2001).

If it is assumed that no single model, and the assumptions upon which it is based, is more fruitful than all the others under all conditions and that different models are not necessarily mutually exclusive, we can examine their variations, shifting significance, scope conditions, prerequisites, and interplay, and explore ideas that can reconcile and synthesize different models. We may enquire how and where different logics of actions are developed, lost, and redefined. We may examine the conditions under which each logic is invoked. We may ask how logics interact, how they may support or counteract each other, and which logics are reconcilable. We may also specify through what processes different logics of action may become dominant.

We may, in particular, explore how different logics of action are formally prescribed, authorized, and allowed, or how they are defined as illegitimate and proscribed, in different institutional settings, for different actors, under different circumstances. We may enquire how institutional settings in practice are likely to prompt individuals to evoke different logics. We may also study which settings in practice enable the dominance of one logic over all others, for example under what conditions rules of appropriateness may overpower or redefine self-interest, or the logic of consequentiality may overpower rules and an entrenched definition of appropriateness (March and Olsen 1998; Olsen 2001).[5]

In the following, focus is on some possible relationships between the logic of appropriateness and the logic of consequentiality. An unsatisfactory approach is to *subsume* one logic as a special case of the other. Within the logic-of-appropriateness perspective, consequential choice is then seen as one of many possible rules that actors may come to believe is exemplary for specific roles in specific settings and situations. From the logic-of-consequentiality perspective, rules of appropriateness may be seen as the result of higher-level or prior utility calculations, choice, and explicit contracts. We see this approach as unsatisfactory because it denies the distinctiveness of different logics.

An alternative is to assume a *hierarchy* between logics. The logic of appropriateness may be used subject to constraints of extreme consequences, or rules of appropriateness are seen as one of several constraints within which the logic of consequentiality operates. One version of the hierarchy notion is that one logic is used for major decisions and the other for refinements of those decisions, or one logic governs the behavior of politically important actors and another the behavior of less important actors. It is, for example, often suggested that politics follows the logic of consequentiality, while public administrators and judges follow the logic of appropriateness. The suggestion of a stable hierarchy between logics and between types of decisions and actors is, however, not well supported by empirical findings.

A more promising route may be to differentiate logics of action in terms of their *prescriptive clarity* and hypothesize that a clear logic will dominate a less clear logic. Rules of appropriateness are defined with varying precision and provide more or less clear prescriptions in different settings and situations. For instance, rules are in varying degrees precise, consistent, obligatory, and legally binding. There are more or less specified exceptions from the rules and varying agreement about who the authoritative interpreter of a rule is. Likewise, the clarity of (self-)interests, preferences, choice alternatives, and their consequences varies. Bureaucrats, for example, are influenced by the rules and structural settings in which they act, yet they may face ambiguous rules as well as situations where no direct personal interest is involved (Egeberg 1995, 2003). In brief, rules and interests give actors more or less clear behavioral guidance and make it more or less likely that the logic of appropriateness or the logic of consequentiality will dominate.

Even when actors are able to figure out what to do, a clear logic can only be followed when available resources make it possible to obey its prescriptions. Following rules of appropriateness, compared to predicting the future, clarifying alternatives and their expected utility, partly requires different abilities and resources. Therefore, variation and change in the relative importance of the two logics may follow from variation and change in the resources available for acting in accordance with rules of appropriateness and calculated (self-)interest.

---

[5] Such questions are raised in several disciplines and subdisciplines, for example by Fehr and Gächter 1998, 848; Finnemore and Sikkink 1998, 912; Clayton and Gillman 1999; van den Bergh and Stagl 2003, 26; Jupille, Caporaso, and Checkel 2003.

Examples are shifting mixes of public and private resources, budgetary allocations to institutions that traditionally have promoted different logics, and changes in recruitment from professions that are carriers of one logic to professions that promote the other logic. Tight deadlines are also likely to promote rule following rather than the more time- and resource-demanding calculation of expected utility (March and Simon 1993, 11). The relation between level of societal conflict and logics of action is not obvious, however. In democratic settings, confrontations and conflicts usually challenge existing rules and possibly the logic of appropriateness. But protracted conflicts also tend to generate demands for compromises and constitutive rules that can dampen the level of conflict.

Lack of resources and understanding may also be one reason why different logics of action are used for different *purposes*, such as making policies and justifying policies. In institutional spheres and societies where policy making is prescribed to follow the logic of appropriateness, the rule of law, traditions, and precedents, and the prescriptions are difficult to implement, the logic of appropriateness is likely to be used to justify decisions also when it is not used to make them. Likewise, in institutional spheres and societies where policy making is prescribed to follow the logic of consequentiality, rational calculation, and an orientation towards the future, and where following the prescription is difficult, the logic of consequentiality is likely to be used for justifying decisions, whatever the underlying logic of making them. We hypothesize, however, that rationality and the logic of consequentiality is more easily used to justify decisions. This is so because consequentiality is behaviorally more indeterminate in its implications than rule following and the logic of appropriateness in situations of even moderate ambiguity and complexity. It is easier to rationalize behavior in terms of one interest or another, than to interpret behavior as appropriate, simply because rules of appropriateness are collective, publicly known, and fairly stable.

The time dimension is also important. A polity may institutionalize a *sequential* ordering of logics of action, so that different phases follow different logics and the basis of action changes over time in a predictable way. In democracies, an example is the vision of an institutionalized demand for expert information and advice as a precondition for informed political decision, followed by technical-logical implementation, monitoring, and adjudication of decisions. Another example is the Habermasian vision of an institutionalized public sphere, providing an ideal speech situation that makes it necessary even for self-interested, utility-calculating actors to argue in universal rather than particularistic terms. Over time deliberation and reasoned arguments become habitualized and normatively accepted, turning egoists into citizens (Habermas 1989). More generally, Mills (1940: 908) hypothesized that the long acting out of a role or rule of appropriateness 'will often induce a man to become what at first he merely sought to appear.'

Finally, change between logics of action may be the result of *specific experiences*. Rules of appropriateness are likely to evolve as a result of accumulated experience with a specific situation over extended time periods. Therefore, rules and standard operating procedures are most likely to dominate when actors have long tenure, frequent interaction, and shared experiences and information; when they share accounts and institutionalized memories; and when environments are fairly stable. Consequences are fed back into rules and rules are likely to be abandoned and possibly replaced by the logic of consequentiality, when rule following is defined as unsatisfactory in terms of established targets and aspiration levels.

In particular, rules are likely to be abandoned when rule following creates catastrophic outcomes, and in periods of radical environmental change, where past arrangements and rules are defined as irrelevant or unacceptable. Similarly, recourse to rules and standard operating procedures is likely when consequential calculations are seen as having produced catastrophes. In particular, rational calculation of consequences is easiest when problems are of modest complexity and time perspectives are short. When applied to more complex problems and longer time perspectives they are more likely to create big mistakes, afterwards seen as horror stories (Neustadt and May 1986).

As these speculations show, the scope conditions and interaction of different logics of action and types of reason are not well understood. Accomplishments are dwarfed by the large number of unanswered questions. Nevertheless, the gap may also be seen as providing a future research agenda for students of democratic politics and policy making.

# REFERENCES

APTER, D. A. 1991. Institutionalism reconsidered. *International Social Science Journal*, 43: 463–81.

ARBLASTER, A. 1987. *Democracy*. Milton Keynes: Open University Press.

ARISTOTLE. 1980. *Politics*. Harmondsworth: Penguin.

BERGER, P. L., and LUCKMANN, T. 1967. *The Social Construction of Reality*. New York: Doubleday, Anchor.

BERMAN, H. J. 1983. *Law and Revolution: The Formation of the Western Legal Tradition*. Cambridge, Mass.: Harvard University Press.

BERSCHEID, E. 1994. Interpersonal relationships. *Annual Review of Psychology*, 45: 79–129.

BIDDLE, B. J. 1986. Recent developments in role theory. *Annual Review of Sociology*, 12: 67–92.

BRENNAN, G., and BUCHANAN, J. M. 1985. *The Reason of Rules: Constitutional Political Economy*. Cambridge: Cambridge University Press.

BRUNSSON, N. 1989. *The Organization of Hypocrisy*. Chichester: Wiley.

CHECKEL, J. T. 2001. Why comply? Social learning and European identity change. *International Organization*, 55: 553–88.

CLAYTON, C. W., and GILLMAN, H. 1999. *Supreme Court Decision-Making: New Institutionalist Approaches*. Chicago: University of Chicago Press.

CRICK, B. 1983. *In Defense of Politics*, 2nd edn. Harmondsworth: Penguin.

CYERT, R. M., and MARCH, J. G. 1963. *A Behavioral Theory of the Firm*. Englewood Cliffs, NJ: Prentice Hall. 2nd edn., 1992.

CZARNIAWSKA, B., and JOERGES, B. 1995. Winds of organizational change: how ideas translate into objects and action. *Research in the Sociology of Organizations*, 13: 171–209.

deLeon, P. 2003. On acting responsibly in a disorderly world: individual ethics and administrative responsibility. Pp. 569–80 in *The Handbook of Public Administration*, ed. B. G. Peters and J. Pierre. London: Sage.

Dworkin, R. 1986. *Law's Empire*. Cambridge, Mass.: Belknap, Harvard University Press.

Eder, K. 1999. Societies learn and yet the world is hard to change. *European Journal of Social Theory*, 2: 195–215.

Egeberg, M. 1995. Bureaucrats as public policy-makers and their self-interest. *Journal of Theoretical Politics*, 7: 157–67.

—— 2003. How bureaucratic structure matters: an organizational perspective. Pp. 116–26 in *The Handbook of Public Administration*, ed. B. G. Peters and J. Pierre. London: Sage.

Eisenstadt, S. 1965. *Essays on Comparative Institutions*. New York: Wiley.

Elias, N. 1982/1939. *The Civilizing Process: State Formation and Civilization*, 2nd edn. Oxford: Basil Blackwell.

Elster, J. 1989. Demokratiets verdigrunnlag og verdikonflikter. Pp. 77–93 in *Vitenskap og politikk*. Oslo: Universitetsforlaget.

Fehr, E., and Gächter, S. 1998. Reciprocity and economics: the economic implications of *homo reciprocans*. *European Economic Review*, 42: 845–59.

Finnemore, M., and Sikkink, K. 1998. International norm dynamics and political change. *International Organization*, 52 (4): 887–917.

Fuller, L. L. 1971. *The Morality of Law*. New Haven, Conn.: Yale University Press.

Goldstein, J. L., Kahler, M., Keohane, R. O., and Slaughter, A.-M. (eds.) 2000. Legalization and world politics. *International Organization* (Special Issue). Reprinted Cambridge, Mass.: MIT Press, 2001.

Goodin, R. E. (ed.) 1996. *The Theory of Institutional Design*. Cambridge: Cambridge University Press.

Habermas, J. 1989. *The Structural Transformation of the Public Sphere*. Cambridge, Mass.: MIT Press.

—— 1996. *Between Facts and Norms*. Cambridge, Mass.: MIT Press.

—— 1998. *The Inclusion of the Other: Studies in Political Theory*, ed. C. Cronin and P. de Greiff. Cambridge, Mass.: MIT Press.

Hechter, M., Opp, K. D., and Wippler, R. 1990. *Social Institutions: Their Emergence, Maintenance and Effects*. New York: de Gruyter.

Heclo, H. 2002. The spirit of public administration. *PS: Political Science & Politics*, 35: 689–94.

Herrmann, R. K., Risse, T., and Brewer, M. B. (eds.) 2004. *Transnational Identities: Becoming European in the EU*. Lanham, Md.: Rowman and Littlefield.

Huntington, S. P. 1965. Political development and political decay. *World Politics*, 17: 386–430.

Joerges, C. 1996. Taking the law seriously: on political science and the role of law in integration. *European Law Journal*, 2: 105–35.

Jupille, J., Caporaso, J. A., and Checkel, J. T. 2003. Integrating institutions: rationalism, constructivism, and the study of the European Union. *Comparative Political Studies*, 36: 7–41.

Kaufman, H. 1960. *The Forest Ranger*. Baltimore: Johns Hopkins University Press.

Lefort, C. 1988. *Democracy and Political Theory*. Minneapolis: University of Minnesota Press.

Levitt, B., and March, J. G. 1988. Organizational learning. *Annual Review of Sociology*, 14: 319–40.

Loewenstein, K. 1951. Reflections on the value of constitutions in our revolutionary age. Pp. 191–224 in *Constitutions and Constitutional Trends since World War II*, ed. A. Z. Zurcher. New York: New York University Press.

Macintyre, A. 1988. *Whose Justice? Which Rationality?* 2nd edn. Notre Dame, Ind.: University of Notre Dame Press.

MARCH, J. G. 1981. Footnotes to organizational change. *Administrative Science Quarterly*, 16: 563–77.

—— 1994. *A Primer on Decision Making: How Decisions Happen*. New York: Free Press.

—— 1999. *The Pursuit of Organizational Intelligence*. Oxford: Blackwell.

—— and OLSEN, J. P. 1975. The uncertainty of the past: organizational learning under ambiguity. *European Journal of Political Research*, 3: 147–71.

—— —— 1989. *Rediscovering Institutions*. New York: Free Press.

—— —— 1995. *Democratic Governance*. New York: Free Press.

—— —— 1998. The institutional dynamics of international political orders. *International Organization*, 52: 943–69.

—— SCHULZ, M., and ZHOU, X. 2000. *The Dynamics of Rules: Change in Written Organizational Codes*. Stanford, Calif.: Stanford University Press.

—— and SIMON, H. A. 1958. *Organizations*. New York: Wiley.

—— —— 1993. *Organizations*, 2nd edn. New York: Wiley.

MERTON, R. K. 1938. Social structure and anomie. *American Sociological Review*, 3: 672–82.

MEYER, J., and ROWAN, B. 1977. Institutionalized organizations: formal structure as myth and ceremony. *American Journal of Sociology*, 83: 340–63.

MILL, J. S. 1962/1861. *Considerations on Representative Government*. South Bend, Ind.: Gateway Editions.

MILLS, C. W. 1940. Situated actions and vocabularies of motive. *American Sociological Review*, 5 (6): 904–13.

NEUSTADT, R. E., and MAY, E. R. 1986, *Thinking in Time: The Uses of History for Decision-Makers*. New York: Free Press.

OFFE, C. 1996. Designing institutions in East European transitions. Pp. 199–226 in *The Theory of Institutional Design*, ed. R. E. Goodin. Cambridge: Cambridge University Press.

OLSEN, J. P. 1997. Institutional design in democratic contexts. *Journal of Political Philosophy*, 5: 203–29.

—— 2001. Garbage cans, New Institutionalism, and the study of politics. *American Political Science Review*, 95: 191–8.

—— 2003. Towards a European administrative space? *Journal of European Public Policy*, 10: 506–31.

—— and PETERS, B. G. (eds.) 1996. *Lessons from Experience: Experiential Learning in Administrative Reforms in Eight Countries*. Oslo: Scandinavian University Press.

ORREN, K., and SKOWRONEK, S. 1994. Beyond the iconography of order: notes for a "new" institutionalism. Pp. 311–30 in *The Dynamics of American Politics: Approaches and Interpretations*, ed. L. Dodd and C. Jillson. Boulder, Colo.: Westview.

POWER, M. 1994. *The Audit Explosion*. London: Demos.

ROUSSEAU, J.-J. 1967/1762/1755. *The Social Contract and Discourses on the Origin of Inequality*, ed. and introd. L. G. Crocker. New York: Washington Square Press.

ROWE, N. 1989. *Rules and Institutions*. New York: Philip Allan.

SARBIN, T. R., and ALLEN, V. L. 1968. Role theory. Pp. 488–567 in *The Handbook of Social Psychology*, ed. G. Lindzey and E. Aronson, 2nd edn. Reading, Mass.: Addison-Wesley.

SCOTT, J. C. 1976. *The Moral Economy of the Peasant: Rebellion and Subsistence in Southeast Asia*. New Haven, Conn.: Yale University Press.

SCOTT, W. R. 1992. *Organizations: Rational, Natural, and Open Systems*, 3rd edn. Englewood Cliffs, NJ: Prentice Hall.

STINCHCOMBE, A. L. 1997. On the virtues of the old institutionalism. *Annual Review of Sociology*, 23: 1–18.

—— 2001. *When Formality Works: Authority and Abstraction in Law and Organizations*. Chicago: University of Chicago Press.

SVERDRUP, U. I. 2000. Precedents and present events in the European Union: an institutional perspective on Treaty reform. Pp. 241–65 in *European Integration after Amsterdam*, ed. K. Neunreither and A. Wiener. Oxford: Oxford University Press.

THOMPSON, D. F. 1987. *Political Ethics and Public Office*. Cambridge, Mass.: Harvard University Press.

TUSSMAN, J. 1960. *Obligation and the Body Politic*. London: Oxford University Press.

TYLER, T. R. 1990. *Why People Obey the Law*. New Haven, Conn.: Yale University Press.

UGLAND, T. 2002. *Policy Recategorization and Integration: Europeanization of Nordic Alcohol Policies*. Oslo: Arena Report 02/3.

VAN DEN BERGH, J. C. J. M., and STAGL, S. 2003. Co-evolution of economic behavior and institutions: towards a theory of institutional change. *Journal of Evolutionary Economics*, 13 (3): 289–317.

VAN MAANEN, J. 1973. Observations on the making of policemen. *Human Organization*, 32: 407–18.

VIROLI, M. 1992. *From Politics to Reason of State: The Acquisition and Transformation of the Language of Politics 1250–1600*. Cambridge: Cambridge University Press.

WEBER, M. 1978. *Economy and Society*, ed. G. Roth and C. Wittich. Berkeley: University of California Press.

WHEELER, H. 1975. Constitutionalism. Pp. 1–91 in *The Handbook of Political Science: Governmental Institutions and Processes*, vol. v, ed. F. I. Greenstein and N. W. Polsby. Reading, Mass.: Addison-Wesley.

WOLLMANN, H. 2006. Executive trajectories compared. In *Governing after Communism: Institutions and Policies*, ed. V. Dimitrov, K. H. Goetz, and H. Wollmann. Lanham, Md.: Rowman and Littlefield.

CHAPTER 35

# ETHICAL DIMENSIONS OF PUBLIC POLICY

## HENRY SHUE

IF one perused the professional backgrounds of the faculties of many of the most prominent schools of public policy, one could be forgiven for believing that one was looking at lists of the faculty members of economics departments, leavened to some degree by other social scientists whose methodologies are nevertheless heavily influenced by various forms of economic analysis. Any specialists on ethics or normative issues generally tend to be peripheral, served on the side like the wilted salad that comes whether requested or not, or perhaps sprinkled on top like the pepper that is entirely optional. I think this helps to explain the superficiality of much analysis of public policy—not, of course, because individual economists have particularly superficial minds and ethics specialists have deep ones, but because the most fundamental decisions must already be made before economic analysis can be valuable. And those less easily manageable decisions concern the considerations that can be systematically weighted only after ethical assessment.

Most important of all is the deceptively simple question of who, and what, counts (Sneed 1977; Barnett 2002; N. Crawford 2002; Finnemore 2003). This question must be decided before any useful calculations of costs, benefits, or risks can be made. Whose costs shall we count? And whose shall we ignore? Whose count fully, and whose are to be discounted? Only members of the constituency of the policy maker or also others who are deeply affected—sometimes more deeply affected (Scheffler 2001)? Only those alive today or those alive a century from now too (Barry 1991)? Only human society or also some or all aspects of the natural world, such as the pattern of changing seasons that in the temperate zones has guided farmers and inspired poets but is now being undermined by the climate change being accelerated by human economic activity (McKibben 1990)?

These are "messy" questions in the sense that they are not amenable to precise calculation. Any precise calculations, however, will mislead the makers of public policy to the extent that they omit matters that ought to be included. Not only is it true that the rule "garbage in, garbage out" prevails, but it is also true that "arbitrary features considered, arbitrary decisions made." Obviously the alternative to analyses that are arbitrarily partial is not analyses that are literally comprehensive—no analysis could consider everything, and analyses can be arbitrarily inclusive as well as arbitrarily exclusive. This makes ethical analysis difficult. Selective judgements must be made, not least because an analysis that is to be useful in the choice of policy must focus attention sharply on whatever matters most in the area affected by the policy. So, what matters most? And what matters not at all? These selective judgements are ethical judgements.

The beginning of wisdom here is the realization that the most fundamental judgements, most especially the decisions about who and what to take into consideration in the first place, are judgements about relative importance—"value judgements." However contentious or inconclusive ethical debates may be—and it is not obvious that they need be any more indecisive than debates among economists themselves—they are the debates that need to be conducted at the outset of well-grounded policy analysis. It is worth looking at a few typical instances of the rock-bottom choice about inclusion/exclusion. The purpose here is not to offer solutions, but simply to demonstrate why the choices need to be confronted in the fundamental ethical terms in which they arise and dealt with as the ethical issues they are.

# 1. Who's In? Who's Out? Across Time

Most economists do recognize that decisions about how far forward in time to run their calculations have enormous consequences; and different choices about how many generations to consider, and how heavily to consider those more distant in time, are understood to skew analyses completely. Yet, economists are amazingly quick to decide that the solution is to use wholesale discounting of total future welfare. Since most likely the numbers of people yet to live—let us temporarily indulge the customary arbitrary exclusion of the entire universe apart from humans—or even the numbers in future generations of one's own community—now indulging the customary exclusion of strangers, without worrying just yet about how to specify relevant communities—will dwarf the number of people currently alive, consideration of all aspects of the welfare of all of them would overwhelm the welfare of the current generation. So selectivity of some kind is unavoidable. But indiscriminately discounting all aspects, major and minor, vital and optional, of the welfare of future generations is only one familiar, and comfortable way to proceed (Cowen and Parfit 1991; Broome 1994).

The arbitrariness of discounting as a general technique is a separate issue from the arbitrariness of the rate of discount selected. Three per cent seems to be highly popular in practice, and it does have a nice round appeal. Usually some reference point is used in a gesture at justification of the number chosen, such as some current interest rate. But why, if some discount rate is to be adopted in our calculations about the welfare of people in future, should this particular rate be the one?

What is even less adequately discussed is why we ought to reduce the weight attributed to absolutely everything about future generations and why the extent of that reduction has any rational relation to any dimension of our economy, like some current interest rate. It tends simply to be assumed that the only issue is how much future generations would have to pay to provide for themselves something to substitute for something else we did not provide for them. This of course assumes we are always concerned with substitutable, marketable commodities, like the cost of medical care for adverse health effects. For instance, it is sometimes argued as follows. Suppose we plan to leave behind some only temporarily secure hazardous nuclear waste that can be expected to cause malignancies, some fatal, among members of a distant future generation. If a public policy resulted in fatal illnesses among people living today, we would want to compensate their families for the loss of life. No one is claiming that a human life is worth only so much money and that the compensation is fully adequate; however, acknowledging the inadequacy and the incommensurability between life and money, it is still far better than nothing if compensation is provided, and even an inadequate gesture may symbolically express our respect. Since, in the case of the hazardous waste, we assume the illnesses will not occur for several generations, the rational path, it is argued, is to provide not the full amount of compensation but that amount suitably discounted.

However, in the current generation we compensate people for unavoidable deaths. We do not, by contrast, adopt a public policy in full knowledge that it is likely to kill a number of people and then at the same time set aside full (since they are contemporaries) compensation. Choosing to cause deaths and at the same time to compensate for the lives lost looks much too much like buying the right to kill the people, or purchasing their right to life with the amount of the compensation. We take all reasonable measures to avoid unnecessary deaths; when nevertheless some people unavoidably die, which may in practice be when the prevention of their deaths would be prohibitively expensive (e.g. requiring accident-free highways), we compensate their families for the loss.

It is important to be clear about precisely what is the blind spot in conventional calculations about future generations, and unfortunately what we do entirely within the current generation is rather complicated. As indicated by the notorious example of straightening the curves in highways in order to reduce accidental deaths, it may be that until all the highways have the ideal amount of curvature, we could save another life by eliminating, or softening one more curve. Yet at some point, what can be thought of as the cost of saving an additional life becomes unreasonably high, and we stop spending money on it. In a sense, this can be described as choosing to allow the person whose death could have been prevented to die. But if the cost of saving the additional life has become astronomical, and especially if the same amount of money invested in safety elsewhere (say, shoring up the coal mine ceilings; or even better emergency room care for the people who do run off the less-than-perfect road) would save many more lives, we decide that, crudely put, more expenditure on curve adjustments is "unreasonable" (Sunstein 1996). One implication of its being unreasonable is that we do not judge ourselves bound to compensate those who then die because we stopped spending on highway safety. So, of course, costs come into it. The question is how and where costs come into it.

What we do not do within the current generation is simply decide that allowing people to be killed and compensating their families would be cheaper than saving their lives, and so choose to let them be killed when their deaths could still be prevented at a higher but perfectly reasonable cost. We do not stop spending on the highways as soon as deaths-plus-compensation would be less. In short, we often decide that death-plus-compensation as an alternative to life is not simply inadequate but unacceptable, provided the cost of saving lives, although considerably more, is still "reasonable."

The issue about the conventional economic approach to future generations is that it is incapable of even considering a policy toward people in the future analogous to the policy toward people today that says: it would be cheaper not to spend any more on saving lives in this policy realm and simply compensate for all the unprevented deaths, but we cannot do that because these are human lives of more than economic value—we cannot simply buy, with our compensation, the right to let them be killed. The analogous policy toward people in future generations would say the following. If we adopt nuclear power and leave behind only temporarily secure hazardous nuclear waste (because we do not have a safe disposal technology for any waste we generate), we can save enough money on energy to compensate members of future generations who develop fatal cancers from exposure to our waste, even if we discount the appropriate level of compensation at an extremely low rate. We will, however, not choose this policy of death-plus-[discounted]compensation because these will be human lives of more than economic value—we cannot simply buy, with our compensation, the right to kill them with our radioactive waste. Nor, if we avoid nuclear power by burning coal, can we simply buy the right to inflict the deaths caused by the more severe climate change produced by the increased carbon emissions. If our policy should observe a minimal constraint against the infliction of death and severe bodily harm, the challenge is not to find the correct rate at which to discount the compensation for absolutely any avoidable deaths we choose to inflict, but to find a way not to inflict the deaths, for example, generate neither the deadly waste, as long as we do not know how to handle it, nor the increased emissions. The fundamental failure in conventional analyses, then, flows from the unargued ethical assumption that in the future, unlike the present, everything can be compensated for, not in the arbitrariness of particular assumptions about rate of compensation (Shue 1999).

This indicates the need at least to consider approaches other than discounting. Perhaps at least some of the constraints on what can be done to human beings that apply to people alive today apply as well to any people who will live, irrespective of their identities. If we must not, for example, allow the torture of prisoners now, perhaps we should not allow the torture of prisoners later either, insofar as we have anything to say about it. Then we should not sponsor political choices now that make it highly likely that a succeeding regime will torture its prisoners, at least not if the costs to us of not sponsoring such choices are not prohibitively high. To put the point more generally, if all human beings have some basic rights, then human beings in future generations will then have the rights as fully as humans alive at the moment do now. Since we do not think that the appropriate policy now toward the right not to be killed is violation-plus-compensation, no reason is apparent why that would be the appropriate policy toward humans yet to be born. This means that there are fatality-producing outcomes that it would be wrong to choose and then compensate for. The objection is not that the compensation is inadequate; insurance policies today often pay only inadequate sums to compensate for deaths. Compensation for many human losses is inadequate. The objection is that one may not purchase an insurance policy on someone's life, with her family as beneficiaries, and then kill her because her death serves some purpose of one's own. The issue is not the adequacy of the compensa-tion—it is making specific avoidable choices to end human lives. Why should it matter that the life, and the premature death brought about by our policy choice now, lie in the future? Matter so much that not even minimum standards of treatment apply? But we must move on to other cases, since our cases are after all intended only as illustrations of underlying ethical assessments typically left undefended.

# 2. WHO'S IN? WHO'S OUT? ACROSS SPACE: EQUALITY OF HARM

One might call the problem sketched above transgenerational minimization: redu-cing (often to the vanishing point) the significance of people who will be profoundly affected at a distant time by policy choices made now. A somewhat similar, but often much more extreme form of conventional reasoning might be called transnational minimization: effectively ignoring people in a distant place, even while deeply shaping their fates. In many of the calculations concerning public policy the welfare of persons outside whatever is taken to be the relevant constituency is not discounted but completely ignored. And this partiality is not only not always wrong but indeed sometimes required, which adds fascinating complexity to the policy choices. In the instance of transgenerational minimization I suggested merely that we should critically examine the strikingly extreme and simple, but completely standard as-sumption that absolutely all aspects of the welfare of persons who come to live in later times may be discounted. I did not even discuss whether on some points we not only may but ought to favour our contemporaries. In the case of transnational minimization we must take very seriously the spatial version of favouring our own (Goodin 1985; Miller 1995; J. Crawford 2002; Buchanan 2004).

The fundamental tension consists in the following. On the one hand, there is a global consensus, with very few significant holdouts, on the view that all human beings are equal in a fundamental dimension, although there are differing views about whether to understand the dimension as dignity, worth, value, fundamental rights, or some combination of the preceding. For our purposes we can simply call this the consensus on human equality. On the other hand, it is nonsense to say, as surprisingly many theorists do, that if there are universal rights, there are universal duties, where "universal duties" are duties that fall upon every person and are more than a merely negative duty not to violate the rights. If every person has some fundamental entitlements, then for every person there must be some other persons who bear the positive duties to protect and if necessary, fulfill the rights. But those "other persons" certainly need not be all other persons. It is not even clear what it could mean in operational terms for every person to be carrying out duties toward every other person—this would not even be physically possible in a world of six billion people. If, for example, every child's dignity demands that he not be left hungry and naked, there must be for every child, one or more persons bound to step in as long as the child is helpless. But it might be that for every child with living parents, the relevant other persons are in the first instance at least, its own parents. This is simply a division of labor in the moral realm—a division of moral labor. No child is less worthy of food and shelter than any other child—all have an equal claim. But not all are specifically your responsibility. So even with a universality of rights there is—indeed, there really must be—some division of responsibility. Naturally, one crucial question is: upon whom does responsibility fall when those with the primary responsibility fail? But whatever the correct answer is, an important matter that we cannot pursue here, it is not: everyone else. Some specific assignment must also be made of default, or back-up responsibilities.

Given that a division of moral labor is unavoidable, it is not at all surprising that the division that arises often takes the form: "we will look after ours, and you look after yours." And, to emphasize, for me to believe, for example, that I ought to feed and clothe my child but not yours, because you ought to do the same for yours, in no way whatsoever commits me to believing that my child is of greater worth, or has more rights, than yours. In general, a division of responsibility does not presuppose a hierarchy of value (Miller 2001; Scheffler 2001; Green 2002; Caney 2005).

When one turns to specifics, matters again become richly complex. One might expect that in war, the ultimate recourse on behalf of the national interest of sovereign states, and perhaps in security policy generally, the commitment to universal human equality would play little to no role. Yet the persons on the other side count, and sometimes count fully, in perhaps surprisingly many respects—at least four: in the firm requirement that only those who have committed a wrong may be attacked, in the requirement that military force must prevent more harm than it causes for all concerned, in the strict equality of non-combatants, and in the strict equality of combatants.

First, although the decision to go to war is ordinarily made only if doing so appears to be in the national interest, it is not sufficient justification that war would be in the interest of the nation that initiates the use of force. It is a legal as well as a moral requirement that the adversary targeted must have acted wrongly; more specifically, must have committed aggression or otherwise be, in the judgement of the UN Security Council, an active threat to international peace (Roberts and Guelff 2000). The simple fact that, if one attacked and defeated a rival, one would be much better off than otherwise is not a good enough reason for launching a war. This clearly presupposes that the interests of the people in the adversary nation, and of other people who would be affected by the war, are being given at least some weight. Otherwise, if war were strongly in the interests of one's own people, and only their interests counted, one could simply go ahead and start the war.

Second, the kind of proportionality that must, again both legally and morally, be considered as part of any justified resort to the use of force internationally similarly includes the interests, or welfare, of everyone affected (Henckaerts and Doswald-Beck 2005). "Proportionality" is used equivocally in norms concerning war (Shue 2003). What has been called "micro-proportionality," and might equally well be termed intra-war proportionality, applies to the conduct of war (in medieval terms, *jus in bello*). Since the applications of this version of proportionality are made when the war is already under way and each side is attempting to defeat, if not destroy, the forces of the other, it would be ridiculous to suggest that each side should give weight to the interests of the other. By contrast, what has been called "macro-proportionality," and could be termed pre-war proportionality, is the norm applicable to the decision whether to resort to war (*jus ad bellum*). This proportionality norm is highly universalistic and takes into account all interests affected, including the interests of people of neutral nations, the interests of at least the non-combatants in the potential adversary (and possibly the potential combatants even), the interests of allies, and the interests of all people who would be affected by the precedents set regarding acceptable grounds for the resort to war and by the effects of the war on the international system (e.g. encouragement of appeasement or deterrence of aggression). Resort to war is justified only if, all these things considered, it would be a proportional act (bearing in mind the kinds of military actions that would be permitted on both sides by intra-war proportionality, which is justifiably not universalistic in its counting of interests). I believe, although space to go into it is not available here, that these two points are closely related. One reason why only an adversary which has acted wrongly—usually, committed aggression—may have force used against it is that pre-war proportionality can be satisfied only if the war serves an end like the deterrence of aggression and/or the entrenchment of the norm against aggression in addition to any national interests it may advance. These considerations centrally ground the unacceptability of preventive war (Crawford 2003; Luban 2004).

Both of these first two points indicate that interests of outsiders are to be given significant weight, but not necessarily equal weight with interests of insiders. Even more surprisingly, there are two more points in the ethics of war where equal weight is given to one's own people and the adversary's people. The first of these, and the third point overall about war, is equality of consideration of non-combatants. Non-combatants retain all pre-war—that is, general human—rights. They are, therefore, like all persons immune to violent assault; the immunity of non-combatants is the fundamental principle for the conduct of war. And although less thoughtful commentators sometimes fall into inappropriate terminology like "enemy non-combatants," a non-combatant is simply a non-combatant, reflecting what is in principle at least an extraordinary commitment to equality.

The complementary form of equality, and fourth point about war, is the odd but real form of equality of combatants. In one respect obviously the combatants on the two sides could not have more unequal status: the combatants on this side are allowed to try to kill the combatants on the other side. But of course the combatants on the other side are allowed to try to kill the combatants on this side. In vulnerability to attack combatants on both sides are equal. This equality in the conduct of war is extraordinary in light of the fact that the resort to war can be justified only if one side is taken to be so seriously in the wrong that the other side is right to use military force against them. How can the combatants on two sides taken to be so unequal in justification—one in the wrong, one in the right— have such equal entitlements in the conduct of the conflict? Some moralists find this troubling: surely, they argue, those fighting for the unjust cause should not be allowed to kill those fighting for the just cause (McMahan 2004). Although I think this is rather like asking, "why do guilty defendants receive the same procedural rights as innocent defendants?" in that at the relevant time no one is in an authoritative position to do the moral sorting, what is important for present purposes is that in international law and in the generally accepted understanding of the ethics of war, the interests of people on both sides are counted to some degree in all four of the ways listed above, and counted equally in at least the last two ways (Walzer 2000).

Now, one might reasonably contend that since the one kind of duties that are literally universal are negative duties, supreme among which is the duty not to harm, and since war is the supreme institution for the infliction of harm, it is not surprising that war is hedged about with some strong negative duties—most obviously perhaps, the prohibition against (intentionally) harming non-combatants. The positive weight given to the interests of outsiders prior to the resort to war is, equally unsurprisingly, not equal. It is often assumed that since economic policies are, broadly speaking, intended positively to benefit the interests of insiders, or constituents, national economic policies are free to consider only the interests of insiders. Let us now as usual look a little more concretely at specific illustrative policy areas.

# 3. WHO'S IN? WHO'S OUT? ACROSS SPACE: INEQUALITY OF BENEFIT

The presupposition that inflicting harm is so sharply and significantly distinguishable from refraining from providing benefit that the two can be governed by radically different principles—namely the infliction of harm is universally prohibited in a manner that treats all humans equally, while the provision of benefit may be selectively focused on "one's own"—is a major ethical assumption with powerful implications that is regularly adopted, rarely defended, and usually not even made explicit. A failure to provide a benefit can have exactly the same results as the infliction of a harm. Yet policy analysts, whose calculations otherwise simply measure results by whatever process the results are arrived at, here use a difference in process—this difference between harming and not helping—-to draw a radical distinction between what counts regarding outsiders (only harm) and what counts regarding insiders (net benefit). Whether this rigid distinction between what counts for outsiders and insiders is arbitrary is a more foundational ethical issue, however, than we can take up here, beyond noting its importance, which will in the following simply be assumed.

So it is typically assumed that domestic economic policies may properly focus on promoting the welfare of domestic constituents exclusively. Policy A, which greatly promotes the welfare of insiders, may be preferred to policy B, which still promotes the welfare of insiders but not quite as much as policy A does while greatly benefiting outsiders. Policy A may be preferred to policy B in spite of the fact that the overall human benefits of policy B would be much greater. The possible benefits to outsiders of policy B may thus be discounted totally—ignored. In some cases this may again be a kind of division of labor—a division concerning the objects of responsibility—that is unobjectionable. If the widely shared political convention is that each government will promote the economic interests of only its own people, one government's efforts might be thrown into disarray if some other government arbitrarily adopted policies also intended to benefit the first government's constituents. Of course, instead of one government's unexpectedly launching attempts to benefit other governments' constituents, explicit agreements on shared policies can be made among governments in cases where the cooperative policies would be more beneficial to each state considered separately than any uncoordinated efforts at mutual benefit would be likely to be. Presumably this is the underlying idea of a regime like the WTO: wide agreements in a broad range of areas will enable each state to do better than it could do if each pursued the interests of its own constituents in uncoordinated and unrestrained ways. Some shared constraints are thought to be generally and over the long run beneficial to all.

The underlying ethical commitment of each state, however, is still taken to be to its own constituents. Neither the WTO nor other economic regimes represent commitments by every nation to promote the welfare of humanity generally; they simply reflect the judgements that cooperative and coordinated policies subject to shared constraints are better for each separately than autarkic policies could be, especially given the broad cooperation of others. A state that thinks it can do better outside the WTO is free to leave (after due notice and so forth). The point is this: one ought not to confuse a belief that general cooperation will promote the interest of each separately with a (non-existent, I believe) commitment by each to promote the interest of all. It is, of course, imaginable that the cooperative pursuit by each of its own interest in cooperation with the others will happen in fact also to promote the interest of all—this would, in effect, be the Global Invisible Hand at work. But perhaps one can be forgiven for believing that the greatest benefit for all, if that were the proper goal, would be more likely to result from conscious efforts to design institutions so that it would result. If, however, individual states have obligations to promote only the interests of their own constituents, they have no obligation to design, much less implement such universally beneficial institutions.

The arrangement just sketched, on which each person belongs to a political unit like a state, and each state exclusively promotes the interests of its own people, while abiding by constraints generally beneficial to people of multiple (if not necessarily of all) states, will seem familiar and perhaps commonsensical to many. A powerful case can be made that the primary moral purpose that the contemporary state is generally assumed to serve, and thus to have its sovereignty justified by, is the promotion of the well-being, especially the economic well-being, of the individual persons who are its constituents (Reus-Smit 1999). Such an institutional system of self-interest-serving sovereign states is, however, only one of the imaginable options for the international arena and may be only one of the feasible options. For we do have some accumulated knowledge about how social institutions function.

One fact we know is that the promotion of any given aggregate effect at the national level is compatible with an extremely wide range of distributive effects. The clichés claiming definitive reliable connections, like "a rising tide lifts all boats," are often false; aggregate gross national product can, and often does rise while the worst-off individuals in the aggregate become still worse off. If there is some reason to attain, or to avoid certain distributive effects, the relevant social institutions need to aim at the distributive goals as firmly and explicitly as they aim at the aggregate goals. If we briefly turn from abstract theoretical considerations to global reality, it is perfectly evident that the lives of many humans, especially children, are nasty, brutish, and short. Deaths from starvation and from cheaply and easily preventable diseases are reliably in the millions annually, and infant mortality rates in many of the international system's constituent states are many multiples of what is regularly attained by best practice (Pogge 2002).

Earlier it was noted that divisions of labor, and allocations of responsibility are often sensible, so that it was conceivable that the current international system's assignments of largely national responsibility for human welfare generally, and for preventing easily preventable deaths of children and other recurrent human traged-ies, are a good arrangement or even the best feasible arrangement. Even a cursory glance at what would once pretentiously have been called the "human condition," and specifically at the chronic death and disease among utterly faultless children in the poorest states in the system, makes it extraordinarily difficult to convince oneself that our social institutions are the best achievable. It is barely conceivable that every feasible institutional change would make matters worse, but it would strain credulity to the breaking point to try to take that possibility seriously. It is reasonable to believe that we could do better institutionally if we actually tried harder.

We must not, however, lose our grip on the fact noted earlier, that the virtually universal commitment to human equality is fully compatible with a division of moral labor: I do not by implication deny the equal worth of your child if I deny primary responsibility for your child and attribute to you the primary responsibility for its care, which includes the practical possibility that you will fail in that responsibility and your child will suffer. It may seem—it is in fact often claimed—that by analogy, however tragic chronic starvation and the other elements of absolute poverty may be, it does not follow from the extent of the evil involved that it is the responsibility of me, or of anyone else in particular, to deal with it; I can recognize that great evil befalls fellow humans and still believe, without denying that their lives and welfare are of equal value with mine, that I have no responsibility toward them. My responsibility stops short of their tragedy, equal in worth and dignity though we are. It cannot be that all human problems are problems for me to deal with.

One respect in which there is an analogy between the individual case and the international case is that the options are not limited to the two extremes consisting, in the individual case, of your doing everything for your child and my doing everything for your child and in the international case, of each state's providing fully for all the children in its territory or a "world government" operating a global welfare system covering the entire human species. One can apply a little bit of imagination in order to formulate less extreme alternatives for the international case, especially if one notices the assumptions about the capacity and desire of parents in the individual case and the numbers of "orphans" in the international case.

First, the usual view of the individual case tacitly assumes ability or capacity. If one's neighbor has lost her money or her mind, or otherwise completely lost her way, one does not simply insist that "it is still her child to look after." At the international level there are undeniable cases of what have come to be called "failed states;" the explanation for the failure may be internal or external, and the explanations and prospects for improvement vary from case to case. But some states plainly lose control of their own economies and are in remotely no position to provide for the welfare of their citizens. It would be pure self-deception to claim that one was turning over to them responsibilities that are obviously impossible for them to fulfill (Goodin 1985).

Second, the usual view of the individual case tacitly also assumes will or desire. Parents who have murdered their first child are not simply assigned responsibility for the care of their second. At the international level, besides failed states, one regularly finds predatory states, such as states engaged in genocide or ethnic cleansing against segments of their own citizenry. In the case of predatory states one cannot without self-deception simply claim that it is sensible to leave matters in their hands nevertheless. Consequently, at an absolute minimum the international system needs some provision for failed states and predatory states, exactly as domestic systems provide for the children of parents who are unable or unwilling to provide for their own.

Third, if one thinks of refugees as roughly analogous to orphans—people lacking a state to be responsible for them—one finds millions more children for whom some provision ought to be made, and for whom in fact some responsibility is already in practice acknowledged, however inadequate the actual provisions currently are. Then, in addition to states that have failed generally, there are the many states torn by civil wars and secessions where only some neutral third party could possibly provide welfare support. All such provision is groundless without acknowledgement of some responsibility for fellow humans outside one's own state.

What is not compatible with a commitment to human equality is a willingness simply to write off millions of children who are unable to provide for themselves. It is one matter to believe that one need bear no responsibility toward even some desperate people because, by means of a reliably functioning division of labor, those people will mostly—one cannot of course demand perfection in social institutions—be provided for. It would be a totally different matter to know full well that existing institutions are so grossly inadequate that tens of millions of children annually and predictably fall through the (gigantic) institutional cracks and then to do nothing, as if one had compelling evidence that existing international institutions are the best of all possible institutions. This attitude does seem tantamount to a denial that the millions now neglected matter as much as other people. One can reasonably say: "I respect your worth as a human being, but I leave to others the responsibility, in which I realize they may fail, to provide essentials that you cannot provide for yourself." But one cannot reasonably maintain: "I respect your worth as a human being, but I leave to others the responsibility, in which I know from repeated experiences they are certain to fail, to provide essentials that you cannot provide for yourself." The latter level of unconcern bespeaks contempt.

The point might be put more abstractly as follows. A commitment to human equality is inconsistent with a ready acceptance of social institutions that are demonstrably inadequate to provide basic necessities for tens of millions of humans unable to provide for themselves, as demonstrated by chronic annual failures over decades, when adequate alternative institutions could be designed and implemented without imposing excessive burdens on anyone. Therefore, divisions of moral labor, yes. But the inherited division structured along national lines, no. It is a demonstrated failure.

## 4. Who's In? Who's Out? Across Space: Equality of Harm Revisited

The immediately preceding discussion of economic desperation tacitly adopted a kind of no-fault picture of absolute poverty, presenting human misery as if it were essentially a natural condition not produced by failures in policy. While natural factors, including scarcity and diversity of natural resources, certainly play a role in world poverty, it would nevertheless be implausible to suggest that policies and institutions will play no part in determining the fate of the globe's poorest. It is again best to consider a concrete instance.

As noted above, "it is typically assumed that domestic economic policies may properly focus on promoting the welfare of domestic constituents exclusively." But virtually all economic activity produces what economists call "negative externalities," like environmental damage from which many people who do not benefit from the economic activity may suffer. In practice it may be possible to prevent environmental damage at the source, but impossible for those who will otherwise be its victims to protect themselves if the damage is not prevented. If state A allows its firms to emit dangerous substances into the air up-wind of state B, what is state B supposed to do: filter all the air as it crosses the border? And transborder pollution is widely recognized to be unacceptable, and the various types of such otherwise invasive pollution are regulated to various degrees (Franck 1995; Sands 1995). The greenhouse gases (GHGs) that are accelerating the rate of climate change, however, raise special and urgent policy questions, the central ones of which are precisely ethical questions about who counts and for whom they count (Drumbl 2002; Eckersley 2004; Gardiner 2004).

Climate change is an extraordinarily complex phenomenon within which the effects of many human activities are intersecting with multiple natural processes of radically different timescales. This makes predictions difficult. The climate is, however, demonstrably changing, with a long-measured rising trend in annual global temperature that is unprecedented in the human era, although not unprecedented in planetary history (Alley 2000; United States, National Academy of Sciences 2002; Parmesan and Galbraith 2004). One major GHG, water vapour is almost entirely outside human control. Of the GHGs that are under human control, the carbon dioxide produced by the burning of fossil fuels (coal, gas, and oil) is unrivalled in its importance and unrivalled in the increases in the rate at which it is being injected into the atmosphere (Houghton et al. 2001). Modern industrial economies are driven by fossil fuel—electricity generation and combustion-engine-powered transportation are the primary sources of carbon dioxide—and the byproducts of burning fossil fuel drive climate change. This means that energy policy is climate policy: the choices that could slow the rate in the increase in climate change are choices about energy: how much to consume and how to generate it (McCarthy et al. 2001).

Energy policy is also, of course, fundamental to economic policy generally. And we have tended to assume in the past that economic policy may permissibly be set with a view exclusively to the benefits for the unit setting the policy, with some relatively minor constraints about inflicting damaging pollution upon people in other units. Now, however, we understand that the principles guiding our decisions have presupposed a grossly misleading picture of some of the most fundamental processes on the planet. Industrial processes—and, of course, agricultural practices as well—do not simply episodically generate a few types of transborder pollution here and there. The so-called externalities are at the heart of the energy consumption that fuels modern economies. The cheap price of fossil fuel was indeed a key element in the economic growth of the last century and a half, and a major reason for contemporary affluence. Today we realize that the same fossil fuel that was the abundant cheap energy that enabled (some of) us to become rich is undermining the stable natural environment that is another necessary condition for our economic lives, especially for abundant, relatively cheap food.

Therefore, while we have assumed that economic activity may, without doing any wrong, be aimed at benefiting whomever one takes to be one's own constituents, as long as one watched out for the most severe externalities, it turns out in fact that the energy policy at the base of economic strategies is producing an effect that is very severe indeed—doing what it was always assumed humans could not do: change the weather. "Weather" is, in a sense, the local bit of climate; the fundamental changes now speeding up go far beyond weather. Every person on the planet—and virtually every species (except perhaps for the deep-ocean worms living in the darkness near the thermal vents)—will be affected, many profoundly.

Some of the more hysterical commentators on climate change suggest that it requires an ethical revolution. This is nonsense. One of the most widespread and most deeply held ethical principles has long been that one is at liberty to pursue benefits for oneself, as one understands them, as long as one limits one's pursuit of one's own interest by the constraint of not inflicting severe harm on vulnerable others. This "no-harm principle," as it is usually called, is fine. No new ethic is needed for application to the threat of rapid anthropogenic climate change, and in fact it is difficult to imagine a genuine society among individuals as predatory as those who had given up the bare principle of no-harm.

We simply need to understand that we have here a global—literally planetary— application of the no-harm principle. We are merely discovering, once again, that a process that we assumed for no particular reason perhaps other than basic optimism, to be safe is in fact dangerous. It is only the public policy, not the ethical principles, that is primitive and needs updating, whether or not revolutionizing.

Who would have thought that enjoying the occasional cigarette could inflict severe health problems on one's children? Now we know, and policies about smoking are changing. Who would have thought that handling the asbestos needed in the ships for the Second World War and the building boom afterwards would cause fatal malig- nancies? Now we know, and asbestos is on the way out, where it is not already gone. Who would have thought that the lead additive that made combustion engines run more efficiently would prevent children's brains from developing fully? And so on: our technology is spectacularly innovative, and along with the many pleasant surprises are unpleasant, and sometimes fatal surprises. The understanding arising from the study of climate change—that the astoundingly cheap fuel that allowed us to adapt our- selves so beneficially to our environment is now changing that environment toward one to which we are not adapted—is one of the most unpleasant surprises of all.

Many discussions of policy toward climate change have so far missed the point. Some assume that climate change is one of many subcategories under environmental policy, where "environmental policy" is taken to have the same level of urgency as, say, architectural policy. Many others who understand that it is as central as energy policy ask, in effect: would it benefit this nation's economy on the whole now if it took certain measures designed to slow rapid climate change? Would, for example, reducing energy waste not only reduce emissions somewhat but add to general efficiency? Such questions miss more than one critical point. One missed point was already introduced in Section 1: it might well be that, apart from the elimination of sheer waste of energy, plus perhaps enough marketing of GHG emissions permits that most emissions reductions are the least-cost ones, any more serious policies to reduce fossil-fuel consumption would entail net costs for the present generation and immediately succeeding generations. But energy policies that continue to rely on ever-increasing consumption of fossil fuel are likely to lead to more human disruption, and indeed more human deaths, from more severe climate change than policies that restrain fossil-fuel consumption (Mahlman 2001). What if the ultimate harms for more distant generations will sharply increase in severity if responsive policies are initiated only later? What if more people will starve because of crop failures if the same measures are launched later rather than sooner? Does one choose the policy that leads to the additional deaths as long as that policy is the most beneficial to the current generation? This has already been briefly discussed.

Another point often missed is yet to be noted. One critical factor affecting how bad the worst will be—how severe the severest climatic disruptions will be—is the absolute amount of the carbon now sequestered under the earth's surface in the forms of coal, gas, and oil that is moved instead into the earth's atmosphere in the form of carbon dioxide. In particular, if virtually all the carbon in the ground is moved into the atmosphere through combustion of fossil fuel, the concentration of carbon dioxide in the atmosphere will become several times the concentration prior to the Industrial Revolution. Today it is already practically certain that the atmospheric concentration will double. If it redoubles—to quadruple the level it was in 1850—the effects on the surface will very likely be significantly more severe than if it "merely" doubles (Kasting 1998).

The critical feature of all this is that climate change is a truly global phenomenon in every important respect. Most critically, there is no natural correlation between those who benefit from the fossil-fuel consumption that dominates the global atmospheric level of GHGs—the concentration results from a thorough global mix of emissions from all points on the surface—and those who suffer from climate change. For example, one of the undoubted effects of climate change will be sea-level rise (McCarthy et al. 2001; McElroy 2002). Those who will suffer most from sea-level rise will, other things equal, be those who live, or farm on land at the lowest elevations above sea level, such as the people of Bangladesh. How likely are Bangladeshis to benefit most, or even equally from additional global aggregate consumption of fossil fuel? But it is likely to matter vitally to Bangladeshis whether the total atmospheric concentration of GHGs "only" doubles or quadruples.

In more abstract terms, the people most likely to suffer the severest effects from national energy policies—US policy, Chinese policy—are for the most part not residents of the nations whose energy policies will dominate the effects. The most vulnerable have almost no voice; hence, this can also reasonably be understood as a problem about voice, representation, and democracy as well as the problem about the infliction of harm on which this discussion focuses. The absence of voice is a central element in the explanation of why the process must be described as the *infliction* of harm. Harm is not occurring naturally, as from the Asian tsunami at the end of 2004. And harm is not being suffered as part of the cost of benefits by those who are choosing to pursue the benefits. The lion's share of the benefits is going to people other than those vulnerable to the severest bad effects.

Further, many of those most vulnerable to the bad effects of climate change are also least able to afford to mitigate the effects. When sea-level rise affects East Coast ports in the United States, the wealth of the USA will be available to pay for the measures necessary. But one has no reason to believe that Bangladesh will even begin to have the resources to try to mitigate the effects it will suffer. Yet there is no comparison between per capita fossil-fuel consumption in the USA and in Bangladesh.

In this crucial respect, energy policies in particular can no longer be treated as domestic policies. When the USA or the PRC makes energy policy, it makes climate policy for the globe. Whose interests should count? On perfectly ordinary, conservatively traditional, commonsense ethical principles, everyone who stands to be severely harmed. To write off the interests of distant strangers, in the sense of ignoring the harms one's own public policies threaten them with, is incompatible with a commitment to fundamental human equality. Worse, it is a form of compound injustice: the use of the power that flows from existing unjust advantages to impose additional unjust disadvantages, including fatal harms (Shue 1992).

# 5. WHO'S IN? WHO'S OUT? WHO'S WHO?

The most unobtrusive, and thus most difficult to resist of the assumptions made so far here is the assumption that only the interests of humans matter. We have briefly considered present humans and future humans, and fellow citizens inside the state and strangers outside the state, but always humans only. What about the bullfinch near the top of the hazel in the garden? He certainly brightens my day, but that is still about me, making it an instance of anthropocentric value: the value that something has for humans (Norton 1986). And of course I do not know this particular bullfinch intimately—I do not even know if it is the same bullfinch who came, at roughly the same time, yesterday, so it may well be the species bullfinches, not this bullfinch, that is the source of delight, making this the anthropocentric value of a species, not of individuals as such. One of the issues, which cannot of course be pursued here, is: what are the units that count from an anthropocentric point of view? I certainly would not object if the garden contained hummingbirds and falcons, and tortoises and gazelles. So this may not be about birds, but about animals, and plants, and

trees—perhaps natural species more generally or more generally still, natural processes that are not subject to human manipulation but confront us humans with
independent worlds we can explore but not master (Scarry 1999). Perhaps it is
valuable for humans to understand that much of the universe does not share our
interests and is not interested in us.

Do some aspects of nature count intrinsically, or at least independently of their
anthropocentric value, their interest for us? Suppose I were out of the picture entirely
and the world could either contain bullfinches or not. Is there any reason to think
that the universe with the bullfinches is superior in value to the universe without the
bullfinches? Superior for whom? For the bullfinches, for a start, and for any other
species, including plant species, which benefit from the activities of the bullfinches—
worse, it is true, for the bullfinches' competition. Ethical theorists sometimes debate
whether there is any reason why "the last man" should not, if he felt like it, dynamite
Victoria Falls or the Grand Canyon before he dies, apart from the fact that he would
have been a better man if he had not been so pointlessly destructive. Obviously it was
not "Victoria Falls" until some European with a queen on his mind thought so; if
there were no people at all, it might be an arbitrarily designated unit of wet rocks. If
there were no fish in the river and no birds in the sky, as well as no people on the cliff,
would it matter whether this water's running over these rocks continued or ceased?
Perhaps value depends upon conscious, or sentient, or at least animate beings that
can in some sense value. But must it depend exclusively upon human consciousness?

For public policy, two things matter. There is, of course, a gigantic spectrum
between nothing but humans counting (all value is anthropocentric, including
what economists call the amenity value of the natural) and everything counting
(every natural "unit" has intrinsic value). The first question that concerns public
policy is whether anything has value apart from the value humans attach to it and
then, if so, how our policies affect the other things that count in their own right. The
question cannot be answered here, but I would say that it strikes me as the height of
self-absorbed arrogance simply to take for granted that nothing counts unless it
counts for some person.

The second question for public policy is how our policies affect the natural
systems, species, and/or individuals that humans do as a matter of fact value.
Questions of intrinsic value apart, humans do value magnificent waterfalls and
canyons, wildernesses, coral reefs, urban parks, gardens, whales, tigers, and
bullfinches. And beyond particular objects, even very large ones like wildernesses,
many humans have found inspiration in natural patterns like the changing of the
seasons in the temperate zones and the less obvious patterns of change in the polar
and tropical zones. Much of what might be considered the least natural activity of
humans—art, poetry, and religion—has in fact drawn upon aspects of the natural
world. Many exalted artefacts make essential reference to nature.

Notions of "sustainable development" have been formulated in attempts to integrate narrowly economic interests focused on human consumption and some degree
of regard for the natural world (World Commission on Environment and Development 1987; Daly and Cobb 1994). Economic development for humans tends to destroy

habitat for other species. But "sustainable development" in the abstract means only that economic development and environmental protection are somehow to be balanced, and where precisely the balance is struck is highly significant. One can make environmental protection the priority and then develop as much as is compatible with adequate protection, or one can make economic development the priority and then protect the environment as much as is compatible with the preferred development. The distance between these polar interpretations of "sustainable development" is vast, and the choice of the location on this spectrum for public policy turns in part on the value, instrumental or intrinsic, attributed to the natural environment itself.

The most obviously unsustainable current policy is the energy policy that consists of the rapid acceleration in consumption of fossil fuel that is producing climate change, the purely human dimensions of which have already been mentioned above. But rapid climate change could become the greatest destroyer of existing habitat and thus the greatest source of species extinction. If the human destruction of non-human species involves a loss of value, this is yet another reason to conclude that current energy policies are misguided. At the extreme, climate change could violate the very integrity of the seasons themselves, changing their length and depth and transforming, say, spring, from an autonomous natural phenomenon into a partial artefact (McKibben 1990).

# 6. Conclusion

The preceding illustrates some of the major points on which public policy unavoidably makes ethical judgements. These judgements can be made on the basis of media fashion, public opinion, conventional wisdom, personal bias, religious tradition, or systematic ethical analysis. But there is no way not to make them, because all choices of policy presuppose that some things matter and other things do not, and that some matter a lot and others matter only a little. Ethics is the attempt to reflect systematically about relative importance and arrive at judgements that can be public and reasonable (Gutmann and Thompson 2005; Mills 1992). Ethics can provide public policy with reasonable grounds.

## References

ALLEY, R. B. 2000. *The Two-Mile Time Machine: Ice Cores, Abrupt Climate Change, and our Future*. Princeton, NJ: Princeton University Press.

BARNETT, M. N. 2002. *Eyewitness to a Genocide: The United Nations and Rwanda*. Ithaca, NY: Cornell University Press.

BARRY, B. 1991. The ethics of resource depletion. Pp. 259–73 in *Liberty and Justice: Essays in Political Theory 2*. Oxford: Clarendon Press.

BROOME, J. 1994. Discounting the future. *Philosophy & Public Affairs*, 23: 128–56.

BUCHANAN, A. 2004. *Justice, Legitimacy, and Self-Determination: Moral Foundations for International Law*. Oxford: Oxford University Press.

CANEY, S. 2005. *Justice beyond Borders: A Global Political Theory*. Oxford: Oxford University Press.

COWEN, T., and PARFIT, D. 1991. Against the social discount rate. Pp. 144–61 in *Justice between Age Groups and Generations*, ed. P. Laslett and J. S. Fishkin. New Haven, Conn.: Yale University Press.

CRAWFORD, J. 2002. *The International Law Commission's Articles on State Responsibility: Introduction, Text and Commentaries*. Cambridge: Cambridge University Press.

CRAWFORD, N. C. 2002. *Argument and Change in World Politics: Ethics, Decolonization, and Humanitarian Intervention*. Cambridge: Cambridge University Press.

—— 2003. The best defense: the problem with Bush's "Preemptive" war doctrine. *Boston Review*, 28; available at: http://bostonreview.net/BR28.1/crawford.html.

DALY, H., and COBB, J. B., Jr. 1994. *For the Common Good: Redirecting the Economy toward Community, the Environment, and a Sustainable Future*. Boston: Beacon Press.

DRUMBL, M. A. 2002. Poverty, wealth, and obligation in international environmental law. *Tulane Law Review*, 76: 843–960.

ECKERSLEY, R. 2004. *The Green State: Rethinking Democracy and Sovereignty*. Cambridge, Mass.: MIT Press.

FINNEMORE, M. 2003. How purpose changes. Pp. 141–61 in *The Purpose of Intervention: Changing Beliefs about the Use of Force*. Ithaca, NY: Cornell University Press.

FRANCK, T. 1995. *Fairness in International Law and Institutions*. Oxford: Clarendon Press.

GARDINER, S. M. 2004. Ethics and climate change. *Ethics*, 114: 555–600.

GOODIN, R. E. 1985. *Protecting the Vulnerable: A Reanalysis of our Social Responsibilities*. London: University of Chicago Press.

GREEN, M. 2002. Institutional responsibility for global problems. *Philosophical Topics*, 30: 1–28.

GUTMANN, A., and THOMPSON, D. 2005. *Ethics and Politics: Cases and Comments*, 4th edn. Chicago: Nelson Hall/Thomson.

HENCKAERTS, J.-M., and DOSWALD-BECK, L. 2005. *Customary International Humanitarian Law*, i: *Rules*. Cambridge: Cambridge University Press.

HOUGHTON, J. T., DING, Y., et al. (eds.) 2001. *Climate Change 2001: The Scientific Basis*. Cambridge: Cambridge University Press.

KASTING, J. F. 1998. The carbon cycle, climate, and the long-term effects of fossil fuel burning. *Consequences: The Nature & Implications of Climate Change*, 4: 15–27; available at: www.gcrio.org/CONSEQUENCES/vol4no1/carboncycle.html.

LUBAN, D. 2004. Preventive war. *Philosophy & Public Affairs*, 32: 207–48.

MCCARTHY, J. J., CANZIANI, O. F., et al. (eds.) 2001. *Climate Change 2001: Impacts, Adaptation, and Vulnerability*. Cambridge: Cambridge University Press.

MCELROY, M. B. 2002. *The Atmospheric Environment: Effects of Human Activity*. Princeton, NJ: Princeton University Press.

MCKIBBEN, B. 1990. *The End of Nature*. London: Penguin.

MCMAHAN, J. 2004. The ethics of killing in war. *Ethics*, 114: 693–733.

MAHLMAN, J. D. 2001. *The Timing of Climate Change Policies: The Long Time Scales of Human-Caused Climate Warming—Further Challenges for the Global Policy Process*. Arlington, Va.: Pew Center on Global Climate Change.

MILLER, D. 1995. *On Nationality.* Oxford: Clarendon Press.

—— 2001. Distributing responsibilities. *Journal of Political Philosophy,* 9: 453–71.

MILLS, C. (ed.) 1992. *Values & Public Policy.* Fort Worth, Tex.: Harcourt Brace Jovanovich.

NORTON, B. (ed.) 1986. *The Preservation of Species: The Value of Biological Diversity.* Princeton, NJ: Princeton University Press.

PARMESAN, C., and GALBRAITH, H. 2004. *Observed Impacts of Global Climate Change in the U.S.* Arlington, Va.: Pew Center on Global Climate Change.

POGGE, T. 2002. *World Poverty and Human Rights.* Cambridge: Polity Press.

REUS-SMIT, C. 1999. *The Moral Purpose of the State.* Oxford: Princeton University Press.

ROBERTS, A., and GUELFF, R. (eds.) 2000. *Documents on the Laws of War,* 3rd edn. Oxford: Oxford University Press.

SANDS, P. 1995. *Principles of International Environmental Law,* i: *Frameworks, Standards and Implementation.* Manchester: Manchester University Press.

SCARRY, E. 1999. *On Beauty and Being Just.* Princeton, NJ: Princeton University Press.

SCHEFFLER, S. 2001. Four essays. Pp. 32–47, 82–130 in *Boundaries and Allegiances: Problems of Justice and Responsibility in Liberal Thought.* Oxford: Oxford University Press.

SHUE, H. 1992. The unavoidability of justice. Pp. 373–97 in *The International Politics of the Environment: Actors, Interests, and Institutions,* ed. A. Hurrell and B. Kingsbury. Oxford: Oxford University Press.

—— 1999. Bequeathing hazards: security rights and property rights of future humans. Pp. 38–53 in *Limits to Markets: Equity and the Global Environment,* ed. M. Dore and T. Mount. Malden, Mass.: Blackwell.

—— 2003. War. Pp. 734–61 in *The Oxford Handbook of Practical Ethics,* ed. H. LaFollette. Oxford: Oxford University Press.

SNEED, J. D. 1977. A utilitarian framework for policy analysis in food-related foreign aid. Pp. 103–28 in *Food Policy: The Responsibility of the United States in the Life and Death Choices,* ed. P. G. Brown and H. Shue. New York: Free Press.

SUNSTEIN, C. R. 1996. Health–health tradeoffs. *University of Chicago Law Review,* 63 (4: Fall): 1533–72.

UNITED STATES, NATIONAL ACADEMY OF SCIENCES, NATIONAL RESEARCH COUNCIL 2002. *Abrupt Climate Change: Inevitable Surprises.* Washington, DC: National Academy Press.

WALZER, M. 2000. *Just and Unjust Wars,* 3rd edn. New York: Basic Books.

WORLD COMMISSION ON ENVIRONMENT AND DEVELOPMENT (G. H. Brundtland, Chair) 1987. *Our Common Future.* Oxford: Oxford University Press.

CHAPTER 36

..............................................................................................................

# ECONOMIC
# TECHNIQUES

..............................................................................................................

## KEVIN B. SMITH

EVEN a cursory rummage through the tool kit of policy scholars should be enough to reveal a dominant manufacturer's label: "Made in Economics." For or good or bad, much of quantitative policy analysis rests squarely on a set of concepts and techniques that are imported directly from economics.

Policy analysts borrow so heavily from economics for their conceptual and analytic gear for good reasons. Public policy can be thought of as a purposive course of action undertaken by public authorities, specifically some action designed to resolve some problem or produce some desirable state of affairs that would not occur without government intervention (Anderson 1994, 5–6; for broader introductions to the assumptions underlying policy analysis, see Haveman and Margolis 1970; Knetsch 1995). Such actions invariably involve allocating scarce resources, an issue of central concern to the discipline of economics. Much of the conceptual and analytical tool kit economists employ for understanding and explaining how markets allocate resources—efficiency, the notion of the rational actor, the importance of marginal analysis—are readily transferable to public policy.

These tools are applied to a broad variety of tasks in policy analysis and detailing all of them and their uses would require a book unto itself. Accordingly, this chapter has more limited aims. What I intend to accomplish here is to provide a basic introduction to some of the conceptual and analytical tools borrowed from economics to understand and assess questions of social choice.

The reason for this focus is simple. At the heart of most public policy making is a fundamental question: What should we do? In other words, given the scarce resources government has at its disposal, to what purposive action or actions should those resources be dedicated? It is the job of all *ex ante* policy analysis to provide answers to such questions. Economics provides a set of tools well suited to that job.

These tools are both conceptual and analytic. They provide a theoretical basis for judging the relative worth of competing policy alternatives, and a set of methodological techniques for calculating and analyzing that worth. What follows is a basic tour of these economic tools and how they can be usefully applied to study policy questions centered on social choice problems.

# 1. Conceptual Tools

A fundamental contribution of economics to the study of public policy is a set of conceptual tools readily transferred from the market to questions of social choice. These tools mostly originate in the discipline of welfare economics, which is the branch of economics concerned with the normative properties of markets (see Zeckhauser and Schaefer 1968; Just, Hueth, and Schmitz 2004). The main objective of welfare economics is to assess the impact of economic activity (or economic policy) on the well-being of society.

This focus on society's well-being provides a strong parallel with the study of public policy. Presumably, governments enact public policies with the general objective of serving the public interest and promoting social welfare. One of the difficulties faced by governments, and by policy analysts is determining what actions will best accomplish this goal. This is the classic conflict of social choice: How should government employ its limited resources? In other words, what purposive actions will best serve the public interest?

Welfare economics helps analysts systematically answer such questions by providing a set of conceptual tools to define and measure the impact of policy alternatives on social welfare. Collectively, these tools represent what has been termed the "welfare economics paradigm" of policy analysis, and they serve as the theoretical and methodological foundation for a broad range of policy scholarship (Munger 2000, 24).

This foundation rests on two core normative assumptions. First, an individual's welfare is best defined by, and only by, that individual. The assumption is that individuals can best decide for themselves their own wants, needs, and levels of satisfaction (Campen 1986, 28). Social welfare in turn is simply the aggregation of these individual-level perceptions of satisfaction. Second, that the "basic goal of society is assumed to be the maximization of social welfare" (Halvorsen and Ruby 1981, 13). These assumptions provide the value-based benchmark for assessing alternative courses of action: Given a choice, the preferred course of action is the one that contributes most to the maximization of social welfare. This will be the choice that maximizes individual levels of utility or satisfaction.

Welfare economics puts this notion of social welfare into practice using the concept of efficiency. The latter is a much misunderstood and maligned term, and is often seen as reflecting anti-democratic tendencies. Yet from the perspective of welfare economics, efficiency carries surprisingly little normative baggage: it is simply a characteristic of a distribution of resources. To welfare economics, the most efficient distribution of resources is one that maximizes consumer (or citizen) preferences.

Economists have long argued that markets are the most effective means of maximizing those preferences, and thus maximizing social welfare. A market can be thought of as any social arrangement (formal institutions and/or a set of social norms) that promotes exchange. Markets, at least under certain conditions, pull off the remarkable trick of allocating resources in a way that maximizes social welfare, without requiring much in the way of coordinated collective action. Markets, then, share some of the functions, if not the intent and process of government and public policy, which also exist to allocate scarce resources and promote the social good.

At least as far back as Adam Smith, economists have recognized that allowed to barter and truck as they please, individuals pursuing nothing but their own self-interest can produce positive collective outcomes. Supermarket chains, for example, are in a fairly cutthroat business. Given a choice, customers will patronize stores that have the most appealing combination of price, quality, and convenience. Supermarkets compete ferociously to provide the best combination of those factors. The collective outcome of this process of exchange is wide availability of high-quality foodstuffs at reasonable prices—social goods that benefit all and are produced with little in the way of central coordination or goals.

The technical definition of efficiency welfare economics uses for judging the collective outcome of market exchange is the Pareto criterion. A Pareto outcome is an allocation of resources where "no alternative allocation can make at least one person better off without making anyone worse off" (Boardman et al. 2001, 26). In other words, a Pareto outcome represents a universally desirable equilibrium where everyone, more or less, is satisfied with how resources are distributed (Weintraub 1983). A central principle of economic theory is that markets produce Pareto outcomes when certain conditions exist (these including these include perfect information, free entry and exit to the market, and no negative externalities—see Nas 1996, 19).

These conditions are generally recognized to be theoretical ideals rather than factually descriptive. Assumptions of perfect information, free entry and exit, etc. are virtually never fully realized in systems of exchange. In other words, while markets in theory produce Pareto outcomes, in practice they rarely do so. Markets for many goods, however, approximate these conditions closely enough to allocate resources reasonably efficiently (think supermarkets). And even though Pareto outcomes are hard to achieve fully in practice, the Pareto criterion is still valuable because it serves as a benchmark to measure the extent to which a market maximizes social welfare. The Pareto criterion can be pressed into the same service for judging the outcomes of public policy, i.e. providing a conceptual basis for measuring the relative change in social welfare.

Governments, of course, are very different beasts from markets, and even in theory we cannot just assume efficient outcomes are a natural product of democratic decision making or bureaucratic implementation. In making public policy, government allocates resources through a process of centralized coordination backed by the coercive powers of the state. Contrast this with a market, where (in theory) there are no collective decisions, collective outcomes being the product of accumulated, individual actions. Public policy on the other hand, represents a collective decision that government will impose on individuals whether it suits their interests or not.

These differences are exacerbated by the type of goods that markets and government actually produce and distribute. Governments deal primarily with public goods such as clean air and law enforcement, i.e. goods that are non-rivalrous (one person can consume the good without preventing another from consuming) and non-exclusionary (excluding people from consuming is costly or impractical). For private goods, individuals can decide how much they want to consume and markets will set the price based on supply and demand. For public goods, government decides how much they will pay for a set quantity that will be consumed by all (Nas 1996, 32–3).

Despite these differences, there is a fundamental similarity here: Both markets (through a process of free exchange) and governments (through the policy-making and implementation process) allocate scarce resources. Despite the difference in the means of allocation, the Pareto criterion can be used to judge the ends in both cases. The Pareto notion of efficiency provides the conceptual means to assess a collective outcome, to judge how well it serves the ultimate objectives of society, regardless of whether it is a product of a market or a public policy.

All these theoretical differences between market and government approaches are not as clear-cut in practice as they are in theory. There exists a large class of quasi-public goods that both government and the market play a hand in providing. Public and private schools provide educational services, for example. The existence of these quasi-public goods has provided a fertile ground to develop economic theory as democratic theory. Public choice, for example, is basically neoclassical economic theory translated into a normative theory of democratic politics (Ostrom 1973; Buchanan and Tullock 1962; Friedman 1962). In the policy realm, public choice emphasizes creating market-like conditions for the provision of public goods and services through programs such as contracting out, school choice, pollution credits, and the like. Foundational to such arguments is the notion that social welfare is maximized when individuals are allowed greater freedom to make the choices they believe will increase their own utility—in other words, efficiency is already a driving justification for a broad range of public policies and programs (for a overview see Frederickson and Smith 2004, 185–206).

In short, there already exists both in theory and in practice, a considerable overlap between markets and governments. At least in theory, and perhaps in practice it is a straightforward matter to transfer the concept of efficiency from the market production and distribution of private goods to the government production and distribution of public goods. Under the Pareto criterion an efficient public policy is one that alters the status quo such that at least one person is better off, and no one is worse off. In practice, of course, the task is considerably more complex.

The central obstacle with making the economic concept of efficiency the basis for assessing policy alternatives or outcomes is that public policies rarely hold even the theoretical possibility of a true Pareto outcome. A good deal of public policy is deliberately redistributive in nature, meaning that by design it imposes costs on one group to provide benefits to another. In other words, government action may improve the welfare of some individuals at the expense of the welfare of others. These sorts of situations are obviously at odds with the Pareto criterion.

Such situations are also exceedingly common elements of the political arena. A lot of political conflict centers on the question of who will bear the costs and who will reap the benefits of policy decisions. As virtually all policy options will produce losers as well as winners, the Pareto criterion is of little practical help in assessing which policy option best serves the overall goal of maximizing social welfare.

Because of these difficulties, efficiency is typically transferred to questions of social choice using a modified concept called the Kaldor–Hicks compensation principle, which was independently formulated by two British economists (Kaldor 1939; Hicks 1939). This principle defines efficiency using the concept of net benefits; it judges the social worth of a policy by looking at whether it creates more gains than losses. Technically, Kaldor–Hicks states that if those who benefit from a policy can use their gains to offset the losses borne by those who bear the costs of the policy, then that policy is *potentially* a Pareto outcome. As Boardman et al. (2001, 27) succinctly put it: "If a policy has positive net benefits, then it is possible to find a set of transfers, or side payments, that makes at least one person better off without making anyone else worse off."

It is important to recognize that such side payments are purely theoretical—the winners do not actually have to compensate the losers for the policy to be judged efficient. In layman's terms, Kaldor–Hicks means a policy whose benefits are greater than its costs is deemed efficient, and thus helps maximize social welfare.

This notion of efficiency is controversial for obvious reasons. Policies may yield a positive net benefit, yet bring misery to those who bear the costs. Those who have their communities cut in two by highway projects, for example, may find small comfort in the argument that their loss is outweighed by the benefits to passing motorists. While there is an undeniable logic to the notion of judging social welfare from the Kaldor–Hicks perspective, such situations would strike many reasonable people as unfair.

Given this, it is unsurprising that the Kaldor–Hicks notion of efficiency is criticized as a highly subjective notion of social welfare. It represents a not insignificant modification of the normative assumptions underpinning that notion of social welfare sketched above (especially in terms of social welfare being an aggregation of individual welfare), and there are reasonable criticisms that this recalculated notion of the social good sits uneasily with other values highly prized by democratic systems such as equity and minority rights (for discussions of such issues, see Williams 1972; Kelman 1981; Goodin and Wilenski 1984).

In response to such criticisms, welfare economists defend Kaldor–Hicks as closely allied to the philosophy of utilitarianism. Utilitarianism essentially argues for pursuing public policies that increase the *average* utility of citizens, and doing so is assumed to promote the greatest good for society. Around an average increase, however, individual utility can vary considerably, from healthy gains to devastating loss. Utilitarianism is often criticized on the grounds that it offers individuals no guarantee of a minimum allocation of resources, a criticism that is equally applicable to Kaldor–Hicks. As a basis for judging public policy, both Kaldor–Hicks and utilitarianism weight the aggregate gain over the loss of any particular set of individuals (Weimer and Vining 2005, 135; Posner 1983).[1]

Philosophical pros and cons aside, the big advantage in using Kaldor–Hicks as the basis for policy analysis is sheer practicality. This concept of efficiency provides a straightforward benchmark for judging public policies: Given a set of policy alternatives, choose the option that produces the greatest net benefit. Though substituting the notion of a potential Pareto outcome for an actual Pareto outcome, this approach boils the challenge of measuring changes in social welfare down to something that is analytically manageable. To figure out which policy best maximizes social welfare an analyst simply needs some means to calculate the net benefits of the alternatives.

Under Kaldor–Hicks, then, measuring relative changes in social welfare comes down to measuring net benefits. Yet in order to calculate the relative costs and benefits of a given policy alternative, it is first necessary to have some understanding of what costs and benefits are and how (economic) values should be attached to them. The basic conceptual tool for achieving these goals and measuring changes in social welfare is willingness to pay (WTP).

WTP is an intuitive way to attach values to costs and benefits. WTP is simply the maximum amount that an individual would be willing to pay for a good or a benefit, or how much they would want in return for giving up the utility derived from that good or benefit (these are assumed to be the same thing). WTP thus attaches an economic value to the utility of a good or service being consumed (Campen 1986, 29).

WTP is similarly used for valuing costs. Economics conceives of costs as opportunity costs, which are defined as the benefits that could be gained by putting resources to their next best use (Stokey and Zeckhauser 1978, 151–2; Fuguitt and Wilcox 1999, 46). For example, let's say I have enough money to buy a pint of beer or a bag of peanuts. I opt for the beer. The opportunity cost of the beer is the benefit, or satisfaction I give up by not consuming the peanuts. That cost, i.e. the benefit I would derive from the peanuts, is defined by my WTP for the peanuts.

WTP thus provides the means to measure changes in individual welfare by providing a conceptual basis to attach values to costs and benefits. Aggregate these concepts to the collective level, and WTP provides a way to measure social welfare. Let's say a public body is faced with two alternatives, A and B. If at least one person has a higher WTP for alternative A, and no one has a higher WTP for B than for A,

---

[1] This chapter is designed to explicate the basic conceptual and analytical tools policy analysis borrows from economics. It is not designed to provide a full-blown critique of the normative implications of putting those tools into practice. Readers interested in those implications are directed towards Haubrich and Wolff, this volume, which is devoted to just such a critique.

then alternative A is more efficient and maximizes social welfare (this situation represents a Pareto outcome). If we add up the WTP for every individual for each alternative both in a positive and negative sense—i.e. we measure the costs and benefits each individual attaches to the two alternatives and subtract costs from benefits—the alternative with the highest net positive total is efficient under the Kaldor–Hicks compensation principle (Campen 1986, 29–30).

This basic idea of valuing social welfare can be readily conveyed by the notion of consumer surplus. Consumer surplus is simply the difference between WTP for a good or a service and what they actually pay for that good or service (Mishan 1975, 24; see also Willig 1976; Harberger 1971). So if I am willing to pay five dollars for a beer and the beer actually costs two dollars, the consumer surplus in this transaction is three dollars. In theory, there is no obstacle to aggregating willingness to pay and applying it to public policy. In comparing policy alternatives, the option that maximizes consumer surplus is more efficient and makes the greater contribution to social welfare.

Despite its theoretical simplicity, consumer surplus is complicated in practice by several factors. One such factor is that willingness to pay for most goods and services is variable. The maximum amount I am willing to pay for one beer after a hard day's teaching is different from the maximum amount I'm willing to pay for a second beer. Technically, this is what's known as diminishing marginal utility, which simply means the personal satisfaction I get from consuming beer diminishes with each pint I put away. The same principle applies in the aggregate. For example, consider a program to build parking garages to ease a shortage of parking spaces in a central city. As more and more parking spaces become available, the social utility of each additional parking space diminishes, and therefore so does the willingness to pay. The value of the parking garages, in other words, is not simply a matter of subtracting the costs of construction and operation from the estimated revenue from parking fees. The social value of the parking garage depends on what motorists are willing to pay for a parking space, and what they are willing to pay will vary based on how many parking spaces are available.

All this variability, at least in theory, is relatively easy to deal with through marginal analysis. Imagine a graph where the x-axis represents units of a good, and the y-axis represents the maximum amount the individual is willing to pay for that good. A basic demand curve can be drawn connecting the WTP for the first unit of the good all the way down to where consuming one more unit has no utility at all and willingness to pay for that additional unit drops all the way to zero.

Assuming a linear demand curve, the resulting picture should look like a right-angled triangle with the demand curve sloping from the y-axis downward and to the right where it connects to the x-axis. Now, go up the y-axis to the actual price paid for the good and draw a horizontal line out to the demand curve. This dissects the larger triangle into two smaller shapes, the upper being a triangle with the horizontal line representing price paid as its base. The area represented by this triangle represents consumer surplus—the net value to the individual of consuming the good to the point where the price of the good and willingness to pay intersect, and consumption stops.

The same basic principle can be applied to public polices or programs by simply aggregating demand curves relative to public goods or programs. Imagine the $y$-axis representing parking fees and the $x$-axis representing parking spaces. As long as there is some reasonable estimation of aggregate demand (the collective willingness to pay for each additional parking space), the consumer surplus is calculated in exactly the same way, i.e. as the area above the parking fee charged and below the willingness to pay represented by the demand curve.

The practical challenge and the real complicating factor for putting the welfare economics notion of social welfare into analytic practice is the fact that WTP is generally unobserved. It is easy to observe what is charged for a good. The WTP for an individual—let alone a municipality or a county or a country—is rarely immediately evident. Much of the methodology of the welfare economics paradigm is employed to generate estimates of WTP, to in effect produce reliable demand curves for the consumption of public goods and services (for a detailed survey of such techniques, see Boardman et al. 2001).

Despite the methodological challenges, what should not be lost is that there is an underlying intuitive simplicity to the conceptual tools welfare economics uses to define and measure social welfare. Certainly all of the ideas represented in this section can be summarized very succinctly: Efficiency is nothing more than a characteristic of the distribution of resources. The optimal distribution of resources to maximize social welfare is a Pareto-optimal distribution, which can be roughly thought of as the distribution that maximizes the preferences of all citizens. Because the opportunities to maximize the preferences of all citizens are rare (especially with public policy) a more practical modification—the Kaldor–Hicks compensation principle—is used. Kaldor–Hicks recognizes that altering distributions of resources will often result in winners and losers. Kaldor–Hicks adopts the utilitarian perspective that if the gains of the winners outweigh the losses of the losers, society gains in the aggregate and such a distribution can thus be viewed as efficient. These conceptual tools can be used to fashion a set of practical analytic tools to study public policy.

## 2. Basic Analytic Tools: Cost Analysis

The conceptual tools discussed in the previous section can be applied analytically using a number of different methodologies. One of the most common approaches to applying the Kaldor–Hicks concept of efficiency is cost analysis. Indeed, cost analysis can generally be thought of as a methodology to calculate the efficiency of policy alternatives.

Cost analysis is not a technique, but rather an umbrella term for a variety of techniques that include cost–benefit analysis (CBA), cost–effectiveness analysis (CEA), cost utility analysis (CUA), and cost feasibility analysis (CFA). These techniques (especially CBA) constitute the primary economic tools used by policy scholars to analyze problems of social choice (Levin and McEwan 2001, 27–8 provide an excellent summary of the various cost analysis approaches). Though readily adaptable to *ex post* policy studies, the most commonly employed cost analysis techniques—especially CBA and CEA—are used almost exclusively as *ex ante* techniques (Boardman et al. 2001).

Essentially, the big attraction of cost analysis is that it offers a way systematically (and its most fervent proponents would argue, objectively) to judge the social worth of alternative policy options. If, for example, policy makers are focused on the problem of high secondary school dropout rates, there will undoubtedly be a constituency for a wide range of responses to this problem: smaller classes, vouchers, more qualified teachers, after-school programs, a back-to-basic curriculum; the potential policy permutations are virtually endless. Given limited resources, which of these alternatives should policy makers pursue?

Such problems of social choice are common in public policy decision making and represent a significant challenge to policy analysts for two reasons. First, there are high levels of uncertainty in *ex ante* analysis. Exactly what a program or policy will achieve is unknown until it is implemented and its outcomes analyzed. Proponents of, say, vouchers may argue their favored policy will result in fewer dropouts, and will cut educational costs with no adverse consequences. Until a voucher system is actually in place and given time to work, however, the empirical merits of such a claim are unknown.

Second, the notion of what best serves the public interest or makes the greatest contribution to social welfare is very much in the eye of the beholder. Partisan or ideological preference—even outright self-interest—can heavily influence perceptions of what policy is judged to be the best use of public resources. Given this, on what objective basis can policy analysts claim to rank the merits of one policy option over another?

Cost analysis is designed to provide one potential answer to this question. Distilled to its essence, the central objective of most forms of cost analysis is to estimate the relative efficiency (of the Kaldor–Hicks variety) of competing policy alternatives. This is practically achieved by calculating ratios of policy inputs to some measure of outcomes. The inputs represent the resources a program or policy consumes, which theoretically (though not always in practice) are valued as opportunity costs. The outcomes represent the expected real-world impacts or performance of the program or policy. The latter are actually translated into economic values using the WTP approach in CBA, though in other forms of cost analysis theoretical purity typically bows to a more rough and ready notion of efficiency (though one still that clearly springs from the Kaldor–Hicks principle). The logic is simple: however calculated, these ratios allow a comparative judgement of which policy option will provide more of the desired outcomes at the least cost. In economic terms, these are viewed as measures of the relative efficiency of the policy alternatives.

In addition to providing a practical basis for calculating the efficiency of policy alternatives, cost analysis can also address (though not fully solve) the uncertainty problem. Part and parcel of any good cost analysis is an accompanying sensitivity analysis. The latter involves varying input and outcome estimates across some range of reasonable possibilities. This helps assess how robust any estimate of efficiency is relative to the assumptions underpinning the calculation of inputs and outcomes. This does not remove uncertainty from policy analysis, but it does provide a basis for assessing how the unknowns of the future may influence the efficiency of any given policy alternative. In short, sensitivity analysis allows us to capture the potential consequences of uncertainty across the best- and worst-case estimates of inputs and outcomes (Manning, Fryback, and Weinstein 1996; Drummond et al. 1997).

All forms of cost analysis share this basic conceptual approach, and all commonly use market (monetary) values to quantify the input side of ratio. Cost analysis techniques differ mainly on how they attempt to quantify the costs of policy outcomes. The simplest (and most limited) is cost feasibility analysis, which is simply a ratio of the estimated costs of a policy option relative to the resources available. If the ratio of available resources to estimated costs is greater than 1.0, the project is judged to be feasible given the available resources. The main objective of conducting a CFA is simply to assess whether a particular policy alternative is possible given available resources (for an introduction to CFA see Levin and McEwan 2001, 22–6; for an example see Brewer et al. 1999).

Cost effectiveness analysis evaluates policies on the basis of costs relative to some measure of policy or program effectiveness (i.e. a quantitative outcome measure that reflects the relative achievement of the desired policy goal). Dividing costs by the outcome measure yields a ratio that can be interpreted as the cost per unit of effectiveness (good primers on CEA include Fuguitt and Willcox 1999, 276–95; Weinstein and Stason 1977; examples include Quinn, Van Mondfrans, and Worthen 1984; Levin 1988; Weinstein 1996). For example, in the dropout scenario above an obvious effectiveness measure would be the estimated number of dropouts prevented by each policy option in a given timeframe. Dividing the costs of each policy option by the estimated number of dropouts prevented provides an intuitively easy way to rank the options in "bang for the buck" terms (for good introductions to CEA see Levin 1991, 1995).

For programs or policies that share a single objective, cost effectiveness analysis provides an intuitive way to rank alternatives on the basis of their cost effectiveness. The obvious drawback of CEA is that many policies have more than one objective, or at least have more than one expected outcome, and CEA assesses alternatives on the basis of a single outcome. Cost utility analysis offers a partial solution to the problem. CUA assesses the utility of policy alternatives relative to their costs.

The "utility" of Cost Utility Analysis is generally thought of as "satisfaction" or "preference" and is often operationalized by combining a series of outcome or effectiveness measures into a weighted utility score. A good example is the quality-adjusted life year (QALY) that has been used in a number of health research studies. QALY is a utility measure that assesses a medical treatment by looking at how long it extends life and the health-related quality of life during that time. The concept of

QALY allows health researchers to assess medical treatments on a more holistic level than a single outcome (see Drummond et al. 1997; Nord 1999).

By far the most flexible and most commonly used form of cost analysis, however, is cost–benefit analysis (see Haveman and Weimer 2001). CBA was originally developed in the 1930s to aid decision making about federal water resource projects in the United States. The Flood Control Act passed by Congress in 1936 began applying economic principles to policy analysis by requiring federal agencies to calculate the costs and benefits of water resource projects (McKean 1958).

From those beginnings CBA spread to other policy areas and other countries. By the 1960s the British government, for example, was using basic CBA methodology to help inform decisions about transportation investments and nationalizing industries (Fuguitt and Wilcox 1999, 8–9). This general spread of CBA methods progressed through the 1970s, 1980s, and 1990s, its main attraction being its ability to fill a practical decision-making need: "how to assess and prioritize policy alternatives that generate benefits or costs not priced in markets" (Fuguitt and Wilcox 1999, 13). CBA is currently one of the most widely employed forms of *ex ante* policy analysis and is employed across a wide variety of policy fields at all levels of government.

CBA represents the most direct attempt to put the conceptual tools described above into methodological practices. It does this by using the concepts of WTP and opportunity cost to place monetary values on both the inputs and the outcomes of policy alternatives. Once this is accomplished, CBA provides a very straightforward measure of a given policy alternative's economic efficiency. A benefit–cost ratio (BCR) can be interpreted as the monetary units of benefit produced for each monetary unit of cost. Assuming the monetary units are dollars, then, a ratio of 1.0 indicates a project that produces a dollar's worth of benefits for every dollar's worth of costs invested. A ratio above 1.0 indicates a more efficient option, i.e. an option that returns more benefits for every dollar of cost. A ratio below 1.0 indicates an inefficient alternative, one that has more costs than benefits (basic introductions to the methodology of CBA include Boardman et al. 2001; Layard 1974).

In CBA it is also common to produce an even more direct measure of the Kaldor–Hicks notion of efficiency: net benefits. Net benefits are simply the total benefits of an alternative in monetary terms minus total costs. A positive number indicates a project that meets the efficiency threshold set by Kaldor–Hicks, i.e. it is a project where society gains overall.

One of the huge advantages of CBA over other forms of cost analysis is that it can weigh any policy alternative on a common metric of economic efficiency. Thus CBA can be employed to judge the relative merits of projects as disparate as, say, a new road, an after-school tutoring program, and a tax cut. Given that set of choices, which option best maximizes social welfare? CBA has no problem answering this question as long as an analyst can figure out whose benefits and costs should be counted (not a trivial problem—see Whittington and MacRae 1986) and is able to translate the costs and benefits of these programs into monetary terms. Once this is done the economic efficiency of each option is readily calculated and under the welfare economics paradigm the most efficient contributes the most to the social welfare.

As long as the inputs and outcomes of a policy can be reasonably translated into monetary units, CBA thus offers an unparalleled tool to assess the efficiency of various policy options. The rub, of course, is accurately translating the value of things like less traffic congestion and fewer dropouts into monetary terms. There is no shortage of CBA critics who cringe at the notion of putting dollar figures on the worth of clean air, reduced crime, or even life itself. Much of the analytic horsepower used in CBA analyses is expended in estimating the WTP for things that are not traded in efficient markets, things such as clean air and occupational risk.

There are a number of methodologically creative ways to get such estimates. Hedonic pricing, for example, is built on the notion that while we cannot observe WTP for things like the value of green space, we can observe what people are willing to pay for things whose value is partially driven by such non-observables. The price of a house, it is well known, is driven by location. Proximity to a good view or a park will help drive the price of real estate. Given this it is possible to decompose the price of houses in a given geographical area into its constituent parts using basic regression analysis. Market price of the house is the dependent variable, and characteristics of the house (e.g. size, number of bedrooms) and neighborhood (e.g. median income, crime rates), function as independent variables.

It is also possible to include on the right-hand side of the equation things like proximity to a park, the test scores of local schools, and quality of air in the neighborhood. The resulting coefficients can be used to estimate the WTP for the value of green space, a good education, and clean air. Essentially hedonic pricing values things that are not traded in markets by decomposing the values of goods that are traded in reasonably efficient markets (see Rosen 1974 for the theoretical case for hedonic pricing; for primers on techniques see Boardman et al. 2001, 340–4; Lancaster 1966; examples include Uyeno, Hamilton, and Biggs 1993; Smith and Huang 1995).

Other approaches include contingent valuation, which is essentially surveying people on their WTP for goods and services, and market analogy or intermediate good methods. The latter methods rely on estimating WTP by finding some private good that is either analogous to a public good or is actually produced by a public program. An example of the market analogy approach would be using rents charged in the private housing market to put a value on the benefits of a public housing program (for overviews and examples of these and similar methods, see Mitchell and Carson 1989; Bishop and Heberlein 1990; Nelson 1981; Brown and Mendelsohn 1984; Arrow et al. 1992). While these and other approaches can produce the monetary estimates CBA requires to gain its analytical traction, there will always be questions about their reliability and validity (see Self 1975).

For example, can you really put a value on human life (Zeckhauser 1974)? Is the "cost" of a rape to the victim really equivalent to $81,200 (Miller, Cohen, and Rossman 1993)? Is the "benefit" of a day of fishing really $45 (Walsh, Johnson, and McKean 1992)? To literally put a price on being the victim of a violent crime, the pleasure of a day spent with a rod and reel, or even life itself strikes many as requiring a questionable philosophical leap of faith. Is there, quite literally, a market value for everything? If your answer to that question is no, it is unlikely you will be persuaded by monetary estimates to the contrary, regardless of their underlying methodological creativity or sophistication.

Yet while acknowledging that critics may have a point, CBA has become the Swiss army knife of *ex ante* policy analysis for good reasons. Many of the targets of policy analysis involve things that are reasonably amenable to economic valuation. The benefits of a job training program, for example, can be reasonably monetized by looking at the earnings difference between those who have the training and those who do not. The difference is presumed to be WTP, i.e. the amount participants would want in order to give up the benefits they received from the program. Once costs and benefits are transformed into monetary units, CBA provides the most direct way of assessing any given alternative's impact on social welfare as it is conceived by the welfare economics paradigm.

Perhaps the ultimate defense of CBA is that when costs and benefits can be reasonably quantified in monetary terms it provides a robust and systematic assessment of social welfare. This does not have to be the end all and be all of policy analysis, and does not automatically have to exclude other views from being taken into account. CBA simply represents an effective means of evaluating public policies on the basis of economic efficiency. The latter represents important information when confronting questions of social choice, and CBA along with other forms of cost analysis, are analytical tools well suited to producing that information.

# 3. CONCLUSION

There is no doubt that economics, welfare economics in particular, is a primary supplier of the conceptual and analytical tools used in policy analysis. The reason for this is simple: welfare economics makes available a robust set of theoretical and methodological frameworks that are readily adaptable to problems of social choice. A key challenge in policy analysis is coming up with some systematic answer to the question: what should we do? Given scarce resources, and a range of alternatives to address a problem or issue of concern, how can those resources be expended to best serve the public interest?

Conceptually, the welfare economics paradigm answers these questions by starting with a clear notion of what constitutes the public interest. Public interest is conceived of as social welfare, which is nothing more than the aggregation of individual perceptions of their own levels of utility or satisfaction. The normative benchmark welfare economics provides for judging the public interest is this: given a choice of policy alternatives, the most preferred is the choice that maximizes social welfare.

To measure changes in social welfare, the concept of efficiency is employed, which defines a particular characteristic of a distribution of resources. The conceptual modifications of efficiency, let alone the methodological calculations, can seem complex to those uninitiated into the welfare economics paradigm. Yet the basic idea of how efficiency is practically employed as a benchmark of social welfare is intuitive and can be usefully captured in lay terms: social welfare is improved if a policy or program results in a situation where those who benefit from the policy could, at least in theory, compensate the losers and still come out ahead. This represents a net gain to society, and thus advances social welfare.

Methodologically, the concepts underpinning the welfare economics paradigm are readily translated into applied analytic tools through approaches such as cost analysis. Among the family of cost analytic techniques, cost–benefit analysis represents the most straightforward attempt to measure the economic efficiency of policy alternatives.

There exist criticisms of both the concepts and the methods that point out legitimate limits of the welfare economics paradigm of policy analysis. Other conceptions of social welfare can be formulated that pay greater attention to minority rights, or more egalitarian distributions of resources than the efficiency benchmark of welfare economics. Putting monetary figures on intangibles such as the value of a human life or the worth of clean air may strike some as normative navel gazing regardless of the econometric sophistication that generates such efforts.

Such criticisms, however, should not obscure the fact that a policy analyst's tool kit would be very minimal if these conceptual and analytical approaches were removed. Economics provides the means to generate systematic analysis to inform policy-making decisions. Ultimately the value of these tools is practical: they provide "a hard number... of the net value of an investment, project, or activity" (Munger 2000, 376). As long as policy makers and policy scholars see value in knowing such hard numbers on net values, the welfare economics paradigm will continue to provide the tools to get that particular job done.

## References

ANDERSON, J. E. 1994. *Public Policymaking: An Introduction*, 2nd edn. Princeton, NJ: Houghton Mifflin.

ARROW, K., SOLOW, R., LEARNER, E., PORTNEY, P., RADNER, R., and SCHUMAN, H. 1992. *Report of the NOAA Panel on Contingent Valuation*. Washington, DC: National Oceanic and Atmospheric Administration.

BISHOP, R. C., and HEBERLEIN, T. A. 1990. The contingent valuation method. Pp. 81–104 in *Economic Valuation of Natural Resources: Issues, Theory and Application*, ed. R. Johnson and G. Johnson. Boulder, Colo.: Westview.

BOARDMAN, A. E., GREENBERG, D. H., VINING, A. R., and WEIMER, D. L. 2001. *Cost–Benefit Analysis: Concepts and Practice*. Upper Saddle River, NJ: Prentice Hall.

BREWER, D. J., KROP, C., GILL, B. P., and REICHARDT, R. 1999. Estimating the cost of national class size reductions under different policy alternatives. *Educational Evaluation and Policy Analysis*, 21: 179–92.

BROWN, G., and MENDELSOHN, R. 1984. The hedonic travel cost model. *Review of Economics and Statistics*, 66: 427–33.

BUCHANAN, J., and TULLOCK, G. 1962. *The Calculus of Consent*. Ann Arbor: University of Michigan Press.

CAMPEN, J. T. 1986. *Benefit, Cost, and Beyond: The Political Economy of Benefit–Cost Analysis*. Cambridge, Mass.: Ballinger.

DRUMMOND, M. F., O'BRIEN, B., STODDART, G. L., and TORRANCE, G. W. 1997. *Methods for the Economic Evaluation of Health Care Programmes*, 2nd edn. Oxford: Oxford University Press.

FREDERICKSON, H. G., and SMITH, K. B. 2004. *The Public Administration Theory Primer*. Boulder, Colo.: Westview.

FRIEDMAN, M. 1962. *Capitalism and Freedom*. Chicago: University of Chicago Press.

FUGUITT, D., and WILCOX, S. J. 1999. *Cost–Benefit Analysis for Public Sector Decision Makers*. Westport, Conn.: Quorum.

GOODIN, R. E., and WILENSKI, P. 1984. Beyond efficiency: the logical underpinnings of administrative principles. *Public Administration Review*, 44: 512–17.

HALVORSEN, R., and RUBY, M. G. 1981. *Benefit–Cost Analysis of Air Pollution Control*. Lexington, Mass.: Heath, Lexington Books.

HARBERGER, A. C. 1971. Three basic postulates for applied welfare economics. *Journal of Economic Literature*, 9: 785–97.

HAVEMAN, R., and MARGOLIS, J. (eds.) 1970. *Public Expenditure and Policy Analysis*. Chicago: Markham.

—— and WEIMER, D. L. 2001. Cost–benefit analysis. Pp. 2845–51 in *International Encyclopedia of the Social and Behavioral Sciences*, ed. N. Smelser and P. Baltes, Oxford: Elsevier Science.

HICKS, J. R. 1939. The foundations of welfare economics. *Economic Journal*, 49: 696–712.

JUST, R. E., HUETH, D. L., and SCHMITZ, A. 2004. *Welfare Economics of Public Policy: A Practical Approach to Project and Policy Evaluation*. Cheltenham: Edward Elgar.

KALDOR, N. 1939. Welfare propositions of economics and interpersonal comparison of utility. *Economic Journal*, 39: 549–52.

KELMAN, S. 1981. Cost–benefit analysis: an ethical critique. *Regulation* (Jan.–Feb.): 33–40.

KNETSCH, J. L. 1995. Assumptions, behavioral findings and policy analysis. *Journal of Policy Analysis and Management*, 14: 68–78.

LANCASTER, K. L. 1966. A new approach to consumer theory. *Journal of Political Economy*, 74: 132–57.

LAYARD, R. (ed.) 1974. *Cost–Benefit Analysis*. Harmondsworth: Penguin.

LEVIN, H. M. 1988. Cost-effectiveness and educational policy. *Educational Evaluation and Policy Analysis*, 10: 51–69.

—— 1991. Cost-effectiveness at quarter century. Pp. 188–209 in *Evaluation and Education at Quarter Century*, ed. M. W. McLaughlin and D. C. Phillips. Chicago: University of Chicago Press.

—— 1995. Cost-effectiveness analysis. Pp. 381–6 in *International Encyclopedia of Economics of Education*, ed. M. Carnoy. Oxford: Pergamon.

—— and McEWAN, P. J. 2001. *Cost Effectiveness Analysis*, 2nd edn. Thousand Oaks, Calif.: Sage.

McKean, R. N. 1958. *Efficiency in Government through Systems Analysis with Emphasis on Water Resources Development.* New York: John Wiley and Sons.

Manning, W. G., Fryback, D. G., and Weinstein, M. C. 1996. Reflecting uncertainty in cost-effectiveness analysis. Pp. 247–75 in *Cost-Effectiveness in Health and Medicine,* ed. M. R. Gold, L. B. Russell, J. E. Siegel, and M. C. Wienstein. New York: Oxford University Press.

Miller, T. R., Cohen, M. A., and Rossman, S. 1993. Victim costs of violent crime and resulting injuries. *Health Affairs,* 12: 186–97.

Mishan, E. J. 1975. *Cost–Benefit Analysis: An Informal Introduction.* London: George Allen and Unwin.

Mitchell, R. C., and Carson, R. T. 1989. *Using Surveys to Value Public Goods: The Contingent Valuation Method.* Washington, DC: Resources for the Future.

Munger, M. 2000. *Analyzing Policy: Choices, Conflicts and Practices.* New York: W. W. Norton.

Nas, T. F. 1996. *Cost–Benefit Analysis: Theory and Application.* Thousand Oaks, Calif.: Sage.

Nelson, J. P. 1981. Airports and property values: a survey of recent evidence. *Journal of Transport Economics and Policy,* 14: 37–51.

Nord, E. 1999. *Cost–Value Analysis in Health Care: Making Sense of QALYs.* Cambridge: Cambridge University Press.

Ostrom, V. 1973. *The Intellectual Crisis in American Public Administration.* Tuscaloosa: University of Alabama Press.

Posner, R. 1983. *The Economics of Justice.* Cambridge, Mass.: Harvard University Press.

Quinn, B., Mondfrans, A. V., and Worthen, B. R. 1984. Cost-effectiveness of two math programs as moderated by pupil SES. *Educational Evaluation and Policy Analysis,* 6: 39–52.

Rosen, S. 1974. Hedonic price and implicit markets: product differentiation in pure competition. *Journal of Political Economy,* 82: 34–55.

Self, P. 1975. *Econocrats and the Policy Process: The Politics and Philosophy of Cost–Benefit Analysis.* London: Macmillan.

Smith, V. K., and Huang, J.-C. 1995. Can markets value air quality? A meta-analysis of hedonic property value models. *Journal of Political Economy,* 103: 209–27.

Stokey, E., and Zeckhauser, R. 1978. *A Primer for Policy Analysis.* New York: Norton.

Uyeno, D., Hamilton, S. W., and Biggs, A. J. G. 1993. Density of residential land use and the impact of airport noise. *Journal of Transport Economics and Policy,* 27: 3–18.

Walsh, R. G., Johnson, D. M., and McKean, J. R. 1992. Benefit transfer of outdoor recreation demand studies: 1968–1988. *Water Resources Research,* 23: 943–50.

Weimer, D. L., and Vining, A. R. 2005. *Policy Analysis: Concepts and Practice,* 4th edn. Upper Saddle River, NJ: Prentice Hall.

Weinstein, M. C. 1996. From cost-effectiveness ratios to resource allocation: where to draw the line? Pp. 77–98 in *Valuing Health Care: Costs, Benefits and Effectiveness of Pharmaceuticals and Other Medical Technologies,* ed. F. A. Sloan. New York: Cambridge University Press.

—— and Stason, W. B. 1977. Foundations of cost-effectiveness analysis for health and medical practices. *New England Journal of Medicine,* 296: 716–22.

Weintraub, E. R. 1983. On the existence of a competitive equilibrium: 1930–1954. *Journal of Economic Literature,* 21: 1–39.

Whittington, D., and MacRae, D., Jr. 1986. The issue of standing in cost–benefit analysis. *Journal of Policy Analysis and Management,* 5: 662–82.

Williams, A. 1972. Cost–benefit analysis: bastard science? And/or insidious poison in the body politick? *Journal of Public Economics,* 1: 199–226.

WILLIG, R. D. 1976. Consumer surplus without apology. *American Economic Review*, 66: 589–97.

ZECKHAUSER, R. 1974. Procedures for valuing lives. *Public Policy*, 23: 419–64.

—— and SCHAEFER, E. 1968. Public policy and normative economic theory. Pp. 27–101 in *The Study of Policy Formation*, ed. R. Bauer and K. J. Gergen. Glencoe, Ill.: Free Press.

# CHAPTER 37

# ECONOMISM AND ITS LIMITS

## JONATHAN WOLFF

## DIRK HAUBRICH

## 1. INTRODUCTION

In its broadest sense, "economism" is the claim that decision makers and theorists have overestimated the contribution that the economic realm can make to policy making. Given a society's limited resources, public policy often requires taking decisions among conflicting desires and goals. How best to make such choices—the "allocation of scarce resources among competing ends"—has troubled analysts for quite some time, and economics has been a sought-after discipline to provide guidance in that endeavor. Government agencies, unlike private corporations do not face the danger of bankruptcy when implementing a policy that is not efficient and often find their budget constraints "softened" (Kornai 1986). While private firms have to minimize their costs due to external market pressures exerted upon them, few such pressures exist for government agencies. Hence, inefficiency tends to be more severe and prolonged than in the private sector (Leibenstein 1966). Given that in some welfare states the allocative sector can be as large as half of GDP and that its administration requires an extensive bureaucracy with a plethora of laws and regulations, the quid pro quo question of how most efficiently to organize it is undeniably imminent.

* The authors are grateful to Donald Franklin, Bob Goodin, Michael Moran, Camilla Needham, Jesse Norman, Martin Reid, and Grant Venner for helpful comments on earlier drafts. The research has been supported by AHRB Innovation Grant No. AR15635.

Privatization, the paticipation of the private sector in the delivery of public services, and the application of private sector management techniques, discussed in Chapters 24, 32, and 36 in this volume, have been heralded as pointing in the right direction. The incorporation, privatization, marketization, and deregulation of public services and the reassigning of policy responsibility from bureaucratic administrators to the most cost-effective private bidder through "temporary contracts" were seen as methods to ascertain the desired levels of efficiency. They were based on economic evaluation techniques that enabled policy makers to identify, measure, value, and compare the consequences of alternative policy programs.

These economic evaluations can be seen as proceeding through a number of stages. First, for any proposal under consideration, including the option of doing nothing, a qualitative statement of its expected costs and benefits is to be provided. Second, each cost and benefit should be rendered in quantitative form. Third, each quantity should be translated into a common currency (usually monetary values). Fourth, the total expected costs or benefits should be calculated. Finally a decision should be taken on the basis of which proposal produces the greatest sum of benefits over costs, so understood. The first stage seems essential to any rational decision-making process, but each further stage is highly contested.

This chapter will address the difficulties that these phases give rise to in theory and practice. We will do so against the background of the most popular economic evaluation technique currently employed in policy making, that of cost–benefit analysis (CBA). After setting the scene, in Section 2, with a brief outline of the meaning of economism as a term and concept, Section 3 will explore the issues related to the measurement and monetary valuation of the items that are to be included in economic evaluations (what we might call the valuation problem). To be sure, if the methodology of economic evaluations is not to be arbitrary or fetishistic, some connection between the currency of evaluation and human well-being, at least broadly conceived, must be established. After all, the monetary value of a good reflects the strength of individuals' preferences for that good, which in turn is a measure of the welfare provided by it. Implementing this rationale exposes serious weaknesses, however. They must not go unnoticed and require comprehensive exploration. Section 4 will then deal with the problem of comparing costs and benefits across lives (what we might call the commensurability problem), while Section 5 outlines the issue of how the intrinsic value of human beings might be overridden by economic evaluations (the intrinsic value problem). Although these charges can be brought against any policy domain to a greater or lesser degree we will place them into the specific context of health care provision and environmental regulation to make the discussion more tangible. In Section 6 we will then briefly develop some alternatives and propose a set of recommendations that we would want economic approaches to public policy to follow if the pitfalls of economism are to be avoided.

## 2. ECONOMISM AS A TERM AND CONCEPT

Claims of economism can come in two disguises. The first is a psychological account about the motivation that drives human action, which is assumed to be predominantly spurred by economic motives so as to improve one's own material well-being. First introduced in this sense by communist intellectuals at the beginning of the twentieth century, economism as a term and concept was seen as an antipode to class-consciousness, ideology, and political activity. Sections within the socialist movement were accused, for example, by Lenin (1964, 29) and much later, Gramsci (1971, 165) of betraying their common cause because they were too happy to settle for better economic terms and conditions on which to sell their labor power, found cozy arrangements with capitalist industrialists, and generally refused to engage in the more demanding revolutionary struggle to obtain political power. More muted instances of this account are still heard today: trade unions are said to direct their behavior depending on the extent to which employers are willing to raise salaries for their members; and political parties are accused of obtaining funds from pressure groups to sponsor the voting campaigns of their candidates—in exchange for which they support policies that these economic interests favor and at the expense of satisfying the preferences of their constituents.

The second account, which we are henceforth concerned with in this chapter, refers to the theoretical foundations on which public policy is and should be built. Economism understood in this political theory sense lays blame on public policy for delineating economic efficiency as the predominant policy objective; for applying elaborate economic tools to identify the policy option best suited to achieve that goal; and for relying on the market, or some proxy as the institution best equipped to set the required framework. The policy choices made as a result, so the claim goes, trump, or at least reduce other important values that guide human behavior and that society might therefore uphold, such as solidarity, community, equality, or friendship (Henderson 1996).

The emphasis on economic efficiency became particularly noteworthy in the 1980s, when the new center-right governments that had come into power in the USA, the UK, and Germany started to subject their public expenditures to much more stringent economic scrutiny. They saw the expansion of the welfare state in previous decades as having had adverse effects on economic efficiency and international competitiveness, which has thus become a source of major economic problems, including declining productivity growth and high levels of unemployment (Okun 1975). Hence, governments decided to cut public spending and taxes and to reassign responsibility for individual well-being from the state to the individual. Investments into public services such as health, transport, and education dropped dramatically and were kept at low levels for many years to come.

Two decades later many industrialized countries were rewarded in their economic policies with substantial increases in output of products and services as well as greater international competitiveness. However, these successes came at a considerable price in terms of the domestic distribution of income. For although the causal link between high levels of equality and low levels of efficiency has been contested as "elusive" (LeGrand 1991, ch. 3), the two countries most concerned about efficiency and the free market experienced above-average shifts in income distribution from the poor to the rich: in the UK, the so-called "Gini coefficient," a common statistical index in the social sciences to measure diversity and inequality in income and wealth within a society, rose from 0.25 in 1979 to 0.35 in 2000, while the USA saw an increase from 0.36 to 0.43 over the same period (Coudouel and Hentschel 2000).[1]

The ramifications of greater inequality and competitive pressure were not only felt by the poor and vulnerable. A general dissatisfaction grew among citizens with the absence of rewards that they, at least in the long run, anticipated in exchange for the sacrifices and hardships they increasingly incurred in daily life. The discontent became widespread, uniting individuals with diverse agendas against the ramifications of domestic as well as international economic policies. The unprecedented demonstrations the world saw at the end of the millennium in Prague, Seattle, Genoa, and Washington, among others united the most unlikely bedfellows: farmers complaining about the decline of rural communities found themselves standing shoulder to shoulder with "deep ecologists" demanding sensible stewardship of the resources and value that nature offered. And while feminists decried the absence of the value of household labor in economic calculations, religious leaders raged against the portrayal of human beings as intrinsically motivated by hedonistic interests. By that time, then, the claim of economism no longer emanated from within the political left, as it had done during Marx's and Lenin's time, but cut well across the political left–right spectrum.

The methodological and philosophical difficulties that we will draw out in this chapter will go some way to shed light on the reasons for the public's discontent with economistic policy approaches. A suitable starting point to do so is to examine the evaluation method most commonly employed to ensure that desired efficiency levels are achieved, that of cost–benefit analysis (CBA).[2] CBA enables analysts to exploit a set of analytical tools used in economics and econometrics to evaluate project investments and policy options and has been made a legal prerequisite in most countries. In the USA, for example, a comparison of costs and benefits has been recommended since the Roosevelt administration. Executive order 12991, signed by President Reagan in 1981, later codified CBA as a requirement for agencies when conducting risk assessments in health, safety, and environmental regulation (Smith 1984; PCCRA 1997; for the UK: HM Treasury 1997).

---

[1] The Gini coefficient varies between the limits of 0 (perfect equality) and 1 (perfect inequality) and is best understood as the geometrical divergence in a diagram between a 45 degree line on the one hand, which represents perfect equality, and the Lorenz curve beneath it on the other, which measures percentage income distribution (as plotted on the $y$-axis) across the percentage of the population (as plotted on the $x$-axis).

[2] In some (mostly US) literature the method is also referred to as "benefit–cost analysis."

There is a large body of literature available dealing with CBA, some of which dates back to the 1920s, when large-scale engineering projects in the USA required some type of project evaluation. Although CBA is not really a self-contained field of economics but sits somewhat uneasily between several scholarly discourses including philosophy, psychology, and politics (Adler and Posner 2001; Layard and Glaister 2001), the central procedures of CBA have been predominantly defined by economists. The standard introductory textbook, too, has been written by an economist (Mishan 1972) and is now available in its eighth imprint. While the scope of CBA was often confined to costs and benefits that accrued to a single enterprise only, Mishan soon demanded that CBA be carried out in such a way as to include all known costs, external or internal, and be "concerned with the economy as a whole, with the welfare of a defined society, and not any smaller part of it" (1972, 11).

Appreciating the effects on the welfare of the whole society, however, required policy makers to apply ever greater levels of analytical sophistication so to be able to capture the additional dimensions by which societies have come to define said welfare—such as the environment, health, and safety, to mention but a few. As the remit for economic methodologies became therefore ever more expansive, additional problems, at operational as well as conceptual level, presented themselves. Sections 3 to 5 will outline one of them each.

# 3. THE VALUATION PROBLEM

Economism, we have pointed out, is the charge that a theorist or policy maker has overestimated the significance of the economic realm. To accuse followers of CBA of economism is, then, to suppose that they have made some sort of mistake in applying their economic rationale; most likely one of reductionism, in which some value important to societal well-being is either incorrectly reduced to a monetary metric or ignored altogether. This is what we might call the valuation problem, and one area in which this issue has often been raised is the policy domain of environmental regulation.

When public policy involves decision making about ecological systems, the prices for the natural services and goods required to implement a policy option need to reflect the *true* costs incurred in their creation, not only those that are reflected in market prices. Through an analysis of costs and benefits that incorporates these externalities, policy makers try to ensure that a certain stock of natural resources can be maintained, including the quality of soil, ground and surface water, land biomass, and possibly, the waste-assimilation capacity of the receiving environments (Hanley and Spash 1993). As part of a CBA, the costs and benefits of alternative policy options need to be measured. To do so, quantitative relationships between, for example, pollution exposure on the one hand and some human or ecological response on the other, are needed to estimate the marginal change the policy will bring about.

This can be a substantial endeavor because, contrary to a CBA carried out by a firm, public policy decisions have to include the impact not only on a corporate entity but on wider society as well. The crucial feature of some of the goods in need of valuation is that we care about them—such as clean air and water, the countryside, etc.—but they are not traded in commercial markets and therefore have no market price. Many of nature's services fall into this category of public goods (Hardin 1982): while they are consumed jointly, no one can be excluded from using them ("non-excludability"), and one person's use does not limit another's ("non-rivalry" or "non-divisibility"), at least up to some congestion point. Tangible natural resources that are traded in a market represent only a small part of the services that nature provides. Our ecosystem, with its abiotic (i.e. non-living) and biotic (living) components such as climate, soils, bacteria, plants, and animals, provides additional services from which the human population, either directly or indirectly derives benefits. They include raw materials and waste assimilation of course, but also entail functions usually not included in CBAs, such as hydrological flows, regulation of global temperature, biological control, nutrient cycling, to mention just a few.

The reason for their absence is due to problems economists and policy makers face with the accurate estimation of the value of these services. In the past decades, several attempts have been made to address this issue, and a number of valuation techniques have been advanced that examined revealed behavior in a market. The intention has been to assign a monetary value to both the stocks of natural assets and their use as material inputs and sinks for waste residuals. Most of these methods are only applicable to limited contexts and therefore have their particular strengths and weaknesses. Such is the case for the "travel cost method," which establishes a relationship between the costs individuals are willing to incur to visit resources with recreational functions; "hedonic pricing" for goods the value of which can be inferred from a proxy good in the market—such as property values indicating the costs of noise levels in a given neighborhood; and "opportunity costs" where one resource use precludes another (for a concise overview see Turner, Pearce, and Bateman 1994, 114–27).

A significant advance towards a more universally applicable method was made when from the 1960s onwards, "contingent valuation" (CV) was introduced as another valuation technique, which was not based on individuals' *revealed* but on their *stated* preferences. With CV, economists sought to create *hypothetical* markets for all goods traded outside the market system, by asking people what they *would* pay, if there was a market and they had to (Arrow et al. 1992). Contingent valuation is an umbrella term that covers divergent methodological approaches but usually employs surveys to elicit respondents' value for a commodity and their willingness to pay (WTP) for the satisfaction of a preference or accept compensation (WTA) for forgoing its satisfaction. With the help of CV, considerations of what policy choice might be in society's overall interest can be informed by economic evaluations such as CBA of how these values balance up.

These surrogate valuation methods established themselves very quickly in the academic and policy-making communities. They constituted a paradigm shift in economic theory, away from the study of actors' revealed preferences in the market (Robbins 1932) towards the study of stated preferences and human behavior in experimental settings. CV experienced continuous methodological improvements throughout the 1980s and 1990s reaching ever higher levels of sophistication and purported objectivity. Leading environmental economists such as Pearce (1993) in the UK and Kneese (1984) in the USA endorsed the suitability of this approach for public policy.

In the mid-1990s a team of researchers around Robert Costanza was then able to consolidate more than 100 of such CV analyses so to produce the most comprehensive study to date on the value of nature (Costanza et al. 1997). They estimated that the annual value of seventeen different ecosystem services is equivalent to $US33 trillion, with nutrient cycling (17,075 bn) and waste treatment (2,227 bn) at the top of the price list. The success of CV was not only confined to academic studies such as Costanza's, however. In the USA, it also became a legally binding procedure on which, for example, compensation payments for the environmental damage inflicted by the 1989 *Exxon Valdez* tanker catastrophe were based. But as sophistication advanced, so did the controversies and debates surrounding the method, some themes of which are worth summarizing here.

First, there is the criticism advanced, for example by Diamond and Hausman (1993), that WTP is an inadequate proxy for market prices because of the ambiguity and limited reliability of the stated preferences used in CV, as opposed to those revealed in a market. A price is the economic value beyond which people would cease to demand a good and spend their money on some other source of satisfaction instead. In an actual market, consumers' willingness and financial constraints sets the price at which goods are exchanged in such a way. In a CV setting this is not necessarily the case. The $US33 trillion price tag that Costanza et al. have put on nature does not fulfill this requirement. If these ecosystem services were actually be paid for, the global price system would be very different from what it is today. The implication of Costanza's analysis is that in trying to replace these services, global GDP, which currently stands at $US18 trillion, would need to increase by a further $US33 trillion, without immediate increase in material possessions that individuals would be able to experience qualitatively or quantitatively in exchange for the higher prices that they would have had to pay.

This objection has some merit because CV is by definition a hypothetical approach, with hypothetical markets, a hypothetical provisioning of commodities, and hypothetical payments. As Hayek (1975) had already explained for the related case of collectivist economic planning, individuals cannot articulate their preference independent of the context for action that the marketplace supplies. The difference between hypothetical statements of value and those that are obtained when real economic commitments would have to be made can never be known.

Hypothetical bias is not the only weakness of CV, however. There is, secondly, a set of criticisms directed at the assumption underlying survey methodologies that coherent preferences on policy issues are susceptible to valuation and extractable through interviews or questionnaires. However, uncertainty, the novelty of the survey situation, question construction, and phrasing often make public opinion on policy issues unintelligible if not misleading. Once a particular machinery for making social choices from individual tastes is established it might be in the individual's strategic interest not to reveal her real preferences (von Neumann and Morgenstern 1947). To borrow a well-known example from another subfield of political science, once a society has established a first-past-the post electoral system, citizens are likely to vote for the less desirable major party candidate instead of the minor party candidate they really favor. Underestimating the methodological difficulty of encoding such context-laden statements is therefore difficult, and CV could not possibly do justice to policy proposals aiming to launder them.

Third, the deficiencies of applying CV to economic decision making points to the more fundamental issue whether public policy should be sensitive to preference satisfaction at all—no matter whether hypothetically stated or actually revealed in a market (Sagoff 1988). CBA functions on the basis that an allocation of resources is preferable if people's preferences are better met. This view is founded on the economic assumptions inherent in consumer choice theory that first, an individual consistently knows what she needs (usually referred to as the "rationality" ideal), and second, that her well-being depends on her subjective sense of satisfaction, which is best achieved by letting her preference determine the use of a society's resources (the "consumer sovereignty" ideal). It is then possible to define an economic function for that individual such that the benefit of an alternative is greater than other alternatives over which it is preferred. These assumptions underpin not only the branch of economics, usually referred to as "normative welfare economics," that we are concerned with in this chapter; general economic theory, too, has relied on these assumptions to explain why the autonomous consumer acting in the free market is a better judge of her utility than a central planner. These assumptions have allowed practitioners and theorists in the field to derive the shape of demand curves and explain the efficient functioning of the market (Samuelson 1948; Lipsey and Chrystal 1999).

Scholars critical of the idea's moral credentials have attacked the naive form of subjectivism inherent in the theory, which conceals well-known facts about human nature: that the psychological mechanisms by which social causes are transformed into beliefs and preferences let individuals adjust their aspirations to their perceptions of possibilities, giving rise to the phenomenon of "adaptive preference formation" (Elster 1983); that they might be malformed so that their satisfaction will inflict harm on themselves (the heroin addict; the gambler) or others (the murderer) and should therefore not be accepted as legitimate input into economic evaluations (Sen 1987); that preference satisfaction fails to accord the proper moral status to those beings—both human (e.g. children) and non-human (e.g. animals)—that are incapable of expressing a preference; that people wrongly predict the effects of their own choices on their future well-being (Kahneman 2003); and that finally, preference satisfaction endorses individual choice based on errors, ignorance, or misinformation, as it is incapable of distinguishing them from those based on knowledge.

Consumers are, then, not always the best judges of their preferences, and WTP is a poor proxy for market prices: Policies should not always satisfy what respondents have stated as preferences at the outset. To Richardson (2001), these phenomena are understandable and can be attributed to consumers' "incomplete thinking:" As consumers' experience grows, "practical intelligence" allows them to continue deliberating about the pros and cons of policy options. They then expectedly overturn their preferences in light of new and better information, a fact about human nature that economic tools such as CBA are incapable of factoring in.

To be sure, some economists have concerns about the morally questionable results produced by the equal treatment of uninformed or malevolent preferences in their models. Yet they have failed to command widespread assent in the discipline. Mishan's standard textbook, for example, seems to be unsure whether, or how questionable preferences should be treated (Mishan 1972, 386–8). These preferences are methodologically too meddlesome to deal with. As a minimum he is prepared to exclude from economic evaluations states of mind such as "envy" or mere "dislike." Yet, as Rhoads (1999, ch. 9) shows, even that concession is not accepted among the majority of economists, who insist that no principle or law should constrain consumers' will and sovereignty.

Fourth, the valuation of nature begs the more fundamental and therefore rather well-rehearsed question how to understand the concept of value in the first place. Assigning a value to nature requires the appraisal of fundamental philosophical issues about the role of economic value and human well-being. Economics and the market system, as the basis from which costs and benefits are imputed, are cultural phenomena that reflect just one way of perceiving the world, which is not necessarily shared by all. Nature can also be attributed what Krutilla (1967) has called "existence value" whereby the survival of species itself is deemed to be worth protecting. Often, that value cannot be priced in real or hypothetical markets because the expected benefits do not accrue to those who might be asked to reveal or state a WTP for their preference. Respondents would have to perform the difficult conceptual exercise to determine the residual value of a good that they never have used and never will be using. Existence value is therefore not intelligibly assessed by either WTP, CV, or markets.

Fifth, even if we cast aside the debate about existence value and assume that human well-being *is* accepted as the determining objective of valuation, it is still not clear that market prices indicate or reveal anything about the contribution they make to that goal in a substantive sense. As the eighteenth-century economist Adam Smith (1979) remarked with his "water–diamond paradox," the term "value" has two distinct meanings: sometimes it expresses the utility of some particular object, at other times the power of purchasing other goods which the possession of that object conveys. He called the former "value in use" and the latter "value in exchange," and observed that the things which have the greatest value in use (water) have frequently little or no value in exchange; and conversely, those that have the greatest value in exchange (diamonds) have frequently little or no value in use. Exchange value bears no necessary connection to value in use. Yet, while the latter produces the benefit to individuals and thus augments society's well-being, it is the former that is used to impute values into economic evaluations such as CBA or at the most aggregate level, into a nation's gross domestic product (GDP).

It did not take long for economists to develop "marginalism" as an attempt to resolve the paradox: as water is not very costly to acquire and therefore consumed at high volumes (at least in developed economies), the marginal use value we obtain from an additional bottle is rather low; and so is the exchange value, the price, we are willing to pay for it. The exchange value of diamonds, in turn, is high due to the good's scarcity and the comparatively higher marginal cost an increase in its supply incurs. We consume diamonds at low volumes as a result and are afforded a high marginal use value for every additional unit we consume. Hence, exchange value and use value are, it is said, identical, provided we assess both at the margin and not in total. For the total value of water is, so the argument concludes, of course very high when a large volume of it is consumed, while the total value received from diamonds is relatively low when few diamonds are consumed.

This argument does not hold up to rigid scrutiny, however, as marginalism seems an odd concept to apply to many goods we use in daily life. The value (in affording happiness and contentment) of a teddy bear to a child, for example, or that of a wedding ring to its bearer cannot be adequately expressed by the exchange value that these items command in retail. Their use value is not meaningfully assessed through reference to the scarcity of teddy bears or the marginal value that a second or third ring might provide. For the particular case of environmental goods the additional problem presents itself that as mentioned before, they are, for the most part, not traded in markets at all. There is no exchange value for the air that we breathe or the solar energy that heats our planet, although both are required for our survival and are therefore of high use value to us. They are, in fact, so-called "essential goods:" the demand for air, water, and the sun is never zero, even at extreme prices. Under essentiality, the maximum value in use of one additional unit of these goods is equal to total income, an assessment that is not true for most other goods that are used in the production process. It is therefore misleading to treat them in the same way as other goods. Hence, while exchange value and use value at the margin might be synonymous for some goods, they are not so for others, including those provided by nature.

In concluding this section, we should acknowledge, then, that the economic value of some goods cannot be ascertained; that for those goods for which valuation is possible, economic value might not be a correct indicator for preference satisfaction or well-being; and that even if it were, preferences are not always a suitable basis for public policy. The undermining of these assumptions calls into question the tools economists use to study efficiency. Conventional economic valuation is deficient and in need of improvement, or replacement by a model that better reflects the interaction between the economy and the physical and biological world. Some important work has still to be done. At this point in time, policy makers need to be aware of the limits of the valuation of costs and benefits. Before we indicate some ways out of this impasse in Section 6, a second issue area is worth being carved out.

# 4. THE COMMENSURABILITY PROBLEM

Once attributes of well-being have been valued in the way discussed above, policy makers have to compound these attributes into a single aggregated standard so as to decide who in a society should be given scarce resources. To do so, various attributes of individual well-being need to be commensurate across lives so that an increase in well-being for individual A can be weighed against the forgone improvement individual B would have experienced. This next phase in public decision making, however, gives rise to various issues that we will draw out against the background of health care as the second policy domain that governments tend to subject to economic evaluations.

The provision of health care is an activity different from other policy domains on many levels, with important ramifications for the applicability of economic evaluations. Individuals do not willingly enter the health care market as they do for other services that governments might provide. Nor do they know when they will be in need of health care or what form of health care they will then require (Arrow 1963). As patients rarely have experience from previous purchases of health care, these decisions are in general not made by the consumer either but by a doctor. The doctor is also seen to be better equipped to calculate the many probability terms involved in the health prospects of alternative treatments. In economic parlance, she acts for the patient as an *agent*, a special relationship that creates two important dissociations.

First, the consumer becomes dissociated from the market. Health care services are sought after not based on preferences of the consumer alone, as indifference map demand theory in economics would assume, but they are either split or based solely on those of the agent (Mooney 1992, 67–82). Price formation theory, too, is repudiated as the consumer is rarely able to make a rational, informed choice in the market. He has only little information about the level of benefit or well-being various health care services and medical treatments might provide. These information asymmetries might be brought about consciously—by the doctor withholding information from his patient or vice versa, by the patient concealing the true nature of her illness—or are merely due to the highly specialized knowledge required to understand the causes and effects of illnesses. The claim that consumers seek health care is therefore misleading too: individuals do not seek *health care*. Rather their goal is *health*. This is an important distinction: while health care resources are consumed by medical personnel, it is the patient who experiences the anticipated improvements in health and welfare that the resource consumption promises.

Second, the government as financial supplier becomes dissociated from the market also. Doctors as street-level providers possess significant discretion over the health care resources that governments have to pay for. Policy makers have therefore only limited possibilities to control the expenditure for these services. In an effort to regain that control some governments have attempted to challenge, with various degrees of success, the clinical autonomy of doctors through the creation of internal markets and other measures inspired by the New Public Management approach.

Shortcomings in economic assumptions notwithstanding, economic evaluations in health care provision are more in demand than ever before, greatly spurred by the ever-growing share of GDP that is absorbed by the treatment of nations' aging populations. Carrying out CBAs in such policy contexts promises guidance for decision makers as to the optimal distribution of medical manpower, R&D funding, reimbursement practices, capital controls, and safety regulations. Costs and benefits accrue at three different points, or channels where health care is provided: cure (to improve health), care (to retain dignity for those who are sick), and prevention (to reduce the probability of illness or premature death). The benefits in these channels are established by valuing the respective effects a policy has on the state of health of the individual(s) in question. The methods used to conduct this activity have attracted their own set of criticisms. They are similar to the charges elucidated in Section 3 above and will therefore not be rehearsed here.

Rather, we direct our attention to a related issue, the aggregation of attributes of well-being, which represents itself as soon as health improvements *have been* valued. Aggregation is a task not confined to health care but is pursued in all policy domains and for all goods and services that governments provide. Aggregation needs to be done over different outcomes of varied interventions undertaken on different problems. Staying with health care as a policy domain, for life-threatening diseases such as coronary bypass surgery or tetanus the primary outcome will obviously be defined as death or survival. Case fatality rate and survival rate may in such cases be good indicators of the achievements of heath care reached. Each survival can then be indexed with the value 1 and each fatality with 0. Treatment of most other illnesses—or for that matter, effects of other policy decisions on well-being—does not result in such binary outcomes, however, and measuring them in such a way means that everyone who survives a medical intervention is given the same value, no matter whether the person is confined to bed or is actively able to play sports. A more accurate measure would be required for these cases, one that is able to capture benefits in the form of subsequent *grades* of well-being between the two end points of the spectrum.

In a move to derive a methodology suitable to develop such an index, scholars began from the 1970s onwards, to define health in terms of "utility of life" (Torrance, Thomas, and Sackett 1972; Zeckhauser and Shephard 1976). Three decades of research and numerous refinements later, utility of life has come to be calculated along two dimensions: (*a*) the duration of life as measured in life years and (*b*) the quality of life as experienced by the individual's physical, social, and emotional functioning. The latter is elicited via patient questionnaires and interviews, where rating scale, time trade-off, or standard gambling techniques (of which more will be heard in a moment) are applied across a multitude of domains—including mobility, emotion, cognition, and pain—so as to arrive at the weighted preference that each domain commands (Drummond et al. 1997, 150–83). The greater the preference for a particular health state, the greater the "utility" associated with it. Utilities of health states are generally expressed on a numerical scale ranging from 0 to 1, in which 0 represents the utility of the state "dead" and 1 the utility of a state lived in "perfect health." Finally, utilities are multiplied by the remainder of an individual's lifetime for each outcome to calculate so-called "quality-adjusted life years" (QALYs). The QALY benefit associated with any given intervention is calculated as the difference between the QALYs available with that intervention and the QALYs available without that intervention. The results can then be used to create "cost-per-QALY" rankings for different interventions which aids in deciding on "best-buy" strategies, and to develop statistics on "disability-adjusted life-year expectancies" (DALYs) across countries (WHO 2000, 176–83; Murray 1996).

The QALYs approach is an exercise in what is commonly called "multi criteria mapping" and thus akin to methods developed to address aggregation issues in other policy domains. It soon established itself as the most sophisticated and therefore default methodology for measuring and aggregating individual levels of human well-being in general and quality of life in health care in particular. In no other policy sector has there been developed a similarly refined approach. And as a non-monetary standard it has the added benefit of bypassing the criticisms about monetary valuation that we elaborated upon in the previous section.

Despite the advantages of using a single indicator to measure the effectiveness of health care interventions, QALYs have been widely criticized on ethical, conceptual, and operational grounds, casting doubts on whether the underlying methodology actually solves the problem of incommensurability. The possibility of combining quantity and quality of life in a single index is rooted in the school of political philosophy known as utilitarianism. It is the foundation for the economic analysis of individual behaviour and emerged in the works of Jeremy Bentham and John Stuart Mill in the eighteenth and nineteenth centuries respectively. Now known as the "interpersonal comparison of well-being" problem, it has kept philosophers on their toes ever since (Elster and Roemer 1991).[3] Bentham's intention was to provide the British Parliament with a political theory that could be used to construct sound and rational policies rather than letting them rely on vague and biased intuitions. The theory's main prescription was to enact laws that are dictated by the principle of utility, when in like manner the tendency which it has to augment the utility (or "happiness" as Bentham called it) of the community is greater than any which it has to diminish (Bentham 1970). In what became later known as classical utilitarianism, this principle directs the policy maker to maximize the utility of the members of a society.

Utilitarian theory has been persistently attractive to generations of policy makers and political theorists because of its simplicity; its scientific allure as a theory that can be written down as a mathematical formula; and its concern for human welfare as the core of moral philosophy. Yet it has also attracted its fair share of criticism, resulting in many authors proposing modifications and redefinitions to make the theory more palatable. This is certainly not the place to rehearse this debate. The reader may refer to the extensive research produced on the topic, with the collection edited, for example, by Glover (1990) providing a good starting point. Sen (1987, 39) is more useful for us in that he has drawn out the elementary requirements of any utilitarian

---

[3] We use "utility" here interchangeably with the terms "welfare" and "well-being" as the satisfaction accruing to an individual from the consumption of a good or service.

moral principle. These are (1) *welfarism*, requiring that the goodness of a state of affairs be a function only of the utility information regarding that state; (2) *sum ranking*, requiring that utility information regarding any state be assessed by looking only at the sum total of all the utilities in that state; and (3) *consequentialism*, requiring that every choice, whether of actions, institutions, motivations, rules, etc., be ultimately determined by the goodness of the consequent state of affairs.

Note that the first requirement about welfarism can only be made to work if individuals are assumed to be able to evaluate their utility; if that utility can be made known to interested third parties, such as policy makers through some sort of valuation; and if that valuation can be measured in quantitative terms. These assumptions have already been questioned in Section 3 when we discussed the case of environmental goods. It is the second requirement on sum ranking which we are concerned with in the current context of aggregation of utilities and QALYs. Bentham insisted that sum ranking is possible because, to him, the item to be aggregated (happiness) denoted only one type of experience (the feeling of pleasure). Hence, utility was in his view easily aggregated across lives, for it was only one, not multiple experiences that people would encounter. It didn't take long before philosophers objected that some pleasures differ in kind according to the value individuals attach to them. And these are not the same across lives.[4]

Given the multiplicity of states of health that individuals might experience, the question then remains whether it is possible to know how much healthier some are compared to others. We are certainly able to make such a comparison in an ordinal sense, e.g. I can stipulate that I feel better than someone who is in great physical pain. However, to compare utilities across lives, I need to be able to make the comparison in a cardinal sense, i.e. I need to know exactly *how much better* I am. Cardinality, in turn, implies two requirements that need to be satisfied (Bossert 1991): (1) a number must be attached to the outcome that represents the strength of the preference relative to others, so that a health state of, say, 0.6 is three times better than one of 0.2; and (2) the scale must have an equal interval property where equal differences at different points along the response scale are equally meaningful, so that boosting a patient from, say, 0.1 to 0.2 on that scale is of equal benefit to raising someone from 0.8 to 0.9.

Health scientists and policy makers have recently started to develop various preference elicitation techniques in an effort to calculate the required QALY weightings. Various psychological studies suggest that because of cognitive limitations in humans, the techniques do not always elicit responses that satisfy the two requirements. With the *rating scale* approach, for example, individuals are asked to rank health outcomes from

---

[4] The utility concept as used by most economists and philosophers in the nineteenth and twentieth centuries is theoretically distinct from the utility used in the QALY methodology. The former describes decisions where goods are received with certainty, whereas the latter does so for probabilistic outcomes under uncertainty. Decision theory under uncertainty aspires to the more rigid requirements as stipulated by the so-called von Neumann–Morgenstern utility theory (von Neumann and Morgenstern 1947), whereas the conventional philosophical/economic understanding sees a utility merely as the satisfaction of preferences. For our discussion this is no relevant distinction, however: NM utilities cover decision-making theory at the individual level only and cannot be used to compare welfare between individuals (Zeckhauser and Schaefer 1975, 41; Drummond et al. 1997, 150).

most preferred to least preferred and to place them on a scale such that the intervals between placements correspond to the differences in preference as perceived by the individual. However, psychologists have challenged the meaningfulness of the cardinal statements thus produced by respondents. As Bleichrodt and Johannesson (1997) argue, subjective impressions cannot be discriminated equally at each level of a scale. Individuals will attempt to use categories equally often and spread their responses when cases are actually close together (the "spacing out" bias), or they compress them when the underlying attributes are actually far apart (the "end-of-scale" bias).

*The standard gamble*, as a second method, induces the individual to choose between two alternatives: (*a*) no treatment at all which will result in a specified state of ill health, or (*b*) treatment that could result in either death or illness-free health, each with a probability of p and 1−p respectively. The probability is then varied until the respondent is indifferent between the two alternatives, thus producing the preference score sought after. Tversky, Slovic, and Kahneman (1990), however, have shown through various laboratory experiments that individuals have the tendency to reverse previously revealed preferences. They might use inappropriate psychological representations and simplifying heuristics that misdirect their decisions. Psychologists have attributed this phenomenon to the serial way by which individuals process information: they use an anchoring technique for the first piece of information and then gradually adjust their decision making with each additional piece of information they obtain.

Finally, the *time trade-off* presents individuals with a choice of living for a defined amount of time in perfect health or a variable amount of time in an alternative state that is less desirable. The time is varied until the respondent is indifferent between the two alternatives. The method's application, however, has found patients to prefer, for example, immediate death to being in a state of mild dysfunction for three months. This suggests that individuals misunderstand the nature of the trade-off, reducing the meaningfulness of the results on a utility scale that ranges between 0 and 1.

Patients' responses as well as the metric underlying their measurement cannot, then, be standardized across individuals. Epistemological difficulties remain when adding up or comparing subjective levels of satisfaction that the consumption of goods gives to individuals (Nord 1999). The preference elicitation techniques used with the QALY approach encounter too many teething problems that prevent policy makers from uncovering stable and consistent preferences revealing true commensurate valuations. Notably, the failure to make attributes of well-being commensurate does not mean that comparisons are futile exercises. Incommensurability does not deny the possibility of comparisons of course. Neither does it need to be inconsistent with fundamental assumptions in decision theory: reason-guided choice is still possible even without commensurability, as the data underlying QALYs are still useful to make more simple comparisons through ordinal rankings (Sunstein 1997, 39). Yet, they lack the precision that is required to impute them into economic methodologies such as CBA.

More exchange between psychologists, economists, and philosophers seems necessary. For the case of health care in the UK, for example, the National Center for Research Methodology (NCRM) and the National Institute for Clinical Excellence (NICE) have recently commissioned joint research projects with the aim of determining the societal value of a QALY.[5] This project addresses, among other issues, the conceptual link between a QALY and an individual's WTP as well as the relative value of health gains to different beneficiaries, according to personal attributes such as age, education, and geography. These initiatives could shed more light on the problem at hand. Until solutions are developed from those (and other) findings, however, the second requirement on sum ranking that Sen specified for utilitarian theory remains unsatisfied.

To be sure, as Kymlicka (2001, 18) rightly reminds us, in daily life practical reasoning constantly requires us to make decisions about how to balance different kinds of goods that are incommensurable, by simply judging what is better or worse overall. While we might go along with his assessment for the individual decisions we make in our personal lives, we believe it is an ill-advised position to take for the analysis of public policy. The economic evaluation techniques used to arrive at policy decisions differ in their level of complexity from the balancing acts between the comparatively few personal values that inform our individual choices. We can revisit and reassess the ordinal rankings we have made in a personal choice situation at any given time. Economic evaluation techniques, by contrast, balance many more preferences and values that are held by markedly more individuals and eventually produce only one (usually quantitative) recommendation. From that moment on, they conceal the complex weighing process between the different cardinal attributes that had been imputed beforehand.

Admittedly, for evaluation techniques to work the imputed preferences and values need to be made explicit in the first place, which is an approach preferable to making policy choices on the basis of decision makers' implicit (and therefore concealed) assumptions and preferences. Yet, once all of the relevant goods are aligned along a single metric, they are no longer visible, or perhaps become invisible (Sunstein 1997, 50). People can no longer make judgements based on qualitative differences. Hence, if we want the policy recommendation to be meaningful and accurate we need to ensure that the numerical values imputed into the analysis at the outset have been compared and aggregated accurately. This demonstrably does not always hold true, in which case the policy choice needs to be made through alternative measures. Some of these we will present in Section 6 below.

## 5. THE INTRINSIC VALUE PROBLEM

At the end of Section 3 we introduced the concepts of "existence value," "exchange value," and "use value" to our discussion. We defined existence value as a value that a good can have independent of the effects it produces for human well-being, such as the survival of species. We also contended that exchange value, as the metric that is

---

[5] See www.publichealth.bham.ac.uk/nccrm/publications.htm for publication of future research results.

imputed into economic evaluations, bears no necessary connection to the value in use that produces the benefit to individuals and thus augments human well-being.

There is a crucial link between these three concepts that merits further exploration: economic evaluations impose a unitary standard (usually money) on the valuation and comparison of goods and thus subordinate both existence value and use value to the new standard of exchange value. While we have already drawn out some aspects of this relationship for *objects* (i.e. environmental goods in Section 3 and health care services in Section 4), we will in this section, develop that point in more detail for *subjects*. We will argue that the intrinsic value of human beings (as the equivalent to the existence value of objects) is crowded out by economic evaluations.

To understand why, let us assume that in some distant future, the problem of valuation and aggregation expounded earlier will have been solved and that it is therefore possible to evaluate policy programs according to the extent to which they maximize benefits to society. Now consider the following simplified case borrowed from Harris (1975): a hospital has admitted four patients who are all bound to die if no suitable organ donor is soon to be found. The next morning, the postman enters the building to deliver his daily load of letters and parcels. From previous conversations the nurse recalls that he would be a suitable donor for all four patients. As a possible route of action she could now kill him, harvest his organs, and thus enable the four patients to survive. If numbers count and we conduct a simple CBA we would have to conclude that sacrificing the postman is the superior alternative: four lives are more valuable than one and the highest aggregate level of welfare is achieved if the postman dies and the four patients live.

Most of us would consider this option as objectionable of course. In most contexts it strikes us intuitively as unfair if a few may be sacrificed for the benefit of the greater good of the many. Yet, given the economic rationale of benefit maximization, it is justifiable, if not mandatory, to proceed that way. The problem we encounter here is caused by the formally equal way by which these evaluations treat human beings: every individual counts as one and can thus be added up to, or traded against somebody else. This observation is akin to the phenomenon of "commodification" originally developed by Karl Marx (1964, 96–105). In capitalist societies, so Marx argued, the mode of production comes under private ownership, commodity production proliferates, and labor division becomes increasingly fragmented. Forced to sell their labor power to survive, workers themselves become akin to a commodity and are reduced from the status of a qualitative individual to mere exchange value in the form of labor. Where once the goal of production was the simple satisfaction of needs, and exchange was driven through the need for the other's use value, capitalism eliminates individual exchange. It subordinates use value to exchange value and establishes exchange value as an independent logic. In the extreme but quite common form of trading stocks, for example, there is no longer a physical referent at all: money is made out of money with no apparent connection to the world of real commodities.

The reduction of human beings to a number—either expressed as a simple unit as in the organ donor case or as a monetary WTP value attached to their preferences—

assumes equivalence between attributes of persons and thus dissolves their qualitative differences into the identity of a single quantitative metric. Such a metric might in general solve the problem of aggregation (how to compare levels of well-being), and the monetary metric as exchange value in particular might solve the problem of exchange (how to trade qualitatively unique goods in equal quantitative ratios), but it transforms subjects into abstract entities that are deprived of their unique characteristics.

One such characteristic is that each individual has intrinsic value: we have an interest in our own continued existence and cannot be used solely as a means for assisting other individuals as ends in themselves. Intrinsic values are non-relational: they are not defined relative to some other human being, species, or object, nor to the benefit it might provide to them. My intrinsic value is the value I have in and of myself, beyond any value I might have as a means to further ends. I am therefore to be respected as a rights bearer proper, as an end in myself. Rights are principles that assign claims or entitlements to someone against someone, and are usually interpreted as "trumping" consequential claims made in the name of welfare (Dworkin 1977). That means that I should never be treated in certain ways, even if the calculation of aggregated individual well-being shows that the action which has these effects would be the most beneficial one overall.

Reducing individuals to a monetary metric might change the way we perceive their value to us. Margaret Jane Radin (1996) illustrates the implications for the trade in "commodities" such as sex, children, and body parts and observes that there are not only willing buyers for such commodities but some desperately poor people are willing sellers, too. To her, this reflects a persistent dilemma in liberal societies: freedom of choice is valued but at the same time, choices ought to be restricted to protect the integrity of what it means to be a person. She views this tension as primarily the result of underlying social and economic inequalities, which need not reflect an irreconcilable conflict in the premises of liberal democracy but a mere setting of the right priorities in distributive policy choices.

Political philosophy has therefore sought to embed intrinsic value and individual rights into some concept of justice, such as a (neo-)Kantian imperative to treat others fairly or Locke's view that people have the right to be protected against the breaches of their rights by the actions of others. Even utilitarians like Mill have endorsed rights and intrinsic values as a possible strategy to maximize utility. Such a position is known as rule utilitarianism, in contrast to act utilitarianism which is the view Bentham originally suggested. It postulates that the principle of utility can yield a notion of "rights" if we appreciate the way a person's rights are defined by rules regarding the treatment of human beings that are by and large utility maximizing.

This is no place to develop the pros and cons of any of these concepts. It is important to note, however, that while constraining economic evaluations through intrinsic values and individual rights can be attractive to a great variety of tradition-ally juxtaposed theories of morality, the resulting consensus in political philosophy cannot be transferred easily to public policy formation or economic evaluation techniques. This follows because, to follow Ruth Chang's (1997, 5–23) helpful distinction, intrinsic values give rise to the problem of ordinal *incomparability*.

The reader might recall from Section 4 that we concluded that attributes of well-being are incommensurable across lives, i.e. that they cannot be compared cardinally for the purpose of aggregation, but that at least ordinal comparisons are available as a basis for rational choice. We now encounter the more severe case where the relevant imputations for the analysis are not even comparable in that latter sense.

This follows because the practical role of intrinsic values is neither to prescribe an end to be maximized nor to prescribe an attitude toward an aggregate. As such there are multiple ways in which we can sharpen our understanding of a person's intrinsic value, such as by love, respect, honor, or admiration. In some cases one understanding might be privileged while in another it isn't. This vagueness disallows for any strand of the usual trichotomy of comparison ("better than," "worse than," "equally good as") to hold, which applies to comparisons between intrinsic values themselves as much as between them and other quantifiable values.

While incomparability might be less of a problem for clear-cut cases such as the life-or-death choices to be made in the organ transplant scenario mentioned earlier, other policy decisions are more clearly subject to this limitation. Health care, to stay in the same policy domain, does not only suffer from a lack of organs, for example. Hospital beds, technical equipment, and medical personnel, too, are scarce resources that can be distributed among patients in different ways. Economic evaluations would recommend that these should be used less intensively for the care of acute or incurable patients as they require far more of them than does the care of convalescing patients. Similarly, applying the QALY approach explicated in Section 4 to the optional treatment of either an elderly person or a young child would result in the preference to be given to the latter, because QALY scores are particularly high for those who still have many years to live and therefore have a greater "capacity to benefit." Economic evaluations applied in an unconstrained way would therefore lead to the marginalization of the incurable, chronically ill, or elderly. They would override individuals' intrinsic value in terms of their dignity and possibly, their right to live.

To be sure, in some contexts an intelligible response that bypasses the intrinsic value problem is possible. The application of distributional weights, for example, can go a long way to ensure an equitable distribution of scarce resources that does not neglect groups who are in need (Layard and Walters 2001). However, while the existence of a tangible criterion to define disadvantage allows us to identify some such groups—e.g. income levels as an indicator that demarcates the needy poor from the non-needy rich—other groups which we deem worthy of special consideration, and would ideally want to apply appropriate distributional weights to, are less lucidly identified. How, for example, should we weigh the feelings of love, respect, honor, or admiration by which we grant a person her intrinsic value? How do we gauge the underlying psychological processes? Our choice between these feelings does not proceed on some measurable comparison but on the more intangible principle of obligation.

Intrinsic values cannot be ranked ordinally in a meaningful way then. There is no way to incorporate them into any type of evaluation. The policy maker is thus faced with a situation in which he can choose to either (1) ignore the intrinsic value, or (2) admit it as a constraint and reject the policy recommendation under review.

The former will then judge the recommendation to be permissible whereas on the latter it is impermissible. Judging the policy as impermissible, in turn, implies that any benefits which would result from rights-incompatible actions must be excluded from the action decision altogether. It places limits on what would otherwise be the implication of aggregative economic evaluations and restricts governmental action.

This is, of course, not a satisfying conclusion to arrive at because our following option 2 puts the whole exercise of economic evaluation into question in the first place while under option 1 intrinsic values are crowded out and "forgotten" by the imperative of identifying, collecting, measuring, and aggregating other values that *are* comparable.

Two alternative and somewhat juxtaposed approaches to the dilemma seem to be on offer both of which, however, require further refinement and specification if they are to provide meaningful solutions. There is, first, the suggestion made by Shrader-Frechette (1991, ch. 11) that each group affected by a proposed policy program should conduct their own economic evaluation as an intermediate stage of a more extensive process of participative justice. This approach would not only allow for a separate assessment of intrinsic values and a weighing of their merits. It would also reflect different methodological, ethical, and social assumptions and thus portray all sides of a given story. The end result would then be likely to be an evaluation with a multidimensional array of benefits and costs. Alternatively, we might want to embrace the work begun by Scanlon (1991) on the compatibility of the ethical and economic conception of value that individuals attach to human well-being. Instead of requiring various stakeholder groups to carry out multiple evaluations that are later democratically deliberated upon, Scanlon suggests a single common index, a shared conception between philosophers and economists of things good and bad in life. These would not only consist of exchangeable goods but could also refer to other levels of development and states of consciousness. If developed further, as suggested by Kopp (1993), to clarify *who* should determine which goods and conditions for a good life make it onto that index, this line of thought could indeed result in a more complete economic theory.

# 6. ALTERNATIVE APPROACHES

In each of the previous three sections we have outlined an issue area that decision makers need to be aware of when devising public policy that is based on economic evaluations such as CBA. That awareness is not equally called for in all policy domains, as policy decisions in some domains are less vulnerable to our criticisms than in others. It remains up to the judgement of the reader to assess the relevance of the three issue areas and possibly, conclude that CBA can be applied unequivocally to help solve a given policy problem. When decisions have to be made in domains such as those referred to in this chapter, however, policy makers are advised to consider other methodological approaches that bypass the pitfalls identified. To that end we briefly offer below two alternative approaches. They are not fundamentally new evaluation techniques but are best seen as less stringent variants of CBA and should therefore be easily comprehensible.

In Section 3 we saw that not all costs and benefits that enter economic evaluations can be measured in monetary terms, as some valuation techniques rest on contestable assumptions regarding the quantification of economic value. As a possible way out of this impasse, the policy maker could replace CBA with a similar technique, that of cost utility analysis (CUA). The difference is that, while CBA converts benefits into a monetary metric as a common unit, CUA expresses benefits in terms of the utility they provide to the individual—such as QALYs in the case of health care. It is a non-monetary concept for estimating the value to society of improvements in a status of well-being and thus sidesteps the problem of monetary conversion.

Its merits as a non-monetary economic evaluation technique notwithstanding, CUA remains, just as CBA is, vulnerable to the criticisms we raised in Sections 3 and 4: calculating utility ratings by quizzing individuals for their preferences of well-being is contestable because these preferences might be non-authentic, malformed, strategically motivated, or simply uninformed. And individuals differ—across lives and across stages of their own life—in how they value particular states of well-being. Any attempt to aggregate such incommensurable attributes into a single standard brings about methodological as well as ethical issues.

To cater to these objections, cost effectiveness analysis, or CEA recommends itself as yet another evaluation technique. Both CBA/CUA as well as CEA are formal methods for comparing the benefits and costs of a policy program. The difference is that, while CBA and CUA convert these benefits into monetary value and utility respectively as a common unit, CEA expresses benefits as such, i.e. in terms of a natural unit as some standard of outcome. In the case of health care such an outcome could, for example, constitute the incremental reduction in mortality rate or the increase in the number of immunizations delivered, rather than the monetary value or utility that CBA/CUA would calculate for each of these effects. In the case of environmental regulation an outcome could, for example, constitute the level of air quality as measured by the ambient ozone level, rather than the economic value or utility it provides to humanity. CEA thus sidesteps the problem of monetary conversion as found in CBA *and* the problem of preference satisfaction and utility aggregation as found in CUA.[6]

The detour comes at a price, however, because CEA is a much less powerful tool than CBA or CUA. It can only assess alternative policies where costs relate to a single common effect as measured on a natural scale (such as mortality rate) which may differ in magnitude among the policy options evaluated. It can then be used to choose among those options in terms of their effectiveness-to-cost ratio. Conversely, if the budget is predetermined, that is the costs are "fixed," it can again, only be used to compare various policy options as to their rate of attaining that non-quantified

---

[6] Note that some authors and literatures treat CUA as a particular case of CEA, or CEA and CUA as particular cases of CBA. The three techniques may therefore appear under different labels.

goal, such as decreasing mortality. What it cannot do is to give an indication *how much* should be spent to achieve a policy outcome. Neither can CEA give guidance whether a policy intervention is worth doing at all, for it tacitly assumes that the objective has been deemed worth meeting beforehand. It therefore does not specify how far a program's ratio of effects to costs can fall before it is no longer worth doing. To determine whether resources have been allocated in such a way that benefits to society have been maximized is not possible with CEA.

What neither CBA, CUA, nor CEA can solve, however, is the intrinsic value problem that we addressed in Section 5. Intrinsic values are not merely not commensurable, they are more fundamentally, also not comparable with other benefits and costs. All too often, they are therefore "forgotten" in economic evaluations although they should be allowed to restrict the projects that government may permissibly carry out. In policy practice, such side constraints can be feasibly implemented by giving a veto power to the individuals impacted by the proposed policy. It does not follow, of course, that such rights automatically override any possible net benefits of a proposed policy, but neither are they morally irrelevant.

# 7. CONCLUSION

In concluding, economic tools are very general techniques that have very stringent information requirements not all of which can always be met. They can therefore not function as a fundamental standard of choice among policy options. This is not a reason to reject economic evaluations per se as they do provide us with information that is morally relevant and thus possibly uncovers hitherto concealed judgements by policy makers eager to cater to special interests. It is, we have argued, both unethical and irrational in general to ignore the cost and benefits of a pending policy decision. Yet, it is a reason to acknowledge that economic evaluations should be understood as an input into, rather than a substitute for political deliberation and judgement (Sunstein 2002). Not all situations call on us to maximize value. Some simply compel us to respect it. Economic evaluations should be seen as a useful heuristic to raise red flags about policy proposals and identify the economic factors involved. Whether economic factors are, in fact, the dominant concern at all in a given situation is a judgement that will have to remain within the realm of responsibility of the policy maker.

## REFERENCES

ADLER, M. D., and POSNER, E. A. (eds.) 2001. *Cost Benefit Analysis: Legal, Economic, and Philosophical Perspectives.* Chicago: University of Chicago Press.

ARROW, K. J. 1963. Uncertainty and the welfare economics of medical care. *American Economic Review,* 53(5): 941–73.

—— SOLOW, R., LEARNER, E., PORTNEY, P., and SCHUMAN, H. 1992. *Report of the NOAA Panel on Contingent Valuation*. Washington, DC: National Oceanic and Atmospheric Administration.

BENTHAM, J. 1970. *An Introduction to the Principles of Morals and Legislation*, ed. J. Burns and H. L. A. Hart. London: Athlone Press.

BLEICHRODT, H., and JOHANNESSON, M. 1997. An experimental test of the theoretical foundation for rating scale valuations. *Medical Decision Making*, 17(2): 208–17.

BOSSERT, W. 1991. On intra- and inter-personal utility comparisons. *Social Choice and Welfare*, 8: 207–20.

CHANG, R. (ed.) 1997. *Incommensurability, Incomparability, and Practical Reason*. Cambridge, Mass.: Harvard University Press.

COSTANZA, R., et al. 1997. The value of the world's ecosystem services and natural capital. *Nature*, 387: 253–61.

COUDOUEL, A., and HENTSCHEL, J. 2000. *Poverty Data and Measurement*. Washington, DC: World Bank; available at: www.worldbank.org/poverty/strategies.

DIAMOND, P. A., and HAUSMAN, J. 1993. On contingent valuation measurement of non-use values. Pp. 170–90 in *Contingent Valuation: A Critical Assessment*, ed. J. Hausman. New York: North Holland.

DRUMMOND, M. F., BRIEN, B., STODDART, G. L., and TORRANCE, G. W. 1997. *Methods for the Economic Evaluation of Health Care Programmes*, 2nd edn. Oxford: Oxford University Press.

DWORKIN, R. 1977. *Taking Rights Seriously*. Cambridge, Mass.: Harvard University Press.

ELSTER, J. 1983. *Sour Grapes*. Cambridge: Cambridge University Press.

—— and ROEMER, J. (eds.) 1991. *Interpersonal Comparisons of Well-Being*. Cambridge: Cambridge University Press.

GLOVER, J. (ed.) 1990. *Utilitarianism and its Critics*. New York: Macmillan.

GRAMSCI, A. 1971. *Selections from the Prison Notebooks of Antonio Gramsci*, ed. Q. Hoare and G. N. Smith. New York: International.

HANLEY, N., and SPASH, C. 1993. *Cost–Benefit Analysis and the Environment*. Aldershot: Edward Elgar.

HARDIN, R. 1982. *Collective Action*. Baltimore: Johns Hopkins University Press.

HARRIS, J. 1975. The survival lottery. *Philosophy*, 50: 81–7.

HAYEK, F. 1975. *Collectivist Economic Planning: Critical Studies on the Possibilities of Socialism*. London: Routledge.

HENDERSON, H. 1996. Fighting economism. *Futures*, 28: 580–4.

HM TREASURY 1997. *Appraisal and Evaluation in Central Government: Treasury Guidance*. London: HMSO.

HOLLAND, A. 1995. Cost–benefit analysis: a philosopher's view. Pp. 21–38 in *Environmental Valuation: New Perspectives*, ed. K. G. Willis and J. T. Corkindale. Wallingford: CAB.

KAHNEMAN, D. 2003. A psychological perspective on economics. *American Economic Review*, 93: 162–8.

KNEESE, A. 1984. *Measuring the Benefits of Clean Air and Water*. Washington, DC: Resources for the Future.

KOPP, R. 1993. Environmental economics: not dead but thriving. *Resources*, 111: 7–12.

—— KRUPNIK, A. J., and TOMAN, M. 1997. *Cost–Benefit Analysis and Regulatory Reform: An Assessment of the Science and the Art*. Discussion Paper 97–19. Washington, DC: Resources for the Future.

KORNAI, J. 1986. The soft budget constraint. *Kyklos*, 39: 3–30.

KRUTILLA, J. 1967. Conservation reconsidered. *American Economic Review*, 57(5): 777–86.

KYMLICKA, W. 2001. *Contemporary Political Philosophy: An Introduction*. Oxford: Oxford University Press.

LAYARD, R., and GLAISTER, S. (eds.) 2001. *Cost–Benefit Analysis*, 2nd edn. Cambridge: Cambridge University Press.

—— and WALTERS, A. A. 2001. Income distribution. In Layard and Glaister 2001, 179–98.

LE GRAND, J. 1991. *Equity and Choice*. London: HarperCollins.

LEIBENSTEIN, H. 1966. Allocative efficiency vs. "X-efficiency." *American Economic Review*, 56: 392–415.

LENIN, V. I. 1964. A caricature of Marxism and imperialist economism. Pp. 28–76 in V. I. Lenin, *Collected Works*, vol. xxiii, 5th edn. Moscow: Progress.

LIPSEY, R. G., and CHRYSTAL, K. A. 1999. *Principles of Economics*, 9th edn. Oxford: Oxford University Press.

McLELLAN, D. 2000. *Karl Marx: Selected Writings*. Oxford: Oxford University Press.

MARX, K. 1964. *Economic and Philosophic Manuscripts*. New York: International.

MISHAN, E. J. 1972. *Cost–Benefit Analysis*. New York: Praeger.

MOONEY, G. 1992. *Economics, Medicine, and Health Care*. London: Harvester Wheatsheaf.

MURRAY, C. J. 1996. Rethinking DALYs. Pp. 1–98 in *The Global Burden of Disease*, ed. C. J. Murray and A. D. Lopez. Cambridge, Mass.: Harvard School of Public Health.

VON NEUMANN, J., and MORGENSTERN, O. 1947. *Theories of Games and Economic Behavior*. Princeton, NJ: Princeton University Press.

NORD, E. 1999. *Cost Value Analysis in Health Care: Making Sense of QALYs*. Cambridge: Cambridge University Press.

OKUN, A. 1975. *Equality and Efficiency: The Big Trade Off*. Washington, DC: Brookings Institution.

PEARCE, D. 1993. *Economic Values and the Natural World*. London: Earthscan.

PRESIDENTIAL/CONGRESSIONAL COMMISSION ON RISK ASSESSMENT AND RISK MANAGEMENT (PCCRA) 1997. *Framework for Environmental Health Risk Management*, 2 vols. Washington, DC: PCCRA.

RADIN, M. J. 1996. *Contested Commodities: The Trouble with the Trade in Sex, Children, and Body Parts*. Cambridge, Mass.: Harvard University Press.

RHOADS, S. E. 1999. *The Economist's View of the World*. Cambridge: Cambridge University Press.

RICHARDSON, H. S. 2001. The stupidity of the cost–benefit standard. In Adler and Posner 2001, 135–68.

ROBBINS, L. 1932. *The Nature and Significance of Economic Science*. London: Macmillan.

SAGOFF, M. 1988. *The Economy of the Earth*. Cambridge: Cambridge University Press.

SAMUELSON, P. A. 1948. *Foundations of Economic Analysis*. Cambridge, Mass.: Harvard University Press.

SCANLON, M. 1991. The moral basis of interpersonal comparison. In Elster and Roemer 1991, 17–44.

SEN, A. 1987. *On Ethics and Economics.*. Oxford: Basil Blackwell.

SHRADER-FRECHETTE, K. 1991. *Risk and Rationality: Philosophical Foundations for Populist Reforms*. Berkeley: University of California Press.

SMITH, A. 1979. *The Wealth of Nations: Books I–III*. London: Penguin.

SMITH, V. (ed.) 1984. *Environmental Policy under Reagan's Executive Order: The Role of Benefit–Cost Analysis*. Chapel Hill: University of North Carolina Press.

SUNSTEIN, C. 1997. Incommensurability and kinds of valuation: some applications in law. Pp. 34–54 in *Incommensurability, Incomparability, and Practical Reason*, ed. R. Chang. Cambridge, Mass.: Harvard University Press.

—— 2002. *Risk and Reason: Safety, Law, and the Environment*. Cambridge: Cambridge University Press.

TORRANCE, G., THOMAS, W. H., and SACKETT, D. L. 1972. A utility maximization model for evaluation of health care programmes. *Health Services Research*, 7: 118–33.

TURNER, R. K., PEARCE, D., and BATEMAN, I. 1994. *Environmental Economics*. Hemel Hempstead: Harvester Wheatsheaf.

TVERSKY, A., SLOVIC, P., and KAHNEMAN, D. 1990. The causes of preference reversals. *American Economic Review*, 80(1): 205–18.

WOODS, N. 2000. Order, globalization, and inequality in world politics. Pp. 8–35 in *Inequality, Globalization, and World Politics*, ed. A. Hurrell and N. Woods. Oxford: Oxford University Press.

WORLD HEALTH ORGANIZATION (WHO). 2000. *The World Health Report 2000: Health Systems: Improving Performance*. Geneva: World Health Organization.

ZECKHAUSER, R., and SCHAEFER, E. 1968. Public policy and normative economic theory. Pp. 27–102 in *The Study of Policy Formation*, ed. R. A. Bauer and K. J. Gergen. New York: Free Press.

—— and SHEPHARD, D. 1976. Where now for saving lives? *Law and Contemporary Problems*, 40 (4): 5–45.

# CHAPTER 38

## POLICY MODELING

### NETA C. CRAWFORD

[A] "decision" is only a part of a decisional process that began long before the specific decision was made.... The momentary act of decision, on which so much of the literature of "decision-making" focuses, may be little more than *pro forma*.   (Green 1966, 205)

Systems analysis takes a complex problem and sorts out the tangle of significant factors so that each can be studied by the method most appropriate to it. Questions of fact can be tested against the available factual evidence; logical propositions can be tested logically; matters of value and uncertainty can be exposed so that decision makers can know exactly where to apply their judgment.   (Enthoven and Smith 1971 61)

From the days when generals used miniature battlefields and maps to analyze, plan, and predict the outcome of battles, to the contemporary use of computer simulations and war gaming, modeling has played a crucial part in the equipment, planning, and conduct of war. Policy modeling is intended to help decision makers and observers make "rational" judgements about complex and technical public policy questions. It uses a variety of techniques ranging from scenarios and simulations to operations research and game theory, but all policy modeling relies on similar inputs: more or less hard data derived from experience or experiments, assumptions about unknown variables, and rules of thumb or formulas for handling data. Climate modelers use a combination of real-world measurement, assumptions about the growth and effects of certain "greenhouse" gases, and computer simulation to predict the effects of human behavior on the climate. Those who prepare for conventional war can rely on thousands of years of experience; modeling nuclear war is necessarily more abstract.

Responding to the charge that the US military was ill prepared for war in Iraq, US Secretary of Defense Donald Rumsfeld said, "As you know, you go to war with the Army you have. They're not the Army you might want or wish to have at a later time"

(Ricks 2004: A1). In other times, the USA has been more than well prepared for "overkill;" at the end of the cold war in 1989, the United States deployed a "triad" of 14,530 strategic nuclear weapons on land-based intercontinental ballistic missiles (ICBMs),[1] submarine-launched ballistic missiles (SLBMs),[2] and long-range bombers.[3] The USA also had tens of thousands of medium-range (theater) and short-range (tactical) nuclear weapons for use in "less than all-out nuclear war" scenarios. From 1940 to 1995 the USA spent over $4 trillion in 1995 dollars making nuclear weapons and preparing for nuclear war (Schwartz 1995). How did the United States come to have these particular weapons, and in numbers that were well in excess of the ability to destroy the other side, the Soviet Union, as a functioning society? How did US cold war nuclear planners answer the question of "how much is enough?"

The reason for the exact number, composition, and quality of United States nuclear weapons during the cold war was overdetermined and could be explained by several theories.[4] But one often overlooked factor was the formal logic of nuclear discourse—known in the nuclear weapons planning community as "operations research" or "systems analysis."[5] Although its methods are not widely known and understood, the practice and assumptions of nuclear systems analysis helped determine the size and capabilities of the US nuclear weapons arsenal. The Pentagon's Systems Analysis Office established in 1961 (renamed Program Analysis and Evaluation in 1973), was just one site of nuclear operations research and systems analysis. Operations research and systems analysis were widely practiced and became

---

[1] On Minuteman II, Minuteman III, and MX (Peacekeeper) missiles.

[2] On Poseidon C-3 and Trident C-4 missiles.

[3] On B-52 and B-1B bombers, which carried both gravity bombs and in some cases, air-launched cruise missiles (ALCM).

[4] On nuclear weapons procurement and the arms race see Brown 1994; Evangelista 1988; Greenwood 1975; Sapolsky 1972; Spinardi 1990; Francis 1995. Rational planning by one state could lead to "action–reaction" phenomena of quantitative and/or qualitative arms racing driven by security dilemma dynamics. "Action–reaction phenomena, stimulated in most cases by uncertainty about an adversary's intentions and capabilities, characterizes the dynamics of the arms race" (Rathjens 1969, 42). Inter-service rivalry among branches of the US military led to a duplication of effort as each service allocated nuclear weapons for targets that had also been identified as targets by other services. Organizational interests within services also led to what critics called "bootstrapping," where "growth of the stockpile was linked to expansion of the target lists, and both were used to justify expansion of SAC [Strategic Air Command]" (Rosenberg 1986, 42). Domestic politics and economics also helped to determine whether or not a nuclear weapons system was purchased: Congressional support sometimes depended more on the clout of a particular Congressperson whose district or state made the weapon than on whether it could efficiently perform its mission. For example, Senator Alan Cranston's (D-CA) support of the B-1 strategic nuclear bomber (manufactured in California) grew during the early 1980s with his presidential aspirations. A "technological imperative" to make nuclear weapons more complex and advanced may also have affected the growth of the arsenal (e.g. Thee 1986; Zuckerman 1983).

[5] "Operations research uses mathematical models to plan real systems that either function optimally or meet some defined performance criterion.... Systems analysis emphasizes a rigorous statement of the goals of the project and a listing of different policies and their consequences. It can handle broader messier problems than operations research, and has often helped in the design and procurement of weapons systems" (O'Neill 1993, 2567–8).

embedded in organizational routines and the work of individual analysts within government and non-government policy organizations.[6] To the extent that the Soviets responded to US weapons developments, systems analysis helped determine the character of the Soviet arsenal as well.[7] Though game theory was used, operations research, or operations research supplemented by game theory, was one of the primary tools, if not the primary technique for nuclear policy modeling.[8] Moreover, operations research and nuclear systems analysis are still used in the post-cold war era by policy analysts inside and outside government (see Wilkening 1994; Larson and Kent 1994; Cimbala 1995; Batcher 2004). According to one analyst who worked in the Pentagon's office from 1969, with the end of the cold war, the techniques of operations research and systems analysis and their importance in the policy process "haven't changed" although because the world has changed, "nuclear things are less important and there is more emphasis on general purpose conventional forces," and counter-terrorism (Yengling 1997). Indeed systems analysis may return to prominence if all the elements of the Bush administration Nuclear Posture Review are implemented.[9] Hence, it is still vital to understand how systems analysis works.

The specific practices of nuclear systems analysis vary depending on the problem at hand. These modeling techniques can be used to estimate the effects of nuclear weapons on particular targets, to estimate the cost of a specific weapons system over time, to assess the cost effectiveness of targeting strategies, to compare the effectiveness of different weapons, to decide how many of which weapons systems to build, to determine the likely number of casualties resulting from a nuclear war, to assess the effectiveness of civilian defense, and to decide how to use nuclear forces in the event of war. The analysis itself can be done with relatively simple formulas on "the back of an envelope," using spreadsheets, or using fairly complex classified or unclassified versions of computer codes such as FAS/CIVIC (Fallout Assessment System/ Civilian Vulnerability Indicator Code) and PDCALC (Batcher 2004; Scouras and Nissen 1994).

Operations research and systems analysis techniques are thus knowledge-making processes that underpinned, rationalized, and to a surprising degree determined the

---

[6] Other institutions and individuals, such as air force Strategic Air Command (SAC), the Congressional Budget Office, analysts at universities, the Brookings Institution, the RAND Corporation, and other private think tanks, used nuclear modeling.

[7] The Soviet Union had 12,403 strategic nuclear warheads, distributed between missiles and aircraft. Totals, using SALT II counting rules, are from IISS 1989, 212. After the cold war, the United States found out that it had underestimated the total number of Soviet nuclear weapons (Broad 1993).

[8] As O'Neill suggests, "One myth about game models and deterrence is worth refuting in detail. It is that in the late 1940s and 1950s thinking on nuclear strategy was molded by game theory. By the end of the Cold War this claim was so widely believed that no evidence was needed to support it.... In fact, with a couple of exceptions, substantial game modeling of international strategy started only in the later 1960s, after the tenets of nuclear strategy had already developed" (1994, 1010–11).

[9] Including deployment of an anti-ballistic missile system; the introduction of "capabilities-based" and "adaptive planning" to allow for limited nuclear strikes; the upgrading of its nuclear weapons (DOD 2002; Woolf 2002).

choice of United States strategic nuclear weapons after 1961. The equations and procedures of systems analysis exemplify instrumental beliefs (causal understandings of how nuclear weapons and nuclear strategy work) and what Eden (2004) calls "organizational frames"—ways of understanding the world. The strategists who use systems analysis constitute an epistemic community of government and private nuclear analysts, with systems analysis constituting a core element of the cultural practices of that community. Being able to use systems analysis, or at least under-standing its formal logic is one of the criteria for membership in this epistemic community understood as "a network of professionals with recognized expertise and competence in a particular domain and authoritative claim to policy relevant knowledge within that domain or issue area." Epistemic communities have "(1) a shared set of normative and principled beliefs... (2) shared causal beliefs... (3) shared notions of validity... (4) a common policy enterprise" (Haas 1992, 3; also see Adler 1992). This epistemic community, above all, sought ways to deal rationally with uncertainty in the scientific-technical-political context created by the develop-ment and deployment of nuclear weapons. Policy modeling in the form of systems analysis became a taken-for-granted part of the Pentagon's organizational culture. Yet as Litfin suggests, "Epistemic community approaches downplay... the ways in which scientific information simply rationalizes or reinforces existing political conflicts" (1994, 12). In other words, scientists have politics too and in any case, their analysis may not be used by neutral observers.

The point of using operations research and systems analysis was and is to make the decision-making process more "rational." The models and the math are supposed to abstract from nuclear reality and to predict the unknowns of nuclear war in order better to represent and understand it. The conclusions might ultimately be distorted in the policy process, but the numbers themselves should be neutral and hard. On the one hand, in some respects the policy modelers failed *by their own criteria* to do an adequate job. Indeed, others have criticized poor applications of nuclear systems analysis techniques and some of those criticisms are discussed below.[10] The logical conclusion of those critiques is to urge more rigorous specification and application of mathematical models.[11] Yet the aim here is not so much a critique of shoddy practices, the provision of remedies, or alternatives, as it is to understand some of the consequences of using this sort of modeling. An examination of nuclear discourse at its most formal, abstract level illustrates unexpected and even frighten-ing aspects and consequences of policy modeling—whether or not the modeling is well executed.

As much as policy modelers were analyzing, describing, or indeed sometimes simply rationalizing the decisions actors wanted to take for other reasons, systems

[10] See, for examples, Green 1966, 15–93; Brewer and Shubik 1979; Postol 1987; Salman, Sullivan, and Van Evera 1989.

[11] Davis and Schilling (1973) is one of the best open source discussions of the analytical techniques of systems analysis, including the formulas. They critique the application of systems analytical techniques, while accepting the logic of systems analytical practices.

analysts also made the nuclear world through their analysis. The ways they did so are uncovered not so much by an attention to the levers through which the systems analysis community influenced policy (which it certainly did) but by attention to the content of the discourse of systems analysis. Thus, I focus on the instrumental beliefs and logic of systems analysis and show how those beliefs and models helped structure the emerging nuclear world and were used in arguments within the US foreign policy decision-making community to develop the strategic nuclear arsenal. Systems analysis was intended to clarify and model the nuclear reality; instead it mystified nuclear reality *among the experts* and led to technically rational, though profoundly unreasonable consequences.

Nuclear operations research and systems analysis was and is a knowledge-making process that began to make its own "reality" more than the reality that was uncovered through the techniques of nuclear modeling. Despite all its pretensions of rationality, the formal discourse is neither rational nor irrational. Systems analysis is a "belief system" (Little and Smith 1988) that depends on and functions within larger foreign policy and scientific belief systems.[12] Others, e.g. E. P. Thompson (1981), Carol Cohn (1987), and Paul Chilton (1985), have shown how nuclear language was mystifying. My focus here is on the supposedly neutral and objective practice of mathematical modeling. Indeed, just as Cohn argues that "learning the language [of nuclear strategy] is transformative" (1987, 716), then engaging in the formal part of strategic nuclear discourse is even more so. The linguistic and mathematical abstractions used by weapons planners remove them from the reality of their plans and practices and thus allow them to "think the unthinkable" and perhaps do the unthinkable (Chilton 1985; Thompson 1981). Thus, the instrumental consequences of the weapons—what the weapons do to bodies, how the weapons help shape our understanding of and relations to others, and how making and preparing to use the weapons structures our ways of organizing ourselves, economically, politically, and militarily—is more often obscured, not revealed by systems analysis.[13]

But the formal mathematical and logical abstractions of nuclear modeling do more than remove planners from realities that are patently ghastly. The abstractions of systems analysis lead to the creation of new material "realities" which in turn demand new conceptual and linguistic abstractions. The way that this formal reasoning, nuclear rationality, begins to make its own cognitive and real world is obscured by the analysis. In other words, when analysts talk and reason abstractly about nuclear weapons through their nuclear models, they are not simply reporting in a precise way, the realities of the nuclear world as they find it. Nor are they simply using abstraction and models as a veil to hide the nuclear world from plain view by non-experts, though that might be a consequence of their discourse. Nor are they simply using abstraction, metaphor, models, and math psychologically to

---

[12] On belief systems, see Little and Smith 1988.

[13] Lifton and Markuson (1990) have argued that living in a world of nuclear weapons and potential nuclear holocaust has important psychological consequences. Systems analysis may inadvertently help planners deal with the psychological stress of planning for mass death.

insulate themselves from realities that they would rather not examine too closely, though this might also be the case. Nor was modeling simply a rationalization for decisions already taken for political or other reason, though this also happened.

Abstractions and forms of reasoning that become embodied in knowledge-making practices, organizational routines, the acquisition of capabilities, the plans for conducting operations, and the criteria for judging the reasonableness of arguments do not simply model the world. They make it. The formal, abstract, and ultimately incomplete models of systems analysis became more complex and simultaneously divorced from political context even as the political context was in part shaped by the practice of policy modeling. Indeed, there was as Freedman argued, "a tendency, which gradually became more acute, to place an extremely sophisticated technical analysis within a crude political framework" (2003, 169). At the same time the decisions based on systems analysis began to shape the arsenals and thus the political world. As Adler (1992, 108) argues, "the science of nuclear strategy has an input in creating the reality it is supposed to explain and predict." The use of systems analysis by US nuclear strategists, arms control analysts, and their critics illustrates the way that particular rationalities and the process of argument work in foreign policy decision making and how abstractions can make a world.[14] Understanding the abstractions, the models, helps explain how the USA acquired the capability to utterly destroy the Soviet Union, not just once, but almost inconceivably, several times, and why nuclear weapons remain in sizeable numbers despite the end of the cold war.

In what follows, I first briefly summarize some of the main strategic nuclear beliefs and arguments held in the USA during the cold war that constituted the taken-for-granted assumptions that underpinned nuclear arguments and systems analysis as a policy-modeling process. Second, I review the origins of systems analysis and summarize the core beliefs that underpin the practice. Third, I explore the abstract and formal world of systems analysis by "walking" through some of its basic techniques. Fourth, I discuss the "scientific seduction" of operations research and systems analysis and review some of the problems of this analytical tool and its relation to the material reality of nuclear weapons. Finally, I return to the question of the consequences of systems analysis—how nuclear abstractions made the world.[15]

---

[14] The consequences of the systems analysis discourse for non-experts are profound but anticipatable, similar to the consequences or effects of technical discourse in other areas of life, for instance in the ability of non-physicians to understand and participate in choices about their medical care. Non-experts may then defer to the experts, trusting in their rationality and their conscious manipulation of the nuclear forces and planning for either good or ill. Alternatively, non-initiates may claim that the system is completely mad, insane, and illogical, that there is some underlying pathology at work in the community. Still some critics of US nuclear policy understood it and nuclear modeling quite well. Even those who criticized nuclear policy using systems analysis, or who charged that nuclear modeling was little more than a rationalization for decisions that were already made, appear to have believed in the legitimacy of this form of rationality.

[15] One could, of course, make similar arguments about conventional force modeling.

# 1. THE CONTEXT: NUCLEAR WEAPONS AND US STRATEGIC NUCLEAR BELIEFS

The policy process can be conceived of as a flow where US nuclear weapons policy and forces are determined in broad outline by presidential, National Security Council, and Defense Secretary directives. The president and NSC also direct policy analysts to study alternative options. Presidential and NSC directives are then fleshed out and implemented by planners and analysts within the Defense Department and the military services. In both official and public discourse, the lingua franca of nuclear arguments was of course deterrence theory, but arguments rested on nuclear modeling—operations research and systems analysis techniques. United States strategic nuclear policy ranged from war fighting to deterrence (Freedman 2003; Glaser 1990; Eden and Miller 1989). The dominant logic of deterrence theory is based on the idea of keeping someone from acting by threatening them with painful punishment if they do act. The Soviet Union, it was supposed, would be deterred from attacking the United States, or its more distant interests, if they knew the United States would attack them in return. The belief was that decision makers would *not* be deterred if they thought they could get away with an attack without being punished or if the punishment were very light. Success in deterring an attack depended on one ensuring that the other side knew that they would, most likely, receive unacceptable damage as retaliation for an attack.

This logic of deterrence and credibility is embedded in other intersubjectively held philosophical, instrumental, normative, and identity beliefs. The core beliefs of nuclear "rationality"—that the Soviets were the enemy, that the best way to deal with them was through threats, that the utility of threats depends on an ability to carry them out, and so on—were rarely challenged. At the beginning of the cold war, the idea of killing tens of millions of the other's populations was acceptable, considered necessary to ensure the survival of one's own state and population—though by the mid-1970s the US government argued that it was not targeting civilian population per se (Ball 1986a, 27). In addition to these core beliefs there were many more context-specific beliefs about how deterrence worked and how to structure nuclear forces so that threats were credible, and so that if war came the mission of destroying the other side could be accomplished (Jervis 1984; Kull 1988). The project of constructing a nuclear arsenal for the United States in part consisted of meeting the "requirements" of deterrence in a nuclear world. Part of the requirement for deterrence during the cold war was to acquire a secure second strike capability—that is, to build enough weapons that could survive a Soviet first strike nuclear attack, and that would be able to retaliate against their cities or remaining nuclear weapons to inflict unacceptable damage.

There were also those who pushed for the United States to develop a nuclear war fighting capability. Indeed, early US nuclear strategy was explicitly focused on developing a capability for pre-emptive nuclear war fighting, targeting Soviet and Chinese conventional military forces and their industrial infrastructure (Rosenberg

1986, 40, 49; CBO 1978a). The USA also acquired weapons that were accurate enough to destroy Soviet nuclear weapons. But, some strategists argued, the USA had to be careful not to build so many of these accurate weapons as to put the Soviet Union in fear that the USA was preparing to attack its weapons and thus vitiate the Soviet Union's ability to deter a USA attack. If the Soviets believed that the USA was planning to strike first and could destroy their weapons (and their ability to the deter the USA), the Soviets might launch their weapons out of the fear of losing them to a US first strike. According to this reasoning, each side must build enough weapons to survive a first strike by the other side, but not so many extremely accurate weapons as to scare the other side into launching a pre-emptive nuclear strike. If both sides had highly accurate weapons, and a policy of aiming them at the other's weapons, a reciprocal fear of surprise attack could be an incentive for both countries to put their nuclear weapons on alert, and perhaps lead to nuclear war. The dilemma of creating a secure second strike force with highly accurate warheads was perhaps most acutely posed during the late 1970s and throughout the 1980s in the "window of vulnerability" debate and by critics of US acquisition of highly accurate land-based MX and submarine-based Trident D5 missiles.

Those charged with developing nuclear weapons, and the external critics of US strategic nuclear policy, sought to make sure that the nuclear policy was rational. By rational they meant that the most cost-effective and survivable weapons were purchased, and that those weapons sent the intended signal to the adversaries of the United States. But there were frequent and often bitter disputes within the armed forces and the Pentagon, among civilian defense analysts, and in the United States Congress about how to best implement nuclear strategy. After 1961, a consensus emerged within the strategic analytical community that the best method for ensuring that the posture was rational, and to constrain procurement by military services, was to use operations research and systems analysis.

# 2. Origins and "Philosophy" of Strategic Nuclear Systems Analysis

Operations research is now widely applied to all sorts of decision problems, as is evident in the journal of the Operations Research Society. Its origins, however, are in a set of mathematical techniques applied by United States and British military analysts during the First World War and applied more widely during the Second World War to improve the efficiency and effectiveness of strategic bombing and anti-submarine warfare (O'Neill 1993; Quade 1968a; Hitch 1965; Freedman 2003 167). After the Second World War, many of the techniques that would become nuclear systems analysis were refined by analysts at the RAND Corporation think tank and at the Strategic Air

Command (SAC) of the air force.[16] Early nuclear modelers relied on the analysis of the effects of nuclear weapons against Hiroshima and Nagasaki, and on data gathered through nuclear weapons tests in the South Pacific and the far West. The public rarely saw those early studies, though they sometimes came to light in popular books such as Herman Kahn's *On Thermonuclear War* (1960).

Systems analysis became a dominant tool in the Pentagon under Kennedy's Secretary of Defense Robert McNamara who hired operations researchers, economists, and RAND Corporation strategists to form the Systems Analysis Office at the Department of Defense in 1961. McNamara "made it clear at the outset that . . . he wanted all defense problems approached in a rational and analytical way, and that he wanted them resolved on the basis of national interests" (Enthoven and Smith, 1971, 31). McNamara's "whiz kids," the bright young men who did the systems analysis for the Pentagon, immediately set about "rationalizing" the different services' military forces, which included eliminating some of the military's favorite programs and weapons. They often won arguments, or at least set the terms of the debate within the Pentagon about nuclear forces, because their analysis seemed more objective and rational than other arguments that the services could put forward. This fact was said to annoy members of the military services who wanted to acquire the weapons they wanted without outside interference. According to Fred Kaplan, "In December 1961, some of the brightest Air Force officers met at Homestead Air Force Base . . . to figure out what they were doing wrong, how they could deal with McNamara and win a few bureaucratic battles. They concluded that they would have to work up their own analytical corps. . . . They too would have to learn the lingo of 'scenarios,' do 'cost-effectiveness' analysis, become their own 'systems analysts' " (Kaplan 1983, 256–7). Thus, the use of systems analysis techniques became essential for analysis of nuclear planning and war inside the Pentagon, as well as at the think tanks which evaluated nuclear strategy.

Basic criteria for the US nuclear arsenal were set and/or evaluated using systems analysis. For example, in the early 1960s, McNamara articulated the requirement that the United States be able to accomplish "assured destruction" of the Soviet Union even after the USA suffered a nuclear strike by the USSR. US strategic planners "calculated that the Soviets would be sufficiently deterred if we could kill 30 percent of their population and destroy half of their industrial capacity, and further that the task could be accomplished with the explosive power of 400 megatons" (Kaplan 1983, 317). In 1967, McNamara reduced this "requirement," arguing that the United States would have the capacity to "inflict an unacceptable degree of damage . . . even after absorbing a first strike" with 200 equivalent megatons[17].

---

[16] As Rosenberg notes, "The JSCP [Joint Strategic Capabilities Plan of 1952] and the operational plans it guided including the SAC Emergency War Plan, were prepared consistently on an annual basis. They fostered a process of debate and analysis that, in the absence of real global conflict, served as a kind of 'surrogate war' for generating and testing forces and concepts." In this context, "Each new planning effort built on the experience gained in the preceding 'war,' thereby creating a dynamic that tended to discourage radical changes" (Rosenberg 1986, 43).

[17] McNamara quoted in Salman, Sullivan, and Van Evera 1989, 209; see also Enthoven and Smith 1971, 207; and Kaplan 1983, 317–18.

The Systems Analysis Office prepared the initial "Draft Presidential Memoran-dums" (DPMs), on issues such as strategic offensive and defensive nuclear forces, tactical nuclear forces, and anti-submarine warfare. The process of drafting the final DPMs, which would serve as the basis for decisions by the Secretary of Defense and the president, included input and review by all the relevant parties within the DOD over several months. Two former members of McNamara's systems analysis team described the DPM procedure this way. "The growth in the number of DPMs reflected McNamara's desire to have all major defense programs considered and analyzed as a whole. This is a good illustration of what we like to call 'McNamara's First Law of Analysis': always start by looking at the grand totals" (Enthoven and Smith 1971, 54). They urged systems analysts to keep the larger context in mind:

Whatever problem you are studying, back off and look at it in the large. Don't start with a small piece and work up; look at the total first and then break it down into its parts. For example, if cost is the issue, look at total system cost over the useful life of the system, not just at this year's operating or procurement costs.... If you are analyzing a particular strategic offensive weapon system, start by looking at the total strategic offensive forces. If you are considering nuclear attack submarines, look at the total anti-submarine warfare force, which includes land- and sea-based patrol aircraft, destroyers, sonars and the like. One simply cannot make sense out of costs, or missiles, or submarines without looking at the totals. The DPMs were a practical result of this principle. (Enthoven and Smith 1971, 54)

The DPMs drew on the work of systems analysis in order to evaluate the compet-ing claims of different actors and devise policy, and calculations were fed into the protocols for nuclear weapons use, the Single Integrated Operational Plan (SIOP). Enthoven and Smith describe systems analysis as a "frame of mind" and a "philosophy:"

Systems analysis is a reasoned approach to highly complicated problems of choice in a context characterized by uncertainty; it provides a way to deal with differing values and judgments; it looks for alternative ways of doing a job; and it seeks by estimating in quantitative terms where possible, to identify the most effective alternative. It is at once eclectic and unique. It is not physics, engineering, mathematics, economics, political science, statistics or military science; yet it involves elements of all these disciplines. It is much more a frame of mind than a specific body of knowledge.... A good systems analyst is a relentless inquirer, asking fundamental questions about the problem at hand.... systems analysis is more a philosophy than a specific set of analytical techniques. (Enthoven and Smith 1971, 61–2)

Operations research and systems analysis applied to nuclear war became a form of nuclear reasoning or rationality, but there was more than one way to analyze nuclear problems. The Joint Chiefs of Staff "Catalogue of Wargaming and Military Simulation" notes eight models which could be used to assess the specific effects of nuclear weapons, estimate civilian fatalities from nuclear war, or model a full-scale nuclear war (Arkin and Fieldhouse 1985, 99). Game theory, computer simulations, and war gaming (where live military forces engage in mock battles under conditions that partially replicate those of a war) are also used to understand the utility of particular forces and strategies against potential adversaries. What is described in this chapter is thus only a snapshot of the use of modeling for nuclear weapons issues.

# 3. Basic Systems Analysis Techniques

Policy modelers are always responding to a problem. In the case of nuclear weapons and nuclear war, the problem is typically understood as a scenario. War scenarios are the political and military conditions in which the system under analysis is assumed to be operating. For example, one classified study produced by the Pentagon's Director of Defense Research and Engineering for Secretary of Defense McNamara considered the problem of damage limitation: "If the Soviets spend $x$ dollars to create damage in the U.S., and the U.S. spends $y$ dollars to limit damage, what is the percentage [sic] U.S. population and industry surviving? What are the results of the mirror imaging problem? (Note: Soviet 'damage limiting' is the same problem as U.S. 'assured destruction.' [sic])" (Director of Defense Research and Engineering 1964b, 14). Other strategic nuclear war scenarios consider using nuclear weapons and the force posture for deterrence or using the weapons to wage a nuclear war should deterrence fail. War fighting scenarios may be "first strike" or "second strike" and they also vary depending on whether the targets are other nuclear weapons or conventional forces (counterforce) or cities and industry (countervalue). Charles Hitch illustrates one use and technique of systems analysis: "To give an oversimplified example, suppose the objective were to achieve an expectation of destroying 97 per cent of 100 targets, using missiles having a per cent single-shot 'kill' capability." He continues:

The traditional requirements study would conclude that 500 missiles were needed because 100 missiles would achieve an expectancy of 50 kills, 200 missiles—75 kills, 300 missiles—87 kills, 400 missiles—94 kills, and 500 missiles—97 kills. This, of course, merely reflects the operation of the familiar law of diminishing returns. But the significant point is that the last 100 missiles would increase the "kill" expectation by only three extra targets, from 94 to 97. Thus we should not only ask the question, "Do we need a capability to destroy 97 percent of the 100 targets?"; we should also ask the question, "Is the capability to raise expected target destruction from 94 to 97 percent worth the cost of 100 extra missiles?" In other words, we must not examine total costs and total products but also marginal costs and marginal products. (Hitch 1965, 50–1)[18]

The particular numerical values used to conduct systems analysis include the quantification of nuclear weapons effects, the capabilities of the weapons and their strategic "delivery vehicles" (aircraft or missiles), and the characteristics and "value" of the target. Table 38.1 summarizes some of the characteristics and their units that are commonly used in basic systems analysis equations that deal with nuclear exchange scenarios.

Analysts also want to know how likely it is that, once launched, the warhead delivered by a missile or aircraft will be able to destroy its intended target. The formulas used to estimate the likelihood of one of these events, and even of a number

---

[18] For example, multiply the number of targets remaining by the SSPK of the missiles. Then add the number of targets killed after each round. If one cannot count on knowing which missiles were successfully destroyed in the first round, one must continue to send missiles to all of the targets.

**Table 38.1** Basic inputs for nuclear modeling

| Type of information | Characteristic measure | Acronym/symbol |
| --- | --- | --- |
| Nuclear explosion effects | blast overpressure | psi: pounds per square inch |
| | heat/thermal radiation (prompt) | temperature calories per square |
| | long-term radiation | centimeter cal/cm$^2$ |
| | | REM and RAD$^a$ |
| | | half life in years |
| Weapon capabilities | delivery vehicles | DV |
| | missile re-entry vehicles | Rv |
| | accuracy | CEP: circular error probable in nautical miles or feet; the radius from the target that a re-entry vehicle would land with 50% probability |
| | yield in megatons TNT equivalent | Y in MT and EMT (scaled to 1MT) where EMT = Y2/3 for yields < 1MT and EMT= Y1/3 where Y is >1MT |
| | overall reliability | OAR or R |
| Target characteristics | hardness | H in pound per square inch or psi |
| | type: area (e.g. city, airbase, factory) or point (missile) or linear (railroad track or road) | |

*Note*: see Glasstone and Dolan 1977 for a more comprehensive discussion of nuclear weapons effects.

$^a$ A rem (reontgen equivalent man) is a measure of biological damage; a rad is a measure of radiation energy absorbed.

of these events, are derived from nuclear weapons test data and from commonly used statistical procedures. One basic problem, of determining the probability of a single nuclear weapon of a certain size destroying a target of a certain size and type, is symbolized in the following formula known as the "single shot kill probability" or SSPK formula: SSPK = 1−0.5(LR/CEP)$^2$ where LR or lethal radius is the radius of (blast) destruction of a warhead (measured in nautical miles) of a certain yield against targets of a particular hardness and CEP is the measure of the warhead's accuracy.[19] If the hardness of a particular target is given as greater than 1,000 psi the lethal radius formula would be:

---

[19] A nautical mile is longer than a standard mile: 1 nm = 6,080 ft; 1 mi = 5,280 ft.

$$LR = \frac{2.62\ Y^{1/3}}{H^{.33}}$$

and if hardness were about 5 psi, the LR formula would be:

$$LR = \frac{6.81Y^{2/3}}{H^{.62}}$$

where Y is Yield in equivalent megatons and H is hardness in pounds per square inch. Overall probability of kill or OPK, is calculated by the equation: OPK = SSPK (OAR) where OAR is the overall reliability of the missile delivery vehicle and warhead. In other words, to determine how likely it is that a nuclear weapon will be able to destroy any particular target, one must determine the destructive capacity of a weapon against a target of a certain hardness, where hardness is the target's ability to withstand the blast effects of a nuclear weapon. For example, each United States MX missile has ten nuclear warheads, each with a yield of 0.45 equivalent megatons and an estimated accuracy of 0.06 nautical miles CEP. The overall reliability of the MX missile delivery vehicle and warhead is often assumed to be 0.81 per cent. The greater the hardness of a target, the less likely it will be destroyed by the blast effects of a nuclear weapon. However, the greater the accuracy and destructive power of a warhead, the more likely that a single shot will destroy the target.

Modeling a nuclear war would involve assessing the probable outcome of using one side's nuclear weapons against another side's nuclear weapons and cities and other targets. This requires figuring out how a number of weapons would perform against many targets and whether more than one nuclear weapon should be used against a particular target to increase the likelihood that the target would be destroyed. And of course it is possible to model a dynamic exchange of weapons between two or more sides assuming various constraints, such as the use of ballistic missile defenses and so on. The results of these calculations are then used in arguments about whether one side's nuclear forces and strategy are adequate for the task (deterrence or war fighting) or whether some change in forces or strategy would be required to meet the task (e.g. see CBO 1978a). The term "damage expectancy" (DE) describes the "probability that the desired level of damage will be achieved against each target or set of targets" and consists of the product of individual probabilities that systems function reliably (PRE), of prelaunch survivability (PLS), of penetrating air defenses (PTP), and the probability of killing the target (PK). Thus, $DE = PRE \times PLS \times PTP \times PK$ (Postol 1987, 379–80). The CBO (1978b, 52) used a different equation for Damage Expectancy: "Mathematically, $DE = 1 - (1 - R \times Pk)^n$." Where R is reliability, P is the probability of successful penetration to target, and n is the number of nuclear weapons of the same type allocated to the target. Other basic formulas and procedures for calculating the activities of nuclear war are dependent upon particular scenarios and target sets. Common scenarios for nuclear war fighting are "area barrage" (against a large area), "linear barrage" (against a linear target such as a railway), "defensive" (where weapons are to be defended against attack), and "counterforce exchange" (targeting each other's nuclear weapons). The assumptions, data, and formula given above are thus intended as simple illustrations for what can be a much more involved and intricate set of calculations.

# 4. RATIONAL REPRESENTATION OR SOCIAL PRACTICE?

The aim of nuclear operations research and systems analysis was to help nuclear strategists make decisions about which weapons to acquire, how to use the weapons, and how to predict how others will likely use their weapons. Practitioners believed that their analysis represented the *realities* of nuclear weapons and war. Indeed, the equations and models seem straightforward enough. And getting the numbers or parameters to put into the equations also seemed simple enough: just do the tests or make observations of the phenomena. Yet practitioners themselves noted that systems analysis regularly suffered from several problems: opaqueness, uncertainty, arbitrariness, and unrealistic scenarios. Thus, the policy modelers, and their critics cautioned that there were limits to individual analyses and to the craft.[20] As noted below, the proposed solution of the practitioners' systems analysis was to ameliorate and correct these problems through better analysis—to make the models more transparent, certain, realistic, and complete. Yet correcting the problems would not necessarily result in better policy modeling. Insiders believed that if the problems discussed below were corrected the models could ultimately accurately model the nuclear world. Yet, something more fundamental emerges when we examine the practice of systems analysis from outside the paradigm. No amount of tinkering could make the systems analysis better for purposes of policy modeling. The nuclear world was not simply re-presented and understood in and through a neutral and scientific policy-modeling process. Rather, nuclear systems analysis itself in part made and remade the nuclear world. As the following discussion of the problems of opaqueness, certainty, omission, arbitrariness, and implausibility shows, the models and abstractions made an already elusive nuclear world more opaque, uncertain, and arbitrary.

*Opaqueness.* Transparency of assumptions and techniques facilitates informed assessments and criticism of the policy process. Perhaps the most common criticism of systems analysis and other techniques of military assessment is that the practitioners have not made their assumptions and procedures transparent so that others (including other experts) can fully understand and evaluate their work. Opaqueness

---

[20] Quade (1968b) summarized several other "pitfalls" that can confound systems analysis such as the failure to specify the problem, adherence to cherished beliefs, parochialism, disregard of the limitations of forces available, and so on.

may also be consciously adopted as a cover for extreme biases in analysis that are used to advance a particular interest (Salman, Sullivan, and Van Evera 1989). In discussing military analysis techniques, models, simulations, and games (MSG), Garry Brewer and Martin Shubik (1979, 225–6) argued that "all such analyses are generated by a program, the workings of which are obscure and often unfathomable... [T]he interested onlooker does not know, for instance, what the structure of the MSG is, what data are assumed to be relevant, what is omitted, what factors influence which others, or how sensitive the outcome is to changes and uncertainty in the assumptions." Like most conscientious scholars and consumers of systems analysis, Brewer and Shubik urge practitioners to make their assumptions and operations "less opaque" and to produce alternative analyses based on "equally plausible assumptions about the performance of weapons and the operational environment." Of course this last piece of advice presumes that there are such things as more or less plausible assumptions and scenarios.

*Certainty and uncertainty.* Systems analysis is specifically intended to model decisions in uncertainty. Systems analysis relies on pre-existing data for inputs and makes assumptions about probabilities of uncertain events. All policy modeling is therefore more or less sensitive to degrees of certainty and uncertainty.[21] Yet, Quade (1968b, 356) has noted that systems analysts sometimes neglect "consideration of the real uncertainties" and focus on uncertainties that have been modeled or simulated although "real uncertainties may have made trivial the effect of any statistical uncertainty." More fundamentally, because of the nature of nuclear weapons and nuclear war, it may not be possible for nuclear systems analysts to even know the degree of uncertainty they are attempting to model. Despite their best efforts to represent, specify, and bracket the range of possible outcomes and uncertainties, analysts were ultimately working in a realm of illusory or even false certainty. Thus, numbers were used as if they were hard, when in fact the values were quite uncertain. Specifically, the numbers used to describe nuclear weapons and their effects—such as hardness, CEP, and reliability—are assumed to be "hard," based on real, observable, and knowable data. Yet, several basic inputs are not hard at all in the sense of being observable and knowable with high degrees of certainty because data used for input are derived from tests under "artificial" conditions that do not approximate the real conditions of nuclear war. Analysis assumed the numbers were "real;" rather, the data that comprised the assumptions and values used in systems analysis were social constructions.

For example, hardness, that is, the ability of an object to withstand the effects of a nuclear weapon to a designated level of blast overpressure, is a crucial input to equations in nuclear systems analysis; results are often quite sensitive to changes in the hardness parameter (recall that $SSPK = 1 - 0.5(LR/CEP)^2$ and lethal radius depends on hardness of the target). Figures for the hardness of objects, especially missile silos, depend on engineering data about the effects of blast overpressure on certain kinds of construction. Many tests of different materials

---

[21] See Bunn and Tsipis 1983, for example.

and construction methods were conducted by placing objects of different types at various distances from nuclear explosions (Glasstone and Dolan 1977) during the period when above ground nuclear testing was conducted. Thus, while there are some real "data," the "hardness" values for an adversary's industries, missile silos, and command bunkers are essentially a guess, assuming that their methods of construction and materials are basically like the systems for which one has data. Then, to be "safe," it seems that planners assumed their construction was just a bit better, more resilient than even the best of the ones that have been "tested" (CBO 1978b, 46–7). Such may be the case with figures for the hardness of Soviet silos, given as very high numbers (1,000 and 2,000 psi) in the late 1970s and early 1980s. These high numbers, with little basis in "reality," were often repeated without the qualifications attached to them by the Congressional Budget Office when CBO first used the estimates (see CBO 1978a, 16).

Donald MacKenzie's work on missile reliability and accuracy demonstrates the softness of these supposedly hard inputs. For instance, the figure used for the overall reliability of US ballistic missiles is a probability that depends on several operations happening in sequence. The land-based missiles must be launched from underground silos and submarine-based missiles must be launched from their submarines. After launch, booster rockets must function successfully, the re-entry vehicle that carries the nuclear warhead must separate from the booster and re-enter the atmosphere, and the nuclear warhead must detonate. High estimates of overall reliability were almost uniformly used in nuclear systems analysis. Yet, despite the importance of missile reliability, there has never been a test of a US nuclear ballistic missile over the same range and gravitational conditions that would be found in an "actual" war. Nor were there many tests of ballistic missiles with "live" nuclear warheads: in testing, ballistic nuclear warheads are removed so that tracking devices can be placed in the missile and re-entry vehicle. Apparently, there was only one test of a nuclear missile that approached operational conditions (although the range and trajectory of the test were not the same as they would be during a nuclear war) in 1962 when a Polaris missile was launched from a submarine and its nuclear warhead detonated at the test range. Air force Chief of Staff Curtis LeMay told members of Congress that even this test "was not under fully operational conditions, we fired one Polaris out in the Pacific with a warhead on it. It was not truly operational. It was modified somewhat for the test" (quoted in MacKenzie 1990, 344). MacKenzie (1990, 343) also notes that because of problems with the Polaris warhead's fusing, "By 1966 it was being estimated by the Livermore nuclear weapons laboratory that between half and three quarters of W47 warheads [used on Polaris missiles] would fail to detonate." Thus, if overall reliability depends on the probability of missile launch, warhead separation, and detonation, the high estimates for reliability given in most systems analysis equations were themselves so optimistic and based on artificial assumptions as to have been nearly fictional. Perhaps such optimistic assumptions were accepted because without them, the deterrence threat became less credible.

Similarly, uncertainty was also elided in the figures for missile accuracy, circular error probable. A supposedly "hard" number, CEP is also based on a relatively few number of artificially simplified tests. Recall that CEP, a distance measured in nautical miles or feet, is the radius of a circle around the target where 50 per cent of the warheads are expected to fall if a large number of test firings were conducted. Some 50 per cent would likely fall outside this radius.[22] Accuracy depends on the gravitational and electromagnetic field of a missile flight path, precise calibration of the inertial guidance system of a weapon, that the re-entry vehicle does not get thrown off course by debris when it re-enters the atmosphere, and so on. The tests that were used to estimate US missile accuracy were conducted on east to west flight paths, over what is known as the Western Test Range, while a US ballistic missile flight against the USSR during the cold war would have gone over the North Pole and over longer ranges—these missiles would experience different gravitational and electromagnetic forces. Moreover, the missiles that are used in these flight tests are specially prepared and "modified" for the tests, so that they are in better working condition than the missiles that actually sit in silos or on submarines (MacKenzie 1990, 344).[23] The missile warhead lands in the test area and the number that is eventually given for CEP of a particular missile type depends on a statistical analysis of a number of these tests. To take uncertainty into account, there are "safety factor" formulas that are apparently used by systems analysts for CEP (MacKenzie 1990, 419). Yet the CEP number is generally taken as a given when inputted into systems analysis calculations.

Ironically, uncertainty, and the sources of uncertainty with respect to CEP were sometimes discussed in great detail by policy modelers and then ignored. For example, the Congressional Budget Office (CBO) produced a number of widely used papers examining US strategic nuclear forces in the 1970s and 1980s. The CBO report was careful to make the problems and uncertainty with the data explicit and also to note that even if more tests were conducted in order to increase confidence in the CEP figures used in the analysis, "actual" nuclear war would be quite different from the tests:

A very significant consideration for attack planning is the great uncertainty surrounding the actual accuracy of any given guidance technology. This uncertainty results in part from the limited number of tests a missile system undergoes to verify its accuracy potential. Gaining high confidence in estimates of a missile CEP would require a large number of tests for each missile and for each change in its guidance system. Such testing is constrained, however, by the limited resources that can be devoted to the very expensive task of missile testing. Moreover, actual operational performance can be degraded by variable atmospheric conditions and small perturbations in the earth's gravitational field. As a result, actual CEPs can only be estimated within a fairly large range of uncertainty, and any assessment of the damage that an

---

[22] Lynn Eden suggested to me that this is an odd locution: it is *circular* error probable although weapons would not fall in a circle but in more of an elliptical pattern.

[23] One could respond that because of these areas of uncertainty, one needs to do more tests. In fact, those who do not want to halt nuclear tests or tests of delivery vehicles and components argue that periodic testing of nuclear weapons and delivery vehicles is necessary to ensure that the weapons will be reliable and that the assumptions about performance are accurate. Yet, even if testing advocates had their way, tests would still be stylized simply because to get the necessary measurements, tests must be conducted under "artificial" and stylized conditions.

attack can be expected to cause must take into account the uncertainties surrounding these operational accuracies. (CBO 1978a, 10–11)

Yet, although data reported by the CBO as the basis for their calculations were frequently used by other analysts, the explicit cautions expressed in the CBO reports, including the one quoted above, are rarely reproduced. Thus, the problem of uncertain inputs being used as hard numbers was exacerbated by the tendency of analysts to simply repeat earlier estimates made or given by respected sources (Crawford 1987). Uncertainty was thus acknowledged and then forgotten or erased and turned into hard and certain numbers which became the basis for other calculations. Simulations were taken to be real and accurate, when they were highly constructed and likely to be far from accurate; the analysts knew this and proceeded anyway.

Further, uncertainty was magnified and masked when classified and public estimates frequently based on projections of *future* capabilities of the USSR rather than on what was known or presumed to be the current capability. There were enormous questions about contemporary Soviet military capabilities; those uncertainties were even greater if Soviet capabilities were projected into the future. For example, projections of future Soviet capabilities that never actually materialized were the basis of the highly publicized bomber and missile gaps. Classified estimates in NIEs and operations research studies also, as a general rule, proceeded on the numbers projecting future capabilities. For instance, the 1964 classified study of damage limitation estimated US and Soviet capabilities for 1970 (DDR&E 1964a) but no one could know for sure what the Soviet arsenal would look like in six years and the basis for such projections was often never specified. Even the use of the term "projection" in the estimates connotes a systematic and empirically based number when what was given was often simply a guess of what the Soviets might be capable of doing in the future.

*Omission and elision.* "It is a serious pitfall," Quade (1968b, 359) argues, "for the analyst to concentrate so completely on the purely objective and scientific aspects of his analysis that he neglects the substantive elements or fails to handle them with understanding." Despite this caution, issues and numbers that are important for understanding the capabilities and effects of nuclear weapons are often omitted during the process of systems analysis. Four examples—the persistence in ignoring or downplaying the thermal effects of nuclear weapons, the omission of command and control in many models, the problem of fratricide, and the lack of reference to human bodies—illustrate the sort of omissions that characterize nuclear modeling.

As Lynn Eden (2004) shows in her masterful account, nuclear planners focused on blast effects, despite the fact that the thermal effects of nuclear weapons are enormous: when combined with the wind that nuclear explosions generate, huge fires would be expected in cities. As Eden demonstrates, blast effects are certainly important, but when trying to model the destruction of nuclear missile silos or other hard structures and when weapons planners talk about targeting cities and industrial targets, they usually took *only* blast effects into account. For example, the RAND Corporation SNAPPER Nuclear Damage Assessment Model focuses on blast effects. SNAPPER was used by the CBO (1978*b*) for its modeling, although the CBO noted that "*Secondary* effects from a nuclear blast, such as fire or shorts in electrical systems, can damage machinery just as effectively as primary effects can" (emphasis added; CBO 1978*b*, 47). Yet, depending on the dominant building materials and other conditions, the area of damage from a nuclear blast in a city and perhaps even against weapons will likely be much smaller than the area damaged by heat and firestorms. Firestorms did significant damage in Hiroshima and Nagasaki and there was other evidence that thermal effects of nuclear weapons would be significant. Still, nuclear modelers preferred to focus on blast because they believed blast effects were easier to predict and model. This example of a preference to model blast effects is taken from a now declassified memorandum to President Kennedy, and occurs in a discussion of the kill distance of anti-ballistic missiles against a swarm of incoming nuclear warheads and decoys by RAND Corporation experts Edward Teller and John Foster:

Suppose the kill distance of the defensive warhead could be vastly increased—made comparable to the size of the swarm. The decoys could become ineffectual.

If there were multiple warheads they could all be killed in one blow....

How can the kill distance of a nuclear warhead be made so large? Is such a warhead development possible? The answer is that it may not be necessary to do anything to the warhead. The kill distance with present warheads might be big enough *and we just don't know it.* It is an important fact that the science of the effects of nuclear explosions on targets is in a much more rudimentary state than the science of nuclear weapons themselves. Because we know so little about effects and because we do not know the detailed construction of the Soviet ICBM, we are forced to base our estimate of the kill distance on the most direct, best understood, and therefore most reliable effects of the explosion. It is this way [deletion]....

Aren't the Soviets, like us, forced to be conservative in their AICBM [anti-ICBM] planning? (Teller and Foster 1961, 3, 5)

Thus as Teller and Foster imply, the fact that a firestorm would likely destroy a vast area was not taken into account because analysts were focused on the blast effects of nuclear weapons, and the result of considering other effects "secondary" is that more nuclear weapons would be targeted on an area such as a city, to produce damage to a certain level of blast. The idea that one needs more weapons often leads to building them, and then the other side may build weapons to be able to target those weapons, and so on.

Command and control of nuclear forces was also often omitted from analysis by the assumption that it would work flawlessly or at least quite well. There were about thirty-six nuclear command posts in the USA and fifty in the USSR in the mid-1980s (Arkin and Fieldhouse 1985, 93; Blair 1985). As Ball (1986*a*, 19) argues, "Escalation Control requires U.S. strategic nuclear forces be supported by a survivable C³I system with sufficient endurance to maintain control through some extended period of protracted conflict." But as Ball shows, US C³I is "subject to certain critical vulnerabilities" which call into question the ability to follow through with war fighting scenarios. Despite command and communication redundancies and other precautions, an attack on all of these command posts would likely hinder political leaders' ability to launch nuclear weapons, assess damage to their own and the other side, or terminate a nuclear war once it was begun. The smooth and effective functioning of C³I, essential for all nuclear war scenarios, is assumed in most systems analysis of second strike retaliation, despite the fact that C³I is quite vulnerable to disruption.[24]

Analysts also sometimes acknowledged and then proceeded to omit from their calculations the possibility of fratricide—that the detonation of one of your weapons could disable another of your weapons—from their analysis. Specifically, to increase the overall probability of kill (OPK) against a target, nuclear weapons planners often allocate more than one nuclear weapon to it. "To hedge against massive failures of an entire weapon type, weapons would be cross targeted by different delivery systems" (Postol 1987, 380). Cross-targeting raises the possibility of fratricide because the first weapon to explode will create a fireball and dust cloud. "If the second cross-targeted booster did not fail in flight to the target, its warheads would arrive next, perhaps minutes or fractions of minutes after the arrival of the first.... Some of the warheads might be damaged or destroyed if they encountered the debris clouds from the earlier detonations, but from the point of view of the targeter that might be unimportant, because the warheads would be cross-targeted mainly to make it highly probable that the targets of interest were struck" (Postol 1987, 389). But according to the CBO, "It is possible that no more than one warhead could be successfully detonated over each target. Other nuclear effects, such as intense heat and dust clouds, could be lethal to subsequent warheads even if first round weapons were burst above the surface to avoid the throwing of ground debris into the air" (CBO 1978a, 12). Moreover, "Uncertainties about fratricide will probably never be settled. For one thing the prohibition on atmospheric testing prevents real world evaluation of a modern warhead's ability to withstand the various effects of a nuclear explosion" (CBO 1978a, 13). Despite these significant concerns, fratricide is often left out, or minimized in calculations by strategists. The result is that the "models" are less and less removed from the "reality" of the weapons effects, even as the conclusions of models based on this optimistic assumption create yet another sort of reality.

Finally, as Cohn (1987) and Gusterson (1996) have noted, one of the most glaring omissions is the frequent lack of clear references to what nuclear weapons do to humans. Of course one of the main points of using nuclear weapons is to kill people. Calculations about "countervalue" strikes against population centers do discuss the casualties associated with nuclear weapons use (e.g. OTA 1979; Batcher 2004). But, apart from the early research on the effectiveness of civil defense, many of the counterforce calculations proceed as if there were no human injuries or deaths from counterforce nuclear exchanges. Indeed, the intentional and inadvertent

---

[24] Though command bunkers and other elements of C3I are "hardened" against blast, transient electronic effects (TREE), and electromagnetic pulse (EMP), they are still vulnerable to direct hits.

release of sometimes high doses of radioactive substances during nuclear weapons tests and as part of the program of human radiation experiments undertaken in the USA during the first fifteen years of the cold war (see Hilts 1994, 1995, 1996; Wald 1997) could lead to speculation that human life itself was discounted by some planners.

*Arbitrariness.* The inputs to policy modeling should be based on non-arbitrary considerations. Yet, modeling inputs used as baselines in nuclear systems analysis, and that seem relatively uncontroversial, such as the size of the ICBM arsenal, for CEP, and the criteria of second strike survivability, were all too often arbitrary. An initial arbitrary assumption may appear uncontroversial, but the effects of the initial policy choice ripple through subsequent analysis.

For example, there was no compelling military or scientific reason why the US ICBM arsenal was set at 1,000 missiles (Ball 1980, 209–10). In 1974 nuclear scientist Herbert York asked Alfred Rockefeller, chief of the Presentations Division of the Space and Missile Systems Organization of the air force, to explain how the size of the US ICBM force was determined to be 1,000 in the mid-1950s, suggesting that its number was essentially "a natural one, and not decided by anybody consciously" (York 1974). Rockefeller replied to York, "I agree with you on the interpretation of the number 1000. Basically, it is a nice round number which would be equally applicable to an aircraft procurement.... the number 1000 was a natural one. A nice base figure to calculate cost on" (Rockefeller 1974).

Similarly, the criterion used by NATO countries for accuracy CEP is 50 per cent probability of the warhead landing within a radius expressed in nautical miles or feet. According to this criterion, 50 per cent of the warheads land somewhere outside that radius. Again, this distance is calculated based on several test firings of the weapon, and the classified results of tests include confidence intervals and an error budget of the causes of inaccuracy (Mackenzie 1990, 348–9).[25] So, although the number for CEP is *expressed* as a distance, the circular error probable figure is a *probability* for landing within a certain distance. Yet, the choice of 50 per cent is essentially arbitrary. Why does NATO use 50 per cent as the probability? Clearly, if a different criterion were used, the distance would be different, altering one's perception of the missile accuracy, and therefore, likely altering the number of weapons procured. Why not use a different criterion, for instance 80 or 90 per cent, which would be more consistent with the numbers for reliability of missiles and warheads? Weapons would appear to be less accurate if CEP were 80 per cent and more accurate if it were 21 per cent, the figure the Soviets used for CEP.[26]

Other figures, taken for granted at the time as not arbitrary but as "reasonable and essential," were the criteria used to assess when deterrence would be accomplished. McNamara's Department of Defense asserted that deterrence would be accomplished

[25] Mackenzie (1990, 367–8) notes how CEP confidence intervals were viewed differently and CEP numbers adjusted when the air force wanted to make their nuclear weapons appear more accurate than navy weapons.

[26] Because the Soviet criterion for CEP was a 21% probability for landing within the radius they could expect 79% of their weapons to land outside that radius.

with the guarantee of 400 (later revised to 200) equivalent megatons for a second strike—that is, the USA should be able to inflict that amount of nuclear damage even after absorbing a first strike by the Soviet Union. McNamara told the Congress in 1965 that "it seems reasonable to assume the destruction of, say, one-quarter to one-third of its population and about two-thirds of its industrial capacity...would certainly represent intolerable punishment to any industrialized nation and thus should serve as an effective deterrent" (quoted in Ball 1986*b*, 69). Plans were developed to accomplish this level of destruction, and it was shown through systems analysis techniques that 400 EMT would do the job of visiting this much destruction on the Soviets. Yet, the number used by McNamara's Pentagon for "unacceptable" damage was essentially pulled out of the air and then the number of equivalent megatons necessary to do the job was calculated by looking at the diminishing marginal returns of doing more damage (Kaplan 1983, 316–18). These criteria were later changed. The *Annual Report of the Secretary of Defense, Fiscal Year 1969* (1969, 50) estimated that 400 EMT would be sufficient to destroy half of Soviet industry. The NUWEP-1 (Nuclear Weapons Employment Policy) of the USA in 1974 required nuclear weapons to destroy 70 per cent of the Soviet economic and industrial base needed to achieve economic recovery (Ball 1986*b*, 74). In 1978 US Secretary of Defense Harold Brown told Congress that it was "essential that we retain the capability at all times to inflict an unacceptable level of damage on the Soviet Union, including destruction of a minimum of 200 major Soviet cities" (quoted in Ball 1986*a*, 27). The CBO suggests that "Destruction of 80 percent of the industrial target set [of their 1,400 industrial target base] appears to be a reasonable objective" (1978*b*, 52).

Where did these numbers, which changed from administration to administration, come from? Why these numbers and not others? The requirements, and the arsenal built to accomplish them, appear to be arbitrary. No one knew for sure—or even with confidence—what would deter the decision makers of the Soviet Union or any other leadership. Maybe more, maybe significantly less destruction would be required. Arbitrariness and uncertainty is then glossed over by the use of words like "requirement," "reasonable," and "essential."

Sometimes opaqueness and arbitrariness were combined. For example, in a discussion of allocating weapons to targets, the CBO gave an example designed to illustrate damage expectancy: "[I]f the first target has a value of 1000 and the weapon Pk is 0.80, then, assuming 100 percent reliability, one bomb would destroy 800 units of target value. Allocating a second weapon to this target would result in additional value destroyed of 160 units. Therefore, this second weapon should be allocated to the first target before a target valued at 159 units is attacked" (CBO, 1978*b*, 53). But what is the unit of target value? A 1,000 what? How *should* targets be valued?

Such precise yet arbitrary inputs have the effect of making the activities of nuclear planners and preparations for nuclear war seem more accurate, but the consequences of the analysis were probably just the opposite. Even as nuclear analysts acknowledged uncertainty, and then developed and refined techniques for identifying and eliminating uncertainties from their models, they minimized the uncertainties that they did count and did not take into account other very important areas of uncertainty. In some equations, the mathematical "precision" of the models was accomplished by inserting numbers with little or no precise, "real" basis.

*Implausible/"unrealistic" scenarios.* Many of the systems analysis scenarios work on paper, but because they leave important effects out, or factor in unlikely events the scenarios are implausible. Three examples—issues of human reliability, the possibility of conducting nuclear and conventional war in an integrated and controlled manner, and the idea of "reprogramming" during nuclear war—are illustrative.

The question of human reliability was rarely discussed, much less factored into systems analysis. For example, there is one missile launch control center, operated by air force officers, for every 10 Minuteman and MX missiles (Blair 1985, 87). Thus, for MX missiles, which each have ten independently targeted warheads, one control center is responsible for launching 100 nuclear weapons. Commanders and systems analysts generally assume that humans will perform in a nuclear war environment as they were trained to function. Yet this is unknown and thus huge potential failures of reliability—humans may become ill or simply refuse to perform their duties—are rarely, if ever considered by systems analysts (see Dougherty 1987, 413–15). Omitting the discussion of human reliability has the effect of making the unrealistic assumption that human reliability will be perfect. Similarly, by not discussing Soviet reliability, one unrealistically assumes perfect reliability on their part.

US war planners also assumed it was possible to control escalation in nuclear war and developed plans for flexible, limited, and theater (local) nuclear war throughout the 1960s, 1970s, and 1980s. For example, Harold Brown presented Presidential Directive 59 in 1980 as a plan that would "integrate" strategic, theater, and tactical nuclear weapons use. "Our planning must provide a continuum of options, ranging from use of small numbers of strategic and/or theater nuclear weapons aimed at narrowly defined targets, to employment of large portions of our nuclear forces against a broad spectrum of targets" (Secretary of Defense 1980, 55). War plans included "integrating" nuclear, chemical, and biological weapons on the battlefield and discussed "selective employment of nuclear weapons against armored thrusts" (Joint Chiefs of Staff 1977, 85). US Army Field Manual 100–50 of March 1980, "Operations for Nuclear Capable Units," talked about training to "disperse" and "issue" tactical nuclear weapons rounds in a combat situation. "The U.S. has reviewed force levels and system requirements in an effort to achieve a TNF [Theater Nuclear Force] posture that will correct existing imbalances and provide credible, flexible responses, particularly at lower levels of nuclear warfare. Such a posture will provide timely accurate nuclear options for reinforcing deterrence outside the NATO area" (Joint Chiefs of Staff 1982, 29–30). The dubious assumption was clearly that the Soviet Union had conventional "superiority" which could be "corrected" by using tactical nuclear weapons. Yet, little attention was paid to the fact that the "employment" of tactical nuclear weapons on the "battlefield" could cause "tactical" nuclear war to escalate to all-out nuclear war.

Planning for "reprogramming" on the fly during nuclear war was also unrealistic. The idea was that nuclear weapons held in reserve would be retargeted to make up for weapons that failed to detonate or to retarget the targets not destroyed by the first round of weapons. Reprogramming is designed to increase the efficiency of nuclear targeting and boost damage expectancy, or the probability that the target will be hit and destroyed by a nuclear weapon. Reprogramming is often considered by nuclear planners who for instance, will make every effort to decrease the probability of fratricide by taking into consideration the height of burst and timing of follow-on nuclear bursts. However desirable it might be to increase efficiency, the scenario is implausible specifically because it assumes functioning damage assessment and command and control in a nuclear environment. On the other hand, the inadequacy of US C³I in such a scenario was highlighted in Presidential Directive 59, where developing the requirements of counterforce were linked to making improvements in command, control, and communications (Ball 1986b, 78).

If the notions that humans were perfectly reliable, that nuclear weapons use could be limited to a battlefield, and that weapons could be reprogrammed in the midst of nuclear war are optimistic, there was also a tendency to emphasize worst-case scenarios—that the other side will do better and your own force worse in a nuclear war. This is known as being conservative or hedging. The tendency to think in terms of worst-case scenarios was reinforced by inferring an adversary's intentions from their military capabilities.[27] And oddly enough, a worst-case bias and hedging often occurs alongside a tendency to assume that things will go according to plan (that your equipment will function according to plan). For example, as mentioned earlier, it is common to omit command, control, and communications from nuclear systems analysis efforts at modeling nuclear war, perhaps because most assume perfect C³I (see e.g. Salman, Sullivan, and Van Evera 1989, 191). "Conservative military planners tend to base their calculations on factors that can be either controlled or predicted, and to make pessimistic assumptions where control or prediction are impossible" (OTA 1979, 3). As Secretary of Defense Caspar Weinberger testified to Congress: "I would rather err on the side of doing too much if that is, indeed, the error, rather than doing to little. It is fire on the side of doing too little" (HASC 1983, 128).

The unanticipated cumulative effect of many "hedges" is a stiffening and enlargement of the requirements for war fighting and deterrence.[28] Hardness numbers were commonly hedged. For example, without giving the evidence for their "hedge" the CBO (1978b, 52) used conservative assumptions about the hardness of Soviet indus-

---

[27] The possibility that one's own actions could be causing defensive reactions by the adversary was rarely explicitly considered, although game theorists, concerned with strategic interaction, do take this into account. Another exception is the discussion in the USA about building new strategic nuclear bombers where the likelihood that the Soviets would have to put resources into air defense systems against bombers (and would therefore not be able to expend vital resources on other, offensive weapons) was used in making arguments about the utility of manned bombers.

[28] While worst-case scenarios and hedging because of uncertainty may unconsciously lead to "threat inflation," deliberate threat inflation to justify strategic plans and programs also occurred.

try: "To hedge against Soviet civil defense measures, it is assumed that half of the Soviet industrial base is hardened to 30 psi..." Hedging also applied to the number of potential targets: "For the purpose of estimating force effectiveness... enough weapons are included in a reserve force to maintain effective retaliatory capability, even if there is such a large growth in the number of industrial targets that, by 1990, there would be a 40 percent increase in the number of weapons required to achieve equivalent damage results" (CBO 1978b, 51). The public version of the 1994 *Nuclear Posture Review* includes a discussion of a "necessary hedge," although it is not clear how that "necessary" hedge is to be determined (DOD 1994, 12, 14, 16, 18, 19). A graph shows that the "Upload Reconstitution Hedge" accounts for thousands more nuclear warheads in the US stockpile than without the hedge, in order to reconstitute US nuclear forces "should political relations with Russia change for the worse" or there are failures in implementation of the START I and START II arms control treaties (DOD 1994, 14, 19).

# 5. THE SCIENTIFIC SEDUCTION OF SYSTEMS ANALYSIS

As noted above, both critics and practitioners of systems analysis raised some of these concerns during the cold war. Practitioners themselves also issued cautionary notes, though such warnings were apparently more common earlier rather than later in the cold war. Sir Solly Zuckerman, an important British nuclear strategist, wrote in 1953 that strategy was "based upon assumptions about human behaviour which seem totally unreal. It neither constitutes scientific analysis nor scientific theorizing, but is a non-science of untestable speculations" (quoted in Freedman 2003, 171). During the 1950s, scholars at the RAND Corporation and elsewhere produced studies emphasizing what they called the "pitfalls" of systems analysis (e.g. Kahn and Mann 1957). Quade (1968b, 363), summarizing these pitfalls argued, "No matter how we strive to maintain standards of scientific inquiry or how closely we attempt to follow scientific methods, we cannot turn military systems analysis into an exact science." Enthoven and Smith (1971, 71) wrote that "Some have criticized systems analysis on the grounds that it tends to overemphasize factors that can be reduced to numbers and underemphasize factors that cannot." They grant that this is a "potential danger," that it is "possible for an analyst to become so intrigued with the measurable aspects of the problem that he gives inadequate attention to nonquantitative factors." Yet, they argue that this is "less likely to occur under systems analysis approaches than under alternative approaches" because in using systems analysis "an individual must lay out all his assumptions, objectives, and calculations." Similarly, Charles Hitch (1965, 57) argues that the "systems analyst, like any other scientist, must be prepared to submit his work to critical scrutiny, and not just by other systems analysts. This is one of the great merits of the scientific method—it is an open, explicit, verifiable, and self-correcting process."

But by the 1980s, there was a sense that assumptions and the models themselves need not be examined. Systems analysis was taken to be policy neutral, a sort of "scientific-technical grounding" that was alluded to in congressional hearings on the MX missile by Scowcroft Commission member John Deutsch as "technical examin-ation" by those who were "more technically inclined" which yielded "net technical judgment" (HASC 1983, 101). Thus, technical analysis and modeling was so taken for granted that it was not necessary to produce the figures. One simply had to believe the more technically inclined. Commission Chairman Brent Scowcroft in explaining his belief that 100 MX was the right number, argued: "There is nothing magic about 100. We felt, first of all, that we wanted a number less than that which in conjunction with the other accurate Minuteman force would constitute a first strike against the Soviet Union, their hard targets, their leadership, nuclear storage and so on" (HASC 1983, 86).

Thus, even the cautions described by the first generations of systems analysts appear to have been mostly forgotten by the 1980s as scholars and practitioners sought ways to sharpen the nuclear debate. In their critical overview of nearly two decades of public assessments within the United States of the US–Soviet strategic balance, Salman, Sullivan, and Van Evera argue that "Discourse succeeds when it rests on sound methods of inquiry; the [nuclear] balance debate has failed as a discourse because its methods have been unsound" (1989, 177). Salman, Sullivan, and Van Evera show how flawed analysis can be used to manipulate the political debate and lead to misleading conclusions. They suggested four common games that analysts play: using static indicators or bean counts; flawed dynamic analysis based on bad numbers or faulty assumptions; using outlandish scenarios; and oracle or *ex cathedra* pronouncements by experts making assertions without evidence.

Like others before them who recognized and detailed some of the pitfalls of certain forms of policy modeling, Salman, Sullivan, and Van Evera urge that the solution is better analysis. They argue that "military strength should be assessed by measuring the capacity of forces to execute strategy.... using data describing the characteristics of the forces on both sides, the analyst measures the strength of the force by asking whether it can perform its assigned missions, and if so, under what conditions and with what degree of confidence." They suggest that: "To be meaningful, measures of the Soviet–American nuclear balance should describe what both sides' nuclear forces can do. This requires dynamic analysis that assesses their ability to perform wartime missions" (1989, 176). They then use "dynamic analysis" to simulate nuclear ex-changes. Their analysis is quite thorough, and to facilitate transparency they provide an appendix discussing the techniques and assumptions of their analysis as well as a computer program so that readers can conduct their own dynamic analysis. They also warn that their analysis should be understood "as an approximation of reality, not a replica.... Nuclear war is a mysterious, unprecedented event" (1989, 213). But, they then suggest that their simulations "probably approximate reality as closely as public data will allow, and our interviews suggest that classified simulations produce similar results" (1989, 213). Salman, Sullivan, and Van Evera conclude their article by arguing that rigorous dynamic systems analysis should "define serious" nuclear discourse and determine what gets published:

Policy concerns will always distort balance assessment to some degree, but scholars of security affairs can mitigate the problem by setting and enforcing higher professional standards. Specifically, they could require that research purporting to measure American nuclear strength, or dealing with issues that require its measurement, provide dynamic analysis that tests the propositions its advances. The provision of such information should define serious work on strategic nuclear issues; manuscripts that omit it should not be published or cited as authority. The academic community can impose such standards if it chooses, and the quality of net assessment will improve if it does. (1989, 244–5)

Thus, even as they document the sloppy use of policy modeling, Salman, Sullivan, and Van Evera simply propose better modeling. They have not, apparently, understood how there was both on the one hand, no way for the modeling to be more accurate, and on the other hand, how the modeling itself began to make the nuclear world.

# 6. Conclusion: How Abstraction Makes a World

Systems analysis was intended to help policy makers understand the complex and essentially unknown nuclear world and assist them in making the policy process more rational. It was intended to produce usable knowledge, to quantify and model the nuclear world. As Enthoven and Smith (1971, 64) say, "In any analysis, the assumptions drive the conclusions:" the virtue of systems analysis was the ability to use it to explore "all assumptions" and, "In this important sense, systems analysis becomes a method of interrogation and debate suited to complex issues....a set of ground rules for a constructive and divergent debate." But while Enthoven and Smith recognize that assumptions drive the conclusions, they and other users of systems analysis were less than attentive to the ways that systems analysis is not simply analysis. The political-military discourse—in the sense of what we do and don't talk about, and how we talk about it—was structured in subtle and not so subtle ways by systems analysis.

As Enthoven and Smith suggest, "The issue here is not numbers versus adjectives, but clarity of understanding and expression. Numbers are an important part of our language. Where a quantitative matter is being discussed, the greatest clarity of thought is achieved by using numbers, even if only expressed as a range" (1971, 69). Yet as one prominent systems analyst wrote, "Quantification is desirable, but it can be overdone; if we insist on a completely quantitative treatment, we may have to

simplify the problem so drastically that it loses all realism" (Quade 1968b, 359).
But systems analysis did more than abridge nuclear reality too far. Systems analysis,
a "knowledge"-making process that is embedded in the organizational routines
of government offices, private think tanks, and sometimes part of public debate,
began to make its own "reality" more than that reality was simply uncovered,
understood, or even obscured through its techniques. How did systems analysis do
this?

As scholars of nuclear discourse have shown, the "clean," precise, sometimes
humorous ways that strategic nuclear planners talk and write to each other
about nuclear weapons and nuclear war distances them from the reality of nuclear
use and enables them to contemplate using nuclear weapons without political
and moral connotations.[29] The abstractions of nuclear discourse also help to "con-
ventionalize" nuclear weapons—that is, make them appear to be more benign, like
non-nuclear weapons. The conventionalization of nuclear weapons is illustrated by
their inclusion in conventional war planning scenarios and of nuclear weapons
among conventional forces. Conventionalization is also seen in the way that blast
effects are "privileged" in systems analysis while thermal and radiation effects are
usually given secondary status if considered at all (Eden 2004).[30] That nuclear
weapons be seen as more like conventional weapons, whose use is more familiar,
whose consequences are believed to be less totally devastating, is important because
the ability to contemplate their use, and actually to use them requires that the users
not be afraid of the violence entailed in making and using the weapons. In this way,
nuclear weapons are demystified, normalized, and familiarized for the specialists in
violence.

On the other hand, the informal and formal systems analysis discourse on nuclear
weapons has the opposite effect when it is used by specialists in violence to mystify
the weapons and the strategy. So, the formal discourse limits those from outside the
strategic nuclear weapons analytical community from understanding, much less
critiquing nuclear arguments on the technical level at which they are conducted. In
this way, the technical discourse of policy modeling decreases the accountability and
transparency of the policy modeling process not only to ordinary citizens and to
non-expert decision makers.

But, the consequences of abstraction go beyond conventionalization and mystifi-
cation. The linguistic abstractions and the mathematical procedures do more than
numb; they also mystify the subject *for and among the experts*. The ways that nuclear
weapons help shape our understanding of and relations to others, what the weapons
do to our own and others' bodies, and how making and preparing to use the weapons
structures our ways of organizing ourselves, economically, politically, and militarily,
is obscured through the practice. In systems analysis, the focus is on technique, and
by using systems analysis, we simultaneously move further from (by omission and

---

[29] See e.g. Cohn 1987; Eden 1991; Green 1966; Gusterson 1996; Nash 1981; Thompson 1981.
[30] The exception is the consideration of radiation effects in the battlefield, and in the case of the
neutron bomb a design where radiation effects are "boosted" over blast effects.

abstraction) and closer to (through a focus on detail and a *sense* of precision) the acts of nuclear violence. It was not just the fact that planners were dealing with a world and conditions that they had never encountered that shaped their conclusions and practices.[31] The formal discourse abstracts the logic and uses of nuclear weapons to the point where the consequences of making and using nuclear weapons are not fully appreciated by the experts, much less raised. Omission, elision, assumption, and false precision were layered upon opacity, hedging, and imprecision. Thus, the most fundamental workings of the logic, belief, and arguments are no longer questioned, debated, re-examined, or perhaps even remembered, much less fully understood by those within the intricate discourse.

Thus, systems analysis became its own baroque and self-fulfilling construction. As a consequence, few analyses looked at the effects of a nuclear "exchange" in the aggregate—counterforce exchange models focus on the effects on weapons, and human deaths are rarely counted in those models (e.g. CBO 1978a; Salman, Sullivan, and Van Evera 1989). Instead, "The question of military or political victory if deterrence fails would depend upon the net surviving destructive capacity of the two sides after the initial counterforce exchanges" (Nitze 1976, 213). Even when numbers of humans injured or killed in a nuclear war are modeled and discussed, analysts have often argued over whether the right assumptions went into the models and the correct quantities were being given in the conclusions (Drell and von Hippel 1976). The debate in other words, was about improving the models so as better to represent the nuclear reality.

But the logic of modeling and its application begins to make its own world, both a cognitive and a real world. Greater numbers of weapons were often "required" as a result of the analysis while the assumptions and results of systems analysis also tended toward increasing the sophistication of weapons and their delivery systems. Thus, systems analysis compounded the effects of other factors that were pushing the development, production, and deployment of ever greater numbers of nuclear weapons—organizational interests, pork barrel politics, technical innovation, and action–reaction dynamics. One had to hedge against failure. Planners assumed that cities would be destroyed with blast (rather than thermal) effects, requiring more and also more accurate nuclear weapons than would otherwise be necessary to destroy a city. In the quest to reduce uncertainty for their own side in a nuclear war scenario, nuclear planners increased the number of nuclear weapons and improved their capabilities (accuracy and range) and this increased uncertainty for the other side, which then boosted as best they could their own nuclear capabilities. Further, these scenarios presume a larger conflictual context, and from within these scenarios of deterrence and war fighting, there is no way out of the conflictual contest. The analysis is often so abstract and disaggregated that the nuclear world is rarely glimpsed for what it is or, more to the point here, how it is

---

[31] Eden (1990) stresses the fact that nuclear outcomes have not been "enacted." Also see Derrida 1984. Adler describes the " 'imaginary' science of nuclear strategy" (1992, 107).

being made.[32] The ways that policy modeling and subsequent preparations for nuclear war reinforce the conflictual context were generally left out of the analysis. Reflexivity was driven out of the process. The unknowable is made known and superficially precise by these formal abstractions, but the price of making it "known" was to paradoxically decrease security.

That there was a nuclear world—nuclear weapons and a nuclear arms race—was *not* the consequence of systems analysis. Nuclear weapons don't just appear out of thin air to meet the requirements of nuclear planners. What humans have done, in their concrete actions in preparing to use nuclear weapons, is to create elaborate systems for the production, further development, stockpiling, transportation, and use of nuclear weapons. Weapons planners and militaries also developed plans and means for the protection of nuclear forces from attack by other nuclear weapons.

In sum, the material and the ideational came together in systems analysis—which should not be surprising since that was the goal of the practice. The nuclear world was in part remade when, based on nuclear "rationality," one side constructed its nuclear forces, thereby mobilizing and making the nuclear world of development, production, stockpiling, and deployment of nuclear weapons. When the other side responded by political or military means, to the forces and policies in part determined by systems analysis, the entire context was further shifted. Good analysts change or redo their calculations when conditions change, and some of the arguments that follow from their analysis may be used to change the world of weapons and strategy yet again. The strategic nuclear belief system existed and elaborated itself, impelled by its own logic, and was only partially stopped by a major shift within the larger political system, the end of the cold war. That the nuclear arms race ended was not the result of some change in systems analytical practices. But nuclear operations research and systems analysis helped make it the kind of nuclear world it became.

Several questions remain. First, in trying to understand the enormous nuclear arsenal of the USA, can one separate the effects of other forces such as organizational biases, from the effects of systems analysis? Was systems analysis too embedded in other processes to be considered as a force on its own? Second, I have not shown why analysts recognized and cautioned against "pitfalls" in using systems analysis, but nevertheless continued to ignore the caveats the best among them would state. Rational actor and cybernetic theories of decision might argue that complex problems will be simplified by decision makers. But why were certain behaviors (such as the tendency to recognize that implausible assumptions were being made, and to make them anyway) so common in systems analysis? Third, why was systems analysis

---

[32] The brilliance of the anti-nuclear activists who argued against all nuclear weapons modernization, and for the abolition of nuclear weapons, was that they drew the whole nuclear "reality," especially the futility of civil defense, to the forefront and ignored arguments about numbers of survivable nuclear forces. Anti-nuclear activists who argued from within the discourse of nuclear planners (see e.g. Forsberg 1982) were sometimes perhaps co-opted in some ways by the logic of nuclear analysis.

adopted over other methods of analysis? Are or were there plausible alternatives to systems analysis? Fourth, to what extent was systems analysis, or something like it a part of Soviet military planning?

Finally, turning to counterfactuals, what would US nuclear planning have looked like in the absence of the practice of systems analysis? Would there have been even more nuclear weapons of greater destructive capability? Did systems analysis actually function as a tool to constrain the organizational and pork barrel elements of the military and politics? Or, would US nuclear weapons policies have been more or differently "rational" without systems analysis? In other words, nuclear forces might have been designed by other criteria, such as Clausewitzian or Just War views of proportionality of political purpose and military means. The best strategists recognized the dilemma of trying to deal with the unknown through policy analysis. As Brent Scowcroft said in congressional testimony on the MX missile that hints at both the role and the limits of any kind of analysis:

We have argued among ourselves for years about what is an adequate deterrence. It doesn't really matter. We will never know what is an adequate deterrence unless these weapons are used, and then we will know what was not an adequate deterrence.

What we have to try to do, though, is to calculate as best we can what is in the minds of the Soviet Union. That is a very difficult thing to do. Deterrence is an attitude, a frame of mind. The best we can do is look at the kind of things they do, the kinds of systems they deploy, the kind of things they rely on, the kinds of defenses that they develop to ascertain what might be an adequate deterrence. (HASC 1983, 95)

Although Scowcroft said, "It doesn't really matter," of course it did matter what the USA built, how much it cost, and how the Soviets reacted. Scowcroft was simply acknowledging the inadequacy and indeed, absurdity of the nuclear policy modeling process. But even Scowcroft failed to recognize that the technical arguments and in particular the policy modeling process itself, were part of the process driving the arms race.

# References

ADLER, E. 1992. The emergence of cooperation: national epistemic communities and the international evolution of the idea of nuclear arms control. *International Organization,* 46: 101–45.
ARKIN, W., and FIELDHOUSE, R. W. 1985. *Nuclear Battlefields: Global Links in the Arms Race.* Cambridge: Ballinger.
BALL, D. 1980. *Politics and Force Levels: The Strategic Missile Program of the Kennedy Administration.* Berkeley: University of California Press.
—— 1986a. Toward a critique of strategic nuclear targeting. In Ball and Richelson 1986, 15–32.
—— 1986b. The development of the SIOP, 1960–1983. In Ball and Richelson 1986, 57–83.
—— and RICHELSON, J. (eds.) 1986. *Strategic Nuclear Targeting.* Ithaca, NY: Cornell University Press.

BATCHER, R. T. 2004. The consequences of an Indo-Pakistani nuclear war. *International Studies Perspectives*, 6 (4): 135–62.

BLAIR, B. 1985. *Strategic Command and Control: Redefining the Nuclear Threat.* Washington, DC: Brookings Institution.

BREWER, G., and SHUBIK, M. 1979. *The War Game: A Critique of Military Problem Solving.* Cambridge, Mass.: Harvard University Press.

BROAD, W. J. 1993. Russian says Soviet atom arsenal was larger than West estimated. *New York Times*, 26 Sept.

BROWN, M. 1994. *Flying Blind.* Ithaca, NY: Cornell University Press.

BUNN, M., and TSIPIS, K. 1983. The uncertainties of a preemptive nuclear attack. *Scientific American*, 249 (Nov.): 38–47.

CARTER, A., STEINBRUNER, J., and ZRAKET, C. (eds.) 1987. *Managing Nuclear Operations.* Washington, DC: Brookings Institution.

—— 1978*b*. *Retaliatory Issues for the U.S. Strategic Nuclear Forces.* Washington, DC: Government Printing Office.

CHILTON, P. (ed.) 1985. *Language and the Nuclear Arms Debate: Nukespeak Today.* London: Frances Pinter.

CIMBALA, S. J. 1995. Deterrence stability with smaller forces: prospects and problems. *Journal of Peace Research*, 32 (Feb.): 65–78.

COHN, C. 1987. Sex and death in the rational world of defense intellectuals. *Signs*, 12: 687–718.

CONGRESSIONAL BUDGET OFFICE (CBO) 1978*a*. *Counterforce Issues for the U.S. Strategic Nuclear Forces.* Washington, DC: Government Printing Office.

CRAWFORD, N. C. 1987. *Soviet Military Aircraft.* Lexington, Mass.: Lexington Books.

DAVIS, L. E., and SCHILLING, W. R. 1973. All you ever wanted to know about MIRV and ICBM calculations but were not cleared to ask. *Journal of Conflict Resolution*, 17: 207–41.

DAVIS, P. (ed.) 1994. *New Challenges for Defense Planning: Rethinking How Much is Enough.* Santa Monica, Calif.: RAND.

DEPARTMENT OF DEFENSE (DOD) 1994. *Nuclear Posture Review.* Unclassified version. Washington, DC: Department of Defense.

—— 2002. *Nuclear Posture Review.* Unclassified excerpts; available at: www.defenselink.mil/news/Jan2002/d20020109npr.pdf;www.globalsecurity.org/wmd/library/policy/dod/npr.htm.

DIRECTOR OF DEFENSE RESEARCH AND ENGINEERING (DDR&E) 1964*a*. Damage limiting: a rationale for the allocation of resources by the US and USSR. 21 Jan.

—— 1964*b*. A summary study of strategic offensive and defensive forces of the U.S. and USSR. 8 Sept.

DERRIDA, J. 1984. No apocalypse, not now (full speed ahead, seven missiles, seven missives). *Diacritics*, 14 (Summer): 20–31.

DOUGHERTY, R. 1987. The psychological climate of nuclear command. In Carter, Steinbruner, and Zraket 1987, 407–25,

DRELL, S. D., and VON HIPPEL, F. 1976. Limited nuclear war. *Scientific American* (Nov.) In Russett and Blair 1978, 144–54.

EDEN, L. 1990 The hypothetical organization: organizational learning and interpretation in U.S. strategic nuclear targeting. Paper presented at the Annual Meeting of the American Political Science Association, Chicago.

—— 1991. Sterilizing destruction: the imaginary battlefield in contemporary U.S. nuclear targeting. Paper presented at the Annual Meeting of the American Historical Association.

—— 2004. *Whole World on Fire: Organizations, Knowledge, and Nuclear Weapons Devastation.* Ithaca, NY: Cornell University Press.

—— and MILLER, S. (eds.) 1989. *Nuclear Arguments.* Ithaca NY: Cornell University Press.

ENTHOVEN, A. C., and SMITH, K. W. 1971. *How Much is Enough? Shaping the Defense Program, 1961–1969.* New York: Harper and Row.

EVANGELISTA, M. 1988. *Innovation and the Arms Race: How the United States and the Soviet Union Develop New Military Technologies.* Ithaca, NY: Cornell University Press.

FORSBERG, R. 1982. A bilateral nuclear-weapon freeze. *Scientific American,* 247 (Nov.): 52–61.

FRANCIS, S. 1995. Warhead politics: Livermore and the competitive system of nuclear weapon design. Ph. D. dissertation, Massachusetts Institute of Technology.

FREEDMAN, L. 2003. *The Evolution of Nuclear Strategy,* 3rd edn. New York: Palgrave.

GLASER, C. L. 1990. *Analyzing Strategic Nuclear Policy.* Princeton, NJ: Princeton University Press.

GLASSTONE, S., and DOLAN, P. J. 1977. *The Effects of Nuclear Weapons,* 3rd edn. Washington, DC: Government Printing Office.

GREEN, P. 1966. *Deadly Logic: The Theory of Nuclear Deterrence.* Columbus: Ohio State University Press.

GREENWOOD, T. 1975. *Making the MIRV: A Study of Defense Decision Making.* Cambridge: Ballinger.

GUSTERSON, H. 1996. *Nuclear Rites: A Weapons Laboratory at the End of the Cold War.* Berkeley: University of California Press.

HAAS, P. 1992. Introduction: epistemic communities and international policy coordination. *International Organization,* 46: 1–35.

HILTS, P. J. 1994. Inquiry links test secrecy to a cover-up. *New York Times,* 15 Dec.

—— 1995. Healthy people secretly poisoned in 40's test. *New York Times,* 19 Jan.

—— 1996. Payments to make amends for secret tests of radiation. *New York Times,* 20 Nov.: A1.

HITCH, C. J. 1965. *Decision-Making for Defense.* Berkeley: Unversity of California Press.

HOUSE OF REPRESENTATIVES, ARMED SERVICES COMMITTEE (HASC) 1983. Hearings on H.R. 2287 Department of Defense authorization of appropriations for fiscal year 1984: part 2 of 8 parts strategic programs. Washington, DC: Government Printing Office.

INTERNATIONAL INSTITUTE FOR STRATEGIC STUDIES (IISS) 1989. *The Military Balance, 1989–1990.* London: Brassey's.

JERVIS, R. 1984. *The Illogic of American Nuclear Strategy.* Ithaca, NY: Cornell University Press.

JOINT CHIEFS OF STAFF 1977. *Military Posture Statement of the Joint Chiefs of Staff, FY 1978.* Washington, DC.

—— 1982. *Military Posture Statement of the Joint Chiefs of Staff, FY83.* Washington, DC.

KAHN, H. 1960. *On Thermonuclear War.* Princeton, NJ: Princeton University Press.

—— and MANN, I. 1957. *Ten Common Pitfalls.* Santa Monica, Calif.: RAND.

KAPLAN, F. 1983. *The Wizards of Armageddon.* New York: Simon and Schuster.

KULL, S. 1988. *Minds at War.* New York: Basic Books.

LARSON, E. V., and KENT, G. A. 1994. *A New Methodology for Assessing Multilayer Missile Defense Options.* Santa Monica, Calif.: RAND.

LIFTON, R. J., and MARKUSEN, E. 1990. *The Genocidal Mentality: Nazi Holocaust and Nuclear Threat.* New York: Basic Books.

LITFIN, K. T. 1994. *Ozone Discourses: Science and Politics in Global Environmental Cooperation.* New York: Columbia University Press.

LITTLE, R. and SMITH, S. (eds.) 1988. *Belief Systems and International Relations.* Oxford: Basil Blackwell.

MACKENZIE, D. 1990. *Inventing Accuracy: A Historical Sociology of Nuclear Missile Guidance.* Cambridge, Mass.: MIT Press.

NASH, H. T. 1981. The bureaucratization of homicide. Pp. 149–60 in *Protest and Survive,* ed. E. P. Thompson and D. Smith. New York: Monthly Review Press.

NITZE, P. H. 1976. Assuring strategic stability in an era of détente. *Foreign Affairs,* 54: 217–18.

O'NEILL, B. 1993. Operations research in strategic warfare. Pp. 2567–73 in *International Military and Defense Encyclopedia,* ed. T. Dupuy. New York: Pergamon.

—— 1994. Game theory models of peace and war. Pp. 995–1053 in *Handbook of Game Theory,* vol. ii, ed. R. J. Aumann and S. Hart. New York: Elsevier Science.

OFFICE OF TECHNOLOGY ASSESSMENT (OTA) 1979. *The Effects of Nuclear War.* Washington, DC: Government Printing Office.

POSTOL, T. A. 1987. Targeting. In Carter, Steinbruner, and Zraket 1987, 373–406.

QUADE, E. S. 1968a. Introduction. In Quade and Boucher 1968, 1–19.

—— 1968b. Pitfalls and limitations. In Quade and Boucher 1968, 345–63.

—— and BOUCHER, W. I. 1968. *Systems Analysis and Policy Planning: Applications in Defense.* New York: Elsevier.

RATHJENS, G. W. 1969. The dynamics of the arms race. *Scientific American* (Apr.). In Russett and Blair 1978, 33–43.

RICKS, T. E. 2004. Rumsfeld gets earful from troops: complaints cite equipment woes, extended tours and pay delays. *Washington Post* (9 Dec.): A01.

ROCKEFELLER, A. 1974. Letter of 24 Apr. to Herbert F. York in reply to his letter of 18 Apr.

ROSENBERG, D. A. 1986. U.S. nuclear war planning, 1945–1960. In Ball and Richelson 1986, 35–56.

RUSSETT, B., and BLAIR, B. 1978. *Progress in Arms Control.* San Francisco: W. H. Freeman.

SALMAN, M., SULLIVAN, K. J., and EVERA, S. V. 1989. Analysis or propaganda? Measuring American strategic nuclear capability, 1969–1988. In Eden and Miller 1989, 172–263.

SAPOLSKY, H. M. 1972. *The Polaris System Development: Bureaucratic and Programmatic Success in Government.* Cambridge, Mass.: Harvard University Press.

SCHWARTZ, S. I. 1995. Four trillion dollars and counting. *Bulletin of the Atomic Scientists* (Nov.–Dec.): 32–52.

SCOURAS, J., and NISSEN, M. J. 1994. *FALCON: A Rule-Based Strategic Force Allocation Model User's Guide.* Prepared for the US Arms Control and Disarmament Agency under AC94OD4112.

SECRETARY OF DEFENSE 1969. *Annual Report, FY 1969.* Washington, DC

—— 1980. *Annual Report of the Secretary of Defense, FY 1981.* Washington, DC

SPINARDI, G. 1990. Why the U.S. Navy went for hard-target counterforce in Trident II. *International Security,* 15: 147–90.

TELLER, E., and FOSTER, J. S. 1961. Some new considerations concerning the nuclear test ban. A RAND Special Report attached to a Memorandum for the President, from Col. (USAF) Godfrey T. McHugh, 7 Apr.

THEE, M. 1986. *Military Technolgy, Military Strategy and the Arms Race.* London: Croom Helm.

THOMPSON, E. P. 1981. A letter to America. *The Nation,* 232 (24 Jan.): 68–93.

WALD, M. L. 1997. U.S. atomic tests in 50's exposed millions to risk. *New York Times,* 29 July: A10.

WILKENING, D. 1994. Future U.S. and Russian nuclear forces: applying traditional analysis methods in an era of cooperation. In Davis 1994, 301–48.

WOOLF, A. 2002. The nuclear posture review: overview and emerging issues. Congressional Research Service.

YENGLING, A. 1997. Telephone interview with the author, 19 Aug.

YORK, H. H. F. 1974. Letter to Albert Rockefeller, 18 Apr.

ZUCKERMAN, S. 1983. *Nuclear Illusion and Reality.* New York: Vintage.

CHAPTER 39

# SOCIAL EXPERIMENTATION FOR PUBLIC POLICY

CAROL HIRSCHON WEISS

JOHANNA BIRCKMAYER

## 1. POLICY EXPERIMENTS

Lift the curtain and "the State" reveals itself as a little group of fallible men in Whitehall, making guesses about the future, influenced by political prejudices and partisan prejudices, and working on projections drawn from the past by a staff of economists. (Enoch Powell in Jay 1996, 297–8)

THE statement, made by the British Conservative politician Enoch Powell, highlights the fact that public policy making involves not only the higher arts of principle, intellect, and persuasion, but also the play of interests and the pushing and hauling of partisans for power and control. While the centrality of interests and prejudices has received a great deal of attention in both the scholarly and popular media, it is Powell's "guesses about the future" and that "staff of economists" that concern us in this chapter.

Policy inevitably deals with an uncertain future. Even with the plethora of statistical series and policy research currently available, policy making has to be based on some degree of guesswork. Powell's economists who project past trends into the future, now supplemented by sociologists and policy scientists of several hues, shed sometimes flickering light on what the effects of policy interventions will be. It is to get closer to understanding the likely effects of a prospective policy that social experimentation was born. The idea is simple: Try out a policy on a small scale and see what happens.

Since the late 1960s, spending on trials of social policy proposals in the USA has consumed over a billion dollars (Burtless 1995). In this chapter we consider the nature of social experiments that have been conducted in the past forty years. We review the efforts of many social scientists and economists to develop systematic empirical evidence about the likely advantages and disadvantages of specific policy proposals through the conduct of social experiments. Then we examine the advantages and disadvantages of social experiments themselves and try to project the current trend line into the hazy future.

# 2. DEFINITION

Social experiments are randomized field trials of a social intervention. Within that rubric, two emphases jostle for primacy (and a third emphasis tags along). Some authors define social experiments (SE) by emphasizing the "trial" in randomized field trial. For them, the hallmark is that a prospective intervention is being tried out on a small scale before it is widely adopted. Not only is it being tried out; it is being studied in its pilot version. The aim is to find out whether the intervention achieves its aims. If so, the assumption is that policy makers should adopt it on a system-wide basis. There is a sense of self-conscious intention to influence policy, and often this intention is accompanied by a sense of urgency as the policy window opens.

Other authors put the stress on randomization. It is randomization that allows experimenters to have confidence that the intervention was the *cause* of whatever changes are observed. In a randomized study, the experimenters select samples from the same population, assign one to the intervention, or "experimental" condition, and the other to a "control" condition. At the end of the period, the groups are compared. Inasmuch as they were very much the same at the start and the only thing that differed over time was exposure to the intervention, any differences at the end are due to the intervention. From a methodological point of view, randomization gives experimenters confidence in their estimates of effects.

The third focus in the definition of social experiments, now widely taken for granted, is that the trial is done in the "field." Gone is the comfortable milieu of the laboratory for studying outcomes. Rather the social scientist conducts the studies in the precincts in which the actual policy will be run. Thus we have randomized field trials.

If the emphasis on randomization is accepted as the guiding principle, then any study of desired outcomes conducted through randomization is an SE. Such a definition sweeps in large numbers of evaluations of existing programs. Many evaluations of social programs are conducted after the programs are enacted, and some of the evaluations (although not nearly as many as evaluators would like) randomize prospective participants into "experimental" and "control" groups. After a period of time, the evaluator compares the status of the two groups on the desired indicators (e.g. health status, earnings, school graduation). To blanket such *post hoc* evaluations into the category of SEs widens the category substantially.

If we confine ourselves to randomized studies undertaken on a test basis to guide adoption of future policy, we have a more focused field of enquiry. It is the definition we adopt here. Of course, the distinctions are not hard and fast. Some evaluations of existing programs are expected to guide future iterations of the program—i.e. to lead to modifications and improvements in the intervention. Sometimes, as in cases where a program at the state level is a possible model for federal policy (states as "laboratories of democracy"), what is an evaluation at one level is an SE at another. Still, the distinction is useful to hold on to. It is important to consider the main purpose for which the SE is done as well as its research design.

# 3. HISTORY

With a little difficulty we could probably trace SEs back to Francis Bacon, but it is sufficiently historical to go back to Sidney and Beatrice Webb. In their 1932 book, *Methods of Social Study* they argue for scientifically based social policy in words that have remarkable resonance for our own times. They advocated research conducted by social scientists trained in experimental methods who conduct independent social investigations and transmit their results to those making social policy. The actual methods, as Ann Oakley (1998a) has pointed out, were developed by educationalists and psychologists in the USA in the late nineteenth and early twentieth centuries. The philosopher Charles S. Peirce, the father of "pragmatism," introduced the idea of randomization into psychological experiments in the 1880s. Some of the early studies dealt with the transferability of memory skills from one subject to another (Oakley cites Thorndike and Woodworth 1901 and Winch 1908). These psychological researchers invented techniques for randomly assigning subjects to experimental treatments. R. A. Fisher who did his research in agriculture and developed much that has become commonplace in statistics, is widely known for championing randomization methods.

With regard to the "field" aspect of policy experiments, Oakley (1998b) reminds us that two US sociologists, Stuart Chapin at the University of Minnesota and Ernest Greenwood at Columbia University, applied experimental methods to the study of social problems in the early years of the twentieth century. Where psychologists tended to work in laboratory settings, pioneering sociologists took their research out into the community. Chapin (1947) describes nine experimental studies that he and others carried out on topics such as recreation programs for delinquent boys, social effects of public housing, and effects of student participation in extracurricular activities. Where others had stated that randomized experiments could be done only under antiseptic laboratory conditions, he was interested in demonstrating that they could be adapted to community settings as well. Greenwood provided a theoretical rationale for applying experimental methods to social issues, described in his book *Experimental Sociology* (1945).

In the first half of the twentieth century, most of the forerunners of current SEs were evaluations of existing programs. They shared many of the characteristics of experiments, but dealt with programs that were already up and running. The intent, nevertheless, was very similar: to see whether a program worked and, if it proved successful to extend and expand it. One evaluation that gained a great deal of attention was the Perry Preschool Project, largely because the preschool participants were followed up into their late twenties and because their lives turned out to be significantly more successful than the lives of kids in the control group (Schweinhart, Barnes, and Weikart 1993). The data provided much of the justification for authorization and reauthorizations of the Head Start program and other early childhood programs. Among other noteworthy early studies were the Eight Year Study of progressive high schools, conducted by Ralph Tyler (unpublished), the Cambridge–Somerville youth worker program that aimed to prevent juvenile delinquency (Powers and Witmer 1951), and the Hawthorne studies of reforms to working conditions in a Western Electric plant (Roethlisberger and Dickson 1939).

A relatively small number of evaluation studies used randomization for assigning participants, but some of them sought to introduce controls in other ways. Campbell and Stanley (1966) wrote a landmark monograph, *Experimental and Quasi-Experimental Designs for Research*, classifying the designs of studies that had been reported. In the language of the time, "experimental" meant that the study had randomly assigned participants to the program (or several variants of the program) and to a control group that did not receive the program. "Quasi-experimental" designs used other strategies to reduce the threat that something other than the program was the *cause* of whatever differences appeared between the groups. Although perhaps not its intent, the Campbell and Stanley book tended to legitimize quasi-experiments for evaluation purposes. Campbell and his collaborators in subsequent versions of the book (Cook and Campbell 1979; Shadish, Cook, and Campbell 2002) have sought to overcome the impression and place randomization back in priority position.

It wasn't until after the Second World War that the three main ideas of SE were combined in large-scale investigations—randomization, study in the field, and intentional preparation for policy change. With the War on Poverty in the 1960s, SEs began their modern history. The first noteworthy SE of the period was the series of income maintenance experiments. They began in 1968 in four sites in New Jersey and were followed by parallel studies in a series of urban and rural locations. The program was an effort to change the existing welfare system by the provision of a guaranteed annual income to poor people (Cain and Watts 1973; Kershaw and Fair 1976; Danziger, Haveman, and Plotnick 1981). The aim of the *experiment* was to test a policy innovation *prior* to enactment.

The income maintenance experiment was followed by experiments with housing allowances (Carlson and Heinberg 1978; Friedman and Weinberg 1983; Kennedy 1980), health insurance (Newhouse 1993), performance contracting in education

(Rivlin and Timpane 1975), and job search (Wolfhagen 1983). Greenberg and Shroder (1997) provide reports on 143 SEs conducted in the USA, one in Canada, and one in the Netherlands. All of them were randomized field trials of prospective new policies (although the policies studied in the later experiments generally represented merely incremental changes in existing programs). Only experiments that had reported results by 1996 are included in the inventory. Their appendix lists seventy-five SEs then still in progress.[1]

To ground the reader in some real examples, Table 39.1 provides information on four SEs which we refer to in the following discussion.

*Income maintenance experiments.* Four income maintenance experiments were run in the 1960s and 1970s at eleven sites to test the impact of variations in a negative income tax program for low-income families. Families were provided with a guaranteed level of benefits and were allowed to earn additional income through work. Program benefits were reduced by a set fraction for each dollar earned. The findings showed that families reduced the number of hours they worked but not by significant amounts. Other results were mixed, with small positive results on many measures. However, by the time results were reported, the political climate had changed. Congress was in no mood to give the poor a blank check. The long and hugely expensive experiment (Greenberg and Shroder 1997 report the cost as $111.7 million) had little policy impact.

*The health insurance experiment* conducted by the RAND Corporation tested the effects of varying levels of cost sharing on the use of health services and health outcomes. It randomly assigned families to one of fourteen fee for service plans or an HMO. A total of 7,708 individuals were tracked in six sites chosen to represent the United States over a period of eight years, making the experiment one of the largest and most expensive in American history. The findings showed that overall, cost sharing reduces use of medical services without substantial negative effects on health. This proved to be a factor in later acceptance of cost sharing as a cost containment strategy in both public programs and private insurance plans.

*Welfare-to-work programs.* In the 1980s, the Manpower Development Research Corporation (MDRC) tested ten specific state programs using random assignment, measuring the impacts and benefit–costs of state welfare-to-work programs, as well as studying their implementation. State and local governments designed, implemented, and operated the programs that were evaluated, and the MDRC developed the evaluation design and conducted the actual evaluation. The findings showed that the tested programs increased earnings and reduced the size of the welfare rolls, the benefits to society as a whole exceeded the social costs of the programs, and the programs usually resulted in net savings for taxpayers. However, the effects were relatively small.

*Nursing home incentive reimbursement experiment.* This experiment, conducted from 1980 to 1983, tested the effects of incentive payments for proprietary nursing homes.

---

[1] A new updated edition of the inventory of social experiments was published in 2004, after we had finished this chapter.

Table 39.1 Four selected social experiments

| Experiment | Tested intervention | Design | Results | Dissemination |
|---|---|---|---|---|
| Income maintenance experiments (1968–78) | Income supplements for welfare recipients with varied tax rate for paid work | Randomly assigned families to varying benefit reduction rates in 11 sites | Payment of income subsidy slightly reduced number of hours worked | Widely published in books, journal articles, and reports |
| RAND health insurance experiment (1974–82) | Varied cost sharing for medical services | Randomly assigned families to different cost-sharing programs in 6 sites | Increases in cost sharing reduced use of health services without significantly affecting health status | Numerous publications, widely disseminated |
| MDRC welfare–to–work experiments (1975–88) | Provided job training and other employment services to AFDC participants | Randomly assigned AFDC recipients to various employment programs in 10 sites | Consistent small positive effects on participants' earnings, reductions in welfare rolls and in cost to taxpayers | Widely disseminated during welfare debates |
| Nursing home incentive reimbursement experiment (1980–3) | Provided reimbursement incentives for nursing homes accepting Medicaid patients | Randomly assigned 36 nursing homes to participate in intervention program or control group | Little effect of reimbursement on health outcomes or discharge of Medicaid patients. Slightly increased admissions of heavy care patients | Not widely disseminated |

The aim was to encourage them to accept more hard-to-care-for Medicaid patients and to discharge patients to lower-care facilities when they had attained acceptable health status. The study was conducted with a total of thirty-six nursing homes in San Diego County, eighteen of which were in the control group. Findings showed that in the first year of the experiment there was no difference between the two groups of nursing homes in the intensity of care that admitted patients required, but in the second year the experimental nursing homes did admit patients in need of more intensive care. No statistically significant differences emerged on achievement of patient health goals or on patient discharges to less expensive facilities. The small size of the sample and the shortness of time over which the experiment was run (thirty months) militated against significant differences. The findings were not disseminated widely, and few people heard about the results.

## 4. THEMES

It seems obvious that social experiments (SEs) are conducted to improve decision making regarding policies under study. However, a direct relationship between the results of SEs and policy decisions presumes a rational policy environment with established pathways for information from experiments to feed into policy decisions. The relationship between the conduct of SEs and the policy environment is more complex than such a simple statement suggests. SEs are generally lengthy and results arrive in changed, sometimes unreceptive policy space. Experiments arise for a variety of reasons and are not always set up to answer directly specific policy questions. And indeed experiments are but one in a multitude of information sources that policy makers must consider when making policy decisions.

In this chapter, we explore the relationship of SEs to policy making. First we look at the advantages of conducting such experiments. We examine contributions to policy and contributions to social science. Then we describe the disadvantages that SEs entail both for the policy process and for social science. Last, we puzzle about their future, in a near-sighted attempt to foresee what use is likely to be made of SEs as political and economic conditions change.

We admit that our view is largely a United States view, but that is not totally our doing. The story of SEs has been largely a US story. The first large experiments were done in the USA and most of the subsequent work has been "made in the USA." In recent years, Canada has jumped on the bandwagon, and the Netherlands has also conducted a few experiments. But most of the experience on which the policy world relies is US work.

Running alongside our discussion of advantages and disadvantages of SEs are three main themes. Hold the pages sidewise and you will see these ideas: (1) The policy world is a complex place. Policy making evolves from ideologies and beliefs, interests, and institutional norms, as well as from competing information. "Scientific evidence" alone will almost never determine the direction of policy making. (2) The research world is no less complex. Technical issues bedevil the study of complex policy issues and affect the extent to which social scientists can derive authoritative evidence. (3) The fit between the worlds of policy and research is inexact. Sometimes the answers that SEs provide bear little resemblance to the questions that decision makers ask. A major misalignment is timing. An experiment may not be completed until long after the questions that provoked the experiment have faded from view. Another issue is the uneasy pattern of communication between researchers and policy makers. Nevertheless, despite all the disabilities that affect SEs, we conclude that a well-done SE provides important information that illuminates the policy field and has at least the potential for influencing policy.

# 5. Advantages of Social Experiments

## 5.1 Policy Advantages

### Provide Data on Likely Outcomes of a Policy Idea

Social experiments are experimental tests of new policy ideas. They provide information to people engaged in the political process of making policy. They advance the *rational component* in policy making (Rivlin 1971). Many policy decisions are made in a relative information vacuum with little known about the actual effects of the policies proposed. Data from well-designed tests of policies under discussion can provide invaluable information about the realities of the expected effects of policy adoption, including the potential for unexpected or negative consequences. In some cases, such information has counted in decisions to adopt a particular policy track. For example, the positive results of the welfare-to-work experiments played a modest role in the further expansion of work requirements in state welfare programs. In addition, the success of state-designed and -implemented welfare-to-work programs may have encouraged later legislation to give states flexibility to design state-specific welfare programs (Greenberg, Linksz, and Mandell 2003; Baum 1991).

Some advocates claim that SEs offer objective information, unsullied by the pull of interests. But objectivity is relative. Social scientists for over a generation have acknowledged that every social science enquiry is inevitably colored by the assumptions, biases, and blinkers of its investigator. Nevertheless, experiments appear less prone to dispute than most other forms of knowledge. They collect information systematically from a known population according to the canons of social science. The element of randomization adds authoritativeness. When there is contention, other social scientists can reanalyze the data to try to support their argument. In resolving disputes, SEs rely on the judgement of the community of social scientists.

(See Howell and Peterson 2004; Krueger and Zhu 2004, on rival interpretations of school choice experiments.) On any reasonable scale, experimental information is credible. In the four experiments that we have cited here, little important disagreement emerged about the interpretation of the findings.

## Clarify Trade-offs

Social experiments can at times clarify the key trade-offs in policy decisions and provide information to debate these trade-offs (Orr 1998). For example, the AFDC Homemaker Home Health Aide Demonstration found that home care did not reduce health costs but did improve clients' sense of well-being. The findings provided policy makers with information to debate the trade-off between the costs and benefits of the program.

## Keep a Policy Idea Alive

One aim ascribed to social experiments is keeping alive a policy idea that cannot muster enough support at the moment to ensure passage. The income maintenance experiments were reportedly undertaken because most members of Congress did not support a negative income tax for the poor to replace the welfare system. The federal Office of Economic Opportunity and academic economists who favored the idea could not carry the day, but they gained support for an experiment (and then additional experiments) in the hopes of making a good case. They might also have hoped that the political winds would change, and members of Congress would come to embrace their idea for income maintenance for the poor. (Despite their efforts, the negative income tax was not to be.)

The contrary assumption, that SEs are used to delay a new policy until the lengthy study is done, does not receive much empirical support. Once a policy proposal has acquired political momentum, it is usually enacted regardless of evidence. Before results were available from the housing allowance experiments, Congress enacted one feature that was still being tested They passed a bill, known as Section 8, that provided subsidized payments for the poor in the private housing market.

## Stock a Library of Information

SEs can create inventories of information for future policy situations (Feldman 1989). Although their sponsors, with their eyes focused on current options, do not intend only to pile up knowledge for the future, that is one likely result. Even if the findings of the experiment have little impact on current discussions, they do provide a stock of information that future political actors and analysts can draw on (Orr 1998). For example, the health insurance experiment notably provided information on elasticities in health care demand that informed later analysis.

## Help to Build Consensus

The focus and intensity of a social experiment, coupled with a general acceptance among researchers of the quality of impact estimates derived through experimental designs, may provide the focal point needed to draw together diverse actors and information sources to agreement. The health insurance experiment finding that cost sharing reduced health care use without harming health led to a fairly broad acceptance among researchers and policy makers of cost sharing as a legitimate cost containment strategy. Similarly, the welfare-to-work experiments broadened acceptance of mandated work requirements in public assistance programs.

## Legitimize Existing Preferences

If the results of an experiment align with preferences of decision makers, they can provide legitimacy to existing policies or preferred alternatives. They can reaffirm policies after the policy has been chosen (Greenberg and Mandell 1991). Some social scientists worry that this kind of after-the-fact legitimization is a misuse of social science. But if the findings support a policy that policy actors have already selected on other grounds, there doesn't seem anything wrong with giving it a social science seal of approval.

At times, social experiments may provide political cover for either difficult or highly contested policy decisions, shifting the onus of decision making onto "science." They may offer policy makers a set of data-driven arguments for or against a particular policy option.

## 5.2 Research Advantages

### Spur the Development of New Research Methods

In order to do the challenging work of SEs, social scientists have had to develop new methods and techniques. They have also had to develop new statistical methods to analyze the data. The field environment, the size of the samples, the rarity of certain groups about whom data is needed, the need to generalize to a larger population, the need to measure difficult concepts—all have contributed to innovations in research methods. Current textbooks bear witness to the methodological advances spurred by decades of social experimentation.

### Real-life Test for Social Theories

Another advantage for social science is that SE gives social scientists the opportunity to test theories in the crucible of real-world settings. They can subject theories and practices based on those theories to actual test. This can help bring abstract theorizing down to a practical level. For example, theories about the value of competition in improving the quality of schools are being tested in a number of SEs that give parents choice of their children's schools (Howell and Peterson 2004). Theories about the positive effects of a non-stigmatizing guaranteed income, implemented through a negative income tax, were studied in urban and rural areas for extensive periods of time.[2]

Many of the pilot ideas that SEs have studied originated not in social science theories but in political or practice settings. For example, the MDRC welfare experiments did not directly test any specific behavioral theory. Nevertheless, they often derived from—or coincided with—theories that were current among social scientists. The studies therefore supported, refuted, or failed to provide convincing evidence regarding the theories to which they were related.

## Provide Interesting Work to Social Scientists

SEs are interesting, frontier studies. They generate considerable enthusiasm among social scientists, especially those who work in research institutes that have the resources to do them well. SEs require skilled staff and the latest statistical know-how to do this kind of demanding work, and only a few organizations have over time been able to establish and maintain the type of expertise needed for such work. An analysis of the 143 SEs identified in *The Digest of Social Experiments* found that three organizations dominate the conduct of SEs in the USA: Abt Associates, the Manpower Demonstration Research Center (MDRC), and Mathematica Policy Research conducted almost half of the experiments reviewed (Greenberg et al. 1999). In Canada, the Social Research and Demonstration Association does most of the social experiments.

One of the interesting things about SEs is that economists are the investigators in most of them. Economists, who haven't been known for their empirical fieldwork, in a sense reinvented survey research for the income maintenance experiments, and developed sampling and analysis techniques from their tradition. Why economists? Many of the topics deal with money. They are testing schemes that expect to reduce government expenditures. Do welfare-to-work programs reduce the welfare rolls and welfare costs? Does nursing home reimbursement increase intake of patients in need of intensive care so that they do not have to stay in (very expensive) hospitals? Do job-finding programs reduce the length of time that unemployed workers receive unemployment compensation? Another reason for the frequent presence of economists is that money is easier to measure than the outcomes that often concern sociologists and psychologists, such as "functional ability" or "age-appropriate childhood development." Policy makers and the public find data on costs and savings more credible than fuzzier concepts. Economists have the techniques to study and model data denominated in dollars.

---

[2] See Kershaw and Fair 1976; Watts and Rees 1976; Palmer and Peckman 1978.

# 6. LIMITATIONS OF SEs

## 6.1 Policy Limitations

### Effects on Decisions

When we review the history of social experiments, we see that they have not had a decisive, direct effect on the ensuing decisions. Of our four examples, only the welfare-to-work experiments were later reflected in policy. Neither the health insurance experiment, the nursing home incentive reimbursement experiment, nor the income maintenance experiments made much of a dent at all, and the findings were relegated to the great analytical storehouse. Even in the welfare-to-work experiments, where experiment results seemed to affect later policy, the result was at best indirect.

Greenberg, Mandell, and their colleagues did a telephone interview study of welfare directors in the states. They found that while most of the state directors knew something about the findings of the welfare-to-work experiments (although not the specifics), they didn't believe the findings had influenced the policies of their own state. What they did value was the demonstration that states could administer the program without much problem and a general sense that work first was better than training first for former welfare recipients. In their 2003 book, Greenberg et al. conclude:

Ironically, however, even though these experiments did have important effects on policy, their role was nonetheless limited ... In particular, many policymakers already viewed the programs tested by the welfare-to-work experiments as attractive on other grounds. Findings from the experiments simply reinforced that view. Consequently, rather than being pivotal to whether the types of programs they tested were adopted, they were instead used persuasively and in designing these programs. In other words, they aided policymakers in doing what they already wanted to do. (2003, 308, 310)

Why should the results of SEs be so marginal? Why doesn't rationality reign?

Social scientists are under no illusions that "scientific evidence" will displace all other sources of understanding. Policy making is also based on ideologies and beliefs, interests, competing information, and institutional norms (Weiss 1983, 1995). The results of social experiments can nudge policy only a small distance, and their influence is dependent in large part on the interplay with the other factors in the policy environment. Social scientists know that legislators and administrative officials have long-standing beliefs and principles that guide much of their orientation toward policy. Their ideological orientation exerts powerful influence over which policy proposals receive even a hearing. Attitudes toward abortion and gay marriage are obviously determined by ideology and principles, but it is not only on such extreme issues that ideology often prevails. For some policy makers, similarly strong beliefs affect their views of the enactment of a draft, the need for standardized performance tests in schools, mandatory sentences for repeat offenders, and needle exchange programs for drug addicts.

Interests are always powerful influences on policy. Drug manufacturers, farmers, radio station owners, state and city service workers, trial lawyers, charities, utility companies, universities, hospitals—almost every organized body in the nation seeks to promote its own well-being through public policy. The jostling among organized interests provides much of the drama in the policy arena. The scene is marked by the formation and dissolution of temporary coalitions of interests as the issues on the agenda shift and change.

Nor does social science represent the only form of legitimate information. The policy world is awash with formation. Lobbyists hawk their own version of past events and futures. Media columnists and editorial writers add to the stew. Many organizations have their own in-house information resources—databases, research units, news services. The availability of 24/7 web-based information in titanic proportions makes getting information much less difficult than interpreting the information with a sense of history and context.

Furthermore, each institution in the policy system has its own set of rules and norms. The US Congress, for example, proceeds according to a system of committee appointments, minority/majority representation on committees, vote taking, reporting to the full body, closing off debate, reconciling different versions of bills passed by the two houses, as well as time schedules, budget limits, pressure group access, and so on, that have major influence on the nature of policy that emerges. Ron Haskins (1991) tracked the instances that the MDRC research was mentioned at various times in the welfare reform policy process and found fewer and fewer specific mentions of the MDRC research as the welfare policy made its way through hearings, bill writing, and consideration in the House and finally in the House–Senate Conference. The internal norms and culture of each institution in the policy system exercise great pressure on its own activities and on the activities of other institutions with which it interacts. These four sets of influences—ideology and beliefs, interests, other information, and institutional norms—set limits to what social science can contribute and how much attention it can mobilize. Social experimentation, as one small subset of social science research, is even further constrained by the surround.

## Misuse of Research Findings

The results of SEs can be misused in policy discussions (Orr 1998). As with any source of information, policy makers may choose to disregard results if they are not congruent with their own beliefs and political agendas. During the congressional welfare reform debates, the welfare-to-work research was used to argue that education and training were effective strategies and that large amounts of federal funding were needed to produce effects. In fact, education and training received little attention in the programs studied, and the experiments showed that relatively low-cost job search and work experience were effective (Haskins 1991).

Policy makers may take note of the general public reaction. If the public is not interested or is skeptical of certain results, policy makers have little incentive to push forward any change based on the results. Results may not even reach the ears of policy makers if the sponsoring agents of the studies themselves do not like the results. What goes to publication can be influenced by the satisfaction (or dissatisfaction) of the agency that asked and paid for the study in the first place. Less insidious is a simple lack of dissemination of experiments' results. In the nursing home incentive study, the departure of the federal staffer who had sponsored the study contributed to the lack of dissemination of the findings. Few people learned of the results, and little use was made of the findings (Greenberg et al. 2003). A reanalysis of the data that showed more positive results from incentives (Norton 1992) went almost totally unnoticed.

Contributing to the risk of misinterpretation or misuse, policy makers may not have a particularly honed sense for the quality of research or indeed have the skills to interpret results correctly when they are presented with them (they are not alone . . . it is difficult for everyone). Policy makers tend to rely on indirect indicators of quality such as the reputation of the researchers, how the research community reacts to the results, and whether the research fits with their own preconceived notions of what the results should be (Orr 1998).

## Simplistic Thinking

SE encourages policy makers to ask a simple question: What works? It leads them to think that social scientists can identify one policy that has the desired results. It discourages them from asking follow-up questions: For whom does it work? Under what conditions? What kind of implementation is necessary? How much difference does it make? What are other alternatives and how effective are they?

## Ability of Researchers to Work in the Policy World

Social experiments take place in the messy world. The kinds of social scientists who have the requisite knowledge of research design, sampling, measurement, and statistical analysis are not always the kinds of social scientists who communicate well with political actors. Experimenters in these circumstances have to listen. They have to be aware of what policy options are feasible. They should know the history of political battles already waged on the turf. And still they have to know the scientific literature and the intricacies of research design and conduct. Such people can be hard to find. In their stead come highly skilled researchers who may have little skill, and often less interest in aligning their experiment with the world of politics.

## Heightened Scrutiny

The results of social experiments may fare somewhat better than other research findings as they are less assailable by opponents. This occurs, in part, as the research community tends to support the results of randomized experiments and thus, may present a more unified front for policy makers trying to understand what researchers believe. Thus, for example, the health insurance experiment produced generalized agreement among the research community that cost sharing could reduce health care without detrimental effects on health—a question that until then no study had adequately answered. And yet, even some of the best social experiments are open to methodological critique and indeed sometimes may be treated to a more rigorous critique than might be expected due to their high visibility in both the research and the policy worlds. The school choice experiments are an example (e.g. Howell and Peterson 2004; Krueger and Zhu 2004). Because parental choice of schools is such a politically loaded issue, studies are scrutinized in meticulous detail.

## 6.2 Research Limitations

Social experiments are not easy to bring off. To be at all persuasive, social experiments require big slugs of time, lots of money, powerful research expertise, and enough flexibility to respond to changing conditions and questions while the experiment is in process. The impact of social experiments on policy making is limited not only by the political process but also by the constraints and limitations of the research world. Social science methods themselves are not always ideal for describing and analyzing complex policy issues.

### Design Challenges

Researchers are plagued by a series of challenges when conducting research in the real world. Experiments pose difficulties all along the way. The first problem is choice of sites. Even though the policy option that an experiment is testing is usually intended to apply to all members of the relevant group in the nation (or the state), the experiment cannot be implemented among a random sample chosen throughout the nation. The intervention can be offered (and studied) in only a few places. Even the most expensive SEs have had to limit the intervention to a few sites. How does the researcher decide what sites are "typical" or "representative" enough to stand in for the nation as a whole? Researchers avoid places with obviously unusual features, but much of the choice depends on which sites agree to cooperate.

Another problem is recruitment. The design demands enlistment of nursing homes or low-income households, and the experimenter has to convince the required number of units to sign on. About half of them have to be told that they will not receive any new services but will be required to give periodic information. Locating participating units, explaining the conditions of the experiment, and convincing them to participate is no small task. Then there is the issue of when to tell participants that they might be in the control group and receive no service at all. Cook and Shadish (1994) provide a balanced discussion of the pluses and minuses of revealing the possibility of control group status at various points in the recruitment process. It is an important issue because if people (or organizations) refuse to participate because they know about the no-service possibility, the randomness of the assignment is compromised.

Another problem is being sure that the program is being implemented as planned. If, say, the state welfare agency is not delivering the job-search services it is supposed to be offering, i.e. the intervention is not on offer, the SE would be testing the effects of a phantom policy or of an unknown intervention of the agency's own devising. Results of the SE would be meaningless. From experience, researchers have learned the importance of monitoring the implementation of the intervention.

Probably the most basic design issue is implementing and maintaining randomization. Often researchers do not do the random assignment themselves. The operating agency selects participants for its programs and in the process is expected to assign participants to intervention and control groups according to the protocols prepared by the researchers. The actual assignment is "often carried out by a social worker, nurse, physician, or school district official" (Cook and Shadish 1994, 558). Sometimes these people misunderstand what they are expected to do, and sometimes they are tempted to use their professional judgement in assignment decisions. Researchers have learned that they must not only train agency staff but also maintain an oversight presence to ensure that assignment is indeed random.

Nor is that the end of the problem. What started as true randomized assignment may become undone as time goes on. In some cases the experiment does not enroll enough participants. Agency staff therefore may raid the control group to fill slots in the program. People labeled "controls" may in truth receive the intervention. Or, and this is inevitable, participants may drop out of the program and the study. That would be fine if they dropped out equally from intervention and control groups for similar reasons. However, it is usually more common for controls to drop out. They are not receiving services and they have less reason to persevere. For example, in the income maintenance experiments, higher drop-out rates were registered in the control group and in some of the experimental groups receiving smaller benefits than in the more generous benefit groups. The effect of differential drop-out is to compromise the equality of the groups. A selection bias is reintroduced.

In other cases, the control group may become contaminated by being inadvertently exposed to the intervention under study. Teachers receiving an experimental professional development course may share some of their new learnings with fellow teachers in their school, regardless of their official "control" status.

The list of complications goes on and on. As researchers have become more sophisticated over time and with experience, they have identified a host of further threats to the validity of SEs. Manski and Garfinkel (1992) suggest that some interventions might cause changes in norms and attitudes in the community, and the changed community attitudes would influence the success of the intervention. Heckman (1992) and Heckman and Smith (1995) have written that people who enlist in SEs may not be representative of people who would participate in full-scale programs. Moffitt (1992, 2004), too, has worried about "entry effects," the conditions of a full-scale program that would affect participants' behavior that do not show up in small-scale experiments.

## Time

The worlds of research and policy do not work in tandem. Social experiments are time consuming, often taking many years to design, implement, and finally analyze and report results. The policy process meanwhile has moved forward and the results of a SE arrive in a new, changed policy environment. Research results may have little or no relevance in this changed policy world. For example, the health insurance experiment began at a time when the development of a national health care system was under active consideration, and the impact of cost sharing had real relevance. By the time the results of the experiment were known, the health care debate had petered out and national health care was no longer an imminent possibility. The relevance of the results was greatly diminished (Greenberg et al. 2003).

In the past it has often taken four or five years (or more) before experimental results were ready. The housing allowance experiment ran much longer. It studied the effect of giving housing allowances to low-income people not only on the families involved but also on the *supply* of housing. It had to go on long enough for landlords to increase the number of housing units available to recipients of allowances. The study ran (in two cities) for eleven years (Bradbury and Downs 1981).

On the other hand, some experiments are too short to produce convincing results. The nursing home incentive study ran for thirty months. Many nursing homes were evidently not willing to change their practices in response to the short-term monetary incentives. One of the sponsoring agency's reports states:

To the participants [nursing homes] . . . it may seem a very brief duration and there may be reluctance to make staffing, policy, and organizational changes which could affect their environment long after the experiment is concluded. (Greenberg et al. 2003, 107)

Yet even within that brief time period, the study was not able to catch the wave. By the time it was completed, political interest had moved away from incentives and toward regulation.

Foresight is not a particularly strong point of social science. Trying to figure out what policy issues will be lively at some future point is an exercise for a soothsayer. Knowing how rapidly the political canvas changes, knowing how volatile the complexion of government is these days with the country divided almost equally between Republicans and Democrats, knowing how policy windows open and shut as the economy changes, can we ever be confident that we are foreseeing an appropriate mix of interventions? Many people worry about issues of causation in experimentation. We worry about the clouded crystal ball. Fortunately or not, in recent years SEs have become more modest. As noted in the next paragraph, they are making do with available data, and they are taking less time to complete. But they are testing more modest initiatives.

## Expense

Expense can limit the value that social experiments can provide to policy making. There is generally a direct relationship between the complexity of a research design and its cost. The more policy alternatives, settings, or types of participants tested, the more expensive is the experiment likely to be. Thus, cost plays a direct role in limiting the relevance of the findings of social experiments to particular policy questions. Over time, social experiments appear to be becoming simpler and consequently cost less. Greenberg et al. (1999) suggest that this is due in part to the increased use of administrative databases rather than special surveys, an increase in the likelihood that organizations that would run the program are the ones involved in the social experiment (as opposed to developing new programs run by the research organization), simpler designs with fewer groups, and shorter tracking periods for participants.

## Limits on How Much Can be Tested

It is a rare experiment that can test all the variations in a particular policy that may be relevant to the question under study. Thus, the findings of social experiments are limited only to specific alternatives tested. SEs take place in a limited number of sites with a particular set of participants, and the findings may not generalize to other settings or participants. The time horizon is often truncated (although not in the health insurance experiment). Only a few social experiments can assess trade-offs among components of the intervention. Almost none are large enough to examine differences among multiple subgroups of the client population (the income maintenance experiments are an exception). Few examine the behavior of the staff implementing the program and so have little to say about practices that are associated with better or worse outcomes. Costs of the intervention are not always carefully calculated (for example, in the nursing home reimbursement experiment, officials were unable to separate costs of running the program from costs of the study (Greenberg and Shroder 1997)).

A distinction can be made between "black box" experiments, which test one or a few treatments, and "response surface" experiments that test a wide range of treatments (Greenberg et al. 2003; Burtless 1995). Examples of the latter are the income maintenance experiments of the 1960s and 1970s in which income guarantees and tax rates were varied across the treatment groups and the health insurance experiment in which cost sharing was varied across the groups. Greenberg et al. (2003) conclude that if the particular intervention that is being tested is still on the policy agenda when the experiment is concluded, the black box experiment would be fine. However, that is almost never the case. The advantage of the "response surface" experiment is that the design allows for the estimation of elasticities over a range of treatment options and its results can be used in later simulation models well into the future.

## Small Effects

Social experiments almost never produce slam-dunk findings. If a proposed intervention were so obviously superior, there would probably be little reason to experiment. Most policy proposals are uncertain. The results of experimentation are often marginal. There are small gains in certain circumstances with some subpopulations. Interpretation becomes critical.

Because experimentation is such a difficult craft, the results are not always authoritative. Decisions about the course of the experiment have to be made all along the way. Compromises are made, sometimes in response to crises in the environment, sometimes to fit within a budget, sometimes to suit the skills of the available staff, sometimes to meet deadlines, sometimes in an attempt to answer new questions that emerge in the course of the study. Other researchers will critique the findings. They may reanalyze the data. They will come up with new models that they claim better account for the patterns in the data. The experiment can get captured by the research experts and become fodder for struggles for dominance.

## Feasibility of Random Assignment for Organizational/Community Interventions

Some innovative policy ideas involve intervening in neighborhoods or systems or states. Rather than giving service to individuals one at a time, the proposed policy is designed to change the practices and culture of a larger entity. Examples include: changing the attitude of welfare offices so that staff priority is to place the client in a job; changing the practices in a neighborhood so that families, restaurants, and law enforcement agencies actively work to prevent youngsters from drinking alcohol; and changing the culture of a school system so that teachers and administrators actively welcome parents to participate in their child's education. To test ideas like these in an SE requires study not so much of individuals as of the units that are being altered— welfare offices, neighborhoods, or school systems. The interest is the behavior of the collectivity.

The obvious solution is to randomize the unit. A certain number of school systems or neighborhoods might be assigned randomly to the intervention or to a control group. However, as the size of the unit increases (say, to counties or states), fewer units can be studied. It is extraordinarily difficult and expensive to study a large number of neighborhoods or counties, and few studies have managed to go beyond ten or twelve. However, with only a limited number of cases, the laws of probability do not necessarily work. Any differences observed between the intervention group and the control group may be the result of chance. There are too few cases to even out the lumps of chance. Therefore, randomization of large units is a partial solution at best. Here is an issue where research innovations are needed and are currently being developed.

Another reason for the objection to random assignment is that a city is not a city is not a city, nor are neighborhoods interchangeable, or health systems or schools. Each of them has a history. Each has a set of established traditions. Each has a culture that has developed over generations. Each has attracted particular kinds of civic organizations and program staff and residents. Harlem is not the South Side of Chicago, which is not Watts. P S 241 in Brooklyn is not the same as the Condon School in Boston (Towne and Hilton 2004). Even if a researcher were randomly to assign neighborhoods, they wouldn't be totally comparable, and differences observed at the end might be due not so much to the intervention as to the whole complex of prior history and culture. For example, an evaluation of a program to promote nutritious food products randomly assigned supermarkets in Washington and Baltimore. The intervention group of markets placed nutritious products in favorable shelf locations and distributed fliers about nutrition. The control group did nothing. The measure of success was the customers' purchase of nutritious foods. Results showed that there were more differences between the two cities than between the experimental and control groups.

## Ethics

Ethical issues have dogged experimentation since its beginning. People have displayed considerable concern with withholding a social good from one group regardless of degree of need. Practitioners are often loath to allow services to be allotted on the basis of chance, without exercise of their own professional judgement. Beneficiaries of service object strongly to being placed in a no-service control group. A host of ethical issues (withholding services for those eligible, full disclosure of experimental procedures, right to refuse, harm to participants) may significantly limit the questions that social experiments can address.

The rebuttal is that no one really knows whether the service is a social "good" until it has been studied. Many experiments find that the intervention is no better than standard service—or even detrimental. Thus, the nursing home reimbursement experiment did not show positive effects from the reimbursement scheme. Bickman's study of intensive mental health service, which included all the professionally fashionable bells and whistles, showed that intensive service did not have better results than regular service (Bickman 1996).

## Complexity of Interventions

Perhaps the most vivid argument against experiments is that they assume that interventions have a simplicity that can be captured in a treatment/no-treatment design. Many interventions are highly complex social interactions, and simple cause-and-effect patterns may not be easily detected. The "program" is often implemented differently by staff, and the desired outcomes are social processes that cannot be readily measured by simple metrics. Studying the effects of psychotherapy, for example, poses all manner of problems because of the inherently personal ways in which therapists work and clients respond. No matter what label one affixes to the "brand" of psychotherapy, or how assiduously one tries to train therapists to use the same procedures, critics argue that quantitative randomized studies cannot yield sensible results.

Similarly, educators often say that interactions within a classroom, such as the introduction of a new teaching method, cannot be studied appropriately by quantitative randomized techniques. The assumption that all teachers trained in the new teaching method will implement it consistently, and that children in all classrooms will react in similar ways, represents a fundamental misunderstanding of the variability of teaching and learning. The rejoinder is that despite the variability, which certainly introduces more error of measurement, large samples should show the extent to which mean scores (of social functioning, of math achievement, of attendance) differ across populations exposed and unexposed to the intervention. In Cook's (2001) words: "It is not an argument against random assignment to claim that some schools are chaotic, the implementation of a reform is usually highly variable, and that treatments are not completely faithful to their underlying theories." There is enough consistency in human behavior, experimentalists claim, to allow an experiment to reach valuable conclusions about whether an innovation is worth adopting.

# 7. Conclusions

We started this chapter with a description of three distinctive traits of SEs: research in the field, conducted through random assignment of samples of prospective beneficiaries to intervention and control conditions, in order to test the probable success of a policy intervention. The first two characteristics are increasingly accepted as viable and necessary. Research in the field has now become mainstream practice. Randomized studies have received considerable support not only from the research community (although some researchers, particularly in the field of education, have lodged vigorous dissents) but also in Congress. For example, the education legislation that Congress passed in 2002 gives preference to evaluation studies with randomized designs. It is the third feature that may no longer be as firmly established: the prospective test of alternative policies.

SE came into prominence in the late 1960s at a time of turbulent policy change. It was part of the climate of innovation and radical reform that was sweeping the country. In the late 1980s and 1990s, as interest in fundamental change lessened, the fortunes of experimentation also shifted. Experiments continued to be done, more of them in fact, but fewer resources were devoted to them. The emphasis changed from major innovations to marginal improvements in existing programs. In Burtless's words, they were "narrower in focus, less ambitious, and less likely to yield major scholarly contributions" (1995, 63). Now, at a time of budget deficits and fiscal stringency in the USA and elsewhere, the likelihood of new domestic initiatives seems low. It is not a time when large new ideas will be tested, at least with government funds. The trend is to test minor modifications, preferably cost-saving modifications, and shifts of activity to the private sector. If you were considering investment in large-scale SEs, our advice would be: hold off. The product is a sound one, with high potential, but the time is not now—at least in the USA. But hang in. Some version of SEs will have their day.

We also began our story with an outline of three themes: the complexity of the policy world, the technical complexity of the research world, and the alignment or misalignment between experimental findings and policy questions. Overall, SEs have showed the possibilities and the limits of affecting policy through social science research. They have contributed considerable new knowledge. Some of their findings have infiltrated the policy arena and are part of policy-speak (Anderson 2003; Weiss 1999). Influentials in Congress, federal agencies, international organizations, interest groups, and the media learn to be conversant with experimental findings in order to take an informed part in policy conversation.

On the other hand, there are no examples of an SE that led directly to policy change. Results of the health insurance experiments were so late and so unfocused on actual legislative proposals that they were pretty much ignored—except by economists, who have used them to model new proposals. The nursing home reimbursement experiment results also arrived late, after the zing had gone out of the incentive idea. Almost nobody was still interested in incentives for nursing homes; the action was in the area of regulation. While widely published, the income maintenance experiments led to little concrete change in policy. The welfare-to-work experiments seemed to have policy consequences. The MDRC study provided support for mandatory work-first requirements and demonstrated the ability of states to design and manage their own welfare programs. All three of these program design aspects ultimately ended up in the Family Support Act of 1998. Nevertheless as we have seen, the experiment merely reinforced what policy makers were planning to do on other grounds.

Because policy making is such a complicated business, with so many players pursuing such divergent interests, it is overly optimistic to expect research information to carry the day. Even the high-quality information supplied by SEs cannot overwhelm all the other forces on the scene. And as we have seen, the timing of SEs is often off. The policy agenda moves on, while the SE is still studying last year's proposals.

Yet, totting up advantages and disadvantages, we come out in favor of further experimentation. The world is in dire need of greater understanding of the consequences of government action. Social experimentation cannot fully satisfy the needs for knowledge about policy outcomes, partly because of the intrinsic nature of social science research and partly because of the limitations imposed by the conditions under which it is done. Still it makes headway. Anything that advances rationality in the messy world of policy is worth supporting. Not venerated or kowtowed to, but cheered on.

But we also need to moderate our expectations of the contributions that SE can make. The notion of basing policy strictly on experimental evidence is wrong-headed. SE doesn't tell everything that a polity needs to know about a pending policy option.

Many other considerations have to go into government action, such as popular demands, costs, capabilities available for implementing the policy, competing needs, effects on neighboring policies, and so on. Resolution comes through politics. Although the word has fallen on evil times, politics is the system we have for resolving differences in our complex societies and reaching decisions that are at least minimally acceptable to all parties (for a resounding affirmation of politics, see Crick 1972).

Evidence of policy outcomes cannot and should not supplant the play of politics as the basis of policy. Of course, we do not want to see policy developed on the basis of faulty understanding of the situation or unrealistic expectations for the effects of action, but it does seem presumptuous to think that experimental data alone can point to the best resolution of complex policy issues. History matters, as do political culture and institutional practices. What SE can do is illuminate the understanding of publics and elites and infuse policy discussion with insight.

Science and politics cohabit in the policy sphere, but their alliance is an uneasy one. Social scientists, to put the best face on the relationship, have pointed to the "value-added" features that social science brings to the table: an inventory of knowledge for the future to draw on, general enlightenment of elites and publics in the present, puncturing of faulty assumptions, and confirmation of wise instincts for action. But for all the understanding and insight contributed by the social sciences—and by SEs in particular—they do not run the show. There is inevitable tension between science and politics, and convergence is usually a happy accident.

## References

ANDERSON, L. 2003. *Pursuing Truth, Exercising Power: Social Science and Public Policy in the 21st Century.* New York: Columbia University Press.

BAUM, E. B. 1991. When the witch doctors agree: the family support act and social science research. *Journal of Policy Analysis and Management,* 10: 603–15.

BICKMAN, L. 1996. A continuum of care: more is not always better. *American Psychologist,* 51: 689–701.

BRADBURY, K. L., and DOWNS, A. (eds.) 1981. *Do Housing Allowances Work?* Washington, DC: Brookings Institution.

BURTLESS, G. 1995. The case for randomized field trials in economic and policy research. *Journal of Economic Perspectives,* 9: 63–84.

—— and ORR, L. L. 1986. Are classical experiments needed for manpower policy? *Journal of Human Resources,* 21: 606–39.

CAIN, G. G., and WATTS, H. W. (eds.) 1973. *Income Maintenance and Labor Supply.* Chicago: Rand McNally.

CAMPBELL, D. T., and STANLEY, J. C. 1966. *Experimental and Quasi-Experimental Designs for Research.* Boston: Houghton-Mifflin.

CARLSON, D. B., and HEINBERG, J. D. 1978. *How Housing Allowances Work: Integrated Findings from the Experimental Housing Allowance Program.* Washington, DC: Urban Institute.

CHAPIN, F. S. 1947. *Experimental Designs in Sociological Research.* New York: Harper and Row.

COOK, T. D. 2001. Sciencephobia. *Education Next,* Fall: 62–9; available at www.educationnext. org.

—— and CAMPBELL, D. T. 1979. *Quasi-Experimentation: Design and Analysis Issues for Field Settings.* Chicago: Rand McNally.

—— and SHADISH, W. 1994. Social experiments: some developments over the past fifteen years. *Annual Review of Psychology,* 45: 545–80.

CRICK, B. 1972. *In Defense of Politics,* 2nd edn. Chicago: University of Chicago Press.

DANZINGER, S., HAVEMAN, R., and PLOTNICK, R. 1981. How income transfer programs affect work, savings and income distribution. *Journal of Economic Literature,* 19: 975–1028.

FELDMAN, M. 1989. *Order without Design: Information, Production and Policy Making.* Stanford, Calif.: Stanford University Press.

FRIEDMAN, J., and WEINBERG, D. H. 1983. History and overview. Pp. 11–22 in *The Great Housing Experiment,* ed. J. Friedman and D. H. Weinberg. Beverly Hills, Calif.: Sage.

GREENBERG, D., LINKSZ, M., and MANDELL, M. 2003. *Social Experimentation and Public Policymaking.* Washington, DC: Urban Institute.

—— and MANDELL, M. 1991. Research utilization in policymaking: a tale of two series (of social experiments). *Journal of Policy Analysis and Management,* 10: 633–56.

—— and SHRODER, M. 1997. *Digest of Social Experiments.* Washington, DC: Urban Institute Press.

—— —— and ONSTOTT, M. 1999. The social experiment market. *Journal of Economic Perspectives,* 13: 157–72.

GREENWOOD, E. 1945. *Experimental Sociology: A Study in Method.* New York: King's Crown Press.

HASKINS, R. 1991. Congress writes a law: research and welfare reform. *Journal of Policy Analysis and Management,* 10: 616–32.

HECKMAN, J. J. 1992. Randomized and social policy evaluation. In Manski and Garfinkel 1992, 201–30.

—— and SMITH, J. A. 1995. Assessing the case for social experiments. *Journal of Economic Perspectives,* 9: 85–110.

HOWELL, W. G., and PETERSON, P. E. 2004. Use of theory in randomized field trials: lessons from school voucher research on disaggregation, missing data, and the generalization of findings. *American Behavioral Scientist,* 47: 634–57.

JAY, A. (ed.) 1996. *The Oxford Dictionary of Political Questions.* Oxford: Oxford University Press.

KENNEDY, S. D. 1980. *Final Report of the Housing Allowance Demand Experiment.* Cambridge, Mass.: Abt Associates.

KERSHAW, D., and FAIR, J. 1976. *The New Jersey Income-Maintenance Experiment,* i: *Operations, Surveys and Administration.* New York: Academic Press.

KRUEGER, A. B., and ZHU, P. 2004. Another look at the New York City School Voucher Experiment. *American Behavioral Scientist,* 47: 658–98.

MANSKI, C. F., and GARFINKEL, I. (eds.) 1992. *Evaluating Welfare and Training Programs.* Cambridge, Mass.: Harvard University Press.

MAYO, S. K., et al. 1980. *Housing Allowances and Other Rental Housing Assistance Programs.* Cambridge, Mass.: Abt Associates.

MOFFITT, R. A. 1992. Evaluating methods for program entry effects. In Manski and Garfinkel 1992: 231–52.

—— 2004. The role of randomized field trials in social science research: a perspective from evaluations of social welfare programs. *American Behavioral Scientist,* 47: 506–40.

NEWHOUSE, J. P. 1993. *Free for All? Lessons from the RAND Health Insurance Experiment.* Cambridge, Mass.: Harvard University Press.

NORTON, E. C. 1992. Incentive regulation of nursing homes. *Journal of Health Economics*, 11: 105–28.

OAKLEY, A. 1998*a*. Experimentation and social interventions: a forgotten but important history. *British Medical Journal*, 317: 1239–42.

—— 1998*b*. Public policy experimentation: lessons from America. *Policy Studies*, 19: 93–114.

ORR, L. L. 1998. *Social Experimentation: Evaluating Public Programs with Experimental Methods*. Cambridge, Mass.: Abt Associates.

POWERS, E., and WITMER, H. 1951. *An Experiment in the Prevention of Delinquency: The Cambridge–Somerville Youth Study*. New York: Columbia University Press.

RIVLIN, A. 1971. *Systematic Thinking for Social Action*. Washington, DC: Brookings Institution.

—— and TIMPANE, P. M. (eds.) 1975. *Planned Variation in Education: Should We Give up or Try Harder?* Washington, DC: Brookings Institution.

ROETHLISBERGER, F. J., and DICKSON, W. J. 1939. *Management and the Worker: An Account of a Research Program Conducted by the Western Electric Company, Chicago*. Cambridge, Mass.: Harvard University Press.

SCHWEINHART, L. J., BARNES, H. V., and WEIKART, D. P. 1993. *Significant Benefits: The High/ Scope Perry Preschool Study through Age 27*. Ypsilanti, Mich.: High/Scope Press.

SHADISH, W. R., COOK, T. D., and CAMPBELL, D. T. 2002. *Experimental and Quasi-Experimental Designs for General Causal Inference*. Boston: Houghton-Mifflin.

TOWNE, L., and HILTON, M. (ed.) 2004. *Implementing Randomized Field Trials in Education: Report of a Workshop*. Washington, DC: National Academies Press.

WEISS, C. H. 1983. Ideology, interests, and information: the basis of policy positions. Pp. 213–45 in *Ethics, the Social Sciences, and Policy Analysis*, ed. D. Callahan and B. Jennings. New York: Plenum Press.

—— 1995. The four I's of school reform: ideology, interests, information, and institutions. *Harvard Education Review*, 65: 571–92.

—— 1999. The interface between evaluation and public policy. *Evaluation*, 5: 468–86.

WOLFHAGEN, C. F. 1983. *Job Search Strategies: Lessons from Louisville WIN Laboratory*. New York: MDRC.

PART IX

# PUBLIC POLICY, OLD AND NEW

CHAPTER 40

# THE UNIQUE METHODOLOGY OF POLICY RESEARCH

## AMITAI ETZIONI

POLICY research requires a profoundly different methodology from that on which basic research relies, because policy research is always dedicated to *changing* the world while basic research seeks to understand it as it is.[1] The notion that if one merely understands the world better, then one will in turn know how to better it, is not supported by the evidence.

Typical policy goals are the reduction of poverty, curbing crime, cutting pollution, or changing some other condition (Mitchell and Mitchell 1969, 393). Even those policies whose purpose is to maintain the status quo are promoting change—they aim to slow down or even reverse processes of deterioration, for instance that of natural monuments or historical documents. When no change is sought, say, when no one is concerned with changing the face of the moon, then there is no need for policy research in that particular area.

Moreover, although understanding the causes of a phenomenon, which successful basic research allows, is helpful in formulating policy, often a large amount of other information that is structured in a different manner best serves policy makers.[2] Policy researchers draw on a large amount of information that has no

---

[1] The first book to deal with policy sciences and consequently often cited is Lasswell and Lerner's *The Policy Sciences* (1951). However this book does not address the methodological issues at hand. For an early treatment of these issues, see Etzioni 1971*b*, 1968.

[2] For an example of how to structure and present policy research and analysis, see Dunn 1981, 322.

particular analytical base or theoretical background (of the kind that basic research provides).[3] In this sense medical science, which deals with changing bodies and minds, is a protypical policy science. It is estimated that about half of the information physicians employ has no basis in biology, chemistry, or any other science; but rather it is based on an accumulation of experience.[4] This knowledge is passed on from one medical cohort to another, as "these are the way things are done" and "they work."

The same holds true for other policy sciences. For instance, criminologists who inform a local government that studies show that rehabilitation works more effectively in minimum security prisons than in maximum security prisons (a fact that can be explained by sociological theoretical concepts based on basic research)[5] know from long experience that they had better also alert the local authorities that such a reduction in security could potentially lead some inmates to escape and commit crimes in surrounding areas. Without being willing to accept such a "side effect" of the changed security policy, those governments who introduced it may well lose the next election and security in the prison will be returned to its previously high level. There is no particular sociological theoretical reason for escapes to rise when security is lowered. It is an observation based on common sense and experience; however it is hardly an observation that policy makers, let alone policy researchers should ignore. (They may though explore ways of coping with this "side effect," for instance by either preparing the public ahead of time, introducing an alert system when inmates escape, or some other such measure.)

The examples just given seek to illustrate the difference between the information that basic research generates versus information that plays a major role in policy research. That is, there are important parts of the knowledge on which policy research draws that are based on distilled practice and are not derivable from basic research. Much of what follows deals with major differences in the ways that information and analysis are structured in sound policy research in contrast to the ways basic research is carried out.

One clarification before I can proceed: Policy research should not be confused with applied research. Applied research presumes that a policy decision has already been made and those responsible are now looking for the most efficient ways to implement it. Policy research helps to determine what the policy decision ought to be.

---

[3] For example many policy makers subscribe to George L. Kelling and James Q. Wilson's criminology theories because they make sense, despite the fact that they are not grounded in academic research. See Wilson and Kelling 1982. For criticisms of this approach to criminology, see Miller 2001.

[4] "Much" of medicine is not scientifically supported (Inglefinger, Relman, and Findland 1966). "85 percent of the problems a doctor sees in his office are not in the book" (quoted from a physician in Schön 1983, 16).

[5] See Etzioni 1971a, 246–7.

# 1. MALLEABILITY

A major difference between basic and policy research is that malleability is a key variable for the latter though not the former (Weimer and Vining 1989; 4). Indeed for policy researchers it is arguably the single most important variable. Malleability for the purposes at hand ought to be defined as the amount of resources (including time, energy, and political capital) that would have to be expended to cause change in a given variable or variables. For policy research, malleability is a cardinal consideration because resources always fall short of what is required to implement given policy goals. Hence, to employ resources effectively requires determining the relative results to be generated from different patterns of allocation (Dunn 1981, 334–402). In contrast, basic research has no principled reason to favor some factors (or variables) over others. For basic research, it matters little if at all whether a condition under study can be modified and if it can how much it would cost. To illustrate, many sociological studies compare people by gender and age and although these variables may seem relevant, they are of limited value to policy research. Other variables used, such as the levels of income of various populations, the extent of education of various racial and ethnic groups, and the average size of cities, are somewhat more malleable but still not highly so. In contrast, perceptions are much more malleable.

One may say that basic research should reveal a preference for variables that have been less studied; however, such a consideration concerns the economics and politics of science rather than methodology. Because all scientific findings are conditional and temporary and often subject to profound revision and recasting, for basic researchers, retesting old findings can be just as valuable as covering new variables. In short, although in principle for basic research the study of all variables is legitimate, in a given period of time or amongst a given group of scientists, some may consider certain variables as more "interesting" or "promising" than others. In contrast, to reiterate, for policy research, malleability is the most important variable as it is directly related to its core reason for being: Promoting change.

Given the dominance of basic research methodology in the ways policy research is taught, it is not surprising to find that the question of which variables are more malleable than others is rarely studied in any systematic way. Due to the importance of this issue for policy research, some elaboration and illustrations are called for. Economic feasibility is a good case in point. Many policy researchers' final reports do not include any, not even crude estimates of the costs involved in what they are recommending.[6] Even less common is any consideration of the question of whether such changes can be made acceptable to elected representatives and the public at large; that is, political feasibility (Weimer and Vining 1989, 292–324). For instance, over the last decades several groups favored advancing their policy goals through constitutional amendments, ignoring the fact that these are extremely difficult to get passed.

---

[6] See for example Free Expression Project 2003; Raver 2002, 3–19.

In other cases, feasibility is treated as a secondary "applied" question to be studied later, after policy makers adopt the recommended policy. However, the issue runs much deeper than the assessments of feasibility of one kind or another. The challenge to policy research is to determine the relative resistance to change according to the different variables that are to be tackled. And this question must be tackled not on an ad hoc basis, but rather as a major part of systematic policy research. Moreover, if the variables involved are studied from this viewpoint, they themselves may be changed; that is, feasibility is enhanced rather than treated as a given.

Another example of the cardinal need to take malleability into account when conducting policy research concerns changing public attitudes. Policy makers often favor a "public education" campaign when they desire to affect people's beliefs and conduct. Policy makers tend to assume that it is feasible to change such predispositions through a way that might be called the Madison Avenue approach, which entails running a series of commercials (or public service announcements), mounting billboards, obtaining celebrity endorsements, and so on.

For example, the United States engaged in such a campaign in 2003 and 2004 to change the hearts and minds of "the Arab street" through what has also been termed "public diplomacy."[7] The way this was carried out provides a vivid example of lack of attention to feasibility issues. American public diplomacy, developed by the State Department, included commercials, websites, and speakers programs that sought to "reconnect the world's billion Muslims with the United States the way McDonald's highlights its billion customers served" (Satloff 2003, 18). It was based on the premiss that "blitzing Arab and Muslim countries with Britney Spears videos and Arabic-language sitcoms will earn Washington millions of new Muslim sympathizers" (Satloff 2003, 18). A study found that the results were "disastrous" (Satloff 2003, 18). Some countries declined to air the messages and many Muslims who did see the material viewed it as blatant propaganda and offensive rather than compelling.

Actually, policy researchers bent on studying feasibility report that the Madison Avenue approach works only when large amounts of money are spent to shift people from one product to another when there are next to no differences between them (e.g. two brands of toothpaste) and when there is an inclination to use the product in the first place. However, when these methods are applied to changing attitudes about matters as different as condom use,[8] the United Nations,[9] electoral reform, and so

[7] See, for instance, The Advisory Group on Public Diplomacy in the Arab and Muslim World, "Changing minds, winning peace: a new strategic direction for U.S. public diplomacy in the Arab and Muslim world," Oct, 2003, Edward P. Djerejian, chair.

[8] For instance, the Centers for Disease Control conducted a ten-year ad campaign to educate Americans about condoms and to encourage their use to prevent HIV transmission. After spending millions of dollars on these ads, a CDC study found that only 45 % of sexually active high school students used a condom the last time they had sex: see Scott 1994. A recent evaluation of the program issued an unqualified "no" in answer to the question, "Has the U.S. federal government's HIV/AIDS television [public service announcement] campaign been designed not only to make the public aware of HIV/AIDS but also to provide appropriate messages to motivate and reinforce behavior change?" See DeJong, Wolf, and Austin 2001, 256. Of the fifty-six ads reviewed, fifty were created by the CDC, the other six were created by the National Institute on Drug Abuse.

[9] Star and Hughes 1950, quoted in Berelson and Steiner 1964, 530.

forth, they are much less successful. Changing people's behavior—say to conserve energy, drive slower, cease smoking—is many hundreds of times more difficult. This is a major reason why totalitarian regimes, despite intensive public education campaigns, usually fail. The question of what is most feasible is determined by fiat by policy makers and their staffs rather than by studies that are reported to the policy makers by policy researchers. Hence decisions are often based on a fly-by-the-seat-of-your-pants sense of what can be changed rather than on empirical evidence.[10] One of the few exceptions is studies of nation building in which several key policy researchers presented the reasons why such endeavors can be carried out at best only slowly while at the same time many policy makers claimed that it could be achieved in short order and at low cost.[11]

In a preliminary stab at outlining the relative malleability of various factors, one may note that as a rule the laws of nature are not malleable; social relations, including patterns of asset distribution and power, are of limited malleability; and symbolic relations are highly malleable. Thus any policy-making body that would seek to modify the level of gravity, for example, not for a particular situation (for instance a space travel simulator) but in general, will find this task at best extremely difficult to advance. In contrast, those who seek to change a flag, a national motto, the ways people refer to one another (e.g. Ms Instead of girl or broad), have a *relatively* easy time of doing so. Changes in the distribution of wealth among the classes or races—by public policy—are easier than changes involving the laws of nature, but more difficult than changing hearts and minds.

When policy researchers or policy makers ignore these observations and enact laws that seek grand and quick changes in power relations and economic patterns, the laws are soon reversed. A case in point is the developments that ensued when a policy researcher inserted into legislation the phrase "maximum feasible participation of the poor." This Act was used to try to circumvent prevailing local power structures by directing federal funds to voluntary groups that included the poor on their advisory boards, which thus helped "empower the poor." The law was nullified shortly thereafter. Similarly, when a constitutional amendment was enacted that banned the consumption of alcohol in the United States, it had some severely distorted effects on the American justice and law enforcement systems and did little actually to reduce the consumption of alcohol. It was also the only constitutional amendment ever to be repealed.

Among social changes, often legal and political reduction in inequality is relatively easier to come by than are socioeconomic changes along similar lines. Thus, African-Americans and women gained *de jure* and de facto voting rights long before the differences in their income and representation in the seats of power moved closer to those of whites (in the case of African-Americans) and of men (in the case of women). Nor have socioeconomic differences been reduced nearly as much as legal

[10] Indeed unlike science, Carol Weiss has argued that in the policy field it may be impossible to separate objective knowledge from ideology or interests: see Weiss 1983.

[11] See Carothers 1999; Etzioni 2004.

and political differences, although in both realms considerable inequalities remain. The same is true not just for the United States, but for other free societies and those that have been recently liberated.

In short, there are important differences in which dedication of resources, commitment of political capital, and public education are needed in order to bring about change. Sound policy research best makes the determination of which factors are more malleable than others, which is a major subject of study.

## 2. SCOPE OF ANALYSIS

Another particularly important difference between basic research and policy research methodology concerns the scope of factors that are best encompassed. Policy research at its best encompasses all the major facets of the social phenomenon it is trying to deal with.[12] In contrast, basic research proceeds by fragmenting the world into abstract, analytical slices which are then studied individually.

A wit has suggested that in economics everything has a price; in sociology, nothing has a price. Policy makers and hence researchers are at a disadvantage when they formulate preferred policy alternatives without paying attention to the longer-run economic and budgetary effects—or the effect of such policy on social relations including families (e.g. tax preferences for singles), socioeconomic classes (e.g. estate taxes), and so on.

To put it in elementary terms, a basic researcher may well study only the prices of flowers (together with other economic factors); a physiologist the wilting processes; a social psychologist the symbolic meaning of flowers; and so forth. But a community that plans to grow flowers in its public gardens must deal with most, if not all of these elements and the relations between them. Flowers that are quick to wilt will not be suitable for its public gardens; the community will be willing to pay more for flowers that have a longer life or those that command a positive symbolic meaning, and so on.

Medicine provides another model of a policy science. It cannot be based only on biology, chemistry, anatomy, or any one science that studies a subset of variables relating to the body. Instead physicians draw on all these sciences and add observations of interaction effects among the variables. This forms a medical knowledge base and drives "policy" recommendations (i.e. medical prescriptions). Indeed doctors have often been chastised when they do not take into account still other variables, such as those studied by psychologists and anthropologists. Similarly, international relations is a policy science that best combines variables studied by economists, political scientists, law professors, and many others.

In short, the scope of variables that basic research encompasses can be quite legitimate and effective but also rather narrow. Policy researchers must be more

---

[12] Roe 1998. For an academic policy research perspective, see Nelson 1999.

eclectic and include at least all the variables that account for a significant degree of variance in the phenomenon that the policy aims to change.

## 3. Private and Confidential

Basic research is a public endeavor. As a rule its results are published so that others can critically assess them and piece them together with their findings and those of still others in order to build ever more encompassing and robust bodies of knowledge. Unpublished work is often not considered when scientists are evaluated for hiring and promoting, for prizes, or for some other reason, especially not if the work is kept secret for commercial or public security reasons. Historically, scientific findings were published in monographs, books, and articles in suitable journals. These served as the main outlets for the findings of basic research both because only by making scientific findings public could they become part of the cumulative scientific knowledge base and also because publication indicates that they have already passed some measure of peer review. It is only through peer review that evidence can be critically scrutinized. In recent years findings are still made public but increasingly they are often posted on websites, most of which lack peer review foundations, which is one reason why they are less trusted and not treated as a full-fledged publication. Publication is still considered an essential element of basic research.

In contrast, the findings of policy research are often not published—they are provided in private to one policy maker or another (Radin 1997, 204–18). The main purpose of policy research is not to contribute to the cumulative process of building knowledge but rather to put to service available knowledge. In that profound sense policy research is often not public but client oriented.[13] Although some policy research is conducted in think tanks and public policy schools that may treat it similarly to basic research, more often than not it is conducted in specialized units in government agencies, the White House, corporate associations, and labor unions. And often tools of policy research are memos and briefings, not publications.

Often the findings of policy researchers are considered confidential or are governed by state secret acts (which is the case in many nations that have a less strong view of civil liberties than does the United States). That is, the findings are merely aimed at a specific client or a group of clients, and sharing them with the public is considered an offense.[14]

---

[13] See "Professional practice symposium: educating the client," *Journal of Policy Analysis and Management,* 21 (1: 2002): 115–36.

[14] For instance, the Defense Department has prohibited a Washington think tank from publishing a complete report about the lack of government preparedness for bioterror attacks: see Miller 2004.

# 4. COMMUNICATION

Basic researchers, as a rule, are much less concerned with communicating, especially with a larger, "secular" public than are policy researchers. This may at first seem a contradiction to the previously made point that science (in the basic research sense) is public while policy research is often "private" (even when conducted for public officials). The seeming contradiction vanishes once one notes that basic researchers are obligated to share their findings with their *colleagues*, often a small group, and that they seek feedback from this group for both scientific and psychological valid-ation. However, as a rule basic researchers have little interest in the public at large. Indeed, they tend to be highly critical of those who seek to reach such an audience—as did scholars such as Jay Gould and Carl Sagan (Etzioni 2003, 57–60).

In contrast, policy researchers often recognize the need to mobilize public support for the policies that their findings favor and hence they tend to help policy makers to mobilize such support by communicating with the public. James Fishkin developed a policy idea he called "deliberative democracy," which entailed bringing together a group of people who constitute a living sample of the population for a period of time during which they are exposed to public education and presenta-tions by public figures, and they are given a chance to have a dialogue. By measuring the changes in the views of this living sample, Fishkin found that one is able to learn how to change the public's mind. Fishkin did not just develop the concept and publish his ideas, but conducted a long and intensive campaign through radio, TV, newspapers, visits with public leaders, and much more, until his living sample was implemented in several locations (Fishkin 1997). Indeed, according to Eugene Bardach, policy researchers must prepare themselves for "a long campaign potentially involving many players, including the mass public" (Bardach 2002, 115–17).

Hence, basic researchers are more likely to use technical terms (which may sound like jargon to outsiders), mathematical notations, extensive footnotes, and other such scientific features. On the other hand, policy researchers are more likely to express themselves in the vernacular and avoid technical terms.

One can readily show numerous publications of professors at schools of public policy and even think tanks that are rather similar if not indistinguishable from those of basic researchers.[15] But this is the case because these schools conduct mostly basic, and surprisingly little policy research. For example, on 28 April 2004 Google search found only 210 entries for "policy research methodology," the good part of which referred to university classes by that name. But on closer examination, most entries

---

[15] See for instance the reports of the family research division of the Heritage Foundation, available at www.heritage.org/research/family/issues2004.cfm (accessed 29 Apr. 2004). See also "The war on drugs: addicted to failure," Recommendations of the Citizens' Commission on US Drug Policy, available at www.ips-dc.org/projects/drugpolicy.htm (accessed 29 Apr. 2004).

were referring to basic, not policy research methodology. For instance, a course titled "Cultural Policy Research Methodology" at Griffith University in Australia includes in its course description "basic research techniques, particularly survey methodologies, qualitative methods and a more in depth approach to statistics."[16] Many other entries were for classes in policy *or* research methodology (usually basic). The main reasons for this are (*a*) because few places train people in the special methodologies that policy research requires and (*b*) the reward structure is closely tied to basic research. Typically, promotions (especially tenure) at public policy schools are determined by evaluations and votes by senior colleagues from the basic research departments at the same universities or at other ones. Thus the future of an economist at the Harvard Business School may depend on what her colleagues in the Harvard Economics department think of her work. More informally, being invited to become a member of a basic research department is considered a source of prestige and an opportunity to shore up one's training and research. Conversely, only being affiliated with a policy school (like other professional schools) indicates a lack of recognition, which may translate into objective disadvantages. This pecking order, which favors basic over policy (considered "applied") research, is of considerable psychological importance to researchers in practically all universities. Even in think tanks dedicated to policy research, many respect basic research more than policy research and hope to conduct it one day or regret that they are not suited to carry it out.[17]

People who work for think tanks, which are largely dedicated to policy research, often seek to move to universities, in which tenure is more common and there is a greater sense of prestige. Hence many such researchers are keen to keep their "basic" credentials, although often they are unaware of the special methodology that policy research requires or are untutored in carrying it out in the first place because they were trained in basic research modes instead.

At annual meetings of one's discipline, in which findings are presented and evaluated, jobs are negotiated and information about them shared, and prestige scoring is rearranged, policy researchers will typically attend those dominated by their basic research colleagues. And attendance at policy research associations (such as the Association for Public Policy Analysis and Management) is meager. Most prizes and other awards available to researchers go to those who conduct basic research.

In short, although the logic of policy research favors it to be more communicative than basic research, this is often not the case because the training and institutional formations in which policy research is largely conducted favor basic research.

---

[16] See Griffith University course catalog. Available at: www22.gu.edu.au/STIP/servlet/STIP?s= 7319AMC (accessed 28 Apr. 2004).

[17] This section is based on my personal observations of organizations such as the John F. Kennedy School of Government, the American Enterprise Institute, RAND, CATO, the Heritage Foundation, and many others.

## REFERENCES

BARDACH, E. (2002). Educating the client: an introduction. *Journal of Policy Analysis and Management*, 21 (1): 115–17.

BERELSON, B., and STEINER, G. 1964. *Human Behavior: An Inventory of Scientific Findings*. New York: Harcourt Brace and World.

CAROTHERS, T. 1999. *Aiding Democracy Abroad: The Learning Curve*. Washington, DC: Carnegie Endowment for International Peace.

DEJONG, W., WOLF, R. C., and AUSTIN, S. B. 2001. US federally funded television public service announcements (PSAs) to prevent HIV/AIDS: a content analysis. *Journal of Health Communication*, 6: 249–63.

DUNN, W. N. 1981. *Public Policy Analysis: An Introduction*. Englewood Cliffs, NJ: Prentice Hall.

ETZIONI, A. 1968. *The Active Society: A Theory of Societal and Political Processes*. New York: Free Press.

—— 1971*a*. *A Comparative Analysis of Complex Organizations*, rev. edn. New York: Free Press.

—— 1971*b*. Policy research. *American Sociologist*, 6 (supplementary issue: June): 8–12.

—— 2003. *My Brother's Keeper: A Memoir and a Message*. Lanham, Md.: Rowman and Littlefield.

—— 2004. A self-restrained approach to nation-building by foreign powers. *International Affairs*, 80: 1–17.

FISHKIN, J. S. 1997. *The Voice of the People: Public Opinion and Democracy*. New Haven, Conn.: Yale University Press.

FREE EXPRESSION PROJECT 2003. *The Progress of Science and Useful Arts: Why Copyright Today Threatens Intellectual Freedom*, 2nd edn. New York: Free Expression Project; available at: www.fepproject.org/policyreports/copyright2dconc.html (accessed 27 Apr. 2004).

INGLEFINGER, F. J., RELMAN, A. S., and FINDLAND, M. 1966. *Controversy in Internal Medicine*. Philadelphia: W. B. Saunder.

LASSWELL, H., and LERNER, D. 1951. *The Policy Sciences*. Stanford, Calif.: Stanford University Press.

MILLER, D. W. 2001. Poking holes in the theory of broken windows. *Chronicle of Higher Education* (Feb.): A14.

MILLER, J. 2004. Censored study on bioterror doubts U.S. preparedness. *New York Times* (29 Mar.): A15.

MITCHELL, J., and MITCHELL, W. 1969. *Policy-Making and Human Welfare*. Chicago: Rand McNally.

NELSON, B. 1999. Diversity and public problem solving: ideas and practice in policy education. *Journal of Policy Analysis and Management*, 18: 134–55.

RADIN, B. A. 1997. The evolution of the policy analysis field: from conversation to conversations. *Journal of Policy Analysis and Management*, 16: 204–18.

RAVER, C. 2002. Emotions matter: making the case for the role of young children's emotional development for early school readiness. *Social Policy Report*, 16 (3): 3–19.

ROE, E. 1998. *Taking Complexity Seriously: Policy Analysis, Triangulation, and Sustainable Development*. Boston: Kluwer Academic.

SATLOFF, R. 2003. How to win friends and influence Arabs. *Weekly Standard*, 18 Aug: 18–19.

SCHÖN, D. 1983. *The Reflective Practitioner*. New York: Basic Books.

SCOTT, J. 1994. Condom ads get direct: use them and get sex. *Atlanta Journal and Constitution* (3 Oct.): B1.

STAR, S. A., and HUGHES, H. M. 1950. Report on an educational campaign: the Cincinnati plan for the United Nations. *American Journal of Sociology*, 55: 389–400.

WEIMER, D. L., and VINING, A. R. 1989. *Policy Analysis: Concepts and Practice.* Englewood Cliffs, NJ: Prentice Hall.

WEISS, C. 1983. Ideology, interests and information: the basis of policy positions. Pp. 213–45 in *Ethics, the Social Sciences and Policy Analysis,* ed. D. Callahan and B. Jennings. New York: Plenum.

WILSON, J. Q., and KELLING, G. 1982. Broken windows: the police and neighborhood safety. *Atlantic Monthly,* 249 (3: Mar.): 29–38.

# CHAPTER 41

# CHOOSING GOVERNANCE SYSTEMS: A PLEA FOR COMPARATIVE RESEARCH

## ORAN R. YOUNG

## 1. INTRODUCTION

Studies of public policy typically focus on processes taking place at a single level of social organization—more often than not the national level—and direct attention either to one-off choices (e.g. whether or not the US federal government should open parts of the Arctic National Wildlife Refuge to oil and gas development) or to generic decisions applicable to a relatively well-defined class of situations (e.g. whether or not the US should prohibit or ban the harvesting of marine mammals regardless of the circumstances). There is much to be said for engaging in analyses of this type. They have given rise to an influential stream of research; there is much still to be done to broaden and deepen our understanding of public policy processes approached in this way.

In the discussion to follow, however, I take the view that there is a compelling case to be made for adding to the mainstream of research in this field a second stream of work that directs attention to a different class of public choices and highlights the value of comparing and contrasting policy processes occurring at different levels of social organization. Specifically, I focus on public choices featuring the creation of governance systems or institutional arrangements (e.g. the system of tradeable permits for sulfur emissions established under the US Clean Air Act Amendments of 1990), and I emphasize the added value to be derived from supplementing the normal focus on the national level with comparative studies of the formation, implementation, and adaptation of these regimes at the local and international levels.

In developing this argument, I proceed as follows. The first substantive section provides a map of the relevant conceptual landscape. The next section explores insights about the policy process arising from this approach to public choice. The final substantive section then raises questions about the practical implications of these insights and more specifically about issues of scale and institutional interplay (Young 2002). To illustrate my argument, I resort throughout to examples relating to natural resources and the environment. But the subject is generic; it arises in all issue areas.

## 2. MAPPING THE TERRAIN

There is a natural tendency to equate public policy with the actions of governments construed as organizations that possess the authority to make choices on behalf of societies or in other words, public choices addressing more or less well-defined sets of issues or subjects. This way of thinking is understandable and often useful. But it obscures several important points. The domain or range of issues over which governments can exercise authority is a variable. Actual governments differ widely in these terms, ranging from minimalist arrangements in which the government is limited to maintaining law and order internally and providing for the common defense against external threats, to maximalist arrangements in which the government owns the means of production and possesses authority to intervene deeply in the lives of individual citizens. In most places and during most eras, the boundaries of the authority of governments are contested, with some groups calling for an expansion of the authority of government and others advocating increased restrictions on the authority of government. Under the circumstances, equating public policy with the actions of governments defines a subject whose boundaries are often hard to specify and whose scope varies not only from one society to another but also over time within the same society.

Even more fundamental is the observation that performing the social function of governance in the sense of arriving at public choices that are authoritative and regarded as legitimate by members of the relevant society does not require the existence of a government in the ordinary sense of the term. Many small-scale and especially traditional societies, for instance, rely on the emergence and evolution of social conventions to handle the function of governance (Ostrom 1990). They produce, as Hayek and others have observed, public orders that are spontaneous or self-generating in nature (Hayek 1973). Similar remarks apply to governance in international society, a social system widely construed as a society of states (and increasingly, non-state actors) that is anarchical in character due to the lack of anything resembling a government at the international level (Young 1999). Naturally, there is considerable variation in the methods used to address the functions of governance in small-scale societies as well as in distinct sectors of international society. Valid generalizations in this realm are difficult to construct. The important point, however, is that societies lacking governments in the ordinary sense or in other words, stateless societies still need to find ways to arrive at public choices, a fact that makes them interesting to those seeking to understand public policy processes. My starting point in this regard, is that there is much to be gained from comparing and contrasting the public policy processes characteristic of stateless societies with the more familiar processes centered on the activities of governments at the national level.

Beyond this, it is helpful to draw clear distinctions among major types or classes of public choices emerging from policy processes. On one account, policies are (or should be) generic decisions that can be applied to determine the proper course of action to take in dealing with any member of a well-defined class of issues. A policy that calls for the stationing of observers on board all fishing boats, for instance, can be applied to individual vessels without regard to the details of specific cases. Similarly, a policy requiring all oil tankers to be built with segregated ballast tanks can be applied to individual cases without engaging in any assessment of the circumstances surrounding specific situations.

But this does not exhaust the range of situations that public policy processes address. There are many situations in which issues are framed as one-off choices and the relevant policy process is expected to reach a decision applicable to a singular or unique situation. Issues relating to public lands, for example, are often cast in these terms. Although it is perfectly possible to make generic decisions relating to matters like the establishment of national parks or the creation of wildlife refuges, policy makers regularly find themselves confronted with the need to make choices about the management of places—such as the Arctic National Wildlife Refuge—construed as unique situations rather than as matters to be handled through the application of generic decisions.

Yet another, arguably more important class of issues that arise in public policy processes encompasses those in which the challenge is to create a management regime or governance system that addresses a particular issue area and that is expected to guide human (inter)actions relating to that area for an indefinite period of time. Such regimes may vary widely from spatially limited arrangements like the Colorado River Compact to global arrangements like the ozone regime and from regimes involving a small number of actors like the regime established under the provisions of the Great Lakes Water Quality Agreements to arrangements involving large numbers of actors like the climate regime.

During the course of agenda formation, it is sometimes possible to make conscious choices regarding the framing of an issue as a one-off choice, a generic decision, or a matter of regime formation. But there is no denying that many issues now call for decisions involving the creation of regimes or specialized governance systems and that choices of this sort can and often will produce outputs, outcomes, and impacts whose effects are felt far and wide and over long periods of time. My plea in this short chapter is for a more concerted effort to examine choices of this type and to compare and contrast the policy processes involved in making such choices at the local, national, and international levels.

In thinking about the implications of these distinctions, it may help to visualize the major points outlined in the preceding paragraphs. Table 41.1 highlights the distinction between the mainstream of policy analyses and the supplemental stream I am advocating. To be specific, the center of gravity of mainstream analyses of public policy processes falls into the cells marked "A" in the table. The supplemental stream I am advocating, by contrast, focuses on the cells marked "B." Note that there is no conflict between the two streams, except perhaps with regard to the allocation of scarce resources available to support research. On the contrary, the addition of the second stream provides a new lens for the examination of public policy processes that can sharpen our understanding of these processes at all levels.

# 3. Comparing Policy Processes

Turn now to a comparison of policy processes involving efforts to create institutional arrangements across three levels of social organization: small-scale, largely traditional societies, national societies, and international society. It is apparent at once that small-scale, traditional societies and international society share a fundamental feature that sets them apart from national societies. They are stateless societies in the sense that they do not have well-developed governments possessing the authority to make public choices regarding a range of important matters and the capacity to make them stick (Young 2005). Yet the need to create governance systems or regimes capable of addressing the demand for governance is just as pressing in these settings as it is in national societies. A systematic investigation is needed to understand the implications of this difference—together with a number of lesser differences—for efforts to establish and implement regimes in a variety of issue domains. In addressing this topic here, I draw relatively sharp distinctions among the three levels of social organization. No doubt, some actual societies constitute borderline cases or exhibit

Table 41.1. Policy domains

| | Level of decision making | | |
| Type of decision | Small scale, traditional | National | International |
| --- | --- | --- | --- |
| One-off choices | | A | |
| Generic decisions | | A | |
| Regimes | B | B | B |

complexities that make them hard to place into one or another of the categories I employ. Even so, an analysis of public policy processes in three distinct social settings can generate insights that help to illuminate fundamental features of the processes involved in making public choices about the provisions of institutional arrangements or regimes. I discuss the most significant of these insights in this section and summarize them in Table 41.2.

## 3.1 Policy Products

The provisions of institutional arrangements take distinct forms depending upon the level of social organization at which they operate. We are all familiar with the legislative acts or statutes (e.g. the US Fishery Conservation and Management Act of 1976 or the Outer Continental Shelf Lands Act of 1978) that set forth the principal elements of regimes and provide the administrative arrangements needed to operate them at the national level. Many small-scale traditional societies by contrast, make no use of legislative acts or statutes; their institutional arrangements develop spontaneously and evolve into informal but often well-understood and generally effective social conventions. For their part, international regimes generally find expression in conventions or treaties (e.g. the 1946 International Convention on the Regulation of Whaling, the 1992 UN Convention on Biological Diversity). In some respects, these products differ sharply. Whereas legislation becomes the law of the land upon enactment, for instance, international conventions do not enter into force until they are ratified by some specified number of signatories. The UN Convention on the Law of the Sea, for example, was opened for signature in 1982 but did not enter into force until 1994; the United States has still to ratify the convention.

Table 41.2. Comparing policy processes

| Policy processes | Social settings | | |
| --- | --- | --- | --- |
| | Small-scale societies | National society | International society |
| Policy products | Social conventions | Legislation/statutes | Conventions/treaties |
| Agenda formation | Individual leaders | Interest groups | Civil society/non-state actors |
| Relevant knowledge | Traditional knowledge | Mainstream science | Global science |
| Decision process | Consensus building | Legislative bargaining | International negotiation |
| Implementation | Stakeholders themselves | Government agencies | Two-step processes |
| Sources of compliance | Social pressure | Sanctions | Management |
| Interpretation | Ad hoc tribunals | Courts/litigation | Self-help procedures |

Even so, it would be a mistake to exaggerate these differences. Rules in use at the national level and in international society often differ substantially from the letter of the law (Ostrom 1990); social conventions may become quite clear-cut with the passage of time and the growth of precedents. Although their building blocks are quite distinct, institutional arrangements become successful at all three levels of social organization when they give rise to rules of the game or social practices that subjects follow routinely or out of habit.

## 3.2 Agenda Formation

Recent studies of policy processes have documented the importance of the pathways through which issues are framed, find their way onto policy agendas, and achieve sufficient salience to attract the attention of influential players (Kingdon 1995). In small-scale societies, individuals are apt to champion specific issues and to play essential roles in propelling these issues toward the top of the policy agenda. Surprisingly perhaps, interest groups and various non-state actors loom large in processes of agenda formation at the national and international levels. Naturally, chief executives at the national level and powerful states at the international level can exert considerable influence over processes of agenda formation. Nevertheless, it is uncommon for an issue to move toward the top of the policy agenda in these settings in the absence of one or more groups that provide the intellectual capital needed to cast the relevant issues in an appealing manner and invest the time, energy, and political capital needed to ensure that the issue does not get displaced or over-shadowed by issues of interest to other groups. At all three levels in other words, leadership is essential to framing and promoting issues arising in policy processes. But the forms that leadership takes can be expected to differ substantially from one level of social organization to another.

## 3.3 Relevant Knowledge

Those who focus on policy processes at the national level have become accustomed to focusing on the science/policy interface. But what types of knowledge are most relevant to policy making at other levels of social organization (Jasanoff and Martello 2004)? For the most part, small-scale traditional societies do not rely on scientific knowledge in the sense of mainstream Western science; they base their decisions on traditional ecological knowledge (Berkes 1999) and analogous modes of thinking applicable to other issue areas (Usher 1987; Riordan 1990).

Proponents of science often maintain that the scientific method is international or global in character so that science should play the same role at the international level as it does at the national level. In many cases, however, this is not the case. Not only do non-state actors in international society have their own stables of scientists ready to provide testimony of the desired sort, but also there is no international or global academy of sciences or similar body to evaluate and aggregate the views of the science community regarding matters of policy arising at the international level. The resultant problem has given rise to the creation of blue ribbon panels (e.g. the Intergovernmental Panel on Climate Change, the Millennium Ecosystem Assessment) designed to provide scientific assessments that seek to distill and codify current judgements of the global scientific community (Andresen et al. 2000). But as these examples suggest, the task of developing a consensus regarding the state of knowledge pertaining to global concerns such as climate change or the loss of biological diversity is not an easy one. As a result, policy processes taking place at the international level are particularly susceptible to dissension regarding the knowledge claims that proponents of different plans of action bring to such processes.

## 3.4 Decision Processes

Actual decisions about the creation of institutional arrangements or regimes emerge from different processes at the three levels of social organization. Most familiar perhaps is the process of legislative bargaining that yields outcomes regarding the (re)formation of regimes at the national level. Because it is clear who the players are in legislative bargaining and it is assumed that subjects are likely to comply with the outcomes, analyses of this process typically center on matters like the development of minimum winning coalitions and the opportunities for logrolling or vote trading across two or more distinct issues (Riker 1962).

The decision process in stateless societies differs fundamentally from the process of legislative bargaining. In small-scale traditional societies, every effort is made to craft institutional arrangements capable of producing consensus among the stakeholders themselves (in contrast to their elected representatives). In international society, the weakness of compliance mechanisms generally leads to a process of institutional bargaining in which the goal is to put together maximum winning coalitions in contrast to minimum winning coalitions (Young 1994). Although the formal players in these processes are normally states in contrast to the stakeholders themselves, it is worth emphasizing that the result is a process in which those engaged in bargaining make a concerted effort to arrive at consensual results in much the same way that stakeholders do in devising the terms of institutional arrangements at the level of small-scale societies.

## 3.5 Implementation

How are the provisions of the regimes emanating from these processes implemented? Again, we are most familiar with the national-level process in which legislative provisions assign a public agency (e.g. the US Forest Service, the National Park

Service, the National Marine Fisheries Service) to take the lead in the implementation process, the lead agency prepares and promulgates regulations, and agency personnel serve as what are sometimes called "street-level bureaucrats" in administering the provisions of regimes on the ground

Here again, the processes occurring in small-scale societies and international society are quite distinct. In small-scale traditional settings, stakeholders participating in the process of developing the rules of the game often play key roles in implementing the provisions of regimes as well. Whether the regime focuses on the appropriation of water for agricultural use or the allocation of fishing sites and trap lines, the stakeholders themselves monitor implementation and are the first to spot deviations from the terms of consensus-based rights and rules. Due to the underdevelopment of administrative arrangements at the international level, by contrast, efforts are commonly made to incorporate the provisions of conventions or treaties into the legal and administrative systems of member states. What ensues is a two-step process in which member states ratify conventions or treaties, (typically) pass implementing legislation, and assign the task of administering implementation to specific agencies. On a day-to-day basis, therefore, the implementation of international regimes is apt to resemble the implementation of national-level regimes. Yet, as I discuss below, this similarity can prove illusory when it comes to the resolution of disagreements regarding compliance or the production of authoritative interpretations concerning the meaning of specific provisions embedded in regimes.

## 3.6 Sources of Compliance

At the end of the day, institutional arrangements work at every level of social organization when they evolve into social practices whose participants adhere to the rights and rules embedded in them as a matter of habit or in other words, without making calculations regarding the benefits and costs of compliance on a case-by-case basis (Hart 1961). Beyond this, however, the procedures employed to discourage potential violators differ substantially from one level of social organization to another. In small-scale traditional societies, the essential mechanism involves the application of social pressure. In extreme cases, traditional communities can resort to ostracism, an outcome that is generally costly to the violator and that can amount to a death sentence under some conditions. Lacking the capacity to impose serious sanctions, international society tends toward the use of what have come to be known as management mechanisms in contrast to enforcement mechanisms (Chayes and Chayes 1995). In essence, this means building capacity for compliance in cases where members of regimes are willing to comply once enabled to do so and nurturing the growth of what is often called the logic of appropriateness in contrast to the logic of consequences as a determinant of the behavior of the members of the relevant regimes (March and Olsen 1998).

Once again, there is a clear distinction between these processes and the parallel processes occurring at the national level in which government agencies have the capacity to monitor the behavior of subjects, and public authorities (e.g. the US Department of Justice) can initiate legal action against violators and ultimately impose serious penalties on them. Yet it would be a mistake to exaggerate these differences, especially in terms of day-to-day practices in contrast to the procedures envisioned in constitutive documents. Not only are social pressures and management approaches often quite effective, but also those who violate the provisions of national-level arrangements may get away with their infractions without being caught and often receive no more than symbolic punishments even when they are caught.

## 3.7 Interpretation

One of the more striking differences in the policy processes occurring at the three levels involves the mechanisms available for producing authoritative interpretations when disagreements arise regarding the application of the provisions of institutional arrangements to specific situations. Even the promulgation of detailed regulations cannot prevent the emergence of more or less sharp disagreements concerning the application of regulations to concrete cases. At the national level, this is where the courts enter the picture. In most (but not all) systems, stakeholders can sue the government asserting that the responsible agency has failed to implement the terms of a regime in accordance with the intent of the legislature. Conversely, the government can sue individuals—including corporations treated as legal persons—alleging that the defendants are failing to comply with the relevant rights and rules. Societies in which such procedures work well have a great advantage wherever there is a need to implement the provisions of institutional arrangements in a wide range of circumstances.

By contrast, small-scale societies rely for the most part on ad hoc tribunals, and international society either turns to the domestic systems of individual members for authoritative interpretations or accepts (or tolerates) self-help procedures in the sense of interpretations arrived at by individual member states, often on their own behalf. It would be a mistake to overemphasize these differences. Some national societies do not have a fully independent judiciary. Ad hoc tribunals can produce satisfactory outcomes without incurring the cost to society of creating a permanent judiciary, and international society is engaging in important experiments with tribunals designed to deal with the need to arrive at authoritative interpretations in specific issue areas (e.g. the International Tribunal on the Law of the Sea). Still, differences regarding the production of authoritative interpretations constitute one of the sharper contrasts between policy processes occurring at the national level and their counterparts occurring in small-scale, traditional societies and in international society.

# 4. Exploring the Implications

What are the implications of the differences in public policy processes discussed in the preceding section? Do analytic differences typically wash out in concrete settings or are the effects of these differences amplified as we shift our attention from regimes on paper to regimes in practice? Those who take the view that institutions matter can be counted on to argue that the contrasts described in the preceding section will have a marked impact on the products emerging from public policy processes (Weaver and Rockman 1993). Analysts who claim that other driving forces, such as population, consumption patterns, or technology explain most of the variance in human affairs will take the view that the differences I have described are not likely to explain a significant portion of the variance in the character—much less the impacts—of public choices. I cannot address this issue systematically in these reflections. But I do want to identify and comment on two important aspects of this topic; I describe them as the problem of scale and the problem of interplay (Young et al. 1999).

## 4.1 The Problem of Scale

With regard to public policy processes, the problem of scale is a matter of the extent to which propositions developed in the course of analyses conducted at one level of social organization hold at other levels as well. Are generalizations derived from research on policy processes at the national level, for instance, applicable to parallel processes occurring in small-scale traditional societies or in international society? Can we apply generalizations about policy processes occurring in international society to analogous processes in small-scale societies and vice versa (Ostrom et al. 1999; Young 2002)? The preceding discussion suggests that it is important to avoid both excessive optimism and undue pessimism in this regard. There are obvious differences among the three levels that lead to skepticism about the prospects for scaling up and scaling down in this field of study. The actors involved in policy processes at the three levels—individual stakeholders, elected representatives, appointed representatives of governments—are sufficiently different to raise questions about the applicability of models based on the same behavioral assumptions at the three levels. Similarly, both the decision rules employed and the types of knowledge brought to bear on specific issues differ, often dramatically, across the level of social organization. Yet it would be inappropriate to dismiss the prospects for scaling up and down for these reasons. The policy processes occurring at all three levels address the same basic functional need: how to arrive at public or collective choices in settings involving interactions among a number of actors whose interests overlap but are by no means identical.

One attractive response to this concern features the selection of a particularly important element of policy processes for more thorough investigation. Take the case of the decision process, for instance, where the differences I have noted among consensus building, legislative bargaining, and international negotiation appear to be profound, at least at first glance. Building winning coalitions through vote trading or logrolling across distinct issues certainly seems to differ fundamentally from bargaining over the terms of a single convention or treaty. And both of these processes seem to differ from the consensus-building processes occurring in small-scale societies. On reflection, however, these differences are not so sharp or dramatic. Actors engaged in legislative bargaining frequently strive to put together bipartisan and even maximum winning coalitions rather than minimum winning coalitions. Those engaged in negotiating the terms of treaties are mindful of the importance of consensus building, especially in settings where nurturing a sense of ownership on the part of major constituencies provides the best prospect for securing compliance once a specific treaty has entered into force. More generally, there is a lot to be said for the proposition that a serious concern for consensus building looms large—in fact if not on paper—in policy processes at all three levels. It follows that future research on policy processes may well generate significant payoffs by comparing and contrasting strategies and styles of consensus building under the specific circumstances prevailing at the different levels of social organization.

## 4.2 The Problem of Interplay

The problem of interplay centers on a fundamentally different concern. As the density of institutional arrangements operative in a given social space increases, the probability that individual regimes will affect one another in significant ways rises (Young et al. 1999). In many cases, these interactions, which may be both unintended and unforeseen, are horizontal in nature in the sense that they involve two or more institutional arrangements operating at the same level of social organization. As levels of interdependence among human activities rise, however, vertical interactions—those involving regimes operating at two or more levels of social organization—become more common. Recent developments featuring both globalization and the devolution of authority from central governments to local governments have intensified this trend. Increasingly, actions occurring at the international and global levels affect the results flowing from public or collective choices made at the local level. Far from reducing vertical interactions, efforts to reallocate political authority between the national and local levels regularly intensify interplay, since the growth of functional interactions continues apace without regard to juridical decisions about the allocation of authority. As a result, the need to structure policy processes at different levels of social organization in such a way as to maximize synergy and minimize conflict has emerged as a central concern in the field of public policy.

Yet addressing this need is easier said than done. A particularly striking case in point in the realm of environmental or resource regimes centers on the creation of co-management systems (Singleton 1998). The defining feature of co-management is the sharing of decision-making power (though not necessarily authority) regarding the use of natural resources or environmental services among users and managers who are located at different levels of social organization. Typical examples in the United States involve the establishment of boards whose members include representatives of federal agencies (e.g. the US Fish and Wildlife Service) and representatives of local user communities (e.g. harvesters of migratory birds in western Alaska) (Osherenko 1988). When they are successful, such arrangements can generate a sense of legitimacy that encourages all the stakeholders to comply with their provisions on grounds of appropriateness rather than some utilitarian calculation of the relevant benefits and costs. But how likely are initiatives of this sort to succeed? A consideration of the distinctions discussed in the preceding section should make it clear that achieving success in this realm is a major challenge. Members of local user groups often rely on different types of knowledge (e.g. traditional ecological knowledge) from representatives of federal agencies in arriving at conclusions about harvesting renewable resources (Berkes 1999). What is more, traditional approaches to implementation and compliance bear little resemblance to those characteristic of modern bureaucratic systems. None of this is to argue that co-management cannot work. Several intriguing arrangements that appear to be producing positive results have been established in recent years. But the argument I present in these reflections points to several key issues that must be addressed in a thoughtful and sensitive manner if co-management is to be capable of overcoming divergences in policy processes occurring at different levels of social organization.

# 5. A CONCLUDING OBSERVATION

The comparative approach to the study of public policy processes I recommend in these reflections will not only sharpen our understanding of the production of public choices in specific settings, it can also contribute to the transition from studies of government to studies of governance now occurring in a number of subfields of political science. As the discussion in the preceding sections makes clear, it is a serious mistake to assume that the domain of public choice is confined to the products of governments and that public policy processes do not occur in stateless societies. It goes without saying that this does not mean that research on policy processes centered on the actions of legislatures or government agencies (e.g. studies of legislative bargaining) is no longer relevant. But expanding the analysis of policy processes to encompass stateless systems, including small-scale traditional societies as well as international society, makes it possible both to contrast processes of arriving at public choices with and without the involvement of a government in the normal sense and to identify fundamental features in contrast to idiosyncratic details of policy processes occurring at the national level.

To take a single example, we want to know how much the operation of specific attributes of decision rules affects the substantive character of the regimes or management systems chosen in different settings. One way to approach this concern is to compare and contrast national societies that differ from one another with regard to these attributes. But an alternative—and equally attractive—procedure is to compare and contrast processes of consensus building and institutional bargaining occurring in small-scale societies and international society with the legislative bargaining characteristic of national societies. It is not easy to forecast the results likely to flow from comparisons of this sort. But they may well involve the identification of certain underlying similarities in mechanisms leading to the selection of public choices that are not affected by specific attributes of particular policy processes.

## References

ANDRESEN, S., SKODVIN, T., UNDERDAL, A., and WETTESTAD, J. 2000. *Science and Politics in International Environmental Regimes: Between Integrity and Involvement.* Manchester: Manchester University Press.

BERKES, F. 1999. *Sacred Ecology: Traditional Ecological Knowledge and Resource Management.* Philadelphia: Taylor and Francis.

CHAYES, A., and CHAYES, A. H. 1995. *The New Sovereignty: Compliance with International Regulatory Agreements.* Cambridge, Mass.: Harvard University Press.

HART, H. L. A. 1961. *The Concept of Law.* Oxford: Clarendon Press.

HAYEK, F. A. 1973. *Law, Legislation, and Liberty,* i: *Rules and Order.* Chicago: University of Chicago Press.

JASANOFF, S., and MARTELLO, M. L. (eds.) 2004. *Earthly Politics: Local and Global in Environmental Governance.* Cambridge, Mass.: MIT Press.

KINGDON, J. W. 1995. *Agendas, Alternatives, and Public Policies,* 2nd edn. New York: HarperCollins.

MARCH, J. G., and OLSEN, J. P. 1998. The institutional dynamics of international political orders. *International Organization,* 52: 943–69.

OSHERENKO, G. 1988. Can comanagement save Arctic wildlife? *Environment,* 20 (6): 6–13, 29–34.

OSTROM, E. 1990. *Governing the Commons: The Evolution of Institutions for Collective Action.* Cambridge: Cambridge University Press.

—— et al. 1999. Revisiting the commons: local lessons, global challenges. *Science,* 284: 278–82.

RIKER, W. H. 1962. *The Theory of Political Coalitions.* New Haven, Conn.: Yale University Press.

RIORDAN, A. F. 1990. *Eskimo Essays.* New Brunswick, NJ: Rutgers University Press.

SINGLETON, S. 1998. *Constructing Cooperation: The Evolution of Institutions of Comanagement.* Ann Arbor: University of Michigan Press.

USHER, P. 1987. Indigenous management systems and the conservation of wildlife in the Canadian north. *Alternatives,* 14: 3–9.

WEAVER, R. K., and ROCKMAN, B. A. (eds.) 1993. *Do Institutions Matter: Government Capabilities in the United States and Abroad.* Washington, DC: Brookings Institution.

YOUNG, O. R. 1994. *International Governance: Protecting the Environment in a Stateless Society.* Ithaca, NY: Cornell University Press.

—— 1999. *Governance in World Affairs.* Ithaca, NY: Cornell University Press.

—— 2002. *The Institutional Dimensions of Environmental Change: Fit, Interplay, and Scale.* Cambridge, Mass.: MIT Press.

—— 2005. Why is there no unified theory of environmental governance? Pp. 70–84 in *The Handbook of Global Environmental Politics,* ed. P. Dauvergne. Cheltenham: Edward Elgar.

—— et al. 1999. *Institutional Dimensions of Global Environmental Change (IDGEC) Science Plan.* Bonn: IHDP.

# CHAPTER 42

# THE POLITICS OF RETRENCHMENT: THE US CASE

## FRANCES FOX PIVEN

This chapter reconsiders theories of the political dynamics underlying welfare state development in light of the sharp reversals that have occurred in recent decades, particularly in the United States. I argue that the big theories that have dominated interpretation of the welfare state, with their emphasis on systems, or institutions and their organizational, legal, political, and cultural concomitants, lead us to expect continuity and gradualism, and are not equal to the task of explaining ruptures with past practices. Such ruptures reflect institutional factors to be sure. But they also reflect the exceptional episodes that can occur in politics, including the periodic crusades of powerful interest groups, and the eruption of social movements.

Consistent with an emphasis on systems or institutions, we usually think of the historical development of the welfare state as the gradual creation by governments of categorical exemptions from unregulated markets. By providing income or services, governments constructed protections for specific groups from the penalties they would face if left to fend for themselves and their families in labor markets. Or the protections were constructed with regard to specific needs that could not reasonably be met by markets. Once created, these exemptions became institutionalized, encased in legal rights, in public bureaucracies and their supportive constituencies, and in the ideas and expectations of the broader public.

Some of the categories of people protected by welfare state programs are biological. The aged are supported with pensions to protect them from a penurious old age. Or the sick or the crippled or the orphaned or the widowed who cannot fend for themselves in labor markets are provided with income supports. Other categories reflect gaps in market provision of socially acknowledged necessities that result from market instabilities or market flaws. Thus the unemployed are given income to sustain them through downturns in employment. Or government programs help people who cannot afford market prices for housing or health care to gain these essentials. Whatever the intention, all of these interventions have the effect of shielding substantial numbers of people from participation in markets, or the programs provide subsidies that allow people who otherwise could not to enter markets. Two decades ago, Esping-Andersen coined the term "decommodification" to describe this aspect of the welfare state (Esping-Andersen 1985a). And two decades ago, most welfare state scholars thought that the century-old trend toward decommodification would continue. The welfare state would expand, and as it did, it would generate new and stronger shields from markets for vulnerable groups. Put more simply, we believed that our societies were gradually becoming more benign, more just in their treatment of the vulnerable among us.

No longer. A dramatic shift has occurred in the past two decades in the politics and policies of the welfare state. New welfare state initiatives are now justified not because they protect people who need protection from the harsh terms of labor markets, or because they provide goods or services that markets do not provide on affordable terms, but because the reforms are necessary to promote economic growth and enforce participation in labor markets. Welfare state expenditures, it is said, have become a drag on profits and therefore on economic growth in an era when the internationalization of capital, goods, and labor markets have intensified competitive pressures. And welfare state protections are also a drag on economic growth because the very protections they provide interfere with what is called labor market flexibility, meaning the ability of employers to adapt the terms they offer their own workers to internationally competitive markets.

At the same time, and rollbacks in spending notwithstanding, welfare state programs have become a new frontier for market expansion. The neoliberal rallying cry of deregulation is translated into measures to turn the provision of erstwhile public services over to private entrepreneurs. This shift in ideas from a protective welfare state to a market-friendly welfare state was led by the United States, where the new policies have already had a significant impact. But the ideas that justify welfare cutbacks and work-enforcing policies are spreading across the globe, and especially to Europe, partly as a reflection of the enormous cultural influence of the USA in an era of globalization, and partly as a result of the purposeful efforts of American-based think tanks to promote what has become the new common sense of welfare policy, which I will call the turn from decommodification to commodification (Janiewski 2003).

In fact, the welfare state was never simply "decommodifying," either in the United States or elsewhere. Rather, state interventions were shaped with an acute consciousness of their potential impact on labor markets. The very categories of people designated as eligible for social protections reflected consideration of labor markets. People were eligible for government income supports when they were not considered active labor market participants. Thus income supports for the aged and the disabled were, until recently relatively uncontested. Even so, not all of the aged or the disabled were eligible. In the USA, eligibility for old age and disability insurance depended on a record of steady work in a covered occupation, although the covered occupations have expanded over time, as has the eligible population. Income supports for the unemployed were more elaborately conditioned, in the USA by past work experience and earnings, by evidence of job search, and in any case, benefits were typically available only for the short term. Benefits for children and single mothers were even more stringently conditioned. Not only were grant levels kept very low, but the concern that unearned cash would reach men who were potential workers, as well as the fact that some women and children, particularly black women and children in the south, were considered workers, helps account for the elaborately conditioned system of regulation and surveillance that characterized the American Aid to Families with Dependent Children program.

The old welfare state was also market friendly in another sense. It did not provide public benefits that would compete with market provision. In Europe, the big programs in housing and health were inaugurated only after the Second World War had weakened the private sectors in these industries. In some countries, there were no significant organized health or housing providers to oppose the public or quasi-public programs that were initiated to build housing or provide health care. In the United States, by contrast, where the housing and health markets were vigorous, so was the opposition from industry actors to public intervention that would interfere with private markets. Eventually that opposition succeeded in limiting government intervention largely to measures that shored up markets. The result is that in the United States, both the housing and health sectors function as private markets with minimal government regulation, even though they are heavily dependent on public subsidies.

All this said, the development of the American welfare state did have some decommodifying effects. Until the development of pensions for the old and the disabled, most of the old and the disabled were considered workers, whether they could actually find jobs or not, and they competed with other workers on unfavorable terms. Far fewer worked once benefits became available and as coverage gradually expanded. Similarly, until the unemployment insurance program was inaugurated, workers who lost their jobs were forced to take whatever other work they could find, whatever the terms, since without the cushion of benefits, they could not afford to wait for a job at their customary wage or in their customary occupation. For some of those without the employment and earnings record requisite for unemployment benefits, there was "welfare," the means-tested programs that were the ultimate recourse for the destitute. And then there were the non-cash programs which were really in-kind income programs, such as food stamps, or low-cost housing, or health services for the poor. All of these combined to provide some security for people whose position in the labor market was precarious. This was decommodification, American style.

Now these programs are under attack, and significant rollbacks have occurred. These rollbacks are not readily apparent if we rely on gross data on welfare state expenditures. Rather, it is the decommodifying features of the programs that are under attack, and spending on work-enforcing features, some of them new initiatives, has in fact greatly increased. Thus, cash assistance to poor mothers and children has been slashed; nutritional and housing assistance to the poor is contracting; extended unemployment insurance benefits have been made more difficult to get. Even coverage of social security pensions for the aged, long considered the "third rail" of American politics, is contracting as the age at which people become eligible inches upward. Meanwhile, expenditures on programs that push people into the labor market, or that increase the rewards of low-wage work are growing. Funds that once provided "welfare" now pay for "workfare;" more funds are provided for child care assistance for working mothers; and expenditures are increasing for Earned Income Tax Assistance, a program that provides refundable tax credits, but only for the working poor.[1]

The main theoretical traditions that attempt to account for the development of the welfare state are not adequate to explain this development. Reflecting the dominant perspective of the historical period in which they were developed, the theories explain the genesis, continuity, and expansion of the programs, mainly by fastening on two sorts of assumptions. One assumption is that welfare state programs are broadly functional in an industrial and capitalist society because they solve problems that have to be solved to maintain the stability of such societies. The second assumption to which I turn later focuses on the continuities and vulnerabilities generated by political institutions, including the institutions of the welfare state. Presumably, a developed welfare state gives rise to the constituencies that defend it. But some features of national political institutions, which come to be reflected in welfare state programs themselves, can also generate the political opposition that accounts for retrenchment.

The most ecumenical of the functional perspectives argued straightforwardly enough that the dislocation of traditional village and family arrangements associated with industrialization and urbanization made new forms of public provision necessary, at the same time that the wealth generated by economic growth provided the funds to support public provision. Variants of this approach identified the motor of welfare state development not in a *sui generis* economic growth but more specifically in capitalist economic systems, and the imperatives of accumulation and legitimization that capitalist—and therefore class-divided—economies generate. Thus, welfare state programs promoted accumulation by subsidizing some of the costs of capitalist production, particularly the health, housing, and education costs of "reproducing" labor. At the same time, welfare state programs helped to legitimize a class-divided society by easing the grievances of workers, thus quieting class conflict and creating the illusion of a universalizing political system. Or in feminist variants, the propelling

---

[1] Spending for prisons has also soared. By convention, incarceration is not considered a welfare state activity, although arguably the large-scale incarceration of the minority poor in the USA ought to be examined in the light of theories of welfare state development. See for example Western and Beckett 1999. For the original argument about the labor market functions of prisons, see also Rusche and Kirchheimer 1939.

force for the development of the welfare state was rooted not in the economy but in the imperative of sustaining patriarchy and/or the patriarchal family. Or the development of the welfare state was attributed to the evolution of the electoral-representative institutions which came to characterize North America and Europe. Each of these theoretical traditions allowed for qualification, according to distinctive national cultures, or the peculiarities of national political institutional development, or distinctive state capacities. Nevertheless, the explanatory ambitions of these theories were large for they attributed welfare state development not to these national peculiarities, but to what were perceived as the dominant institutions of contemporary Western societies. Theories of the welfare state echoed Anthony Giddens's definition of structural functionalism as the theory of industrial society (Giddens 1976, 81).

There were problems, however. None of these perspectives could claim a very neat fit between the historical evolution of the big systems of industrialism, or capitalism, or electoral-representative institutions, and the development of welfare state programs. Germany and Sweden, the pioneering welfare states were not the pioneers of industrialization or capitalism or democracy. Nor did these systemic theories explain the significant differences that had emerged among welfare state regimes, differences between, for example, the relatively ample programs in the Nordic states, and the relatively niggardly programs in the United States. Esping-Andersen (1990) was later to dramatize these differences as distinctive "welfare regimes," grouping the Nordic states together as social democratic welfare states, while countries on the European Continent were "conservative," and the nations descended from the British empire, including the United States, were "liberal." None of these perspectives, however, anticipated contemporary reversals in welfare state development.

A potential solution to the theoretical puzzle of accounting for retrenchment is to reconsider the exogenous imperatives generated by the big systems of industrialization—capitalism, democracy, and family—which framed earlier explanations of welfare state development. Perhaps rupture and reversal reflects the evolution of these systems in ways that demand a new kind of welfare state. Consider, for example, the changes associated with the multifaceted developments called economic globalization and post-industrialism. Whatever else is meant by the term globalization, the internationalization of investment, goods and service production, and labor markets has intensified competition for investment, trade, and employment. Intensified competition in turn, generates growing opposition to the fiscal burdens of welfare state expenditures on the national state, which inevitably must join the international competition for investment if it is to sustain its revenues and satisfy mass voting publics. Competition also means rising calls for labor market "flexibility," meaning a rollback of the regulatory measures and the income supports which restrain employer discretion in the workplace and shore up wages. Meanwhile, huge changes have occurred in traditional family structures as women move into the labor market to take jobs generated by expanded public and private service sectors. There is a case to be made, in other words for a reconsideration of the big systemic theories by paying more attention to changes in those systems. "[T]he 'real' crisis of contemporary welfare regimes," writes Esping-Andersen, "lies in the disjuncture between the existing institutional construction and exogenous change" (Esping-Andersen 1999). Still, even the most casual appraisal of the comparative data suggests that this route will not produce an entirely satisfactory explanation of welfare state reversals. The United States is far from the most open or internationalized economy, but it is the pioneer in welfare state retrenchment, and in particular, the pioneer in the commodification of welfare state programs. Indeed, not only is it the pioneer, but it has become an international proselytizer of retrenchment and privatization throughout the world. This anomaly I argue should lead us to attend to the distinctive politics of the USA, and not only the institutionalized politics that welfare state scholars have emphasized, but also the more disruptive and unpredictable politics of mobilized interest groups and social movements.

It is now generally agreed that however satisfying their bold sweep, structural-functional theories of industrial society are inadequate to explain patterns of welfare state development. The solution of choice to solve the problems of historical timing and comparative differences is to focus on national political institutions, including the institutions of the welfare state itself. Political institutions shape the translation of the systemic imperatives of industrialism or capitalism or family reproduction into specific government policies, and into different government policies. The general argument is that specific and nationally distinctive features of political institutions, such as the structure of electoral-representative arrangements or the internal administrative capacity of the state, account for the variable timing of welfare state initiatives, and also explain the variable organization and scope of the programs (Shefter 1979; Evans, Reuschemeyer, and Skocpol 1985; Skocpol 1992; Amenta 1998; Pierson 1994).

And American political institutions are distinctive. For example, the power resources school associated with Walter Korpi has long argued the importance of working-class influence, expressed through the institutionalized political vehicles of unions and labor or socialist parties, in the growth of the Nordic welfare state (Korpi 1983; Shalev 1983, 315; Stephens 1979; Esping-Andersen 1985b). In the USA, however, not only was working-class influence muted, popular influence generally was muffled by the weak and fragmented character of American political parties. And weak parties, in turn, could be traced to the structure of American government, to divided powers in the national government, and to the substantial decentralization of government authority to states and localities. Schattschneider thought these arrangements, embedded in the American constitution, were "designed to make parties ineffective ... [because they] would lose and exhaust themselves in futile attempts to fight their way through the labyrinthine framework" (Schattschneider 1942, 7). Perhaps so; the founders did, it is true, express an antipathy to parties. Weak parties, in turn, simultaneously frustrated the expression of working-class identities and interests and also inevitably opened the way for greater influence by organized interest groups, notably business and farm interest groups, and this also has been a characteristic of American political development that helps account for a stunted welfare state.

Weak and fragmented parties also did not resist the elite disenfranchising movement that swept the American state capitols in the late nineteenth century. In the
south, the reigning Democratic Party led the movement to impose the poll taxes,
literacy tests, and voter registration requirements that stripped blacks and poor
whites of their votes. In the north, where the immigrant working class was the
main target of the disenfranchisers, state Republican parties led the disenfranchising
efforts, but state and local Democratic Party resistance was feeble, notwithstanding
the fact that these state and local parties claimed the immigrant working class as their
constituents. As a consequence, at the very moment when the European peasantry
and working class were gaining the franchise, significant portions of the American
peasantry and working class were losing it (Piven and Cloward 2000, ch. 1–6). The
United States entered the industrial era with a stunted and skewed electorate. This
also was to limit welfare state development.

Another important reason for a limited welfare state in the USA was the influence
of the southern section on welfare state policies, reflecting a sectional political
advantage that was owed to institutional arrangements. The constitutional decentralization of policy authority to the states was importantly the result of the influence
of the wealthy and powerful delegations from the southern colonies who were
determined to protect their distinctive slave-based economy from national interference. To this end, they worked to limit the authority of the national government in
ways that became embodied in the enduring slogan of "states' rights," with pervasive
consequences for the emergence of labor as a force in American politics. Just as
important, southern delegates used constitution making to shore up the power of the
southern section in national government, with a series of rules that weighted
representation in the Congress and in presidential elections toward the south.

The power of the south was tamed by its defeat in the Civil War and later by the
election of 1896 which became a sectional contest pitting largely northern Republicans against a largely southern Democratic–Populist alliance. The south was
defeated, and the Republican Party became the dominant force in national politics.
But shoring up Republican power was a tacit compact permitting southern elites a
large degree of autonomy in the management of their region. The resulting persistence of the southern caste system, and its low-wage and caste-based labor force, had
dramatic consequences in limiting the welfare state initiatives that became possible
during the tumultuous 1930s (Piven and Cloward 1971; Quadagno 1994). The political
upheavals of the Great Depression propelled national politicians to introduce national welfare state programs, but southern congressional delegations made certain
that the programs were narrowly circumscribed so that they would not interfere with
the terms of southern labor, especially the terms of indentured black plantation labor.

Institutional continuities are sometimes described by the phrase "path dependence," meaning that existing institutional arrangements limit the policy options of
political actors at a given historical juncture, and that the resulting policies tend to
reproduce those limitations (Steinmo and Watts 1995; Pierson 2000). Thus in the
American case, a fragmented and decentralized state ensured that mass political
parties would remain weak and fragmented, and ready vehicles not only for local

and sectional interest group influence, but for a political culture stamped with parochial and racist sentiments.

These features of American politics were reflected and reinforced by the welfare state programs that were created under the Social Security Act in the 1930s. To be sure, pensions for the old who had earned eligibility in covered occupations eventually covered a large proportion of the aged, and were administered by the national government. But eligibility for unemployment insurance was conditioned by a record of steady employment and earnings, and the program was administered by the states, although the states were prodded to assume this responsibility by the threat of a new federal payroll tax were any state to demur. Other groups in need were divided among different programs, each with their own conditions of eligibility, and each decentralized. Thus the several means-tested programs, including aid to orphans, to the uninsured aged, and to the disabled who were not covered by disability insurance, were to be administered by the states and counties under broad federal guidelines. (Only in 1975 did the federal government assume responsibility for the impoverished aged and disabled.) In these cases, federal grants-in-aid ensured that the states would create the programs.

These arrangements constituted the skeletal structure of the American welfare state, and a number of its features are noteworthy. One is that it reproduced the decentralization of the American state structure and party system. Another is that it created fragmented programs that also had the consequence of fragmenting the constituencies which institutionalists argue become the political defenders of the programs, ensuring continuity and even expansion (Mettler 2002; Campbell 2003; Soss 2005). And a third is that decentralization granted the states (and the counties) great latitude to craft the unemployment and means-tested programs so that the potentially decommodifying effects of state income supports would not interfere with local labor markets. Put another way, if the institutionalists emphasize that once in existence, welfare state programs generate a politics that sustains them, the US case provides dramatic examples of program structures that inhibit the growth of political support, and also generate political opposition.

A focus on American political institutions helps, in short, to account for a stunted and fragmented American welfare state. And a stunted and fragmented welfare state in turn helps account for public ambivalence toward the welfare state, and outright antipathy toward the means-tested and unemployment programs that are doubly burdened because their constituents are poor, disproportionately racial and ethnic minorities, and because both programs and constituents come to be tainted by the elaborate conditions and monitoring that characterizes decentralized programs crafted with an eye toward their impact on local labor market participation.

The most demeaned of these programs became Aid to Families with Dependent Children. Originally designed as a program for orphaned children and their caretakers, in the 1960s it was the program that was allowed to offer a limited safe harbor for African-American families suffering the multiple distresses of forced displacement from the agricultural south and marginalization from the urban economy. In the face of urban protests and riots, program rules were liberalized, and the program expanded (Piven and Cloward 1971, 1977). Somewhat later, as Hispanic migration increased, many of them turned to AFDC as well. No wonder that this was the program that became the punching ball for the opponents of the US welfare state. But while AFDC figured largely in the rhetorical campaign against social spending, the retrenchment campaign had far broader goals.

The business political mobilization that began in the 1970s, and that came to operate through a new infrastructure of think tanks, policy institutes, and the Republican Party, targeted a number of the New Deal and Great Society welfare state initiatives for rollbacks, partly to justify the tax cuts business was demanding, but more importantly as a component of the effort to roll back labor costs. The reforms, initially advocated by the new business-backed think tanks such as the Heritage Foundation and the Manhattan Institute, were actually a revival of formulas that have existed since the days of poor relief, and were applied most assiduously to the means-tested programs which reach the contemporary poor: welfare, food stamps, and Medicaid. Eligibility for benefits said the reformers, should be more strictly conditioned by work and marital behavior, real benefits should be lowered, states should have a larger role in the administration of benefits, bureaucratic discretion to give or withhold benefits should be increased (and wherever possible, the privatization of the programs should be promoted). Ironically, these are the program features that help explain popular antipathy toward the means-tested programs. Low benefits and intrusive procedures stigmatize both the programs and their beneficiaries, and this cultural stigma is then mobilized in attacks on the programs.

Once Ronald Reagan gained the presidency with the almost undivided support of American business, large-scale action on this agenda became possible. Not only were big cuts made in a range of welfare state programs, but a strategy of what Paul Pierson calls "systemic retrenchment" was inaugurated (Pierson 1994). Huge tax cuts were implemented, while military spending escalated, and this pincer movement limited the revenues available for welfare state spending. (When the strategy was revived with the election of George W. Bush in 2000, leading again to a series of huge tax cuts and a military build-up, Paul Krugman (2004a) called it the "starve the beast" strategy, meaning of course, starve government social spending.)

In 1996, the campaign scored a signal success with the passage of the Personal Responsibility and Work Opportunity Reconciliation Act which eliminated AFDC in favor of a new program called Temporary Assistance to Needy Families that not only granted the states greater administration discretion to limit aid, but by replacing grants-in-aid with block grants, gave the states a financial incentive to lower the rolls and thus lower the amounts they actually spent on assistance (Diller 2000). The Act also introduced new restrictions on eligibility for means-tested health and nutritional programs. These developments surely give credence to an institutionalist perspective. Once they were targeted by the retrenchers, the narrow and marginalized constituencies of these programs, and the cultural stigma encouraged by program procedures did indeed make them excruciatingly vulnerable.[2]

---

[2] Hacker (2004) provides an insightful discussion of the covert strategies by which many of these cuts were accomplished.

But the retrenchers had broader sights from the start. The really big prizes were the huge Medicare and social security programs. In institutionalist terms, the programs are well defended because they are so popular with the broad public. The popularity of the programs is owed in no small measure simply to the fact that they help a lot of people and are not means tested, and thus involve none of the humiliating rituals of certifying need, investigation, and surveillance that characterize means-tested programs. Indeed, social security is widely believed to be a social insurance system, a misapprehension that was in fact carefully cultivated by the proponents of the program during its early years in the 1930s. And then there is the fact that both programs have huge constituencies of supporters among the tens of millions of seniors or soon-to-be seniors who receive benefits. These are exactly the features that, according to an institutionalist perspective, should lead to the continuation and expansion of the programs.

These features have indeed bred caution among opponents of the programs, but it is the persistence of their campaign, and their innovative strategies that I will pause to describe in somewhat greater detail. To be sure, no one proposes to do away with the programs. Rather the argument for change is always on the grounds that the programs are financially unsound and need to be restructured in order to be saved. And the main solution proffered is privatization. In other words, the conservative animus against these programs is forged not only from their general animosity toward social spending; they are also animated by the profits that privatization promises, for health care providers and insurance companies in the case of Medicare, and for Wall Street firms that will handle private pension accounts in the case of social security.

There are in fact financial problems looming for Medicare, which provides federal health insurance for 41 million of the aged, and some of the disabled, and is paid for by a combination of payroll taxes, general revenues, deductibles, and co-payments. The financial problems expected in the future are not simply the result of demography, of the aging of the baby boomer generation, and longer lifespans, but are more importantly the result of anticipated continuing increases in health care costs (CBO 2003). In other words, the Medicare program is affected by the crisis in health care costs that affects all Americans. The Bush tax cuts, by depleting future revenues, of course make this problem much more serious. The recently passed Medicare Prescription Drug Act takes steps toward a market solution to this at least partially manufactured crisis. Well, not really a market solution. Rather, the legislation moves us further toward the creation of an unregulated market in health care, but a market saturated with public funds. The legislation contains subsidies for just about everyone in the health care business, including doctors, hospitals, insurance companies, and for-profit health plans. Moreover, the legislation forbids Medicare from bargaining with the pharmaceutical companies to bring down the cost of prescription medicines.

More than that, the legislation contains what may be important pilot programs that move in the direction of privatization. Private health plans are offered $12 billion in subsidies to compete with traditional Medicare, and are also guaranteed that no

HMO will be paid less for a patient than the provider would receive in the traditional fee-for-service Medicare program. This is called an experiment, and it will be launched in six major cities in 2010 (Meyerson 2003). Tax-free Health Savings Accounts are also introduced, which actually means another tax cut for the better off. And a provision in the legislation requires that a crisis be declared if more than 45 per cent of Medicare funding is expected to be drawn from general revenues in a seven-year budget projection (Skocpol 2004). As for prescription drugs for seniors, the bill provides a decidedly patchy and limited solution. A senior will have to pay $3,600 out of the first $5,100 in annual costs of drugs before the government starts reimbursing costs.

It is noteworthy that the Bush administration and Republican leaders in the Congress were singularly determined to pass this legislation. As Elizabeth Drew reports:

Republicans allowed no House Democrats and only two Senate Democrats, Max Baucus and John Breaux, both of whom supported the Medicare bill, to participate in the House-Senate conference setting its final terms. It had been passed by the house by a five-vote margin (220–215) just before 6:00 AM, after the Republican leaders made extraordinary efforts to persuade reluctant members—a process that took three hours rather than the usual fifteen minutes for a roll-call vote. Republican House leaders made offers of campaign funds to reluctant conservatives; they also threatened one Republican, who was planning to retire, with cutting off money for his son, who was running to replace him. This sort of rough stuff is without recent precedent. (Drew 2004)

There were reasons for the rough stuff. Not least, the legislation allowed the administration to trumpet the new subsidies for prescription drugs in the run-up to the 2004 presidential election, while taking large steps toward the privatization of Medicare.

Social Security is far and away the biggest prize among the social programs, and it will also be the hardest to grasp. The program was initiated during the crisis of the Great Depression, when massive unemployment and its politically destabilizing effects made public solutions imperative. As high levels of unemployment persisted, resistant even to the upturn of the economy in 1934, New Deal politicians became persuaded that it was important to remove the aged from the labor market. They were also helped to reach that conclusion by the huge numbers of the elderly who were mobilizing behind Francis Townsend in a movement that demanded pensions far more generous than social security would ever pay. Once the program was established and eligibility gradually expanded, while benefits rose especially during the tumultuous 1960s, the program became very popular indeed. It helped that the program was widely understood to be "insurance," and therefore not welfare, much as its early proponents intended. Then the tide turned, largely under the influence of the business mobilization that began in the 1970s, and especially of the think tanks that were created with business money. Several arguments against the program emerged. One was that the old were greedy, using funds that should be spent on the young. Another was that old age itself had changed; people lived longer and were healthier, and so they should work longer. And finally, there was the argument that over the long run, the program was not financially sound, an argument that tarnished the program for the simple reason that it spread doubt in the minds of future beneficiaries about whether their pensions were safe (CBO 2003).

Some changes were introduced. The age at which people become eligible for social security is being gradually raised, from sixty-five to sixty-seven. Those currently receiving benefits who were prohibited from working in the original legislation are now encouraged to work by regulations that reduce the penalties on earnings. These changes reveal that the labor market preoccupations that animated efforts to reduce other social programs also affected social security.

But the Bush agenda for social security is far more ambitious. Social security was originally a pay-as-you-go system, where payroll taxes collected each year funded the pension benefits that were paid each year. That changed in 1983 when the large deficits created by the Reagan tax cuts and defense increases were eased by a big increase in payroll taxes for social security. The result is that at least on paper, social security reserves have become enormous, although in actuality, those reserves exist only as Treasury notes, debts of the federal government to the fund. Nevertheless, the existence even in principle of huge public pension funds is ideologically offensive to the right. More than that, were the funds converted to private pensions, a new frontier of millions of individual stock accounts and broker fees would open for Wall Street investment firms, an arrangement naturally favored by the financial firms that backed Bush, including Merrill Lynch & Co., Crédit Suisse First Boston, UBS Paine Webber, and the Goldman Sachs Group, who together with others formed a lobbying group called the Coalition for American Financial Security (Center for Public Integrity 2004). The strident and insistent talk of a long-term crisis in social security financing is the overture to proposals for privatizing the system. Almost as soon as he assumed the presidency, Bush appointed a commission to make recommendations regarding social security that concluded in December of 2001 that any reform of the program should "include a system of voluntary personal accounts" (Center for Public Integrity 2004).

George Bush has long advocated that younger workers be allowed to set aside part of their social security tax payments for private investment accounts. This would be a first step toward the big goal of privatizing the system. There are huge obstacles such a strategy has to overcome. One is simply that the much-hyped crisis in social security financing is at most a far-off and unpredictable event. Thanks to a steep increase in payroll taxes inaugurated in 1983, the system is sound for the next fifty years, and even after that the gap in financing is small relative to the economy, less than three-quarters of 1 per cent of national income (Krugman 2004b; Weisbrot 2004). If there is a fiscal crisis looming in the foreseeable future, it is a crisis of overall federal debt, and the prospect that raises that the Treasury notes now owed to the social security fund will not be honored. Another obstacle is that the step-by-step strategy of partial privatization while honoring existing pension promises means sharply higher costs, since the money redirected to private accounts would come out of the funds now used to pay current retirees. The largest obstacle is that the program continues to have staunch voter support, and the institutionalists may yet be proven at least partly right. Still, with deficits ballooning, no one can safely predict the future of the programs.

Clearly, an institutional perspective yields insights into retrenchment in the US welfare state. A decentralized and fragmented governmental structure was reflected in decentralized and fragmented parties, parties that were easily penetrated by interest group and sectional influences, parties that did not even sustain the mass franchise during the critical early period of industrialization. These political institutions in turn produced the politics that led to fragmented and truncated welfare state programs, helping to account for the exposure of the mean-tested programs when opposition to them was mobilized.

But why did these institutions produce welfare state programs at all? An institutionalist perspective goes far toward explaining the limits on the American welfare state, but it cannot explain the irregular and non-institutionalized political forces that finally made the inauguration of the programs an imperative if domestic stability was to be sustained. After all, employer opposition to social spending is long standing. It was overcome in the United States only during periods when popular economic discontent reached levels that threatened both civil order and the stability of reigning political regimes. During the Great Depression of the 1930s, joblessness and hardship led to demonstrations and riots across the country, and also led to the defeat of the then dominant Republican Party. Programs like emergency relief, and later social security and unemployment insurance, were initiated quickly by Franklin Delano Roosevelt to deal with the immediate threat of popular unrest, and to build longer-term support for his New Deal Democratic coalition. Once trouble subsided, however, most of the social programs atrophied, until a new surge of popular protest erupted in the 1960s, this time spearheaded by the civil rights and urban poverty movements. The New Deal programs were revived and expanded, and new programs were added, most importantly Medicaid and Medicare. It is worth noting that at these peak moments of crisis in the 1930s and 1960s, even leaders of big business supported new social spending.

Similarly, an institutionalist perspective explains the vulnerability of the means-tested programs. Most Americans didn't like the programs they called "welfare." But for the most part, neither were they mobilized to do much about it. That required the emergence of a business-backed campaign that created the new think tanks and policy institutes, paid for the coalitions of organizations of the populist right, funded the campaigns of right-wing candidates, and launched the propaganda campaign that targeted these programs. This too was a kind of social movement, albeit a movement employing the strategies available to well-funded elites.

And the campaign by organized business interests and the right-wing populist groups with whom they have become allied also targeted the more universal programs. The long-term and persistent campaign has scored some considerable successes, and it shows no signs of abating. Moreover, the opponents have succeeded in altering the conditions which will influence the viability of social security over the longer term. Their propaganda has shattered public confidence in the program; they have used tax policy to encourage private pension investment accounts; and they have implemented massive tax cuts to produce the huge deficits that threaten to deplete social security funds.

Many of the arguments developed in the assault against welfare state programs in the United States have spread to Europe, especially to the United Kingdom. Sloganeering about "workfare not welfare" is also widespread on the Continent, and so is the introduction of new "workfare" programs. The similarities to the USA are not accidental. The right-wing think tanks and public intellectuals who played a large role in the campaign to roll back welfare state programs in the USA worked hard to carry their arguments overseas.[3] But while the language of welfare cutbacks, and even some of the model workfare programs, spread relatively easily, overall the cutbacks have remained modest.[4] In some countries, and particular in the social democratic Nordic states, welfare programs have actually continued to expand.[5] Norway's Cash Benefit Scheme is a good example. As Nina Berven has shown, the debates over the new program, which provides cash benefits for stay-at-home mothers, employed language very similar to the language used in the debates over US welfare reform, emphasizing work, family, and responsibility. In Norway, however, this language was used to justify a rather different set of policies. To be sure, the number of years a single mother could receive welfare benefits was reduced. At the same time, however, a new cash allowance program was inaugurated that allows all mothers, whether in single or two-parent households, to either stay at home or pay the costs of child care for children aged one to three (Berven 2004).

Institutional explanations are clearly relevant. The United States exemplifies the "liberal" welfare regimes which Esping-Andersen characterized as highly stratified, with an emphasis on individual self-responsibility and stigmatizing relief for people at the bottom (Esping-Andersen 1990, 65). These characteristics permitted but by no means predicted the contraction and reorganization of recent decades. The European welfare regimes not only generated higher levels of popular support which, at least until now ensured considerable continuity, but they have not experienced the full-scale mobilization against welfare state programs by business and its right-wing populist allies that occurred in the United States.

Institutional perspectives have obviously contributed to our understanding of welfare state developments. Still, theories of the welfare state need to confront more squarely the deep social conflicts that periodically erupt and overflow the channels of institutional politics, driving both the expansion and the contraction of the welfare state. In the United States, ongoing transformations reflect not the

---

[3] Janiewski (2003) discusses this process in some detail.

[4] The German government is, however, currently proposing cutbacks in unemployment benefits, which are now far more generous than unemployment benefits in the USA. The proposals would end unemployment benefits after twelve months, after which the unemployed would receive only basic welfare. The proposals have precipitated modest protests in a number of German cities. See Landler (2004). See also Gangl (2004) for a study that shows that the more generous German unemployment benefits reduce the "scar" of unemployment in comparison with the US system.

[5] See Navarro, Schmitt, and Astudillo 2004. Navarro et. al. cite data from the OECD, *OECD Historical Statistics 1960–1994* (Paris, 1996), and OECD, *OECD Historical Statistics 1970–1999* (Paris, 2000).

relatively comfortable politics of institutional gradualism, but the bold politics of a business class primed for class war.

## References

AMENTA, E. 1998. *Bold Relief: Institutional Politics and the Origins of American Social Policy.* Princeton, NJ: Princeton University Press.

BERVEN, N. 2004. National politics and global ideas? Welfare, work and legitimacy in Norway and the United States. Unpublished dissertation, Sociology Department, University of Bergen.

CAMPBELL, A. 2003. *How Policies Make Citizens: Senior Political Activism and the American Welfare State.* Princeton, NJ: Princeton University Press.

CENTER FOR PUBLIC INTEGRITY 2004. *The Buying of the President.* New York: HarperCollins.

CONGRESSIONAL BUDGET OFFICE 2003. *The Long-term Budget Outlook: A CBO Study.* Congress of the United States, Congressional Budget Office, Dec.

DILLER, M. 2000. The revolution in welfare administration: rules, discretion and entrepreneurial government. *New York University Law Review,* 75: 1121.

DREW, E. 2004. Hung up in Washington. *New York Review* (12 Feb.).

ESPING-ANDERSEN, G. 1985a. *Politics against Markets: The Social Democratic Road to Power.* Princeton, NJ: Princeton University Press.

—— 1985b. Power and distributional regimes. *Politics and Society,* 14: 223–56.

—— 1990. *The Three Worlds of Welfare Capitalism.* Princeton, NJ: Princeton University Press.

—— 1999. *Social Foundations of Postindustrial Economies.* Oxford: Oxford University Press.

EVANS, P., REUSCHEMEYER, D., and SKOCPOL, T. (eds.) 1985. *Bringing the State Back in.* Cambridge: Cambridge University Press.

GANGL, M. 2004. Welfare states and the scar effects of unemployment: a comparative analysis of the United States and West Germany. *American Journal of Sociology,* 109: 1319–64.

GIDDENS, A. 1976. Classical social theory and the origins of modern social theory. *American Journal of Sociology,* 81: 34–57.

HACKER, J. 1998. The historical logic of national health insurance: structure and sequence in the development of British, Canadian, and U.S. medical policy. *Studies in American Political Development,* 12: 57–130.

—— 2004. Privatizing risk without privatizing the welfare state: the hidden politics of social policy retrenchment in the United States. *American Political Science Review,* 98: 243–60.

JANIEWSKI, D. 2003. Making the world safe for "global capitalism:" the new right as a transnational enterprise. Unpublished manuscript, Victoria University of Wellington.

KORPI, W. 1983. *The Democratic Class Struggle.* London: Routledge and Kegan Paul.

KRUGMAN, P. 2004a. Red ink realities. *New York Times,* 27 Jan.

—— 2004b. Social security scares. *New York Times,* 5 Mar.

LANDLER, M. 2004. It's Monday in Germany: time for social protest. *New York Times,* World Business (25 Aug.).

METTLER, S. 2002. Bringing the state back in to civic engagement: policy feedback effects of the G.I. Bill for World War II veterans. *American Political Science Review,* 96 (2).

MEYERSON, H. 2003. Powerlines. *LA Weekly* (28 Nov.–4 Dec.).

NAVARRO, V., JOHN, S., and ASTUDILLO, J. 2004. Is globalization undermining the welfare state? The evolution of the welfare state in developed capitalist countries during the 1990s. *International Journal of Health Services*, 34: 185–228.

PIERSON, P. 1994. *Dismantling the Welfare State? Reagan, Thatcher, and the Politics of Retrenchment*. Cambridge: Cambridge University Press.

—— 2000. Increasing returns, path dependence, and the study of politics. *American Political Science Review*, 94: 251–68.

PIVEN, F. F. and CLOWARD, R. A. 1971. *Regulating the Poor: The Functions of Public Welfare*. New York: Pantheon.

—— —— 1977. *Poor People's Movements: Why They Succeed, How They Fail*. New York: Pantheon.

—— —— 2000. *Why Americans Still Don't Vote*. Boston: Beacon Press.

QUADAGNO, J. 1994. *The Color of Welfare: How Racism Undermined the War on Poverty*. New York: Oxford University Press.

RUSCHE, G., and KIRCHHEIMER, O. 1939. *Punishment and Social Structure*. New York: Russell and Russell.

SCHATTSCHNEIDER, E. E. 1942. *Party Government*. New York: Rinehart.

SHALEV, M. 1983. The social democratic model and beyond: two generations of comparative research on the welfare state. *Comparative Social Research*, 6: 315–51.

SHEFTER, M. 1979. Party, bureaucracy, and political change in the United States. In *The Development of Political Parties: Patterns of Evolution and Decay*, ed. L. Maisel and J. Cooper. Beverly Hills, Calif.: Sage.

SKOCPOL, T. 1992. *Protecting Soldiers and Mothers: The Political Origins of Social Policy in the United States*. Cambridge, Mass.: Harvard University Press.

—— 2004. A bad senior moment. *American Prospect*, Jan.

SOSS, J. 2005. Making clients and citizens: welfare policy as a source of status, belief, and action. In *Deserving and Entitled: Social Constructions and Public Policy*, ed. A. Schneider and H. Ingram. New York: State University of New York Press.

STEINMO, S. and WATTS, J. 1995. It's the institutions stupid! Why comprehensive national health insurance always fails in America. *Journal of Health Politics, Policy and Law*, 20: 329–72.

STEPHENS, J. D. 1979. *The Transition from Capitalism to Socialism*. London: Macmillan.

WEISBROT, M. 2004. Social security doing just fine. *Providence Journal* (23 Jan.).

WESTERN, B. and KATHERINE, B. 1999. How unregulated is the U.S. labor market? The penal system as a labor market institution. *American Journal of Sociology*, 104: 1030–60.

# CHAPTER 43

# REFLECTIONS ON HOW POLITICAL SCIENTISTS (AND OTHERS) MIGHT THINK ABOUT ENERGY AND POLICY

## MATTHEW HOLDEN, JR.

## 1. A PERSPECTIVE OF THIRTY YEARS: PERSONAL HISTORY AS METHOD

In this chapter, I wish to stipulate three important factors that limited space will not allow me to analyze. (1) Energy policy in the next decade or two will be profoundly influenced by China, India, and Russia. China and India are the two biggest energy consumers in the world, and their consumption is growing. This affects both international energy economics and international politics. (2) Unless there are notable economic and technological changes, energy patterns will work hardship upon the poorest countries of the world. (3) Energy policy everywhere will be influenced by climatic events, and policies based upon the proposition that global warming is occurring and that climate change is occurring as a result of activity that human beings can make a decision to control. These three factors must be read "between the lines," though overtly most of this chapter is about the policy of the United States.

By good fortune rather than training or planning, I was led from the 1970s until now, into a series of official and private engagements to do with energy. The first step was purely intellectual. Edwin Young, the Chancellor of the University of Wisconsin in Madison, sponsored a small faculty seminar on "a method for natural resource decision-making" over the same period that the Organization of Petroleum Exporting Countries (OPEC) placed its 1973 embargo on oil sales to the United States and other Western countries.

The year 1973 was a crucial one. Another was 1979, the time of the Iranian revolution. United States policy making and public opinion has been dominated by fears and fantasies of those years and others that might hypothetically be similar to them. Those fears and fantasies have also governed the study of energy policy. It turns out that, after an initial spurt promoted by the 1973 and 1979 crises, students of politics have been little concerned with energy. Apparently, this is not true of political science alone. Judge Richard D. Cudahy (US Court of Appeals, Seventh Circuit) spoke of this to an energy lawyers group: "Energy law, although it is gradually finding a place in the thinking of students of law, is still a rather exotic offering, landing somewhere between regulated industries, environmental, and natural resources law" (Cudahy 2004). When the realistic fears, and the fantasies declined, the subject became less topical. In turning to consider the newest political science on energy, I have been surprised to find less new work focused centrally on energy than expected. There is in my opinion, a serious need for new work. My hoped-for audience is in political science, but also amongst others concerned with energy who need to understand its politics.

# 2. How Political Scientists Have Looked At Energy

Political scientists may understand the energy problem somewhat better if we put it in the simplest human terms, and move thus to the technical. No one can fail to perceive the imperative of physical self-protection. Energy is requisite in some form, lest one die from excessive cold of the Arctic regions or excessive heat of the Australian "Outback" or the arid regions of Arizona and Nevada.

The "new politics of energy" was a function of, or at least brought forcefully to view by the 1973 crisis. This overrode the traditional politics which had mainly to do with limited government regulation of coal, strip mining, government regulation of domestic production in order to maintain oil prices, civilian nuclear power, government regulation of natural gas, and a variety of attempts at deregulation. David H. Davis (1992) ranks "five political arenas of energy—coal, oil, natural gas, electricity, and nuclear energy... in an order based on the degree to which government intervenes." The new energy politics also involves new participants and new issues. The biggest new issue is the attempt at protecting the domestic energy supply from disruptive actions by foreign governments.

The assumption that demand would outrun supply within a quarter-century made the concept of conservation seem imperative. This assumption ran through the National Energy Act, which was a five-part combination of legislation dealing with deregulation of natural gas, conversion from natural gas to coal, windfall profits taxation, legislation to encourage utilities (under state regulation) to allow higher (or more "efficient") pricing.

The political science literature on energy appears notably disenchanted. Robert E. Keohane supposes that the impact of the 1973 crisis could not have been avoided. The problem he saw as inherent in American society. "Fragmentation of public authority, pervasive business influence, and the willingness of public officials to follow the path of least resistance in the short run [were] fatal flaws [that made] it difficult to imagine that the United States could have averted the oil crisis of the 1970s" (Keohane 1982, 183). Others asked, how well was the 1973 crisis managed? Badly, supposes Peter deLeon (1988, 72):

To help unravel the complicated relationships between energy resources and uses, public and private sponsors generated an immense set of research studies, most of them quantitative in nature, which were used as the basis for recommending and formulating energy policy.... Perhaps as many as two-thirds of the models failed to achieve their avowed purposes of direct application to policy problems.

deLeon offered the judgement (which fortunately for the real world has not been tested by experience) that "it is highly likely that the United States will experience another seriously debilitating energy shortfall; the only outstanding questions are of magnitude and timing."

Franklin Tugwell, with about ten years' experience in the State Department, Office of Technology Assessment, and the Congressional Information Service, said he had first thought we had done well. But:

It became evident [upon closer retrospective study] that, though we did avoid some costly mistakes, our policies on balance accomplished little of value. Worse, when they did not cancel one another out, they often increased our economic losses and our strategic vulnerability, and failed to protect the disadvantaged from bearing a disproportionate burden of the costs involved .... The arrangement left after ten years of struggle—"free markets" in energy— likely to work well or endure.   (Tugwell 1988, vii)

Wildavsky, Tenenbaum et al. (1981, 14) make a case more generally, that "U.S. behavior has always been irrational (except in wartime), if by that one means inconsistent policies were followed." One may adapt here the use of the political science word "regime" (Greenstein and Polsby 1975). Tugwell uses the same terminology, with credit to Robert E. Keohane, with perhaps more stringency than the present author uses it here.

Policy analysts within political science have had hardly a good word to say for United States energy policy, and it is doubtful whether the overall assessment of any other policy would be better. Maybe that is correct. But at this stage, recall Baker's

(19\*\*) admonition: "scholars often neglect the hard realities that impinge on ideal solutions and the day-to-day requirements that constrain the statesman's options."

# 3. "Politics," "Institutions," "Interests," and "Energy"

Whatever policy or innovation one may have in mind does depend upon a fourfold connection of technology, economics and finance, law, and politics. If the proposal violates scientific knowledge and the related technology, it will not work. But it will not make any difference either, unless the innovation can be financed by someone, somehow. Finance depends upon defining parties' rights and duties (such as the terms on which the financier can sue if payment is not made). But in the end, there is some point at which those who would do something must resort to politics, trading amongst incommensurable values.

"Politics" is the defining framework of "policy" organizations. "Politics" can mean the use and control of an energy resource in order to achieve some result that has nothing to do with energy per se. It can also mean as the emergent term "the geopolitics of energy" suggests, the ability to interdict because of physical location. So it was in 1973. But the main interest in this chapter is in the making of decisions in order to achieve some result about energy both for now and for the future.

Those who would pay attention to energy would find it useful to know the institutions of energy policy making. Institutions may not be adequate causes to explain results. But the ways they come into existence, gain a presence, and assume functions indicate that decision makers, acting from interests deem them important.

In most countries, an energy decision seems to be a function mainly of the executive—whether this is the political part of the executive or the career/technical bureaucracy—with fairly limited effects from any collective representative body. Equally important is what interests or influence gives the agency its tone and function, and how the agency asserts its self-perceived mission. Perhaps the intense passion that people felt about the discomforts of the 1973 crisis explains why the United States was the only country with a separate Department of Energy, compared with nine IEA countries in 1983 and three in 1976.

As of 2005 the Secretary of Energy, under whose domain some of the major energy industries lie, is head of a department that had been established for a supply objective with responsibility also for collecting data from a national survey of greenhouse gas emissions. It is also the department for weapons development.

The idea of combining functions into one unified department is very influential in American (and possibly other countries') thinking about the organization of government. There is a special set of institutions in the regulatory agencies. These agencies seem to have new roles almost everywhere, or themselves to be new, and studies of them are beginning to become available.

Regulation is a process in which in principle, private parties may be asked to secure prior clearance, to accept concurrent oversight and after-the-fact review, with rewards and penalties being attached.

The role of the judiciary has been a very big factor in American decision making about energy issues. Through judicial decision, the natural gas part of the energy market was put under price regulation.[1] Judicial interpretation of what a statute (the Natural Gas Policy Act of 1938) required an agency (the Federal Power Commission) to do in interpreting a contract (by the Phillips Petroleum Company), imposed legal authority for producer price regulation for almost twenty-four years. Similar phenomena have been major factors in German decision making about nuclear plants, about subsidies to encourage wind and solar electric power, and have some role in the emerging Australian regulatory system. Regulatory systems have existed in some form through much of history, since ancient Rome. But regulatory systems that seem somewhat like the American format have been created in many countries within the past two decades.

Economists under the impact of neoclassical reasoning, talk of "command and control" regulation. In fact, there is not all that much "command" and little "control." The strength and the limitations of a regulatory agency's dealings with regulated firms can be expressed in terms of how much it can actually command the firm, and how much it bargains with the firm on a continuing basis. Four variables determine the strength or weakness of the regulatory agency's actual ability to make decisions. These are: the degree of *complexity* of the subject being regulated; the changing *beliefs, myths, and values* that encourage the society and its political leadership to invest the agency with authority and latitude or to withhold that authority and latitude; the *access of the regulated interests* to other influential decision points that have some control over the regulatory agency; and the *reality of tomorrow* or the expectation of future engagement with the regulated interests.

Federalism can also be extremely important if the political regime allows different national and subnational decision making on energy questions. This has been notably important in the United States and has at least sometimes been important in Canada, and should be taken into account in thinking about Australia and India.

As regards legislative law *making*, it is well known that US party discipline or cohesion is nowhere near that in otherwise similar countries such as the United Kingdom, Canada, and Australia. The US president, powerful as he is, does not control the agenda of either House; nor does either House take precedence over the other.

Political scientists generally find it useful to deal with institutions but the true first principle of political analysis is "interest." Interest is not merely the same thing as "overt attitude." It is the inherent necessity.

---

[1] See below on how this happened.

What we must know is what are the uses and who are the users. We must know the gains and losses *and therefore, the interests likely to be affected, activated, or neutralized politically*, in any set of imagined decisions. From this, we are likely to have some better idea of the likelihood of feasibility and viability.

Energy policy is necessarily involved with the inherent conflict between producer interests and consumer interests. Industrial customers in all sectors have interests that diverge from those who purchase energy in some form to use in their residences, in contrast to those who purchase energy to use in their shops and stores. Political science can take some account of energy issues within the conventional understandings of a petroleum regime. In 1900 total world oil production was something like 150 million barrels annually. In 2002, the world as a whole produced about 30 billion barrels per annum. By that count, the world is 200 times more dependent on petroleum in the twenty-first century than it was at the beginning of the twentieth century.

The importing country—or the importing part of a country with adequate resources—has the necessity of finding a supply of energy. In the circumstances of the early twenty-first century this most often means petroleum or natural gas. There are a variety of other issues that can emerge. In the contemporary United States, one of the contending positions is not to find new physical supply, but to practice conservation and efficiency as an equivalent means of supply (Lovins et al. 2004). Physical protection by force or threat of force is another means. In addition, there is economic protection via purchase contracts, storage mechanisms, and reserves as part of means of doing business.

Implicitly what we have described is the problem of allocating supply. Allocation can be done by a completely free market, by some kind of regulated market, or (in theory) by complete central control. If supply is taken as the objective, what is integral is the question of whether or not money making is also an objective. On the other hand, in exporting countries, money making is a crucial objective, whether for the government or for governmental facilitation so that private persons can make money. This distinguishes such different countries as the former Soviet Union, present Russia or the other of the former Soviet republics, Saudi Arabia, Nigeria, or Venezuela.

There are, especially for exporting countries, the issues of adopting market terms for governmental action, as in the creation of state-operated companies that behave more or less as if they were private companies (Grayson 1981; Scholes 1989, 19–21).

As both the oil and uranium cases show, energy policy has involved a permanent intersection, not only for the United States but also for Britain with military policy. This war/defense-related interest goes back almost a hundred years. The example was set first by the United Kingdom. The naval objective was to convert warships from coal-burning engines to oil-burning engines. The Anglo-Persian Oil Company was set up about 1907, evidently as a private venture (Caroe 1951, 71). In just a few years, Winston Churchill, not yet forty years old, pushed successfully to get the government to take half-ownership of the company.[2]

---

[2] Black (2004, 128–65) offers a detailed discussion of the negotiations and finally, parliamentary sanction of the arrangement that gave the British government a 50% interest in Anglo-Persian Oil Company.

American firms were interested in the Middle East, in competition with their British and Anglo-Dutch rivals. They desired governmental help for their business purposes. But the United States military had no particular interest. The situation changed as of the Second World War. The United States was then the second biggest oil-producing country and domestic United States oil was deemed virtually invulnerable. The Second World War left a strong argument amongst members of American elites, that "resources for America's future" must be conserved, and that Middle East oil should be secured.

The Conservation/Environmental Objective historically may have involved the protection of energy resources. By now, the protection of the total environment from adverse impacts is the bigger political question. As of the 1970s, this meant the "Faustian bargain" concern about permanent custody of supra-dangerous nuclear wastes. Now it also means the global climate change issues that are embodied in the Kyoto Treaty.[3]

The Social Objective is to deal with policies as supplements to presumptive market failure. These may include short-term, sudden, disruptive price changes, even for prosperous and middle-class consumers.[4] They may also involve the issue of distribution of benefits to different classes of owners, such as was undertaken by the Texas system of pro-rationing that protected independent producers and royalty owners from the impact of the major international companies.

What pass as conservation/environmental objectives may in reality be distributive social protection. This may be illustrated when the question of "environmental impact" is advanced to prevent some energy facility, such as a liquified natural gas (LNG), from being developed in what prior users find a desirable area for other purposes.

# 4. Experience from US Policy Making

## 4.1 The Problem of Massive Legislation

Energy legislation at least since the 1973 crisis has two qualities:

1. *The conflicts are so intense and protracted that new legislation appears almost impossible.* During the Carter administration, Speaker Thomas P. O'Neill adopted the tactic of the omnibus bill. "This practicing of 'packaging' or 'bundling' a number of legislative proposals into one legislative measure"— known as "omnibus legislation"—"has been engaged in for about half a century" (Patterson 2001, ix). Glen S. Krutz (2001, 122) "found omnibus use

---

[3] Since the Kyoto Treaty issues are so strongly advocated, one should call attention to one forceful advocate of the other side (Michaels and Balling 2000, 209–13).

[4] See below on the natural gas case.

to be a positive and significant influence on legislative productivity." It worked well for passing the Carter program through the House. It has not worked so well in energy since.

From 1954 onward, the industry aim was get Congress to override the *Phillips* decision and deregulate natural gas. After what was probably the hardest-fought energy battle during the Carter administration, Congress adopted a law (the Natural Gas Policy Act of 1978) that provided for phased price increases.

There followed a tortuous fourteen years until another major energy law was adopted: the Energy Policy Act of 1992, adopted by a Democratic Congress when George H. W. Bush was president. In some respects, it is a far-reaching law. To give some sense of its physical size it amounts to 443 printed pages and, one may estimate crudely about 250,000 words.

In American law-making terminology, a major section of a statute is called a "title." The Energy Policy Act has some thirty titles. Every provision is there for a reason. Or the provision is there because some person of influence or reputation suggested it, or was in any case prepared to sanction it.[5]

The politically salient questions are: "Who was interested in energy efficiency and why? What did they give for it? What has been done with it since the law was adopted?" Title VII deals, as noted with electricity and contains important modifications of the Federal Power Act. That provision more or less assumes the theory that generation is not a natural monopoly that has to be regulated.

Nearly all other energy legislative efforts have been blocked by what Uslaner (1989) calls "destructive coalitions of minorities." The net result has been that there has been no comprehensive energy legislation in the United States since that time.

The Energy Policy Act of 2003 is said to be 900 pages, which means it is about twice the size of the Energy Policy Act of 1992. In 2003, the crucial and difficult features were manifestations of the petroleum regime. One was the proposal for drilling in the Alaskan National Wildlife Reserve (ANWR). This is a high-priority item for the petroleum industry, as the area is estimated to contain about 10 billion barrels.

The other issue was rather technical, involving a chemical known as MTBE (methyl tertiary butyl ether). MTBE was used in reformulated gasoline. Reformulated gas is required in some circumstances, under Act of Congress, to satisfy EPA requirements in cities with the worst smog.[6] On the other hand, MBTE has been found to have leached into the underground water supply in some areas, to be extremely difficult to remove, and apparently to be cancer related. As a result, litigation has been brought against some companies. We would not spend time on so

---

[5] Most students of the legislative process know how important staff is (are), but the present author has never seen a detailed, informed, quantitative study that shows how often legislative provisions result from staff initiatives that members neither know about nor approve nor have left within the scope of the staff.

[6] The summary explanation of MTBE in this paragraph comes from the Environmental Protection Agency: www.epa.gov/mtbe.faq.htm.

arcane a matter as MTBE, except that it illustrates how "technical" matters may become the critical items that jam the entire process. If somewhere in the legislative process, there had not been some actor determined to protect MTBE, the 2003 legislation almost surely would have passed and been signed by the president.

2. *The massive legislation, once adopted is likely to lack intellectual coherence.* The far-reaching effects of energy generate a demand for comprehensive decisions, in contrast to "piecemeal" decisions. It is likely to be so complex that no one understands it, and therefore is likely to be unadministrable.

The two features join to impose special burdens upon the regulatory process, which also plays a large role in energy decision making. United States energy policy also involves "research and development," or the spending of large amounts of money from the federal treasury. That, except for passing references, is one also that is also bypassed in this chapter.

## 4.2 Regulatory Decision Making

Regulation in the United States has been primarily a means of dealing with the social protection objective. In petroleum proper, there has been relatively little governmental regulation over many years, though there have been increases during patent national emergencies (Bradley 1996, vol. i). There was a period in which oil producers were limited in the amount they could pump, theoretically on the ground of protecting the oil source from wasteful or damaging exploitation. But a significant element of this was to protect smaller producers from the really major producers (Bradley 1996). There were also controls for a time, to prevent too much cheaper oil (mainly Middle Eastern) from being imported. The advantage in such regulation was in favor of domestic producers against the international firms that had the money, skill, and diplomatic backing to operate in Saudi Arabia and elsewhere (Engler 1961).

The distributional issue became most apparent in the regulation of pricing in the natural gas market. Natural gas was a fuel not widely marketed before the 1940s. The incentive for investing in long-distance pipeline technology was not very high. Then came the Second World War. The federal government paid for big pipelines to move gasoline run from the producing areas in Texas to the East Coast. After the war, these pipelines were sold, and a company known as the Texas Eastern Transmission Company converted them to carry natural gas (Goodwin 1980, 130–2).

Protection of urban customers, now that gas could become big business in the cities, had a different economic and political meaning. Natural gas policy was one of the matters where technology, economics and finance, politics, and law created an issue in the 1940s that had hardly existed before.

It provided a new reality to test the language of the Natural Gas Act of 1938. Under the law, the prices from the transmission companies to the distributors were regulated by the Federal Power Commission. The producers charged what they saw fit, and these became part of the transmission prices automatically to be passed through to the distributors and, through them automatically to the end-use customers.

The issue arrived in the form of a dispute about what contracts would mean and how to interpret them. Producers (who brought the gas out of the ground) and pipelines (people who bought the gas and transported it to sell to their customers) had contracts with each other. The contract would state that Producer would sell X million cubic feet of gas to Y for price Z. The contract would also say, "if such and such event occurs, then the price will go to 125% of Z."

The fight that began in 1948 in the FPC went on in a virtual thirty years' war. Its settlement came in the form of the Natural Gas Policy Act of 1978, mentioned before, the complex new statute to govern this fuel. The Federal Energy Regulatory Commission had to figure out how to administer this law, and to do so in a way compatible to most of the forces at play in Congress.

In the 1978 legislation, Congress set some higher gas prices than the contracts called for. The question is: did that mean that the existing contracts would have to stay at the old price until they expired, which might mean several years? Within the Commission there were Commissioners and staff members who wanted to move as rapidly as possible to something like deregulation. There was the minority of Commissioners (the present author among them, and sometimes the present author only) and staff who wanted to retain as much as possible of the regulation, in the interest of the household customer. Suffice it to say, the former won and the latter lost.

This discussion is intended to show that the regulatory process has an important part in the United States natural gas policy arena. It has, and characteristically has had a relatively modest role in the petroleum arena. It has a very large part in the electric arena. In the past twenty years, since the Reagan administration officially advocated deregulation, the regulators have been prone to advocate deregulation as well. But reality is much more complicated. The concept of creating a competitive electric power system (or of deregulating the electric system to the extent legally possible) was in motion. In the United States, the Federal Energy Regulatory Commission has argued that Congress required it to follow that path. It is seldom that a simple and patent statement of FERC statutory authority can comfortably be accepted unless the words are so explicit as to admit no doubt.

A claim of mandatory congressional instruction may often be taken as a claim for protection in doing what the agency would itself like to do. In the regulated electric utility industry, the Commission may have acted wisely, or not. It may well have acted within its authority. But, subject to the controversy this may bring, *FERC did not have to do what it did; it chose to do what it did.*

The Commission, having developed a procedure for application to natural gas, could find no basis for not applying the same concepts to electricity. FERC decided a long time ago that it would favor open access when and if it could. After all, the Commission had learned transmission policy in the natural gas area, and it is plausible to think it would try to apply the same principles (or "principles") to electricity. Moreover, the parties ("interests") who had all along wanted wheeling could be expected to bring wheeling cases. They did.

The heavy-duty transmission lines that carry power in bulk have historically been owned by the individual utility companies. Those lines can only be built by going, often for many miles, through other people's real estate. The companies, though privately owned are granted certain rights of eminent domain, which is "the inherent right of a governmental entity to take privately owned property, especially land, and convert it to public use, subject to reasonable compensation for the taking" (Garner 1999, 541).

The battles can be tedious. In the United States at any rate, there are no well-known and systematized data as to the extent of a problem securing transmission routes. The present author stands himself as authority on the point. In 2003, he was a member of the Electricity Advisory Board of the United States Department of Energy. He thought it would aid the board's deliberations if data could obtained, but was unable to find such data. There are some well-known individual cases.

Several years ago, the present author made an error in anticipating the course of action. He thought that FERC action in claiming certain jurisdiction, against the claims of states, would be the next storm on the electric power front. The Commission's actions precipitate a situation that can be restated in the following proposition: every solution produces some new problem.

In this case, the Commission's solution contributed to threats of bulk power system reliability. Bulk power system reliability was undervalued in the FERC's new policy. When the vertically integrated utilities controlled their geographic domains, they also controlled access to their transmission lines. They then began to plan jointly for areas described as "pools." The volume and direction of the traffic increased beyond the planned capacity of the system. Herein lies the threat to bulk power system reliability. There are not many bulk power transmission failures, but they are serious. The evidence is now available in the form of the Lake Erie blackout of 2003.

Life does not remain stagnant. Under its new policies, the Federal Energy Regulatory Commission has sponsored the creation of "regional transmission organizations," which join the transmission facilities of all the companies within a defined area. Under American federalism, one state (Virginia) forbade the utilities under state regulation to do so.

Under this new policy, the Commission has maintained that by virtue of a provision in the Energy Policy Act of 1992, it has that authority to override the state. But behind this is a national concern that becomes global as to how to structure an electric industry. The principle that has already been accepted is that the government should cease utility regulation. The practice has become that of opening the business to others.

## 4.3 What Is the Quality of the Scientific Advice?

Energy policy also forces attention to the quality of scientific advice. It is apparent that over the past three decades, things have not gone very well. The need for "better" is not hard to find. If top-level leaders are not all that good, social scientists (political scientists included) have not much justification in hard criticism. The belief, which is implicit in our criticisms (Davis 1992; Keohane 1982; deLeon 1988; Tugwell 1988), can easily be little more than a conceit, unless we at least face up to the hard problems that policy makers do face.

This allows some reconsideration of Harold D. Lasswell. Most comment on "the policy sciences" appears to wash out the Lasswellian essence. There are certain things that Lasswell knew or believed. Policy, as soon as people get to the hard things over which there is struggle, is enveloped in clouds of pretense. This comes from writing a book on what the young Lasswell then thought of as "the world war." Before there was Rational Choice, easy to learn and apply if you have the mathematics and believe neoclassical economics, there is also Irrational Choice, easy to see and hard to systematize. This comes from the man who sought to bring psychoanalysis into politics.

Then there is politics as struggle, and the expectation of hierarchy (not the same as preference for hierarchy), even if it is not prescribed and proclaimed as formal doctrine. This is the politics: who gets what, when, how (Lasswell 1950); a shorthand phrase that refers to symbols, violence, goods, and practices as means of attaining and maintaining control.

All this must be assumed, for one is aware of no sign that Lasswell renounced any of it. Rather, in an almost Hobbesian understanding that the world needs something better than the mess its top leaders produce, the knowledge for the making and maintaining of commonwealths is framed in the language of "the policy sciences" (Lerner and Lasswell 1951).

The Lasswellian problem, meaning the need for better substantive policy making, is quite real for energy. But it is doubtful if it can ever be applied very well, for it requires too much good knowledge in a time of urgent action, and it also requires people at the highest levels of authority to give up too much authority themselves.

What is more at least as far as energy goes, is the same problem of over-certain belief in the natural science–engineering world and in the world of journalism which has the function of continually re-educating us all.

Policy analysts of the political-science type do not have to decide all the pertinent issues. But as a profession not primarily for hire, and specializing in the governmental process and the evaluation of data, there is at least one crucial role for political science. That is accentuating the needed resolution in the conflicts between the public positions of the experts who are most influential or who make the boldest claims that their opinions should be decisive.

There is a politics of conflict over what is and is not expert that becomes very intense when natural science/engineering policy analysis is involved. The politics of expertise can become a bitter battle in which the holders of approach X give little, if any presumption of competence to the holders of approach Y (Goodstein 2004). We can illustrate this with a number of examples.

## 4.4 Reasoning about Oil Exhaustion

The political science-type policy analyst should recognize that there is considerable debate about the concept both of the exhaustion of oil, and of its consequences for policy. There is intense controversy about this issue. The concept of oil exhaustion has run throughout the history of the industry. Wildavsky, Tenenbaum et al. (1981) demonstrated this quite neatly. Individual reputations and careers are now implicated, at least by the way they handle their materials (Hughes 2005, 12). The lesson that we can project, if there is an audience that is interested at all in what we say, is that much of what is said amounts to scare tactics.

Oil exhaustion has also been a matter of discourse for educated people who conceive themselves as having a "public interest," not an investment interest in energy (Dewhurst et al. 1947, 574–5). This issue also has an interest for people in the oil business. It stands to reason that if you wish to put your effort or your money into place X, you have some desire to know how much you will find and how it will last.

It is important to make clear that the arguments need clarity and resolution.

M. King Hubbert, a Shell geologist, stands out as a forecaster who anticipated in 1956 that United States production would reach its maximum in 1970. Apparently, he is regarded by many observers as having been right. There is nonetheless a conflict between Hubbert Curve advocates and economics, on exhaustion of resources (whether there is an "end of oil," when) and of the policy options attendant to the answer. The National Research Council–National Academy of Engineering (2004) observed that, "For decades, various analysts have predicted petroleum resource constraints. US production peaked in the 1970s, but international production has so far shown no signs of faltering."

The statement that production shows no signs of faltering is clearly opposed by others. That is a central intellectual issue posed by the Hubbert thesis and at the same time, by the emergence of debate about what policies are consequent to a belief in global warming.

Kenneth S. Deffeyes (2001, 186) includes the following sentence in his final chapter: "We could go happily on, pretending either (1) a permanent decline in world oil production won't happen or (2) it doesn't matter.... In 2008 the oil won't be there." As an example, Deffeyes argues that Hubbert's methodology, applied to the whole world, tells us that the peak production year after which the decline of oil would be seen, is at hand. The "peaking" concept is also the intellectual center of a book by Paul Roberts (2005, 47–72). Deffeyes (2001, 149) is emphatic: "No Caspian

Sea exploration, no drilling in the South China Sea, no SUV replacements, no renewable energy project can be brought in at a sufficient rate to avoid a bidding war for the remaining oil.'

Deffeyes pays no attention in his argument, except by a footnote reference, to the economic theory under which the Hubbert estimate has to be rejected.[7] Deffeyes says nothing about why his approach should be regarded as better than Adelman and Lynch's (1997) approach. What is involved, however, is the economists' challenge to the reasoning of Hubbert and others, a challenge grounded in economic theory (Adelman 1997).

At one level, Adelman and Lynch challenge empirically. After the fact they say, Hubbert's numbers were wrong, as were the numbers of others who are respected and influential.

Adelman and Lynch (1997, 56) describe Hubbert's bell-shaped curve of ultimately recoverable reserves (URRs): "Hubbert correctly predicted that US crude oil output would peak in 1970." But they raise the expected economist's question, "was it the result of resource exhaustion *or* of cheaper oil imports now freely available?"

They say that discoveries continue, and the reserve number continues to get bigger. Moreover, they say that the natural gas numbers continued to show production above Adelman and Lynch's estimated peak and continue rising. They, as would be expected for economists, explain it as the result of the Natural Gas Policy Act and the end of end-use regulation.

Hubbert gets emphasis here because his method is so famous, and because it is the vehicle for Deffeyes's analysis. However, they have a trenchant comment on a consulting firm in the industry known as Petroconsultants. Petroconsultants had in 1986, estimated that decline before 1990 was "imminent" and "unstoppable." They say: "This was not only wrong, it was the contrary of truth. Ten years later non-OPEC proved 15% more (where decline had been thought unstoppable); outside the US, 35% more."

Lovins does not expressly take up the question of the end of oil, for he stands as perhaps the most noted exponent of efficiency, for the thesis that the issue does not have to be faced at all. The executive summary of his most recent book claims: "*Winning the Oil Endgame* offers a coherent strategy for ending oil dependence, starting with the United States but applicable worldwide." Lovins (2004) continues:

There are many analyses of the oil problem. This synthesis is the first oil *solution*—one led by business for profit, not dictated by government or for reasons of ideology. This road map is independent, peer reviewed, written for business and military leaders, and co-funded by the Pentagon. It combines innovative technologies and new business models with uncommon public policies: market-oriented without taxes, innovation-driven without mandates, not dependent on major (if any) national legislation, and designed to support, not distort, business logic.

---

[7] "One of the best critical rejections of Hubbert's approach," he says, "is M. A. Adelman and M. C. Lynch (1997)" (Deffeyes 2001, 191 n. 9).

## 5. CONCLUSION

This chapter suggests both a practical challenge and an intellectual challenge. The practical challenge, especially for governments, is that energy depends upon knowledge and upon money.

Choices have to be made.

Each choice has been associated with some significant detriment, though the advocates of each choice will generally tend to minimize the detriment, overstate the advantages. If the Hubbert thesis is basically sound, then an upward pressure on prices is to be expected. Another practical factor relates to the effect in the market of Russia as seller and China and India as buyers. As noted at the outset of the chapter, there are also the considerations of the poor countries.

In this very decade, as well, there is the question of the current policy choices, of the institutions through which choices will be formulated, and of the interests by which choices will be driven. In the European and American context, the issue is: what is the practical future for coal? Is coal sequestration to be taken seriously? There are two levels of consideration. At one level, there is the purely scientific question of whether the sequestration of carbon dioxide makes sense. At another level, there is the question of what degree of policy consideration the idea is receiving. Britain and Europe are contra-carbon which almost surely leads either to "green" policy preferences or to nuclear policy preferences. What also remains is the concept of "The Hydrogen Economy," of whether as an energy matter it is feasible, and of what capital requirements and technological developments are feasible in a period of twenty or thirty years.

Finally, there is "the conceit of journalism." Similarly, the language of crisis and threat is often adopted in an exaggerated way that does not bear close analysis. Deffeyes (2001) for instance, anticipates the decline of available oil and the competition for that oil by money.

As a matter of style, it might not have suited to say the "Hubbert's Peak indicates that oil production will reach its apex some time within the next four years and will begin to decline so that the production level sixty years away will be about 20% of what it now is." But that is what the author, Francis S. Deffeyes (2001) does say. He does say that production will peak and there is nothing anyone can do about it. He estimates the 20 per cent date in a very simple way. It is when his two-year-old granddaughter will reach retirement age, presumably sixty-three years away. "By the time you reach retirement age, Emma, world production of oil (the kind that's fun to drill for) will be down to a fifth of its present size."

Notice, then, the language of alarm that follows: "At least, let's hope that the war is waged with cash instead of nuclear warheads." For what reason, indeed, would it be logical to imagine that oil shortage would lead nations to nuclear struggle? Whether any wars have occurred between major states for oil is debatable, though perhaps a case can be made. What prospect has to do with Hubbert's Curve is most obscure.

I conclude with reference to some other intellectual issues that also relate to energy policy.

1. There is need for some thought about the very meaning of "policy;" and its relation to law and to public–private relationships. *Black's Law Dictionary* defines "public policy" as "broadly, principles and standards regarded by the legislature or the courts as being of fundamental concern to the state and the whole of society" (Garner 1999). For a political scientist, what *is* empirically "of fundamental concern to the state and the whole of society?" Moreover, the dictionary continues quoting an authoritative source, to say, "The policy of the law, or public policy, is a phrase of common use in estimating the validity of contracts." This issue entered natural gas industry politics in the 1980s when some buyers found themselves committed to old contracts under which, as it turned out, the prices they had to pay were well above the prices at which they could sell.

2. The energy arena involves a good deal of reference to "the geopolitics of energy." That may demand new attention to its meaning in political science. This terminology seems to have little or nothing to do with the concept of geopolitics (systematic ability to predict political outcome because of location of conflicting or cooperating parties) as it once existed in such work as that of Halford J. Mackinder (1943) or even in the work of Harold Sprout and Margaret Sprout (1965), who were senior figures in American political science in the 1950s. But there is new thinking along these lines from the left as expressed in the writing of Michael T. Klare (2001) and in research projects such as that currently centered at the Baker Institute of Public Policy, Rice University, which has a project on "The geopolitics of energy in northeast Asia."[8]

3. On a global basis, it is important to recognize something else. While it is not well analyzed in this chapter, or anywhere in political science to the author's knowledge, the energy industries could be described as some mix of oligarchy, oligopoly, and oligopsony. The dominant roles are played by one or two large governments, a small number of medium-sized governments, and the rest of the world. One could repeat the previous sentence substituting the words "sellers" or "customers."

# REFERENCES

ADELMAN, M. A. 1997. My education in mineral (especially oil) economics. *Annual Review of Energy and the Environment,* 22 (Nov.): 13–46.

[8] For details, see www.rice.edu/energy/research/asiaenergy/index.html (accessed 5 Apr. 2005).

—— and LYNCH, M. 1997. Fixed view of resources creates undue pessimism. *Oil and Gas Journal*, 95 (14): 56–60.

BLACK, E. 2004. *Banking on Baghdad: Inside Iraq's 7,000 Year Old History of War, Profits, and Conflict*. Hoboken, NJ: Wiley.

BRADLEY, R. L., Jr. 1996. *Oil, Gas & Government: The U.S. Experience*. Lanham, Md.: Rowman and Littlefield.

CAROE, O. 1951. *Wells of Power: The Oilfields of Southwestern Asia*. London: Macmillan.

CUDAHY, R. J. 2004. *Energy Law Journal*. 25th anniversary celebration, Washington, DC, 28 Apr. *Energy Law Journal*, 25.

DAVIS, D. H. 1992. *Energy Politics*, 4th edn. New York. St Martin's.

DEFFEYES, K. S. 2001. *Hubbert's Peak: The Impending World Oil Shortage*, Princeton, NJ: Princeton University Press.

DELEON, P. 1988. *Advice and Consent*. New York: Russell Sage Foundation.

DEWHURST, J. F., et al. 1947. *America's Needs and Resources: A Twentieth Century Fund Survey*. New York: Twentieth Century Fund.

ENGLER, R. 1961. *The Politics of Oil*. Chicago: University of Chicago Press.

GARNER, B. A., ed. 1999. *Black's Law Dictionary*, 7th edn. St Paul, Minn.: West.

GOODSTEIN, D. 2004. *Out of Gas: The End of the Age of Oil*. New York: Norton.

GOODWIN, C. D. 1980. Truman administration policies toward particular energy sources. Pp. 130–2 in *Energy Policy in Perspective*, ed. C. D. Goodwin. Washington, DC: Brookings Institution.

GRAYSON, L. E. 1981. *National Oil Companies*. New York: Wiley.

GREENSTEIN, F. I., and POLSBY, N. W. (eds.) 1975. *Handbook of Political Science*. Reading, Mass.: Addison-Wesley.

HARRISON, C. 2004. Peer review, politics, and pluralism. *Environmental Science and Policy*, 7: 357–68.

HOLDEN, M., Jr. 1966a. "Imperialism" in bureaucracy. *American Political Science Review*, 60: 943–51.

—— 1966b. *Pollution Control as a Bargaining Process*. Publication No. 9. Ithaca, NY: Cornell University Water Resources Center.

HUGHES, J. R. 2005. Letter: the real oil problem. *Oil and Gas Journal* (17 Jan.): 12.

KEOHANE, R. E. 1982. State power and industry influence: American foreign oil policy in the 1940s. *International Organization*, 36: 165–83.

KLARE, M. T. 2001. *Resource Wars: The New Landscape of Global Conflict*. New York: Henry Holt.

KRUTZ, G. S. 2001. *Hitching a Ride: Omnibus Legislation in the US Congress*. Columbus: Ohio State University Press.

LASSWELL, H. D. 1950. *Politics: Who Gets What, When, How?* New York: P. Smith.

LERNER, D., and Lasswell, H. D. (eds.) 1951. *The Policy Sciences*. Stanford, Calif.: Stanford University Press.

LOVINS, A., et al. 2004. *Winning the Oil Endgame: Innovation for Profits, Jobs and Security*. Old Snowmass, Colo.: Rocky Mountain Institute.

MACKINDER, H. J. 1943. The round world and the winning of the peace. *Foreign Affairs*, 21: 595–605.

MICHAELS, P. J., and BALLING, R. C., Jr. 2000. *The Satanic Gases: Clearing the Air about Global Warming*. Washington, DC: Cato Institute.

NATIONAL RESEARCH COUNCIL AND NATIONAL ACADEMY OF ENGINEERING, Committee on Alternatives and Strategies for Future Hydrogen Production and Use 2004. *The Hydrogen Economy: Opportunities, Costs, Barriers and R & D Needs*.

NEFF, S. 2005. Review of the Energy Policy Act of 2005. Center for Energy, Marine Transportation and Public Policy, Columbia University, August.

PATTERSON. S. C. 2001. Foreword. In Krutz 2000.

ROBERTS, P. 2005. *The End of Oil.* New York: Houghton-Mifflin.

SAVISTSKI, D. 2002. Review of *Pricing in Competitive Electricity Markets,* ed. A. Farqui and K. Eakin. *Review of Industrial Organization,* 21: 329–33.

SCHELLING, T. C. 1960. *The Strategy of Conflict.* Cambridge, Mass.: Harvard University Press.

SCHOLES, W. 1989. Australia's uranium: plenty of it, but not for sale. *Energy Economist,* June: 19–21.

SPROUT, H., and SPROUT, M. 1965. *The Ecological Perspective on Human Affairs.* Princeton, NJ: Princeton University Press.

TUGWELL, F. A. 1988. *The Energy Crisis and the American Political Economy: Politics and Markets in the Management of Natural Resources.* Stanford, Calif.: Stanford University Press.

USLANER, E. M. 1989. *Shale Barrel Politics: Energy and Legislative Leadership.* Stanford, Calif.: Stanford University Press.

WILDAVSKY, A. B., TENENBAUM, E., et al. 1981. *The Politics of Mistrust: Estimating American Oil and Gas Resources.* Beverly Hills, Calif.: Sage.

WILLIAMS, J. H., and DUBASH, N. K. (eds.) 2004. Special issue: the political economy of electricity reform in Asia. *Pacific Affairs,* 77 (3).

# REFLECTIONS ON POLICY ANALYSIS: PUTTING IT TOGETHER AGAIN

## RUDOLF KLEIN

## THEODORE R. MARMOR

THE attempt to pin down a chameleon concept like "public policy" tends all too often to become an exercise in anatomy rather than physiology. The bones are there, right down to joints of the little finger. They can even be put together, rather like an exhibit in a natural history museum. But the creature itself, the sense of what drives it and shapes its actions, remains elusive: a victim of the academic drive to taxonomize everything in sight. To make this point is not to criticize the editors. Their strategy accurately reflects the state of the field and the end product mirrors its diversity. As Robert Goodin has put it in a different context, "theorists are inveterate product-differentiators" (Goodin 2000, 523). Different disciplines, and different sects within disciplines have fought over the body of public policy, all seeking to impose their own definitions of the subject and to patent their own analytic methodology. To set out these varied and competing perspectives is in itself, a valuable pedagogic exercise but risks analyzing the subject out of existence.

In what follows we shall argue for a theoretically less ambitious but (in our view) practically more useful strategy. We define public policy quite simply. It is what governments do and neglect to do. It is about politics, resolving (or at least attenuating) conflicts about resources, rights, and morals. We sideline the issue of whether policy analysis is about understanding or prescribing by claiming that no prescription is worth the paper it is written on if it is not based on an understanding of the world of policy making. If prescription (or advice to policy makers) is not based on such a foundation of understanding, it will either mislead or fall on deaf ears. In turn, understanding depends not just on seeing policy making as a strange form of theater—with the analyst in the first row of the stalls—but on trying to capture the intentions of the authors of the drama, the techniques of the actors, and the workings of the stage machinery. Empathy in the sense of capturing what drives policy actors and entering into their assumptive worlds, is crucial. In adopting this view we place ourselves unapologetically in the tradition of those who see policy analysis as an art and craft, not as a science (to use Wildavsky's 1979 terminology)

By assumptive worlds (Vickers 1965) we mean the "mental models" that "provide both an interpretation of the environment and a prescription as to how that environment should be structured" (Denzau and North 1994, 4). Policy actors have theories about the causes of the problems that confront them. They have theories about the appropriate solutions. To take an obvious example: poverty can be seen as reflecting social factors outside the control of individuals or the result of individual failings, and very different policy responses follow depending on the initial diagnosis made. There is additionally and importantly, a normative component to such mental models. What counts as a problem depends once again on assumptions about the nature of society and the proper role of government. Problems, as the constructivists are the latest to remind us, are not givens but the product of social and political perceptions. If AIDS is seen as a judgement of God punishing sinful behavior, then governments will see this as a matter for the preacher, not for the politician. When such mental model or assumptive worlds are tightly organized, and internally consistent, then traditionally we tend to call them ideologies.

What other fundamental tools of understanding do we need to make sense of what governments do? Parsimoniously, we would suggest only two. First, we need an analysis of the institutions within which governments operate. In contrast to much of the literature, we define "institutions" narrowly: the constitutional arrangements within which governments operate, the rules of the game, and the bureaucratic machinery at their disposal. Self-evidently the process of producing public policy will be very different in a country with a Westminster-type constitution and one with a US-type constitution with its multiple veto points. Second, we need an analysis of the interests operating in the political arena: interests which may be structured around either economic or social concerns (which may be either self or other-regarding) and serve both to organize and articulate demands on governments and to resist measures which are seen to be inimical by those interests.

In what follows, we develop these notions. The first section's starting point is the uncontentious proposition that what (democratic) governments do—that is, the policies they advance and implement—reflect their larger concerns about gaining (and maintaining) office and doing so legitimately. Uncontentious, even banal though this proposition may appear to be, it is much ignored in the more rationalistic conceptions of policy analysis. The second section argues that individual policy outputs need to be interpreted in the context of the overall policy portfolio. That is, governments are almost always engaged in a complex balancing act, given that the demands for policy action usually exceed the supply of the administrative, financial, and political resources required to meet them. The third section explores the importance of taking the historical dimension into account when analysing public policy. The fourth section examines the promise and perils of cross-national analysis, and its role as a check on overdetermined national explanations of why governments do what they do. As a final coda, we briefly restate the case for eclecticism in public policy analysis.

Throughout we illustrate our arguments with examples drawn from history. And even those examples which were contemporary with the writing of this chapter in 2004, will have become history by the time this chapter is read. Accordingly, where appropriate, footnotes provide the necessary background information about the events concerned.

# 1. THE DOUBLE IMPERATIVE

To define public policy as what governments do may seem a rather simple-minded opening gambit. In fact, much follows from it. It suggests that before analyzing the genesis and life-cycle of specific policies—the focus of most of the public policy literature—we should first consider some of the larger concerns of governments: the context in which specific policy decisions are taken and which helps to shape those decisions. Two such concerns, we would suggest, underlie the actions of all governments (at least in Western-style liberal democracies.) The first is to gain office and, having done so, to maintain their own authority and the legitimacy of the political system within which they operate. The second is to stay in office. We explore each of these points in turn.

The authority of governments, and the legitimacy of political systems tends to be taken for granted in the public policy literature. The centuries-old debate among political philosophers about the nature of, and justification for the exercise of political power is left to another branch of the academic industry. And even the more recent political science literature expressing worries about the decline of active support for democratic regimes and engagement in civic participation (Putnam 2001)—as shown, for example, by the fall in voter turnout at election times—has taken a long time to percolate into the academic analysis of public policies, particularly the economistic variety, with some notable exceptions.

Do they, however, figure in the concerns of policy makers? It would be absurd to suggest that presidents and prime ministers spend sleepless nights worrying explicitly about how to maintain their authority and the legitimacy of the political system, though occasionally there are spasms of interest in such notions as social capital.

Indeed it can be argued that it may be in their self-interest to gain short-term advantages for themselves—by deception or concealment—at the price of undermining confidence in the system in the long term. Nevertheless, balancing such incentives, concerns about legitimacy and authority are woven into the fabric of policy making. If they are largely invisible, it is precisely because they are so much part of normal routine. Before governments decide to act, they must first determine whether they are "entitled" to do so: whether a particular course of action conforms to what governments are supposed to do. The fact that their interpretation may be contestable does not detract from the importance of this policy filter. And when they decide to act, they must establish that they are doing so in the right way: whether the proposed policy conforms to contemporary understandings of the requirements of the constitution and the law and whether their implementation has followed the appropriate processes of consultation and legislation.

In short, policy making takes place in a framework of established conventions and normative rules. Governments may at times attempt to stretch those conventions and to sidestep those rules. But governments which are judged to act in an arbitrary fashion, or which threaten the private sphere of the citizen, are rightly seen as undermining the basis of their authority—whose maintenance depends on its exercise conforming to the established rules and conventions. The point is obvious enough. It is emphasized here only because it is so often forgotten—because taken as "read"—in the public policy literature.

There is a further point to note. The legitimacy of any political system depends on its ability to ensure the stability of the social order, as Hobbes (among many others) observed a long time ago. Not only must governments, if they are to justify their authority, be able to defend the state against external enemies. They must also be able to maintain social cohesion at least in the minimal sense of maintaining law and order and protecting the vulnerable. How best to maintain law and order is, of course, another matter, involving disputes about the criteria to be used in framing and judging policies (to which we return later). For example, does it simply require efficient policing and capacious prisons, or does it mean social engineering designed to deal with the sources of crime, disorder, or disaffection? Governments with different assumptive worlds will give different answers to such questions. But however interpreted, the maintenance of social cohesion is surely a fundamental concern of all governments which not only shapes individual policies but also the priorities within any list of candidate policies. And what is more, the apparent responsiveness to these concerns is electorally important in all liberal democracies. Governments face evaluation not only for what they in fact deliver, but whether they do so in ways various publics regard as legitimate.

The other obvious concern of governments once in office, is to keep themselves there: to secure their own re-election. From this perspective, the production of public policy can be seen as an exercise in maximizing their chances of winning office (Downs 1957). This raises both analytical and normative issues. Normatively, the notion that politicians design their policies (and more often still, the presentation of those policies) in order to win votes prompts criticism. It is often seen as an abuse of politics: a misuse of political authority/power. It can suggest bad faith, manipulative cynicism, and the deceptive use of power (Goodin 1980). Far be it for us to suggest that politicians do not engage in manipulation: there is no shortage of examples of "spin," of misrepresentation of the evidence, and of the selective use of data by governments. There are few better examples in recent history than the case made in 2003 by the United States and British governments for invading Iraq: Subsequently no evidence was found to justify the claim that Iraq had the capacity to use weapons of mass destruction (Butler 2004; Woodward 2004). It also provides a warning: whatever the motives that drove Bush and Blair, their policies were not simple exercises in vote maximization (and if so, they turned out to be a massive miscalculation). But, if we change the wording—if instead of talking about vote chasing, we substitute the assertion that in a democracy politicians should be sensitive and responsive to public concerns—we will get approving nods. Politicians are not necessarily or exclusively vote maximizers. They may, for example, be *maximizers of* moral rectitude (or history book reputation).

Moving one step further, let us take a slightly weaker but more realistic definition of the political imperative from which somewhat different normative conclusions follow. If we assume that one of the tests applied to the production of public policies by governments is their acceptability, then we may conclude that this is a perfectly legitimate concern. Not only are governments that produce policies unacceptable to the public less likely to be re-elected. They will also be condemned as foolish or authoritarian, on the grounds that unacceptable policies will also be either not implementable or in breach of the conventions that delineate the proper role of government (or both). The introduction in the 1980s of the poll tax by Mrs Thatcher's government in Britain would be one example of producing an unacceptable policy that was roundly (and plausibly) condemned and subsequently abandoned;[1] the US example of the repeal of catastrophic coverage for Medicare in the late 1980s is more complicated. It was in fact a perfectly sensible policy that was widely misunderstood as unfair (Oberlander 2003).[2]

---

[1] After decades of discussion about reforming Britain's system for funding local government—a mixture of property taxes and central government grants—the government of Mrs Thatcher decided to replace the former by a poll tax, as from 1988. The decision was widely criticized, led to sometimes violent demonstrations, and prompted widespread evasion. While 8 million people gained as a result of the switch from property taxes to the poll tax, 27 million lost. As one of Mrs Thatcher's ministers subsequently commented: "It was fundamentally flawed and politically incredible. I guess it was the single most unpopular policy any government has introduced since the War" (quoted in the classic account of this episode: Butler, Adonis, and Travers 1994, 1). The poll tax fiasco greatly weakened Mrs Thatcher's position and contributed to her subsequent downfall, and her successor's government promptly dropped the poll tax.

[2] The legislation to add catastrophic health insurance and outpatient prescription drug coverage to Medicare in 1987–8 was and is regarded as a debacle. The legislation, repealed within a year, addressed two serious problems, but was financed exclusively by increased premiums on beneficiaries, which in turn was neither explained nor justified well by the Reagan administration and the reform's defenders in Congress. In a memorable incident, the then chairman of the House Ways and Means Committee, Congressman Dan Rostenkowski, was pelted with tomatoes by older constituents in Chicago who were outraged by this unorthodox form of financing a social insurance program. The obvious truth was that while the program had merit, the financing means were genuinely a surprise, not well defended, and

There is a fine borderline between on the one hand, the investment of political capital and the use of rhetoric in persuading the public of the necessity and desirability of policies—in rallying support and making them acceptable, in other words—and on the other hand, manipulative cynicism in their presentation. We praise the former as political leadership—only consider Churchill's use of rhetoric in rallying the British people in the dark days of 1940 or Roosevelt's defense of the Lend-Lease policy—while condemning the latter. Modeling governments as prudential, self-regarding actors does not, therefore, capture the complexity of the real world of public policy. It leaves unexplained, for example, why governments take policy decisions that will only benefit their successors. It also creates a puzzle: why do governments address moral or ethical issues which at best are neutral in their impact on voting behavior or at worst may turn out to be stirring up an angry hornet's nest of opposition?

The case of pension policy in the opening years of the twenty-first century illustrates the first point. Across most OECD countries governments were anxiously addressing the problem of aging populations and the expected (and often exaggerated) burden of meeting the consequent pensions' bill. In doing so, they were looking twenty and more years ahead. Why did they do so when, on the face of it, they had little to gain by such a strategy? After all, no government in office in 2000 would have to answer to the electorate of 2030. One reason may of course be that they were using the future as a pretext for pursuing present reform proposals (such as further pension privatization) which otherwise might be regarded as unacceptable.[3] Ideology is there for sure but so is serving their friends in the finance community. This is a fully defensible interpretation of the Bush administration's embrace of social security pension reform as required by the feared insolvency that population aging foreshadows. The argumentative structure and rhetoric is familiar: actuarial forecasts project increasing pension claims and assuming no change in benefits or contributions, "bankruptcy" at some future date is a mathematical certainty. The fact that "trust fund" language originally was meant to communicate political commitment is lost. Instead, the analogy to private trust funds which can go broke, becomes a contemporary source of public fearfulness (Marmor 2004).

However, even conceding this explanation, invoking the interests of yet to be born voters can be seen (like hypocrisy) as the tribute paid by vice to virtue. Governments rightly presume that they are expected to take a long-term view and the fact that policy makers feel obliged to invoke this justification for their policies illustrates the extent to which public policy is shaped by such normative considerations. Which is not to argue, of course, that governments invariably (or even usually) examine the long-term implications of their policies: witness, for example, the problem of nuclear

especially vulnerable to the claim that they had not been legitimized by broad public discussion and understanding.

[3] There is no question that President Bush was hesitant about direct criticism of the US social insurance pension programs. The use of spectres of an aging America was a vehicle for prompting present adjustments in the name of necessity. The change he proposed—using social insurance contributions for investments in individual risk-bearing accounts—was deeply controversial within the policy analytic community, but amplified rather than ridiculed by the media.

waste that will remain radioactive for generations. Rhetorical long-sightedness can sit alongside policy myopia.

Again, the self-image of policy actors—who want to be seen to be following certain ideal types of behavior—seems to be at least as important as their narrow self-interest when it comes to ethical and moral issues. Only consider President Clinton's ill-fated decision at the very outset of his presidency about how to treat homosexuality in the American armed services. In February 1993, his very first presidential decision on defense matters was to propose that the US military change its long-standing objections to having homosexuals in the services. The presidential suggestion provoked sharp criticism within the military, enthusiastic support from the organized homosexual community, and derision among the chattering classes for its timing, content, and presumed insensitivity to military norms. In terms of self-seeking political behavior this made no sense, as quickly became apparent. But it did make sense in terms of the president's sense of what was right and appropriate in terms of his self-image as a progressive liberal. (It also made Clinton the recipient of substantial financial support from the gay community, which is comparatively rich, ready to spend, and politically active.[4])

The same point could be made about many other governmental "policy outputs." In the case of the UK, for example, successive governments have resisted attempts to restore capital punishment, even though survey evidence suggests that bringing back the hangman would earn them applause from a majority of the population and the tabloids. However, not only would such a move bring them condemnation from the liberal establishment and the broadsheets. But for many legislators opposition to the death penalty is a core value which they are prepared to put before majoritarianism. The 2003 controversy over the religious symbolism of attire in French schools—with the state forbidding the wearing of headscarves—obviously involved ideals of secular republicanism as well as prejudice against Islamic fundamentalism. In short, policy actors have moral constituencies, as well as constituencies of material interest, and follow moral imperatives. It is not unknown for policy actors to congratulate themselves on pursuing unpopular policies for what they consider right. Invoking considerations of moral rectitude earns points in this world as well as (possibly) the next. And any convincing analysis of their assumptive worlds must take this into account.

## 2. THE POLICY PORTFOLIO

Analyzing the genesis, development, and implementation of individual policies is misleading to the extent that it misses out on an important characteristic of public

---

[4] The Clinton suggestion ended up with what came to be known as the "don't ask, don't tell" policy. While not what President Clinton called for, this operational policy has no doubt changed military norms substantially.

policy making. This is that demands for public action tend to exceed any govern-ment's capacity to supply policy responses. The portfolio of policies that eventually emerges therefore is the product of a complex process of bargaining, negotiation, and political calculation. On the one hand, there is competition between and among interest groups and departments pressing for action on their concerns. Governments are not unitary actors, although for convenience we refer to them as a collectivity in the text (Allison 1971; Allison and Zelikow 1999). Cabinet ministers with different and sometimes conflicting priorities jostle for space in the legislative program. On the one hand, there are judgements about where the investment of administrative capacity and political capital will yield the largest returns—judgements which are filtered through the lenses of the "mental models" of the policy actors whose interests will be affected. In short, the launch of a policy may reflect as much the desire to have a "balanced portfolio" (whether in terms of maintaining the legitimacy of the government or in terms of political expediency) as factors intrinsic to the specific policy arena.

The heterogeneity of such a policy portfolio is illustrated by both the British data in Appendix 44.1 and the American counterpart in Appendix 44.2. The first sum-marizes the Queen's speech delivered to the UK Parliament in November 2003, outlining the British government's legislative program for the next year. The US example summarizes the State of the Union speech given by President Bush to the Congress in January 2004. Both examples should be seen as illustrative, not repre-sentative. The contents of these two speeches are time specific. Under different governments, at different stages in the life-cycle of any administration and in a different global environment, they could have been very different. Our concern here, however, is not so much with the details of the policies involved—which are only discussed to the extent that they need to be comprehensible to the reader—but with the overall style and shape of such policy portfolios at one particular historical moment.

Even the long laundry list that is the 2003 Queen's speech greatly understates the extent and variety of British public policy "outputs" in any given year. Most import-antly, it excludes fiscal policies: decisions by the Chancellor of the Exchequer about the level of spending on specific programs and the design of the system of taxes and benefits. And it cannot include, by definition, government policies—whether ad-ministrative, legislative, or judicial—prompted by the outbreak of an epidemic, a natural disaster, or an external threat.

Immediately striking is the prominence in this particular portfolio of what might be called social stability concerns. These included: tightening up the appeal system in asylum cases, working towards the introduction of national identity cards, and modernizing the law and system for protecting women and children. All three examples can be understood as public policy in the responsive mode, reacting to external events and perhaps even more importantly, to public perceptions of those events. The tighten-ing up of the appeals system and the incremental development of identity cards can both be seen as part of a strategy for reassuring the public that the government was acting to stop the UK from being flooded by fraudulent asylum seekers and illegal immigrants. These were concerns with high political salience that had attracted much attention in the media in the UK, as in many other European countries. The improvement of services for protecting children was again a response to an issue with a high public and media profile: a series of appalling cases of child abuse had revealed great shortcomings in the existing system of surveillance and protection.

All three examples also, however, underline the importance of distinguishing between *why* a particular issue makes it onto the agenda for action and *how* it is then translated into a specific public policy measure. In all three cases, the government's decision to respond to public worries could be interpreted either as (three cheers) a demonstration of its sensitivity to public concerns or (boos) as a cynical political maneuver designed to prevent the opposition from exploiting these issues. But all three cases had long histories. The UK system for processing asylum seekers had long been recognized as a shambles (not least because of the hardships inflicted on genuine cases). What is more, previous attempts to improve it had produced meager results. The introduction of identity cards had been debated since at least the 1960s, though the debate was given new impetus after 2000 by both developments in technology and increasing concern (whether justified or not) about illegal immigration. Child protection had been an ongoing worry, with recurring scandals despite a succession of attempts to improve the system, for at least as long. As this historical example shows, a raised sensitivity to public concerns (or pejoratively, political expediency) opened the window for the various government agencies who had long been working on these problems to get their ideas onto the agenda for action (Kingdon 1995). The specific measures that eventually emerged reflect as much bureaucratic bargaining and negotiation, organizational routines, and notions of administrative feasibility, as political-electoral considerations. The factors that influence the timing of public policy do not necessarily determine the contents.

There are some other points to note about this particular British policy portfolio. First, little of the proposed legislation involved classic pressure group activity. Like the three examples already discussed, most of the initiatives represented a response to diffuse public concerns rather than to demands from organized interest groups (though in the case of pension reform the government was involved in tough negotiations with employers, the insurance industry, and the trade unions when it came to the details of the legislation). Second, much of it represented the incremental processes of government rather than policy innovation: for example, the proposals to make the planning system faster and to improve traffic flows—a reminder that public policy is as much drudgery as drama, a constant process of tinkering and repairing. The small print of public policy (we all care about traffic flows) matters if governments want to demonstrate their competence in dealing with the day-to-day concerns of their citizens. Most of public policy is as boring as darning old socks. Third, policy may represent a moral commitment, which has little or nothing to do with political expediency. The proposed legislation to allow the registration of civil partnerships between same-sex couples is a case in point. This was symbolism not as a substitute for action but as a signal that the government's heart was in the right place: that it was a liberal, progressive administration. In this sense, it was an important part of a balanced portfolio, a rebuttal of the charges of authoritarianism prompted by some of the Blair government's law and order policies.

Quite different in kind was one of the most contentious measures in the 2004 Queen's speech: reform of the House of Lords. Here the fissures were as much within the governing Labour Party as between the Labour Party and the Conservative opposition. In the case of the House of Lords, there was cross-party agreement that the hereditary element should be eliminated. But divisions existed within all parties about how the new composition of the second chamber should be determined, whether by election or nomination: a series of votes in the House of Commons on various options had failed to produce a consensus about the composition. This, then, can be seen as an example of a government being able to exploit confusion and disagreement to impose its own preferred option: a second chamber appointed by an independent commission, its party composition reflecting voting patterns. It was an unusual and rare form of public policy making worth noting, however, for demonstrating the difficulty of classifying and anatomizing the variety of activities that go under that label.

The State of the Union speech, given 20 January 2004, set out President Bush's legislative aims for 2004 and beyond. The contents of the list range from announcing broad policy aims to proposing legislative action: It is the breadth of the range—and the loose connection to likely legislative action—that most sharply distinguishes the American practice from that of parliamentary leaders like Blair.

Yet, the similarities of the two forms are striking. The Bush speech offered to its audience just the kind of "balanced portfolio" presented to the Commons. In other words, within the heterogeneous legislative proposals and public policy concerns there were a parallel mix of appeals. For example, all of the funding proposals were incremental, with flourishes about "doubling" efforts to encourage sexual abstinence and to make the world safer for democracy, free markets, and free speech. Evident as well were the responses to what we have characterized as diffuse concerns about social stability. So, we find aspirational gestures towards such difficult subjects as how to control medical inflation with policies as weakly connected to the purpose as tax subsidies for catastrophic plans. Likewise, there was top billing for concerns about terrorism, however uncertain the connection between means and ends. And finally, the speech appealed for support of two very controversial legislative actions: the re-enactment of the Patriot Act (and its attendant conflict with civil liberties) as well as the proposal for a temporary workers program (which excites the ire of the labor movement). Very few of the American proposals looked like simple responses to classic pressure group demands. Or put another way, the language suggested responsiveness to diffuse rather than concentrated organizational concerns.

Institutional structures and the policy context of the moment explain much of the remaining differences between our two illustrations. The most obvious feature of the Bush laundry list is its aspirational character, not its predictive accuracy. In the US system of government, the general rule is that administration proposes, but the Congress disposes. And what the Congress does is not usually decided by general elections, as it is in parliamentary regimes. There is no necessary policy majority in the Congress even when controlled by one party, as it was in 2004. As a result, no one could have said with any certainty in January of 2004 whether any of the actions President Bush proposed would become law that year. In the event, the worsening circumstances in Iraq during the spring and summer of 2004 rendered the president's influence in the Congress less decisive. The electoral context increasingly made the Democrats unwilling to cooperate and fissures within the Republican congressional majority made legislative majorities harder to construct.

This brings us back to the most general conclusion of this section: namely, that it is very difficult to classify (or anatomize) public policy. What counts as an issue, or what similar "issues" evoke, depends, as we have argued, on context, which in turn is filtered through the mental models of actors and audiences. So, for instance, the salience of immigration reform in the UK is not reflected in the modest reference by the Bush administration to a temporary worker program. In 2004, immigration had priority on the policy agendas of the EU generally, reflecting domestic conflict over amnesty programs, EU worker mobility policies, and claims of foreigner "misuse" of welfare state programs. Nothing of that kind is evident in the US document, and the reason is largely institutional rather than ideological. American federalism shapes welfare state disputes in the USA so that conflicts over access to medical care programs (like Medicaid) or educational expenses of newcomers (local and state funding issues) are channeled away from national debates. The same range of sentiments that excited debate in the UK during the first years of the twenty-first century did appear in the USA, but not during those years, on the national agenda. California enacted measures limiting the access to social programs by foreign, largely Mexican workers; Texas confronted cross-border concerns in state legislation. And at the national level, the federal Immigration and Naturalization Service increasingly used helicopters to interdict workers crossing deserts and rivers to enter the southwest. But the "face" of immigration policy looked different across the Atlantic, which illustrates our classificatory caution.

# 3. THE HISTORICAL DIMENSION

Much is made in the literature of path dependency, variously defined. At one level this is simply another way of describing the incremental, adaptive nature of much policy making: that (as we have seen in our case study) public policy consists to a large extent of patching and repairing, building on and learning from experience (Heclo 1974). Again, the fact that policy makers faced with a new problem tend to draw on an established repertory of tools reinforces the bias of public policy against radical innovation, as does dependence on existing organizations for delivery. Initial policy reactions to AIDS were a case in point (Fox, Day, and Klein 1989). More narrowly and rigorously, path dependency is seen as flowing from the structure of interests created by policy (Tuohy 1999; Hacker 2002). Decisions taken at point A in time entrench—sometimes indeed create—interests that come to constrain decisions at point B. Either way, what is interesting and appears to call for explanation is the rare occasion when public policy takes a new turn, whether successfully or not, rather than the sock-darning dimension of public policy.

So history matters. But we would suggest, it matters in a more profound sense still. Not only are policy makers obliged to work within the context of inherited institutions—constitutional arrangements and conventions and the administrative machinery of government—as well as the structure of interests created by previous policies, as noted. But their world of ideas is also the product of history. This is so in a double sense. On the one hand, their notions are likely to be shaped by early experience and the culture of their time, as with all of us. On the other hand, they are likely to use history (or rather their own interpretation of it) as a quarry for policy exemplars or warnings.

From this wider perspective, history can be used to explain change and divergence from existing paths as well as continuity. Consider, for example, the generation of politicians who grew to maturity in the years of slump and mass unemployment of the 1920s and 1930s. The experience persuaded even those in the middle of the political spectrum (Roosevelt in the USA; Macmillan in the UK) to adopt radical social and economic policies. And to underline the importance of ideas, they could draw on Keynesian theory to justify their policies. In short, there was not only a change in what was considered politically important but also in what was considered to be possible in practice. The converse applies to the next generation, who grew up in a period of unprecedented economic growth and full employment. They proved, when in power, less sensitive to unemployment statistics. And again, they could turn for justification to the new economic paradigm (Hall 1993) which challenged Keynesian notions by arguing that there was a natural rate of unemployment about which governments could do little and only at the risk of fueling inflation.

What matters in all this, of course, is not history as written in academic textbooks but the interpretations put on it by policy makers: the lessons they choose to draw from the past (Neustadt and May 1988). So, for example, the nebulous Third Way as espoused by Clinton and Blair in the 1990s—the latest in a long line of attempts to find a middle way (Macmillan 1938)—cannot be understood without taking into account their diagnosis of the mistakes made by their predecessors as party leaders. The interpretation of history need not be correct. Some disastrous policy decisions have flown from the misapplication of supposed historical lessons, largely as a result of mis-specifying the similarity between past and present situations. The conclusion that it never pays to appease dictators drawn from the abject surrender of the Western powers to Hitler at Munich in 1938, plus the equation of Nasser with Hitler, was used to justify Britain's disastrous Suez adventure in 1956. And Bush's initiation of the 2003 Iraq War may also, in part at least, have reflected a misreading of history. Bush's Iraq policy appeared to some a reaction against his father's "failure" to topple Saddam. Whatever the president's motives, the justifications offered—that weapons of mass destruction in the hands of a dictator will be used and therefore must be "taken out" preventively—relied on historical claims. In another sense, the Iraq policy was an earlier conviction searching for an occasion, a commitment to get rid of Saddam by officials from Bush I's presidency acted upon in Bush II's administration (Woodward 2002, 2004; Dean 2004).

Particular readings of history may also persuade policy makers to diverge from the trodden path. Policy change is not only the result of windows of opportunity suddenly opening as the result of some upheaval in the economic or political environment. Policy change itself may open such windows by demonstrating that the previously unthinkable has become doable. A case in point is the repudiation in the 1980s by Mrs Thatcher of the assumption shaping the policies of all post-1945 British governments that they needed the cooperation of the trade union movement to manage the economy. Instead, she was prepared to confront and fight the unions (Young 1989). The skies did not fall in. And Tony Blair, as Labour Prime Minister, shaped his policies accordingly, largely sidelining the unions when he took office in 1997 and making a political virtue of his independence of them.

The Bush II 2004 administration's approach to old-age and retirement policy illustrated similar risk taking. By suggesting that what Americans call social security retirement pensions should be partially privatized, President Bush repeatedly risked identification as an enemy of a public policy "sacred cow." The cliché has been that "social security is the third rail of American politics, electrocuting all those who touch it." Yet, throughout his administration's first term, Bush called for private, individual pension accounts funded by a proportion of the compulsory "contributions" that all Americans pay. This innovation, the president claimed, was the right response to the fiscal strains the aging American society faces. Leaving aside the merits of this view—which are few if any—this bold rhetoric in presidential speeches and proposals did not provoke the public condemnation pundits anticipated on the basis of social security's status as a supposed "sacred cow." In turn, the rhetoric emboldened the interest groups who would gain financially if the American government required some share of social insurance taxes to be invested in the stock and bond markets. As a result, the presidential election of 2004 was replete with references to the differences between the traditional defense of social insurance (largely by Democrats) and the call for private individual accounts (largely by Republicans).

Innovation occurs, but not as commonly as appeals to its possibility (Baumgartner and Jones 1993, 2002). Nonetheless, without history there can therefore be no understanding of public policy. And without history there can also be no realistic evaluation of public policy. For if evaluation does not take into account what policy makers were trying to achieve, if the criteria used in judging the success or otherwise of policies are those of the evaluator rather than those of the originator, the result will at best yield a very partial, perhaps anachronistic verdict. By this we do not claim a historical monopoly on either the understandings or the evaluation of public policy. But we do connect our insistence on the explanatory importance of the assumptive world of policy actors with the truism that all our assumptions incorporate historical understandings, both biographical and cultural.

# 4. THE COMPARATIVE DIMENSION

This chapter has so far emphasized the importance of context—institutional, ideological, and historical—in the understanding of policy making in modern polities. Here we turn to another important way to understand and to evaluate policy making: namely, the use of cross-national policy studies. There is little doubt such work has mushroomed in recent decades, partly no doubt, because of technological innovations that have speeded up the transfer of information about what is happening abroad. Indeed, none of us can escape the "bombardment of information about what is happening in other countries" (Klein 1995). The pressing question, however, is whether this informational dispersion is a help or a hindrance to understanding what governments do and why.

There are at least three obvious ways in which policy analysis might be improved by cross-national understanding. One is simply to define more clearly what is on the policy agenda by reference to quite similar or quite different formulations elsewhere. The more similar the problems or policy responses, the more likely one can portray the nuanced formulations of any particular country. The more dissimilar, the more striking the contrast with what one takes for granted in one's own policy setting. This is the gift of perspective, which may or may not bring with it explanatory insight or lesson drawing. A second approach is to use cross-national enquiry to check on the adequacy of nation-specific accounts. Let's call that a defense against explanatory provincialism. What precedes policy making in country A includes many things—from legacies of past policy to institutional and temporal features that "seem" decisive. How is one to know how decisive as opposed to simply present? One answer is to look for similar outcomes elsewhere where some of those factors are missing or configured differently. Another is to look for a similar configuration of precedents without a comparable outcome. A third and still different approach is to treat cross-national experience as quasi-experiments. Here one hopes to draw lessons about why some policies seem promising and doable, promising and impossible, or doable but not promising. All of these approaches appear in the comparative literature. And with the growth of such writing, one senses an optimism about the possible improvement of comparative learning and lesson drawing. But is the optimism justified? That question is what interests us here.

The interest, however, is not in addressing the broad topic of the promise and perils of cross-national policy studies (Klein 1991; Marmor, Okma, and Freeman 2005). Rather, it is to offer some illustrations of how comparative understanding can advance the art and craft of policy analysis. This requires some examples of each of these approaches, positive or negative. A useful starting point would be to take a misleading cross-national generalization that upon reflection, helps to clarify differences in how policy problems are in fact posed. A 1995 article on European health reform claimed that "countries everywhere are reforming their health systems." It went on to assert that "what is remarkable about this global movement is that both the diagnosis of the problems and the prescription for them are virtually the same in all health care systems" (Hunter 1995). These globalist claims, it turns out, were mistaken (Jacobs 1998; Marmor 1999). But the process of specifying exactly what counts as health care problems—whether of cost control, of poor quality, or of fragmented organization of services—is helpful. The comparative approach first refutes the generalization, but it also enriches what any one analyst portrays as national "problems." So, for instance, the British health policy researcher coming to investigate Oregon's experiment in rationing would have soon discovered that it was neither restrictive in practice nor a major cost control remedy in the decade 1990–2000 (Jacobs, Marmor, and Oberlander 1999).

Offering new perspectives on problems and making factual adjustments in national portraits are not to be treated as trivial tasks. They are what apprentice policy craftsmen and -women might well spend a good deal of time perfecting. That is because all too many comparative studies are in fact caricatures rather than characterizations of policies in action. A striking illustration of that problem is the 2000 World Health Organization (WHO) report on how one might rank health systems across the globe. Not only was the ambition itself grandiose, but the execution of it would be best regarded as ridiculous (Williams 2001). The WHO posed five good questions about how health systems work: are they fair, responsive, efficient, and so on. But they answered those questions without the faintest attention to the difficulties of describing responsiveness or fairness or efficiency in some universalistic manner. What's more, they used as partial evidence the distant opinions of Geneva-based medical personnel to "verify" what takes place in Australia, Oman, or Canada. With comparativists like that, one can easily understand why some funders of research regard comparative policy studies as excuses for boondoggles. But mistakes should not drive out the impulse for improvement.[5]

The most commonly cited advantage of comparative studies, however, is as an antidote to explanatory provincialism. Once again, a health policy example provides a good illustration of how and how not to proceed. There are those in North America who regard universal health insurance as incompatible with American values. They rest their case in part on the belief that Canada enacted health insurance and the USA has not because North American values are sharply different. In short, these comparativists attribute a different outcome to a different political culture in the USA. In

---

[5] There are, of course, other interpretations of the WHO action, however unreliable the precise evaluations of national performance. One such interpretation, offered by one of the *Handbook*'s editors, is that the ranking of countries on the basis of specious data surely would provoke local political interest in gathering and presenting more reliable data about health across the globe. In the case of Australia for instance, the civil servant in charge of the federal health department did in fact challenge the WHO report; in other capitals outrage did lead to condemnation and the provision of counter-evidence. This was certainly one result of the exercise, and there is reason to believe this aim was in the mind of the WHO study director, Murray. One of this chapter's authors confronted Murray in London during the spring of 2001 at a conference with the inaccuracies and absurdities of this ranking. Murray responded by invoking the experience of national income accounts. No one, he said, thought GDP measured income perfectly or did so correctly at the outset. But Murray went on to add, "we would not want to go back on GDP measures, would we?" The notion that producing junk science energizes better science may have some empirical backing, but it is the weakest possible defense of any particular, flawed study.

fact, the values of Canada and the United States, while not identical, are quite similar. Canada's distribution of values is closer to that of the United States than any other modern, rich democracy. Like siblings, differences are there. In fact, the value similarities between British Columbia and Washington state are greater than those between either of those jurisdictions and, say, New Brunswick or New Hampshire along the North American east coast. Similar values are compatible with different outcomes, which in turn draw one's attention to other institutional and strategic factors that distinguish Canadian from American experience with financing health care (Maioni 1998; White 1995). One can imagine multiplying examples of such cautionary lessons, but the important point is simply that the lessons are unavailable from national histories alone.

The third category of work is not so directly relevant to our enquiry. But it is worth noting that drawing lessons from the policy experience of other nations is what supports a good deal of the comparative analysis available. The international organizations have this as part of their rationale. WHO, as noted, is firmly in the business of selling "best practices." The OECD regularly produces extensive, hard to gather, statistical portraits of programs as diverse as disability and pensions, trade flows and the movement of professionals, educational levels, and health expenditures. No one can avoid using these efforts, if only because the task of discovering "the facts" in a number of countries is daunting indeed. But the portraiture that emerges requires its own craft review. Does what Germany spends on spas count as health expenditures under public regulation or should it, as with the United States be categorized differently? The same words do not mean the same things. And different words may denote similar phenomena. For now, it is enough to note that learning about the experience of other nations is a precondition for learning from them. A number of comparative studies fail on the first count and thus necessarily on the second. On the other hand, if one were to look for exemplary instances of cross-national learning, one would turn quite quickly to Japan, Taiwan, and Korea. All have sent first-rate civil servants abroad to find promising models, have worried about the barriers to transplantation, and have when using these apparent models, worked carefully on issues of adaptation, transformation, and implementation.

## 5. THE CASE FOR ECLECTICISM

One reaction to our chapter may well be to dismiss it as an exercise in trying to have it all ways: eclecticism as a substitute for intellectual rigor. However, we make no apology for this. In practice, no public policy analyst can use all the tools of the trade all the time: a rational choice analyst in the morning, a psycho-biographer in the afternoon, a historian in the evening, and a political theorist in the hours when sleep does not come. However, our contention throughout has been that the attempt to draw on all these disciplines is essential. Trying to understand and explain public policy as a whole—making sense of what governments do, rather than analysing specific election results or policy outputs—has to be in our view, an exercise in synthesis.

The point can be simply illustrated, bringing together many of the issues previously discussed. Central to most public policy analysis (including our own) is the notion of self-interest. We invoke the self-interest of politicians in getting elected and staying in office. We invoke the self-interest of lobbies in pressing for their share of pork or in pursuit of some ideology. Yet as Thomas Macaulay (cited in Wildavsky 1994, 155) pointed out some 150 years ago in his critique of utilitarianism:

One man cuts his father's throat to get possession of his old clothes; another hazards his own life to save that of an enemy. One man volunteers on a forlorn hope; another is drummed out of a regiment for cowardice. Each of these men has no doubt acted from self-interest. But we gain nothing from knowing this, except the pleasure, if it be one, of multiplying useless words.

In short, much of public policy analysis involves giving meaning to what, in the absence of background knowledge, is indeed an empty word. How people define their self-interest (their assumptive worlds) depends on culture and history. How people in turn, act to further that self-interest will depend on the institutions within which they operate. And the definitions, and the way in which they are translated into practice, will vary and evolve over time as the intellectual, social, and economic environment changes. So, for example, no one can understand the evolving history of Britain's National Health Service (Klein 2001) without taking into account the changing environment in which it operates.

In summary then, we have argued that no sensible understanding of what liberal democratic governments should do, have done, or will do is possible without attention to the realities of office seeking and office keeping, and how those realities are perceived by those involved. This theme—stunningly obvious in one sense—is nonetheless all too frequently ignored. The history of efforts to make the analysis of public policy more scientific, rigorous, and thereby more helpful for policy development is a fascinating (and controversial) one, but has not been our concern here. Rather our contribution is to insist that whatever technical improvements are possible—in polling accuracy, in economic modeling, in the simulation of policy options, and so on—it remains essential to emphasize the centrality of the most basic features of governmental policy making in democratic polities. These, we have suggested, include the need to maintain regime legitimacy, the competitive struggle to achieve (and keep) office, and the search for a balanced policy portfolio.

Beyond that we have emphasized the importance of understanding the constellation of ideas, institutions, and interests that converge in any policy activity. Here the focus is, as argued above, on how historical evidence—and evidence about history—shapes the options available to policy makers, their understanding of the material (and other) interests at stake, and their interpretation of what contemporary audiences will make of their ideas. Throughout we have illustrated our claims about historical understanding by citing examples that appear to tell an apt illustrative story—in line with our contention that the analysis of public policy, like policy making itself is an exercise in persuasion (Majone 1989). Hence the importance of examining critically the rhetoric of persuasion used by both policy makers and public policy analysts.

The discussion of comparative policy emphasizes still another element in the art and craft of policy analysis. Comparing formulations of policy problems across national borders illustrated the degree to which the mental worlds of actors are shaped by their distinctive historical understandings and the ideas that stakeholders in particular settings take for granted, as well as being a protection against explanatory provincialism. Finally, we note the complexities of evaluating public policy making once the perspectives of policy makers are taken as central to understanding their options and choices. Put another way, an appreciation of what policy makers believe they are doing is a necessary—albeit far from sufficient—condition for understanding and evaluating their actions.

# APPENDIX 44.1  THE QUEEN'S SPEECH, NOVEMBER 2004

## THE UK GOVERNMENT'S LEGISLATIVE PROGRAMME

The Queen's speech announced the following planned legislation, for the 2004/5 session of Parliament. The bills announced would:

- Enable young people to people to benefit from higher education and abolish up-front tuition fees.
- Encourage employers to provide good-quality pensions and individuals to save for retirement, and set up a Pension Protection Fund to protect people when companies become insolvent.
- Allow registration of civil partnerships between same-sex couples.
- Establish a single tier of appeal against asylum decisions.
- Take forward work on an incremental approach to a national identity cards scheme.
- Modernize the laws on domestic violence and improve services designed to protect children.
- Remove hereditary peers and set up an independent Appointments Commission.
- Enable a referendum on the single currency, subject to the government's five economic tests being met.
- Make the planning system faster and fairer with greater community participation.
- Improve traffic flows and manage road works more effectively.
- Modernize charity law and allow for the creation of Community Interest Companies.

*Source*: Adapted from *The Queen' Speech* 2004.

# APPENDIX 44.2 BUSH'S 2004 STATE OF THE UNION ADDRESS

## Summary of Contents

- Continue support for the War on Terror; a peaceful, stable, and democratic Iraq; and homeland security.
- Renew the Patriot Act, which is set to expire in 2005.
- Put pressure on regimes that support and harbor terrorists and seek to obtain weapons of mass destruction.
- Double the budget for the National Endowment for Democracy to help it develop free elections, free markets, free press, and free labor unions in the Middle East.
- Give students the skills they need to succeed in the workplace with Jobs for the Twenty-First Century, a series of measures that includes extra help for students falling behind in reading and math, greater access to AP programs in high schools, private sector math and science professionals teaching part-time in high schools, larger Pell grants for college students, and increased support for community colleges.
- Make the temporary tax cuts permanent to keep the economy going strong.
- Help small business owners and employees find relief from excessive federal regulation and frivolous lawsuits.
- Enact energy-related measures to modernize the electricity system, protect the environment, and make America less dependent on foreign oil.
- Create Social Security Personal Retirement Accounts.
- Cut the federal deficit in half over five years with a budget that limits growth in discretionary spending to 4 per cent.
- Reform immigration laws to create a temporary worker program allowing illegal immigrants to obtain temporary legal status.
- Control medical costs and expand access to care by letting small businesses collectively bargain with insurance companies, giving refundable tax credits to low-income Americans so they can buy their own health insurance, computerizing health records to improve quality and reduce cost, reforming medical malpractice law, and making the purchase of catastrophic health care coverage 100 per cent tax deductible.
- Increase funding to combat drug use through education, drug testing in schools, and asking children's role models to set a good example.
- Double federal funding for abstinence programs to reduce the incidence of sexually transmitted diseases.
- Prevent same-sex marriages, using the constitutional process if necessary.
- Codify into law the executive order allowing faith-based charities to compete for federal social service grants.
- Enact a prisoner re-entry program providing better job training and placement, transitional housing, and mentoring.

*Source*: Adapted from Bush 2004.

# References

ALLISON, G. 1971. *Essence of Decision: Explaining the Cuban Missile Crisis*. Boston: Little, Brown.

—— and ZELIKOW, P. 1999. *Essence of Decision: Explaining the Cuban Missile Crisis*, 2nd edn. New York: Longman.

BAUMGARTNER, F., and JONES, B. 1993. *Agendas and Instability in American Politics*. Chicago: Chicago University Press.

—— —— 2002. *Policy Dynamics*. Chicago: Chicago University Press.

BUSH, G. W. 2004. State of the Union Address, Jan. 20. Available at: www.whitehouse.gov/news/releases/2004/01/20040120-7.html.

BUTLER, D., ADONIS, A., and TRAVERS, T. 1994 *Failure in British Government: The Politics of the Poll Tax*. Oxford: Oxford University Press.

BUTLER, R. 2004. *Review of Intelligence on Weapons of Mass Destruction*. London: HMSO.

DEAN, J. 2004. *Worse than Watergate: The Secret Presidency of George W. Bush*. New York: Little, Brown.

DENZAU, A. T., and NORTH, D. C. 1994. Shared mental models: ideologies and institutions. *Kyklos*, 47 (1): 3–31.

DOWNS, A. 1957. *An Economic Theory of Democracy*. New York: Harper and Row.

FOX, D., DAY, P., and KLEIN, R. 1989. The power of professionalism: policies for AIDS in Britain, Sweden and the United States. *Daedalus*, 118 (2): 93–112.

GOODIN, R. E. 1980. *Manipulative Politics*. New Haven, Conn.: Yale University Press.

—— 2000. Institutional gaming. *Governance*, 13: 523–33.

HACKER, J. S. 2002. *The Divided Welfare State*. New York: Cambridge University Press.

HALL, P. A. 1993. Policy paradigms, social learning and the state. *Comparative Politics*, 25: 275–96.

HECLO, H. 1974. *Modern Social Politics in Britain and Sweden*. New Haven, Conn.: Yale University Press.

HUNTER, D. 1995. A new focus for dialogue. *European Health Reform: The Bulletin of the European Network and Database*, 1 (Mar.):.

JACOBS, A. 1998. Seeing difference: market health reform in Europe. *Journal of Health Politics, Policy and Law*, 23 (1): 1–33.

—— MARMOR, T., and OBERLANDER, J. 1999. The Oregon Health Plan and the political paradox of rationing: what advocates and critic have claimed and what Oregon did. *Journal of Health Politics, Policy and Law*, 24 (1): 161–80.

JACOBS, L. R., and SHAPIRO, R. Y. 2000. *Politicians Don't Pander: Political Manipulation and the Loss of Democratic Responsiveness*. Chicago: University of Chicago Press.

KENNEDY, J. 1964. *Profiles in Courage*. New York: Harper and Row.

KINGDON, J. W. 1995. *Agendas, Alternatives and Public Policies*, 2nd edn. New York: Harper-Collins.

KLEIN, R. 1991. Risks and benefits of comparative studies. *Milbank Quarterly*, 69 (2): 275–91.

—— 1995. Learning from others: shall the last be the first? Pp. 95–102 in *Four Country Conference on Health Care Reforms and Health Care Policies in the United States, Canada, Germany and the Netherlands: Report*, ed. K. Okma. The Hague: Ministry of Health.

—— 2001. *The New Politics of the NHS*, 4th edn. Harlow: Prentice Hall.

MACMILLAN, H. 1938. *The Middle Way*. London: Macmillan.

MAIONI, A. 1998. *Parting at the Crossroads: The Emergence of Health Insurance in the United States and Canada*. Princeton, NJ: Princeton University Press.

MAJONE, G. 1989. *Evidence, Argument and Persuasion in the Policy Process.* New Haven, Conn: Yale University Press.

MARMOR, T. 1999. The rage for reform: sense and nonsense in health policy. Pp. 260–72 in *Health Reform: Public Success, Private Failure,* ed. D. Drache and T. Sullivan. London: Routledge.

—— 2000. *The Politics of Medicare.* 2nd edn. New York: Aldine de Gruyter.

—— 2004. The US Medicare programme in political flux. *British Journal of Health Care Management,* 10: 143–7.

—— OKMA, K. G., and FREEMAN, R. 2005. *Health Policy, Comparison and Learning.* New Haven, Conn.: Yale University Press.

NEUSTADT, R. E., and MAY, E. R. 1988. *Thinking in Time: The Uses of History for Decision Makers.* New York: Free Press.

OBERLANDER, J. 2003. *The Political Life of Medicare.* Chicago: University of Chicago Press.

PUTNAM, R. 2001. *Bowling Alone: The Collapse and Revival of American Community.* New York: Simon and Schuster.

THE QUEEN'S SPEECH 2004. *Hansard's Parliamentary Debates* (Lords), 467: cols. 1–4. Available at: www.publications.parliament.uk/id19900/dlhansard/pdvn/ldso4/41123-01.htm.

TUOHY, C. H. 1999. *Accidental Logics.* New York: Oxford University Press.

VICKERS, G. 1965. *The Art of Judgment.* London: Chapman and Hall.

WHITE, J. 1995. *Competing Solutions: American Health Care Proposals and International Experience.* Washington, DC: Brookings Institution.

WILDAVSKY, A. 1979. *The Art and Craft of Policy Analysis.* London: Macmillan.

—— 1994. Why self-interest means less outside of a social context. *Journal of Theoretical Politics,* 6: 131–59.

WILLIAMS, A. 2001. Science or marketing at WHO? A commentary on World Health 2000. *Health Economics,* 10 (2): 93–100.

WOODWARD, B. 2002. *Bush at War.* New York: Simon and Schuster.

—— 2004. *Plan of Attack.* New York: Simon and Schuster.

WORLD HEALTH ORGANIZATION 2000. *The World Health Report 2000, Health Systems: Improving Performance.* Geneva: World Health Organization.

YOUNG, H. 1989. *One of US: A Biography of Margaret Thatcher.* London: Macmillan.

# NAME INDEX

Note: Includes all referenced authors and organizations.

# SUBJECT INDEX